MTV

Europe

1st Edition

by Lauren Berger, Naomi Black, Ari Cohen,
Valerie Conners, Christi Daugherty, Taryn
Firkser, Fernando Gayesky, Kitty Hall, Sylvie
Hogg, Andre Legaspi, Hana Mastrini, John
Moretti, Clare O'Connor, Jennifer Reilly &
Colleen Taylor

Wiley Publishing, Inc.

Lauren Berger

Lauren Berger (Austria) has written for *US Weekly,* *Nickelodeon Magazine,* Nordstrom.com, and other publications. She hopes to pursue a career in entertainment reporting, freelance writing, and television development.

Naomi Black

Naomi Black (editor) has written or contributed to eight books on travel and food. Her anthropology degree has served her well working in and around Manhattan, especially during her stint as editor at Frommer's. As a freelance writer, she's placed work in *Travel & Leisure, Brides,* and other travel-related magazines. She dives, caves, and hikes when she can, when she's not being called on to get something from the kitchen by her two wonderful children, Katherine and Thomas.

Ari Cohen

Ari Cohen (Croatia, Hungary, Turkey) enjoys the fortune and glory of living in exotic war zones and drinking shaken martinis. When he is not doing covert private-sector work, he attends university in Israel, aiming for a degree in international relations. Although he has won myriad awards and accolades, his favorite is his number-one spot on the "Most Interesting People to Ever Come from Menlo Park, California" list.

Valerie Conners

Valerie Conners (Portugal, Greece) has taught writing in Italy and spent the past 6 years working as a freelance writer and producer for the Travel Channel online. She has a BA in writing from Loyola College in Baltimore and an MA in journalism from Boston University.

Christi Daugherty

Christi Daugherty (Ireland) is an American expat living in London. She is the author of *Frommer's Ireland 2006,* *Frommer's Paris Day by Day,* and *MTV Ireland.* Before emigrating, she worked as a journalist in New Orleans. She attended Texas A&M University.

Taryn Firkser

Taryn Firkser (Denmark; Iceland; Sweden; and Venice and Campania, Italy) has studied geography at Simon Fraser University in Vancouver and Tibetan studies at Indiana University. She presently lives in Ottawa, Canada, where she is beginning her career as a diplomat in the Foreign Service. She has also contributed to *MTV Italy*.

Fernando Gayesky

Fernando Gayesky (Spain) moved from Argentina to New York City to study film when he was 21 with $800 in his bank account, which was good fodder for his first travel article on meals for under $5. He's since traveled throughout South America and Europe before settling down in Barcelona, Spain. He's also a contributor to *MTV Spain*.

Kitty Hall

Kathleen "Kitty" Hall (France) has studied at the Sorbonne and in Aix-en-Provence at the Université Aix-Marseille. She graduated in 2004 from Indiana University with degrees in French and anthropology. Kitty is currently living in Marseille, France, working on a master's degree in public health in developing countries at the Faculté de Médecine de Marseille.

Sylvie Hogg

Native Californian Sylvie Hogg (Rome, Florence, Venice, and Naples, Italy) took her totally practical Dartmouth degree in Classical studies to Rome, where she lived and worked as a travel writer and tour guide for 5 years. She is the lead author of *MTV Italy* and also wrote *Frommer's Rome Day by Day* and *Frommer's Irreverent Guide to Rome*. Sylvie now resides in sexy New York City.

Andre Legaspi

Andre Legaspi (The Netherlands; Germany; and Florence, Italy) was born and raised in Queens, New York, and attended McGill University in Montreal, where he wrote CD reviews and covered the music scene. He has also contributed to *MTV Italy* and *MTV Spain*, as well as *Frommer's Montreal Day by Day*.

Hana Mastrini

Hana Mastrini (Czech Republic) is a native of the western Czech spa town of Karlovy Vary and became a veteran of the "Velvet Revolution" as a student in Prague in 1989. She is a regular contributor to *Frommer's Europe* and *Frommer's Europe from $70 a Day*.

John Moretti

John Moretti (Florence, Milan, and Venice, Italy) has written for the *International Herald Tribune, The Independent on Sunday, Italy Daily, New York Sun,* the Associated Press, and FT Online. He has also co-edited *Rome in Detail,* contributed to the *Time Out* city guides to Milan and Naples and to *MTV Italy,* and written *Living Abroad in Italy.*

Clare O'Connor

Clare O'Connor (England, Scotland) is a global nomad, born in Bermuda and educated in England and Philadelphia, where she graduated from the University of Pennsylvania in 2005. She hopes to someday edit a travel magazine and retire to the Dalmatian Coast, but for now she lives and works in London. Clare also contributed to *MTV Ireland.*

Jennifer Reilly

Jennifer Reilly (Best of Europe, editor) lives in New York City but spends her days editing travel guides in Hoboken, New Jersey. In her opinion, all of Europe is a "best of," but she's especially eager to visit Croatia, Greece, Iceland, and Turkey because she hasn't had her passport stamped in those countries yet. She has a BS from Boston University and an MA from Columbia University.

Colleen Taylor

Colleen Taylor (Belgium, Greece) hit the road as *CosmoGIRL!* magazine's first-ever political correspondent during the 2004 presidential campaign, prompting the Youth Vote Coalition to honor her as one of the "30 Most Influential People in Politics Under 30."

Published by:
Wiley Publishing, Inc.
111 River St.
Hoboken, NJ 07030-5774

ISBN-13: 978-0-7645-8499-2

ISBN-10: 0-7645-8499-5

Editors: Naomi Black and Jennifer Reilly

Production Editor: Suzanna R. Thompson

Cartographer: Elizabeth Puhl

Special thanks to Andrew Murphy and Guy Ruggiero

Cover and Interior Design: Eric Frommelt

Wiley Anniversary Logo: Richard Pacifico

Production by Wiley Indianapolis Composition Services

For information on our other products and services or to obtain technical support, please contact our Customer Care Department within the U.S. at 800/762-2974, outside the U.S. at 317/572-3993 or fax 317/572-4002.

Wiley also publishes its books in a variety of electronic formats. Some content that appears in print may not be available in electronic formats.

Manufactured in the United States of America

5 4 3 2 1

Table of Contents

The Best of Europe   1

The Best European Experiences   1
The Best Nightclubs   2
The Best Bars & Pubs   2
The Best Live Music   3
The Best Hostels   4
The Best Deal & Big-Deal Hotels   5
The Best Cheap Eats   5
The Best Cafes   6
The Best Dining Spots   7
The Best Things to Do for Free or Dirt Cheap   7
The Best Panoramas   8
The Best Offbeat Tours   9
The Best Markets   9
The Best Water Activities   10
The Best Outdoor Activities   10

The Basics: Planning Your Trip to Europe   11

The Stuff You Need to Figure Out before You Go   12
Money (Makes the World Go Round)   21
Getting In & Out   26
Health & Safety   29
Getting Wired   33
Getting to Europe   36
Getting Around Europe   40
For Travelers with Special Interests or Needs   48
Surf the Turf   52

Amsterdam   54

The Best of Amsterdam   55
Getting There & Getting Around   56
Amsterdam Basics   61
Sleeping   66
Eating   71
Partying   73
Performing Arts   77
Sightseeing   77
Playing Outside   81
Shopping   82

Antwerp   86

The Best of Antwerp   87
Getting There & Getting Around   87
Antwerp Basics   88
Sleeping   91
Eating   93
Partying   94
Performing Arts   96
Sightseeing   97
Playing Outside   99
Shopping   99

Athens   101

The Best Of Athens   102
Getting There & Getting Around   102
Athens Basics   104
Sleeping   107
Eating   111
Partying   112
Performing Arts   113
Sightseeing   114
Playing Outside   117
Shopping   117

Barcelona   118

The Best of Barcelona   119
Getting There & Getting Around   119
Barcelona Basics   121
Sleeping   126
Eating   131
Partying   133
Sightseeing   136
Playing Outside   141
Shopping   142

Berlin   144

The Best of Berlin   145
Getting There & Getting Around   145
Berlin Basics   148
Sleeping   152
Eating   159
Partying   161
Performing Arts   163
Sightseeing   165
Playing Outside   170
Shopping   170

Brussels   172

The Best of Brussels   173
Getting There & Getting Around   173
Brussels Basics   175
Sleeping   180
Eating   181
Partying   183
Performing Arts   185
Sightseeing   186
Playing Outside   189
Shopping   190
Road Trip   191

Budapest   194

The Best of Budapest   194
Getting There & Getting Around   195
Budapest Basics   198
Sleeping   202
Eating   206
Partying   208
Sightseeing   210

CONTENTS

Performing Arts   216
Playing Outside   217
Shopping   218

Copenhagen   221

The Best of Copenhagen   222
Getting There & Getting Around   223
Copenhagen Basics   225
Sleeping   229
Eating   233
Partying   235
Performing Arts   236
Sightseeing   237
Playing Outside   241
Shopping   242
Road Trip   242

The Dalmatian Coast   244

The Best of the Dalmatian Coast   244
Dalmatian Coast Basics   245
Split   246
Hvar   254
The Island Brač   258
The Island Korčula   262

Dublin   266

The Best of Dublin & Galway   267
Getting There & Getting Around   268
Dublin Basics   271
Sleeping   276
Eating   281
Partying   285
Performing Arts   292
Sightseeing   293
Playing Outside   300
Shopping   303
Road Trip   305

Dubrovnik   320

The Best of Dubrovnik   320
Getting There & Getting Around   321
Dubrovnik Basics   321
Sleeping   324
Eating   326
Partying   327
Performing Arts   328
Sightseeing   328
Playing Outside   331
Shopping   332

Edinburgh   333

The Best of Edinburgh   334
Getting There & Getting Around   335
Edinburgh Basics   337
Sleeping   340
Eating   344

Partying 346
Sightseeing 350
Shopping 354

Florence 355

The Best of Florence 356
Getting There & Getting Around 356
Florence Basics 359
Sleeping 365
Eating 372
Partying 376
Performing Arts 379
Sightseeing 380
Playing Outside 389
Shopping 390
Road Trip 392

The French Riviera 394

The Best of the French Riviera 395
French Riviera Basics 395
Nice 398
St-Tropez 406
Cannes 410
Road Trip 415

Glasgow 417

The Best of Glasgow 418
Getting There & Getting Around 418
Glasgow Basics 420
Sleeping 423
Eating 428
Partying 431
Performing Arts 433
Sightseeing 434
Playing Outside 437
Shopping 438

The Greek Islands 440

The Best of The Greek Islands 440
Santorini 442
Ios 453
Mykonos 459

Ibiza 465

The Best of Ibiza 466
Getting There & Getting Around 466
Ibiza Basics 467
Sleeping 469
Eating 472
Partying 473
Performing Arts 477
Playing Outside 477
Shopping 478

Interlaken 480

The Best of Interlaken   **481**
Getting There & Getting Around   **481**
Interlaken Basics   **482**
Sleeping   **483**
Eating   **485**
Partying   **486**
Sightseeing & Playing Outside   **487**
Shopping   **487**
Road Trips   **488**

Istanbul 491

The Best of Istanbul   **491**
Getting There & Getting Around   **492**
Istanbul Basics   **494**
Sleeping   **499**
Eating   **503**
Partying   **505**
Performing Arts   **508**
Sightseeing   **508**
Playing Outside   **512**
Shopping   **512**
Road Trip   **514**

Lisbon 517

The Best of Lisbon   **518**
Getting There & Getting Around   **518**
Lisbon Basics   **521**
Sleeping   **524**
Eating   **527**
Partying   **530**
Performing Arts   **532**
Sightseeing   **533**
Playing Outside   **536**
Shopping   **538**
Road Trip   **539**

London 541

The Best of London   **542**
Getting There & Getting Around   **543**
London Basics   **550**
Sleeping   **559**
Eating   **562**
Partying   **565**
Performing Arts   **568**
Sightseeing   **570**
Playing Outside   **577**
Shopping   **578**
Road Trip   **581**

Madrid 585

The Best of Madrid   **586**
Getting There & Getting Around   **587**
Madrid Basics   **589**
Sleeping   **593**
Eating   **599**
Partying   **602**

CONTENTS

Performing Arts   605
Sightseeing   606
Playing Outside   608
Shopping   609

Milan   611

The Best of Milan   612
Getting There & Getting Around   612
Milan Basics   616
Sleeping   618
Eating   620
Partying   622
Performing Arts   624
Sightseeing   624
Playing Outside   626
Shopping   627

Munich   629

The Best of Munich   629
Getting There & Getting Around   630
Munich Basics   632
Sleeping   636
Eating   642
Partying   643
Performing Arts   646
Sightseeing   647
Playing Outside   651
Shopping   652
Road Trips   653

Naples, Capri & the Amalfi Coast   655

The Best of Campania   655
Naples   656
Capri   671
The Amalfi Coast   679

Paris   689

The Best of Paris   690
Getting There & Getting Around   691
Paris Basics   694
Sleeping   701
Eating   707
Partying   711
Performing Arts   716
Sightseeing   718
Playing Outside   725
Shopping   727
Road Trips   730

Prague   732

The Best of Prague   733
Getting There & Getting Around   733
Prague Basics   736
Sleeping   743
Eating   747
Partying   750

Performing Arts 755
Sightseeing 758
Playing Outside 763
Shopping 764
Road Trip 766

Reykjavík 770

The Best of Reykjavík 771
Getting There & Getting Around 771
Reykjavík Basics 772
Sleeping 775
Eating 778
Partying 779
Performing Arts 781
Sightseeing 781
Playing Outside 784
Shopping 785
Road Trips 785

Rome 787

The Best of Rome 788
Getting There & Getting Around 789
Rome Basics 792
Sleeping 799
Eating 806
Partying 812
Performing Arts 817
Sightseeing 818
Playing Outside 832
Shopping 834

Seville 837

The Best of Seville 838
Getting There & Getting Around 839
Seville Basics 840
Sleeping 844
Eating 849
Partying 851
Performing Arts 853
Sightseeing 855
Playing Outside 858
Shopping 858
Road Trip 860

Stockholm 861

The Best of Stockholm 862
Getting There & Getting Around 862
Stockholm Basics 863
Sleeping 866
Eating 870
Partying 872
Performing Arts 874
Sightseeing 874
Playing Outside 877
Shopping 878
Road Trips 878

CONTENTS

Venice 881

The Best of Venice   882
Getting There & Getting Around   883
Venice Basics   887
Sleeping   890
Eating   897
Partying   902
Performing Arts   906
Sightseeing   907
Playing Outside   918
Shopping   920

Vienna 922

The Best of Vienna   922
Getting There & Getting Around   923
Vienna Basics   925
Sleeping   929
Eating   934
Partying   935
Performing Arts   937
Sightseeing   938
Playing Outside   943
Shopping   945
Road Trip   946

Zurich 951

The Best of Zurich   952
Getting There & Getting Around   952
Zurich Basics   954
Sleeping   957
Eating   960
Partying   961
Performing Arts   963
Sightseeing   963
Playing Outside   965
Shopping   967

Appendix 968

Tourist Offices   968
Airlines   970
Rail & Ferry Lines   973
Conversion Charts   974

Index 976

CONTENTS

List of Maps

Europe   14
Amsterdam   68
Antwerp   92
Athens   108
Barcelona   128
Barcelona Metro   130
Berlin-Mitte   153
West Berlin   155
Berlin U-Bahn & S-Bahn   156
Brussels   176
Budapest   204
Copenhagen   230
The Dalmatian Coast   245
Split   247
Hvar   255
Dublin Sleeping & Eating   277
Dublin Partying & Sightseeing   286
Dubrovnik   325
Edinburgh   342
Florence   366
The French Riviera   397
Nice   399
Cannes   412
Glasgow   424
The Cyclades   443
Santorini   445
Ibiza   471
Interlaken   484
Istanbul   500
Lisbon   525
London   544
West London   546
Madrid   594
Madrid Metro   596
Milan   614
Munich   638
Munich U-Bahn & S-Bahn   640
Naples   661
The Amalfi Coast   681
Paris Sleeping & Eating   702
Paris Partying & Sightseeing   712
Prague   744
Reykjavík   777
Rome   800
Rome Metropolitana   803
Seville   846
Stockholm   868
Venice Sleeping & Eating   892
Venice Partying & Sightseeing   908
Vienna   930
Vienna Public Transport   932
Zurich   959

Acknowledgments

Many people helped out on this book, and special thanks should go to Darwin Porter and Danforth Prince, John S. Bowman, Sherry Marker, Rebecca Tomin, Haas Mroue, George McDonald, Lynn A. Levine, Karen Tormé Olson, Donald Olson, Joseph S. Lieber, and Christina Sheal, as well all the *Hanging Out* authors. We're also very grateful to Stephen Bassman, Alexis Lipsitz, Anuja Madar, Andrew Murphy, Marc Nadeau, Melinda Quintero, Guy Ruggiero, and Megan Murray for their editorial and/or map prowess—and, of course, to Suzy Thompson and Liz Puhl, for performing a multitude of miracles.

An Invitation to the Reader

In researching this book, we discovered many wonderful places—hotels, restaurants, shops, and more. We're sure you'll find others. Please tell us about them, so we can share the information with your fellow travelers in upcoming editions. If you were disappointed with a recommendation, we'd love to know that, too. Please write to:

MTV Europe, 1st Edition
Wiley Publishing, Inc.
111 River St.
Hoboken, NJ 07030-5774

An Additional Note

Please be advised that travel information is subject to change at any time—and this is especially true of prices. We therefore suggest that you write or call ahead for confirmation when making your travel plans. The authors, editors, and publisher cannot be held responsible for the experiences of readers while traveling. Your safety is important to us, however, so we encourage you to stay alert and be aware of your surroundings. Keep a close eye on cameras, purses, and wallets, all favorite targets of thieves and pickpockets.

A Note on Prices

The MTV Guides provide exact prices in each destination's local currency. The rates of this exchange as this book went to press are listed in the table below. Exchange rates are constantly in flux; for up-to-the-minute information, consult a currency-conversion website such as www.oanda.com/convert/classic.

Euro €	US $	UK £	Canadian $	Australian $	New Zealand $
1€ equals	US$1.20	£.68	C$1.35	A$1.60	NZ$1.75

Star Ratings, Icons & Abbreviations

Every hotel, restaurant, and attraction listed in this guide has been ranked for quality, value, service, amenities, and special features using a star-rating system. Hotels and restaurants are rated on a scale of zero (recommended) to three stars (exceptional). Attractions, shopping, and nightlife are rated according to the following scale: zero stars (recommended), one star (highly recommended), two stars (very highly recommended), and three stars (must-see). In addition to the star-rating system, we also use three feature icons that point you to great deals, in-the-know advice, and unique experiences. Throughout the book, look for:

 The most-happening restaurants, hotels, and things to do—don't leave town without checking these places out

 When cash flow is at a trickle, head for these spots: no-cost museums, free concerts, bars with complimentary food, and more

 Savvy advice and practical recommendations for students who are studying abroad.

The following abbreviations are used for credit cards:

AE American Express	DISC Discover	V Visa
DC Diners Club	MC MasterCard	

The Best
of Europe

Choosing what destinations to include in a guide to Europe is a downright dizzying task. Zurich or Geneva? Iceland or Norway? Prague or Krakow? We wish we could fit in *all* the continent's cities and countries, but a limited page count has forced us to discriminate. The destinations covered in this book have therefore been winnowed down to only the hippest and the hottest—consider this our opinionated take on where you *really* must go.

What follows are some even more opinionated views on the best of what each carefully vetted destination in this book has to offer.

The Best European Experiences

○ **Seek Out the Best Neighborhoods:** Copenhagen's Christiania, Dublin's Temple Bar, Barcelona's Barri Gòtic, Amsterdam's the Jordaan, Galway City's Eyre Square, Paris's Marais, London's Islington, Berlin's Kreuzberg, Istanbul's Ortaköy, Lisbon's Barrio Alto and the Alfama, and Florence's Santa Croce are some of the best places for people-watching in Europe—perfect places to put up your feet and watch locals interact.

○ **Get a Caffeine Fix:** The occasional Starbucks pops up throughout Europe, but Italy, France, Spain, and Austria all have such raging cafe cultures that it's simply inexcusable not to try the local brew. If you fancy tea instead, London and Edinburgh are the best places to sip a cuppa and sample a scone. Throughout Scandinavia, you simply can't leave home without 1 or 10 Red Bulls to keep you dancing all night.

○ **Celebrate Carnival:** Most of western Europe celebrates Carnival, 3 days of pre-Lenten festivities that pit one outrageously dressed celebrant against another. The most famous festivities are hosted by Nice, Milan, and Venice, but you'll also find quirky local celebrations in cities like Copenhagen and Vienna.

○ **Listen to Local Tunes:** From Portugal's *fado* (sorrowful singing accompanied by guitar and viola players) to Iceland's electronic bands to Berlin's cabaret, tune in to the music of whatever country you're visiting. It'll bring you that much closer to the soul of its people. See p. 532.

○ **Get Outside:** Europe isn't only about standing in line for hours, waiting to view historic cathedrals and museums. It doesn't matter if you play chess in an Italian square, swim in Capri, or catch a cricket match in England—the point is to be active. See "Best Water Activities" and "Best Outdoor Activities," below, for some adventurous ideas.

○ **Crack Open a Book or Catch a Flick:** Trust us on this one: Reading a book or watching a movie set in the country you're visiting will enhance your experience there tenfold. See "Recommended Books, Music & Movies" throughout this book's chapters.

The Best Nightclubs

○ **Café d'Anvers** (Antwerp, Belgium): Haven't managed to squeeze any cathedrals into your busy clubbing schedule? Then head to Café d'Anvers, where you can dance the night away in a gorgeous converted monastery. See p. 94.

○ **A-38** (Budapest, Hungary): Break out the Dramamine. One of the hippest clubs in Europe is on this ship, anchored at the Buda side of the Danube River. See p. 208.

○ **Pachá** (Ibiza, Spain): One of the finest nightclubs, anywhere. This place has pumped up the hits to crowds of sweaty, sexy hipsters since 1975. Dance here, and be part of history. See p. 475.

○ **Carpe Diem Cocktail Bar/Nightclub** (Hvar, Croatia): Yes, Tara Reid once came here, but don't hold that against this club. Although the surroundings are fabulously posh, this place somehow attracts both the superfamous and your everyday backpackers. See p. 256.

○ **Fabric** (London, England): Three floors, a 2,500-person capacity, and big-name DJs. The scene at Fabric is hopping no matter the night. The fine tunes complement the stylish, industrial space. See p. 566.

○ **Atomik Café** (Munich, Germany): Retro paradise. Atomik Café's 1920s night features big-band tunes that will get your inner flapper dancing. On non–theme nights, the club boasts a mellow vibe and a selection of cutting-edge indie rock tunes. See p. 645.

○ **Pravda** (Reykjavík, Iceland): At Pravda, a club converted from police department offices, outrageous fashion and cutting-edge dance music now rule. In a city filled with hot clubs, this is the hottest. See p. 780.

The Best Bars & Pubs

○ **The Long Hall** (Dublin, Ireland): Tuck into one of the traditional snugs of this gorgeous Victorian and order a pint or two of Guinness. The mellow atmosphere and friendly bartenders make this one of the best places in Ireland to try the dark brew. See p. 289.

○ **Pavilhão Chinês Bar** (Lisbon, Portugal): At this drinking playground, you'll find everything from boy toys to actual toys. The walls are lined with G.I. Joe figures and other kitschy dolls, though you may be too distracted by the sexy clientele to notice. See p. 531.

○ **Hofbräuhaus** (Munich, Germany): It's the world's most famous beer hall, so it's gonna be crowded. Plow through the crowds of up to 4,500, though, and you'll be rewarded with live oompah music and mug after mug of some of Germany's best beer. See p. 644.

○ **Tropical Bar** (Santorini, Greece): Proof that it's the people—not the bar—that makes the scene, Tropical Bar compensates for its lackluster decor with a crowd of hot tourists who break out the occasional table dance. The amazing beachside location doesn't hurt. See p. 450.

○ **Habanilla Café** (Seville, Spain): Run out of a former whorehouse, Habanilla boasts a supernatural setting and trippy jam music. No matter the time of day, this place is bumping. See p. 852.

○ **Naranzaria** (Venice, Italy): We challenge you to find a more fabulous, unpretentious spot in all of Italy. This wine bar features 50 exclusive-feeling seats on the wide-open Erbaria esplanade, and it faces the Grand Canal just north of the Rialto Bridge. See p. 905.

The Best Live Music

○ **Melkweg** (Amsterdam, Holland): If you can't find something to suit your tastes here, you won't find it anywhere. Melkweg has a restaurant, a coffee shop, a bar, an art center, a dance floor, a photo gallery, and an exhibition space. The live acts are just as eclectic, influenced by art forms as varied as world beat music and gay/lesbian theater. See p. 77.

○ **Razzmatazz** (Barcelona, Spain): This mega warehouse complex can house 10,000, and it boasts five clubs under one roof, as well as a concert space for indie rock. See p. 135.

THE BEST OF EUROPE

The Top 16 Attractions

→ **The Acropolis** (Athens, Greece; p. 114)
→ **Sagrada Familia** (Barcelona, Spain; p. 139)
→ **Charlottenburg Palace** (Berlin, Germany; p. 166)
→ **Grand-Place** (Brussels, Belgium; p. 187)
→ **Tivoli** (Copenhagen, Denmark; p. 238)
→ **Diocletian's Palace** (Dalmatian Coast, Croatia; p. 252)
→ **Edinburgh Castle** (Edinburgh, Scotland; p. 351)
→ **Santa Croce** and **The Duomo** (Florence, Italy; p. 384 and p. 382)
→ **Monte-Carlo Casino** (Monte-Carlo, France; p. 416)
→ **Hagia Sophia** (Istanbul, Turkey; p. 509)
→ **Westminster Abbey** (London, England; p. 572)
→ **Pompeii** (Pompeii, Italy; p. 670)
→ **Notre-Dame** and **Tour Eiffel** (Paris, France; p. 722)
→ **Prague Castle** (Prague, Czech Republic; p. 760)
→ **Roman Forum** and **St. Peter's Basilica** (Rome, Italy; p. 821 and p. 826)
→ **Alcázar** (Seville, Spain; p. 856)

○ **The Crane** (Galway City, Ireland): Trad Irish music complete with old men dressed in tweed sporting scruffy old beards. This is the genuine article. Sessions can occur at any time, but the Sunday afternoon one is the most religious experience. Worship at the altar of folk. See p. 314.

○ **Royal Albert Hall** (London, England): If, like John Lennon, you've wondered "how many holes it takes to fill the Albert Hall," check out this curious circular domed building just off Kensington Gardens. The music—everything from the summer Proms (p. 572) to classical and rock concerts—is as great as the architecture. See p. 568.

○ **Le Blue Note** (Paris, France): This cozy little spot mixes Brazilian music, jazz, and blues into its nightly repertoire. Tasty Brazilian cocktails help enliven the shows. See p. 715.

○ **El Tamboril** (Seville, Spain): El Tamboril will make you a flamenco convert. Male and female performers stamp, clap, and exude rigidly controlled Iberian passion, and then make way for you to try out your own moves. See p. 854.

○ **Vienna Boys Choir** (Vienna, Austria): In a city steeped in musical traditions and institutions, this group stands out. Created in 1498, the choir still performs Masses by Mozart and Haydn at the Hofburgkapelle on Sundays and holidays from September through June. See p. 938.

The Best Hostels

○ **Albergue de Juventud Kabul** (Barcelona, Spain): This is *not* the place for rest. Two hundred young backpackers can cram into this hostel's rooms, which sleep from four to eight. The hostel is smack dab in the city's best nightlife area. See p. 126.

○ **Hotel mitArt** (Berlin, Germany): Tired of not being able to actually sleep in your hostel? Then head to Hotel mitArt, which boasts extremely quiet rooms and an arty decor that will help you snooze in style. See p. 154.

○ **Charlie Rocket's** (Bruges, Belgium): Charlie Rocket's is converted from what was once Bruges' largest cinema. The cheap, clean rooms and bonus amenities, including a game room and restaurant, guarantee that you won't feel cheated on the price of admission. See p. 191.

○ **Isaacs Hostel** (Dublin, Ireland): Calling itself "Dublin's first V.I.P. hostel," Isaacs adds a full restaurant and an attractive sauna to the usual mix of TV rooms, lockers, and bunk beds. See p. 276.

○ **Balmer's Herberge** (Interlaken, Switzerland): Right in the middle of the city's younger, sports-friendly Matten 'hood, Balmer's has an activities office that can book you on the spot for skydiving and whitewater-rafting trips. Or, you can try to make your way through the hostel's crowded Metro Bar—an adventure in its own right. See p. 483.

○ **Wake Up! London** (London, England): You may not rise early if you stay at Wake Up! London. That's because London's best hostel is regularly packed with a mix of punk-rockish Aussie and European guests who are primed to party. See p. 560

○ **The Beehive** (Rome, Italy): Pardon the pun, but this buzzing place features artfully decorated rooms, a beautiful garden, free Wi-Fi, and organic food at the cafe. The vibe is also thankfully mellower than the city's more frat-worthy hostels. See p. 799.

○ **Hostel Af Chapman/Skeppsholmen** (Stockholm, Sweden): This hostel was converted from an authentic three-masted schooner. Land lubbers can dock in one of the more spacious rooms located off the ship. See p. 866.

The Best Deal & Big-Deal Hotels

○ **Hotel Arena** (Amsterdam, Holland): A converted Roman-Catholic orphanage built in 1890, the Hotel Arena now features spare, modern guest rooms styled by young Dutch designers. Need convincing? You can check out the rooms online at www.hotelarena.nl. See p. 67.

○ **Hotel Burchianti** (Florence, Italy): This is one of the most sought-after little hotels in Florence, and for good reason—from its incredible frescoes to its all-in-the-family service it is that rare combination: classy and cheap. See p. 370.

○ **Pension Unitas** (Prague, Czech Republic): All the guest rooms here used to be holding cells for the secret police. Don't worry—they're actually plusher than the average cheap hotel. With its unbeatable location, the Pension Unitas is a great value for the money. See p. 746.

○ **Hôtel Byblos** (St-Tropez, France): Attached to one of the best nightclubs in St-Tropez, Byblos is where the hot and hip come to preen before heading out to dance. The hotel is pricey, so you may want to simply check out the nightclub. See p. 408.

○ **Astra Apartments** (Santorini, Greece): Try one of the luxury studios, which room up to three to four people. The kitchenette and pool only add to the deal, though the real reason to stay here is the amazing view—the hotel is perched on the dramatic cliffs of Imerovigli. See p. 448.

○ **Hotel Amadeus** (Seville, Spain): This peaceful haven of high culture is run by a family of music lovers. Music is everywhere, from the periodic concerts to the soundproofed practice rooms with pianos. See p. 845.

○ **X-Tra Hotel Limmat** (Zurich, Switzerland): X-tra literally rocks. The management organizes some of Switzerland's best rock concerts, and the nightclub on the ground floor is one of the hottest in the city. Rooms are basic, but who cares when you'll be spending all your time at shows? See p. 958.

○ **L'Hôtel** (Paris, France): Once a 19th-century fleabag, its major distinction used to be that Oscar Wilde died in one of its rooms. Today's guests, however, aren't anywhere near destitute; this place isn't cheap. The seriously Parisian bar is worthy of a drink or two. See p. 706.

The Best Cheap Eats

○ **Frites** (Antwerp, Belgium): Otherwise known as french fries, these tasty treats are best served with mayo. Some of Beligum's best can be found at **Frituur Nº1** in Antwerp. For around 2€, you'll get a big old order of fries with sauce. See p. 93.

○ **Döner Kebab** (Barcelona, Spain): Barcelona's **King Döner** in the Rambla de Raval manages to outdo all kebab shops in a city chock-full of them. For 3.50€, you'll get a *schawarma*, a tasty "Arab taco" filled with heaping portions of lamb or chicken and fresh veggies. They also

have falafel for those PETA card–holding members. See p. 129.

○ **Irish stew** (Dublin, Ireland): On a cold day in Dublin, get thee to **The Porterhouse.** For about 6€, you can get a heaping bowl of stew that will warm you up immediately. See p. 285.

○ **Gelato** (Florence, Italy): If you're human, you'll succumb to at least one gelato (ice cream) a day in Italy. The stuff served up at **Vivoli**, the most famous gelateria in Florence, is among the city's best. See p. 376.

○ **Tapas** (Madrid, Spain): These minitreats are your best bet for cheap food throughout Spain. Madrid's **Automático Bar** dishes up some of the county's most delicious, including dates with bacon and a bunch of homemade pâtés. See p. 600.

○ **Pizza** (Naples, Italy): Naples is the home of Margherita pizza—your standard slice with dough, cheese, tomatoes, and basil— and the city's **Brandi** restaurant claims to have invented it. It's certainly perfected it. See p. 664.

○ **Falafel** (Paris, France): You'll find falafel—fried balls of chickpeas in a pita— all over Europe, but they're especially omnipresent in Paris. At the chain **Maoz** you can load your sandwich with toppings from a self-serve bar. See p. 709.

○ **Gyros** (Santorini, Greece): There are exactly 15,000 trillion gyro places in Greece. **Lucky's,** a tiny stand in Fira's main square, is among the best. The meat-packed gyros are topped with an unreal tzatziki and french fries, and they're worth the wait. See p. 449.

The Best Cafes

○ **Attanasio** (Naples, Italy): Come here for Europe's best *sfogliatelle* (triangles of lay-ered puff pastry, filled with delicious ricotta). See p. 665.

○ **Le Fumoir** (Paris, France): Right off the rue de Rivoli, with a view of both the Seine and the dome of the Institut de France, Le Fumoir is how you imagined Paris would be. This long, ersatz-'30s speakeasy is peopled with just about everyone who's anyone. See p. 710.

○ **Café Slavia** (Prague, Czech Republic): Former President Havel loves this place, open since 1863. He even intervened to keep it in business back in the 1990s. Once you've had a chance to soak in its history and sample the shop's affordable coffee and snacks, you'll understand why. See p. 749.

○ **Kaffi Hljomalind** (Reykjavík, Iceland): This laid-back, unpretentious cafe boasts

The Best 13 Festivals

→ Carnival (throughout Europe). See "The Best European Experiences," above.

→ Amsterdam Pride (Amsterdam, Holland; p. 79)

→ Barcelona street festivals (Barcelona, Spain; p. 137)

→ Love Parade (Berlin, Germany; p. 166)

→ Bloomsday (Dublin, Ireland; p. 294)

→ The Fringe Festival (Edinburgh, Scotland; p. 347)

→ Galway Arts Festival (Galway City, Ireland; p. 316)

→ Oktoberfest (Munich, Germany; p. 647)

→ Rock en Seine (Paris, France; p. 720)

→ Prague Spring Festival (Prague, Czech Republic; p. 759)

→ Feria de Abril (Seville, Spain; p. 855)

→ Stockholm Jazz Festival (Stockholm, Sweden; p. 874)

→ Walpurgis Eve (Uppsala, Sweden; p. 880)

delicious organic eats from pasta dishes to pies. The crowd mainly consists of New Age hippie types, mothers with young children, and serious-looking intellectuals. See p. 779.

○ **Café Latte** (Seville, Spain): This place takes "dinner and a movie" to a whole new level. Settle into one of the cafe's designer chairs, order some delicious macchiatos or mojitos, and watch the music videos and movies shown on the dining area's big screen. See p. 851.

○ **Café Sacher** (Vienna, Austria): Sacher-torte fans, welcome home. The decadent chocolate layer cake was created here in the 1880s, and this cafe is still the perfect old-world setting in which to satisfy all your chocolate cravings. See p. 935.

The Best Dining Spots

○ **Restaurante Olivier** (Lisbon, Portugal): This is the Barrio Alto's hottest spot, so you'll need reservations. You'll also have to knock to gain entry which lends this stylish, small spot—serving delicious Mediterranean cuisine—a definite speakeasy vibe. See p. 528.

○ **Cocoon** (London, England): This Pan-Asian restaurant offers an enticing mix of tasty cocktails and inventive dishes like jungle curry with seafood. See p. 562.

○ **Louisiana Bistro** (Milan, Italy): Head to this converted brothel for some traditional American grub. If you can tear your eyes from all the models, you'll be rewarded with a big-screen TV that shows music videos. See p. 622.

○ **Mandala Ray** (Paris, France): One of the city's most popular see-and-be-seen spots, Mandala Ray serves small portions at big prices. The haute Asian-fusion cuisine goes perfectly with the haute fashion on the attractive clientele. See p. 708.

○ **Supper Club** (Rome, Italy): For a transporting experience into modern Euro-fabulousness, check out this über-trendy spinoff of the original joint in Amsterdam. Barely clad waiters serve tasty Mediterranean- and Asian-inspired dishes—good fuel for dancing in the restaurant's swank club area. You can even get a massage here. See p. 807.

○ **Grand Veranda** (Stockholm, Sweden): You'll get grand views of the harbor and the Royal Palace, as well as truly grand traditional Swedish food (yes, reindeer is on the menu). See p. 871.

THE BEST OF EUROPE

The Best Things to Do for Free or Dirt Cheap

○ **Picnic:** There's no better way to mingle with the natives than to stop at a market and grab some food for a picnic. You'll save money and you'll be able to savor the parks, lakes, or other green areas of wherever you're visiting. Going to market is a sightseeing venture in its own right.

○ **Visit a Museum:** Some cities offer free admission to their museums (like London), and many more offer free days. You also may want to keep an eye out for notices for gallery openings. These are usually free and open to the public, and some include complimentary drink and food.

○ **Get a City Pass:** Many European cities offer special deals with free or discounted admission to attractions, along with public transport access, if you buy a 1-, 2- or 3-day pass. Check with the local tourist board for details.

○ **Attend a Summer Festival:** You may pay more money to fly to Europe during the summer, but you'll be rewarded with all sorts of free theater, dance, and music performances. See "The Best 13 Festivals," earlier in this chapter, to get some idea of all that the continent has to offer.

○ **Go Underground for Art:** For roughly 1€ (the average Métro fare), you'll gain instant access to Paris's Art Nouveau subway entrances, Brussel's metro murals, and Budapest's labyrinthine subway passages, to name just a few.

The Best Panoramas

○ **Mount Tibidabo** (Barcelona, Spain): Unbelievable views of Montserrat and the Pyrenees. On a clear day, you can see as far as Mallorca. See p. 141.

○ **Fisherman's Bastion** (Budapest, Hungary): This place is pure romance, with sweeping views of Pest and the Danube. See p. 212.

○ **The City Wall** (Dubrovnik, Croatia). A work of art in its own right, the city wall also offers a prize-worthy vista of greater Dubrovnik. See p. 329.

○ **Top of Jungfraujoch** (Interlaken, Switzerland): Once you're done marveling at how a train could climb up such a steep mountain, take some time to admire the worthy view. See p. 488.

○ **Castelo de São Jorge** (Lisbon, Portugal): This castle looms over Lisbon, so it's not surprising that it serves as a great vantage point to look out over the city. See p. 534.

○ **Tour Eiffel** (Paris, France): It's cheesy, but you *have* to go. The views are simply great. See p. 722.

○ **The Prater Ferris Wheel** (Vienna, Austria): Take a spin around this 65m-tall (213-ft.) Ferris wheel, and you'll get an aerial view of the whole city. (Watch *The Third Man* first, if you can—it'll enhance the ride.) See p. 944.

The Top 12 Museums

→ Anne Frankhuis **(Anne Frank House)** and **Rijksmuseum** (Amsterdam, Holland; p. 79 and p. 81)

→ **Erotik Museum** and **Museuminsel** (Berlin, Germany; p. 166 and p. 167)

→ **Museo Tattile di Pittura Antica e Moderna** (Bologna, Italy; p. 393)

→ **Uffizi Gallery** (Florence, Italy; p. 387)

→ **The Burrell Collection** (Glasgow City, Scotland; p. 435)

→ **Tate Modern** and **The British Museum** (London, England; p. 576 and p. 574)

→ **Museo del Prado** (Madrid, Spain; p. 607)

→ **ZAM** (Munich, Germany; p. 650)

→ **Museo Archeologico Nazionale** (Naples, Italy; p. 668)

→ **Centre Pompidou** and the **Louvre** (Paris, France; p. 723)

→ **Vatican Museums/Sistine Chapel** (Vatican City; p. 827)

→ **Kunsthistorisches Museum** (Vienna, Austria; p. 941)

The Best Offbeat Tours

- **Heineken Experience Tour** (Amsterdam, Holland): An insufferable tourist trap. For 10€, you get a chance to see how the amber brew in the green bottle is made, via amusement rides and touch-screen exhibits. See p. 79.

- **Ghosts and Gore Tour** (Edinburgh, Scotland): They're a bit overacted and cheesy, but once you get past that, you'll find these tours of Edinburgh's darker side fun and informative. See p. 337.

- **Whale-Watching Tour** (Reykjavík, Iceland): Reykjavík offers a ton of whale-watching tours, all of them great. Chances are, you'll see over a dozen leviathans

and, during the summer, you even might spot a puffin or two. See p. 784.

- **Underground Tour of the Catacombs of San Callisto** (Rome, Italy): Rome's subterranean world is a veritable street labyrinth, so it really helps to have a guide. Though the Catacombs of San Callisto are often packed with tour-bus groups, they're also phenomenal. See p. 822.

- **Original *Sound of Music* Tour** (Salzburg, Austria): Musical fans, this 4-hour tour pays homage to one of the most-watched American musicals ever, and by golly, it's a damn good time. See p. 949.

The Best Markets

THE BEST OF EUROPE

- **Monastraki Flea Market** (Athens, Greece): At this Athens shopping institution, you'll see knockoffs galore. But you'll also find everything from touristy gifts to antiques. See p. 117.

- **Las Ramblas** (Barcelona, Spain): Although not technically a market, this promenade crams enough street entertainers, news vendors, and flower vendors into one street to qualify as one. See p. 121.

- **Marché-aux-Puces** (Brussels, Belgium): Every weekday from 7am to 2pm, the Marché-aux-Puces in place du Jeu-de-Balle hosts a big old flea market. Memorize a few French phrases and see how low you can talk someone down. See p. 189.

- **San Lorenzo street market** (Florence, Italy): This queen of Florentine markets fills up Piazza San Lorenzo and surrounding side streets with a chaotic and colorful array of stands. Merchants hawk T-shirts, silk scarves, and lots and lots of leather. See p. 390.

- **The Grand Bazaar** (Istanbul, Turkey): This bazaar is a grand collection of over 2,600

shops (at last count); 24 *hans* (privately owned marketplaces); 65 streets; 22 gates; two *bedestens* (covered markets); and sundry restaurants, mosques, fountains, and tea houses. Prepare for an exhausting day of shopping and some major haggling. See p. 514.

- **Portobello Market** (London, England): Portobello is most famous for its antiques stalls and shops. It also sells fruits and vegetables and some innovative fashion. See p. 580.

- **Marché aux Puces St-Ouen de Clignancourt** (Paris, France): Paris's most famous flea market is actually a grouping of more than a dozen markets. This complex of 2,500 to 3,000 open stalls and shops sells everything from antiques to junk, from new to vintage clothing. See p. 729.

- **Naschmarkt** (Vienna, Austria): If you like to haggle, come to Vienna's outdoor food-and-produce market. It's a perfect place to stock up before picnicking. See p. 946.

The Best Water Activities

○ **Beach Excursions:** Whether you decide to swim off the Amalfi Coast or to sun on the man-made Paris Plage, just be sure to check out one of Europe's beaches. You need to get *some* sun in between all the museum-seeing and clubbing, after all.

○ **Boat Rides:** A boat offers the perfect vantage point to take in whatever city you're visiting on the continent. Our favorite journeys include a gondola ride in Venice, chugging down the Danube in Budapest, and rowing a boat down the Vltava River in Prague.

○ **River Strolls:** Amble along the banks of certain European rivers, and an amazing cathedral or breathtaking building is sure to come into view. Europe's most

romantic and scenic strolls are along the Seine in Paris, the Danube in Budapest, and the Thames in London.

○ **Surf Spots:** From windsurfing along the Dalmatian Coast to plain old surfing off the French Riviera, Europe offers some incredible opportunities to break out your board. Even better are the lesser-known surfing spots, like the Galway Coast in Ireland, which boast great waves and no crowds.

○ **Water Workouts:** You might want to try some of Europe's more unique ways to break a sweat: soaking in Iceland's thermal pools, ice climbing in London, biking on the water in Amsterdam, or skinny dipping in the Vltava.

The Best Outdoor Activities

○ **Parks:** Berlin's Tiergarten, London's Hyde Park, Dublin's St. Stephen's Green, Rome's Villa Borghese, Zurich's Botanischer Garten, and Paris's Jardins du Luxembourg are some of the best green spaces on the continent, if not anywhere. Run, walk, or sit—just take the time to experience them.

○ **Urban Sports:** If you're tired of sightseeing, try rock climbing in Paris; spelunking in the Buda Castle Labyrinth in Budapest, bungee jumping in Vienna, or biking outside Zurich.

○ **Spectator Sports:** The best way to get to know a city is to root for its teams. Rally behind Wimbledon tennis matches in London, *calcio* (soccer) games in Italy, bullfighting in Spain, or curling in Glasgow.

○ **Winter Sports:** Everyone knows that Switzerland, Austria, and northern Italy have amazing skiing and snowboarding trails. Less famous, but equally worthy, are London's Somerset House, which boasts a first-rate ice-skating rink, and Interlaken, Switzerland, where you can hike on a glacier.

The Basics: Planning Your Trip to Europe

You're going to Europe! By now, you've started daydreaming about all the beautiful things you'll see, all the amazing things you'll consume, and all the romantic things that will happen to you. Guess what? In all likelihood, all of the above will come true without your planning a damn thing. No matter how hard you prepare, one of the best things about traveling is encountering the unexpected—both good and bad.

That said, going to Europe is infinitely more complicated—and ultimately more rewarding—than just going on your standard road trip. Without some help, you may repeatedly find yourself surrounded by a numbed-out tour group, scratching your head and wondering what all the fuss is about. So, plan for the worst-case scenarios (rain, pickpockets, and so on), expect the best (fine weather, no hassles), and consider the surprises as small gifts that, if not appreciated at the time, will become fodder for a grand tale to tell back home.

Sometimes, finding your way around is a matter of asking the right question; other times, finding the right guide is key. Between the info in this section and that in the appendix, you should have more than enough material to start your research. We've provided some overall planning suggestions and then get into the nitty-gritty details. You'll find info on how to plan your trip, what to pack, where to get a rail pass, and who to contact for more info.

The more you plan ahead, even if that means plotting time that's flexible, the more carefree you can be once you step off the plane. You'll also find, below, a roundup of different traveling personalities—the student, the tourist, the partyer, the wanderer, the anthropologist, and the fashionista. Take the time to figure out what's most important to you before you go, and then you can hone in on that when you're there. Read on, and we hope you'll minimize those "I can't believe I didn't think of that" moments that can stress you out and throw a wrench into your otherwise "perfect" trip.

The Stuff You Need to Figure Out before You Go

○ **Figure out how to get there.** For the best airfare and flight structure, get to know the big travel websites and shop around. Try sites like Kayak, Orbitz, and Priceline, but also be sure to check budget carrier sites like Easyjet. In general, try to book your flights well in advance—at least a month before you depart, more for summer travel. While airfares to Europe do occasionally go on sale at the last minute, the savings are usually not enough to offset the anxiety of wondering whether you'll get a seat.

○ **Find a place to sleep.** In a perfect world, you would book your hotel reservations in Europe even before you booked your flight there—during high season, it can be tough to find good-value accommodations on the spot. However, it's not a perfect world. You'll probably end up changing your travel plans somewhat while abroad, and furthermore, some hostels don't accept reservations until the day before your intended arrival. So, even if you can't book all your accommodations before you leave home, you'll find plenty of helpful tips in the "Staying There" section, below, which will give you a feeling for the lay of the land, accommodations-wise, in Europe.

○ **Know what to expect at different times of the year.** Tourism throughout Europe has a rather entrenched seasonal cycle, and depending on when you go, you're likely to have quite different experiences. Weather, of course, is the most obvious variable. There are also significant differences in traveler demographics during the year: Droves of North American college kids come in the summer, while older, more budget-oriented travelers tend to come in the off-peak months of February and November. (Fall and winter are also the cheapest times to travel throughout Europe, except in the ski destinations of Austria and Switzerland.) And in some parts of Europe (such as Greece), many island accommodations and restaurants close in the off season; and boat schedules are often erratic, depending on weather and demand.

○ **Pay attention to opening hours.** The majority of Europe's museums are closed according to a schedule that is posted—on websites, in books, and so on. A few countries, though, are more lax in their scheduling, so it's always good to call ahead and confirm hours. Most countries also have 1 day of the week when museums shut their doors. It's often either Monday or Tuesday, when tourist traffic is lighter. We'll also give you advice about the best days of the week and the best times of day to visit different sights. Where possible (at such top attractions as the Uffizi in Florence or the Louvre in Paris), book your tickets online in advance.

○ **Embrace the cultural differences.** You won't find all the conveniences of home in much of Europe, and the language barrier

Itinerary Tips

When you first sit down to plan where to go, look at how many days you have. Take the time to write down each day you'll be away, even your travel days, and the days you'll be in the same town (unless you're going for more than a month or two). I pencil in the all the info I can. It's spotty at first, but it begins to look like a grid. Usually, I also divide each day into AM (which town I'll be in during the day) and PM (where I'll be sleeping).

I find that the fewer places I visit, the happier I am. Less is often more, and it allows for those unexpected and good surprises mentioned earlier. If you have 14 days, for example, spend 5 in one city, get to know its cafe culture, walk, and walk some more. Plan for 3 days in another town, and maybe a sightseeing day out of town. Add 1 rest or buffer day at the beginning of your trip, so that you can more easily deal with jet lag (doing this by the water is always fun). Add in your travel days, and you're already up to your limit.

We recommend spending a few days in less touristy areas or neighborhoods. Seek out the charming medieval centers but also check out the university (if the town has one). In warm weather, definitely dedicate at least 1 full day, if not several, to a beach or island.

can be frustrating, but part of why you flew thousands of miles to get here was to experience something different, right?

○ **Be realistic about how much you can do on your trip.** Time flies when you're having fun, and you'll be having a lot of fun. Don't rush through the continent in your quest to send postcards from 10 different cities—or even worse, 10 different countries. Leave the *veni, vidi, vici* to Julius Caesar, and allow yourself some idle *dolce vita.*

How Much Time Do I Need in Europe?

To get a sense for the best that Europe has to offer, we recommend that you spend at least 2 weeks here. If you're content to visit only a few cities or regions, a week to 10 days is great. If you're only visiting one city, you'll probably find that a long weekend is quite satisfying. However long you stay, wherever you go, you'll leave wanting more. Also, when you factor in travel time between destinations, checking in at hotels, arriving at the train station in time for your next train out, and so on, you lose a lot of valuable hours that you might

have originally dedicated to hanging out, sightseeing, or partying. Moral of the story? You need more time than you think.

We especially recommend that you resist the temptation to do a whirlwind London-Paris-Rome-in-a-week scenario. Lots of people do it, sure, but it's far more fun to spend more time in each place and get your bearings before you pack up and head for the next city. Unless you're an experienced traveler—and even if you are an experienced traveler—you'll be wiped out and overwhelmed if you try to see too much too quickly. For itinerary tips, see the box above.

WHEN TO GO

Europe's **high season** lasts from mid-May to mid-September, with the most tourists hitting the continent from mid-June to August. In general, this is the most expensive time to travel, except in Austria and Switzerland, where prices are actually higher in winter during the ski season. And because Scandinavian hotels depend on business clients instead of tourists, lower prices can often be found in the fleeting summer, when business clients vacation and a smaller number of tourists take over.

Europe

You'll find smaller crowds, relatively fair weather, and often lower prices at hotels in the **shoulder seasons,** from Easter to mid-May and mid-September to mid-October. **Off season** (except at ski resorts) is from November to Easter, with the exception of December 25 to January 6. Much of Europe, Italy especially, takes August off, and August 15 to 30 is vacation time for many locals, so expect the cities to be devoid of natives but the beaches to be packed.

Weather

BRITAIN & IRELAND Everyone knows it rains a lot in Britain and Ireland. Winters are rainier than summers; August to mid-October are the sunniest months. Summer daytime temperatures average from the low 60s (10s Celsius) to the mid-60s (20s Celsius), dropping to the 40s (5s Celsius) on winter nights. Ireland, whose shores are bathed by the Gulf Stream, has a milder climate and the most changeable weather—a dark rainy morning can quickly turn into a sunny afternoon, and vice versa. The Scottish Lowlands have a climate similar to England's, but the Highlands are much colder, with storms and snow in winter.

CENTRAL EUROPE In Vienna and along the Danube Valley, the climate is moderate. Summer daytime temperatures average in the low 70s (20s Celsius), falling at night to the low 50s (10s Celsius). Winter temperatures are in the 30s Fahrenheit (below 0 Celsius) and 40s (10s Celsius) during the day. In Budapest, temperatures can reach 80°F (25°C) in August and dip to 30°F (0°C) in January. Winter is damp and chilly, spring is mild, and May and June are usually wet. The best weather is in the late summer through October. In Prague and Bohemia, summer months have an average temperature of 65°F (18°C) but are the rainiest, while January and February are usually sunny and clear, with temperatures around freezing.

FRANCE & GERMANY The weather in Paris is approximately the same as in the U.S. mid-Atlantic states, but like most of Europe, there's less extreme variation. In summer, the temperature rarely goes above the mid-70s (mid-20s Celsius). Summers are fair and can be hot along the Riviera. Winters tend to be mild, in the 40s (10s Celsius), though it's warmer along the Riviera. Germany's climate ranges from the moderate summers and chilly, damp winters in the north to the mild summers and very cold, sunny winters of the Alpine south.

NORTHERN EUROPE In the Netherlands, the weather is never extreme at any time of year. Summer temperatures average around 67°F (20°C) and the winter average is about 40°F (5°C). The climate is rainy, with the driest months from February to May. From mid-April to mid-May, the tulip fields burst into color. The climate of northern Germany is very similar. Belgium's climate is moderate, varying from 73°F (23°C) in July and August to 40°F (5°C) in December and January. It does rain a lot, but the weather is at its finest in July and August.

SCANDINAVIA & ICELAND Summer temperatures above the Arctic Circle average around the mid-50s (mid-10s Celsius), dropping to around 14°F (−10°C) during the dark winters. In the south, summer temperatures average around 70°F (22°C), dropping to the 20s (below 0° Celsius) in winter. Fiords and even the ocean are often warm enough for summer swimming, but rain is frequent. The sun shines 24 hours in midsummer above the Arctic Circle, where winter brings semipermanent twilight. Denmark's climate is relatively mild by comparison. It has moderate summer temperatures and winters that can be damp and foggy, with temperatures just above the mid-30s (just above 0° Celsius).

SOUTHERN EUROPE Summers are hot in Italy, Spain, and Greece, with temperatures around the high 80s (30s Celsius) or even higher in some parts of Spain. Along the Italian Riviera, summer and winter temperatures are mild, and except in the Alpine regions, Italian winter temperatures rarely drop below freezing. The area around Madrid is dry and arid, and summers in Spain are coolest along the Atlantic coast, with mild temperatures year-round on the Costa del Sol. Seaside Portugal is very rainy but has temperatures of 50°F to 75°F (10°C–25°C) year-round. In Greece there's sunshine all year, and winters are usually mild, with temperatures around 50°F to 54°F (10°C–12°C). Hot summer temperatures are often helped by cool breezes. The best seasons to visit Greece are from mid-April to June and mid-September to late October, when the wildflowers bloom and the tourists go home.

SWITZERLAND & THE ALPS The Alpine climate is shared by Bavaria in southern Germany and the Austrian Tyrol and Italian Dolomites—winters are cold and bright, and spring comes late, with snow flurries well into April. Summers are mild and sunny, though the Alpine regions can experience dramatic changes in weather any time of year.

Visit **www.weather.com** for weather forecasts throughout Europe.

WHERE TO GO

It's good to figure out in advance what kinds of places you want to hit in Europe. No matter what articles and guidebooks tell you, you still have to determine what's best for you. If you don't mind crowds, go for the big-draw cities, such as London and Paris and Rome, but if you want a quieter, less bustling look at the continent, try Zurich, Seville, Lisbon, Edinburgh, or Copenhagen. And if you really just want to party, look into Ibiza, Barcelona, Madrid, or Dublin. Sports aficionados might want to add Interlaken, the Greek Isles, or Reykjavík to their lists. For cities with a school offering language courses you can take, see p. 51.

What Kind of Traveler Am I?

When planning a trip to Europe, or anywhere for that matter, one of the most important questions to consider is, "What kind of traveler am I?" Take a moment and think about the statements below to pinpoint your traveling persona. The unfortunate reality is that you can not see it all, so focus your desires and hone in on what's most important to you.

THE TOURIST

- ◑ I feel as if I must see everything I possibly can while in Italy.
- ◑ I am less focused on historical details, and more interested in grabbing that photo and heading on to the next major attraction.
- ◑ I am likely to be the first one up in the morning, ready to grab my espresso and hit the Barri Gòtic or Christiania.
- ◑ I am likely to plan out my stay prior to arriving to maximize my travel route, excursions, and attractions.
- ◑ If I could have it my way, I would hit the beach on the Dalmatian Coast, ski the Italian Alps, shop in Paris, hike in the Swiss Alps, go museum-hopping in Berlin, grab a souvenir at Big Ben, and tour Edinburgh Castle before stopping in Dublin for a pint of ale.
- ◑ I would feel as though I was missing out if I were to have a 3-hour dinner. After resting my feet for a few minutes, I would be anxious to hit the road again and see and do more sights.
- ◑ If I could, I'd rent a car, but more so because it is a quick way to get to the next city on my itinerary.
- ◑ Where is the shopping center? I want to see all the stores!

THE STUDENT

- ◑ I am likely to study the history behind major attractions.
- ◑ When visiting an attraction, I ask questions and explore the architect/painter/sculptor behind it all.

- When in a museum, I rent the audio tour that explains what I'm seeing.
- I am likely to buy a book and read about what I saw upon returning home.
- I would prefer to see fewer attractions and hear more details.
- I am more likely to study a few paintings that grab me in a museum than skip over them all to get to the *Mona Lisa* or the statue of *David.*
- I prefer to see the city by way of guided tours.
- I am likely to wake up early and spend the first hour of my day with a leisurely cup of coffee while planning the day ahead.
- I must have a travel book with me so that I can read up on the attractions as I see them.
- I prefer to see fewer cities or regions and spend more time in each.
- I'd rent a car to travel to a nearby city, and enjoy the countryside on my way.
- I can always come back!

THE WANDERER

- I am less likely to read up on my city prior to arriving.
- I feel that a map is merely a tool to get you home at the end of the day.
- I am more focused on the aesthetics of a city and its treasures than its details and history.
- I can spend a day in a museum enjoying the art without having to memorize the artists' names.
- I look forward to capturing the feel of my destination as opposed to the best photos of its tourism icons.
- When choosing a restaurant, I walk around in the less touristy part of town until I see something that inspires me.
- I would enjoy spending an afternoon of my trip with a bottle of wine and a book in a Renaissance garden.
- I like to get out of the city center and explore the outer limits of the town.

- I would like to take a leisurely drive through the countryside with no particular agenda.
- If I wake up late because I was out the night before, I won't be anxious about what I might have done that morning.
- I am not likely to wait in line for 4 hours to see any attraction.
- I am more likely to shop if I stumble on an outdoor market than if I pass a high-end boutique.

THE PARTYER

- The first things I look for in a travel guide are the hot clubs and bars.
- When packing, I think mostly about what I will be wearing at night.
- I would rather stay out late and sleep in. I can see the attractions in the afternoon.
- Do they have a booze cruise?
- I plan on getting drunk on the plane ride over! I'm on vacation!
- I'll have more money for the cover at the club if I don't spend money on entrance to this museum.
- I really want to hook up with a local guy/girl!

THE ANTHROPOLOGIST

- I started learning a new language when I decided to go to Europe.
- I really want to make local friends and let them show me around.
- I don't want to go to bars that are going to be filled with Americans.
- What do the locals do on the weekend?
- How do I get away from the tourists?
- I would hate to be in a European city in August when everyone is on holiday.
- I would prefer a home-stay setup over a hotel of my own.
- I would rather eat in an ancient family-owned restaurant and have dinner for hours than swing by a hot spot in the middle of town.

THE FASHIONISTA

○ Where's Chanel, Vivienne Westwood, or Dries Van Noten?

○ Is there a gift shop here?

○ Is this on sale?

○ Will you come down 10€ on the price?

○ I would rather take the bus to the Versace outlets outside of Florence than read a book by the Arno—or hit Antwerp instead of touring historic Bruges.

Now that you've determined the type of traveler you are, it's important to think about *who* you will be traveling with. Choosing a travel buddy is a lot like finding a new roommate. Traveling with your closest friend always seems like the best option, but make sure he/she wants to do the same of types of things that you do and has the same type of travel style! It's also a good idea to think about your travel budget and match yourself with someone whose budget is comparable. Your time may be limited, so minimizing potential for debate and conflict is a great way to maximize your experience.

Passports & Visas

PASSPORTS

For up-to-date passport requirement info, visit the passport Web page of the U.S. State Department at **http://travel.state.gov**. This site will be your key to updated travel advisory information and passport requirements/application downloads.

If you don't have a passport yet, allow *plenty* of time before your trip to get one; passport processing normally takes 3 weeks but can take longer during busy periods (especially spring). And keep in mind that if you need a passport in a hurry, you'll pay a higher processing fee.

Before your trip, **make a few copies** of the critical front pages of your passport, with your photo, passport number, and issuing agency info. Keep one copy with you, in a separate place from the passport itself—for

example, the bottom of your suitcase—and leave a copy with a trusted friend or family member at home. If you lose your passport, you'll need to visit the nearest consulate or embassy of your native country as soon as possible for a replacement. **Replacement passports** will be issued much more quickly if you have a photocopy of the vital info passport page handy. Note that there are varying requirements to obtain a passport for travelers under 14 or depending on whether you are renewing your passport or applying for one for the first time.

When traveling between destinations (on planes, trains, boats, and so on), safeguard your passport in an inconspicuous, inaccessible place like the inside pocket of your handbag or daypack. When you've arrived at your destination, it's best to stow your passport in the hotel safe. Even if your individual room doesn't have a safe, the reception desk usually does. *Note:* Many hotels and hostels require a passport (or European Union ID card, for European citizens) with you whenever you're checking in.

When you clear customs and immigration at most European airports, your passport should be stamped with an entry date.

VISAS

From the date that's stamped in your passport, most foreign citizens are automatically given a 3-month "tourist visa." A visa is basically official permission to go into a country. It can be a piece of paper inserted into a passport, or it can look like a postage stamp, or just be the imprint from a stamp-pad stamp. Of the countries covered in this book, the tourist visa applies to Austria, Belgium, the Czech Republic, Denmark, France, Germany, Greece, Hungary, Iceland, Italy, the Netherlands, Portugal, Spain, and Sweden, and you can travel freely among them with the visa.

When you enter a country by train and stay in a private home or apartment, there will be no official record of your arrival in most countries. The start of your 3-month visa will be the date of your first check-in at a hotel or hostel.

WHAT IF I WANT TO STAY LONGER?

If you'd like to stay in one of the countries listed above for more than 3 months, and you want to do it legally, you'll need a proper visa first. You must do it from your home country and provide required documentation. Depending on whether you're extending your stay as a student, a temporary worker, or a tourist, the paperwork can vary from government-approved letters of employment to letters of enrollment in study programs (good for 3 months to 2 years) to showing that you have medical insurance, no criminal record, and no intentions to get a job while visiting. Contact the country's consulate for further information on obtaining a visa.

Customs Info
WHAT CAN I TAKE WITH ME?

When entering Europe, your luggage is subject to search and held to specific import customs regulations. As a general rule, you are allowed to bring all personal items, and means for entertainment such as music, sporting equipment, computer, and so on, as long as they will not be sold once in your chosen country. Also, strict guidelines define the quantity of alcohol, tobacco, coffee, and so on, that can be brought into each country duty-free. Please make sure to check with each country's Tourist Board for specific info. (See the appendix for a list of the tourism boards.)

WHAT CAN I BRING HOME WITH ME?

Returning U.S. citizens who have been away for at least 48 hours are allowed to bring back, once every 30 days, $800 worth of merchandise duty-free. You'll pay a flat rate of duty on the next $1,000 worth of purchases. Any dollar amount beyond that is subject to duties

at whatever rates apply. On mailed gifts, the duty-free limit is $200. Be sure to keep your receipts or purchases accessible to expedite the declaration process. *Note:* If you owe duty, you are required to pay on your arrival in the United States—either by cash or check, and, in some locations, a Visa or MasterCard.

To **avoid paying duty** on foreign-made personal items you owned before your trip, bring along a bill of sale, insurance policy, jeweler's appraisal, or receipts of purchase. Or you can register items that can be readily identified by a permanently affixed serial number or marking—think laptop computers, cameras, and iPods—with Customs before you leave. Take the items to the nearest Customs office or register them with Customs at the airport from which you're departing. You'll receive, at no cost, a Certificate of Registration, which allows duty-free entry for the life of the item.

With some exceptions, you cannot bring fresh fruits and vegetables into the United States. For specifics on what you can bring back, download the invaluable free pamphlet *Know Before You Go* online at **www.cbp. gov**. Or contact the **U.S. Customs & Border Protection (CBP;** 1300 Pennsylvania Ave., NW, Washington, DC 20229; ☎ **877/287-8667)** and request the pamphlet.

For a clear summary of **Canadian** rules, write for the booklet *I Declare,* issued by the **Canada Border Services Agency (☎ 800/461-9999** in Canada, or 204/983-3500; www.cbsa-asfc.gc.ca). Canada allows its citizens a C$750 exemption, and you're allowed to bring back duty-free one carton of cigarettes, one can of tobacco, 40 imperial ounces of liquor, and 50 cigars. In addition, you're allowed to mail gifts valued at less than C$60 to Canada each day, provided they're unsolicited and don't contain alcohol or tobacco (write on the package "Unsolicited gift, under $60 value"). All valuables should be declared on the Y-38 form before departure from Canada, including serial

What to Bring & What to Put It In!

Backpacker is a figurative term. You can be a young, carefree, budget-oriented traveler even if you carry a rolling suitcase. In most cases, a rolling bag is just as convenient to carry around as a backpack, if not more so, and it can be easier to keep organized. However, when it comes to climbing stairs and covering longer distances on foot, the classic backpack can't be beat.

To maximize the space in any bag, the key words are **roll** and **compartmentalize**. Roll your clothes as if you were rolling a poster. Rolling versus folding is more space-efficient, and stuff wrinkles less. To compartmentalize, you want to be able to more readily access those things that you need most, and others not so much. Put toiletries and such near the top or in their own compartment. Keep film, camera, and so on in a separate compartment that is easily accessible, and make sure that you have a separate compartment for dirty clothes. You can **create your own compartments**—whether you pack in a suitcase, a backpack, or a duffel—by using different-sized plastic bags.

And keep in mind, you don't have to look like a schlep to be a backpacker! Nice(r) clothes don't necessarily take up more room, so pack some wrinkle-free items so that you can look presentable when you hit the town. High-end, travel nylon is also good for misty weather.

Depending on your itinerary—you know how much actual hiking you want to do—you may not need your grungiest clothes. You'll most likely be traipsing around cities where the locals look effortlessly chic year-round.

Lastly, think about your footwear. Shoes can take up the most room in your bags. Many backpackers travel in their hiking boots so that they don't have to pack them. (When you choose a backpack, make sure that there are straps on the outside for larger items such as shoes, a fleece, a towel, and/or a blanket.) Regardless of whatever else you pack, you'll want that favorite, flattering pair of jeans; a pair of non-denim pants for rainy days; sneakers or other supportive walking shoes (comfortable but cool); comfy, non-skimpy sleepwear (for those shared hostel rooms); and a pair of rubber flip-flops for the shared bathrooms and showers you'll encounter at hostels and other budget hotels.

Keep some room inside of your bag free for anything fragile that you might need to protect. And, you may want to bring a few things home; it doesn't hurt to leave space in your bag (or bring an extra, empty bag) for the goodies.

numbers of valuables you already own, such as expensive foreign cameras. **Note:** The C$750 exemption can only be used once a year and only after an absence of 7 days.

Money (Makes the World Go Round)

Less than a decade ago, you might have arrived in Europe, changed money, and brought back to the hotel enough paper lira to fill a bathtub—almost. And you would have found francs in Belgium, gulden in the Netherlands, escudos in Portugal, and on down the list. As of 2002, however, the euro has taken over much of Europe. The boring euro (€) is standard currency in all the European Economic Community countries except for Britain, Denmark, and Sweden. (The Czech Republic and Hungary are recent members, and Croatia, Switzerland, and Turkey are not part of the E.U.) For more information, visit **http://europa.eu.int/euro/entry.html**.

Kunas, Korunas, Krones & Other Currency

Most countries in this book use the euro, but we've provided info on the holdout countries below.

Note that Europe uses commas instead of periods when denoting price denominations, so £3.50 will be written £3,50. Bear in mind, too, that exchange rates fluctuate daily so the below conversions aren't guaranteed.

- **British pounds sterling:** England and Scotland both use pounds sterling. At press time, £1 = $1.85.
- **Croatian kuna:** $1 = approximately 6kn (or 1kn = approximately 17¢). Many Croatian establishments express prices in both euros and kunas.
- **Czech koruna:** 80¢ = 30Kč.
- **Danish krone:** $1 = 6DKK.
- **Hungarian forint:** $1 = 219 FT.
- **Icelandic krona:** $1 = 73ISK.
- **Swedish krone:** $1 = 8SEK.
- **Turkish new lira:** $1 = about 1.60TRY.

There are eight euro coins in circulation, ranging from 1-cent pieces to 2€ coins, as well as seven different euro bills from 5€ to 500€. Every country in the European Economic Community mints its own euro coins (which are standardized in color and shape, but differentiated by images of national landmarks or historical figures on the reverse), so you might come across a French or German 2€ coin here and there, but for the most part, euro coins tend to stay in their country of origin. All euro coins, regardless of the country where they were minted, are good throughout the E.E.C. At this writing, US$1 is approximately .82€; and 1€ is $1.22. This will fluctuate of course, so make sure to check the exchange rates at **www.oanda.com/convert/classic** to see how your money will hold up during your stay. Europe is not exactly cheap right now, so make sure that you budget accordingly. It is all too easy to think that US$1 is *more or less* equal to 1€ and get yourself into trouble. Those decimals make a big difference.

Cash

Except at high-end hotels, fancier restaurants, and mass retailers, cash is still the preferred method of payment in many European destinations, especially smaller towns and cheaper places. Some smaller hotels, restaurants, and boutiques will accept credit cards (or debit cards with the Visa or MasterCard symbol), and they're used to dealing with tourists who only have plastic, but they'll love you forever if you can flash some cash. They may even offer a modest discount for cash payment, too. However, carrying mass quantities of cash is neither smart nor practical. So use your card where you can—just be prepared for a little attitude from time to time (as well as the all-too-common "our credit card machine is out of order" line).

That said, you will definitely need to have cash on hand for the following: local public transportation (including buses and taxis); museum and monument admissions; on-the-go snacks and drinks; and other small incidentals like postcards and postage. (*FYI:* I always got cash from ATMs that spit out euros, and I made it a point to break down the 50€ and 100€ notes into smaller bills as soon as possible. Museum admissions and restaurant checks are good for this.) The quickest way to piss off a small-business cashier is to present a 50€ bill when paying for a 2€ coffee.

It's more expensive to purchase foreign currency in your own country than to do so once you've reached your destination. But it's a good idea to arrive in Europe with a little bit of the local currency—at least enough to get you from the airport to your hotel. While traveling, either withdraw local currency from an ATM (see below) or convert your cash or traveler's checks at a bank whenever possible. Banks invariably give better rates than tourist offices, hotels, travel agencies, or exchange booths.

ATMs

The easiest and best way to get cash when you're in Europe is from a local ATM. You can ask at the tourist info offices what ATMs are called locally. Smaller, more rural towns may not have ATMs, so if you're going to the Dalmatian Coast and the back roads of Greece, you might want to pick up some cash before you go. Most bank cards can be used to withdraw cash as long as you have a compatible PIN (some ATMS require a four-digit PIN).

Because your bank will likely impose a fee of $5 or more every time you withdraw from an international ATM (and the bank from which you withdraw cash may charge its own fee), be strategic about how much you withdraw and how often. (The minimum withdrawal is usually 50€; the maximum is usually 300€.) Start by withdrawing, say, 200€ or 250€ at the airport or train station,

From Cheap to Splurge: From Low-Rent to Top-Euro

Throughout the book we divide the hostels/hotels and restaurants by price range, from "Hostels" to "Cheap" to "Doable" to "Splurge."

You know what your budget is, and what's important for you to experience on your trip, so you can plan accordingly.

And even if most of your nights will be spent in hostels or budget hotels, and your meals eating pizza and gyros, we also think you should budget for and treat yourself to something deluxe that you *know* you will enjoy, whether it's a meal at a world-class restaurant, or a night in a *grande dame* hotel. A constant stream of second-class travel, shared bathrooms, and meals consumed standing up can wear you out.

Here is a very general price range for each category (and prices can, of course, vary widely depending upon what city or town you are in, the season, and even the day of the week):

Accommodations
→ Hostel: Dorm-style, 20€–25€; single/double/triple, 30€–75€.
→ Cheap: Single 65€–100€; double 75€–150€; triple/quad 100€–300€.
→ Doable: Single 75€–120€; double 100€–200€; triple/quad/suite 150€–250€.
→ Splurge: Single 150€–220€; double 200€–350€; triple/quad/suite 300€–1,000€ and (way) up.

Dining
The ranges below do not include the purchase of wine.
→ Cheap: 5€–12€.
→ Doable: Lunch 7€–15€; dinner 10€–25€.
→ Splurge: Lunch 10€–25€; dinner 25€–50€ and up.

and see how much of that you're spending on average per day. If you're using a credit or debit card to pay for your bigger-ticket expenses like hotel bills and restaurant meals, you may well find that you only need to make two or three trips to the ATM (spending $15–$25 in fees) over the course of a 10-day trip. Some cities, such as Stockholm, will bleed you more quickly and others, such as those along the Dalmatian Coast, will let you coast a while longer.

Credit Cards

Credit cards are another safe way to carry money. They also provide a convenient record of all your expenses, and they generally offer relatively good exchange rates. You can also withdraw cash advances from your credit cards at banks or ATMs, provided you know your PIN. It usually takes 5 to 7 business days, though some banks will provide the number over the phone if you tell them your mother's maiden name or the last four digits of your Social Security number.

MasterCard, Visa, and American Express cards are commonly accepted throughout Europe, and as in the U.S., most storefronts will post the logos of the cards they accept in the windows. Do note, however, that small businesses, even in big cities, far prefer cash payment. Keep in mind that many banks now assess a 1% to 3% "transaction fee" on all charges you incur abroad (whether you're using the local currency or U.S. dollars). But credit cards still may be the smart way to go when you factor in things like exorbitant ATM fees and the higher exchange rates and service fees you'll pay with traveler's checks.

Traveler's Checks

Back before there were international ATMs and global bank networks—when Pan Am was still in business—you'd go to your bank or American Express office before a trip and buy traveler's checks and bring them with you on vacation. You could use them to pay for things

like train travel and hotel bills, or you could trade them in for cash at the local bank or Amex office in your destination. Because the traveler's checks were numbered and protected, even if you lost them or they were stolen, your money would be protected.

Well guess what? Good old traveler's checks are still out there! They're less widely accepted at hotels and other businesses, but the fundamental idea behind traveler's checks is still a good one: You can cash them as you go along, and your money is protected in case of loss or theft of the checks. And, given the fees you'll pay for ATM use at banks other than your own, this old-fashioned method of carrying money on the road isn't such a crazy idea.

You can get traveler's checks at almost any bank. **American Express** offers denominations of $20, $50, $100, $500, and (for cardholders only) $1,000. You'll pay a service charge ranging from 1% to 4%. You can also order American Express traveler's checks over the phone by calling ☎ 800/221-7282; Amex gold and platinum cardholders who use this number are exempt from the 1% fee.

Visa offers traveler's checks at Citibank locations nationwide, as well as at several other banks. The service charge ranges from between 1.5% and 2%; checks come in denominations of $20, $50, $100, $500, and $1,000. Call ☎ 800/732-1322 for information. **AAA** members can obtain Visa checks for a $9.95 fee (for checks up to $1,500) at most AAA offices or by calling ☎ 866/339-3378. **MasterCard** also offers traveler's checks. Call ☎ 800/223-9920 for a location near you.

Foreign currency traveler's checks might be useful when traveling to some countries in Europe, as they're accepted at locations where dollar checks may not be, such as bed-and-breakfasts, and they minimize the currency conversions you'll have to perform while you're on the go. American Express, Thomas Cook (☎ 800/223-7373; www.thomascook. com), Visa, and MasterCard offer foreign

Before You Leave: The Checklist!

Here are a few things you might want to do before you walk out the door to ensure that you get the most efficient and drama-free trip to Europe.

→ Write down or type up a copy of all the **embassy and consulate phone numbers** for each country you're visiting. There's a list of addresses/phone numbers of the consulates in the "Nuts & Bolts" section in each chapter, or you can visit www.usembassy.it/acs.

→ Check online to see if you can book any museum, theater, or special travel in advance. Almost all tourist attractions now have websites. It can't hurt to check! From the Louvre to London's West End and beyond.

→ Check the weather on www.weather.com. Pack accordingly.

→ Make sure all of your favorite hot spots and tourist destinations are open. Is *David* being restored? Is Christiania still a free state? Is Akrotiri (on Santorini) still covered in scaffolding? Is Mount Vesuvius planning on erupting any time soon? You never know!

→ Check the current exchange rate at www.oanda.com/convert/classic.

→ Call your bank. Find out your daily ATM withdrawal limit. Do you have your credit card PIN? If you have a five- or six-digit PIN, you might need to get a four-digit number from your bank.

→ Notify your bank and/or credit card company that you will be traveling overseas to avoid automatic account freezes for suspicious activity.

→ **This one is essential.** Make sure you have the credit card you used to purchase your ticket. And some rental car and other companies do not accept debit cards, so make sure that you have an actual credit card, if it's at all possible.

→ Record your traveler's checks numbers and store the documentation separately from the checks.

→ Pack your camera, an extra set of batteries, and enough film/memory.

→ Pack (or get) an international power converter to charge your iPod, computer, and other gadgets.

→ Assess yourself. Do you have a safe, accessible place to store money?

→ Bring any ID cards that could entitle you to discounts, such as student ID cards, ISIC Cards, and so on.

→ Bring emergency drug prescriptions and extra glasses and/or contact lenses.

→ Leave a copy of your itinerary with someone at home, preferably not the ex who just got a shredder.

→ If using a mobile phone from the U.S., check to make sure you can make/receive calls to/from whichever countries you'll be visiting. Ask your carrier about international long distance rates.

THE BASICS

currency traveler's checks. You'll pay the rate of exchange at the time of your purchase, and most companies charge a transaction fee per order (and a shipping fee if you order online).

Getting In & Out

Staying There: Tips on Accommodations

Read this section carefully: Knowing the lay of the accommodations land in Europe (and being a bit anal about it) will be one of the most important factors in making your trip a stress-free success. Some key points to keep in mind:

○ **It pays to book early.** We can't stress this enough. Europe is a popular tourist destination, and rooms book up year-round in places like Italy, Paris, and London. The good, affordable beds go fast. If you know you'll be leaving in 3 months, get on the Internet *now* and start sending e-mails to prospective hotels and

hostels. You can always cancel, penalty-free (with enough notice; read the fine print), if your plans change.

○ **Reconfirm** all bookings several days before you arrive, and **carry documentation** (that is, a printout of the e-mail the hotel sent you) to prove your reservation exists.

○ **What cheap sleeps?** In the bigger cities, the northern cities, and the most touristy cities—even those that we categorize as "cheap" in this book (such as 80€ for a no-frills double room with shared bathroom down the hall)—might strike you as pricey if you're used to what similar lodging costs in Colorado or Cambodia.

Playing the Hostel Game

With prices starting at 18€ per night, dorm beds in hostel-style accommodations are the cheapest way to go in top tourist destinations (and often in smaller towns as well).

Hostel booking policies vary dramatically. Some allow reservations and you can pay by credit card; others don't accept reservations and you have to pay cash. Many hostels do not accept reservations more than 12 or 24 hours before your planned check-in time. (This is not because they're deliberately being pains in the ass—it's because they don't know how many beds they'll have free until their current guests inform them that they're moving out.) The best way to handle this is to call the hostel first from home (if you can) and then again a few days before you're thinking of staying there, and get a clear understanding of how their reservations system works. Often, they'll ask you to call back at 9pm the night before your arrival to make a reservation, and to arrive by 3pm the next day to pay for your bed. Play by their rules, and everybody wins.

If you're a member of **Hostelling International** (www.hihostels.com), you can often book days or even weeks in advance, but many private hostels don't offer the same service. Also, hostels often take only cash (even if they accept credit cards for reservations).

Once there, you'll notice that hostels also vary in what services they offer. Lockouts, when the whole place is closed during the day, used to be the norm. That's not the case now, but you should always ask. Most hostels also have laundry facilities (but not detergent), lockers (but not locks), kitchens (but not food), beds (but no bedding)—you get the picture. You might also be able to rent for a low fee many of the things that they don't officially have. Ask, ask, and ask again, if you have any questions. It's best not to be surprised.

Know what to expect and plan accordingly, and you won't be blindsided by your cumulative hotel expenses, which may be anywhere from 25% to 50% of your daily budget.

○ **Location, location, location.** We're all for saving money, but we're also for living the European dream, which often means forking over a little extra cash for a room in a great location. It doesn't have to be fancy, but life's too short to sleep by the train station when you could wake up next to the Pantheon. So even if you're traveling on a tight budget, try to plan for at least one "splurge."

○ **Skip the breakfast club.** Many hotels offer some kind of small, often buffet breakfast, at no extra charge, to their guests. This is not necessarily a good thing, as most breakfast rooms are depressing salons of tourists talking in too-soft voices and noshing on wooden croissants. Instead, get your day going at a local coffee bar or cafe. And sit—or sometimes stand—next to bright-eyed locals as you sip.

○ **Consider short-term apartment rentals.** As more and more center-city dwellers move into the more livable and affordable suburbs, there are more vacant apartments in the heart of some cities than ever before. Some of these apartments are rented out as (furnished) short-term tourist accommodations. These properties, which were probably someone's family home for generations, can be booked through tourism and accommodations agencies easily found online. Simple Internet searches (for example, Google the city and "apartments") will yield hundreds of results, with pictures and prices usually clearly posted.

Booking Your Hotel Online

Shopping online for hotels is generally done by booking through the hotel's own website or through an independent booking agency (or a fare-service agency like Priceline; see below). These Internet hotel agencies have multiplied in mind-boggling numbers, competing for the business of millions of consumers surfing for accommodations around the world. This competitiveness can be a boon for those who have the patience and time to shop and compare the online sites for good deals—but shop you must, for prices can vary considerably. And keep in mind that hotels at the top of a site's listing may be there for no other reason than that they paid money to get the placement. In our experience, most hotels offered in package deals to Europe are soulless chain-style monstrosities far removed from the city center.

The most popular online travel agencies are **Travelocity** (www.travelocity.com or www.travelocity.co.uk), **Expedia** (www.expedia.com, www.expedia.co.uk, or www.expedia.ca), and **Orbitz** (www.orbitz.com).

In addition, most airlines now offer online-only fares that even their phone agents know nothing about. For the websites of airlines that fly to and from your destination, see the appendix.

Other reliable online booking agencies include **Hotels.com** and **Quikbook.com.** An excellent free program, **TravelAxe** (www.travelaxe.net), can help you search multiple hotel sites at once—even ones you may never have heard of—and conveniently lists the total price of the room, including the taxes and service charges. Another booking site, **Travelweb** (www.travelweb.com), is partly owned by the hotels it represents (including the Hilton, Hyatt, and Starwood chains) and is plugged directly into the hotels' reservations systems—unlike independent online agencies, who have to fax or e-mail reservation requests to the hotel, a good portion of which get misplaced in the shuffle. More than once, travelers have arrived at the hotel, only to be told that they have no reservation. To be fair, many of the major sites are improving in service and ease of use, and Expedia will soon be able to plug

FYI: Stars

When booking a hotel through an online agency, keep in mind that their star ratings are subjective, and that comments in the feedback section are often listed by the hotels themselves. Although a picture is worth 1,000 words, it can also be very deceiving. A bigger issue is that often you don't get a sense of how well located a hotel is from these websites because everyone advertises that their hotel is "steps from the Prague castle" or "minutes from the Prado." But how many minutes is it?

Also, in some countries, star ratings do have specific criteria (and not always what you'd expect). So, in Scotland, a dumpy, dirty B&B might get a better star rating than an impeccable neighbor because one has a TV and full breakfast in the morning, while the other opts not to have media or a full spread.

directly into the reservations systems of many hotel chains—none of which can be bad news for consumers. In the meantime, you should definitely get a confirmation number and bring along a printout of any online booking transaction.

See p. 27 for website recommendations for apartment shares.

SAVING MONEY WHEN YOU'RE THERE

○ Before you start dialing away on the in-room phone, find out from hotel staff how much they charge per call. Some hotels charge astronomical rates, while other, more honest hotels only charge you what the phone company charges them—that is, a humane .10€–.20€ for a local call. In the former case, use prepaid phone cards, pay phones, or your own cellphone instead of dialing direct from hotel phones.

○ If your hotel offers Internet access (in-room broadband or Wi-Fi, or a public terminal in a common area), find out if there's a charge for using it. Some hotels don't disclose that they charge 10€ an hour for online access; so you stay logged on for hours, and then they slap you with an outrageous bill upon checkout.

○ In summer, if your hotel has air-conditioning, be sure to find out upfront if there's an additional charge for using it. (At smaller, budget hotels, it's usually something like 10€–15€ per day.)

○ Stock the minibar yourself. If, like us, you can't resist the siren song of the minibar, just remember that hotels charge through the nose for water, potato chips, and those little bottles of Jack Daniels. If you want to keep food and drink in the room, buy your own snacks and drinks and store them in the minibar. (But do it on the sly: Most hotels don't condone this behavior.)

○ Always ask about local taxes and service charges, which can increase the cost of a room by 15% or more. Some hotels include the tax in the room charge, while others (often the larger, more expensive hotels) tack taxes/charges on top of the already exorbitant room rate, so check it out before you check in.

○ If a hotel insists upon tacking on any surprise charges that weren't mentioned at check-in or prominently posted in the room, or a "resort fee" for amenities you didn't use, you can often make a case for getting them removed. You can always take any accommodations-related complaints to the local tourism board—mention that to an ornery hotel staffer, and they're sure to back down.

TIPS ON DINING

○ Order the house wine by the half-bottle or bottle. It is usually the most inexpensive wine on the menu, but not at the expense of taste.

Questions to Ask about Your Accommodations

→ Will I be sharing a room with someone (as with most hostels)? How many people?

→ Will I be sharing a bathroom? Where is the bathroom?

→ Are there safes or lockers for my personal valuables?

→ Is there a curfew (a few hostels or small hotels still have lock-in or lockout)?

→ Is there air-conditioning or ceiling fans? (June–Aug, this is key.)

→ Does the hotel serve breakfast, and if so, is there an extra charge?

→ Are there airport transfers to and from my hotel?

→ How far is the hotel from the train station? If it's not walking distance, how will I get there?

→ What is check-in/checkout time? Is there an hour after which they'll cancel my reservation if I haven't arrived yet?

→ Is there Internet access—either a public terminal in the lobby or Wi-Fi throughout the property?

Note: If you aren't happy with your room when you arrive, politely ask for another one. Most lodgings will be willing to accommodate you if they have something else available.

○ Buy a bottle of wine and take it with you! Yes, open containers are permitted on the street in some countries. Sitting on a bench with a pal and a bottle of wine can be a good way to pass hours of downtime. Just remember to be respectful, and if it's not the custom of the city, just wait until you get home.

○ Most cities in this book have restaurants where you can get good food cheap. You really don't have to turn to global fast food (unless you want to, of course).

○ Note that some restaurants, especially those in Italy, charge a cover charge of anywhere from .50€ to 10€ for the mere privilege of sitting at a table. Some places also charge extra for bread, so ask if you're unsure.

Also see "The Best Cheap Eats" in chapter 1 for specific dining recommendations.

Health & Safety

Staying Well

Most illnesses experienced by travelers are caused by food and water that your digestive system isn't accustomed to—loosely translated as: Bring diarrhea medicine! Even in cities with extremely high standards of culinary hygiene and where the tap water is perfectly safe to drink, there are always going to be those miniscule microbes in the local tomatoes, or whatever, that can throw off your foreign gastrointestinal system for a few hours. In all likelihood, if you experience any, uh, *discomfort,* it will probably be mild and pass in less than 24 hours.

In most of Europe, the tap water is generally safe to drink—except on trains and wherever it's marked as nondrinking (or nonpotable) water—the milk is pasteurized, and health services are good.

Although there are no required vaccinations when entering Europe, it is important that you are up-to-date with all immunizations as defined by the Advisory Committee on Immunization Practice (ACIP). Major

THE BASICS

Your Portable Medicine Cabinet

The following is a list of medications and health aids to bring with you when traveling to Europe, as suggested by the CDC:

→ Sunblock (as well as sunglasses and a wide-brimmed hat) during summer months.

→ Enough prescription medication to last your entire trip and a copy of your prescription(s)—Italian pharmacists can fill almost all foreign prescriptions, on the spot, and at a very low cost.

→ Anti-diarrhea medication.

→ Stomach-calming medication like Pepto-Bismol or Gaviscon.

→ Insect repellent containing DEET during the summer.

→ A pain reliever like aspirin, acetaminophen, or ibuprofen.

→ Antifungal or antibacterial cream or ointment.

With the exception of high-SPF waterproof sunblock, all of the above are readily available at many overseas supermarkets and pharmacies, but do you really want to be in the position of having to track down some Imodium AD when you're about to hike a glacier on the Jungfraujoch? Pack a small medicine kit with some basics, and you'll always be prepared.

vaccinations include tetanus, Hepatitis B, MMR, and chickenpox if necessary. It is also always a good idea to see your doctor 4 to 6 weeks prior to your departure for a regular checkup and to make sure that you have enough prescription medications to last your entire stay.

For more information, contact the **International Association for Medical Assistance to Travelers (IAMAT;** ☎ 716/754-4883, or 416/652-0137 in Canada; www.iamat.org) for tips on travel and health concerns in the countries you're visiting, and for lists of local, English-speaking doctors. The United States **Centers for Disease Control and Prevention** (☎ 800/311-3435; www.cdc.gov/travel) provides up-to-date information on health hazards by region or country and offers tips on food safety. The website **www.tripprep.com**, sponsored by a consortium of travel medicine practitioners, may also offer helpful advice on traveling abroad. You can find listings of reliable clinics overseas at the **International Society of Travel Medicine** (www.istm.org).

If you suffer from a chronic illness, consult your doctor before your departure. For conditions like epilepsy, diabetes, or heart problems, wear a **MedicAlert identification tag**

FYI: Just Say "No"

Drug laws are strictly enforced in most parts of Europe, and being a foreigner does little to exempt you from abiding by those laws. Possession of an illegal substance, regardless of quantity, is a criminal offense in some countries and punishable by anything from deportation to up to 20 years in jail! Be smart and do not attempt a drug purchase or transaction. The consequences are hardly worth it.

There are a few exceptions to the above, very few, and even in a city like Amsterdam, using drugs is officially illegal. Check out the "Culture 101 Tips" section in each chapter or relevant boxes throughout the book for specific drug and drinking info.

(☎ 888/633-4298; www.medicalert.org), which will alert doctors to your condition and give them access to your records through MedicAlert's 24-hour hot line.

Pack **prescription medications** in your carry-on luggage, and carry prescription medications in their original containers, with pharmacy labels—otherwise they may not make it through airport security. Also carry copies of your prescriptions in case you lose your pills or run out. Know the generic name of prescription medicines, just in case a local pharmacist is unfamiliar with the brand name. It's also a good idea to pack an extra pair or two of **contact lenses** or **prescription glasses.**

What If I Get Sick?

Any foreign consulate can provide a list of area doctors who speak English. If you get sick, consider asking your hotel concierge to recommend a local doctor—even his or her own. Emergency care at many European hospitals is free to everyone, regardless of insurance status, but you will be charged for other office visits and examinations. That said, it is always good to make sure that you have a U.S. or other home country health-insurance policy and that you have checked with the company to see how it may or may not cover medical attention abroad. Most health plans (including Medicare and Medicaid) do *not* provide coverage, and the ones that do often require you to pay for services upfront and reimburse you only after you return home. As a safety net, you may want to buy travel medical insurance, particularly if you're traveling to a remote or high-risk area where emergency evacuation is a possible scenario. If you require additional medical insurance, try **MEDEX Assistance** (☎ 410/453-6300; www.medexassist.com) or **Travel Assistance International** (☎ 800/821-2828; www. travelassistance.com; for general information on services, call the company's Worldwide Assistance Services, Inc., at ☎ 800/777-8710).

THE BASICS

How to Say Condom (& Some Other Useful Stuff) in Four Languages

Hello
→ Bonjour (French)
→ Hallo *or* Guten Tag (German)
→ Ciao (Italian)
→ Hola (Spanish)

Goodbye
→ Au revoir (French)
→ Auf Wiedersehen (German)
→ Arrivederci (Italian)
→ Adiós (Spanish)

Thank You
→ Merci (French)
→ Danke (German)
→ Grazie (Italian)
→ Gracias (Spanish)

Please
→ S'il vous plaît (French)
→ Bitte (German)
→ Per favore (Italian)
→ Por favor (Spanish)

Do you speak English?
→ Parlez-vous anglais? (French)
→ Sprechen Sie Englisch? (German)
→ Parla Ingelse? (Italian)
→ ¿Habla inglés? (Spanish)

Condom
→ Préservatif (French)
→ Kondom (German)
→ Condom (Italian)
→ Preservativo (Spanish)

Safety Tips

→ Never give out your credit card information unless you're using it to pay for something.

→ Solo travelers, beware of those who are very eager to befriend you in a crowded tourist area. Just as in the U.S., if someone seems abnormally nice or generous, you should smell a rat.

→ Always stay by your drink. It's rare, but we've heard a few stories about someone being slipped a roofie or other substance in their drink and having their stuff stolen (or worse). Stay aware.

→ Watch how much you drink. Being drunk makes you an even easier target.

→ Stay in well-lit, populated areas at night. You don't want to find yourself alone and far off the beaten path.

→ Keep your money, any papers, and passport in a secure location, preferably on your body and not in a secondary bag or backpack.

→ Always keep copies of your passport, visa, and so on in a location other than that of the originals.

→ Use common sense.

→ Most important, maintain respect for the country and its moral and legal statutes. Tourists may have reputations as partyers, but that does not allow you carte blanche to behave like animalistic idiots, nor does it exempt you from being held accountable for your actions under a law that may be different from your own.

Playing Safely

With so many young, good-looking natives (and fellow backpackers) on the loose, hooking up is as time-honored a tradition on European vacations as seeing the masterpieces of the Renaissance. If you're going to partake, just remember that they have sperm and STDs all over the E.U., too. And that Dutch hottie from the hostel in Budapest might be a walking gonorrhea case. *Always* use a latex condom (or polyurethane, if you're allergic) when engaging in sexual activity abroad (or anywhere for that matter).

Condoms that are not latex are less effective against disease transmission and pregnancy and should be avoided. If you are unsure as to what the condom is made of or it is not clearly marked, it's not worth the risk. Latex condoms are widely available in Europe at supermarket checkout lines or any pharmacy.

As with any destination, you should always avoid shared needles for tattoos, piercings, or injections of any kind. Always make sure that you watch the establishment open a fresh needle—again, it's not worth the risk.

Personal Safety

On the whole, Europe is relatively safe, when you compare it to other hot spots around the world. The main thing you need to watch out for is petty theft—unfortunately, **pickpockets** and **bag-snatchers** are a very real problem in the bigger cities, especially Naples, Paris, and Rome. The streets and public transportation are crawling with sleight-handed miscreants, but locals rarely get pickpocketed. How is this? The city's petty thieves prey on you, the unwitting *gringo*, who is naïve enough to leave your wallet in your jeans pocket.

Also, be alert to people stealing your bag while you dine in a crowded restaurant or have another drink at the bar. Anyone eating or drinking alfresco is a target for thieves on the prowl, so be sure to keep your bags and other valuables (cameras and such) well away from the side of the table that faces the street. Truly ballsy thieves have been known to go inside a crowded, casual restaurant (like a lively pizzeria) and take handbags that have been hung on the backs of dining chairs.

As with any part of the world, you should also keep an eye out for other scams and use common sense to avoid any situations that could sacrifice your safety.

Getting Wired

Whether or not you bring your own computer, you'll have many opportunities to check your e-mail, update your travel blog, tweak your MySpace page, or whatever while in Europe. If you feel like toting your Power-Book along, you'll find Wi-Fi coverage in a lot of places, and broadband cable connections in some hotels, but chances are your backpack is stuffed enough without having to squeeze in your laptop (and worry about its theft). If you don't bring your own computer, you'll still find plenty of Internet points, Internet cafes, and kiosks.

If you don't already have one, you may want to open a free, Web-based e-mail account with Yahoo, Hotmail, or Gmail, which you can access from any computer in the world with an Internet connection. If you already have an AOL account, you can log on to www.aol.com and check your AOL mail from there.

Without Your Own Computer

Many hostels and some budget hotels have at least one Internet terminal set up for guests' use. Some places offer this service for free; others charge up to 5€ an hour or even more. (Whatever you do, avoid logging on at any large hotel's business center—their rates for Internet use are ridiculously high, and usually not very well posted.)

If your hotel does not have a public computer, you'll need to track down an Internet cafe. See the "Nuts & Bolts" section in the specific chapters for local info.

Most major airports now have Internet kiosks scattered throughout their terminals. These kiosks, which you'll also see in hotel lobbies and tourist information offices around the world, give you basic Web access for a per-minute fee that's usually higher than regular Internet cafe prices. The kiosks' clunkiness and high price means you should avoid them whenever possible.

With Your Own Computer

If you're going to haul along your laptop, make sure that at least some of the places you'll be staying offer in-room broadband

What Time Is It, Anyway?

Based on U.S. Eastern Standard Time, Britain, Ireland, and Portugal are 5 hours ahead of New York City; Greece is 7 hours ahead of New York. The rest of the countries in this book are 6 hours ahead of New York. For instance, when it's noon in New York, it's 5pm in London and Lisbon; 6pm in Paris, Copenhagen, and Amsterdam; and 7pm in Athens. The European countries now observe daylight saving time. The time change doesn't usually occur on the same day or during the same month as in the U.S.

If you plan to travel to Ireland or continental Europe from Britain, keep in mind that the time will be the same in Ireland and Portugal, 2 hours later in Greece, and 1 hour later in the other countries in this guide.

THE BASICS

Number, Please: Calling Europe

To make a phone call **from the United States to Europe,** dial the international access code **(011),** then the **country code** for the country you're calling, then the **city code** for the city you're calling, and then the regular phone number. For an operator-assisted call, dial **01,** then the country code, then the city code, and then the regular phone number; an operator will then come on the line.

Note: The dial tone for Europe is different than the standard American dial tone—you'll hear long beeps, with a series of even longer pauses in between.

The following are the codes for the countries and major cities in this guide. These are the codes you use to call from overseas or from another European country.

European phone systems are undergoing a prolonged change. **Italy, France, Spain, Monaco, Copenhagen, and now Portugal no longer use separate city codes.** The code is now built into all phone numbers, and you must always dial the initial 0 or 9 (which was previously—and still is in most other countries— added before a city code only when dialing from another city within the country). Also, be aware of these two recent changes: The city codes for London (171 and 181) have been replaced by a new single code (20), which is then followed by an eight-digit number beginning with either 7 or 8; and the city code for Lisbon has changed from 1 to 21.

Austria	3	**Czech Republic**	420
Salzburg	62	Prague	2
Vienna	1	**England**	44
Belgium	32	London	20
Antwerp	03	**Germany**	49
Brussels	2	Berlin	30
Croatia	385	Munich	89
Dubrovnik	020	**Greece**	30
Dalmatian Coast	021	Athens	1

connections or Wi-Fi coverage on the property. Hotels that offer Wi-Fi often have some convoluted password-protected network that may be down half the time; in fact, hotels that offer the somewhat more old-fashioned broadband/Ethernet cable connection are often more reliable. If you have a wireless card, just open your laptop and see what happens. With so many unprotected wireless networks in such close proximity, you'll often be able to get online automatically.

Although they're not nearly as widespread as in the U.S., there are more and more Wi-Fi "hot spots" cropping up at cafes and bars throughout Europe. In 2005, the city of Rome, for example, launched free Wi-Fi access in over 20 public parks and piazzas throughout the city. Logging on in one of these hot spots requires a simple, one-time registration.

The website **Wi-Fi411.com** has a remarkably comprehensive list of all the wireless Internet networks throughout the world: Select your desired city, and then select "All Networks" and "All Locations," and you'll get dozens of results.

Some airports also have wireless hot spots where access costs $6.95 per day—of course, you only end up using it for an hour, so it ends up being a bit of a rip-off.

Hungary	36	Spain	34
Budapest	1	Barcelona	93
Iceland	354	Ibiza	97
Ireland	353	Madrid	91
Dublin	1	Seville	95
Monaco	377	Sweden	46
Netherlands	31	Stockholm	8
Amsterdam	20	Switzerland	41
Scotland	44	Zurich	01
Edinburgh	131		
Glasgow	141		

The easiest and cheapest way to call home from abroad is with a calling card. On the road, you just dial a local access code (almost always free) and then punch in the number you're calling as well as the calling-card number. If you're in a non–touch-tone country, just wait for an English-speaking operator to put your call through. The "Telephone" entry in the "Nuts & Bolts" section of each chapter gives the AT&T, MCI, and Sprint access codes for that country (your calling card will probably come with a wallet-size list of local access numbers). You can also call any one of those companies' numbers to make a collect call; just dial it and wait for the operator.

When it comes to dialing direct, calling from the United States to Europe is much cheaper than the other way around, so whenever possible, have friends and family call you at your hotel rather than you calling them. To dial direct back to the **United States** and **Canada** from Europe, the international access code is often, but not always, 00; the country code is **1**, and then you punch in the area code and number. For **Australia** and **New Zealand**, the access code is also 00; the country codes are 61 and 64, respectively.

THE BASICS

Mobile Phones

Yes, you can totally get through your trip without having a cellphone, but let's face it— it's incredibly handy to have at least one between you and your traveling companions for when you need to make hotel reservations, coordinate travel plans with other people, and, of course, for when you meet someone cute and need to exchange numbers!

Most of the world, it seems, is on **GSM** (Global System for Mobiles), a big, seamless network that makes for easy cross-border cellphone use throughout Europe and dozens of other countries worldwide. In the U.S., T-Mobile, AT&T Wireless, and Cingular use

this quasi-universal system; in Canada, Microcell and some Rogers customers are GSM, and all Europeans and most Australians use GSM. If your cellphone is on a GSM system, and you have a world-capable multiband phone such as many Sony Ericsson, Motorola, or Samsung models, you can make and receive calls across civilized areas around much of the globe. Just call your wireless operator and ask for "international roaming" to be activated on your account. Unfortunately, per-minute charges can be high—usually $1 to $1.50 in western Europe. When you speak to your service provider, make sure you check to see if there is a per-month charge for international calling capability. T-Mobile, for example, doesn't charge you a per-month fee; Cingular does. If your provider does charge you for this service, remember to call and cancel it when you return from your trip.

If you don't have a GSM phone, you can always **rent a mobile phone** for your trip. There are dozens of cellphone rental outfits on the Web—including www.planetfone.com, www.worldcell.com, www.cellhire.com, www.cellularabroad.com, and www.rentcell.com—which are all pretty competitive with each other. You'll fill out an online form (or call their toll-free customer service line) and provide your credit card number, and they'll ship you a box that contains your rental cellphone, extra battery, charger, and dorky heavy-duty nylon cases, to the address of your choice. When you've returned from your trip, you just put everything back in the same packaging and ship it back to them in the pre-addressed and pre-paid FedEx or UPS package. The whole process couldn't be easier—just remember to do it at least a week in advance of your trip. Phone rental isn't cheap, however. You'll usually pay around $50 per week, plus airtime fees of anywhere from 15¢ to a $1 a minute. (Most

have free incoming calls, however.) The bottom line: Shop around for the best deal.

While you can rent a phone from any number of overseas sites, including kiosks at airports and at car-rental agencies, we suggest renting the phone before you leave home. That way you can give loved ones and business associates your new number, make sure the phone works, and take the phone wherever you go—especially helpful for overseas trips through several countries, where local phone-rental agencies often bill in local currency and may not let you take the phone to another country.

For trips of more than a few weeks, **buying a phone** makes more economic sense than renting one. Once you arrive on the continent, stop by a local cellphone shop—Vodafone and T-Mobile are the big names in cellular service throughout Europe—and ask about the cheapest package; you'll probably pay less than $100 for a phone and a starter calling card. Most providers have plans where calls to land lines and text messages are as low as 10¢ per minute, and all incoming calls, even from outside the country (whichever country you happen to be in), are free.

Getting to Europe

Flying from North America

Most major airlines charge competitive fares to European cities, but price wars break out regularly and fares can change overnight. Tickets tend to be cheaper if you fly midweek or off season. **High season** on most routes is usually from June to mid-September—the most expensive and most crowded time to travel. **Shoulder season** is from April to May, mid-September to October, and December 15 to December 24. **Low season**—with the cheapest fares—is from November to December 14 and December 25 to March.

All major airline flights from North America to continental Europe are overnight flights; flight time from anywhere on the East Coast of

Building a Multicity Itinerary

If you're planning to visit several European cities or regions, multicity flight structures (for example, flying into Rome and out of London) are a great option. All the big online travel agencies have a function that allows you to build a multicity itinerary. Best of all, multicity trips are priced about the same as regular round-trips—great news because you used to pay quite a premium for this convenience.

the U.S. is about 8 hours. Because most hotels and hostels won't let you check in until lunchtime or later, try to book a flight that arrives in Europe in the mid- or late morning. If you arrive at 7 or 8am, you'll have several uncomfortable hours before you can shower, change, and freshen up. As for the trip back, flights from Europe to the U.S. depart in the late morning or early afternoon. Do your best to book a return flight that leaves at 10am or later—the only way to get to the airport in the early morning is by taxi, which is much more expensive than the airport train or bus services, which start running at 6:30am or so.

For those whose trips originate on the East Coast, keep in mind that nonstop flights to Italy and other southern destinations don't cost much more than flights that connect through a European hub like London, Paris, Frankfurt, Amsterdam, or Munich. So, if at all possible, we recommend that you go nonstop from the U.S.: You'll obviously get there faster (and get a decent night's sleep, if sleeping on planes is one of your talents), and you'll eliminate the risk of your luggage not making its connection at Heathrow (all too common, unfortunately).

See the appendix for specific info on carriers to Europe.

Getting to the Continent from the United Kingdom

BY TRAIN Many rail passes and discounts are available in the United Kingdom for travel in continental Europe. One of the most complete overviews is available from **Rail Europe Special Services Department** (10 Leake St., London SE1 7NN; ☎ **0870/584-8848**). This organization is particularly well versed in information about discount travel as it applies to persons under 26, full-time or part-time students, and seniors.

The most prevalent option for younger travelers, the **EuroYouth passes,** are available only to travelers under 26 and entitle the pass holder to unlimited second-class rail travel in 26 European countries.

BY CHUNNEL The **Eurostar** train shuttles between London and both Paris and Brussels; trip time is under 3 hours (compared to 10 hr. on the traditional train-ferry-train route). **Rail Europe** (☎ **877/272-RAIL;** www.raileurope.com) sells tickets on the Eurostar between London and Paris or Brussels (both $312 one-way).

For Eurostar reservations, call ☎ **800/ EUROSTAR** in the U.S., 0870/5104-105 in London, or 08-92-35-35-39 in Paris; or log on to www.eurostar.com. Eurostar trains arrive at and depart from Waterloo Station in London, Gare du Nord in Paris, and Central Station in Brussels.

BY FERRY & HOVERCRAFT **Brittany Ferries** (☎ **08703/665-333;** www.brittanyferries. com) is the largest British ferry/drive outfit, sailing from the southern coast of England to five destinations in Spain and France. From Portsmouth, sailings reach St-Malo and Caen; from Poole, Cherbourg. From Plymouth, sailings go to Santander in Spain. **P&O Ferries** (☎ **0870/520-2020;** www.poferries.com) operates car and passenger ferries between Portsmouth and Cherbourg (three departures a day; 5–7 hr.); between Portsmouth and Le Havre, France (three a day; 5 hr.); and between Dover and Calais, France (25 a day; $1^1/_4$ hr.).

What's in a Name?

Note that some European cities are spelled quite differently in their native language: Copenhagen is Kobenhavn, Florence is Firenze, Munich is München, Prague is Praha, Venice is Venezia, and Vienna is Wien.

Some countries are very different, too: Austria is Osterrecih, Germany is Deutschland, Italy is Italia, Spain is España, Sweden is Sverige, Switzerland is Schweiz or Suisse, and Turkey is Turkyie.

THE BASICS

Unless you're interested in a leisurely sea voyage, passengers without cars might be better off using the quicker, and slightly cheaper, **Hoverspeed** (☎ 0870/5240-241; www.hoverspeed.com). Hoverspeeds make the 35-minute crossing between Calais and Dover 7 to 15 times per day, with the more curtailed schedule in winter. Prices are £26 adults on foot or £13 children; vehicle fares are £122 to £143. Prices are one-way.

See the appendix for more ferry route options.

BY CAR Many car-rental companies won't let you rent a car in Britain and take it to the Continent, so always check ahead. There are many "drive-on/drive-off" car-ferry services across the Channel; see "By Ferry & Hovercraft," above. There are also Chunnel trains that run a drive-on/drive-off service every 15 minutes (once an hour at night) for the 35-minute ride between Ashford and Calais.

BY COACH Though travel by coach is considerably slower and less comfortable than travel by train, if you're on a budget you might opt for one of Eurolines's regular departures from London's Victoria Coach Station to destinations throughout Europe. Contact **Eurolines** at 52 Grosvenor Gardens, Victoria, London SW1W OAU (☎ 020/7730-8235; www.eurolines. co.uk).

Booking Your Flight Online

Of the big online travel agencies—**Expedia. com, Travelocity.com,** and **Orbitz.com**— we've had the best experience with Orbitz. We also like **Kayak.com,** an under-the-radar travel-booking site that uses a sophisticated search engine (developed at MIT). Each has different business deals with the airlines and many offer different fares on the same flights, so take the time to shop around. Open several Web browsers at once and do side-by-side searches for the same destination and dates, and you'll get a feel for how different sites behave. A nice feature of Expedia, Kayak, and Travelocity is that you can sign up for e-mail notification when a cheap fare becomes available to your favorite destination.

Also remember to check the individual websites for carriers that fly from your home country to Europe. (See the appendix for this info). If you want to get really creative (and you don't mind changing planes several times), you can scout out low-fare carriers such as **easyJet** (www.easyjet.com) or **Ryanair** (www.ryanair. com), which can take care of your short hops in Europe but not the transaatlantic or transpacific leg of your trip.

Great last-minute deals (for example, half of what you'd pay by booking in advance) are often available through free weekly e-mail services provided directly by the airlines. Most of these are announced on Tuesday or Wednesday and must be purchased online. Most are only valid for travel that weekend, but some (such as British Airways) can be booked weeks or months in advance. Sign up for weekly e-mail alerts at airline websites or check megasites that compile comprehensive lists of last-minute specials, such as Smarter Travel (www.smartertravel.com). For last-minute trips, **www.site59.com** and **http:// us.lastminute.com** often have amazing air-and-hotel package deals, for much less than the major-label sites (however, 90% of the hotels they offer are located miles from the heart of town).

If you're willing to relinquish some control over your flight details, use what is called an "opaque" fare service like **Priceline**'s "Name-Your-Own-Price" feature (www.price line.com). Opaque travel sites offer rock-bottom prices in exchange for travel on a "mystery airline" at a mysterious time of day, often with a mysterious change of planes en route. The mystery airlines are all major, well-known carriers—and the possibility of being sent from Philadelphia to Bruges via Dallas is remote; the airlines' routing computers have gotten a lot better than they used to be. Your chances of getting a 6am or 11pm flight, however, are still pretty high. If all this seems

Travel in the Age of Bankruptcy

Airlines sometimes go bankrupt, so protect yourself by buying your tickets with a credit card, as the Fair Credit Billing Act guarantees that you can get your money back from the credit card company if a travel supplier goes under (and if you request the refund within 60 days of the bankruptcy). Travel insurance can also help, but make sure it covers against "carrier default" for your specific travel provider. And be aware that if a U.S. airline goes bust midtrip, a 2001 federal law requires other carriers to take you to your destination (albeit on a space-available basis) for a fee of no more than $25, provided you rebook within 60 days of the cancellation.

too complicated, **BiddingForTravel** (www.biddingfortravel.com) is an online forum of experienced travel bidders that helps demystify Priceline's inner workings and offers strategic advice on how to get the best fare. Priceline also offers a non-opaque service where you can pick the exact flight/time for a specific price, if you don't feel like gambling with your time.

OTHER CASH-SAVING TRAVEL IDEAS

○ Keep an eye on local newspapers for **promotional specials** or **fare wars,** when airlines lower prices on their most popular routes.

○ Several reliable consolidators are worldwide and available online. **STA Travel** (☎ 800/781-4040; www.statravel.com) is the world's top consolidator for students, but their fares are competitive for travelers of all ages. **ELTExpress** (☎ 800/TRAV-800; www.flights.com) has excellent fares worldwide, particularly to Europe. It also has "local" websites in 12 countries.

○ Join **frequent-flier clubs.** Accrue enough miles, and you'll be rewarded with free flights and elite status. It's free, and you'll get the best choice of seats and prompter service.

○ Passengers who can book their ticket **long in advance,** who can **stay over Saturday night,** or who **fly midweek** or **at less-trafficked hours** may pay a fraction of the full fare. If your schedule is flexible, say so, and ask if you can secure a cheaper fare by changing your plans.

Package Tours

Package tours aren't the same thing as escorted tours. They're simply a way of buying your airfare and accommodations at the same time and getting an excellent rate on both. Your trip is your own. In many cases, a package including airfare, hotel, and transportation to and from the airport costs less than the hotel alone if you booked it yourself. The downside is that many stick you in large international-style hotels (which in Europe are often outside the historic city center). You do get a good rate for that sort of hotel, but with a little more work (and the hotel reviews in this book), you can easily find on your own a midrange pension or friendly B&B for the same price or less—and right in the heart of the action.

All major airlines flying to Europe sell vacation packages. The best place to start looking for independent packagers is the travel section of your local Sunday newspaper and national travel magazines. **Vacation Together** (☎ 800/839-9851; www.vacation together.com) allows you to search for and book packages offered by a number of tour operators and airlines. **Liberty Travel** (☎ 888/271-1584; www.libertytravel.com) is one of the biggest packagers in the Northeast and usually boasts a full-page ad in Sunday papers. **Kemwel** (☎ 800/678-0678; www.kemwel.com) is a reputable option, too.

THE BASICS

Escorted Tour Groups

With a good escorted group tour, you'll know ahead of time what your trip will cost, and you won't have to worry about transportation, luggage, hotel reservations, communicating in foreign languages, and other basics—an experienced guide will take care of all that and lead you through all the sightseeing. The downside of a guided tour is that you trade much of the freedom and personal time independent travel grants you and often see only the canned, postcard-ready side of Europe through the tinted windows of a giant bus. You get to *see* Europe, but rarely do you get the chance to really *know*

it. Consult a good travel agent for the latest offerings and advice.

The two largest tour operators conducting escorted tours of Europe are **Globus/Cosmos** (☎ **800/338-7092;** www.globusandcosmos. com) and **Trafalgar** (www.trafalgartours. com). Both companies have first-class tours that run about $100 a day and budget tours for about $75 a day. The differences are mainly in hotel location and the number of activities. There's little difference in the companies' services, so choose your tour based on the itinerary and preferred date of departure. Brochures are available at travel agencies, and all tours must be booked through travel agents.

Getting Around Europe

By Train

In Europe, often the shortest—and cheapest—distance between two points is lined with rail tracks. European trains are less expensive than those in the United States, far more advanced in many ways, and certainly more extensive. Modern high-speed trains (209kmph/130 mph) make the rails faster than the plane for short journeys, and overnight trains get you where you're going without wasting valuable daylight hours—and you save money on lodging to boot.

If you have a **Eurailpass** (see box below), you can use it for most second-class travel on any train throughout Europe, without paying a supplement.

SOME TRAIN NOTES Many European high-speed trains, including the popular EC (EuroCity), IC (InterCity), and EN (EuroNight), require you to pay a **supplement** in addition to the regular ticket fare. It's included when you buy tickets but not in any rail pass, so check at the ticket window before boarding; otherwise, the conductor will sell you the supplement on the train—along with a fine. **Seat reservations** ($20–$50 or more, when a meal is included) are required on some high-speed runs—any marked with an R on a printed train

schedule. You can usually reserve a seat within a few hours of departure, but be on the safe side and book your seat a few days in advance. You need to reserve any sleeping couchette or sleeping berth, too.

With two exceptions, there's no need to buy individual train tickets or make seat reservations **before you leave the United States.** However, on the high-speed Artesia run (Paris–Turin and Paris–Milan), you must buy a supplement, on which you can get a substantial discount if you have a rail pass, but only if you buy the supplement in the United States along with the pass. It's also wise to reserve a seat on the Eurostar, as England's frequent "bank holidays" (long weekends) book the train solid with Londoners taking a short vacation to Paris.

The difference between **first class** and **second class** on European trains is minor—a matter of 1 or 2 inches of extra padding and maybe a bit more elbowroom. European **train stations** are usually as clean and efficient as the trains, if a bit chaotic at times. In stations, you'll find posters showing the track number and timetables for regularly scheduled runs (departures are often on the yellow poster). Many stations also have tourist offices and hotel reservations desks, banks with ATMs,

Behold! The Legendary Eurailpass!

Many travelers to Europe take advantage of one of the great travel bargains of our time, the **Eurailpass,** which permits unlimited rail travel in any country in western Europe (except the British Isles) and Hungary in eastern Europe.

The advantages are tempting: There are no tickets; simply show the pass to the ticket collector, and then settle back to enjoy the scenery. Seat reservations are required on some trains (see the table, below). Many trains have couchettes (sleeping cars), for which an extra fee is charged. Obviously, the 2- or 3-month traveler gets the greatest economic advantages. To obtain full advantage of a 15-day or 1-month pass, you'd have to spend a great deal of time on the train.

Eurailpass holders are also entitled to considerable reductions on certain buses and ferries as well.

In **North America,** you can buy these passes from travel agents or rail agents in major cities such as New York, Montreal, and Los Angeles. Eurailpasses are also available from **Rail Europe** (☎ 877/272-RAIL; www.raileurope. com). No matter what everyone tells you, you *can* buy Eurailpasses in Europe as well as in America (at the major train stations), but they're more expensive. Rail Europe can give you information on the rail/drive versions of the passes.

A **Eurailpass** is $605 for 15 days, $785 for 21 days, $975 for 1 month, $1,378 for 2 months, and $1,703 for 3 months. If you're under 26, you can buy a **Eurail Youthpass,** entitling you to unlimited second-class travel for $394 for 15 days, $510 for 21 days, $634 for 1 month, $897 for 2 months, and $1,108 for 3 months. Even more freedom is offered by the **Saver Flexipass,** which is similar to the Eurail Saverpass, except that you are not confined to consecutive-day travel. For travel over any 10 days within 2 months, the fare is $608; any 15 days over 2 months, the fare is $800.

Eurail Saverpass, valid all over Europe for first class only, offers discounted 15-day travel for groups of three or more people traveling together from April to September, or two people traveling together from October to March. The price is $498 for 15 days, $648 for 21 days, $804 for 1 month, $1,138 for 2 months, and $1,408 for 3 months.

The **Eurail Flexipass** allows you to visit Europe with more flexibility. It's valid in first class and offers the same privileges as the Eurailpass. However, it provides a number of individual travel days you can use over a much longer period of consecutive days. That makes it possible to stay in one city and yet not lose a single day of travel. There are two passes: 10 days of travel in 2 months for $715, and 15 days of travel in 2 months for $940.

Having many of the same qualifications and restrictions as the Flexipass is the **Eurail Youth Flexipass.** Sold only to travelers under 26, it allows 10 days of travel within 2 months for $465, and 15 days of travel within 2 months for $612.

Eurail countries: Austria, Belgium, Denmark, Finland, France, Germany, Greece, Hungary, Ireland, Italy, Luxembourg, the Netherlands, Norway, Portugal, Spain, Sweden, and Switzerland.

THE BASICS

and newsstands where you can buy phone cards, bus and metro tickets, maps, and local English-language event magazines.

You can get many more details about train travel in Europe and automated schedule information by fax by contacting **Rail Europe**

Train Tips

→ Keep your schedule somewhat flexible: Some countries in Europe have near perfect on-time records; others are prone to strikes or general delays.

→ For train trips longer than 4 or 5 hours, consider booking your travel overnight. This will help you maximize your daylight time and save you money that you'd otherwise have spent on a night's lodging. Overnight train trips must be booked at least 24 hours in advance to guarantee a seat or sleeping compartment. Some train buffs, however, would argue just the opposite. And some exceptions stand out; trains in the Bernese Oberland in Switzerland, for instance, have such spectacular scenery that it's best to see it fully awake.

→ Some European trains have smoking sections, so if you're going to smoke, be sure to smoke in the special smoking cars only, not in the corridor of a non-smoking car with the window open.

→ If you're trying to hoard your cash, banish all thoughts of the faster and cleaner Eurostar trains from your mind. Intercity trains are covered by rail passes, and they're not that much slower than Eurostars.

→ Unfortunately, theft can be a problem on trains. Keep your bags near you at all times, and if you're going to sleep, make sure you have a hand or arm on valuables.

(☎ 877/272-RAIL; fax 800/432-1329; www.raileurope.com). If you plan on doing a lot of train travel, consider buying the *Thomas Cook European Timetable* ($29 from travel specialty stores; or order it at ☎ 800/FORSYTH; www.forsyth.com). Each country's national railway website, which includes schedules and fare information, occasionally in English, is listed at **Mercurio** (http://mercurio.iet.unipi.it).

RAIL PASSES The greatest value in European travel has always been the **rail pass,** a single ticket allowing you unlimited travel (or travel on a certain number of days) within a set time period. If you plan on going all over Europe by train, buying a rail pass will end up being much less expensive than buying individual tickets. Plus, a rail pass gives you the freedom to hop on a train whenever you feel like it, and there's no waiting in ticket lines. For more focused trips, you might want to look into national or regional passes or just buy individual tickets as you go.

Passes Available in the United States
The granddaddy of passes is the **Eurailpass,** covering 17 countries (most of western Europe except Britain). It has been joined by the **Europass,** covering 5 to 12 countries (depending on which version you buy); this pass is mainly for travelers who are going to stay in the heart of western Europe. See "Behold! The Legendary Eurailpass," above, for more details on specific passes.

There are also **national rail passes** of various kinds and **regional passes** like ScanRail (Scandinavia), BritRail (Great Britain), and the European East Pass (Austria, Czech Republic, Slovakia, Hungary, Poland). Some national passes you have to buy in the United States, some you can get on either side of the Atlantic, and still others you must buy in Europe. Remember: Seniors, students, and youths can usually get discounts on European trains—in some countries just by asking, in others by buying a discount card good for a year or for some other period of time. Rail Europe or your travel agent can fill you in on all the details.

See the appendix for links to national rail sites.

High-Speed Trains in Europe

Nation & Train Name	Route	Time	One-Way Fare (2nd Class)	Pass Fare/ Res. Fee (1st Class)	Reservations
Belgium					
Thalys	Brussels– Paris	1 hr. 25 min.	$43–$188	$18	Yes
Denmark					
X2000	Copenhagen– Stockholm	5 hr. 18 min.	$171	$11	Yes
England					
Eurostar	London– Paris	2 hr. 35 min.	$90	$75	Yes
	London– Brussels	2 hr. 15 min.	$90	$75	Yes
France					
Artesia	Paris/Lyon– Milan	6 hr. 50 min.	$123	$11	Yes
TGV	Paris to many major cities	Varies	Varies	$11	Optional
Germany					
ICE	All major cities	Varies	Varies	Free	Optional
Italy					
Cisalpino	Florence– Zurich	6 hr. 52 min.	$83	$15	
	Milan– Stuttgart	6 hr. 48 min.	$94	$15	Optional
	Milan– Basel	4 hr. 30 min.	$73	$15	Optional
	Venice– Geneva	6 hr. 48 min.	$84	$15	Optional
Eurostar Italia	All major cities	Varies	Varies	$20	Yes
Netherlands					
Thalys	Brussels– Amsterdam	2 hr. 39 min.	$28–$72	$18	Yes

continues

High-Speed Trains in Europe

Nation & Train Name	Route	Time	One-Way Fare (2nd Class)	Pass Fare/ Res. Fee (1st Class)	Reservations
Portugal					
Alfa	Lisbon–Porto	3 hr.	$29	$11	
Spain					
AVE	Madrid–Cordoba	1 hr. 45 min.	$53–$59		
	Madrid–Seville	2 hr. 30 min.	$72–80	$29	Yes
Talgo	Barcelona–Montpellier	7 hr. 30 min.	$58	$11	Yes
	Cartagena-Montpellier	4 hr. 30 min.	$102	$11	Yes
Talgo 200	Madrid–Malaga	4 hr. 10 min.	$59–$67	$29	Yes
Alaris	Madrid–Valencia	3 hr. 50 min.	Varies	Varies	Yes
Altaria	Madrid–Alicante	3 hr. 45 min.	Varies	Varies	Yes
Euromed	Barcelona–Alicante	4 hr. 30 min.	Varies	Varies	Yes
Arco	Barcelona–Valencia	Varies	Varies	Yes	
Sweden					
X2000	All major cities	Varies	Varies	$11	Yes
Switzerland					
Served by Cisalpino trains from Italy, TGV trains from France, and ICE trains from Germany					

By Car

Road-tripping throughout Europe is great if you plan to delve into the continent's rural areas that aren't well served by rail (such as smaller hill towns); otherwise, you'll probably find trains an easier beast to tame. Driving in urban areas is a nightmare, but once you're outside the cities, the highways and state roads are well marked and easy to use.

Many rental companies grant discounts if you **reserve in advance** (usually 48 hr.) from your home country. Weekly rentals are almost

The Rules of the Road: Driving in Europe

- First off, know that European drivers tend to be more aggressive than their American counterparts.

- Drive on the right except in England, Scotland, and Ireland, where you drive on the left.

- If someone comes up from behind and flashes his lights at you, it's a signal for you to slow down and drive more on the shoulder so he can pass you more easily (two-lane roads here routinely become three cars wide).

- Except for the German autobahn, most highways do indeed have speed limits of around 100 to 135kmph (60–80 mph).

- Remember that everything's measured in kilometers here (mileage and speed limits). For a rough conversion, 1km = 0.6 miles.

- Be aware that although gas may look reasonably priced, the price is per liter, and 3.8 liters = 1 gallon. So multiply by four to estimate the equivalent per-gallon price.

- Never leave anything of value in the car overnight, and don't leave anything visible any time you leave the car (this goes double in Italy, triple in Naples).

- Only use the left lane if you are passing someone. If you and your little Fiat hatchback make the mistake of hanging out in the left lane, you'll find an endless convoy of black BMW SUVs crawling up your ass (at about 145kmph/90 mph).

always less expensive than day rentals. Three or more people traveling together can usually get around cheaper by car than by train (even with rail passes).

When you reserve a car, be sure to ask if the price includes the E.U. value-added tax (VAT), personal accident insurance (PAI), collision-damage waiver (CDW), and any other insurance options. If not, ask what these extras cost because at the end of your rental, they can make a big difference in your bottom line. The CDW and other insurance might be covered by your credit card if you use the card to pay for the rental; check with the card issuer to be sure.

If your credit card doesn't cover the CDW (and it probably won't in Ireland), **Travel Guard International** (1145 Clark St., Stevens Point, WI 54481; ☎ 800/826-1300 or 715/345-0505; www.travelguard.com) offers it for $7 per day. Avis and Hertz, among other companies, require that you purchase a theft-protection policy in Italy.

The main car-rental companies are **Avis** (☎ 800/331-1212; www.avis.com), **Budget** (☎ 800/472-3325; www.budget.com), **SIXT** (known as Dollar in the U.S.; ☎ 800/800-3665; www.dollar.com), **Hertz** (☎ 800/654-3131; www.hertz.com), and **National** (☎ 800/227-7368; www.nationalcar.com). U.S.-based companies specializing in European rentals

FYI: Hope You Can Drive a Stick!

When renting cars in Europe, make sure that you have a valid driver's license and remember that most rental cars are manual transmission (stick shift). Automatic transmission can be prohibitively expensive, or not available at all.

THE BASICS

are **Auto Europe** (☎ 800/223-5555; www. autoeurope.com), **Europe by Car** (☎ 800/ 223-1516, or 212/581-3040 in New York; www.europebycar.com), and **Kemwel Holiday Auto** (☎ 800/678-0678; www. kemwel.com). Europe by Car, Kemwel, and **Renault USA** (☎ 800/221-1052; www. renaultusa.com) also offer a low-cost alternative to renting for longer than 15 days: **short-term leases** in which you technically buy a fresh-from-the-factory car and then sell it back when you return it. All insurance is included, from liability and theft to personal injury and CDW, with no deductible. And unlike at many rental agencies, who won't rent to anyone under 25, the minimum age for a lease is 18.

The **AAA** supplies good maps to its members. **Michelin maps** (☎ 800/423-0485 or 864/458-5619; www.michelin.com) are made for the tourist. The maps rate cities as "uninteresting" (as a tourist destination); "interesting"; "worth a detour"; or "worth an entire journey." They also highlight particularly scenic stretches of road in green, and have symbols pointing out scenic overlooks, ruins, and other sights along the way.

U.S. and Canadian drivers don't need an **International Driver's License** to drive a rented car throughout most of Europe. However, if you're driving a private car, you need such a license. You can apply for an International Driver's License at any **American Automobile Association (AAA)** branch. You must be at least 18 and have two 2-by-2-inch photos and a photocopy of your U.S. driver's license with your AAA application form. The actual fee for the license can vary, depending on where it's issued.

By Plane

Though trains are often the cheapest and easiest way to get around in Europe, air transport options have improved drastically in the past few years. Intense competition with rail and ferry companies has slowly forced airfares into the bargain basement. **British Airways** (☎ 800/AIRWAYS in the U.S., or 0870/850-9850 in the U.K.; www.british airways.com) and other scheduled airlines fly regularly from London to Paris for only £107 ($171) round-trip, depending on the season. Lower fares usually apply to midweek flights and carry advance-purchase requirements of 2 weeks or so.

The biggest airline news in Europe is the rise of the **no-frills airline** modeled on American upstarts like Southwest. By keeping their overheads down through electronic ticketing, forgoing meal service, and flying from less popular airports, these airlines are able to offer low fares. Most round-trip tickets are $40 to $170. This means now you can save lots of time, and even money, over long train hauls, especially from, say, London to Venice or from central Europe out to peripheral countries like Greece and Spain. Budget airlines include **easyJet** (☎ 0870/6-000-000 in England; www.easyjet.com); **Ryanair** (☎ 0870/333-1231 in England; www.ryanair. com) in Ireland; and **Virgin Express** (☎ 020/ 7744-0004; www.virgin-express.com), an off shoot of Virgin Air, in Belgium. Be aware, though, that the names might change because these small airlines are often economically vulnerable and can fail or merge with a big airline. Still, as quickly as one disappears, another will take off. See the appendix for info on other budget carriers.

Lower airfares are also available throughout Europe on **charter flights** rather than regularly scheduled ones. Look in local newspapers to find out about them. Consolidators cluster in cities like London and Athens.

American citizens can contact **Europe by Air** (☎ 888/387-2479; www.europebyair. com) for their Europe flight pass serving 30 countries, 30 airlines, and 150 European cities. It costs only $99 to travel one-way between these cities.

Because discount passes are always changing on air routes within Europe, it's best to check in with **Air Travel Advisory Bureau** in London (☎ **020/7636-5000;** www.atab.co.uk). This bureau offers a free service directory to the public for suppliers of discount airfares from all major U.K. airports.

By Ferry

Many ferries are covered by the Eurailpass, including international routes from Italy to Greece, from Germany to Sweden, from Denmark to Norway, and from Germany and Sweden to Finland. The Eurailpass also offers discounted fares on several other routes, including ferries from Ireland to France. On many routes—especially the Scandinavian and Adriatic ones—the modern, comfortable ferryboats are great ways to cross borders while you sleep.

European ferries are generally even more plush than European trains. They may have onboard swimming pools, movie theaters, sit-down restaurants, or even casinos. On the Adriatic ferries, accommodations range from chaise longues on the deck to luxurious, hotel room–like private cabins equipped with showers, refrigerators, and TVs, with views of the water. In colder waters, nobody's forced to sleep on the deck—accommodations start with reclining, airline-style seats or four-berth cabins and work their way up to two-berth cabins with a view. ·

Note however, that your rail pass usually covers only the lowest possible fare. Depending on the route, that may give you an unreserved seat, a bed in a four-berth cabin, or a little space on the deck overnight. If you want better accommodations, you'll have to pay more. You'll also likely have to pay port fees (ranging 6€–20€) and/or high-season supplements, even if you have a rail pass. These fees are usually payable at the port when you're about to board the ferry, so have some cash on you.

By Bus

BETWEEN CITIES

Bus transportation is readily available throughout Europe; it sometimes is less expensive than train travel and covers a more extensive area but can be slower and much less comfortable. European buses, like the trains, outshine their American counterparts, but they're perhaps best used only to pick up where the extensive train network leaves off. One major bus company serves all the countries of western Europe (no service to Greece): **Eurolines** in London (☎ **0870/514-3219;** www.eurolines.com), whose staff can check schedules, make reservations, and quote prices.

IN THE CITIES

Once you're in a city, the most efficient and cost-effective way to get around, other than using your own two feet, is by bus, metro, or tram. Pick up a public transit map and head on out. Bus lines are named by numbers and the piazza, street, or landmark that is their final destination. Choose the destination that lies in your desired general direction, and get on that bus—it's usually that simple. Even though different local agencies operate each city's public transit system, no matter where you are, bus tickets can be purchased at a newsstand, and they usually cost about 1€ for a ride in one direction (they cannot be purchased onboard). Make sure you validate your bus ticket as soon as you get on the bus. Just stick it in the timer as you'll see others doing. Often, your bus trip becomes invalid after 1 hour or 75 minutes. Bus authorities do random checks and if you're caught without a ticket, you'll get a hefty fine and heaps of public embarrassment.

For Travelers with Special Interests or Needs

Student Travelers

Before you leave, get an **International Student Identity Card (ISIC;** www.myisic.com), which offers substantial savings on rail passes, plane tickets, and many entrance fees. It also provides you with basic health and life insurance and a 24-hour help line. The card is available for $22 from **STA Travel** (☎ 800/781-4040 in North America; www.statravel.com). If you're no longer a student but are under 26, you can get an **International Youth Travel Card (IYTC)** for the same price from the same people, which entitles you to some of the same discounts. **Travel CUTS** (☎ 800/667-2887 or 416/614-2887; www.travelcuts.com) offers similar services for both Canadians and U.S. residents.

Many monuments and museums throughout Europe offer reduced rates to students—the trouble is, many of these reductions are reserved for E.U. citizens only. Still, bring along your regular university ID, which often works just as well.

Single Travelers

Solo travelers can have a grand old time in Europe. You can choose your own adventure and follow your own itinerary, without the tension that inevitably arises from making sure your traveling companions want to do exactly what you want to do, and without the distraction of your friends' constant chit-chat that can keep you from fully absorbing the local sights and sounds.

Be mindful of safety issues and use common sense. Check what the more dangerous areas are in a city before you go; local tourist boards can help, if you tell them you're traveling by yourself. If you stay at hostels and go on group walking tours, bike tours, and such, you're bound to meet a ton of young, like-minded people, whom you can join for dinner and nights on the town and such. In every major city, there are also plenty of bars and pubs that have a high backpacker or expat quotient. We've listed the best ones in each city in this book. Don't feel weird about hitting the town on your own—it'll give you an exhilarating sense of freedom, and you might stumble into adventures that never would have happened if you'd just stayed at the hostel reading a book.

Many Europeans are incredibly open and are more likely to strike up a conversation with you if you're by yourself. (So, if part of your plan overseas is to meet some fine young locals, going around solo can be a great strategy!) One exceedingly common pitfall of traveling for too long on your own, however, is that when you do finally interact with people, you're so relieved for the human contact that you tend to talk too much. Don't let this happen to you—you'll come off as a crazy person, even if you're not!

To save money as a solo traveler, always stay in hostels, as single rooms in budget hotels usually cost almost as much as double rooms.

Travelers with Disabilities

Many travel agencies offer customized tours and itineraries for travelers with disabilities. **Flying Wheels Travel** (☎ 507/451-5005; www.flyingwheelstravel.com) offers escorted tours and cruises that emphasize sports and private tours in minivans with lifts. **Access-Able Travel Source** (☎ 303/232-2979; www.access-able.com) offers extensive access information and advice for traveling around the world with disabilities. **Accessible Journeys** (☎ 800/846-4537 or 610/521-0339; www.disabilitytravel.com) caters specifically to slow walkers and wheelchair travelers and their families and friends.

Avis Rent a Car has an "Avis Access" program that offers such services as a dedicated 24-hour toll-free number (☎ 888/879-4273) for customers with special travel needs;

special car features such as swivel seats, spinner knobs, and hand controls; and accessible bus service.

Organizations that offer assistance to disabled travelers include **MossRehab** (www.mossresourcenet.org), which provides a library of accessible-travel resources online; the **American Foundation for the Blind** (**AFB**; ☎ 800/232-5463; www.afb.org), a referral resource for the blind or visually impaired that includes information on traveling with Seeing Eye dogs; and **SATH** (Society for Accessible Travel & Hospitality; ☎ 212/447-7284; www.sath.org; annual membership fees: $45 adults, $30 seniors and students), which offers a wealth of travel resources for all types of disabilities and recommendations on destinations, access guides, travel agents, tour operators, vehicle rentals, and companion services.

For more information specifically targeted to travelers with disabilities, the community website **iCan** (www.icanonline.net/channels/travel) has destination guides and several regular columns on accessible travel. Also check out the quarterly magazine *Emerging Horizons* (www.emerginghorizons.com; $14.95 per year, $19.95 outside the U.S.); and *Open World* magazine, published by SATH (see above; subscription: $13 per year, $21 outside the U.S.).

Gay & Lesbian Travelers

As a general rule, when it comes to gay and lesbian travel, the bigger metropolitan areas seem to have more gay bars and clubs than outlying towns and villages. In general, you won't see a lot of same-sex couples walking hand-in-hand down the street. Homosexuality is a more personal rather than public issue in many of the cultures here. Most chapters list a gay bar or two, and in cities where openness and tolerance rule, we've included more info.

Because you've already picked up one of our guides, we'd like to recommend *Frommer's Gay & Lesbian Europe* (Wiley Publishing, Inc.), which is an excellent travel resource for the top gay and lesbian cities and resorts in Europe.

The International Gay and Lesbian Travel Association (IGLTA; ☎ 800/448-8550 or 954/776-2626; www.iglta.org) is the trade association for the gay and lesbian travel industry, and offers an online directory of gay- and lesbian-friendly travel businesses; go to their website and click on "Members."

Many agencies offer tours and itineraries specifically for gay and lesbian travelers. **Above and Beyond Tours** (☎ 800/397-2681; www.abovebeyondtours.com) is the exclusive gay and lesbian tour operator for United Airlines. **Now, Voyager** (☎ 800/255-6951; www.nowvoyager.com) is a well-known San Francisco–based, gay-owned and operated travel service. **Olivia Cruises & Resorts** (☎ 800/631-6277; www.olivia.com) charters entire resorts and ships for exclusive lesbian vacations and offers smaller group experiences for both gay and lesbian travelers.

Gay.com Travel (☎ 800/929-2268 or 415/644-8044; www.gay.com/travel or www.outandabout.com) is an excellent online successor to the popular *Out & About* print magazine. It provides regularly updated information about gay-owned, gay-oriented, and gay-friendly lodging, dining, sightseeing, nightlife, and shopping establishments in every important destination worldwide. It also offers trip-planning information for gay and lesbian travelers for more than 50 destinations, along various themes, ranging from "Sex & Travel" to "Vacations for Couples."

The following travel guides are available at many bookstores, or you can order them from any online bookseller: *Spartacus International Gay Guide* (Bruno Gmünder Verlag; www.spartacusworld.com/gayguide) and *Odysseus: The International Gay Travel Planner* (Odysseus Enterprises Ltd.), both good, annual, English-language guidebooks focused on gay men; and the *Damron* guides (www.damron.com), with separate annual books for gay men and lesbians.

Women Travelers

As a rule, the farther south you go in Europe (and this is a very general statement), the more liberal the men get about flexing their machismo, which often translates to harassment. Note that blondes and anyone dressed skimpily are often a greater target for harassment or negative attention. The sensibility among many men sometimes characterizes foreign (and particularly American) women as "easy." When fraternizing with local boys, make sure you keep this in mind. As crass as it sounds, most men are not interested in a female backpacker's intellect. **If you are ever in a situation that makes you feel uncomfortable, walk away from it.** If you need to, turn to another woman for help.

As for general safety precautions, women should always use common sense when walking alone at night, just as you would in any metropolitan area.

Minority Travelers

The attitudes towards people of color vary from city to city and country to country. Even though a given European area is not nearly as ethnically diverse as the U.S., it is unlikely that you'd encounter any problems. More often than not, it's ignorance that you'll come up against, even more so than prejudice. One thing that can take some getting used to is how ignorant/curious some Europeans are about how integrated other ethnicities are in other countries. As more and more cities become well integrated, problems tend to dwindle.

COOKING 101

We recommend some European cooking schools throughout this book, but check out http://cook forfun.shawguides.com for a more extensive list of options.

Some white Europeans have a hard time thinking of Asians as "Americans" even if, like so many Chinese Americans or Indian Americans, they were born and bred in the U.S. And if you're an African American, you might find people asking you about "what that's like" and assuming you are an aspiring hip-hop artist or something. This curiosity isn't meant to be offensive.

On the Net, there are a number of helpful travel sites for African-American travelers in particular: **Black Travel Online** (www.black travelonline.com) posts news on upcoming events and includes links to articles and travel-booking sites. Agencies and organizations that provide resources for black travelers include **Rodgers Travel** (☎ 800/825-1775; www.rodgerstravel.com), a Philadelphia-based travel agency with an extensive menu of tours in destinations worldwide, including heritage and private-group tours.

Then there are the following collections and guides: *Go Girl: The Black Woman's Guide to Travel & Adventure* (Eighth Mountain Press), a compilation of travel essays by writers including Jill Nelson and Audrey Lorde, with some practical information and trip-planning advice; *Travel and Enjoy Magazine* (☎ 866/266-6211; www.travelandenjoy.com; subscription: $38 per year), which focuses on discounts and destination reviews; and the more narrative *Pathfinders Magazine* (☎ 877/977-PATH; www.pathfinderstravel. com; subscription: $15 per year), which includes articles on everything from Rio de Janeiro to Ghana as well as information on upcoming ski, diving, golf, and tennis trips.

Ecotourists

The International Ecotourism Society (TIES) defines ecotourism as "responsible travel to natural areas that conserves the environment and improves the well-being of local people." You can find eco-friendly travel tips, statistics, and touring companies and associations—listed by destination under "Travel Choice"—at

ᴹᵀⱽ🆄 Language Study

If you want to get fluent and have fun doing it, take a language course in the country you're visiting. There are countless language schools throughout Europe, but we've listed some better-known options below. You can explore other options at **www.language-directory.com** or **www.languageschoolsguide.com**, or find an online partner to practice your new skills with at **http://mylanguage exchange.com**.

→ **Don Quijote** (www.donquijote.org) offers Spanish classes, both Castilian and Catalan, in Barcelona and Madrid, as well as other cities in Spain. You can choose between intensive classes, four or six classes daily for a few weeks, or longer semester courses. The cheapest option is a 1-week course with 10 language lessons and 5 culture lessons for 130€.

→ The venerable **Dante Alighieri** language school (www.dantealighieri.it), which is based in Florence, has affiliated locations in Rome, Bologna, Milan, Siena, and Venice. Dante Alighieri has flexible class structures; for example, an intensive 1-week, 20-hour course starts at 195€; a part-time 4-week, 40-hour course starts at 295€.

→ **L'Atelier Privé des Langues** (www.latelierdeslangues.fr) offers French courses in the heart of Batignolles, Paris. Classes are limited to six students and prices start at 10€ an hour with no registration fee.

→ If you'd rather learn French closer to the beach, check out **Atoll** (www.atoll-france.com). Classes are taught in Cannes and Nice and they have a special program for teens, costing 585€ per week with full board. Also try the **Centre International d'Antibes (C.I.A)**, which hosts courses in the south of France at a rate of 410€ per week with board included.

→ Learn German in Berlin at **Akkusativ** (www.akkusativ.de). Classes never go over six students, and they offer private lessons or intense courses for 4 weeks, with 20 lessons per week (for 699€).

→ The U.K.-based company **Language Courses Abroad** (www.languages abroad.co.uk) offers a number of language programs, including a Portuguese program in Lisbon and a Greek course in Athens. Check out the website for prices and course info.

the TIES website, **www.ecotourism.org**. **Ecotravel.com** is part online magazine and part ecodirectory that lets you search for touring companies in several categories (water-based, land-based, spiritually oriented, and so on). Also check out **Conservation International** (www.conservation.org), which, with National Geographic Traveler, annually presents World Legacy Awards (www.wlaward.org) to those travel tour operators, businesses, organizations, and places that have made a significant contribution to sustainable tourism.

Visit http://whc.unesco.org/en/list for information on Europe's many UNESCO-protected World Heritage Sites.

Work or Volunteer Abroad

A number of agencies help students and recent grads (within 6 months of schooling) get special visas allowing them to work or volunteer abroad. Most agencies charge a fee (about 400€) to secure you a visa. It's up to you to find a job once you've landed in the foreign country, though agencies do provide listings to get you started. Just be warned that, if you're

¿Habla Inglés?

If you're looking for work while in Europe, why not teach English? The pay is decent and you'll probably pick up some of the local language during the lessons. Some training is necessary for placement, though: You can take lessons before your journey through the **University of Cambridge** (www.cambridge-efl.org) or you can take a **CELTA** (Certificate in English Language Teaching for Adults) course in the city where you want to work. **Dave's ESL Café** (www.eslcafe.com) is a good place to hunt for advice on the subject.

searching for a paid position, chances are you might be placed into either au pair work or a minimum wage position in a restaurant or bar. Volunteer programs tend to be more exciting.

○ **www.amscan.org**: Summer work programs for Americans 21 and up; specializes in engineering, chemistry, business, and computer science placements.

○ **www.bunac.org**: Flexible work programs in Britain and Ireland.

○ **www.ciee.org**: Work assignments in Germany, France, and Ireland.

○ **www.interexchange.org**: Belgium work programs for Americans and Canadians over 18.

○ **www.anyworkanywhere.com**: Job postings throughout Europe, and assistance with getting a visa.

○ **www.jobsabroad.com**: Listings for jobs throughout Europe, as well as links to study and volunteer options.

○ **www.transitionsabroad.com**: Advice on working abroad, along with postings on short- and-long term positions.

○ **www.idealist.org**: Resources and tips on volunteering abroad, along with volunteer and paid postings.

○ **www.volunteerabroad.com**: Extensive listings for European volunteer opportunities. Possible trips include working with wildlife in Greece, camp counseling in Croatia, and researching glacial conditions in Iceland.

Surf the Turf

Useful & Necessary Sites to Check Out

Here's a list of sites you might want to bookmark as you plan your trip to Europe.

ACCOMMODATIONS

○ **www.couchsurfing.com** and **www.hospitalityclub.com**: Land free apartments during your trip, as long as you're willing to share your home space with other travelers.

○ **www.tripmates.com**: Interactive site that enables you to meet locals, find traveling partners, and read destination reviews.

○ **http://friends.roadjunky.com/public/home.jhtml**: Meet other cool folks to travel with, and research travel spots.

○ **www.travelpackers.com**: Tips on backpacking, from finding a place to stay to meeting fellow travelers.

○ **www.hiayh.org**: Info on Hostelling International cards, and links to buy cards online.

GOVERNMENT

○ **www.usembassy.com**: The United States Diplomatic Missions website gives information regarding U.S. embassies, consulates, and travel information for U.S. citizens abroad.

○ **www.state.gov**: The U.S. Department of State website has information regarding

THE BASICS

passports, visas (including forms and applications), travel advisories, and much more.

○ **http://travel.state.gov**: Travel warnings issued by the U.S. State Department.

○ **www.cdc.gov**: Info on vaccinations and outbreaks from the U.S. Centers for Disease Control and Prevention.

OFFICIAL TOURIST BOARDS

See the appendix for addresses and phone numbers of each country's (or city's, in some cases) tourism boards.

TRANSPORTATION

See the appendix for airline, train, and ferry websites.

○ **www.airlineairportlinks.com**: Links to Europe's many airport websites.

○ **www.sleepinginairports.com**: Exactly what it sounds like: advice on sleeping in airports.

○ **http://flightview.com/traveltools**: Enables you to look into the status of any flight in the world.

○ **www.travel-watch.com/airlink.htm**: Links to all airlines worldwide.

○ **www.interrail.co.uk**: Rail fare and timetable information.

○ **www.railserve.com**: Links to European rail services.

○ **www.horizonsunlimited.com**: Advice on motorcycling around Europe.

○ **www.maporama.com**: Online map site with extensive maps of Europe.

MONEY

○ **www.x-rates.com/calculator.html**: Get the most up-to-date exchange rate and see how far your home currency will take you.

○ **www.westernunion.com**: Send money overseas.

○ **www.moneygram.com**: Allows you to send money and pay urgent bills.

LIFESTYLE

○ **http://esl.meetup.com/2**: Students abroad who want to rub elbows with locals and other students can meet online here.

○ **www.dinnerpoint.com/index.jsp**: Brings strangers together over a meal.

○ **www.foreignword.com**: Translations from English to about 73 other languages.

Travel Blogs & Travelogues

More and more travelers are using travel Web logs, or **blogs,** to chronicle their journeys online. You can search for other blogs about specific cities in Europe at **Travelblog.com** or post your own travelogue at **Travelblog. org.** For blogs that cover general travel news and highlight various destinations, try **Writtenroad.com** or Gawker Media's snarky **Gridskipper.com.** For more literary travel essays, try Salon.com's travel section (**Salon.com/Wanderlust**), and **Worldhum. com,** which also has an extensive list of other travel-related journals, blogs, online communities, newspaper coverage, and bookstores.

THE BASICS

Amsterdam

So rich culturally, this town generates its own, unique kind of culture shock. Think beyond mind-bending drugs and paid fellatio to a city that boasts more canals and bridges than Venice, a city that welcomed artists from Rembrandt and Vermeer to van Gogh to Mondrian, a place where you can step back into history through Anne Frank's attic hideaway or Rembrandt's bedroom.

A'dam's growing up and away from its 1960s hippie paradise image. The city embraces what it can't outlaw. Prostitution gets a clean bill of health through laws that regulate it—to the point where the Red-Light District has become a tourist attraction (more on that later). Drugs are illegal officially, but if you go to a coffee shop, you'll see hash or cannabis on the menu (more on that later, too). That same mind-set also propelled the Netherlands to the top of the green environmental scale. The tiny country, the most densely populated in Europe, is in the middle of a greener-is-better political/economic 25-year makeover. You'll still see construction all around A'dam, but on closer inspection outside the city, you're likely to see rainwater-flushed toilets, recycled manure biofuel, sod roofs, and solar panels. Add low unemployment and a stable economy to the mix, and you come out with a city that's relatively safe considering it's known for its drugs, sex, and rock 'n' roll.

You don't need a car to see the city. Use the bus and the tram—and a bike. You can cover a lot of territory, and you'll have worked up a thirst that you can quench at one of the famed brown cafes. These convivial haunts, where tourists and locals come face to face, take their beverages seriously. There's no better place to learn the art of the perfect pour.

For cheap eats, Amsterdam's got variety, in part because the city has become a multicultural mecca: fish stands with raw herring, salmon, or crab salad; Dutch sandwich places (try the smoked eel); traditional cafes that give you a plate with the daily special; Asian restaurants; and eateries that specialize in Indonesian *rijsttafel*, a buffet that features several small plates of meats, rolls, and rice, an especially good choice if you've picked up a buddy or two at the local hostel.

Most Amsterdammers speak English and, especially when it's sunny, are happy to help inquiring tourists. The Dutch use the word *gezelligheid* to describe something that is warm, cozy, friendly, and welcoming. Spend a little time in Amsterdam, and you'll see why the word easily applies to this wonderful, vibrant city.

The Best of Amsterdam

○ **The Best Tourist Trap: Cruising the canals** gives you a different perspective—it makes you realize how much revolves around the water here. A typical tour on a glass-topped boat lasts an hour and takes in Centraal Station, the floodgates that flush the canals nightly, houseboats, the narrowest building in the city, the mayor's residence, and the harbor. See p. 59.

○ **The Best Museums:** Make time to see all "The Big Three" museums. The Rijksmuseum is a college course in art history. The Van Gogh Museum will tempt you to break the law and touch a canvas. The Anne Frankhuis (Anne Frank House) is a powerful, sobering lesson in freedom and injustice. See p. 81, p. 81, and p. 79.

○ **The Best Off-Beat Museum:** You might as well learn what drugs do to a body, especially the lungs. The **Hash Marijuana & Hemp Museum** isn't as gimmicky as you'd think. Their displays do a good job explaining how one goes from being a respectable, sober individual to giggling, red-eyed druggie. See p. 80.

○ **The Best Hostel:** It costs a little more than a standard hostel, but it's worth every euro. I'd give up my own shower and a private room any day, if it meant

hunkering down for a few nights in the sociable and ultraclean **Flying Pig Hostel.** See p. 66.

○ **The Best Hotel for Bikers:** Even bicycles need a place to rest their sprockets. The **Bicycle Hotel Amsterdam** rents bikes and bike shelters in addition to housing butt-weary travelers. Some rooms are no better than a hostel's, but you're assured clean sheets, a secure feeling, and chill roommates. See p. 67.

○ **The Best Hotel When You're Homesick:** Pepijn and Rachel have decked out six funky but tastefully designed rooms with names like "Rembrandt" and "Afrika" in the **Hotel Misc.** Each has either a charming canal view or a balcony overlooking the garden. The rooms are great, but the hosts are what make the place. You'll quickly feel as if you're one of the family and Pepijn and Rachel are those cool older sibs you wished you had. See p. 70.

○ **The Best Minimalist Hotel: Hotel Arena**'s undergone several radical changes in the last century or so (it once housed an orphanage), and in the latest one, it has turned into a wonderfully urbane hotel that won't destroy your

AMSTERDAM

bank account. Up-and-coming young Dutch designers had a hand in creating each individually decorated, minimalist-yet-comfy, room. See p. 67.

○ **The Best Cafe:** It's tough to say which is better, sitting outside on the terrace, checking out the canal directly in front of you, or hunkering down inside and taking in the college students cramming for their exams at the shared "international reading table." **Café de Jaren** is a great people-watching cafe near the university, but it gets a mixed clientele that comes for traditional European sandwiches (cheese, ham, jam), soups, and couscous. See p. 71.

○ **The Best Alternative Music Bar:** Don your vintage metal T-shirt and enjoy the soothing sounds of hard rock, alternative, and industrial at **Soundgarden.** Nothing feels better than downing a pint and kicking back to the Clash. See p. 76.

○ **The Best Clubbin' Crowd Bar:** It's not nearly as over-hyped as Sinners or Jimmy Woo's and it has a much better sound system, with speakers never more than a few feet away from the movers and

shakers. To add to the **Odeon**'s atmosphere, the super-slick murals add a splash of sophistication and give you something to think about while grinding to insane beats meticulously chosen by the resident DJs. See p. 75.

○ **The Best Excuse for a Drink:** For 10€, submit to Amsterdam's most elaborate advertisement: **Heineken Experience.** Interactivity is their sales pitch, and their product is, of course, the amber ale in that notorious green bottle. Touch screens, amusement rides, and audio-visual treats galore make the price of admission more than bearable. The "free" beer at the end *could* be bigger, but no self-respecting drinker goes here for the sampling. See p. 79.

○ **The Best Street to Meet Locals:** Think of them as happy hipsters. The locals here at **Haarlemmerdijk,** on the **Jordaan,** are approachable and friendly. Stroll into a cafe, laundromat, or bookstore and strike up a conversation with the first person you run into. I guarantee you'll at least get a smile. See p. 61.

Getting There & Getting Around

Getting into Town

It's always a good idea to ask questions before you get to the city; one of the staff at your hotel or hostel can usually tell you the best ways to get into town.

BY AIR

Pilots heading to Amsterdam land in one of the most beautiful and efficient airports in the world: **Schipol Airport** (☎ 0900/0141 for flight information; www.schipol.nl). Its innovations offer a model other international hubs try to imitate. It handles the huge numbers of commercial planes with such relative ease that delays are rare (and they're usually attributed to the connecting airport rather than Schipol). When you exit Customs, you'll be in **Schipol**

Plaza, a combined arrivals hall and mall, with a tourist information desk, ATMs, bars, restaurants, and more.

The airport is 13km (8 miles) southwest of the city. You can enter A'dam by train, public bus, private bus, or taxi. A 20-minute **train** ride links the airport to Centraal Station (2.95€). Metro trains depart from **Schipol Station,** a floor below Schipol Plaza, about every 20 minutes at peak times and about once an hour at night. If your hotel is near De Pijp, Leidseplein, the Museumplein area, or Rembrandtplein, you might want to take the train to Amsterdam Zuid/WTC (World Trade Center) station or RAI station (beside the RAI Convention Center). The fare is 2.95€; the trip takes about 15 minutes. From

Amsterdam Zuid/WTC, take tram no. 5 for Leidseplein and the Museum area; from RAI, take tram no. 4 for Rembrandtplein.

The **Connexxion Hotel Bus** (☎ 0900/9292) shuttles between the airport and 16 hotels, but you can get to many more hotels if you don't mind walking a block or two. It leaves from the airport every 20 minutes from 7am to 5pm, every 30 minutes from 5 to 7pm, and every hour from 7 to 9pm. The fare is 8.50€ to 11€ one-way. You don't need a reservation; just show up. If you're not sure if where you're staying is on the route, ask at the Connexxion Desk inside the airport and one of the clerks will tell you where to get off. Also, bus no. 197 connects the airport and the center city, runs every half-hour, and costs 3.40€. Shell out about 45€ to 50€ for a metered taxi into town; the tip is included in the fare. The **Schipol Taxi** (☎ 020/653-1000) stands are in front of Schipol Plaza. *Tip:* You'd be wise to take the train, however, because the bus can take as long as an hour to reach town.

BY TRAIN

Centraal Station, a beautiful 19th-century architectural landmark, is an elegant welcome for travelers. Expect fast, frequent rail service throughout the Netherlands and this part of Europe. Three types of trains feed into Centraal Station: the Thalys high-speed train from Brussels or Paris (www.thalys.com), the regular international trains (☎ 0900/9296), and trains from elsewhere in the Netherlands (☎ 0900/9292; www.9292ov.nl).

From London's Waterloo Station to Brussels Midi Station (the closest connecting point for Amsterdam), the travel time on Eurostar is 3¹/₄ hours. A one-way, weekend fare, for example, runs from 100€ to 140€. For **Eurostar** reservations, call ☎ 8701/606600 in Britain (☎ 020/423-444 in Holland).

BY BOAT

If you're traveling from the U.K. or from port cities in Europe, a boat can be a relaxing alternative to the roads or rail, provided you have the time and the Dramamine. Unfortunately, most of the trips are overnight affairs that can range from 10 to 15 hours (except for the Harwich to Rotterdam route).

The **DFDS Seaways**'s (☎ 08705/333111 in Britain, or 0255/534-546 in Holland; www.dfdsseaways.co.uk) 15-hour, overnight trip offers daily car-ferry service between **Newcastle** and **IJmuiden** (on the North Sea coast west of Amsterdam). From IJmuiden, take the train to Centraal Station. Or, if you're flush, hop a **Fast Flying Ferries** jetfoil that will take you to a pier behind Centraal Station (see "Cool Jets" on p. 85 for more info).

P&O Ferries (☎ 08705/202020 in Britain, or 0181/255-555 in Holland; www.poferries.com) has daily car-ferry service between **Hull,** England, and **Rotterdam (Europoort).** The overnight trip takes 10 hours, but on arrival, the company's coach takes passengers from the Europoort terminal to Rotterdam Centraal Station. From there, frequent trains leave for Amsterdam.

Stena Line (☎ 08705/707070 in Britain, or 0174/389-333 in Holland; www.stenaline.com) has twice-daily fast car-ferry service between **Harwich,** England, and **Hoek van Holland (Hook of Holland)** near Rotterdam. Travel time is only 3 hours and 40 minutes (plus the time it takes to get to Amsterdam by train).

BY BUS

I've never been a fan of buses in Europe, but they're not a bad option when you're hurting financially or if everything else is booked. From England, try **Eurolines** (☎ 08705/808080 in Britain, or 020/560-8788 in Holland; www.eurolines.com). You'll arrive in Amsterdam via ferry, not Chunnel. All in all, the leg-atrophying trip should take 12 hours and cost from about 35€ for a one-way ticket.

Amsterdam's **bus station** is at the **Amstel rail station** (Metro: Amstel), in the south of the city. Getting to the city proper is a breeze; the subway and train connect Amstel and Centraal stations.

BY CAR

Driving to Amsterdam is straightforward. A handful of European highways converge here; the one road you need is the **A10,** Amsterdam's main highway. The surrounding highways connect to the A10. The road names on the signs include both the European and Dutch designations. The European labels start with an E; the Dutch, with an A. For example: E19 (A4). But, be forewarned: Driving in Amsterdam is no picnic (see "By Car" in "Getting Around," below).

Getting Around

BY CAR

Ditch the engine outside of Amsterdam or at the nearest rental-car office in town. The only thing worse than the headache of navigating through the tiny streets, narrow bridges, and heedless crowds is finding parking. It's tough, and the ticket and towing regs are even tougher: 68€ to have a wheel-clamp removed, 154€ a day if your car's been towed. *Tip:* Take everything out of your car, even from the trunk; you don't want to tempt the nearest junkie.

If you had to drive from your last destination or must rent a car to get to your next stop or just want to drive into the countryside, you'll find all the major rental companies here: **Avis** (Nassaukade 380; ☎ **0800/235-2847** or 020/683-6061; tram: 1 or 6), **Budget** (Overtoom 121, ☎ **020/612-6066;** tram: 1 or 6), **Europcar** (Overtoom 19, ☎ **020/683-2123;** tram: 1 or 6), and **Hertz** (Overtoom 333; ☎ **020/201-3512;** tram: 1 or 6).

BY BUS, TRAM & METRO

The **GVB** (☎ **0900/9292;** www.gvb.nl) deals with public transportation in this diminutive city, and it does a good job, even if much of it isn't necessary. The tram is by far the most convenient of the bunch. It covers many of the well-traveled areas, following major veins of the city's street plan. There's also a

bus system that reaches the back streets of the city, complementing the tram system perfectly. Given the city's size and the prevalence of those quirky little waterways, an underground doesn't make much sense. But, logic be damned, higher-ups in the city pushed for and got a subway system, albeit a rather wimpy one. The simple line can be convenient if you're heading for the area around Oosterpark and anywhere upstream on the Amstel. Otherwise, you're better off—and it's more scenic—taking the aboveground trams.

You can purchase tickets from bus and tram drivers, vending machines in the subway stations, tourist offices, post offices, and several supermarkets. If you're near Centraal Station, however, you can also get your tickets—sometimes at a discount—in the **GVB Tickets & Info** office (Mon–Fri

Validating Your Tickets

To validate a strip card on a **tram,** ask the conductor or use the yellow machines in the front, middle, and rear of the car. Fold the card, count down the number of strips you need, and punch it in so the last strip you need is the one that gets punched. At **Metro** stations, use the machines at platform entrances and on the platforms (you must have a valid ticket to be allowed on the Metro platforms). Double-check to make sure that the machine stamped the correct date and that it stamped the ticket properly. On **buses,** the driver stamps your card.

If your tram doesn't have a conductor, it operates on the honor system. Inspectors travel around, and if you're caught without a ticket (or a properly stamped card), you have to pay up on the spot: 30€ plus the cost of the ride.

7am–9pm, Sat–Sun 8am–9pm) in front of the station. Amsterdam is divided into 11 fare zones for public transportation. Buy a map for 1€ at the office; the tram map is free.

It's a little confusing at first, but we recommend buying a **strippenkaart (strip card).** To use it, you have to cancel one or more of the ticket's strips based on how far you're going (the number of zones). To validate it (see the box above), you cancel two strips for one zone, three strips for two zones, and so on. The card is good for all transfers on trams, buses, and Metro trains within one hour of when it is stamped (up to $3^1/_2$ hr. if you're going farther away). More than one person can use a strip card, as long as it is stamped for each passenger. Strip cards are available with 8 strips (6.40€; can be used as a one-day ticket and is the only one available for purchase on the tram or bus), 15 strips (6.50€), and 45 strips (19€).

If you plan on rarely using public transportation, purchase **single tickets** (1.60€ for one zone, 2.40€ for two zones). **Day cards** (6.40€) are good for unlimited travel for 24 hours, 2 days (10€), or 3 days (13€). The **All Amsterdam Transport Pass,** at 17€, is even more expensive, but it includes the Canal Bus (see below). If you want to walk around the city, though, it's probably cheaper to buy a strip card.

When you don't want to walk, the **trams** work well and are a good option. Of the 16 tram routes, 11 begin and end at Centraal Station.

Many **buses** depart from Centraal Station, and they're slower than the tram, so use them advisedly. The **Metro** serves commuters more than it does tourists. Few of the sights on the lines are worth going out of your way for. On these lines, validate your strip card on the platform before boarding.

BY TAXI

In the past, you couldn't hail a cab from the street; now you can—sometimes. If you don't want to chance it, look for one of the taxi stands throughout the city, generally near the luxury hotels or at the major squares (the Dam, Stationsplein, Spui, Rembrandtplein, Westermarkt, and Leidseplein). Metered taxis have blue license tags and rooftop signs.

For a generally reliable service, call **Taxi Centrale Amsterdam** (☎ 020/677-7777). TCA's fares begin at 2.90€ when the meter starts and run up at 1.80€ a kilometer, and after 25km, the fare changes to 1.30€ a kilometer; waiting time is 32€ per hour. The fare includes a tip, but you may round up or give something extra if you had a friendly chat or the driver helped with your bags.

BY WATER TAXI

Because you're in the city of canals, you might want to round up a few buddies and splurge on a water taxi. These launches do more or less the same thing as landlubber taxis, except they do it on the canals and the Amstel River and in the harbor. You can move faster than on land, and you get your very own canal cruise. To order one, call **Watertaxi** (☎ 020/535-6363), or pick one up from the dock outside Centraal Station, close to the VVV office. For up to eight people, the fare is 60€ for 30 minutes, plus an additional 25€ if they need to collect you.

BY WATER BUS

You'll rarely find a local on board, but the water buses probably travel to (or close to) many of the destinations on your to-do list: museums, shopping, clubs. Two different companies run the buses. **Canal Bus** (☎ 020/623-9886; www.canal.nl) has three routes—Green Line, Red Line, and Blue Line—with stops that include Centraal Station, Westermarkt, Leidseplein, Rijksmuseum (with an extension to the RAI Convention Center when big shows are there), Waterlooplein, and East Amsterdam. Hop one between 10am and 6:30pm; two buses an hour ply the waters at peak times. A day pass, valid until noon the next day and including a discount on some museum and attraction admissions, is 14€.

The 🆃🆅 ‍ Best ‍ **Museumboot** (☎ 020/530-1090; www.lovers.nl)—pronounced "museum boat"—transports weary tourists on their pilgrimages from museum to museum. Being on the water is an end unto itself. Boats depart from the Rederij Lovers dock in front of Centraal Station daily from 10am to 5pm, every 30 minutes in summer, and every 45 minutes in winter. They stop at seven key spots that will take you to or near the Rijksmuseum, Van Gogh Museum, Stedelijk Museum, Anne Frankhuis (Anne Frank House), Leidseplein, Vondelpark, Flower Market, Museum Het Rembrandthuis, and the Muziektheater, among other places. A day ticket is 14€; after 1pm, the price drops to 13€. Tickets include discounted admissions to some museums and other sights.

BY BIKE

Walking through the narrow streets and canal-side paths, it's easy to see why 90 percent of the locals get around by bicycle. The slim vehicle scoots through the crowds on the tight roads with amazing deftness. When you're walking, keep your ears perked for that distinct bicycle bell ringing in the background. And avoid walking down the middle of the street, if you can.

Bicycle rental shops are almost as prevalent as coffee shops, but the best place to get some wheels is **Mike's Bike Tours** (Kerkstraat 134; ☎ 020/622-7970; www.mikesbiketours.com) It'll run you 5€ for a half-day, 7€ for 1 day, 10€ for 24 hours, or 12€ overnight; insurance is an additional 3€. They also run great 4-hour, show-up-and-ride tours for 22€. These depart from outside the Rijksmuseum, May to August, at 11:30am and 4pm; times vary in other seasons.

Grandmother bikes don't attract attention (or thieves, usually), but if you'd like to try a tandem or a touring bike, call **MacBike,** which rents a variety of two-wheeled vehicles. Rental outlets are at either side of

Bike Sense

Sunday is a particularly good day to bike in the city. The city's quieter, and you can practice riding on cobblestones and in bike lanes, crossing bridges, and dodging trams before venturing forth into the fray of an Amsterdam rush hour.

Navigating the city on two wheels may seem suicidal at first. But thanks to a vast network of dedicated bike lanes, it's not quite so crazy. Bikes even have their own traffic lights. Amsterdam's battle-scarred bike-borne veterans make it almost a point of principle to ignore every safety rule ever written. Though they mostly live to tell the tale, don't think the same will necessarily apply for you.

For less treacherous biking, head to **Vondelpark** (p. 81).

Centraal Station, at Stationsplein 12 (☎ 020/624-8391) or Stationsplein 33 (☎ 020/625-3845), and at Weteringschans 2 (☎ 020/528-7688). Alternatively, you can rent from **Zijwind Fietsen,** a women's cooperative at Ferdinand Bolstraat 168 (☎ 020/673-7026), though it's a bit out from the center of town.

Make sure you park your bike securely—bike frame and wheel—on one of the racks or the railings on the canal edge. Bike theft has become a major problem in A'dam. Be wary of the entrepreneurial thief who tries selling you a freshly stolen bike.

See also "Playing Outside" (p. 81) for bike rentals in Vondelpark.

ON FOOT

Some clogs aren't meant for walking, but the streets of Amsterdam definitely are. This pedestrian paradise isn't without its dangers, however. The canals have no guardrail or barrier. Pub patrons and folks stumbling out of the coffee shops are most susceptible to an evening dip, but anyone can venture too close, trip, and fall in. When you're not watching out for suspicious, smelly canals, be on the lookout for something that is more likely to get you: Locals rarely pick up after their dogs.

Use your third eye to look out for vehicles. Many of the sidewalks are extremely narrow, and the crowds of people inevitably spill over onto the street. It bears repeating, keep your ears open as well for those bicycle bells. Keep in mind that drivers won't stop for pedestrians. Don't get furious if you almost get hit by them rounding the corner; they have right of way.

Amsterdam Basics

Orientation: Amsterdam Neighborhoods

Here's a rundown of the areas that you'll probably be hitting up during your jaunt:

THE OLD CITY (THE CENTER) Arrive in Centraal Station and walk down **Damrak** to get your first taste of the Old City—where most of the hotels, restaurants, historical buildings, and notorious coffee shops are. Damrak overflows with tourists, and navigating the sea of bodies can get rather disorienting. Veer off into one of the side streets and explore the rest of the Old City, including the **Red-Light District,** by walking along the aged, tiny canals. A little trivia: The main square of the Dam is the site of the original dam across the Amstel River.

THE JORDAAN Every city has a new trendy spot every 5 years, but it seems the Jordaan has held that honor for a while. The Jordaan, west of the Old City, is home to a community of hipsters, trendy businesses, and yuppies. If you're looking for a chill cafe or bar to spend your night, look no further than **Haarlemmerdijk,** one of the Jordaan's most interesting streets to explore.

THE CANAL BELT Within the Old City, canals haphazardly weave in and out of the streets. A few minutes' walk from the Old City, however, lies a much more symmetrical, circular network called the Canal Belt. The **Anne Frankhuis (Anne Frank House)** is here, among many quaint storefronts. Anyone looking for a charming hotel or dinner should make their way to this area just west of the Old City.

MUSEUMPLEIN Follow the tour buses south to get to Museumplein, where you'll find (what else?) museums, including the **Rijksmuseum** and the **Van Gogh Museum.** Make a day of it, at the very least. Better yet, book a hotel in the area for a couple of nights. The Rijksmuseum and Van Gogh Museum each can easily take an entire day.

DE PIJP The inhabitants of De Pijp are making it hard for those in the Jordaan to keep their cool reputation. De Pijp is quickly growing as a diverse community of ethnicities with little restaurants and bars reflecting the incredible mix of cultures. Your palette will have a field day, and your credit card signature may rub away in the off-beat stores on **Albert Cuypstraat.** De Pijp is just to the east of Museumplein, bordered by Stadhouderskade, Van Woustraat, Ceintuurban, and Ruysdaelkade. Simply put, it's sandwiched between the Heineken Experience and Sarphatipark.

Tourist Offices

Before you leave home, contact one of the following offices for the most up-to-date information. **For the U.S. and Canada:** The **Netherlands Board of Tourism (NBT;** 355 Lexington Ave., 19th floor, New York, NY 10017; ☎ **888/464-6552** or 212/557-3500) offers advice in person as well as by phone and letter. **For the U.K. and Ireland:** NBT has a mailing address only (P.O. Box 30783, London WC2B 6DH; premium-rate brochure order line: ☎ **09068/717-777**).

Once there, you may find the slew of canals and streets that make up the tangled pathways of Amsterdam confusing. Grab a map and some free touristy brochures at one of the two **VVV** Amsterdam tourist information offices at Centraal Station. VVV stands for Vereniging voor Vreemdelingenverkeer (**Association for Foreigner Travel;** ☎ **0900/400-4040**). One is located on platform 2; the other, in front of the station at Stationsplein 10 (Mon–Fri 9am–5pm). Both offices have hotel reservation desks. There are more scattered throughout the city.

Recommended Websites

○ **www.visitholland.com** or **www. visitholland.com/uk**: Check out the official tourist sites for Amsterdam.

○ **www.visitamsterdam.nl**: Has good info on hotels, sightseeing, and side trips.

○ **www.amsterdamhotspots.nl**: A decidedly less official site, this one has everything from webcams and an event calendar to reviews of the smoking coffee houses.

○ **www.channels.nl**: This site can give you a virtual tour and boasts photos of most tourist areas and links so that you can direct your own route; visitors to the site give their impressions of restaurants, hotels, museums, and hash houses.

○ **www.amsterdammuseums.nl**: Discover Amsterdam's 35 museums on the Web before you see them in person.

○ **www.go-amsterdam.org**: A good site to book a hotel online.

○ **www.specialbite.nl**: This site is only about the food.

Recommended Books & Movies

BOOKS

If you didn't read *The Diary of a Young Girl* by Anne Frank (Viking, 1997) in school, it's a must-read before you hit Amsterdam. Checking out her house is much more fulfilling after you've read this teen's thoughts. The sobering visit will haunt you long after you've left the Netherlands, but the book leaves an even larger impression. You won't soon forget what the Frank family, and others throughout Europe, had to endure during World War II. Anne's diary is a series of letters to herself, which she wrote while in hiding for 2 years. It ends when she's arrested on August 4, 1944. The book includes a map of the house and photos of Anne and her family. Her thoughts on being a teenager—from the boredom to the anguish—make the book particularly moving.

For a lighter look at history, turn to native Amsterdammer Geert Mak's *Amsterdam*

Talk of the Town

Three ways to start a conversation with a local

The Dutch are friendly and incredibly multilingual—many can switch seamlessly from conversations in Dutch to English, French, and German. Here are a few topics to get going:

1. **Do you think the European Union is going to put a stop to the city's more liberal laws about sex and drugs?** There is a feeling of inevitability among some citizens that it's just a matter of time before the E.U. clamps down on them.

2. **So which countries have you visited?** The Dutch are notoriously well traveled.

3. **Which football team do you follow? Who were you rooting for in the World Cup?** If you know anything about European soccer, pull out that knowledge now; it's always a good lead-in topic.

Culture 101: **The Grass Is Greener**

Let's get one thing straight: Technically, it is *not* legal to buy and smoke cannabis. Rather, like many other things in the city, it's widely tolerated. That means that cops usually won't cuff people for indulging in a little marijuana or hash, if they follow the rules: Don't light up in the open, don't carry more than 30 grams (1.2 oz.), and smoke only in a **coffee shop** or the privacy of your own room (if the hostel or hotel doesn't frown upon smoking on their property).

Coffee shops that sell **hashish** and **marijuana** are licensed and controlled. Each coffee shop has a menu listing the different types of hashish and marijuana it sells (and the THC, or tetrahydrocannabinol, content of each). Patrons can sit and smoke for however long they want. The menu typically offers white and black hashish. The black is usually more powerful, but both are potent. Local producers, who are tolerated as long as they don't go in for large-scale production (some of their crop is used for drug therapy), have developed a Super Skunk hash that is said to be better than imported stuff from Lebanon and Morocco. Connoisseurs say the best has a strong smell and is soft and sticky. A 5-gram bag costs from 4€ to 10€, depending on the quality. Hashish joints, rolled with tobacco, are also for sale.

Most coffee shops sell drinks in one area, marijuana in another. Drugs are often ordered by potency. It's common for first-timers to ask which is weakest; it's less embarrassing than passing out on the premises.

The coffee's generally good, but don't expect food or alcohol. Coffee shops usually aren't allowed to sell either, although you will find hash-laced brownies, milkshakes, and spacecakes, along with coffee, tea, and fruit juices. If you choose to smoke in a coffee shop, you'll be smart to order a drink to go with your joint. Chill music, dimmed lights, and comfy couches are staples of every joint (pun intended).

Some of the most popular smoking coffee shops are the crowded but good, award-winning **De Dampkring** (Handboogstraat 29; ☎ 020/638-0705); patio-blessed **Rokerij** (Singel 8; ☎ 020/645-432-567); pool table– and dart-friendly **Rookies** (Korte Leidsedwarsstraat 145–147; ☎ 020/694-2353); not touristy, laid-back **Paradox** (Eerste Bloemdwarsstraat 2; ☎ 020/623-5639); and the frat-boy, club-like shops of the **Bulldog** chain, which has branches around the city, including the **Bulldog Palace** (Leidseplein 15; ☎ 020/627-1908).

Finally, just like your momma told you: Don't talk to strangers or get a bag of reefer from them. It's sound advice because street peddlers like to throw in random ingredients that may give consumers unpleasant side effects.

(2002), a readable "history" of anecdotes that touches on such varied stories as Rembrandt's painting of a hanged girl to finding medieval artifacts during recent construction projects. Other, even lighter, views of A'dam come from foreigners who've stayed a while, including Bill Bryson's *Neither Here Nor There: Travels in Europe* (1999), where he retraces his 1972 to 1973 backpacking route, and Sean Condon's *My 'Dam Life: Three Years in Holland* (2003), an autobiography of sorts that details, among other things, what it's like to be unemployed and employed (the oddball jobs!) in the city.

Amsterdam: A Traveler's Literary Companion, edited by Manfred Wolf, is organized by area. The chapters, 17 stories by residents, include "The Canals," "The Red-Light District," "Gay Amsterdam," and "Jewish Amsterdam."

The Girl with a Pearl Earring (1999) by Tracy Chevalier (author of the book and co-scriptwriter) takes place in Delft, but it's all about Vermeer, and it's like watching a Dutch painting come to life. Although the painting that it's based on is in New York City, there are only 36 Vermeers known to exist, and many are in Amsterdam.

MOVIES

You can always find a Bond movie that's shot in a city you're traveling to; in Amsterdam's case, it's *Diamonds Are Forever* (the beginning). *Ocean's Twelve* is a love letter to the city. *The Bourne Supremacy*, in contrast, is supposed to be set in Amsterdam, but the filmmakers used German cities as stand-ins.

An earlier thriller, Hitchcock's *Foreign Correspondent* (1940), uses Amsterdam well.

Keep an eye out for *Nightwatching*, Peter Greenaway's movie about Rembrandt's classic painting, *The Nightwatch*, due to start filming as we go to press. The movie will peer behind the scenes of the people depicted, not all of whom want to be painted. There's even a murder. You might want to compare this to Jean-Luc Godard's *Passion* (1982), if you can get your hands on a copy, which also tells the story about *The Nightwatch*. *Prospero's Books*, Peter Greenaway's version of Shakespeare's *The Tempest* is also partly filmed in Amsterdam.

Lovers of stupid comedy should note that Harold and Kumar (of *Harold & Kumar Go to White Castle*, 2004) are due to arrive in Amsterdam in 2007.

Amsterdam Nuts & Bolts

Cellphone Providers & Service Centers   If your phone has GSM (Global System for Mobiles) capability and you have a world-compatible phone, you should be able to make and receive calls from Holland. Or you could rent a phone through Cellhire (www.cellhire.com or www.cellhire.co.uk). After a simple online registration, they will ship a phone, usually with a U.K. number, to your home or office. Usage charges can be astronomical, so read the fine print. U.K. mobile phones work in Holland; call your service provider before departing from home to ensure that the international call bar has been switched off and to check call charges, which can be extremely high.

Currency   Exchange your cold, hard American cash for some colorful, happy euros at the currency exchanges at Centraal Station, Schipol Airport, or any of the VVV tourist offices.

Embassies   All of the embassies are in the Hague. You can reach an official at the **U.S. Consulate** (Museumplein 19; ☎ **020/575-5309**). It's open from Monday to Friday 8:30am to noon and 1:30pm to 3:30pm. The **U.K. Consulate** (Koningslaan 44; ☎ **020/676-4343**) is open Monday to Friday 9am to noon and 2 to 4pm.

Emergencies   For all emergencies, police, ambulance, and fire department, call ☎ **112**. Some local hospitals are Academish Medisch Centrum (Meibergdreef 9; ☎ **020/566-9191**), Onze Lieve Vrouwe Gasthuis (1e Oosterparkstraat 279; ☎ **020/599-9111**), and Sint Lucas Ziekenhuis (Jan Tooropstraat 164; ☎ **020/510-8911**). The Rape and Sexual Abuse (De Eerste Lijn) hot line is at ☎ **020/612-7576**. The Drug Prevention Center is at ☎ **020/626-7176**.

Internet/Wireless Hot Spots   God knows how many windmills power the **easyInternetcafe** on Damrak 33 (www.easyinternetcafe.com; daily 9am–10pm). The 144 computers on the premises draw tourists trying to figure out train schedules or hostel accommodations online. If you walk down Damrak from Centraal Station, the easyInternetcafe will be on your right.

Laundry   Throw your smelly duds in a washer at **Wash and Mail** (Amstel 30) and check your e-mail while they go through the cycle. If you're in the western section of town, **The Wash Company** (Haarlemmerdijk 32, ☎ 020/625-3672) will make your skunky clothes snuggly fresh.

Luggage Storage   Centraal Station has great facilities that will stow your luggage while you figure out your transportation situation or look for a bed for the night. The cost is 4€ to 5€ for self-service lockers of various sizes (storage time of up to 24 hr.).

Narcotics   The use of narcotic drugs is officially illegal in the Netherlands, but Amsterdam allows the sale in licensed premises of up to 5 grams (.2 oz.) of hashish or marijuana for personal consumption, and possession of 30 grams (1.2 oz.) for personal use. Not every local authority in the Netherlands is as liberal-minded as Amsterdam when it comes to smoking pot—and Amsterdam is not so tolerant that you should just light up on the street, in regular cafes, and on trams and trains (though enough dopey people do). The possession and use of hard drugs like heroin, cocaine, and ecstasy is a serious offense, as is peddling any kind of drugs.

Pharmacies   A list of pharmacies can be found at www.fbadam.nl. While closing times are not consistent throughout the different locations, at least one pharmacy is always open on nights and weekends (based on a rotating schedule). To determine which pharmacy is open, call ☎ **020/694-87-09.**

Post Offices   Mail your postcards at the post office on Singel 250–256 (☎ **020/556-3311**). It's open Monday to Friday from 9am to 6pm (Thurs till 8pm) and on Saturday from 9am to 3pm.

Restrooms   What looks like a church statue may actually be a beautiful, freestanding, four-person urinal. Municipal officials have sprinkled a few of these around town (oddly enough, some in front of churches). When night falls, they drop off the portable, outdoor pissoirs to prevent revelers and drunk folk from doing their business in public. In the morning, they get picked up for emptying and to get them out of sight of tourists. Unfortunately, unless you're desperate, incredibly drunk, or both, women still have to beg coffee shop or bar staff to let them use the facilities.

Safety   In between the side streets and canals are hundreds of small alleyways where anything or anyone can be waiting, so use your common sense to get back to your hotel or hostel. Avoid sketchy areas and keep your guard up. The fact that drugs and prostitution are somewhat regulated doesn't mean that the streets are safer. Aside from the occasional pickpocket and the rare mugger, tourists are relatively secure in the city. You will be approached once in a while by someone trying to sell you some random drug or Viagra, but these people are mostly harmless and should leave you alone if you answer them with a simple and direct "no."

AMSTERDAM

Telephone Tips For **information** in Holland, call ☎ **0900/8008.** Watch out for special Dutch numbers that begin with 0900. Calls to these are charged at a higher rate than ordinary local calls. It could be as much as .90€ a minute. If you plan to use pay phones, get a KPN or a Telfort *telekaart* (phone card) that sells for 5€ and up to 25€. Note that neither company's cards will work with the other company's phones. Cards are sold at post offices, train ticket counters, VVV tourist information offices, some tobacconists, and newsstands. Some pay phones take credit cards, and a few take coins, of .10€, .20€, .50€, and 1€. No coins are returned. Both local and long-distance calls from a pay phone are .30€ a minute.

Tipping The Dutch government requires that all taxes and service charges be included in the published prices of hotels, restaurants, cafes, discos, and sightseeing companies. Even taxi fare includes taxes and a standard 15% service charge. In a restaurant, you can look for the words *inclusief BTW en service* ("BTW" is the abbreviation for the Dutch words that mean value-added tax), but not every place uses the written note. To tip like the Dutch, in a cafe or snack bar, leave small change on the counter or table. In a restaurant, leave 1€ to 2€, and up to a generous 5€ per person or 10% of the tab if the service was good. Should you feel an irrational compulsion to tip taxi drivers, on in-town rides either round up a euro or two or splurge with up to 5% or 10%.

Sleeping

When you emerge from Centraal Station and walk down Damrak, the crowds of people and the overabundance of hotel signs might give you the wrong impression. Hotels and hostels in central Amsterdam can get full rather quickly, especially in the summer. Don't fret, however; just outside of the city center you can find other options, most with better amenities at a lower price.

Also, most hotels and hostels do not have an elevator. If you book a room on the sixth floor, be prepared to climb the wonderfully narrow steps to reach your room. Many of the rooms are in houses that could never accommodate an elevator. What you lack in convenience is made up for in charm.

Hostels

→ **Bulldog Hotel** The enterprising Bulldog name has spread from its busy hostel to cafes, coffee shops, and bars all around Amsterdam. Look no further than Bulldog for new buddies and a raucous time. It's advertised as a hotel, but it really is just a hostel. Rooms are relatively clean and the entire thing is run efficiently, constantly welcoming hordes of eager college kids itching to rock it out in A'dam and sweeping out the ones who've had their fill. As a result, sleeping shouldn't be much of a priority if staying here. The entire hostel hums with guests partying until the wee hours of the morn. *Oudezijds Voorburgwal 220.* ☎ *020/620-3822. www. bulldog.nl. 22€–26€ single bed (8- to 12-person room); private room (with private bathroom and TV): 77€–85€ double, 99€–108€ triple, 115€–125€ quadruple. Amenities: Bar; cafe; outdoor patio.*

[MTV] [Best] → **Flying Pig Hostel** ★ It's by far the best hostel in Amsterdam, in terms of comfort and social opportunities. Beds are cushy, superclean, and crab free. Here you'll actually get a decent night's rest; the only drawbacks are that it's a bit pricier than other hostels and it fills up quickly. Meeting people here is a breeze in their phenomenal bar, and sketchy folks rarely frequent the building.

Compared to Bulldog and Meeting Point, Flying Pig is the Ritz-Carlton of hostels. *Nieuwendijk 100.* ☎ *020/420-6822. www. flyingpig.nl. Single bed with shared bathroom: 22€–23€ (18- to 26-person dorm), 25€–26€ (8- to 10-person dorm), 28€–30€ (4–6 person dorm). Rates include breakfast. Amenities: Bar; Internet; kitchen; lockers; luggage storage.*

→ **Hostel Meeting Point** Several hostels outshine the scruffy Meeting Point. Guests either hate the hostel with a vengeance or they don't mind the place at all. Rooms come stocked with 12 or 18 beds; huge oil barrels function as lockers. The system, though relatively simple, is sometimes stinky. The musty bins can be a pain to open, for the lids weigh about 15 pounds each and have a 5-pound padlock that makes it even heavier. Beds are smooshed so close together, don't be surprised if you roll over and find yourself nose to nose with a 25-year-old Brazilian. Unless you packed a biohazard suit, brush your teeth on the first floor. In fact, use the bathroom on the first floor for everything. The redone room is leaps and bounds cleaner than its second-floor counterpart. Guests smoke whatever they want freely in the hostel bar. Couple that with a pool table, foosball table, Sublime on the P.A., and the hostel almost redeems itself for its less-than-stellar accommodations. *Warmoesstraat 14.* ☎ *020/627-7499. www.hostel-meetingpoint.nl. 16€–21€ single bed. Amenities: Bar; Internet.*

Cheap

🎵 Best → **Bicycle Hotel Amsterdam** ★ Even bicycles need a place to rest their sprockets. Clemens Marjolein and Clé run this hotel/bike rental in the south of Amsterdam. Guests can rent a two-wheeler for 5€ and park it inside their shelter. Finding the hotel is a breeze: Look for the bicycles hanging on the brick face of the building on Van Ostadestraat. Plan to spend a lot of time in the quirky reception area when you're not riding around outside. The rooms can

sometimes feel like a hostel dorm (walls and doors a tad run-down), but the accommodations are acceptable. The common area near the entrance has Internet access, couches to rest your bike-butt, trippy lighting, and a cool cactus. *Van Ostadestraat 123.* ☎ *020/679-34-52. www.bicyclehotel.com. 61€–70€ double with shared bathroom, 70€–100€ with private bathroom. Rates include breakfast. Amenities: Bike rental; Internet. In room: TV.*

→ **Hotel Acro** The probability of renting a room with elevator access for less than 100€ in Amsterdam is close to nil. The Hotel Acro defies those odds. Guests get a lift and inexpensive rates. Its rooms are more than livable. Simple beds are surprisingly soft. And it's a stone's throw from Museumplein. *Jan Luijkenstraat 44.* ☎ *020/662-5538. www.acro-hotel.nl/index.php. 65€–110€ single, 75€–130€ double, 90€–165€ triple, 105€–185€ quad. Rates include breakfast. Tram: 2, 3, 5, or 12 to Van Baerlestraat. Amenities: Bar; Internet point (for a fee). In room: TV.*

🎵 Best → **Hotel Arena** ★ The Arena has matured greatly since its days as an orphanage. As a hotel, it now welcomes anyone looking for a decently priced room with a bit of style. The place oozes class, with minimalist, but comfortable, high-ceilinged rooms that up-and-coming young Dutch designers created. In the reception area, the walls are draped from floor to ceiling in black and red. Add a slick but casual restaurant (called TODINE), an urbane bar (TODRINK), and a trendy nightclub that was once a chapel (TONIGHT), and you have no reason to leave the grounds. If you can, try scoring at least a double room; many of the singles are slightly larger than closets. Aside from that, the only negative is its distance (30 min. by foot or 15 min. by Metro) to central Amsterdam. The only time you should ever use the underground public transportation in the city is to get to and from this chic hotel.

Amsterdam

SLEEPING

Agora **27**
Bellevue Hotel **3**
Die Port Van Cleve **17**
Flying Pig Hostel **5**
Hostel Bulldog **11**
Hostel Meeting Point **6**
Hotel Arena **40**
Hotel Misc **10**
Le Meridien **39**
Rho Hotel **13**
Winston Hotel **9**

EATING ◆

Albert Heijn **28**
Brasserie de Poort **19**
Cafe de Jaren **33**
Gelateria
  Italiana Peppino **41**
Green Planet **18**
Le Relais **32**
Pianeta Terra **25**
Tibet Restaurant **7**
Van Kerkwijk **14**

SIGHTSEEING ●

Ann Frankhuis **20**
Hash Marijuana
  Hemp Museum **12**
Huis Marseille **35**
Madame Tussaud's **16**
Stedelijk Museum CS **8**

PARTYING ★

Bulldog **35**
Cafe Chris **21**
De Dampkring **29**
De Drie Fleschjes **15**
De Duivel **30**
Hoppe **24**
Jimmy Woo **37**
Melkweg **38**
Odeon **26**
Papeneiland **1**
Paradox **22**
Rokerij **2, 31, 36**
Sinners **34**
Soundgarden **23**
Tonight **40**

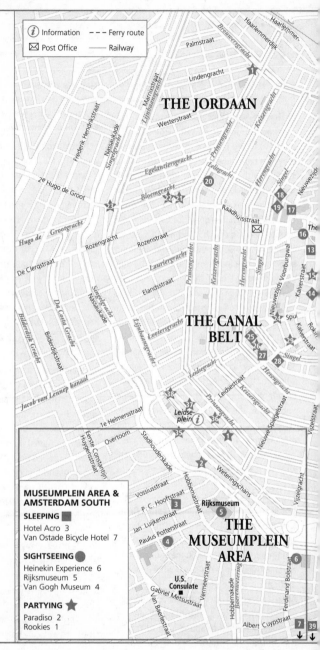

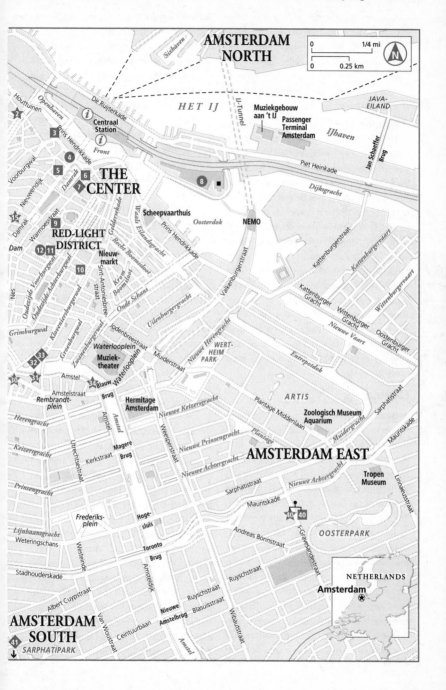

Gravesandestraat 51. ☎ *020/850-2400. www. hotelarena.nl. 80€–110€ standard double, 115€–150€ large double, 135€–165€ triple, 165€–200€ extra large room, 185€–235€ junior suite, 225€–275€ suite. Tram: 7 or 10 to Korte 's-Gravesandestraat. Amenities: Restaurant; bar; Internet. In room: TV.*

➜ **Winston Hotel** Quirky art adorns the walls, though you'll have to make it out through a few centimeters of hash tar. Once you get past the reception area and head for the hallways, a dank skunk smell radiates from the walls. Smoking is wholeheartedly permitted in the Winston. Stench aside, groups of friends will enjoy the relatively spacious dorm-like rooms. The place bills itself as an art gallery, too; the smallest gallery room is the toilet in the nightclub on the premises (use the website to check out the art before you book). A lounge provides further distraction. *Warmoesstraat 131.* ☎ *020/623-1380. www. winston.nl. 45€–55€ single, 56€–76€ double, 81€–105€ triple, 100€–128€ quad. Tram: 4, 9, 14, 16, 24, or 25 to the Dam. Amenities: Bar. In room: TV.*

Doable

➜ **Bellevue Hotel** Living in a Skyy Vodka ad would be an amazing experience: Imagine spending your days barely clothed with scantily clad and perfectly bronzed models lounging on sleek blue and white furniture. If the latter sounds good to you, you can at least live half of the fantasy at the Bellevue Hotel. The modern Bellevue is tastefully furnished with avant-garde beds that could have been designed by Frank Lloyd Wright and a slick blue-and-white color scheme. There's also enough lights (hidden track lighting), gizmos, and gadgets (LCD TVs) to keep many a tech head happy. *Martelaarsgracht 10.* ☎ *020/ 707-4500. www.bellevuehotel.nl. 110€ single, 155€ double, 210€ triple, 240€ quad. Amenities: Bar; Internet; luggage storage. In room: A/C, TV, hair dryer, safe.*

➜ **Hotel Agora** Symmetry isn't the Agora's strongest suit. Thanks to its being deemed "historical" by municipal officials, each of the 16 scattered rooms is uniquely shaped. You'll have to buzz in to get inside the hotel, but security in the immediate area isn't much of an issue. The quarters are pleasant with simple decorations and furniture. The airy, homey breakfast room is a great place to slurp your orange juice and inhale your cereal in relative comfort. *Singel 462.* ☎ *020/627-2200. www.hotelagora.nl. 72€ single with shared bathroom, 103€ with private bathroom; 88€ double with shared bathroom, 120€ with private bathroom, 135€ with canal view; 158€ triple; 185€ quad. Rates include buffet breakfast. Tram: 1, 2, or 5 to Koningsplein. Amenities: Breakfast room. In room: TV, hair dryer, safe.*

MTV Best ➜ **Hotel Misc** ★ Spending a couple nights at Hotel Misc is like crashing at the home of the cool older siblings you wish you had. The young, down-to-earth owners, Rachel and Pepijn, make you feel like part of their family. Friends of the two come in regularly to chat, and the ensuing laughter adds an element more calming than any couch or wallpaper pattern. Inside, the design and architecture magazines littering the lobby/restaurant area reinforce the fact that the couple go to extraordinary lengths to make every piece of furniture chic and chill, yet cozy. Together, the duo makes an incredible team. While they split most of the hotel duties, Pepijn is usually the handyman and Rachel the unbelievably warm host. Each of the six rooms is uniquely themed with names like "Afrika" and "Wonders." "Zen," perhaps their quirkiest and most interesting room, is adorned with African-influenced pieces and anchored by a wall mural depicting a beautiful beach during sunset. Half the rooms overlook the canal; the others have balconies over the quiet garden/ courtyard in back. *Kloveniersburgwal 20.*

☎ 020/330-6241. www.hotelmisc.com. Thurs–
Sun 135€ garden-view room, 155€ canal-view
room; Mon–Wed 125€ garden-view room, 145€
canal-view room. Rates include breakfast.
Amenities: Restaurant; bar. In room: TV,
minibar, safe.

Splurge

→ **Hotel Die Port Van Cleve** Brag to your
friends that you spent a few nights in the
Heineken brewery, and they'll try to call your
bluff the second you utter "Heine." If you
want to prove them wrong, gather the euros
to book a few nights in the Hotel Die Port Van
Cleve, 5 minutes from Centraal Station. The
19th-century building housed the first
Heineken brewery in the world. Much of the
regal exterior is matched inside its rooms.
Beds are draped in nicely patterned fabric
and the matching draperies give off a
soothing royal feel. Treat your stomach as
well by ordering one of their famous juicy
steaks at the Brasserie De Poort (see "Eating,"
below) inside the building. Nieuwezijds Voorburgwal 176–180. ☎ 020/624-4860. www.
dieportvancleve.com. Single 200–285€, executive single 250–340€, double 220–300€,
executive double 250–350€, suite 350–525€.
For the most up-to-date rates, call the hotel.
Breakfast buffet 18€. Tram: 1, 2, 5, 6, 13, or 17 to
the Dam. Amenities: Restaurant; bar. In room:
TV, hair dryer, living room, minibar (on
request), safe.

Eating

Dutch cuisine serves to warm and nourish.
One practical dish, erwtensoep, is a pea soup
with bacon or sausage. Traditional restaurants will always have it listed as a starter,
and while it may not be the most flavorful
dish, it sure satisfies any hunger. Herring,
another staple in Dutch cuisine, is sold on the
street in herringhuis stands throughout Amsterdam and is not expensive. Another, more
substantial and flavorful alternative is the
rijsttafel. Brought from Indonesia in the East
India Company's day, this meal can easily
feed a small group of people. The buffet
features several small plates of meats, rolls,
and rice.

Amsterdam's culinary and drinking
choices go beyond the conventional and the
upscale. This is a city of places that invite
you to sit a while. The bruine kroeg (brown
cafes) aren't cafes at all; these are usually
wood-paneled, traditional bars where you
can sit at a bar and taste gin (see "Partying"
below). Cafes and eetcafes are not just for
coffee; there you'll find simple sandwiches
and other light food that the Dutch typically
eat for lunch. And the "coffee shops" attract
customers who want to smoke pot and hash;
they do serve coffee, but they don't serve
food.

Hot Spots

🎬 **Best** → **Café de Jaren** ★ CONTI-
NENTAL Satisfy your eyes *and* your
stomach at the Café de Jaren. The menu prof-
fers hot dishes like couscous with lamb, but
the cafe mostly serves sandwiches and salads
along with its coffee. Come here to enjoy the
outdoor patio and the terrace along the canal.
Very few places can match this view, even
when the patio is closed in the winter. The
high ceilings and enormous windows treat
diners inside the cafeteria-like cafe to the
same beautiful panorama. The adjacent university guarantees a steady stream of undergrads to chat up at the bar or at the
"international reading table" when you're
swigging your espresso. Nieuwe Doelenstraat
20–22. ☎ 020/625-57-71. www.cafe-de-jaren.
nl. Main courses 12€–16€. Daily 10am–1am
(Fri–Sat till 2am; food served until 10:30pm,
drinks until 1am). Tram: 4, 9, 16, 24, or 25 to
Muntplein.

Cheap

➔**Restaurant Rozenbloom** DUTCH
Rozenbloom's homey, comfortable dining area
complements the hearty, traditional dishes
they offer on their reasonably priced menu.
The typical Dutch plate of marrow peas with
salty bacon, pungent onions, pickles, and
a single meatball is a great choice for the indecisive eater, and it won't leave your equally
indecisive stomach in knots. *Zit Plaatsen 60.*
☎ *020/622-5024. Main courses 11€–13€. Mon–
Sat noon–9pm. Tram: 1 or 2 to Spui.*

📺 Best ➔ **Tibet Restaurant** ★ CHI-
NESE Among the coffee shops in the
northern section of Warmoesstraat (just east
of Damrak) are a number of Asian kitchens and
sit-down restaurants. Most of them offer salty,
over-fried, cheap eats, but a few gems stand
hidden among the greasy joints. This one
whisks you to its wooden tables for perfectly
cooked Asian fare and temporarily transports
you from the noisy, congested streets. If you're
not drawn into the dining room by the sumptuous aromas, the low prices will get you to a
seat. For the same price as a meal in one of the
other nearby eateries, you can get a wonderfully prepared dinner in a relaxing environment. *Warmoesstraat 17.* ☎ *020/420-7833.
Main courses 7€–14€. Daily 1:30pm–1:30am.
Tram: 4, 9, 14, 16, 20, 24, or 25 to Dam Sq.*

➔ **Van Kerkwijk** FUSION A variety of
cuisines influence this tiny haunt: Indonesian, Vietnamese, Mexican, and Indian in particular. Walking past the Van Kerkwijk is
difficult without noticing the aromas of the
Indonesian chicken cooked in coconut milk,
for instance. Submit to this temptation and
sit down at one of the simple wooden tables.
You won't be disappointed when they start
bringing out the overflowing plates. *Nes 41.*
☎ *020/620-33-16. Main courses 9€–13€.
Daily noon–10pm. Tram: 1, 2, 5, 14, 16, 24, or 25
to Dam Sq.*

Doable

➔**Green Planet** VEGETARIAN/ORGANIC
The organic and vegetarian Green Planet uses
a liberal assortment of herbs in its original
recipes. The strudel filled with rosti, spinach,
goat cheese, asparagus, other veggies, and
tzatziki will make you forget how delicious
cooked cow can be. To make earth-conscious
folks even more comfortable, their dishes can
be adjusted to satisfy vegans, and nothing is
ever nuked (not a microwave in sight). Cap
off your meal with the tofu lemon "cheese"
cake and figure out how to convert your significant other to the vegetarian world. *Spuis-
traat 122.* ☎ *020/625-8280. Main courses
9€–16€. No credit cards. Mon–Sat 5pm–midnight, kitchen 5:30–10:30pm.*

➔ **Le Relais** ★ INTERNATIONAL This is
where you can sate your craving for high-
class munchies, and if you're so inclined,
book a room in a five-star hotel (the restaurant is inside the Hotel de l'Europe). Don
your finest duds and prepare your wallet for
fine Dutch dining. The menu here changes
more often than hostels change their sheets.
All the dishes are top-notch, particularly
the succulent pan-fried halibut with fennel
and fresh spinach. *Nieuwe Doelenstraat 2–8.*
☎ *020/531-1705. Main courses 18€–20€.
Mon–Fri noon–2:30pm and 7–11pm; Sat–Sun
7–11pm.*

➔ **Sama Sebo** ★★ INDONESIAN Many
locals consider this the best Indonesian
place in town. A 23-plate *rijsttafel* sets the
standard that others try to match. The very
Indonesian environment means rush-mat
and batik decor. You can make your own
mini-*rijsttafel* by putting together a selection from the a la carte menu. When you
order either of the two lunch specials, you
get a heaping mound of food that's more like
a one-plate *rijsttafel* than anything else. It's
cramped but convivial indoors, and the sidewalk terrace is equally as area-challenged as
the interior. The takeout service is a good

AMSTERDAM

option if you want to eat in your hotel room or maybe even snack on a bench on nearby Museumplein. *Pieter Cornelisz Hoofstraat 27 (close to the Rijksmuseum).* ☎ *020/662-8146. Main courses 14€-20€; rijstaffel 25€. Mon–Sat noon–2pm and 6–10pm. Tram: 2 or 5 to Hobbemastraat.*

Splurge

→**Brasserie De Poort** ★★ DUTCH/ INTERNATIONAL   If it's meat you're craving, look no further than Brasserie De Poort. The restaurant, part of the Hotel Die Port Van Cleve, gives a number to every steak it sells. If you're lucky enough to have a steak with a number that's a multiple of 1,000, you get a free bottle of vino. So far, they say they've served about six million steaks. Be forewarned: Wear a napkin bib. *Nieuwezijds Voorburgwal 176–180.* ☎ *020/ 624-4860. www.dieportvancleve.com. Main courses 16€–22€. Daily 7am–10:30pm. Tram: 1, 2, 5, 13, 14, or 17 to the Dam.*

→**Pianeta Terra** ITALIAN/ORGANIC Everything that used to have a pulse in this Italian restaurant (waitstaff excluded) is advertised as being "free range," and the leafy dishes are all organic. It's hard to make a bad choice with this menu; if you're particularly adventurous, order the octopus and potato terrine. I'm pretty sure *that* was free range— though I don't exactly know what an octopus farm would look like. *Beulingstraat 7.* ☎ *020/626-1912. Primi 12€–13€, secondi*

Picnic Pick-Ups

The **Albert Heijn** supermarket, at the corner of Leidsestraat and Koningsplein, near Spui (Mon–Fri 9am–8pm, Sat 9am–6pm; tram: 1, 2, or 5), stocks almost anything you might crave for a picnic, including cold cuts, sandwiches, and a bottle of wine. Take the 10-minute walk to Vondelpark, if the weather's nice, and you might even time it right to catch a free concert there.

At the Museumplein branch of the store, across the street from the Concertgebouw (tram: 3, 5, 12, or 16), you can climb to the sloping, grass-covered roof with your goodies and sunbathe there.

19€–24€. Tues–Sun 6–10:30pm. Tram: 1, 2, or 5 to Koningsplein.

Cafe

→**Gelateria Italiana Peppino** ★★ ICE CREAM   Considered the best homemade ice cream in town by many, this family-run parlor serves about 100 flavors. If you've walked around the Albert Cuyp market, this is the place to go for a refreshing break. The cappuccino's good, too. *Eerste Sweelinckstraat 16.* ☎ *020/676-4910. Daily 11am–11pm. Closed Nov–Apr. Tram: 4 or 20.*

Partying

Save the Funyuns, Visine, and ruminating for the day, and hit the streets at night to experience Amsterdam's killer bar and club scene. The city's tolerance also carries over to its bars and clubs, most of which are open until a respectable 2am (later for several clubs). In addition, international DJs regularly visit Amsterdam, making the coastal city a venerable hot spot for electronica and techno. Tsk, tsk, and you thought the city was good for only one thing.

Clubs and bars are scattered throughout the city and especially around **Leidseplein, Rembrandtplein, Rosse Buurt (Red-Light District),** and nearby **Nieuwmarkt.** If you find yourself in the northwest part of A'dam, look no further than **Haarlemmerdijk** (the street) for nightlife info. Almost any store, coffee shop, or bar should have employees happy to help you find some nocturnal action. If you're wandering in central Amsterdam, stroll around the **university**

AMSTERDAM

📻 That's the Ticket
m t v

If you're 25 or younger, you can buy a **CJP (Cultural Youth Pass)** at the **AmsterUit Buro (AUB) Ticketshop** (Leidseplein 26; ☎ 0900/0191; www. uitburo.nl). It entitles you to free or reduced admission to most museums and discounts on many cultural events, including theatre and concerts. The Ticketshop can reserve tickets for almost every venue in town, for 2€ a ticket. You can even get in touch with them before your trip, and reserve tickets from abroad. The office is open Monday to Wednesday and Saturday from 10am to 6pm, Thursday from 10am to 9pm, and Sunday from noon to 6pm.

AUB also publishes the free monthly magazine *Uitkrant* (it's in Dutch, but it isn't difficult to understand the listings info). For a similar charge (2.50€), the VVV Amsterdam tourist info office (p. 62) can also reserve tickets.

area (south of Kloveniersburgswal and north of Singel). Cafes and busy university buildings are usually stocked with flyers and cards advertising special student nights in the city's hottest clubs.

Don't worry too much about dress code. Most clubs will let you in with whatever you're wearing (as long as you're not barefoot or topless). Pricier joints like Jimmy Woo's or Sinners, on the other hand, keep you out if you're not in decent threads.

Brown Cafes & Tasting Houses

Even if you don't drink, look in on a *bruine kroeg* (brown cafe) and order something. The tradition goes back to the 1600s. These bars serve alcohol and get their name as much from the wood furnishings inside as from the tobacco residue on the walls. They tend to be older, more traditional places where you can sip a glass of beer or maybe even get a cheap meal. You might find sand on the floor or a snooker table and locals who act surprised when a tourist walks in. Many often begin to get busy after 8pm, but they usually open around noon and stay open all day.

Proeflokaal (tasting houses) are basically brown cafes, but in these establishments, customers traditionally order *jenever* (Dutch gin, taken "neat" without ice) or another product of the distillery that owns the place.

Ritual demands that you drink the first sip with your hands behind your back as you lean over the bar. Order like the locals: A *borrel* is the most common term for a glass of *jenever*. When it's filled to the brim, as tradition dictates, it's called a *kamelenrug* (pronounced "cam-*ay*-len-rookh," meaning "camel's back"). The *kopstoot* (literally "knock on the head") that comes next is a beer chaser. Regular beer is a *pils,* and you can ask for one in four different sizes from "dwarf" to half-liter size.

Some of the more popular cafes are listed below.

➜ **Café Chris** One of the oldest—possibly *the* oldest—of the brown cafes, Café Chris tends to attract a blue-collar crowd. Beer mugs hang from the ceiling, the pool table is always busy, and the old toilet has a pull-chain that you work from the main room. *Bloemstraat 42.* ☎ *020/624-5942. Tram: 6, 13, 14, or 17.*

➜ **De Drie Fleschjes** Journalists and other businesspeople gravitate here to taste the wide variety of *jenevers* (gins). "The Three Little Bottles" began 300 years ago as a tasting house, where customers could try liqueurs distilled and aged on the premises. *Gravenstraat 18 (between the Nieuwe Kerk and Nieuwendijk).* ☎ *020/624-8443. Tram: 1, 2, 4, 5, 6, 9, 13, 14, 16, 17, 24, or 25.*

→**Hoppe** Tourists mix with locals here. Hoppe opened in 1670; its dark walls and low ceiling seem unchanged from when it first opened. If you find you've come when it's standing room only, you can just spill out onto the sidewalk along with the many other customers who'd rather wait than leave. *Spui 18–20.* ☎ *020/420-4420. Tram: 1, 2, or 5.*

→**Papeneiland** While you're in the Jordaan, check out the beautiful Delft tiles in here. The cast-iron stove adds to the atmosphere. *Prinsengracht 2 (at the corner of Brouwersgracht).* ☎ *020/624-1989. Tram: 1, 2, 5, 6, 13, or 17.*

Coffee Houses

Although you will find coffee here—and tea and juice—these coffee houses sell mostly marijuana and hash. See "Culture 101: The Grass Is Greener" on p. 63 for legalities and a list of popular hangouts.

Comedy Club

→**Boom Chicago** The place to go for a good dose of British and American humor that's partly scripted and partly improvised. The targets: Amsterdam, the Dutch, tourists—nothing is sacred. The restaurant opens at 7pm; meals will run you 16€ to 20€ per person. The box office is open daily from noon to 8:30pm. *Leidseplein Theater, Leidseplein 12.* ☎ *020/423-0101. www.boomchicago.nl. Cover 12€–32€ (doesn't include dinner). Tram: 1, 2, 5, 6, 7, or 10 to Leidseplein.*

Dance Clubs

→**De Duivel** The best (and sometimes only) place in A'dam for hip-hop and rap oldies. Wear your jeans baggy and low, and you'll fit right in. *Reguliersdwarsstraat 87.* ☎ *020/850-2400. Tram: 16, 24, or 25 to Keizersgracht.*

→**Jimmy Woo** Overhyped? Maybe. Overrated? A smidge. Oriental and swank? Check and check. Jimmy Woo still has enough draw to lure big-name Dutch, as well as international, celebrities into its genteel atmosphere. The Far East theme extends to its ornately decorated furniture and to the exotic cocktails whipped together at the bar. It's not the best value when clubbing, but value will be the last thing on your mind when you see all the pretty partyers on the dance floor as you kick back on your plush couch. *Korte Leidsedwarsstraat 18.* ☎ *020/626-3150.*

📺 Best →**Odeon** ★ The owner of Hotel Arena did a heck of a job revamping Singel 460. The building dates back to 1663, when it began as an unsuccessful brewery. In its awkward adolescence, it went through several identity crises: a mansion in the late 1600s, a bank in the 1780s, a concert hall in the 1830s, a theater in 1900, and an auction house in 1920. In 2005, it reopened as a trendy club and bar. The architects restored the place from 2003 to 2004, keeping bold, old architectural details like exposed brick vaulted ceilings, and added the best of modern design. The four baroque representations of the seasons surround the contemporary wall murals. Owner Paul Hermanides lowers the speakers each evening, bringing the patrons up close and personal with the big beats. Not just any run-of-the-mill electronica is allowed through the booming boxes; only the most cutting-edge tracks engulf the dancers below. *Singel 460.* ☎ *020/521-8555. www.odeon amsterdam.nl. Cover 3€–8€. Tram: 1, 2, or 5 to Koningsplein.*

→**Paradiso** Electronica in Amsterdam is basically a religion for the thousands of 20-somethings skittering between the city's canals and coffee shops. These devout followers can practice their faith in Paradiso. Whenever possible, a DJ is spinning some hard-core jungle, industrial, or electro-disco. It's only fitting that the building that the club invaded was an old, converted church. If you feel dirty and impure after a rip-roaringly immoral time in Sinners (see below), bring your penitent self to the cathartic Paradiso. The power of disco compels you! *Weteringschans*

6–8. ☎ *020/626-4521. www.paradiso.nl. Cover 8€–22€. Tram: 1, 2, 5, 6, 7, or 10 to Leidesplein.*

→ **Sinners** It's officially known as Sinners in Heaven. After only one night, you can scratch off four of the seven deadly sins from your life list. If you're not dressed to the nines, the surly doormen won't hesitate to toss you off the queue: Say hello to Sin Number One: wrath. Once inside, gluttony takes over as you grab a few liters of perfectly mixed, expensive cocktails. A glance at the dance floor will take care of lust. This overly popular joint is rife with young, lithe revelers shimmying to the latest R&B hits from the West. Occasionally, some big shots from European cinema, radio, and TV come here to wallow in each other's bling. If you're not careful, envy might just get the best of you. *Wagenstraat 3–7.* ☎ *020/620-1375. Cover 6€–12€. Tram: 4, 9, or 14 to Rembrandtplein.*

📺 **Best** → **Soundgarden** ★ Chris Cornell, long before his little tryst with

Audioslave, named his band after a Seattle outdoor exhibition that made fantastically eerie sounds when the wind blew through its various sculptures. The Amsterdam bar is no different. Anyone looking for a break from the repetitive and brain-splitting effects of insipid techno will find relief in the speakers at Soundgarden. Here, hard and alternative rock (both new and old) are the tune-du-jour every jour. The grungy 1993 atmosphere will

Red Light, Green Light!

Wide-eyed and eager sightseers visit the area just west of Damrak in the Old City to indulge their curiosities and their hormones. Amsterdammers call their infamous, well-visited **Red-Light District** "Rosse Buurt." For most modest tourists, an evening stroll through the area is completely harmless. Stick to the well-lit main paths and you'll find many other tourists simply getting a kick out of seeing who comes staggering out of the peep shows.

Do not take pictures, though. The women, behind large windows, might be knitting, reading, or doing their nails. For some, this is a second job, complete with good benefits, including regular medical checks, welfare eligibility, and their own trade unions. They work in clean premises, pay taxes, and expect a certain level of respect from the—mostly—tourists who come to call.

Some do, however, try to get the attention of potential customers. Don't be surprised to hear tapping on the glass. Among the women's storefronts, you'll find peep-show joints with private areas, dark and noisy bars, theaters offering off-color performance art, adult bookstores and video shops, and appliance stores.

Be careful, though, of the "heroin whores" who are wild cards and not part of the legal prostitution scene. They tend to hang out on the bridges just outside of where their more professional counterparts are working. And keep your wallet well covered; this is also pickpocket and junkie territory.

Tip: Women who come might want to hook up with a buddy—male or female—before visiting. A solo female might be harassed.

make any fan of flannel happy. *Marnixstraat 164–166.* ☎ *020/620-2853.*

→**TODINE/TONIGHT** You probably will spend less time admiring the frescoes on the orphanage chapel's walls (if you even notice them) than bouncing off them. But when the bright lights hit the dance floor just so, the aura of the chapel adds to the intimate environment. If you can notice it, kudos to you. Now stop spacing out, get back to the task at hand, and work that gorgeous crowd. *Gravesandestraat 51.* ☎ *020/850-2400. Cover 6€–10€. Tram: 7 or 10 to Korte 's-Gravesandestraat.*

Performing Arts

→**Concertgebouw** ★ Designed by the same architect as the Rijksmuseum, this 1888 building is said to be one of the most acoustically perfect concert halls in the world. You probably won't hear Marley here (although they do occasionally have world music scheduled), but it is home to the Royal Concertgebouw Orchestra and host to many classical and jazz ensembles. Within the Main Hall, classical's heavy hitters bring crowds to standing ovations. The smaller Recital Hall is used for more intimate sessions and solo concerts. *Concertgebouwplein 2–6.* ☎ *020/ 671-8345. www.concertgebouw.nl. Tickets from 15€; ask about student concerts and free rehearsals. Tram: 3, 5, or 12 to Museumplein; 16 to Concertgebouwplein.*

→**Heineken Music Hall** A mega-hall for mega stars, from LL Cool J to Radiohead to Elvis Costello to Pink. Ticket prices vary; check the website for details on schedule and price. *Arena Boulevard 590. www.heineken-music-hall.nl. Metro: to Bijlmer.*

📺 **Best** →**Melkweg** ★★ Melkweg is basically a Chuck E. Cheese's for college kids. Instead of a furry rodent leading you around, quality international bands and DJs take on most of the entertainment responsibilities in this enormous complex. A cinema and theater replaces plastic ball pits and arcades.

Melkweg's eclectic collection of artsy performances are influenced by art forms as varied as world-beat music and gay/lesbian theater. In between shows or before, don your party hat and check out the rest of Melkweg's offerings: a restaurant, a coffee shop, a bar, an art center, a dance floor, a photo gallery, and an exhibition space. You'll have to pay a nominal membership fee in addition to the performance ticket, but given the endless number of amusements, it's worth every euro. The box office is open Monday to Friday from 1 to 5pm and Saturday to Sunday from 4 to 6pm. *Lijnbaansgracht 234A.* ☎ *020/531-8181. www.melkweg.nl. Cover 5€–10€.*

→**Musiekgebouw** ★ This concert hall focuses on jazz, modern, and experimental music, as a complement to its more staid sister, the Concertgebouw. The 2005 building is a showcase of glass and steel and uncompromisingly modern lines. The menu is varied, including an annual Jew's Harp Festival in July. Look for late-night concerts in the summer, too. And if you just want to gawk at the building, reserve space on one of the Saturday morning tours (11am); it's well worth the 7.50€ tag if you like architecture. *Piet Heinkade 1.* ☎ *020/788-2010 (box office). www. muziekgebouw.nl.*

Sightseeing

The Big Three. No, it's not a legendary team member on the Netherlands' national basketball team. It's the Rijksmuseum, the Van Gogh Museum, and the Anne Frankhuis (Anne Frank House). Their combined powers attract thousands of tourists to the city. Two of the

Free & Easy

The free **ferries** are ideal microcruises for the cash-strapped. With fine views of the harbor, these short crossings connect the city center with Amsterdam Noord (North), across the IJ channel. They're free for passengers on foot and bicyclists. There's little of interest in Noord, though, so the crossing is its own attraction. Ferries depart from piers along De Ruyterkade behind Centraal Station. One route connects Pier 7 and Buiksloterweg on the north shore, with ferries every 10 to 15 minutes. A second route links Piers 8 and Uplein, a more easterly point on the north shore, with ferries every 10 to 15 minutes. Both services operate round the clock. (A third service costs 1.30€ for a half-hour trip that provides an even better view of the harbor. The exact route varies, but it generally runs from Pier 9 to Java Island in the Eastern Docks and across to points on the north shore; it departs about every half-hour.)

→ Stroll along the canals at night, especially by the **Skinny Bridge.** The white fairy lights make it particularly romantic.

→ Check out the city's **narrowest house** (just 1m/3 ft. wide) at Singel 7. It's a cheat, though, because it's only the facade that's so narrow. The house broadens in the back.

→ Visit the **flower market** on Singel (p. 84). The flowers will cost you, though!

→ Take in a lunchtime rehearsal concert at the **Muziektheater** (Tues; www.hetmuziektheater.nl) and the **Concertgebouw** (Wed; p. 77) from 12:30 to 1pm every week from October to June.

big three are in Museumplein, an area south of central Amsterdam where art reigns supreme. You'll find heaps of other fantastic museums there, ranging from the off-beat (Hash Marijuana & Hemp Museum) to the avant-garde (Stedelijk). To find out which exhibitions are in town and which galleries are worth missing, visit the tourist offices near Centraal Station. You may find discounts for the major attractions there, too.

The University Scene

Head to the university area (southern part of Kloveniersburgwal and north of Singel) and ask where students hang out. Schmooze in Café de Jaren, and you may discover that the Stedelijk is having a Warhol exhibition—and that your new buddy has time to show you around. Students in the area are incredibly chill and approachable, so don't be shy to strike up a conversation while you're exploring the area.

Festivals

April

Queen's Day. This is the definitive Dutch celebration for a queen who justly should be celebrated for environmental do-gooding, if for nothing else. Call the tourism office (p. 61) for info. April 30.

May

Liberation Day. An annual celebration of the anniversary of the liberation of Holland from the Germans in World War II. Call the tourism office (p. 61) for info. May 5.

National Cycling Day. Throughout the city and the rest of the country, the Dutch people get on their bikes and pedal. So what else is new? Call the tourism office (p. 61) for info. Second Saturday in May.

June

Holland Festival. An arts fest that highlights new developments in theater, dance, opera, pop music, film, and photography in various locations throughout the city. Call ☎ 530/7111 for more info. Throughout June.

Amsterdam Roots Festival. The city plays host to a wide range of music, theater, and cultural events with an international flavor in different venues within the city. Call Uit Boro (☎ 621/1211) or Melkweg (☎ 020/624-1777) for more info. June 5 to 13.

July

Over Het IJ Festival. Avant-garde theater, music, and dance are performed in Amsterdam-Noord, beside the IJ channel, at the old NDSM Wharf. Contact Over Het IJ Festival (TT Neveritaweg 15; ☎ 020/624-6380) for more info. Around the last 2 weeks of July.

August

Amsterdam Pride. This is a big event in Europe's most gay-friendly city. A crowd of 150,000 people turns out to watch the highlight: the Boat Parade's display of 100 or so outrageously decorated boats cruising the canals. Add to the mix street discos, open-air theater, sports, and a film festival. Contact Gay Business Amsterdam (☎ 020/620-8807) for more info. First weekend in August.

September

Jordaan Festival. This loosely organized festival in the trendy Jordaan neighborhood features food, games, fun, and lots of drinking and music in the streets. Contact Stichting Jordaan Festival (☎ 020/624-6908) for more info. Early September.

Top Attractions

🎬 Best → **Heineken Experience** ★ You don't need a travel guide to understand that this multimedia museum is a tourist trap. It's still a trap worth visiting, though, because the sensory overload hits all the right spots. The few "educational" displays are the products of a mass-marketing effort that cooked up as many short-attention span attractions as possible. One ride simulates what it would feel like to be a beer bottle (not for the queasy), another puts you in the driver's seat of a horse-drawn carriage (that carries the beer, of course) in Amsterdam, and heaps of touch-screens quiz visitors about the bubbly beverage. It's just barely worth the price of admission. *Stadhouderskade 78.* ☎ *020/523-9666. www.heinekenexperience.com. Admission 10€. Tues–Sun 10am–6pm (last entrance at 5pm). Closed Dec 25 and Jan 1. Tram: 16, 24, or 25 to Stadehouderskade.*

→ **Madame Tussaud's** A ton of things from my childhood still freak me out. Clowns take the top spot, but wax museums are a close second. This Madame Tussaud's has specimens so lifelike that I was able to enjoy it. In addition to dead-on representations of Gandhi, Bowie, van Gogh, and Ah-nold the Governator, interactive spots like the Music Zone encourage you to belt out a few tunes (do you have the chops to be the next Idol—American *or* Dutch?). Not a karaoke fan? Bike beside Lance Armstrong on a virtual bike in the Sports Zone, and compare your ride times with that of other visitors. Unlike boring wax museums where you're limited to taking cheesy photos alongside an awful replica of Joe Pesci, here you may feel as if you're hanging out with glitterati. *Dam 20.* ☎ *020/522-1010. www.madametussauds. nl. Admission 23€. Daily 10am–6:30pm (last entrance at 5:30pm). Tram: 4, 9, 14, 16, 24, or 25 to the Dam.*

Museums

🎬 Best → **Anne Frankhuis (Anne Frank House)** ★★★ Reading her diary is one thing, but walking through Anne Frank's actual home is something else. Climbing the narrow stairs and halls is an emotionally wrenching experience as you put yourself in the little Dutch girl's shoes. Everything has been relatively untouched, from the trick bookcase door to the pictures that Anne put up in her shared bedroom. Even if you've

12 Hours in Amsterdam

1. **Admire Centraal Station.** Architect Petrus Josephus Hubertus designed this classic Dutch structure (ca. 1884–89) on three artificial islands supported by 30,000 pilings. At the time, it was not well received. Now its detailed facade is considered a classic example of the Dutch neo-Renaissance.

2. **Explore the Big Three.** Even if you get allergic in museums, go, go, and go.

3. **Rent a bike.** Life is faster in the bike lane.

4. **Ride a canal boat.** Missing it would be like missing a ride on one of London's double-decker buses.

5. **Go to Boom Chicago.** Funny, creative, and guaranteed to give you the giggles, even after all these years. It's Amsterdam's best English-language comedy show.

6. **Chill in Vondelpark.** No chaos, no trams, no cars, no crowds, few tourists, and a little peace of mind.

7. **Hang out at a brown cafe.** No games, no gimmicks, no nonsense, just locals and beer.

8. **Experience Bimhuis.** A no-brainer for a night of impressive live music.

AMSTERDAM

never picked up the international bestseller, you won't be completely lost here, as tours and displays bring to life the suffering the Frank family endured in their 2 years of hiding during the Nazi occupation. *Prinsengracht 263.* ☎ *020/556-7105. www.annefrank.nl. Admission 7.50€ adults, 3.50€ kids 10–17. Apr–Aug daily 9am–9pm; Sept–Mar daily 9am–7pm; Jan 1 and Dec 25 noon–7pm; May 4 9am–7pm; Dec 16 and Dec 31 9am–5pm. Closed Yom Kippur. Tram: 6, 13, 14, or 17 to Westermarkt.*

MTV Best → **Hash Marijuana & Hemp Museum** ★ Check it before you wreck it. By "it," I mean your brain. The informative displays describe the chemical affects of THC on the body, the weed's history in various countries and eras, and how it's grown/cultivated. Unlike the Heineken Experience, you won't be given a free sample at the end of your tour. *Oudezijds Achterburgwal 130.* ☎ *020/623-5961. www.hashmuseum.com. Admission 5.70€ adults, 3.85€ per person for groups larger than 10 people. Daily 11am–11pm. Closed Jan 1, Apr 30, and Dec 25. Tram: 4, 9, 14, 16, 24, or 25 to the Dam.*

→ **Huis Marseille** After taking dozens of photos on your digital of your buddies exhaling clouds of smoke into various lights, you probably think you have pretty good camera chops. Before you declare yourself the next Ansel Adams, though, see how true artists frame their compositions, from Cecil Beaton to Lee Friedlander. *Keizersgracht 401.* ☎ *020/531-8989. www.huismarseille.nl. Admission 5€ adults, 3€ students. Tues–Sun 11am–6pm. Closed Jan 1, Apr 30, and Dec 25. Tram: 1, 2, or 5 to Keizersgracht.*

→ **Museum Het Rembrandthuis (Rembrandt House Museum)** ★★ To see the artist's greatest works, get thee to the Rijksmuseum. This house, which dates from 1606, offers a more intimate, personal look at the artist himself. Rembrandt bought the three-story, 10-room house at the height of his fame, in 1639. His wife died here; his son was born here. And the artist went bankrupt here. It wasn't until 1906 that the house became a museum, which now looks the way it did when the painter lived here. See his artist's cabinet, walk where his students walked, and try to imagine what his printing press must have been like when he was working on it. *Jodenbreestraat 4–6 (at*

Waterlooplein). ☎ *020/520-0400. www. rembrandthuis.nl. Admission 7€ adults, 5€ students. Mon–Sat 10am–5pm; Sun and holidays 1–5pm. Closed Jan 1. Tram: 9 or 14 to Waterlooplein; 16, 24, or 25 to Keizersgracht.*

MTV Best → Rijksmuseum ★★★ The savvy curators here culled the most impressive masterpieces from their collection of seven million artifacts to bring you, for a limited time only (until summer 2008), "Rijksmuseum: The Greatest Hits!" Enjoy crowd pleasers such as Rembrandt's *The Night Watch,* Vermeer's *The Kitchen Maid,* and much, much more! A single wing (Philips Wing) is chock-full of Dutch masters, from Vermeer to Frans Hals to de Hooch. A renovation has closed much of the rest of the museum to the public. *Jan Luijkenstraat 1 (Museumplein).* ☎ *020/647-7000. www.rijksmuseum.nl. Admission 9€ adults, free for visitors under 19. Combination meal and ticket 12€–14€. Daily 9am–6pm. Closed Jan 1. Tram: 2 or 5 to Hobbemastraat.*

→ Sexmuseum Amsterdam Behind its faux-marble facade, this museum is not as sleazy as you might expect, apart from one room covered with straight-up pornography. Otherwise, the presentation tends toward the tongue-in-cheek. Exhibits include erotic prints and drawings from around the world and trinkets like tobacco boxes decorated with naughty pictures. *Damrak 18.* ☎ *020/622-8376. www.sexmuseumamsterdam.com. Admission 2.50€. Must be 16 to enter. Daily 10am–11:30pm. Tram: 1, 2, 4, 5, 9, 13, 16, 17, 24, or 25 to Centraal Station.*

→ Stedelijk Museum CS ★★ The Rijksmuseum and Van Gogh Museum are fine and all, but anyone jonesin' for something a little more contemporary should seek out the Stedelijk Museum. While the main building undergoes renovation, Amsterdam's modern art museum can be found east of Centraal Station, a perfect spot for lazy art hounds who don't want to trek down to Museumplein (its permanent address). When the Stedelijk will move back to its original location is anyone's guess, but it's a museum that's worth visiting after you've hit the Big Three. Here, the walls are home to works by modern icons such as Warhol, Calder, and Appel. You may find a van Gogh or two; the exhibits change regularly. *Oosterdokskade 5 (until 2008, then moves back to Paulus Potterstraat, Museumplein).* ☎ *020/573-2911. www.stedelijk.nl. Admission 9€. Daily 10am–6pm. Closed Jan 1. Tram: 1, 2, 4, 5, 6, 9, 13, 16, 17, 24, or 25 to Centraal Station.*

MTV Best → Van Gogh Museum ★★★ That Vincent is a pretty popular guy. He took some magical swipes with a paintbrush, took another swipe at his ear, and now he rates an entire museum. In his lifetime, the artistic genius went through hundreds of canvases and sketch pads, each of which thousands of people would now line up to see. While he bartered many of them for everyday necessities back in the day, a good number of them ended up in the hands of his family. The Van Gogh Museum is the final resting place for the pieces his family donated to Holland. You can view sketches, letters, paintings, and prints in the extensive exhibition. *Paulus Potterstraat 7.* ☎ *020/570-5200. www.vangoghmuseum.nl. Admission 13€ adults, 2.50€ kids 13–17. Sat–Thurs 10am–6pm, Fri 10am–10pm. Closed Jan 1. Tram: 2, 3, 5, or 12 to Baerlestraat.*

Playing Outside

Easygoing Amsterdam sports a few places where you can clear your head and get your heart pumping. Finding large parks, though, is harder than you'd think. The miles of canals snaking through the compact city make spacious green spaces hard to come by.

Vondelpark ★★★ Look to the west of Museumplein for the one exception:

AMSTERDAM

Vondelpark. The warm weather and sun bring out the Frisbee tossers, in-line skaters (see rental info below), and sunbathers. If you're feeling particularly active, drop in on one of the pickup games of soccer or basketball. Vondelpark also offers open-air concerts and theater performances, most of which are free of charge.

Best Canal Bikes ★★ If water's your scene, don your floaties and try these quirky canal vehicles that seat two to four people. Most folks associate the plastic pedal boat with quiet lakes, but here you can pedal under the city's bridges. Rent from **Canal Bike** (various locations: Anne Frankhuis, Rijksmuseum, and Keizersgracht/Leidsestraat; ☎ **020/626-5574;** www.canal.nl; 7€–8€ per hour per person). The bike comes with a map, but check out "Biking on Water" (below) for a suggested tour route. You can also rent the bike at one mooring and leave it at another. Keep in mind that you need to leave a deposit of 50€.

Ice-Skating Almost everyone skates in the winter, but it's not easy finding a skate shop that rents. Try **Jaap Edenbaan** (Radioweg 64; ☎ **020/694-9894**), which is open from November to February, and has an outdoor rink that attracts casual skaters as well as speed skaters practicing for the next big race. If it's cold enough, the frozen canals become sparkling highways through the city. You can take the rental skates to the canals, where little kiosks dispense heart-warming liqueurs. Follow the Dutch and be careful of thin ice under the bridges!

In-Line Skating The Friday Night Skate can attract up to 3,000 skaters some nights. It starts at 8pm at the Filmmuseum in

BIKING on Water

A suggested tour by **MTV** **Best** water bike: Start at the Canal Bike mooring on Prinsengracht (at Westermarkt, near the Anne Frankhuis). Pedal south along Prinsengracht, past Lauriergracht, Looiersgracht, and Passeerders-gracht, maybe diverting into one or more of the quiet side canals. At Leidsegracht, go straight ahead under the Leidsestraat Bridge until you come to Spiegelgracht, where you turn right. Continue to the end, then left under the bridge into Lijnbaansgracht.

Turn right at the first corner into narrow connecting canal that merges with Singelgracht in front of the Rijksmuseum. Go right along this canal, which is bordered by overhanging trees.

Keep going, past the Bellevue Theater and the De la Mar Theater, and turn right into Leidsegracht, which brings you back to Prinsen-gracht and the long home stretch back to Westermarkt.

Tip: Don't leave the bikes unat-tended. They'll get taken away.

Vondelpark and wends its way through 15km (9 miles) of the city. **Rent a Skate** (☎ **020/ 664-5091**) does what its name suggests—at the Amstelveenseweg entrance of Vondel-park. It costs 5€ to rent gear for an hour and 15€ for a day; you need to leave an ID with them and a 20€ deposit that is refundable when you return the skates.

Shopping

Amsterdam's known for its flower bulbs, dia-monds, and pottery. The list below takes a different approach to shopping in the city: You'll find shops for books, clothes, music, condoms, and the artful souvenir (including chocolate and cheese). Regular shopping hours are Monday, Tuesday, Wednesday, and Friday from 9 or 10am to 6pm (although some stores don't open until 1pm on Mon); Thursday to 9pm; and Saturday to 5pm. Many stores stay open on Sunday as well, usually from noon to 5pm, and more and more supermarkets are staying open daily from 8am to 8pm, or even to 10pm.

Amsterdam also has *avondwinkels,* "evening stores," which can prepare takeout meals on the cheap and sell deli items and other munchies that you can take home to your hotel room. Hours are usually from 5 to 11pm or midnight.

Even if you don't want to buy anything at the markets, you might want to stroll through one or two. They are free, interesting, and often in a neighborhood that merits exploration.

→ **Athenaeum Boekhandel B.V.** English versions of the classics are usually easy to find in European bookstores, but works by contemporary authors are often scarce. Athenaeum sells both with a decent selection in Dutch and English. *Spui 14–16.* ☎ *020/ 622-62-48. www.athenaeum.nl.*

→ **Betsy Palmer** Clogs make for decent, albeit lame attempts at souvenirs, but if you're looking for something you'll actually put on your feet, Betsy Palmer has a line of kooky cowboy boots, galoshes, slides, heels and flip-flops for women. *Rokin 9–15.* ☎ *020/422-10-40. www.betsypalmer.nl.*

→ **Boudisque** This music depot probably pays by the word on its advertisements, given the signage inside the shop. CDs and vinyl from amalgamated genres like "allpoprockdance" and "reggaeworldhiphop" fill the bins here. They also sell a bunch of DVDs. *Haringpakkerssteeg 10–18.* ☎ *020/623-26-03. www.boudisque.nl.*

→ **Brutus** Of all the music vendors in Amsterdam, Brutus might be the smallest of them all. What it lacks in size, it makes up for in the selection. The tiny staff has an amazing ear for indie rock and underground hip-hop.

Brutus is the place to go for those hard-to-find EPs and rare releases by labels like DefJux, SubPop, and Matador. *Molsteeg 8.* ☎ *020-420-61-05. brutus@xs4all.nl.*

→ **Condomerie Het Gulden Vlies** The Golden Fleece stocks a vast range of condoms—all shapes, sizes, and flavors, from regular brand labels to flashy designer fittings. It just happens to be on the edge of the Red-Light District. *Warmoesstraat 141 (behind De Bijenkorf department store).* ☎ *020/627-4174. Tram: 4, 9, 14, 16, 24, or 25 to the Dam.*

→ **Fame Music** Sometimes those little hole-in-the-wall CD stores just don't have what you want because they carry a limited selection and at most, two of each CD. If The Killers, Kelly Clarkson, and Kanye West all have new releases coming out while you're traipsing around Holland, you're sure to find a hefty cache of each artist in this Dutch chain. Apologize to the small businesses that you squash on your way out. *Kalverstraat 2–4.* ☎ *020/ 638-25-25. www.fame.nl.*

→ **Het Grote Avontuur** It's hard to categorize exactly what Het Grote Avontuur sells. Maybe it's because half of the products hang off the ceilings or sit on the floor. You'll find pieces to brighten up your living room or trinkets to give as souvenirs. Lampshades, nesting dolls, and stationery all look like party favors with a colorful, 1920s Art Nouveau spin. *Haarlemmerstraat 25.* ☎ *020/ 626-85-97. www.hetgroteavontuur.nl.*

→ **Kinki** Your shaggy mane should fit in just fine with the rest of the unkempt folks in the coffee shops, but if you want to impress the sober cutie behind the counter, shed a few pounds of locks at Kinki. The small Dutch chain is basically a Supercuts, only hipper. Walls are purposely shoddy, the staff's amiably sassy, and the styles are incredibly punk-chic. Unfortunately, this wonderfully trashy dive needs to fund itself somehow, and customers sometimes feel mugged by the bill.

AMSTERDAM

Haarlemmerdijk 17. ☎ *020/625-6000. www. kinki.nl.*

➜**WE** That tie-dyed shirt might help you score with that hippie chick/dude, but the standards of the clubbing crowd in Amsterdam is slightly more refined. WE, a Dutch chain based in Utrecht (think H&M with a haughty twist), has a sizeable branch in Amsterdam located on Kalverstraat. The friendly and shiny staff will help you pick out some threads to impress even the snootiest of dancers in Jimmy Woo's. *Kalverstraat 87.* ☎ *020/626-34-52. www.wefashion.com.*

➜**Wini** The closest beach for Amsterdammers is on the Ijburg Lake, a mere 20 minutes by bus. The next best option: Go to Wini on trendy Haarlemmerstraat. It's mostly stocked with Hawaiian shirts, flip-flops, and flowing dresses, but you'll also find a strange but good assortment of secondhand clothes and accessories, including a rack of trackjackets, some designer jeans, rugged cowboy boots, and a ton of used/retro threads. *Haarlemmerstraat 29.* ☎ *020/427-93-93.*

➜**Zipper** I haven't seen crisper used clothing anywhere. I'm convinced that Zipper treats the things it buys with some magical chemical that gives the well-chosen T-shirts and pants a starchy texture. Zipper takes the fun out of snagging a sweet vintage shirt in a huge Salvation Army store. It's as if they've taken everything cool from those thrift stores and

AMSTERDAM

Market Makers

The city hosts more than 50 MTV (Best) **outdoor markets** ★ every week, some of them permanent or semipermanent, and others that just pass through. Three of the best are the floating 15-stall Bloemenmarkt (Flower Market), the Waterlooplein Flea Market, and the 350-stall Albert Cuyp Market.

The **Waterlooplein Flea Market** on Waterlooplein (tram: 9 or 14) is a mix of junk and nicer things amid a constant press of people. You might find a cooking pot or a Dutch print among the CDs, bargain watches, and leather jackets. For a snack, try the *patates frites met mayonnaise* (french fries, Dutch style, with mayo). The market's open Monday to Saturday from 10am to 5pm.

Don't expect all the stalls at the **Bloemenmarkt** (floating flower market) on Singel (tram: 4, 9, 14, 16, 24, or 25 at Muntplein) to be floating, or you'll be disappointed. Many of them are moored or on land, but the place is still heavy in atmosphere. The flowers are gorgeous, and the tulips will cost just a little less here than in town. It's open daily from 8am to 8pm.

You'll find just about anything and everything at the **Albert Cuyp Market** on Albert Cuypstraat (tram: 16, 24, or 25), including different types of foods, clothing, textiles, flowers, and plants. The market's open Monday to Saturday from 9am to 6pm.

Another market, the Friday **book market** at Spui (tram: 1, 2, or 5), usually has about 25 different booksellers. You might even be able to pick up a few books in English. It's open Friday from 10 to 6pm.

Antique-hunters, be forewarned: The **Kunst- & Antiekcentrum De Looier** at Elandsgracht 109 (tram: 7, 10, or 17) is an enticing collection of old warehouses overflowing with dealers showing their wares. You can salivate over the armoires and other big pieces, but you'll have to make do with toting home smaller items: jewelry, prints, porcelain, knickknacks, tin toys, and Delft tiles, to name a few.

cool Jets

Take a ride to the seacoast by jetfoil. **Fast Flying Ferries** (☎ 020/639-2247) run between Amsterdam and IJmuiden (on the North Sea Canal), a seaport known for its fish auctions (at Halkade 4; Mon–Fri 7–11am) and the three great locks that manage the water flow to Amsterdam (Amsterdam lies up to 5.5m/18 ft. below sea level). The 30-minute ride starts from a pier behind Centraal Station. The boats leave every half-hour from 7 to 10am and 4 to 7:30pm, and every hour from 10am to 4pm. Fares are 4.50€ one-way and 7.75€ round-trip for adults.

marked up the price by a few euros. Anyone looking to forgo the gratifying feeling of scoring an obscure, yet funky, shirt after hours of searching will find *exactly* what they're looking for at Zipper in about a minute. *Nieuwe Hoogstraat 8.* ☎ *020/627-03-53.*

Antwerp

Once neglected by travelers, the port town of Antwerp (Anvers in French, Antwerpen in Flemish) has been seeing more visitors in recent years. Antwerp is 48km (30 miles) from Brussels, but don't come expecting to see wooden shoes or milkmaids here: Antwerp's become a fashion curiosity, a mecca that draws followers who come to see the work of the Antwerp Six—the group of clothing designers, including Dries van Noten, Ann Demeulemeester, and Dirk Bikkembergs, that started shaking up runways in the 1980s. Belgium's largest and edgiest city, Antwerp (pop. 450,000) is also beginning to rival Berlin and Amsterdam as a hotbed for clubs. Always a popular road trip destination for Bruxellois looking for a real party, the city has slowly been coming up from under the radar for international travelers, too.

It's not Antwerp's first run as a European "It" city. Once home to Flemish master painters such as Peter Paul Rubens and Anton van Dyck, Antwerp was an active stage in the Renaissance-era art world. And Antwerp's long-time status as the "Diamond Capital of the World," and home to DeBeers, certainly hasn't scaled back its cache in Europe and beyond: Tucked away in tiny Belgium is the world's leading market for cut diamonds, a $25 billion-per-year industry.

In some ways, Antwerp feels like an extension of Brussels—its big sibling 45 minutes to the south—except that Antwerp leans decidedly more Dutch than French Brussels. You'll also find that it's mainly the misfits of Brussels (those who dare to speak Flemish instead of French) who thrive in the Antwerpian scene. Mix that rebellion with the tons of young, fashionable people here, and you've got a laid-back city that really knows how to party.

The Best of Antwerp

● **The Best Hotel Breakfast:** In the hopping Het Zuid neighborhood—a playground for artists, hipsters, and their Starbucks-toting yuppie-wannabe fans— **Hotel Rubenshof** is great in its own right. The breakfast in the morning, however, is divine—with a wide choice of cheeses, fruits, breads, eggs, and meats— served with a smile in a gorgeous dining nook with stained-glass windows and elegant woodcarvings. See p. 91.

● **The Best Cheap Eats:** As the name suggests, **Frituur Nˈi** is best for a big old heap of Belgian frites (those tasty fried potatoes that you must not, under any circumstances, call "french fries"). Resist the urge to douse them in Heinz, and eat them like the locals do, with mayonnaise or spicy cayenne ketchup. See p. 93.

● **The Best Splurge Meal:** If a restaurant has a couple Michelin stars, it's gonna be good, and **t'Fornuis** is no exception. In a sea of kitschy restaurants that charge a bit too much for mussels and stews, this French restaurant in a 16th-century stone mansion is a standout. The cuisine and decor have an understated elegance. See p. 94.

● **The Best Club Scene:** The top nightspot in Belgium for years, **Café d'Anvers** is a former monastery with Gothic-medieval decor. It's where the most beautiful denizens of the fashion and music worlds get crunked and show off their labels. Wear something nice (at least a decent knockoff) if you want to get past the doorman. See p. 94.

● **The Best Bar for Beer Lovers:** A classic place to start your night and find like-minded friends is **The Kulminator.** This rustic bar has staggering options— 700 types of beer—and staggering consequences: Belgian ales can have double the alcohol content of their American counterparts, so pace yourself. See p. 95.

Getting There & Getting Around

Getting into Town

BY PLANE

The closest major airport is **Brussels National Airport** (☎ 02/753-45-50), about 40 minutes away by train, which you can catch at Centraal Station. The **Sabena Airport Express Bus** (☎ 02/511-90-30; 7.50€ one-way) runs to and from Antwerp every hour.

Antwerp has its own airport, **Deurne Airport** (☎ 03/285-65-00), but the flight schedule is scant, with few international flights. It's generally cheaper and more sensible to fly through Brussels National. If you do fly into Deurne, **De Lijn** bus no. 16 shuttles between the airport and Pelikaanstraat, outside Centraal Station in Antwerp center. Taxi fare to the center is around 12€.

BY TRAIN

From the train, you'll see the city's Flemish name—ANTWERPEN—on the boards at **Centraal Station.** The city's gorgeous main rail depot, built between 1895 and 1905, Centraal Station is 1.5km (1 mile) east of the Grote Markt, on the edge of the city center. The neighborhood is the typically seedy, bustling part of town where train stations are often located. For your security, Centraal Station has coin-operated luggage lockers. Antwerp's other mainline rail station is **Berchem,** 4km (2¹/₂ miles) south of the city center. For schedule and fare information for both stations, call ☎ 03/240-20-40.

ANTWERP

Trains arrive about every half-hour from Brussels and Ghent. The trip time from both cities is around 30 minutes. Antwerp is on the **Thalys** high-speed train network that connects Paris, Brussels, and Amsterdam (and Cologne via Brussels). From Paris, you can take the Thalys high-speed trains through Brussels direct to Antwerp, or the slower and cheaper International trains, changing in Brussels. From Amsterdam, you can go direct, either on the Thalys or the normal International and Inter-City trains. Reservations are required for Thalys. Most Thalys trains stop at **Berchem,** but a few serve **Centraal Station.** For all schedules, fares, and reservations, call ☎ 02/528-28-28.

BY BUS

Most long-distance buses arrive and depart from the bus station on Franklin Roosevelt-plaats, a short distance northwest of Centraal Station. Timetables and fare information are available from a kiosk in Centraal Station, or by calling ☎ 070/22-02-00. The Eurolines company operates a daily service from London's Victoria Coach Station—via the Dover-Calais (France) ferry or the Channel Tunnel's Le Shuttle train—to Antwerp, stopping at Bruges and Ghent. The city can also be reached from around Europe on the Eurolines network, direct or via Brussels or Amsterdam. For schedule and fare information, contact **Eurolines** at ☎ 08705/808080 in Britain (☎ 02/274-13-50 in Belgium).

Getting Around

ON FOOT

Even though Antwerp is a fairly large city, walking is a great way to get around in good weather. Streets are wide, with sidewalks everywhere. One major street threads through the city and accesses most points of interest. Its name changes along the way, however, so don't forget your map. (*Tip:* The names are based on nations, so look for signs such as Belgiëlei and Amerikelei.)

BY TRAM

Antwerp's mass transit system is run by **De Lijn** (☎ 070/22-02-00; www.delijn.be). There is an underground Metro, but for visitors, the tram is the best way to get around. A single fare is 1€. The most useful trams for tourists are lines 2 and 15, which run between Groenplaats and Centraal Station. Full public transportation information is available from a De Lijn kiosk inside Centraal Station.

BY TAXI

You can't hail taxis on the street; you must go to a stand (found all over town) or call ☎ 03/646-83-83 or 03/238-38-38.

BY BIKE

If you're a very confident city cyclist (or a thrill seeker) you can rent bicycles at Centraal Station for around 8€ a day. Check out Antwerp's chaotic traffic scene, though, before you plunk down a deposit. I'd highly recommend hoofing it or taking public transport instead.

Antwerp Basics

Orientation: Antwerp Neighborhoods

Legend has it that Antwerp was deliberately laid out to confuse outsiders, to stave off potential plunderers who might invade the city from the port. Sound far-fetched? Try finding your way around Antwerp for a couple of hours.

The good news is that most places you'll want to visit (bars, pubs, watering holes, maybe a museum or a cathedral, more bars) are within a pretty concentrated area.

Talk of the Town

Four ways to start a conversation with a local

1. **Parlez vous français?** Most likely, the answer will be no. French is the official language here, but it's just not spoken in this part of Belgium. While this is too bad for the French, it's cool for the English speakers.
2. **Couture or vintage?** Runway chic rules the city's formidable fashion schools, but ask around to find out what sartorial taste has trickled down to the masses.
3. **How many carats do you like?** Seeing as how Antwerp is the diamond capital of the world, diamonds are bound to come up in conversation. Artificially price-inflated lumps of glorified coal mined using labor enforced by child mercenaries, or the scintillating embodiment of two hearts beating as one? Discuss.
4. **Dark or light beer?** Ask your neighbor to decipher a menu or recommend a frothy brew, and you'll find yourself on the receiving end of a treatise. Avoid mention of Budweiser at all costs.

Opposite Centraal Station, at the heart of a bustling area, is **Koningin Astridplein;** from here De Keyserlei runs toward the river and joins the **Meir,** one of Antwerp's main shopping streets. The Meir leads into **Schoenmarkt,** which heads into a large square called **Groenplaats**—hard to miss, as it is home to the tallest cathedral in the low countries, the Cathedral of Our Lady. Steps away from Groenplaats is Antwerp's main square, the **Grote Markt (Market Square)**— a colorful, banner-filled hub with Renaissance buildings such as the majestic Town Hall and 16th-century guild houses. It's also lined with sidewalk cafes and bars, and hosts lots of outdoor concerts and festivals in summer. In the square's center, it's worth checking out the fountain-statue of the Roman soldier Brabo— interesting for the fact that there's no pool to catch the water. From here, you can walk down the **Suikerrui** to the river, where you'll find a Mario Bros.—style medieval fortified castle, the Steen, which houses the maritime museum.

Tourist Information

The **Antwerp Tourist Office** (Grote Markt 15; ☎ 03/232-01-03; toerisme@antwerp.be;

Sun–Fri 9am–6pm; Metro: Groenplaats) is smack in the middle of things. Here you can find maps and information on local goings-on during your stay, as well as detailed public transportation fares and updates.

Recommended Websites

○ **www.visitantwerpen.be**: This site by the Antwerp tourist office is the go-to spot for info on the city.
○ **www.visitflanders.com**: One stop shopping for answers to any question you might have about traveling throughout Flanders.
○ **www.trabel.com/antwerp.htm**: Breaking details on events in the city, as well as in-depth history and sightseeing information.

Culture Tips 101

Antwerp is definitely not all gloss and glam. You don't have to look hard to find the seediness you'd expect from a port town, red-light district and all. It's more important than in other Belgian cities to bring your street smarts to Antwerp, along with your cutting-edge club wear. Although it's not particularly dangerous, it's safe to say you're not in Bruges anymore.

ANTWERP

You're not in Brussels either. French may be the official language of Belgium, but don't try *bonjour*-ing your way around Antwerp. Locals are proud of their provincial Flemish roots and local Dutch language. But the average Antwerpian's borderline disdain for all things French is good news for you: Most of them speak English as a second language, and will be more than happy to practice with you.

See "Rules of the Game" below for tips on Antwerp's drinking and drug scene.

Recommended Books, Movies & Music

See p. 178 in the Brussels chapter for recommendations on Belgian books, movies, and music.

Antwerp Nuts & Bolts

Cellphone Providers & Service Centers Belgium's largest cellphone provider, **Proximus,** sells phones throughout Antwerp. Call ☎ **32-78-05-6030** or visit www.proximus.be for info.

Currency Banks give the best exchange rates, but they are open only Monday through Friday from 9am to 1pm and 2 to 4:30pm. Street bureaus are open later, especially around the train station, but your best bet is to tote around your debit or credit cards and use them whenever possible. Antwerp accommodates plastic more than most Flemish cities.

Embassies All embassies are in Brussels; see p. 178 for info.

Emergencies For a medical emergency, dial ☎ **101.** For the fire department or police, call ☎ **100.** The police station is at Oudaan 5 (☎ **03/202-55-11**).

Internet The cheapest, best Internet access is at 136 Nationale, for only about 1.50€ an hour. It's not the cleanest place in town, but it's far from the dirtiest—and they have American keyboards available.

Laundry There's a shortage of laundromats in Antwerp, but one to try is **Cleaning Masters NV** (2170 Merksem; ☎ **03/645-01-02**).

Luggage Storage Lockers are available at the train station, Centraal, at Koningin Astridplein.

Pharmacies Look for neon-green crosses. Pharmacies take turns on the midnight shift, so every area should have a drugstore that's open 24 hours. Most pharmacies will post a sign directing you to the store on duty that night.

Post Office The main post office is at Groenplaats 42. It's open Monday to Friday from 9am to 6pm and Saturday from 9am to noon.

Restrooms Should you need to go while in the center of Antwerp, try the Astrid Park Plaza Hotel (Koningin Astridplein 7; ☎ **03/203-12-34**), across the square from Centraal Station. See p. 87 for more info.

Safety Antwerp is generally a safe city, but crime is more prevalent here than it is in Brussels or Bruges. It's a good idea to take the sensible precautions as you would in any major city: Watch your wallet and purse, don't go out alone at night, and watch your back in any areas that seem seedy—especially around Centraal Station and in the red-light district north of the Grote Markt.

Telephone Tips   You can reach a local operator by dialing ☎ **1207** and an international operator with ☎ **1204.**

Tipping   The prices on most restaurant menus already include a service charge of 16%, so it's unnecessary to tip. However, if the service is good, it's usual to add something extra by rounding up the bill to the nearest convenient amount. Otherwise, 10% is adequate, and more than most Belgians would leave. A service charge is included in your hotel bill as well. Taxis include the tip in the meter reading. You can round up the fare if you like, but you don't need to tip unless you've received an extra service, such as help with luggage. Here's a general guide to tipping for other services: Give 1€ to ushers in some theaters and cinemas, 20% of the bill for hairdressers (leave it with the cashier when you pay), and 1€ or 2€ per piece of luggage for porters.

Sleeping

Antwerp's hostel and hotel owners and employees are generally warm and hospitable—thanks in part to the many young adults who come here from Holland looking to break into the travel industry. Chances are you'll come across quite a few ridiculously polite, blond-haired, blue-eyed receptionists who are gung-ho to give you advice and recommendations about the city they now call home. That said, "Princess and the Pea" types looking for luxury hotels are better off staying in Brussels and commuting into Antwerp, a half-hour away.

For travelers who would gladly sacrifice five-star digs for a good party, here are a few of the better places to hang your hat between club hopping.

Hostels

→ **Den Heksenketel Hostel** For location alone, steps away from Groenplaats, this is your best bet for cheap lodgings in Antwerp. It's a 2-minute walk from the Cathedral of Our Lady, which is visible from all over the city—key for finding your way home after a long night. It's one of the most popular hostels in the city, so you're sure to find pals at the bar downstairs. (Don't miss the House Brew beer before you head out for a night; it's especially good.) Dorms are coed, and security and supervision are minimal, which means you've

got to be alert and safeguard your stuff and your personal space. *Pelgrimsstraat 22.* ☎ *03/226-19-128. www.hostelworld.com. 16€ dorm. Rates include breakfast. Metro: Groenplaats. Amenities: Cafe; 3am curfew; kitchen; laundry service; shared bathrooms.*

Doable

📺 Best → **Hotel Rubenshof** ★★ In the hopping Het Zuid neighborhood, the refreshingly old-fashioned Hotel Rubenshof has simply decorated, clean, comfortable rooms with high ceilings and hardwood floors. Plain, crisp sheets and blankets cover the beds. In the former residence of the Belgian cardinal, dating back to 1860, this hotel still feels like a home. The main room of the lobby has a fireplace, newspapers, and many well-used board games for guests. And breakfast, served in a dining nook with stained-glass ceilings and woodcarvings, is amazing—with plenty of cheeses, fruits, breads, eggs cooked various ways, and meats. *115–117 Amerikalei.* ☎ *03/237-07-89. www.rubenshof.be. 28€ single with shared bathroom, 50€ with private bathroom; 40€ double with shared bathroom, 65€ with private bathroom; 55€ triple with shared bathroom, 80€ with private bathroom. Tram: 12 or 24 to 1st stop in Brederodestraat. Rates include breakfast. Amenities: Breakfast room; shared bathrooms (in some).*

Antwerp

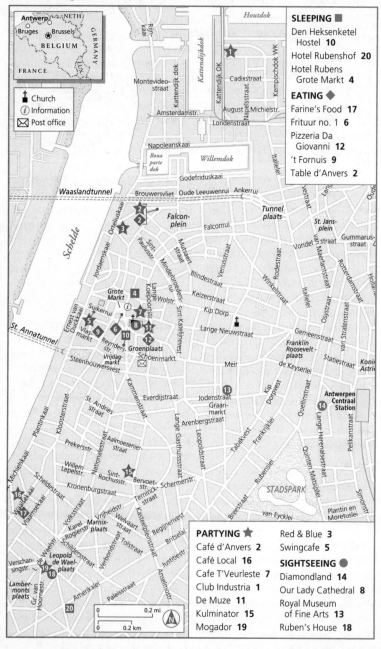

SLEEPING ■

Den Heksenketel
  Hostel **10**
Hotel Rubenshof **20**
Hotel Rubens
  Grote Markt **4**

EATING ◆

Farine's Food **17**
Frituur no. 1 **6**
Pizzeria Da
  Giovanni **12**
't Fornuis **9**
Table d'Anvers **2**

PARTYING ★

Café d'Anvers **2**
Café Local **16**
Cafe T'Veurleste **7**
Club Industria **1**
De Muze **11**
Kulminator **15**
Mogador **19**

Red & Blue **3**
Swingcafe **5**

SIGHTSEEING ●

Diamondland **14**
Our Lady Cathedral **8**
Royal Museum
  of Fine Arts **13**
Ruben's House **18**

† Church
ⓘ Information
✉ Post office

Splurge

→ **Rubens Grote Markt** The Hotel Rubens goes a long way to ensure your stay in Antwerp is comfortable. It's a splurge, but you get what you pay for—a complimentary cocktail at check-in, individually decorated rooms, bathrooms with marble fixtures, the best hangover-curing breakfast in town, and a courtyard garden with architecture from the 16th century—including Pagaddertoren, the oldest tower in Antwerp. Best of all, it's 1 block from Grote Markt square, the centuries-old center of Antwerp. *Oude Beurs 29.* ☎ *03/222-48-48. www.hotelrubensantwerp.be. 145€–255€ double, 445€ suite. Tram: 10 or 11 to Wolstraat. Amenities: Bar; limited room service; laundry service. In room: A/C, TV, dataport, minibar, hair dryer, safe.*

Eating

A hot-button topic in Antwerp is the recent influx of immigrants from all over, but it's good news for the tourist on a budget looking for a cheap meal. Little no-name ethnic dining spots abound, especially in the area just south of the red-light district on Paardenmarkt and on the outskirts of Het Zuid. Antwerp also has the second largest Hassidic Jewish population after New York City, so there are lots of kosher restaurants. If you're not dead set on classic Belgian cuisine, you can still count on having a full belly during your stay.

One classic Belgian dish that's popular here is mussels and frites—you can find it at practically any restaurant in the city, regardless of the price range. The little shops around Grote Markt or Groenplaats also feature simple Belgian classics, from frites to omelets.

People in Antwerp tend to sit down to dinner after the sun goes down—after 7:30pm.

Hot Spots

MTV **Best** → **Table d'Anvers** ★★ FRENCH Just down the block from Farine's, the cellphone-for-pleasure-not-business crowd heads to this spot for fine French cuisine, such as rack of lamb and filet of sole. Exposed brick, light woods, and faux cracked ceilings give the place a casually elegant feel. Situated along the trendy southern quays, and with only 40 seats inside and 12 outside, this place books solid days in advance, so call for reservations. *43 Vlaamse Kaai.* ☎ *03/248-51-51. www.tabledanvers.be. Main course 8.75€–19€ per entree. Tues–Fri noon–2:30pm and 6–11pm, Sat–Sun 6–11pm. Tram: 8 to Museum.*

Cheap

MTV **Best** → **Frituur N°1** ★ FRITES As its name suggests, Frituur N°1 serves the best frites in town. But whatever you do, don't call them french fries, and don't douse them with ketchup. Eat them like the locals do, with mayonnaise or spicy cayenne ketchup. *Hoogstradt at Oude Koornmarkt. No phone. 3€ for an order of fries with sauce. Tram: 2, 3, or 15.*

→ **Pizzeria Da Giovanni** ITALIAN Had your fill of frites? Can't shake your Domino's habit, even overseas? Then make your way to this pizza joint, in the shadow of the cathedral at Groenplaats. Sure, the waitstaff may hit on you or your date, but the pizza is good, the bread is homemade, and everything is served super quickly. Don't forget your student ID—it'll get you a 20% discount. *Jan Blom Straat 7.* ☎ *03/226-74-50. Pizzas 4.50€–13€, pastas 6€–13€. Daily 11am–midnight. Metro: Groenplaats.*

Doable

→ **Farine's Food** BELGIAN/VEGETARIAN With its communal, family-style tables, Farine's is good for some fun as well as great food. It's a safe pick for even the most picky vegetarian and/or foodie, with its menu of classic, hearty Belgian fare and some international dishes, all prepared with fresh, often organic ingredients in an open kitchen. It's not a place where diners tend to mind their own business; be ready to converse with whichever artsy-fartsy Belgian or in-the-know globetrotter ends up seated next to you. *40 Vlaamse Kaai.* ☎ *03/238-37-76. Main courses 10€–16€. Wed–Mon 7am–10:30pm. Tram: 8 to Museum.*

Splurge

🎵 Best →**t'Fornuis** ★★ BELGIAN Widely known as Antwerp's best restaurant, t'Fornuis isn't riding on the strength of its Michelin stars. The waitstaff is extremely skilled and accommodating, and the decor manages to be understated despite being set in a 16th-century stone mansion. The place has no menus, but trust me when I say the French food will be amazing. Chef Johan Segers will actually visit your table to talk with you about your meal. How's that for service? *Reyndersstraat 24.* ☎ *03/233-62-70. Main courses 24€–52€. Mon–Fri noon–3pm and 7–10pm. Metro: Groenplaats.*

Partying

Nightlife is the real reason most travelers come to Antwerp. But I've got a secret for you: I didn't find anything special about Antwerp's clubs and bars, in and of themselves, compared to nightclubs elsewhere in Europe. If you've seen one neon glow stick, you've seen them all, right? What makes clubbing in Antwerp great fun is the buzz. Everyone comes here expecting to have a blast, and they make it happen.

Because hot spots in a city like Antwerp fluctuate more than a Hollywood starlet's bra size, you've got to check out a website such as **www.amphion.be** to find out what's happening. Do your research because the rumors are true—Antwerp has no legal minimum drinking age—and you may end up at a club that resembles a lame version of your junior prom. Don't be afraid to ask around. Most Antwerpians are happy to have a new club-hopping partner for the night, or at least give you the dirt on what's happening. It also doesn't hurt to have a local help you get past the doorman. Even if your backpack wouldn't fit your hottest club gear, a Flemish-speaking person in your posse might help stand in for those Gucci loafers that you left at home.

Clubs don't get started here till at least 1am, and wind down sometime around sunrise; most dance spots also have about a 10€ cover.

Clubs

🎵 Best →**Café d'Anvers** ★★ In a former monastery, with Gothic medieval decor, Café d'Anvers is without a doubt the trendiest nightspot in town. Dress to kill. The doorman can be absolutely brutal, especially if you're not a regular, a rock star, a model, or a mogul.

Rules of the Game

In a country that prides itself on its beer above all else, it's not really surprising that there's no official minimum drinking age—so, if you have a younger sibling along, you can legally be the bad influence he/she has always needed. As for the other flavors of the substance rainbow, Antwerp is not quite as forthcoming as its Netherlandic neighbors. Hash is illegal, but cops don't usually expend much energy pursuing dope smokers. Naturally, in the city's heavy rave scene, there's a lot of E around. A word to the wise: True, you're not in Singapore, and in general, Antwerp PD isn't looking to hassle tourists, but be careful about where and with whom you expand your mind.

Verversrui 15. ☎ *03/232-147-112. www. cafe-d-anvers.com. Tram: 2, 3, 7, 8, 10, or 15.*

➔ **Café Local** A spacious, Latin-themed dance club with a more easygoing door policy and relaxed clientele. In the hipsterhaven Het Zuid area, salsa and meringue beats move the crowd of collegiate Corona swillers and laid-back young professionals. *Waalse Kaai 25.* ☎ *03/238-50-04. www.cafe local.be. Tram: 8 to Museum.*

➔ **Club Industria** This club in a former warehouse is still solidly in second place—the pre- or post-game to the Café d'Anvers scene—but its sights are set on being the number-one spot. The heady mix of Euro house attracts world-famous DJs. *Indiestraat 8–10.* ☎ *03/234-109-192. www.clubindustria. be. Bus: 27 to Indiestraat.*

Bars & Lounges

On your first night in town, you might settle down into the nearest cool-looking bar only to wonder, "So where is everybody?" The first thing you need to know about Antwerp bars is that they don't fill up until well past 11:30pm. This isn't to say there's no fun to be had before the crowds thicken; Belgians love beer, and you're sure to find yourself a buddy at any time of day, no judgments cast.

➔ **Café T'Veurleste** This is the place for the 25-and-under crowd. You'll find miniskirted coeds and Belgian frat boys who love to throw back cheap brews, tequila shots, and the oh-so-exclusive Bacardi and Diet Cokes. It's just a block from the Grote Markt, so you'll have lots of other options if the debauchery and thumping Top 40 get to be too much. *Lijnwaadmarkt 4.* ☎ *03/231-97-92. Metro: Groenplaats.*

📺 **Best** ➔ **The Kulminator** ★ A classic place to start your night and find likeminded friends is The Kulminator, a rustic bar with 700 types of beer. Just beware that Belgian ales are much more potent than their American counterparts. Even if you're the reigning champ of your college's kegstand

parties, avoid chugging here in A-town. *Vleminckveld 32.* ☎ *03/232-45-38. Tram: 12 or 24 to Bank.*

➔ **Mogador** Savvy Antwerpians with some cash come to this swank pre-club party to see and be seen. The crowd is young, manicured, and professional; the cocktails are top-shelf; and the music is soul and funk, spun by a DJ. It's in the Het Zuit, a bit off the beaten path between Grote Markt and Groenplaats. *Graaf van Egmontstraat 57.* ☎ *03/238-71-60. www. mogador.be. Tram: 8 to Egmonstraat.*

Gay Clubs

San Francisco has the Castro. New York City has Christopher Street. Antwerp has . . . well, nothing. There is no geographic or metaphoric center of Antwerp's gay scene—a few gay and lesbian bars are tucked in between straight bars, and the best dance parties find their homes on certain nights in come-one-come-all clubs just to the west of the red-light district. Many of the city's hotties have split for Amsterdam, so, with the exception of the raging weekend club nights when those hotties come back, the scene tends to be a little bit older and mellower. Also, Antwerp is not the greatest place to go walking hand in hand; the narrow, dark streets of this conservative city offer easy hiding spots for those whose attitudes are as ancient as the architecture.

➔ **Hessenhuis** The staple of the scene is Hessenhuis, a bar in an old museum that draws the most chiseled features in town. The crowd is often a little mature and a lot upscale, with potential partners loitering around the bar with martinis surgically attached to their hands. If this place is too swank for you, the bartenders will be happy to turn you on to the best underground gay party or newest trendy gay bar. *Falconrui 53.* ☎ *03/231-13-56. Bus: 6, 9, or 34 to Falconplein. Tram: 4 or 7 to Huikstraat.*

➔ **Red & Blue** For a colorful gay scene, the Red & Blue, in the red-light district, is the place to be. It's owned by the same pros that

Boy Meets Girl Meets Wallet

Prostitution in Belgium is illegal, but the government tolerates it as long as it stays in one place: the **red-light district.** Once home to the scurviest ruffians just into port, the area hasn't come far. A quick jaunt up Sint-Paulusstraat will take you into the lion's den, a small ganglion of miscreancy that's less campy and more down-to-business than its Amsterdam counterpart. Lingerie-clad women of all races, ages, and degrees of heft roost in closet-size window cabins, leering back at the groups of men that saunter up the sidewalk. A male passerby with an averted gaze will incite the prostitutes to rap their rings on the glass in a shrill chorus of ill repute. Potential customers (there are more than you'd think) wave the women from the window to a side door, where prices can be haggled over. If successful, the curtain is drawn over the front window and, well, the deal is sealed. The district, which dates back to the city's rise as an international port centuries ago, is most densely concentrated around Oude Manstraat, Leguit, and Verversrui.

Exuding a different breed of bad karma is the neighborhood just to the east of the red-light district, which locals have dubbed **"Red Square."** The Mercedes quotient skyrockets on Falconplein, a shabby street where enterprising Russian immigrants (read: mobsters) have built up a bargain-basement shopping street de résistance. Browsing through the convincing knockoffs of name-brand televisions, video recorders, and purses is a lesson in intimidation, as heavily jeweled front men scowl from their stoops. Not for the nighttime—this place can get properly scary.

run Brussels' Le Fuse, and lots of Bruxellois gay glitterati make the drive into Antwerp for Saturday night here. Sorry *Will & Grace* duos—the crowd is strictly men only. *Lange Schipperskapelstraat 11–13.* ☎ *03/232-47-12.* *www.redandblue.be. Tram: 2, 3, 7, 8, 10, or 15.*

Live Music

Live music in Antwerp? Not so much. In this clubby atmosphere, most nightlife revolves around a DJ spinning vinyl. If you're looking for the next big thing in, say, rock or jazz, look elsewhere. Brussels is the place to be for Belgian live acts, and most touring musicians don't have gigs to play in Antwerp. It's not a completely dry scene, though—you can find someone strumming an instrument if you look hard enough.

➔**De Muze** A longtime leader in the live jazz scene, De Muze boasts a cozy, inviting atmosphere where tourists and natives of all ages drink beer and eat snacks in a truly charming environment, right in the center of town. *Melkmarkt 15.* ☎ *03/226-01-26. Metro: Groenplaats.*

➔**Swingcafe** In nice weather, try for a spot on the terrace for prime people-watching in the area between the Grote Markt and the river. They often have live bands playing typical rock and pop, but it's a mixed bag—the selections of songs chosen by bands can be decent or awful, depending on their interpretation of "American music." *Suikerrui 13.* ☎ *03/223-14-78. Metro: Groenplaats.*

Performing Arts

Antwerp takes pride in being a citadel of Flemish culture. Two of the region's stellar companies are based here: the **Vlaamse**

Opera (Flanders Opera; Frankrijklei 3; ☎ **03/233-66-85);** and the **Koninklijk Ballet van Vlaanderen (Royal Flanders**

Ballet; Kattendijkdok-Westkaai 16; ☎ 03/234-34-38).

To house its vibrant cultural life, the city has no shortage of performance venues. Top of the line for theater and classical music is the **Stadsschouwburg** (Theaterplein 1; ☎ 03/227-03-06). For music and ballet, there's the classically oriented **Queen Elisabeth Concert Hall** (Koningin Astridplein 23–24; ☎ 03/203-56-00) and the more modernist **deSingel** (Desguinlei 25; ☎ 03/248-28-28).

Antwerp has more theaters than any other Flemish city, as well as two excellent theater companies: **Jeugdtheater** and **KNS**, the Royal Flemish Theater. Though most plays are in Dutch, you can often understand the plot regardless of language difficulties, and the quality of these shows merits attendance.

For information and reservations for the city's performing arts options, contact the **Cultural Information Desk** (Grote Markt 40; ☎ 03/220-81-11).

Sightseeing

Although much of Antwerp is purely functional commercial space (the port, the industrial warehouses, the red-light district), the city still has some important historical and cultural things to check out. If you're a dedicated do-it-yourselfer, you can get maps and sightseeing booklets from the tourist office to guide you. Walking trails marked within the city will lead you through typical streets and squares to find the main points of interest.

Many of Antwerp's museums and churches are open to the public for free or at a minimal charge. Also note that nearly all museums are closed on Monday. You can get info for many of the museums and churches reviewed below at http://museum.antwerpen.be.

Festivals

July & August

Zomer van Antwerpen (Summer of Antwerp). This huge summer festival includes circuses, theater and film showings, and museum nights. Call ☎ 03/224-85-28 or visit www.zva.be for info. Throughout July and August.

Navigaytion. This huge dance party on the water, complete with party boats and drag queens galore, takes place at the Willemdok harbor. It's the largest event for gays and

lesbians in Belgium, so expect a crowd. www.navigaytion.be. July 1.

Sinksenfoor. One of the biggest fairs in Belgium, it runs for about 6 weeks at de Vlaamse en Waalse kaai. More than 1.5 million people visited the fair last year, so come early to avoid lines. www.sinksenfoor.tk. Throughout July and August.

Polé Polé. This festival in nearby Ghent (www.gent.be) is the only floating festival in Europe. Over a period of 10 days, Polé Polé offers free world music performances; you can fill the time between sets with trips to the many cocktail bars and exotic foodstands. www.polepole.be. Mid July.

September

Laundry Day. Each year around Labor Day, Antwerp airs out its laundry at this street party in de Kammenstraat: From 10am till 10pm, the street is filled with about 30 DJs playing loud house, techno, and R&B music to keep the thousands of hipsters in attendance happy. www.laundryday.be. Early September.

December & January

Ice-Skating. During the last 3 weeks of the year and the first week of the new year, Antwerp transforms the Grote Markt in front of the city hall into an ice-skating paradise. Visit www.antwerpen.be for info. Mid-December to early January.

ANTWERP

New Year's Eve. Fireworks are displayed over the harbor every year. Visit www.antwerpen.be for details. December 31.

The University Scene

Universiteit Antwerp (☎ 03/220-49-99; www.ua.ac.be) is the city's main university, with a student body that is about 12% international. Its four campuses are located around the city center; the main campus is about a 15-minute walk from the Centraal Station. Because the university is so integrated within the city, your best bet to mingle with some Antwerp students is to go to the city's hot spots. Most of the city's hangouts are clustered **between the River Scheldt** (aka the Schelde River) and the city's two main squares, **Groenplaats** and **Grote Markt** (use the towering spire of Our Lady's Cathedral, which sits between the two squares, as a landmark). Overpriced cafes along the squares also offer decent people-watching for the patient pickup artist (the place isn't crawling with hotties, but they're around).

A notable exception to the between-the-river-and-the-squares rule is the **Meir** (running west from Grote Markt to Centraal Station), the city's main shopping drag. Ernest van Dijkckkaai (a block east of Grote Markt, along the river) offers a stroll along the disappointingly homely river, but the strip throbs with Latin and disco clubs at night. For a cool place to chill, head about a mile south of Groenplaats to **Het Zuid** (tram: 8), the South District. The quays on this industrial-zone-turned-artists'-quarter-turned-hot-spot are lined with bars, restaurants, and clubs. The district is walking a tightrope between laid-back hipness and yuppified gentrification, but the total sellout shouldn't hit full swing for another decade, so enjoy it while you can.

Top Attractions

→**Diamondland** Learn how stones are polished into gems in the largest diamond

showroom in Antwerp. *Appelmasstraat 33A.* ☎ *03/234-36-12. Free admission. Apr–Oct Mon–Sat 9:30am–5:30pm, Sun 10am–5pm (closed Nov–Mar). Tram: Centraal Station.*

MTV Best →**Koninklijk Museum voor Schone Kunsten Antwerpen (Royal Museum of Fine Arts)** ★★ Antwerp was once the artistic center of Belgium and a huge contender in Europe—which is evident in this museum; it houses the world's most impressive collection of works by Flemish Old Masters. Rubens (whose voluptuous nudes inspired the term "Rubenesque") made his home in Antwerp, and a sizeable collection of his works is here. So are paintings by Jan van Eyck, Rogier van der Weyden, Dirck Bouts, Hans Memling, the Brueghel family, and Rembrandt. If you want something a little more recent, you're in luck: The modern wing houses works by Ensor, René Magritte, Permeke, and Delvaux. Wear comfortable shoes because it's easy to lose track of time walking around this massive neoclassical building. *Leopold de Waelplaats 2.* ☎ *03/238-78-09. http://museum.antwerpen.be/kmska. Admission 5€ adults, 4€ students (free admission last Wed of the month). Tues–Sat 10am–5pm, Sun 10am–6pm. Tram: 12 or 24.*

→**Onze-Lieve-Vrouwekathedraal (Our Lady Cathedral)** ★★ A building you couldn't miss if you tried, this church is the tallest in the Benelux region, boasting a spire more than 122m (400 ft.) tall. Completed in the early 16th century, it houses no fewer than four Rubens masterpieces: *The Raising of the Cross* (1610), *The Descent from the Cross* (1614), *The Resurrection of Christ* (1612), and *The Ascension of the Virgin* (1626). *Handschoenmarkt, off the Grote Markt.* ☎ *03/213-99-51. www.dekathedraal.be. Admission 2€. Metro: Groenplaats.*

→**Rubenshuis (Rubens's House)** If you can't get enough art, head to where the Flemish Renaissance magic happened—Peter Paul Rubens' 17th-century crib. No starving

12 Hours in Antwerp

1. **Pay your respects to Rubens.** You could easily spend a couple of hours touring the exhibits at the Antwerp Royal Museum of Fine Arts. If you just have time to catch the highlights, visit the Peter Paul Rubens gallery and then compare and contrast his work to the more modern exhibitions by Magritte and Ensor.

2. **Partake of a golden brew.** Find a seat at one of the outdoor cafes surrounding Grote Markt and the cathedral and pour any of (or many of) Belgium's plethora of brews down your hatch as you watch the not-so-local crowd bum about the square.

3. **Shop till you drop.** Even if you go easy on the liquid and heavy on the lunch, the wares on Kammenstraat will appear no less funky. A veritable strip mall of psychedelica, this run of music stores, clothing shops, and tattoo parlors is a must-see.

4. **Dine at Frituur N°1.** You've got to get your necessary daily intake of frites.

5. **Head to Café d'Anvers.** Where else but in a monastery would you find the hippest place to sip red wine and mingle with the Euroflash?

artist type, Rubens bought this mansion when he was only 33. The house features some of his own paintings, his collections of other artists' work, and a restored version of his garden. *Wapper 9–11.* ☎ *03/201-15-55.*

http://museum.antwerpen.be/rubenshuis. Admission 5€ adults, free for visitors under 19. Tues–Sun 10am–5pm. Tram: 2, 3, or 15 to Meir; 4, 7, or 8 to Meirbrug/Katelijnevest; 12 or 24 to Frankrijklei.

Playing Outside

Antwerp isn't much of a lounge-in-the-great-outdoors kind of city, but Groenplaats (tram stop of the same name) and Grote Markt (a few blocks to the northwest) are where you're most likely to find grungy teens and travelers strewn under the Rubens monuments on sunny days.

Get your tush in prime clubbing form for those long Antwerp nights by renting a bike. Go to **De Windroos** (Steenplein 1; ☎ **03/480-93-88;** daily 9am–6pm; Metro: Groenplaats) or **Cyclorent** (Sint-Katelijnevest 19; ☎ **03/226-95-59;** cyclorent@ping.be; Mon–Sat 10am–6pm, Sun by appointment; tram: 7 or 4).

For a walk on the wild (and kind of expensive) side, head to the **Zoo Antwerpen** (Koningin Astridplein 26; ☎ **03/202-45-40;** www.zooantwerpen.be; daily Nov–Feb 10am–4:45pm, Mar–Apr and Oct 10am–5:30pm, May–June and Sept 10am–6pm, July–Aug 10am–7pm; admission 14€ adults; Metro: Centraal Station). The place dates back to 1843, and contains no less than an aquarium, winter garden, Egyptian temple (which houses elephants), anthropoid house, museum of natural history, deer parks, Kongo peacock habitat, and planetarium.

Shopping

Let's face it, you didn't come all the way to Antwerp to shell out dough for stuff you could get elsewhere. And unless you're into high-quality diamonds, Antwerp doesn't offer much in the way of unique wares. The Meir, a ritzy pedestrian street running from the Centraal Station to Groenplaats, features most of your basic chain stores, from Armani to European Gap knockoffs. The Groenplaats end of the Meir, on such streets as Nationalestraat and Lombardest, plays host to Antwerp's famed fashion houses. There sure are a ton of designer shops catering to the elite here—it's fun to crash the party and window-shop for a few hours, regardless of your own buying power.

➜**Ann Demeulemeester** The boutique of one of the "Antwerp Six" is a vast space that used to be a seaman's academy in the 19th century. The chick has attitude—she once turned down Naomi Campbell as a model because she wasn't "elegant" enough—that shows through in her designs. This is the only place in the world (really) that features her complete line of men's and women's clothing, shoes, and accessories. *Verlatstraat 38.* ☎ *03/ 216-01-33. Tram: 8 to Leopold de Waelplaats.*

➜**Coccodrillo** The place to be for the Carrie Bradshaw—type, where you can find shoe designs from all the top Belgian designers like Dries Van Noten and Ann Demeulemeester. *Schuttershofstraat 9A/B.* ☎ *03/233-20-93. Tram: 2, 3, or 15 to Meir.*

➜**Fish & Chips** ★★ To pick up fashionable, one-of-a-kind Antwerpian fashions without totally breaking the bank, head to Fish & Chips. With achingly hip, cutting-edge clothing, shoes, and accessories, a hair salon, a DJ, Internet access, a coffee shop, and, yes, even a bar—you might feel as if you've stepped into the dreamland of every indie band that's ever been featured on an O.C. soundtrack. If you're not in the shopping frame of mind, it's still a great place to find out what's going on at night: Club and party flyers are posted throughout, and you can chat up the hip sales staff for ideas. *Kammenstraat 36–38.* ☎ *03/ 227-08-24. www.fishandchips.be. Tram: 8 to Kammenstraat.*

Read All About It

English-language books are available from **FNAC** (Groenplaats 31; ☎ 03/231-20-56) and **Staandard** (Huidevetterstraat 57; ☎ 03/231-07-73).

➜**Taboo Records** This centrally located store serves as headquarters for the local Goa and psychedelic trance scene. The place is tiny, with a few racks of CDs on the main floor and milk crates of albums in the brick-walled basement. *Kammenstraat 66.* ☎ *03/ 233-39-73. www.tabooproductions.com. Tram: 8 to Kammenstraat.*

➜**Verso** ★ The best of the best—a place that looks more like a museum than like your local Macy's. With hand-picked selections from top Belgian designers as well as collections by the likes of Dolce & Gabbana, Giorgio Armani, Versace, and Valentino, don't forget to walk in like you mean it—the super-snobby staff can smell fear, I swear. If you don't have a couple hundred euros to plop down on designer jeans, you don't have to feel left out of the Verso party—you can nurse an espresso at the super trendy Verso Café and fake it. *Lange Gasthuisstraat 9–11.* ☎ *03/226-92-92. www. verso.be. Tram: 2, 3, or 15 to Meir.*

Markets

For the bargain-loving grandma in all of us, head to one of Antwerp's unique markets. **Antiques Market** at Lijnwaadmarkt is on Saturdays from Easter to October from 10am to 6pm. The **Bird Market** sells food, textiles, and, yes, live animals; it takes place Sunday mornings in Oude Vaartplaats near the City Theater. Also check out the **Friday Market,** on Wednesday and Friday mornings on Vrijdagmarkt facing the Plantin-Moretus Museum, a public auction for household goods and furniture.

Athens

A thens has growing pains. You can see its potential and the full grown global metropolis it will become, but it's just not quite there yet. The massive restructuring the city went through to prepare for the 2004 Summer Olympic games left the city better off than it was before (except for its debt). Renovations included revamped public transportation, remodeled hotels, and a more up-to-date airport—but something about Athens hasn't quite gotten used to its big makeover. Traces of grime stubbornly remain. Stray dogs and cats are, well, *everywhere.*

A bit of the old grunginess still lurks in Athens—but no one ever said that was a wholly bad thing. The city is a must-see for its ancient, crumbling ruins, including the world-renowned, not-to-be-missed Acropolis. Many people visit, stay 2 or 3 days seeing the old stuff, and then head out to the islands or to some of the historic sites inland. Especially in August, when more than half the city skips town for vacations elsewhere, you might do as others do and stay for a short while. But, there are others who say that Athens is worth more time and attention. If you stay longer, you won't be bored: Athens's chic cafe, bar, and club scene is growing, and shopping now gets you appropriately trendy attire. Plus, Athenians in general are warm and talkative, and are always eager to flex their English skills and help give you recommendations and directions. But really, who needs words when the legendary ruins of monuments like the Acropolis really do just speak for themselves?

The Best Of Athens

○ **The Best Place to Pick Up a Sugar Daddy or Momma:** In the lobby of the **Grande Bretagne Hotel,** everybody is *somebody,* or is at least trying to look like one—from movie stars to politicians to CEOs. Stop by the bar, drop a few euros on a coffee frappe, and bat those eyelashes. See p. 110.

○ **The Best One-Stop Sightseeing: The Acropolis** is a focal point of the city and pretty much the cornerstone for all Western art. If you take the time to see one thing besides your hostel and the bottom of your bottle of Mythos beer, the Acropolis should be it. See p. 114.

○ **The Best Museum:** History is alive at the **National Archaeological Museum,** and you shouldn't miss it, no matter how much you suffer from museum fatigue elsewhere. See p. 116.

○ **The Best Place to Get Naked:** Okay, so Poseidon's Temple is a big deal, a major archaeological relic and all, but trek down the hill to **Cape Sounion** to find some after-temple water fun. See p. 116.

○ **The Best Place to Shop:** You might actually find something at a fair price at **Monastiraki Flea Market.** Search for good vintage clothes and sunglasses amid the Greek bric-a-brac. See p. 117.

Getting There & Getting Around

Getting into Town

BY PLANE

The **Athens International Airport Eleftherios Venizelos** (☎ 210/353-0000; www.aia.gr), 27km (17 miles) northeast of Athens, opened in 2001. A modern, large international hub, Venizelos has good services, big restrooms, and a wide selection of shops.

Most international carriers have ticket offices in or near Syntagma Square. Just a tip: The hours aren't exactly always "businesslike"—3-hour lunch breaks are not uncommon in Greece, so call before you hoof it over there.

The easiest way into Athens is to take a taxi from outside the terminal. The cost is approximately 30€ to 37€, and more between midnight and 5am. Extra fees include a 2€ airport surcharge and a charge of 1€ per suitcase. Depending on traffic, the cab ride can take from 30 minutes to more than an hour.

A taxi from the airport to Piraeus, south of Athens, should cost 15€ to 25€. If you are making a connection, this is probably the best way to go, as public transportation in Athens is a bit less than reliable. There is bus service from the airport to Piraeus every hour (4€)—go to the ground transportation desk near baggage claim at the airport and ask for information on the bus to Piraeus. The bus usually leaves passengers in Karaiskaki Square near the harbor. The official schedule for **Spata-Piraeus (E96)** is every 20 minutes from 5am to 7pm; every 30 minutes from 7 to 8:30pm; and every 40 minutes from 8:30pm to 5am. Bus service from the airport to Syntagma Square or to Piraeus costs 4€, but bus schedules are less than dependable and the journey can be very long. Ask the driver where the bus is headed—sometimes buses can be incorrectly marked. Bus no. 019 runs to Syntagma and Omonia squares every half-hour from 7am to 10pm (1€), and then every hour from about 10:15pm to 6:30am (3€).

BY TRAIN

Trains from the south and west arrive at the **Peloponnese Station (Stathmos Peloponnisou;** ☎ 210/513-1601). Trains from the north arrive at **Larissa Station (Stathmos Larissis;** ☎ 210/529-8837), just across the tracks from the Peloponnese Station. The

Larissa Station is a big, modern facility that was renovated for the Olympics; it's got an exchange office that is usually open daily from 8am to 9:15pm, and luggage storage is usually open from 6:30am to 9pm.

To get to both train stations, take the Metro to Larissa (line 2).

BY BOAT

Piraeus, the main harbor of Athens' principal seaport, 11km (7 miles) southwest of central Athens, is a 15-minute Metro ride from Monastiraki and Omonia squares. The subway runs from about 5am to midnight and costs 1€.

If you take a taxi from the boat to the nearest subway terminal or bus stop, which can be a hike if you are weighed down with baggage, be ready to bargain with the taxi driver. The normal meter fare from Piraeus to Syntagma should be about 6€ to 10€, but often drivers simply offer a flat fare, which can be as much as 20€. Address the fare situation before you get in the cab and ask your driver to turn on the meter—and make sure that he does.

Getting Around

BY TAXI

Taxis are plentiful, but empty taxis are not. At least not when you need one. It costs 2€ extra to reserve a cab, The minimum fare is 2€, and it's best to pay the cost of a licensed cab. Pirate taxis might also be gray, like the licensed cabs. The difference: A pirate cab won't have a photo ID and a meter.

Get in the cab and check first to make sure that the meter is turned on and set on "1," which means that it's before midnight and you're within city limits. The "2" (double fare) is for fares between midnight and 5am. Sometimes drivers will pick up other passengers; let it slide. Round up the fare if you want to give a tip. Two of the companies are **Athina** (☎ 210/921-7942) and **Parthenon** (☎ 210/532-3300). Tell drivers where you want to go before you get in. If you have any problems communicating, you can solve the

problem with help from someone at the hotel or restaurant before you get in the taxi.

BY METRO

The **Attiko Metro** (☎ 210/679-2399; www.ametro.gr), the north-south subway line that runs through both Omonia and Monastiraki squares, costs 1€. Tickets are sold inside Metro stations. They're rarely checked, and it's an honor system of sorts when you buy them. Just shell out the change, though—if you're caught without a ticket, you can face a fine. The Syntagma Square and Acropolis stations are mini-museums, with displays of artifacts dug up during the subway excavations.

BY BUS

Blue buses (☎ 210/513-6185) run throughout Athens and its suburbs. Tickets are .70€, and available at most news kiosks. Again, these run on sort of an honor system—you punch the ticket yourself in the machine on the bus—but don't try to be sneaky and dodge the fare because fines are hefty if you're caught riding without a ticket.

There are also orange electric trolley buses that run in the center of the city from 5am to midnight, and green buses that shuttle between central Athens and Piraeus every 20 minutes (or so) 6am to midnight and hourly after that.

BY CAR

Do not drive in Athens—Athenians aren't much for following rules of the road, and traffic is almost always heavy. Parking spots are impossible to find, too.

If you must rent a car, it'll set you back anywhere from 50€ to 100€ a day. Some agencies with offices around Syntagma Square include **Budget Rent a Car** (8 Leoforos Syngrou; ☎ 210/921-4771 to -4773); **Eurodollar Rent a Car** (29 Leoforos Syngrou; ☎ 210/922-9672 or 210/923-0548); **Hellascars** (148 Leoforos Syngrou; ☎ 210/923-5353 to 5359); and **Hertz** (12 Leoforos Syngrou;

☎ 210/922-0102 to -0104) and 71 Leoforos Vas. Sofias (☎ 210/724-7071 or 210/722-7391).

ON FOOT

The best way to explore Athens really is on foot. The city has pedestrian zones in sections of the Commercial Triangle (the area bounded by Omonia, Syntagma, and Monastiraki squares), the Plaka, and Kolonaki. Even though the city might recognize the importance of pedestrians, sometimes drivers do not: Be careful when walking as Athenian motorists and cyclists can be a tad, well, aggressive.

Athens Basics

Orientation: Athens Neighborhoods

From almost anywhere in the city, you can put where you are in perspective by looking for either the **Acropolis** or **Lykavitos** Hill.

The most touristy area, the **Plaka district,** hugs the eastern side of the Acropolis. This area is rife with trinket stands, cheap jewelry shops, and scores of cafes and bars. Hotels, restaurants, and Internet cafes abound here. Most streets in Plaka are closed to cars, and because it's considered a historical district, strict laws govern each shop's appearance (for instance, awnings aren't allowed on the windows). Cozied up to Plaka's northwest border is **Monastiraki Square,** another touristy area.

Head to **Psiri,** just north of Monastiraki, for nighttime entertainment. After dark, blocks of upscale restaurants and bars cater to Athens' young wannabes—a mostly all-Greek crowd. During the day, however, most of these cafes and bars are closed, making this area little more than a promenade with a good view of the Acropolis.

Kolonaki, a 15- to 20-minute walk east of Psiri, is the most upscale, Euro neighborhood in Athens, with many government buildings, designer shops, and expensive watering holes.

Glyfada, a 30-minute bus ride from the center of Athens, is a summertime favorite on the coast, with lots of beaches and nightclubs.

Tourist Offices

The **Greek Tourist Organization (EOT)** is at Othos Amerikis 2 (☎ 210/331-0437). It's open Monday through Friday 8am to 3pm, but don't be surprised if no one picks up the phone. You can also try the main office (☎ 210/870-0000; www.gnto.gr), which is out of town a bit. Info from them includes transportation schedules (ha!) and maps, hotels lists, and a free city map.

Recommended Websites

○ **www.athensguide.com**: Known for its off-the-beaten-path tips and detailed reviews.

○ **www.gnto.gr** and **www.greece.gr**: Check out these government-operated tourism sites for general info.

Culture Tips 101

Services and schedules, including hours when stores are open, are not set in stone. Depending on the whims of the workers, the weather, or whatever, changes occur.

There is no minimum drinking age in Greece. Listen up, though: Be careful with ouzo. Locals place a few cubes of ice in a tumbler, and then pour the ouzo (there are five brands that all taste like liquid licorice) and watch as it changes from clear to milky white. They *sip* the ouzo and wait. This stuff can wreak havoc on your digestive system, and it can pack one hell of a hangover. *Be forewarned:* Treat this drink with respect.

12 Hours in Athens

1. **Go to the Acropolis.** It is, after all, the birthplace of Western Civ, and you should see it before sulfurous smog destroys it.

2. **Take the tram to the top of Likavitos (Lycabettus) Hill.** This spot is home to one of the best views of the city. The tram to the top is cheap and well worth it if you do nothing else.

3. **Shop at Monastiraki Flea Market.** The best market and shopping in general, as we've mentioned before, is at this market, which has the feel of the bazaar scene in *Raiders of the Lost Ark.*

4. **Hang out in Pisri, the coolest new neighborhood in town.** You'll find some of the best bars and restaurants here. By the time this hot little book is in your hands, the scene is sure to have gotten even better.

5. **Hobnob with the beautiful people in Kolonaki.** Between the cafes in the square and the ubiquitous art galleries, Kolonaki is where many monied Europhiles alight.

6. **Explore the National Gardens.** An enchanted little forest in the middle of the city, this is a great place to go to get out of the bustle. Be on the safe side and leave well before dark.

7. **Laze about among the poppy fields of the Roman Forum.** See if you start feeling like Dorothy in *The Wizard of Oz.*

ATHENS

There is also definitely a drug culture in Athens, which is centered, of course, around the club scene, but getting a local to trust you with info is a task worthy of Hercules. Plus the somewhat draconian drug laws make it very risky: Possession of narcotic substances, including marijuana and E, gets users an *automatic* 7-year-minimum sentence.

Recommended Books & Movies

BOOKS

Do your homework before you hit these shores. Read anything by Homer—the *Iliad,* the *Odyssey*—to get into the groove of what's shaped not only Greek literature, but the literature of the entire Western Hemisphere. And it wouldn't hurt to look through Edith Hamilton's classic *Mythology.* For a more modern take, check out Nikos Kazantzakis; his *Zorba the Greek* is a classic in its own right, but he also wrote a book on his travels through other parts of Europe and the Middle East. *Eleni,* by Nicholas Gage, is a heartbreaking book that shows what some Greeks had to live through during World War II.

MOVIES

Start with *Never on a Sunday,* a movie from 1960 that stars one of the country's proudest Greek exports, movie star glam-girl Melina Mercouri, who is now a minister in the Greek government. In this referenced-all-the-time flick, Mercouri portrays a prostitute in Athens who charms a visiting American who is obsessed with all things Greek. Practically as much a part of Greek pop culture as Coca-Cola is to the U.S.

Zorba is also a great movie. Although it's an American film, *My Big Fat Greek Wedding* is fun to watch just to familiarize yourself with the warmth and humor of the Greek people. Don't expect to find many chubby goofballs in Athens. This is a major city, darling, and the look for young people is definitely chic and thin.

Athens Nuts & Bolts

Cellphone Providers   The situation changes regularly. Call the tourist information office for current options.

Currency   The Greek unit of currency is the euro. For exchanges, go to the central post office, in the southwest corner of Syntagma Square. As usual, ATMs are common, and credit cards are widely accepted, although you may find that at smaller shops the owners don't accept plastic. The National Bank of Greece operates a 24-hour ATM next to the tourist information office on Syntagma Square.

Embassies & Consulates   **Canadian** citizens can consult at their embassy at 4 Ionnou Yenadiou (☎ 210/727-3400 or 210/725-4011). **U.K.** citizens can receive emergency aid at their embassy at 1 Ploutarchou (☎ 210/727-2600 during the day and 210/723-7727 at night). The **U.S.** embassy is at 91 Leoforos Vas. Sofias (☎ 210/721-2951; emergency number 210/729-4301).The **Australian** embassy is at 37 Leoforos Dimitriou Soutsou (☎ 210/645-0404 or -0505), and the **New Zealand** embassy is at 24 Xenias (☎ 210/771-0112).

Emergencies   Police are at ☎ 100, fire at ☎ 199, and ambulance at ☎ 166. Or go to the **Hygeia Diagnostic and Therapeutic Center** (Othos Erythrou 4; ☎ 210/682-7940).

Internet/Wireless Hot Spots   The best and cheapest Internet terminal, **EasyInternet-access,** is on the second floor of the Everest fast-food restaurant, attached to the McDonalds in Syntagma Square. It's open from 10am to 2am, and costs about 2€ per hour for high-speed Internet access. Most cybercafes now charge about 6€ an hour. The **Hellenic Cosmos Museum** also has a cafe where you can log on; check out www.fhw.gr for museum hours.

Luggage Storage   You can find lockers at the Metro station in Piraeus and at both train stations. If you are taking a jaunt to the islands and are using Athens as a central hub, it might be a good idea to store whatever luggage you don't need in the city rather than lugging it while you island-hop. A company like **Pacific Ltd.** (26 Nikis, near Syntagma Sq.; ☎ 210/324-1007 or 210/322-3213) has a per-piece charge and is open Monday through Saturday from 8am to 8pm. They will store your things by the day, week, or month.

Laundry   Try the **National Dry Cleaners and Laundry Service** (17 Apollonos; ☎ 210/323-2226). They charge 5€ per kilo of laundry including wash, dry, and soap. They are open Monday and Wednesday from 7am to 4pm and Tuesday, Thursday, and Friday from 7am to 8pm.

Pharmacies   Generally, all pharmacies keep the same hours (Mon and Wed 8:30am–2pm; Tues and Thurs–Fri 8:30am–2pm and 4:30–8:30pm). However, there are always a few pharmacies open 24 hours. Most pharmacies post the emergency hours schedule on the door. Or you can call ☎ 107.The English-language *Athens News* often has a list of pharmacies.

Post Offices   Post offices can be found at 100 Eolou and in Syntagma Square at the corner of Mitropoleos. Hours are Monday through Friday from 7:30am to 8pm, Saturday from 7:30am to 2pm, and Sunday from 9am to 1pm.

Restrooms   You'll find public restrooms in the Metro stations at Omonia and Syntagma squares and beneath Kolonaki Square. In most parts of Athens, you shouldn't flush the toilet paper down the toilet—throw it into the trash.

Safety   Athens is very safe in terms of violent crimes, however, pickpocketing is definitely a concern, particularly in touristy areas like the Plaka. Keep your eyes open and your money close by, and definitely utilize the safe in your hostel or hotel for your passport and other valuables.

Telephone Tips   Public phones now often accept only phone cards, which are available at newsstands.

Tipping   Most restaurants have the service charge included in the bill. It's nice to leave a 10% tip if the service has been good. In taxis, do as the locals do, and round up to the nearest euro, adding more for a higher fare.

Sleeping

Unfortunately, some budget hotels and hostels are where the seedy underbelly of Athens can be most apparent. Brochure-waving hotel and hostel owners will likely be waiting as your train or ferry pulls into town, but I recommend that you make reservations before you come to the city. Most of these people are legit, but you never know what you're getting for sure until you're already roped in—play it safe and have a room waiting for you somewhere.

Hostels

→ **Athens Backpackers Hostel** This hostel, which opened in 2004, touts itself as "Athens' only Australian-style hostel." Upon check-in the staff gives you a "welcome shot" of alcohol to warm you up to the city—and if that's what Aussie manager Ed Fischer means by down-under hospitality, so be it! The hostel does its best to cultivate a young, partying, adventurous atmosphere: The rooftop bar has a great view of the Acropolis and is an excellent place to kick off the night and meet some fellow travelers. The rooms are bare with dorm-style new, firm, and comfy bunk beds and en suite bathrooms, most likely the best you'll get for the price in the city. Also, the volume level in the rooms is

strictly kept low, and it enforces a "no alcohol, no smoking" policy. A small library has good sightseeing info. *12 Makri St. (near Plaka).* ☎ *210/922-4044. www.backpackers.gr. 18€ dorm bed. Metro: Acropolis. Amenities: Bar; Internet; kitchen; library; 24-hr. reception; meals available; TV. In room: A/C, linens, lockers.*

→ **Hotel Carolina** A longtime favorite for travelers on a budget, the Hotel Carolina, on the outskirts of the Plaka, is within walking distance of many Athenian sightseeing musts. Every room has air-conditioning, a TV, a safe, double-glazed windows, a toilet, and a shower. Some rooms have up to five beds. The hotel's vibe isn't quite that of a hostel's but it's close: A lot of young people come here. *5 Kolokotroni (off of Stadiou St.).* ☎ *210/324-3551. www.hotelcarolina.gr. 75€–100€ double. Breakfast 5€. Metro: Monastiraki. Amenities: Internet. In room: A/C, TV, hair dryer, safe.*

→ **Student and Traveller's Inn** Unlike a lot of inexpensive, sometimes sketchy lodgings in the outskirts of Athens, this well-run, clean but spare renovated hostel sits right in the heart of Plaka. The real draw here is the hostel's friendly, tightly knit, and helpful staff members. They speak English and are eager

Athens

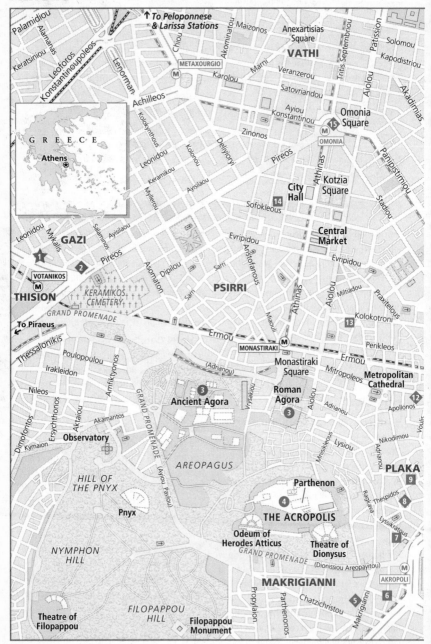

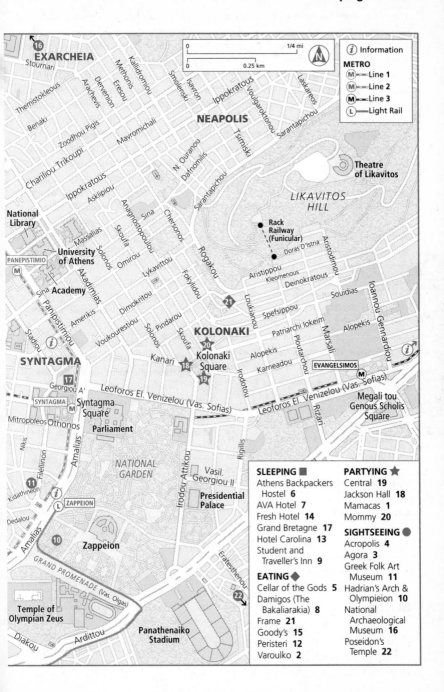

SLEEPING ■
Athens Backpackers
  Hostel **6**
AVA Hotel **7**
Fresh Hotel **14**
Grand Bretagne **17**
Hotel Carolina **13**
Student and
  Traveller's Inn **9**

EATING ◆
Cellar of the Gods **5**
Damigos (The
  Bakaliarakia) **8**
Frame **21**
Goody's **15**
Peristeri **12**
Varoulko **2**

PARTYING ★
Central **19**
Jackson Hall **18**
Mamacas **1**
Mommy **20**

SIGHTSEEING ●
Acropolis **4**
Agora **3**
Greek Folk Art
  Museum **11**
Hadrian's Arch &
  Olympieion **10**
National
  Archaeological
  Museum **16**
Poseidon's
  Temple **22**

to give you inside tips and information about sightseeing and planning your stay. This place is popular with travelers who are gung-ho for sightseeing and don't spend much time at the hostel, so if you're looking for a backpacker, party atmosphere, you're in the wrong place. The hostel offers singles, doubles, triples, quads, and dorms. Some rooms come with private bathrooms, others with hallway-style bathrooms and showers, and some have balconies. *16 Kydathineon.* ☎ *210/324-4808. www.studenttravellersinn.com. 20€ per person dorm bed with shared bathroom, 50€ single with private bathroom, 55€ double with private bathroom, 69€ triple with private bathroom. Metro: Syntagma Sq. Amenities: Internet; 24-hr. reception; safe; storage. In room: A/C.*

Doable

→ **Fresh Hotel** A brand-new hotel in downtown Athens with sleek, minimalist designs and bright color schemes, the hip Fresh Hotel's 133 rooms come with crisp white linens and accents like magenta throw pillows or bright green curtains. The hotel's modern touches are definitely New Age (a Zen rock garden is a standard feature in the Executive rooms, for example), and the staff is attentive and friendly. And price-wise, it's a pretty good deal. The breakfast is one of the best you'll find in the city: a buffet-style spread with gourmet cheeses, fruits, eggs, and breads. *26 Sofokleus St.* ☎ *210/524-8511. www.freshhotel.gr. Around 140€ single, around 160€ double. Rates include breakfast. Metro: Omonoia. Amenities: Restaurant; bar; fitness center; laptop rental; outdoor pool (May–Oct, weather permitting); sauna; steam room. In room: A/C, TV, minibar, Wi-Fi.*

Splurge

→ **AVA Hotel and Suites** A quiet and sophisticated hotel in the heart of the Plaka, AVA offers apartments and suites that are great options for a longer stay in Athens. Each

unit has its own kitchen, private balconies, and free Internet access, and can accommodate from three to five people—so if you are rounding up your friends, want a cushy place to stay, and aren't planning on throwing any parties (this place is filled with families and businesspeople), an apartment here should be first on your list. Lucy Van Alphen, the hotel owner, has made sure her renovated hotel is run as she would operate her own home, with gracious, helpful 24-hour staff. The hotel is also in a perfect location for sightseeing—steps away from the Acropolis, Hadrian's Arch, and Zeus's temple. Ask for a front apartment if you can—they have great views. *9–11 Lyssikratous St.* ☎ *210/325-9000. www.avahotel.gr. 140€–175€ regular apt, 190€–240€ executive apt, 230€–310€ AVA suite. Extra person 20€ per night. Rates include buffet breakfast. Metro: Acropolis. In room: A/C, Internet, kitchenette, minibar, safe, TV.*

📺 Best → **Grande Bretagne Hotel** ★ *The* place to go in Athens, the Grande Bretagne's ornate 19th-century building assumes a stately stance on Syntagma Square, right across from the Parliament building. The hotel underwent a massive $70-million renovation in preparation for the Olympics, and it has all the splendor you'd imagine from a hotel that was a favorite of the likes of Winston Churchill. Now, political, entertainment, and just plain fabulous heavyweights stay here while in Athens. Rooms are decorated in old-school 19th-century British fashion, with mahogany desks and thick tapestry-like draperies, but have all the best in modern amenities, including marble bathrooms with whirlpools. Some rooms have balconies overlooking the square with views of the Acropolis. *Syntagma Sq.* ☎ *210/333-000. www.grandebretagne.gr. 350€–800€ double. Metro: Constitution Sq. Amenities: 2 bars; 2 restaurants; hairdresser; 2 pools (1 indoor, 1 rooftop); world-class spa. In room: A/C, TV, minibar.*

Eating

Greek food: You either love it or you hate it. Typical fare can be heavy—souvlaki, moussaka, gyros, and baklava—or light, with choices such as fresh grilled fish, cucumber salads, and veggie appetizers. And there's always a standard Greek salad.

A couple more FYIs about dining in Greece: No, it isn't just you the waiters are ignoring. It's everyone. Service in Athens is hands-off, to say the least. Also, most Greeks don't even think about dinner until 9 or 10pm, and then they linger until close to midnight.

Countless options exist for cheap eats in Athens. At any given corner of the city, you'll find a kiosk serving gyros and souvlaki for a euro or two, and McDonalds are everywhere, including on Syntagma Square. Or try one of dozens of Goody's fast-food restaurants. Greece's answer to McDonalds.

Mezedes are Greece's answer to tapas or dim sum, appetizers of a sort. Don't feel obliged to order a whole meal; there's a world of tastes from cucumber-yogurt dip to eggplant to squid to little sausages, big ~~beans~~, and octopus.

Spots

~~Frame~~ CONTEMPORARY GREEK A ~~depart~~ure from the typical heaviness of some ~~Greek~~ food, Frame's menu focuses on ~~the~~ modern cuisine and a holistic, feel-~~good appr~~oach to the dining experience. Dec-~~orated in~~ a relaxed, chic, 1970s throwback ~~style, with~~ white canvas chairs, geometri-~~cally tile~~d tableware, and groovy, vivid ~~color~~s—this is one of the trendiest ~~spots in~~ Athens. Lounge music wafts ~~from the~~ speakers as the beautiful ~~people—Greek an~~d foreign—nosh on seafood ~~and~~ the delicious, fresh baked ~~brea~~d that comes with dinner. ~~The~~'s bar area buzzes with ~~the~~ sexy "in" crowd. *1 Dinokra-~~tous (Hotel~~ Lycabettus), Kolonaki.*

☎ *210/721-4368. Main courses 20€–30€. Daily 11am–midnight.*

Cheap

→ **Damigos (The Bakaliarakia)** GREEK This little cozy tavern, in a basement in the super-busy Plaka area, serves traditional Greek fare such as deep-fried codfish and homemade stews—and they've been doing it since the middle of the 19th century. The real treat here is the selection of Greek wines, many of which come from the family's own vineyard. Make sure to bring cash—they don't take credit cards. *41 Kidathineon, Plaka.* ☎ *210/322-5084. Main courses 4€–10€. Daily 7pm–midnight.*

Doable

→ **Cellar of the Gods** GREEK Traditional, casual, home-cooked Greek fare like moussaka (a casserole-like dish) and tzatziki (a cucumber, onion, and yogurt dip for pita bread) is the specialty at this small, family-run restaurant. Owner Vangeli is a sweetheart, an amicable Athenian who is happy to tell you about his favorite parts of the town over a glass of one of his great (and quite affordable) house wines. *23–27 Makrigianni.* ☎ *210/923-3721. Main courses 7€–8€, wines 3€–5€ a glass. Daily 6pm–midnight.*

Peristeri GREEK Probably the only restaurant actually frequented by locals in the entire super-touristy Plaka area, Peristeri offers good, cheap, hearty Greek food, beer, and wine. Try the basics—chicken and potatoes, for example—and a glass of house wine. The inside is air-conditioned during the summer, and there are little tables set up outside for those who want to dine al fresco and watch the tourist action on the street. *Patroou St., Plaka. Main courses 5€–9€. Daily noon–3pm and 6pm–midnight.*

ATHENS

Splurge

→ **Varoulko** ★★★ GREEK/SEAFOOD
Widely regarded as one of the best restaurants in Athens, if not the best, Varoulko is under the supervision of Lefteris Lazarou, the only Greek chef to be awarded a prestigious Michelin star. The food is beautifully presented; the decor, the best in minimalist chic; and the seafood and wine, top-notch. And, this is no nose-in-the-air place. The gracious, multilingual staff explains each course in English, and the restaurant's sommelier answers any questions about the bottle she will pick to complement your meal. Try their specialty, seafood moussaka. Chances are, the highlight of your visit will be a chat with Lazarou—he ambles around the restaurant nightly, joking with his patrons in many languages. During the summer, get a table on the rooftop—the view of the Acropolis is unparalleled. *80 Piraeus St. (next to Hridanos hotel), Piraeus.* ☎ *210/522-8400. www.varoulko.gr. Dinner with wine 70€. Daily 7:30pm–midnight.*

Partying

Greeks, on the whole, tend to be welcoming and warm—and really do believe in "the more the merrier"—so most places you go, you'll probably feel included. Even at the most see-and-be-seen clubs in upscale Kolonaki, the attitude is more high-five than high society. And age here really is nothing but a number: There's no minimum drinking age in Greece. You probably won't see anyone younger than 18 making it into most clubs in downtown Athens, however; many clubs enforce their own guidelines as to who can and can't party there.

Athenians like to party. Dinner often starts at 9pm (10pm in the summer), so don't expect clubs to get going until much later. Nightlife happens throughout the city, but your two best bets for finding a bar or club are the scenester-rich, trendy Kolonaki; the more down-to-earth, industrial-area-turned-hipster-hangout, Gazi; and the up-and-coming Psirri district.

To fit in with the metropolitan Athenian crowd, ladies and gentlemen: Think tight and black. Partygoers take their roles as glamorous urbanites very seriously. Outfits are chic and far from conservative, regardless of gender. Weather in Athens can get hot, hot, hot, and people dress accordingly: In Athens, skin is definitely in.

To find out what's going on during your stay, pick up a copy of *Now in Athens*, published monthly and available at kiosks on the street. There you'll find listings for clubs and events going on all over the city.

→ **Central** Along the same young, chic lines is Central, which is a restaurant and a lounge. The cool crowd here indulges in cappuccino and biscotti by day and pricey mixed drinks and sushi at night. The music is usually ambient—think subdued funk and house.

Summer Nights

Glyfada is a South Beach–esque mecca for Athenians who've haven't escaped the city in the summer. (Most residents head for the islands or beyond.) During the day, you'll find Greeks of all ages and degrees of dress and undress—bathing-suit tops are optional in these parts, and Speedos are more popular than you'd think. Every season, the hot spots in this area open or close for good, or become cool or lame, so it's best to ask around with in-the-know locals to see where you should head during your stay. Check bus schedules; you can take a city bus to the shore, and buy tickets at any kiosk.

14 Platia Kolonaki. ☎ *210/724-5938. www. island-central.gr.*

➔ **Island Central** For a Kolonaki-gone-wild experience, head to Central's May-through-August home on the coast: Island Central moves out to the water for the summertime and brings its chic clientele along for the ride. This isn't some dive-y tequila-shot strewn beach bar, though. It's got mod lighting, funky decor, and a wine-and-cigar cellar. Despite its upscale details, this place welcomes non-regulars with open arms—just don't expect to speak English to the bartenders and waiters here. Something in me says they know the language, but they're just too cool to be bothered to speak it. Pointing and smiling works just fine. To get to the coast, take a city bus; check kiosks for tickets and schedules. *Athens-Sounio Ave., Varkiza.* ☎ *210/892-5000. www.island-central.gr.*

➔ **Jackson Hall** Athenians like the American vibe here at Jackson Hall, a bar, restaurant, and club space in Kolonaki. For dinner, the kitchen serves hamburgers, steaks, and fries, and after the sun is well down, hip locals and tourists down beers and typical clubby cocktails like vodka and Red Bulls while swaying to the rock-'n'-roll/pop soundtrack. *4 Milioni St., Kolonaki.* ☎ *210/361-6098.*

➔ **Mamacas** First stop for everyone who's anyone in Athens is a drink or dinner at Mamacas, a taverna that's known for its updated Greek dishes, until around 11pm or midnight, when the lights get darker and the place turns into a full-on bar and lounge. Squint and see if you recognize anyone lounging among the modernist, white decor: This place is ground zero for Greek celebs. *14 Persoponis, Gazi.* ☎ *210/346-4984.*

➔ **Mommy** For a more Euro-chic experience, head to Mommy, an upscale nightspot that's a fave hangout for those in the fashion and media scene. Snooty but gorgeous waiters and waitresses serve up fancy martinis and Cosmos along with Chinese-fusion bar food. *4 Delpon St., Kolonaki.* ☎ *210/361-9682.*

ATHENS

Performing Arts

Find out what's going on in *Athens News* and *Now in Athens*, available at the Greek Tourist Organization. Most Athenians can speak at least a little English, but it is most certainly not the language of the theater; plays are performed in Greek almost without exception. Still, if you like the idea of being in the country of Aristophanes and Sophocles, you might give it a whirl. Otherwise, try these options below.

➔ **Ergostasio** Check out the dance, usually modern, at this place. Don't dress like a slacker. *268 Leo. Vouliagmenis.* ☎ *210/973-1993. Tickets prices vary.*

➔ **Megaron Musikis** This acoustically good concert hall hosts all sorts of classical music.

Try the box office on weekdays 10am to 6pm, Saturday 10am to 2pm, and Sunday 6 to 10:30pm. Call first, though, because it's not always open during these hours; this is Greece, after all. You can also try their downtown ticket kiosk in the Spiromillios Arcade. *89 Vas. Sopias Ave.* ☎ *210/729-0391. www.megaron.gr. Tickets usually 5€ and up.*

➔ **Opera Assos Odeon** The theater runs good American movies that are only a few months old. *Othos Akadimias 57.* ☎ *210/362-2683.*

➔ **Pallas Theater** Head here for the major jazz and rock concerts. *1 Voukourestiou.* ☎ *210/322-8275.*

Sightseeing

Even if you don't know the difference between Socrates and the Simpson sisters, it's hard to not be impressed by the importance and just the sheer *oldness* of the monuments in Athens. Whether you're an archaeology buff or on a layover to Mykonos, you won't regret lacing up your New Balances, slathering on your SPF, and hiking up to check out attractions like the Acropolis and the Agora. Just remember to stay more hydrated that you think you need to be, especially during the summer. The sun is hot, the climate is arid, and the hike up the hill to the Parthenon is doable, but certainly not a walk in the park.

Festivals

February & March

Carnival. This midwinter celebration is when most of Athens gets wasted enough to send Dionysus into rehab. During February and/or March.

May

Annual Tattoo Expo. A different club hosts this gathering each year. It features an army of artists, hairstylists, piercers, jewelers, and live music. Ask Kostas at Lazy Dayz Juggling (www.lazydayz.gr) for the exact dates each year.

June to September

Athens and Epidaurus Festival. It's known by many names, and the real draw is the roster of national and international artists who get to perform in ancient (and sometimes modern) venues, including the Odeon of Herodes Atticus. For details, see www.hellenicfestival.gr. June to September.

Likavitos Festival. This multimedia festival offers modern plays, dance, and musical performances in the Likavitos (aka Lycabettus) Theater. Call ☎ 322/14-59 for details. June to August.

MTV Best → **The Acropolis** ★★★ The Acropolis is actually not the name for the monument you see perched on top of that hill—it's the hill itself. The marble-columned building perched atop is Greece's most famous temple, the **Parthenon.** People lived on the Acropolis as early as 5,000 B.C.; the great view provided good defense against any invaders. The Acropolis remained the city's religious center after the population spread out to other areas surrounding the hill. The city's civic and business center, the **Agora,** is just below the hill.

The first thing you'll hit when you enter the Acropolis is **Beulé Gate,** which was built by the Romans and named for the French archaeologist who discovered it in 1852. Next, walk through the **Propylaia,** the 5th-century B.C. entranceway.

You can then ascend the steps to the temple of **Athena Nike (Athena of Victory),** an Ionic temple built in 424 B.C. in honor of the goddess of wisdom.

Ahead of Athena Nike, to the left of the Parthenon, is the **Erechtheion,** constructed to be the tomb of Erechtheus, a legendary king of Athens. Look for the carved figures that act as columns holding up the roof on the outside of the temple: These are called the **Caryatids** and are actually replicas. The original statues are safe, away from the city's smog, in the Acropolis museum. The hole in the ceiling and floor of the northern porch is meant to represent the spot where the sea god Poseidon's trident struck during his mythical contest with Athena to have the city named in his honor. Obviously, Athena was the victor. The olive tree, which was her answer to Poseidon's hissy fit, is planted beside the Erechtheion as a reminder of who won the contest.

But it's that big, old, columned behemoth—the Parthenon—that's the main event. Dedicated to Athena Parthenos (Athena the Virgin), patron goddess of Athens, the temple was only for priests and honored visitors. Visitors, even in antiquity, were not allowed inside to see the monumental 11m-tall (36-ft.) statue of Athena. Bummer, because nothing but stories remain of the gold-and-ivory statue today. Use your imagination to conjure up how the Parthenon must have looked in ancient times—it wasn't always a serene, ivory marble—when it was painted in bright colors.

The Parthenon has been undergoing serious restoration for many years now, a large-scale project that has been typically delayed. Much of what visitors will see when visiting the Parthenon in the near future, however, will be additions from this restoration, which is attempting to transform the ruins into exactly what the building looked like in its heyday.

Although you might be pooped after just gawking at the sights on the hill, it's worth it to cool down in the blessedly air-conditioned **Acropolis Archaeological Museum,** at the foot of the hill, to see the original artifacts that aren't subjected to the weather and the pollution. It houses four original Caryatids from the Erechtheion along with other original statues.

And have no fear, gossips: The story of the Parthenon isn't complete without serious drama-rama. After a 17th-century attack on the Acropolis, many of the hill's monuments were destroyed. Most of the remaining sculptures of the Parthenon were "rescued" and brought to London by Lord Elgin in the early 19th century. Those surviving sculptures—known as the Elgin Marbles—are on display in the British Museum, which ticks off the Greeks to this day. In 1988, a historian alleged that the British Museum carelessly cleaned the Marbles during the 1930s, resulting in irreparable damages. Greeks still clamor for the Marbles to be returned to their homeland, but the Brits haven't budged yet. *Dionysiou Areopayitou.* ☎ *210/321-0219. www.culture.gr. Admission 12€ adults, free Sun and national holidays. Ticket (valid 1*

Free & Easy

➔ Check out the **walk along the Acropolis to Hadrian's Arch** and beyond. This may very well be the best freebie in the whole country.

➔ The **National Archaeological Museum** is free on the first Sunday of the month. Don't miss it! It's a history book come alive.

➔ Go to the **War Museum** (Othos Vas. Sofias, right next to the Byzantine Museum; ☎ 210/725-2975; Tues–Sun 9am–2pm). Take a trip through the history of Greek warfare. The jet plane in the courtyard alone is worth the trip.

➔ Buy a coffee or juice at any **cafe** in town and nurse it till the cows come home. Bring a book. You won't be bothered.

➔ Take the no. A2 or A3 bus to **Glyfada** and lie on this tiny strip of a beach. Don't expect any surfable waves, though.

week) includes admission to Acropolis, Acropolis Museum, Ancient Agora, Theater of Dionysus, Karameikos Cemetery, Roman Forum, Tower of the Winds, and Temple of the Olympian Zeus. Summer daily 8am–7pm; winter daily 8:30am–2:30pm. Acropolis Museum usually closes at least 30-min. earlier than the Acropolis. Metro: Acropolis.

➔ **The Agora** Admittedly, there's not much here to see anymore—and some of it is even defaced by graffiti—but the Agora used to be Athens' commercial and civic center. Now it seems like a mishmash of ruins and labeled leftovers, but you have to use your imagination and picture Socrates and Plato strolling through this area that once would have been filled with merchants, politicians, and other local celebrities. Still pretty intact, though, is the 5th-century B.C. **Thesion (Temple of Hephaistos and Athena).** Another juicy tidbit of ancient Greek gossip: In 399 B.C., Socrates was accused of "introducing strange gods and corrupting youth," and sentenced to death. He drank the famous cup of hemlock poison in a prison in the southwest corner of the Agora.

Also in the Agora is the 2nd-century B.C. **Stoa of Attalos,** a large building which requires no imagination because American archaeologists reconstructed it in the 1950s. On the ground floor is a museum with tons of trinkets dating back 5,000 years, artifacts including dishes, eating utensils, voting machines, and ballots—all with labels in English. *Below the Acropolis on the edge of Monastiraki entrance on Adrianou.* ☎ *210/ 321-0185. www.culture.gr. Admission (including museum) 4€. Tues–Sun 8:30am–3pm. Metro: Maroussi station, then take the municipal minibus (free ticket) no. 060 in the direction of Paradissos Amaroussiou.*

→ **Greek Folk Art Museum** ★ For a smaller, more navigable Athenian museum experience, head to the Greek Folk Art Museum. Not as much a madhouse or tour-group destination as the National Archaeological Museum, it still has many cool things on display, including colorful clothing and embroidery exhibits, along with work from 20th-century Greek artist Theofilos Hadjimichael. *17 Kidathineon, Plaka.* ☎ *210/ 322-9031. www.culture.gr. Admission 2€. Tues– Sun 10am–2pm. Metro: Syntagma or Acropolis.*

(FREE) → **Hadrian's Arch and Temple of the Olympian Zeus** ★★ The Roman emperor Hadrian wasn't exactly the strong silent type, as evidenced by the statements made by (and on) the massive arch entrance to Athens that he had constructed along with many other monuments in the city. An inscription facing the Acropolis side reads THIS IS ATHENS, THE ANCIENT CITY OF THESEUS. Just in case there was any confusion among his

constituents as to who was really in charge, on the other side it states, THIS IS THE CITY OF HADRIAN, NOT OF THESEUS. That cleared things up. Hadrian's Arch leads into this temple, which the Roman emperor also had constructed. At 110 by 44m (360 by 143 ft.), this was one of the largest temples in the ancient world. There are 13 17m-high (56 ft.) Pentelic marble columns that remain standing, and a horizontal one on the ground. Inside the temple were statues of Zeus and of Hadrian. *On Leoforos Amalias, easily visible from the street. www.culture.gr. Free admission. Metro: Syntagma or Acropolis.*

MTV Best → **National Archaeological Museum** ★★★ Even if museums aren't exactly your bag, this place is a must-see. The Olympics prompted a large-scale renovation here, too, and its collection is one of the best in the world. From looming bronze sculptures and ancient frescoes to teensy artifacts of jewelry and housewares, the collection offers thousands of different ways to become completely absorbed in the country's history by checking out these original ancient items first-hand. You won't be on a solitary journey to the olden, golden days of Greece, however; this place gets absolutely packed on most days, especially in the summer. Arrive really early or during lunchtime to dodge the tour-group crowds. *44 Patission St.* ☎ *210/ 821-7717. www.culture.gr. Admission 7€ adults, 3€ students. Free admission 1st Sun of the month. Mon 1–7:30pm, Tues–Sun 8:30am–3pm. Metro: Omonia Sq.*

→ **Poseidon's Temple** ★★ MTV Best **Cape Sounion,** 69km (43 miles) east of Athens, is worth the bus ride not just for the visit to the Temple but also for hitting the prime real estate on which it's located. On the southernmost point of Attica, the temple is perched with an amazing view of the Aegean Sea and its yachts and boats. Over the centuries, this spot was used in the Peloponnesian war as a lookout (the area's most important sea routes were below). It was so well protected that 15 of the temple's original 34 columns are still standing. Sounion is an inspiration to many, and a favorite of poets through the ages—try to find the spot on one of these columns where Lord Byron allegedly carved his name. There is no shortage of places to eat and hang out around the temple: Souvenir shops, restaurants, and cafes are all around, but expect to pay a bit more because of all the tourists as well as the gorgeous views.

Go ahead and walk down the hill from the temple to enjoy the sea for yourself—the rocks are great for sunbathing and the clear, warm water is perfect for a dip. Yachters like this spot and the monied Europeans who gather here won't bat an eyelash if you lose your suit. *Cape Sounion, 69km (43 miles) east of Athens.* ☎ *0292/39-363. www.frommers.com for more info. Admission 4€. Daily 10am–sunset. Take the Sounion bus leaving from Mavromateon along the west side of the Pedion tou Areos Park. Buses leave about every half-hour, taking 2 hr. to reach Sounion, and round-trip tickets cost 6€.*

Playing Outside

For a cheap thrill and to rest your feet before or after a hike up the Acropolis, check out the public **National Garden,** between Leoforos Amalias and Irodou Attikou. Here you'll find a park, a garden, and a zoo—you can nosh at one of the overpriced cafes in the garden or bring your own food for a picnic. The garden is open daily from 7am to 10pm.

You can't miss Mount Lycabettus, the highly visible spot in the northeast of the city—it's the large hill rivaling the Acropolis for great views of Athens and its surroundings. Hike on up the hill from Dexa Meni Square or shell out the 2€ to take the funicular from Ploutarchou. Just make sure you make it up in time to see the sunset. Also, check out the Chapel of St. George and the Lykavitos Theater, which hosts concerts in the summer.

Shopping

The look in Athens is designer, designer, designer—remember, this is the biggest city around, and young people especially can take themselves quite seriously when parading down those historic streets. The bad news for those designers is that, in Greece, it's easy to just fake it: Designer knockoffs are everywhere, often sold out in the open. "Dior" and "Chanel" sunglasses and purses are sold at nearly every convenience store or shop corner.

For the real thing, go to **Kolonaki,** the haven of beautiful people (or just those who go into debt to appear that way), which has all the designer stores you'd ever need.

Best **Monastiraki Flea Market** (daily 9am–6pm; Metro: Monastiraki) is the place to be for cool, unexpected shopping finds. Every day, shops sell touristy stuff, such as worry beads (strings of beads that you'll see every man over 50 juggling in cafes and bars while ranting about the weather and their wives) and leather sandals. The place gets amped up on Sunday, though; get there before 11am because the swarm of Athenians buying and selling can get to be deafening. Everything from antiques to clothing to housewares, you can haggle for here.

Music buffs should head off of Monastiraki Square to teensy Ifaistos Street, where many little record stores sell hard-to-find used and new vinyl and CDs. Check out **Jimmy's Inferno** (24 Ifaistos St.). Jimmy's a scary-looking metal head, but he's a nice guy who speaks impeccable English and can give you some tips on the underground scene in Athens, as well as info you never knew about metal and rock music.

Barcelona

I heard folks in Barcelona are more interested in being clear-headed at work the next day than they are in downing their fifth whiskey and Coke. Yet it's 4am on a Wednesday morning and the colorfully decorated streets of the bohemian Gràcia neighborhood are still packed with kids jumping in the rain. Huge speakers blast ska music, wet curls and soggy dreads slosh atop bouncing heads, and everyone but me seems to know the words. I can't help but wonder, "Don't these people have to work in the morning?"

Good thing I don't have to clock in anytime soon. Since my wanderings through Barcelona began, I've partied from Thursday through Monday morning, hit the beach, and sat at cafes to drink up the electric Kool-Aid that is Barcelona along with thousands of other travelers and expats who invade this cosmopolitan city each summer. Invasions are nothing new to Barcelona, which has been dealing with travelers for the last 1,500 years thanks to its prime location on the Mediterranean. Therefore, becoming friends with out-of-towners and non-Spanish locals is an inevitable part of an authentic local experience.

I came to Gràcia's yearly street fest with a Colombian, an Argentine, a dreadlocked Cuban, and a proud *gitano* (gypsy). I've met more kids from Latin America in Barcelona than actual Catalans—maybe the Catalans are as cold as they say—or maybe there are just so many South Americans here.

Other Spaniards say that Barcelona is the most European of Spain's cities—and it's not always said in a complimentary manner. But the people here are proud of their rebellious, edgy coolness that traces its routes back to ancient history. Wander the Barri Gòtic, one of the best-preserved medieval quarters in Europe, and then take in Gaudí. Check out the city's amazing street murals, and then Goya. Fado, bullfights, and now *mestizaje* and hip-hop enrich this city that's so close to the beach it hurts.

The Best of Barcelona

○ **The Best Hotel:** The quirky boutique **Hostal Gat Xino** will give you a flavor of Barcelona's minimalist style without breaking the bank. See p. 127.

○ **The Best Unusual Meal:** Keep your balls intact at **Foodball,** a new dining concept pioneered here by the Camper shoe company. You can get balls—whole-grain rice balls, that is—stuffed with organic mushrooms, chicken, chickpeas, or tofu and alga. It's near the MACBA, and the crowd is as interesting as the food. See p. 131.

○ **The Best Cafe:** Follow the trails of incense onto the patio of the Maritime Museum for a late-night cup of savory tea at the **Spiritual Café** in Raval. Breathe in the rich surroundings and smoke of the hookahs. See p. 133.

○ **The Best Sunset Cocktails:** Visit Gaudí's masterpiece, **La Pedrera (Casa Milà),** and watch the sunset as you drink *cava* (chilled wine) from the whimsical rooftop terrace bar. Time it so you can catch the live music at 9pm from July to September. See p. 138.

○ **The Best Mega-Club:** Partying with a group? **Razzmatazz** has several rooms playing different styles that will please nearly everyone bumping and grinding in this huge entertainment complex. See p. 135.

○ **The Best Music:** Immigration from both within and abroad has created the Barcelona sound, *mestizaje,* a multicultural blend of Latin, Spanish, and African rhythms with a dose of hip-hop and electronica. See p. 134.

○ **The Best View:** Take a funicular ride up **Mount Tibidabo,** which forms the northwestern boundary of the city. When the weather's good, you can catch breathtaking views of Montserrat and the Pyrenees—and even Mallorca on the clearest days. See p. 141.

○ **The Best Photo Op:** Explore the nooks and crannies of Gaudís strange and enchanting **Parc Güell** that sits atop a hill and offers great views of the city. See p. 139.

BARCELONA

Getting There & Getting Around

Getting into Town

BY PLANE

El Prat de Llobregat Airport (☎ 93/298-38-38; www.barcelona-airport.com or www.aena.es) is 13km (8 miles) southwest of the city. Most people fly to Madrid and change plans there for Barcelona, although Delta has direct flights to Barcelona.

The **Aerobús** is the easiest way to get into town from El Prat; it leaves from all three terminals (A, B, and C) every 12 minutes from 6am to midnight Monday through Friday and 6:30am to midnight Saturday, Sunday, and holidays. It costs 3.60€ one-way and takes about 30 minutes to get to Plaça Espanya, Plaça Universitat, and Plaça Catalunya.

The **train** (☎ 90/224-02-02) also connects the airport to town. It runs from El Prat to Estació Central de Barcelona-Sants, daily from 5:38am to about 10pm. The half-hour ride costs 2.25€.

Talk of the Town

Four ways to start a conversation with a local

1. **Do you speak Catalan as well as Spanish?** Ask this, sit back, and let your new Barcelona buddy go on about how the Catalans are truly bilingual. If you really want to set them off (and don't mind risking your rep), just add, "So why don't y'all just speak Spanish?" (see "Cata-*What*?" below).

2. **Do you think Catalonia should separate from Spain?** In this fiercely independent state, separatist politics remain a hot-button issue.

3. **My *amigo* in Madrid said that people in Barcelona are close-minded and snooty. Why is that?** After cursing the "ignorant monkeys that spawned" the Madrileños, they'll say it's not true and counterpoint that Madrid has no sense of art, fashion, or business—especially business. As the epicenter of trade for over 2,000 years, Catalonia has been a thriving economic region that has circumvented the political bungles of Madrid.

4. **What's your favorite museum?** If you're lucky, maybe they'll even take you there. If your new friend doesn't have a favorite, shake 'em off because in the home of some of the last century's most influential artists, everyone ought to have a *número uno*.

A 20-minute **taxi** ride from El Prat into town will cost about 20€ to 30€.

BY TRAIN

RENFE (☎ 90/224-02-02) is Spain's national train line. **Estació Sants** (Metro: Sants-Estació) handles most trains traveling within Spain. Although if you're leaving for or coming from elsewhere on the continent, you'll usually end up at the **Estació de França** (Metro: Barceloneta); look for showers, visitor info, first aid, and shops there. The Metro goes to both stations, so you can hop aboard, get off in the Barri Gòtic (either the Liceu or Plaça Catalunya stops), and start hunting for hostels.

BY BUS

Take a bus to Barcelona only if you have time to spare. The main station, at **Estació del Nord** (Alí Bei 80; ☎ 93/265-65-08), is the arrival and departure point for **Entecar** (☎ 90/242-22-42), buses that come from southern France, Italy, and Madrid. **Linebús** (☎ 93/265-07-00) makes the Paris run, while **Julià Via** (☎ 93/490-40-00) caters to travelers from Frankfurt and Marseille. Estació del Nord's Metro stop is the Arc de Triomf.

BY BOAT

Barcelona's harbor is the biggest in the Mediterranean, with passenger services to the Balearic Islands and Genoa, Italy. **Transmediterránea** (Moll de Barcelona Station; ☎ 93/295-91-00 or 902/45-46-45) is the major ferry line between Barcelona and the Balearic Islands (about 8 hr.). There's no Metro stop here, but it's only a 10-minute walk from the Drassanes Metro stop at the base of Las Ramblas. Take a taxi if you're lugging around a lot of stuff. *Tip:* Make your reservation as far in advance as you can, especially in the summer.

BY CAR

Driving tip number one: Do not drive here! As in Madrid, it's not worth the hassle—too much traffic, no parking, and Spanish drivers. If you do decide to take the coast road during the high season, expect to be slogging through bumper-to-bumper traffic at times.

Cata-what?

Barcelona is the capital of **Catalonia** (Catalunya in Catalan, Cataluña in Castilian), a region that continues to forge its identity apart from that of Spain. Many Catalans think of their region as a separate country, with its own language, traditions, and turbulent history. In the late 19th and early 20th centuries, Catalonia was a hotbed of socialist and anarchist activity. Catalan separatists established an autonomous republic (1932–38) that opposed Francisco Franco's loyalist forces during the Spanish Civil War (1936–39). Over 65 years after the end of the Spanish Civil War, Catalonia is dominated by leftists, and officials are debating a proposal that says the region has a right to separate from Spain. However, most Spaniards do not agree with recognizing Catalonia as a separate nation.

Getting Around

BY SUBWAY

The Metro (subway) is clean and efficient, but doesn't have any stops in the Ciutat Vella, so the stops closest to where you want to get on/off are on Las Ramblas or Port Olímpic. A single ticket (valid for both the Metro and buses) costs 1.15€, but if you intend to take more than five journeys, it's best to buy the T-10 ticket for 6.30€, which is good for 10 trips. And yes, as in just about every city, you'll see locals jump the turnstiles. Before you're tempted, keep in mind the squares in the red pinstripe shirts. If you're caught by them without a Metro ticket, you'll be fined 40€. The Metro runs from 5am to midnight Sunday through Thursday and 5am to 2am Friday and Saturday.

BY BUS

There are plenty of buses with routes and timetables clearly marked at each stop. Be aware that most buses stop running well before the Metro closes and you'll be at the mercy of nasty traffic jams. As with the Metro, a single ticket costs 1.15€.

BY BICYCLE

There are a few bicycle lanes in the center of the city, along with places that will rent them, including **Un Coxte Menys** (Espartaria 3; ☎ 93/268-21-05), and **Biciclot** (Verneda 16; ☎ 93/307-74-75). You are not required by law to wear a helmet, so you don't have to worry about smashing your weave—just your brains.

Barcelona Basics

Orientation: Barcelona Neighborhoods

Pushing up against the Mediterranean Sea, Barcelona's coastline runs from southwest to northeast. It'll only take you 10 minutes to walk from the beach's cool breeze to city-slicker sleaze once you pass the **Mirador de Colón** (p. 138) and hit Las Ramblas.

    📺 Best **Las Ramblas,** a wide promenade that is the city's main artery, stretches all the way to **Plaça Catalunya.** From end to end, it's about a 20-minute walk, but that doesn't count all the time taken to snap a photo with the silver chick statue (how she gets the paint out of her hair is beyond me), peruse the newsstands, buy a gerbil, or just sit at one of the many cafes and watch the herd shuffle along. It can get pretty crowded sometimes. Keep drifting northward on Las Ramblas, and the **El Raval** neighborhood will be to your left and the **Barri Gòtic** to your right. Put the two together and you get a meaty portion of the **Ciutat Vella (Old City),** where most of what you want to see awaits.

El Raval is a multicultural mash of maze-like streets that smell like tandoori chicken and pee. This neighborhood used to be the Dirty South of Barcelona, full of hookers, hard drugs, and muggers. But, like Mariah Carey, this place has experienced a remarkable comeback. Thanks to gentrification (aka "urban renewal") and police crackdowns, the place has been cleaned up. It's still a little grimy, but the construction of the sleek **Museu d'Art Contemporani** (see "Performing Arts," below) brought in trendy new galleries, shops, and artsy bars. You should still keep your eyes open and hold on to your bags on L'Arc del Teatre, which points south in the area known as **Barri Xinès** (literal translation: Chinatown; actual meaning: red-light district). Since the cops came stomping through, the worst that will probably happen to you is an old prostitute named Tita might suck her teeth at you by the port. But still be wary of your wallet, and women should not wander through here alone, especially on Carrer de Hospital.

The 📺 **Best** **Barri Gòtic** is the city's oldest quarter; here you'll find the **Cathedral de la Seu** (see "Performing Arts," below). It's best to wander through the narrow, winding cobblestone streets at dusk when the buildings warm up to the fading Mediterranean light and the street musicians come out to play. On the northeastern edge of Barri Gòtic (about a 15-min. walk northeast from the center of Las Ramblas) is the must-check-out bohemian neighborhood **El Born,** with some good eats and drinks, as well as the **Museu Picasso (Picasso Museum;** see "Museums," below). The Born is the latest up-and-coming neighborhood whose gentrification includes coffee and pastry shops, old-style delis, and designer shops.

Important streets to know about in case you get lost are the east-west **Gran Vía** (officially Gran Vía de les Corts Catalanes), which runs through Plaça Espanya and is just a few blocks north of Plaça Catalunya. **Avinguda Diagonal** runs northwest to southeast and cuts the whole city in half 10 blocks northwest of the Ciutat Vella. Passeig de Gràcia begins at Plaça Catalunya and runs north to Avinguda Diagonal. Besides the Gaudí buildings on Passeig de Gràcia, there really isn't much to see on the other streets.

Gràcia, about an hour's walk to the northwest of Ciutat Vella, was once a separate village outside the city walls erected by the Romans. Those walls are long gone, yet this mildly bohemian and chill community still has a strong sense of identity and neighborhood pride ("Gràcia for life, holmz") marked by their annual street parties in August (p. 138). Grab a drink at the Plaça de Sol and act like you're from *el barrio, vato.*

Savings

The **Barcelona Card** is worth every penny if you plan on hitting up a ot of attractions. It offers steep discounts on admissions and free unlimited use of public transportation. You can buy this card to cover 1 to 5 days. The price ranges from 17€ to 30€. For adults, it's 17€ for 1 day and 22€ for 2 days, for example.

The 24-hour card includes the Metro and the bus, and unlimited travel on all public transport.

You can also use the card to get discounts of 10% to 100% in 29 museums, 10% to 25% off some theaters and shows, and discounts at other venues. In addition, there's a 10% to 12% savings at about 2 dozen stores and 18 restaurants. Check the cards for specifics when you buy one. They're for sale at the tourist offices at the airport, at Sants Station, and in the Plaça de Catalunya. See "The Ruta del Modernisme: L'Eixample & Gaudí" on p. 140 for another discount offering.

North of Plaça Catalunya is **L'Eixample,** which means "the expansion," and is simply a huge grid of commercial streets devoid of any character, with the exception of Gaudí's mutant *modernista* behemoths— **Sagrada Familia, Casa Milà,** and **Casa Batlló**—and the **Quadrat d'Or (Golden Triangle;** see "Performing Arts," below).

Don't bother walking through the **Sants-Montjuïc,** a plain middle-class neighborhood on the west end of the city. Go straight to the summit of Mont Juïc (the big mountain and Barcelona's highest point), which is crammed with museums, botanical gardens, a fortress, and the 1992 Olympic grounds. **Plaça de Espanya** on the southeastern end is also cool, with its wild fountains. The **Poble Espanyol** area has a handful of good clubs—most notable/notorious is La Terrrazza (see "Clubs & Discos," below). And if you must, there's Epcot's unwanted stepchild, the Poble Espanyol mini–theme park (see "Performing Arts," below).

Back to the beach. Following Columbus's lead, head east and cross the Rambla de Mar footbridge to **Maremagnum,** a "waterfront development area" (read: mall with a boardwalk). Here you'll find shops, overpriced restaurants, an IMAX, and pimply teenagers. There are several clubs offering free entrances and drinks, but unless you're broke or a middle-aged white guy looking for prostitutes, it's best to avoid them. Keep walking northeast along the coast for 5 minutes and you'll hit the Port Olímpic. Wow. How terribly *un*exciting. But hey, at least the beach starts here.

TOURIST OFFICES

The main office is located underground at the Plaça Catalunya. Look for the sign with a big, red I. The office has free magazines and fliers, including info on the big clubs and bars, and will make hotel reservations for you. The *Barcelona Card* (see above) can also be picked up here. Call ☎ **80/711-72-22** from inside Spain, or 93/368-37-30 from outside (www.barcelonaturisme.com; daily 9am–9pm; Metro: Catalunya).

Hot Spots

....

You'll find access to the Internet throughout town but especially in Ciutat Vella. Many *locutorios* (see "Barcelona Nuts & Bolts," below) also have Internet access.

easyInternetCafé has over 300 terminals in this modern center. Just don't let the bright orange walls blind you—a few travelers have lost their wallets to thieves here. You can burn CDs, scan, copy, and fax. It's located at Las Ramblas 31 (www.easyinternetcafe.com). The charge is 1.80€ per hour; a 1-day unlimited pass is 4€, a 7-day pass is 10€, 30 days is 20€. It's open daily from 8am to 2:30am (Metro: Liceu). A branch at Ronda Universitat 35 is a little less expensive (daily 8am–2am; Metro: Catalunya).

Bcnet's Internet cafe also doubles as a gallery, at Carrer Barra de Ferro 3, down the street from the Museu Picasso. Call ☎ **93/268-15-07.** It's 2.40€ per hour, and a 10-hour ticket is 18€ (Mon–Fri 10am–10pm and Sat–Sun noon–10:30pm; Metro: Jaume I).

Euro NetCenter is at Carrer Marqués de Barbera 19, a block off Las Ramblas. It charges .50€ per 30 minutes (daily 11am–10pm; Metro: Liceu).

MS Internet, at Carrer Pintor Fortuny 30, is 3 blocks off Las Ramblas in El Raval. Call ☎ **93/317-55-62.** You can surf here for 1€ per hour (Mon–Sat 9:30am–9:30pm; Metro: Liceu or Catalunya).

Recommended Websites

○ **Barceloca.com**: An all-round guide to what's on or available in the city. Restaurants, bars, clubs, and everything else you can think of.

○ **GoGayBCN.com**: In Spanish and Catalan, this caters to LGBT travelers, with apartment listings and a Gay Guide.

○ **Barcelonareporter.com**: A news, opinion, and information resource on Catalonia.

○ **bcn.es**: The city's bilingual website.

○ **Lifestylebarcelona.com**: Specializes in offering "unique experiences" in and around the city, from parachute jumping to chocolate massages.

Recommended Books & Movies

The Madrid chapter talks about Pedro Almodóvar's films. Many of his movies were filmed in Madrid, but Barcelona appears now and then. And Almodóvar is a perfect intro to Spanish movies.

For books, look into the lives of the artists who thrived here. Try *Gaudí: A Biography* by Gijs van Hensbergen; the controversial *Picasso, Creator and Destroyer* by Arianna Huffington; and *Salvador Dalí: A Biography*. History buffs should turn to George Orwell's *Homage to Catalonia* and the more recent *Barcelonas* by native writer Manuel Vázquez Montalbán.

Culture Tips 101

Catalan, is one of Spain's four native languages and the regional (or national,

Rules of the Game

The legal minimum drinking age in Barcelona is 16, but who's counting? Like everywhere else in Spain, no one cares about your drinking problem unless you step out of line and pick a fight or mistake a flower stand on Las Ramblas for the loo. When staggering out of bars or clubs, be courteous to the folks living in Ciutat Vella. If you make too much noise, the club bodyguards will do a good job of shutting you up. It's okay to drink alcohol in public.

As for drugs, the rules are the same as in Madrid; see p. 590.

depending on your politics) language of Catalonia. It's somewhat of a half-Spanish, half-French love child of the Pyrenees and you can get the gist of what's going on if you speak either of the two. After years of being outlawed during the Franco dictatorship, Catalan has returned to Barcelona and the rest of the region in full force. All of the signs, menus, and TV and radio shows are in Catalan. Fortunately, everyone also speaks perfect Spanish. It's totally cool to address someone in *castellano* (Castilian, aka Spanish) without first asking if they speak it, but you'll definitely make them crack a smile if you spit out a few Catalan phrases.

Word of warning: Much of Barcelona closes for 3 weeks during August.

Barcelona Nuts & Bolts

Currency   There are several banks around Plaça Catalunya, Las Ramblas, and Plaça de Sant Jaume in Barri Gòtic. General banking hours are Monday through Friday from 8:30am to 2pm. You'll probably get the best rates at ATMs (you'll need a four-digit PIN, so call your bank before you leave home, if you need one). Many exchange stations stay open late in Las Ramblas, but you won't get a good rate. Hotels should be your last resort; they give the poorest rates.

Embassies   If you lose your passport, get really sick, fall into the hands of the law, or get into some other serious trouble, the embassy can help. See "Madrid Nuts & Bolts" (p. 591) for details.

Emergencies   In an emergency, dial ☎ 112 for the main number for the municipal police, to report a fire, or to request an ambulance. To dial for an ambulance directly, use ☎ 061. If you are the victim of a crime and want to call the police directly, dial ☎ 091. If you've been pickpocketed, go to **Turisme Atenció** at Carrer Nou de la Rambla 80 (☎ 93/344-13-00) in El Raval, 3 blocks from the port; this police station deals specifically with tourists.

Pharmacies   Look for signs with green neon crosses. They rotate the 24-hour shift, so check any pharmacy window to see the nearest one on duty.

Laundry   There are several self-service laundromats and dry cleaners in the Ciutat Vella. Some hostels have laundry facilities and charge an average of 7€ a load, wash and dry.

Lavomatic is at Plaça Joaquim Xirau 1 (☎ 93/344-13-00), 1 block to the right of Las Ramblas and 1 block below Carrer Escudellers. A wash is 3.75€ and a dry is .75€ for 5 minutes of hot air. It's open Monday through Saturday from 10am to 10pm.

Wash ⌀ Net is at Carrer les Carretes 56, near Las Ramblas in El Raval. A wash is 4€ to 6€ and a dry is 1€ every 10 minutes. You can surf the Internet for .50€ per 30 minutes. It's open daily from 10am to 11pm.

Luggage Storage   **Estació Barcelona-Sants** (☎ 93/495-62-00) rents lockers for 4.50€ a day. It is open daily from 5:30am to 11pm. **Estació de França** (☎ 93/496-34-64) rents lockers for 3.50€ per day, daily from 7am until 10pm.

Post Office   The **main post office** is on Plaça d'Antoni López, facing the water at the end of Passeig de Colom (☎ 90/219-71-97), and is open Monday to Saturday 8:30am to 9:30pm and on Sunday from 8:30am to 2:30pm. You can also pick up stamps at *estancos* (the kiosks that say TABACO) and just drop off your postcards or letters in any of the bright yellow mailboxes throughout the city.

Restrooms   Call them *aseos, servicios, lavabos,* or whatever. Make a beeline to the back of any restaurant or bar and be sure to go through the correct door—CABALLEROS or SENORES means men, and DAMAS or SENORAS is for women.

Safety   Unlike the folks in Madrid, Barcelona locals won't constantly remind you to walk with your handbags in front of you—but don't get too comfortable. Tourist-infested zones like the Ciutat Vella and on or around Las Ramblas and on the Metro are prime hunting grounds for pickpockets. Petty theft and pickpocketing are problems, so avoid being a target and keep a limited supply of your money in a secure place on your body. Be especially careful around the Picasso Museum, Parc Güell, Plaza Real, and Mont Juïc.

Telephone Tips   To use a phone booth, it's best to buy a *tarjeta telefónica* from a newsstand or *estanco,* as many do not take coins. All have dialing instructions in English. If your family likes to pass the phone around so everyone in the house can say "hi," it's better you look for a *locutorio* (call center). They're all over Ciutat Vella, give better rates, and offer a booth for privacy.

For **directory assistance,** dial ☎ 1003 for numbers within Spain, 1008 within Europe, and 1005 for the rest of the world. **Toll-free numbers** are phone numbers that begin with 900. Calling an 800 number in the States from Spain is *not* free and costs the same as an international call.

Tipping   Prices shown on menus have to include any service charge. Only when the menu indicates "IVA no incluido" (VAT not included) can this be added to the bill. Tips are not compulsory, but plan to dish out an additional 5% to 10% when you're happy with the service. Taxi drivers don't expect tips.

Sleeping

What is it that makes sleeping in Barcelona so much more expensive than Madrid? Well, it could be that the population nearly doubles with young tourists during the summertime. Expect to pay around 80€ for a double and 50€ for a single, and you'll just have to learn to deal with the cramped, overpriced hostels if you're on a tight budget. If you want to stay in the touristy areas like Las Ramblas or Barri Gòtic, make reservations weeks, even months, in advance. If you didn't plan ahead, your best bet is to show up at hostels around 11am when they know exactly who's sticking around another night and who's taking off (there are several on Carrer de la Unió). You could also try staying in Gràcia, which will have more vacancies and is not too far from Ciutat Vella. If all else fails, go to the tourist office—they can make reservations for you.

Hostels

📺 Best → **Albergue de Juventud Kabul** ★ If you want a good night's rest, steer clear of this animal house. But if it's an all-night party you're looking for, about 200 frat boys and sorority gals are crammed into rooms of four to eight people; you can expect to be awoken in the middle of the night by drunks looking for their bunks. Smack dab in backpacker central, the party leaks in from the streets to the common rooms that blast American music. *Plaça Reial 17.* ☎ *93/318-51-90.*

www.kabul.es. 15€–23€ single bed. Key deposit 15€. Reservations not accepted. Amenities: Bar; free Internet; laundry (2.50€); pool table; TV (in common room). In room: A/C. Metro: Liceu.

→ **Backpackers BCN** This small hostel is far away enough from the center of Barcelona to be safer and quieter, but still within walking distance of Las Ramblas (10 min.). On your downtime, grab a book from their library and chill on the terrace, check out a DVD in the common room, or cook dinner in their full-service kitchen. Nice place to stay if you want to relax and get a good night's sleep. Max four people to a room, 18 beds total. *Carrer Diputación, 323 ppral.1a.* ☎ *93/488-02-80. 22€ single bed. Rates include breakfast. Amenities: Curfew 3am–7:30am; kitchen; lockers (5€ deposit); patio; PlayStation; free sheets; TV (in common room); free Wi-Fi. Metro: Passeig de Gràcia.*

→ **Gothic Point Youth Hostel** Comfy couches, a large TV, colorful decor, and free Internet make the lobby a great place to hang out and meet other backpackers. There are 150 beds in dorm-style rooms, but each bed has its own shelf, plug, and reading light and can be curtained off for added privacy. About a 10-minute walk from the most popular bars. Sea Point Youth Hostel is their sister hostel on the beach nearby. *Plaça del Mar 4.* ☎ *93/224-70-75. www.seapointhostel.com.*

Carrer Vigatans 5. ☎ *93/268-78-08. www. gothicpoint.com. High season 22€ single bed, low season 17€ single bed. Rates include breakfast. Metro: Jaume I. Amenities: Free Internet; lockers (1.20€ per day); refrigerator; rooftop terrace; sheets (1.80€); towels (1.80€); vending machines. In room: A/C.*

Cheap

→ **Hostal La Terrassa** You get what you pay for, so don't expect spectacular views and chocolate on your pillow. The 50 sparely decorated rooms are claustrophobically small. Some rooms have terraces (only .6m/ 2 ft. deep), but you can go to the outdoor terrace on the main floor. The friendly staff speaks English. People gather in the large and impeccably clean eating/chilling area, where you can watch TV, bring in food from outside, or grab a snack from the vending machine. *Junta de Comerç 11.* ☎ *93/302-51-74. 46€–50€ double, 50€–66€ triple. Amenities: Eating area; terrace. In room: A/C, TV. Metro: Liceu.*

→ **Hostal Malda** These are the cheapest, cleanest beds in Barri Gòtic, hands down. The only drawback is that the hotel is on the third floor (no elevator) and they don't give you your own key (you have to be buzzed in), but the location within the hustle and bustle of the Barri Gòtic and the price more than make up for that. No reservations, so show up by 10am to snag one of the 30 rooms. *Carrer Pi 5 (entrance inside small shopping center).* ☎ *93/317-30-02. 15€ single, 30€ double, 45€ triple with shower. Shared bathrooms. Amenities: TV (in common room). Metro: Liceu.*

Doable

[MTV] [Best] → **Hostal Gat Xino** ★★ Centrally located in the Barri Xinès of the Raval district, this modern hostel is stylish and comfortable with its groovy green decor, en suite flatscreen satellite TVs, high-power jet showers, and incredibly soft sheets. The best rooms have private terraces. There's also a breezy breakfast area, a wood-decked patio,

and a roof terrace perfect for an afternoon smoke. *Hospital 155.* ☎ *93/324-88-33. 64€– 75€ single, 96€ double, 1,280€ quad suite. Rates include breakfast. Amenities: Breakfast room; patio; roof terrace. In room: A/C, TV, Internet. Metro: Sant Antoni.*

→ **Hostal Goya** ★★ The address may be posh, but the service is comforting. You can make yourself feel at home—especially when you treat yourself to all the free tea, coffee, and hot chocolate in the Scandinavian-looking communal TV room. Half of the rooms have been renovated and have that minimalist Ikea look, with comfy beds, plush duvets, and throw pillows. The best rooms are doubles with balconies and the worst are small, dark singles. Be sure to reserve in advance because it fills up quickly. *Pau Claris 74.* ☎ *93/302-25-65. www.hostalgoya. com. 34€ single with shared bathroom; 73€ double with shared bathroom, 88€ with private bathroom. Amenities: Terrace; TV (in common room). In room: A/C (in some rooms). Metro: Urquinaona or Catalunya.*

→ **Hotel Peninsular** ★ Maybe it's good karma from once having housed a convent that makes this hotel genuinely one of the nicest places to stay in Barcelona. The iron railings, relaxing courtyard, and plant-draped atrium extending to the glass ceiling make this an oasis within the grimy Barri Xinès. The rooms are spacious and clean, and they also serve a decent continental breakfast. *Sant Pau 34.* ☎ *93/302-31-38. 30€ single with shared bathroom, 50€ with private bathroom; 50€ double with shared bathroom, 70€ with private bathroom. Rates include breakfast. Amenities: Breakfast bar; TV (in common room); safe. In room: A/C. Metro: Liceu.*

Splurge

→ **Hotel Omm** ★★★ With an award-winning design that looks like a space station gone feng shui, the Hotel Omm has quickly become a Barcelona accommodations hot

Barcelona

SLEEPING ■
Albergue de Juventud Kabul **38**
Backpackers BCN **12**
Gothic Point Youth Hostel **41**
Hostal Gat Xino **19**
Hostal Goya **15**
Hostal La Terassa **30**
Hostal Malda **27**
Hotel Omm **9**
Hotel Peninsular **32**

EATING ◆
Agua **45**
Bar Jardí **26**
El Café que Pone
   Muebles Navarro **20**
El Quatre Gats **25**
Foodball **24**
Kashmir **31**
King Döner **35**
La Boqueria/
   Mercat de San Jozep **29**
Pla dels Angels **21**
Romesco **33**
Spiritual Café **44**
Venus **39**

PARTYING ★
Bang Bang **17**
City Hall **16**
Discotheque **5**
Fritz Hot Club **8**
Harlem Jazz Club **40**
Jamboree **38**
La Paloma **18**
La Terrazza **5**
Moog **37**
O'Hara's Irish Pub **36**
Razzamatazz **13**
Salvation **14**
Travel Bar **34**

SIGHTSEEING ●
Casa Milà (La Pedrera) **10**
Catedral de Barcelona **28**
CCCB (Centre de Cultura
   Contemporània de
   Barcelona) **23**
Fundació Joan Miró **2**
Fundació MACBA (Museu
   d'Art Contemporani) **22**
La Font Màgica **6**

La Sagrada Familia **11**
Mirador de Colón **43**
MNAC **3**
Museu Picasso **42**
Olympic Stadium **1**
Parc Güell **7**
Poble Espanyol **4**

Barcelona Metro

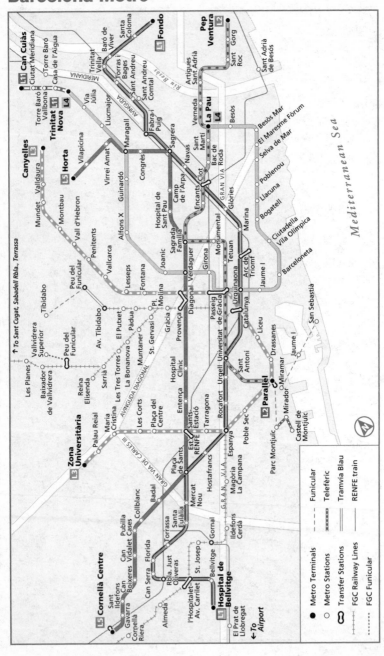

spot. The rooms have a minimalist, "Nordic Zen" feel with two bathrooms and high-tech illumination. Spend an afternoon lounging by the rooftop pool where you can enjoy the spectacular views of Gaudís landmark buildings, or sit in the sleek lobby and gawk at all the fabulous and ridiculously beautiful people

sauntering along. *Rosselló 265.* ☎ *93/445-40-00. www.hotelomm.es. 210€ single, 375€ double, 428€–535€ suite. Metro: Diagonal. Amenities: Bar; fitness center; laundry service/dry cleaning; pool; restaurant; spa. In room: A/C, TV, hair dryer, safe, Wi-Fi.*

Eating

As skinny as the women may be, Barcelona knows how to eat. With Cuban, Indian, Basque, American, or a ubiquitous multinational chain, Barcelona offers every kind of food you could desire, yet at less-than-desirable prices. The cheapest way to fill your belly is to hit up the *mercats* (markets) for fresh foods and pick up other staples at *supermercats/supermercados* (grocery stores).

Another option: Pick up a bocadillo, a no-frills baguette filled with meats, cheese, or an omelet. For late-night snacks (overpriced chips and candy), check out the news kiosks on Las Ramblas. And then there's döner kebabs—everywhere!

It is important to adjust to Spanish time. Lunch is eaten from 2 to 4pm and is followed by a long siesta to rest and digest, drinks at around 10pm, and dinner at 11pm. You'll have more than enough time to make it out to the clubs by 2am when the party starts jumping.

Cheap

🎵 **Best** ➔ **Foodball** ★ HEALTH FOOD Located near the MACBA, this quirky new dining concept by the Camper shoe company caters to the neo-hippies in the neighborhood. The food is presented in, yes, balls. Whole-grain rice balls stuffed with either organic mushrooms, chicken, chickpeas, or tofu and alga, and are actually good. Take a couple to go or plant yourself on the colorful tiered concrete and see which of your friends can stuff the most tasty balls in their mouth. *Elisabets 9.* ☎ *93/270-13-63. Foodballs 1.75€ each; main courses 5€. Daily noon–11pm. Metro: Liceu.*

➔ **King Döner** ★ MIDDLE EASTERN This city has more döner kebab joints than 50 Cent has gunshot wounds, but King Döner in the Rambla de Raval tops them all. Shawarmas, affectionately known as "Arab tacos," come 3.50€ a serving. You can order them with chicken, lamb, or fresh veggies. They also serve veggie falafels for PETA members. *Bajos 39, Rambla de Raval. No phone. Metro: Liceu.*

➔ **Romesco** CATALAN It feels like *abuela* (grandma) is in the kitchen serving up huge portions of home-style food in this small restaurant popular with locals and backpackers on a budget. Try the menú del día, aka the Cuban Grand Slam: Fill up on rice and beans, fried plantains, carne en salsa, and a fried egg for only 4.50€. *Sant Pau 28 (1 block off Las Ramblas).* ☎ *93/318-93-81. Main courses 5€–12€. Mon–Fri 1pm–midnight, Sat 1–6pm and 8pm–midnight. Closed Aug. Metro: Liceu.*

Doable

➔ **Kashmir** PAKISTANI There are plenty of Pakistani and Indian restaurants in Barcelona, but Kashmir tops every local's list. This small, no-frills restaurant serves up great food at a reasonable price and is a good lunch break after a day of gallery walking and thrift shopping in El Raval (it's very busy 2–4pm). They're a little conservative with the *picante*, so you might have to ask them to kick it up a notch if you want enough curry to set your mouth on fire. *Sant Pau 39.* ☎ *93/441-37-98. Main courses 6€–10€. Daily 1–5pm and 8pm–midnight. Metro: Plaça Catalunya*

➔ **Venus** MIDDLE EASTERN/CAFE A vegetarian's paradise—choose from 14 different salads, couscous, and hummus, moussaka, and lasagna. Packed with artists, students, and the sales clerks who work in the trendy shops of the neighborhood, you can feel like part of the gang. Well, almost. You sort of can't help it, as they cram as many tables as physically possible into such a small place. The walls are just as crammed with colorful paintings and artist expos that rotate every 2 months. Try the Alexandria couscous with chicken, chickpeas, raisins, and the works. *Avinyó 25.* ☎ *93/301-15-85. Main courses 4.90€–8.50€. Mon–Sat noon–midnight. Metro: Liceu.*

Splurge

➔ **Agua** ★★ MEDITERRANEAN Whether you sit on the terrace right smack on the beach or inside the sunny dining room with huge windows, simply watching the waves crash ashore from either venue makes this one of the most relaxed places to eat. Order heaping portions of meats and fish to be grilled over an open fire or try the fresh pasta with succulent prawns. Wines are a tad expensive, but the food is reasonably priced for the quality. It's a very popular spot, so make reservations for the weekends. *Passeig Marítim de la Barceloneta 30.* ☎ *93/225-12-72. Main courses 13€–16€. Daily 1:30–4pm and 8:30pm–midnight (Fri–Sat till 1am). Metro: Ciutadella–Vila Olímpica.*

➔ **Pla dels Angels** MODERN INTERNATIONAL Opposite the MACBA, this trendy restaurant explodes with a kooky kaleidoscope of colors and imaginative dishes. Pick up the wine bottle; the menu's glued to it. Take your pick from the high-quality and reasonably priced salads, meat, pasta, and gnocchi. Try the octopus carpaccio or just stick with the bourgeois White Castle miniburgers if you're not as adventurous. You can fill yourself up by ordering one of their generously portioned appetizers. Be sure to book in advance for the weekends.

Ferlandina 23. ☎ *93/329-40-47. Main courses 13€–16€; menu 5.35€. Daily 1:30–4:30pm and 9–11:30pm (Fri–Sat till midnight). Metro: Universitat.*

Cafes & Tearooms

➔ **Bar Jardí** CAFE This outdoor cafe is a refuge from the shopping madness on the street. Look out for the big camel by the doorway, walk through to the back of the market, and head upstairs to an unexpected spot for an afternoon beer and bocadillo. The trees, chirping birds, and hanging surf boards—not to mention the hotties with flared bangs and shaved heads peppered throughout the open courtyard—are a welcomed distraction from the sensory overload on the street. *Portaferrissa 17. No phone. Mon–Sat 11am–9pm. Metro: Universitat.*

➔ **El Café que Pone Muebles Navarro** CAFE If you're wondering where the long name came from (aka Muebles Navarro, Café Muebles), it used to be a furniture store, which explains the bizarre collection of chairs and sofas to sink into with your new Barça-buddy. Grab some coffee and NY cheesecake, and check out the art, the alternacool clientele, or spoken word artists on select nights. *Riera Alta 4–6.* ☎ *607/18-80-96. Tues–Wed 2pm–2am, Thurs 6pm–2am, Fri–Sat 6pm–3am. Metro: Liceu.*

➔ **Els Quatre Gats** ★ CAFE Step back in time at this former turn-of-the-century artist's lair, where Picasso hung his first exhibit and Gaudí chilled out with other members of the Modernista movement. "The Four Cats" (Catalan slang for "just a few people") was a center point in the city's intellectual and bohemian life and its history comes alive on the mosaic tiled walls and dozens of black-and-white pictures of famous past customers. Your best bet is to order a coffee and take in the fin-de-siècle atmosphere, and the mixed crowd, because the prices are inflated and the service is snooty. *Montsió 3.* ☎ *93/302-41-40.*

Daily 1pm–1am; cafe daily 8am–2am. Metro:
Plaça de Catalunya.

[MTV] [Best] →**Spiritual Café** ★★ CAFE
Lounge on comfy cushions, breathe in the
sweet incense, and watch the performers spit
fire, perform Chinese theater and acrobatics,
or even give you a massage. The Chinese pottery, Arabic scrawled tables, hanging plants,
and patterned rugs add to the feeling of an
Oriental oasis. After a few cups of tea and
puffs of the flavored tobacco in the hookahs,
you'll feel like your aura is hot pink with
purple polka dots. *Museu Marítim, Av.*
Drassanes. ☎ *93/317-52-56. Thurs–Sat*
9:30pm–3am. Metro: Drassanes.

Markets

→**La Boqueria/Mercat de Sant Josep**
Be sure to bring your camera to this bustling
market. Dozens of stalls spill over with fresh
vegetables, fruits, nuts, spices, meats, and
seafood, along with hundreds of people chattering and haggling, and it's all packed underneath an impressive vaulted glass and iron
structure. If you or any of your friends get a
kick out of the skinned rabbits, pig heads, and
guts hanging off hooks, seek help. Seriously.
La Rambla 89, between Carrer de Carme and
Carrer de L'Hospital in El Raval. ☎ *93/318-*
25-84. Mon–Sat 8:30am–8:30pm. Metro: Liceu.

Partying

It doesn't match the madness of Madrid and
Ibiza, but you can easily be initiated into the
night owl tribes' ritual club-hopping. Thursdays through Saturdays are the busiest nights,
yet you can find a joint any night of the week.
Clubs open after 11pm but aren't jumping until
3am. You can go to "afters" until 10am—so
don't expect to get much sightseeing done
once you fall into the clubbing cycle.

You can also save beaucoup bucks by
looking for promoters passing out flyers
after 10pm on Las Ramblas (for free or
discounted entrance to the major clubs, such
as Moog and City Hall). Start your search
at Plaça Real and then walk through nearby
Carrer Escudellers in Barri Gòtic, where
you'll find several clubs, bars, and stumbling
drunks, *ahem,* party people.

The club scene relies heavily on
electronica—house and electro, in particular—but hip-hop heads, indie rockers, and
salseros can also find their spots to bug out.
Barcelona isn't really known for its live
music scene, but you can catch some international acts and homegrown talent (p. 136)
in venues half the size of those in major
American cities. For up-to-date listings check
the *Guía del Ocio,* available at newsstands;
snag free mags like *Go, Metropolitan, Mondo*

Sonoro, and *AB* at bars or music shops; or
check out the websites in "Get Connected:
Music & Nightlife Listings," below. Spanish-
titled sites and publications are in Spanish,
but listings are straightforward and easy to
understand.

The dress code isn't nearly as froufrou and
pretentious as in New York or London. Jeans
are the norm, but why be boring? Now is the
time to wear the quirky threads you bought
at the *mercadillo*—you might hesitate to
wear those orange, poofy, Ali Baba pants
at home. You can wear sneakers at most
clubs (be careful at moody Terrrazza and
Discotheque, where bouncers double as the
fashion police), but flip-flops are a definite
ticket back to your hotel room.

Get Connected: Music & Nightlife Listings

→ www.BarcelonaRocks.com
→ Lecool.com
→ Atiza.com
→ Salirenbarcelona.com
→ Clubbingspain.com
→ Guiadelocio.com

Clubs & Discos

Serious drinking at the bars doesn't begin until the clocks strike midnight. Most clubs don't open until 2am, and they are generally empty until the bars close at 3am. Many clubs stay open as late as 6am. Expect to find cover charges of between 5€ and 10€, if there is one, depending on the night, the DJ, and what the bouncer thinks of you (ladies have the upper hand). Some clubs don't charge to enter or you can use flyers (from bars or given out on the street) to get a discounted admission. But a mixed drink can set you back 5€ to 10€. Don't balk at the price; the drinks here are *strong*. If you are charged to get in, ask if it's *amb consumició* (drink included). If so, take your ticket to the bar to get the first drink free. Tipping is not compulsory, although it's common to leave .05€ to .10€ at bars.

Follow those wide-eyed clubbers who just can't stop to after-hours clubs (aka *el after*) like **Fritz Hot Club** (Autovía de Castelldefels Km 12 no. 6; ☎ **93/414-69-90;** bus: L95 from Plaça Universitat and Plaça España) on Monday and Sunday mornings or **Bang Bang** (Gran Vía 580; no phone; Metro: Plaça Universitat) to end or begin your day with electro and Latin house.

➜ **City Hall** *The* place to be partying on Sunday nights. This night is more about the party people than the beautiful people, so leave the heels at home and get ready to jump around until 5:30am. Work up a sweat to electro and deep house sets by resident and international DJs, or chill outside on the comfy sofas. Once you snag a seat, it's hard to give it up. *Rambla de Catalunya 2–4.* ☎ *93/317-21-77. Cover varies. Metro: Plaza de Catalunya.*

➜ **Discotheque** During the winter, the fabulous shift rotates next door from La Terrrazza to Discotheque, known to host glam parties like "F**K Me, I'm Famous!" Expect top international DJs and bags of attitude from the doormen and bartenders.

The Groove

Barcelona's 📺 Best *mestizaje* is a syncretic sound, born in the heart of this city, that taps into global rhythms, layering flavors of funk into a tasty *paella* of beats. It's a fusion, not confusion, of body-moving rhythms. You can catch plenty of *mestizaje* acts during BAM (see "Festivals," below) in the summer.

Check out Ojos de Brujo (Eyes of the Wizard), which spreads hip-hop, funk, and rumba onto a little flamenco to get the crunchy *cachondeo* that reflects the real multicultural Barcelonese identity. Their DIY, anti-corporate approach is very much in line with their egalitarian spirit and lyrics on their albums *Vengue* and *Bari*.

There's also Raval's 08001, a collective of 23 artists that mix reggae, dub, raï, flamenco, and electronic beats with a dose of triphop. Their first work *Raval ta Joie* is the culmination of 10 months of music-making spontaneously combusting in their warehouse studio. Both Ojos and Raval's are worth checking out live—their jam sessions combine tripped out visuals with high-energy beats that guarantee a fun, sweaty show.

Remember, tipping is compulsory. *Poble Espanyol, Av. Marqués de Comillas s/n.* ☎ *93/511-57-64. Metro: Espanya.*

➜ **La Paloma** This elegant restored theatre and dancehall will transport you back to the Belle Epoque with its red velvet foyer and chandeliers. If you get there early enough, stand in the balconies and catch Grandma and Grandpa in full formal regalia practicing their cha-cha until the ballroom session finishes and the house music begins. They have live performances and mix up techno, pop, and hip-hop later in the evening. *Tigre 27.* ☎ *93/301-68-97. Cover 7€. Metro: Universitat.*

➜ **La Terrrazza** This megaclub has reopened its doors, welcoming the buff and the beautiful to romp in its extravagant playground under the stars. Unless you spent all winter in the gym or recovering from plastic surgery, expect a long wait at the door. *Poble Espanyol, Av. Marqués de Comillas s/n.* ☎ *93/423-12-85. www.laterrrazza.com. Cover 18€ (includes 1 drink). Metro: Espanya.*

➜ **Moog** Known as the "catedral del techno" (techno cathedral), this granddaddy of Barcelona electronica clubs is like Mick Jagger—a little old, but can still wiggle and make the girls jiggle. It has deep house and techno on the roster and gets ridiculously packed by 3am, especially on its best nights— Monday and Wednesday. They play NuWave upstairs and the scene is full of alternakids with their printed T-shirts and Converse kicks, so the dress code is cool and comfortable. *Arc del Teatre 3.* ☎ *93/319-17-89. Cover varies. Metro: Drassanes.*

🅼 **Best** ➜ **Razzmatazz** ★ This mega warehouse entertainment complex can house up to 10,000 dilated pupils. About 5,000 clubbers (give or take a few Cyclops and eye patches) can take in the five clubs housed here for just one admission price. The indie rock concert space is considered to be the best venue in town. Concert prices vary; check listings or call ahead. *Almogavers 122.* ☎ *93/272-09-10. Cover 12€. Metro: Marina.*

Bars

➜ **Chiringuitos Beach Bars** At least a dozen of these are scattered along the Barcelona coastline, blasting reggae, house, or chill electronic lounge. During the day, you can rent out chairs and umbrellas on the sand and wait for the girls to come around with free *chupitos* (shots). Stick around after dark, grab a table, and mingle with the mixed tourist-and-local crowd over drinks. **Beach Bar 23** (on

Barceloneta; ☎ **93/319-04-72**) plays a good mix of old-school salsa on Fridays (7–11pm) that gets everyone dancing on the sand. Mixed cocktails go for 6€; canned beer, 2.50€. If you're not down with the 300% markup, pick up cans of beer at the supermarket across the street for .60€ and listen to the music from the shoreline. *Metro: Jaume I.*

➜ **O'Hara's Irish Pub** A good place to congregate with fellow Anglos from around the world. It gets jam-packed with sweaty Brits, Aussies, and Irish folk wiggling their way to the bar. Each night has a different theme, but a cowboy hat apparently is acceptable gear any night of the week. And don't get too excited about the beach party; it just means the bartenders are wearing bikinis—sorry, no foam. *Ferran 18.* ☎ *93/318-53-21.*

➜ **Thiossan** Ya' mon, if you've been techno'd out in this concrete jungle, let the sweet smell of incense and the reggae vibe relax you as you chill with a friendly international crowd. Order a plate of typical Senegalese food—fish and rice—for 5.50€ and then mellow out with smooth African gin. After your third shot, the 4.6m (15-ft.) boa skin will start to creep up the green, red, and yellow walls. *Lidre 5.* ☎ *93/317-10-31.*

➜ **Travel Bar** Depending on your luck, it might be packed with huge British jocks or drunk singing Frenchman on any given night—both are equally entertaining. Decent plates of food like pasta and curry chicken are served every night for 1€ and if you bring in one of their flyers they leave at most hostels, you'll get a two-for-one drink special. If you're lucky, the guy in the gorilla suit will come out and do a table dance, free of charge. They also have Internet access, play movies during the day, and are the jumping-off point for the "Smashed Pub Crawl" on Tuesdays, Thursdays, and Saturdays at 9:30pm. For 18€, drinks included, you're herded to four bars and a nightclub with a group of folks you'll probably be a little *too* familiar with by the end of the night. *Boqueria 27, just off La Rambla.* ☎ *93/342-52-52. Metro: Liceu.*

Gay Bars

➔ **Salvation** Gay boys and their minions strut their stuff on the two floors of this industrial space. Nineties music and house beats throb in the air, so you can "pump the jam" on the packed dance floor or get a little closer to your new boy-toy in the chill-out area. The door policy also isn't as strict as other places, so bring your ugly friends, too. *Ronda Sant Pere 19–21.* ☎ *93/18-06-86. Cover 11€, includes 1 drink. Metro: Urquinaona.*

Other Live Music

➔ **Harlem Jazz Club** One of Barcelona's oldest and best jazz clubs is also one of the smallest and most sterile looking. But you're not here for dorm-room decorating tips, right? Get a little chummy with the international student crowd and enjoy an eclectic variety of music. Despite the name, you can hear everything from live jazz to African rhythms to kelzmer to Romanian gypsy music on any given night. *Comtessa de Sobradiel 8.* ☎ *93/310-07-55. Cover 5€ (includes 1 drink) Fri–Sun. Metro: Jaume I.*

➔ **Jamboree** If you think Barcelona ain't got no soul, come out on Monday nights for the "What the Fuck" (WTF) jazz jam session that gets packed with a wild, funky crowd and b-boys/girls getting ready to mash up the dance floor during the funk/hip-hop DJ set that follows. Daily jazz or blues performances. The drinks run from 8€ to 10€ each, so pregame it. Upstairs, the attached club Tarantos (☎ **93/318-30-67**) has flamenco shows (3€). *Plaça Real 17.* ☎ *93/301-75-64. Cover 3€ Mon, 8€ Tues–Sun. Metro: Liceu.*

Sightseeing

Barcelona transforms the most ordinary of objects into works of art—benches, sidewalks, and even light posts have a subtle aesthetic quality, not to mention the wild architecture of Gaudí and the Modernistas concentrated in L'Eixample (see the walking tour on p. 140). Barri Gòtic is one of the best-preserved medieval quarters in Europe, with quiet plazas, lofty palaces, and a maze of narrow streets. Take a stroll down Carrer

12 Hours in Barcelona

1. **See La Sagrada Família.** It is the coolest. We'll write it over and over again.

2. **Go to the beach.** It's free and it's fun.

3. **Walk the Manzana de la Discordia (Block of Discord).** Just a 5-minute walk from Plaça Catalunya on the Passeig de Gràcia, this group of three modernista houses look nothing alike. Five blocks up, you'll get to La Pedrera. Don't miss any of them.

4. **Relax at Parc Güell.** It's the best place to get out of the city. Period.

5. **Get your kicks at Barcelona's famed soccer stadium.** Camp Nou stadium (Travessera de les Corts 65; Metro: to Les Corts) is one of the greatest soccer stadiums in the world. Barcelona's team, C.F. Barcelona (Barça, for short), celebrated its 100th season in 1999.

6. **Hit the Picasso Museum.** So many museums here are great, but this one tells the story of a single individual in addition to sharing captivating art.

7. **Party hearty.** Even if you're normally a stay-at-home type at night, go out.

Festival Frenzy

That day in Gràcia with my friends, we toasted and sloshed our foamy beer when suddenly a wave of bodies rushed down the narrow street. Some mugs were laughing, most were cursing, and I felt my stomach drop to my knees as I was swept away by the crowd. I had no idea what we were running from or where my friends were, but within seconds the stampede flowed out into the main avenue. The situation was as absurd as the wildly monstrous architecture towering over the crowd. I crossed the street as a van labeled GUARDIA URBANA screeched to a halt and spit out six masked guards swinging batons and shields at anyone running from them.

Some punks threw whatever they could at the cops, but I sat still and watched. I thought violence and the police state were something of the Franco era; apparently, Barcelona kept that tradition when it tried to revive its Catalan identity. The van then left as quickly as it came and I looked around for some recognizable faces. "Let's go to the after-party," said the Colombian as he ran up to me. The madness never ends in "Barce-loca."

Avinyó to see major landmarks and lunch in some of the area's most popular restaurants and bars.

Festivals

The year-round schedule of unique neighborhood *festes* share traditions like the *castelles*, or castles, where groups of up to 400 people pit their strength and balance against each other to build human towers up to 10 stories high; and, of course; the *gegantes* (giants) that lead processions; and finally, the freaky *capgrossos* (fatheads) that spark up mischief. Check out www.festivales.com and the cultural agenda section of www.bcn.es for dates and general info.

April

Sant Jordí. The red-and-gold Catalan flag decorates every inch of the city during this celebration of patron saint, St. George. The equivalent of Valentine's Day in the United States (sans corporate takeover), lovers exchange gifts—a man gives a rose and a woman gives a book. Most enlightened couples give both. April 23.

June

Marató de L'Espectacle. Locals love this event that packs in theater, skits, animation, dance, movies, music, and circ (circus-related performances, like fire-eating and such) into this 2-day "marathon of the spectacle." Performances, at Carrer de Lleida 59, begin around 10:30pm and don't let up until dawn in the historic and beautiful Mercat de les Flors. Second week in June.

Sónar. If you're into electronic music, multimedia technology, and contemporary urban art, this 3-day international festival of advanced music and multimedia art is a must. There are exhibitions, record fairs, and soundlabs by the CCCB by day, and concerts and DJs play at SónarNight. For more info, go to www.sonar.es. Tickets 20€–105€. Mid-June.

Sant Joan. It's the summer solstice and Barcelona's burning up. Check out the fireworks at Montjuïc, Tibidabo, or L'Estació del Nord. Later, head to the beach for Barceloneta's pyromaniac orgy Nit del Foc (Night of Fire), dance around bonfires until dawn, and then follow the drunken lemmings into the ocean for some skinny-dipping fun. June 23.

GREC Festival. This 5-week summer event brings theater, dance, and music performers from all over the world to over 50 different venues. Pick up a free schedule at the big booth in Plaça Catalunya and try to see at

BARCELONA

least one show at the beautiful theatre at Montjuïc, aka Teatre Grec. For more info, go to www.barcelonafestival.com. End of June and all of July.

August

Festa Major de Gràcia. The most popular neighborhood party is distinctive for its wildly decorated streets. Bands play on small stages throughout Gràcia as young crowds sing and scream along, drinks in hand. Just get out before the Guardia Urbana slams through in the wee hours. For more info, go to www.festamajordegracia. com. Third week in August.

September

Festa de la Mercé. This weeklong celebration of Barcelona's patron saint, Our Lady of Mercy, features human towers, *gegantes* and *capgrossos,* dazzling fireworks, and general drunken revelry. Check out BAM (Barcelona Acció Musical; www.bam.es), which hosts free concerts. September 19 to 25.

Top Attractions

🎥 **Best** **FREE** → **Casa Milà (La Pedrera)** ★★★ The last work of Gaudí's before he turned to the Sagrada Familia. The

That's the Ticket

Don't expect a tour guide and bus on this route—the **Ruta del Modernisme.** It's actually a ticket for discount admission at dozens of Modernista buildings in the city and includes a map and guide booklet detailing the history of different sites. Passes are 3.60€ for adults and 2.60€ for students, are valid for 30 days, and can be bought at Casa Amatller (Passeig de Gràcia 41; ☎ 93/488-01-39). See "The Ruta del Modernisme: L'Eixample & Gaudí" on p. 140 for info on walking the route.

building seems to have washed ashore with walls that mimic the ocean's waves and balconies tangled like seaweed. Check out the whimsical rooftop with its views of Barcelona. It's a great place to see the sunset. Live music at 9pm from July to September adds to its charm. *Provença 261–265.* ☎ *93/ 484-59-80. Admission 7€ adults, 3.50€ students. Daily 10am–7:30pm. English tours Mon–Fri 6pm. Metro: Diagonal.*

FREE → **Catedral de Barcelona** ★★ It's near Las Ramblas, so you can take your picture and go on with your day. If you stick around, you can catch a performance of the *sardana* in front of the cathedral on Sunday after Mass; services begin at noon and 6:30pm. *Plaça de la Seu s/n.* ☎ *93/315-15-54. Free admission to cathedral; museum 1€ ($1.15). Cathedral daily 9am–1pm and 5–7pm; cloister museum daily 10am–1pm and 4– 6:30pm. Metro: Jaume I and Liceu.*

FREE → **La Font Mágica (Magic Fountain)** ★★ Designed for the 1929 World's Fair, this enormous fountain comes to life during weekends when streams of water shoot in the air in sync with colored lights and dramatic music. The colorful clouds of mist can be frighteningly trippy, but the hundreds of camera-snapping tourists ferried in by the busload will kill any buzz. *Plaça Carles Buïgas 1 (in front of the Palau Nacional). Free admission. Shows May to early Oct Thurs–Sun every ¹/₂ hr. 9:30–11:30pm; mid-Oct to April Fri–Sat every ¹/₂ hr. 7–8:30pm. Metro: Espanya.*

→ **Mirador de Colón** This tower with a statue of Columbus on top is a city landmark. Pay 2€ and take the elevator to the top to catch a great view of the urban sprawl and the ocean. *Portal de la Pau s/n.* ☎ *93/302- 52-24. Admission 2€. June–Sept 9am–8:30pm; Oct–May 10am–6:30pm. Metro: Drassanes.*

→ **Poble Espanyol** ★★ Built for the 1929 World's Fair, this "Spanish Village" represents each region in Spain with scaled-down versions of their most recognizable attractions.

It's definitely a tourist trap with plenty of overpriced souvenir shops, but it's a great stop if you want to fill your scrapbook with funny, cheesy pics. *Av. Marqués de Comillas.* ☎ *93/508-63-00. www.poble-espanyol.com. Admission 7€ adults, 5€ students. Sun 9am–midnight, Mon 9am–8pm, Tues–Thurs 9am–2am, Fri–Sat 9am–4am. Ticket booth closes 1 hr. before park. Metro: Espanya.*

➜**Sagrada Familia** ★★★ If you see only one thing in this town, it has got to be this glorious, spiraling drippy sand castle in the sky. Love it or hate it, Gaudí's enormous masterpiece, started in 1882 and still incomplete, is an architectural monument to the absurd. Climb up the narrow spiral staircase or wait in line and take an elevator to catch the view from the top of the towers. *Majorca 401.* ☎ *93/207-30-31. Admission 8€ adults, 5€ students, 3€ guide/audioguide, 2€ elevator ride. Nov–Mar daily 9am–6pm; Apr–Sept daily 9am–8pm. Metro: Verdaguer or Sagrada Familia.*

Gaudí

The most famous of the Modernisme architects, Antonio Gaudí i Cornet's wildy amorphous designs have sparked debate for years. He infuses Gothic influences with inspiration from nature and innovative materials into colorful untraditional forms. He constructed two of Barcelona's most visited sites—the Casa Milà (p. 138) and the Sagrada Familia (see above)—although he wasn't well appreciated during his lifetime. He died penniless at the age of 76 and today some still consider his work a little too, well, gaudy. Yet the city of Barcelona has certainly come around in recent years, even going as far as to proclaim 2002 the Gaudí International Year.

☒ Best FREE ➜**Parc Güell** ★★★ In true Gaudí fashion, construction of the tripped-out park he designed wasn't finished until after his death. The park was initially intended to be a miniature garden city for the rich, but only one of his intergalactic gingerbread houses was completed and is now the Casa-Museu Gaudí. Try to get here early in the morning if you plan on taking pictures of the colorfully tiled serpentine structures—you'll be fighting with dozens of parents and their toothless kids to snap a picture of the iguana fountain seen on every postcard. (*Tip:* If you take the Metro, prepare to trek up a huge hill. Pack some water and snacks because a lot of the shops on the outskirts of the park are overpriced.) *Carrer del Carmel 28.* ☎ *93/424-38-09 or 93/219-38-11. Free admission. Daily 10am–sunset. Metro: Lesseps (then a 15-min. walk). Bus: 24.*

FREE ➜**Olympic Stadium** See where all the action took place at the 1992 Olympics. The stadium was originally built in 1929, was remodeled for the Games, and now hosts the RCD Espanyol (team of the Professional Spanish Football League). Perched atop the Montjuïc, it overlooks Barcelona from the southwest. ☎ *93/426-20-89. Free admission. Sept–Mar 10am–6pm; May–Sept 10am–8pm. Metro: Espanya (then a 20-min. walk).*

Museums

➜**Centre de Cultura Contemporània de Barcelona (CCCB)** ★ Spain's largest cultural center is dedicated to exploring how the urban landscape catalyzes cultural development—highbrow talk for how cities shape art and media, and vice versa. The CCCB has regular multimedia exhibits, including film series and music performances. *Montalegre 5.* ☎ *93/306-41-00. www.cccb.org. Admission 4.40€ 1 exhibit, 6€ 2 or more exhibits, free 1st Wed of month. June 21–Sept 21 Tues–Sat 11am–8pm, Sun 11am–3pm; Sept 22–June 20 Tues and Thurs–Fri 11am–2pm and 4–8pm,*

BARCELONA

The Ruta del Modernisme: L'Eixample & Gaudí

By the mid–19th century, an overcrowded, old Barcelona was bursting at the seams with crime and cholera when it was decided that the city walls had to come down and make way for the "expansion" (*l'eixample* in Catalan). Ildefons Cerdà designed a plan for a utopian space with gridded streets, ample park space, and low buildings that was later ignored by developers who erected tall, fortress-like buildings. However, the building boom coincided with Barcelona's golden age of architecture and provided the setting for Modernist experimentation, with its over-the-top curvilinear designs and bright colors.

Grab your camera and get ready to walk the **Ruta del Modernisme.**

1. **Plaça Catalunya:** Start off here at the lower edge of L'Eixample. Get your last dose of A/C at the Corte Inglés shopping mall and pick up a free map.

2. **Passeig de Gràcia:** Walk up the main artery of L'Eixample and you can already notice a big difference from cramped Barri Gòtic. Do some window-shopping at the designer boutiques and check out the wrought-iron lamp-posts and the spiral, trippy slabs of pavement that were originally designed for the patio of Gaudí's Casa Batlló.

3. **Manzana de la Discordia:** The "Block of Discord" is one of the most notable Modernist landmarks, home to three flamboyantly clashing designs—Casa Amatller, Casa Lleó, and Casa Batlló—between Carrer Aragó and Carrer Consell de Cent. You can buy a Ruta del Modernisme pass (p. 138) in Casa Amatller.

4. **Carrer Aragó:** Head east off of Passeig de Gràcia to take a lunch break in one of the affordable restaurants. It's also a great spot for people-watching.

5. **Casa Milà (La Pedrera):** Get back on Passeig de Gràcia and head 3 blocks north to one of Gaudí's signature works, La Pedrera, which you should go out of your way to see. The building seems to have washed ashore with walls that mimic the ocean's waves and balconies tangled like seaweed. Check out the whimsical rooftop and its views of Barcelona.

6. **Sagrada Familia** (see "Top Attractions," above): Get ready for a walk. Turn right on Carrer Provença and follow it for 11 blocks (don't turn on slanted Av. Diagonal). Gaudí's masterpiece-in-the-making sticks out like a sore thumb.

There's a Metro stop here (L5 and L2) to take you back into the city.

Wed and Sat 11am–8pm, Sun 11am–7pm. Metro: Plaça Catalunya or Universitat.

➜ **Fundació Joan Miró** ★★★ Joan Miró is yet another Spanish artist who made an impact on the modern art scene. If you find yourself thinking, "I could've painted this with my eyes closed," think of it this way—his surreal, simple forms and primary colors collaborate to create vitality and spark the imagination (so use it!). If you're still confused, check out the cool Mercury Fountain. The permanent collection is well worth a trip. *Parc de Montjuïc s/n.* ☎ 93/443-94-70. *www. bcn.fjmiro.es. Admission 7.20€ adults, 5€ students. Oct–June Tues–Sat 10am–7pm; July–Sept Tues–Sat 10am–8pm, Thurs 10am–9:30pm, Sun 10am–2:30pm. Metro: Parallel, then Funicular de Montjuïc. Bus: 50 or 55.*

➔**Museu d'Art Contemporani (MACBA)** ★★ If you're into modern art, you'll totally fall in love with this museum. The temporary exhibitions are innovative, even more so than the permanent ones, which focus on avant-garde art between World War I and World War II, and include paintings, sculpture, and photography. The building itself, designed by Richard Meier, is a gargantuan anomalous work of art—it's like a space station landed in El Raval. The plaza in front attracts dozens of fledgling skaters busting their stuff. (If you skate by the entrance, you *will* get yelled at!) *Plaça dels Angels 1.* ☎ *93/412-08-10. www.macba.es. Admission 7€ adults, 5.50€ students. Mon–Fri 11am–7:30pm, Sat 10am–8pm, Sun and holidays 10am–3pm. Metro: Plaça Catalunya or Universitat.*

➔**Museu Nacional d'Art de Catalunya (MNAC)** ★★ Learn the history of Catalonia through its art and artifacts, like Romanesque frescoes and Gothic paintings. Modern art from the Museu d'Art Modern complements the collection. *Palau Nacional, Parc de Montjuïc.* ☎ *93/622-03-76. www.mnac.es. Admission 8.50€ adults, 6€ students. Tues–Sat 10am–7pm, Sun and holidays 10am–2:30pm. Metro: Espanya.*

➔**Museu Picasso** ★★★ Whether or not you're a Picasso buff and are familiar with the works that made him famous (cubism, Blue and Pink periods), consider what you'll see at this museum. It doesn't have any of his masterpieces. Most of the work here is from his younger and older years, so if you're interested in seeing how his technique and style evolved, it's worth a visit. If for nothing else, you can pick up some cool mugs, tees, and general Picasso goodies at the gift shop. *Montcada 15-23.* ☎ *93/319-63-10. www.museupicasso.bcn.es. Admission 6€. Tues–Sun 10am–8pm. Metro: Liceu or Jaume I.*

Playing Outside

PARKS Visit the city's main park, **Parc de la Ciutadella** (daily 8am–9pm; Metro: Ciutadella or Arc de Triomf), and jog, ride a bike, or simply veg out by the fragrant gardens or tranquil ponds; just be sure to check out the funky fountain that Gaudí helped create. There are plenty of families with rug rats in tow heading to the city zoo in the park. It's safe during the day.

BICYCLING Bike Tours Barcelona (Esparteria 3; ☎ **93/268-21-05;** www.biketoursbarcelona.com; admission 22€, includes 1 drink; Metro: Jaume I or Liceu) is a guided bike tour that will take you to all the major sites, like the Barri Gòtic, the Old Harbor, Ciutadella Park, the Sagrada Familia, the Port Olímpic, and Gaudí's architectural landmarks, in 3 hours. No reservations needed; just show up at 11am at the meeting point, the Tourist Office of Plaça Sant Jaume, and grab a bike (closed Dec 24–25).

BEACHES The **beaches** are quite nice for a city, but are crowded at all hours. The most popular spot is **Barceloneta,** and the promenade from here to Port Olímpic is a great place to walk and people-watch.

🎬 Best MOUNTAINS At **Mount Tibidabo,** breathe in some fresh air, take in Barcelona, and then go scream your guts out on the rides at the theme park, **Parc d'Atraccions Tibidabo** (Plaça Tibidabo 3; ☎ **93/211-79-42;** 22€ for all rides, 11€ for six rides; summer daily noon–10pm, off season Sat–Sun noon–7pm; bus: 58 to Avinguda Tibidabo Metro, then take the Tramvía Blau, which drops you at the funicular, round-trip 3.10€).

Hanging Out

If you want to get away from the crowds, walk from Las Ramblas (more than 15 min.) and just keep walking (and walking) until you hit the nudist beach Platja Mar Bella.

Even if you prefer to keep the family jewels under wraps, Mar Bella is worth the trek to check out skaters peeling their skin on the popular half-pipe.

In true Spanish fashion, the best places to chill with a bottle and a group of friends are at the plazas; yet don't let the names fool you. Plaça George Orwell in the Barri Gòtic is anything but Big Brother. Also known as the "Plaza del Trippy," there really isn't anything psychedelic about this grimy concrete enclave at the end of Carrer Escudellers. It's a prime spot for *botellón* (passing around a bottle among friends outdoors), but the crowd can be a bit shady.

The Jardins Rubio i Lluch is the perfect spot for bringing a bocadillo and a book. Sit underneath the many trees or archways of the Escola Massana, the neighboring school of art and design, and check out the art students smoking cigarettes between classes. Feel free to wander through the two-room student gallery and try to be there around 1pm during their midday break if you're looking to meet José or María del Arte. (Metro: Liceu).

Shopping

Most shops don't open until 10am and they close for lunch roughly between 2 and 5pm. Large shops don't take the siesta, though; most stay open until 8pm (and an hour later on Sat).

➜ **Adolfo Domínguez** Called "The Spanish Armani," the store, one of many throughout Spain, cuts clothes for people—men and women—with hips. They make clothes for kids, too, so if you want to spend, it's likely you'll find something that works. *Passeig de Gràcia 32.* ☎ *93/487-41-70. Metro: Passeig de Gràcia.*

➜ **Central Bookstore** Stocked with goods by liberal arts and philosophy heavyweights in several languages, this is the place to come if you have to finish up a late paper during spring break. A good place to study or fish for cute bookworms at the cafeteria in the back of the Raval locations. *Three locations. Check www.lacentral.com for details.*

➜ **Coses de Casa** The store dates from the 19th-century, but the goods are modern, mostly hand-woven fabrics and weavings from Majorca. The appealing textiles, many

with bold, geometric patterns, take inspiration from centuries-old Arab motifs. *Plaça de Sant Josep Oriol 5.* ☎ *93/302-73-28. Metro: Jaume I or Eliceo.*

➜ **El Mercadillo** Also known as the "Camello" because of the life-size camel standing guard below the alien spaceship at the entrance to this indoor flea market. It's a great place to get those Turkish MC Hammer pants and whatever else is trendy at the moment at a cheaper price. There's a tattoo and piercing parlor, as well as the chill Bar Jardí (see "Cafes & Tearooms," above) upstairs. *Porta Ferrissa 17.* ☎ *93/301-89-13. Metro: Universitat or Liceu.*

➜ **Etnomusic** Pick up some old-school salsa, klezmer, or dub reggae at this small shop that has been catering to eclectic music tastes since 1991. Don't know how to pronounce Youssou N'Dour? Think djembe is a typo? Don't fret—the friendly staff will help guide you through stacks of world music CDs. *Bonsucces 6.* ☎ *93/301-18-84. Metro: Catalunya.*

Road Trip

Come to the hometown of Salvador Dalí and check out his museum, the **Teatre-Museu Dalí** (Plaça de Gala-Dalí 5; ☎ **97/267-75-00**; admission 9€ adults, 6.50€ students; July to mid-Sept daily 9am–7:45pm, mid-Sept to June Tues–Sun 10:30am–5:15pm; visits available various nights July–Aug, call for information). The city itself is pretty dull, but the trippy museum is worth the short excursion. The huge museum plays enough tricks on your perception that you'll begin to understand the surrealist master when he said, "I don't do drugs. I am drugs."

When the mayor of Figueres asked native Salvador Dalí to donate a painting to a museum the town was planning, the artist in turn donated an entire museum. He insisted on using the ruins of an old theater that burned down in 1939 (hence the name: theater-museum), which was where he showed his first exhibition as a teenager. The reconstructed theater is huge and infused with Dalí's character, studded with giant eggs and loaves of bread, and is full of his paintings, sculptures, jewelry, and other creations—even his own tomb.

If you thought Diddy was a shameless self-promoter, the rapper pales in comparison to the self-proclaimed genius Dalí's personally designed museum/mausoleum/monument to himself. Check out the remarkable Sala de Mae West—when viewed from the plastic camel, the furnished room resembles Mae West. But don't just focus on the enormous paintings; take in every square inch of the floor, wall, nooks, and crannies, to absorb all the decorative touches and surprises.

➜ **Overstock** This store stands out from the other five record stores on the same street because it definitely lives up to its name. Pick up magazines, biographies, DVDs, apparel, footwear, patches, pins, concert tickets—you name it, they've got it. Oh yeah, they also have CDs and vinyl that you'd have a tough time finding at home in Wichita. *Calle Tallers 9.* ☎ *93/318-20-41. Metro: Catalunya.*

Markets

El Encants is an **antiques market** held during the day every Monday, Wednesday, Friday, and Saturday in Plaça de les Glòries Catalanes (Metro: Glòries). For **coins** and **postage stamps,** check out the trading at Plaça Reial on Sunday from 10am to 8pm (Metro: Drassanes). A **book** and **coin** market is held at the Ronda Sant Antoni every Sunday from 10am to 2pm (Metro: Universitat).

BARCELONA

Berlin

"Berlin ist arm, aber sexy." Translation? "Berlin is poor, but sexy."

You might guess that legendary Berlin babe, Marlene Dietrich, uttered the above phrase. She did, after all, exemplify everything great about the German capital, which is beautiful, urbane, and down-to-earth. Yet it was Klaus Wowereit, mayor of Berlin, who deserves credit for putting into words how many of the city's residents feel about their home: Whether you're in the cosmopolitan West or the grungy East, you'll find that Berlin exudes sexiness everywhere, from its restaurants to the very strut of passing pedestrians, and yet the city suffers from a noticeable inferiority complex.

The city's reluctance to brag is not surprising considering that 60 years ago, Berlin was a pile of rubble with a few skeletal buildings to call a skyline. Since the end of the cold war and the fall of the Berlin Wall, though, the city has had plenty to crow about. Berlin has not only recouped its status as a political behemoth, but it has also become one of the biggest party cities in Europe. Just check out the city's Love Parade, an annual 24-hour orgy that cranks up the municipal mojo to record levels. During the parade, partyers from every part of the world flock to Berlin's streets to kick back, take in some techno, and let endorphins do their thing, often helped by alcohol that flows as freely as the nearby Spree River.

Measuring in at an expansive 343 square miles, Berlin is a gargantuan, living, breathing dive bar, both literally with its hundreds of unique bars, and figuratively, with an unassuming, relaxing character that has persisted despite all the new construction of the past few decades. The end result is a city that is decidedly the opposite of poor—one that is richly endowed with glitzy nightlife, amazing food, and world-class museums.

The Best of Berlin

○ **The Best Hotel Room for Sleep:** At **Hotel mitArt**, you won't find TVs, radios, or noise. Just an extremely quiet room with an extremely beautiful and unique piece of art. Fall asleep to the sound of absolutely nothing while you try and figure out what the extremely bright yellow blob on your wall is supposed to represent. Oh wait . . . that's just the light fixture. See p. 154.

○ **The Best Hotel for Not Sleeping:** Considering how many beautiful, young travelers frequent **Circus Hostel** and how close the nightlife is, your bed might be rendered useless because you'll be out partying with other guests. Come to think of it, if you play your cards right, you (and your new friend) might actually get some use out of it. See p. 154.

○ **The Best Form of Potty Training:** Toilets galore make for an interesting drinking environment at **Klo.** Choose carefully when you relieve yourself. That might not be a working john you're unloading on. See p. 162.

○ **The Best Off-Beat (or Vice Versa) Museum:** Let's face it: Visitors aren't looking for enlightenment at the **Erotik Museum.** Chuckle over the phalluses and mannequins featured over three floors of sex displays. See p. 166.

○ **The Best Train Station:** Sure, Bahnhof Zoologischer Garten has the zoo, luggage storage, and the Erotik Museum nearby, but **Ostbahnhof** is much prettier (especially during sunset). When it comes to train stations, who are you trying to fool? No one *really* likes them for their personality. See p. 146.

○ **The Best Classy Restaurant: Lindenlife** combines the high-class feel of West Berlin with the creative styles of East Berlin, and it does it while producing some mouthwatering dishes. Open your ears to some acid jazz and open your stomach to interesting takes on old ingredients at the elegant Lindenlife. See p. 161.

○ **The Best Lunch Spot:** There's no better place to spend your 3pm Saturday late lunch than the casual **St. Oberholz.** The waiters and waitresses are easy on the eyes, as well as extremely amiable, but the interior is what makes St. Oberholz so comfortable. High ceilings, equally high windows, and amazingly plush pillow-covered corners will make that afternoon whiz right by. See p. 159.

○ **The Best Half of Berlin: East Berlin** is the hands-down winner. West Berlin is old and stuck up. Gimme grime anytime!

BERLIN

Getting There & Getting Around

Getting into Town

BY AIR

Most direct flights from the United States arrive in Frankfurt. If you'd rather not make the 7-hour train trip from Frankfurt to Berlin,

you can fly to Berlin's **Tegel Airport.** Most flights from the U.K., Canada, Australia, and New Zealand arrive here, too. **Schönefeld,** the airport in the eastern sector, is used primarily by Russian and eastern European airlines. Private bus shuttles among the airports operate constantly, so you can make connecting flights at a different airport. For flight information at all airports, call ☎ 01805/000186 or visit www.berlin-airport.de/PubEnglish.

A **cab ride** from Tegel can cost anywhere from 15€ to 25€. The airport is also accessible by both bus and U-Bahn, with tickets at a fraction of a taxi fare (around 3€ for a one-way trip). **BVG bus** nos. X9 and 109 run every 10 to 15 minutes from the airport to Bahnhof Zoo in Berlin's center, departing from outside the arrival hall; a one-way fare is 3€. The **JetExpressBus TXL,** operated by Berlin's public transport provider, BGV, leaves the airport for Potsdamer Platz, Friedrichstrasse, and Unter den Linden (trip time: 20–25 min.), at a cost of 3€. It runs Monday to Friday every 15 minutes from 6am to 7pm and every 20 minutes from 7 to 11pm;

Saturday every 20 minutes from 6am to 11pm; Sunday every 20 minutes from 6am to 2pm and 6 to 11pm, every 15 minutes from 2 to 6pm. It departs daily from Berlin City Center from the Underground Station U Alexanderplatz starting at 5:23am.

See "Getting Around" below for info on the U-Bahn.

BY TRAIN

Berlin is well connected to Europe's extensive rail system. If you're coming in from Munich, Brussels, or any point west of the city, you can get off at **Bahnhof Zoologischer Garten** rail station, which lies in the center of the city. Most lines continue to East Berlin's 🏧 Best **Ostbahnhof** station 15 minutes farther down the line. Both stations are connected to town by the S-Bahn, so if you'd rather take the slower but more frequent form of public transportation to either hub, you can

Talk of the Town

Four ways to start a conversation with a local

1. **Does Heidegger completely blow your mind, like he does mine?** Back in the day, when we weren't connected to the Internet by some information-umbilical cord, students and intellectuals used to gather in Berlin's cafes for philosophical debates and political discussions. Widely regarded as the breeding ground for Germany's geniuses, cafes are still popular among the undergrad population in Mitte.

2. **Has anyone ever told you that you'd make a great Warhol subject?** The city has its fair share of museums showcasing artists from hundreds of years ago, but Berlin is a contemporary art behemoth. From the Guggenheim on Unter den Linden to the bohemian artist community of Tacheles, you'll easily find someone to discuss the latest and most creative trends among Berlin's vibrant art community.

3. **Notice the infestation of colorful, life-size bears throughout the city?** Vendors and locals can buy a bare bear for about 1,000€, and then hire some artist to give it a splash of paint. The Berlin mascot is then auctioned off for charity, but owners seem to have grown attached to the animals and few have actually been sold.

4. **Don't you look good on the dance floor!?** This question serves two purposes: (1) It might get your intended target to grind with you, and (2) if they get the Arctic Monkeys lyric, you know you can talk to them for hours about music.

take the state-run S-Bahn instead of shelling out extra euros for a 10-minute trip on the InterCity train. For specific train schedules, call ☎ 0180/599-66-33 or check out www.bahn.de for station info.

BY BUS

Travel to nearby German cities is really the only reason bus lines are still in business. Long-distance journeys are usually extremely uncomfortable in the cramped coaches. For information on buses, contact **Deutsche Touring** (☎ 069/7-90-32-40; www.touring-germany.com).

Getting Around

BY PUBLIC TRANSPORTATION

The Berlin transport system consists of buses, trams, and U-Bahn (underground) and S-Bahn (elevated) trains. The network is run by the **BVG**, or Public Transport Company Berlin-Brandenburg. Public transportation throughout the city operates from about 4:30am to 12:30am daily (except for 68 night buses and trams, and U-Bahn lines U-9 and U-12). For information about public transport, call ☎ 030/1-94-49 or visit www.bvg.de.

The **BVG standard ticket (Einzelfahrschein)** costs 2.30€ to 2.60€ depending on the zones traveled, and is valid for 2 hours of transportation, transfers included. A 24-hour ticket for the whole city costs 5.70€ to 6€. Only standard tickets are sold on buses. Tram tickets must be purchased in advance. All tickets should be kept until the end of the journey; otherwise, you'll be liable for a fine of 40€ .

If you're going to be in Berlin for 3 days, I recommend purchasing a 22€ **Berlin-Potsdam Welcome Card,** which entitles holders to 72 free hours on public transportation in Berlin and Brandenburg. You'll also get free admission or a price reduction of up to 50% on sightseeing tours, museums, and other attractions, and a 25% reduction at 10 theaters as well. The card is sold at many hotels, visitor information centers, and public-transportation sales points.

Whether you pick up a Welcome Card or a single trip fare, remember to validate it before you scoot off to your destination. For the U-Bahn and S-Bahn, the validation points are on the platforms, whereas the bus and trams have them inside the vehicle.

BY BICYCLE

The speed and efficiency of the U-Bahn and S-Bahn make using a bicycle to get around less handy, though the city's flat streets are ideal for cruising around and taking in the sights. While most thoroughfares are cycle friendly, some can be dangerous and chaotic, especially in East Berlin or on Ku'Damm in West Berlin. Still, several companies offer bike tours that cover a great deal of ground and usually provide you with the company of a group of youngish sightseers. **Fat Tire Bike Tours** (Panorama Strasse 1a; ☎ 030/24-04-79-91; www.fattirebiketoursberlin.com) offers two routes: a city tour and a Berlin Wall Tour, both of which cover different points and paths. The former is a daily affair, leaving at 11am (as well as a 4pm tour June–Aug) while the Berlin Wall tour is available on Monday, Wednesday, Friday, Saturday, and Sunday (May 15–Sept 15). Both originate from the TV Tower in Alexanderplatz; either tour costs 20€ (17€ for students; rates include a cup of hot tea).

If you'd rather explore by yourself, Fat Tire also rents out bicycles for a reasonable rate (7€ for 4 hr., 12€ for 1 day, 9€ for the second day, and 6€ each subsequent day). In addition, the small store offers Internet access and laundry facilities.

BY CAR

I don't recommend driving in Berlin. Traffic is heavy, and parking is difficult to come by. Use the excellent public transportation instead.

BY TAXI

Taxis frequently cruise the major boulevards, indicating their availability by an illuminated roof light. The meter begins ticking at 2.50€. A 1.55€ supplement is added if you call a cab to a specific address by phone. Within the city center, each kilometer costs around 1.50€, depending on the time of day. Prolonged taxi rides that you arrange to distant suburbs are factored at a per-kilometer rate of 1€. Staff members at hotels and restaurants can easily summon a cab for you, in some cases simply by throwing a switch on their phone. Otherwise, dial ☎ **030/21-01-01,** 030/26-30-00, or 030/44-33-22.

ON FOOT

The German capital is one of the largest cities in Europe, not just population-wise, but also in square kilometers. An adventurous tourist *could* cover each half of Berlin with Kevlar runners, but most will likely succumb to fatigue and settle for a U-Bahn ticket. While there are better ways to explore the city, walking is the only way to enjoy certain areas like Tiergarten, Kurfürstendamm, Unter den Linden, and Nikolaiviertel.

Be careful at crosswalks. Ignore the zebra-lines and you'll likely get a substantial fine. It sounds ridiculous, but the police are extraordinarily tenacious when it comes to petty pedestrian crimes. Locals know their doggedness all too well (the 50€ fine isn't worth the 20 seconds saved).

Berlin Basics

Orientation: Berlin Neighborhoods

Berlin is an expansive city, so it's worth getting your bearings before exploring it. Aside from its obvious east/west division, the city is separated into several diverse neighborhoods. For the most part, East Berlin is home to a distinctly more alternative and younger population than its Western counterpart. The stores, buildings, and bars here are characteristically trendier and grungier. On the flipside, West Berlin is much more urbane. Older tourists and families on vacation usually spend their time in this classier area, but that's not to say that West Berlin is without its sketchy areas. The region around the Bahnhof Zoologischer Garten, especially near the Erotik Museum, can get rather chaotic and seedy. Below is a quick rundown of the city's major districts.

WEST

CHARLOTTENBURG The swank section of West Berlin is pumping with high-end stores and pricey hotels along the main artery of Kurfürstendamm. Most of the region, like much of Berlin, was obliterated during the war. Bling-ridden storefronts aside, you'll also find the Schloss Charlottenburg, the royal residence and cultural focal point of the area here.

KU'DAMM The immediate area around the Bahnhof Zoologischer Garten can be off-putting to some, but the commercial heart of West Berlin is chaotic for a reason. No, it's not because of the Erotik Museum. Rather, it's where capitalism reigns supreme and where West Berlin businessmen thrive. Couple that with the thousands of tourists pouring through the train station . . .

📺 Best **KREUZBERG** ★★ If you squint really, really hard, you might mistake the neighborhood along the Spree for an over-hyped NYC borough. Click your Converse Chuck Taylors three times and transport yourself to Berlin's hipster haven, a predominantly Turkish neighborhood that has quietly accepted its status as home to the trendiest of the trendy in Berlin. Chill cafes and unique bars like the lovely **Freischwimmer** makes it a far superior choice to hang.

TIERGARTEN One-third of Berlin is made up of natural attractions, but the Tiergarten is truly the city's green lung, providing both the East and West with a beautiful square mile of grass and trees. The wide boulevard of Strasse des 17 Juni cuts it in half, and the street ends with one of Berlin's main landmarks, the Brandenburg Gate. The Reichstag and the Berlin Zoo bookend the park on the east and west ends, respectively.

EAST

ALEXANDERPLATZ Thoughts of East Berlin during the Cold War instantly stir images of this wide, scruffy square. The TV tower, with its huge spherical dome/observatory platform on the top, sits in the middle of Alexanderplatz and can be seen from almost any part of East Berlin. It's slowly undergoing reconstruction.

MITTE Unter den Linden, the main street of Berlin-Mitte, used to be the pride and joy of communist Berlin, but it's since become an urbane boulevard that captures much of East Berlin's attitude. Some of Berlin's most recognizable sights sit in this area, sandwiched between the dingy Alexanderplatz to the east and Potsdamer Platz, with its advanced architecture, to the west.

MUSEUMINSEL The tiny island is home to Berlin's best museums. The Alte Nationalgalerie and Pergamon Museum make it the most-visited island on the Spree.

POTSDAMER PLATZ Enough antiques and historical crap! Come to Potsdamer Platz for a peek at the architectural present and future. The ultramodern square to the southeast of Tiergarten is a collection of metal and glass structures that would make the architect I. M. Pei proud (he designed the German Historical Museum in Mitte). Corporate cultivation has led to the development of an IMAX theater, a futuristic U-Bahn station (not yet functional as of this writing), and a massive shopping area.

Tourist Offices

Let's face facts: Berlin is huge, and you're gonna need some help getting around. The first order of business for any visitor is to head to the main tourist office in the Europa Center on Budapesterstrasse. There you'll find the **Berlin Tourist Information Center** (☎ 030/25-00-25 within Germany), where you can stock up on city maps, museum brochures, and hotel information. It's open Monday to Saturday from 8am to 8pm and Sunday from 10am to 6:30pm.

If you're lost in East Berlin, ask for directions to the Brandenburg Gate. Another tourist information center is open at the south wing of the gate every day from 9:30am to 6pm.

Recommended Websites

○ **www.berlin-tourism.de**: Basic info, information about local events, and a slew of other links.

○ **www.bahn.de**: Germany's well-organized rail system has an equally efficient website.

Culture 101

Berlin's relatively young population makes conversing with locals a pleasure rather than a process. English is widely understood and spoken in both West and East Berlin. And although U.S. and U.K. fashion, movies, and music have obviously influenced pop culture here, Berliners put a wholly unique and industrial twist to whatever they poach. There are two noticeable schools of fashion among the locals, especially in the refreshingly arty East: retro-punk and military-chic. Some straddle the line and others take small bites of both, but 20-somethings tend to sport things like studded belts, Mohawks, and arena-rock T-shirts, or Doc Martens.

On the heels of its totalitarian history, Berlin has become quite forgiving when it

BERLIN

comes to those healthy habits of yours. Drinking: The legal minimum age is 18. Marijuana possession: It's technically illegal, but if you're caught with a small amount (under 10 grams/¹/₃ oz.), the cops will often snatch your stash and leave you alone—but you can't count on this. Particularly popular herb-friendly venues include parks and the outdoor movie theaters that open up in the summer. Harder substances, like ecstasy and coke: There are fines for having small quantities, but nobody seems to be doing hard time for it. Ecstasy is common in clubs and especially during the Love Parade (p. 166).

Overall, Berlin is a friendly and inviting place, and despite nasty stories of xenophobic neo-Nazi movements, you don't need to be too concerned here. Yes, there's definitely a contingent of stuffy old cranks who can get belligerent with you for no good reason, but the Nazi thing is really not a presence in the city (at least not for short-term visitors). Berlin has just become too international for skinhead freaks to get too much play. Travelers from all over the globe have become a welcome ingredient in the melting pot that is Germany's capital.

Recommended Books, Movies & Music

BOOKS

For an uninhibited look into the effect that Berlin has had on its people, as well as on the people of the world, David Clay Large penned the divisive book simply called *Berlin* (2000). For an even heavier read, both physically and mentally, try your hand at Arthur Schopenhauer's *World as Will and Representation: Vol. 1.* The legendary philosopher was once a figure in Berlin's Humboldt University.

MOVIES

The fantastic indie flick *Goodbye Lenin* gives viewers an idea of what East Germany was like for a 20-something during the tumultuous year of 1989. The main character, Alex, tries to protect his mother from the drastic reality of a reunified Germany after she wakes up from a coma. To protect her, he and his sister work diligently to create a false world around her where the wall still stands and where Berlin is still divided. Another rental that'll help prepare you for Berlin's streets is the frantic *Run Lola Run,* which showcases multiple landmarks within the city.

MUSIC

Kraftwerk's *Autobahn* is the album that put electronic Krautrock on the map. Berlin, more so than Munich, has always embraced the group's influence. For irrefutable proof, walk into any nightclub. The prevalence of electronica, techno, and drum 'n' bass is a product of Kraftwerk's popularity and importance.

So authoritative were the four German musicians in Kraftwerk that David Bowie, a legend in his own right, wrote a song called "V₂-Schneider" (one of Kraftwerk's members was Florian Schneider) in honor of their contributions to rock. During his stay in Berlin, he put together *Heroes* with Brian Eno and, if you listen closely enough, you'll hear bits of German synth-pop floating among the 10 tracks of the amazing album. Equally great are Bowie's two other albums in the so-called "Berlin Trilogy," *Low* and *Lodger,* which were also partially recorded in Berlin.

Berlin Nuts & Bolts

Cellphones & Service Providers   You'll find **Vodafone** (☎ 0800/1721234) and **T-Mobile** (www.t-mobile-international.com) offices throughout Berlin, where you can purchase a local SIM card or a cellphone.

Currency **Deutches Bank** and **Dresdner Bank** both do a stand-up job in making sure that Berlin has no shortages of ATMs. Drawing money from one of these machines is a lot cheaper and easier than exchanging cash or traveler's checks at a currency exchange. Most banks are open Monday to Friday 9am to either 1pm or 3pm. If convenience is more important than a few percentage points, you can buy euros at the currency exchange in Bahnhof Zoologischer Garten (Mon–Sat 8am–9pm, Sun 10am–6pm).

Embassies Someone swipe your passport at the Love Parade? Man, they just don't make the zippered pockets on leather fetish outfits like they used to. Strut over to the **U.S. Embassy** (you might want to change into more suitable clothes) in Dahlem (Clayallee 170; ☎ 030/832-92-33; U-Bahn: Dahlem-Dorf). They're open Monday to Friday from 8:30am to noon. The **U.K. Embassy** is at Unter den Linden 32–34 (☎ 030/20-18-40; U-Bahn: Unter den Linden), open Monday to Friday 9am to 4pm. The **Australian Embassy** is at Wallstrasse 76–79 (☎ 030/8800880; U-Bahn: Spittel-markt), open Monday to Thursday 8:30am to 5pm and Friday 8:30am to 4:15pm. The **Canadian Embassy** is at Friedrichstrasse 95 (☎ 030/203120; U-Bahn: Friedrichstrasse), open Monday to Friday 9am to noon. The **Irish Embassy** is at Friedrichstrasse 200 (☎ 030/220720; U-Bahn: Uhlandstrasse), open Monday to Friday 9:30am to noon and 2:30 to 3:45pm. The **New Zealand Embassy** is at Friedrichstrasse 60 (☎ 030/206210; U-Bahn: Friedrichstrasse), open Monday to Friday at 9am to 1pm and 2 to 5:30pm.

Emergencies For an ambulance or a fire truck, call ☎ **112.** If you need the police, they can be reached at ☎ **110.**

Internet/Wireless Hot Spots There are several Internet cafes scattered around the city, but the best deal is found in a bicycle rental store near the TV tower. For a flat fee of 2€, you choose the "all-you-can-surf" option and spend your entire day scoping out eBay auctions, e-mailing friends, or updating your blog. Contact **Fat Tire** at Panorama Strasse 1a (☎ 030/24-04-79-91; www.fattirebiketoursberlin.com).

Over in the West, you can use the Internet terminals in the **Information Call Center** located on the ground floor of the Europa Center (Tauentzienstrasse 9–12; infi@europa-center-berlin.de; daily 10am–8pm).

Laundry You can only reuse your underwear for so long. Let your nose breathe easy and get your threads clean and fresh by tossing them in the machines at **Wascherei Lindenberg** (Curtiusstrasse 13–14; ☎ 030/833-10-56). Another option is along Torstrasse. There are a couple of places to get your threads fresh, but you're better off at the **Waschsalon** on Torstrasse 114. It's open from 6am to midnight, and you'll pay 1.50€ for a load of about 6.5 kilograms (14 lb.).

Luggage Storage Luckily, Bahnhof Zoologischer Garten has a luggage drop-off where you can drop off your bags while searching for hotels. Shed 50 pounds of extra weight for a small fee of 2€. The drop-off is open daily from 6:15am to 10:30pm, but you can also use the smaller luggage lockers nearby for 1€ to 2€ per day.

Post Offices Bahnhof Zoologischer Garten has the most conveniently located post office branch. Drop off your postcards or parcels anytime Monday to Saturday from 6am to midnight as well as Sunday from 8am to midnight. If you need to get a package sent to you, they also receive incoming mail for visitors. Have your parcels addressed to:

Hauptpostlagernd, Postamt 120, Zoologischer Garten, D-10612, Berlin. Contact ☎ **030/ 31-00-80** for info.

Restrooms   Use the word *Toilette* (pronounced "twah-*leh*-tah"). Women's toilets are usually marked with an F for *Frauen*, and men's toilets with an H for *Herren*. Germany, frankly, doesn't have enough public toilets, except in transportation centers. The locals have to rely on bars, cafes, or restaurants—and using them isn't always appreciated if you're not a paying customer.

Safety   For the most part, Berlin is a relatively safe city. You still need to be alert, however, of muggings, pickpockets and, very rarely, hate crimes. Be particularly vigilant in extremely crowded areas like the Europa Center in West Berlin or Alexanderplatz in East Berlin.

Telephone Tips   Local and long-distance calls may be placed from all post offices and coin-operated public telephone booths. The unit charge is 15€. More than half the phones in Germany require an advance-payment telephone card from **Telekom**, the German telephone company. Phone cards are sold at post offices and newsstands; they cost 6€ to 25€. Rates are measured in units rather than minutes. The farther the distance, the more units are consumed. Telephone calls made through hotel switchboards can double, triple, or even quadruple the regular charge, so try to make your calls outside your hotel.

Tipping   If a restaurant bill says *Bedienung*, a service charge has already been added, so just round up to the nearest euro. If not, add 10% to 15%. Round up to the nearest euro for taxis. Bellhops get 1€ per bag, as does the doorperson at your hotel, restaurant, or nightclub. Room-cleaning staffs get small tips in Germany, as do concierges who perform some special favors. Tip hairdressers or barbers 5% to 10%.

Sleeping

In West Berlin, the bulk of the sleeping spots are scattered all along Kurfürstendamm. However, if you're looking for the best night's rest, you're better off getting a room toward the southwest of the busy street, particularly near the gay neighborhood. Get a little too close to the bars near Nollendorfplatz and it's a different story: Raucous partying usually spills out onto the street. In Berlin-Mitte, it's even tougher to find quiet quarters. If you have the opportunity to scout around for a place, look for a hotel on a side street along the busy avenues of Rosenthaler Strasse and Oranienburgstrasse, closer to the Prenzlauer Berg part of Berlin.

Hostels

➜**AO Hostel** If you can't score a room at the Circus (see below), try the AO. Of its three locations (Friedrichshain, Mitte, and Zoo), the Bahnhof Zoologischer Garten rail station one is the most oddly situated. The immediate area around the zoo isn't exactly tranquil. Below the hostel are three different sex shops and the Erotik Museum is just down the block. The reception at times feels like a waiting area—with so many guests checking in, and drinking going on at the lobby bar and hobnobbing in the common area, this place is better for socializing than sleeping. The proximity to the rail station is a big plus, though, and rooms are clean The other two locations offer

Berlin-Mitte

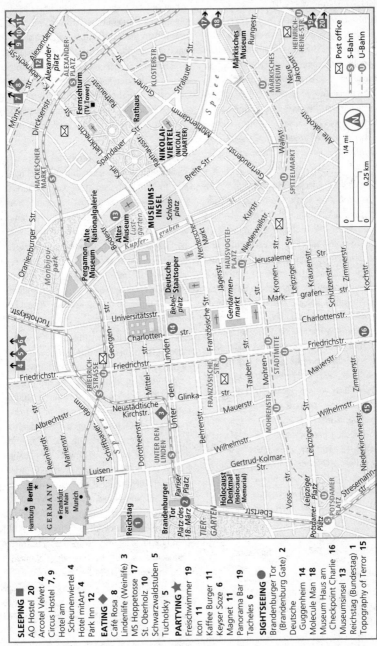

SLEEPING ■
AO Hostel **20**
Arcotel Velvet **4**
Circus Hostel **7, 9**
Hotel am
  Scheunenviertel **4**
Hotel mitArt **4**
Park Inn **12**

EATING ◆
Café Rosa **8**
Lindenlife (Weinlife) **3**
MS Hoppetosse **17**
St. Oberholz **10**
Schwarzwaldstuben **5**
Tucholsky **5**

PARTYING ★
Freischwimmer **19**
Icon **11**
Kaffee Burger **11**
Keyser Soze **6**
Magnet **11**
Panorama Bar **19**
Tacheles **6**

SIGHTSEEING ●
Brandenburger Tor
  (Brandenburg Gate) **2**
Deutsche
  Guggenheim **14**
Molecule Man **18**
Museum Haus am
  Checkpoint Charlie **16**
Museumsinsel **13**
Reichstag (Bundestag) **1**
Topography of Terror **15**

BERLIN

quieter alternatives. *Hostel am Zoo: Joachimstalerstrasse 1–3.* ☎ *030/88-91-35-0. U-Bahn/S-Bahn: Bahnhof Zoo. Hostel Mitte: Köpenikerstrasse 127–129.* ☎ *030/809-47-0. U-Bahn: H-Heine Strasse. S-Bahn: Ostbahnhof. Hostel Friedrichshain: Boxhagenerstrasse 73.* ☎ *030/29-77-81-0. S-Bahn: Ostkreuz. www. aohostels.com. 10€–11€ single bed in an 8- to 10-person dorm, 11€–13€ in a 4- to 6-person dorm. Shared bathrooms in the hallways for dorms. Buffet breakfast 5€; sheets 3€. Amenities: Bar; game room; Internet; luggage storage; TV (in common room).*

Ⓜ Best → **Circus Hostel** ★★★ The Circus should be at the top of your accommodations list. This hostel has two locations in the city—the Weinbergsweg and the Rosa; both are relatively close to each other and equally as cushy. The Weinbergsweg hostel also has a bar and street cafe. At both you'll find a clean, well-furnished room waiting for you, including sturdy, wooden Ikea beds with sheets that are changed every morning. The young, attractive staff is top-notch: They'll be happy to recommend nightspots, give you info about museums, or serve you up a beer. *Rosa-Luxemburg-Strasse 39 or Weinbergsweg 1a.* ☎ *030/28-39-14-33. www. circus-berlin.de. 15€–17€ single bed in 7- to 8-person dorm, 18€–19€ in 4- to 5-person dorm, 20€–21€ in 3-person dorm; 32€–33€ single with shared bathroom, 45€–46€ with private bathroom; 48€–50€ double with shared bathroom, 60€–62€ with private bathroom. U-Bahn: Rosa Luxemburg Platz (Rosa) or Rosenthaler Platz (Weinbergsweg). Amenities: Breakfast room (2€–4.50€ in Circus Café Weinbergsweg); shared bathrooms in the hallways for dorms; sheets 2€ (1-time fee).*

Cheap

→ **Arco Hotel** West Berlin's gay neighborhood is chock-full of small, fantastic restaurants and stores. It's also home to the cozy Arco Hotel. Rooms are situated off the main building in what used to be a Berlin apartment complex and sport basic but arty furnishings. When the weather is agreeable, breakfast is served in the quaint courtyard situated in the rear. Given the quiet and friendly neighborhood and appealing rooms, guests are assured a relaxing stay. *Geisbergstrasse 30.* ☎ *030/23-51-48-0. www.arco-hotel.de. 57€–85€ single, 75€–102€ double. Rates include breakfast. U-Bahn: Wittenbergplatz. Amenities: Breakfast room; garden; Internet; safe. In room: TV, hair dryer.*

→ **Hotel am Scheunenviertel** Hotel am Scheunenviertel is a small, budget hotel nestled in the lively street of Oranienburger Strasse. Large groups of travelers tend to rent rooms here. When this happens, the hotel takes on a dorm-like feel, with college kids lounging in the halls. *Oranienburger Strasse 38.* ☎ *030/282-21-25. 70€–90€ single, 80€–100€ double, 100€–130€ triple. Rates include breakfast. U-Bahn: Oranienburger Tor. S-Bahn: Oranienburger Strasse. Amenities: Breakfast room. In room: TV, Internet.*

Ⓜ Best → **Hotel mitArt** ★★★ Can't catch any Zs because the guest watching German game shows next door has his volume knob turned up to 11? Book a room in Hotel mitArt. The hotel is located within a secure courtyard, and there's not a radio or TV to be found anywhere. Instead, each room features a unique canvas painted by one of the 30 artists hired by mitArt owner Christiane Waszkowiak. Their entire credo revolves around the organic ideal. Rooms are minimalist and functional—bed, chair, wooden table, and clean bathroom—which allows the single original piece of artwork to be focal point of each quarter. The organic breakfasts of fresh fruit, squeezed juices, and cereals or oatmeal, were the best I had in Berlin. *Linienstrasse 139–140.* ☎ *030/283-90-43. www.mitart.de. 88€–110€ single, 105€–140€ double. Rates include breakfast. U-Bahn: Oranienburger Tor. Amenities: Breakfast room; organic cafe/bar; elevator; in-house gallery; Internet.*

West Berlin

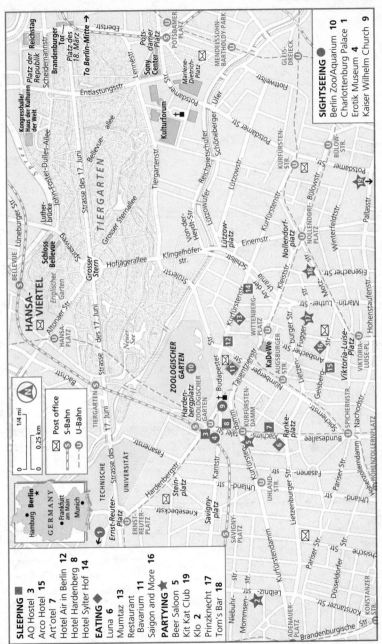

SIGHTSEEING ●
Berlin Zoo/Aquarium **10**
Charlottenburg Palace **1**
Erotik Museum **4**
Kaiser Wilhelm Church **9**

SLEEPING ■
AO Hostel **3**
Arco Hotel **15**
Art'otel **7**
Hotel Air in Berlin **12**
Hotel Hardenberg **8**
Hotel Sylter Hof **14**

EATING ◆
Luna **6**
Mumtaz **13**
Restaurant Bavarium **11**
Saigon and More **16**

PARTYING ★
Beer Saloon **5**
Kit Kat Club **19**
Klo **2**
Prinzknecht **17**
Tom's Bar **18**

Berlin U-Bahn & S-Bahn

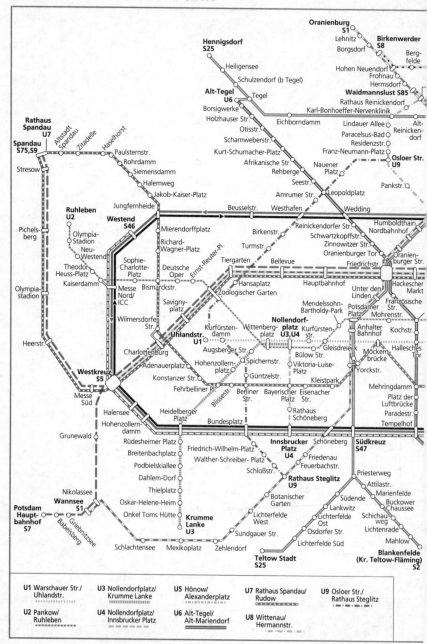

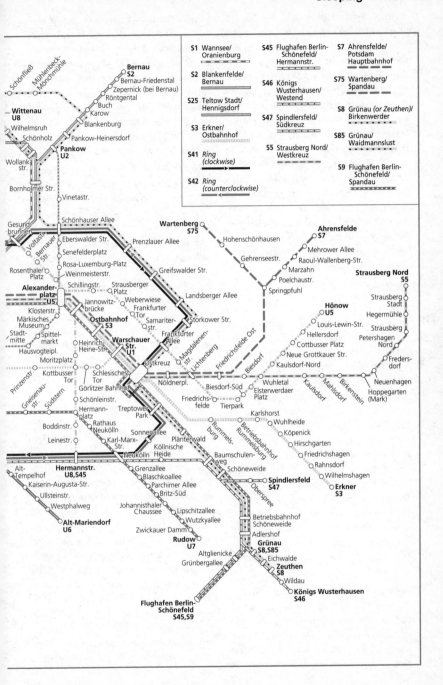

➜**Hotel Sylter Hof** ★ Built in 1966, this hotel is dripping with old- (not cold-) world comfort. Antique-themed rooms complement the regal reception area, and most of the bathrooms have tubs in which you can actually take a bubble bath. On arrival, the amiable staff and management will make sure you're completely at ease; they even provide ashtrays next to the urinals in the ground floor men's bathroom. *Kurfürstenstrasse 114–116.* ☎ *030/21-20-0. www.sylterhofberlin.de. 79€–99€ single, 109€–139€ double, 139€–159€ junior suite, 159€–179€ business suite. Rates include breakfast. U-Bahn: Wittenbergplatz or Bahnhof Zoologischer Garten. S-Bahn: Bahnhof Zoologischer Garten. Amenities: Bar; breakfast room; laundry service. In room: TV, minibar.*

Doable

➜**Arcotel Velvet** ★★ It doesn't take an Einstein to realize what a steal this urbane hotel is. That's probably why his mug, along with JFK's, Marlene Dietrich's, and those of other international and local legends, is patterned a la Warhol all over the slick black-and-red interior. The accommodations feature floor-to-ceiling windows, flatscreen LCD TVs, ultramodern bathrooms, and cushy beds, making it hard to believe that a single in this joint is less than 150€. Try to book one of the 85 rooms the minute you decide to visit Berlin. *Oranienburger Strasse 52.* ☎ *030/27-87-530. www.arcotel.at. Rates subject to change daily. 100€ single, 115€ double, 175€ suite. U-Bahn: Oranienburger Tor. Amenities: Bar/lounge (Velvet Lounge); breakfast room. In room: Flatscreen TV, DVD/CD player, Internet, minibar, safe.*

➜**Art'otel** ★ There's no shortage of color in the aptly named Art'otel. The sassy accommodations are a welcome change from the sterile environs of other West Berlin hotels. Case in point: Rather than opt for some humdrum sign, room numbers are displayed along the festively decorated hallways by an overhead light. Guest quarters are a mix of retro furniture and funky patterns. *Joachimstalerstrasse 29.* ☎ *030/88-44-70. www.sorat-hotels.com. 118€–148€ standard single, 138€–168€ double; 128€–158€ superior single, 148€–178€ double; 138€–168€ deluxe single, 158€–188€ double. Rates include breakfast. U-Bahn: Kurfürstendamm. Amenities: Breakfast room. In room: AC, TV, hair dryer, minibar.*

➜**Hotel Air in Berlin** I spent the same inordinate amount of time wondering if the Hotel Air's interior decorator was colorblind as I did thinking about what exactly inspired them to choose their cryptic name. Fortunately, if you can get past the mustard-and-maroon color scheme of the reception, a stay here can be quite rewarding. Rooms are light and airy, as is the breakfast area. Rates are a good deal. *Ansbacherstrasse 6.* ☎ *030/212-992-0. www.hotelairinberlin.de. 60€–125€ single, 80€–150€ double, 115€–300€ apt for 3–8 people. Rates include breakfast. U-Bahn: Wittenbergplatz. Amenities: Breakfast room; travel desk. In room: TV, Internet, minibar.*

➜**Hotel Hardenberg** Walking into the Hardenburg is like walking into a trashy museum. Unusually colored marble columns and walls lead to the cramped reception area, dispelling any misconceptions of grandeur. Most singles are constricting, but the doubles—well worth the extra 30€—are much more spacious and even include an opulent bathroom with a large bathtub and separate shower. The huge, ornate bed in the double will leave you snug as a bug while some poor soul rolls off his tiny cot in the nearby single. *Joachimstalerstrasse 39–40.* ☎ *030/882-30-71. www.hotelhardenberg.de. 100€–130€ single, 130€–150€ double. U-Bahn: Bahnhof Zoo or Kurfürstendamm. S-Bahn: Bahnhof Zoo. Amenities: Breakfast room; travel desk. In room: TV, hair dryer, minibar, safe.*

Splurge

→ **Park Inn** ★ The Park Inn near Alexanderplatz affords guests the same comforts of higher class inns that you'd find in the West. The only downside is the price tag; rates are a little high. The Park Inn tries to make the cost worth your while by cramming the hotel with bonuses like a sauna and casino. *Alexanderplatz.* ☎ *030/238-90. www. parkinn.de. 110€–130€ standard single, 125€–140€ double; 120€–145€ business single, 130€–145€ double. U-Bahn: Alexanderplatz. Amenities: Bar; breakfast room; casino; massage room; sauna; travel desk. In room: TV, hair dryer, Internet, minibar, trouser press.*

Eating

Examples of traditional German dishes are the Berliner *Schlachteplatte* (cold plate); pigs' trotters cooked with sauerkraut and pea purée; and *Eisbein* (pickled knuckle of pork with sauerkraut). Venison, wildfowl, wild boar, carp, and trout also appear frequently on menus, along with an infinite variety of sausages. But Berlin does not limit itself to traditional cuisine. A new wave of restaurants has swept across the city, from east to west. More and more are going ethnic, serving everything from Indonesian or French to Thai or Japanese. Eastern European wines are now almost as popular as those from Germany itself.

Head to Kreuzberg to find the city's best international restaurants. The combination of trendy, radical youth and a motley assortment of ethnicities makes it one of the most mouthwatering neighborhoods outside of Berlin-Mitte. The gay neighborhood around Lietenburgerstrasse is another area for great little eateries, ranging from Vietnamese to seafood spots.

Hot Spots

→ **Café Rosa** ★ CAFE Anyone staying at the Circus Hostel will recognize this place as their little breakfast spot, though locals also enjoy their coffee and toast here in the mornings. At night the cafe plays host to underground events like poetry readings or open mic nights. The main area is ridiculously tiny and the performance area can, at most, fit 16 average-size Americans or 30 average-size Europeans, but this is still a fun joint. The singer/songwriter nights are especially worth checking out, with locals doing their best Joan Baez or Bob Dylan impersonations. Breakfast here, and you might be left with enough cash for the 4€ beers they serve at night. *Rosa-Luxemburgstrasse 41.* ☎ *0172/390-67-52. www.cafe-rosa.com. Mon–Sun 8:30am–noon, Wed–Sun 9pm–late. Breakfast 7€. U-Bahn: Rosa Luxemburg Platz.*

→ **Schwarzwaldstuben** GERMAN If the syndicated sitcom *Friends* picked up and moved to Berlin, this, without question, would be its "Central Perk." The cast of *Freunde* would be completely at home in Schwarzwaldstuben. The dark digs; wood-paneled walls; and antique, velvet couch in the corner are almost identical to the set of the long-lived show. If you're famished, try some of their savory spätzle. Otherwise, hop on a barstool, and let the bartender pour you a nicely proportioned cocktail. *Tucholskystrasse 48.* ☎ *030/28-09-80-84. Main courses 5€–11€. Daily 9am–2am. U-Bahn: Oranienburger Tor.*

MTV Best → **St. Oberholz** ★★★ CAFE So you managed to get a number from that hottie the night before, but you have no idea where to meet him or her for lunch. St. Oberholz is the ideal spot to sit down to a flatbread sandwich and chat with friends or possible mates. If you find out that he/she is an absolute wacko, the spacious interior offers an unobstructed escape route and

BERLIN

you can quickly flee to the Rosenthaler Platz U-Bahn station (just outside of the exit). Otherwise, the bi-level cafe features lofty ceilings and enormous windows where, on sunny days, the bright interior of St. Oberholz is almost as pleasant as the staff. *Rosenthaler Strasse 72.* ☎ *030/240-855-86. www.sanktoberholz.de. Main courses 5€–10€. Daily 8am–midnight. U-Bahn: Rosenthaler Platz.*

Cheap

➜ **Luna** BREAKFAST Nothing works up a craving for bagels more than a museum full of penises. Half a block away from the Erotik Museum is the tiny breakfast nook Luna. It's open in the afternoon, too. *Joachimstalerstrasse 13.* ☎ *030/88-70-26-17. www.luna-bagels.de. Mon–Fri 8:30am–8pm; Sun 10am–6pm. Bagels 1–2€. U-Bahn: Kurfürstendamm.*

➜ **Saigon and More** VIETNAMESE Vietnamese food works wonders when you want to purge your body of all the alcohol and poisons you've accrued the night before. Head to Geisbergstrasse, find a seat in the kitchenlike dining area, order some hot pho or the tasty *mi xao* (chicken and noodles), and bid *auf Wiedersehen* to your hangover. The trinkets and cheap decorations will go unnoticed once you slurp down your soup. *Geisbergstrasse 12.* ☎ *030/236-260-90. Main courses 6€–9€. Mon–Sat noon–11pm. U-Bahn: Viktoria-Luise-Platz.*

Doable

➜ **MS Hoppetosse** ★ INTERNATIONAL Everything on this boat-restaurant's fish-heavy menu is succulent, savory, and relatively easy on the wallet. Menus change every week, but you can score more traditional lunches like spätzle or spaghetti for about 6€ on the weekdays. The bi-level riverboat hearkens back to the 1960s and the interior looks as if it hasn't changed since then. Owners of the club/restaurant seem to

rely on the novelty of clubbing and dining on a boat to draw patrons to the Hoppetosse. Perhaps they should recruit the decorator of the nearby Freischwimmer for some Martha Stewart–like advice. *Eichenstrasse 4.* ☎ *030/533-20-340. www.arena-berlin.de. Main courses 8€–12€. Tues–Fri noon–late, Sat 2pm–late. Sun 11am–late. U-Bahn: Schlesisches Tor.*

➜ **Mumtaz** INDIAN Get your curry in a hurry or sit down to an aromatic meal in a quiet section of Ku'Damm. Mumtaz serves Indian dishes with a punch and it won't bruise your budget. While the traditional interior may look dated and somewhat cheap, it doesn't compromise the quality of the food. The chicken tikka alone is worth a return trip. *Bayreuther Strasse 3.* ☎ *030/211-22-36. Main courses 8€–13€. Daily 11:30am–midnight. U-Bahn: Wittenbergplatz.*

➜ **Restaurant Bavarium** BAVARIAN By the name alone, you should be a little wary of Restaurant Bavarium. It's a few hundred miles from Bavaria and a few yards away from the tourist office. To be more precise, it's in the basement of a shopping complex. Despite this, the grub is surprisingly edible and satisfying and the dining area is deceptively spacious. You can choose to sit in a semi-intimate booth or, if you have a large group, reserve one of the party rooms. Bavarium does an honorable job preparing their schnitzel, a dish usually associated with Austrian fare, and guests will not be disappointed when ordering the fried pork. *Tauentzienstrasse 9–12 (inside the Europa Center).* ☎ *030/261-43-97. www.bavarium-berlin.de. Main courses 11€–16€. U-Bahn: Kurfürstendamm.*

➜ **Tucholsky** GERMAN Berlin's dynamic duo, pork knuckles and ham with plum sauce, are two of the more popular dishes at Lutz Keller's restaurant. The knuckles may not sound appetizing but Tucholsky prepares them so that you'll enjoy them. Choose between the inside space, with dark-wood furniture and fake ivy running rampant on the ceiling, or the outdoor patio with real greenery on the trellises. The catch is that this place only accepts cash in exchange for those salty knuckles. *Torstrasse 189.* ☎ *030/281-73-49.* *www.restauration-tucholsky.de. Daily noon–midnight. Main courses 8€–13€. U-Bahn: Oranienburger Tor.*

Splurge

📺 Best → **Lindenlife (Weinlife)** ★★ GERMAN/INTERNATIONAL Most of the clientele is office peons looking to take the edge off after a long day at work. This is a great place to indulge your taste buds while unwinding to the chill acid-jazz of St. Germain. There's a baby grand in the corner, and the lighting's different shades of soft neon along the walls. If the roasted wild salmon with rice or garlicky prawns Provençal ain't your thing, choose from three-course menus (17€–83€). *Unter en Linden 54.* ☎ *030/20-62-90-333. www. lindenlife.de. Main courses 9€–19€. U-Bahn: Friedrichstrasse or Franzosische Strasse.*

Partying

I wouldn't do the club and bar scene any justice if I had 200 pages. I highlight 10 of Berlin's wackiest, most exciting nightspots below. Bars and clubs gain and lose popularity on a monthly basis, so to find out where the hottest haunts are, hang out in Kreuzberg or Berlin-Mitte. The cafes and stores have flyers, posters, and tons of locals just waiting to endow their party knowledge onto you.

Another place in Mitte to check out is the area around the Oranienburger Tor U-Bahn stop in the northeast. Nearby, you'll find the arty Tacheles complex surrounded by spunky bars and exotic—at least by regular Berlin standards—restaurants. Just to the north of this square-mile grunge is Torstrasse, an oasis of classier coffee shops and boutiques. While they may be a bit more proper, they also reek of youthful verve that's quite contagious—independent stores are popping up at the rate that would make even the most finicky of hipsters jealous.

Berlin's nightlife, especially on weekends, runs until the wee hours of the morning. By the time revelers pass out and call it quits, half of Europe is on its lunch break. Partying in Berlin is also relatively cheap. Most, if not all bars, have no cover charge and while it varies from club to club, you won't pay more than 10€ unless you decide to go to one of the few super-glitzy hot spots. Just be sure to glance at a calendar before you decide to party: During the summer, many clubs stay open only on the weekends while a few others shut down completely.

Finally, before you hit the streets, don't stress out over the contents of your suitcase. Few establishments will turn you down based on what kind of shirt you're sporting. The only exception to this is at a place like the oversexed Kit Kat Bar, where the dress code is, um . . . rather rigid.

Bars

→ **Beer Saloon** Frat guys travel, too. Get obnoxious and drunk without drawing any attention in this English bar/pub. Tons of foreigners flock here, but if there's an important football (soccer) match, you can be sure that it'll be playing on Beer Saloon's big screen. You and your cronies can enjoy the game from the privacy of your own little booth, or you can kick and scream with the other fans at the bar. *Kurfürstendamm 225.* ☎ *030/88-43-99-28. U-Bahn: Kurfürstendamm.*

➔**Freischwimmer** Thankfully, you won't need Dramamine to enjoy yourself in Freischwimmer. While the entire bar sits on a small canal in East Berlin, the place is rather stable considering it's essentially a booze servin' barge. Get here early on Liquid Mondays and claim the couches to enjoy tunes ranging from "electric future sound" to "modern Oriental music." The festive Christmas lights along the water's edge create a fantastic environment for flirting and mingling. *Vor dem Schlesischen Tor 2a. ☎ 030/61-07-43-09. www. freischwimmer-berlin.de. Cover 6€ only on Liquid Mondays, free on other days. U-Bahn: Schlesisches Tor.*

➔**Kaffee Burger** ★ Poetry slams serve as appetizers to the various main dishes served by the DJs. Most often, anything goes for the spinners, from salsa-techno to Dick Dale surf rock. If there's a night to head to Kaffee Burger, though, it's definitely on Russian Disco (Russendisko) night. Socialist beats never sounded so good. *Torstrasse 60. ☎ 030/28-04-64-95. www.kaffeeburger.de. Fri 7pm–3am and Sat 9pm–5am. U-Bahn: Rosa-Luxemburg-Platz.*

➔**Keyser Soze** If you were so inclined, you could spend 19 hours of the day sitting on one of the comfy couches in this restaurant/bar. Up until 11pm, the menu features tasty dishes, but the incredible bar really comes to life around midnight. The young crowd is laid-back and you won't find some middle-aged sap trying to relive his/her college years here. *Tucholskystrasse 33. ☎ 030/ 28-59-94-89. U-Bahn: Oranienburger Tor.*

🆄🆅 **Best** ➔**Klo** ★★★ Klo means "toilet" in German, a conclusion you might draw on your own the second you walk through the door and face the vast homage to the porcelain potty. Don't spend too much time inspecting your surroundings though; chances are the DJ or waiters are sneaking up behind you to pull some prank. A mix of tourists and locals enjoy a night full of whoopee cushion sounds, water dousings, and everything in a clown's practical-joke book. If you're a good sport, you're guaranteed a great time. *Leibnizstrasse 57. ☎ 030/32-70-26-92. www. klo.de. U-Bahn: Adenauerplatz.*

Clubs

➔**Icon** The dance floor of this converted brewery is guaranteed to be packed on Friday and Saturday nights. The former finds Berliners drowning in the latest electronica and hip-hop beats while Saturdays feature international DJs spinning insane house and drum 'n' bass for the masses in the ancient cellar. I urge anyone jonesin' for some rhythms on the weekend to head to Icon. *Cantianstrasse 1. ☎ 030/48-49-28-78. www.iconberlin.de. Cover 3€–6€. U-Bahn: Eberwalderstrasse. S-Bahn: Schönhauser Allee.*

➔**Kit Kat Club** ★ Leave your inhibitions, as well as your trousers, at the door. The best way to get into this infamous club is to sport your finest fetish gear. Baring as much skin as possible will help you get past the velvet rope. The regular dress code, according to Kit Kat's website, is: "fetish, latex and leather, kinky, stylish, glamour, costume and elegant evening dresses—*no* regular street wear and *no* underwear." I'm assuming they mean not wearing *just* underwear. The more reserved should avoid Saturdays when the club throws its "Slut Night." *Bessemerstrasse 2–14. ☎ 030/21-73-680. www.kitkatclub.de. U-Bahn: Tempelhof.*

➔**Magnet** ★★ If I didn't live 5,000 miles away, I'd probably try to swipe Magnet's sound system. The awesome setup plays host to various rock and indie acts coming to town. After shows or on concertless nights (there's usually *some* band performing every night, though), the speakers spew a killer selection of indie rock. Anyone with an ear for music won't be disappointed. *Greifswalderstrasse 212. www.magnet-club.de. U-Bahn: Senefelderplatz.*

➔ **Panorama Bar** "Panorama" couldn't be a bigger misnomer. More disco than bar, it's not much to look at from outside; the real draw is the crowd within the concrete walls. Stroll down Strasse der Pariser Kommune, hang a right, and crawl past the warehouse complex. Once you've reached the end (you'll know when you see grassy fields ahead and a torn-down chain link fence), hang a left after the last building and walk straight for 20 yards. Directly ahead of you is a crummy shell of what used to be some industrial building. You've arrived. The popular club is regularly packed on Fridays and Saturdays with an attractive alternative mob groovin' to the latest beats. *Am Wriezener Bahnhof. No phone. www.berghain.de. Cover 8€–10€. U-Bahn: Ostbahnhof.*

➔ **Tacheles** Trashy clubs are where East Berlin gets its marvelously scruffy reputation, and if you want to get down and dirty, Berlin-Mitte is where it's at. Tacheles, a four-story, converted, squatters haunt, is the mother of all dingy discos. The first few floors are littered with various bars, but the top floor is home to the booty shakers. Luckily, in the dark and crowded spaces, you can't make out the details that make Tacheles so wonderfully filthy. A night in the club is a ridiculously good time: There's cheap beer, a great crowd, and kinky music; but by day, the bare interior reeking of dry urine and the grafittied walls give off a more decidedly squatter feel. *Oranienburger Strasse 54–56a.* ☎ *030/282-61-85. U-Bahn: Oranienburger Tor.*

Live Music

➔ **Wild at Heart** This club, with its kitschy knickknacks, colored lights, and wine-red walls, is dedicated to the rowdier side of rock. Hard-core punk, rock, and rockabilly bands from Germany and elsewhere are featured. Live performances take place Wednesday to Saturday nights. It's open Monday to Friday 8pm to 3am, Saturday and Sunday 8pm to 10am (yes, you may miss breakfast). *Wienerstrasse 20.* ☎ *030/6-11-70-10. Cover 8€ for concerts only. U-Bahn: Bahnhof.*

Gay Nightlife

Given the city's exhaustive options for nocturnal partying, it's not surprising that Berlin has some of the best gay and lesbian nightspots in Germany, and perhaps in all of western Europe. Whether you're a fetish connoisseur or simply looking to dance off 5 pounds in sweat with a newfound friend, you'll find something to your liking near Nollendorfplatz.

➔ **Prinzknecht** The low-key clientele here can be a little disarming, especially for someone looking for a rowdy, oversexed crowd. Down-to-earth may be the best way to describe the men mingling over colorful drinks. People rarely leave without a smile and a phone number. *Fuggerstrasse 33.* ☎ *030/23627444. U-Bahn: Viktoria-Luise-Platz.*

➔ **Tom's Bar** Prinzknecht's more popular and badass little brother is Tom's Bar. You're almost guaranteed a bar chock-full of 20-something gay men who revel in rowdy surroundings. Monday nights have the perfect recipe for an even more debaucherous evening: two-for-one drink specials. *Motzstrasse 19.* ☎ *030/213-4570. U-Bahn: Nollendorfplatz.*

Performing Arts

If you have both the time and the cash to visit at least one of the places below, your ears will thank you.

➔ **Berliner Ensemble** Even if you don't understand German, you may enjoy a production of a familiar play or musical at this theater—one of the best in a city known for its theater. It was founded by the late playwright Bertolt Brecht, and works by Brecht and other playwrights are presented here today. *Am Bertolt-Brecht-Platz 1.* ☎ *030/284-08-155. Tickets 6€–30€. U-Bahn/S-Bahn: Friedrichstrasse.*

→**Berliner Philharmonisches Orchester (Berlin Philharmonic Orchestra)** Few orchestras can compare to the one found on Herbert-von-Karajan-Strasse. Among the many reasons to visit are Claudio Abbado directing the orchestra and the venue itself. From the 2,218 possibilities of where you can park your bum, you'll find that you're never farther than 30m (98 ft.) from the stage. *Herbert-von-Karajan-Strasse 1.* ☎ *030/254-880. www.berlin-philharmonic.com. Tickets 18€–83€. U-Bahn: Potsdamer Platz.*

→**Deutsche Staatsoper (German State Opera)** This world-renowned opera venue is also home to awe-inspiring concerts and some brilliant ballet. However, the building itself has had a rough life. Erected in the 1700s, it became an architectural casualty in World War II. It's since been rebuilt to resemble the original 18th-century opera house. *Unter den Linden 7.* ☎ *030/20-35-45-55. www.staatsoper-berlin.org. Tickets: opera 7€–63€; concerts 5€–38€. U-Bahn: Französische Strasse. S-Bahn: Friedrichstrasse.*

→**Konzerthaus Berlin** The Konzerthaus Berlin has a performance space for chamber music where you can experience some of the most exciting concerts this side of the classical genre. The other space, Grosser Konzertsaal, is used for orchestras, often

Life is a Cabaret

Berlin perfected the 📺 **Best** cabaret, a showcase of singing, dancing, and theater, between World War I and II, but the art form lives on with floor-show patter and acts that make fun of the current political and social scene. These emporiums of schmaltz have been reborn in the former East Berlin—though the satire may be a bit less biting than it was during the Weimar Republic. Today's cabaret shows may remind you of Broadway blockbusters, without much of the intimacy of the smoky and trenchant cellar revues of the 1930s. (Not surprising, considering that the 1970s Liza Minelli movie *Cabaret* was made into a Broadway musical in the 1990s.) Following are two of the city's best cabaret venues:

Die Stachelschweine Since the beginning of the Cold War, the "Porcupine" has poked prickly fun at the German and American political scenes. The performance is delivered in rapid-fire German. Shows take place Tuesday to Friday at 8pm and Saturday at 8 and 9:30pm. *Tauentzienstrasse and Budapesterstrasse (in the basement of Europa Center).* ☎ *030/2614795. Box office Tues–Fri 11am–2pm and 3–7:30pm, Sat 10am–2pm and 3–8:45pm; shows Tues–Fri 8pm, Sat 8 and 9:30pm. Closed in July. Tickets 12€–25€. U-Bahn: Kurfürstendamm.*

Wintergarten Varieté The largest and most nostalgic Berlin cabaret, the Wintergarten offers a variety show every night, with magicians, clowns, jugglers, acrobats, and live music. The most expensive seats are on stage level, where tiny tables are available for simple suppers costing from 13€ to 24€. Balconies have conventional theater seats, but staff members pass frequently along the aisles selling drinks. Shows last around 2¼ hours each. *Potsdamer Strasse 96.* ☎ *030/23088230. www.wintergarten-berlin.de. Shows Mon–Fri 8pm, Sat 5 and 9pm, Sun 6pm. Tickets Fri–Sat 25€–55€, Sun–Thurs 15€–45€. U-Bahn: Kurfürstenstrasse.*

the Deutsches Sinfonie-Orchester. *In the Schauspielhaus, Gendarmenmarkt.* ☎ *030/* *203-09-21-01. www.konzerthaus.de. Tickets 10€–90€. U-Bahn: Französische Strasse.*

Sightseeing

Given the sheer size of the German capital, you'll no doubt need a little help finding out what events are going on and which exhibitions are in town. As with any other city, your best resource is the tourist office (in this case either in the Europa Center or near the Brandenburg Gate); see "Visitor Information" earlier. They're well equipped with info about any show, gallery, or attraction in town. Hotels and hostels (especially the incredible staff at Circus Hostel), are fantastic sources as well, and they'll usually have better knowledge of nearby museums and events.

Festivals

February

International Film Festival. At this well-attended festival, the unusually cold atmosphere of Potsdamer Platz is replaced by the chatter and applause of film fans from all across Europe. It lasts for about 2 weeks, but by the end of the festival, participants usually clamor for more. Contact the Full

House Service (☎ **030/25489-100**) or go to www.berlinale.de for info. Mid-February.

June

Christopher Street Day Parade. The Love Parade's competitor in the "shock-and-awe" category. This gay-and-lesbian parade is a sight to behold for some, but it may be a little too ostentatious for others. Start the celebration near Kurfürstendamm and follow the train of revelers all the way to the Victory Angel in Tiergarten. Mid-June.

November

Jazz-Fest Berlin. The year is closed out in style with this annual festival. International jazz musicians and fans travel to Berlin to catch the various shows, workshops, and festivities in early November. Check out www.berlinerfestspiele.de for the different venues and dates. Early November.

December

New Year's Eve. Come party at the Brandenburg Gate. December 31.

Top Attractions

→ **Berlin Zoo/Aquarium** Löwen, tiger, und bären—oh my! In addition to those three furry animals, the Berlin Zoo is also home to the largest number of animal species in the world. Watch lions shag like minxes, and then check out deep-sea creatures in the neighboring Aquarium. The admission to the liquid menagerie is worth it just to watch massive stingrays gracefully fly by in their 35,000 gallon tank. *Berlin Zoo- Hardenbergplatz 8.* ☎ *030/25-40-10. www.zoo-berlin.de. Mon– Sun 9am–6:30pm (till dark in winter). Admission 11€ adults, 8€ students. Combination tickets for Zoo and Aquarium 16€ adults, 13€ students. U-Bahn: Bahnhof Zoologischer Garten or Kurfürstendamm.*

Free & Easy

→ Admission to the **Reichstag, Brandenburg Gate, Kaiser Wilhelm Church,** and the **Topography of Terror** will cost you absolutely nothing.

→ The first Sunday of the month is a great day for admiring ancient relics: The **Pergamon** and the **Ägyptisches museums** offer free admission then.

→ For more contemporary pieces, the **Guggenheim** opens its doors to anybody every Monday.

S-Bahn: Bahnhof Zoologischer Garten. Berlin Aquarium: Buda-pester Strasse 32. ☎ *030/ 25-40-10. www.aquarium-berlin.de. Daily 9am— 6pm. Admission 11€ adults, 8€ students. U-Bahn: Bahnhof Zoologischer Garten or Kurfürstendamm. S-Bahn: Bahnhof Zoologischer Garten.*

MTV **Best** → **Charlottenburg Palace** ★★ Museuminsel aside, the cultural heart of Berlin resides west of the Tiergarten in the Charlottenburg Palace, an expansive area that's home to a number of museums and royal residences.

The main attraction for most tourists is the **Schloss Charlottenburg,** the excessively plush summer pad of King Friedrich I was built for his wife, Sophie Charlotte. You can either explore the grounds yourself or take a tour to guide you through the miles of opulent statues, rich tapestries, priceless porcelain, and other extravagant art.

The **Ägyptisches Museum** is another worthy stop within the Charlottenburg complex. The collection of ancient Egyptian artifacts is impressive, but it pales in comparison to the grandeur of the museum's centerpiece: the bust of Queen Nefertiti. Like the statue of *David* in Florence's Galleria dell'Accademia, the ancient queen's noggin has a room all to itself and is constantly surrounded by a swarm of admirers. *Schloss Charlottenburg: Luisenplatz.* ☎ *030/32-09-1275. Admission to all buildings 7€. Palace Tues–Fri 9am–5pm, Sat–Sun 10am–5pm; museum Tues–Fri 10am– 6pm; gardens (free admission) daily 6:30am– 8pm. U-Bahn: Sophie-Charlotte-Platz or Richard-Wagner-Platz. Ägyptisches Museum: Schlossstrasse 70.* ☎ *030/32-09-11. www.smpk. de. Admission 6€; free for everyone 1st Sun of the month. Tues–Fri 10am–6pm, Sat–Sun 11am–6pm. U-Bahn: Sophie-Charlotte-Platz or Richard-Wagner-Platz.*

→ **Deutsche Guggenheim** This tiny gallery opens its walls to contemporary art and usually only showcases one or two

particular artists at a time. Warhol, Picasso, Cezanne, and Man Ray are a few that have been highlighted in the two main spaces. Some exhibitions, such as Douglas Gordon's 2005 "VANITY of Allegory," feature a small theater in the rear where you can sit back and watch the films by or about the artist. *Unter den Linden 13–15.* ☎ *030/20-20-930. www.deutsche-guggenheim.de. Daily 11am– 8pm (Thurs till 10pm). Admission 4€, free on Mon. U-Bahn: Französische Strasse.*

MTV **Best** → **Erotik Museum** ★★ Seek true sensual enlightenment in Berlin's Erotik Museum. Start by grabbing a ticket (and maybe a tape or two) in the sex shop on the

Mardi Whaaa?

Break out your glow sticks, kiddies! Accept no imitation, and, trust me, there are tons, and come to Berlin at least for 1 day in July. Wait, you'll most likely need an extra day for your ears to recover from the intense music and, come to think of it, another day to adjust your eyes after being exposed to miles upon miles of bare flesh—so really, you'll need 3 days to enjoy the 24-hour party known as the **MTV** **Best** Love Parade, held the second weekend of July.

Although several international cities got ants in their municipal pants and couldn't hold themselves back from having their own Love Parade, these other celebrations don't hold a candle to the mutha-of-all-love-parades in Berlin. The original procession takes place yearly (although in 2004 and 2005 it was canceled for the first times since its creation in 1989 due to sponsorship problems). Just listen and watch when half-naked dancers in bondage gear scoot by as the floats of monstrous speakers spit out meaty electronica.

ground floor and follow the signs to the top floor. Several floors cover the exploits of man throughout history. Chronologically ordered displays showcase forbidden ancient Japanese illustrations, chastity belts, eerie wax representations of famous sex figures in history, and penis sculptures of all shapes and sizes. If you elect to actually read the accompanying descriptions, you'll be happy to find that they're provided in both German and English. *Joachimstalerstrasse 4.* ☎ *030/ 88-60-666. Mon–Sat 9am–11pm, Sun 1–11pm. Admission 5€ adults, 4€ students. U-Bahn/ S-Bahn: Zoologischer Garten.*

→ **Museum Haus am Checkpoint Charlie** ★ The infamous crossing for Berliners is also the spot where Russian and American tanks took part in a tenuous Cold War standoff in 1961. East Berliners tried various methods to escape into the West, mostly in vain. In 1962, the world was made brutally aware of the situation when bricklayer Peter Fechter bled to death after being shot by DDR (German Democratic Republic) soldiers at the border trying to gain his freedom because neither side offered medical help. The museum built at the site explores the checkpoint's history in depth, providing mock-ups of the different vehicles (hot-air balloons, minisubs, and modified trucks) used in escape attempts by East Berliners. *Friedrichstrasse 43–45.* ☎ *030/25-37-25-0. www.mauermuseum.de. Admission 9.50€ adults, 5.50€ students; free lockers available. Daily 9am–10pm. Films shown throughout the day as well as feature films shown every 2 hr. 9:30am–5:30pm. U-Bahn: Kochstrasse or Stadtmitte.*

MTV Best → **Museuminsel** ★★ Pitch a tent somewhere close because you could spend days wandering the several notable museums on the island. If you're short on time, two in particular shouldn't be missed. First, the **Alte Nationalgalerie,** which houses some of the most extraordinary works of 19th-century German and French artists.

The other is the **Pergamon Museum.** Artifacts from ancient civilizations are showcased here, but the Pergamon Altar (located in the Greek and Roman wing) is the only can't-miss. The enormous work contains so many intricate details that it's hard to

BERLIN

MTV The University Scene

Much of Berlin's energy is easily traced to the city's youth. The underground cafes that nurtured past intellectuals now swarm with students from **Humboldt University,** by far the best institution of higher education in Berlin. On Unter den Linden 6, the university is one of the oldest in Germany; since 1810, the likes of Hegel, Einstein, Marx, and Schopenhauer have walked through its halls. Anyone looking for inside information on the university's social scene can walk through Humboldt's buildings and scan the bulletin boards. Don't be afraid to approach students on their way to class. Undergrads here speak English almost flawlessly.

For some good East Berlin crowd-watching, the view from any of the outdoor cafes on Oranienburger Strasse is one of the most entertaining. If you linger into the early evening, you'll see prostitutes reporting for duty. In the afternoon, the nearby Tacheles Courtyard is popular with a student and young artist crowd. Another East Berlin hangout on a warm weekend night is the corner of Tucholsky Strasse and August Strasse, where young, hip-dressing, good-looking types take expensive mixed drinks out of trendy local bars to mingle in the street.

believe they've stayed intact for 2,000 years. If you have time after visiting the remarkable altar, be sure to walk through the departments devoted to Persian, Assyrian, Babylonian, and Islamic relics. *Alte Nationalgalerie: Museuminsel.* ☎ *030/209-055-55. www.smpk.de. Admission 6€. Tues–Sun 10am–6pm. S-Bahn: Hackescher Markt. Pergamon Museum: Kupfergraben, Museuminsel.* ☎ *030/20-90-50. www.smpk.de. Admission 6€; free admission 1st Sun of the month. Tues–Sun 10am–6pm (Thurs till 10pm). U-Bahn/S-Bahn: Friedrichstrasse.*

FREE → **Topography of Terror** A few blocks away from Checkpoint Charlie is this open-air exhibition dedicated to the Berlin Wall. The Topography of Terror was once an ambitious project that has since been ignored. What now stands on the corner of Niederkirchnerstrasse and Wilhelmstrasse is an abandoned stretch of independent displays. It chronologically explains not only the wall's beginnings, but also the history of events that preceded the wall's construction. The outdoor museum stands on what used to be the old National Socialist and SS Police Headquarters and is open year-round. *Niederkirchner Strasse 8.* ☎ *030/25-48-47-03.*

May–Sept 10am–8pm; Oct–Apr 10am–dark. Free admission. U-Bahn: Potsdamer Platz.

Churches

FREE → **Kaiser Wilhelm Church** Most of Berlin has been, or is in the midst of being, rebuilt. In West Berlin, however, the once glorious Kaiser Wilhelm Church was reduced to a few wall fragments by Allied bombers. Rather than demolish the scant remains and start from scratch, officials decided to keep the ruins as a ghostly reminder. A newer, more modern chapel was erected adjacent to the ruins and it holds small services at the end of the day for West Berliners. A stop here is definitely worth your time while you explore the Ku'Damm area. *Breit-Scheidplatz.* ☎ *030/218-50-23. Free admission. Ruins Mon–Sat 10am–4pm, church daily 9am–7pm. U-Bahn: Bahnhof Zoologischer Garten or Kurfürstendamm.*

Landmarks

FREE → **Brandenburger Tor (Brandenburg Gate)** ★★ Carl Langhans designed one of Berlin's most recognizable structures: the Brandenburg Gate. The six-columned gate was once incorporated into the Berlin

The Wall

After World War II, the city of Berlin was occupied by four separate powers: the U.S., France, Britain, and the Soviet Union. Each held a section of the city, but the Soviets decided to close off their portion of Berlin. Known as the German Democratic Republic (aka DDR), it was sealed off in 1949 after the Soviet Union constructed a wall along the borders, prohibiting any of its residents from leaving. The stone obstruction was emblematic of the Cold War tension that was beginning to build in eastern Europe and that would last another 40 years. In 1989, with the fall of communism in other parts of Europe, the wall also followed and crumbled at the feet of exuberant Berliners.

Total unification finally became official the following year, in the fall of 1990. Parliament then decided in 1991 to vacate Bonn and re-establish Berlin as Germany's capital. It would take some time before the government recovered from the radical changes made to the country (the city is still in a constant state of rebuilding), but it didn't take long for Germans to embrace the long-forgotten feeling of unity.

12 Hours in Berlin

1. **Go to the top of the Alexanderplatz for some of the best views in the city.** This centerpiece of East Berlin is chock-full of photo ops, but nowhere more so than the intimidating TV tower that looms above the S-Bahn station. The observation platform is about 186m (610 ft.) tall and is worth the admission price of around 7€.

2. **Hit the Museuminsel.** Just west of Alexanderplatz, on the easternmost end of Berlin's famed Unter den Linden, sits a cache of museums containing everything from 19th-century Impressionist works to Greek relics. The area is home to the Alte Nationalgalerie, the Altes Museum, and the Pergamon Museum. Each can easily take up a full day to explore, but if you're on a tight schedule you're better off simply taking in the Alte Nationalgalerie with its great collection of 19th-century art.

3. **Take a walk on the Unter den Linden.** Stroll west on this street until you find yourself at the **Brandenburg Gate,** once part of the infamous Berlin Wall. Not far away, you'll find Germany's parliament, the **Reichstag.** Visitors can tour parts of the building or go to the roof for some more camera fodder.

4. **Visit Charlottenburg Palace, Western Berlin's cultural center.** This place also happens to be the old royal Prussian residence. The Schloss Charlottenburg is perhaps the palace's crown jewel but if bling's not your thing, there are several other attractions. One museum, in particular, should not be missed: the **Ägyptisches Museum.** Within the walls of this converted guardhouse is the bust of Queen Nefertiti.

5. **Spend time on the Ku'damm.** The wide avenue with a wide name is home to some of West Berlin's best shops and restaurants.

BERLIN

Wall and is now the subject of countless tourist photos. The most notable feature is the goddess Nike atop her chariot, which was once stolen by the impulsive Napoleon. Upon its return in 1814, the olive wreath in her hand was replaced by the Iron Cross. When reunification occurred in 1990, they restored the wreath to Nike's outstretched arm. After you admire the gate from afar, pay homage to those who suffered in the Room of Silence, a converted guardhouse at the base of the gate. *Pariser Platz. Free admission. Room of Silence daily 11am–6pm. S-Bahn: Unter den Linden.*

FREE ➔ **Molecule Man** Artist Jonathon Borofsky built this massive structure on the Spree and it was commissioned by Allianz GmbH. It was initially slated to be erected in the middle of the river, but that proved to be a logistical nightmare; it now sits just off the shore. Still, from a distance, the three monstrous figures, seeming to float precariously on the Spree, are quite a sight. Borofsky wanted to show that the molecules of every person on earth constitute our existence as human beings. *Elsenbrücke (Kreuzberg, on the Spree River). U-Bahn: Schlesisches Tor.*

FREE ➔ **Reichstag (Bundestag)** ★★ Parliament sessions returned to the Reichstag in 1999, but the building is better known for the famous fire that sparked the beginnings of Nazi rule in Germany. A fire in 1933 engulfed the Reichstag, and the German Communist party was blamed, even though it was clear that Hitler's underlings were the ones who set it ablaze. Soon after, the Nazi party took over. Decades followed and the Reichstag was used mainly as a conference center. Finally, in the '90s, it was restored and Parliament returned. Get there early to avoid the lengthy lines. *Platz der Republik 1.* ☎ *030/22-73-21-52. www.bundestag.* *de/htdocs_e/info/visit/vberl.html. Free admission. Daily 8am–midnight. Last admission at 10pm. U-Bahn: Unter den Linden.*

Playing Outside

Berlin boasts a surprising number of grassy spots (a third of the city is made up of gardens, lakes, and parks), but the city's most popular grassy oasis is the modestly sized (1.6 sq. km /1 sq. mile) **Tiergarten** ★★. The Tiergarten has gone through many changes after its beginnings as a private park. The war destroyed most of the trees and plants and it now serves as a refuge for joggers, strollers, and locals hanging out. Sunbathers emerge during the summer months, and while some decide to go commando, you won't see as many nude sunbathers as in Munich's Englischer Garten.

Also worth checking out is the smaller **Bahnhof Zoologischer Garten** (see earlier in this chapter for zoo and aquarium info). All streets converge at the golden centerpiece of the park: the Siegessäule (Victory Column). If you want to catch a better view of the park, climb the 290 steps to the top of the observation platform for 1€ (Mon 3–6pm, Tues–Sun 9:30am–6:30pm). Continue east until you reach the famous Brandenburger Tor (see "Sightseeing" earlier) where you can snap a few pictures of the famous landmark.

Fortunately, the two parks mentioned above are a small sampling of places where you can breathe in some fresh air. Give your senses an aromatic and visual treat by visiting Berlin's **Botanischer Garten** (Königin-Luise-Strasse 6–8; ☎ 030/8385o111; www. bgbm.org/BGBM). If you opt for a trip on the S-Bahn, get off at the Botanischer Garten or Rathaud Steglitz stop. Once there, you can relax in the peaceful arboretum or wander through the various exotic plant displays. Adults get in for 5€, and while the museum is open daily (10am–6pm), the garden's closing hours vary. It's open daily at 9am, but in April and August it closes at 8pm; at 9pm in May, June, and July; at 7pm in September; at 6pm in March and October; at 5pm in February; and at 4pm from November through January.

The best way to get some physical activity *and* take in some sightseeing is to rent a bike and explore alone or with a bike group. **Fat Tire Bike Tours** (p. 147) is the best place to rent bikes and meet other cyclists looking to pedal around the city. If you'd rather escape the confines of the city, make your way west to **Grunewald**. Yet another vast expanse of forest and grass, Grunewald has plenty of biking and hiking paths that snake through its 20 sq. km (13 sq. miles) of fresh air.

Shopping

Berlin's stores pander to everyone's vices. If you've got your penny loafers on, West Berlin is where you'll want to pull out the plastic; Kurfürstendamm here is the Madison Avenue of Berlin. Otherwise, East Berlin is an oasis for creative and kooky shops, especially around Torstrasse or Oranienburger Strasse. The influence of the under-30 crowd is heavy in the grungier part of town, thankfully so. Among the vendors, you'll find independent clothing labels, small record stores that have impeccable aural styles, and a slew of wonderfully kitschy specialty stores. Stores generally close at a reasonable 6pm and open around 10am.

➔ **Der Weinkeller** Choose from an extensive selection (over 10,000 bottles) of wine at Der Weinkeller. *Linienstrasse 147.* ☎ *030/246-320-65. derweinkeller@gmx.net. U-Bahn: Oranienburger Tor.*

➔ **Dig a Little Deeper** ★ Bringing records on a commercial jet or through Customs can be a big pain. Finding that rare EP by DJ Shadow, though, could make it worth the hassle. Dig A Little Deeper is a small independent shop where you'll find a few hard-to-find gems. Most of the LPs are underground hip-hop, electronica, jazz, funk, and indie rock but they do have a few mainstream discs floating around. *Torstrasse 102.* ☎ *030/970-051-06. www.digalittledeeper.net. U-Bahn: Rosenthaler Platz.*

➔ **Kalerie** Kemal Cantürk works on his metal art in a small workshop/showroom in the Kunsthaus Tacheles (Art Gallery of Tacheles) where he welds fantastic robotic figures, wacky furniture, and trippy light fixtures. While many of his pieces are hefty, you can purchase some smaller works from the man himself. Even if you're not planning on buying anything, drop in and take a look. *Oranienburger Strasse 54–56a.* ☎ *0162/23-86-084. www.kalerie.de. U-Bahn: Oranienburger Tor.*

➔ **KaDeWe** Kaufhaus des Westens (KaDeWe), an exclusive seven-floor shopping center has high-class labels, designer furniture, and specialty electronics in its sprawl. While the price tags may be a little out of your range, wandering the walkways of KaDeWe is the perfect respite for the rare times that the mercury rises above 32°C (90°F). *Tauentzienstrasse 21.* ☎ *030/212-10. www.kadewe.de. U-Bahn: Wittenbergplatz.*

➔ **Kaufhaus Schrill** Few stores mingle junkiness and kitsch with such artful abandon. Stock here would gladden any punk-rocker's heart, especially if he or she were on the lookout for Elvis-era memorabilia, hair barrettes that glow in the dark, and jewelry that may appeal to Courtney Love for her date with a group of bikers. Don't expect anything tasteful—that isn't its style. *Bleibtreustrasse 46.* ☎ *030/8824048. S-Bahn: Savignyplatz.*

➔ **Musik Unter den Gleisen** There aren't rows upon rows of used CDs and vinyl here, but the friendly and knowledgeable staff does a good job of weeding out the worthless albums from the quality ones. The store is also stocked with a couple of listening stations where you can sample classic rock and indie electronica titles. New releases can run up to 18€, but you're better off looking for more obscure discs at a consumer-friendly price of 10€. Bring cash because they don't take credit cards. *Friedrichstrasse 128.* ☎ *030/285-91-44. U-Bahn: Oranienburger Tor.*

➔ **Trash** ★ East Berliners love to recycle old communist uniforms and pass them off as war-chic. For all their military needs, they rummage around a trendier-than-usual surplus store called Trash. The boots and supplies might not be your cup of tea, but an army green officer's jacket might be the perfect complement to that shirt you picked up at the Checkpoint Charlie gift shop. *Torstrasse 59.* ☎ *030/417-253-16. www.trash-clothing.de. U-Bahn: Rosa Luxemburg Platz.*

BERLIN

Brussels

Brussels has changed a lot within the past few years—what was once regarded as a quaint, lace-making, beer-nursing town of chocolate shops and wood-paneled bars has transformed into a savvy, bustling metropolis, with surprisingly high-octane nightlife options. We can thank the European Union for the makeover. Ever since Brussels (pop. 140,000 in the city proper) became the official headquarters of the E.U. in the 1990s the city has grown increasingly more willing to modernize—so much so that locals are complaining that massive construction projects have dampened the city's old Flemish charm.

Despite recent changes, Brussels maintains a distinct, provincial flavor. The upside of all those years heading up Europe's equivalent to your junior high's "nerd table"? Even in the most cosmopolitan nightspots, the vast majority of the Belgian people you'll meet will be ridiculously down-to-earth and proud of their country's accomplishments. Brussels also remains *the* place to indulge in the best of typically old-school Belgian treats, from traditional "frites" (do *not* call them french fries) to fluffy waffles to hundreds of beers (you'll never reach for a Miller Lite again) to lace products that would make your grandma proud. It's just that now there are more wide-ranging alternatives defining Brussels, especially after the sun goes down. So, really, who could complain? Truth is, most critics of the city's recent developments come from older generations. The majority of people under 35 I chilled with in Brussels love the luxuries that accompany the city's modernization, and the new-found street-cred that comes with hailing from the "Capital of Europe."

The Best of Brussels

◦ **The Best Cheap Sleep:** You won't feel like a starving artist at **The Centre Vincent Van Gogh**—it's conveniently located, clean, and home base for tons of hip backpackers. See p. 180.

◦ **The Best Chocolates:** In a country where chocolate is thought of more as a fine art than a guilty pleasure, being the royal court's chocolate provider is a pretty big deal. **Chocolatier Mary,** a small shop on rue Royal, holds that title—and lives up to the hype that goes along with it. Head on in with a few euros and pick up a few truffles. Just be warned that they can be seriously habit forming. See p. 190.

◦ **The Best Nightclub:** Without a doubt, the hot spot of the moment is **Le You.** You know it's a cool place when it's not even labeled on the outside, right? Belgian celebrities, socialites, and club kids party here until the wee hours—feign an accent, order a vodka Red Bull, and you'll fit right in. See p. 184.

◦ **The Best Cheesy Photo Op:** Yes, **Manneken-Pis,** that statue of the shameless little boy relieving himself, calls Brussels home. Don't be shy—get right up next to him and do a shameless pose of your own. Hey, you're a tourist—go ahead and act like one for a few seconds! See p. 187.

Getting There & Getting Around

Getting There

BY AIR

If you're flying, you'll likely touch down in **Brussels National Airport** (☎ 02/753-39-13), a large, international hub of sorts. It's located in Zaventem, 14km (9 miles) northeast of the city center. From here you can easily hop on an Airport Line Bus (head to the airport bus terminal on Level 0 and look for the no. 12 to take you right into town) for 3€. There's also an Airport City Express train service, departing from the airport's train station at Level 1, which shuttles directly to Brussels' three main stations, Gare du Nord, Gare Centrale, and Gare du Midi. Taxis are pretty pricey, but you can get one from a taxi stand outside the airport—a ride into the heart of the city should cost you around 30€.

BY TRAIN

Flying into another major European city and then taking a train to Brussels might be the best and cheapest option for getting into town. Brussels is well served by high-speed trains—the Eurostar arrives through the Channel Tunnel from London and Thalys offers connecting service with Paris, Amsterdam, and Cologne. There are five big train stations in the Brussels metropolitan area. Travelers arriving from other European countries will probably want to get off at one of the three main stations: **Gare Centrale,** Carrefour de l'Europe 2; **Gare du Midi,** rue de France 2 (which is also the Eurostar and Thalys terminal); and **Gare du Nord,** rue du Progrès 86. Trains traveling within Belgium may also stop at **Gare du Quartier Léopold,** place du Luxembourg; and **Gare de Schaerbeek,** place Princesse Elisabeth 5 (which also is the international auto-rail terminal). A train ticket to or from *Bruxelles agglomération* (Brussels metropolitan area) is valid for any of the city's five stations. For train information and reservations, call ☎ **0900/10-177;** for international trains, call ☎ **0900/10-366.**

BY BUS

Eurolines (www.eurolines.com) has service three times daily from London's Victoria

Benelux Saving Pass

You might want to consider a **Benelux Tourrail pass** if you're traveling throughout Belgium, Amsterdam, and Luxemburg. It's sold by Rail Europe (www.raileurope. com) and you can get tickets for both classes. Passes cost $176 (second class) and $263 (first class) for 5 days of unlimited rail travel in all three countries during 1 month. If you're traveling with someone else, you'll pay only $132 (second class) and $198 (first class) each.

Coach Station, via the Channel Tunnel's Le Shuttle train, to Brussels. For schedule and fare information on this, and on Eurolines service from all other major towns and cities in Europe, contact Eurolines at ☎ **099/080-8080** in Britain and ☎ **02/203-07-07** in Belgium. Most buses from continental destinations arrive on **rue Fonsny** beside Gare du Midi, though some stop at various city center locations around **place de Brouckère.**

BY CAR

If you drive to Brussels, I recommend parking your car at your hotel and leaving it there. You won't need a car to get around the city, so spare yourself the hassle.

Getting Around

BY PUBLIC TRANSPORTATION

The **Société des Transports Intercommunaux de Bruxelles (STIB;** ☎ **02/515-20-00;** www.stib.be) runs the city's dependable network of underground Métro trains, street-level trams, and buses. The **Métro** (subway) system is quick and efficient, and covers many important city-center locations, as well as reaching out to the suburbs. You can spot a Métro station entrance by its sign: a white M on a dark blue background.

Tram or **bus** stops are marked with red-and-white signs and often have a shelter. Trams are generally faster and more comfortable than buses.

You can buy 1.40€ single ride tickets from bus drivers or Métro stations, which can be used on the Métro, trams, and buses. Also available are 6.50€ 5-ride tickets, and 9.80€ 10-ride tickets. 3.80€ buys you an all-day pass.

You validate your ticket by inserting it into the orange electronic machines that stand inside buses and trams and at the access to Métro platforms. Though the ticket must be revalidated each time you enter a new vehicle, you are allowed multiple transfers within a 1-hour period of the initial validation, so you can hop on and off Métros, trams, and buses during that time and only one journey will be canceled by the electronic scanner. If more than one person is traveling on one ticket, the ticket must be validated each time for each traveler.

Check out www.urbanrail.net/eu/bru/brussels.htm for more info.

BY CAR OR MOTORCYCLE

Thinking about **renting a car or motorcycle** to zip around Brussels? You should really think again. Belgians somehow morph into take-no-prisoners road warriors when they're behind the wheel of their Peugeots. If your need for speed is too great to heed my warning, you can find rental places at Gare du Midi or at the airport. Or contact **Hertz** (bd. Maurice Lemonnier 8; ☎ **800/654-3001** in the U.S., or 02/720-60-44); or **Avis** (rue de France 2; ☎ **800/331-2112** in the U.S., or 02/527-17-05).

BY BICYCLE

Bicycles aren't nearly as popular in Brussels as in other European cities, probably due to reckless car drivers and the lack of bike paths in the city center. Most streets in the city center are also paved with cobblestones, which aren't exactly a biker's best friend. If you insist on pulling a Lance Armstrong, you can rent a bike at **Pro Vélo** (rue de Londres 15; ☎ 02/217-01-58; www. provelo.be; Métro: Porte de Namur). It's open Monday to Friday from 9am to 6pm. Rental is 12€ per day.

BY FOOT

If the weather is nice, try getting around the old-fashioned way—on foot. The only time it's really necessary to use public transport in Brussels is if you're heading to the European District or the Bruparck.

Brussels Basics

Orientation: Brussels Neighborhoods

Although Brussels proper is actually a 161 sq. km (62 sq. miles) area, most attractions are located within a small central section of the city. Brussels-dwellers generally refer to locations within this city center as being either in the "Upper Town" or the "Lower Town."

The cobblestone-paved, older area that includes the town square Grand-Place, the restaurant-packed Ilôt Sacré by the Métro stop Ste-Catherine, hipster and bar-hopper friendly St-Géry, and the more working class Marolles neighborhoods all comprise the Lower Town.

The Upper Town has a completely different feel; it's home to Brussels' answer to New York City's 5th and Madison avenues—the boulevard de Waterloo and the avenue Louise. If you can navigate west through the poodles and the Botox, you'll arrive at the place du Grand Sablon, which is where the city's upper crust dines. Southeast of the city's center, outside the Upper and Lower towns, is the European Union quarter—big-wig central, and home of the E.U. Parliament buildings.

Tourist Offices

You can pick up maps, make hotel reservations, and look into tours and pub-crawls at the **Brussels International Tourist Office** (Town Hall, Grand-Place 1000; ☎ 02/ 513-89-40; www.brusselsinternational.be; summer daily 9am–6pm; winter Mon–Sat 9am–6pm, Sun 10am–2pm; Métro: Gare Centrale) and the **Belgian Tourist Information Center** (rue du Marché aux Herbes 63; ☎ 02/504-03-90; www.visitflanders.com; Métro: Gare Centrale). The Belgian Tourist Information Center is open June to September, Monday to Saturday from 9am

BRUSSELS

Talk of the Town

Three ways to start a conversation with a local

1. **How about that traffic?** You don't need to put a Belgian behind the wheel to incite a nasty case of road rage.

2. **What's the lowdown on local food and beer?** The Belgians' stomachs are near and dear to their hearts, and with hundreds of bars serving as many different types of brew and new restaurants going in and out of style daily, every local has an opinion they're dying to share.

3. **Who's your favorite to win this year's football match?** It's important to realize that in Europe, where the next-best sports are cricket and rugby, you've got to make the best of what you have. If you do try to talk sports with a local, the most important thing to know is: Anderlecht rules! Rooting for anyone else could be hazardous to your health.

Brussels

SLEEPING ■

Aris Centre Hotel **5**
The Centre
  Vincent Van Gogh **8**
Hotel George V **1**
The Stanhope Hotel **17**

EATING ◆

Cafe Metropole **6**
Chez Leon **31**
Comme Chez Soi **2**
Oh! La La Tearoom
  & Cafe **22**
Plaka **24**
Pulp **29**
Quick Burger **28**
't Kelderke **25**
Yasmina **23**

PARTYING ★

AB **10**
A La Mort Subite **30**
Le Botanique **9**
Le You **15**
Louise Gallery **20**
Le Fuse **18**
New York Café Jazz Club **21**
People **19**
Roy d'Espagne **27**
Zebra **11**

SIGHTSEEING ●

Atomium **4**
Brussels Park **14**
Cathedrale des Sts. Michel
  et Gudule **12**
Centre Belge de
  la Bande Déssinée
  (Belgian Center for
  Comic Strip Art) **7**
Mannekin-Pis **13**
Mini Europe **3**
Musée de la Ville Brussels **26**
Musees Royaux des
  Beaux Arts, including
  Musee d'Art Moderne
  & Musee d'Art Ancien **16**

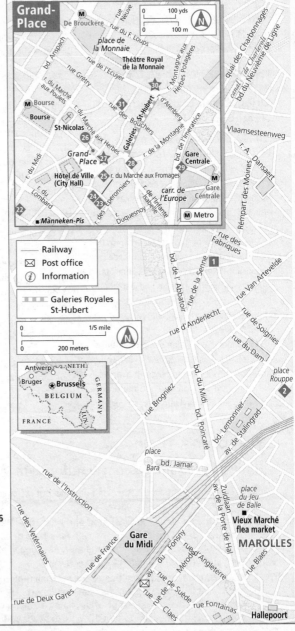

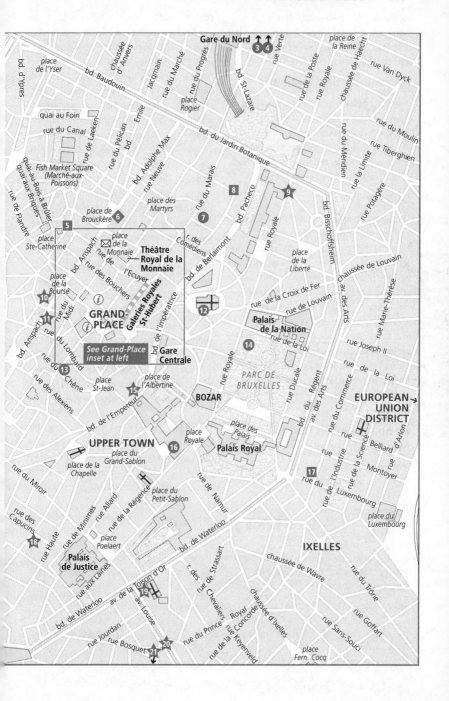

to 7pm, Sunday from 9am to 6pm; October to March, Monday to Saturday from 9am to 6pm; and April, May, and October, Sunday from 9am to 6pm (to 5pm Nov–Mar).

Recommended Websites

◦ **www.opt.be**: The definitive travel site on Brussels, through the tourist office.

◦ **www.brusselscitytourist.com**: Another informative site on goings on in Brussels.

◦ **www.use-it.be**: Hip tourist information on Brussels and the rest of Flanders.

Culture Tips 101

The local language in Brussels is French but most natives speak English fluently. Belgians also take their boozing very seriously, and they start training early: The legal minimum age to buy is 18. You may see the patrons of a crowded bar spilling into the street—hittin' on a brew in public is A-OK here. Hittin' the pipe, on the other hand, is *not* legal.

One annoying quirk of Belgian law: You're required to carry your passport or some form of national identification at all times. Unless you want to risk a police escort to your hotel to retrieve your ID, don't leave home without it.

Recommended Books, Music & Movies

Belgium has cranked out quite a few well-known books, many of them by the very prolific George Simenon. He amassed over 450 written works in his lifetime, but is best known for the 75 novels and 28 short stories from the 1930s to 1970s featuring Commissaire Maigret, a police detective who was also popularized in a number of French films. Poet and playwright Maurice Maeterlinck won the Nobel Prize in Literature in 1911; he achieved his greatest fame for his fairy play *L'Oiseau Bleu* (*The Blue Bird,* 1909), which was later made into a movie starring Judy Garland. The best-known piece of Belgian writing probably remains Hergé's *The Adventures of Tintin,* though. It'll be hard to miss the colorful Tintin comic books, centered on a cartoon reporter Tintin and his handy dog Snowy, during your visit.

In the past, Belgium's film industry floundered because the country doesn't have a major film studio. Recently, though, Belgian directors like Luc and Jean-Pierre Dardenne have overcome this obstacle to win worldwide acclaim; the two recently won the top prize at Cannes (the Palme d'Or) for their film *L'Enfant* (*The Child,* 2005) about a poor couple struggling with the birth of their child.

Jacque Brel gained acting fame in films like 1969's *Mon Oncle Benjamin,* but is better known for penning songs, which inspired the 1970s song revue *Jacques Brel is Alive and Well and Living in Paris.* Check out the 1975 movie if you want an introduction to Brel's music—just be warned that it's pretty dated.

Brussels Nuts & Bolts

Cellphone Providers & Service Centers   Belgium's largest cellphone provider, **Proximus,** sells phones throughout Brussels. Call ☎ **32-78-05-6030** or visit www. proximus.be for info.

Currency   ATMs are everywhere in Brussels, and most major places take credit cards. Banks (most are open Mon–Fri 9am–1pm and 2–4:30pm) give the best exchange rates. An **American Express** location is at 100 bd. de Souverain (☎ **02/676-21-11;** Métro: to Hermann Debroux; Mon–Fri 9am–1pm and 2–5pm).

Embassies   The **U.S. Embassy** is at bd. du Régent 25–27 (☎ **02/508-21-11;** www. usembassy.be; Métro: Arts-Loi). It's open for visa applications Monday to Friday from

9am to noon, and for assistance to U.S. citizens, from 1:30 to 4:30pm. The **Canada Embassy** is at av. de Tervuren 2 (☎ 02/741-06-11; www.canadianembassy.org; Métro: Merode), and it's open Monday, Wednesday, and Friday from 9am to noon and 2 to 4pm, Tuesday and Thursday from 9am to noon. The **U.K. Embassy** is at rue Arlon 85 (☎ 02/287-62-11; www.britishembassy.gov.uk; Métro: Maalbeek). It's open for visa applications Monday to Friday from 9:30am to noon, and for other matters, from 9:30am to 12:30pm and 2:30 to 4:30pm. The **Australia Embassy** is at rue Guimard 6–8 (☎ 02/286-05-00; www.austemb.be; Métro: Arts-Loi), and it's open Monday to Friday from 9am to 12:30pm and 2 to 4pm. The **New Zealand Embassy** is at square de Meeûs 1 (☎ 02/512-10-40; www.nzembassy.com; Métro: Trone). It's open Monday to Friday from 9am to 1pm and 2 to 3:30pm. The **Ireland Embassy** is at rue Wiertz 50 (☎ 02/235-66-76; http://foreign affairs.gov.ie; Métro: Schuman), and it's open Monday to Friday from 10am to 12:30pm.

Emergencies   Accidents or fire: ☎ 100; police assistance: ☎ 101; emergency medical service: ☎ 02/479-18-18 or 02/648-80-00; emergency dental service: ☎ 02/426-10-26 or 02/428-58-58.

The main hospitals are **Hôpital Universitaire Saint Luc** (10 av. d'Hippocrate; ☎ 02/764-11-11; Métro: to Alma), **Hôpital Saint Pierre** (322 rue Haute; ☎ 02/535-31-11; Métro: to Porte de Hal), and **Hôpital Brugmann** (2 place Van Gehuchten; ☎ 02/477-21-11; Métro: to Houba-Brugmann).

Internet/Wireless Hot Spots   Brussels, like most major European cities, has Internet cafes pretty much everywhere. Your best bet is to keep your eyes peeled for signs or to ask around in your area—there should be a few cheap places for an e-mail fix within the radius of a block or two. In the center, the large Internet center **easyEverything** (place de Brouckère 9–13; ☎ 02/211-08-20; www.easyeverything.com; Métro: De Brouckère) is open 24 hours a day; access begins at 2.50€.

Laundry   A major laundromat chain in Brussels is **Ipsomat** (☎ 02/512-61-71), which has a branch at rue Blaes 193 (Métro: Louise). It's open daily 7am to 10pm. There are other locations in the city—ask your hostel or hotel for info on the closest one.

Luggage Storage   Lockers are available at Brussels three main train stations, **Gare Centrale,** Carrefour de l'Europe 2; **Gare du Midi,** rue de France 2 (which is also the Eurostar and Thalys terminal); and **Gare du Nord,** rue du Progrès 86.

Post Offices   There are several post offices in Brussels. The office at Centre Monnaie, place de la Monnaie (☎ 02/226-21-11; Métro: De Brouckère), is open Monday to Friday from 9am to 5pm and Saturday from 9:30am to 3pm. The office at Gare du Midi (av. Fonsny 1E/F; ☎ 02/538-33-98; Métro: Gare du Midi) is open 24 hours.

Restrooms   Most restrooms will sport an H or HOMMES for men, and an F or FEMMES for women. Be sure to pay the person who sits at the entrance—the cost is usually about .30€. The best place to find immediate relief is at the **Hotel Metropole** (place de Brouckere 31; Métro: De Brouckere).

Safety   Brussels is a very safe city, but no one is immune to pickpockets and muggings, especially in tourist areas and in Métro trains and stations. Take precautions, especially when alone or at night.

BRUSSELS

Tipping In restaurants, taxis, and hotels, a 16% service charge is usually added in with the total—extra tipping isn't customary. Rounding up (giving 20€ for a 19€ bill) isn't unusual, but it's not at all expected. Hotel porters may expect a small tip per item of luggage they carry.

Sleeping

A lot of hotels have been renovated recently due to a surge in business clientele. You'll probably get a great deal on the weekends, summer, and holidays, times when all the suits leave town. Don't be afraid to do a little haggling when making reservations. Pretty much no matter where you stay (or how little you pay) in Brussels, you'll find a friendly and approachable hotel staff and should have no problem speaking English to whomever is at the front desk.

Hostels

MTV **Best** → **The Centre Vincent Van Gogh/C.H.A.B.** ★ Your best hostel bet in all of Brussels, the Vincent Van Gogh has a really laid-back atmosphere; clean, tastefully decorated rooms; and super-friendly staff. It's also really youth-oriented—most people who stay here are around college age, and it feels a lot like a dorm. The bar is well stocked by any standards, with more than 20 Belgian brews. There's also a beautiful courtyard open during spring and summer. The central location, an easy walk across the park to the Grand-Place, is one more bonus. *Rue Traversière 8.* ☎ *02/217-01-58. www.chab.be. 28€ single, 21€ per person double or triple, 17€ per person quad, 16€ per person in 6-person room, 14€ per person in 8- to 10-person room. Métro: Botanique. Amenities: Internet; kitchen; laundry facilities; luggage storage; 24-hr. access. In room: Shared bathrooms; sheets (4€).*

Cheap

→ **Hotel George V** This small, cozy, family-run hotel is actually a renovated 19th-century house. Rooms are basic and small, but clean and definitely adequate for the price—essentially just beds, chairs, and a bedside table or two adorn most units. It's located near the fish market and the port, which makes for a quieter area. *Rue t' Kint 23.* ☎ *02/513-50-93. www.georges.com. 64€ single, 75€ double or twin, 86€ triple, 97€ quad. Rates include breakfast. Métro: Ste-Catherine. Amenities: Bar. In room: TV.*

Doable

→ **Aris Centre Hotel** Location, location, location—this moderately priced hotel sits 2 blocks away from the Grande Centrale and only 1 block away from the Grand-Place. Although it may be a bit noisier if you have a room with views from the front, overall the hotel has a feeling of being the calm at the center of the Brussels storm. As far as amenities go, you're getting what you pay for—it's not a hostel, but it's obviously not a five-star. *Marché aux Herbes 78–80 Grasmarkt.* ☎ *02/514-43-00. www.arishotel.be. Weekdays 125€ single, 160€ double or twin; weekends 87€ single, double, or triple. Call or check website for seasonal and holiday rates. Rates include taxes and buffet breakfast. Métro: Gare Centrale. Amenities: Business services; car rental; concierge; currency exchange; dry cleaning; luggage storage; wheelchair friendly. In room: A/C, TV, hair dryer, radio, safe, Wi-Fi.*

Splurge

→ **The Stanhope Hotel** ★★ If you're gonna splurge, you might as well go for the best—and this is the city's best. A sophisticated boutique hotel near the ultrafashionable avenue Louise area, the Stanhope has a homey, personal feel that's mainly due to its former use as, well, a home. The hotel is actually three 19th-century town houses, with a convent thrown in for good measure. You'll be rewarded with a beautiful room, decorated in Old English style, and an in-house restaurant serving tasty French food. *Rue du Commerce 9.* ☎ *02/506-90-30. www.* *stanhope.be. 120€–325€ double. Métro: Trone. Amenities: Bar; business center; Internet; health club; dry cleaning/laundry services; restaurant; room service; sauna; solarium; wheelchair friendly. In room: A/C, TV, bathrobe, hair dryer, Internet, minibar, radio, safe, slippers, trouser press, umbrella.*

Eating

Prepare to be spoiled. Tasty, high-quality food, affordable prices, and service with a smile is the standard in Brussels—Belgians are pretty hard core about their cuisine, and many have the love handles to prove it. After munching on crispy frites (eat them like the Belgians do with a dollop of mayo—*trust* me on this one), breakfasting on piping hot waffles, and swilling the world's best milkshake-thick

Trappist ales, I can definitely say I left Brussels fatter and happier than I came.

The only catch to eating here is that you have to put your rip-off radar on high, especially when dining along the restaurant-laden streets of the Ilôt Sacré district. If you get the feeling a place might be trying to jack up prices for starry-eyed tourists, you're probably right—keep walking. Overall, the

Beer 101

> **Lambic ale** is known as the "pink champagne" of Belgian brews, as it's the crispest and fruitiest. Some examples are Gueuze, Faro, and Kriek.

> **Trappist ales** are strong, very flavorful brews made in abbeys. This stuff is a national treasure: There are only six brewing monasteries in the world, and they are all in Belgium. They are Westmalle, Westvleteren, Chimay, Rochefort, Orval, and Achel. By law, no other breweries in the world may label their product as a "Trappist" beer.

> **Abbey ale** is beer brewed in the Trappist style, but by non-monastic breweries—these often have names of now-defunct monasteries in their titles, such as St. Bernardus or Affligem. Witbier is a pale (*wit* means white), thick, refreshing style of beer that is often served with a slice or two of lemon. Hoegaarden and De Kluis are two popular Witbier breweries.

> **Belgian Pils,** or **Pilsner** beer, is the closest thing you can get to American style beer in Belgium—mild, not bad, but nothing special. These are usually the cheapest offerings in any bar—like Stella Artois and Jupiler.

> **Amber ales** are basically stronger, more flavorful, slightly darker versions of Pilsner brews. These include Artevelde Grand Cru, De Koninck, and my fave, Kwak, which is served in a tall test tube–like glass that requires its own wooden stand.

> **Golden ales** are almost always on the stronger end of Belgian beers— usually no less than 9% alcohol. You can usually spot these by the name, which implies that it'll knock you on your rear—Duvel, Lucifer, Straffe Hendrick, and Delerium Trements, to name a few.

Belgian Fries

Belgium has bragging rights to inventing what Americans call "french fries"—the legend is that the misnomer came about when American soldiers in Europe were served the snack by Belgian waiters who spoke, you guessed it, French.

vast majority of Brussels' restaurants are pretty darn good, though. You can't go wrong if you order the Plat du Jour (usually less than 10€) or a pot of mussels and some frites.

For a late-night greasy-food fix, try the rue Marché aux Fromages 1 block away from the Grand-Place. Here you'll find a cluster of Greek and Turkish joints, serving up cheap gyros, fries, and soda until the wee hours. Although these places are pretty much indistinguishable from one another, a couple I tried and liked were **Yasmina** (rue Marché aux Fromages 7–9) and **Plaka** (rue Marché aux Fromages 6).

Hot Spots

➜ **Café Metropole** ★★ BISTRO   Opened in 1895, this cafe at the luxury Hotel Metropole has hosted the chicest Bruxellois and world travelers ever since. Steps away from the glittering chandeliers of the hotel lobby, the scene consists of crisply dressed, multilingual waiters serving up highballs and hors d'oeuvres for the hotel's Vuitton-toting clientele. Don't be too intimidated, though— the menu itself is casual and relatively inexpensive, the beer and drink selection is expansive, and the staff isn't nearly as snobby or frigid as you might expect. Though the food is good (try their shrimp salad for a satisfying snack), the people-watching from the heated sidewalk terrace is the real reason to eat here. Think of your order as rent-to-sit at one of the best seats in Brussels. *Place de Brouckère 31.* ☎ *02/219-23-84. Plat du Jour 11€, light snacks/appetizers 10€–17€. Daily 9am–2am. Métro: De Brouckere.*

Cheap

➜ **Chez Leon** ★   BELGIAN/SEAFOOD Bustling and no-nonsense, Chez Leon, in the heart of the restaurant district "Ilôt Sacré" has been the best at what it does—mussels— since 1893. This place is an establishment and they know it, so I'd recommend deciding on your order before the waiter asks. While the waitstaff isn't exactly *mean,* they're not charmed by indecisive tourists mulling over the menu. Once the ordering is out of the way, though, they're chill about letting you take your time polishing off their huge pots of signature mussels. *Rue des Bouchers 18.* ☎ *02/511-14-15. www.chezleon.be. Main courses 9.90€–23€, prix fixe 14€. Métro: Gare Centrale.*

➜ **Quick Burger** FAST FOOD   Although the fast food leader throughout Europe is McDonalds, Belgium's Quick Burger dominates the market in its own country. Expect the standard burgers and fries, but also, surprise—beer. There are a few of these franchises scattered throughout Brussels, but the most central is at rue du Marché-aux-Herbes 103. ☎ *02/511-47-63. Métro: Gare Centrale.*

Doable

➜ **'t Kelderke** FRENCH/BELGIAN   Even though it's smack in the middle of the Grand-Place, 't Kelderke is a genuine Belgian restaurant that's as popular with locals as it is with fanny pack–wearing tourists. You may feel like you're stepping into the pages of *The Hobbit* as you descend the narrow staircase and duck through the entrance into the cozy dining room—a 17th-century cellar with vaulted ceiling and long wooden tables. Even if you're not exactly the Tolkien type, this old-school atmosphere is definitely a plus. The unmistakably Belgian vibe might just embolden you to try the menu's seriously traditional specialties, like *lapin à la gueuze* (rabbit in local Belgian beer). *Grand-Place 15.* ☎ *02/513-73-44. Main courses 9.50€–19€, Plat du Jour 9€. Métro: Gare Centrale.*

Splurge

→ **Comme Chez Soi** ★★ FRENCH If you're looking to spend serious cash and get a top-rate meal in return, head to Comme Chez Soi. The restaurant's French title means "Just Like Home," which is accurate only if your home sports Art Nouveau decor, has received three Michelin stars, and requires reservations at least a month in advance. Yeah—this place is a pretty big deal. The chef, world-famous Pierre Wynants, changes his classic French menu frequently, but when you're paying this much for grub, you won't feel badly taking time to discuss meal choices with the über-knowledgeable servers. If you're in a group, try to reserve a spot at the table in the kitchen, where you can squeeze in among other awestruck diners to watch the chef at work. *Place Rouppe* 23. ☎ *02/512-29-21. www.commechezsoi.be. Main courses 34€–62€, prix fixe 56€–124€. Métro: Anneessens.*

Cafes & Tearooms

A quick, inexpensive spot (think the love child of Starbucks and Jamba Juice) with coffees, teas, juices, and sandwiches is **Pulp** (bd. de l'Imperatrice 60; ☎ 02/502-72-82). A more upscale, sit-down place is **Oh! La! La! Tearoom and Café** (rue du Midi 71; ☎ 02/503-29-00), which offers more than 70 kinds of teas, with prices ranging from 2.50€ to 11€ per cup. Coffee is a more forgiving 1.55€ to 3€. The cute college-aged counter staff shuffles fresh baked bread in and out of the ovens nonstop and can offer great personal suggestions on things to do in the city.

Partying

Although it's true that the posh Euro club scene is making inroads in increasingly metropolitan Brussels, the city's specialty when it comes to nightlife remains its plethora of Bruncafés (French for "brown cafe"—think lots of oak furnishings, frothy mugs filled with hundreds of varieties of local beer, and wisecracking older men tending bar). Belgians don't mess around when it comes to beer: Each variety is served in its own specially shaped and monogrammed glass, and the varieties available at even the smallest of dive bars will put your local pub to shame. It's a good plan to start the night early with a local beer at a traditional haunt (sip, don't chug—Belgian beers are deceptively strong, up to triple the alcohol content of, say, their American counterparts) and see where the evening takes you from there. Most of the best clubs don't even *open* until after midnight, giving you plenty of time to warm up.

To find out what's up during your stay, pick up a copy of the weekly English-language magazine *The Bulletin* at any newsstand, which has an extensive "What's On" section. Overall, despite its status as a center for European culture and politics, Brussels is a pretty casual city, clothing-wise. Even at the most upscale clubs, jeans and nice shoes will have you fitting in with the natives just fine.

Bars & Lounges

Somewhere in between the old-fashioned appeal of the city's Bruncafés and the Manolo-heeled tapas bars lies the scene found in the area around **place St-Géry,** near the Bourse Métro station. Any one of the bars along this street is great for a drink or two while rubbing elbows with young Bruxellois in the know. A standard in this area is **Zebra** (place St-Géry 33–35; ☎ 02/511-09-01), the go-to spot for laid-back but well-heeled teens and 20-somethings that features a great bar selection, dessert menu, and live jazz on Thursdays.

→ **A la Mort Subite** A classic stop that's pretty much a fixture in every Brussels travel guide is A la Mort Subite, in business since 1928. Far from being a tourist trap, this is a local hangout where folks from all walks of Brussels life cozy into wooden booths alongside tourists to down bottles of dark Trappist selections like Chimay Brune, Orval, Rochefort, or glasses of the signature "Mort Subite" (translation: Sudden Death) brew. Also on tap are lighter, fruitier lambic brews. *Rue Montagne-aux-Herbes Potagères 7.* ☎ *02/513-13-18. Métro: Gare Centrale.*

➜ **People** ★ The trendiest place to start out the evening is at this bar in the designer-laden avenue Louise area. It's the perfect place to linger and psych yourself up for a night of club-hopping. Hone your Zoolander-worthy pout while nibbling on selections from the tapas menu (6.50€–13€). Better yet, get liquid courage from the 8€ mojito, and then chat up the designer-clad, model-esque waitstaff to get the inside scoop on which club's VIP room they're headed to after work. *Av. de la Toison d'Or 11.* ☎ *02/534-72-74. Métro: Louise.*

➜ **Roy d'Espagne** ★★ Because of its prime Grand-Place location, the second floor views at this classic Bruncafé are unparalleled. The building dates back to 1697, when it was a guildhouse for bread bakers. You may pay a euro or two more for a beer here than you would in a less central, less storied bar, but that won't matter if you think of the added tab as the price of admission for your table's great real estate. *Grand-Place 1.* ☎ *02/513-08-07. Métro: Gare Centrale.*

Live Music

The cozy, underground feel of most clubs and bars in Brussels makes for tons of great jazz venues. A lot of bars and clubs have jazz jam sessions once a week—check local newspapers to get specific info on the wheres and whens. The **New York Café Jazz Club** (chaussée de Charleroi 5; ☎ *02/502-02-97*) is a safe bet for good jazz.

When it comes to the rock/pop/hip-hop scene, two of the most important live music venues in Brussels are **AB** (**Ancienne Belgique;** Anspachlaan 110; ☎ *02/548-24-24;* www.abconcerts.be) and **Le Botanique** (rue Royale 236; ☎ *02/218-37-32*), which also hosts a weeklong rock/pop festival every September. Give these places a call for info on who's playing during your stay.

Nightclubs

Before you squeeze into your vinyl pants for a night of clubbing, keep in mind these need-to-knows: When the Belgians put on their club wear, it generally doesn't get peeled off until after daybreak—the action starts late and ends late here. Most nightclubs in Brussels also charge a 5€ to 15€ cover fee, depending on the night.

➜ **Le Fuse** ★ A bit edgier than Louise Gallery, Le Fuse is historically the most gay-friendly of all Brussels' standard clubs. Its three floors pulse with techno, house, and reggae, and the already flamboyant crowd is liable to get even crazier as the night wears on. It's located in Marolles, a slightly more downtrodden district of town, so it's probably a good idea to spring for a cab back to your hotel or hostel if you're planning on staying late. *Rue Blaes 8.* ☎ *02/511-97-89. www.fuse.be. Free before 11pm. Bus: 20 or 48.*

🎬 Best ➜ **Le You** ★★ At press time, the hippest, poshest place to be seen hanging by the bar and toastin' the good life was Le You. Don't even think about approaching the door before midnight, and make sure you're wearing your understatedly luxurious best if you want to get past the hulking doorman. Cover is around 10€, and a vodka Red Bull (the club's most popular drink by far) will set you back 9€. Celebrity DJs from all over Europe spin a mix of funk, electronic, disco, and lots of house to the delight of the cream of the young, rich, and fabulous Euro crop. *Rue Dusquenoy 18.* ☎ *02/639-14-00. www.leyou.be. Métro: Gare Centrale.*

→ **Louise Gallery** The crowd here is pretty much a crapshoot—sometimes it's hot, sometimes it's not—you've really gotta ask around to find out what night is the night to go in any given week. As a rule, though, coming here anytime before 3am will guarantee a crowd of fake ID–wielding Bruxellois high schoolers. *Av. Louise, Galerie 1.* ☎ *047/879-79-79. www. louisegallery.com. Métro: Louise.*

Gay Bars & Nightclubs

Rue des Riches-Claires and **rue du Marché-au-Charbon** host some gay and lesbian bars. **Macho 2** (rue du Marché-au-Charbon 108; ☎ **02/513-56-67**; Métro: Bourse), a block from rue des Riches-Claires,

houses a gay men's sauna, pool, steam room, and cafe. It's open Monday to Thursday noon to 2am, Friday and Saturday noon to 4am, and Sunday noon to midnight. Admission is 12€, or 8€ for men under 25 (on Thurs, it's 8€ for everyone); students enter for 5€. **Le Fuse** (see above) has gay nights as well.

For more information, contact **Infor Homo** (av. de Roodebeek 57; ☎ **02/733-10-24**; Métro: Diamant), open Tuesday to Friday 8am to 6pm. Or stop by the gay-and-lesbian community center, **Telsquels** (rue du Marché-au-Charbon 81; ☎ **02/512-45-87**; Métro: Bourse), which is open Saturday to Thursday 5pm to 2am and Friday 8am to 4am.

Performing Arts

You would think the international contingent in Brussels would give birth to some sort of regular English-language theater, but you would be wrong. An amateur comedy troop looking for an audience is usually the most you'll find advertised in the English section of *The Bulletin,* which lists plays by language.

The thirst for culture is better quenched by catching a dance performance. The Brussels dance scene is lively and innovative, as small venues draw contemporary dance troops from across the world. The 743-seat **Lunatheater** (place Sainctellette 20; ☎ **02/201-59-59**; www.kaaitheater.be; Métro: 2; tram: 18 to Yser; 12€–20€ adults, 7€–12€ for those under 26), known also by its Dutch name Kaaitheater, regularly features stars from renowned troupes. Its smaller companion theater, **Kaaitheater Studios** (rue Notre Dame du Sommeil 81; ☎ **02/201-59-59**; tram: 18 to Porte de Ninove), with only 100 seats, hosts lesser-known faces in an intimate setting. Performance art also finds a home in the two venues.

Great fun can be had watching puppeteer José Géal's marionettes bust a wooden move in **Théâtre Toone VII** (Impasse

Schuddeveld 6, off Petite rue des Bouchers; ☎ **02/217-27-53**; Premetro 1a, 1b to de Brouckère; 8:30pm Tues–Sat; 10€ adults, 6€ students [except Fri–Sat]), just a block north of Grand-Place. Performing the satirical stylings of Faust, The Three Musketeers, and Hamlet, the performances are usually in French or Flemish, but are not too difficult to follow. Now in its seventh generation under the control of the Toone family, this puppet show has become one of Brussels' most famous (if most clichéd) attractions.

Brussels is one of the best cities in Europe in which to catch a flick. The huge international community ensures that films are nearly always shown in their original languages with French and Flemish subtitles. Must-see films come in from Brazil, France, Germany, and the United States (though U.S. flicks arrive a few months after their original release).

For the least-outdated American blockbusters, head for **UGC de Brouckère** (place de Brouckère 38; ☎ **02/218-57-25**; www. cinebel.com/ugc; admission 6€; Métro: 1a or 1b to de Brouckère). For you film buffs, the **Musée du Cinéma** (rue Baron Horta 9; ☎ **02/507-83-70**; from 5:30pm daily; 2€ entry fee, 1.50€ if you reserve ahead; Métro:

1a or 1b to Gare Centrale; bus: 30, 60, or 71 to Beaux-Arts) brings back the timeless classics by the world's preeminent filmmakers. Black-and-white masterpieces by Fritz Lang, Frank Capra, Akira Kurosawa, and Federico Fellini fill one tiny theater, while the other features silent movies accompanied by a live pianist. The entry fee also gains you entry to the museum, which exhibits equipment from the first days of film. Unfortunately, most displays are only in French and Flemish.

For the latest in indie celluloid, the bomb shelter–esque back-alley venue **Nova** (rue d'Arenberg 3; ☎ 02/511-27-74; www.nova-cinema.com; 6€ adults, 3.70€ students; Métro: Gare Centrale) screens mostly foreign projects in formats ranging from 35mm to VHS. Once a month, Nova offers a free Open Screen event, where you get to watch Joe Wannabe fill 15 minutes with sometimes brilliant home-movie bytes. Below the cinema is a bar, about as underground as you can hope for, where Nova's turtleneck-clad, bed-headed artist crowd talks shop and listens to discordant, borderline-demented industrial music.

Sightseeing

For newcomers to Brussels, just walking around the city is a sightseeing experience in itself. As the birthplace of Art Nouveau and a world center for comic strip art, Brussels boasts aesthetic stimulation to suit all tastes. You'll spot cobblestone streets, exquisitely detailed baroque architecture, and centuries-old cathedrals—all with nary a strip mall in sight.

Festivals

January

Brussels International Film Festival. New international releases and Belgian films are shown at Cinema Porte de Namur. Contact **Tourist Information Brussels** (☎ 02/513-89-40). Late January.

March

Brussels International Fantasy Film Festival. This film fest screens science fiction and fantasy films at Auditorium du Passage 44. Contact **Tourist Information Brussels** (☎ 02/513-89-40). Late March.

April

Sablon Spring Baroque Music Festival. This music fest features open-air concerts in place du Grand-Sablon. Contact **Tourist**

That's the Ticket

Students with appropriate ID can get **half-price tickets** to many cultural events, and discounts on train and plane fares and certain tours. **Acotra** (rue de la Madeleine 51; ☎ 02/512-86-07; Métro: Gare Centrale) sells discount student train, plane, boat, and bus tickets and books places in youth hostels and private rooms. It also sells the ISIC (International Student Identity Card). Across a small park from Gare Centrale, toward the Grand-Place, it's open Monday to Friday from 8:30am to 12:30pm and 1:30 to 5:30pm.

One of the city's best discounts is the **Brussels card** available from the Brussels International tourist office in the Grand-Place, and from hotels, museums, and offices of the STIB city transit authority for 30€. Valid for 3 days, it allows free use of public transportation, free and discounted admission to around 30 of the city's museums and attractions, and discounts at some restaurants and other venues, and on some guided tours.

Information Brussels (☎ 02/513-89-40). April or May.

May

KunstenFESTIVALdesArts (KFDA). KFDA is an arts festival renowned across the cultural universe for its irritatingly scrunched-up name, which means—brilliantly original, this—Arts Festival, in both Dutch and French. It spotlights stage events, putting an emphasis on opera, theater, and dance, but also finds space for cinema, music concerts, and fine arts exhibits. Various auditoriums and venues around town. Contact **KFDA** (☎ **02/219-07-07**). Throughout May.

Brussels Jazz Marathon. This annual 3-day-long event boasts appearances by 400 artists and over 120 free concerts at open-air venues around town. Contact ☎ **02/456-04-75** for info. End of May.

July

Belgian National Day. This holiday is celebrated throughout Belgium but is especially important in Brussels, which hosts a military procession and music concerts at the Royal Palace. Contact **Tourist Information Brussels** (☎ 02/513-89-40). July 21.

December

Christmas Market. The city's annual Christmas celebration includes an open-air ice-skating rink in Grand-Place. Contact **Tourist Information Brussels** (☎ 02/513-89-40). Throughout December.

Historic Structures

→ **Atomium** ★ It's well worth the risk of ninth-grade science-fair flashbacks to visit this 101m-tall (335-ft.) metal structure: a model of an atom that's 165 billion times bigger than the real thing. Constructed for the 1958 World's Fair, the building recently underwent a massive reconstruction project. Head up to the highest deck and check out the amazing view of the whole city. *Square Atomium, bd. du Centenaire, Heysel.* ☎ *02/475-47-77. www.atomium.be. Admission 9€ adults; 6€ with student ID. Apr–Aug daily*

9am–8pm; Sept–Mar daily 10am–6pm (Panorama to 9:30pm). Métro: Heysel.

FREE → **Cathédrale des Saints Michel et Gudule** ★ Saints Michel is a must see, if only to marvel at how old the massive Gothic cathedral is—it was built in 1226. The ornate stained-glass windows and the architecture epitomize the Gothic movement. In fact, writer Victor Hugo once proclaimed this church as the "purest flowering of the Gothic style." Although it's been around for a long time, the building wasn't officially consecrated as a "cathedral" until 1961. Make sure to check out the amazing stained-glass windows: They were a gift from the 16th-century Habsburg emperor, Charles V. *Bd. de l'Impératrice.* ☎ *02/217-83-45. Free admission. Daily 7am–7pm (Oct–Mar till 6pm). Métro: Gare Centrale.*

FREE → **Grand-Place** ★★★ The most obvious center of everything, sightseeing-wise, is Brussels' famous town square, where former baroque-style guildhalls now house buzzing cafes and restaurants. During the day, street artists and musicians dot the square, and by night, clusters of local teenagers and college-aged international backpackers swill Stella Artois and Jupiler, swapping stories and strumming the occasional guitar. The way the Grand-Place looks now dates mostly from the late 1690s, thanks to rebuilding and protection from France's Louis XIV, so the square remains more neo-Gothic than neon, more jumbo bell tower than Jumbo-tron. Make sure to note the Gothic Hôtel de Ville (Town Hall) and the neo-Gothic Maison du Roi (King's House), two of the most famous buildings in the square. During the summer, a free light-and-music show is shown at the square. *Métro: Gare Centrale.*

MTV **Best** **FREE** → **Manneken-Pis** ★★ Yep, Brussels is the home of the tinkling little boy fountain, a cheeky devil of a statue. It's touristy, sure, but you know you wanna snap a photo. You won't be looking at the real thing. Because the fountain dates perhaps as far back as the 8th century, it's been the subject of many a kidnapping. Don't get any of your own ideas: One criminal who stole and shattered the statue back in 1817 was sentenced to a lifetime of hard labor. *Corner of rue de l'Étuve and rue du Chêne. Métro: Gare Centrale.*

→**Mini-Europe** Here you'll find mini-renderings (the scale is 1:25) of European Union's most notable landmarks, including London's Big Ben, Berlin's Brandenburg Gate, the Leaning Tower of Pisa, the Bull Ring in Seville, and an erupting Mount Vesuvius. *Bruparck, Heysel. ☎ 02/478-05-50. www.minieurope.com. Admission 12€. Late Mar–June and Sept daily 9:30am–5pm; July–Aug daily 9:30am–7pm (mid-July to mid-Aug Fri–Sun 9:30am–11pm); Oct–Dec and 1st week Jan 10am–5pm. Métro: Heysel.*

Museums

→**Centre Belge de la Bande Déssinée (Center for Comic Strip Art)** ★ Belgians of all ages are absolutely nuts about Tintin, a comic book character dating back to 1929. Check him and other colorful creations out at this comic strip museum. You'll probably never get why Belgians are so into cartoons, but it's still fun to look around. *Rue des Sables 20. ☎ 02/219-19-80. Admission 6.25€ adults, 5€ students/seniors, 2.50€ children under 12. Tues–Sun 10am–6pm. Métro: Rogier or Botanique.*

→**Musée d'Art Ancien** ★★ If you can head to only one museum in Brussels, come here. The museum showcases works from the 15th to the 18th centuries, in the expansive Musées Royaux des Beaux-Arts complex, which also contains Musée d'Art Moderne (see below). The collection's gems are indisputably two of Brueghel's most famous works, the *Adoration of the Magi* and *Fall of the Rebel Angels,* and the museum also contains works by Rembrandt and Rubens. *Rue de la Régence 2. ☎ 02/508-32-11. Admission 5€; free on 1st Wed of the month. Tues–Sun 10am–5pm. Tram: 92–94.*

→**Musée d'Art Moderne** Housing Brussels's largest collection of modern art, this museum also boasts a great collection of

12 Hours in Brussels

1. **Park yourself at one of the chocolatiers around Grand-Place and go cuckoo for Cocoa Puffs.** What better excuse to rot your teeth than engaging in an indigenous cultural practice?

2. **Go on a walkabout.** Brussels is so charming and Old World that you could just puke. Wander around and do some exploring, but wear comfy shoes—cobblestones are rough on the feet.

3. **Get pissed.** Or watch a little kid do it. Yes, it's cheezy and touristy . . . but could you really come all this way and not check out Manneken-Pis, the world's most famous monument to incontinence?

4. **Okay, actually get pissed.** Brussels is a town that rewards the drinker . . . with another round! The beer here is tasty, plentiful, and damn cheap.

5. **Jump around.** Party like it's 2999 at Le Fuse, techno mecca of Europe. This place is wall-to-wall dancing, and the beats come fast and furious, so get ready to sweat out all that chocolate.

6. **Get your finger-lickin' on.** Dine in swank style at Comme Chez Soi, where the waitstaff is as yummy as the food.

surrealist works from hometown favorite Magritte and others. *Rue de la Régence 2.* ☎ *02/508-32-11. Admission 5€; free on 1st Wed of the month. Tues–Sun 10am–5pm. Tram: 92–94.*

→**Musée de la Ville Brussels** In the Grand-Place, inside the neo-Gothic Maison du Roi this collection displays art and artifacts especially dedicated to the history of Brussels. You can get a feel for the old days of Brussels by perusing the collection of maps and photos or the intricate tapestries that date from the 16th century. Also showcased are more than 650 costumes that have been sported by the Manneken-Pis statue on different national holidays. *Grand-Place 1.* ☎ *02/279-43-50. Admission 3€ adults, 2.50€ students. Tues–Fri 10am–5pm; Sat–Sun noon–5pm. Métro: Gare Centrale.*

The University Scene

Brussels has two main universities, the French **Université Libre de Bruxelles (Free University of Brussels)** in the far southeastern Vogelzang neighborhood, and the Flemish **Vrije Universiteit Brussel,** in the Elsene neighborhood south of the center city. You'll certainly stumble upon students if you wander through either of these campuses, but they're both far from the city center. If you want to ingratiate yourself with local students without making an extra trek, check out the huge Sunday morning flea market called the 🅼🆅 (Best) **Marché-aux-Puces** ★★ (place du Jeu de Balle; daily 7am–2pm). Young hipsters come here to amuse themselves by snooping through the deer antlers, old tubas, and broken-in bras on sale. Come early and claim a seat at one of the many surrounding cafes to take in the sound of accordion music and the scent of *escargots* wafting through the square.

Playing Outside

Cycling is a national sport for the Belgians, so bike paths are set up throughout the city and its surroundings. **Pro Vélo** (rue de Londres 15; ☎ **02/217-01-58;** www.provelo.org) rents bikes and gives guided tours. It's open Monday to Friday from 9am to 6pm. Road bikes will run you 2.50€ for an hour, 9.90€ for a day, and 50€ for a week.

Spin your wheels in the **Bois de la Cambre** (main entrance on av. Louise 1050; tram: 23, 90, 93, or 94), a lush green forest about a half-hour's pedal to the southeast of the city. The closer **Parc de Bruxelles** (between the Palais du Roi and rue de la Loi, 1 block east of Gare Centrale) is one of the few patches of green within city limits, good for emergency sunbathing or a quick jog around the mile-long perimeter.

The terrace in front of the **Palais des Congrès** (on rue Royal at rue de Congrès), near the Gare Centrale, draws the city's skate rats. Those little rebels love to show off under the nation's political hero, riding their rails along the base of King Albert I.

Brussels has a few indoor **pools,** but nothing as impressive as the ocean water park the **Océade** (Bruparck, bd. du Centenaire 20; ☎ **02/478-43-20;** Premetro 1a to Heysel; Apr–June Tues–Fri 10am–6pm and Sat–Sun 10am–9pm, July–Aug daily 10am–9pm, check website for off-season hours; 15€ for 4 hr.). The park attracts a family-centered crowd, but it could be worth an afternoon trip if the heat's wilting your spirits.

The **Maison du Football** (av. Houba de Strooper 145; ☎ **02/477-12-11**) can arrange tickets for international soccer matches if you phone Monday to Friday between 9am and 4:15pm. The local team is FC Anderlecht, which is always in contention for Belgian prizes and usually in the running for European honors as well. During continental tournaments some of the crack European soccer squads can often be seen in action in Brussels.

Shopping

Clothes

Brussels generally gets the short end of the stick when it comes to its reputation for shopping, especially when compared to nearby Paris, but for most of us, Brussels is no slouch when it comes to standard clothing stores. The hoity-toity **avenue Louise** area boasts shops from the likes of Gucci, Tod's, and Chanel with the odd midpriced store like Zara (av. Louise 8) tossed into the mix.

The **rue Neuve** area is home to the more wallet-friendly offerings of H&M (rue Neuve 36–38) and department store Galleria Inno (rue Neuve 112–123) The indoor shopping area **Galeries St-Hubert** (Métro: de Brouckère) dates from 1847 and carries the title of being Europe's first shopping center. It has shops by high-end Belgian designers Mer du Nord, *the* place where well-heeled young Bruxellois snap up cute T-shirts and pairs of 110€ designer jeans.

For personal recommendations from a really hip, really hot staff, duck into **Kozmic Music** record store (rue du Midi 36; ☎ 02/511-66-07). Browse through the hipster music scene weeklies, along with their serious collection of vinyl and CDs of all genres. Most of the staff members are in bands—chat them up and get the inside scoop on where to see shows during your stay.

Markets

Every neighborhood in Brussels is host to its own quirky market. Seriously—there's a bird market, a flower market, an antiques market, a flea market, and a horse market. If you only have a day or two of shopping in Brussels, I'd head to a market instead of taking in the too-posh avenue Louise scene. Check out the weekend antiques market at the **place du Grand-Sablon.** Here you can pick up high-quality antiques like silverware, pottery, paintings, and jewelry. The market is open Saturday 9am to 6pm and Sunday 9am to 2pm. Also, the **Grand-Place** has a daily flower market, and at the top end of **rue du Marché-aux-Herbes,** there's a weekend crafts market, with lots of jewelry and cheap knickknacks. For more refined art picks, head to the **Marché d'Art** at Parvis St-Pierre, Uccle. The market is open from May to September on Sundays only from 10am to 1pm. Here you'll find painters, sculptors, potters, and photographers selling their wares.

Place du Jeu de Balle is one of the city's best flea markets (see "University Scene" earlier in this chapter for info).

Sweet Stuff

Foodies usually agree that Belgian chocolatiers churn out the world's finest truffles. Some world-famous native Belgian brands are **Godiva** (Grand-Place 22), **Neuhaus** (bd. Waterloo 1), and **Leonidas** (bd. Anspach Laan 46).

Because you probably didn't come all the way to Brussels for chocolate you can get in your local mall, you might want to head to **Chocolatier Mary** (rue Royal 73) for a really exclusive Belgian chocolate experience. They supply pralines to the Belgian royal court, and are just as attentive to their day-to-day customers as they are to the royals.

Road Trip

Often called "the Venice of the North," **Bruges** is Belgium's most-visited town. During the summer, sunburned tourists of all ages tote their Nalgene bottles and fanny packs all the way from Brussels, Amsterdam, and beyond, to fawn over exquisitely preserved medieval buildings and to tour the two historic central squares, the Markt and the Burg. Unscathed by the wars that have gutted other European cities since the Middle Ages, Bruges' city center joined UNESCO's World Heritage List in 2000 and reinforced the town's reputation as a living, breathing museum of history.

A day trip here is better than nothing, but it's best to spend a couple of days to ease into the city's rhythms. And if you can stay longer, all the better. Bruges' romantic, tranquil, hospitable environment makes it a perfect pit stop on an adrenaline-charged Eurotrip.

Getting into Town

The closest big airport to Bruges is **Brussels National Airport,** about an hour away by train, the best means of mass transit to Bruges. Trains arrive into Bruges hourly from Brussels, Antwerp, Ghent, and Ostend. The journey is about 1 hour from Brussels and Antwerp, 30 minutes from Ghent, and 15 minutes from Ostend. From Paris, you can take the Thalys high-speed trains through Brussels direct to Bruges, or change to a cheaper and slower International train in Brussels. From Amsterdam, you can go through Antwerp or Brussels, either on the Thalys or on International trains.

Central Bruges is a compact area bordered by a moat and filled with mostly pedestrian-only streets—watch out for all those bicycles! In the heart of town are two side-by-side historic squares, the Markt and the Burg. The southern edge of Bruges' central area is a scenic, tranquil park that includes

Minnewater Park—home to the "Lake of Love," a famously romantic picnic area, and Begijnhof, a preserved town that was home to the Begijns, a group of 17th-century nun-like women. South of this area lies the train station. Many of Bruges' narrow cobblestone streets are navigable only on foot and by bicycle. Bruges has no public subway or tram system, and buses primarily run from the Markt to the Stationsplein. For information on bus service, operated by the **De Lijn** company, call **070/22-02-00.**

The tourist office, **Toerisme Brugge** (Burg 11; ☎ **050/44-86-86;** fax 050/44-86-00; www.brugge.be), is right in the center of town, in the Palace of the Liberty of Bruges. Here you can gather information on walking tours, bike rentals, out-of-town tours, and goings-on about town.

Sleeping

📺 Best → **Charlie Rocket's Youth Hostel** ★★ The most centrally located hostel in town, Charlie Rocket's is run by the same local family that owns the ultraposh Die Swaene. Although the accommodations are inexpensive, they're quite impressive by hostel standards. Pool tables, stacks of magazines, and a Tex-Mex bar/restaurant make the lobby a happening place in the early evening. *Hoogstraat 19.* ☎ *050/33-06-60. www.charlierockets.com. Some of the rooms have private bathrooms. 15€ single dorm bed, 42€ private double with bathroom. Amenities: Breakfast room/restaurant; laundry service; shared bathrooms (in some); sheets.*

📺 Best → **The Pand-Romantik Hotel** ★★★ Close to the Markt, this lovely 18th-century mansion surrounded by plane trees is an oasis of tranquillity. Although it provides modern conveniences, its exquisite, old-fashioned furnishings lend special grace to comfortable rooms. *Pandreitje 16.*

☎ 050/34-06-66. *www.pandhotel.com. 125€–170€ standard single or double, 155€–200€ superior single or double, 225€–325€ Ralph Lauren Jr. suites. Amenities: Internet. In room: A/C, TV, Internet (in lobby), Jacuzzi (in some), minibar.*

Eating

MTV **Best** ➔ **Arthies** ★★ BELGIAN/ASIAN FUSION   Different from Bruges' typical old-world restaurants, Arthie's has pictures of Che Guevara on the walls, black lights, and other touches that say Greenwich Village more than medieval village. But it's no mere gimmicky hipster lounge; Arthie's serves some of the best food in town. Arthie himself whips up classic Belgian dishes with fusion touches borrowing from Asian cuisine. His pots of mussels (served six different ways) are some of Bruges' most generous. Try them with freshly made fries, or go for whatever's on the daily lunch menu. If Arthie's around, he won't mind chatting about his visit to Cuba or his successful interior design business. *Wollestraat 3.* ☎ *050/33-43-13. www.arthies.com. Main courses 12€–20€. Wed–Mon 11:30am–3pm and 5–11pm.*

➔ **Brasserie Erasmus** ★ FLEMISH/BELGIAN   Word of mouth has done this little place right: On any afternoon you're bound to find lots of locals and tourists alike imbibing 1 (or more) of the 150 available beers. Make yourself at home with them, and try a seriously Belgian dish such as *lapin à la bière:* rabbit cooked with—take a wild guess—beer. *Wollestraat 35* ☎ *050/33-57-81. Main courses 13€–18€. Tues–Sun noon–4pm (summer also Mon) and 6–11pm.*

Partying

Let's face it: Bruges is no Rock 'n' Roll High School. When the sun goes down, so do most of the residents of Bruges. That said, there are more fun nightspots than may initially meet the eye—especially in the spring, summer, and fall, when tourism is at its peak.

Think about it: All those cute college-aged waiters and waitresses need somewhere to party after the day-trippers board their buses, and the shops close their doors. Backpackers and locals flock to the **Eiermarkt** area, filled with bars, just a block behind the Markt square. It can actually get pretty bumping after 11:30pm or midnight. Later in the evening (read: very early morning), the crowd moves farther outside the town center, to **'t Zand** square, near the western edge of Bruges. People can get noisier there without consequence, making it popular with the younger crowd.

Sightseeing

The real reason Bruges gets four million visitors per year is the sightseeing. It's one of Europe's most picture-perfect cities; it doesn't seem to have a bad angle. Make sure you bring your camera and a pair of comfortable shoes, because there's a lot worth seeing in this little town. Beyond the sites listed here, check out the four **windmills** that line the canal there at the northeastern edge of town, accessible by bike or on foot.

The Markt & the Burg

Bruges' two main squares, the **Markt** and the **Burg** ★★, sit next to each other in the center of town. The Markt is the old market square, the site of the 83m (270-ft.) Belfort (Belfry) tower, with a 47-bell carillon. In the center of the Markt are memorial statues of Jan Breydel and Pieter De Coninck, medieval Flemish war heroes. Here you'll find a handful of sidewalk cafes, and even the Belgian fast-food chain Quick Burger.

From the southeast corner of the Markt, you can turn onto Breidelstraat and follow it to the Burg, the smaller of the two squares and also the site of **Heilig Bloed Basiliek (Holy Blood Basilica).** Here you'll also find the **Landhuis van het Brugse Vrije (Palace of the Liberty of Bruges;** Burg 11; ☎ **050/44-87-11;** free admission to courtyard; Renaissance Hall 2.50€ adults, 1.50€ seniors and visitors 13–26; Tues–Sun 9:30am–5pm), a 16th-century government structure that now houses the city-council administration. (Don't miss the Liberty's council chamber, the best restored part of the building.) Next door is Belgium's oldest town hall, from the 13th century—**Stadhuis (State House;** Burg 12; ☎ 050/44-87-11; admission and hours are the same as the Palace of the Liberty of Bruges). Among all the Burg's old grandeur, you'll find a small modernist bridge by Japanese artist Toyo Ito, built in 2002.

 Best → **Onze-Lieve-Vrouwekerk** ★★ The ornate Onze-Lieve-Vrouwekerk (Church of Our Lady) gives a glimpse into Bruges's glory days, during the Renaissance, when it was one of the wealthiest towns in Europe. Constructed over the course of 2 centuries, from the 1200s to the 1400s, the church's 118m (387 ft.) spire can be seen for miles around. Inside, it would be impossible to miss Michelangelo's 1504 statue *Madonna and Child*. Just look for the throng of people trying to politely throw elbows for a good view of the only Michelangelo statue to leave Italy during his lifetime. *Onze-Lieve-Vrouwekerkhof Zuid.* ☎ *050/34-53-14. Free admission. Mon–Fri 9am–12:30pm and 1:30–5pm; Sat 9am–12:30pm and 1:30–4pm; Sun 1:30–5pm.*

BRUSSELS

Budapest

Budapest is a city in which it seems, at times, as if time has stood still. Walking through its broad boulevards lined with stoic statues, soaking in the waters at a traditional bath, or getting a caffeine fix at one of its classic coffee houses, you may feel as if you've been transported to an era long gone. At other times, the city feels ruthlessly progressive, eager to shed its bloody history of over 1,000 years of rule by the Habsburgs, Turks, and Russians in favor of partying the night away.

This fascinating contradiction between the old and the new makes Budapest one of the most beautiful and vibrant cities in the world. And there's no better time to visit than now: Hungary's successful push to join the European Union in 2004 has rejuvenated the city in a way not seen since the fall of communism in 1989. The city is currently experiencing a new Golden Age, with hotter than ever nightlife, and new restaurants and cultural attractions opening regularly. The most amazing part about all these new developments, though, is that the city has not lost any of its singular flavor. There's always time for a 3-hour espresso at a grand coffee house or for a tall cold one on a shady patio. My suggestion? Go now, before it changes.

The Best of Budapest

○ **The Best See-and-Be-Seen Restaurant:** On the Pest side of the city, docked three boats from the Chain Bridge, is the trendiest new restaurant in the city—**Spoon Cafe.** The food and the atmosphere are excellent, so it's worth coming here at least once even though the prices are high. See p. 206.

○ **The Best Local Disco:** If you're tired of dancing with English speakers and want to hit a club with cheap drinks, head through the maze of alleys to get to **Holdudvar,** the favorite club among the young local crowd, presumably because there are no tourists here. On Wednesdays, club employees hand out free coupons so that drinks are two for 1,000 Ft. See p. 208.

○ **The Best Free Booze:** While you're exploring the **Buda Castle Labyrinth,** an ancient cave system that spans 20,000 miles under Buda, do your best to find the wine room. It's the only room not on the map (which you get when you buy a ticket), so you'll have to search. You'll be rewarded with the sight of an ivy-covered fountain that spurts red wine. Bring an empty water bottle and fill it up for an intriguing souvenir. See p. 211.

○ **The Best Photo Op:** Get your camera at the ready and head to the immense, white structure that used to house the Fisherman's Guild, next to St. Matthias Church. Called the **Fisherman's Bastion,** it makes for an excellent photo op because of its sweeping, fairy-tale arches, and views of the Chain Bridge and Parliament. See 212.

Getting There & Getting Around

Getting into Town

BY AIR

All international flights fly into **Ferihegy International Airport;** for general information, call ☎ 1/296-7155. The airport is about 40 minutes outside the city center. The best way to get into town is via the **Airport Minibus.** Tickets for the minibus run 2,100 Ft one-way, 3,000 Ft round-trip, and can be purchased from the booth at the end of Terminal 2; call ☎ 1/296-8555 for info. After you buy a ticket, take a seat and the driver will call your hotel when he is ready to go. The shuttle service will take you right to the door of your hotel; factoring in stops along the way, the ride might take up to an hour.

Taxis are available at the front of the airport, but they charge way too much—between 4,000 Ft and 5,000 Ft. However, dozens of cabs from the cheaper fleets that we recommend (p. 198) are stationed at roadside pullouts just off the airport property, waiting for radio calls from their dispatchers. All it takes is a phone call from the terminal and a cab will be ready for you in a matter of minutes. For three or more people traveling together, it makes sense to take a dispatched taxi into the city; at approximately 4,500 Ft, it's substantially cheaper than the combined minibus fares. A taxi from the airport to downtown takes about 20 to 30 minutes.

For the true penny pincher, another option into town is the **bus/train combination.** Take the Red line bus no. 93 to the last stop, Kobanya-Kispet, and then pick up the Blue line Metro to the city center. The total cost is a mere 500 Ft, but the entire route from the airport into town will set you back about an hour and 10 minutes on a good day.

BY TRAIN

Budapest has three major train stations: Keleti pályaudvar (Eastern Station), Nyugati pályaudvar (Western Station), and Déli pályaudvar (Southern Station). The stations' names, curiously, correspond neither to their geographical location in the city nor to the origins or destinations of trains serving them. Each has a Metro station beneath it and an array of accommodations offices, currency-exchange booths, and other services.

If you are backpacking through Europe and are headed to Budapest by Eurail, you'll arrive into the **Keleti Station** (☎ 1/314-5010) in the center of Pest. The hostels in this area send representatives to the station to solicit you for reservations and to provide rides if you have already made reservations. The Metro's Red line is below the station; numerous bus, tram, and trolleybus lines serve the station as well.

Some international trains arrive at **Nyugati Station** (☎ 1/349-0115). It's located on the

BUDAPEST

Outer Ring, at the border of the V, VI, and XIII districts. A metro station for the Blue line is beneath Nyugati, and numerous tram and bus lines serve the busy station (formerly called Marx tér). A few international trains also arrive at **Déli Station** (☎ 1/375-6293), an ugly modern building in central Buda; the terminus of the Red Metro line is beneath this train station.

MÁV operates a **minibus** that will take you from any of the three stations to the airport for 2,100 Ft per person, or between stations for 1,200 Ft per person. To order the minibus, call ☎ 1/353-2722. Often, however, a taxi fare will be cheaper, especially for groups of two or more travelers. See "Getting Around," below, for taxi info.

Getting Around

BY FOOT

The best way to see the city is with a good pair of walking shoes and a map. Most city maps are free and can be found at all tourist offices (p. 199) as well as in hotels and hostels. The city tends to be clustered around the Danube and even if you have an awful sense of direction you can stay on course if you just follow the river.

BY BIKE

Plan to bike around Budapest only if you want to endanger your life. The city is decidedly not bike friendly. Sidewalks are open to bikers, though, which seems like a safer alternative to the streets. **Margaret Island** (p. 217) is a very popular place for biking—there are no cars and the shady lanes make for a soothing ride. Bike rental is available at the **Corinthia Grand Royal Hotel** (☎ 1/436-4100) for 3,000 Ft for the entire day.

BY BUS

There are about 200 different bus *(busz)* lines in greater Budapest. Many parts of the city, most notably the Buda Hills, are best reached by bus. Although the bus system here is complicated, with patience (and a BKV map), you'll be able to get around in no time.

Népliget Station is the city's modern main bus terminal on the Red Metro line at the **Népstadion stop.** The Blue line goes to the much smaller **Árpád híd bus station** that caters to domestic bus service only. For bus info call (☎ 1/219-8080).

BY TRAM OR METRO

Budapest's 34 bright-yellow **tram lines** (known as *villamos* in Hungarian) are useful, particularly **nos. 4** and **6,** which travel along the Outer Ring (Nagykörút), and **nos. 47** and **49,** which run along the Inner Ring. Tram no. 2, which travels along the Danube on the Pest side between Margit híd and Boráros tér, provides an incredible view of the Buda Hills, including the Castle District, and is far better than any sightseeing tour on a bus.

Talk of the Town

Three ways to start a conversation with a local

1. **How much do you love the 40% or more personal income tax?** Far from a boring question, this is guaranteed to get any Magyar (aka Hungarian) really going. It will also open your eyes to a few facts of life here.

2. **Do you have a favorite night at Holdudvar?** Once you've determined what the most popular night is at this popular club (p. 208), go check it out.

3. *Unicum or palinka?* Find out which local drink the actual locals prefer. Sampling is allowed for research purposes, of course.

My Metro Is Older than Yours

Budapest's three Metro lines are universally known by color—Yellow, Red, and Blue. Officially, they have numbers as well (1, 2, and 3, respectively), but all Hungarians refer to them by color, and all signs are color coded. All three lines converge at **Deák tér**, the only point where any lines meet.

The **Yellow (1) line** is the oldest Metro on the European continent. Built in 1894 as part of the Hungarian millennial celebration, it has been refurbished and restored to its original splendor. Signs for the Yellow line, lacking the distinctive colored M, are harder to spot than signs for the Blue and Red lines. Look for signs reading *földalatti* (underground). Each station has two separate entrances, one for each direction. The Yellow line runs from Vörösmarty tér, the site of Gerbeaud's Cukrászda in the heart of central Pest, along the length of Andrássy út, past the Városliget (City Park), and ends at Mexikói út, in a trendy residential part of Pest known as Zugló. So, depending on the direction you're heading, enter either the side marked IRANY MEXIKOI UT or IRANY VOROSMARTY TER. Incidentally, somewhere in the middle of the line is a stop called Vörösmarty utca; this is a small street running off Andrássy út and should not be confused with the terminus, Vörösmarty tér. It's worth taking a ride on this line, if only to soak in its distinct 19th-century atmosphere.

The **Red (2)** and **Blue (3) lines** are modern Metros and to reach them you must descend on long, steep escalators. The Red line runs from Örs vezér tere in eastern Pest, through the center, and across the Danube to Batthyány tér, Moszkva tér, and finally Déli Station. Keleti Station is also along the Red line. The Blue line runs from Kőbánya-Kispest, in southeastern Pest, through the center, and out to Újpest-Központ in northern Pest. Nyugati Station is along the Blue line.

All public transport tickets cost 185 Ft for a single, one-way ride. Although many locals don't get tickets because ticket-taker sightings are rare, riding sans ticket is *not* recommended. Should you be approached by a ticket checker (you'll recognize them by the red bands around their upper left arms), they'll hit you with a hefty 10,000 Ft fine.

We recommend that you purchase a day pass or multiday pass; they're still rather inexpensive and only need to be validated once, saving you the hassle of having to validate a ticket every time you board the Metro. Day passes (napijegy) cost 1,150 Ft and are valid until midnight of the day of purchase. Buy them from Metro ticket windows; the clerk validates the pass at the time of purchase. A 3-day pass (turistajegy) costs 2,500 Ft and a 7-day pass (hetijegy) costs

3,400 Ft; these have the same validation procedure as the 1-day pass.

Single tickets can be bought at Metro ticket windows, newspaper kiosks, and the occasional tobacco shop. There are also automated machines in most Metro stations and major transport hubs.

The **Budapest Card,** a tourist card that we do not particularly recommend (it does not pack any value), combines a 3-day turistajegy (transportation pass) with free entry to certain museums and other discounts.

Most of the Budapest transportation system closes down between 11:30pm or midnight and 5am. There are, however, 17 night routes (13 bus and 4 tram), and they're generally quite safe. A map of night routes is posted at many central tram and bus stops, and a full listing appears on the BKV

BUDAPEST

transportation map. Visit www.urbanrail.
net/eu/bud/budapest.htm for info.

BY TROLLEYBUS

Budapest's red trolleybuses are electric
buses that receive power from a cable above
the street. There are only 14 trolleybus lines
in Budapest, all in Pest. Of particular interest
to train travelers is no. 73, the fastest route
between Keleti Station and Nyugati Station.
See "By Tram or Metro" earlier for info on
fares and hours.

BY CAR

I don't recommend driving through Budapest's
chaotic and unfamiliar traffic. If you have your
heart set on renting a car and driving
around, rent either at the airport or through
Fox Auto Rental (☎ 1/382-9000), which
will deliver your rental car to wherever you
may be after you pay a relatively inexpensive fee. On almost every city block you can
find somewhere to rent a car, from big name
agencies to ones operating out of the back of
a hair salon.

BY TAXI

Because taxi regulations permit fleets (or
private drivers) to establish their own rates,
fares vary greatly between the different fleets
and among the private unaffiliated drivers.

The best rates are invariably those of the
larger fleet companies. I recommend **Fő
Taxi** (☎ 1/222-2222). Other reliable fleets
include **Volántaxi** (☎ 1/466-6666), **City
Taxi** (☎ 1/211-1111), **Tele5** (☎ 1/355-
5555), and **6x6** (☎ 1/266-6666). You can
call one of these companies from your hotel
or from a restaurant—or ask whoever is in
charge to call for you—even if there are
other private taxis waiting around outside.
You will seldom, if ever, wait more than 5
minutes for a fleet taxi in any but the most
remote of neighborhoods.

Beware that you may have a dishonest
driver if you're asked to pay for his or her
return trip, asked to pay with anything but
forints, or quoted a "flat rate" in lieu of running the meter.

Budapest Basics

Orientation: Budapest Neighborhoods

The city is divided into two sections, inter-
sected by the river Danube and linked by the
Chain Bridge. **Pest** is the larger of the two: It
contains most of the city's hostels, restaurants, and nightclubs. **Buda** is smaller and
older—it sits on top of the hill and holds a
good deal of the museums in its walled grasp.

PEST

LIPOTVAROS (LEOPOLD TOWN) Home
to much nightlife, this part of town stretches
from Margit Bridge to the outskirts of
the Inner City. Here you'll also find the
Parliament Building, a few museums, government buildings, antiques shopping street
Falk Miksa út, and extraordinary views
over the Danube.

BELVAROS (INNER CITY) You'll likely
spend a good deal of time here because this
is still considered the heart of Budapest,
with the city's best shopping, dining, and
partying found within the neighborhood limits. Most hotels and hostels in the area are a
stone's throw from the Danube, which borders the Inner City to the west.

TEREZVAROS (THERESA TOWN) You'll
find the city's main artery here, the
Andrássy út, the tree-lined boulevard with
some of the best shopping and sightseeing in
the city. The neighborhood begins at Heroes
Square, continues through Oktogon, and
ends at the **inner city.**

ERZSEBETVAROS (ELIZABETH TOWN) En-
compassing the town's formerly large Jewish
community and the much smaller current

one, Erzsébetváros is also where Nazi forces housed Jews in a ghetto between 1944 and 1945. One of the main attractions in this neighborhood is the graceful **Dohány Synagogue and Jewish Museum.**

JOZSEFVAROS (JOSEPH TOWN) Because most of Budapest is beautiful and charming, you might begin to wonder where all of the dodgy inhabitants have gone. You'll find them in Józsefváros: This area is rife with prostitutes, drug dealers, and other crooked sorts. If for any reason you find yourself here, be careful, especially at night.

MARGARET ISLAND

The long, thin island that lays dead-center of the Danube just up the river from the Chain Bridge is known as Margeret Island. It's non-residential but home to two hotels, a lovely park, a bath complex, and the best **langos** (p. 207) in town.

BUDA

VARNEGYED (CASTLE DISTRICT) The oldest and loveliest section of the city (dating from the 13th c.) is also the most expensive. It contains a variety of museums, including the **Royal Palace, Buda Castle Tunnels, St. Matthias Church,** and **Fisherman's Bastion.** Avoid staying in this area if you're traveling on a budget or looking for nightlife; the hotels are overpriced and the neighborhood locks up at night.

VIZIVAROS (WATERTOWN) A long, narrow neighborhood wedged between the Castle District and the Danube, Vízíváros is the stamping ground for the city's literati, whom you'll spot hobnobbing at the local cafes.

BUDA HILLS The Buda Hills are numerous remote 'hoods that feel as if they're nowhere near, let alone within, the capital city. Neighborhoods here are generally known by the name of the hill on which they stand.

Tourist Offices

There are seven tourist offices scattered across the city but the three that follow are the most conveniently located. Call ☎ 1/317-9800 or visit www.hungarytourism. hu for more info.

○ Near **Oktogon,** VI. Liszt Ferenc Sq. 9–11: The most centrally located of the offices, located just at the head of Andrássy út.

○ **Buda Varinfo** in the Buda Castle, I. Szentharomsag tér: The only office on the Buda side of the city, conveniently right inside the not-to-miss site that is Buda Castle.

○ **Ferihegy Airport, Terminal 2A, Arrivals:** When you arrive in Budapest, head to this booth and pick up a map; on the 40-minute ride into town, you can start getting acclimated to the city. The staff here is also great at suggesting ways to budget your time during your stay.

Recommended Websites

○ **www.budapestinfo.hu**: The information website of the Tourism Office of Budapest. You'll find a good deal of what you need to know here—where to go, what to see, and where to eat—although they tend to be a little biased.

○ **www.ohb.hu**: Includes maps, contact info for hotels and hostels, and basic facts about the region.

○ **www.backpackers.hu**: Great for making hostel reservations online.

○ **www.budapestsun.com**: Budapest's leading English-language newspaper's website, with info on upcoming events and general news.

Culture Tips 101

Though Budapest is inching toward complete Westernization, it's not quite there yet. An older sense of cultural mores still prevails, and tourists are expected to take heed. Here

BUDAPEST

are some basic rules to follow to avoid getting stuck in awkward situations. **Club wear is nice—in the club.** At restaurants, appropriate tire is important—some restaurants won't even let you in if you do not meet their dress code. **Respect the elderly.** Old people will frequently cut you off in line at the supermarket, or at stores. Just take it in stride.

The Magyar (aka Hungarian), who may have Asian, Roman, Slavic, and/or Ottoman roots, is pretty hard to categorize. The average Budapester you'll likely connect with is working full-time, saving for a rickety apartment in the center, a fanatic nationalist who nevertheless gripes about everything Hungarian (but don't you try it!), a party animal of epic proportions, extremely well read, and just as well turned out. They are also usually more than willing to speak English.

The legal minimum drinking age here might as well be 15 (IDs are never checked) and people smoke everywhere except inside the Metro. All recreational drugs are illegal here, but people still do manage it. Excerise caution wherever you are, but in a District VII club, a lot more discretion should be exercised. Periodic raids have been known to happen in clubs and the penalties are strict, with no presumption of innocence.

Recommended Books, Movies & Music

BOOKS

Be sure to read *A History of Hungary*, by Laszlo Kontler, to get briefed on the country's complicated history. *The Habsburg Monarchy from 1809–1918* by A. J. P Taylor is an interesting profile on the Habsburg monarchs. I also enjoyed Michael Farquhar's *A Treasury of Royal Scandals;* although it's not devoted to Hungary, a good part of the book deals with the Habsburg dynasty and reads like a trashy magazine. Lastly, check out *Prague,* by Arthur Phillips, a novel about life as an expat in Budapest right after 1989.

MOVIES

If you want a sneak peak of the Budapest subway system before your trip, definitely rent *Kontroll* (2003), a thriller about Metro ticket inspectors. *I Love Budapest* (2001) is the East's answer to *Flashdance;* it's just campy enough to make it worth renting.

MUSIC

If you're in a classical music mood, you should definitely give anything by Béla Bartók and Zoltán Kodály, two of Hungary's most famous composers, a listen. Few rock bands have made it outside of Hungary, though the '70s band Omega has had modest success in Europe. Their 1969 hit song "Gyöngyhajú lány" was later covered by the Scorpions (renamed "White Dove"), so that gives you some idea of their influence.

The international DJ conspiracy is slowly assassinating live music here, but a few patches of ground are still holding out. Jazz, soul, folk, world music, and indie rock are all seemingly safe, at least for now, while much of the pop rock (both Hungarian and international) that tours here might actually benefit from being replaced by electronic beats. In any case, they say Hungarians are born with fiddles under their chins (and this must be the world capital of Gypsy bands in restaurants): There's always a jam in progress here somewhere.

Budapest Nuts & Bolts

Cellphone Providers & Service Centers   SIM cards can be purchased at the **T-Mobile** store (☎ 1/265-9210) on Vörösmarty tér across the plaza from Gerbeaud.

Currency   You can take out cash via ATM or exchange cash at the **Citibank** office next to the Herend store on Vörösmarty tér.

Embassies   The embassy of **Australia** is at XII. Királyhágó tér 8–9 (☎ 1/457-9777); the embassy of **Canada** is at XII. Budakeszi út 32 (☎ 1/392-3360); the embassy of the **Republic of Ireland** is at V. Szabadság tér 7 (☎ 1/302-9600); the embassy of the **United Kingdom** is at V. Harmincad u. 6 (☎ 1/266-2888); and the embassy of the **United States** is at V. Szabadság tér 12 (☎ 1/475-4400). New Zealand does not have an embassy in Budapest, but the U.K. embassy can handle matters for New Zealand citizens.

Emergencies   There are four main emergency numbers to enter into your phone: police ☎ 107; ambulance ☎ 104; fire ☎ 106; and emergency ☎ 112.

Internet/Wireless Hot Spots   Budapest is, in general, wired for the digital age, and most Internet places won't charge you more than 1,000 Ft for a half-hour. **Café/Bar Wins** (1061 Jokai tér) has free Wi-Fi for customers and is open every day from 9am to midnight.

Another option is **Internet Café** (V. Kecskeméti u. 5; ☎ 1/328-0292), near Kálvin tér (Blue line), which is open daily from 10am to 10pm. This drab space has about 20 terminals in a basement room, and the cost is 900 Ft for an hour, with pricing by 30-minute intervals (except 10 min. or less, which costs 150 Ft).

Laundry   The best place to do laundry is in your hotel or hostel because self-service laundromats are scarce. The **Mister Minit** chain, a locksmith and shoe repair service located in all large shopping centers throughout the inner city area, offers laundry service. For 1-hour dry cleaning, try **Ruhatisztító Top Clean,** at the Nyugati Skála Metro department store (across the street from Nyugati train station; no phone); they are open Monday through Friday from 7am to 7pm, and Saturday from 9am to 2pm.

Luggage Storage   If you are headed somewhere by train for a few days and don't want to bring all your belongings, you can store your luggage at the **Keleti railroad station** (☎ 1/314-5010) for 250 Ft for as long as you like (you need exact change). Your bags will be surprisingly safe, and while the lockers can only be opened once, you can leave your stuff in there as long as you need to.

Post Offices   Most post offices are open Monday to Friday from 8am to 6pm. The main post office (near Keleti Train Station at VI. Terz krt. 51; ☎ 1/312-1480) is open Monday to Saturday from 7am to 9pm.

Restrooms   The word for toilet in Hungarian is *WC* (pronounced "*vay*-tsay"). *Női* means "women's;" *férfi* means "men's." For free and generally clean, well-stocked toilets, try any of Budapest's ubiquitous McDonald's or Burger King locations, except for the Burger King at Astoria.

Safety   All in all, Budapest is a very safe city. However, you still need to be aware of pickpockets, the biggest problem. Watch out for them in crowded shopping areas and on public transport. They will rarely resort to force, so just keep your valuables close to you at all times and keep your eyes open. In taxis and restaurants, make sure you know what final bill to expect—otherwise, the employees may tack on extra charges. Taxi drivers also may use the night charge during the day, so check the meter. If you are on public transportation, make sure you have validated your ticket so that the ticket controllers cannot bully you into giving them money.

Tipping   Tipping is expected for waiters, hairdressers, masseuses, hotel employees, taxi drivers, and the like. Pay what you want, but the norm is between 10% and 15%.

BUDAPEST

Sleeping

Location plays a significant role in the cost of a room here—you'll pay much more for something centrally located. Buda may have the castle but it also has the misfortune of being a walled city, which means it locks up at night. With that in mind, I recommend staying in Pest, where you'll find better nightlife and restaurants.

Accommodations agencies can help you narrow down your choices even further. The main **Ibusz reservations office** is at Ferenciek tér 10 (☎ 1/485-2700; www. ibusz.hu), accessible by the Blue Metro line. This office is open year-round Monday through Friday 8:15am to 5pm. All major credit and charge cards are accepted. **Cooptourist** (Nyugati Station; ☎ 1/458-6200) is open 9am to 4:30pm Monday through Friday and does not accept credit cards. **Budapest Tourist** (Nyugati Station; ☎ 1/318-6552) is open 9am to 5pm Monday through Friday and 9am to noon Saturday. The agency does not accept credit cards. **MÁV Tours** (Keleti Station; ☎ 1/382-9011) is open 9am to 5pm Monday through Friday and does not accept credit cards.

Hostels

→ **Caterina Guesthouse and Hostel** Some of the cheapest beds in the city are also conveniently located, and this is one of them. Caterina's place on Andrássy, next to the Oktogon Metro stop, is invaluable if you plan to get out and see the city. It's always bustling with hordes of backpackers and budget travelers, so book your room before showing up. Once inside, you'll appreciate the full-service kitchen and copious hot water available for showers at night. *VI. Andrássy út, 47, 3rd floor, bell 10. ☎ 1/466-5794. 3,500 Ft single; 5,000 Ft double. Metro: Oktogon (Yellow line). Amenities: Bar; kitchen; Internet; lockout 10am–2pm; shared bathrooms.*

→ **Marco Polo Hostel** ★★ The Marco Polo can attract an older crowd, but the decor is definitely "hostel." Given the primo location in the center of town, the large rooms, and the reasonable prices, though, I can deal with the sparse decor. In addition to squeaky-clean rooms, the hostel also has a restaurant, bar, and nightclub—though the latter seems to be popular only with the older guests looking to relive their youth. *VII. Nyar utca 6. ☎ 413/25/55. www.hotelmarco polo.com 5,000 Ft dorm bed; 13,750 Ft single. Ask about discounts. No credit cards. Metro: Blaha Lujza tér (Red line). Amenities: Restaurant; bar; shared bathrooms; swimming pool and recreation center; nightclub. In room: TV, safe.*

<u>MTV</u> **Best** → **Mellow Mood Central Hostel** ★★ Centrally located, cheap, clean, and spacious, this home base of the Mellow Mood Hostel Group (they own many hostels and discount hotels in town) gives backpackers the most bang for their buck. Ceilings are high, everyone gets a secure locker and the beds are sturdy. Although it costs about the same as other hostels in the city, you get a variety of special services here, including 24-hour reception and bar, a coin-operated washer/dryer, and coin-operated Internet corner. It's a great place to meet people. *Becsi út 2, H-1052. ☎ 1/413-2062. www. mellowmoodhostel.com. 3,200 Ft–5,000 Ft dorm bed; 5,700 Ft–7,900 Ft private double. Metro: Deák Ferenc tér. Amenities: Bar; Internet; laundry facilities; shared bathrooms; safe.*

→ **Yellow Submarine Youth Hostel** ★ One of Budapest's most popular hostels, Yellow Submarine is one of the few hostels in this (or most other) cities that includes breakfast with the price of the bed. The backpacking crowd jumped right on that freebie, and now this place has become one of the city's definite "party hostels." Rooms are clean, and laundry facilities, a kitchen, Internet access, and round-the-clock beer and soda selections are available. Although the hostel is full of young people, lots of them are visitors—most people who stay here are more into leaving the hostel than spending their time mingling. *Terez korut 56, district VI.* ☎ *1/331-9896. www.yellow submarinehostel.com. 3,500 Ft single, 5,000 Ft double. Rates include breakfast. Metro: Nyugati pu (Blue line). Amenities: Breakfast room; Internet; kitchen; laundry; sheets; shared bathrooms (in some); towels; stocked beverages; TV (in common room).*

Cheap

➜ **Hotel Baross** An imposing gray mansion that would look completely out of place in any city but Budapest, the Baross Hotel is a relatively good buy. The rooms are quite spacious for the price and the hotel's attempt at elegance—the stone mansion features a courtyard in the center and an old-school elevator—almost works. If you're traveling through Europe and just have the night to spend, you may want to stay here because the train station is across the street. *Baross tér 15, 1077.* ☎ *1/461-3010. www.budapestpensions.hu. Low season: 16,700 Ft single, 20,000 Ft double. High season: 22,500 Ft single, 26,000 Ft double. Metro: Keleti pu (Red line). Amenities: Breakfast room; elevator; Internet; laundry; room service; wheelchair friendly. In room: A/C, cable TV, minibar, safe.*

Doable

➜ **Danubius Grand Hotel Margit-sziget** Located about 100m (328 ft.) away from the Thermal Hotel, the Grand Hotel is a good deal more dour than the bright, airy Thermal, but thankfully it's linked to that hotel's spa facilities. The oldest hotel in Budapest, at over 150 years, the Grand Hotel is chock-full of works by famous Hungarian artists and architects. I'm not sure that excuses its musty atmosphere, though. *XIII, Margit-sziget 1138.* ☎ *1/889-4752. www.danubiushotels.com/grandhotel. 120€–165€ single, 138€–208€ double. 20% discount in low season. Rates include breakfast. Amenities: Restaurant/bar; gift shop; laundry and dry cleaning services; fitness center and spa (at adjacent Thermal Hotel); room service; wheelchair friendly. In room: A/C, TV, minibar, safe.*

➜ **Danubius Health Spa Resort Margit-sziget** ★★ A government-rated four-star hotel on charming Margaret Island in the middle of the Danube, the Thermal Hotel comes complete with free visits (for guests) to thermal pools. The hotel is a wellness spa, and the airy and warm yellow, brown, and white painted rooms create a vibe of spiritual as well as physical wellness. *XIII, Margit-sziget, 1138.* ☎ *1/889-4700. www.danubiushotels.com/thermalhotel. 138€ single, 208€ double. Rates include breakfast. Amenities: Restaurant/bar; gift shop; laundry and dry cleaning services; fitness center and spa; Internet; room service; wheelchair friendly. In room: A/C, TV, minibar, safe.*

Splurge

➜ **Corinthia Grand Hotel Royal** ★★ This creamy yellow building on Erszébet was remodeled at the end of 2002, resulting in a delightful baroque-style jewel. If you can stop gawking at the ornate lobby, make your way to one of the enormous rooms, which feature eye-catching light fixtures and marble bathrooms with a separate tub and shower. The hotel offers a massive breakfast spread (not included in the rates) and a luxurious spa with a pool. *Erszébet körút 43–49, H-1073.* ☎ *1/479-4000. www.corinthiahotels.com. 186€ double, 381€ junior suite. Metro: Oktogon (Yellow line). Amenities: 3 restaurants; bar; concierge; health club; lounge; massage; pool; sauna; shopping arcade; steam room; spa. In room: A/C, TV, hair dryer, iron.*

BUDAPEST

Budapest

SLEEPING ■
Caterina Hostel **39**
Corinthia Grande Hotel
  Royale **29**
Danubius Grand Hotel
  Margitziget **1**
Danubius Thermal Hotel
  Margitziget **2**
Four Seasons
  Gresham Palace **12**
Hotel Baross **27**
Marco Polo Youth Hostel **25**
Mellow Mood
  Youth Hostel **24**
Yellow Submarine
  Youth Hostel **36**

EATING ◆
Amstel River Café **23**
Csesmge Bakery **41**
Dunacorso **15**
Gerbeaud House **13**
Gundel Restaurant **45**
Gyros **48**
Múvész Kávéház **31**
Spoon **14**
Szent Jupat **4**
Wins Bar/Cafe **38**

PARTYING ★
A-38 Concert Ship **18**
Action Bar **21**
Angel **28**
Beckett's Irish Bar **35**
Birdland Restaurant
  and Bar **30**
Café del Rio **17**
Coxx Club **26**
Eklektika Cafe **37**
Holdudvar **22**
Morrison's Music Pub **32**
Mystery Bar **34**

SIGHTSEEING ●
Buda Castle Labyrinth **9**
Buda Palace **10**
Chain Bridge **11**
Fisherman's Bastion **7**
Gellért Bathhouse **16**
Heroes' Square/
  Millenium Monument **43**
House of Terror **40**
Hungarian National
  Museum **20**
Király Bathhouse **3**
Múcsarnok Museum
  (Museum of Modern Art) **42**

Museum of Ethnography **5**
Museum of Fine Arts **44**
Parliament **6**
St. Matthias Church
  (Church of Our Lady) **8**
St. Stephen's Basilica **33**
Statue Park **19**
Széchenyi Baths &
  Thermal Pools **49**
Vidámpark **47**
Zoo **46**

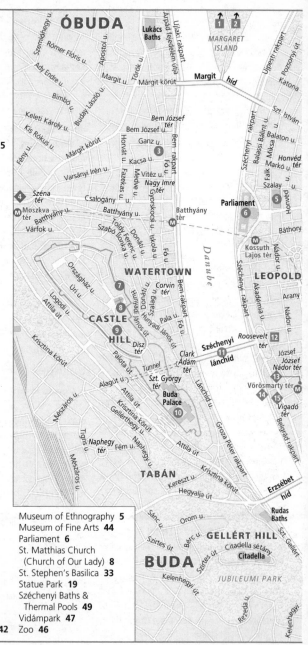

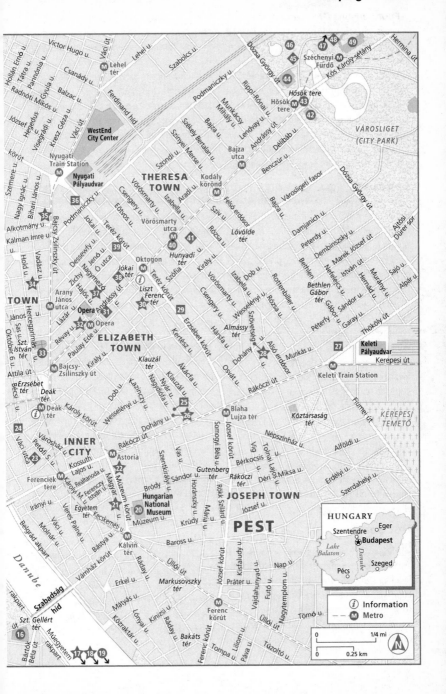

→**Four Seasons Gresham Palace** ★★★
I guess they could have had a fire-red Lamborghini pickup and drop-off service. That's the only thing missing from this palatial, glamorous hotel in the center of Budapest. Mirroring the opulence of the Royal Palace, located on the other side of the Lion's Bridge, the Four Seasons really has everything and it boasts the guest list to prove it. The Gresham hosts monarchs from around the world, movie stars, and rock stars. Rooms are immense. If you have 1 night to splurge, do it here, and if you don't, at least try to stop in and take in the 19th-century building. *Roosevelt tér 5–6, H-1051.* ☎ *1/268-6000. www. greshampalace.com. From 300€ single. Metro: Vörösmarty tér (Yellow line). Amenities: Restaurant; cafe; bar; gym; health club; indoor pool; Internet; laundry and dry cleaning service; nonsmoking floors; room service; sauna; shops; spa; steam room; travel services. In room: A/C, cable TV, dataport, minibar, safe.*

Eating

Hungary is not a land for the weak—if you doubt that, look at the name: *Hun*-gary points to how big a role the Huns, who ravaged Europe a millennium ago, played in this country's heritage. Cold, dark winters led the Hungarians to make food that's everything Western doctors warn against: high calorie, high carb, and high fat. A heavy use of shortening, cream, paprika, and especially onions dominates most meals.

Dishes here change drastically from summer to winter. During the warm summers, you can expect cold, creamy, sweet fruit soups—the most traditional is sour cherry soup—and the favorite of Emperor Joseph II, *wienerschnitzel,* which is veal lightly fried in spiced batter. In the winter, menus instead tend to feature thick *goulash*—a traditional stew that is a meal in itself. In all seasons, you will find chicken *paprikas*—a delicious chicken-and-dumplings dish.

Hot Spots

MTV **Best** →**Spoon Cafe** ★★★ ASIAN
To experience Budapest's trendiest dining, head straight to Spoon. This posh restaurant-cum-boat offers an Asian-fusion menu filled with sushi and other Asian-inspired dishes. You'll pay more here than at other restaurants, but the food quality, on-the-river atmosphere, and service make it worth the splurge. The entire staff speaks English, so ask for recommendations—they're more than willing to advise. *Docked, at the Chain Bridge.* ☎ *1/411-0933. www.spooncafe.com. Main course, soup, and wine 7,000 Ft. Noon–2am daily. Metro: Vörösmarty tér (Yellow line).*

Cheap

→**Csemege Bakery** CAFE If a Hungarian grandmother's baking is what you crave, look no further than the Csemege. This tiny bakery holds no more than four people at any one time. It serves up such scrumptious delights, though, that you won't mind being cramped. Try the Turos Tarka, a croissant-like creation stuffed with sweet cheese, and the Finom Pesti Azelet, a decadent cake layered with sweetened chocolate and topped with crunchy white sugar. *94 Izabella út. No phone. Daily 5am–8pm. Metro: Lehel (Red line).*

→**Gyros** GYROS This tiny stall in the upper level of the Déli railway station lacks a name but makes up for it with its cheap, tasty gyros. A word to the wise: When the server asks if you want spicy sauce, take heed—the sauce is *flaming. Déli Station.* ☎ *1/375-6293. Metro: Déli palyaudvar (Red line).*

BUDAPEST

Doable

→ **Amstel River Café** CONTINENTAL/ DUTCH   A delightful little spot with reasonably priced food, the Amstel River Café sports a decidedly old-world, tavern-like atmosphere (think dark-wood paneling). It's the only cafe on the street, so you can't miss the chattering folks clustered around the outdoor tables when you walk down Parizsi út. The house wines are wonderful, particularly the Konyari Chardonnay, and the Continental-infused fare includes everything from chicken *paprikas* to plain old hamburgers. *V Parizsi u. 6.* ☎ *1/266-4334. Main courses 400 Ft–2,000 Ft; wine starts at 300 Ft. Daily 11am–midnight. Metro: Ferenciek tere (Blue line).*

→ **Gerbeaud House** ★★ CAFE/HUNGARIAN   All your food desires will be sated in the mind-blowing Gerbeaud. Opened in 1870 as a *patisserie* under the name Kugler, today Gerbeaud houses a brewery and a restaurant in renovated rooms. If you want sweet, go to the confectionary and sample their famous candies. If you want savory, head to the Lion Fountain Restaurant for authentic Hungarian cuisine, such as the *paprikas csirke tohasos galuskaval* (chicken stew with egg dumplings). *V. Vörösmarty tér 7.* ☎ *1/429-9000. www. gerbeaud.hu. Lunch main courses 1,900 Ft; dinner main courses 2,900 Ft. Daily 9am–9pm. Metro: Deák tér (all lines).*

→ **Szent Jupat** ★ HUNGARIAN   Got the late-night munchies something fierce? Head over to Szent Jupat for relief. Massive, inexpensive portions await diners at this restaurant catering to a young, tipsy, and/or foreign crowd. When you go, go hungry; portions include mountainous piles of excellent Hungarian cooking: Thick goulash, piping hot country bread, and baked chicken take the cake (which is also excellent) at this locale. *Retek út 16, district II.* ☎ *1/212-2923. Main courses 1,600 Ft. Daily 24 hr. Metro: Moszkva tér (Red line).*

Splurge

→ **Dunacorso** ★ HUNGARIAN   If you have some extra cash to spare, head to Dunacorso. Overlooking the water, this restaurant serves Hungarian delicacies. You can order the Hungarian country bread, a meal on its own: Thick, hearty, and filling, it's a perfect complement to a shot of Unicum (a liquor found only in Hungary that supposedly has medicinal and digestive benefits) or a hot cup of coffee. *3 Vigado Sq, district V.* ☎ *1/318-6362. www.dunacorso.hu. Prix fixe 16,000 Ft. Apr–Oct daily 10am–midnight, Nov–Mar daily noon–midnight. Metro: Vörösmarty tér (Yellow line).*

→ **Gundel Restaurant** ★ HUNGARIAN FUSION   Although the food remains as good as locals have proclaimed it to be for around a century, the service at Gundel has started to suffer. When I visited, the waiters were stuck up, slow, and sullen. My advice is to come here with friends so that you can laugh off the attitude and still enjoy a great meal. Penny pinchers, take note: Gundel is the city's most expensive restaurant. *XIV. Allatkerti út 2.* ☎ *1/468-4040. www.gundel.hu. Reservations highly recommended. Main courses 4,500 Ft–8,900 Ft. Daily noon–4pm and 6:30–midnight. Metro: Hősök tere (Yellow line).*

Go for Langos

Langos are crispy pieces of fried potato dough. Look for them in tourist spots throughout the city (City Park, Margaret Island), although local gossip holds that the best langos are at the **Ecseri Flea Market** (XIX. Nagykorosi út; ☎ 1/ 280-8840; Mon–Fri 8am–4pm, Sat 6am–3pm, Sun 8am–1pm).

BUDAPEST

Partying

So many clubs and bars have popped up throughout Budapest in the last decade that you're sure to find something to suit your mood. From the casual bars on Andrássy (dress code: casual European) to the super-trendy summer clubs on the river shore (dress code: tight designer wear), Budapest is certainly not lacking in nightlife. Most bars open in the early afternoon and stay open till dawn, but a few hard-core ones disguise themselves as coffee shops so that they can open in the early morning.

Clubs start late here and last until morning, and the club scene tends to shift a lot. You'd be wise to check out a *Pesti Est* visitor guide from one of the tourist offices or ask a local for the latest info.

Clubs

📺 **Best** → **A-38** ★ Good-looking locals flock to A-38 for its cheap food, hopping dance floor (on an old ship docked in the Danube), and Foosball machine. *Buda, Petőfi Bridge.* ☎ *1/464-3940. www.a38.hu. Metro: Bororos tér (Yellow line).*

📺 **Best** → **Holdudvar** ★★ To reach this popular club filled with young Hungarians, look for the orange HOLDUDVAR

The Silent "Toast"

When in Budapest, you may find yourself celebrating some accomplishment with friends over a cold beer. *Never* clink your glasses of beer when toasting. Why? After the unsuccessful 1848 revolt against the Habsburgs, the ringleaders were sent to hang. To celebrate their win, the Habsburgs clinked their glasses. More than a century and a half later, Hungarians associate beer glasses clinking with the tyranny of the Habsburg monarchy.

signs that will lead you down a driveway, through an alleyway, and around some bends until you finally hear the beats of American Top 40 remixes. If you go on a Wednesday, snap door prizes will be doled out: The martini stirrer, for example, will get you two drinks for 1,000 Ft (by far the cheapest in town). Just don't expect to hear any English spoken, and consider heading here with friends: Hungarian kids travel in packs and tend to stay with those packs. *8th district, Múzeum krt.* ☎ *1/485-5270. Metro: Astoria (Red line).*

Bars & Lounges

→ **Beckett's Irish Bar** One of the seemingly ubiquitous "Irish" pubs that have popped up all over the world, Beckett's goes beyond the call of duty with a full bar and live music every night. The musical styles change regularly. *Bajcsy Zsilinszky út 72.* ☎ *1/311-1033. Metro: Arany Janos utca (Red line).*

→ **Café del Rio** ★★ If you head to Café del Rio, try to snag one of the bar's luxurious white leather booths with pillows. Regardless of your seat, enjoy the multicultural meals and original cocktails—a medley of Mexican, Hungarian, American, and Japanese food that somehow works. The "Speed" cocktail—a healthy mix of guarana, Red Bull, strawberry and pomegranate juice, vodka, tequila, and pure caffeine—is not recommended for those with weak hearts or asthma. In the height of the summer, this place teems with pretty people dancing on tables and living *la vida loca.* This place is open daily 2pm to 4:30am. *Goldman Gyorgy tér 1.* ☎ *1/297-2158. www.rio.hu. Metro: Astoria (Red line).*

→ **Eklektika Café** This cafe is wonderfully appointed with 1950s Socialist Realist furnishings, and features live jazz on Wednesday, Friday, and Sunday. A quiet, intimate place, Eklektika hosts a women-only night every

The Local Brew

Craving something stronger than cocktails or beer? Try some Budapest specialties: *unicum* and *palinka*. The thick, sweet herbal brew that is *unicum* comes in a round, green cross-covered bottle and starts with a somewhat medicinal taste that quickly grows on you. *Palinka,* a clear brandy-like spirit produced from a medley of fruits (local favorites are plum and apricot) is consumed like a shot—all at once. Be careful, though; it's not called "kerités-szaggató" (Hungarian translation: to tumble over palisades) for nothing: Most types are 120-proof alcohol.

second Saturday from 10pm on. It's open Monday through Friday noon to midnight, and Saturday and Sunday 5pm to dawn. *Semmelweis u. 21. ☎ 1/266-3054. Metro: Deák tér (all lines).*

→ **Morrison's Music Pub** An almost-20-something crowd packs this casual pub every night of the week. There's a small dance floor, an eclectic variety of loud live music, and a number of beers on tap. It's open Monday through Saturday 8:30pm to 4am. *VI. Révay u. 25. ☎ 1/269-4060. Metro: Opera (Yellow line).*

Live Music

→ **Birdland Restaurant and Bar** A snazzy American jazz–themed bar, Birdland dishes out hearty food and stiff drinks. If you call ahead to check the schedules, you may catch some jazz covers by Hungarian musicians. With its central location near the Opera House, this bar is an excellent place to unwind after a long day of touring the city. *Liszt Ferenc tér 7. ☎ 1/413-7983. www.birdlandcafe.hu. Cover 4,500 Ft–6,400 Ft. Metro: Bajcsy-Zsilinszky út.*

→ **Fonó** Something almost totally unknown outside this part of Europe is the Carpathian folk, Gypsy, and klezmer traditions of small villages to the east, and the fine souls at Fonó actually scour these towns, bringing musicians to Budapest, putting them on the stage, and recording and distributing them. It's open daily 8pm to midnight. *XI. Sztregova u. 3. ☎ 246/53-33. www.fono.hu. Prices vary. Metro: Deák tér (all lines).*

Gay Nightlife

As with the capricious dance club scene, gay "in" bars become "out," or even close down, at a moment's notice. The gay bar scene in Budapest is largely male-oriented at this point, though this is starting to change. For reliable information, visit the first Hungarian GLBT website: www.pride.hu (not in English).

→ **Action Bar** It won't get packed until midnight—right around the time the two-man strip show begins. Housed in a cellar complete with low ceilings, red paint, and flashing lights, Action gets the party started with funky rap/foreign remixes. Upon entering, you'll be handed a consumption card for listing what you've had to drink, which you must have when you leave; keep it close, or you'll have to pay a hefty 10,000 Ft tab. *District V. Magyar u. 42. ☎ 1/266-9148. Cover 700 Ft; 1,300 Ft drink minimum. Metro: Blaha Lujza tér (Red line).*

→ **Angel** A nondescript basement establishment with a bar, a restaurant, and a huge dance floor, Angel has been around for a while now and is definitely here to stay. The clientele is not exclusively gay, particularly on Friday and Saturday nights, when Angel hosts its now-famous transvestite show starting at 11:45pm, and Sunday nights, which is an "open day" (straights welcome). It's open Thursday through Sunday 10am to dawn. *VII. Szövetség u. 33. ☎ 1/351-6490. Cover 600 Ft. Metro: Blaha Lujza tér (Red line).*

→ **Coxx Club** Scores of men gyrate to pounding techno beats and consume alcohol

BUDAPEST

Coffee Talk

The Budapest coffee house is a venerated tradition.

Gerbeaud House ★ Probably Budapest's most famous coffee house, and as such, it deserves to be mentioned twice. *See p. 207 for complete info.*

Művész Kávéház ★★ Just across Andrássy út from the Opera House, Művész (Artist) was (and still is) one of Budapest's finest traditional coffee houses; it was around even in communist times. The lush interior features marble table tops, crystal chandeliers, and mirrored walls. Despite its old-world grandeur, however, Művész retains a casual atmosphere. Decaffeinated cappuccino, which is still a rarity in Budapest, is available here. Elaborate ice-cream sundaes seem to be a favorite with locals and travelers alike. There are tables on the street, but sit inside for the full coffee house effect. *VI. Andrássy út 29.* ☎ *1/352-1337. No credit cards. Daily 9am–11:45pm. Metro: Opera (Yellow line).*

Wins Bar/Café Tucked into a little park, this low-key bar/coffee shop teems with friendly expats from all over the world. You'll appreciate the competent, English-speaking staff, although the bar's biggest plus may well be the free Wi-Fi for customers. *1061 Jokai tér.* ☎ *1/331-1955. Mon–Sat 9am–midnight. Metro: Nyugati pu (Blue line).*

hand over fist at this self-proclaimed "boys only" bar/nightclub. The club is underground. *FYI:* They only let guys inside, so if you come with a lady friend, prepare to leave her at the door. Don't be surprised if it looks empty when you walk in—the upper floor is an Internet cafe/gallery called **Chaos**. *38 Dohány St.* ☎ *1/344 48 84. www.coxx.hu. Metro: Astoria (Red Line). Night bus: 78é.*

Sightseeing

The best place to find out what is going on in town is the Tourist Office at Liszt Ferenc square 9–11, near the Oktogon tram stop. The staff is more than happy to oblige your questions and they can give you the tourist guide for the month and sometimes sell you tickets to events and goings on about town. See "Tourist Offices," earlier in this chapter.

Festivals

March

Budapest Spring Festival. For 2 weeks, opera, ballet, classical music, and drama are held at all the major halls and theaters of Budapest. Simultaneously, temporary exhibitions open in many of Budapest's museums. Tickets are available at the **Festival Ticket Service** (V. 1081 Rákóczi út 65; ☎ 1/486-3300; Metro: Blaha Lujza tér [Red line]), and at the individual venues. Mid- to late March.

June to August

Open-Air Theater Programs. A rich variety of open-air performances are given throughout Budapest during the summer. Highlights include opera and ballet at the Margeret Island Open-Air Theater, folklore and dance at the Buda Park Theater, musicals in Városmajor Theater, and classical music recitals in the Dominican Courtyard at the Hilton Hotel. For information, contact the **Hungarian Arts Festivals Federation** (☎ 1/318-8165; www.artsfestivals.hu). June through August.

"Budafest" Summer Opera and Ballet Festival. This festival is the only time to see a summer performance at the wonderful Hungarian State Opera House in Budapest. Tickets are available at the **Opera House box office** (VI. Andrássy út 20; ☎ 1/353-0170) or at the **National Philharmonic Ticket Office** (V. Vörösmarty tér 1; ☎ 1/318-0281). 10 days in August.

Formula One Grand Prix. One of the European racing circuit's most important annual events is held at Budapest's HungaroRing in Mogyoród. Call ☎ 36/2-844-4444 or check out www.hungaroring.hu. Second weekend in August.

St. Stephen's Day. This is Hungary's national day. The country's patron saint is celebrated with cultural events and a dramatic display of fireworks over the Danube at 9pm. Hungarians also celebrate their constitution on this day and ceremonially welcome the first new bread from the recent crop of July wheat. August 20.

National Jewish Festival. In 1999, this annual festival arrived on the Hungarian cultural scene. The festival features a variety of Jewish culture–related events—from klezmer music to a book fair, from ballet to cabaret—held in "Gödör," a cultural center that opened

in Deák tér in 2004 (on the site of the former central bus station). For information, contact the **Tourism and Cultural Center of the Budapest Jewish Community** (Síp u. 12; ☎ 1/343-0420; the not-quite-up-to-date website is at www.interdnet.hu/Zsido/zsikk/festival_en.html). Late August or early September; call for exact dates.

September

Budapest Art Weeks. In celebration of the opening of the fall season, special classical music and dance performances are held for 3 weeks in all the city's major halls. For information, contact the **Hungarian Arts Festivals Federation** (☎ 1/318-8165; www.artsfestivals.hu). Starts September 25 (the day of Béla Bartók's death).

Contemporary Music Weeks. Held in conjunction with the Budapest Art Weeks, this 3-week festival features contemporary music performances in all the capital's major halls. For information, contact the **Hungarian Arts Festivals Federation** (☎ 1/318-8165; www.artsfestivals.hu). Starts September 25.

Top Attractions

📺 **Best** → **Buda Castle Labyrinth** ★
Though on the touristy side, the Buda Castle Labyrinths are nevertheless beloved by locals, who refer to the attraction in unnervingly awe-inspired tones. Making up a small part of the natural tunnels that extend under Buda for hundreds of miles, these catacombs were used for war storage as well as secret military planning during World War II. Today, they serve as a good test of your nerves because the museum is filled with partially hidden and lifelike terra-cotta statuary that may give you quite a start. The labyrinths are split into five sections: Prehistoric, Historical, Otherworld, Bravery, and two special evening exhibits. The Labyrinth of Bravery uses techniques that

BUDAPEST

Free & Easy

→ Spend the day **photographing** some of the most photogenic scenery in the world, favorites being **Margeret Island** and **Fisherman's Bastion.**

→ Window-shop on **Falk Miksa út.** Some of the best antiques are for sale here.

→ People-watch on **Andrássy Boulevard.** Pick a bench, take a seat, and watch the masses stream by.

Another Amazing View

Gellért Hill, towering 230m (754 ft.) above the Danube, offers one of the best panoramas of the city. The hill is named after the iron-fisted Italian Bishop Gellért, who assisted Hungary's first Christian king, Stephen I, in converting the Magyars. Gellért became a martyr when vengeful pagans killed him by rolling him down the side of this hill in a barrel. An enormous statue of Gellért now stands on the hill, with the bishop defiantly holding a cross in his outstretched hand.

On top of Gellért Hill you'll find the **Liberation Monument,** built in 1947 supposedly to commemorate the Red Army's liberation of Budapest from Nazi occupation, though many believe that Admiral Horthy, Hungary's wartime leader, had planned the statue prior to the liberation to honor his fighter-pilot son, who was killed in the war. Also atop Gellért Hill is the **Citadella** (☎ 1/365-6076), a symbol of power built for military control by the Austrians in 1851, shortly after they crushed the Hungarian War of Independence of 1848 and 1849. It costs 1,200 Ft ($6) to enter the Citadella, which is open daily from 9am to 7pm. There are several exhibitions to see here, but the main attraction is the great view. To get here, take bus no. 27 from Móricz Zsigmond körtér or hike up on any of the various paved pathways that originate at the base of the hill.

would definitely not fly in the U.S. If you don't like dark, enclosed places, I would not recommend this one, unless you want to have a massive coronary. *Tip:* There's an ivy-covered fountain in the museum that spouts a good red wine. If you can find it, feel free to sample it. *Várnegyed, Úri u. 9. www.labirintus.com.* ☎ *1/489-3281. Admission 1,400 Ft adults; 1,100 Ft students. Daily 9:30am–7pm; night tours at 6pm. Metro: Batthyany tér (Red line).*

⚑ Best FREE → Halászbástya (Fisherman's Bastion) ★★ Once the site of the city fish market, the Fisherman's Bastion is now one of the most-photographed monuments in the city, and for good reason. Depending on when you visit, the walls change color with the rising and falling sun, and the view of Pest and the Danube from the ramparts is one of the most romantic settings in the city. To get to the Fisherman's Bastion, take the Várbusz from Moszkva tér or bus no. 16 from Deák tér, or funicular from Clark Ádám tér to Castle Hill.

FREE → Hősök tere (Hero's Square) ★★ At the entrance to City Park, Hero's

Square is one of Budapest's most famous sites, mainly because this wide open space has been home to most of the city's major political rallies over the years. The enormous **Millenium Monument** stands proudly in the middle of the square and was erected to mark the 1,000th anniversary of the Magyar conquest of Hungary. The archangel Gabriel stands as the tallest figure in the middle surrounded by seven chieftains. *End of Andrássy Ave. Metro: Hősök tere (Yellow line).*

→ Mucsarnok Múzeum (Museum of Modern Art) If modern art is your thing, look no further than the columned building to the right of the Millenium Monument. The Mucsarnok houses myriad contemporary Hungarian artists. The Museum also hosts performing arts at intervals throughout the year; call for a schedule. *Budapest XIV Hősök tere.* ☎ *1/460/7000. www.mucsarnok.hu. Tues–Wed and Fri–Sun 10am–6pm; Thurs noon–8pm. Admission 900 Ft adults, 500 Ft students. Metro: Oktogon (Yellow line).*

→ Nemzeti Múzeum (Hungarian National Museum) ★★ The Hungarian

National Museum, an enormous neoclassical structure built from 1837 to 1847, was one of the great projects of the early-19th-century Age of Reform, a period that also saw the construction of the Chain Bridge and the National Theater (no longer standing), as well as the development of the modern Hungarian national identity.

The museum's main attraction is the replica of the so-called crown of St. Stephen (King Stephen ruled A.D. 1000–38). The two main museum exhibits on view are "The History of the Peoples of Hungary from the Paleolithic Age to the Magyar Conquest," and **"The History of the Hungarian People from the Magyar Conquest to 1989"** ★, which includes artifacts and documents relating the story of the Hungarian people from their arrival in this area up to the system change in 1989. *VIII. Múzeum krt. 14.* ☎ *1/338-2122. www.hnm.hu. Free admission. Tues–Sun 10am–6pm (to 5pm in winter). Metro: Kálvin tér (Blue line).*

➜**Néprajzi Múzeum (Museum of Ethnography)** Across the square from the Parliament sits the grand museum of ethnography. The building once housed the royal court, which isn't surprising considering how opulent it is. Although some of the museum artifacts come from outside Hungary, the permanent exhibit, "From Ancient Times to Civilization," is of local interest. The exhibit is also free, provided you go to no other halls. If you have the time, though, I recommend paying the 500 Ft fee to wander the great marble halls for a few hours. *V. Kossuth tér 12.* ☎ *1/473-2400. www.neprajz.hu. Free admission for permanent exhibits; 1,200 Ft for temporary shows. Tues–Sun 10am–6pm. Metro: Kossuth tér (Red line).*

➜**Statue Park** ★ Statue Park is where the Hungarian government placed the enormous statues that once decorated the city during its communist years. Although it sits a good deal away from the city center, the spectacle of a park filled with stone-faced men is worth the trip. *Balatoni út (road no. 70; corner of Szabadkai út).* ☎ *1/424-7500. Admission 200 Ft–600 Ft. Daily 10 am–nightfall. Bus: 14, 50, or 114.*

FREE ➜**Széchenyi Lánchíd (Chain Bridge)** The first permanent bridge connecting Buda and Pest was completed in 1849. The present bridge is a remake; the Nazis blew up the original during their retreat from Hungary. The Chain Bridge is one of the most romantic places in Budapest—especially, at night. *Roosevelt tér.*

➜**Szépművészeti Múzeum (Museum of Fine Arts)** An imposing structure to the left of the Millenium Monument, the Museum of Fine Arts hosts occasional special exhibits in addition to a permanent collection of Spanish Masters unrivaled outside of Spain. If you have an International Student Card, entrance is 800 Ft for all exhibits. *XIV. Hősök tere.* ☎ *1/469-7100. Free admission for permanent collection; other exhibits 1,000 Ft–1,800 Ft. Tues–Sun 10am–5:30pm. Free guided tours in English Tues–Fri at 11am, Sat 11am and 3pm. Metro: Hősök tere (Yellow line).*

➜**Terror Háza (House of Terror)** In the old headquarters of the Secret Police, the House of Terror is an excellent, eye-opening museum experience. Thousands of Jews were executed by the Nazis in the basement and an unknown number of dissenters were tortured into making false confessions here when the communists took over. All the exhibits are in Hungarian; English speakers will have to pick up the information sheets at the entrance to each room or listen with the English audio headphones that can be picked up at the entrance. *VI. Andrássy út 60.* ☎ *1/374-2600. www.houseofterror.hu. Admission 1,200 Ft. Tues–Fri 10am–6pm; Sat–Sun 10am–7:30pm. Metro: Oktogon (Yellow line).*

BUDAPEST

Historic Buildings

In addition to the buildings below, we definitely recommend stopping by **Dohány Synagogue** ★★ (VII. Dohány u. 2–8; ☎ 1/ 342-8949; Tues–Thurs 10am–5pm, Fri and Sun 10am–2pm; Metro: Astoria/Red line). It's the world's second-largest synagogue, so prepare to snap some photos.

➜ **Királyi Palota (Buda Palace)** ★★ Housing a tremendous collection of artistic masterpieces, Buda Palace is itself an artistic wonder. The Palace is separated into four floors, including the Nemzeti Galéria, a repository of Hungarian art from medieval times through the 20th century; the Budapesti Történeti Múzeum (Budapest History Museum), devoted to the history of medieval Buda; and the Ludwig Múzeum (Ludwig Museum of Contemporary Art), which houses a so-so collection of contemporary Hungarian and international art. *Nemzeti Galéria: District I, Királyi Palota (entrance in Wing C), Dísz tér 17.* ☎ *1/375-5567. www.mng.hu. Free admission to museum; special exhibits 600 Ft; photos 1,500 Ft; videos 2,000 Ft. Tues–Sun 10am–6pm. Bus: Várbusz (5th stop from M2: Moszkva tér/Red line). Budapest History Museum: District I, Királyi Palota (Wing E), Szt. György tér 2.* ☎ *1/ 224-3700. www.btm.hu. Admission 800 Ft. Mar to mid-May and mid-Sept to Oct Wed–Mon 10am–6pm; mid-May to mid-Sept daily 10am– 6pm; Nov–Feb Wed–Mon 10am–4pm. Bus: Várbusz (5th stop from M2: Moszkva tér/ Red line). Ludwig Museum: District I, Királyi Palota (Wing A), Dísz tér 17.* ☎ *1/375-9175. www. ludwigmuseum.hu. 600 Ft; free admission to ground-floor exhibits. Tues–Wed and Fri–Sun 10am–6pm; Thurs 10am–8pm. Metro: Moszkva tér (Red line).*

➜ **Mátyás Templom (St. Matthias Church)** ★★ The Renaissance king who was twice married here added the gorgeous white tower that stretches into the sky. When the Turks conquered the city, they transformed this beautiful building into a mosque, but it was converted into the monument it is today after their departure in the 1400s. Don't miss the treasures inside the church: It houses a lapidarium (stone and gem work), reliquary, and some beautiful coronation memorabilia. *I. Szentháromság tér 2.* ☎ *1/355-5657. Admission 600 Ft. Daily 9am–6pm. Bus: Várbusz from Moszkva tér or 16 from Deák tér Castle Hill. Funicular: from Clark Ádám tér to Castle Hill.*

➜ **Parliament** ★ This permanent seat of the national assembly and the largest building in the country cannot be missed. Looming over the banks of the Danube on the Pest side, the neo-Gothic Parliament building was started in 1884 and finished in 1902. Between then and 1989, the assembly convened only once before the communist takeover. Most of the interior art is by famous Hungarians. Since 2000, the general public has been invited to view the royal coronation relics: St. Stephen's crown, the scepter, orb, and the Renaissance sword. *V. Kossuth tér.* ☎ *1/441-4415. www.parlament. hu. Admission (by guided tour only): 2,300 Ft 60-min. tour in English, 1,150 Ft for students. Tickets are available at Gate X. Tours are given Mon–Fri 10am, noon, and 2pm (but not on days in which Parliament is in session, usually Tues–Wed, or during protocol events); Sat 4pm; Sun 2pm. Metro: Kossuth tér (Red line).*

FREE ➜ **St. Stephen's Basilica** ★★★ You simply can't miss St. Stephen's, the largest church in Budapest. This monstrous, domed church is so big that locals have dubbed it a "basilica." The building took three architects and more than 50 years to build, and is dedicated to King St. Stephen, the first Christian king of Hungary. Although there are guided tours, you are free to wander about. Donations are requested to light a candle (200 Ft) or to view the holiest of Hungarian relics: the "Holy Right" hand of King St. Stephen (head all the way to the back of the back chapel). *V. Szent István tér*

33. ☎ 1/317-2859. www.basilica.hu. Free admission to church; 300 Ft treasury; 500 Ft tower. Church daily 7am–6pm, except during services; treasury daily 9am–5pm (10am–4pm in winter); Szent Jobb Chapel Mon–Sat 9am–5pm (10am–4pm in winter), Sun 1–5pm; tower Apr–Oct Mon–Sat 10am–6pm. Metro: Arany János utca (Blue line) or Bajcsy-Zsilinszky út (Yellow line).

Other Attractions

→ **Állatkert (Zoo)** The owners of this zoo seem to be under the impression that the animals (elephants, zebras, and the other usual zoo suspects) miss their homes, so they've styled the buildings according to the animals' native countries. Be prepared to see arabesque, Indian, and Spanish-style buildings throughout the zoo, which starts to feel like a miniature golf course after a while. The **Nagy Cirkusz (Great Circus)** is situated next to the zoo, and might be worth a stop afterwards if you're enjoying the grade school–appropriate sightseeing. XIV. Állatkerti krt. 6–12. ☎ 1/273-4900. www.zoobudapest.com. Admission 1,300 Ft adults. Mon–Thurs 9am–5pm; Fri–Sun 9am–7pm (varies according to month, verify with

Lost & Found

The two-tiered crown that sits in the case at the Parliament building never belonged to St. Stephen, who died in 1038. Its lower part was evidently a gift to King Géza I (1074–77), and its upper part was built for Stephen V, who reigned almost 250 years after the first Stephen's death.

website). Metro: Hősök tere or Széchenyi fürdő (Yellow line).

→ **Vidám Park (Amusement Park)** Large cartoon graphics and technological throwbacks (creaky wooden rides, bumper cars that are more bumper than car these days, and others) fill the park. Like most theme parks, expect to be overcharged. XIV. Állatkerti krt. 14–16. ☎ 1/363-8310. www.vidampark.hu. Admission 300 Ft ($1.50) adults; rides 300 Ft–600 Ft ($1.50–$3); your best bet is to buy a stack of 20 tickets (plus 2 "free" extra tickets) on entry for 6,000 Ft ($30). Mar–Nov Mon–Fri 10am–8pm, Sat–Sun to 8pm (summer hours; see website for other periods). Metro: Széchenyi fürdő (Yellow line).

BUDAPEST

12 Hours in Budapest

1. **Start with coffee.** Cruise through an old-world coffee house like **Gerbeaud House.**
2. **Take in the country's largest church.** You can't miss a trip to **St. Stephen's Basilica** and its treasury.
3. **Soak in the view.** Hit the **Royal Castle** grounds across the river in Buda to take in the view of Pest through the battlements.
4. **Soak.** Swing a visit to the **Gellért baths** for a steam and a soak before they close for the day.
5. **Grab some grub.** Once thoroughly purged of your toxins, you'll be feeling strangely hungry. Hit **Spoon** early, and beat the crowds to get the best view of the **Chain Bridge.**
6. **"Hydrate."** After dinner, wander to whichever of the other pubs on **Dohány u.** has the most interesting crowd, and cap your night off by buying a *unicum* or *palinka* shot.

The University Scene

Budapest is home to the **CEU** (Central European University), a prestigious school that is an American-accredited university. CEU attracts students from over 80 countries and its political science program is quite well known. The main information building is at Nador u. 9. For more information, call ☎ 1/327-3000 or check out www.ceu.hu.

If you're strolling around Pest's inner city, you can't miss Budapest's largest and oldest university: Eötvös Loránd University (ELTE). The campus is concentrated around university square, along Karolyi Mihaly utca. Stop by to chat up a hot student or two, or at least come to peek into the baroque University Church.

Performing Arts

Budapest is now on the touring route of dozens of major European ensembles and virtuosos. Check out *Budapest Program, Budapest Panorama, Pesti Est,* and *Budapest in Your Pocket,* which are all helpful English-language entertainment guides. They're available at major hotels and tourist offices.

Budapest's gallery scene is hopping. Galleries tend to keep normal store hours (Mon–Fri 10am–6pm, Sat 10am to 1 or 2pm and sometimes as late as 6pm). They're concentrated in two areas: the Inner City of Pest and Buda's Castle District. If you want to browse, the art and antiques area of Budapest runs along Falk Miksa, from Jászai Mari tér down to the Parliament. Also check out the virtual galleries found at Artpool (www.artpool.hu).

→ **Budai Vigadó (Buda Concert Hall)** The Budai Vigadó is the home stage of the Hungarian State Folk Ensemble (Állami Népi Együttes Székháza). This ensemble is the oldest in the country and includes 40 dancers, a 20-member Gypsy orchestra, and a folk orchestra. It performs folk dances from all regions of historic Hungary. Tickets can be reserved by telephone. The box office is open 10am to 6pm daily. Performances usually start at 8pm on Tuesday, Thursday, and Sunday. *I. Corvin tér 8.* ☎ *1/317-2754. Tickets 5,500 Ft. Metro: Batthyány tér (Red line).*

→ **Magyar Állami Operaház (Hungarian State Opera House)** ★★ Designed to emulate the Vienna Opera House in its sheer magnificence, the State Opera House was completed in 1884 by Hungarian architect Miklos Ybl. The result employs arching columns of white marble and plush red velvet decor to create a gem of a building. In addition to the State Opera and State Ballet, the Opera House is home to a bevy of statues of famous composers. The only way to get inside is to take a guided tour (1,500 Ft at 3 and 4pm) or to see one of the performances, which generally run all year, except August. Tickets start at about 600 Ft, but if you have some spare cash, see the opera the way the Habsburgs did—in one of the boxes, which cost around 8,500 Ft. Just remember that opera wear means dressy (no tux, but no jeans either). *22 Andrássy út.* ☎ *1/331-2550. Box office: Mon–Fri 11am–6pm. Metro: Opera (Yellow line).*

→ **Zeneakadémia (Ferenc Liszt Academy of Music)** The Art Nouveau Great Hall (Nagyterem) of the Academy of Music, with a seating capacity of 1,200, is Budapest's premier concert hall. Unfortunately, the Great Hall is not used in the summer months; the smaller Kisterem, also a fine hall, is used at that time. In addition to major Hungarian and international performances, you can attend student recitals (sometimes for free). A weekly schedule is posted outside the Király utca entrance to the academy. The box office is open Monday through Friday from 2pm to showtime. Performances are frequent. *VI. Liszt Ferenc tér 8.* ☎ *1/341-4788 or 1/342-0179.*

Tickets 1,000 Ft–8,000 Ft. Metro: Oktogon or Opera (Yellow line).

Theaters

Budapest has an extremely lively theater season from September through June. For productions in English, try the **Merlin Theater** (V. Gerlóczy u. 4; ☎ 1/317-9338 or 1/266-4632), located on a quiet street in the heart of the Inner City. It's the only primarily foreign-language theater in Budapest. Tickets cost 1,800 Ft; box office hours vary. Take the Red line Metro to Astoria or any Metro line to Deák tér.

Dance

Taking in a traditional Hungarian dance performance is good way to up your trip's cultural ante, and there are several dance houses to choose from throughout the city. My personal favorite is the **Kalamajka Dance House** (Molnár utca 9, ☎ 1/371-5928; Sept–June Sat 8pm–1am). The second floor has dancing and dance lessons while the fourth floor has jam sessions and oceans of *palinka*.

Playing Outside

If you're feeling cooped up, Budapest is a wonderful city to just walk around in. It's enjoyable whatever the weather, which tends to be somewhat fickle—always bring an umbrella.

Gardens, Parks & Labyrinths

→ **City Park** If you keep walking along Karoly Kos (the street behind Millennium Monument, and the street the Andrássy turns into) you'll eventually walk into City Park, Budapest's all-in-one answer to a theme park. It has everything from baths to a zoo and circus (p. 215) to a lake, where you can go boating during the summer or ice-skating during the winter. You may not think the activities are worth the price of admission. *Varosligtet. Park open Apr–Aug daily 9am–6pm; Sept–Mar 9am–3pm. Pedal boat rentals May–Aug daily 10am–8pm; 980 Ft per hour. Rowboat rental May–Aug daily 10am–9:30pm; 500 Ft per hour. Ice skate rental Oct–Feb daily 10am–2pm and 4–8pm; 500 Ft per 4 hr. Metro: Széchenyi Furdo (Yellow line).*

→ **Margaret Island** This long, thin island sits in the middle of the Danube, simply calling out for you to bike, run, or do other outdoorsy things. Random ruins are strewn about the island, making any trip here feel like a scavenger hunt of sorts—see how many ruins you can find. There are no cars here, and while buses can get you to the outskirts, they can't infiltrate the island's interior. The best way to navigate the island is to rent a bike. One of the most affordable places to do so is at the Corinthia Grand Hotel Royal (p. 203), which rents even to non-guests. If you get hungry after all the biking, one of the city's best langos stands is behind the Magitszigent Danubius Thermal Hotel in a dilapidated stone building. You can't miss the smell (and the line).

→ **Roosevelt Tér** Located in front of the **Four Seasons Gresham Palace** and the **Chain Bridge,** Roosevelt tér was set to be torn down for a parking lot, but the Four Seasons spared it and built their garage under the hotel. Now, a very green, very relaxing little park sits in the middle of the city, so that tired tourists can have someplace to sit and watch the sun go down over the castles of Buda.

BUDAPEST

Make a Splash

Budapest has gained fame throughout the centuries for its supposedly healing waters. Things to know before you take the plunge: Only a few city baths are open at any one time (many are being renovated), so check before venturing out. The baths' obscenely high mineral content gives the body what it needs, but locals also drink the water. Nude bathing depends on where you are; observe what the majority of other people are doing and do the same if you feel comfortable.

Gellért Bathhouse ★★ The most beautiful, famous bathhouse in Budapest, the Art Nouveau–style Gellért building is housed in the Hotel Gellért. In addition to two thermal baths (single-sex), Gellért also has a pool complete with soaring ceilings and gorgeous statuary, open to both sexes. The roof has sunbathing decks (nude and single-sex) in addition to an outdoor pool that generates waves every 50 minutes. *XI. Kelenhegyi út 4.* ☎ *1/466-6166. Thermal baths: admission 3,000 Ft for 4 hr. or more, 2,300 Ft for a 15-min. massage; lockers or cabins included. Pools and baths (no cabin, communal dressing rooms): admission 2,500 Ft adults and children for 4 hr. or more. Prices and the lengthy list of services, including the complicated refund system, are posted in English. Thermal baths: Summer daily 6am–7pm; winter Mon–Fri 6am–7pm, Sat–Sun 6am–5pm, with the last entrance 1 hr. before closing. Tram: 47 or 49 from Deák tér to Szent Gellért tér.*

Kiraly Bathhouse ★ An architectural ode to the Turks who built it, the Kiraly Bathhouse was built in the 16th century by the ruling Ottomans. Today, sunlight spirals down through the domed ceiling, and the quiet baths house sauna and steam room facilities. The thermal baths are some of the cleanest in the city, but the only towel you'll receive comes at the end of your bath (you're welcome to bring your own). Women can use the baths on Monday, Wednesday, and Friday from 7am to 5pm. Men are welcome on Tuesday, Thursday, and Saturday from 9am to 7pm. *I. Fő u. 84.* ☎ *1/201-4392. Admission 1,100 Ft for 1½ hr. Metro: Batthyány tér (Red line).*

Szechnyi Baths & Thermal Pools ★ The baths in this monstrous yellow-and-white building in City Park are the largest baths in the country and among the largest in Europe. A favorite of Budapest natives, the baths are expensive, but a quick soak could make you feel like a million bucks. Some thermal baths are in underground chambers; these are considered the hottest baths in Budapest, drawn from a well more than 4,602m (100 ft.) deep. *XIV. Állatkerti út 11–14, in City Park.* ☎ *1/363-3210. www.szechenzifurdo.hu. Admission 2,000 Ft; dressing cabins are extra. Daily 6am–7pm, except Sat–Sun in winter, when the complex closes at 5pm. Metro: Széchenyi fürdő (Yellow line).*

Shopping

Shopping in Budapest leaves only one thing to be desired: A true, inexpensive souvenir that can not be eaten. If you have the means, Budapest is known for its graceful Herend porcelain that is worth its weight in gold (almost). Other popular items include pillowcases, pottery, dolls, dresses, skirts, and sheepskin vests. Hungarian food and wine also make great gifts; standouts are Herz Salami and chestnut and paprika paste.

Most stores are open Monday through Friday from 10am to 6pm and Saturday from

9 or 10am to 1 or 2pm. Some shops close for an hour at lunchtime, and most stores are closed Sunday, except those in the central tourist areas.

→ **Akt.Records** Once known as Afrofilia, this cozy shop in the heart of Budapest stocks an impressive collection of minimal, hip-hop, electro, jazz, and folklore records. Open Monday through Friday 11am to 7pm, Saturday 11am to 4pm. *V. Múzeum körút 7.* ☎ *1/266-3080. www.manamana.hu. Metro: Astoria (Red line).*

→ **Ciánkáli** ★★ Called the Anti-Fashion Shop, this "high-quality" secondhand shop chain sells vintage junk and alternative-punk modish collections and accessories. They also display a large selection of funky brand-new items. Look for the wide selection of

On Váci Utca

The shopping lane running from Gerbeaud Confectionary to Vamhaz krt used to be filled with bookshops, but it's become Budapest's answer to Rodeo Drive and Madison Avenue in these more capitalist times. The long, crowded street is an interesting place no matter if you intend to shop or simply people-watch. Metro: Vörösmarty tér (Yellow line).

leather clothing. Open Monday through Friday 10am to 7pm, Saturday 10am to 2pm. *VII. Dohány u. 68.* ☎ *1/341-0540. Metro: Blaha Lujza tér (Red line).*

Road Trips

Venture just 40km (25 miles) north of Budapest to **Visegrad,** and you'll find yourself knee-deep in legends involving the first monarchs of Hungary, the Romans, and King Solomon, not to mention soaring castles and perhaps the most picture-perfect photo ops around. Visegrad once served as a border town for the Roman empire, and it still holds some of the watchtowers that helped defend the borders of Rome, as well as an amazing Royal Palace. I recommend taking the **hydrofoil** (V. Vigadoter) here, which runs between June 6 and September 6, and will shuttle you quickly off to the beautiful Danube Bend. It costs just under 2,000 Ft for a round-trip ticket, which can be purchased on the boat. Contact **MAHART** (☎ 1/318-1880) for info on the hydrofoil. You can also take the train; train timetables are at www.elvira.hu. The tourist office, **Visegrad Tours** (REV u. 15; ☎ 26/398-160; www.visegrad.hu) is located across from the ferryboat landing. It's open weekdays April through October 9am to 6pm, and November through March 10am to 4pm.

A 20-minute train ride from Budapest, **Szentendre** is an artist's colony visited by more and more people every year. Amazingly, it hasn't lost any of its Mediterranean charm. The town is packed with mouthwatering restaurants, and art galleries abound. A train runs from I. Batthyany tér to Szentendre every 20 minutes and the ride takes around 20 minutes. Tickets cost 268 Ft. Or you can take a boat that departs the station (V. Vigadoter) every morning at 9am and leaves Szentendre at 11:45am and 5:55pm. Round-trip tickets cost 1,200 Ft. Visit www.elvira.hu for train info, or call ☎ 43/729-2161 for ferry info. The main **tourist office** is at Dumtsa Jeno u. 22 (☎ 26/317-965), and it's open April to October Monday to Friday from 9am to 7pm and Saturday and Sunday 9am to 2pm; in the off season, the office is closed on weekends but open weekdays from 9am to 5pm.

➜ **Herend Porcelain Company** ★ First produced in the little town of Herend in 1826, the thin, opaque, and almost crystalline textured porcelain produced by this company quickly rose through the ranks to become what it is today: beautiful, lavish, wonderful pieces that cost a small fortune. *V. József nádor tér 11.* ☎ *1/318-9200. www.herend.hu. Metro: Vörösmarty tér (Yellow line) or Deák tér (all lines).*

➜ **Írók Boltja** ★★ This is the center of the Magyar lit scene and feels like it, with dark paneling, author readings (once in a blue moon there's actually one in English), and little tables where you can camp out with a coffee for as long as you like and spy on the hyper-intellectual set who constantly flow through here. Open Monday through Friday 10am to 6pm, Saturday 10am to 1pm. *VI Andrássy út 45.* ☎ *1/322-1645. www.irok boltja.hu. Metro: Oktogon (Yellow line).*

Markets & Centers

➜ **Ecseri Flea Market** Informed locals have told me that this flea market reached its peak 10 years ago and is on a downward spiral. Most things at this market are plain junk, so prepare to dig. Just beware of pickpockets during your search. The market runs Monday through Friday 8am to 2pm, Saturday 6am to 2pm, and Sunday 8am to 1pm. *XIX. Nagykörösi út.* ☎ *1/280-8840. Take bus no. 54 from Boráros tér.*

➜ **Központi Vásárcsarnok (Central Market Hall)** ★ A trip to Central Market Hall, the largest of the city's food markets, is a half- or full-day activity. Shoppers can find whatever they need, be it wines, fish, flowers, or tablecloths. Take a rest from buying souvenirs for everyone you know by eating at any of the food stands or inexpensive buffet-style restaurants on the top floor. Open Monday 6am to 5pm, Tuesday to Friday 6am to 6pm, and Saturday 6am to 2pm. *IX. Vámház körút 1–3.* ☎ *1/217-6067. Metro: Kálvin tér (Blue line).*

➜ **Westend City Center** This behemoth mall came into being at the end of 1999, when it moved in next to the Western Railway Station. Designed by Gustave Eiffel, the complex houses a 14-screen movie theater, offices, and a 5,574 sq. m (60,000 sq. ft.) shopping center complete with waterfall. Open daily 8am to 11pm. *VI. district. Váci út 1–3.* ☎ *1/238-7777.*

Copenhagen

Arriving in Copenhagen, visitors will emerge into a city rich in contradictions—little surprise, considering this is the culture that produced both the Vikings (more on that later) and some of the world's most beloved, innocent fairy-tale characters, the Little Mermaid and Thumbelina. This historic dichotomy persists into the present; to see the city, travelers need to look beyond the stereotypes and embrace the new as well as the old. Gorgeous old Copenhagen, with its picturesque harbors and colorful buildings that crowd tiny cobblestone alleyways, is now surrounded by a bustling modern metropolis complete with neon signs, fashionable shopping streets, and towering office buildings. Yet the city, the largest in Scandinavia, maintains an almost villagelike feel.

Denmark, with the world's oldest monarchy, is also noted for its political progressivism and tolerance, including being home to Christiania, a self-governing state run by former hippies where certain drugs are tolerated and violence of any kind is not. Yet this is also a system of law-abiders, for the most part. Pedestrians, for example, wait at crossings even when no cars are coming; no one jaywalks.

You can see that Denmark is a small peninsula (it's the smallest of the Scandinavian countries). What's hard to see—or even imagine—are the 400 small islands that make this country a homeland. Greenland and the Faroe Islands are still technically considered Danish territory, as was Iceland until the 1940s. Copenhagen (pop. 1.7 million), whose name comes from the word *koben-havn* meaning "merchants' harbor," sits on the island of Zealand—the largest, wealthiest, and most populated of Denmark's islands.

It's also a country with one of the highest standards of living in the world, which for kids, means free universities and, for the entire state, means insane taxes, universal health care, generous pensions, and a good public transportation system.

And even though Copenhagen can be cold in the summer—from the ever-present wind and rain—press on; beyond this cold exterior lies a fun, beautiful, impressive city with some very interesting people.

The Best of Copenhagen

○ **The Best Boho Bar Area:** The **Nørrebro** neighborhood, popular with young bohemian types, is not surprisingly also home to the city's most happening nightlife. For a mellow evening, have a drink at **Barcelona** or **Pussy Galore's.** For a full-on night on the town, follow that with some dancing at **Rust.** See p. 226 and p. 235.

○ **The Best Street Food:** Tourists shell out big bucks to dine on restaurant terraces along the Strøget. For a fraction of the cost, grab a **hot dog** or **falafel** from one of the vendors on the street and soak up the atmosphere from a free seat in the square.

○ **The Best Splurge:** Nothing spells Copenhagen like a seafood dinner by the harbor. Feast on fresh fish and smørresbrod along the Nyhavn harbor. For the full experience, try the herring buffet at **Nyhavns Færgekro.** See p. 234.

○ **The Best Tourist Attraction:** Let your inner child roam wild at **Tivoli,** Copenhagen's fairy-tale amusement park, that boasts roller coasters and puppet shows, as well as orchestra concerts and striking gardens. Be sure to catch the nightly light show. See p. 238.

○ **A Utopia:** To the east of the city center lies the Freetown of **Christiania.** Once the site of military barracks, the area was occupied by frustrated hippies in the 1970s who proceeded to set up their own state. Today, Christiania still maintains its own government, which has combined various philosophies of alternative living to create its own little version of utopia. See p. 238.

○ **The Best Deal:** The city provides **bikes** for free (with a 20DKK deposit). Take your cue—it is the best way to see the city. More than 125 city bike parking places

Great Danes

Hamlet: Shakespeare wrote one of his most famous works about this Danish king.
Hans Christian Andersen: This 19th-century author created some of our most memorable fairy-tale characters: the Little Mermaid, Thumbelina, the Ugly Duckling, and so on.
Søren Kierkegaard: A 19th-century philosopher best known for founding the Existential movement, the oh-so-uplifting philosophy that argues that life is essentially meaningless.
Carlsberg Beer: According to the modest Danish slogan, it's "possibly the best beer in the world."
Helena Christiansen: Denmark's hottest export is the supermodel and sexy star of a steamy Chris Isaak music video.

operate from May through mid-December, distributing 1,300 bikes. See p. 224.

○ **The Best Lazy Activity: Picnicking** in a city park on a sunny day. When the weather is good, locals congregate in Copenhagen's parks and spend the day lounging, drinking beer, and chatting with friends. See p. 241.

Getting There & Getting Around

Getting into Town

BY AIR

Flights arrive at **Kastrup Airport** (☎ 32-31-32-31; www.cph.dk), about 12km (7½ miles) from Copenhagen. The airport has luggage storage, restaurants and shops, money exchange, and amenities such as wireless Internet, sauna, shower, and solarium. Trains go from the airport's Air Rail Terminal (a short escalator ride down from the gates) to Copenhagen's central railway station. The trip takes from 11 to 15 minutes, usually, and departs several times an hour. It costs 26DKK.

You can also take an SAS bus to the city terminal; the fare is the same (26DKK). A taxi to the city center will run about 150DKK.

BY TRAIN

Trains arrive at the **Hoved Banegaård** (the central railroad station; ☎ 70-13-14-15 for rail info) in the center of Copenhagen, near Tivoli Gardens and the Rådhuspladsen. International trains connect Copenhagen with Malmö, Sweden, and several points in Germany. Inside the station, you'll find luggage storage, a small tourist office, currency exchange, Internet, post office, restaurants, and cafes. For trip planning, see the DSB (Danish State Railway) website at www.dsb.dk. You might want to consider getting a Scanrail pass (see box for more info).

You can connect with the **S-tog**, a local commuter train, here, and local buses depart from outside the station. There's an information desk near tracks 5 and 6.

BY BUS

Buses arrive behind the Central Railroad Station on Ingerslevsgade. For bus info, call ☎ 36-13-14-15. Also, **Eurolines** runs buses; purchase tickets on board, online at www.eurolines.com, or by calling ☎ 33-88-70-00.

BY FERRY

There are direct ferries to Denmark from Sweden, Norway, and Germany, though they won't take you right to Copenhagen; most only go as far as Helsingør, although some come as far in as Havnegade, which is at the southern end of Nyhavn and is a short walk from the center of Copenhagen. It's a scenic way to go, but cost and logistics make it a bit more inconvenient than other types of transport.

The Scanrail Pass

If you plan to visit Scandinavia primarily, look into the Scanrail Pass, which allows tourists a designated number of days of free rail travel within a larger time block, so you can sightsee in between days of moving around. (There is a consecutive 21-day pass if you're interested.) The Flexi passes, as they're called, allow 5 to 10 days of travel; give you the choice of first- or second-class travel; and offer free or discounted travel on some ferries, boats, and buses. The Scanrail Youth pass is a boon for wanderers who are 26 and under. For example, the second-class youth fare for any 5 days within 2 months is $203; any 10 days within 2 months is $273. Buy these before you fly to Europe. The Scanrail site, www.scanrail.com, has links to travel agents who sell the passes.

COPENHAGEN

DFDS Seaways (☎ 33-42-30-00; www. dfdsseaways.com) operates a line from Oslo, Norway, to Copenhagen and back to Oslo (via Helsingør) from 398DKK, with discounts for travelers under 26 years old or those who book online. It also operates out of Harwich, England. Otherwise, **Scandlines** (☎ 33-15-15-15; www.scandlines.dk) runs ferries from Sweden and Germany to Helsingør, which is a port town very close to Sweden and about 65km (40 miles) from Copenhagen.

Getting Around

BY CAR

Copenhagen's various walkways and pedestrian streets are best suited to walking or biking. We recommend parking your car in one of a dozen city parking lots, then retrieving it when you're ready to leave the city. Many of the lots are open 24 hours, but a few close between 1 and 7am; some close on Saturday afternoon and on Sunday. It'll cost about 23DKK to 25DKK per hour or 240DKK for 24 hours.

If you do want to drive in the city, you can rent a car at one of the various international car-rental agencies located at the airport, such as **Hertz** (☎ 32-50-30-40), **Avis** (☎ 32-51-20-99), and **Budget** (☎ 32-52-39-00). Prices vary depending on length of rental and type of vehicle, but generally run around 1,300DKK per day. Some agencies also have satellite companies in the city itself. Note that the government imposes a hefty 25% tax on all car rentals.

BY PUBLIC TRANSPORTATION

Copenhagen has a very reliable, extensive public transit system: buses, the S-Tog (subway), and a new Metro line. The city is divided into zones, and riders must pay based on the number of zones they enter: Most places in Copenhagen are accessible with a two-zone ticket for 26DKK, which you can buy at machines at bus stations and train stations, or on the bus. Tickets are valid for

Discount & Student Cards

The **Copenhagen Card** entitles you to free and unlimited travel by bus and rail throughout the metropolitan area (including North Zealand), 25% to 50% discounts on crossings to and from Sweden, and free admission to over 60 sights and museums. You can opt to get a 1- or 3-day version (199DKK and 399DKK, respectively). Buy the card at tourist offices, at the airport, at train stations, and at most hotels or online at www.woco.dk/tourist. For more info, contact the Copenhagen Tourist Information Center (p. 226).

Students who have a current **International Student Identity Card (ISIC),** are eligible for discounts around town. See p. 48 for info on how to get the card before you begin your trip.

1 hour and allow riders to transfer (within the same zone) between bus, subway, and Metro. For information, visit the HT information hub at Rådhuspladsen (☎ 36-13-14-15; www.hur.dk).

BY PRIVATE BUS

A 2¹/₂-hour **City Tour** makes stops at a brewery (during the work week only), *The Little Mermaid,* the Rosenborg Castle, and the Amalienborg Palace, among other places. A **City and Harbor Tour** offers a slightly different itinerary, going along the city's canals and stopping at the Old Fish Market. **Shakespeare** tours take in the castles of North Zealand on a 7-hour excursion. For more information, call **Copenhagen Excursions** (☎ 32-54-06-06; www.cex.dk).

BY BICYCLE

Free bikes! Yep. Most people in the city 🅜 Best **bike,** so the bikes lanes are great.

(You do have to put down a 20DKK deposit that will release a city bike from the locker, which will then be returned to the renter when the bike is locked up again.) These aren't hotshot titanium superbikes; they are sturdy wheels (with advertisements), though. And you can find them near major tourist sites in central Copenhagen from May 1 through December 15—for use only within the city center (check the map on the bike). Bike service is run by **Byckyckler** (☎ 35-43-01-10).

If you feel the need to actually pay for a bicycle rental, the best option in town is Rent a Bike, which has two branches: **Kobenhavns Cykler** (Reventlowsgade 11; ☎ 33-33-86-13) and **Østerport Cykler** (Oslo Plads 9; ☎ 33-33-85-13; www.rentabike.dk). Rentals are from 75DKK per day, plus deposit.

You'll also see bicycle taxis, sort of like modern-day rickshaws. The drivers can take you on a specific tour—Danish Design, for example—or you can design your own. Prices vary.

BY TAXI

Taxis can be flagged down anywhere in Copenhagen. The basic fare is 19DKK when hailed on the street and 32DKK when you book over the phone, plus at least 10DKK per kilometer, depending on time of day. If you need to call a taxi, some companies operating in the city center include **Codan Taxi** (☎ 70-25-25-25), **Hovedstadens Taxi** (☎ 38-77-77-77), and **Taxamotor** (☎ 35-35-35-35).

ON FOOT

Other than biking, this is the best way to get around, as Copenhagen is small and easy to navigate by foot. You can wander along the water or through alleyways and really explore the city. Pick up a free map of the city at the tourist office.

Copenhagen Basics

Orientation: Copenhagen Neighborhoods

Copenhagen is located on the east coast of Zealand Island, to the north of Germany, and across the Øresund Straight from Sweden (a new bridge connects Copenhagen with Malmø in Sweden).

OLD COPENHAGEN The historical heart of Copenhagen, it sits in the middle of the city, and the long pedestrian street **Strøget** runs from north to south through the middle of the town. To the south of the Strøget lies **Hans Christian Andersen Boulevard,** which is the main thoroughfare that crosses through the city from east to west. To the south of this street is **Tivoli Gardens,** and beyond that the train station. Bridges along major arteries connect the eastern and western neighborhoods, which are separated from the center by canals.

THE OLD CITY This area centers around **Strøget,** Copenhagen's pedestrian shopping street—the longest in the world—which runs through the center of Old City from Rådhuspladsen (City Hall) to Kongens Nytorv. The street changes names several times. Smaller streets branch off and wind through the Old City leading to narrow alleyways and squares, more shopping, and the **Latin Quarter,** where the **University of Copenhagen** is. Christiansborg Palace, the seat of the Danish government is on Slotsholmen Island on the east side of the Old City, and to the north of that is Amalienborg Palace, where the Denmark royal family resides.

NYHAVN Just beyond Kongens Nytorv, sailors once hung out in this harbor area waiting to ship out. Today, it remains a popular place for tourists to eat along the waterfront. It's now considered chic. A central canal, with 19th-century boats in it and overlooking 18th-century building facades, makes it all the more charming.

CHRISTIANSHAVN Considered the "new town"—though it was built in the early 1500s to house the city's working class—today Christianshavn remains a mainly residential area with its own shopping street, **Torvegade.** The "free state" of **Christiania** (see later in this chapter) lies in the northwestern corner of this neighborhood.

VESTERBRO This hip and funky neighborhood was once Copenhagen's red-light district—and traces still remain, particularly in the area behind the train station. Restaurants, cafes, and bars line the main street, **Istedgade.** Otherwise, the neighborhood is mainly residential and quiet.

NØRREBRO This multicultural neighborhood in the eastern part of the city is home to many immigrants, but it's also become a popular spot for students and artists, and is home to funky bars and restaurants, and many of Copenhagen's most popular clubs—especially the area bound by **Assistens Kirkegård, Nørrebrogade, Åboulevard,** and the canal to the east. It's a bit run-down compared to some other 'hoods, but that's part of its charm.

Tourist Offices

The main tourist office is located near the train station, across from the main entrance to Tivoli. It's at Vesterborg 4a (☎ **70-22-24-42;** www.woco.dk/tourist). It is open January 2 through April 30 Monday to Friday 9am to 4pm, Saturday 9am to 2pm; May 1 through June 30 Monday to Saturday 9am to 6pm; July 1 through August 31 Monday to Saturday 9am to 8pm, Sunday 10am to 6pm; and September 1 to December 30 Monday to Friday 9am to 4pm, Saturday 9am to 2pm.

An even better option for those on a budget is the **Use-It Information Office,** which books budget accommodations, has free Internet, and offers information on various attractions and events in the city. Make sure to pick up their excellent magazine, *Playtime,* which includes information on attractions, restaurants, and nightlife as well as general information on the city itself. It's located at Radhusstræde 13 (☎ **33-73-06-20;** www.useit.dk). Hours are June 15 through September 14 daily 9am to 7pm; September 15 through June 14 Monday to Wednesday 11am to 4pm, Thursday 11am to 6pm, and Friday 11am to 2pm.

Recommended Websites

Copenhagen's got a number of sites to choose from; all are good in their own way.

○ **www.woco.dk**: The official tourism site of Copenhagen offering information on the city's attractions, as well as accommodations and general practical information.

○ **www.denmark.dk**: The official website of Denmark, run by the Ministry of Foreign affairs.

○ **www.copenhagen.com**: A website for information on Copenhagen, where you can even take a virtual tour of the city.

○ **www.cphpost.dk**: The online version of the *Copenhagen Post,* for all the latest news in English.

○ **www.useit.dk**: Look for the list of free events for the week and a guide to architecture in the city.

Culture Tips 101

The legal minimum drinking age here is 18, but the age restrictions are for the most part only enforced at bars. If you're obnoxious or endangering someone else, the police may show up; otherwise, they probably won't hassle you.

Things are tougher when it comes to drugs, hard and soft. They are illegal in Copenhagen, and you can get in big trouble with the authorities if you're snared with anything—even a gram of hash. The situation

Talk of the Town

Three ways to start a conversation with a local

1. **What do you think of your neighbors to the north?** The Swedes have to deal with a government-controlled alcohol monopoly in their own country, so they come to Copenhagen to get smashed on cheap booze, basically using the city as a resort for indulging. The indignant Danes view the Swedes as immature brats who can't hold their liquor.

2. **And what do you think of your neighbors to the south?** The Germans don't do comedy, and the Danes pride themselves on their sense of humor. Just wait till you see your first German sitcom.

3. **What do you think of all this rain?** Locals are obsessed with the weather — maybe because it's so rotten in Denmark!

in Christiania (p. 238) is also risky and even more complicated.

Recommended Books, Movies & Music

To be or not to be: Check out Shakespeare's *Hamlet.* The original rocks in its own certain way. For bedtime stories, check out Hans Christian Andersen's fairy tales. His stories present a troubled side of childhood: The original *Little Mermaid* is a lot darker and more cynical than the Disney version, for instance.

The list of movies you could associate with Copenhagen is a good one, beginning with the old *Hamlets;* moving on to *Pelle Erobreren (Pelle the Conqueror),* a story of father-son Swedish immigrants looking for a better life in Denmark, which won an Oscar for best foreign language film in 1988; and then on to *Babette's Feast,* another Oscar-winning flick in which a French housekeeper is sent to a small town to aid a pair of religious Danish sisters.

Download Aqua's *Barbie Girl* for some cheesy fun; for something a little less mainstream, try listening to the Raveonettes (garage pop), Junior Senior (dance), or the Horrorpops (punk).

Copenhagen Nuts & Bolts

Cellphone Info   Sonofon, TDC, and Orange are three of the best-known telecoms.

Currency   The Danish currency is the krone (DKK) which is divided into smaller øre. Bank notes are issued in denominations of 50DKK, 100DKK, 200DKK, 500DKK, and 1,000DKK, and coins are issued in 1DKK, 2DKK, 5DKK (all decorated with hearts, with a hole in the center), as well as 10DKK and 20DKK. Øre coins come in 25 and 50 denominations.

Banks are generally open Monday to Friday from 9:30am to 4pm (till 5:30pm on Thurs). There are many ATMs throughout the city, as well as exchange offices, open on weekends.

Embassies   The **U.S.** office is at Dag Hammerskjölds Allé 24 (☎ **35-55-31-44**); the **U.K.,** Kastelsvej 40 (☎ **35-44-52-00**); **German,** Stockholmsgade 57 (☎ **35-45-99-00**); **Canadian,** Kristen Bernikowsgade 1 (☎ **33-48-32-00**); and **Australian,** Dampfaergevej 26 (☎ **70-26-36-76**).

Emergencies   In an emergency dial ☎ 112 to contact the police or ambulance and fire service. Emergency calls from public pay phones are free. If you need a doctor, call the medical hot line at ☎ 70-13-00-41 weekdays from 8am to 4pm, or ☎ 38-88-60-41 from 4pm to 8am. On weekends or in an emergency, try **Bispebjerg Hospital** at Bispebjerg Bakke 23 (☎ 35-31-23-73).

Internet/Wireless Hot Spots   **Boomtown,** Scandinavia's largest Internet cafe, is across from Tivoli's main entrance, at Axeltorv 1 (☎ 33-32-10-32). The cost is 20DKK for 30 minutes, 30DKK for 60 minutes. It's open 24 hours. **Faraos Cigarer** is a small Internet cafe above a comic-book store. You can catch up on your Spider-Man and IM your pals about it at Skindergade 27 (☎ 33-32-21-11, ext. 5; www.faraos.dk). It's 10DKK for 30 minutes and 20DKK for an hour; it's open Monday to Tuesday 11am to 11pm, Wednesday to Thursday 11am to 5:30pm, Friday 11am to 6pm, and Saturday 10am to 7pm. You can also check your e-mail for free at the **Use-It Information Office** (see listing under "Tourist Offices," above), 20 minutes maximum.

Laundry   The **Laundromat Café** (Elmegade 15, in Nørrebro; ☎ 35-35-26-72) makes laundry fun. Put your clothes in a machine in the back, and have a drink or snack in the cozy cafe up front. A wash costs 32DKK; a dry is 1DKK per minute. In the cafe, salads and sandwiches run from 65DKK and up. It's open 8am to midnight.

Luggage Storage   You can store your luggage for free at the **Use-It Information Office** (see "Tourist Offices," above), but beware of their early closing time. At the train station, lockers cost from 25DKK. The office is open Monday through Saturday 5:30am to 1am and Sunday 6am to 1am. The HT information hub at Rådhuspladsen also has lockers to rent for 20DKK (daily 8am–10pm).

Pharmacies   If you need a pharmacy, look for an Apotek, usually accompanied by a green A sign. One 24-hour pharmacy is **Steno Apotek** at Vesterbrogade 6C (opposite the train station; ☎ 33-14-82-66).

Post Offices   It costs 7.50DKK to send a postcard to North America, and 6.50DKK to Europe. You can post them at the train station location, which is open weekdays 8am to 9pm, Saturday 9am to 4pm, and Sunday 10am to 4pm. Another office, at Købmagergade 33, off the Størget, is open Monday to Friday 10am to 5:30pm and Saturday 10am to 2pm.

Restrooms   Public toilets are available all over town, including inside the train station and at Rådhuspladsen. *Damer* is women; *Herrer* is men.

Safety   Copenhagen is a relatively safe city, though you should watch out for pickpockets and petty thieves in dimly lit or otherwise empty places and in areas around the train station. As with any place, use common sense if you're walking alone.

Telephone Tips   Public pay phones accept coins or prepaid Telecards. Telecards come in denominations of 30DKK, 50DKK, and 100DKK and are available from kiosks and post offices. *Note:* Phones don't give back change—even if you don't get connected. For international calls, use a Telecard. For number information, dial ☎ 118 for Denmark and ☎ 113 for international information and assistance.

Tipping   Service is usually included in the restaurant bill, so you don't have to leave a tip. Most people do round up, however.

Sleeping

Rooms may be hard to find from May to September, the high season, when Tivoli Gardens is open. Make sure to ask about off-season discounts if you come in fall or winter. The dates for each hotel's high- and low-season rates change every year. So, do ask. Also ask about two other things: whether breakfast is included (usually it isn't) and whether a bathroom means a tub or a shower. In most of the cheaper hotels, if you ask for a room without a bathroom (meaning you'll share a common bathroom with other boarders), you'll get a better price. And, in some hotels, the private bathrooms are so teeny, you may as well share. The rates below reflect a range from without bathroom to en suite bathrooms.

Hostels

→ **DanHostel** A modern, high-rise hostel, and reportedly Europe's largest with 15 stories and 1,020 beds. Rooms with 4 to 10 beds and clean bathroom are spotless and are furnished to look like they're straight out of an Ikea catalogue. It's in a great location, just a few minutes from Tivoli and the Strøget. *Hans Christian Andersen Blvd. 50.* ☎ *33-11-85-85. www.danhostel.dk/copenhagencity. Low season 130DKK shared room, 520DKK–780DKK 1- to 6-person family room; high season 150DKK shared room, 600DKK–900DKK 1- to 6-person family room. HI membership required. Amenities: Internet; kitchen; laundry facilities; sheets and towels (60DKK); TV (in common room).*

→ **Sleep-in Green** An "ecological hostel" that seeks to minimize the impact of its guests on the local environment. Organic snacks and drinks are sold at the reception. The three rooms—with 8, 20, and 38 bunks—all feel friendly and social. And it helps to have clean bathrooms. *Ravnsborggade 18, 2200 Copenhagen N.* ☎ *35-37-77-77. www.sleep-in-green.dk. 100DKK dorm bed. Breakfast*

40DKK. Late May to late Oct. Metro: Nørreport Station. Amenities: Blanket and pillow rental (30DKK).

→ **Sleep-in Heaven** A fun, social place to stay that attracts an international backpacking crowd that's especially convenient if you plan on hitting the bars in Nørrebro. The lounge area's pool table gets more play than the board games. And if you're in the mood, they offer a bridal suite. Open 24 hours. *Struenseegade 7.* ☎ *35-35-46-48. www.sleepin heaven.com. 130DKK dorm bed, 500DKK double with shared bathroom. Breakfast 40DKK. Bus: 250S. Amenities: Bar; free lockers; games room; Internet; sheets (30DKK).*

Cheap

→ **Hotel Jørgensen** A popular hotel with both private rooms and dorm beds, although its reputation is undeserved: The rooms are dark and dingy, and many rules must be followed regarding lockouts, quiet hours, door codes, and so on. However, the hotel is centrally located and does make for a good budget option when the others are full. It became the city's first gay hotel in 1984, although the white stucco building dates from 1906. The hotel also welcomes straight guests. *Rømersgade 11.* ☎ *33-13-81-86. www.hotel joergensen.dk. 135DKK dorm; 475DKK–575DKK single; 575DKK double with shared bathroom, 700DKK double with private bathroom; 170DKK per person for family room (4-person) with shared bathroom. Rates include buffet breakfast. Metro: Nørreport. Amenities: Breakfast room; bar; cafe; pool table. In room: TV (singles and doubles).*

Doable

→ **City Hotel Nebo** In a restored building, this hotel, whose website says it is "run on a Christian foundation," is behind the train station. Its philosophy is to offer rooms for everyone. The rooms are clean but small,

Copenhagen

SLEEPING ■
City Hotel Nebo **12**
DanHostel **44**
DGI-byens Hotel **9**
Hotel Jørgensen **16**
Hotel Selandia **11**
Saga Hotel **10**
Sleep In Green **5**
Sleep-In-Heaven **7**
The Square **13**

EATING ◆
Café Globen **14**
Domhusets Smørresbrød **39**
Ida Davidsen **25**
Kate's Joint **6**
La Glace **35**
Nyhavns Færgekro **26**
Riz Raz **38**
Samsara **27**
Vero Italiano (aka
  Honky Tonk's Café) **36**
Wienerbageriet **30**

PARTYING ★
Barcelona **4**
Copenhagen JazzHouse **33**
Det Lille Apotek **31**
Mojo Blues Bar **40**
PAN Club and Café **37**
Pussy Galore's Flying Circus **3**
Rust **2**
Studenterhuset **29**
Vega **8**

SIGHTSEEING ●
Amalienborg Slot
  (Amalienborg Castle) **24**
Assistens Kirkegård **1**
Botanisk Have
  (Botanical Gardens) **17**
Carlsberg Visitors Center **8**
Christiania **45**
Copenhagen Opera House **23**
Den Lille Havfrue (The
  Little Mermaid Statue) **21**
Det Kongelige Theater
  (Royal Theater) **28**
Frihedsmuseet
  (The Museum of Danish
  Resistance 1940-1945) **22**
Kongenshave **19**
Nationalmuseet **41**
Ny Carlsberg Glypototek **43**
Ørsteds Parken **15**
Østre Anlæg **20**

Rosenborg Slot
  (Rosenborg Castle) **18**
Strøget **34**
Tivoli **42**
University of Copenhagen **32**

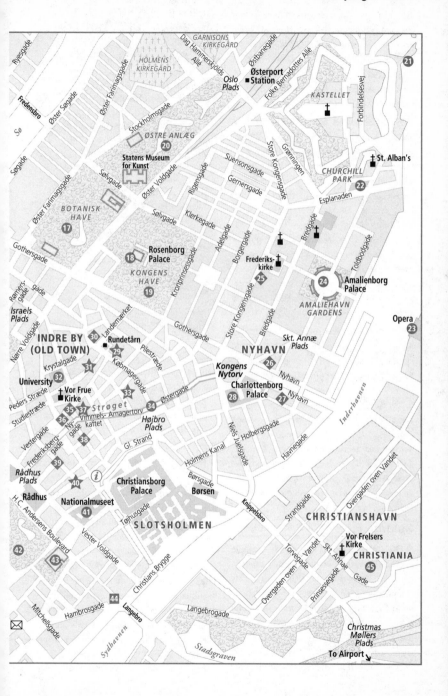

especially the so-called low-economy rooms that are cell-like in size. *Istedgade 6.* ☎ *33-21-12-17. www.nebo.dk. 360DKK–790DKK single; 690DKK–860DKK double; 840DKK–1,140DKK family (3–5 people); 950DKK suite. Bus: 1, 6, 16, 28, or 41. Amenities: Bike rental. In room: TV (in some).*

→ **Hotel Selandia** One of the nicer choices among the hotels behind the train station. The lobby was refurbished with, among other things, funky orange chairs and lacy curtains with butterfly decals. Some of the rooms repeat the orange theme. Most are furnished in a simple, modern Scandinavian style. *Helgolandsgade 12.* ☎ *33-31-46-10. www.hotel-selandia.dk. High season 575DKK–995DKK single, 695DKK–1,195DKK double; low season 450DKK–800DKK single, 540DKK–900DKK double. Extra bed 200DKK. Rates include breakfast. Amenities: Internet. In room: TV, fridge (in some), Internet.*

→ **Saga Hotel** One of several affordable hotels in the seedy area behind the train station (a sometimes troublesome area). Furniture and design are straight out of the 1970s; you'll feel like you've stepped back in time. *Colbjørnsensgade 18–20.* ☎ *33-24-49-44. www.sagahotelcopenhagen.com. High season 480DKK–695DKK single, 720DKK–950DKK double; low season 400DKK–525DKK single, 600DKK–720DKK double. Book online and save up to 38% off rack rates. Bus: 6, 10, 16, 28, or 41. Amenities: Breakfast room; lounge; nonsmoking rooms. In room: TV.*

Splurge

→ **DGI-byens Hotel** ★ Another example of Scandinavian minimalism, this modern hotel is attached to the DGI-byens sports complex, so you can swim for free (check online for swim center hours). The hotel also has a cafe and free Internet access in the rooms. *Tietgensgade 65.* ☎ *33-29-80-50. www.dgi-byen.dk. 825DKK–1,295DKK single, 1,025DKK–1,495DKK double. Rates include*

Reservations Service

The Tourist Information Center across from Tivoli Gardens' main entrance maintains a helpful hotel-booking service, Værelsænvisningen (☎ 70-22-24-42). You can book into a private home, a hostel, or a luxury hotel, and the price is the same: 60DKK per person. You must pay a deposit, which will later be deducted from your room fee (it's about 8.6% of your room's cost). You'll also get a city map and bus directions. This office doesn't accept advance reservations, and it's open April 19 to September 30, daily 9am to 9pm, and October 1 to April 18, Monday to Friday 9am to 5pm, and Saturday 9am to 2pm.

If you want to book in advance, try the **Hotel Booking Service** (☎ 33-25-38-44).

breakfast, entry to swim center, and spa certificate. Amenities: Restaurant; bar; lounge; laundry service; dry cleaning; room service; 5 indoor heated pools; sports center; sauna; spa; nonsmoking rooms; wheelchair friendly rooms. In room: TV, hair dryer, free Internet, safe, VCR.

→ **Hotel Skt. Petri** ★★ From the 1930s until recently, this was the site of a much-loved department store. Today, in an amazing reincarnation, it's become one of the grandest hotels in Copenhagen. Modern Danish design is showcased here. The 270 rooms are individually done—minimal yet elegant—with bright, cheerful colors and small touches, such as Mondrian-inspired headboards. The beds are exceedingly comfortable, with down mattress pads, soft pillows, Angora blankets, and comfy duvets. The lobby rises three floors, with an atrium garden. Musicians, artists, and designers are among those who frequent the fashionable

Bar Rouge, or dine at **Brasserie Bleu.** *Krystalgade 22.* ☎ *33-45-91-10.* *www.sktpetri.dk.* *998DKK–2,695DKK double, from 3,095DKK suite. S-tog: Nørreport. Amenities: Restaurant; bar; fitness room, laundry and dry cleaning services; nonsmoking rooms; 24-hr. room service; wheelchair friendly. In room: A/C, TV, Internet access, minibar, safe.*

➔ **The Square** ★★ This new, ultramodern 268-room luxury hotel is in tourist central, right in front of Rådhuspladsen. It's like stepping into a design store, especially in the common areas. The rooms are a bit small, but the beds are incredibly comfortable—and this kind of modern is comforting. The staff is friendly, too. *Rådhuspladsen 14.* ☎ *33-38-12-00. www.thesquarecopenhagen.com. 1,360DKK–2,325DKK single, 1,635DKK–2,325DKK double, 2,840DKK–3,255DKK suite. Rates include breakfast. Amenities: Bar; car rental; dry cleaning; Internet; laundry service; nonsmoking rooms. In room: A/C, TV, hair dryer, Internet, minibar, radio, trouser press.*

Eating

If you're not careful, dining in Copenhagen can be extremely costly, especially if you make a habit of eating in the trendy areas like the Strøget and Nyhavn.

It's possible to still eat well for an affordable price, though, if you grab a hot dog (around the Rådhuspladsen); you might want to try it with shredded onions on top and french fries on the side. Copenhagen's also got delicious pickled herring. If that doesn't grab you, wander into one of the groceries for sliced meats and bread and make your own picnic. A few of the best places to go are Kongsgarten near Kongens Nytorv, the Kastellet area near *The Little Mermaid* statue, Botansik Have (site of the Botanical Gardens), the lakeside promenades in southeastern Copenhagen, and the old moat at Christianshavn.

For dinner, the Danes tend to keep farmers' hours: 6:30pm is common, although restaurants remain open much later.

Hot Spots

➔ **La Glace** ★ CAFE This is Copenhagen's oldest confectioner, and it's easy to see why it's still in business: cozy atmosphere, cheerful staff, and delicious eats such as layer cakes, pies, and pastries. *Sportskage,* their specialty, is heaven on a plate! A large piece of this crushed nougat, caramelized choux pastry, and whipped-cream cake with a macaroon bottom is a bit pricey at 36DKK, but it is enough to share and is well worth the cost. It was originally produced for a play in 1891. *Skoubagade 3.* ☎ *33-14-46-46. Menu items from 7DKK. Mon–Thurs 8:30am–5:30pm, Fri 8:30am–6pm, Sat 9am–5pm.*

🎶 Best ➔ **The Strøget** ★★★ Grab some takeout and have a seat in a nearby square—a perfect people-watching spot, without the hefty cost. Besides the usual fast-food joints, Italian, Chinese, and Middle Eastern fare are available along the street, as well as cheap hot dogs.

Cheap

➔ **Domhusets Smørresbrød** DANISH For a light lunch or snack, the smørrebrød sandwiches here are delicious; the shrimp and egg was surprisingly tasty. *Kattesundet 18. Sandwiches from 10DKK.*

➔ **Vero Italiano (aka Honky Tonk's Café)** ITALIAN A tiny place that faces the busy square Gammel Torv, with friendly Italian owners. Grab a cheap meat or vegetable sandwich or a pizza to go. *Gammel Torv 2.* ☎ *33-70-00-04. Sandwiches 35DKK, pizza 25DKK. Daily 8am–8pm.*

Smørrebrød

We like splurging occasionally on traditional smørrebrød, an open-face sandwich topped with various ingredients from simple cheese to caviar and smoked salmon. The purest form is made with dark rye bread, called *rugbrød*. Other versions might include liver paste and cucumber, sliced pork (with or without a prune on top), or roast beef with béarnaise sauce. The high-end and most popular type is with tiny Danish shrimp topped with fresh dill or caviar. Most taverns and cafes offer smørrebrød. It also works well as picnic takeout.

Doable

➜ **Kate's Joint** MODERN INDIAN A groovy hangout in trendy Nørrebro, which fills up quickly with young locals for dinner. Huge portions of warm, nutritious food such as curries, noodle dishes, and stir fries. Out-of-date fashion magazines are on hand for some light reading. *Blågårdsgade 12.* ☎ *33-37-44-96. Main courses 59DKK–90DKK. Daily 6pm–10pm.*

➜ **Riz Raz** MEDITERRANEAN A wonderful place to chow when your body is begging for a large, nutritious vegetarian meal. Fill yourself up at the buffet with delicious salads, tasty falafel, mousaka, and other vegetarian delights—and the inattentive service only means more time to eat. Have a seat outside or on the upstairs level, but avoid the area around the buffet table. *Kompagnistræde 20 (at Knabro St.).* ☎ *33-15-05-75. Lunch buffet 59DKK, dinner buffet 69DKK, main courses 120DKK. Daily 11:30am–11pm.*

➜ **Samsara** TIBETAN For something a little different, try this restaurant on a quiet street off of Nyhavn. Try the *momos* (Tibetan dumplings) or the *Thangtuk* (noodle soup): traditional Tibetan fare. Other dishes include

soups, curries, and noodles. *Herßluß Trolles Gades 5.* ☎ *33-32-37-08. Main courses 69DKK–85DKK. Tues–Sun 3–11pm.*

Splurge

➜ **Det Lille Apotek** PUB This is a good spot for English-speaking foreign students to meet their Danish counterparts. Although the menu varies from week to week, keep an eye out for the prawn cocktail and tenderloin, both highly recommended. *St. Kannikestræde 15.* ☎ *33-12-56-06. Main courses 88DKK–188DKK. Mon–Sat 11am–midnight, Sun noon–midnight; closed Dec 24–26.*

➜ **Ida Davidsen** ★ DANISH Known as the spot for smørresbrød (traditional open-face sandwiches), this trendy spot caters to a mainly business crowd—they're only open for weekday lunch. Order your food from the huge selection at the counter, and don't worry if the decision seems daunting—the staff members are more than happy to help. Reservations are a must: I saw dozens of people turned away at the door. *St. Kongensgade 70.* ☎ *33-91-36-55. www.idadavidsen.dk. Sandwiches 65DKK–155DKK. Mon–Fri 10am–4pm. Closed July.*

📺 **Best** ➜ **Nyhavns Færgekro** ★ DANISH One of several restaurants set up along the water on Nyhavn. Here, you pay not just for the food but for the location; both are worth the splurge. You can go for various smørresbrød but the main draw here is the herring buffet served daily for lunch. *Nyhavn 5.* ☎ *35-15-15-88. Herring bußßet 98DKK, smørresbrød 54DKK–150DKK. Daily 11:30am–4pm and 5–11:30pm. (Call ßor hours iß you're interested in weekend brunch.)*

Cafes & Tearooms

➜ **Café Globen** CAFE A comfy spot to duck in from the rain for a coffee or beer, with friendly staff and an international feel, this cafe is owned by an organization of travelers. With free Internet and a Wi-Fi connection, happy hour (4–6pm) takes on a new meaning.

If you're interested in the group that runs the cafe, check out www.berejst.dk; it explains how well traveled these "shareholders" are. If you're lucky, someone will be sharing info about an exotic trip. *Turesensgade 2b.* ☎ *33-93-00-77. www.cafesloben.dk. Coffee and tea from 10DKK, beer from 25DKK. Mon–Wed 4–10pm, Thurs 4pm–midnight, Fri 3pm–1am, Sat 4pm–1am.*

➔ **Wienerbageriet** CAFE A busy cafe near the old university, and a good place to rest your legs after climbing the nearby round tower. Order something sweet at the counter and then take a seat in the adjacent room and watch local students stroll by outside. It's known for its "weinerbrod" (Danish pastries). *Købmagergade 67. Daily 6am–6pm.*

Partying

While Copenhagen will never be known as a wild and crazy place to party, Danes do like to get out, and there are pockets of nightlife in the city, mainly in young and trendy areas of Nørrebro and Vesterbro.

A great source of information is the magazine *Playtime*, available at the Use-It Information Office, or alternatively check out *Copenhagen This Week*, available in the Tourist Information Office. The big clubs have websites listing upcoming shows and events (see listings below). Check out the websites listed above (p. 226) for weekly listings, too.

Bars and clubs are usually dead Sunday through Tuesday, then a bit busier Wednesday and Thursday, and then packed on the weekend. If you don't mind sitting around in an empty club for a while, you can go early and often avoid both the line and cover charge; things heat up at around midnight. Copenhageners party well into the night, with things winding down at 4 or 5am in the hottest spots, although some places close at 1am.

Copenhageners are definitely up on all the latest fashion trends. While you can probably get away with jeans in the bars, it might be difficult to get into the fancier clubs dressed that casually. Also, if you go early in the week or early in the night, the clubs might not charge a cover at the door.

Clubs

➔ **PAN Club and Café** Copenhagen's most well-known gay club has two dance floors, six bars, a karaoke bar, as well as rooms for chilling out and an open yard. Every night is gay night, but a lot of straights come for the music. *Knabrostræde 3.* ☎ *33-11-37-84. www. pan-cph.dk. Cover charge 55DKK.*

MTV **Best** ➔ **Rust** ★ One of the most popular clubs in Copenhagen, with two floors where a trendy young international crowd grooves the night away. Hosts both DJs and live music. No one under 21 is admitted to the nightclub, but you'll spot very few people over 45. And anyone can go hear the live music. The range: reggaeton, funk, garage/grime, tech/house, post-punk, cutting-edge artsy. *Guldbergsgade 8.* ☎ *35-24-52-00. www. rust.dk. Cover 30DKK on Thurs (or free with student ID), 50DKK–110DKK on Wed and Fri–Sat.*

➔ **Vega** Concert hall and nightclub in an old but well-preserved building in Vesterbro catering to a slightly older (20 and up) crowd with local artists to players from all over the world. *Enghavevej 40.* ☎ *33-25-70-11. www. vega.dk. Cover 60DKK after 1am.*

Bars & Lounges

➔ **Barcelona** Popular with a young crowd, in Nørrebro. There's a small dance floor in back with a DJ on weekends. The beer is cheap (from 30DKK), but you're just as likely to see someone ordering martinis, mojitos, and champagne. *Fælledvej 21.* ☎ *35-35-76-11. www.restaurantbarcelona.dk.*

MTV Best → **Pussy Galore's Flying Circus** ★ The most creative bar/restaurant name in the city. Located on a central square in Nørrebro, it's a good place to have a drink before heading to a club. In summer, tables overflow onto the sidewalk. From juicy burgers to fresh salads, the menu makes it a good place to fill your tum, too. Prince Frederik, the playboy heir to the throne, reportedly shows up here now and again. *Sankt Hans Torv 30.* ☎ *35-24-53-00. www.pussy-galore.dk.*

Live Music

→ **Copenhagen JazzHouse** On a little street right off of the Strøget, the JazzHouse is the primo jazz club in Denmark. Various styles of jazz, world music, and improv are performed by talented Danish and international artists every Thursday, Friday, and Saturday, and additional shows are held during the week from September to April. During the Jazz Fest, the place stays open even later and gets even livelier. *Niels Hemmingsensgade 10.* ☎ *33-15-26-00. www. jazzhouse.dk. Cover 70DKK–260DKK. Bus: 10.*

→ **Mojo Blues Bar** Also in the Ströget area, the small, cozy, and candlelit Mojo features mostly Scandy blues every night of the week. Get here early—drafts are half-price from 8 to 10pm, and you might actually score one of the precious few seats. The music is mostly classic Delta blues played by guys named Lars and Anders. Go for the experience. It's open daily 8pm to 5am. *Løngangstræde 21C.* ☎ *33-11-64-53. www. mojo.dk. Cover 50DKK Fri–Sat. Bus: 2, 8, or 30.*

Late-Night Bites

→ **Studenterhuset** A student hangout, and a popular place for international students to mingle with their local counterparts. Occasional live music. *Købmagergade 52.* ☎ *35-32-38-61. www.studenterhuset.com.*

Performing Arts

For **discount seats** (sometimes as much as 50% off), go in person to a ticket kiosk at the corner of Fiolstraede and Nørre Voldgade, across from the Nørreport train station. Discount tickets are sold the day of the performance, Monday to Friday noon to 5pm and Saturday noon to 3pm.

→ **Det Kongelige Teater** ★★ The queen opened the 1,700-seat steel-and-glass **Copenhagen Opera House** in 2005 to much fanfare. It's the home of the **Royal Danish Opera,** one performance site for the **Royal Danish Ballet,** and a venue for visiting international artists. The foyer is open to anyone Monday to Friday 10am to 9pm, except before and during a performance (the lobby closes 4 hr. prior). Guided tours cost 100DKK and run Saturday and Sunday at 9:30am and 4:30pm. The other stages include the **Old Stage,** which opened in 1748; the **Stærekassen,** which is an Art Deco beauty next to the Old Stage; and a converted power station called the **Turbine Halls** that is now a theater. You can dine on-site at the restaurant before curtain time or opt for the lighter fare at the Opera Café. The season runs from August until the beginning of June. *Ekvipagemesteruej 10 (and other addresses).* ☎ *33-69-69-33. Tickets 70DKK–440DKK. Box office:* ☎ *33-69-69-69 (Mon–Sat noon–6pm.) Check out www.kglteater.dk and click on the English link to get full info on the various venues and programs.*

Sightseeing

The best way to explore Copenhagen is to walk through it, soaking up the atmosphere, admiring the architecture, and smelling the ever-present saltiness of the sea.

Copenhagen's rich history plays out on the streets in a display of diverse, beautiful attractions: palaces, jeweled treasures, and pretty cobblestone neighborhoods. And, although highly overrated, a visit to *The Little Mermaid* statue is like a right of passage in the city, and therefore a must. Tivoli Gardens is another. For something a little different, spend some time in a cafe in Christiania (which may not be independent for too much longer if the city government gets its way).

Festivals

May

Carnival in Copenhagen. A citywide event featuring musical acts and fantastic costumes celebrating local culture. For more info, call ☎ 33-38-85-04 or go to www.karneval.dk. Mid-May.

June

Midsummer's Night. A traditional event throughout Scandinavia, with music, bon-

Cellphone Tourism

A new, free service allows travelers to use mobile phones to get tourist info. The information, divided by districts, includes cafes, restaurants, movies, theaters, nightlife, shopping, and sightseeing.

Send an SMS with the text WOCO to ☎ 45-22-90-40-00, and the service will forward a link to your mobile. You might also want to connect directly via mobil.woco.dk. (*Remember:* Although the service is free, you do have to pay your regular cellphone rates.)

fires, and fireworks to mark the longest day of the year. June 21.

July

Copenhagen Jazz Festival. An annual music event in the city that draws huge crowds to performances by both local and international artists. For more info, call ☎ 33-93-20-13 or go to www.jazzfestival.dk. Mid-July.

August & September

Copenhagen International Film Festival. The city's annual movie shindig, with films from around the world, and often a celebrity or two. For more info, call ☎ 33-45-47-49 or go to www.copenhagenfilmfestival.dk. August or September.

The Little Mermaid's **Birthday.** Celebrations mark the anniversary of the raising of the famous statue. August 23.

Top Attractions

→**Amalienborg Slot (Amalienborg Castle)** ★★ The Buckingham Palace of Denmark, Amalienborg Castle has been the home of the royal family for over 200 years, since they moved from Christianborg when that palace was damaged by fire. Besides the attractive courtyard, there are two main things to see: the changing of the guard and the museum. The Royal Life Guard leaves Rosenborg Slot at 11:30am and marches to Amalienborg Slot, arriving at noon. When the Queen is in residence, they are accompanied by a band. The official "changing" only lasts a few minutes and while interesting to watch, should not be a priority on a busy day. The museum acts as a contemporary continuation of the Rosenborg collection, including a section of the palace with several rooms left as they were when the royals lived there from the 1860s to the 1940s. The museum gets crowded just after the changing of the guard, so try to see it before the

COPENHAGEN

event. ☎ 33-12-08-08. *Museum admission:
50DKK adults, 30DKK students. Photo permit
20DKK. Combo ticket with Rosenborg Slot:
80DKK. May–Oct by guided tour only, daily at
1pm. Bus: 1, 6, 9, or 10.*

Ⓜ️ Best → Tivoli ★★ Don't be turned off
by the costly entrance fee; walking into Tivoli
amusement park is like entering a living,
breathing fairy tale. Indulge your inner child
with amusement park rides, games, puppet
shows, cotton candy, and daily performances
guaranteed to delight even older souls. But be
prepared to spend: Rides cost between 15DKK
and 60DKK in addition to the entrance fee!
Happily, most of the outdoor performances
are free. Check the schedule at the entrance
for the day's itinerary. Tivoli is even more
beautiful in the evening, when it twinkles with
lights, and especially during the light-and-laser
shows performed nightly 15 minutes before
closing. *Vesterbrogade 3. ☎ 45-33151001. www.
tivoligardens.com. Admission 75DKK adults,
35DKK children. Ride tickets 15DKK each
(with rides requiring up to 4 tickets), or
purchase a multiride ticket (adults 195DKK,
150DKK children). Apr 15–Sept 25 Sun–Wed
11am–11pm, Thurs 11am–midnight, Fri 11am–
1am, Sat 11am–midnight. June 17–Aug 21 Wed–
Sat open 1 hr. later.*

Ⓜ️ Best FREE → Christiania ★★
Originally a 19th-century military barracks,
Christiania is now a self-defined free-state
utopia. The government abandoned this site
in 1971, and a group of young, liberal squatters moved in and proceeded to lay claim to
the area, coining it "the free state of
Christiania." Christiania still manages to be
self-governed (see the sign upon exit: NOW
ENTERING THE E.U.), but in the past few years,
police have cracked down on the open tolerance of drugs in the area, and the government is looking to reclaim the land it "lent"
the residents. Christiania is a bit seedy,
particularly Pusher Street, where people

Free & Easy

→ Take a ride on a free **bike.** (Note that you do have to put down a deposit
   that will be returned to you when you bring back the bike.)

→ See *The Little Mermaid* statue.

→ Visit **Christiania.**

→ Visit the **Ny Carlsberg Glyptotek** for free on Wednesday or Sunday.

→ Go to the **Nationalmuseet** or the **Frihedsmuseet,** which welcome visitors
   for free on Wednesday.

→ Take a **Tour of Parliament** in the Christianborg Palace.

→ Visit the **botanical gardens,** with everything from cacti to Alpine plants.

→ Wander with the locals on **night walks.** Favorite haunts include Nyhavn
   Quay and Christianshavn by the castle, which is lit at night.

→ **Some clubs** are free to students with ID or before 1am.

Bevar Christiania!

The residents of Christiania, both past and present, migrated to the free state to participate in an experiment in communal living and freedom. Nobody owns individual property, and a Citizens Council self-governs the town, ruling by consensus instead of majority. No written laws guide the residents of Christiania; people prefer to base their actions on common sense. There are only four rules: (1) no hard drugs, (2) no weapons, (3) no violence, and (4) no trading residences. While clearly not the most modern, prosperous place on earth, Christiania has done quite well for itself over the years: It is fully self-sustaining, providing sufficient electricity and water services to its residents; runs a successful recycling program; and even provides low-cost high-speed Internet. Residents of Christiania take pride in the success of their experiment and encourage visitors to see this success for themselves. The Danish government, however, is not a huge fan of the place. From the start, there have been disputes between the free state and the city of Copenhagen, and today, cries of *"Bevar Christiania"* ("Save Christiania") are heard loud and clear in Copenhagen as the government seeks to ultimately dismantle the community.

sometimes still do sell marijuana. Don't even think of taking photos here; you're likely to upset residents. Amid the worn down and dirty bits are colorful cafes, restaurants, and crafts stalls. The website (or your feet) will lead you to a nonalcoholic cafe, a women's smithy, and bikes designed specifically for the area (with a big basket). For a guided tour, meet by the entrance off Prinsessegade (June 26–Aug 31 daily at 3pm, Sept 1–June 25 Sat–Sun at 3pm; 30DKK). *Information office: New Forum.* ☎ 32-95-65-07. *www.christiania. org. Mon–Thurs noon–6pm, Fri noon–4pm.*

FREE ➜ *Den Lille Havfrue (The Little Mermaid)* **Statue** ★ In 1909, the Danish brewer Carl Jacobson attended a performance of the *Little Mermaid* ballet, which so moved him that he commissioned sculptor Edvard Eriksen to create a statue of the title character. Eriksen's bronze version of the maiden sits on a boulder on the shoreline, where she longingly looks out to the sea. The statue itself may be a bit of a disappointment if you're required to fight through a mob of tourists to get a glimpse of it, but it is, after all, the thing to see in Copenhagen as well as an important part of Danish heritage, and

would be a shame to miss. A more interesting sculpture is *Gefion Springvandet* (Gefion Fountain), just to the south. The powerful goddess Gefion is depicted in all her glory, reigning in her sons, who have been turned into oxen in order to plow Zealand from Sweden. She is majestic.

In summer, a special "Mermaid Bus," leaves from Rådhuspladsen (Vester Voldgade) at 9am and then at half-hour intervals until 5:30pm. On the "Langelinie" bus, there's a 20-minute stop at *The Little Mermaid.* If you want more time, take bus no. 1, 6, or 9. *www.mermaid sculpture.dk.*

➜ **Rosenborg Slot (Rosenborg Castle)** ★★ This castle, built by King Christian IV in the early 17th century, was initially used as a summer castle and then later for official functions and as an heirloom storehouse. Today, the castle is unimpressive from the outside. But don't be deceived. Grab a map from the entrance and stroll through the various rooms whose furnishings and accessories epitomize royalty. If you are impressed by material wealth, visit the cellar and the treasury of the Danish monarchy to see even more treasures, including the crown

ᴹ ᵀ ᵛ 🎓 The University Scene

The **University of Copenhagen** is the largest in Denmark, with over 30,000 students, and a hefty number of international students. Founded in 1497 and originally located in the Old City, it has since expanded to various locations throughout Copenhagen. The website has good links to a handbook on studying abroad, other courses of study in the country, and info on student life; visit www.ku.dk/english.

Student life centers on three areas of the city: the so-called Latin Quarter, in the Old City near the university's original location, and the trendy neighborhoods of Nørrebro and Vesterbro. A good place to meet local as well as international students is at Studenterhuset and Det Lille Apotek (see listings earlier in this chapter).

jewels. You might be overwhelmed. *Øster Voldage 4a.* ☎ *33-15-32-86. www.rosenborg slot.dk. Admission 65DKK; combo ticket with Amalienborg Slot 80DKK. Photo pass 20DKK. Jan–Apr Tues–Sun 11am–2pm; May and Sept daily 10am–4pm; June–Aug daily 10am–5pm; Oct daily 11am–3pm; Nov–Dec 17 Tues–Sun 11am–2pm. Bus: 5, 10, 14, 16, 31, 42, 43, 184, or 185. S-tog: Norreport.*

Museums & Galleries

➔ **The Carlsberg Visitors Center** Tour the new Jacobsen Brewhouse to learn how that yummy Carlsberg beer is turned from barley into delicious brew. It also has an exhibit of the history of Carlsberg, horse stables with horses still used to transport beer today, a sculpture garden, and kiosks to send e-mail to friends and family straight from the factory. Be sure to stick around for the sampling at the Jacobsen Bar. *Gamle Carlsberg Vej 11.* ☎ *33-27-13-14. www. carlsberg.dk. Admission 40DKK (includes samples). Tues–Sun 10am–4pm. Bus: 18 or 16. S-tog: Vesterþaelleddvej Station.*

12 Hours in Copenhagen

1. **Take a walk.** Make your way up Vesterbrogade, past Tivoli to the right, to Rådhuspladsen (City Hall Square). And walk some more: up the **Strøget** as it winds through the Old City.

2. **Check out the Royal Guards.** Arrive at 11:30am and follow the parade on their procession from Rosenberg Castle to Amalienborg Palace. Get there at noon to watch the changing of the guard.

3. **Walk even more.** Stroll along trendy Torvegade until you get to Prinsessegade. Go left and walk up to the entrance of Christiania, a good place to stop for a drink or bite to eat.

4. **Go to Tivoli Gardens.** Okay, so it's the biggest tourist attraction in Denmark—still, it's got its charm.

5. **Grab a seat along Copenhagen's beautiful waterfront at Nyhavn.** Old wooden sailboats, the setting sun, a drink in hand, and lots of smiles.

6. **Hop on a free bike and explore by pedal power.**

7. **Go to the Copenhagen Jazzhouse.** The place is packed, unassuming, and affordable—and pure Copenhagen.

➜**Frihedsmuseet (The Museum of Danish Resistance 1940–1945)** This museum highlights the period during World War II when Denmark found itself under German occupation. Rather than focusing on the era as one of sorrow, the museum documents the resistance movement and its activities, which included helping Jews escape the country. Exhibits include photos, letters, and video footage. *Churchillparken.* ☎ *33-13-77-14. www.natmus.dk. Admission (includes entry into Nationalmuseet) 40DKK adults, 30DKK students and seniors, free on Wed. May 1–Sept 30 Tues–Sun 10am–4pm, Sun and public holidays 10am–5pm; Oct 1–Apr 30 Tues–Sat 10am–3pm, Sun and holidays 10am–4pm. Free guided tours May–Sept Tues, Thurs, and Sun at 2pm. Bus: 1, 6, or 9.*

➜**Nationalmuseet** ★★★ To avoid being totally overwhelmed in this enormous museum, begin your exploration by watching the introductory video shown across from the entrance desk. It introduces visitors to the various exhibits. I'd recommend also getting the guide to "The History of Denmark in 60 Minutes" and follow it through an extensive—and sometimes long-winded—history of the country from 13,000 B.C. to the present. I skipped through the collection of Near Eastern and Classical Antiques (and you might also unless you're dying to see hundreds of pieces of very similar looking pottery), but I took more time in the Ethnographic collection, which showcases a brief tour of the traditional cultures of the world. *NY Vesterdage 10.* ☎ *33-13-44-11. www. natmus.dk. Admission 50DKK adults, 40DKK students, free on Wed. Tues–Sun 10am–5pm. Bus: 1A, 6A, or 15.*

➜**Ny Carlsberg Glyptotek** ★★ Carl Jacobson, of Carlsberg Brewery fame, founded this museum when he donated his huge art collection to the public in the 1880s. His treasures run the gamut from Roman sculpture to French post-Impressionist paintings. The building itself is a work of art: marble stairs; great lighting; and warm, earthy colors. There's also a pleasant winter garden and a rooftop terrace. *Dantes Plads 7 (just past Tivoli off of Hans Christiansen Andersen Blvd.).* ☎ *33-41-81-41. www.glyptoteket.dk. Admission 40DKK (50% discount until renovations are complete), free on Wed and Sun. Tues–Sun 10am–4pm. Bus: 1A, 2A, or 15.*

Playing Outside

Gardens & Parks

Copenhagen has a huge amount of free and clean 🎵 **Best** **green space.** Take a stroll in one of the gardens or **pack a picnic** and spend the afternoon lounging on the grass. Check out the suggestions below, or stumble upon your own pieces of Eden.

Probably the nicest, and most popular, park in the city is **Kongenshave,** surrounding the Rosenborg Slott, with well-manicured lawns and trees just begging you to sit under them. The **botanical gardens** across the street also make for a pretty haven. To the south is **Ørsteds Parken,** and to the north **Østre Anlæg,** both with trails and grassy knolls surrounding a duck-filled pond.

Bicycling

If the weather holds out, a great way to see the city is by bicycle (see p. 224 for rental information). You'll be following in the pedals of many city-dwellers.

Beaches

On a sunny day, visit the new beach in Amalgar, on the outskirts of the city: Metro to Lergravspaken or the beach in Bellevue. Catch the S-tog to Klampenborg.

Ice-Skating

In the winter, you can skate on the several free outdoor rinks in the city: at Blågårds Plads, Kongens Nytorv, or Frederiksberg Runddel. Skates are available for rental.

Shopping

In general, stores are open at the following hours: Monday to Friday 9:30 or 10am to 6 or 7pm; Saturday 9am to 3 or 4pm. On Sunday, only bakeries, florists, and souvenir shops are open, except for several Sundays in the summer, when all stores are permitted to open.

For trendy, but expensive, threads look no further than fashionable Strøget and the surrounding streets. For secondhand goods, try the Nørrebro area, especially around Ravnsborgade and along Elmegade, Guldbergsgade, and Blågårdsgade. If modern Danish designs are what you're after, check out Bredgade.

A good place to shop for unique souvenirs, and kitschy memorabilia, is at the weekend flea markets in the city: Israel Plads Flea Market (May–Oct Sat 9am–3pm), Gammel Strand Flea Market (May–Sept Fri 9am–5pm, Sat 9am–3pm), and Nørrebro Flea Market (along the cemetery wall in Nørrebro; May–Sept Sat 8am–2pm).

Road Trip

Founded in the 10th century as the first capital of Denmark, **Roskilde** recently celebrated its 1,000th anniversary. Undoubtedly, the city is full of historic landmarks, including authentic Viking ships that were resurrected and reassembled in the 1950s. But today the city is probably better known for its huge annual rock festival.

Roskilde Basics

Trains and buses both leave frequently from the central station in Copenhagen for the 35-minute ride out to Roskilde.

The tourist information office is located at Gullandsstræde 15 (☎ **46-35-27-00**). It's open January 1 to March 31 and August 23 to December 1 Monday to Thursday 9am to 5pm, Friday 9am to 4pm, and Saturday 10am to 1pm; April 1 to June 27 Monday to Friday 9am to 5pm and Saturday 10am to 1pm; June 28 to August 22 Monday to Friday 9am to 6pm and Saturday 10am to 2pm. Info is lso available at the city's website: www.roskilde-info.dk.

Exploring Roskilde

The Roskilde Festival is one of Europe's massive annual summer music festivals, attracting an enormous crowd and big-name international artists: The 2005 lineup included Green Day, Foo Fighters, and Black Sabbath. It's usually held at the beginning of July. For more information call ☎ **46-35-27-00**, or check the website at www.roskilde-festival.dk.

➜ **Roskilde Domkirke (Cathedral)** Upon arrival in Roskilde, the first thing you will notice is the cathedral, which, with its twin towers, dominates the landscape. Construction on the cathedral began in 1170, and finished a whopping 200 years later. The interior is also impressive: The tombs of previous Danish monarchs are here, and their final resting places are lavishly decorated. *Domkirkestræde 10.* ☎ *46-31-65-65. Admission 35DKK adults. Apr–Sept Mon–Fri 9am–4:45pm, Sat 9am–noon, Sun 12:30–4:45pm; Oct–Mar Tues–Sat 10am–3:45pm, Sun 12:30–3:45pm.*

COPENHAGEN

➜**Viking Ship Museum (Vikingeskib-shallen)** ★ When the Vikings first inhabited Roskilde 1,000 years ago, they planted several ships in the fiord to ward off attacks. These ships have since been painstakingly recovered and are now on display at this museum. Visit the boatyard to watch the restoration of old boats, and the creation of new ships based on Viking design. You can even embrace the Viking spirit by taking a ride in a traditional Nordic boat. *Vindebader 12.* ☎ *46-30-02-00. www. vikingeskibsmuseet.dk. Admission May–Sept 75DKK adults, 55DKK students. Boat rides 50DKK adults; must also purchase admission to museum. Daily 10am–5pm. The boats run May 1–Sept 30.*

Sleeping

➜**DanHostel Roskilde (HI)** Centrally located hostel, and the only budget place to stay in town. *Vindeboder 7.* ☎ *46-35-21 -84. www.danhostel.dk/roskilde. Low season: 150DKK shared room, 400DKK–720DKK 1- to 6-person family room; high season: 150DKK shared room, 600DKK–900DKK 1- to 6-person family room. Breakfast 45DKK. Amenities: Bike rental; laundry; TV. In room: Sheets (45DKK), towels (15DKK).*

➜**Hotel Prinsden** ★ A renovated hotel whose foundations date back to the late 17th century, its rooms are cozy and nicely furnished. *Algade 13.* ☎ *46-30-91-00. www. hotelprindsen.dk. 1,225DKK single standard, 1,425DKK business; 1,325DKK double standard, 1,525DKK business; 1,725DKK deluxe; 2,150DKK– 6,000DKK suite. Extra bed 250DKK. Rates include breakfast. Bus: 602 or 603. Amenities: Restaurant; bar; dry cleaning; laundry service; nonsmoking rooms; 24-hr. room service; sauna. In room: TV, hair dryer, Internet access, mini-bar, trouser press.*

Eating

Plenty of affordable restaurants, as well as several supermarkets, are located on Algade and Skomagergade streets.

➜**La Brasserie** DANISH/INTERNATIONAL One of the finest dining venues in town, with friendly staff and Parisian-like decor. *Algade 13.* ☎ *46-30-91-00. Main courses from 120DKK. Daily noon–10pm.*

The Dalmatian Coast

Countless publications have proclaimed that the Dalmatian Coast is the world's "next French Riviera." I disagree: The Croatian coast is its own animal. Few other destinations have such a long history of political turmoil, and yet the Dalmatian Coast is thriving. Tens of thousands of tourists flock to the islands here each summer. The reason? Reaching from Split to Dubrovnik, this craggy coast boasts an ample supply of ancient ruins and natural beauty (with vineyards, lavender fields, and olive groves) that appeals to both jetsetters and backpackers. The coast is also home to the world's hippest nightlife. If you're not impressed with the area's surprising beauty and super-stylish parties, I'd be seriously shocked—the Dalmatian Coast possesses too much history and too much life *not* to be exhilarating.

The Best of the Dalmatian Coast

○ **The Best Place to Feel like a King or Queen:** Tucked inside Diocletian's palace, the **Hotel Peristel** in Split has witnessed 1,500 years of history. Though the facade is respectful of the magnificent Roman ruin, its interior is brand new, with *tons* of creature comforts. See p. 250.

○ **The Best Place to Feel House Envy:** What remains of **Diocletian's Palace** and what has been built out of its remains is now Split's Old Town. In order to comprehend Diocletian's enormous ego, you have to walk around it, through it, and under it. See p. 252.

○ **The Best Town for Water Lovers:** **Bol** has a worldwide reputation as a windsurfer's paradise, but it's also a great place to try scuba diving, parasailing, and jet-skiing. See p. 258.

○ **The Best Club: Carpe Diem** in Hvar packs an amazing amount of friendly revelers into its swank space. The best part is that both (suitably dressed) backpackers and rich folks are at home here. See p. 256.

The Dalmatian Coast

Primošten
Podorljak
Prapatnica
Kaštel Stari
Trogir
Okrug Gornji
Rogač
Split
Solin Klis
Stobreč
Podstrana
Jesenice
ŠOLTA
Supetar
Nerežišća
Pučišća
BRAČ
Bol
Sumartin
Hvar Town Stari Grad
Komiža
Vis
VIS
HVAR
Vrboska *Hvarski Channel*
Jelsa
Zavela
Poljica
Igrane
Bogomolje
Sućuraj
Korčulanski Channel
ADRIATIC SEA
Vela Luka
Blato
Brna
KORČULA
Korčula
Lovište
Pelješac Pen.
Orebić
Trpanj
Potomje
Lastovo
LASTOVO
MLJET N.P.
MLJET
Sobra
Konta
Hrvače
Sinj
Brnaze
Trilj
Dugopolje
Omiš *Cetina R.*
Cista Provo
Brela
Baška Voda
Makarska
Runović
Drvenik
Gradac
Ploče
Opuzen
Drače Klek
Janjina
Dubrava
Luka Mali Ston
Ston
Livno
Podgradina
Buško L.
Tomislavgrad
Imotski
Vrgorac
Ljubuški
Međugorje
Čaplinja
Metković
Gornji Vakuf
Ravnica
BOSNIA– HERCEGOVINA
Siroki Brijeg
Mostar
Stolac
Topolo
Doli
Slano
Trsteno
Orašac
Dubrovnik
Mljetski Channel

⊛ **Zagreb**
CROATIA
Area of detail

0 ——— 10 mi
0 ——— 10 km

Dalmatian Coast Basics

Recommended Books, Movies & Music

One movie classic set in the area is 1981's *Velo Misto*, which offers a portrait of Split between 1910 and 1947.

Considered to be the "Elvis of Dalmatia," Oliver Dragojević is hugely popular in this area. As in Dubrovnik, folk music rules in coffee bars and restaurants, but clubs groove to a decidedly more techno and rap driven beat.

See the Dubrovnik chapter for more Croatian book, movie, and music picks.

Festivals

January

Old Christmas. Roman Catholic Croatians, about 90% of the population, celebrate Christmas on December 25. Serbian Croatians who follow Eastern Orthodox rules, however, celebrate Christmas 2 weeks later by taking a day off from work. January 7.

February

MTV Best **Carnival.** Break out your costumes to parade in this festival—various towns throughout Croatia put their own spin on the country's carnival celebrations, but Split's is especially memorable. Shrove Tuesday.

May

Feast of St. Domnius. This is a public holiday for the patron saint of Split. Market stands line the town's streets, and the saint's bones are displayed in the Cathedral. May 7.

June to August

Split Summer Festival. The arts take center stage, usually in the beautiful Croatian National Theater or in the Peristil, in addition to other venues around town. Be sure you have hotel reservations. Contact the Croatian National Theater (Gaje Bulata 1; ☎ **021/585-999;** www.hnk-split.hr) for information and tickets to various performances. July to August.

Sword Dance Festival. An annual spectacle that recalls a battle between Christians and "infidels" that was fought over a woman. Visit www.visitkorcula.com for info. In Korčula, every Monday and Thursday at 9pm in July and August; several times on July 29, the town's festival day; on Thursdays in June and September; and other times when tourist traffic is heavy.

The University Scene

Split has a university with about 11,000 students; it's located at Livanjska 5 (☎ **021/558-200;** www.unist.hr).

Split

The old city of Split is beautiful, especially the justifiably famous remains of **Diocletian's Palace** (p. 252). Yet the town's population swells in the summer, making it feel overrun. I eventually wanted to flee for a smaller, less trampled town. The city is a good base for seeing the rest of the coast, though, because the rail station and ferry and catamaran terminals are here.

BY AIR Split's **airport** (☎ 021/203-171; www.split-airport.hr) is 26km (16 miles) northwest of the city center between Kaštela and Trogir. Flights from all over Croatia as well as from many European cities fly in and out on regular routes. Service is more frequent in the summer months, and an airport bus shuttles passengers between the airport and Split's main bus station for 30kn each way. Contact the **main bus station** (next to the train station, at Obala Kneza, Domogoja 12; ☎ 021/203-305; www.ak-split.hr) for schedule information.

BY TRAIN Split's main train station is next door to the main bus station at Obala Kneza Domogoja 10 near the town center. It runs between Split and Zagreb, Knin, and Šibenik. There is also an overnight train between

Split and Zagreb. Call the **Split train station** (☎ 021/338-535) or the **national train office** (☎ 060/333-444; www.hznet.hr) for schedule and fare information. *FYI:* This route is not covered by the regular Eurail pass, so you will need to pay an extra fee.

BY BOAT Except for its historic core, Split's port is the busiest part of town because international, local, and island ferries move in and out here almost constantly. The port also accommodates daily fast catamarans to the islands of Brač, Hvar, Vis, Korčula, Lastovo, and Šolta, as well as huge ferries that make overnight runs to Ancona, Italy. Contact the local **Jadrolinija** office (☎ 021/338-333; www.jadrolinija.hr), **Sem Marina** (☎ 021/338-292; www.sem-marina.hr), or **Adriatica** (☎ 021/338-335) for schedule and price information.

The catamaran only takes 50 minutes for Brač and Hvar as opposed to the ferry, which takes $1^1/_2$ hours. Generally speaking, the catamaran to Hvartown leaves at 2pm while the ferry leaves at 2:30pm. Check out the schedule at the Jadrolinija booth near the F-Café. The ferry and catamaran schedules are fickle, so times listed may not be accurate

Split

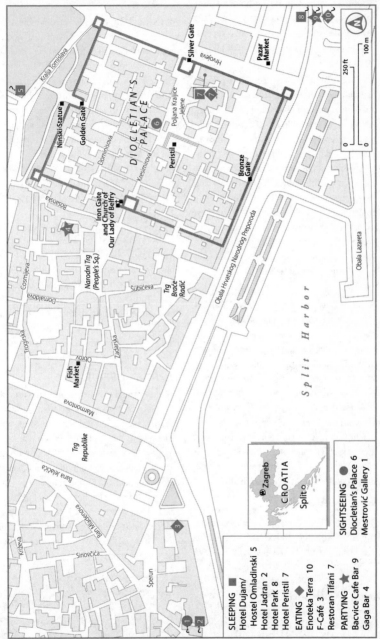

Silver Gate

Hrvojeva

Pazar Market

Kralja Tomislava

Ninski Statue

Golden Gate

DIOCLETIAN'S PALACE

Dominisova

Pojana Kraljice Jelene

Peristil

Kresimirova

Bronze Gate

Iron Gate and Church of Our Lady of Belfry

Bosanska

Narodni Trg (People's Sq.)

Cosmjeva

Domaldova

Šubićeva

Trg Braće Radić

Obala Hrvatskog Narodnog Preporoda

Obala Lazareta

Trogijska

Zadarska

Obrov

Fish Market

Marmontova

Split Harbor

Trg Republike

Bana Jelačića

Ban Mladenova

Križeva

Sinovčića

Šperun

CROATIA

Zagreb

Split

SIGHTSEEING
- Diocletian's Palace 6
- Meštrović Gallery 1

SLEEPING ■
- Hotel Dujam/ Hostel Omladinski 5
- Hotel Jadran 2
- Hotel Park 8
- Hotel Peristil 7

EATING ◆
- Enoteka Terra 10
- F-Café 3
- Restoran Tifani 7

PARTYING ★
- Bacvice Cafe Bar 9
- Gaga Bar 4

when you go. In summer, from June to September, a high-speed **catamaran** runs between Split and Ancona, Italy, on a daily basis. **SNAV,** an Italy-based transit company, can be reached locally at ☎ **021/322-252** (www.snav.it).

BY BUS   Split is well served by local, national, and international buses. Local bus lines run through Split and its suburbs, including Salona, Klis, Omiš, and Trogir, while others travel many times a day to Zagreb, Zadar, Rijeka, Dubrovnik, and destinations beyond. International buses provide daily service to Slovenia, Germany, and Italy, and weekly service to Austria and England. This is the easiest and quickest route to **Dubrovnik,** and the tickets for such a trip generally run around 100kn for a one-way trip. Schedule and fare information is available at ☎ **021/338-483.**

BY CAR   Before May 2005, it took 5 hours or more to drive from Zagreb to Split. But that changed when Croatian officials cut the ribbon to open the new Zagreb-Split Autocesta that flows through mountains and bypasses country roads running through smaller villages and towns. The new route isn't quite as scenic as the old, but this toll way has cut about an hour from the trip. Except for weekends in July and August, the 364km (226-mile) drive from Zagreb to Split now takes less time than the 217km (135-mile), south-to-north drive from Dubrovnik to Split on the Adriatic Coastal Highway.

Getting Around

ON FOOT   The best way to get around the city is by foot. The walled city is limited to pedestrians; even the street skirting the Riva

immediately outside the palace walls is closed to motorized vehicles.

BY CAR & SCOOTER   I rented a moped for venturing outside the Old City. It costs 300kn for 24 hours and makes transport between the beaches, hotels, and nightclubs far more accessible. Mopeds can be rented from any of the travel agencies up and down the main street, **Obala Hrvatskog.** You could rent a car from the same agencies that hawk scooters, but I recommend going with Avis or Hertz instead. **Avis** has an office inside the Hotel Marjan at Obala kneza Branimira 8, and can be reached at ☎ **021/399-000. Hertz** has an office at Tomića stine 9 (☎ **021/360-455**).

Split Basics

ORIENTATION: SPLIT NEIGHBORHOODS

Split is divided into two neighborhoods: the tourist-saturated **Old City,** and the rest of town. The **Old City** is recognizable by its stone streets and its proximity to the sea, while the rest of the city looks typically Eastern European with dour, five-story or more modern buildings.

TOURIST OFFICE

The main **tourist office** is in the center of the plaza outside of Diocletian's Palace (☎ **021/342-666;** www.visitsplit.com), and it doubles as an excellent meeting place for any new backpacker friends. It's open June to September Monday to Friday from 8am to 8pm, Saturday from 8am to 7pm, and Sunday from 9am to 1pm; October to May Monday to Friday from 9am to 5pm. Pick up a copy of the free *Split Guide,* which has listings for most of the attractions in town; the office also has free maps.

Split Nuts & Bolts

Cellphone Providers & Service Providers   There are three mobile operators in Split: **T-Mobile** (098, 099), **VIP** (091), and **Tele 2** (095); all have stores in Old Town. The

T-Mobile store, located at the end of Obala Hrvatskog, has a huge pink sign and a cafe out front that serves gelato and pastries.

Currency   Always carry cash because some smaller places do not have the capability to deal with credit cards. The main bank in Split is **Splitska Bank.** They have a partnership with Visa, so if you forget to bring your ATM card, you can get cash through your credit card here.

Embassies   There are no embassies in Split, but consulates from major tourist countries are available. See "Dubrovnik Nuts & Bolts" on p. 323 for info.

Emergencies   You can call for police at ☎ **92;** a fire truck at ☎ **93;** an ambulance at ☎ **94;** and road assistance at ☎ **987.** For general information call ☎ **981.**

Internet/Wireless Hot Spots   There are Internet centers all over the city; most will charge 5kn to get access and another 5kn every additional 10 minutes. You'll get the cheapest rates at **Mriza** (Kruziceva 3; ☎ **321-320)** and **Issa** (Dobric 12; ☎ **341-050).**

Laundry   There's a laundromat called **Galeb** at Viseslava 3 (☎ **589-297);** it's open Monday to Friday from 7am to 8pm.

Luggage Storage   Most luggage storage places are located around the bus station and train station. Look for a sign that says GARDEROBA, store your luggage, and you will receive a slip of paper with the time you deposited and the number of your luggage. *Note:* Garderobas close at around 10pm, so be sure to have your stuff out by then unless you want it left overnight.

Post Offices   Split's main post office is at Kralja Tomislava 9 (☎ **021/356-990).** It's open Monday to Friday 7am to noon and 1 to 6pm.

Restrooms   See p. 323 in the Dubrovnik chapter for info.

Safety   Generally speaking, Croatia is a very safe country and violent crime is rare. Tourists aren't particularly targeted for pickpocketing, but it has been known to happen. As a rule, don't flash around your money, especially on public transportation, and you should be fine.

Tipping   See p. 323 in the Dubrovnik chapter for info.

Sleeping

Hotel rooms in Split are scarce, and reasonably priced ones almost nonexistent, though private accommodations are easy to secure. Split has never been known as a vacation "destination." Rather, its reputation has been as a gateway to points south along the Dalmatian coast. But that attitude is changing, and hotels are renovating, while small boutique hotels are entering the market.

HOSTELS

➔**Hostel Omladinski** Omladinski is the best bet in Split for a budget stay. Depending on when you come, the pleasant staff members (who are fluent in English) will hook you up with room rates that rarely surpass 80kn. Despite the "hostel" in the name, most of the rooms only have two to three beds. In addition, it has an easy-to-find location, close to the supermarket **Kerum,** which will help stretch your budget even further. *Velebitska 27, Split, 21000.* ☎ *021/538-028. www.hoteldujam.com. High season from 80kn double; lower low-season rates vary. Amenities: Shared bath-rooms; kitchen; TV (in common room).*

DOABLE

➜ **Hotel Dujam** ★★ The Hotel Dujam is like the richer, prettier cousin of Hostel Omladinski. The rooms are more spacious and better decorated, and there are bath-rooms in the rooms. Because it's situated on the top floor (the penthouse if you will) the hotel also has excellent views of the moun-tains and the sea. *Velebitska 27, Split, 2100.* ☎ *021/538-025. www.hoteldujam.com. 37kn–74kn single, 25kn–54kn double. Amenities: Restaurant; conference hall; laundry service. In room: A/C, cable TV, Internet.*

➜ **Hotel Jadran** This hotel, tucked about 15 minutes away from the city center on a secluded beach, is a great choice if you crave quiet. The rooms are relatively small, but they are clean. Everything here is decorated in deep, dark blue to match the seaside views—combined with spotless white walls, the color scheme actually works. The staff is eager to please but they speak little English. *Sustjepanski put 23.* ☎ *212/398-622. www. hoteljadran.hr. 73€ single, 108€ double. Amenities: Restaurant; beauty salon; wellness center with swimming pools and tennis courts. In room: TV.*

SPLURGE

➜ **Hotel Park** ★ This is one of the nicest hotels in town, and the staff knows it. (They tend to be a little snooty.) Housed in a lovely pink sandstone building and close to the city's best nightclubs and beaches, the hotel boasts some of the largest, best-equipped rooms in town. The hotel's restaurant also serves good grub and occasionally has per-formers; you might want to stop by to eat even if staying here is out of your price range. *Hatzeov perivoj 3.* ☎ *021/406-400. www.hotelpark-split.hr. 103€–127€ single, 130€–157€ double. Amenities: Restaurants; salon; wellness center. In room: A/C, TV, Internet, minibar, safe.*

➜ **Hotel Peristil** ★★ The Peristil opened in April 2005, giving guests a place to sleep smack in the middle of Diocletian's former living room and next door to the Cathedral of St. Domnius. The Peristil is just inside the Silver Gate and, in fact, the hotel shares walls with the palace, which puts guests in literal touch with history. The Peristil's own-ers worked with conservators for 6 years to come up with a design that respects the sur-rounding ancient architecture before they were able to build and open their hotel, and they have done an excellent job. All guest rooms are comfortably sized and have origi-nal artwork on the walls. Most have showers rather than tubs. **Restoran Tifani** ★★ (p. 251) downstairs is great. *Poljana Kraljice Jelene 5.* ☎ *021/329/070. www.hotelperistil. com. July–Aug from 120€ double; off-season rates vary. Rates include breakfast. Amenities: Restaurant; bar. In room: A/C, TV, hair dryer, Internet access.*

Eating

Beware dining in Split: Some restaurants overcharge. Though the ambience is perfect at all the city's seaside restaurants, few are worth the price of a second bite of food. To save money, plan to supplement your din-ners and late lunches with pastries and fresh fruits from the city's market. Also, note that if a place calls itself a "cafe," it usually only serves ice cream.

HOT SPOTS

MTV Best ➜ **Bar Gaga** ★ SALADS/ SANDWICHES This coffee house/bar is lively all the time, but especially after mid-night when everything else closes down. Crammed into a narrow street junction, Gaga by day is a crowded coffee stop, and by night is a collection of tables on the street where wall-to-wall people try to hold conversations over throbbing disco music. *Iza Loža 5.* ☎ *021/342-257. Entrees 20kn–40kn. Daily 7am–whenever (officially 11pm).*

CHEAP

➜**F-Café** ★ ICE CREAM If you're craving a scoop of icy goodness, F-Café is Split's front for ice-cream trafficking. Though it may look like a restaurant, in reality you'll encounter only coffee, beer, and ice cream. Get ready to empty your pockets, though, as an ice cream concoction will set you back 60kn. The cafe's locale by the waterfront is the perfect place to wait for your ferry out of Split, or simply to take a seat and watch the ships roll into town. *Obala Hrvatskog 1.* ☎ *021/612-324. Ice cream 60kn. Daily 8am–9pm.*

DOABLE

➜**Enoteka Terra** ★ WINE BAR/CROATIAN Enoteka Terra is really only moonlighting as a restaurant. In addition to dishing up food, it also serves as a wine shop (there's an amazing wine cellar). When it's not busy, take a minute to converse with the waiters who are more than willing to answer any questions. The best part? It costs about the same (perhaps less) than most of the restaurants in town. *Prilaz bracé Kaliterna 6.* ☎ *021/ 314-800 or 021/314-801. www.vinoteka.hr. Main course 20kn. Daily 4pm–midnight.*

➜**Restoran Tifani** ITALIAN/CROATIAN This restaurant, in the Hotel Peristel, is a pleasant enough place to stop for lunch, though it's a little overpriced. The food is typical of what is found throughout the coast—seafood with an Italian spin—but the real reason to come is for the atmosphere. The restaurant is surrounded by ancient walls and heavy foot traffic—if you score an outside seat, you'll get some prime people-watching accomplished. *Poljana Kraljice Jelene 5.* ☎ *021/329-070. www.hotelperistil. com. Main course 45kn–160kn. Daily 7am–midnight.*

Partying

➜**Bacvice Café Bar** ★ This is really the only club in the city worth going to—or at least the locals who crowd in here seem to think so. Bacvice is in the mega-mall of all club scenes, housed inside a promenade-like complex with multiple dance floors, blasting all types of music. Despite being the place where all the well-dressed, pretty people come, the club still doesn't buy its own soundtracks; they are all illegally downloaded. *Kaliterna setaliste, on the beach. No phone.*

➜**Bar Gaga** ★ In addition to being a great place to eat, Gaga may very well be Split's hottest bar. The service is slow, but that's because it's always packed with every young, hip person in town. Grab a seat outside if possible, as the inside gets awfully sweaty with all of the barely clothed club-goers. See the dining review, earlier in this chapter, for info.

Performing Arts

➜**Croatian National Theater** ★★ The theater is outside the walls directly north of the intersection of Marmontova and Kralja Tomislava. Once a nondescript mousy brown, the exterior of this beautiful 19th-century building has been restored to Habsburg-yellow splendor. The cool, dark interior is no less impressive, and is the setting for assorted performances during Split's summer festival and periodically during the rest of the year. *Trg Gaje Bulata 1.* ☎ *021/585-999. www.hnk-split.hr.*

Sightseeing

The main attraction in Split is **Diocletian's Palace** and its surrounding environs. Locals have mapped out a 19-point plan to highlight the palace and its nearby attractions, and you'll find the starting map outside the entrance to the Old City. If the signs prove too confusing, follow "Exploring the Palace," below.

Before leaving Split, try to amble down **Riva,** one of Croatia's busiest promenades. At any time of day, you'll catch folks drinking coffee at the street's sidewalk tables. The strip is busiest at night, though, when people come to linger over dinner, stroll the concrete length with their ice-cream cones, and arrive or depart on the late ferries.

MTV **Best** → **Diocletian's Palace** ★★★

The Roman Emperor Diocletian's heavily protected enclave is basically a military installation whose footprint covered nearly 3 hectares (10 acres) and included the emperor's apartments, several temples, and housing for soldiers and servants.

Diocletian lived in this palace built of local limestone (mostly from the island of Brač) after abdicating his throne in A.D. 305 following a reign of 21 years. Immediately following Diocletian's death in A.D. 316, the immense palace was used as government office space, but it inadvertently became a city of refugees in the early 7th century when threatened inhabitants of a nearby city fled to the security of the palace walls here, which were 2m (6 ft.) thick and nearly 30m (100 ft.) high at points.

This huge influx of refugees overcrowded the palace compound, and the new settlement spread outside its walls. Successive rulers, including the Byzantine emperors, the Croatian kings, the Hungarian-Croatian kings, and the Venetians, later built structures within and outside the complex, changing it so much that its Roman character has almost disappeared.

After the fall of Venice in 1797, the Austrians took over, ceded control of the city to France for a short time in the early 19th century, and then took over again until World War I, when control reverted to the Yugoslav government and ultimately Croatia. *Historic center of town. Hours run according to the Cathedral of St. Domnius: Kraj Sv. Duje 5.* ☎ *021/342-589. Admission 5kn. July–Aug daily 8am–8pm; other times daily 7am–noon*

and 5–7pm. You can see the cathedral treasure for an extra 5kn: saints' heads done in silver, body-part reliquaries, and such. The adjacent campanile: another 5kn 8am–noon and 4–7:30pm daily. Free admission to see the rest of the palace.

→ **Meštrović Gallery** ★ The Meštrović Gallery is housed in the magnificent mansion built as a home/atelier for Croatian sculptor Ivan Meštrović and his family. Meštrović's religious art comprises most of the gallery's permanent exhibits, but traveling exhibitions from Croatia and other locations are periodically on display. Walk up the road to Šetalište Ivana Meštrovića 39 to visit the 16th-century **Kaštelet,** a summer house on the gallery property purchased and remodeled by Meštrović in 1939 as a showcase for his "Life of Christ" reliefs. There is no extra charge to enter Kaštelet if you have a ticket to the main gallery. *Šetalište Ivana Meštrovića 46.* ☎ *021/358-450. Admission 15kn adults. Summer Tues–Sun 9am–9pm; winter Sat 9am–4pm; Sun 10am–3pm.*

Shopping

A must shopping stop is **Marmontova Street,** a broad, brick-paved pedestrian street that forms Old Town's western border. You won't find too many quaint shops here, but you will see some international retail outlets (Tommy Hilfiger, Benetton) and a set of McDonald's golden arches. There are smaller shops, too, and some stalls selling Croatian crafts and handiwork at the northern end of the street.

Pazarin (aka **Pazar**) is reminiscent of a Turkish bazaar in looks, sounds, and smells; booths and tables line both sides of Hrvojeva Street outside the east wall of Diocletian's Palace from the Riva to the Silver Gate. You'll find the usual assortment of produce here. You'll also find a large variety of textiles and some of the most persuasive vendors anywhere.

Exploring the Palace

You can choose among several entrances to enter Split's historic core, but perhaps the best place to begin is the **Bronze Gate** where the sea once came right up to the palace's back walls. Today, the Bronze Gate opens outward from the palace's southern flank to Split's Riva and the ferry port beyond; and inward toward the **podrum** or basement area that meanders under the palace. The podrum was the palace's "plant" where support staff cooked meals for Diocletian and his guests, fixed palace equipment, and took care of day-to-day maintenance. The space was sadly neglected until the mid-1950s, and parts of it have yet to be restored and cleared of centuries of debris. The **cryptoporticus (gallery)** that runs east and west from the Bronze Gate was an open promenade and probably the site where Diocletian went to catch a sea breeze and take his daily constitutional. Today, the outdoor promenade can only be imagined from the form of the long corridor beneath it. The part of the podrum that extends from the Bronze Gate toward the steps to the Peristil above it is a brick-lined mini-mall filled with merchants and craftspeople selling jewelry, maps, and souvenirs.

At the far end of the aisle that runs through this section of the podrum, you'll find a staircase that leads up to the **Peristil,** which was the palace's main courtyard and the place where Diocletian received important visitors. Today, the Peristil is one of the busiest spots in the historic city and home to cafes, a hotel, the cathedral, and passages leading to the heart of Old Town. It also functions as a stage during the Split Summer Festival, and on May 7 when the city celebrates the feast of St. Domnius.

Note the black granite sphinx standing guard outside the cathedral. It was 1 of 11 acquired by Diocletian during battle in Egypt and it is the only one still standing.

If you are approaching the palace from the Riva and entering through the **Silver Gate** on the eastern wall, you first must walk through the jumble of stalls that is the **city fruit and vegetable market (Pazar).** Making this walk is fine during the day, but it can be a little dicey at night, even though the market often stays open until 10pm or later during the summer (despite the posted signs that say it closes at 2pm). The Silver Gate leads directly to **Decumanus,** the original east-west street that intersects with **Cardo,** the original north-south artery, at the Peristil. These former thoroughfares sectioned the palace into quadrants, which, in turn, became districts. The medieval **Cathedral of St. Domnius** outside the Silver Gate was completely rebuilt in the 17th century and is home to several good pieces of sacral art.

The **Golden Gate** at the north end of the wall was the portal to Salona and was the most ornate gate into the palace. It has a guardhouse that contains the 9th-century **Church of St. Martin.** Ivan Meštrović's largest **statue of Bishop Grgur (Gregorius of Nin) Ninski,** a 9th-century bishop who defended the church's use of the Glagolitic script and Slav language, towers over visitors approaching the gate. The sculpture is entirely black except for one toe, which visitors rub for good luck as they pass. To the west, the **Iron Gate**'s guardhouse is the site of the oldest Romanesque belfry in Croatia and the 10th-century **Church of Our Lady of Belfry.**

The **Cathedral of St. Domnius** is on the eastern side of the Peristil. The **Temple of Jupiter** (now the cathedral's baptistry) and what's left of the small, round **temples of Venus** and **Cybele** are on the Peristil's western side.

Playing Outside

The best beach in the city is at **Bacvice**. It's always jammed with people even though the sand is lined with trash—the water, at least, is beautiful. There are **tennis courts** here, and visitors are welcome if you pay 40kn an hour. It's at Put Firule, close to Bacvice Bay (☎ 389-576).

You can also go **sailing** 1km southwest of the city center, at ACI Marina (Uvala Baluni bb; ☎ 298-599; www.aci-club.hr); it's open all year. For **diving** in the area, contact Issa (☎ 536-806; www.diving.hr/idc).

Hvar

Declared one of the world's top 10 most beautiful islands by *Condé Nast Traveler*, **Hvar** ★—with its crystal clear Adriatic sea, hugging a coast lined with fields of lavender and high craggy cliffs—easily lives up to the hype. Its ability to meld ancient architecture with an exploding mod nightclub scene makes this the best island to hit on the Dalmatian Coast. Hvar has been occupied since the Romans came here in the 3rd century, and has undergone rule by the Venetians, Hungarians, Habsburgs, Russians, and the Croats, to name just a few. Now that its stormy political history is behind it, Hvar lies firmly in the hands of the pervasive yacht owners who control the marina.

Getting There

There's only one way to get to the island: by boat. **Jadrolinija** (☎ 021/741-132; www.jadrolinija.hr) runs a ferry service (from Split) and a catamaran. The catamaran is quick and painless for those who don't sail well, while the ferry is choppy enough that it might result in 2 hours of seasickness. From Split, the catamaran to Hvar town leaves at 2pm and the ferry leaves at 2:30pm.

Getting Around

Hvar is closed to motorized traffic from the bus station to the Riva, which is also the busiest thoroughfare until after nightfall, when the long, rectangular main square, Trg Sveti Stjepana, becomes a circus. If you want to see anything besides Hvar town and Stari Grad, a car is necessary, but the town is best covered on foot.

Hvar Basics

TOURIST INFO

Hvar town's principal **tourist office** is at Trg Sveti Stjepana bb, Hvar's main square (☎ 021/741-059; www.tzhvar.hr). Stari Grad's tourist office is at Nova Riva 2 (☎ 021/765-763; www.hvar.hr).

Hvar Nuts & Bolts

Currency   There's a **Splitska Banka** on Riva that's open 8am to 11:30am and 6pm to 8pm Monday to Friday, 8am to 11:30am Saturday.

Emergencies   For a doctor or ambulance, call ☎ 741-111.

Luggage Storage   The restroom attendant by the bus station holds luggage for 15kn a bag; it's open from 7am to 9pm daily.

Post Office   The post office is on the harbor and is open 7am to 8pm from Monday to Friday, 7am to 5pm Saturday.

See "Split Nuts & Bolts" (p. 249) for more info.

Hvar

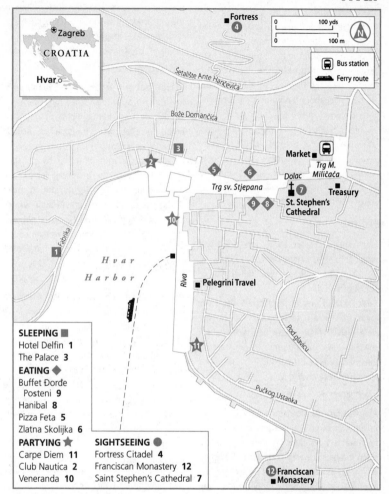

SLEEPING ■
Hotel Delfin 1
The Palace 3
EATING ◆
Buffet Đorđe
  Posteni 9
Hanibal 8
Pizza Feta 5
Zlatna Skolijka 6
PARTYING ★
Carpe Diem 11
Club Nautica 2
Veneranda 10
SIGHTSEEING ●
Fortress Citadel 4
Franciscan Monastery 12
Saint Stephen's Cathedral 7

Sleeping

Your best bet for finding cheap accommodations is to follow one of the, CAMERE/ZIMMER/ROOM/SOBE signs that are posted by the ferry stop. Rooms generally cost about 100kn per person per night, but can cost as much as 200kn or as little as 80kn. Just make sure that you and your host decide on a price beforehand, and find out what time you need to leave to avoid paying for another night. If you rent a room in a private residence through the tourist information shop, you will pay higher rates.

➔**Hotel Delfin** This modest hotel on the sea is essentially a hostel with a face-lift and a high price tag. Location makes this place stand out, especially for partyers. It's a 2-minute walk to **Veneranda** (p. 257). *Far side of the port.* ☎ *021/741-168. www.suncanihvar.com. 69€–79€ double. Rates include breakfast. Amenities: Restaurant; bar; sundries shop;*

tennis courts nearby; TV (in common room); video games; Wi-Fi.

→ **The Palace** ★★ In a converted Venetian palace built in the 1600s, The Palace is easily the nicest hotel in the area, though it could stand some renovations. The hotel spares no expense to make their guests feel at home. The best part about the hotel is the location. The Palace sits in the direct center of Hvar. *Trg sv. Stjepana bb.* ☎ *021/741-966. www. suncanihvar.hr. 85€–115€ double. Rates include breakfast. Amenities: Bar; Internet; massage; pool; restaurant; sauna; sundries shop; tennis courts nearby; wheelchair friendly; Wi-Fi. In room: TV.*

Eating

Hvar's specialties are twofold: seafood and pizza. A freshly caught meal will cost you, but it's worth a splurge, especially if you're sick of pizza.

The restaurants up and down the Hvar Town harbor all serve pretty much the same dishes—pizza, pasta, and grilled fish. However, some restaurants in the narrow, unnamed streets off the main square and Riva offer distinctive cuisine.

HOT SPOTS

→ **Buffet Đorđe Pošteni** ★ PIZZA One of the many pizza/grill restaurants on the square, this one is next door to Hanibal and the outdoor tables are almost always full. Pošteni is as much a place to see and be seen as it is a restaurant. The pizza is nonetheless quite good. Service can get bogged down on busy nights. *Trg Sv. Stjepana 13.* ☎ *021/741-138. posteni-hvar@hi.htnet.hr. Entrees 50kn–95kn. Daily 10am–midnight. Closed Oct 15–May 15.*

CHEAP

→ **Pizza Feta** PIZZA Serving what's probably the best pizza in Hvar, and easily the most affordable, Pizza Feta could be your main restaurant spot while in Hvar (supplemented with daily trips to the supermarket next door). Sassy waitresses and a pizza-maker

who never seems to get your order right somehow enhance the experience. Indulge in the mushroom pizza, and eat it seaside for an unforgettable experience. *Off Ivan Novak. No phone. Pizza 11kn–80kn. Daily 1pm–midnight.*

DOABLE

→ **Hanibal** ★★ DALMATIAN Hanibal has been a fixture in Hvar since 1997 and it's a good choice no matter what you're in the mood for. The tables outside are usually crammed until midnight, so you might have to settle for a spot in the spiffy polished wood interior, where model ships are mounted on Plexiglas. Try the stuffed squid, the scampi risotto, or the grilled lamb. Service is exceptionally attentive. *Trg Sv. Stjepana 12.* ☎ *021/742-760. Reservations recommended. Entrees 70kn–140kn. Daily 10am–midnight.*

→ **Zlatna Skoljka** ★★ SLOW FOOD The affable owner says that slow food is the opposite of fast food, which doesn't begin to explain this Croatian style of dining. It's really a leisurely presentation of courses. Start with Dalmatian ham and goat cheese in olive oil, and follow that with steak stuffed with goat cheese and capers, the excellent lamb stew, or grilled fish. This is a place where food is an art form. *Petra Hektorovica 8.* ☎ *098/1688-797. Entrees 75kn–175kn. Daily noon–3pm and 7pm–midnight. Closed Jan 5–Mar 31.*

Partying

Just how hot is Hvar? The nightlife on this Dalmatian Coast island has become so legendary that party princess Tara Reid showed up at the local club, **Carpe Diem,** in 2005. Plan on a late outing—places only get hopping here around midnight.

MTV **Best** → **Carpe Diem** ★★ Super-famous and super-posh, Carpe Diem attracts both international backpackers and rich yacht bums, but it manages to avoid the worst of both. Carpe Diem is one of the best places to meet new friends. Dress to impress here; though there's no cover or wait, you will feel mighty awkward if you show up in dirty pants and a faded T-shirt. *Riva bb.* ☎ *742-369. www.carpe-diem-hvar.com.*

➔**Club Nautica** Under other circumstances, this cocktail bar—with rockin' music and hefty cocktails—would be amazing. Due to competition from hot spots Carpe Diem and Verandera, it's simply good. That doesn't mean it's not a fun place to hang out, plus the cocktails are a good deal cheaper than they are at other clubs. Ladies: Flaunt those skimpy bikini tops and miniskirts because the dress code here is somewhat lax. If you don't like what the DJ is playing, locals say he can be bribed with drinks. *Near Hvar's main square. No phone.*

➔**Veneranda** Contained within a fortress on a hill, just a short hike from the Hotel Delfin, Verandera is your average club . . . until 3am, when Carpe Diem closes. All of the drunk, barely clad young people then head over here, pay the 50kn cover, and that's when the after-hours outdoor club gets started. Bring your swimsuit: Verandera has a pool. *Just west of town. No phone. Cover 50kn. Open-air films are shown at 9:30pm during the summer.*

Sightseeing

➔**The Fortress Citadel** Cresting the hill overlooking the town of Hvar, the Fortress Citadel was built in the 1550s by the Venetians but remained unused until after the Turkish invasion when Uluz Ali destroyed the town. The Citadel was strengthened and subsequently reinforced by various owners, including the Habsburgs and Napoleon, who managed to overcome its defenses and conquer Hvar. Today, it serves as a small museum and weather station. To find it, walk straight up one of the narrow streets to the left of The Palace and just keep trekking. *North of Hvar Town center.* ☎ *021/741-816. Admission 10kn. Summer daily 8am–midnight; winter by appointment only.*

➔**Franciscan Monastery** ★★ Concerts are held every 2 days during the summer at this lovely 15th-century monastery. An art museum inside opens to an idyllic garden with a view of the sea. The adjacent church, Our Lady of Mercy, also dates from the 15th century and it is home to many pieces of religious art. *Hvar Town.* ☎ *021/741-123. Admission 10kn. Summer daily 10am–noon and 5–7pm; winter daily 10am–noon. Performance times and prices vary.*

FREE ➔**St. Stephen's Cathedral** ★★ The looming church at the far end of Hvar's main square is impossible to miss. Built in the 15th century on the remains of another late Gothic cathedral, St. Stephen's lends a certain imposing sort of mood over Hvar. The bell tower was built in the 16th century and the Cathedral now houses a few interesting Christian reliefs. Musical festivals sometimes take place inside; check at the tourist office. *Trg Sv. Stjepana bb. Daily 7am–noon and 5–7pm. Hours sometimes extended during tourist season.*

Playing Outside

MTV Best **Hvar's Beaches** ★ follow some basic standards: They're either very pebbly or composed of hard-core rocks. Don't let that deter you from the aquamarine beauty that lies just off the shore. This part of Croatia is home to some of the best conditions in Europe for windsurfing, kite boarding, jet-skiing, sailing, diving, and swimming. Some of the best diving centers are noted below.

From Hvar, you can walk around the Marina to get to some very lovely but large rock beaches. There is also a beach just past **Carpe Diem** that has relatively small pebbles, but huge crowds. However, for a mere 10kn, you can hop a taxi boat to nearby **Pakleni Otoci,** a cluster of pine-forested, uninhabited islands whose coastlines are alternately rimmed with rocks and little pebble beaches.

➜ **Dive Center Hvar** This large professional dive center near the Hotel Amfora runs diving trips between Hvar and the island of Vis. The Dive Center offers a long menu of dive services and trips and supports other watersports such as water-skiing, snorkeling, kite boarding, windsurfing, and banana boating. It also rents boats, kayaks, and equipment to go with all its sports. Dives run from 250kn for a single dive including equipment to an all-inclusive certification course for 2,360kn. *At the Hotel Amfora.* ☎ *021/741-503. www.divecenter-hvar.com.*

➜ **Viking Diving Center** The Petrinovic family runs this establishment right next to the Podstine Hotel, and it can supply equipment, instruction, and even rooms. Many of Viking's diving excursions go to the waters off Pakleni Otoci. Viking offers a wide range of options: from a single dive at 220kn, to a package of 5 days and 10 dives for 1,720kn, to a full-day trip with cave diving for 490kn. Equipment rental is extra. *Podstine bb.* ☎ *021/742-529. www.viking-diving.com.*

Boat Trips

Head to the main marina in Hvar for a slew of boat tour excursions around the area.

Most tours leave around 7am, and include a fish lunch with wine. You can buy tickets through the tourist office.

ZLATNI RAT The boat to the "Golden Horn" beach in Bol, on Brač, leaves daily in the early morning; the ride is around 1 hour (40kn; no lunch). See more info in the section on the island Brač.

BISEVO The famed "Blue Grotto" here is a rare geological wonder in which sunlight is reflected off the bottom, covering the walls of the cave with blue-silver streaks. It can only be reached by small fishing boats and is near the island of Vis, a common second stop for this boat (75kn with fish lunch).

KORČULA & MLJET This all-day tour first chugs to Korčula (p. 262), where legend holds that the famed adventurer Marco Polo was born. From there, you will continue to Mljet National Park, where the main attractions are "Great Lake" and "Small Lake." On the banks of the "Great Lake," you'll stop to see the remains of a Benedictine monastery from the 12th century (60kn with lunch).

The Island Brač

The largest island on the Adriatic Sea, Brač (pronounced "brach") is a rocky, seemingly inhospitable island. Closer inspection, though, shows that throughout thousands of years, peasant farmers have wrested crops and wine from the barren soil. Most of the attractions lay either on, or very near the sea. The real attraction, at least for young people, can be found on the sunny, exuberant beach "capital" of this island, 📺 Best **Bol.** This town center is literally swimming with beautiful young natives and tourists, in addition to a wide range of watersports and nightlife.

Getting There

Almost all ferries land in Brač's main port town, **Supetar.** Because the ferry arrives here relatively late, I'd plan to stay here for the night and then make my way to the other side of the island the next morning. In the summer, more than a dozen car ferries make the daily hour-long journey from Split to Supetar on Brač's northern shore, and high-speed catamarans travel to Bol on the southern shore. Car ferries from the resort area of Makarska south of Split run to Sumartin on Brač's eastern shore. Several independent ferry services run between Brač and Hvar. See p. 254 for info.

Getting Around

Buses run from Supetar to Bol six times a day and to several other towns and villages on Brač three times daily, but making connections can be limiting. The best way to explore more than one town per visit is to rent a car, a scooter, or even a bike (in Supetar) and explore the island independently. If you plan to stay in one place on Brač, walking is probably best. A limited number of bikes and mopeds are available for rent in Supetar, but no cars—unless you arrange to have one available before you arrive.

If you're traveling between Supetar and Bol, you have two options: Rent a car (300kn for 24 hr.) and navigate the roads (the signs are remarkably clear). Otherwise, take the bus; the (very) flexible schedule means you should pick up one of the free timetables from wherever you are staying, or at any of the hotels in the area.

Check with the tourist office (see below) for schedule and fare info for all these transport options.

Brač Basics

TOURIST INFO

Supetar's **Turistička Zajednica Grada Supetar** is at Porat 1 (☎ 021/630-551; www. supetar.hr). From June to the end of September, hours are 8am to 10pm daily. At other times, it's open 8am to 4pm Monday through Friday. Bol's tourist office is at Porat Bolskih Pomoraca bb (☎ 021/635-638; www. bol.hr). Both offices can help you locate private accommodations, provide you with maps, and even suggest excursions and walking routes.

Brac Island Nuts & Bolts

Currency   There's a **Splitska Bank** at Frane Radica 16. If you have a Visa card, Bank Splitska will charge your card and give you back cash—just bring your passport and ask about the fees.

Internet/Wireless Hot Spots   M∂3X **Internet Café** (Rudina 6, Bol; ☎ 021/718-877) doesn't have the fastest connections—especially if there are other people using the computers—but that's because all of Croatia is still operating on a 56K network. It's open from 7am to 11pm and charges a flat rate of 5kn for the first 5 minutes, and then 5kn for every 10 supplementary minutes.

Emergencies   The police can be reached at ☎ 021/635-207; the fire department at ☎ 021/635-582; and ambulance service at ☎ 021/635-112.

See "Split Nuts & Bolts" (p. 249) for additional information.

Sleeping

In **Supetar,** most of your accommodations choices are the package hotels at the west end of town, though you can secure private accommodations at the tourist office near the dock (see above). Or inquire wherever you see a SOBE sign. Bol has its share of rooms in well-equipped resort hotels, too, but it also has some charming private accommodations. *FYI:* The main ferry terminal is positively swarming with hotel reps who you can haggle with for a room.

If you really look, you can find accommodations in a pinch, but **Bol** makes this task a good deal more difficult than in other places in Croatia. Few hotel reps are sent out to solicit guests, so you will likely have to go through the tourist office if you haven't booked a room in advance.

➜ **Hotel Riu Borak** A very family-friendly Majorcan chain hotel, Borak has a resort-like atmosphere: It's all-inclusive if you can afford the price to get yourself a room. As we all know, nothing in this world is free, but if you decide to splurge for a night and come here, you will end up saving some money on alcohol and food. *Bracka cesta 13, Bol.* ☎ *021/306-202. www.zlatni-rat.hr. High season 108€ double; call for low-season rates. Rates include breakfast. Amenities: Restaurant; bar; beach volleyball; business facilities; health club; live entertainment; massage; 2 pools; tennis courts nearby. In room: A/C, TV, hair dryer, minibar, refrigerator (apts and suites), safe (for a fee).*

➜ **Villa Adriatica** This cute, personal hotel sports a maritime theme, and clean, spacious rooms. As a bonus, breakfast is provided (the croissants are amazing) and the staff goes out of their way to help you sort out your trip, from calling a car to scheduling excursions. *In Supertar Vele Luke 31.* ☎ *021/ 343-806. www.villaadriatica.com. 40€–67€ double. Rates include breakfast. Amenities: Restaurant; Jacuzzi; pool. In room: A/C, cable TV.*

Eating

Restaurants in both Bol and Supetar are pretty predictable, though Bol has a better selection. Most of the folks who book rooms on Brač stay in the resort complexes and take advantage of the all-inclusive deals, so the restaurants in both towns are few and far between except for cafes and pizzerias.

➜ **Bistro Palute** ★ DALMATIAN You can watch locals demolish huge plates of fish at this local hangout with tables inside and out. *Janjetina* (roasted or grilled lamb) is one of the specialties. Palute also operates a bed-and-breakfast. *Put Pašike 16, Supetar.* ☎ *021/ 631-730. palute@st.htnet.hr. Main courses 35kn–49kn. Daily 8am–3am.*

➜ **Bistro/Pizzeria Riva** ★ DALMATIAN/ PIZZA Riva's menu has a respectable selection of grilled fish, but lots of grilled meat is

Game On!

You may notice a Croatian ball game with kids (and sometimes adults) running around wildly after a speck of a ball. This is Picigin, which is kind of like hacky sack played near and in the water. The goal is to keep the ball from touching the water. Usually played in a circle, it's not uncommon for players to throw themselves into the sand to save the fist-size ball.

available here, too. In addition, Riva offers pizza, a staple among Supetar's restaurants. *Riva bb. Supetar.* ☎ *021/631-155 or 091/ 580-1950. Main courses 40kn–60kn. Daily 7am–midnight.*

➜ **Konoba Mlin** ★★ CROATIAN One of the most expensive restaurants in Bol, Konoba Mlin is housed in the Old Town mill. Decorated in rustic hues, this "home-style" restaurant serves delightful native Croatian food like Dalmatian ham, grilled meats, seasoned seafood, and excellent homemade "black wine." *Ante Starcevica 11, Bol.* ☎ *021/ 635-376.*

➜ **Skalinada** PIZZA Even though this entire restaurant is the size of a shoe closet, the delicious smells emanating from the kitchen and the weathered wooden booths make clear that this pizzeria is a real establishment. The service is slow, the crust is thin and crispy, and the sauce is pungent and flavorful—well worth the wait. *Rudina 30, Bol.* ☎ *021/635-727. Pizza 50kn.*

Partying

Bol is the undisputed king of Brač's nightlife scene, partially because it *has* a nightlife scene. In the height of the summer, you can expect all clubs and bars to be packed, but expect a mellower flavor as it cools down—no matter the season, though, don't plan on arriving before midnight. If you are headed to a bar, you can dress casually; nightclubs are less fancy than those on Hvar, but still demand some dressing up. Remember that you may be in the company of mainland Europe's best-dressed, young elite.

➔**Faces Disco** ★ This massive outdoor club claims to hold up to 2,000 young, sweaty dancers. It's owned by the same company that owns the mediocre **Master's Club** in Split, but the vibe is much better here. During the summer, it gets so packed, it's downright steamy. *Bracke ceste bb, Bol.* ☎ 021/635-410.

➔**Moby Dick Bar** This fun, somewhat touristy little bar boasts a variety of beers and a warm place to take a seat if the weather's nippy. English speakers tend to congregate here, so the bar is a good place to meet fellow travelers. *Loa 13, Bol.* ☎ 021/635-281.

➔**Varadero Bar Lounge** Invoking the spirit of the aquamarine waters a few meters away, this oasis features thatched huts where you can rest and soak in the pervasive Spanish tunes. The bartenders are skilled at their craft; you'll discover drinks here unknown in the rest of the country. *Riva, promenade by the main marina, Bol.* ☎ 021/635-996.

Sightseeing

Despite its air of newness, Bol is not a recently popular destination. Illyrians (of Shakespeare fame) and ancient Romans flocked here way back when. Though ownership has changed hands over the years, Brač's attractions have stayed pretty much the same.

Supetar's tourism revolves around its beach, which arcs away from the ferry port and is the center of almost all activity. The town does have a few other sites that can keep anyone busy for an afternoon. The best of these is the baroque **Church of the Annunciation,** which is a short uphill walk from the port toward the city center.

Rat Race

If you've been in Croatia more than a few hours, you'll have seen the many postcards depicting Croatia's most famous beach—Zlatni Rat, or the "Golden Horn." The Golden Horn stretches along the ocean for 100m (328 ft.) I think that the beach is a bit overrated. It's so packed with tourists and locals that finding an unoccupied spot is a huge task. You should go for a quick visit just so you can say you did . . . but Zlatni Rat looks far better on that postcard than it does on closer inspection.

Supetar's **cemetery** and its ornate **Petrinović Mausoleum** are other attractions worthy of a stop. The cemetery is at the far end of the beach on a small, eerie-looking peninsula draped with cypress trees.

➔**Branislav-Dešković Modern Art Gallery** Even if sun worship is your cup of tea, you might want to duck into Branislav-Dešković Modern Art Gallery at Porat Bolskih Pomoraca bb near the tourist office in Bol. It has a fine collection of Brač landscapes from such renowned Croatian artists as Ivan Rendić, the man who created much of the sepulchral art in Supetar's lovely cemetery. *Porat Bolskih Pomoraca bb, Bol. July–Aug daily 6pm–midnight.*

➔**Dominican Monastery** Sitting on the ruins of a 11th-century Episcopal palace that once hosted a prince—if you choose to believe the ancient manuscripts that claim such things—the present Dominican Monastery was built in 1475, though the belfry was completed in the 18th century. Take note of the church's paving, made out of tombstones, and the glowing collection of art housed inside the Monastery Museum. *Somostan Dominikanaca, Bol.* ☎ 635-132. *Open for Mass only.*

Party Island

The island Pag is the fifth largest off Croatia's coast, and it also lays claim to having one of Croatia's most happening beaches: **Zrce beach** ★★, a little over a mile south of Novalja. Almost every bar in town has set up shop on this stretch of real estate, which vibrates with nonstop rock music and gyrating bodies during the day but doesn't *really* get going until about 10pm. Zrce draws hordes of the 18- to 29-year-old demographic through the summer and has become Croatia's answer to "Where the Boys Are" in the Balkans. Visit www. psh-tourism.hr for info on getting to the island.

➔ **Dragon's Cave** While not technically in the town of Bol, the Dragon's Cave is a must-see. Situated west of Bol in the village of Murvica, this cave has beautiful reliefs carved into the stone that depict a variety of mythical creatures, including dragons. *5km to Murvica, plus a 1-hr. walk to the cave. Tours organized by tourist office for 100kn.*

Playing Outside

Generally, Bol is a water-lover's heaven on earth. It's a great place to sign up for water-sports classes. It's not unusual to see "schools" of boarders riding the waves around the island, especially near Potočine beach, west of Bol. If your interest lies under the sea, Bol also offers **scuba-diving** trips. If

you aren't licensed, you can get certified here by taking a course.

Check out these reputable companies: **Big Blue Sport** has beginner **windsurfing classes** (139€), or if you just want to rent a board it will cost 15€ every hour or 35€ for a half-day. Scuba will cost either 40€ (discovery dive with a guide, no license needed); if you want to go by yourself it will cost 25€ to 35€ for a half-day. Big Blue Sport is located at Podan Glavice 2, Bol (☎ 021/635-614; www.big-blue-sport.hr). **Nautic Center Bol** pretty much covers all of ground that Big Blue Sport fails to, such as **banana-boat rides, tubing, jet-skiing,** and **parasailing**. It's located at M. Marulic 3, Bol (☎ 021/635-367; www.nautic-center-bol.com).

The Island Korčula

With its dark, thick forests of pine trees and foreboding mountains, **Korčula** (*core-cha-la*) is the only Dalmatian Coast island almost untouched by tourists. You won't find bright umbrella stands by the rocky beaches, nor will you find flashy nightclubs. In lieu of packed bars and banana boats, there's beautiful architecture, good food, and a sense of Croatian culture.

The town of Korčula is the island's main tourist site, famed for being the birthplace of Marco Polo. If you have the time, be sure to explore the island: Highlights include **Lumbarda** and its exclusive "Grk" white wine; the tiny island of **Vrnik** with ancient

stone quarries and clear blue seas; and **Pupnat,** a town which boasts lots of Illyrian architecture. Although Korčula could technically be seen in a day (minus travel), I recommend staying here overnight.

Getting There

If you are coming from Split by ferry, you'll dock in **Vela Luka,** an easily forgotten town. Once you dock, expect to encounter apartment hawkers; walk through them, and board the bus that journeys to the town of Korčula. It costs 25kn, and another 5kn to store a bag under the bus (if you have a big bag, you have to do this).

For ferry information, contact the Jadrolinija office in Korčula Town at ☎ **020/ 715-410**. It is open from 8am to 8pm Tuesday through Thursday; and from 8am to 9pm Monday, 8am to 1pm Saturday, and from 6am to 2pm Sunday. Ferry service runs from Orebić through **Mediteranska Plovidba** in Orebić at ☎ **020/711-156**. Bus schedule and fare information can be obtained at the Korčula Town bus station (☎ **020/711-216**).

Getting Around

Local buses make five runs daily from one end of the island to the other. You can also rent a bike and easily pedal the 6km (4 miles) between Korčula Town and Lumbarda (where the best beaches are). At its widest point, Korčula is about 8km (5 miles) wide and less than 32km (20 miles) long.

Korčula Basics

TOURIST OFFICE

The tourist office is next door to the Hotel Korčula at Obala Dr. Franje Túmana bb (☎ **020/715-701**; www.korcula.net). The office is open Monday to Friday 9am to 6:30pm.

Korčula Town Nuts & Bolts

Currency   The post office changes money (see below), or you can head to the Splitska Banka or Dubrovacka Banka in town.

Emergencies   Call for an ambulance at ☎ **94**. In case of fire, dial ☎ **93**, and for police, call ☎ **92**.

Internet/Wireless Hot Spots   Tino's Internet (☎ **091-509-1182**; 30kn per hour) is on Ul Tri Sulara. It's open Monday to Saturday 8:30am to 1pm and 5:30pm to 9pm, and 5:30 to 9pm on Saturday.

Post Office   The post office (adjacent to the stairs up to Old Town) is open Monday to Friday from 7am to 8pm and Saturday 7am to 2pm.

See "Split Nuts & Bolts" (p. 249) for more information.

Sleeping

As always, home stays are an option if you are on a tight budget and if the islands' hostels are full. Just get off the bus and follow the sign that says ROOMS, SOBE, CAMERE, ZIMMER. Be sure to bargain and agree on a price with a hawker beforehand.

➜**Happy House Korčula** ★ In addition to being housed in a renovated 200-year-old villa, the Happy House also boasts a beachfront location, a bar, kitchens, spacious rooms, and a young crowd that likes to party at night. Unfortunately, as far as hostels go, this one is a tad expensive. *Hrvatske bratske zajednice 6.* ☎ *020/716-715. www.happyhouse korcula.com. From 12€ dorm bed. Amenities:* *Bar/restaurant; Internet; kitchen; movies; planned activities; shared bathrooms; TV (in common room). In room: Sheets.*

➜**Hotel Marco Polo** Decorated in 1970s style (think: linoleum and yellows and greens), the Hotel Marco Polo impresses guests with its efficient service and coziness. *Šetalište F. Kršinića 10.* ☎ *020/726-336. www. marcopolo.hr. 41€–94€ per night for 1 person in double-occupancy room (depends on season and view); 32€–68€ per person per night for 2 people in double-occupancy room (depends on season and view). Rates include breakfast. 3-night minimum stay. Add 20% to rates if staying less than 3 nights. Amenities: Bar; billiards; business facilities; currency* *exchange; mini-golf; pool; restaurant; table tennis; tennis courts. In room: Hair dryer.*

Eating

As with every town in the Croatian islands, if you are looking for expensive seafood and a medley of pastas and other Italian delicacies, you will not go hungry in Korčula. The pizza is also pretty much the same all over the town—it's the cheapest bet.

➔ **Fresh** ★ Owned by a Canadian couple who came to Korčula because of a missed ferry, Fresh is the only wraps place I saw during my travels. Its food is healthier than at other Croatian restaurants and everything generally costs under 5€. I highly recommend the Asiana, a chicken-and-vegetables wrap. Fresh also serves smoothies. *Hrvatske Bratske Zajednice, 1 Kod Kina Liburne.* ☎ *091/ 896-7509. Wraps 5€. Daily 8am–2am.*

Partying

Unlike the other Adriatic islands, Korčula caters mainly to older people. This means there are some good bars around town but very little in the way of clubs. The best option is in the basement of **Happy House Korčula** (p. 263), where most of the island's young travelers stay. Also, **Fresh** (see above) serves sangria and pitchers of beer until the wee hours of the morning.

➔ **Disco Gaudi** ★ Once you're ready to shake your groove thing, find this little disco, which is far too small to accommodate the number of people trying to enter and have a rollicking time. The trick here is to realize that you really have nowhere else to go, and learn to love the space. *Inside Korcula Arsenal. No phone.*

➔ **Dos Locos** The island's pre-gaming hub, Pub Dos Locos also serves as a pleasant meet-and-greet place before the club to encounter those of the opposite or same sex before moving on to dancing. *I Setaliste Frana. No phone.*

Sightseeing

FREE ➔ **Cathedral of St. Marco** Construction of the Cathedral of St. Marco commenced in the 15th century and continued on for more than a century as the original architects died and were replaced with fresh faces. Built mostly out of the characteristic Korčula stone (which comes not from Korčula, but from a small island called Vrnik near Korčula) the building is a Gothic structure punctuated with ornate reliefs and statues. Dedicated mainly to three saints—St. Rocco, St. Marco, and St. Bartholomew—the entire church houses different pieces from different eras spanning around 400 years. The museum staff is helpful and speaks some English, so if you have a question, don't hesitate to ask. *Strossmayer Trg. Summer daily 7am–9pm; winter daily 7am–7pm.*

➔ **House of Marco Polo** Don't believe everything you read/see/hear/are told in this town. Although Korčula swears up and down that it was the birthplace of Marco Polo, the famous traveler and writer, the only proof it has is the fact that "DePolo" is a common name and that Korčula is good at building ships. Don't let that discourage you from sightseeing, though; it's a fun legend even if it proves not to be true someday. The house that supposedly belonged to Marco Polo is presently being renovated into a new Marco Polo museum and should be reopening in 2007. *Put Sv. Nikol bb. No phone. Admission 10kn. Summer daily 9am–1pm and 5–7pm; closed in winter.*

➔ **Korčula Museum** ★ In the 16th-century Gabrielis Palace, the Korčula Town museum exhibits the island's changes over its 2 millennia of inhabitation. One of the more interesting artifacts here is a carved stone agreement between Greek settlers from the island of Vis and the local heads of Korčula. Dating from the 4th-century B.C., the tablet is written in ancient Greek and depicts a loyalty agreement between the newcomers and the Illyrian heads of the community. In addition, you can find trinkets from all over Europe, famous Croatian art, examples of the "Korčula stone" used to construct many famous buildings (Hagia Sophia, Vienna Parliament, to name a couple), and other items that demonstrate what Korčula has been up to in the last 2,500 years. *Trg Sv. Marka Statuta.* ☎ *020/711-420. Admission 10kn. Daily June–Aug 9am–1:30pm.*

→**Town Treasury** ★★ This place is like the historical equivalent to the biggest Goodwill store ever. You can find everything from Mother Teresa's Nobel Prize medal to sketches by Leonardo da Vinci to an alabaster statue of Mary Stuart from the 15th century to a grand collection of Croatian masterpieces dating from 600 years ago. *Trg Sv. Marka Statuta. Admission 15kn. Daily May 1–Oct 31 9am–8pm.*

Dublin

Funky, trendy, modern, sophisticated . . . Dublin? Oh, yes.

Don't tell us, let us guess—the picture of Dublin you have in your head is of a kind of rock-solid, old-fashioned, quaint place, where Irish Colleens smile shyly as they pour you a pint of Guinness, and men in wool caps sit at the bar, a pipe clenched between their teeth as they talk about the horse races.

Please. That's so 1930. Things have changed around here, you know.

Twenty-first-century Dublin is a rocking place, one of Europe's top city-break destinations, a favorite spot for European urbanites, who come for a weekend of drinking, dining, and partying, and then jet off back home. Property sells for millions of euros for even the tiniest closet-size flat, millionaires sip vintage champagne in private clubs here, and dinner out in even a casual-nice restaurant will set you back €82.

But don't let that intimidate you. It's also a young city, ambitious and energetic, packed with international students here to study at its many universities and language schools. So, you'll find great bars, cheap hostels, nightly gigs, slammin' dance clubs, and lots of free stuff to do with your time.

This town is compact and walkable—you can easily stroll from Parnell Square in the north down to the Grand Canal on the south side without breaking a sweat—and it's as friendly as an international city can be. Give yourself a few days to get your bearings and you'll be navigating the place like a pro.

In the summertime, its lush, green squares and parks open up as vast, breezy picnic grounds, where you can loll in the sunshine and watch the girls and boys go by. In the winter, the pubs look particularly inviting, as fires roar and crackle at the grate, and you can settle down into an easy chair with a creamy pint of stout and read the local papers.

So, whatever you like, and whatever brought you here, get ready to have a great time. This is a buzzing, happening, *living* city. You're going to have a great time. And while you're at it, check out the music and arts scene in smaller but not too far Galway.

The Best of Dublin & Galway

○ **The Best Place for a Pint of Guinness:** With its old-fashioned bar, fancy Victorian decor and quirky paraphernalia—check out those muskets and chandeliers—**The Long Hall** is a great place to grab a pint of the black stuff with some newfound friends. See p. 289.

○ **The Best Bargain Meal:** When you get caught out in a Dublin rain shower—trust me, you will—warm up with a bowl of steaming Irish stew at **The Porterhouse** for only €6. It's a great big rambling pub, with wooden floors and endless rooms. See p. 285.

○ **The Best Bed with Extras:** No, not *those* sorts of extras. Taking the novel approach that cheap doesn't need to mean grim, the **Isaacs Hostel** has lots of frills including a sauna and a restaurant. Add in a bright and friendly atmosphere and it's easy to forget this is just a hostel. See p. 276.

○ **The Best Place to Snog:** With a decor designed to summon images of naughty harems, the **Zanzibar** nightclub provides a place for young professionals to meet other young professionals and fall helplessly in lust. See p. 289.

○ **The Best Free Show:** On a sunny Saturday, **Grafton Street**'s mimes, musicians, and artists are legion, and

just watching them interact with the hassled shoppers and baffled tourists is a joy. See p. 272.

○ **The Best Places to Hear Music:** Everybody who was ever anybody has played in rock-cool **Whelan's,** a historic music pub in Dublin. And when they're not playing, they're hanging out at the bar. The excellent **Roísín Dubh** is *the* place to go in Galway and is one of the country's top venues—not to be missed. See p. 290 and p. 314.

○ **The Best Place for a Shopping Spree:** The many tiny, quirky boutiques on this little lane are owned by locals, who design and make the one-of-a-kind fashions. Whatever you buy here on **Cow Lane,** you're unlikely to ever run into someone else wearing the same thing. See p. 297.

○ **The Best Show Put On by Druids:** Don't get too excited. You're not going to get a weird pagan ritual performed for you. But you will get the world-renowned **Druid Theatre Company,** home to some of Ireland's top actors. See p. 315.

○ **The Best Arts Festival:** Being in Galway in July for the massive **Galway Arts Festival** is unforgettable. Famous for its street carnival, music, theater, and great atmosphere. Possibly the best all-round summer festival in Europe. See p. 316.

DUBLIN

○ **The Best Adrenaline Adventure:** Hook up with **Delphi Adventure Holidays,** which offers plenty to set your hair on end, from sailing to sea kayaking to water-skiing, by way of abseiling, archery, and pony trekking. See p. 317.

Getting There & Getting Around

Getting into Town

BY PLANE

Dublin International Airport (☎ 01/814-1111; www.dublin-airport.com) is 11km (6³/₄ miles) north of the city center. A Travel Information Desk in the Arrivals Concourse provides information on public bus and rail services throughout the country.

An excellent airport-to-city shuttle bus service called **AirCoach** (☎ 01/844-7118; www.aircoach.ie) operates 24 hours a day, making runs at 15-minute intervals. Its buses run direct from the airport to Dublin's city center and south side, stopping at O'Connell Street, St. Stephen's Green, Fitzwilliam Square, Merrion Square, Ballsbridge, and Donnybrook—that is, all the key hotel and business districts. The fare is €7 one-way or €12 round-trip; buy your ticket from the driver. Although AirCoach is slightly more expensive than the Dublin Bus (see below), it is faster because it makes fewer intermediary stops and speeds you right into the hotel districts.

If you need to connect with the Irish bus or rail service, the **Airlink Express Coach** (☎ 01/844-4265) provides express coach service from the airport into the city's central bus station, Busáras, on Store Street, and on to the two main rail stations, Connolly and Heuston. Service runs daily from 7am until 11pm (Sun 7:30am–8:30pm), with departures every 20 to 30 minutes. One-way fare is €5 for adults.

Finally, **Dublin Bus** (☎ 01/872-0000; www.dublinbus.ie) runs services between the airport and the city center from 6am to 11:30pm. The one-way trip takes about 30 minutes, and the fare is €5. Bus nos. 16a, 33, 41, 41a, 41b, 41c, 46x, 58x, 746, 747, and 748 all serve the city center from Dublin Airport. Consult the Travel Information Desk in the Arrivals Concourse to figure out which bus will bring you closest to your hostel.

For speed and ease—especially if you've brought your entire extreme sports kit—a taxi is the best way to get directly to your hostel or hotel. Depending on your destination in Dublin, fares average between €18 and €25. Surcharges include €.50 for each additional passenger and for each piece of luggage. Depending on traffic, a cab should take between 20 and 45 minutes to get into the city center. A 10% tip is standard. Taxis are lined up at a first-come, first-served taxi stand outside the arrivals terminal.

Major international and local car-rental companies operate desks at Dublin Airport. For a list of companies, see "Getting Around," below.

BY FERRY

Passenger and car ferries from Britain arrive at the **Dublin Ferryport** (☎ 01/855-2222), on the eastern end of the North Docks, and at the **Dun Laoghaire Ferryport** (☎ 01/204-7700). Call **Irish Ferries** (☎ 01/661-0511; www.irishferries.ie), **P&O Irish Sea** (☎ 01/800-409-049; www.poirishsea.com), or **Stena Line** (☎ 01/204-7777; www.stenaline.com) for bookings and information. There is bus and taxi service from both ports.

BY TRAIN

Irish Rail (☎ 01/836-6222; www.irishrail.ie), also called Iarnród Éireann, operates daily train service to Dublin from Belfast, Northern Ireland, and all major cities in the Irish Republic.

Are We Lost Yet?

In the town center just south of the river, **Dame Street,** which changes its name to College Green, Westmoreland Street, and Lord Edward Street at various points, is the main east-west artery connecting **Trinity College** with **Dublin Castle** and **Christ Church Cathedral.** On one side of Dame Street, the winding medieval lanes of Temple Bar are jam-packed with nightclubs, pubs, and bars. This is Dublin's party central, and we have a feeling you'll spend some time there at one point or another.

On the other side of Dame Street are lots of tributary streets lined with stores and cafes. The best of these—**Great Georges Street**—arcs off toward the south, with many good coffee shops and a few bars.

Where Dame turns into College Green, the sturdy gray stone walls of Trinity College make an excellent landmark and a great place to hang out, watching Irish students walk by on their way to class. At its southwest corner is the top of **Grafton Street,** a crowded pedestrianized shopping lane with tourists, musicians, and artists. It leads to the peaceful statue-filled park, **St. Stephen's Green.**

From there, heading back up via **Kildare Street** will take you past **Leinster House,** where the Irish parliament meets, while a turn to the right brings you to **Merrion Square,** another of Dublin's extraordinarily well-preserved Georgian squares, with a *louche* statue of Oscar Wilde, who once lived there.

The street running along the Liffey's embankment is generally referred to as the **North Quays,** although it changes its name on almost every block reflecting the long-gone docks that once lined it. This is an increasingly hip area for pubs, hotels, and restaurants.

BY BUS

Bus Éireann (☎ 01/836-6111; www.bus eireann.ie) operates daily express coach and local bus service from all major cities and towns in Ireland into Dublin's central bus station, Busárus, Store Street.

BY CAR

If you are arriving by car from other parts of Ireland or on a car ferry from Britain, all main roads lead into the heart of Dublin and are well signposted to An Lar (City Centre).

Getting Around

BY BUS

Dublin Bus operates a fleet of green double-decker and single-deck buses, and cute little minibuses called "imps." Most originate on or near O'Connell Street, Abbey Street, and Eden Quay on the north side, and at Aston Quay, College Street, and Fleet Street on the south side. Bus stops, which resemble big blue or green lollipops, are located every 2 or 3 blocks on main thoroughfares. To tell where the bus is going, look at the destination streets and bus numbers above each bus's front window; those heading for the city center say so, but in Gaelic: VIA AN LAR.

Bus service runs daily throughout the city, starting at 6am (Sun at 10am), with the last bus at 11:30pm. On Thursday, Friday, and Saturday nights, the Nitelink night buses take over, ferrying people from the city center to the suburbs from midnight to 3am. Buses operate every 10 to 15 minutes for most runs; schedules are posted on revolving notice boards at bus stops.

Inner-city fares are based on distances traveled. The minimum fare is €.90; the maximum fare for journeys in the city center is €1.85. The Nitelink fare is a flat €4. Buy your tickets from the driver as you enter the bus; exact change is required, so have some change available. Notes of €5 or higher may not be accepted. Discounted 1-, 3-, 5-, and 7-day passes are available in advance. The 1-day bus-only pass costs €5; the 3-day pass costs €10; the 5-day pass goes for €16; and the 7-day pass costs €19. For more information, contact **Dublin Bus** (59 Upper O'Connell St.; ☎ 01/873-4222; www.dublinbus.ie).

BY DART

While Dublin has no subway in the strict sense, there is an electric rapid-transit train, known as the **DART** (Dublin Area Rapid Transit). It travels mostly at ground level or on elevated tracks, linking the City Centre stations at **Connolly Station, Tara Street, and Pearse Street** with suburbs and seaside communities as far as Malahide to the north and Greystones to the south. Service operates roughly every 10 to 20 minutes Monday to Saturday from 7am to midnight and Sunday from 9:30am to 11pm. The minimum fare is €1. One-day and 10-journey passes, as well as student and family tickets, are available at reduced rates from ticket windows in stations. For further information, contact **DART** (Pearse Station; ☎ 1850/366222 in Ireland, or 01/836-6222; www.irishrail.ie).

BY TRAM

The newest addition to Dublin's public transportation network, the sleek light-rail tram system known as **LUAS** first opened in the summer of 2004. With trams on two lines traveling at a maximum speed of 70kmph (45 mph) and departing every 5 minutes in peak hours, LUAS has already made an impact on Dublin's appalling traffic congestion. The lines link the city center at **Connolly Station** and **St. Stephen's Green** with the suburbs of Tallaght in the southwest and Dundrum and Sandyford to the south. For visitors, one of the handiest reasons to use the LUAS is to get between Connolly and Heuston stations. The one-way fare within the city center is €1; 1-day and multiple-day passes are also available. For further information, contact LUAS (☎ 01/703-2029; www.luas.ie).

BY TAXI

You don't usually hail taxis on the street here; instead, they line up at taxi stands (called "ranks") outside major hotels, at bus and train stations, and on prime thoroughfares such as upper O'Connell Street, College Green, and the Northside of St. Stephen's Green.

You can also phone for a taxi. Some of the companies that operate a 24-hour radio-call service are **Co-Op** (☎ 01/676-6666), **Shamrock Radio Cabs** (☎ 01/855-5444), and **VIP Taxis** (☎ 01/478-3333).

Taxi rates are fixed by law and posted in each vehicle. The following are typical travel costs in the city center: A 3.3km (2-mile) journey costs €8 by day and €10 at night; an 8km (5-mile) journey runs €10 by day and €12 at night; and a 16km (10-mile) journey costs €20 by day and €22 at night. There's an additional charge of €.50 for each extra passenger and for each suitcase. And it costs an extra €1.50 for a dispatched pickup. **Be forewarned:** At some hotels, staff members will tack on as much as €4 for calling you a cab, although this practice violates city taxi regulations.

On Your Own Two Feet

While driving in the city is intimidating, in general, getting around Dublin is not at all daunting. Public transportation is good and getting better, taxis are plentiful and reasonably priced, and your own two feet can easily carry you from one end of town to the other. In fact, with its current traffic and parking problems, it's a city where the foot is mightier than the wheel. If you can avoid it, don't use a car while you're in the city.

BY CAR

Getting around the city is much easier without a car. If you must drive in Dublin, free parking on Dublin streets is almost nonexistent, but throughout the city there are "pay and display" **parking** facilities. The best places to park are surface parking lots and multistory car parks in central locations such as Kildare Street, Lower Abbey Street, Marlborough Street, and St. Stephen's Green West. Expect to pay €1.90 per hour and €19 for 24 hours. Night rates run €6 to €9 per hour.

Never park in bus lanes or along a curb with double yellow lines. City officials will either clamp or tow errant vehicles. To get your car declamped, the fee is €85; if your car is towed away, it costs €165 to reclaim it.

BY BICYCLE

The relentless flow of Dublin traffic rushing down one-way streets might look a little scary for most cyclists, but there are many opportunities for more chill pedaling in residential areas and suburbs, along the seafront, and around Phoenix Park. The Dublin Tourism office can supply you with bicycle touring information and suggested routes.

Bicycle rental averages €20 per day, €80 per week, with a €65 deposit. The one-way rental fee is €100. In the downtown area, bicycles can be rented from **Raleigh Ireland** (Kylemore Rd.; ☎ 01/626-1333).

ON FOOT

Marvelously compact, Dublin is ideal for walking, as long as you remember to look right and then left (in the direction opposite your instincts if you're from North America) before crossing the street. Pedestrians have the right of way at specially marked, zebra-striped crossings (there are usually two flashing lights at these intersections).

DUBLIN

Dublin Basics

Orientation: Dublin Neighborhoods

Dublin is sliced down the middle by the River Liffey, which empties into the sea at the city's farthest edge. To the north and south, the city center is encircled by canals: The Royal Canal arcs across the north, and the Grand Canal through the south. For years, the section just south of the river has been Dublin's buzzing, trendy hub. It still holds most of the best hotels, restaurants, shops, and sights, but the Northside is on the move, with hip new bars and chic hotels making it the new cool place to hang. Both north and south, Dublin is compact and easily walked in an hour. In fact, a 25-minute walk from the bucolic peace of St. Stephen's Green, up Grafton Street, and across the Liffey to the top of O'Connell Street offers a good overview of the city's prosperous present and troubled past.

Don't overlook the city's waterfront suburbs, easily reached by tram. These are (heading north on the tram) Drumcondra, Glasnevin, Howth, Clontarf, and Malahide; and (heading south) Ballsbridge, Blackrock, Dun Laoghaire, Dalkey, Killiney, Rathgar, and Rathmines.

TRINITY COLLEGE AREA On the south side of the River Liffey, Trinity College is an Ivy League–style university with shady quadrangles and atmospheric stone buildings. It's just about the dead center of the city, and is surrounded by bookstores, shops, and noisy traffic. It's a handy meeting place, fun to wander, and sort of the center of everything.

📺 Best **TEMPLE BAR** Wedged between Trinity College and the Old City, this is Dublin's party hub, packed with noisy bars, clubs, and pubs. There are also a few good shops, two worthwhile art galleries, recording studios, and theaters. This is largely the stamping ground of young people on the hunt for lots of alcohol.

OLD CITY   Dating from Viking and medieval times, the cobblestone streets of this historic area include Dublin Castle, the remnants of the city's original walls, and Christ Church and St. Patrick's cathedrals. Recently, Old City has also gained cachet for its hip boutiques, mostly on Cow Lane, where local designers sell their clothes. It encompasses the Dublin 8 and 2 zones.

THE LIBERTIES   Adjacent to Old City, the Liberties district takes its name from the fact that it was once just outside the city walls, and, therefore, exempt from Dublin's jurisdiction. Although it prospered in its early days, Liberties fell on hard times in the 17th and 18th centuries and is only now feeling a touch of urban renewal. Its main claim to fame is the Guinness Brewery.

MTV Best ST. STEPHEN'S GREEN/GRAFTON STREET AREA   The biggest tourist draw in town, this district is home to Dublin's finest (and priciest) hotels, restaurants, and shops. The neighborhood is filled with impressive Georgian architecture, and is primarily a business and shopping zone.

FITZWILLIAM & MERRION SQUARE   These two little square parks between Trinity College and St. Stephen's Green are surrounded by grand Georgian town houses. Some of Dublin's most famous citizens once lived here; today many of the houses are offices for doctors, lawyers, and government agencies. This area is part of the Dublin 2 zone.

O'CONNELL STREET (NORTH OF THE LIFFEY)   The epicenter of Dublin's stormy political struggles, the north was once a fashionable area, but it lost much of its charm and became run-down in the 20th century. Now it's rebounding with high-profile hotels, plenty of shops, and a few top-rated restaurants. With four theaters in

walking distance of O'Connell Street, this is Dublin's theater district.

NORTH QUAYS (THE LIFFEY RIVERBANKS ON THE NORTHSIDE)   Once the grubby center of Dublin's shipping industry, this is now one of Dublin's trendier addresses for hotels, bars, and clubs. The quays are actually a series of streets named after the wharves that once stood at the water's edge, starting near the mouth of the Liffey and ending in the green peace of Phoenix Park.

BALLSBRIDGE/EMBASSY ROW   Immediately south of the Grand Canal, this wealthy suburb is just barely within walking distance of the city center. Primarily a residential area, it is also home to expensive hotels, restaurants, and embassies, including the U.S. embassy.

TOURIST OFFICES

Dublin Tourism operates six useful walk-in visitor centers in greater Dublin, and they're open every day except Christmas. The biggest is on Suffolk Street near Trinity College, and it has a decent currency exchange counter, a car-rental counter, an accommodations-reservations service, bus and rail information desks, desks where you can book tickets to upcoming events, tour operators, helpful people wandering around who can give you directions or advice, a gift shop with reasonable prices, and a cafe. It's open from June to August Monday to Saturday from 9am to 8:30pm, Sunday and national holidays 10:30am to 3pm, and the rest of the year Monday to Saturday 9am to 5:30pm, Sunday and national holidays 10:30am to 3pm.

The five other centers are in the Arrivals Hall of Dublin Airport; at Exclusively Irish, O'Connell Street; at the Baggot Street Bridge, Baggot Street; at The Square Towncentre, Tallaght; and in the ferry terminal at Dun Laoghaire Harbor. All centers are open year-round with at least the following hours: Monday to Friday 9am to 5:30pm and

Saturday 9am to 5pm. To reach any of them, call ☎ **01/605-7700** or www.visitdublin.com.

For information on Ireland outside of Dublin, call **Bord Fáilte** (☎ **1850/230330** in Ireland; www.travel.ireland.ie).

At any of these centers you can pick up the free *Tourism News;* or the free *Event Guide,* a biweekly entertainment guide, online at www.eventguide.ie. Alternatively, you could do what the locals do and pick up a copy of *In Dublin,* a very useful arts-and-entertainment magazine that sells for €3 at most newsstands.

Recommended Websites

○ **www.eventguide.ie:** Go here for up-to-date local listings for gigs, theater, clubs, and restaurants.

○ **www.hotspots.ie:** This site lists clubs and pubs and gives good descriptions and basic guidance for most worthwhile places in the city.

○ **www.hostel.com/ie.html:** If you need advice on possible cheap places to stay, check out this site.

○ **www.visitdublin.com:** This is one of the best sources for last-minute rooms (often at a discount).

Culture Tips 101

Dublin may be a party town, but Ireland's a conservative country. Given its reputation as a fun-loving, hard-drinking place, this island just might surprise you with its collective habit of clucking its tongue. A combination of strong religious mores and a largely rural environment make this a cautious, old-fashioned place. So no public drinking, no drugs, no PDAs.

Starting at age 18, you can buy alcohol in liquor stores (which are called "off-licenses" here) and drink in pubs. Some nightclubs are exceptions to that rule, though, and voluntarily set higher age limits of 21 or even 23, so check with the venue before you go if you're at the lower end of the age range.

Other age limits for the young and hopeful: You must be at least 16 to buy cigarettes and 17 to drive.

Dublin police, called the Gardai (that's "Gardee" or usually just "the Guard"), are a pretty straightforward, helpful bunch. Feel confident going to them if you need assistance, but also keep in mind that they can search anyone on reasonable suspicion of drug possession and hold them in jail for 7 days without charging them.

The streets of Temple Bar crawl with sweat-suited teenage touts selling hash and other drugs of questionable quality. As in many other countries, buying and carrying drugs is illegal and, if caught, you will most likely land in jail.

Recommended Books, Movies & Music
BOOKS
When you go to Ireland, read up on Joyce (try *Dubliners* first), Yeats, Brendan Behan, and old George Bernard Shaw. Pack in a little Jonathan Swift while you're at it.

Ireland is loaded with good, living writers, and they all merit your attention just as much as its classical writers do. A good place to start is with Roddy Doyle. His novels are clever, quick, and often hilarious. If you haven't discovered *The Commitments, The Van,* and *The Snapper* yet, you really should.

If you've been there and read that, move on to Colm Tóibín. One of Ireland's leading journalists and best young writers, he received good reviews around the globe for his first two books. *The Blackwater Lightship,* which tells the fictional history of a young Irishman's family as he dies of AIDS, was short-listed for Britain's Booker Prize, and is beautifully written in a short, spare, honest style. His other book is a kind of shortcut to Irish writing, the *Penguin Book of Irish Fiction,* a massive 1,000-page anthology of Irish lit. Read some of it, and you'll make just about everyone happy.

DUBLIN

Another writer to look out for as you make your way through the shelves of the Winding Stair bookshop, is Dermot Bolger, a Dublin native who has written numerous books, plays, and film scripts. Colum McCann is another Irish writer worth tracking down. Frank McCourt, who wrote *Angela's Ashes* was clearly blown away. He wrote, "The language you find in Colum McCann's novel, *This Side of Brightness,* makes you claw at yourself with pleasure."

Other writers making headlines include playwright Marina Carr, who wrote *Portia Coughlan* and *By the Bog of Cats,* and novelist Anne Enright whose quirky novels *What Are You Like?* and *The Pleasure of Eliza Lynch* are both enjoyable reads. And Sean O'Reilly has been creating a real stir with his angry, clever Dublin thriller *The Swing of Things.*

MOVIES

Although lots of movies have been made about Ireland, not very many *good* movies have been made about Ireland. A few exceptions follow. *Michael Collins* (1996) is a great biopic about the Irish rebel, with Liam Neeson taking fine command of the lead; it's filmed largely on location. *Nora* (2000) is a good take on James Joyce's fascinating and long-suffering wife. *Maeve* (1982) is considered one of Ireland's first independent films. Cate Blanchett plays the main character in *Veronica Guerin,* a dark, fact-based movie about a troubled investigative reporter.

You'll also find *Bloom* (2004), a brave adaptation of *Ulysses,* with Steven Rea. And *Intermission* (2003) has Colin Farrell romancing using his real accent.

MUSIC

Music is inescapable in Ireland, and if you hear a band playing somewhere, ask if they have a CD for sale. Some home-grown heroes, besides U2, Van Morrison, and Sinéad O'Connor are Damien Rice ("O"), folk singer Christy Moore ("Live at the Point"), the Undertones ("Teenage Kicks"), and The Pogues ("The Band Played Waltzing Matilda").

For the up and coming, look to Snow Patrol and the Thrills. The band Bell X1 plays music with a soft lyrical grace. Based in Dublin, Blink is a jobbing band with a gentle indie sound and sharply creative lyrics. Their records are popular in Ireland, Europe, and the U.K., and they've had four Irish top 10 singles.

Loud, brash, and defiant, the three-piece Dublin-based band Future Kings of Spain has been receiving critical acclaim since it formed in 2000. Check them out if you get the chance.

Another to check out is the tousle-haired singer-songwriter Damien Dempsey, whose alt-country sound has been getting quite a bit of airtime in Ireland and the U.K. recently. If you like Dempsey's thoughtful lyrics, you should also track down the Dublin-based singer-songwriter Paddy Casey, who's rockin' 2005 album "Amen (So Be It)" was a hit with European music critics.

Dublin Nuts & Bolts

Cellphone Providers & Service Centers   There are companies selling cellphones and related equipment all over town. Try **Carphone Warehouse** (30 Grafton St.; ☎ 01/670-5265; www.carphonewarehouse.ie).

Currency   Currency-exchange services are at the airport, in most Dublin banks, some hotels, and at many branches of the Irish post office system. The best rate of exchange is usually when you use your bank card at an ATM. Most banks are open Monday to Friday

10am to 4pm (Thurs to 5pm) and have ATMs. Convenient locations include the **Bank of Ireland** (1 Ormond Quay and 34 College Green) and the **Allied Irish Bank** (64 Grafton St. and 37 O'Connell St.).

Embassies & Consulates   The **U.S. Embassy** is at 42 Elgin Rd., Ballsbridge (☎ 01/668-8777); the **Canadian Embassy** at 65–68 St. Stephen's Green (☎ 01/417-4100); the **British Embassy** at 31 Merrion Rd. (☎ 01/205-3700); and the **Australian Embassy** at Fitzwilton House, Wilton Terrace (☎ 01/664-5300). There is a **U.S. Consulate** at 14 Queen St., Belfast (☎ 028/9032-8239).

Emergencies   For police, fire, or other emergencies, dial ☎ **999.** If you need to see a doctor, ask at your hostel for help, contact your embassy for a list of doctors, or call either the **Eastern Health Board Headquarters** (Dr. Steevens Hospital; ☎ 01/679-0700), or the **Irish Medical Organization** (10 Fitzwilliam Place; ☎ 01/676-7273). For dental emergencies, contact the **Eastern Health Board Headquarters,** Dr. Steevens Hospital (James' St.; ☎ 01/679-0700). For emergency care, two of the most modern hospitals are **St. Vincent's University Hospital** (Elm Park, on the south side of the city; ☎ 01/269-4533) and **Beaumont Hospital** (Beaumont, on the north side; ☎ 01/837-7755).

Internet/Wireless Hot Spots   Internet access is everywhere in Dublin; look for signs in cafes, pubs, shopping malls, hotels, and hostels. Like all of Dublin's public libraries, the **Central Library** (in the ILAC Centre, off Henry St.; ☎ 01/873-4333), has a bank of PCs with free Internet access. Three centrally located cybercafes are the **Central Cybercafe** (6 Grafton St.; ☎ 01/677-8298), **Planet Cyber Café** (13 St. Andrews St.; ☎ 01/670-5182), and **The Connect Point** (33 Dorset St. Lower; ☎ 01/834-9821). Spending a half-hour online averages €3.50. Students might want to pop in at the **Oz Cybercafé** (39 Abbey St. on the north side), as they get Internet access for €1 per hour, while mere mortals must pay double that.

Laundry   **Laundrette** (Pearse St., past Goldsmith on left side of the road) is where most Trinity College students get their laundry done. It's not self-service—expect to pay €5 to €10 to have your clothes washed, dried, and folded.

Luggage Storage   The best places to store luggage are at the main bus station, **Busáras** (Store St.; ☎ 01/703-2436); at **Connolly Station** (the "Left Luggage" office is on Platform 2); at **Heuston Station** (left luggage is near the ticket office); and at **Dublin Airport** (☎ 01/814-4633).

Pharmacies   Centrally located drugstores, or chemist shops, include **Dame Street Pharmacy** (16 Dame St.; ☎ 01/670-4523). A late-night chemist shop is **Hamilton Long & Co.** (5 Lower O'Connell St.; ☎ 01/874-8456), and its sister branch at 4 Merrion Rd. (☎ 01/668-3287). Both branches close at 9pm on weeknights and 6pm on Saturday.

Post Office   The Irish post office is best known by its Gaelic name, An Post. The **General Post Office (GPO)** is located on O'Connell Street (☎ 01/705-7000; www.anpost.ie). Hours are Monday to Saturday 8am to 8pm, Sunday and holidays 10:30am to 6:30pm. Branch offices, identified by the sign OIFIG AN POST/POST OFFICE, are open Monday to Saturday, 9am to 5pm.

Telephone Tips   For directory assistance, dial ☎ 11811. If you need to make international calls, get a phone card—you'll see them in newsstands and shops.

Tipping The standard rate in restaurants is 12%. You don't tip in pubs, but you do in upscale bars, as you would back home. Cab drivers should get 10% to 12%, although most people just add a euro to their fare. If anybody helps with your bags, tip whatever your conscience tells you to.

Youth Information Services Contact the **Union of Students in Ireland Travel** (☎ 02/602-1600; www.usit.ie) for help arranging travel from and around Ireland at cheaper rates; its notice boards are filled with flat-shares, language classes, jobs, and cheap flights. Its offices are on Aston Quay (on the South side of the Liffey about 46m/150 ft. from the O'Connell St. Bridge).

For gay and lesbian issues, contact the **Gay Switchboard Dublin** (Carmichael House, North Brunswick St.; ☎ 01/872-1055); the **National Lesbian and Gay Federation** (**NLGF**; 6 S. William St.; ☎ 01/671-0939); or LOT (Lesbians Organizing Together; 5 Capel St.; ☎ 01/872-7770).

Sleeping

Dublin is packed with housing options, from cheap hostels to moderately priced B&Bs and lavishly expensive boutique hotels.

In general, hotel rates in Dublin do not vary as much with the seasons as they do in the countryside, although some charge slightly higher prices during special events, such as St. Patrick's Day and the Dublin Horse Show. It pays to book well in advance: Either call and book before you come, or do it online—many hotels and some B&Bs offer Web-only deals.

Hostels

→**Dublin International Hostel** Open year-round and run by An Óige, the Irish Youth Hostel Organization, this hostel is in a historic stone building smack in the city center. Good-looking public rooms feature stripped wooden floor boards, a huge old kitchen, an Internet cafe, newly renovated TV/game room, garden, laundry, and a handsome restaurant where a continental breakfast is served for free (if you want the full Irish, it will cost you extra). Dinner is available June through August. Rooms are small and basic but clean. The hostel is open 24 hours and the front desk is always staffed. Members of An Óige/Hostelling

International will receive a €2 discount on the rates listed below. *61 Mountjoy St.* ☎ *01/830-4555. www.anoige.ie. €18–€21 dorm, €48–€52 double. Rates include continental breakfast. Amenities: Restaurant; game room; Internet; kitchen; laundry; TV (in common room). Bus: Any City Centre service.*

→**The Four Courts** Set in some mighty pretty Georgian buildings overlooking the Liffey, this friendly hostel has all the basics, and a few frills. Its setting, at the edge of the river, is top-notch. Inside, the rooms have big windows, stripped wooden floor boards, desks, and other sweet touches that make the plain, metal bunk beds slightly more bearable. It has 24-hour access, good security, free Internet access, a place to park your car, and, in general, more than most hostels will give you for your dosh. *15–17 Merchants Quay.* ☎ *01/672-5839. www.fourcourtshostel.com. €10–€19 dorm, €48 double. Rates include continental breakfast. Amenities: Game room; Internet; laundry. Bus: Any City Centre service.*

MTV Best →**Isaacs Hostel** ★ This is the champagne of hostels. Isaacs is turning the backpacker concept of cheap and cheerful right on its head. Calling itself "Dublin's first V.I.P. hostel," it adds to the usual mix of

DUBLIN

Dublin Sleeping & Eating

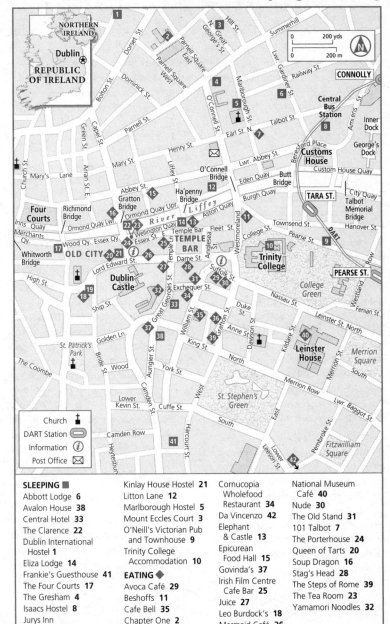

SLEEPING ■

Abbott Lodge **6**
Avalon House **38**
Central Hotel **33**
The Clarence **22**
Dublin International
  Hostel **1**
Eliza Lodge **14**
Frankie's Guesthouse **41**
The Four Courts **17**
The Gresham **4**
Isaacs Hostel **8**
Jurys Inn
  Christchurch **19**

Kinlay House Hostel **21**
Litton Lane **12**
Marlborough Hostel **5**
Mount Eccles Court **3**
O'Neill's Victorian Pub
  and Townhouse **9**
Trinity College
  Accommodation **10**

EATING ◆

Avoca Café **29**
Beshoffs **11**
Cafe Bell **35**
Chapter One **2**
Chompy's **36**

Cornucopia
  Wholefood
  Restaurant **34**
Da Vincenzo **42**
Elephant
  & Castle **13**
Epicurean
  Food Hall **15**
Govinda's **37**
Irish Film Centre
  Cafe Bar **25**
Juice **27**
Leo Burdock's **18**
Mermaid Café **26**

National Museum
  Café **40**
Nude **30**
The Old Stand **31**
101 Talbot **7**
The Porterhouse **24**
Queen of Tarts **20**
Soup Dragon **16**
Stag's Head **28**
The Steps of Rome **39**
The Tea Room **23**
Yamamori Noodles **32**

bunk beds, lockers, and TV rooms a heady cocktail of extras including a full restaurant and, the newest addition, an attractive sauna. It's a thoughtful hybrid hostel, then, with Internet access, a kitchen, pool tables, and a laid-back atmosphere. *2–5 Frenchman's Lane.* ☎ *01/855-6215. www.dublinbackpacker. com. €12–€25 4- to 16-bed rooms, €32–€39 single, €58–€72 double/twin. Amenities: Restaurant; Internet; kitchen; lockers; pool tables; sauna; TV (in common room). Bus: 41, 41B, or 747.*

→ **Kinlay House Hostel** Open year-round and run by USIT, Kinlay House occupies a beautiful redbrick town house in one of Dublin's oldest neighborhoods, which the oldies will tell you is steps from Christ Church Cathedral; but who cares about that when it's right on the edge of the trendy Temple Bar area? There's a large self-catering kitchen and dining room, a TV room, and colorful hangout room. Dorm rooms are small but clean, and the front desk is open 24 hours. Toast and coffee are served each morning until 9:30am. *2–12 Lord Edward St.* ☎ *01/679-6644. www.kinlayhouse.ie. €16–€20 dorm, €40–€50 single, €50–€62 double. Private en suite bathrooms add €2 to price. Rates include continental breakfast. Amenities: Kitchen; TV (in common room). Bus: 21A, 50, 50A, 78, 78A, or 78B.*

→ **Litton Lane** Just a 2-minute walk across the river from Temple Bar, this hip hostel was once a recording studio where legends like Van Morrison, Sinéad O'Connor, Bob Geldof, and others recorded their tunes. Today, it's a small hostel in a cute row of stone buildings, just off O'Connell Street and handy for everything. Rooms are tiny but neatly furnished. Along with 8- and 10-bed dorms, there are twin and double rooms. *2–4 Litton Lane.* ☎ *01/872-8389. www.litton lane.hostel.com. €12–€19 dorm, €70–€80 double or twin. Amenities: Bedding; kitchen. Bus: All O'Connell St. buses.*

→ **Marlborough Hostel** This handy, northside hostel doesn't look like it's up to much from the outside, but inside is a good, sound hostel, with plenty of extras for the underfunded but fussy international traveler. There are dorms with four or eight beds, as well as a few private rooms. This place offers clean shower rooms, and—for those who are about to rock—no curfew. *81–82 Marlborough St.* ☎ *01/874-7629 or 01/874-7812; www.marlboroughhostel.com. €15–€20 dorm, €51–€60 double or twin. Amenities: Game room; garden; Internet; kitchen; TV (in common room). DART: Connolly. Bus: All O'Connell St. buses.*

→ **Mount Eccles Court** This is a beautiful small hostel in a Georgian building on the north side of the river—a great option for those who find themselves freaked out by the bigger facilities. Its 10 bedrooms and 10 dorms are secured with keycard locks and neatly decorated with neutral walls and homey touches, such as plants flourishing in pots. All the extras are there—24-hour access, bedding (including sheets), luggage lockers, Internet access, bike storage, free hot showers, and TV and music lounges. *42 N. Great Georges St.* ☎ *01/873-0826. www. eccleshostel.com. €12–€19 dorm, €32–€34 double or twin. En suite bathrooms add €1–€2 to price. Amenities: Internet; lockers; TV (in common room). Bus: All O'Connell St. buses.*

Cheap

→ **Abbott Lodge** ★ Budget travelers just keep on trotting through the Abbott Lodge's doors. Pop by and you'll see why. The place fairly brims with historical atmosphere, from the huge high ceiling and original cornices to the mahogany beds. And the best bit, it's really near all the bars and eateries of the city center. If you can't decide where to go, the staff will point you in the direction of their favorites. *87–88 Lower Gardiner St.* ☎ *01/836-5548. www.abbott-lodge.com. €45*

ᴹᵀⱽ🎺 Trinity College Accommodations

During the summer months, **Trinity College** (☎ 01/608-1177; www.tcd.ie; bus: all City Centre buses) rents student rooms to visitors by the night, putting you right in the center of the city's action. Forget Ivy League and get a load of the ivy-covered Trinity College, the oldest university in the country. Most of its rooms are inside the college grounds. Ask if you can go in the 19th-century buildings; otherwise, you might get put in the new dorms built in 1990. Most rooms have a twin bed, a desk, plenty of built-in cupboards, and a compact bathroom with shower. Other room breeds include suites with two (or four) single rooms, a living room, one (or two) shared bathrooms, and minimal kitchen facilities (perfect for friends traveling together). The best rooms are in the Graduate Memorial Building—prepare for buckets of character, high ceilings, and views across the green to the Old Library. The biggest rooms can be found in Goldsmith Hall, the newest dorm on campus. A generous continental breakfast is served cafeteria-style in The Buttery, a student eatery. Rooms are available June 7 to September 30 for €42 to €69 per person; rates include continental breakfast.

single, €90 double. Rates include full Irish breakfast. Amenities: Lounge. In room: TV (cable). DART: Connolly. Bus: All City Centre buses.

➜ **Avalon House** This warm and friendly guesthouse in a beautiful old redbrick building is well known among those who travel to Dublin on a budget. Its pine floors, high ceilings, and open fireplace make it a top chillout spot, and its cafe is a popular hangout for international travelers. Rooms range from dorms to doubles, and it's got all you really need—clean, cheerful rooms in a safe location at a cheap price. 55 Aungier St. ☎ 01/475-0001. www.avalon-house.ie. €30–€34 dorm, €28–€32 double. En suite bathrooms add €4 to price. Amenities: Cafe; currency exchange; Internet; kitchen; luggage storage; nonsmoking rooms; safe; TV (in common room). Bus: 16, 16A, 19, 22, or 155.

➜ **O'Neils Victorian Pub and Townhouse** Perched Victorian style above a pub, this inn has been putting up budget travelers for more than a century. The location, just across from Trinity College can't be beat, although some older travelers have complained about street noise in the past. But,

hey, if you're out most of the night, what do you care? Otherwise shove in some earplugs. The eight rooms are tiny but neat, and the full Irish breakfast in the morning will see you through the day. 36–37 Pearse St. ☎ 01/671-4074. www.oneillsdublin.com. Rates include full Irish breakfast. €35–€65 per person double or twin (rate depends on room, time of week, and season). Amenities: Restaurant; bar. Buses: All City Centre buses.

Doable

➜ **Central Hotel** ★ This rambling, eccentric old hotel has enough quirky personality to make up for what it lacks in modernity. The public areas have a laid-back, Victorian atmosphere enhanced by a divine collection of original Irish art. Bedrooms have high ceilings and carved cornices but are let down by cheap-and-cheerful fabrics. Its atmospheric Library Bar is your new favorite place—a truly cool haven for a cappuccino or a pint and a bit of calm. 1–5 Exchequer St. (at the corner of Great Georges St.). ☎ 800/780-1234 in the U.S. or 01/679-7302. www.centralhotel.ie. €135–€175 double. Rates include service charge and full Irish breakfast. Amenities:

DUBLIN

Restaurant; bar; laundry service; lounge; nonsmoking rooms; room service. In room: TV, coffee/tea maker, garment press, hair dryer, iron, minibar, voice mail. Bus: 22A.

➜**Eliza Lodge** ★★ This bijou hotel opened a few years ago right beside the Liffey and immediately staked out a place among the coolest options in Temple Bar. Okay, so it looks like a motel from the outside and the reception rooms aren't much to write home about, but the 18 guest rooms are just fine in neutral creams and blond wood, with big floor-to-ceiling windows—all the better to take in the riverside views. *23 Wellington Quay.* ☎ *01/671-8044. www.dublinlodge.com. €110–€130 double. Amenities: Restaurant; bar; coffee/tea maker; nonsmoking rooms. In room: A/C, TV, hair dryer, iron. Bus: 51B, 51C, 68, 69, or 79.*

➜**Frankie's Guesthouse** ★ Billed as Dublin's only guesthouse exclusively for lesbians and gays, Frankie's is a charming, mews-style building with a wonderful address in the heart of Georgian Dublin. Set on a quiet back street, the house has a Mediterranean feel, with fresh whitewashed rooms and simple furnishings. Book well in advance, especially for a weekend stay. *8 Camden Place.* ☎*/fax 01/478-3087. www.frankiesguesthouse.com. €100 double with private bathroom, €82 with shared bathroom. Rates include breakfast. Amenities: Roof terrace; sauna; TV (in common room). In room: TV, coffee/tea maker. Bus: 16, 16A, 16C, 19A, 22, or 22A.*

➜**Jurys Inn Christchurch** ★ A fab location in the Old City, near all the nightlife, and frequent special offers that keep the price in the bargain-basement arena, make this a budget option. The rooms are larger than many in the city, though the decor disappoints with the same naff polyester floral bedspreads and framed watercolors as every other chain hotel you've ever visited. Make your reservations early and request a

fifth-floor room facing west for a view to remember. *Christ Church Place.* ☎ *800/44-UTELL in the U.S. or 01/454-0000. www.jurys-dublin-hotels.com/jurysinn_christchurch. €117–€130 double. Rates include service charge. Breakfast €9.50. Amenities: Restaurant; bar; laundry/dry cleaning; nonsmoking rooms. In room: A/C, TV, coffeemaker, hair dryer. Bus: 21A, 50, 50A, 78, 78A, or 78B.*

Splurge

➜**The Clarence** ★★★ This has been the most famous hotel in Dublin since 1992, when U2's Bono and the Edge bought it. Its rock-'n'-roll pedigree aside, this is also the most stylish hotel in the city. Rooms are designed with lush fabrics in neutral tones of oatmeal and chocolate, light Shaker-style oak furniture, and ultracomfy, king-size beds. It may be expensive, but it's not snobby—the hip staff members are on top of things. The Tea Room restaurant is one of the best in town for contemporary Irish cuisine, while the Octagon Bar is a favorite with visiting celebrities. *6–8 Wellington Quay.* ☎ *01/670-9000. www.theclarence.ie. €330 double, €640 1-bedroom suite. Amenities: Restaurant; bar; laundry/dry cleaning; nonsmoking rooms. In room: A/C, interactive TV/DVD/broadband system, hair dryer. Bus: 51B, 51C, 68, 69, or 79.*

➜**The Gresham** ★★ This big, historic hotel has been here for nearly 200 years, and it's one of the city's most famous hotels. **Tip:** It's a relaxing place to hang out even if you're not staying here—the vast lobby is ideal for a cup of tea or a pint of beer and people-watching. The whole place is currently undergoing a much-needed makeover. *23 Upper O'Connell St.* ☎ *01/874-6881. www.gresham-hotels.com. €150–€220 double. Amenities: 2 restaurants; 2 bars; Internet; laundry/dry cleaning; nonsmoking rooms. In room: A/C, TV, hair dryer, safe. Bus: 11 or 13.*

Eating

Let's just say it plain: Eating out in Dublin is expensive. Most restaurants are pricey, and even restaurants that *should* be cheap—Chinese restaurants, Indian restaurants, and the like—cost more than you might expect. In fact, restaurant prices in Dublin are considerably more than you'd pay in a comparable U.S. city, or even in Paris or London. The problem, it seems, is a pesky combination of high taxes and a bit of nouveau-riche overenthusiasm among restaurant owners for charging a lot.

Luckily, you can get a cost break in the city's many cafes and coffee shops, where you can pick up sandwiches and hot lunches at reasonable prices, as well as from pubs, which offer big Irish lunches (stews, meat pies, sausages, and mashed potatoes) at more old-fashioned prices. If you really want to save money, try buying sandwiches to go in grocery stores or street-corner delis at lunchtime and only eat out one meal a day. Read menus before you go in, and order carefully. Wine, in particular, can really raise the bottom line.

Hot Spots

➔ **Chapter One** ★ MODERN IRISH Arguably the city's most atmospheric restaurant, this stunner fills the vaulted basement space of the Dublin Writers Museum. Artfully lighted and tastefully decorated, it's one of the top restaurants in town. Meals are prepared with local, organic ingredients, all cleverly used in incredible dishes like the ravioli with Irish goat cheese and warm asparagus, and the Irish beef with shallot gratin. You may want to make reservations if you want to get in. *18–19 Parnell Sq.* ☎ *01/873-2266. www.chapteronerestaurant. com. Main courses €20–€35; fixed-price dinner €52. Tues–Fri 12:30–2:30pm and 6–11pm; Sat 6–11pm. Bus: 27A, 31A, 31B, 32A, 32B, 42B, 42C, 43, or 44A.*

➔ **The Tea Room** ★★★ INTERNATIONAL This ultrasmart restaurant, ensconced in the U2-owned Clarence hotel, is guaranteed to deliver one of your most memorable meals in Ireland. This gorgeous room's soaring yet understated lines are the perfect backdrop for Antony Ely's complex but controlled cooking, which takes form in dishes like loin of Finnebrogue venison with celeriac purée, or the roasted organic salmon with lentils and red wine *jus.* Desserts can wax creative, as in the basil crème brûlée. Reservations are required. *In The Clarence, 6–8 Wellington Quay.* ☎ *01/670-9000. Fixed-price 2-course dinner €48, 3-course dinner €55. Mon–Fri 12:30–2pm; Mon–Sun 6:30–9:45pm. Bus: 51B, 51C, 68, 69, or 79.*

Cheap

➔ **Beshoffs** FISH AND CHIPS This is fish and chips gone up in the world. Recently renovated in Victorian style, it has a chill atmosphere and a simple self-service menu. Crisp chips are served with a choice of fresh fish, from the trad cod to classier options using salmon, shark, prawns, and other local sea life—some days there are as many as 20 different varieties. The potatoes are grown on a 120-hectare (300-acre) farm in Tipperary and freshly cut each day. A second shop is just south of the Liffey at 14 Westmoreland St. (☎ **01/677-8026**). *6 Upper O'Connell St.* ☎ *01/872-4400. All items €3–€7. Mon–Sat 10am–9pm; Sun noon–9pm. DART: Tara St. Bus: Any City Centre bus.*

➔ **Cafe Bell** IRISH/SELF-SERVICE In the cobbled courtyard of early-19th-century St. Teresa's Church, this gem of a place has high ceilings and an old-world decor, providing calm after the bustle of Grafton Street just a block away. The menu changes daily but usually includes thick and tasty homemade soups, thick-cut sandwiches, fresh salads, quiches, lasagna, sausage rolls, scones, and other baked goodies. *St. Teresa's Courtyard, Clarendon St.* ☎ *01/677-7645. All items €3–€6.*

Mon–Sat 9am–5:30pm. Bus: 16, 16A, 19, 19A, 22A, 55, or 83.

➔**Chompy's** ★ BREAKFAST/LUNCH
Perched high above the attractive Powerscourt Centre, this is a favorite place for many
Americans living in Dublin to stop in for a
familiar breakfast of pancakes with maple
syrup, French toast, eggs Benedict, or bagels.
It's a brill lunch spot too, churning out big,
fresh sandwiches and soups. *Powerscourt
Townhouse Centre, Clarendon St.* ☎ *01/
679-4552. Main courses €4–€9. Daily noon–
5:30pm. Bus: Any City Centre bus.*

➔**Cornucopia Wholefood Restaurant**
★ VEGETARIAN This little cafe just off
Grafton Street is one of the best veggie
restaurants in the city. It also serves wholesome meals for people on various restricted
diets (vegan, nondairy, low sodium, low fat).
Soups are particularly good here, as are the
salads and the hot dishes, like the baked
lasagna made with eggplant. A delish healthy
alternative. *19 Wicklow St.* ☎ *01/677-7583.
Main courses €4–€10. Mon–Thurs 8am–7pm;
Fri–Sat 8am–10pm. Bus: Any City Centre bus.*

➔**Epicurean Food Hall** ★★ GOURMET
FOOD COURT This first-rate food hall sells
mountains of yummy artisan foods, local Irish
meats, and regional dishes. Shops to keep an
eye out for include **Caviston's,** Dublin's
fave deli, for smoked salmon and seafood;
Itsabagel, for just-like-home bagels, imported
from H&H Bagels in New York City; **Crème de
la Crème,** for French-style pastries and cakes;
Missy and Mandy's, for American-style ice
cream; **Nectar,** for a flood of healthy juice
drinks; and **Aroma Bistro,** for Italian panini.
There is limited seating but this place gets
jammed during lunchtime midweek, so go
off-peak if possible. *Middle Abbey St. No phone.
All items €2–€12. Mon–Sat 10am–6pm. Bus: 70
or 80.*

➔**Juice** ★ VEGETARIAN If nobody told
you Juice was a veggie restaurant, you'd
probably never guess. Yes, the food is *that*

good. The interior is also beautifully
designed, with soaring 9.1m (30-ft.) ceilings
and oh-so-classy decor. Brunch is classic
here: pancakes, *huevos rancheros,* and
French toast topped with fresh fruit or
organic maple syrup. The rest of the day you
can sample the homemade dips—hummus,
baba ghanoush, tapenade, roasted carrot
pâté—with crudités and pita-bread strips.
And, yes, there are about 30 different types
of juices and smoothies on offer. *Castle
House, 73 S. Great Georges St.* ☎ *01/475-7856.
Reservations recommended Fri–Sat. Main
courses €7–€10. Daily 11am–11pm. Bus: 50, 54,
56, or 77.*

➔**Leo Burdock's** ★ FISH AND CHIPS
From the first fish slapped in batter in 1913,
this Irish takeout shop across from Christ
Church Cathedral is a Dublin institution.
Cabinet ministers, university students, and
businesspeople can all be spotted at the
counter waiting for fish bought fresh that
morning and good Irish potatoes, both
cooked in "drippings" (none of that modern
cooking oil nonsense here). There's no seating, but you can grab a nearby bench or
stroll down to the park at St. Patrick's
Cathedral. *2 Werburgh St.* ☎ *01/454-0306. Main
courses €6–€7. Mon–Sat noon–midnight; Sun
4pm–midnight. Bus: 21A, 50, 50A, 78, 78A, or
78B.*

➔**National Museum Café** ★ CAFETERIA
A great place to nab a cheap meal. The cafe is
pretty casual but not ugly thanks to a mosaic
floor, marble tabletops, and tall windows
looking across the cobbled yard. Everything is
made fresh: beef salad, chicken salad, quiche,
an Everest of pastries. The soup of the day is
often veggie, always good. Admission to the
museum is free, so you can take a tour for
afters. *National Museum of Ireland, Kildare St.*
☎ *01/677-7444. Soup €3; lunch main courses
under €8. Tues–Sat 10am–5pm; Sun 2–5pm.
Bus: 7, 7A, 8, 10, 11, or 13.*

➜ **Nude** ★ VEGETARIAN This small chain with sleek little outlets all around town is an excellent place to grab lunch or a snack without blowing your diet. The emphasis here is on healthy, from the freshly squeezed juices down to the wraps (chickpea and chili is a longtime favorite), sandwiches, soups, salads, and sweets. The prices aren't too chunky either. Other branches are at 103 Lower Leeson St., 38 Upper Baggot St., and 28 Grafton St. *1 Suffolk St., Trinity College.* ☎ *01/672-5577. Main courses €5–€6. Mon–Sat 7:30am–8:30pm; Sun 10am–6pm. Bus: 50, 54, or 56.*

➜ **Soup Dragon** SOUP Soup has become the healthy, hip alternative to stodgy sandwiches and fast food, and the Soup Dragon leads the way for cheap and cheerful chow in Dublin. It's a tiny place, with less than a dozen stools alongside a bar, but it's big on drama. Think blue walls, black and red mirrors, orange slices and spice sticks flowing out of giant jugs, and huge flower-filled vases. The menu changes daily. It's also a good place for dessert. Try the bread-and-butter pudding or the yummy banana bread. *168 Capel St.* ☎ *01/872-3277. All items €3–€8. Mon–Sat 9:30am–6pm; Sun 1–6pm. Bus: 70 or 80.*

➜ **The Steps of Rome** ITALIAN/PIZZA Word is out that this restaurant—just off the busy shopping thoroughfare of Grafton Street—offers some of the best simple Italian fare in Dublin. Large, succulent pizza slices available for takeout are one way to enjoy the wonders of this authentic Italian kitchen when the dining room is full—the seven tables huddled within this tiny restaurant seem to be forever occupied. The potato, mozzarella, and rosemary pizza, with a thick crust resembling focaccia, is particularly delish. Although the pasta dishes are also quite good, nothing tops those pizzas. *Chatham Court, off Chatham St.* ☎ *01/670-5630. Main courses €8–€11; pizza slices €3.50. No credit cards. Mon–Sat 10am–midnight; Sun 1–11pm. DART: Pearse. Bus: Any City Centre bus.*

➜ **Yamamori Noodles** ★ JAPANESE This Japanese restaurant is so fun and bouncy you might just be startled by how good the food is. Prices range from bargain to splurge for dishes like chili chicken ramen, and the yamamori yaki soba with a mound of wok-fried noodles, piled high with prawns, squid, chicken, and roast pork. Lunch specials are outstanding here; work your day around it. *71–72 S. Great Georges St.* ☎ *01/475-5001. Reservations for only parties of 4 or more. Main courses €11–€18. Sun–Wed 12:30–11pm; Thurs–Sat 12:30–11:30pm. Bus: 50, 50A, 54, 56, or 77.*

Doable

➜ **Da Vincenzo** ITALIAN Occupying a storefront within a few minutes of St. Stephen's Green, this friendly, owner-run bistro creates a chill atmosphere with brick fireplaces, pine walls, dried flower arrangements, modern art, and a busy open kitchen. Pizza, with a light, pita-style dough cooked in a wood-burning oven, is a specialty here. Other main courses range from pastas to veal and beef dishes, including an organically produced filet steak. You may want to make reservations. *133 Upper Leeson St.* ☎ *01/660-9906. Fixed-price lunch €11; dinner main courses €12–€22. Mon–Fri 12:30–11pm; Sat 1–11pm; Sun 3–10pm. Bus: 10, 11A, 11B, 46A, or 46B.*

➜ **Elephant & Castle** AMERICAN You might think you could find this kind of food—burgers, chicken wings, omelets—at any old Yankee-style joint, but Noel Alexander lifts everyday American cooking to an art form, working a stove like he was raised in American diners. His chicken wings are admired citywide and his burgers are out of this world. This place fills up fast for breakfast, brunch, lunch, afternoon nibble, dinner, and late dinner. Expect to wait for a table. *18 Temple Bar.* ☎ *01/679-3121. Main* courses €8–€22. *Mon–Fri 8am–11:30pm; Sat 10:30am–11:30pm; Sun noon–11:30pm. Bus: 51B, 51C, 68, 69, or 79.*

→ **Govinda's** ★ VEGETARIAN The motto here is healthy square meals on square plates for very good prices. The meals are generous, belly-warming concoctions of vegetables, cheese, rice, and pasta. Every day, 10 main courses are offered cafeteria-style. Some are Indian, others are your usual Euro dishes like lasagna or macaroni and cheese. Veggie burgers are prepared to order. For dessert, try a rich wedge of carrot cake with a dollop of cream or homemade ice cream. *4 Aungier St.* ☎ *01/475-0309. Main courses €8–€13. Mon–Sat noon–9pm. Closed Dec 24–Jan 2. Bus: 16, 16A, 19, or 22.*

Splurge

→ **Mermaid Café** ★★ MODERN Owned by a chef and an artist, this fashionable eatery is a mixture of good restaurant and classy hangout. A lunchtime favorite of local professionals, and a good place to take a date in the evening, dishes often found on the frequently changing menu range from slow-roasted pork belly, to an array of first-rate seafood dishes, including a luxe Atlantic seafood casserole. If you want to eat here, you'll have to make reservations. *70 Dame St.* ☎ *01/670-8236. www.mermaid.ie. Dinner main courses €18–€30. Mon–Sat 12:30–2:30pm and 6–11pm; Sun 12:30–3:30pm (brunch) and 6–9pm. Bus: 50, 50A, 54, 56A, 77, 77A, or 77B.*

→ **101 Talbot** ★★ INTERNATIONAL This second-floor eatery above a shop might not look like much from the outside but don't be conned—it's actually a bright beacon of good cooking on the Northside. The menu features light, healthy food, with a focus on veggie dishes. These change all the time but could include seared filet of tuna, roast duck breast, or Halloumi cheese and mushroom brochette. The dining area is casually funky, with contemporary Irish art, big windows, and newspapers scattered about. The staff is effortlessly friendly.

Reservations are recommended. *101 Talbot St. (at Talbot Lane near Marlborough St.).* ☎ *01/874-5011. Dinner main courses €14–€19. Tues–Sat 5–11pm. DART: Connolly. Bus: 27A, 31A, 31B, 32A, 32B, 42B, 42C, 43, or 44A.*

Cafes & Patisseries

→ **Avoca Café** ★★ MODERN IRISH A polished, casual cafe perched above the vibrant pinks and reds of the knitted wools and painted doodads in the cutesy Avoca shop near Trinity College is one of Dublin's fave lunch spots. If you can rip yourself away from the shops, there are thick homemade soups, fresh salads, and chunky sandwiches in this buzzing cafe. *11–13 Suffolk St., Trinity College.* ☎ *01/672-6019. www.avoca.ie. Main courses €9–€13. Mon–Wed and Fri 10am–6pm; Thurs 10am–8pm; Sat 10am–6:30pm; Sun 11am–6pm. Bus: 50, 54, or 56.*

→ **Irish Film Centre Cafe Bar** ★ IRISH/ INTERNATIONAL One of the hottest drinking spots in Temple Bar, the hip Cafe Bar (in the lobby of the city's coolest place to watch a movie) features an excellent, good-deal menu that changes daily. Expect plenty of veggie dishes and a smattering of Middle Eastern attitude. *6 Eustace St., Temple Bar.* ☎ *01/677-8788. Main courses €6–€10. Mon–Fri 12:30–3pm; Sat–Sun 1–3pm; daily 6–9pm. Bus: 21A, 78A, or 78B.*

→ **Queen of Tarts** ★★ TEA SHOP A top spot to blow your diet on decadent cakes and cookies. The cake counter is dizzying— we challenge you to come here and not order something sweet, like the luscious blackberry pie or the rich chocolate cake, with cream bursting from its seams. The scones are tender and light, dusted with powdered sugar and accompanied by little pots of jam. *4 Corkhill, Dame St.* ☎ *01/670-7499. Baked goods and cakes €1.25–€4. No credit cards. Mon–Fri 7:30am–7pm; Sat 9am–6pm; Sun 10am–6pm. Bus: Any City Centre bus.*

Pubs

→The Old Stand TRADITIONAL One hundred fifty years ago, this was a forge; now the horses have gone and been replaced with sporting celebs munching on pub grub. Choose from a daily special of soup, meat, and vegetables, with tea or coffee, or omelets, salads, chicken, steak, or fish. *Note:* This is one of few pubs serving food during evening hours. *37 Exchequer St. (just off Great Georges St.).* ☎ *01/677-7220. www. theoldstandpub.com. Lunch main courses €10; dinner main courses €8–€13. Daily noon–9pm. DART: Pearse or Tara St. Bus: Any City Centre bus.*

Ⓜ Best →The Porterhouse ★ TRADITIONAL One of Dublin's first microbrewery pubs and still a star, bang in the middle of the Temple Bar action. Prepare to get your lips round a constantly changing range of home-brewed ales, lagers, and stouts, all served up in a laid-back folksy atmosphere. Pull up one of the many pews and order some traditional chow. Irish stew, bangers and mash, and steak pie are all for the taking at rather attractive prices. *16–18 Parliament St., Temple Bar.* ☎ *01/679-8847. www.porterhousebrewco.com. Pub food €5–€14. Daily 11am–midnight. Bus: Any City Centre bus.*

→Stag's Head TRADITIONAL Built in 1770, the Stag's Head had its last "modernization" in 1895. Wrought-iron chandeliers, stained-glass skylights, huge mirrors, gleaming wood, and mounted stags' heads set the mood. Prep for soup and toasted sandwiches or heaping platters of bacon, beef, or chicken plus two veggies. The pub is just off Exchequer Street (from Great Georges St.)—look for the mosaic depicting a stag's head, embedded in the sidewalk of Dame Street, in the middle of the second block, on the left side coming from College Green, then turn onto the small lane that leads to Dame Court—a complicated journey, but worth the effort. *1 Dame Court.* ☎ *01/679-3701. Main courses €5–€11. Mon–Fri 12:30–3:30pm and 5–7pm; Sat 12:30–2:30pm. DART: Pearse or Tara St. Bus: Any City Centre bus.*

DUBLIN

Partying

Nightlife in Dublin is a well-shaken cocktail of traditional pubs, where the Irish music swirls and jangles, and cool modern bars, where the latest techno rhythms fill the air, and the crowd knows more about Prada than the Pogues. There's little in the way of crossover, although there are a couple of quieter bars and a few pubs with a rock music angle, should you be in a hybrid mood.

If you're here to dance, keep an eye on local-listings magazines and websites because things change constantly. The same club could be a gay fetish scene one night and techno-pop dance the next, so you have to stay on your toes. Pick up a copy of *In Dublin* and the *Event Guide* at local cafes and shops if you're looking for the latest on the club scene. Or check out the website of the *Irish Times* (www.ireland.com), which offers a "what's on" daily guide to cinema, theater, music, and whatever else you're up for. The **Dublin Events Guide** (www.dublinevents.com) also provides a comprehensive listing of the week's entertainment possibilities.

The hottest clubs have a "strict" (read: unfriendly) door policy of admitting only "regulars." Your chances of getting past the door increase if you're female and wear your hippest clothes.

Cover charges tend to fluctuate from place to place and from night to night and even from person to person (some people can't buy their way in, while others glide in gratis). Cover charges range from nothing to €15.

One key difference between pubs, bars, and clubs is open hours. Pubs tend to be

Dublin Partying & Sightseeing

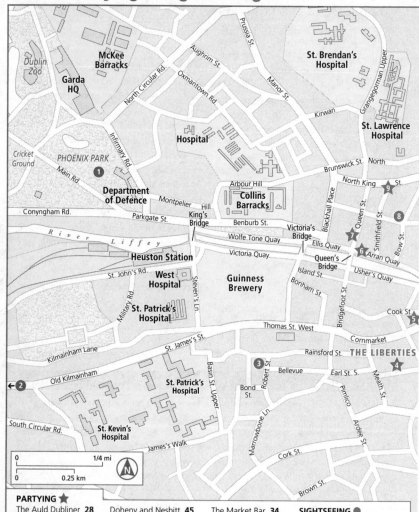

PARTYING ⭐

The Auld Dubliner **28**
Ba Mizu **37**
The Bank **29**
Brazen Head **5**
Bruxelles **38**
Café en Seine **41**
Carnival **46**
The Cobblestone **9**
Copper Face Jacks **48**
Crawdaddy **49**
Davy Byrnes **40**
Dice **7**

Doheny and Nesbitt **45**
Eamonn Doran's **27**
The Front Lounge **21**
The George **36**
GUBU **14**
Ha'Penny Laugh
  Comedy Club **25**
International Bar **31**
Karma **20**
Lillie's Bordello **39**
The Long Hall **35**
The Lower Deck **50**

The Market Bar **34**
O'Donoghue's **44**
Octagon Bar **22**
Out on the Liffey **16**
Rí-Rá **32**
Temple Bar
  Music Centre **26**
Vicar Street **4**
The Village **47**
Voodoo Lounge **6**
Whelans **47**
Zanzibar **15**

SIGHTSEEING ⬤

The Book of Kells/
  Trinity College **30**
Chester Beatty Library **33**
Christ Church Cathedral **18**
Dublin Castle **19**
Dublin Writers Museum **11**
General Post Office
  (GPO) **12**
Guinness Storehouse **3**
Hugh Lane Municipal
  Gallery of Modern Art **10**

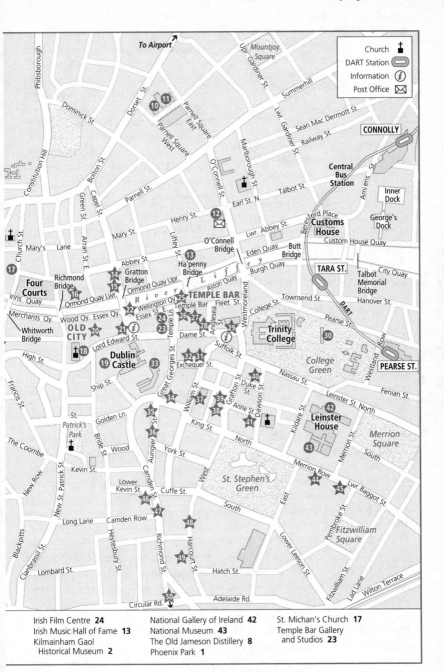

Irish Film Centre **24**
Irish Music Hall of Fame **13**
Kilmainham Gaol
  Historical Museum **2**

National Gallery of Ireland **42**
National Museum **43**
The Old Jameson Distillery **8**
Phoenix Park **1**

St. Michan's Church **17**
Temple Bar Gallery
  and Studios **23**

open all day and almost all close at 11pm, based on long-standing tradition more than anything else. Bars and music clubs usually open at 7pm and stay open until 2am, while nightclubs open even later, and stay open as long as there are dancers on the floor.

Bars & Wine Bars

Going to a bar is the best way to get a cocktail you'll recognize from home—in fact, bars here are cocktail crazy. Flaming Nipples and Curvy Hips—if it has a dumb name, it's going to be on the menu. Prices have risen in recent years, so expect to pay anything from €4.50 for a basic gin and tonic to €12 for a fancy tall cocktail with fruit and an umbrella.

➜**Ba Mizu** This bar draws the young, glamorous set. The clientele includes a regular smattering of models (both male and female) and trendy urbanites. *Powerscourt Townhouse Centre, S. William St.* ☎ *01/674-6712. Bus: 16, 16A, or 65.*

➜**The Bank** As the name implies, this bar is in a converted bank building, and that is somehow appropriate, given that the crowd is made up largely of professionals in very expensive shoes. It's got a good reputation, and it's a gorgeous, vast space. *20–22 College Green.* ☎ *01/677-0677. Dart: Tara St. Bus: 48A.*

➜**Bruxelles** This is one of Dublin's late-night bars, staying open until 2:30am on weekends, and its crowd tends to be well lubricated and therefore somewhat overly friendly. It's not a beautiful place, but it's very popular with locals. Somewhere to get off your face and embrace someone you've never met before. *7–8 Harry St., off Grafton St.* ☎ *01/677-5362. Bus: 14, 14A, 15A, 15B, or 48A.*

➜**Café en Seine** This vast bar packs in thousands of young, well-dressed, well-paid local professionals, and yet it never seems crowded. It's a gorgeous turn-of-the-century building, with plenty of architectural detail, but nobody who comes here regularly much cares. They're here for the booze and each other. Get a load of both. *40 Dawson St.* ☎ *01/677-4567. Bus: 10, 11, or 51X.*

➜**Copper Face Jacks** Locals believe this busy club is *the* Dublin pickup joint. Everybody here is on the make, they say, and everything is physical—it's not how smart you are that counts; it's how good you look. The young crowd (most are in their early 20s) are here to chat, drink, and meet members of the opposite sex. It's loud, steamy, and crowded, but my-oh-my it's a fine looking place. *29 Harcourt St.* ☎ *01/475-8777. www. jackson-court.ie/copper.html. Bus: 14, 14A, 15A, 15B, or 48A.*

➜**Karma** In the George Frederic Handel Hotel at the edge of Temple Bar, Karma is easy to find, and hugely popular for such a small club. Its DJ lineup is solid—this place is serious about music and dancing. Karma is a favorite of expats and students, so it's a good place to meet other Americans. Those in the know often stop in for dinner between 5:30 and 8:30pm, and the food is okay, as are the prices. *In the George Frederic Handel Hotel, 16–18 Fishamble St.* ☎ *01/670-9400. Bus: 41, 41C, or 16A.*

➜**The Market Bar** Around here, this is what they call a "superpub." It's not really a pub at all, just a big, laid-back bar, with a soaring ceiling, gorgeous design, a good beer and wine list, and friendly bar staff. This is the kind of place where you could sit in the late afternoon and have a solitary pint and nobody would bother you. Its no-music policy means it's quiet enough to hear yourself drink. *Fade St., off S. Great Georges St.* ☎ *01/613-9094. Bus: 15E, 15F, 16, 19, or 83.*

➜**Octagon Bar** This incredibly trendy bar on the ground floor of The Clarence hotel is one of the hottest places in town. It's got an eight-sided bar, which the bartenders handle with aplomb, and you don't have to be rich or beautiful to get in the door. There's a quieter back room, and prices are not as high as they might be. A fave celeb hangout. *The*

Clarence, 6–8 Wellington Quay. ☎ *01/670-9000. Bus: 11, 121, 122, 13, 13A, 16, 16A, 3, or 746.*

→ **Voodoo Lounge** Partly owned by New York's Fun Lovin' Criminals, this hip, Northside joint is a hard-core music and dance bar, and a popular late-night hangout for those who are not into the normal techno-pop mix. Given its roots, it's unsurprising that the music here is the latest and best stuff around, with an emphasis on hip-hop and R&B. This place isn't pretty, but it's cool. *38 Arran Quay.* ☎ *01/873-6013. Bus: 37, 39, 70, or 70N.*

📺 Best → **Zanzibar** ★ This, like The Market Bar, is one of Dublin's "superpubs"—a big, sleek bar, with a relaxed publike atmosphere. In its extravagant, vaguely North African–style setting, a huge crowd of young professionals mixes with local university students, and looking good is what it's all about. It's a well-known "meat market," so be prepared for that level of interaction. You can't miss its huge purple facade on Ormond Quay—inside it has multiple levels, multiple bars, and DJs spinning tunes every night from 9pm. *Ormond Quay.* ☎ *01/878-7212. Bus: 25 or 26.*

Pubs

Pubs generally serve beer and liquor, but most don't do much in the way of cocktails beyond a vodka tonic or rum and Coke. Ask for a cosmopolitan, and you'll likely get a blank stare. Beer is generally sold by the pint and half-pint. Prices are pretty uniform in the city center: A shot of whiskey runs around €3.50, a pint of stout about €3.50, and lager €3.70.

The **Stag's Head** and **The Porterhouse** (see "Eating," above) both make classic drinking stops, too. See also "Pubs for Traditional & Folk Music," below.

→ **Davy Byrnes** In *Ulysses,* Leopold Bloom describes this place as a "moral pub," and stops in for a Gorgonzola sandwich and a glass of burgundy. It has drawn poets, writers, and readers ever since. It dates from 1873, when Davy Byrnes first opened the doors—he presided over it for more than 50 years, and visitors can still see his likeness on one of the turn-of-the-20th-century murals hanging over the bar. *21 Duke St. (off Grafton St.).* ☎ *01/677-5217. www.davybyrnes. com. Bus: 14, 14A, 15A, 15B, or 48A.*

→ **Doheny and Nesbitt** Competition is stiff, but this may well be the best-looking traditional pub in town. The Victorian bar houses two fine old "snugs"—small rooms behind the main bar where women could have a drink out of the sight of men in days of old—and a restaurant that's good for traditional Irish food. *5 Lower Baggot St.* ☎ *01/676-2945. Bus: 10, 10A, 15X, 18, 25X, 49X, or 50X.*

📺 Best → **The Long Hall** ★ This is Doheny and Nesbitt's main competition in the Prettiest Pub Contest. With a beautiful Victorian decor of filigree-edged mirrors, polished dark woods, and traditional snugs, this place is like a theater of beer. The atmosphere is great, and bartenders pour a good pint. *51 S. Great Georges St.* ☎ *01/475-1590. Bus: 15E, 15F, 16, 19, or 83.*

→ **O'Donoghue's** Tucked between St. Stephen's Green and Merrion Street, this touristy, smoke-filled enclave is the grand-daddy of traditional music pubs in Dublin, and it's usually packed with Americans. A spontaneous session is likely to erupt at almost any time of the day or night. *15 Merrion Row.* ☎ *01/676-2807. Bus: 10, 10A, 15X, 18, 25X, 49X, or 50X.*

Pubs for Traditional & Folk Music

If you're here for the more old-fashioned Irish music, there are quite a few alternatives. Generally the band plays in the main bar for tips, although sometimes there's a separate room for music, and an entrance

DUBLIN

fee is paid at the door (in cash)—usually €5 to €8.

→**The Auld Dubliner** A pub for people who don't normally go to pubs. It's in Temple Bar, so it's central. It's completely relaxed, with bands playing traditional music upstairs, Irish stew on the stove, and quiet pints at the downstairs pub. *17 Anglesea St.* ☎ *01/677-0527. Bus: 63 or 84.*

→**Brazen Head** In its time, revolutions were plotted in this brass-filled, lantern-lit pub. The Head was first licensed in 1661, which makes it one of the oldest pubs in Ireland. Nestled on the south bank of the River Liffey, it is at the end of a cobblestone courtyard and was once the meeting place of rebels Robert Emmet and Wolfe Tone. Trad music sessions start at 9:30pm nightly. *20 Lower Bridge St.* ☎ *01/677-9549. Bus: 2 or 3.*

→**The Cobblestone** This is the most Irish of Irish pubs, with a musicians' corner downstairs where traditional Irish music is played for free, and a proper music hall upstairs where you have to buy tickets but the bands are top-notch. It's one of the places the locals go to hear music, so expect to find none of what they call "paddy-whackery." *77 King St. North.* ☎ *01/872-1799. Bus: 10, 10A, 15X, 18, 25X, 49X, or 50X.*

Music Clubs

The best place in town to catch an up-and-coming band is always going to be in one of these music bars. Most have been around for years, and all have excellent reputations for attracting bands with a top potential to rock your world.

→**Crawdaddy** Dublin's most intimate live music venue, Crawdaddy has a classy look—like a chilled-out House of Blues. Its good acoustics and fab indie gigs make it one of the hottest places in town to catch a band. The staff is friendly. The atmosphere is deeply casual. Open nightly from 5pm. *Old*

Harcourt Station, Harcourt St. ☎ *01/478-0166. Bus: 14, 14A, 15A, 15B, or 48A.*

→**Eamonn Doran's** This Temple Bar hefty is one of the city's top music bars, with regular gigs by local and national acts. Rock music dominates here, but you can also catch cool jazz from time to time. A great place to hang out and catch an up-and-coming act. *3A Crown Alley.* ☎ *01/679-9114. Bus: 63 or 84.*

→**Temple Bar Music Centre** One of Dublin's hugest names in music, the TBMC attracts both Irish and international bands. The emphasis here is vaguely on indie sounds, but its booking policy is wide ranging, so arrive open-minded. Late on weekend nights it converts into a dance club, while on Saturday afternoons it features local musicians. *Curved St., Temple Bar.* ☎ *01/670-9202. www.tbmc.ie. Bus: 63 or 84.*

→**Vicar Street** Part of the holy music trilogy (along with Whelans and The Village), Vicar Street is a busy, multifarious bar and music club, with a constant stream of Irish, British, and international bands gracing its stage. A great place to know about and an even better place to hang out. *99 Vicar St.* ☎ *01/454-5533. www.vicarstreet.com. Bus: 122, 150, 17, 19, 210, 50, 56A, 77, or 77A.*

→**The Village** This modern music venue and bar within stumbling distance of Whelans is a first-rate place to have a drink and chill, and maybe catch some amazing new Irish band. The very best Irish and international indie bands play here, so you can hardly go wrong popping by to see who's on stage. *26 Wexford St.* ☎ *01/475-8555. www.thevillagevenue.com. Bus: 16, 16A, 19, 19A, or 83.*

MTV **Best** →**Whelan's** ★ This relaxed, colorful bar has been nurturing young musicians for decades now, and it's still one of the top three places in Dublin for live gigs by Irish bands. In a pre-Victorian building

DUBLIN

decorated inside with murals inspired by the Book of Kells, it packs in crowds to hear acts with the potential to make it big. It's also a friendly place and a top spot for meeting locals. *25 Wexford St.* ☎ *01/478-0766. www. whelanslive.com. Bus: 16, 16A, 19, 19A, or 83.*

Clubs

The area around Grafton Street remains the hottest section of town for nightclub action, which is handy as there are ample bars and pubs around there if you want to gather with friends first before heading out to a nightclub.

➜ **Lillie's Bordello** Open more than a decade and still the hippest of them all, Lillie's breaks the rule that you've got to be new to be hot. Paintings of nudes hanging on whorehouse-red walls is the look that's made Lillie's a surprisingly unraunchy icon of kitsch. The door policy can best be described as callous, except on Sundays. If you don't feel like dancing, head for "The Library," whose floor-to-ceiling bookcases and well-worn-leather Chesterfields evoke a Victorian gentlemen's club. Open daily from 11pm to 3am. *Adam Ct., off Grafton St.* ☎ *01/679-9204. Bus: 14, 14A, 15A, 15B, or 48A.*

➜ **Rí-Rá** The name means "uproar" in Irish. If fits. Though trendy, Rí-Rá has a friendlier door policy than most of its competition, so this may be the place to try first. Open nightly from 11:30pm to 4am or later. *1 Exchequer St.* ☎ *01/677-4835. Bus: 16, 19, or 83.*

Gay Bars

The gay scene in Dublin has expanded by leaps and bounds in the last decade, from absolutely nothing at all, to small but determined. Due to the country's traditional conservatism, it's unlikely this will ever be a Miami-level gay zone, but at least there are high-quality gay bars, and regular gay nights at local dance clubs. Cover charges range from €5 to €15, depending on the club or venue, with discounts for students and seniors.

Check the *Gay Community News, Free!,* and *Scene City* to find out what's going on in town. The most comprehensive websites for gay organizations, events, issues, and information are **Gay Ireland Online** (www. gay-ireland.com) and **Outhouse** (www. outhouse.ie). Another good resource is the site **Ireland's Pink Pages** (www.pinkpages. org). Folks on the help lines at **Lesbians Organizing Together** (☎ 01/872-7770) and **Gay Switchboard Dublin** (☎ 01/872-1055) are also extremely helpful in directing you to activities of particular interest. (See "Specialized Travel Resources," in the "Basics" chapter, for details on many of these resources.)

➜ **The Front Lounge** This big, modern bar sprawls across several floors, with wide windows overlooking the hustle and bustle of Temple Bar outside. The crowd is a friendly, mixed gay/straight clientele. The look here is nice shoes, just the right amount of stubble, and expensive hair gel. *33–34 Parliament St.* ☎ *01/670-4112. Bus: 150, 49, 49A, 49X, 50, 50X, 54A, 56A, or 77X.*

➜ **The George** This is Dublin's most established gay bar, and it tends to be packed most nights with a laid-back, cheerful crowd, mixing mostly locals with savvy tourists. It's a quiet haven during the day, and a good place to sit and have a coffee, but late at night there's a DJ, and tables are pushed back for dancing. *89 S. Great Georges St.* ☎ *01/ 478-2983. Bus: 15E, 15F, 16, 19, or 83.*

➜ **GUBU** This mixed gay/straight Northside dance club, with an emphasis on gay, is filled to the bursting most nights, with a casually but beautifully dressed, laid-back, enthusiastic crowd drawn by its party-pop music and "it's a gay thing" attitude. *7–8 Capel St.* ☎ *01/874-0710. Bus: 90.*

DUBLIN

➜**Out on the Liffey** This relaxed, friendly pub caters to a balance of gays and lesbians (except for Sat, which is men only) and serves up pub food with good conversation. In 1998, it expanded to include a happening late-night venue, Oscar's, where you can dance (or drink) until you drop. *27 Upper Ormond Quay.* ☎ *01/872-2480. DART: Tara St. (walk up the Liffey and cross at Parliament Bridge). Bus: 34, 70, or 80.*

Comedy Clubs

Along with the clubs listed below, **Vicar Street** (p. 290) tends to get many of the international comics. As always, check the latest listings magazines for details. Admission ranges from €5 to €20 depending on the act and the night.

➜**Ha'Penny Laugh Comedy Club** Ha'Penny plays host to some of Ireland's funniest people, many of whom are in theater. The Battle of the Axe is a weekly show in which comedians, singers, songwriters, musicians, actors, and whoever storm the open mic in pursuit of the Lucky Duck Award. *Ha'penny Bridge Inn, Merchant's Arch, 42 Wellington Quay.* ☎ *01/677-0616. Bus: 3, 11, 13, 13A, 16, 16A, 121, 122, or 746.*

➜**International Bar** This legendary bar hosts comedy clubs 3 nights a week: Thursdays and Saturdays it's Murphy's International Comedy Club, and Wednesdays it's the Comedy Cellar (which, you'll be un-surprised to learn, is held upstairs). While Murphy's International is more established comedians, the Cellar is young and unpre-dictable. *23 Wicklow St.* ☎ *01/677-9250. Bus: 16, 19, or 83.*

Performing Arts

Classical Concerts, Dance & Theater

The online booking site **Ticketmaster** (www.ticketmaster.ie) is an excellent place to get a quick look at what's playing where and also to buy tickets. In addition to the major theaters listed below, other venues present fewer, although on occasion quite impres-sive, productions. They also book music and dance performances. They include the **Focus Theatre** (12 Fade St.; ☎ **01/671-2417**), the **Olympia** (72 Dame St.; ☎ **01/679-3323**), **Project: Dublin** (39 E. Essex St.; ☎ **01/679-6622**), and the **Tivoli** (135–138 Francis St., opposite Iveagh Market; ☎ **01/454-4472**).

➜**Abbey Theatre** For more than 90 years, the Abbey has been the national theater of Ireland. The original theater, destroyed by fire in 1951, was replaced in 1966 by the current functional, although uninspired, 600-seat house. The Abbey's artistic reputation in Ireland has risen and fallen many times, but is reasonably strong at present. *Lower Abbey St.* ☎ *01/878-7222. www.abbeytheatre.ie. Tickets €15–€26. Student discounts are available.*

➜**Andrews Lane Theatre** This relatively new venue has a rising reputation for fine theater. It consists of a 220-seat main theater where contemporary work from home and abroad is presented, and a 76-seat studio geared for experimental productions. *9–17 St. Andrews Lane.* ☎ *01/679-5720. Tickets €13–€20.*

➜**Gaiety** The elegant little Gaiety holds a varied array of performances, including everything from opera to classical Irish plays to Broadway-style musicals and variety acts. *King St. South.* ☎ *01/677-1717. Tickets €21–€25 or €15 for previews.*

➜**The Gate** Just north of O'Connell Street off Parnell Square, this recently restored 370-seat theater is a venue for a broad range of plays—a blend of modern works and the classics. Although less known by visitors, The Gate is easily as distinguished as the

Abbey. *1 Cavendish Row.* ☎ *01/874-4368. Tickets €21–€25, or €15 for previews.*

→ **The Peacock** In the same building as the Abbey, this 150-seat theater features contemporary plays and experimental works. It books poetry readings and one-person shows, as well as plays in the Irish language. *Lower Abbey St.* ☎ *01/878-7222. www.abbeytheatre.ie. Tickets €10–€20.*

Performance Halls

Bigger, international bands and classical music orchestras generally play in a handful of larger venues scattered around the city and its suburbs. Check local magazines and newspapers to see what's coming up. For most of these performances, tickets need to be rchased weeks, if not months, in advance.

→ **The Helix** This massive auditorium at University College Dublin hosts many concerts throughout the year. The box office is open Monday to Saturday 10am to 6pm. *Collins Ave., Glasnevin.* ☎ *01/700-7077. www. helix.ie. Tickets €13–€60. Bus: 3, 16, 20B, 42A, 103, or 105.*

→ **National Concert Hall** This 1,200-seat hall is home to the National Symphony Orchestra and Concert Orchestra, and hosts dozens of international orchestras and performing artists. In addition to classical music, there are Broadway-style musicals, opera, jazz, and recitals. The box office is open Monday to Friday from 10am to 3pm and from 6pm to close of concert. Open weekends 1 hour before concerts. Parking is available on the street. *Earlsfort Terrace.* ☎ *01/417-0000. www.nch.ie. Tickets €10–€35. Lunchtime concerts €5. Bus: 14, 14A, 15A, 15B, 15C, 27C, 44, 48A, 127, or 129.*

→ **The Point Depot** With a seating capacity of 3,000, The Point is one of Dublin's larger indoor theater/concert venues, attracting Broadway-caliber shows and international stars such as Justin Timberlake and Tom Jones. The box office is open Monday to Saturday 10am to 6pm. Parking is €4 per car. *East Link Bridge, North Wall Quay.* ☎ *01/ 836-3633. Tickets €13–€65. Bus: 53A.*

DUBLIN

Sightseeing

The best way to really discover Dublin is to grab a map and start walking. This city was made for aimless strolling.

Don't worry too much about cost—many of its museums and sights are free, and all of those that charge have student discounts. Bring your international student card or hostel ID with you just in case. Tickets for everything can be purchased at the sight in question, or you could purchase tickets in advance for most sights at the main Dublin Tourism office.

Festivals

February

Six Nations Rugby Tournament. Lansdowne Road, Ballsbridge, County Dublin. This annual international tourney features Ireland, England, Scotland, Wales, France, and Italy. It's a brilliant atmosphere, be it at Lansdowne Road or a neighborhood pub. Contact the Irish Rugby Football Union (62 Lansdowne Rd.; ☎ **01/668-4601**). Alternate Saturdays in February.

March & April

St. Patrick's Dublin Festival. Held around St. Patrick's Day itself, this massive 4-day festival is open, free, and accessible to everyone. Street theater, carnival acts, sports, music, fireworks, and other festivities culminate in Ireland's grandest parade, with marching bands, drill teams, floats, and delegations from around the world. Call ☎ **01/ 676-3205** or go to www.stpatricksday.ie for info. On and around March 17.

12 Hours in Dublin

1. **Take the double-decker Dublin Bus tour.** Don't be embarrassed to do what everyone else either does or wants to do. The ticket lets you get on and off as much as you like during the day. See p. 299 for details.

2. **Go shopping.** Find just what you're looking for at one of the city's many markets (p. 305).

3. **Have a pint at a pub!**

4. **Take in great music at Whelan's.** See p. 290 for details.

5. **Hang out in Eyre Square.**

6. **Have another pint!**

7. **Take in a theater performance.**

8. **Ease that hangover at Café en Seine.** Billie Holiday, eggs Benedict, and a Bloody Mary are just what the doctor ordered.

9. **Learn the words of "Molly Malone" by heart.** Her well-endowed statue stands at the north end of Grafton Street.

Dublin Film Festival. Catch the movies at the Irish Film Centre and various cinemas in town. More than 100 films are featured, with screenings of the best in Irish and world cinema, plus seminars and lectures on filmmaking. Call ☎ 01/679-2937 or go to www.dubliniff.com for info. Throughout March and April.

May

Diversions Temple Bar. This is an all-free, all-outdoor, all-ages cultural program, featuring a combination of day and night performances in dance, film, theater, music, and visual arts. Beginning in May, the Diversions program includes live music, open-air films, and a circus. Call ☎ 01/677-2255 or go to www.temple-bar.ie for info. May to August.

June

Bloomsday. An annual, 24-hour party for James Joyce worshipers and anyone else who cares to join in. Call ☎ 01/878-85-47 or visit www.jamesjoyce.ie for info. June 16.

July

Oxegen. This (mainly rock) music festival is now one of Europe's premier summer music fests, with nearly 100 acts playing on five stages at the Punchestown Racecourse over the duration of a weekend. Previous headliners have included ColdPlay and Counting Crows. Tickets can be obtained through Ticketmaster at www.ticketmaster.ie (☎ 01/836-3222). Early July.

September

All-Ireland Hurling and Gaelic Football Finals. The finals of Ireland's most beloved sports, hurling and Gaelic football, are Ireland's equivalent of the Super Bowl. If you can't be at Croke Park, experience this in the full bonhomie of a pub. Tickets can be obtained through Ticketmaster at www.ticketmaster.ie (☎ 01/836-3222). Early September.

October

Dublin Theatre Festival. Theaters in town showcase new plays by every major Irish company (including the Abbey and the Gate), plus a range of productions from abroad. Call ☎ 01/677-8439 or go to www.dublintheatrefestival.com for info. First 2 weeks in October.

Top Attractions

→ **The Book of Kells** ★★ This extraordinary hand-drawn manuscript of the four Gospels, dating back to A.D. 800, is one of Ireland's true jewels, and with elaborate scripting and colorful illumination, it is undeniably magnificent. Unfortunately, the need to protect it for future generations means that there's little for you to see. It's very small and displayed inside a wooden cabinet shielded by bulletproof glass. So what you really see here are the backs of a lot of tourists, leaning over a small table, trying to see two pages of an ancient book. Along with another early Christian manuscript, the Book of Kells is on display at Trinity College in the Colonnades, an exhibition area on the ground floor of the Old Library. It's quite disappointing. Also housed in the Old Library is the **Dublin Experience,** a multimedia introduction to the history and people of Dublin, which is informative, if a bit basic. *College Green.* ☎ *01/608-2320. www.tcd.ie/Visitors/ attractions.html#book. Admission to Book of Kells €7.50 adults, €6.75 seniors and students. Combination tickets for the Library and Dublin Experience also available. Mon– Sat 9:30am–5pm; Sun noon–4:30pm (June– Sept from 9:30am).*

FREE → **Chester Beatty Library** ★★★ Sir Alfred Chester Beatty was an Irish-American who made a fortune in the mining industry, and spent his spare time collecting rare manuscripts. In 1956, he left his extensive collection to Ireland, and this fascinating museum inside the grounds of Dublin Castle is the ultimate result of that gift. The awesome array of early illuminated gospels and religious manuscripts outshines the Book of Kells, and there are endless other goodies here: ancient editions of the Bible and other religious books; beautiful copies of the Koran; and endless icons from Western, Middle Eastern, and Far Eastern cultures. Best of all: It's free. *Clock Tower Building, Dublin Castle.* ☎ *01/407-0750. Free admission. Tues–Fri 10am–5pm; Sat 11am– 5pm; Sun 1–5pm. Free guided tours Wed and Sat 2:30pm. DART: Sandymount. Bus: 5, 6, 6A, 7A, 8, 10, 46, 46A, 46B, or 64.*

→ **Christ Church Cathedral** ★★ This magnificent cathedral is difficult to appreciate fully if you walk up the street that runs in front of it, as it is actually below street level. It was designed to be seen from the river, so walk to it from the river side in order to truly appreciate it. It dates from 1038, when Sitric, Danish king of Dublin, built the first wooden Christ Church here. The present structure dates mainly from 1871 to 1878, when a huge restoration took place that is controversial to this day, as much of the old detail was destroyed in the process. The best way to get a glimpse of what the building must originally have been like is to wander the crypt. *Christ Church Place.* ☎ *01/677-8099. Admission €5 adults, €2.50 students. Daily 10am–5:30pm. Closed Dec 26. Bus: 21A, 50, 50A, 78, 78A, or 78B.*

→ **Dublin Castle** This 13th-century structure was the seat of British power in Ireland for more than 7 centuries, until the new Irish government took it over in 1922. You can walk the grounds for free, although as this is largely municipal office space now, it's a bit disappointingly dominated by parking lots. *Palace St. (off Dame St.).* ☎ *01/677-7129. Admission €4.50 adults, €3.25 students. Mon–Fri 10am–5pm; Sat–Sun and holidays 2–5pm. Guided tours every 20–25 min. Bus: 50, 50A, 54, 56A, 77, 77A, or 77B.*

FREE → **Hugh Lane Municipal Gallery of Modern Art** ★ This cute but hard-hitting gallery has a brilliant collection of Impressionist works including Degas's *Sur la Plage* and Manet's *La Musique aux Tuileries,* and also holds sculptures by Rodin and lots of other stuff by modern Irish artists. One room holds the complete studio of the Irish painter Francis Bacon, which the

DUBLIN

gallery purchased and moved to Dublin piece by piece from London, then reconstructed it behind glass. Everything was moved, right down to the dust. *Parnell Sq. North.* ☎ *01/874-1903. www.hughlane.ie. Free admission to museum; Francis Bacon studio €7.50 adults, €3.50 students. Tues–Thurs 9:30am–6pm; Fri–Sat 9:30am–5pm; Sun 11am–5pm. DART: Connolly or Tara stations. Bus: 3, 10, 11, 13, 16, or 19.*

→**Kilmainham Gaol Historical Museum** ★★★ If you're interested in Ireland's fight for freedom from British rule, you've got to stop by this museum. Within these walls, political prisoners were incarcerated, tortured, and killed from 1796 until 1924. The leaders of the 1916 Easter Uprising were executed here, along with many others. Future *Taoiseach* (Prime Minister) Eamon de Valera was its final prisoner. To walk along these corridors, through the grim exercise yard, or into the walled compound is a moving experience that lingers in your memory. *Kilmainham.* ☎ *01/453-5984. www.heritage ireland.ie. Guided tour €5 adults. Apr–Sept daily 9:30am–4:45pm; Oct–Mar Mon–Fri 9:30am–4pm, Sun 10am–4:45pm. Bus: 51B, 78A, or 79.*

FREE →**National Gallery of Ireland** ★★ This museum is where you'll find Ireland's national art collection, along with a pile of great European art from the last 600 years. All the top schools of art are represented from Italian Renaissance artists (especially Caravaggio's *The Taking of Christ*) to French Impressionists, and Dutch 17th-century masters. The highlight of the Irish collection is the room dedicated to the mesmerizing works of Jack B. Yeats, brother of the poet W. B. Yeats. All public areas are wheelchair accessible. The museum has a shop and a first-rate help-yourself **cafe** (see "Eating," above). *Merrion Sq. West.* ☎ *01/661-5133. www.nationalgallery.ie. Free admission with free guided tours (meet in the Shaw*

Room) Sat 3pm; Sun 2, 3, and 4pm. Mon–Sat 9:30am–5:30pm (Thurs till 8:30pm); Sun noon–5:30pm. Closed Dec 24–26 and Good Friday. DART: Pearse. Bus: 5, 6, 7, 7A, 8, 10, 44, 47, 47B, 48A, or 62.

FREE →**National Museum** ★★★ This museum is a tutorial in ancient Irish history. It holds the country's most amazing historical finds, including a huge collection of Irish Bronze Age gold and the Ardagh Chalice, Tara Brooch, and Cross of Cong, as well as artifacts from the Wood Quay excavations of the Old Dublin Settlements. The only place where it falls flat is on interactive exhibits. The museum has a shop and a cafe. *Note:* The National Museum includes two other sites, Collins Barracks and the Natural History Museum. *Kildare St. and Merrion St.* ☎ *01/677-7444. Free admission. Tours (hours vary) €2 adults. Tues–Sat 10am–5pm; Sun 2–5pm. DART: Pearse. Bus: 7, 7A, 8, 10, 11, or 13.*

FREE →**Phoenix Park** ★★ The vast green expanses of Phoenix Park are Dublin's playground. It's easy to see why. This is a brilliantly designed park, scored with roads and pedestrian walkways cutting right into the heart of its 704 hectares (1,739 acres). Rows of oaks, beech trees, pines, and chestnut trees make for shady hideaways. The homes of the Irish president and the U.S. ambassador are both in the park, as is the Dublin Zoo. Livestock graze peacefully on pasturelands, deer roam the forested areas, and horses romp on polo fields. The Phoenix Park Visitors Centre, adjacent to Ashtown Castle, has an audiovisual presentation on the park's history. The cafe/restaurant is open 10am to 5pm weekdays, 10am to 6pm weekends. The park is 3km (2 miles) west of the city center on the north bank of the River Liffey. *Phoenix Park.* ☎ *01/677-0095. www.heritageireland.ie. Visitors Centre admission €2.75 adults, €2 students. June–Sept 10am–6pm (call for off-season hours). Bus: 37, 38, or 39.*

ᴍ ᴛ ᴠ 🎵 Hanging Out with Dublin's Students

Students are everywhere in town, but there are a few places where you can almost always find them. They catch bands at **Whelan's** and **The Village** (see "Music Clubs," above), as well as at a bar called **The Lower Deck** (1 Portobello Harbour; ☎ 01/475-2041).

On a weekend night, you're likely to find a youngish crowd in the **Dice Bar,** the sister bar to the **Voodoo Lounge** (p. 289), and at the **Octagon Bar** at The Clarence hotel (p. 288), as well as at **Carnival** (11 Wexford St.; ☎ 01/405-3604), which has guest DJs, and packs in the Whelan's crowd before or after a gig.

Cow Lane's many tiny boutiques and markets draw students in for the good deals on one-of-a-kind fashions, and they keep record and book stores like **Road Records** (16B Fade St.; ☎ 01/671-7340) and **The Secret Book and Record Store** (15A Wicklow St.; ☎ 01/679-7272) alive and kicking. Finally, students get their cheap vintage clothing at shops like **Harlequin** (Castle Market; ☎ 01/478-4122) and the **Eager Beaver** (17 Crown Alley; ☎ 01/677-4332).

Dublin's schools include four major universities and a number of smaller arts colleges and international schools that keep the place young and in a perpetual state of metamorphosis. The most famous, **Trinity College** (www.tcd.ie), is Ireland's oldest university, right in the heart of the city. Upscale Trinity has a great vibe, with its ivy-covered stone buildings, but it is besieged by tourists.

Looming larger on the student scene is **University College Dublin** (www.ucd. ie), the country's biggest university. It has a broad prospectus and is located in Belfield, about 15 minutes by bus from the city center. Compared to Trinity, UCD is more diverse.

DUBLIN

(FREE) → **Trinity College** ★★★ The oldest university in Ireland, Trinity was founded in 1592 by Queen Elizabeth I to educate the children of the upper classes and protect them from the "malign" Catholic influences elsewhere in Europe. Luckily it didn't quite work. It's now simply the top uni in Ireland. Ex-students include Bram Stoker, Jonathan Swift, Oscar Wilde, and Samuel Beckett, and an array of rebels and revolutionaries who helped create the Republic of Ireland. The campus bulges out into central Dublin just south of the River Liffey, with cobblestone squares, gardens, a sweet quadrangle, and lots of buildings, some over 300 years old. This is also where you'll find the **Book of Kells** (p. 295). *College Green. ☎ 01/6008-2308. www.tcd.ie. Free admission.*

Other Attractions

→ **Dublin Writers Museum** This place is for everybody who ever paid attention in English class. The attraction is more than just seeing Joyce's typewriter, or reading early playbills for the Abbey Theatre when Yeats was involved in running it; the draw is also long letters from Brendan Behan talking about parties he was invited to with the Marx Brothers in Los Angeles after he hit the big time, and scrawled notes from Behan, Joyce, and Beckett about work, life, and love. *18–19 Parnell Sq. N. ☎ 01/872-2077. www. writersmuseum.com. Admission €6.50 adults, €4 students. Mon–Sat 10am–5pm (June–Aug till 6pm); Sun and holidays 11am–5pm. DART: Connolly Station. Bus: 11, 13, 16, 16A, 22, or 22A.*

(FREE) → **General Post Office (GPO)** ★ Ah, yes. It looks just like a post office and it was once a post office. So why have we brought you here? Because it's also a symbol of Irish freedom. It was the main stronghold of the Irish Volunteers during the Easter Uprising in 1916. On Easter Sunday, Patrick Pearse stood on its steps and declared a free Irish Republic. Then he and his army barricaded themselves inside. A siege followed that destroyed much of the building. Just when it was looking good again, the Civil War broke out in 1922 and beat it up some more. Today, you can put your fingers into the bullet holes that riddle its columns. Its steps are still a rallying point for demonstrations and protests. In the vast, somber interior, a series of paintings tell the tale of the Easter Uprising. A massive bronze statue of Cúchulainn, the legendary knight of the Red Branch who is used as a symbol by both Loyalist and Republican paramilitary groups, stands proudly in the middle of things. *O'Connell St.* ☎ *01/705-8833. www.anpost.ie. Free admission. Mon–Sat 8am–8pm; Sun 10:30am–6:30pm. DART: Connolly. Bus: 25, 26, 34, 37, 38A, 39A, 39B, 66A, or 67A.*

FREE ➔ **Irish Film Centre** ★ This art-house film institute is a hip hangout for cinephiles in Dublin's artsy Temple Bar district housing two cinemas, the Irish Film Archive, a library, and a small but comprehensive bookshop. The cafe here is a great place for a cup of coffee on a cold afternoon, and the busy bar is one of the city's coolest hangouts. *6 Eustace St.* ☎ *01/679-5744, or 01/679-3477 for cinema box office. www.irishfilm.ie. Free admission; cinema tickets €6.50–€8. Centre open daily 10am–11pm; cinemas daily 2–11pm; cinema box office daily 1:30–9pm. Bus: 21A, 78A, or 78B.*

➔ **Irish Music Hall of Fame** ★ This museum takes you through the entire history of Irish music, from traditional and folk through pop, rock, and dance. There's are bits and pieces from U2, Van Morrison, the Chieftains, the Dubliners, Thin Lizzy, the

Cranberries, and Sinéad O'Connor, right up to Boyzone, Westlife, and Samantha Mumba. *57 Middle Abbey St.* ☎ *01/878-3345. Admission €7.60. Daily 10am–5:30pm. DART: Connolly. Bus: 25, 26, 34, 37, 38A, 39A, 39B, 66A, or 67A.*

FREE ➔ **St. Michan's Church** This is the church that inspired Bram Stoker to write *Dracula*. St. Michan's has a burial vault where, because of the dry atmosphere, bodies have lain for centuries without really decomposing. Little Bram was brought to the spooky vaults filled with perfect corpses as a child and, unsurprisingly, the experience stayed with him. School trips just ain't as good as they used to be. *Church St.* ☎ *01/872-4154. Free admission. Guided tour of church and vaults €3.50 adults, €3 students. Nov–Feb Mon–Fri 12:30–2:30pm, Sat 10am–1pm; Mar–Oct Mon–Fri 10am–12:45pm and 2–4:45pm, Sat 10am–1pm. Bus: 134 (from Abbey St.).*

FREE ➔ **Temple Bar Gallery and Studios** More than 30 Irish artists work here at a variety of contemporary visual arts, including sculpture, painting, printing, and photography. Only the gallery section is open to the public, but you can make an appointment in advance to view individual artists at work. *5–9 Temple Bar.* ☎ *01/671-0073. Free admission. Tues–Wed 11am–6pm; Thurs 11am–7pm; Sun 2–6pm. Bus: 21A, 46A, 46B, 51B, 51C, 68, 69, or 86.*

Breweries & Distilleries

➔ **Guinness Storehouse** ★ Head here to find out how that distinctive dark stout, with its thick, creamy head, is actually made. Founded in 1759, the Guinness Brewery is now world famous. You can explore the Guinness Hopstore, a 19th-century building with multimedia lessons on Guinness brewing. Stop in at the breathtaking Gravity Bar where you can grab a glass of the black stuff in this glass-enclosed bar 61m (200 ft.) above the ground with knock-you-over views of the city. *St. James's Gate.* ☎ *01/408-4800.*

*www.guinness-storehouse.com. Admission €14
adults, €9 students. Daily 9:30am–5pm.
Guided tours every ¹/₂ hr. Bus: 51B, 78A, or 123.*

→ **The Old Jameson Distillery** ★ Irish
whiskey is considered by many the best in
the world. Learn to love it at this museum
telling the history of the stuff known in Ireland
as *uisce beatha* (the water of life). Take as
much as you can bear of the inevitable film,
then move on to the whiskey-making exhibition and right-in-front-of-your-eyes demonstrations. *Bow St., Smithfield Village.* ☎ *01/807-
2355. Admission €8 adults, €6.25 students.
Mon–Sat 9:30am–6pm (last tour at 5pm); Sun
11am–7pm. Bus: 67, 67A, 68, 69, 79, or 90.*

Organized Tours
BUS TOURS

Not got the energy to trot around the
streets? The city bus company, **Dublin Bus**
(☎ **01/873-4222**; www.dublinbus.ie), operates several tours of Dublin, all departing
from the Dublin Bus office at 59 Upper
O'Connell St. Buy a ticket from the bus driver
or book in advance at the Dublin Bus office
or at the Dublin Tourism ticket desk on
Suffolk Street. The following are the best
options:

The 1¹/₄-hour guided **Dublin City Tour**
does the hop-on, hop-off thing, connecting 10
major interesting spots, including museums,
art galleries, churches and cathedrals,
libraries, and historic sites. Rates are €13 for
adults, €11 students. Tours operate daily from
9:30am to 6:30pm.

The 2¹/₄-hour **Dublin Ghost Bus** is a
spooky evening tour run by Dublin Bus,
departing Monday to Friday at 8pm and
Saturday and Sunday at 7 and 9:30pm. The
tour does the rounds of felons, fiends, and
phantoms. You'll see haunted houses, learn
of Dracula's Dublin origins, and even get a
crash course in body snatching. Fares are
€22 for adults only.

The 3-hour **Coast and Castle Tour**
departs daily at 10am, traveling up the north

coast to Malahide and Howth. Fares are
€20 for adults. Visiting Malahide Castle will
require an additional charge.

The 3³/₄-hour **South Coast Tour** departs
daily at 11am and 2pm, traveling south
through the seaside town of Dun Laoghaire,
through the upscale "Irish Riviera" villages of
Dalkey and Killiney, and farther south to
visit the vast Powerscourt Estate. Fares are
€22 for adults.

Gray Line (☎ 01/605-7705; www.guide
friday.com) does a similar thing to the Dublin
City Tour above. The first tours leave at 10am
from 14 Upper O'Connell St., running every 10
to 15 minutes afterwards. The last departures
are 4:30pm. You can also join the tour at any
of a number of pickup points along the route
and buy your ticket from the driver. Gray
Line's Dublin city tour costs €14 for adults,
€12 for students. Gray Line also does day
trips from Dublin to nearby sights like
Glendalough, Newgrange, and Powerscourt.
Fares stretch from €20 to €30.

HORSE-DRAWN CARRIAGE TOURS

Come on, you know you want to do it. It's the
quintessential tourist thing: You can tour
Dublin in a handsomely outfitted horse-
drawn carriage with a driver who will com-
ment on the sights as you clip-clop through
the streets and squares. Drivers are stationed with carriages at the Grafton Street
side of St. Stephen's Green. Rides range from
a short swing around the green to an extensive half-hour Georgian tour or an hour-long
Old City tour. Rides are on a first-come, first-
served basis from approximately April to
October (weather permitting) and will run
you between €15 and €50 for one to four
passengers.

WALKING TOURS

Small and compact, Dublin was made for
walking. If you prefer to set off on your
own, the **Dublin Tourism** office, St. Andrew's
Church, Suffolk Street, has maps for four

tourist trails signposted throughout the city: Old City, Georgian Heritage, Cultural Heritage, and the "Rock 'n' Stroll" music tour.

If you'd like more guidance, more info, or just some fellow walkers to chat with, try one of the following:

→ **Historical Walking Tours of Dublin**
★★ Tours with this award-winning outfit are like cheat sheets on Dublin's history. Lasting 2 hours, they take in medieval walls and Viking remains, posh Georgian houses, and the juiciest bits of Irish history. Guides are historians. *Tours leave from the gate outside Trinity College.* ☎ *01/878-0227. www.historical insights.ie. Tickets €10 adults, €8 students. May–Sept daily 11am and 3pm; Oct–Apr Fri–Sun at noon.*

→ **Literary Pub-Crawl** ★ Walk in the footsteps of Joyce, Behan, Beckett, Shaw, Kavanagh, and other Irish literary giants. This tour joins up the dots between Dublin's pubs and its writers. There is a literary quiz throughout the evening. *The tour assembles at the Duke Pub, 9 Duke St. (off Grafton St.).* ☎ *01/670-5602. www.dublinpubcrawl.com. Tickets €10. Apr–Nov Mon–Sat 7:30pm, Sun noon and 7:30pm; Dec–Mar Thurs–Sat 7:30pm, Sun noon and 7:30pm.*

→ **1916 Rebellion Walking Tour** ★ Head into the heat of the action at the General Post Office, find out how the anger rose until the rebellion exploded on Easter Sunday in 1916. The tour is run by local historians who make things interesting. *Tours begin at the International Bar, 23 Wicklow St.* ☎ *086/ 858-3847. www.1916rising.com. Tickets €10. Mar–Nov Tues–Wed 11:30am; Thurs–Sat 11:30am and 2:30pm; Sun 1pm. Phone or check the website for the winter schedule.*

→ **Traditional Irish Musical Pub-Crawl**
★★ If you can handle the embarrassment, this tour explores and samples the traditional music scene, and the price includes a songbook. Two professional musicians sing as you make your way from one famous pub to another in Temple Bar. It lasts 2¹/₂ hours. *The tour leaves from Oliver St. John Gogarty Pub and Restaurant (upstairs), 57–58 Fleet St. (at Anglesea St.), Temple Bar.* ☎ *01/478-0193. Tickets €12 adults, €10 students. Apr–Oct daily 7:30pm; Nov–Mar Thurs–Sat 7:30pm. Tickets on sale at 7pm or in advance from Dublin Tourism office.*

→ **Walk Macabre** ★ The Trapeze Theatre Company offers this 90-minute walk past the homes of famous writers, while reconstructing scenes of past murder and intrigue. It includes some of the darker pages of Yeats, Joyce, Bram Stoker, and Oscar Wilde. Back home, it would get an "R" for violent imagery. Advance booking is essential. *Tours leave from the main gates of St. Stephen's Green.* ☎ *087/677-1512 or 087/271-1346. Tickets €12 adults, €10 students. Daily 7:30pm.*

→ **The Zozimus Ghostly Experience** ★ A cocktail mix of ghosts, murderous tales, horror stories, humor, circus, history, street theater, and whatever's left, all within the precincts of medieval Dublin. The blind and aging Zozimus is your storyteller and you help guide him down the dark alleyways. It's essential to book in advance, when you'll receive the where (outside the pedestrian gate of Dublin Castle) and the when (time varies according to nightfall). The experience lasts approximately 1¹/₂ hours. *28 Fitzwilliam Lane.* ☎ *01/661-8646. www.zozimus.com. Tickets €10. Daily at nightfall, by appointment.*

Playing Outside

From late spring to early fall, all of Dublin prefers to be out of doors. Summer here is glorious, warm but not hot, breezy and pleasant.

For the rest of the year, however, forget about it. Outdoors might as well not exist.

BEACHES   Plenty of fab beaches are accessible by city bus or DART, which follows the coast from Howth, north of the city, to Bray, south of the city in County Wicklow. Some popular beaches include Dollymount, 5km (3 miles) away and Sutton, 11km (6³/₄ miles) away. But the most popular beaches for the young, tanned, and fit are to be found at Howth, 15km (9¹/₃ miles) away, and Malahide 11km (6³/₄ miles) away. Arguably the most popular is in the southern suburb of Dun Laoghaire, 11km (6³/₄ miles) away, at Sandycove Beach, which can get really packed on warm weekend afternoons. Prepare to get close.

BICYCLING   If you want to get out from the smoke, hire a bike from **Irish Cycle Hire** (☎ **041/685-3772;** www.irishcyclehire.com) for €70 for the week or €15 for the day. You can take a spin around the local area or for an extra €20 you can ride it on to one of their other depots across Ireland in Drogheda, Donegal, Westport, Galway, Ennis, Dingle, Killarney, or Cork. They've got mountain bikes and touring bikes and they're all usually new. A good way to go.

FISHING   Wanna hook your supper from the deep blue sea? **Charles Weston**'s guide service (☎ **01/843-6239**) will take you out to fish the depths off the shores of Malahide, just north of the city. In addition, the **Dublin Angling Initiative** (Balnagowan, Mobhi Boreen, Glasnevin; ☎ **01/837-9209**), will take you out for a bit of deep-sea fishing in Dublin Bay from Dun Laoghaire. Or you can pick up their brochure—the *Dublin Freshwater Angling Guide*, available for €2— to learn all you need to know about local fishing. Agency prices start at around €50 per person.

HORSE RIDING   It's easy to put your legs on either side of a pony near Dublin. Prices start at €25 an hour, with or without instruction. Many stables offer guided trail riding. To do this through Phoenix Park, **Ashtown Riding**

Stables (☎ **01/838-3807**) is ideal. They're in the village of Ashtown, adjoining the park and only 10 minutes by car or bus (no. 37, 38, 39, or 70) from the city center. Among the other riding centers within easy reach of downtown Dublin are **Calliaghstown Riding Centre** (Calliaghstown, Rathcoole, County Dublin; ☎ **01/458-8322**), and **Carrickmines Equestrian Centre** (Glenamuck Rd., Foxrock 8; ☎ **01/295-5990**).

ICE-SKATING   The Dublin Ice Rink (Dolphin's Barn, South Circular Rd.; ☎ **01/453-4153**) will have you skidding across the rink on your behind in no time flat. A quick lesson (€4 for a 20-min. session) should see your behind less bruised.

SKATEBOARDING   Skateboarders in Ireland get quite intense when asked about persecution of the sport in the country. Ireland is the only country in Europe without a public skateboarding park. Because skateboarders tend to be harassed when skateboarding on public streets, this seems to set them up for trouble. Plans are underway to build a skatepark at Bushy Park on the southside, but recent controversy has slowed the process. Until then, most skateboarding in Dublin is done at Phoenix Park.

SWIMMING   Dublin has quite a few public pools. Here are a couple where you can swim for a few euros: **Markiewicz Centre** (Townsend St.; ☎ **01/672-9121**), or **Sean McDermott Street Pool** (Sean McDermott St.; ☎ **01/872-0752**). Commercial pools, which cost slightly more, include **Oasis Swimming Pool** (River Ct., 17–19 Rogerson's Quay; ☎ **01/670-9778**), and **St. Paul's Swimming Pool** (Sybil Hill, Raheny; ☎ **01/831-4011**).

WALKING   Need to get some fresh air? The Royal Canal and Grand Canal, skirting the north and south city centers, are ideal. Both are flat trails and are marked. Both routes pass some small towns and villages where you

DUBLIN

can start or stop, or just sneak in a quick a beer. For more information, contact the Waterways Service at **Dúchas the Heritage Service** (☎ **01/647-6000**).

If you're after something a little more bracing, the walk from Bray (the southern terminus of the DART) to Greystones along the rocky promontory of **Bray Head** is great, with beautiful views back toward Killiney Bay, Dalkey Island, and Bray. Follow the beachside promenade south through Bray; at the outskirts of town, the promenade turns left and up, beginning the ascent of Bray Head. Shortly after the hill begins, a trail branches to the left—this is the cliffside walk, which continues another 5km (3 miles) along the coast to Greystones. From the center of Greystones, a train will take you back to Bray. This is an easy walk, about 2 hours each way. In bad weather or strong winds, the **Cliffside** path can be dangerous. Seriously.

Dalkey Hill and **Killiney Hill** drop steeply into the sea and give stunning views of Killiney Bay, Bray Head, and Sugarloaf Mountain. To get there, leave the Dalkey DART station, head into the center of Dalkey

and then south on Dalkey Avenue (at the post office). About 1km (¹/₂-mile) from the post office, you'll pass a road going up through fields on your left—this is the entrance to the Dalkey Hill Park. From the parking lot, climb a series of steps to the top of Dalkey Hill; from here you can see the whole bay, the Wicklow Hills in the distance, and the obelisk topping nearby Killiney Hill. If you continue on to the obelisk, there is a trail leading from there down the seaward side to Vico Road, another top place for a wind-blown seaside walk. It's about 1km (¹/₂-mile) from the parking lot to Killiney Hill.

Yearning for the great outdoors? Then get out of town with **Dirty Boots Treks** (☎ **01/ 623-6785**; www.dirtybootstreks.com), an outfit offering full-day excursions into the mountains south of Dublin. These guys really know what they're doing, and they'll take you to places you would never find without them, including spots in Wicklow Mountains National Park. A full-day trek, including round-trip transportation and lunch costs €45 for adults, €39 for students. For €11,

You Make Me Want to Hurl

This country is sports crazy. Absolutely nuts for athletic events.

The only problem is, most of the sports they're crazy for, you've never heard of. Consider this: The number-one sport in Ireland? Hurling. Number two? Gaelic football. Soccer's a weak number three.

These are wild and crazy sports, and they're well worth seeing. Gaelic football is a cross between rugby and soccer, while hurling closely resembles a kind of hockey hybrid. And, this is no laughing matter—as Ireland's national sports, they are treated with near reverence.

Gaelic football's closest living relative is Australian Rules Football—like soccer on speed with referees in weird hats, which gives you an idea of what to expect.

Hurling is much more ancient and just as fast. Reference is made to hurling in Ireland's ancient Brehon laws, which date to the 8th century, so this is a truly old, truly Irish sport. It was so popular during the English occupation that it was banned for a time by the British killjoys, who thought if it was popular it must be subversive, but in villages around the country the playing never really stopped.

If you want to find out more, check out the **Gaelic Athletic Association** website (www.gaa.ie). It oversees all the major teams in the country.

Dirty Boots will provide hiking boots, gaiters, and waterproofs. It's essential to book ahead, either by phone or online.

WATERSPORTS Sign up for certified level-one and level-two instruction and equipment rental for kayaking, sailing, and windsurfing at the **Surfdock Centre** (Grand Canal Dock Yard, Ringsend; ☎ 01/668-3945; www.surfdock.ie). It offers surfing weekends, where small groups of would-be surfers spend a weekend learning the art of surfing a wave—prices start at around €180. Dublin Bay is filled with sealife and old wrecks, making it ideal for cold-water diving. To try it out, get in touch with **Oceantec Adventures** in Dun Laoghaire (☎ 01/280-1083; toll-free within Ireland 1800/272-822). It offers a five-star PADI diving school and

arranges dive vacations on the west coast. Or try **Irish Divers** (☎ 01/278-2732; www. irishdivers.com), which offers guided wreck dives in Dublin Bay, as well as guided dives all around the country. If **kitesurfing** is your thing, check out the website www. kitesurfing.ie. It offers advice on where to buy or rent boards, the best locations, weather conditions, and it hooks you up with other kitesurfers.

You can spend a day on a high-speed boat, jetting around the bay startling seals, porpoises, and dolphins, as well as roaring past cormorants and kittiwakes. One of the most popular boating companies is **Sea Safari** (☎ 01/806-1626; www.seasafari.ie). Prices vary depending upon the trip involved, but start at around €25 per person.

Shopping

Dublin has become an excellent shopping city. This is surprising because it used to be a wasteland of chunky white sailor sweaters and bad Irish joke T-shirts. Now you won't find many bargains, but you will find great designer gear, fab vintage items, and some decent well-made knickknacks to take back home. The student population also ensures there are plenty of thrift, book, and record stores scattered across town.

The area of little streets around **Grafton Street** is definitely the city's coolest shopping zone. If you're looking for hip clothes, the latest jewelry, used books, or shoes, check out **William Street South, Castle Market,** and **Drury Street,** all of which have tiny boutiques and lots of funky little shops. The hottest address in the city for shopping right now is **Cow's Lane,** in the Old City, behind Christ Church Cathedral. It's filled with great local boutiques.

On William Street South, pop into the **Powerscourt Townhouse Centre** (59 S. William St.; ☎ 01/679-4144), which is like a little shopping mall in a big Georgian town

house—it's got some of the city's trendiest cafes, cheap antiques shops, good shoe stores, and, on the top floor, the Design Centre, which sells jewelry and clothes by young Irish designers, often at reasonable prices.

If you're looking for used books, cheap vintage clothes, and the latest boho jewelry, pop into the **Georges Street Arcade,** which is just a few minutes' walk from the Powerscourt Townhouse.

If you need to do major industrial shopping (like if you forgot your underwear), go to **Marks and Spencer** on Grafton Street, or dive into one of the city's big(ish) department stores: On the Northside there's **Arnotts** (12 Henry St.; ☎ 01/805-0400) and **Clerys** (Lower O'Connell St.; ☎ 01/878-6000). If you have money to burn (lucky you), and you feel like hitting a department store, you'll definitely want to darken the doorway at **Brown Thomas** (15–20 Grafton St.; ☎ 01/605-6666).

Dublin also has a slew of charity second-hand shops. There are a couple just around

The Winding Stair

This relaxing **bookshop** is a great place to hang out with like-minded literature and caffeine fans, and its self-service **cafe** is a real refuge from the noisy street below. Indulge in a snack while browsing for second-hand gems among the three floors of books, all connected by the winding 18th-century staircase. Tall windows provide light and expansive views of the Ha'penny Bridge and River Liffey, and the food is simple and healthy—sandwiches made with additive-free meats or fruits (such as banana and honey), organic salads, homemade soups, and natural juices. If you come in the evening you might catch a poetry reading or recital. It's at 40 Lower Ormond Quay (☎ 01/873-3292; Mon–Sat 9:30am–6pm, Sun 1–6pm; bus: 70 or 80). All items are between €2 and €8.

the corner from Trinity College including **Oxfam** (S. Great Georges St.). On the Northside, there's **C.A.S.A.** (26 Capel St; ☎ 01/872-8538), which benefits the Caring and Sharing Association.

There are even a couple of cheap second-hand shops in touristy Temple Bar. The **Eager Beaver** (17 Crown Alley; ☎ 01/677-3342) has two floors of unisex secondhand. **Damascus** (2 Crown Alley; ☎ 01/679-7087) has men's and women's secondhand, plus some weird totems from Indonesia and a fleet of wind chimes that's threatening to collapse the ceiling.

Dublin shops are open from 9am to 6pm Monday to Saturday, and Thursday until 9pm. Many of the larger shops also have Sunday hours from noon to 6pm, but most small shops are closed Sundays.

➜**Big Brother Records** Calling all vinyl junkies and beat freaks, Big Bro sells hip-hop,

jazz, techno, funk, reggae, electronica, and so much more. It's snuggled in a basement under Selectah records, in the midst of all the Temple Bar action. The staff members really know their stuff and owner Gerry will always tell you what's rockin' his world that week. *4 Crow St.* ☎ *01/672-9355. www.big brotherrecords.com. Bus: 3, 11, 13, 13A, 16, 16A, 121, 122, or 746.*

➜**BT2** This offshoot of Brown Thomas, the high-end department store, across the street on Grafton, is Dublin's top shop for hip designer labels for both boys and girls. The look is sporty, chill, and geared to the hopelessly cool. The prices are nearly as crazy as in BT. *Grafton St.* ☎ *01/605-6666. Bus: All cross city buses.*

➜**Claddagh Records** Traditional Irish musicians get excited when you mention this shop; this is the real deal in Celtic music and the place to find yourself a new favorite band. Not only are the staff members knowledgeable and enthusiastic about new artists, but they'll tell you the best place to head for live music that week. *Dame St.* ☎ *01/677-3644. www.claddaghrecords.com. Bus: 50, 50A, 54, 56, or 77.*

➜**Flip** This little gem was one of the first Temple Bar shops and it's still putting out a great vintage clothing from the '50s and the '60s. Popular with students. Does boys' and girls' gear. *4 Fownes St., opposite Central Bank, Temple Bar.* ☎ *01/671-4299. Bus: 3, 11, 13, 13A, 16, 16A, 121, 122, or 746.*

➜**Forbidden Planet** Cartoon and sci-freaks can let out a squeal of joy. There's a Forbidden Planet store—just like the one in New York—here in Dublin. Yes, it's a chain but we think it's a good one. *5–6 Crampton Quay.* ☎ *01/671-0688. Bus: 150, 49, 49A, 49X, 50, 50X, 54A, 56A, or 77X.*

➜**Greene's Bookshop Ltd.** Established in 1843, this shop near Trinity College is one of Dublin's treasures for scholarly bibliophiles.

It's chock-full of new and secondhand books on every topic from religion to the modern novel. A catalog of Irish-interest books is issued five to six times a year. *16 Clare St.* ☎ *01/676-2554. www.greenesbookshop.com. DART: Pearse. Bus: 5, 7A, 8, or 62.*

→ **Hodges Figgis** Bookworms, you've found a juicy fruit here. This enormous bookstore has books on almost every topic and is Dublin's go-to store for absolutely everything literary. It's so big you can almost get lost in it. Well worth an afternoon wander. *56–58 Dawson St.* ☎ *01/677-4754. DART: Pearse. Bus: 10, 11A, 11B, 13, or 20B.*

→ **Jenny Vander** This is where actresses and supermodels come to find extraordinary and stylish antique clothing. Dream of grabbing yourself a bejeweled frock, then take a peek at the price tag and back away in shock. If you've got the cash, this is a fabulous place to find a one-of-a-kind stunner. If not, it's still worth a saunter. *20 Georges St. Arcade, S. Great Georges St.* ☎ *01/677-0406. DART: Pearse. Bus: 10, 11A, 11B, 13, or 20 B.*

→ **Tulle** A small but hugely hip shop selling contemporary clothing designs. It's filled with scrummy works by hot new designers, such as Joanne Hynes, and international designers, such as Pink Soda and Stella Forest. Still not cheap. *28 Georges St. Arcade.* ☎ *01/679-9115. Bus: 10, 11A, 11B or 13.*

Markets

Dubliners love a good old-fashioned market.

There are workaday markets like the **Moore Street Market** (bus: 21A or 123), where fruit, vegetables, fish, and bread are sold every weekday from 10am to 2pm, on Moore Street on the Northside (a great place to pick up some hostel provisions). Then there are more upscale, gourmet markets, like the **Temple Bar Food Market** (bus: 3, 11, 13, 13A, 16, 16A, 121, 122, or 746) every weekend from 10am to 5pm in Meeting House Square. Here you can nab yourself some splurge picnic supplies like farmhouse cheeses and fresh, homemade breads, jams, and chutneys. For books, try the **Temple Bar Book Market** (see transport info for Food Market, above) weekends in Temple Bar Square from 11am to 4pm—every imaginable topic is wrapped in its pages, and prices are very good.

If you're looking for bargain antiques, head south of the city center to the **Blackberry Fair** (42 Rathmines Rd., south of the Grand Canal; bus: 14, 14A, 15A, 15B, 15C, 15N, 18, 49N, 65X, or 83). This market, every weekend from 10am to 2pm, gathers equal amounts of discoveries and discardables, and weeding through it all is half the fun.

For a genuine flea market stroll over to the "mother of all markets," **Mother Red Caps Market** (Back Lane, off High St.; ☎ 01/453-8306; bus: 123). You know the drill: stalls selling the usual garage-sale junk mixed in with the occasional treasure (some more in hiding than others), including antiques, old books, coins, silver, leather stuff, clothes, music, and furniture. There's even a fortuneteller.

Finally, if it's all about fashion for you, try the **Cow's Lane Market** (on Cow's Lane in the Old City; bus: 83.). Here local designers try out their work on a savvy crowd, who pack in knowing they'll get the clothes at much lower prices than in a boutique. It's held every Saturday from 10am to 4pm.

DUBLIN

Road Trip

Artsy, funky, laidback **Galway City** is to Dublin what San Francisco is to New York. On a much smaller scale, of course. Sitting on one of Ireland's most dramatic stretches of coastline, tucked between the Atlantic and the blue waters of Lough Corrib, Galway's setting could not be better, and the sheer beauty of the place has attracted a burgeoning

Talk of the Town

Four ways to start a conversation with a local

1. **How about those horse races?** The Galway Races is one of the biggest events of the year for locals. Find out more about it.

2. **What's your favorite band?** This town's nuts about music. Bands play constantly. Ask around for the best options, and who knows where the conversation might lead.

3. **What's up with this town's obsession with JFK and Che Guevara?** Parks are named after the former and murals abound of the latter—what's that about?

4. **Anyone for surfing?** The coast around Galway is great for surfing, and young locals are really into it.

community of artists, writers, and musicians to the west coast town. They feed its lively arts scene and funky nightlife, and keep the city youthful and constantly changing. They also ensure that the bars stay open late at night.

In fact, the little city (pop. 70,000) has some of the best bars and cafes in Ireland, as well as tons of live music, jam-packed clubs, internationally renowned theaters, and a summer-long schedule of kick-ass events including the Galway Arts Festival—one of the most energetic and down-to-earth arts fests in Europe.

Still, even with all that, the pubs are the heart of this city, and you'll find them full of former travelers who came here for a weekend, and loved the vibe so much they never left.

Getting into Town

GETTING THERE

BY AIR **Aer Aran** flies from Dublin into Galway Airport (Carnmore, about 16km/10 miles east of the city; ☎ 091/755569; www.galwayairport.com). A taxi to the city center costs about €16; the occasional bus, if it coincides with your arrival, costs €4 and drops you off at Galway Rail Station.

BY RAIL Irish Rail trains from Dublin and other points arrive daily at Ceannt Station

(☎ 091/561444; www.irishrail.ie), off Eyre Square, Galway.

BY BUS **Buses** from all parts of Ireland arrive daily at **Bus Éireann Travel Centre,** Ceannt Station, Galway (☎ 091/562000; www.buseireann.ie).

GETTING AROUND

BY BUS Galway has excellent local bus service. Buses run from the **Bus Éireann Travel Centre** (☎ 091/562000) or Eyre Square to various suburbs, including Salthill and the Galway Bay coastline. The flat fare is €1.20.

BY TAXI There are taxi ranks at Eyre Square and all the major hotels in the city. If you need to call a cab, try **Abbey Cabs** (☎ 091/569369), **Cara Cabs** (☎ 091/563939), or **Galway Taxis** (☎ 091/561112).

BY CAR If you must bring your car into the center of town, park it and then walk. There is free parking in front of Galway Cathedral, but most street parking is not free. Drivers will need parking "disks" (which can be purchased from the tourism office) in order to park on the street. Expect to pay €.60 per hour. Multistory parking garages average €1.50 per hour or €11 per day.

BY BICYCLE Cycling is a bit tough in the city itself because of the rough stone roads, however all around the edges conditions are outstanding. Most hostels, including Kinlay House and Salmon Weir Hostel, rent bicycles. If you need to rent a bike, check out the **Mountain Trail Bike Shop** (St. Augustine St.; ☎ 091/569888) or **Celtic Cycles** (Queen St., Victoria Place; ☎ 091/566606). Rates start at around €10 for 24 hours.

Galway City Basics

ORIENTATION: GALWAY CITY NEIGHBORHOODS

Galway is small but all the streets are winding ancient paths and you'll get disoriented in no time, so get yourself a good street map from the tourist office as soon as you can. The hub of the city is the big bustling park in [M Best] **Eyre Square** (pronounced "air Square"), officially called the John F. Kennedy Park in commemoration of his visit here in June 1963, a few months before his assassination. A bust of JFK shares space in the park with hundreds of people relaxing, flying kites, kicking balls around, busking—just generally kicking back.

Shop Street at the center of town is, as the name implies, loaded with shops. It's a good place to look for just about anything. It's also dominated by **Lynch's Castle,** which dates to 1490 and is watched over by excellently hideous gargoyles. One block away on Market Street the **Lynch Memorial Window** above a built-up Gothic doorway commemorates the tragic story of a 16th-century Galway mayor, who condemned his son to death for the murder of a wealthy Spanish man. After finding no one to carry out the deed, he executed his own son.

Heading down to the city docks, you can still see the area where Spanish merchants once unloaded cargo from their galleons. The **Spanish Arch** there is another local gathering place (it dates to 1594), and next to it is the **Spanish Parade,** a small open square that is one of the city's most popular hangouts.

TOURIST OFFICE When you first arrive in Galway, drop by the **Ireland West Tourism office** (Aras Fáilte; Foster St.; ☎ 091/537700; www.westireland.travel.ie) and pick up a map and brochures about what's on in town during your stay. Hours are May, June, and September daily 9am to 5:45pm; July and August daily 9am to 7:45pm; October to April Monday to Friday 9am to 5:45pm, Saturday 9am to 12:45pm. For current tourist news and a good calendar of events, go to www.galway.net.

CULTURE TIPS 101

Public drinking, locally called "busking," doesn't seem to get anyone too nervous in Galway. Still, it's best to keep it mellow (and in a paper bag, if necessary). Favorite spots include Eyre Square and along the banks of the Corrib, preferably on the down-low. As with the rest of Ireland, the minimum drinking age is 18, all recreational drugs are illegal, and walking down the street with a joint will likely get you in big trouble.

Galway Nuts & Bolts

Crisis Centers The **Galway Rape Crisis Centre** is at 7 Claddagh Quay (☎ 091/589495). Victims of sexual assault can report an incident using the 24-hour Emergency Callout Service listed above and receive information for counseling services. For information, gay and lesbian travelers might contact **Galway Gay Help Line** (☎ 091/566134; Tues–Thurs 8–10pm) or **Galway Lesbian Line** (☎ 091/566134; Wed 8–10pm).

DUBLIN

Emergencies   In the event of an emergency, call ☎ **999**. Local hospitals include **Galway University College Hospital** (Newcastle Rd.; ☎ **091/580580**), and **Merlin Park Regional Hospital** (Merlin Park; ☎ **091/757631**).

Internet/Wireless Hot Spots   Despite the silly name, **Net@ccess Cyber Café** (The Olde Malte Arcade, High St.; ☎ **091/569772;** www.netaccess.ie) is open for surfing Monday through Friday from 10am to 10pm, Saturday from 10am to 7pm, and Sunday from noon to 6pm. Their rates are €4 per hour for adults and €3.50 for students. They also sell international calling cards with good rates. There's free Internet access at the **Galway Public Library** (Cathedral Sq.; ☎ **091/562471**), but you have to book a day in advance, and you only get the computer for an hour. **Hotlines** (4 High St.; ☎ **091/562838**) offers Internet access and low-cost international phone calls and is open daily.

Laundry   Wash-and-fold service costs about €7 per load at **Laundrette** (4 Sea Rd.; ☎ **091/584524**) and **Bubbles Laundrette** (19 Mary St.; ☎ **091/563434**).

Luggage Storage   The best (and possibly only) option for luggage storage is at the train station, which is located south of Eyre Square.

Pharmacies   If you need a drugstore, try **Flanagan's Pharmacy** (32 Shop St.; ☎ **091/562924**), **Matt O'Flaherty Chemist** (16 William St.; ☎ **091/561442** or after hours 091/525426), or **Whelan's Chemist** (Williamsgate St.; ☎ **091/562291**).

Post Offices   The post office (Eglinton St.; ☎ **091/562051**) is open Monday to Saturday 9am to 5:30pm.

Safety   Galway has a very low crime rate and no particular hot spots. Follow the usual safety advice.

Telephone Tips   International and local phone cards can be purchased in almost any shop. The green-and-pink Spirit cards have the best international rates. There are pay phones in the main pedestrian mall and on the south side of Eyre Square. Eircom calling cards are sold in convenience stores and supermarkets.

Youth Information Service Offices   You can get help and check out the bulletin boards at **Galway Youth Information Centre** (Ozanam House, St. Augustine St.; ☎ **091/562434**), which also has a "Eurodesk Information" point with info on traveling and working in Europe, as well as Internet access and the like. Open Monday through Friday 9am to 4:45pm.

Sleeping

Given its funky atmosphere and bohemian spirit, it's unsurprising that Galway has a wide range of good digs, from super-cheap to absolutely opulent. You're not the only one who wants to hang out in this cool city, so you definitely need to book ahead, especially during the high season, and even in the off season for weekends and during festivals.

Most hostels are clustered near Eyre Square in the city center, as are most of the expensive hotels. Cheaper guesthouses are to be found in the Salthill neighborhood, a couple of miles from the city center, down by the seafront. If you find yourself bedless on a packed weekend, try the reservations center upstairs at the Tourist Office. For a few euros they'll call around until they find you something.

HOSTELS

For the most part, the hostels in Galway are clean and well run. The ones listed here all have laundry services, comfy TV lounges, and well-equipped kitchens.

➜ **Barnacles Quay Street House** ★ This is an attractive and clean hostel right on the main pub drag. Most rooms are bright, spacious (by hostel standards), and airy with polished wood floors, and the added ambience of busker music drifting up from the street. There's international pay phones, free toast and tea in the morning, and no curfew or lockout. *10 Quay St.* ☎ *091/568644. www.barnacles.ie. €11–€13 dorm, €13–€16 per person twin or double. From train station: Walk across Eyre Sq., turn left onto Williamsgate St. (turns into Shop St.); at King's Head Pub bear left and walk down High St onto Quay St. (the hostel is located on the right). Amenities: Bike storage, bureau de change, Internet, kitchen, laundry service.*

➜ **Corrib Villa** This chilled-out hostel epitomizes the laid-back, boho lifestyle of Galway. A Georgian town house with neat, simple rooms, cool artwork, a cozy atmosphere, and a friendly staff, Corrib Villa is located on the river on the grounds of Galway University a couple of miles from the city center. It has a crowd of devoted regulars who make the place warm and homey. Open 24 hours. *4 Waterside.* ☎ *091/562892. €10–€14 dorm. Bus: 36.*

➜ **Salmon Weir Hostel** One of the city's quirkier hostels, Salmon Weir has a cheery, party-loving atmosphere. This place has such a good vibe, one-time guests long since settled into Galway regularly come by just to hang out. It's a clean and cozy converted house with free-flowing tea and coffee, and mucho mayhem. Be warned, though, the dorm rooms here are so tiny, not only is there no room to swing a cat, you'd do damage if you tried to swing a *kitten*. The whole place, including the slacker-paradise TV room with VCR/DVD, is totally nonsmoking. Not for introverts or claustrophobics. *3 St. Vincent's Ave., Woodquay.* ☎ *091/561133. www.*

salmonweirhostel.com. €10–€17 dorm, €18–€20 per person twin or double. Bus: 37. Amenities: Internet; kitchen; laundry service.

➜ **Sleepzone** This is the latest and greatest hostel in Galway. A few minutes' walk from the train and bus terminals, Sleepzone is one of the new "super-hostels," meaning that it's big, it's attractive, and it has plenty of extras. Private rooms are as good as any you're likely to find in a B&B, and the staff is unfailingly friendly, there's no curfew or lockout. Recent visitors have raved about the place. *Bothar Na mBan, Woodquay.* ☎ *091/566999. www.sleepzone.ie. €13–€20 dorm; €18–€50 per person single, double, or triple. Bus: 37. Amenities: Electronic lockers; Internet; kitchen; laundry; safe-deposit boxes; TV (in common room).*

CHEAP

➜ **Clare Villa** ★ This spacious, modern house steps from the beach is very popular in summer, and that's as it should be. Its six pleasant rooms all have firm, comfortable beds, and the owners are as helpful as they can be. The biggest attraction, though, is waking up so close to the seafront, and taking in that fresh salt air every morning. *38 Threadneedle Rd., Galway, County Galway.* ☎ *091/522520. clarevilla@yahoo.com. €60 double. Rates include full breakfast. Bus: 33. Amenities: Sitting room. In room: TV, hair dryer.*

➜ **Devondell** ★ You'd be hard-pressed to find a better B&B in Galway than Berna Kelly's popular house in the Lower Salthill residential area, about 2km (just over a mile) from Galway's city center. It's a modern house, and the four guest rooms are spacious and done up with period furnishings and crisp Irish linens. Breakfasts are big enough to get you through the day, with cereals and fresh fruit, yogurt and cheese, hash browns and kippers, and eggs and French toast. Devondell is walking distance from the seafront. *47 Devon Park, Lower Salthill, County Galway.* ☎ *091/528306. www. devondell.com. €80 double. Rates include full breakfast. Closed Nov–Feb. Bus: 33. Amenities: Sitting room. In room: TV.*

DOABLE

→ **Brennans Yard Hotel** ★ One of the cleverest restorations in Galway's historic area, right next to the Spanish Arch, this four-story stone building was formerly a warehouse. It has compact, skylit public areas enhanced by modern Irish art. The 45 guest rooms overlook the city's Spanish Arch area and are decorated in a hip, contemporary style, with Irish pine furnishings, designer fabrics, and locally made pottery. *Lower Merchant's Rd., Galway, County Galway.* ☎ *800/44-UTELL in the U.S., or 091/ 568166. www.brennansyardhotel.com. €95– €137 double. Rates include full breakfast. Bus: 33. Amenities: Restaurant; bar. In room: TV, coffee/tea maker, hair dryer.*

→ **Eyre Square Hotel** ★ This place is a great find: It's not as expensive as some of the other hotels in this neighborhood and has a convenient address (right on Eyre Sq.), spacious rooms, helpful staff, and a good Irish breakfast each morning. The decor in the 60 bedrooms is a little boring, with lots of dark wood and unimaginatively patterned bedcovers, but the place is kept in good condition with frequent refurbishments, and feels well tended. *Forster St., Galway, County Galway.* ☎ *091/569-6333. www.eyresquare hotel.com. €80–€130 double. Rates include full breakfast. Bus: 33. Amenities: Restaurant; bar; nightclub. In room: TV, coffee/tea maker.*

Eating

Galway is the west coast's foodie capital, so it's jammed with good restaurants, bakeries and cafes, providing a wide variety of food at varied prices. Its proximity to the sea means seafood is very big here—and it's hard to go wrong when you can get a huge order of fish

and chips for under €6. The best seafood is to be found at places down by the waterfront, while the cheapest food is found in cafes and bakeries scattered around Eyre Square and near the hostels.

HOT SPOTS

→ **Home Plate Organics** ORGANIC Possibly the most popular place for travelers to have lunch in Galway. Huge, fresh, tasty helpings of organic pasta, burgers, or sandwiches in a homey little place across from the post office with friendly staff and good service. There are lots of veggie options here as well. *13 Mary St.* ☎ *091/561475. Lunch main courses €3.50–€7, dinner €5.50–€12. Daily 10am–8pm.*

→ **McSwiggans** ECLECTIC A big, friendly pub with good, Irish lunches at reasonable prices, so just about everybody comes here for lunch at one point or another. *3 Eyre St., Woodquay.* ☎ *091/568917. Main courses €5– €10. Sun–Wed 10:30am–midnight, Thurs–Sat 10:30am–1am.*

CHEAP

→ **Busker Brown's** CAFE/BAR A modern cafe in a medieval building, Busker Brown's is a favorite of locals and travelers for its funky decor that mixes ancient stonework with modern tables and art, as well as for its big breakfasts and homemade, inexpensive lunches and dinners. It offers everything from hamburgers and sandwiches to fresh stews and pasta. It also stays open late—one of few Galway eateries that do. *Upper Cross St., Galway, County Galway.* ☎ *091/563377. Main courses €5–€12. Mon–Sat 10:30am– 11:30pm; Sun 12:30–11:30pm.*

→ **The Cobblestone** ★ VEGETARIAN Tucked away on a winding, medieval lane, this casual eatery is a bright light on Galway's cuisine scene. Proprietor Kate Wright serves excellent fresh salads, soups, quiches, and pastas. Their fresh croissants, breads, muffins, cakes, and cookies are good, too. *Kirwan's Lane, Galway, County Galway.* ☎ *091/567227. Main courses €6–€15. Daily 9am–7pm.*

→ **Couch Potatas** CAFE With home-made soups and big baked potatoes stuffed with a ton of different fillings, this place is a good, warming option on a rainy day. Try the Hawaii 5-0, with ham, onion, pineapple, peppers, and melted cheddar cheese. Every 'tater comes with a generous side salad, as well. It's a great spot for lunch, although it does get quite crowded at midday. *Upper Abbeygate St.* ☎ *091/561664. All items under €7. Mon–Sat noon–10pm, Sun 1–10pm.*

→ **Da Tang Noodle House** NOODLES This tiny place on a quiet street off Shop Street, has just a few tables inside, but it's got that great hole-in-the-wall atmosphere. The menu here is all about cheap, tasty noodles. Everything is simple but good, and there are plenty of veggie options. *2 Middle St.* ☎ *091/561443. Main courses €7–€12. Mon–Sat noon–3pm and 5:30–10pm (Fri–Sat till 10:30pm), Sun 5:30–10pm.*

DOABLE

→ **Conlon** SEAFOOD If you love seafood, head here to find Galway's seafood specialists. The house specialties are wild salmon and oysters, so that's not a bad place to start. Entrees include the salmon, grilled; steamed Galway Bay mussels; and fishermen's platters with a bit of everything—smoked salmon, mussels, prawns, smoked mackerel, oysters, and crab claws. *Eglinton Ct.* ☎ *091/562268. Seafood bar items €4–€8; main courses €7–€25. Mon–Sat 11am–midnight; Sun 5pm–midnight.*

→ **McDonagh's** FISH AND CHIPS/SEAFOOD For seafood straight off the boats, this is Galway's best choice. The place is divided into three parts: a cheap "chippy" for fish and chips, a smart restaurant in the back, and a fish market where you can buy raw seafood. Crowds line up every night to get in. In the back restaurant, you can crack your

own prawns' tails and crab claws in the shell, or tackle a whole lobster. *22 Quay St.* ☎ *091/565001. Main courses €8–€34. Daily noon–10pm.*

→ **The River God Cafe** IRISH/CONTINENTAL The portions are huge and the prices are small at this chill cafe. The River God is all about Irish comfort food. The casserole of cod and potatoes Connemara style will put color back in your cheeks, while the large slab of wild-mushroom tart with paprika potatoes will rejuvenate vegetarians. *Quay St. (at Cross St.).* ☎ *091/565811. Fixed-price 3-course dinner €16; dinner main courses €10–€18. Daily 5–10:30pm.*

CAFES & TEAROOMS

→ **G.B.C. (Galway Bakery Company)** ★ BAKERY/BISTRO This place is two eateries in one: The ground-level coffee shop is cheap and cheerful, with steaming fresh coffee and melt-in-your-mouth pastries, while upstairs is a bistro offering quiches, omelets, salads, and stir-fried veggies. The coffee shop gets packed at peak breakfast and lunch times. *7 Williamsgate St., Galway, County Galway.* ☎ *091/563087. www.gbcgalway.com. Coffee-shop items under €7; dinner main courses €10–€20. Coffee shop daily 8am–10pm; restaurant daily noon–10pm.*

→ **Goya's** TEAROOM/BAKED GOODS This small, casual place has a great bakery, so it's often mobbed. Stop in for tea and a scone, or buy a loaf of the rich soda bread for lunch. *Kirwan's Lane, Galway, County Galway.* ☎ *091/ 567010. All items under €8. Mon–Sat 10am–6pm.*

Partying

In Galway, there's no such thing as a dead night out, and there's never a night without music. Just about every pub in town hosts nightly gigs, usually trad sessions or cover bands. Most young travelers in Galway gravitate toward the tourist-oriented "superpubs" of Shop and Quay streets. Sardine-packed with drunken hordes of university students in winter months and tipsy tourists in summer, they're definitely good, in that beer-blast kind of way. For a more mellow, local feel, try the cluster of bars around Dominick Street, on the west side of the River Corrib.

Galway's drink prices are country-cheap compared with Dublin. The general price for a pint in a pub hovers around €3, or €2.75 for a shot. Drink prices at clubs are a bit higher across the board. *Tip:* Bring cash—most bars and pubs don't take cards.

Pub hours are the same here as in the rest of Ireland (Mon–Sat 10:30am–11pm or till 11:30pm in summer, and Sun 12:30–2pm and 4–11pm year-round), but it's standard publican practice to shut the front doors at the prescribed closing time, then let the party roll on inside for another hour or so. You won't get in off the street anywhere after legal closing, so if you're still doing the crawl at 11pm, give it up quick and settle into your favorite pub.

CLUBS

Like the town itself, Galway's clubs are a no-stress affair. Some fashion victims don the full get-up, but the guy in Birks just behind them gets in, too. With a little straightening, your grungy travel gear might even pass muster.

The size of these places may surprise you—no shortage of floor space here. For a night-by-night breakdown, pick up the ever-present *Galway List*. Covers run from €5 weeknights to €8 weekends. Clubs are open from 11pm till 2am, but the crowds, and the lines, arrive as soon as the pubs clear out at midnight. Make an early dash out of the pub on weekends, or take the chance of waiting outside in a line half the night.

→ **Alley** This is youthquake central in a converted warehouse. At the door, they claim to be over-21-only, but the dance floor and three bars are packed with the youngest club crowd in town—seems to be a don't-ask-don't-tell policy. Mostly college pop tunes:

the cheesier the better. The theme from *Friends* gets everybody dancing—yikes!—early on, with the dance stuff coming on later in the night. *Ball Alley Lane, off Williamsgate St. ☎ 091/563173.*

→ **Central Park** One of the city's most obvious meat markets—lots of makeup, lots of very short skirts, *hundreds* of belly buttons . . . you get the picture. The music is cool, and the look of the place is space age. *36 Upper Abbeygate St. ☎ 091/565974. www.central parkclub.com.*

→ **Cuba** Big, blue, and three stories high with a lounge bar on the first floor, DJs on two, and live bands on three. Indie Mondays; Latin jazz, funk, and soul Saturdays; and a healthy mix of chart, disco, and dance for the rest of the week. This place is hot with the cool crowd, and the blue lighting and Latin rhythms get the co-eds *en fuego*. Public displays of lust abound. Passes for free evening admission are behind the bar during daytime hours; ask the bartender to give you a few. *Eyre Sq. ☎ 091/565991.*

→ **GPO** This club does its best to keep the western flame of trendiness alive, trying just a little harder than the rest to be hip. Wear black to match the inky dark interior and the rest of the patrons. The Drum Bar is downstairs; a dance space the size of a four-car garage is upstairs. Home of local heroes, the Disconauts duo, spinning soul and funk-infused house to loving crowds, GPO also regularly hosts hip-hop and drum 'n' bass nights. Daytime bar staff often have free passes to gain admission in the evening hidden behind the jungle-gym piping—just ask sweetly. *Eglinton St. ☎ 091/563073.*

BARS & PUBS

→ **Blue Note** In the same neighborhood, this is the committed clubber's pre-club hangout. Here, as local DJs spin the sounds, you'll find the town's greatest density of hair gel. Go for the great barbecue deal on

Tuesday nights in the summer: Buy a Heineken, get a free burger, repeat. *William St. West.* ☎ *091/568347.*

➜ **Front Door** Just to confuse you, Front Door announces itself as "Tomás ó Riada: Draper, Grocer, Matchmaker" over its other entrance on High Street (which turns into Shop St.). The best bar in town for playing hide-and-seek with its maze-like layout, it's also the mellowest of the superpubs, catering to an unpretentious just-post-university crowd. *Cross St. No phone.*

➜ **Hole in the Wall** Right on Eyre Square. It is the kind of chilled out, friendly pub where you wish you could be a regular: low-beamed ceiling, a jukebox with the standard rock classics, a sunny beer garden out to the side, and just enough off the beaten track so you can always find a seat. The Hole ain't fashionable, but it fits. One warning: The owner is big into horses, so madness reigns during the July races. *9 Eyre St.* ☎ *091/586146.*

➜ **Le Graal** On the alternative side of town, Le Graal is popular with Galway's international and gay crowds, who come to drink wine and lounge about on the red felt couches while candelabras flicker against the rough stone walls. Dance to sounds of Latin, jazz, salsa, and world music, or grab a bite—the relaxed staff also serve up food until last call. Sometimes there's a cover of €2 to €3. *38 Lower Dominick St.* ☎ *091/567614.*

➜ **Tigh Neachtain** Despite its ground-zero location in Galway's teeming tourist hub, this scrappy little bar attracts a nice mix of locals and scruffy beatnik travelers. Allen Ginsberg was known to enjoy a pint (and maybe an occasional joint) here, when in town, and that should give you an idea of what kind of fashions (casual) and attitudes (laid back) to expect. On warm afternoons, drinkers take to the tables outside, to drink in the sun. *17 Cross St.* ☎ *091/568820.*

➜ **Superpubs** The other "superpubs" include **The Quays** (Quay St.; ☎ **091/568347**), which looks like church at sea, and frequently hosts traditional Irish music; the **King's Head** (15 High St., ☎ **091/566630**), which also often has bands playing; **The Skeff** (Eyre Sq.; ☎ **091/563173**) with six different bars on two floors; and **Busker Brownes** (Cross St.; ☎ **091/563377**) with its medieval "Hall of Tribes." These are the pubs with the highest pickup potential.

DUBLIN

Coffee Houses & Late-Night Bites

Two cafes reign over Galway's late-night scene. Both serve good cafe food, with soundtrack, to a student/backpacker crowd. **Apostasy** (56 Lower Dominick St.; ☎ **091/561478**) is a funky little chamber with a wall shrine to the genius of espresso. It's open until 4am, as is **Java** (17 Upper Abbey St.; ☎ **091/567400**), which takes up two floors. The long kitchen-style tables upstairs are great if you're doing the late shift with posse in tow. Do not be surprised if a soft-spoken guy wearing a spiked dog collar serves you your skim latte.

For after-midnight wine, candles, and weirdness, try **O'Ché's** (3 Francis St.; ☎ **091/585126**) also open until 4am. This place is a remnant of Galway's bizarre Che obsession—check out the cosmic-erotic entrance mural starring the "Commie Christ" and his pal Fidel, and then submerge yourself in the slightly eerie underground atmosphere of this up-all-night wine bar. Glasses of house wine run €3.50, pitchers of sangria keep the crowd happy, and the little stage hosts live acts almost every night, starting around midnight.

LIVE MUSIC

For the most part, trad rules the night in Galway (see also "Performing Arts" on p. 315). The remaining slots on local dance cards tend to be filled with your standard rock cover bands. It's sort of like college parties all over again—which makes sense, given the overwhelming size of the university crowd in Galway.

You can hear your basic trad Irish music almost anywhere in town, but the place to go for the real stuff is 📺 Best **The Crane** (2 Sea Rd.; ☎ **091/567419**). It's what the Irish would call an "old man's pub" a little out on the west side of town, so the dress code is a lot of old tweed and a scruffy beard. A session could occur at any time, but a good bet is the one casually "scheduled" nightly at 9:30pm. The Sunday afternoon session here can be a religious experience.

The wood-lined 📺 Best **Roísín Dubh** (Dominick St.; ☎ **091/586540;** www.roisin dubh.net; cover free–€25)—that's "rawsheen dove" to you—happens to be one of the best places in Ireland for all that other music, hosting local and international names in rock, folk, indie, blues—and trad—on the little stage in back. Definitely a musicians' hangout, the pub fills with a good, healthy bohemian blend every night. Check out the website to see listings for what's coming up.

The King's Head (High St.; ☎ **091/566630**) is elbow-to-elbow most nights with the young and drunk, all staggering along to the daily parade of (actually, pretty good) cover bands. A summer meat market is provided courtesy of weekly tour bus shipments of eager young backpackers. The chilled-out Dixieland jazz session, summer Sunday afternoons at 12:30pm, is a local institution.

Catch an excellent (and very well attended) set-dancing session at **Monroe's** (Upper Dominick St.; ☎ **091/583397**) every Tuesday night. And you can hear trad, trad, and more trad every night of the week,

beginning at 9:30pm Irish time, which is to say "sometime after dark." Although relatively spacious for a pub (and charming, too, with murals covering the walls), there's almost never any room to sit down when the music starts, so get here early, around 8 to 9pm, for a seat. Monroe's also serves good pub grub at breakfast and lunch times, and you can get above-average pizzas beginning at 4pm at the little hole-in-the-wall pizzeria next door. Aside from a few well-informed hostellers, the crowd here's exclusively local.

GAY BARS

Galway has a small (okay, *tiny*) scene. If what you're looking for is a comfortable place to meet locals and to just be yourself, check out **Le Graal** (see "Bars & Pubs," above).

Keepers of the faith often congregate in other hip spots, such as **Café du Journal** (The Halls, Quay St.; ☎ **091/568426**), a chilled-out coffee bar filled with chaotic piles of books and daily papers stacked on wooden church pews. It's a bit literary for some—big with grad students and journalists—but pretty much everybody (straight and gay) hangs out here at some point or another. **Apostasy** (56 Little Dominick St.; ☎ **091/561478**) is another funky little coffee shop that attracts a delightfully mixed up crowd. You might also check out **Nimmo's Long Walk Wine Bar** (Spanish Arch; ☎ **091/561114**). This is a romantic little bistro to take your Irish love when you find him/her.

The **Galway Gay Help Line** (☎ **091/566134**) and **Galway Lesbian Line** (☎ **091/564611**) are good resources, or check out the monthly free sheet, *GCN (Gay Community News)* and look for Galway listings in the back.

If you happen to be here on Friday or Saturday night, Club Mix in The Attic at **Liquid** (Salthill; ☎ **088/2691412;** doors open 10:30pm; €5 cover) draws every lonely farm boy from the western hinterlands. It's

Out in Ireland

You want the good news first, or the bad? Let's start with the good news: Ireland has come a very long way in terms of accepting homosexuality. The bad news is that it started out *way* behind most of Europe on this one. In fact, homosexuality was a crime in Ireland until 1993. That, as you might imagine, put quite a damper on coming-out parties.

After Ireland joined the E.U., things began to change. Once gay sexuality was decriminalized, gay bars could finally come out of the closet, and there are a quite a few of them now. Still, it's a very small gay scene.

Generally speaking, you should not be hassled when asking for a room with a double bed for you and your partner in Galway, Belfast, Tipperary, or any major tourist town.

The problems might come in smaller towns or out in the countryside. Our gay friends here highly recommend no public hand-holding, definitely no public displays of affection. Unfortunately, there have been incidents of attacks on same-sex couples who didn't abide by these rules, and although such crimes are rare, we don't want anybody to get hurt.

not only *the* place to meet other guys, it's kind of the *only* place to be guaranteed a meeting with other guys because just about every other gathering spot is mixed.

Performing Arts

For a small town, Galway's theater scene is kickin'. Some of Ireland's finest have come out of this artistic hotbed.

MTV Best → **Druid Theatre Company** ★ If you're lucky enough to be in Galway when the Druids are here, go to a show. They're old hands in London and on Broadway, have won several Tonys, and are considered by many to be the best theater company in Ireland. Their own theater—in a converted grain warehouse—is pretty small, so they also use the Town Hall Theatre on Courthouse Square for their larger productions. Performances are unique and original, focusing on Irish folk dramas and Anglo-Irish classics. Book well in advance. *Flood St.* ☎ *091/ 568617 or 091/569777. www.druidtheatre.com. Evening tickets €11–€20.*

→ **Macnas** This is another company you should catch if they're in town when you are

(they travel worldwide, but are based here). Known for mind-blowing costumes and sets, these are the people who put on the surreal parade at Galway Arts Fest. *Fisheries Field, Salmon Weir Bridge.* ☎ *091/561462. www. macnas.com.*

→ **Siamsa, The Galway Folk Theatre** This touristy blend of traditional Irish music, dance, and folk drama is a kind of guilty pleasure. It's like Riverdance . . . but it's not Riverdance. Shows take place June through early September, Monday to Friday at 8:45pm. *Claddagh Hall, Nimmos Pier, Galway, County Galway.* ☎ *091/755479. http://home page.tinet.ie/~siamsa. Tickets €20.*

→ **Town Hall Theatre** It's the big theater in town, just across from the courthouse. It hosts anything that fills seats: Irish or international theater, dance, opera, music, and readings, and serves as main venue for the Cúirt Festival. The box office is open Monday to Saturday, 10am to 7:30pm. The Town Hall people also run the **Studio** (on the same site), for smaller productions, and the **Black Box** (Dyke Rd.; ☎ **091/568151**), which does everything from theater to music to comedy

DUBLIN

to circus in a big school gymnasium—looking space. *Courthouse Sq.* ☎ *091/569777. Tickets €5–€28.*

Sightseeing

The absolute best way to explore Galway is on foot. It's too small to justify tour buses, and the winding, narrow streets are a nightmare if you're driving. So get a good map at the tourism office and put feet to concrete. Or cobblestones, really.

Many of Galway's sights are outdoors and free—you can have the most fun just strolling around the Spanish Arch and through the shops around Eyre Square, chilling in the John F. Kennedy Park, or picnicking on the banks of the River Corrib.

Festivals

The schedules on these festivals vary, so call for exact dates.

July

Galway Film Fleadh. Your standard film festival, with past appearances by famous Irish actors, including Gabriel Byrne. Call ☎ **091/569777** or go to www.galwayfilm fleadh.com for more information. Early July.

Galway Arts Festival. This is the Big One. Famous for its street carnival, music, theater, and much more. Could be the best summer festival in Europe. Like Mardi Gras with art instead of parades. Call ☎ **091/562480** or go to www.galwayarts festival.com for more information. Mid-July.

Galway Races. A Bukowski-like horse-racing bacchanal that utterly transforms the town. Many businesses shut down for the week as everybody goes to the track and/or pub. You won't find a vacancy in a Limerick broom closet, let alone in Galway. Call ☎ **091/753870** or go to www.galway races.com for more information. Late July.

September

Galway International Oyster Festival. Besides lots of oyster-eating, this festival includes, among other things, a golf tournament and yacht race to celebrate Ireland's favorite bottom-feeding mollusk. Call ☎ **091/527282** or go to www.galway oysterfest.com for more information. Late September.

TOP ATTRACTIONS

FREE ➔ **Galway Arts Centre** Once the home of W. B. Yeats's patron, Lady Gregory, this attractive town house for many years housed local governmental offices. Now those have been kicked out, it's all about posh concerts, readings, and exhibitions by Irish and international artists. Lady Gregory would surely have approved. *47 Dominick St. and 23 Nuns Island.* ☎ *091/565886. www. galwayartscentre.ie. Free admission to exhibits. Mon–Sat 10am–6pm.*

FREE ➔ **Galway Irish Crystal Heritage Centre** Don't go swinging your arms wildly in this place, where craftsmen blow, shape, and hand-cut the glassware. Hang out and watch those glassmakers do their thing. The shop and restaurant are open daily. *East of the city on the main Dublin road (N6), Merlin Park, Galway, County Galway.* ☎ *091/757311. Free admission. Guided tour €4 adults, €3 students. Mon–Fri 9am–5:30pm; Sat 10am–5:30pm; Sun 11am–5pm.*

FREE ➔ **St. Nicholas' Collegiate Church** This is Galway's oldest church—it's said that Christopher Columbus prayed here in 1477 before setting out for the New World. Established about 1320, it has changed from Roman Catholic to Church of Ireland and back again at least four times and is currently the latter. Inside are a 12th-century crusader's tomb with a rare Norman inscription, a carved font from the 16th or 17th century, and a stone lectern with barley-sugar twist columns from the 15th century. Guided tours, conducted by Declan O Mordha, a knowledgeable and enthusiastic church representative, depart from the south porch according to demand, except on Sunday morning. *Lombard St., Galway, County Galway.* ☎ *091/564648. Free admission to church; donations of €2 adults, €1.30 students requested. Tours €3 (reservations required). Mid-Apr to Sept Mon–Sat 9am–5:45pm, Sun 1–5:45pm; Oct to mid-Apr Mon–Sat 10am–4pm, Sun 1–5pm.*

Playing Outside

BEACHES   This is not Greece, but you can walk 20 minutes to Salthill, a hotel- and amusement-gorged suburb west of the city center, home to Galway's closest beach and bathing-suited beauties. It's almost always teeming with humanity's ritzier half. That said, you can probably find nicer strands among Galway's outermost reaches, or try the beach at Spiddal, a short Bus Éireann (route 424) ride west of Galway, past Salthill. It's actually nicer than Salthill's beach: clean, sandy, and perfect for swimming.

BOATING   Take some friends and head up the River Corrib in a rented boat on a sunny afternoon. Try **Corrib Boat Hire** (Brando Screen Printing, Waterside St. across from the old Galway Rowing Club; no phone; 9am–8pm daily; rowboats €8 per hour). Row up the river to the ruins of an old castle surrounded by fields of grazing horses, and then drop anchor and picnic in the sunshine.

If you prefer more powerful vessels, and more exhilarating options, contact **Best** **Delphi Adventure Holidays** (Leenane, County Galway; ☎ 095/42208; www.delphiadventureholidays.ie), which offers a wide variety of activities, from sailing to sea kayaking to water-skiing, abseiling, archery, and pony trekking.

If sailing is your thing, contact the **Galway Sailing Centre** (Renville, Oranmore, County Galway; ☎ 091/794527) for advice on the best rates for renting sail boats in the area. One option is **Bow Waves,** the Galway sailing and powerboat school (Galway Mayo Institute of Technology, Renmore, Galway; ☎ 091/560560; www.bowwaves.com).

CYCLING   Most hostels rent bicycles, particularly Salmon Weir Hostel. For a bigger selection of bikes contact **Richard Walsh Cycles** (Headford Rd., Woodquay; ☎ 091/565710). You can also try **Europa Bicycles** (Hunters Building, Earls Island, across from Galway Cathedral; ☎ 091/563355). Prices average €15 per day or €75 per week.

FISHING   Dotted beside the River Corrib, Galway City and nearby Connemara are popular fishing centers for salmon and sea trout. For the latest information on requirements for licenses and local permits, check with The Western Regional Fisheries Board (WRFB; Weir Lodge, Earl's Island, Galway; ☎ 091/563118; www.wrfb.ie), which also offers free consultation on where to go for salmon or trout, where to find the best *ghillies* (guides), and which gear to use. Maps and brochures are available on request. For gear and equipment, try **Duffys Fishing & Shooting** (5 Mainguard St.; ☎ 091/562367), or **Freeney Sport Shop** (19 High St.; ☎ 091/568794).

Deep-sea fishing is famously good off of Galway's west coast. Numerous boat companies offer fishing tours for about €500 for a 1-day charter. Stop by the tourist office, which will have loads of brochures for you to choose from.

HORSEBACK RIDING   To take a turn on one of those famed Galway horses, try **Aille Cross Equestrian Centre** (Aille Cross, Loughrea, County Galway; ☎ 091/841216; www.aille-cross.com), about 32km (20 miles) east of Galway. Run by personable Willy Leahy, this facility is one of the largest in Ireland, with 50 horses and 20 Connemara ponies. For about €25 to €35 an hour, you can ride through nearby farmlands, woodlands, forest trails, and beaches.

HORSE RACING   This is one of the most famous racetracks in Europe—the subject of fable and song—and when (in July and Sept–Oct) horses pound the track at the

Galway Racecourse (Ballybrit; ☎ 091/ 753870; www.galwayraces.com), less than 3km (2 miles) east of town, it's an event known simply as the **Galway Races.** It brings in horse lovers and high rollers from around the country. Tickets aren't expensive and it's an Irish event well worth catching if you happen to be in town when the races are on. Admission is €10 to €15, depending on the event and the day of the week.

MTV **Best** SURFING Since Ireland hosted the European surfing championship in '98, word's gotten around about the good Irish surf. The Atlantic swells come year-round, but the best are in April/May and September/ October. Sampling Ireland's tubular bounty is easy in Galway: Just call the **Irish Surfing Association** (☎ 096/49428; www.isasurf. ie). Schools often will pick up beginners and provide board, wetsuit, and an hour and a half of individual instruction followed by a full day of surfing. It usually includes a beach barbecue lunch and a scenic return through the desolately beautiful landscape of the Burren. For gear, check out the **Lahinch Surf Shop** (The Promenade, Lahinch; ☎ 065/708-1543; www.lahinch surfshop.com). Owners Tom and Rosemarie Buckley rent and sell beginner surfboards, boogie boards, and full-length wetsuits. They also offer lessons and give a daily surf report on the phone (☎ 0818/365180).

WINDSURFING If you feel like you're tough enough for Ireland's vicious cold-water windsurfing, check out **Rusheen Bay Windsurfing** (☎ 087/260-5702; www. rusheenbay.com), which offers advice, equipment, lessons, and an introduction to the bitchin' conditions on the waves off the Galway coast. Lessons start at €40 per hour.

Shopping

This is a deeply cool town, and with that comes deeply cool shopping. You can get funky clothes, beautiful antiques, and original artwork at vaguely reasonable prices. And it's just a lot of fun to shop here in the tiny malls of small shops clustered in historic buildings, such as the **Cornstore** on Middle Street, the **Grainstore** on Lower Abbeygate Street, and the **Bridge Mills,** a 430-year-old mill building beside the River Corrib. **Eyre Square Centre,** the downtown area's largest shopping mall, with 50 shops, is where you go when you actually *need* something.

Most shops are open Monday to Saturday 9 or 10am to 5:30 or 6pm. In July and August, many shops stay open late, usually until 9pm on weekdays, and some also open on Sunday from noon to 5pm.

If you're here on a weekend, start at the **Galway Market** (Market St.; Sat 9am–5pm) for stands of fruit, organic veggies, pottery, clothes, jewelry, and trinkets. They've got good eats here: Look for the "Curryman" and the stand selling sweet and savory crepes.

In the taxi rank area at the top of Eyre Square, stalls sell clothes, jewelry, and even horse and bridle stuff from 9am till 5pm every Monday through Saturday.

Don't let the slightly precious exterior fool you, 'cause **Kenny's Book Shop and Gallery** (Corner Middle and High sts.; ☎ 091/562507) is the grand old man of Galway books. The three floors are packed with all sorts of subjects and titles, both rare and budget-bin, with a specialty in (what else?) Irish literature.

Conveniently opposite the back door of Kenny's, there's **Charlie Byrne's Bookshop** (The Cornstore, Middle St.; ☎ 091/561766). Just a big, comfy ol' horde of used, remaindered, and discounted books. This is the one in town with that stay-all-day vibe.

Besides being the only place in town where you can score secondhand vinyl, **Mulligan** (5 Middle St. Ct.; ☎ 091/564961) boasts of having "everything" in Irish and Scottish trad, along with respectable collections of jazz, blues, soul, and ethnic music. Tickets for Roísín Dubh (see "Live Music," above) shows, other biggish local gigs, and charity events are all on sale here.

Half-looking like yet another cheesy tourist-drag souvenir shop, **Zhivago Records** (5 Shop St.; ☎ 091/509960) has the Ticketmaster outlet for all major shows nationwide. And you can pick up a "Guinness Is Good For You" T-shirt while you're getting your tix.

If you want a glittering souvenir to take home with you, stop in at **Fallers of Galway** (Williamsgate St.; ☎ **091/561226;** www.fallers.com), which has been a prime source of Claddagh rings, many made on the premises, since 1879. It also sells Celtic crosses and contemporary Irish jewelry designs.

Dubrovnik

Dubrovnik's nickname is "the Pearl of the Adriatic," but this town is better than any gem I've ever encountered. Scarred by the bombs that fell during the 1990s Balkans War, Dubrovnik has emerged to become one of the choicest destinations to summer in Europe. Today, the only people advancing on Dubrovnik are legions of hip tourists, attracted by the UNESCO World Heritage City's mix of old and new attractions, from its historic city wall and modern galleries to old-school restaurants and bustling nightclubs. The added bonus is that Dubrovnik's attractions all come at a cheaper price than most other cities in Europe. That may not last though: On October 3, 2005, Croatia received the go-ahead to begin talks for membership in the European Union, which means its currency may soon be a thing of the past.

The Best of Dubrovnik

○ **The Best Excuse for Breaking Out Your Checkbook:** If you have the cash to spend, splurge for a night at the **Hotel Grand Villa Argentina.** You'll be treated like royalty—Prince Rainier was once a guest here, after all. See p. 326.

○ **The Best Reason to Lace Up Your Sneakers:** A walk around Dubrovnik's **City Wall** is simply not to be missed: The 2km (1¹⁄₄-mile) circuit atop the wall affords some of the best views of the city. See p. 329.

○ **The Best Place to Sport Leather:** The aptly named **Bikers Caffe** attracts

motorcycle enthusiasts from all over, so it's a great place to stop by for a drink if you ever wanted to hop on a Harley. If viewing the Hogs fails to impress, know that the bar boasts a great view of the Old City. See p. 328.

○ **The Best Place to People-Watch:** Spend some time lingering along **Placa** and you're guaranteed to spot some interesting characters. You'll also take in most of the city's major sites, which run along this main street. See p. 328.

Getting There & Getting Around

Getting into Town

BY AIR

Planes land at **Dubrovnik International Airport (Zracna Luka),** located at Čilipi, 18km (11 miles) from the city center (www. airport-dubrovnik.hr).

Croatia Airlines operates a shuttle bus to and from Dubrovnik Airport at Čilipi, 24km (15 miles) south of the city. Buses are coordinated with incoming flights and meet all Croatia Airlines' flights, even the late ones. Buses leave the main terminal in Dubrovnik at Gruž Port every 90 minutes. They say they leave 90 minutes before each flight, but there is no posted schedule and this applies only to Croatia Air flights, though anyone can ride the bus. Cost is 30kn one-way; it takes about 25 minutes.

There is also taxi service to and from the airport. Taxi cost is metered at 25kn and then 8kn per kilometer. Twenty-four kilometers (15 miles) from the airport to Dubrovnik costs 217kn, so that's about 242kn one-way, and it could be more if you don't settle on the price and terms before you get in the cab. The taxi company's website (www.taxiservice dubrovnik.com) tells you not to pay if the driver doesn't turn on the meter, but that could get ugly.

BY BOAT

Every 3 or 4 days, **Split** has a ferry (operated by Jadrolinija) that goes to Dubrovnik, stopping on all three islands on the way. It is a long ride (around 8 hr.) and costs around 50kn. In addition, **Korčula** has a ferry that goes to Dubrovnik every few days—times are sporadic. Buy tickets and obtain schedule information at the Dubrovnik Jadrolinija office in Gruž (☎ 020/418-000) or at Jadroagent at Radića 32 (☎ 020/419-000).

BY BUS

Daily buses operate between the Dubrovnik ferry port at Gruž and Zagreb, Zadar, Split, Šibenik, Rijeka, Orebić, and Korčula in Croatia, as well as Mostar and Sarajevo in Bosnia and Međugorje in Herzegovina. The main Dubrovnik bus terminal is at Put Republike 19 (☎ 020/357-020).

BY CAR

The A1 autocesta between Zagreb and Split opened in June 2005, reducing travel time between the two cities to 3 hours; however, the leg of the highway between Split and Dubrovnik is still under construction. Consequently, if you travel by car down the coast from Split to Dubrovnik, you still have to take the much slower E-65 for the entire 217km (135-mile) trip, which can take as long as 4 hours. If you drive straight from Zagreb to Dubrovnik, it will take approximately 7 hours—more during summer gridlock—so plan to take 2 days for this trip.

Getting Around

Dubrovnik is a compact city, with its main sites clustered around the Old Town, so most of its attractions can be seen on foot. If you're venturing farther afield, buses are the easiest way around. See "By Bus," above, for information.

Dubrovnik Basics

Orientation: Dubrovnik Neighborhoods

OLD TOWN   The area within Dubrovnik's walls is known as Old Town. Most of the city's main attractions can be found here. Besides historic buildings, you will find restaurants, cafes, shops, and services on the side streets that connect with Stradun—a long (just under $1/4$ mile) and wide street that runs from the Western Gate (Pile) to the Eastern Gate

Talk of the Town

Three ways to start a conversation with a local

1. **How do you think the transition from a totalitarian society to a market-driven, democratic society is going?** To the surprise of many Westerners, young Croatians frequently voice their ambivalence about the new lifestyle that has been thrust upon them. Of course, they'll also remind you that life was no day at the beach under the Yugoslavs.

2. **Pop, rap, or house?** Music is another hot topic here. If you know anything about the latest craze, let the local kids know.

3. **Shall we toast to Croatian perseverance?** The Croatians are very proud that they're finally in control of their own destiny, despite getting trounced by their enemies over the centuries.

(Ploče). The Stradun is lined by a mixture of historic buildings and shops, with a cafe or ice-cream shop tucked here and there.

PLOČE   Ploče is the neighborhood just outside Old Town's Eastern Gate. Most of the city's upscale hotels are located on beachfront property in this area, as is the city's main public beach, Banje.

LAPAD   There are no big-time historic sites in Lapad, just a long, leafy promenade lined with hotels and restaurants backed by a residential area on the Lapad Peninsula west of Old Town. Lapad abuts Lapad Bay, so it has some beach area, but Lapad's main attraction is its moderately priced hotels—moderate in comparison with the luxury hotels in Ploče and Old Town. The no. 6 bus connects Lapad with Old Town at the Pile Gate; the ride takes about 15 minutes.

BABIN KUK   On the Lapad Peninsula, at some indeterminable point less than 6.4km (4 miles) from Dubrovnik's center and bordered on three sides by the sea and pebble beaches, the Babin Kuk neighborhood ends and the Lapad neighborhood begins. Babin Kuk has several hotels in various price ranges. It also has access to rocky coves with what optimists call beaches (read: major pebbles/rocks, no sand), as well as to

scores of restaurants, shops, and services. Babin Kuk is connected to Dubrovnik by the city's efficient bus system. Autocamp Solitudo, Dubrovnik's only campground, is here.

Tourist Office

The **Dubrovnik Tourist Board** is at ½ C. Zuzuric (☎ **020/323-887;** www.dubrovnik-online.com). The office has the most helpful staff members I encountered during my travels—they'll tell you honestly where you should go, who to call, and how to schedule your time in town.

Culture Tips 101

Croatian culture has been fairly influenced by Italian culture. One result: People take siestas, sometimes, around 2 to 4pm, so check before shopping then. Other working hours are also generally lax. Croatia is also a predominantly Catholic country. On Sundays, some places shut down for religious services—this is mainly in small towns, though.

The Croatian language is a hard one to master, but most folks here speak at least some English or another foreign language. You should be able to get by if you memorize *"Dobar dan"* (Hello) and *"Govorite il engleski?"* (Do you speak English?) and are prepared for some hand gesturing.

You can drink throughout Croatia if you're 18, and you'll certainly have ample opportunities to get crazy with the energetic, curious, vodka-soaked young Croats during the summer months (locals hibernate in the winter). The drug scene, although largely hidden, is pretty active. Cocaine is reportedly the drug of choice for avid club-goers, along with meth and ecstasy. Due to a recent spate of overdoses in clubs, the police are cracking down on drug use now more than ever.

Recommended Books, Movies & Music

BOOKS

For a good historical overview of the country, try *Croatia: A Nation Forged in War* by Marcus Tanner (2001), which chronicles the beginning of Croatia's history in A.D. 800 through the start of the millennium and includes good coverage of the 1991 to 1995 Homeland War. Rebecca West's *Black Lamb and Grey Falcon: A Journey Through Yugoslavia* (1994) is a graceful history/travel journal that portrays Croatia in a Balkan context. West, who was a journalist, novelist, and critic, undertook her research in the Balkans with the idea of writing a travel book, but the result turned out to be a seminal work that illuminates the tangled history of the former Yugoslavia.

Jan Morris' *The Venetian Empire* features a chapter about Venetian port towns along the Croatian coast. Robert Kaplan's *Balkan Ghost* provides insight into 1980s and 1990s Yugoslavia. Misha Glenny's *The Balkans: Nationalism, War, and the Great Powers, 1804–1999* offers a more comprehensive take on all of Croatian history.

MOVIES

When Croatia was still part of Yugoslavia before the 1990s, its movie industry enjoyed a period of success—*The Road One Year Long* (1958), *Ninth Circle* (1960), and *The Battle of Neretva* (1969) were all nominated for Oscars. Films are picking up steam again, though no one movie has really taken off internationally. The actor Goran Visnjic is the country's most famous recent export; he appeared in *Welcome to Sarajevo* (1997) about British journalists during the Yugoslav war, and *The Peacemaker* (1997) a thriller about Bosnian-Croatian terrorists who plot to bomb New York. He also plays a Croatian immigrant doctor on *ER*.

MUSIC

Folk music dominates in Dubrovnik; the city is home to Lindo, a regional ensemble specializing in Croatian folk songs and ancient courtship dances, and any decent coffee bar or *konoba* (tavern) will feature *klapa* (a Croatian spin on a capella singing). Most clubs and lounges will play Euro dance tunes, though, so you'll still get your daily intake of techno and house music. You can buy albums by artists exclusive to Croatia at www.croart.com.

Dubrovnik Nuts & Bolts

Cellphone Providers & Service Centers   T-Mobile sells SIM cards (80kn), and recharges them as well; call ☎ 020/098 1550 or visit www.t-mobile.hr for info on locations.

Currency   Dubrovnik has many banks, but I recommend using ATMS at **Splitska Bank** (Put Republike 32; ☎ 020/357-160) because it allows you to charge your Visa card for cash.

Embassies   All embassies are in Zagreb, the capital of Croatia: **United States** (Andrije Hebranga 2; ☎ 01-66-12-200), **Australia** (Krsnjavoga 1; ☎ 01-48-36-600);

DUBROVNIK

United Kingdom (Vlaska 121; ☎ 01-45-55-310; also in Split at Obala hrvatskog narodnog preporoda 10, ☎ 021-341-464), **Australia** (Third Floor, Kaptol Center; Nova ves 11; ☎ 01/48-91-2000), **Canada** (Prilaz Gjure Dezelica 4; ☎ 01/48-81-200), and **New Zealand** (Trg S. Radica 3; ☎ 01/61-51-382).

Emergencies   For police, dial ☎ 92. To report a fire, dial ☎ 93. For an ambulance, dial ☎ 94. The public emergency hot line is ☎ 985.

Internet/Wireless Hot Spots   Most Internet shops are open from 10am to midnight daily, and most start with a 5kn charge and then charge 5kn every 5 to 10 minutes you stay on the Internet. **DU net** (Put Republike 7; ☎ 020/356-894) is conveniently located in the same plaza as the Treasury and is nearby tons of restaurants. Get here early, though, because it fills up quickly. Another option is **Netcafe Internet Bar** (no. 21 in the middle of Prijeko St.'s restaurant block). Connections are fast, the coffee is excellent, and the place is air-conditioned. Open 9am to 11pm daily.

Luggage Storage   You can leave luggage at the bus station (p. 321) from 4:40am to 9:30pm.

Post Offices   Post offices are open from 8am to 8pm everyday except Sunday. You might have to wait a while for service, especially between noon and 6pm. Try your luck at 20107 Dubrovnik, Babin Kuk, Mali Stradun (☎ 020/437-677). Right off the main street running through the Old City, this post office is open from 8am to 7pm.

Restrooms   There are no free-standing public restrooms in Croatia, but most restaurants and public buildings have them.

Safety   Dubrovnik is generally very safe, but you should still exercise caution whenever you're out and about in an unfamiliar area—especially after dark.

Tipping   Tips aren't included in bills because they're not expected. If you have good service, leave 10% at restaurants. Bartenders shouldn't get tipped, and it's up to your discretion whether or not to tip taxi drivers.

Sleeping

There's a conspicuous lack of budget accommodations in Dubrovnik. Even moderately priced rooms are difficult to find unless you opt for private accommodations in Lapad or Gruž. Try the tourist office or look for signs in windows that say SOBE (room available), if the places below are booked.

Hostel

→ **Youth Hostel** The general vibe at this hostel is cookie-cutter, but the beds are clean, the bathrooms have showers, and the food is edible. The hostel is also an excellent place to meet other party-loving travelers. *V. Sagrestana 3, Dubrovnik 20000.* ☎ *020/423-241. www.hfhs.hr. 15€ per person. Amenities: Breakfast room; 2am curfew; kitchen; TV room.*

Cheap

→ **Autocamp Solitudo** ★ The bathrooms at this campground outside Dubrovnik are like new. If you don't hate the outdoors, it's worth pitching a tent here to save money for more important things. Who needs a comfy bed when you'll be out late clubbing, anyway? *Vatroslava Lisinskog 17, Babin Kuk.*

DUBROVNIK

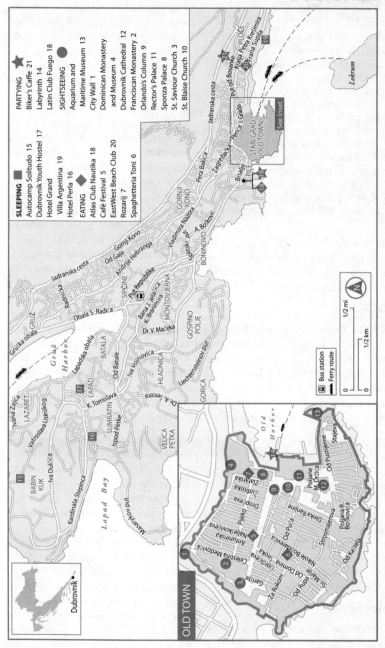

PARTYING
Biker's Caffe 21
Labyrinth 14
Latin Club Fuego 18

SIGHTSEEING
Aquarium and
Maritime Museum 13
City Wall 1
Dominican Monastery
and Museum 4
Dubrovnik Cathedral 12
Franciscan Monastery 2
Orlando's Column 9
Rector's Palace 11
Sponza Palace 8
St. Saviour Church 3
St. Blaise Church 10

SLEEPING
Autocamp Solitudo 15
Dubrovnik Youth Hostel 17
Hotel Grand
Villa Argentina 19
Hotel Perla 16

EATING
Atlas Club Nautika 18
Café Festival 5
EastWest Beach Club 20
Rozarij 7
Spaghetteria Toni 6

Bus station
Ferry route

OLD TOWN

DUBROVNIK

Private Homes

If you arrive at the ferry or bus terminal, you'll be greeted (or accosted) by men and women waving photos of lodging options—mainly rooms in private homes. In general, the cheapest offers will come from the old ladies asking you if you need a place to sleep. You never know what you'll get—perhaps a dirt-cheap find in the center, or a tiny bed (sharing a bathroom with the owner) on the outskirts of town. If you're not in a gambling mood, go to the tourist office (p. 322) to ask for advice.

☎ 020/448-686. www.babinkuk.com. 166 campsites. 16€ site with electricity and 2 persons. Apr 1–Oct 15. Amenities: Restaurant; excursions; laundry; market; pool.

Doable

→ **Hotel Perla** ★ This is a relatively new (Apr 2005) hotel on the Lapad promenade and is still evolving. Guest rooms are spacious and quiet; most have balconies that look onto the hotel's landscaping. Bathrooms are good-size and well equipped, but there is no elevator. Once you check in, your location is excellent, but you cannot drive up to the Perla to unload your luggage because of its position on the promenade: You need to park a couple of blocks away and schlep. *Lapad Mali Stradun bb, Lapad.* ☎ *020/438-244. www. perla-dubrovnik.com. From 120€ double. Rates include breakfast. Amenities: Restaurant; bar. In room: A/C, TV, balcony, hair dryer.*

Splurge

MTV Best → **Hotel Grand Villa Argentina** ★★ Want to get a feel for the Dubrovnik aristocracy and have some kunas left to spend? Then head to the Grand Hotel Argentina. The feel here is definitely old money. The property (the hotel consists of four distinct "villas") is set on sprawling palace grounds, and has welcomed a variety of important dignitaries. The staff is fluent in English and constantly buzzes about the premises to see if guests need help. *Frana Supila 14, Dubrovnik 20000* ☎ *020/440-555. www.gva.hr. July 1–Sept 30: from 320€ double with sea view and balcony, from 500€ suite. Other times: from 250€ double with sea view and balcony, from 420€ suite. Rates include breakfast. Amenities: 3 restaurants; bar; health club; Internet; indoor and outdoor pools; Jacuzzi. In room: A/C, TV, hair dryer, minibar.*

Eating

Dubrovnik meals, as in the rest of Croatia, are all about food from the sea. The restaurants here are counted among the country's best, but expect to pay more for the same stuff because tourists have driven prices up. I recommend grabbing food from the supermarkets around town and having picnic lunches. That way you can save your money for a night out at a truly top-notch restaurant.

Hot Spots

→ **EastWest Beach Club** INTERNATIONAL ★ The hottest restaurant/bar under the scorching sun, EastWest Beach Club bills itself as a "resort." I think they only do this to emphasize the wide range of services they offer: cocktail bar, the nicest beach in Dubrovnik, and assorted rental services. The restaurant, though, is reason enough to come to this tastefully decorated, beachside haunt. The wraparound windows allow you to better enjoy the vistas of the Old City of Dubrovnik and the sea while you eat. The food is uniformly fresh, and the chef has played around with some of the native Croatian dishes to create meals like the spaghetti with lobster and chicken salad. *Frana Supila bb.* ☎ *020/412-220. www. ew-dubrovnik.com. Main course 181kn (for 2 courses and wine). Daily 6am–2am; cocktail bar closed Sept–May.*

Cheap

→ **Café Festival** SANDWICHES This is the ideal place for a light lunch or a cool drink in the Old City. If it's too hot to dine at the tables outside this smart cafe near the Pile Gate, simply grab a seat inside to try the salads, pastas, fancy drinks, and homemade pastries. *Stradun bb, Old Town.* ☎ *020/420-888. www.cafefestival.com. Main courses 15kn– 45kn. Daily 8am–11pm.*

→ **Konoba/Spaghetteria Toni** ★ PASTA/ PIZZA This colorful sidewalk *konoba* (tavern) serves pasta under massive umbrellas that keep the place cool. Try the *macaroni arrabiata* with tomatoes and peppers as a pasta choice with a little kick to it. *Nikole Božidarevića 14, Old Town.* ☎ *020/323-134. Main courses 30kn–59kn. Daily noon–11pm.*

Doable

→ **Rozarij** ★ DALMATIAN SEAFOOD Rattan tables outside this tiny dining room are arranged on steps around Rozarij's entrance, set on a hard-to-find corner of restaurant-clogged Prijeko (corner of Prijeko and Zlatarska). But Rozarij and its impeccable seafood are worth searching out. Try the shrimp with white risotto or the mixed *buzzara,* a combination of mussels and scampi cooked in a fragrant court bouillon. *Prijeko 2, Old Town.* ☎ *020/321-257. Main courses 50kn– 120kn. Daily 11am–midnight.*

Splurge

🅼🆅 **Best** → **Atlas Club Nautika** ★★ DALMATIAN SEAFOOD Prepare yourself for one of the best meals of your life. Club Nautica promises a "light lunch," but in reality, this lunch is exquisitely heavy—both in quality and on your checkbook. The chef cooks innovative dishes centered on the fishermen's most recent catch, and this seems to be the only restaurant in Dubrovnik with lobster on call. The seafood is always excellent, but the other dishes are good, too. Add to that a clifftop location, elegant decor, and an attentive staff, and you'll understand why this is often called Dubrovnki's finest restaurant. *Brsalje 3.* ☎ *020/442-526. Dinner entrees 148kn–380kn. 7-course menu 99€ per person without wine. Daily noon–midnight.*

Partying

Dubrovnik's hot young tourist crowd hits Croatia's most happening nightclubs and bars a bit on the early side. Many places shut down between 11pm and 1am, though some exceptions are noted below.

Nightclubs

→ **Labyrinth** During the day, Labyrinth is an upscale eatery which opens at 9am and offers patrons a lovely sea view and hearty dishes. As the sun goes down and young, rich tourists come out to play, Labyrinth gets a good deal naughtier. The complex's nightclub opens at 10pm, and stays open until 5am. Due to the exorbitant cover charge, all but the wealthiest enter, but those who stay are treated to a free show of "Rich Europeans Gone Wild." There are occasional live performances by Croatian artists, too. *Sv. Dominika 2.* ☎ *020/ 322-222. www.labirint-dubrovnik.com. Cover 100kn; sometimes free.*

→ **Latin Club Fuego** ★ Don't come here expecting to hone your salsa skills: They don't actually play very much Latin music. But if you are interested in hordes of people, unbelievably yummy drinks, and a sweaty, pulsing dance floor, this is your mecca. If you come before midnight (they open at 10pm) you get a free drink. I doubt you'll ever see a cocktail this big again: They make them in 1-liter flower vases. You can work off your buzz on the dance floor until 4am. *Pile, Brsalje 11. www.fuego-dubrovnik.com. Cover 60kn.*

Bars

🎬 **Best** → **Bikers Caffe** ★ Bikers Caffe is a hot spot for the Libertas Bike Riders, Croatia's answer to the Hell's Angels. In addition to witnessing an unusual cadre, you can listen to real rock 'n' roll—a great bonus. Regardless of what you come for, the view from the bar—perched above the Old City—is incredible. *Petra Kresimira VI/39.* ☎ *020/ 680-771. www.bikers-caffe.com.*

Performing Arts

For information on Dubrovnik's Summer Festival, see below.

→ **Trubadur** Trubadur is a jazz club where you can jam to the music inside or sit back on comfy chairs outside and let the music wash over you. Performing groups change almost nightly. The owner, Marko, is a musician and longtime jazz fan who performed at the Eurovision Song Contest in 1968. Hours vary, but it's open very late. *Bunićeva 2, Old Town (near Gundulić Sq.). No phone.*

Sightseeing

Dubrovnik is a tourist's dream, with monuments, museums, and other historical sites galore. Depending on how long you stay, you probably won't see all the attractions. With some good planning, though, you should be able to fit in the highlights below .

Festivals

February

Feast of St. Blaise. The people of Dubrovnik revere St. Blaise—known to Catholics as the patron saint of people with throat problems—as the hero who saved their city from a sneak attack by Venetian galleys in the 10th century. To show their appreciation for his help, the city also celebrates with food and festivities. Reliquaries purportedly containing several of the saint's body parts are carried through the city in a parade, and people line up to have their throats blessed by local priests. February 3.

May

Dubrovnik International Film Festival. This festival showcases the work of Croatian filmmakers as well as internationally produced films. Annual showings are in theaters across the city in late May.

July & August

Dubrovnik Summer Festival. This is the largest arts festival in the country. Libertas, as the festival is affectionately called, has been held annually since 1950 in churches, squares, museums, and other historic sites all over the city. Book rooms well in advance. For more information, go to www. dubrovnik-festival.hr. From the second week of July to the third week of August, every evening at 9:30pm.

Monuments & Historical Buildings

Start at Dubrovnik's main drag, the **Strada** (aka **Placa**). It's been pounded by thousands upon thousands of feet since it was created in the 11th century. Running from **Pile Gate** straight through the city to **Ploce Gate,** the street takes in **Luza Square**—the center of the city's medieval town—and is home to **Onofrio's Fountain,** one of the city's most famous landmarks. It is also lined with neat, uniform buildings housing shops and restaurants.

Dubrovnik History in 500 Words or Less

After being self-ruled for about 1,000 years, Dubrovnik fell to Napoleon's army in 1806, and in 1808, the Dubrovnik Republic was dissolved. Eight years later, Dubrovnik leadership changed forces when the Habsburg Austro-Hungarian army took control of the country, due to the Vienna Congress. It remained part of this country for 100 years. After World War I, Croatia became part of the Kingdom of Serbs, Croats, and Slovenes, only to lose its independence in 1941 when the Italians took control. They held the city until 1944 when Dubrovnik was freed—that is, until it became part of Yugoslavia in 1945. It remained under Yugoslav rule until 1990, when the Socialist Government of Yugoslavia fell due to civil war. The elusive peace that the city enjoys now only lasted 1 year. In 1991, the Serbian army attacked and put a 7-month siege on the city. Even after the siege was lifted, the threat remained for another 3 years. You can still see bomb markings on some of the buildings in the Old City if you need a reminder of the city's turbulent political history.

FREE → **Church of St. Blaise** St. Blaise is the patron saint of Dubrovnik, said to protect against whooping cough and a variety of other things that people do not generally contract anymore. Now the Church of St. Blaise serves a more aesthetic purpose: The church is one of the most stunning buildings constructed after the great earthquake of 1667, which destroyed a good deal of the great Renaissance buildings in town. *Luža Sq. Free admission. Daily 8am–7pm.*

MTV Best → **City Wall** ★★★ The wall and its fortresses and towers are works of art built in medieval times; they undulate around Old Town in a protective embrace, creating an architectural frame for the historic city. As you make the 2km (1¼-mile) circuit atop the wall, which is 25m (82 ft.) high and 6m (20 ft.) thick at some points, with fortresses at intervals along the span, you'll see greater Dubrovnik and its landmark rooftops from every conceivable angle. The imposing 12th-century **Lovrijenac Fortress** was the lookout station for sea attacks. The **Pile Gate** is one of three entry points to the wall's top, and you'll walk up a steep flight of stairs through an arch topped by a statue of St. Blaise to get there. A quarter of a mile on, you'll reach the 16th-century **Revelin Fort,** which guards

the **Ploce Gate** on the eastern side and offers a great view of the port. The guns of **St. John** guarded the port, and **Bokar Fortress** guarded against sea incursions at the city's southwestern corner. *Gradske Zidine. 30kn adults. Apr–Oct daily 9am–7:30pm; Nov–Mar Tues–Sun 10am–3pm.*

FREE → **Clock Tower** This clock tower was first built in 1444 and has since been torn down, rebuilt, and remade too many times to count. The clock that crowns it now is an exact copy of the one that was there from 1478; the original can still be seen in the **Sponza Palace** (see below). You can't see it from the bottom, but pieces of the clock are actually shaped like bronze soldiers. The only piece from the original tower is the bell, cast in 1506. *Luža Sq.*

→ **Dubrovnik Cathedral (Church of the Assumption)** ★★ The original Church of the Assumption was built between the 12th and 14th centuries atop the ruins of a 6th- or 7th-century Byzantine basilica. The original cathedral was an elaborate Romanesque affair so severely damaged in the 1667 earthquake that it had to be restored. The cathedral was rebuilt following the quake in the au courant baroque style and it thus became the third church to be constructed on that site. In fact, remnants of both earlier churches are still visible in the present-day cathedral, which is a three-nave structure in the shape of a cross. The cathedral also has a rich treasury, which includes the skull, arm, and leg of St. Blaise, all plated with gold. Don't miss Titian's polyptych *The Assumption of the Virgin* (1552) in the church's apse. *Poljana Marina Držica. Treasury admission 10kn. Mon–Sat 9am–5:30pm; Sun 11am–5:30pm.*

FREE → **Orlando's Column** Having served as a meeting place for about eight generations of Dubrovnik people, the Orlando Column has stood firm for around 400 years. What is now one of the main symbols of Dubrovnik's independence (the flag flew here for almost 400 years, and the column was built in 1419), used to be the place where criminals were tied for varying lengths of time, according to their crimes. The actual man on the column is Roland, a legendary knight (some say the nephew of Charlemagne) who met his death returning from Spain in 778.

→ **Rector's Palace** ★ For just 15kn, you can guide yourself around the place that formerly held the government of Dubrovnik and which incorporates baroque, classical, and Renaissance designs that were added after several unfortunate gunpowder "accidents." A far cry from the bureaucratic headquarters it used to be, the Rector's Palace currently holds musical events (the acoustics are amazing) and has a tiny, mildly boring City Museum. Most people will find the jail cells the coolest highlight here. *Pred Dvorom 3.* ☎ *020/321-497. Admission 15kn. Summer daily 9am–7pm; winter Mon–Sat 9am–2pm.*

FREE → **Sponza Palace** ★★ The Sponza Palace—directly at the eye-line of the **Orlando Column** (see above)—was never actually an abode. It was constructed in 1516 and served as a customhouse, which means

that this is where all of the goods being traded through Dubrovnik formerly passed through. The lofty, airy atrium was also once where town meetings were held, and it now houses an art museum. In addition, one wing of the Palace held the Dubrovnik Republic mint, until the Republic was dismantled by Napoleon. *Luža Sq.* ☎ *020/321-032. Free admission, except for some exhibitions. Daily 9am–2pm, though times vary during exhibitions.*

FREE → **St. Savior Church** One of the city's few remaining Renaissance structures, this little church was built in 1520 on order from the rulers of Dubrovnik. It's stood intact for almost 500 years, even through the huge earthquake in the 17th century. Be sure to check out the carvings above the door. *Stradun 2 (between the Pile Gate and the Franciscan Monastery). Free admission. Daily 9am–7pm.*

Museums & Art Galleries

→ **Aquarium and Maritime Museum** This aquarium shouldn't amaze the average tourist, but many of the animals on display are only found in this area. There are also delightful displays of colorful sea anemones, corals, shells, sea urchins, and sea horses. The tanks are fed by a constant stream of fresh sea water. The maritime museum has charts, documents, boat models, and artifacts related to Ragusa's sea industry. *Damjana Jude 2, St. John's Fortress.* ☎ *021/427-937. Combined museum/aquarium admission 20kn adults. Aquarium summer daily 9am–9pm; winter Mon–Sat 9am–1pm. Maritime Museum summer daily 9am–6pm; winter Tues–Sun 9am–6pm.*

→ **Dominican Monastery and Museum** ★★ You'll find Dubrovnik's Dominican Monastery off a narrow passageway behind the Sponza Palace leading to the

12 Hours in Dubrovnik

1. **Sip coffee along the Placa.** You'll stumble upon countless cafes while on the city's main strip. Pick one with outdoor seating.
2. **Walk the City Wall.** The city's wall is a work of art in its own right, but the most amazing view is from the top.
3. **Visit the Dominican Monastery.** Head to this 14th-century monastery to get your fill of religious art.
4. **Chill at Café Festival.** Inexpensive, charming, and downright mouthwatering, this is a good place to stop for a much needed food break.
5. **Heat things up at Latin Club Fuego.** Romp with the creative crowd into the wee hours at this hopping late-night stamping ground.

Ploče Gate. The monastery, built in the 14th century, is positioned against the city wall to strengthen the ramparts' northeastern flank. An impressive stairway leads to the church doorway, decorated with a statue of St. Dominic; the door opens to a 15th-century Gothic cloister. The monastery's rooms circle the cloister, whose graceful triple arches frame a garden heady with Mediterranean plantings. But architecture aside, the real reason to visit here is the museum, which holds some fine religious art from Dubrovnik and elsewhere. *Sv. Dominika 4.* ☎ *020/426-472. Museum admission 10kn. Daily 9am–6pm.*

➔ **Franciscan Monastery** ★ Across from the Onofrio Fountain you will find the Franciscan Monastery, which was constructed in 1317. The structure was destroyed in the earthquake of 1667, but later rebuilt. Although the external architecture is very interesting, the one-of-a-kind interior holds the real gems. The Library houses a valuable collection of writings and other works from the 13th century onward, and the pharmacy at the back is the oldest functioning pharmacy in Europe and the third oldest in the entire world. *Muzej Franjevackog Samostana.* ☎ *020/426-345. Admission 10kn adults. Summer 9am–6pm. Erratic hours other times of the year.*

The University Scene

The **University of Dubrovnik** has only been around since 2003, but has a respectable student body of about 3,000. The main campus building is at Ćira Carića 4 (☎ **020/445-744**).

Playing Outside

You can't help but notice long, forested **Lokrum Island,** which sits a short distance from the Old City of Dubrovnik. This little island is a resort for tourists and Dubrovnikians who want to escape the city proper. Chock-full of heritage trees and pebbled beaches, Lokrum attracts those looking for a full day of sun and an ideal picnic spot. The only restaurants sit at the port, and boats run here almost continuously (until 8pm) from the Dubrovnik harbor. It's only a 15- to 20-minute ride.

Every beach in the country belongs to the people. Nonetheless, several of the hotels east of the port have staked out sections of the beach for their guests. Dubrovnik's main public beach, **Banje,** exists as a beach club (see below).

Bobin Kuk's **Copacabana Beach** is a pebble-and-concrete beach with a view of the

DUBROVNIK

graceful Dubrovnik Bridge and part of the Elaphite Islands. It is one of the few beaches in Dubrovnik with facilities for kids, sports enthusiasts, and swimmers with disabilities. Here you can ride a jet-ski, get whipped around on a banana-boat ride, or go airborne with a parachute boat. There are also sea slides for kids. A lift on the concrete part of the beach gives seniors and people with disabilities easy access to the water. Grownups can relax in a beach bar or a beach restaurant. At night, the beach bar becomes a cocktail bar and disco.

Day or night, the **Eastwest Beach Club** is Dubrovnik's answer for people who want to experience the luxury of a beach hotel without paying beach-hotel prices. At Banje, the club has a restaurant with a view and a sophisticated Dalmatian menu, a cocktail bar with space for dancing, watersports galore, a beach with crystal-clear water, beach attendants, and the unique *baldachin*. This "bed" on the beach looks like a raised four-poster hung with gauzy curtains that blow in the breeze. You can rent the *baldachin* for 200kn per day.

Shopping

You'll find lots of souvenir shops along the Stradun, and a big concentration of designer shops in the center of the Old City. Dubrovnik isn't known for any particular ware, but shops here have a good supply of nice embroideries and jewelry. If you're desperate for a cheap memento, try **Aquarius** (Polijana Paskala Millicevica 4), a record shop with a good selection of Croatian CDs, or **Dubrovacka kuca** (Svetog Dominika bb), which has a variety of souvenirs from olive oil to art prints.

Road Trips

The **Elafiti Islands** are so called because "elaphite" means "deer" and the islands once were the deer hunting grounds for the Dubrovnik aristocracy. Now, it requires a good deal less work to get to one of the five islands in the archipelago; boats leave around every hour from the Dubrovnik Harbor. Check with the tourist offices for exact scheduling info. Offices for the islands are on Lopud and at Šipanska Luka. Both are open June to September, Monday through Saturday from 8am to 1pm and from 5 to 8pm, on Sunday 9am to noon. Lopud's office can be reached at ☎ 020/759-086, and Šipanska Luka's at ☎ 020/758-084.

Of the five islands, three are inhabited and, depending on what sort of tour you take, you may only see some of them. **Kalamoto** is the smallest of the inhabited islands; it's closest to Dubrovnik and has a very laid-back, sleepy beach town vibe. **Lopud**—the middle island—is the most visited in the archipelago, and is famed for its Sunj beach and sun-soaked afternoons. If you get peckish while you are here, head for the restaurants *behind* the beachside strip: The ones directly on the beach are huge tourist traps. The farthest island is **Sipan,** the playground of rich Dubrovnik families (you can still see the manor houses that have stood here for hundreds of years).

Edinburgh

Edinburgh's a small enough big city that going at the height of the season is still the best way to see it—if you're interested in music and theater, that is. In August, Edinburgh hosts a world-class performing arts festival, with an accompanying Fringe Fest that is considered by some to be the best in the world.

The rule of thumb for visiting Great Britain is see London first and Edinburgh second, and it's no wonder that this beautiful, historic city is near the top of the list. From its famous Edinburgh Castle to the misty Firth of Forth and all the fabulous pubs in between, this is a city that is comfortable with itself, embracing its past yet open to what's new. You may notice the disparity between Edinburgh's Old Town and New Town, although both areas will attempt to part you with your cash, whether in one of scores of souvenir tourist traps on the Royal Mile and toward the Palace of Holyroodhouse or in a trendy boutique on Princes Street. Dubbed the "Athens of the North," Edinburgh's sights extend beyond the city's boundaries. Outside the city center, you can travel a short distance to the dramatic ruins of Linlithgow Palace, birthplace of Mary Queen of Scots, and to small towns with thatched-roof buildings that look as if they're hundreds of years old.

If you have only 3 or 4 days, you can begin to settle in. Edinburgh feels like home pretty quickly. But to spend more time here is to get the best out of Edinburgh and the surrounding countryside. Some things you absolutely have to do? Watch the sun set from the top of the hill at Edinburgh Castle. The Scots call the fading of the light "the gloaming," and you'll have unparalleled views of the city. Go on one of the touristy walking tours of the Old Town—the ghost tour, for one, can be lots of fun, showing you haunted places you wouldn't see otherwise. Take a double-decker bus tour; it's worth the price of the ticket to see all the local sights in one go, from the offensively ugly Scottish Parliament to the myriad churches and gardens that make Edinburgh the most attractive city in Scotland—perhaps in the whole of Britain. And it will help you decide where you want to spend your time. While in town, check out Rose Street if you want to confirm the rumor that it has more pubs and bars than on any other street in the U.K. Although it used to be a red-light district, today it's very tourist-friendly. Whatever you do in Edinburgh, don't call it "Edin-berg;" it's pronounced "Edin-burra," and you better get it right if you want respect from the locals!

The Best of Edinburgh

○ **The Best Cheap Veggie Meal: Susie's Diner** is neither a greasy spoon nor your typical diner. The vegetarian specials here are wide-ranging, from moussaka to cashew flan to sweet-and-sour tofu. Instead of a milkshake, order a smoothie. The counter staff is pretty friendly, too. See p. 345.

○ **The Best Pig's Cheek:** At the fashionable Leith docklands, restaurant **Martin Wishart** is the proud recipient of a coveted Michelin star. Chef Martin Wishart cooks up delicious and unusual treats like pot-roast pig's cheek with panache. The meal will set you back a few days' wages, unless, you've inherited your lot. See p. 346.

○ **The Best Pub:** Hunker down at one of the spacious booths at **Cafe Royal Circle Bar,** a Victorian-era pub that's a favorite with a trendy young crowd who works nearby in the New Town. Luckily, the food comes courtesy of the oyster bar next door. See p. 349.

Talk of the Town

Three ways to start a conversation with a local

Edinburgh natives are, as a rule, polite but incredibly reserved. As a result, they can be seen as rather aloof. For instance, if an American walks into a bar, many Scots won't automatically give a warm smile and invite him over to chat, as doing so falls in the "it's-rude-to-stare" category. However, there are a few surefire ways to get a Scot talking:

1. **Do you like Edinburgh during the summer months of the Festival or when it's quieter?** Many residents love that their city is so popular with visitors and so cosmopolitan.

2. **Glaswegians seem to think their city is culturally superior to Edinburgh. True or false?**

3. **The new Scottish Parliament building—architectural masterpiece or heinous eyesore?** This multimillion-pound structure always gets tongues wagging.

○ **The Best View of a Virgin:** The collection at the **National Gallery of Scotland** doesn't rival that of other European countries in its size, but it does in quality. Take some time away from the pubs to contemplate Botticelli's *The Virgin Adoring the Sleeping Christ Child,* as well as other master paintings by Titian, Velázquez, and van Dyck. See p. 351.

○ **The Best Place to Shop:** Pristine dressing gowns from the '30s, elegant dresses from the '40s, all the way up to '70s club chic—this is what **Elaine's Vintage Clothes** has to offer. Elaine, the store owner, has brought back the art of mending and tailoring. And the shop is a pleasure to walk into, whether you're spending money or window-shopping. See p. 354.

○ **The Best Outdoor Activity:** The **Rose Street pub-crawl** is some people's ideal way to spend an 18th or 21st birthday. Hell, for some, it's an ideal way to spend any old Friday night. Regulars start at one end of the pub-laden street and attempt to have a half pint of lager in as many pubs as possible before they end up reeling. Favorite watering holes on the crawl include Milne's, the Kenilworth, and the Abbotsford. You can also do the crawl drinking bottled water, just don't tell anyone. See p. 348.

Getting There & Getting Around

Getting into Town

BY PLANE

Getting to Edinburgh couldn't be easier. From London, it's about an hour's flying time (633km/393 miles) to the north. **Edinburgh Airport** (☎ 0131/333-1000) is about 10km (6 miles) west of the center. Direct flights come in from all over Europe and from Newark, New Jersey, in the U.S. The **information and accommodations desk** (☎ 0131/473-3800) is a good stop before you leave the airport; it's open Monday to Saturday 8am to 8pm and Sunday 9am to 4:30pm.

To get into town, you can hop a double-decker Airlink bus that makes the trip from the airport to the city center every 15 minutes and lets people off near Waverley Bridge, between the Old Town and the New Town; the fare is £3.30 one-way or £5 round-trip, and the trip takes about 25 minutes.

A taxi into the city should cost £12 or more, depending on the traffic, and the ride will also be about 25 minutes.

BY TRAIN

Fast, efficient, and air-conditioned InterCity trains link London with Edinburgh, with restaurant and bar service on board. Trains from London's Kings Cross Station arrive in Edinburgh at **Waverley Station** (at the east end of Princes St.; ☎ 08457/484950 in London for rail info). Trains depart London every hour or so; it takes about 4½ hours and costs £41 to £91 one-way. Overnight trains have a sleeper berth, which is always fun, but it will run an extra £35. Taxis and buses are right outside the station in Edinburgh. *FYI:* Your Eurailpass is *not* valid on trains in Great Britain.

BY BUS

Roughly, coach/bus fares are about one-third of the rail charges for comparable trips to Scotland. It's the cheapest—and the longest—way to go. A bus from London to Edinburgh, for example, costs £27, but it takes 8 hours. Scottish CityLink coaches depart from London's Victoria Coach Station and deliver you to Edinburgh's **St. Andrew Square Bus Station,** St. Andrew Square; call ☎ 0870/550-5050 or visit www.citylink.co.uk for timetables. Most travel agents in London sell coach seats and can make reservations for you. Using the buses to get from Glasgow to

Freedom Pass

If you plan to travel exclusively in Scotland, look into the **Freedom of Scotland Travelpass,** which offers unlimited transportation on trains and most ferries and discounts on bus travel throughout the country. The Travelpass is available for 4 days' travel over an 8-day period for £87; 8 days' travel over a 15-day period for £112. When you validate your pass at the beginning of your trip, you'll get a complete packet of rail, bus, and ferry schedules. For more info, contact Britrail ☎ **877/677-1066** in the U.S., or www.britrail.net.

Alternatively, if you want to travel by train but don't want the Travelpass, get a **young person's rail card** (for ages 16–25), sold at major stations. You'll need two passport-size photos—it costs £18—and reduces all fares by about a third for 1 year.

Edinburgh is much more reasonable; travel is fast and prices are low.

Getting Around

BY CAR

Driving a car in Edinburgh can be difficult and frustrating, especially if you're not used to driving on the left-hand side of the road. Also, finding parking can be problematic; many areas have parking just for permit holders.

If you must rent a car, get one at the airport or try **Avis** (5 W. Park Place; ☎ **0870/153-9103;** www.avis.co.uk), **Europcar** (☎ **0131/333-2588**), **Thrifty** (42 Haymarket Terrace; ☎ **0131-337-1319;** www.thrifty.co.uk), **Hertz** (10 Picardy Place; ☎ **0870/846-0013;** ww.hertz.co.uk), **National** (☎ **0870/400-4502**), **Budget** (☎ **0870/156-5656**), or **Alamo** (☎ **0870/599-3000**).

BY BUS

You won't find a subway in Edinburgh, so go by bus if don't want to walk. The bus system is simple and easy to use and bus stops are absolutely everywhere—you won't be able to make it up Princes Street without tripping over people queuing every 100m (328 ft.). The fare you pay depends on the distance you ride; the **minimum fare** (single, one-way, for up to three stages) is 80p. The **maximum fare** is £1 for 44 or more stages. (A stage isn't a stop but a distance of about .8km/$^1/_2$ mile with a number of stops.) The **Edinburgh Day Saver Ticket** allows 1 day of unlimited travel on city buses at a cost of £1.50 to £2.50 for adults. If you're in Edinburgh for a while, buy a **RideaCard** for £12 per week (travel has to start on Sun). For details on fares and timetables go to www.lothianbuses.co.uk or call ☎ **0131/555-6363.**

BY TAXI

If you're coming from London, you'll find taxis in Edinburgh a bargain. However, from any other perspective, it's a rip-off. However, after a few drinks in the Old Town, you really won't want to walk over the bridge back to your hotel. Call ☎ **0131/228-1211** for **City Cabs** or ☎ **0131/229-2468** for **Central Taxis.** You can also hail a cab or simply pick one up at a stand. Meters begin at £2 and increase every 1km ($^1/_2$ mile). Fares are displayed in the front of the taxi and charges posted, including extra charges for night drives or destinations outside the city limits.

BY BICYCLE

You'd better be in good shape to rent a bicycle in Edinburgh as there are lots of cobblestone streets and steep hills to navigate. Try the **Rent-a-Bike Edinburgh** at 29 Blackfriars St.—check out their site (www.cyclescotland.co.uk). The same company organizes bike tours of the city and across Scotland. It costs about £15 a day to hire a bike, and a deposit of £100 is usually required.

ON FOOT

Most of Edinburgh's major tourist attractions are within walking distance of one another. For instance, you could start at the Castle and walk down the Royal Mile to the Palace of Holyroodhouse. If you want a more organized experience, try a walking tour like the Witchery Tours, where you can expect to see some of the city's haunted spots. Check out their ⭐ Best **Ghosts and Gore** tour, where you'll meet characters "summoned from the mists of time," such as body snatchers Burke and Hare, while you explore the city. Go to www.witcherytours.com or call ☎ 0131/225-6745—booking is essential (it's available May–Oct), and a ticket costs £7.50. If you'd like to learn something about Edinburgh's history, try one of six **Mercat Tours,** often led by tour guides with masters degrees or doctorates. Check out their site at www.mercattours.com or call ☎ 0131/225-5445. Different themed tours, including Secrets of the Royal Mile and The Vaults, emphasize different things; don't choose the latter if you're claustrophobic, as you'll be exploring narrow spaces under the South Bridge. Tours costs between £6 and £7; some are running year-round and others only in the summer and fall, so calling first is essential.

Edinburgh Basics

Orientation: Edinburgh Neighborhoods

The oldest part of Edinburgh is, quite obviously, the Old Town, with the **Royal Mile** being the most ancient—it originated in medieval times. The main thoroughfares here are Castlehill, Lawnmarket, Canongate, and High Street. Here you'll find sights like the legendary **Castle** and the **Palace of Holyroodhouse.** Old Town is the tourist heart of Edinburgh, so in the summer you'll find huge groups navigating the cobblestone streets or stopping in at famous restaurants like the Witchery. New Town dates to the 18th century, its most famous artery being **Princes Street.** Some of the most fabulous local hotels and shops can be found on Princes Street—check out the Balmoral Hotel for sheer luxury, and Jenners for the best department store in town. In the heart of the New Town is Stockbridge, which feels like a town-within-a-town. Here you'll find a few surviving bars from the hippie era, plus an up-and-coming food scene. Just west of the city center are Haymarket and Dalry, which are currently being gentrified—real estate prices are skyrocketing. West of the Castle you'll find Tolcross and the West End, home to the conference center and theater district, respectively. The gay neighborhood in Edinburgh is called Calton—also known as the Pink Triangle; it's full of lively gay bars and bistros. Leith is the city's major port, and is becoming very trendy. Many of its cute restaurants focus on seafood.

Tourist Offices

Stop by the **Edinburgh Information Center,** centrally located at Princes Mall (3 Princes St.). You can arrange a hotel room, get info on sights to see, buy tickets for bus tours or plays, and grab some brochures on things to do while in Scotland. It's open 9am to 7pm Monday through Saturday and 10am to 7pm on Sundays, but you'll find extended hours during the Festival. Call ahead ☎ 0131/473-3800 or see their website, www.edinburgh.org.

Recommended Websites

○ **www.visitbritain.com** and **www. visitscotland.com**: The best sites on Edinburgh include these official pages from the British Tourist Authority; they

EDINBURGH

include info for finding accommodations at any price.

- ○ **www.edinburgh.org**: The virtual office of the Edinburgh Information Centre—good for special offers or new tours.
- ○ **www.travelbritain.com**: The Scotland section has good tips on visiting the city.
- ○ **www.netcafes.com**: Lists where to find Internet cafes in the city.
- ○ **www.edinburgh-festivals.com**: Lays claim as the only website that covers *all* of Edinburgh's festivals.
- ○ **www.edinburgh247.com**: News of the day plus links to what's on, with listings as diverse as a Buddhist meditation class to a performance of Luciano Pavarotti.
- ○ **www.edinburgh-pubs.com**: Gives a brief description and pic. Enough said.

Culture Tips 101

Nothing much changes in Edinburgh. It's a deeply conservative, highly traditional city where few things culturally are any different than they were in the 1970s. Except, of course, for a certain huge multimillion-pound building at the bottom of the Royal Mile, the new Parliament building, which has just won the Stirling Prize for best new building in the U.K. (although many Scots would beg to differ).

Edinburgh natives—generally—are hard workers who value the simple things in life: having a "wee dram," a small glass of whiskey, in front of the fire in winter, watching the rugby in a local pub, or playing golf on the weekends. There are, of course, some ways the Scots keep themselves entertained that might not go over well on the other side of the pond! There's reeling—something sort of like country-and-western line dancing but a lot more difficult and with old-fashioned tartan outfits, to boot. There are some similarities to American culture: Edinburgh natives feel the same way about their rival football teams, Hibernian and Hearts, as New Yorkers feel about the Jets and the Giants. When in doubt, follow the general rule of thumb for

Harry Potter's Magic

The Harry Potter franchise—it's big enough and well-known enough that you can call it that now—has sold 250 million books in 61 languages, with movie sales at about £1 billion globally, and that doesn't include DVD and merchandise sales. So, I'm assuming you know that Harry Potter gets much of his magic from Scotland. Here in Edinburgh, it is common knowledge that author J. K. Rowling sat within view of Edinburgh Castle and penned a lot of the first book while soaking up the local culture. A walk within the city yields all sorts of treasures: names of pubs, streets, and stores that Rowling borrowed. If you walk by the university, you may even come across the potter's field for the town, and you might then make the association that dear Harry's last name comes from the fact that he's "unknown" as most of the paupers are in the small cemetery.

polite chitchat when talking to a Scot—don't bring up sex, religion, or politics.

Strictly speaking, the minimum drinking age is 18, but no one usually asks for ID. Kids under 16 are barred from many drinking institutions, with the exception of those serving food. The penalties for driving under the influence are strict. As for drugs, the Scottish take the same pragmatic attitude as the English. Drugs are strictly illegal, yet the government does provide lots of information on rehabilitation instead of draconian punishments.

Recommended Books, Movies & Music

BOOKS & MOVIES

Sir Walter Scott's *The Heart of Midlothian* is a classic—so much so that the novel's title is the name of an Edinburgh football club, nick-named the Hearts. The story focuses on heroine Jeanie Deans and her suitor Reuben Butler, and includes various dialects. For a more modern take on the city of Edinburgh, try Ian Rankin novel's *Black and Blue,* which follows native son Detective Rebus as he solves serial murders. Get your hands on *The Prime of Miss Jean Brodie* by Muriel Spark—or rent the film version starring Dame Maggie Smith—for another contemporary look at the city.

Another book-turned-movie is *Greyfriar's Bobby,* a true story about a dog who sat on his master's grave for years and now has a statue dedicated to him not far from where J. K. Rowling supposedly penned the first Harry Potter (see "Harry Potter's Magic" on p. 338). The 1961 movie has a loyal but small following.

Edinburgh is an excellent backdrop for all sorts of films, from costume dramas such as 2000's *The House of Mirth* starring Gillian Anderson and 1997's *Mrs. Brown,* the story of Queen Victoria starring Dame Judi Dench, to modern black comedies such as *Trainspotting,* action-packed flicks like *Rob Roy,* and weepies like *Chariots of Fire.* There's such diversity in the local scenery, from the cute port town of Leith to the dramatic Forth Bridge to bustling Princes Street. The stately homes and castles on the city's outskirts are perfect for period pieces. A comprehensive website (www.edinfilm.com) for film buffs gives details of films shot here and shows photos of locations.

MUSIC

In summer, the Festival (p. 351), takes over, and there's music everywhere. During the rest of the year, Edinburgh's live music scene suffers at the hands of Glasgow, where the biggest shows and venues are. For more info, see "Partying" below.

Edinburgh **Nuts & Bolts**

Cellphone Providers & Service Centers   You may well find your cellphone switches over to a British network like Vodafone, 3, O2, T-Mobile, or Orange as soon as your plane lands. If not, get a SIM card at one of the following places on Princes Street: T-Mobile (Princes Mall, 3 Princes St.; ☎ **0131/556-3777**), Vodafone (24 Princes St.; ☎ **0845/440-0194**), or The Carphone Warehouse (25 Princes St.; ☎ **0870/168-2026**).

Currency   In Scotland, pounds sterling are used, just as they are all over the U.K. You can change your dollars to pounds at ATMs or exchange bureaus all over the city, at any bank, or at the airport.

Embassies   For lost or stolen passports or other tourist emergencies, contact **U.S. Consulate General Edinburgh** (2 Regent Terrace; ☎ **0131/5568315;** fax 0131-557-6023). The **Canadian High Commission** is at MacDonald House, Standard Life House (30 Lothian Rd.; ☎ **0131/220-4333**), and is open Monday to Friday 8am to 4pm. The **Australian High Commission** is at 37 George St. (☎ **0131/624-333**), and is open Monday to Friday 9:30am to 3:30pm. The **New Zealand Commission** is at New Zealand House (80 Haymarket at Pall Mall, London SW1y 4TQ; ☎ **020/7930-8422**) and is open Monday to Friday 9:30am to 1pm and 2:15 to 5pm.

Emergencies   Dial ☎ **999** for police, ambulance, or the fire service. The best hospital in Edinburgh is the **Royal Infirmary** at 1 Lauriston Place. Call ☎ **0131/536-1000** for their main switchboard.

Internet/Wireless Hot Spots There are **EasyInternetCafes** at three locations, one at 58 Rose St., by the National Gallery, one at 137 Princes St., and one at 67a Raeburn Place. They're distinguishable by their garish orange awnings; go to www.easyinternet cafe.com for maps of each location. You'll also find a couple of cafes on the Royal Mile with signs advertising Wi-Fi service.

Laundry Laundry services are few and far between. If your hotel doesn't provide facilities, ask at a nearby hostel to use its washers and dryers for a fee. Or go to **Bendix Self-Service Launderettes** (342 Leith Walk; ☎ 0131/554-2180). **Euroclean** has dry-cleaning services on 17 Newington Rd. in Dunbar. If you have a student card they give discounts. Go to www.euroclean.org.uk for details.

Luggage Storage Lockers for general use are in Waverly Station at a cost of £3.50 per item for 24 hours. **Excess Baggage** is another option; call ☎ 0131/558-3829 for details.

Pharmacy The city hosts a number of **Boots** outposts. One of the easiest to find is at 48 Shandwick Place, on the west end of Princes Street (☎ 0131/225-6757). It's open Monday to Saturday 8am to 9pm and Sunday 10am to 5pm.

Post Offices The Edinburgh Branch Post Office is located at 8–10 St. James Centre, and is open Monday through Saturday from 9am to 5:30pm. Call ☎ 0845/722-3344. If you need to receive mail here, give your friends/family the address of this post office, and have them write "Poste Restante" on the envelope—with your name, of course. You can collect the mail any time.

Restrooms Look for the boxes marked WC on street corners; it stands for "Water Closet" and it's a free restroom, which is usually safe and relatively clean.

Safety Edinburgh is generally much safer than Glasgow; central tourist areas are crowded and well lit until late at night. This doesn't mean you can leave bags on tables and act like a fool—everything your mother taught you holds true even when on holiday. As in every big city, pay attention and use street smarts.

Telephone Tips A reliable service for directory assistance is ☎ 118, although it can be expensive. You can also visit them online at www.118118.com. Some telephone booths in Edinburgh now have Internet access available so look carefully when you pass them.

Tipping Generally, Edinburgh restaurants include a tip with the VAT charge. If not, a 15% tip is the norm. Tip your taxi driver between 10% and 15%, and leave a few pounds for housekeeping if you stay in a nice hotel. The standard tip for bellhops is 50p to £1 per piece of luggage. It is *not* customary to tip at a British pub. It is, however, normal to tip the lady in the club bathroom who spritzes you with perfume and gives you a lollipop.

Youth Information Service Offices The city has three main switchboards if you run into trouble. Edinburgh and Lothian Woman's Aid: ☎ 0131/229-1419. Lothian Gay and Lesbian Switchboard: ☎ 0131/556-4049. Rape Crisis Centre: ☎ 0141/3311990.

Sleeping

Edinburgh's got a full-range of accommodations, from hostels to trendoid new hotels. It's a good idea to reserve your place in advance, and it's absolutely necessary to reserve during the Festival.

Hostels

→ **Caledonian Backpackers** Just a short walk from bus and train stations and with views of the Castle, this may be your best bet for a hostel in Edinburgh. Their Swamp Bar is a well-known venue for live music acts and thankfully you don't have to bring your own sheets. Wi-Fi access is pretty cheap too. If you want to explore the nightlife in Edinburgh, go ahead—there are no curfews or lockouts at Caledonian Backpackers. *3 Queensferry St.* ☎ *0131/476-7224. www. caledonianbackpackers.com. £11–£15 dorm bed (depending on number of beds in room), £36 double or twin, £51 triple. Light Rail: Haymarket Station. Amenities: Bar; fax; Internet (£1 per hour); kitchens; laundry facilities; library; mail service; safe; tour desk; TV (in common room); Wi-Fi (£1 per hour). In room: Free sheets/duvet; lockers.*

→ **St. Christopher's Inn** This hostel, part of a well-known chain across the U.K. and western Europe, has won awards. Its rooms are bright and airy, and free breakfast is provided. Like their London hostel, the Edinburgh St. Christopher's is attached to Belushi's Bar, where you can drunkenly sing karaoke or watch American sports on the huge TVs. The rooms range from a private room with one twin bed and a shared bathroom to 14-bed dorm rooms with en suite bathrooms. Bed linens are included but you'll have to bring your own towel. *9–13 Market St.* ☎ *0207/ 407-1856. www.st-christophers.co.uk. £12–£17 dorm, £23 double. Rates include breakfast. Light Rail: Waverly Station. Amenities: Restaurant; bar; Internet; kitchen; laundry facilities; storage; TV (in common room); travel desk; wheelchair friendly. In room: Free sheets, lockers.*

Cheap

→ **A-Haven Townhouse** In newly cool Leith, the A-Haven boasts views of the Firth of Forth on one side and hilly Arthur's Seat on the other. Owner David Kay offers a warm welcome and you'll find the rooms a good size for the price. Bonus: Internet is available. *180 Ferry Rd.* ☎ *0131/554-6559. www.a-haven. co.uk. £30–£75 single, £60–£99 double. Rates include breakfast. Bus: 7, 14, or 21. Amenities: Bar; Wi-Fi. In room: TV, coffee/tea maker, hair dryer, Internet, trouser press.*

Doable

→ **The Bank Hotel** You can tell this building used to be a bank, with its high ceilings, Grecian design elements, and a reception area that used to be the bank manager's office. You'll get value for money here and be smack in the middle of the action on the Royal Mile. Enter the nine-room hotel through the crowded Logie Baird bar and enjoy the complimentary full Scottish breakfast. *1 S. Bridge St.* ☎ *0131/622-6800. www. festival-inns.co.uk. £40–£55 single, £110 double. Rates include breakfast. Bus: 35. Amenities: Restaurant; bar. In room: TV, CD player (in some), coffee/tea maker, hair dryer, refrigerator (in some), trouser press.*

→ **Walton Hotel** This small, friendly hotel is a real find. A restored town house in the center of the New Town, the Walton is cozy without seeming old-fashioned, thanks to its refurbished rooms and young, gregarious staff. The bathrooms are so comfortable, with their log-cabin feel and big bathtubs, that you'll want to sleep there. The hotel is entirely nonsmoking. *79 Dundas St.* ☎ *0131/ 556-1137. www.waltonhotel.com. £50–75 single, £89–£145 double, £99–145 triple. Bus: 23 or 27. In room: TV, coffee/tea maker, hair dryer.*

Splurge

→ **The Glasshouse** After you stay a night in this hotel, it'll undoubtedly become one of your favorites in the world. A modern boutique hotel, the Glasshouse is impressive to look at: The facade of an old church has been updated with glass accouterments. The room furnishings are as hip as they come, and

Edinburgh

SLEEPING ■
A-Haven Townhouse **10**
The Bank Hotel **21**
Caledonian
  Backpackers **37**
The Glasshouse **2**
Mansfield House **5**
Prestonfield House **48**
St. Christopher's Inn **26**
Walton Hotel **4**

EATING ◆
Atrium **39**
Baked Potato Shop **22**
Barioja **20**
Bell's Diner **3**
Chocolate Soup **22**
Clarinda's Tearoom **14**
Dusit **33**
Favorit **42, 44**
Gordon's Trattoria **23**
Kebab Mahal **45**
Martin Wishart **11**
Number One **38**
O'Briens **30**
Oloroso **35**
Plaisir du Chocolat **15**
Sea Breeze Café **11**
Susie's Diner **46**

PARTYING ★
The Abbotsford **31**
Black Bo's **17**
Bongo Club **16**
C.C. Bloom's **10**
Café Royal Circle Bar **7**
Corn Exchange **41**
The Honeycomb **19**
Jongleurs **10**
Liquid Room **27**
Opal Lounge **32**
The Outhouse **8**
Planet Out **9**
Po Na Na **34**
Pond Bar **11**
Queen's Hall **47**
The Stand **6**
Usher Hall **40**
Venue **13**

Church
Information
Railway

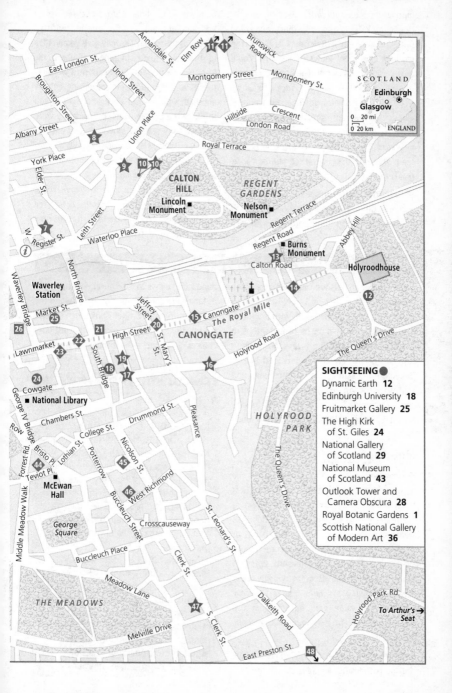

SIGHTSEEING ●

Dynamic Earth **12**

Edinburgh University **18**

Fruitmarket Gallery **25**

The High Kirk
of St. Giles **24**

National Gallery
of Scotland **29**

National Museum
of Scotland **43**

Outlook Tower and
Camera Obscura **28**

Royal Botanic Gardens **1**

Scottish National Gallery
of Modern Art **36**

manage to look cool without being pretentious (think flatscreen TVs that swivel and nude photographs). Balconies and rooftop gardens give great views of the city. You'll never want to check out. The hotel is entirely nonsmoking. *2 Greenside Place.* ☎ *0131/ 525-8200. www.theetoncollection.com/hotels/ glasshouse. £210–£270 double, £345–£450 suite. Bus: 5, 14, or 22. Amenities: Complimentary business cards; roof garden. In room: A/C, TV, coffee/ tea maker, hair dryer, Internet, minibar, safe, trouser press.*

➔ **Prestonfield House** Set in 13 acres of gardens, this 17th-century manor is home to various actors and luminaries when they're in town. Walls lined with blood-red velvet and opulent yet tasteful rooms outfitted with plasma-screen TVs may give you an idea of the kind of luxury to expect. Rhubarb, the in-house restaurant, is decadently wonderful, as is the staff. I felt something ghostly about this place after dark—I caught myself thinking the people in the oil portraits were tracking my every move. *Priestfield Rd.* ☎ *0131/225-7800. www.prestonfield.com. £195–£225 double, £295 suite. Rates include breakfast and champagne. Bus: 2, 14, or 30. Amenities: Restaurant; park views. In room: A/C, TV/DVD, Bose sound system, coffee/tea maker, hair dryer, Internet, iron/ironing board, minibar, safe, Wi-Fi.*

Eating

With national dishes like haggis (see "Deconstructing Haggis," below), which nobody's borrowing or fusing with anything, Scotland's not known for its contributions to the culinary world. There are, however, a few exceptions, which are included below. Baked potatoes and pizza are cheap; beyond that, look for the growing number of ethnic spots (including Mexican, Thai, and Indian) that have good, solid fare for not too much cash.

Hot Spots

➔ **Number One** ★★ EUROPEAN The address of this place says it all: It's the best hotel in the best part of the city. With a Michelin star and a menu filled with delicious treats like Dover sole with langoustine or mulled wine parfait, it's no wonder many consider this a destination restaurant. *Balmoral Hotel, 1 Princes St.* ☎ *0131/557-6727. www. roccofortehotels.com. Main courses average £25. Mon–Fri noon–2pm and 7–10pm (till 10:30pm on Fri); Sat 7–10:30pm; Sun 7–10pm. Bus: 3, 8, 25, or 29.*

➔ **Oloroso** ★★ MODERN SCOTTISH This rooftop restaurant can claim one of the best panoramic views in Edinburgh—you can see as far as the Forth River on one side and the Castle on the other. Chef Tony Singh's menu is imaginative, with out-of-the-ordinary choices like pan-seared pigeon. Anything

Deconstructing Haggis

A quintessential part of Scottish culture, haggis is even the subject of an ode by poet Robert Burns, "Address to a Haggis." Yet to the outsider, few things seem more, well, disgusting than this national culinary treasure. While most Scots eat it only around Burns's birthday in late January, haggis is always available from fish and chips shops, butchers, and tons of restaurants.

So, what the hell is it, anyway? Made from finely chopped sheep's heart, lungs, and liver; oatmeal; and pepper; and cooked within a batter-fried sheep's stomach, haggis is customarily served with "tatties and neeps," or potatoes and turnips. Mmm, mmm, good. Vegetarians: Wipe that smug smile off your face!

from the grill menu will set you back plenty, but there's a cheaper snack menu with choices like fish cakes and burgers. Pop up to the bar if you're in the mood for a strong cocktail. *33 Castle St.* ☎ *0131/226-7614. www. oloroso.co.uk. Main courses £8–£23. Mon–Sun noon–2:30pm and 7–10:30pm. Bus: 13, 19, or 41.*

Cheap

→ **Baked Potato Shop** SCOTTISH If you like baked potatoes and sausages, you won't go hungry in Edinburgh. This worker's favorite lunch place offers—guess what?—with over a half-dozen fillings to choose from. The flaky potatoes go well with the chili and salads also on the menu here. The shop opens early, but the potatoes aren't usually ready till about 11am. *56 Cockburn St.* ☎ *0131/225-7572. Filled potatoes about £3. Daily 9am–9pm. Light Rail: Waverly Station.*

→ **Bell's Diner** AMERICAN Open for dinner only (except Sat, when you can get lunch), Bell's would do well to increase its hours. This American-style diner is markedly better than the greasy spoons you'll find at home. You can get whatever you'd like on your burger, like garlic butter, and for once you'll get salad on the side. You can expect to pay between £6 and £9 for a meal at Bell's. *17 St. Stephen St.* ☎ *0131/225-8116. Sun–Fri 6–10:30pm; Sat noon–10:30pm. Bus: 24, 29, or 42.*.

→ **Kebab Mahal** ★ INDIAN Don't eat at the Kebab Mahal if you need to chase your Indian meals with a few beers: The owner of this Southside establishment is Muslim, so you won't find booze on the premises. The real draw of this restaurant isn't just the tasty, traditional menu but the diversity of the patrons—from dustmen to professors and everything in between. As a bonus, most meals are under £5. *7 Nicolson Sq.* ☎ *0131/ 667-5214. Sun–Thurs noon–midnight; Fri–Sat noon–2am. Bus: 3, 8, or 29.*

📺 Best → **Susie's Diner** ★★ VEGETARIAN Don't let the name of this student establishment fool you: You won't find greasy "diner" food or milkshakes here. What you will find is friendly counter service, decor with a worn-in feel, and veggie specials like moussaka, cashew flan, or sweet-and-sour tofu, with large portions costing under £6. Still craving something sweet like a chocolate shake? Order a healthy smoothie instead. *51 W. Nicolson St.* ☎ *0131/667-8729. Mon noon–8pm; Tues–Sat noon–9pm. Bus: 7, 14, 3, 33, or 37.*

Doable

→ **Barioja** ★ SPANISH Barioja is better than the average tapas bar, but retains the casual, fun atmosphere associated with such places. You'll get a heaping plate for around £9, whether you order seafood like king prawns or traditional dishes like chorizo. A real find. *19 Jeffrey St.* ☎ *0131/557-3622. Mon–Sat 11am–11pm. Bus: 35.*

→ **Dusit** ★ THAI This Thai spot on restaurant-packed Thistle Street is one of the best of its kind in the city. You'll find more than the usual chicken pad Thai, and menu items have cutesy, colorful names like Lady in the Garden (king scallops with garlic and coriander) and Party Girls (mixed fruit and pommelo salad with nut dressing). Fresh local produce has been lovingly incorporated into the menu—for instance, all the veggies and herbs are from a local garden, and a dash of whisky is added to some dishes for a truly Scottish flavor. Main courses start at £7.95. *49a Thistle St.* ☎ *0131/220-6846. Mon–Sat noon–3pm and 6–11pm; Sun noon–11pm. Bus: 24 or 42.*

Splurge

→ **Atrium** ★★ SCOTTISH/INTERNATIONAL Atrium is an eclectic place, with elements of South America, Europe, and Scotland colliding to make your food selections, like loin of Inverary venison served with dauphinoise potatoes, kale, and bacon jus. The terra cotta–washed walls and modern, almost

Moorish decor is stylish without being over the top. The menu is fantastic, including lots of seafood prepared creatively (think sea bass with fennel caponata and tapenade) and a well-put-together wine list that covers the globe. *10 Cambridge St. Main courses £17–£21.* ☎ *0131/228-8882. www.atriumrestaurant.co. uk. Mon–Fri noon–2pm and 6–10pm; Sat 6–10pm. Bus: 2 or 8.*

MTV **Best** → **Martin Wishart** ★★★
MODERN FRENCH   More than one gourmet association has awarded this wonderful place "Scottish Restaurant of the Year," and the chef is rightly proud of his Michelin rating. The menu is short but sweet, taking advantage of the best of the season. Gratin of sea bass, for example, comes with a soft, herby crust; partridge breast arrives paired with black truffle and foie gras. And then there's the pig's cheek. Make reservations because you won't get in without them. *54 The Shore.* ☎ *0131/553-3557. Main courses £19–£24; fixed-price lunch £19 (3 courses). Tues–Fri noon–2pm; Tues–Thurs 6:30–10pm; Fri–Sat 6:30–10:30. Bus: 22 or 36.*

Cafes & Tearooms

You'll find a bunch of cute cafes dotted along the Royal Mile and its side streets. The best two can be found in Canongate: **Clarinda's Tearoom** and **Plaisir du Chocolat.**

→ **Chocolate Soup** If you want coffee and a snack—maybe something covered in fudge—then try this favorite of cappuccino enthusiasts and chocoholics alike. *2 Hunter Sq.* ☎ *0131/225-7669. Bus: 7 or 57.*

→ **Clarinda's Tearoom** This place is staunchly British, with Wedgwood china,

Late-Night Bites

If you crave food and it's past midnight, head to **Favorit,** an American-style diner with two locations: one at 30–32 Leven St. (☎ **0131/221-1800**), and one in the university area at 19 Teviot Place (☎ **0131/220-6880**). They're open till 1 and 3am respectively. If you have a hankering for a greasy pizza, you could try **Gordon's Trattoria** on the High Street, in the Old Town (231 High St; ☎ **0131/225-7992**).

tasty homemade cakes (the scones are the best), and a variety of teas, including a good Earl Grey to wash your fattening treats down. *69 Canongate.* ☎ *0131/557-1888. Bus: 35.*

→ **O'Briens** If you don't mind a more corporate atmosphere, one of the many franchises of this so-called Irish Starbucks offers good all-round snacks and drinks. The most central shop is in the Princes Street Mall. ☎ *0131/557-1444. Bus: 1, 3, 4, 31, 33, or 44.*

→ **Plaisir du Chocolat** As Clarinda's is British, this hot-chocolate paradise is decidedly French. You'll find the act of drinking hot chocolate raised to an art form here. The owners call it "haut chocolat." You'll also find hundreds of varieties of tea and snacks. *251 Canongate.* ☎ *0131/556-9524. Bus: 35.*

→ **Sea Breeze Café** For an older, quainter place to take a coffee break, try this Leith hangout where you can eat a sandwich and chat with locals. *261 Leith Walk.* ☎ *0131/467-7889.*

Partying

As in Glasgow, the best way to find out what's on and all the details for each event is to pick up *The List* magazine for £2 at any newsagent, book shop, or post office. This is a particularly useful guide during the

Festival—there's always far too much going on, and *The List* will rate each show and give a synopsis so you don't waste your time.

As for what's on during the week, there's always something happening in Edinburgh if

The Fringe Festival

The highlight of Edinburgh's year comes in the last 3 weeks of August, when the city hosts the Edinburgh International Festival (☎ **0131/225-1188; www.eif.co.uk**). It is predictably good: There's music, opera, dance, and theater.

But what's most fun is the 📺 **Best** **Fringe Festival** that runs simultaneously. The performances can be spotty but have great heart. The venues are as interesting as the city itself (the performances are held all over the city, including in fields, churches, graveyards, and so on). Anybody can be in the Fringe—professional or not. But what you'll usually find is cutting-edge comedy, political farce, outrageous contemporary drama, and university theater. And the ticket prices are always reasonable.

The first weekend of the festival, hawkers stand along the Royal Mile and perform samples of their art. You might listen to a classical violin trio performing next to a full-ensemble cast of *Once on this Island* next to a serious play about crimes in Bosnia.

For more info on the Edinburgh International Festival, the Fringe Festival, and the accompanying film, jazz, and television festivals, go to www.edinburgh festivals.co.uk, or call ☎ **0131/473-2000** (International Festival) or ☎ **0131/226-5257** (for the Fringe). Young people and full-time students receive a 50% discount, with tickets for most shows as low as £3 to £3.75. Also, £6 youth tickets are available for anyone under the age of 26 on the day of the performance.

EDINBURGH

you know where to go. For pub and clubs, your best bets are the areas around Cowgate and Grassmarket in the Old Town and Broughton Street in the New Town. Don't forget about up-and-coming Leith, particularly the Shore area. For theater and music, head for the West End, where you'll also find independent cinema.

You may notice that a few teens and 20-somethings in Edinburgh are well dressed, but not everyone dresses up. If you're anywhere near the campus on the south side, you might want to dress accordingly. If you're just going to a pub on Rose Street, jeans are fine.

Live Music

Edinburgh doesn't rival Glasgow for live music (except during the Festival), and most big, recent Scottish acts were discovered in Glasgow rather than here. However, Edinburgh does host major musicians, like Robbie Williams at the Murrayfield Stadium, Murrayfield (☎ **0131/346-5000;** walking

distance from Haymarket Station), where the national rugby team plays. For smaller acts with more of a cool quotient like rapper The Streets, check out the Corn Exchange (11 New Market Rd.; ☎ **0871/700-0090;** bus: 4 or 28). The 3,000 seat capacity means it's a hot spot for up-and-coming indie bands too. Smaller still is the Liquid Room (9c Victoria St.; ☎ **0131/225-2564;** bus: 35). To see a schedule for this intimate venue go to www.liquidroom.com. Of course, as it gets closer to the busy Festival month of August, you'll find the music scene is better and more varied.

Nightclubs

Clubbing may be pretty passé at this stage, but the Edinburgh nightclub scene is still lots of fun if you want to sweat the night away on a dance floor.

→ **Bongo Club** If indie tunes are more your scene, check out Bongo Club. The music is less mainstream than elsewhere and drinks won't burn a hole in your wallet. The club showcases young talent, like bands from the music school at nearby Napier University. *37 Holyrood Rd.* ☎ *0131/558-7604. www.the bongoclub.co.uk. Cover £3–£5. Bus: 35.*

➜ **C.C. Bloom's** For the best of the gay club scene, look no further than C.C. Bloom's, aptly named after Bette Midler's character in *Beaches*. It's open daily till 3am and charges no cover, so expect it to be totally packed. The music is varied, although you can definitely be sure you'll hear some crowd-pleasing, staple faves from Kylie Minogue. *23–24 Greenside Place.* ☎ *0131/556-9331. Bus: 7 or 21.*

➜ **The Honeycomb** This is the place to see famous DJs from London and farther afield. Be warned that you might pay up to £15 at the door. The Honeycomb is best known for Manga, the longest running Drum-and-Bass night in the U.K. *15–17 Niddry St.* ☎ *0131/556-2442. www.the-honeycomb.com. Cover £5–£15. Bus: 35.*

➜ **Po Na Na** Always a safe bet as its part of a successful chain. The Moroccan theme is a tad overdone and you certainly won't feel you're in Marrakech, but the music is the real draw: chart-topping hip-hop, or sometimes '80s hits. *438 Frederick St.* ☎. *0131/226-2224. Cover £2.50–£5. Bus: 80.*

➜ **Venue** Located on Calton Road, Venue seems to be the most popular club at the moment, with three floors of different music and often live acts. They operate a popular School Disco night, where everyone wears their old—you guessed it—school uniform. Cue lots of Britney impersonators in pigtails and really, really short kilts. *15–21 Calton Rd.* ☎ *0131/557-3073. www.edinvenue.com. Cover £8. Bus: 2 or 35.*

Bars & Lounges

➜ **Black Bo's** Black Bo's is close to local hostels so you'll find the usual traveler types—Euros, plus Australians and South Africans—enjoying the relaxed atmosphere and good DJs. Because of the vegetarian restaurant attached to Bo's, expect a few pseudo-intellectual types milling around. *57–61 Blackfriars St.* ☎ *0131/557-6136. www. blackbos.com. Bus: 35.*

➜ **Opal Lounge** If you're in search of a hot Edinburgh Uni student to take home with you, check out the chic Opal Lounge, a favorite of Prince William when he attended St. Andrew's. It's on George Street and stays open till 3am every day, serving sugary cocktails to couture-wearing rich kids. Oh, and such is the glamour and sophistication of Opal Lounge that you wouldn't dare call the bartenders anything but Mixologists! *51 George St.* ☎ *0131/226-2275. www.opallounge. co.uk. Bus: 13, 19, or 41.*

➜ **The Outhouse** Located on pub-laden Broughton Street, The Outhouse is modern and stylish. The decor is all chocolaty brown with cube seats, and there's a beer garden for the odd hot day. The clientele is young, good-looking, and often of the Cute Gay Boy variety. *12a Broughton St.* ☎ *0131/557-6668. Bus: 8 or 17.*

➜ **Pond Bar** A bit farther out in Leith, on Bath Road, is the Pond Bar, so called because of the large fish pond out back. The coolness quotient is increased here with the odd mix of furniture and European beers. You'll feel like you've walked out of Edinburgh and into Amsterdam for the night. *2–4 Bath Rd.* ☎ *0131/467-3825. Bus: 12.*

Pubs & Pub-Crawls

If you don't fancy a pub-crawl down **Best Rose Street,** there are some more organized ways to see the best pubs in the city. One fun way to do it is to go to www. electrum.co.uk/pubs, an amusing site with a few virtual pub tours guided by students or history buffs depending on your preference. Once you've decided which tour looks best online, you can join the fun in real life.

Even more entertaining is the **Edinburgh Literary Pub Tour.** You'll be guided by professional actors, and over the course of 2 hours you'll see historically important pubs while hearing the stories of their patrons or the famous novels and plays in which they are featured. You'll hear all about the back story for beloved tales, such as that of Dr. Jekyll and Mr. Hyde, and you might be shocked by the meaning behind Robert Burns' erotic poetry. Go to www.edinburgh literarypubtour.co.uk for more information on the tour and how to book.

→ **The Abbotsford** For a more traditional experience—it's been around since 1887—head to The Abbotsford at the eastern end of Rose Street, a pub mecca. The gaslights and wood paneling have been preserved, and the menu of beers on tap changes weekly. The pub food is reasonably priced. Drinks are served Monday through Saturday from 11am to 11pm. Platters of food are dispensed from the bar Monday through Saturday from noon to 3pm and 5:30 to 10pm. *3 Rose St.* ☎ *0131/ 225-5276. Bus: 3, 31, or 33.*

📺 Best → **Cafe Royal Circle Bar** ★ Edinburgh's most famous pub now shares space with the Oyster Bar of the Cafe Royal, but life continues as usual, especially for the regulars who don't always seem to fit with the opulent Victorian trappings here. Hours for the bar are Monday through Wednesday from 11am to 11pm, Thursday from 11am to midnight, Friday and Saturday from 11am to 1am, and Sunday from 12:30 to 11pm. The restaurant is open Sunday through Wednesday from noon to 2pm and 7 to 10pm, Thursday till midnight, and Friday and Saturday till 1am. *17 W. Register St.* ☎ *0131/556-1884. Bus: 3, 31, or 33.*

Gay Bars

The heart of the gay community is centered on **Broughton Street,** near the Playhouse Theater (bus: 8, 9, or 19). Be sure to check "Nightclubs" for the heavily gay crowd at **Po Na Na.**

→ **Planet Out** If it's a gay bar you're looking for, go to Planet Out, which has more of a lesbian following than most of the local LGBT establishments and it's a good place to warm up before hitting the clubs. The music is the perfect volume for chatting without screaming, and the leopard-print decor hints at the bar's gay-hey-day in the '80s. *6 Baxters Place.* ☎ *0131/524-0061. Bus: 7 or 22.*

Performance Halls

Usher Hall (Lothain Rd; ☎ **0131/228-1155;** bus: 1, 10, 15, or 34) is Edinburgh's answer to Carnegie Hall. During the Festival in August, it may play host to prestigious groups like the London Philharmonic Orchestra. At other times of the year, you might find Joan Rivers dispensing humor or Paul Weller screaming the house down. Go to www.usherhall.co.uk to see a schedule of performers; tickets cost anywhere from £10 to £30. The **Queen's Hall** (Clerk St.; ☎ **0131/668-2019;** bus: 5, 7, 8, or 29) has traditionally hosted classical acts, but lately their new cool website boasts contemporary bands like Elbow and Turin Brakes. See a full list of dates at www.thequeenshall.net; tickets cost up to £15 for the best seats.

Comedy Clubs

There isn't really a thriving comedy club scene in Edinburgh. You'll find **Jongleurs** (at Greenside Place at the top of Leith Walk; ☎ **0870/011-1965;** tickets from £10; bus: 7 or 22), part of a successful chain of clubs where touring acts from all over the world perform as well as in-house acts. After the comedy, there's dancing till the wee hours of the morning. You could also try **The Stand** (5 York Place; ☎ **0131/558-7272;** tickets £1–£10; bus: 8 or 17) known as the top spot for comedy in the city and an important venue during the Fringe Festival. Go on Sunday at lunchtime to get some free laughs with your brunch. Check out www.thestrand. co.uk for more details.

EDINBURGH

Sightseeing

Edinburgh has it all, from ancient buildings (Edinburgh Castle, for one) to verdant parks such as the Princes Street Gardens to top museums, including the National Portrait Gallery. The Old Town and the Royal Mile—so called because the mile-long high street is home to both the Castle and the Palace of Holyroodhouse at either end—are the most tourist-friendly locations, but there's a lot to see a bit farther afield. If you have some time on your hands, venture out to the port town of Leith, stroll in the Botanic Gardens, or head to the futuristic building that houses Our Dynamic Earth, which traces the world's history since the Big Bang. Take in the view from the top of Calton Hill or the surrealist art at the Dean Gallery. With so much to see and do, you'll need to rest every few hours, so it's a good thing that Edinburgh is home to a great variety of evocative, historic pubs.

If you want to find out just about anything that's going on in Edinburgh, buy *The List* magazine from any newsagent, bookshop, and so on. You'll find info on current exhibitions and performances, among other attractions, for both Edinburgh and Glasgow. Otherwise, you could head to the Edinburgh Information Center, on the top level of the Princes Street Mall, right in the heart of the New Town. Their website is www.edinburgh.org so save some time and check that out first.

ᴍ ᴛ ᴠ🎓 The University Scene

Edinburgh University is the most posh "uni" in the country, with wealthy boarding-school brats in designer garb quaffing champagne at local bars and shopping at expensive boutiques like Cruise and Corniche. If you want to meet teens with triple-barrel surnames, head to the south side of town or to upmarket watering holes like the Opal Lounge.

To meet the rest of the student population, check out **Potterow**, a 1,000-person nightclub run by the students in the student union building, which also houses STA travel. One DJ spins oldies and bills himself as "The Big Cheese," so expect (what else?) cheesy music. On weekends, the beat leans more to rock and current radio faves. **Teviot,** another campus building with a big draw, has five bars over seven floors. The fare there includes indie music, pub quizzes, stand-up comedy, and ceilidhs. Call ☎ 0131/650-9195 or log on to www.eusa.ed.ac.uk for current info on what's going on. It will take you to the Student Association front page, and it also links with their fortnightly online magazine, *Hype.* You might also check out www.studentnewspaper.org for the local student newspaper, *The Independent Voice,* which publishes every Tuesday, September through May.

The University itself is located at South Bridge. Call ☎ 0131/650-1000 or see www.ed.ac.uk for general info or to find out whether the dorms will be renting out for the Festival.

While Edinburgh is the best known and most academically rigorous uni in the city, there are others, like **Napier University** (Craiglockhart; ☎ 0500/353-570; www.napier.ac.uk), which has special innovative degree programs like Built Environment, for civil engineering and surveying.

Festivals

January

Burns Night. People around the world toast the bard of Scotland, beloved native poet Robert Burns, and eat some haggis (p. 344), which you might compare to the American dish scrapple. January 25.

March

Ceilidh Culture Festival. This monthlong event features concerts, recitals, workshops, dances, and more. Go to www.ceilidh culture.co.uk. The word *ceilidh* (pronounced "*kay*-lee") translates as "Gaelic social dance," and before the days of disco, ceilidhs were held in village halls on weekends. Throughout March.

April

Beltane. This festival celebrates paganism and the coming of summer. Festivities atop Calton Hill usually include torches, a maypole, the beating of drums, and perhaps some naked dancing. Late April.

June

Royal Highland Show. In Ingliston, near Edinburgh, this agricultural fair is one of the best in Scotland. Come for the food as well as the livestock, flowers, horse jumping, and crafts. For more info, call ☎ **0990/803-0444** or go to www.royalhighlandshow.org. Last week in June.

July

Edinburgh International Jazz & Blues Festival. Billed as the longest-running jazz festival in the U.K., during which the entire city opens its doors to host the best jazz and blues players from all over the world. For more info, call ☎ **0131/667-7776** or check out www.jazzmusic.co.uk. Last week of July and into August.

August

Festival Month. You'll be able to experience the **International, Fringe, Film, Book,** and **Jazz festivals** all over the city. All told, there are over 1,000 shows in the 4-week period, including big-name acts from across the world. Go to www.edinburgh festivals.co.uk for more details. Also, try www.eif.co.uk and www.edfringe.com. Throughout August.

October

International Storytelling Festival. Come celebrate the age-old oral tradition in Edinburgh. Visit www.scottishstorytelling centre.co.uk for more info. Late October.

December

Hogmanay. The New Year's Eve fest is bigger in Edinburgh than in most other cities. Check out the carnival, outdoor theater, fire festival on Princes Street, and torchlight procession. For info, call ☎ **0131/473-2001** or go to www. edinburghshogmanay.org. Last week in December.

Top Attractions

FYI: Note that during the Edinburgh Festival, some of the museums that are usually closed on Sunday *are* open on Sunday. Some museums that are only open in summer may also be open on public holidays. It's worth checking with the tourist office (p. 337) before you head out.

Best → **Edinburgh Castle** ★★ The most famous building in Edinburgh is also the biggest tourist draw. First founded in the 11th century, the only remaining part of the original structure is St. Margaret's Chapel, named after the Saxon wife of the first inhabitant. The role of the Castle over the last few hundred years was one of defense, so many of the displays you'll see are devoted to military history. Visit the spooky castle vaults that were home to prisoners, or see Mons Meg, a 5-ton cannon. *Royal Mile.* ☎ *0131/225-9846. www.historic-scotland.gov.uk. Admission £9.80. Daily 9am–6pm (till 5pm Oct–Mar). Closed Dec 25–26. Bus: 1 or 6.*

Best **FREE** → **National Gallery of Scotland** ★★★ In the center of Princes Street Gardens, this gallery is small as national galleries go, but the collection has been chosen with great care. Cezanne, Renoir, Degas, Tiepolo, El Greco, Velázquez—these are only a few of the masters whose work now resides here. *2 The Mound. ☎ 0131/624-6200. www.nationalgalleries.org. Free admission. Fri–Wed 10am–5pm (extended hours during the festival); Thurs 10am–7pm. Closed Dec 25–26. Bus: 3, 21, or 26.*

FREE → **National Museum of Scotland** ★★★ In an imposing building right off the Royal Mile, the Museum traces the history of Scotland from millions of years ago with displays featuring archaeology, geology, and science. You'll see exhibits on the shipping industry, whiskey distillery, and tartan—everything that makes this country unique. *Chambers St. ☎ 0131/247-4422. www.nms.ac.uk. Free admission. Mon–Sat 10am–5pm (till 8pm Tues), Sun noon–5pm. Walk south from Waverley Station for 10 min. to reach Chambers St. or take bus no. 3, 7, 21, 30, 31, 53, 69, or 80.*

→ **Palace of Holyroodhouse** ★★ The Palace, at the end of the Royal Mile, was built by James IV in the 16th century. Many of Scottish history's most notorious events have transpired here, including the stabbing murder of Mary Queen of Scots' lover by her jealous husband. Check out the Picture Gallery and the Queen's Gallery for portraits of monarchs and the royal collection. HRH Queen Elizabeth still does some entertaining here when in Scotland. *Royal Mile. ☎ 0131/556-5100. Admission £8.50, £7.50 with student ID. Daily 9:30am–6pm (last entry 5pm). Bus: 35 or open-top tours.*

Other Attractions

→ **Dynamic Earth** ★ This former brewery is now a stone amphitheater capped by a translucent futuristic tent. Inside, the galleries celebrate the natural diversity of the Earth. You'll learn about geology, astronomy, and biology here—from the Big Bang to our current high-tech maelstrom. This is an interactive place: Push buttons to make meteor showers, jump onto platforms to simulate earthquakes, stand as a tropical shower creates a rainforest-like effect (including creepy crawlies underfoot). Wander through simulated terrains: polar ice caps, tundra, deserts, and grasslands. There are also specialized aquariums, including some with live sharks, dolphins, and coral. Grab lunch at the restaurant or cafe. *Holyrood Rd. (10-min. walk from Waverley Train Station). ☎ 0131/550-7800. www.dynamicearth.co.uk. Admission £8.45 adults, £4.95 students. Easter–Oct daily 10am–6pm; Nov–Easter Wed–Sun 10am–5pm. Bus: 35 or 36.*

FREE → **Fruitmarket Gallery** The city's leading contemporary art gallery is the Fruitmarket by Waverley Station. You'll find works by leading conceptual artists like Simon Patterson, the Londoner who became famous by adding celeb names to the London tube map in 1992. Also on show here? Works by Beatle wife Yoko Ono. *45 Market St. ☎ 0131/225-2383. www.fruitmarket.co.uk. Free admission. Mon–Sat 11am–6pm; Sun noon–5pm.*

→ **The High Kirk of St. Giles** Just down the street from the Castle is this famous church where Reformation preacher John Knox spoke to crowds. It is considered the Mother Church of Presbyterianism—that is, the Church of Scotland's special, austere brand of Protestantism. Its Chapel of the Order of the Thistle is where the Queen heads for knighting ceremonies in Scotland. *Royal Mile. ☎ 0131/225-9442. Admission £2. Mon–Fri 9am–7pm; Sat 9am–5pm; Sun 1–5pm. Bus: 35.*

→ **Outlook Tower and Camera Obscura** ★ You'll either love this or hate it. You climb to the top of a tower and wait until the group before you is done. Once inside, you're in a room with a periscope-like invention that was built in 1853. From inside, you can see what's happening on nearby rooftops and even on the street below. The scope throws the images onto a circular table while guides

12 Hours in Edinburgh

1. **Sit on the top deck of the double-decker tour bus.** Pick one up at Waverly Station. It's a good way to get oriented.
2. **Climb the path to Edinburgh Castle and check out the impressive views.** Spring for the tour. You'll soak up a little history.
3. **Walk the Royal Mile, starting at the Castle.** Resist buying a sword at one of the tacky souvenir shops.
4. **Head to George IV Bridge and Greyfriars Courtyard beyond.** On the way, have coffee at one of the pubs on this street. This is Harry Potter territory. Look for things that may have influenced J. K. Rowling as she wrote the first volume.
5. **Check out Our Dynamic Earth.** Have lunch at the cafe on the premises.
6. **Take a stroll around the grand Palace of Holyroodhouse.** Allow yourself to be impressed. From here, hike up to Arthur's Seat for a grand view of the Highlands.
7. **Take a taxi to Princes Street.** Try not to spend too much money on the two-for-one book sales at the chain store.
8. **Wander through the National Gallery.** The collections are truly wonderful.
9. **Window-shop on George Street.** Afterwards, dine at one of the upscale little bistros.
10. **Have a pint (try McEwan's ale or Tennent's lager) in one of the numerous pubs on Rose Street.** Strike up a conversation with a local (see "Talk of the Town," earlier in this chapter, for tips on what to say).
11. **Put your glad rags on and head to Opal Lounge.** This is a great spot to party with the uni students.

EDINBURGH

talk about what you're seeing. Another exhibit that covers optical illusions is also fun. *Castlehill.* ☎ *0131/226-3709. Admission £5.75 adults. Apr–Oct Mon–Fri 9:30–6pm, Sat–Sun 10am–6pm, until 7:30pm in July and 7pm in Aug; Nov–Mar daily 10am–5pm. Bus: 1 or 6.*

FREE → **Scottish National Gallery of Modern Art** ★ The NGMA concentrates on the art of the 20th century, and includes works by Miró, Picasso, and Hockney. The outside grounds themselves are works of modern art, with a dramatic "landform" including sculpted mounds of grass and pools designed by acclaimed artists. *75 Belford Rd.* ☎ *0131/624-6200. www.natgal scot.ac.uk. Free admission. Daily 10am–5pm. Closed Dec 25–26. Bus: 13 stops by the gallery* *but is infrequent; nos. 18, 20, and 41 pass along Queensferry Rd., a 5-min. walk up Queensferry Terrace and Belford Rd. from the gallery.*

Gardens & Parks

There's no shortage of gardens or parks in Edinburgh. The most beautiful and peaceful place to hang out in Edinburgh is the 70-hectare (173-acre) Royal Botanic Gardens. Have a cappuccino in Inverleith House, where you'll find the Terrace Café and contemporary art exhibitions, or stroll through the rock gardens or the greenhouses full of exotic plants. If you find yourself exhausted after a day of shopping in the New Town, head to Princes Street Gardens, popular with sun seekers in the summer and autumn months. You can have a 99p flake cone (a British institution when it comes to ice cream—a cone of vanilla topped with a Cadbury Flake bar) while gazing up at the formidable Castle above. Check out the carousel, too; you're never too old. There's also The Meadows, south of the Old Town, which separates the bustling city from the leafy suburbs. The park dates from the 1700s, and you'll be able to imagine little children and their nannies flying kites 100 years ago. This makes the perfect place for a picnic or an impromptu game of football.

Shopping

Edinburgh has trinket shops and places to get a spectacular one-off outfit for a night out. For the best clothes in town, head to George Street, which has the monopoly on chic, with pricey boutiques and jewelers. For more typical high street fashions from national chains like Marks and Spencer and Topshop, head to Princes Street, the long stretch of shops overlooking the Castle in the New Town. Cockburn Street is Edinburgh's indie strip, with three record/CD stores: Underground Solu'shun, Fopp, and Avalanche.

→ **Corniche** If it's sophisticated and slightly offbeat, expect to find it at Edinburgh's coolest boutique. It is filled with designs by Vivienne Westwood, Jean-Paul Gaultier, and Yohji Yamamoto among others. *2 Jeffrey St. (near the Royal Mile).* ☎ *0131/556-3707.*

MTV **Best** → **Elaine's Vintage Clothes**
★ With a following that's been loyal for more than 20 years, Elaine's store gathers together well-made, beautifully tended vintage clothing from the '30s through the '70s. The boho sensibility includes silk scarves, boas, and the articles themselves. *55 St. Stephen St.* ☎ *0131/225-5783.*

→ **Harvey Nichols** The ultimate department store moved into Edinburgh in 2002—known as Harvey Nicks, it is an exclusive London-based landmark selling high-end wares like Jimmy Choo shoes, plus clothes ranging in style from Juicy Couture sweats to amazing Lanvin gowns. Its Forth Floor restaurant (spelling intentional—get it? Firth of Forth?) is worth the trip in itself. *30–34 St. Andrew Sq.* ☎ *0131/524-8388. www.harvey nichols.com.*

→ **Jenners** This is Edinburgh's favorite department store and a Scottish landmark, selling everything including wonderful gifts like Dundee marmalade and shortbread. Right in the heart of Princes Street, Jenners is the reason this area is so well known for shopping. *48 Princes St.* ☎ *0131/225-2442. www. jenners.com.*

→ **Ness** This small chain store is a haven of taste amid the tacky shops on the Royal Mile. If you don't want to take a kilt home but still want something with a Scottish flavor, check out the one-of-a-kind jewelry, scarves, and whimsical Wellington boots here. Everything in Ness has been sourced from various parts of Scotland, so it's authentic without being cheesy. *367 High St.* ☎ *0131/226-5227.*

→ **One World Shop** This Fair Trade shop sells things you probably didn't know you wanted—a white-shell picture frame from India or woven Vietnamese boxes—but once you've had a look at the posters of children slaving away in fields, you'll be parting with your hard-earned cash. *St. John's Church, Princes St.* ☎ *0131/229-4541. www.oneworld shop.co.uk.*

Florence

There's something about the cradle of the Renaissance and the capital of Tuscany that makes you want to stand up straighter as you traipse from sight to sight, or strike your best sophisticated-person pose as you idle on a street corner, trying to read your map. Italy's most refined big city, Florence has roots that go back several thousand years to Etruscan and Roman times, but it's the golden age of Firenze—the 14th and 15th centuries—that is the overriding theme, and it's preserved in incredibly sharp focus here today. From the medieval stage set of Piazza della Signoria to graceful Renaissance churches and squares to grids of narrow, noble streets lined with sandstone *palazzi*, walking around the historical center of Florence is like time-warping back to the fabulous 1400s.

Though its greatest art and architecture might have been created half a millennium ago, Florence is far from over the hill. The Tuscan gregariousness of its residents gives the city plenty of Italian vitality, and a large student population keeps the nightlife going strong year-round. Everywhere you go in Florence, there's a mash-up of ambient noise: the beeping of scooters, the idle chatter seeping out of the ubiquitous gelato shops, the clinking of wine glasses in the open-air restaurants, the classical guitarist busking in Piazza della Repubblica. When darkness falls on Florence, the city takes on a stunning, mystical aura unlike anything you'll experience during the bustle of daytime. The monuments are floodlit, and the streets seem haunted by the ghosts of Florence's illustrious and sometimes violent past. It's not too hard to imagine a Renaissance prince walking by and tipping his hat to you on

Via dei Calzaiuoli; the din of marble hoists and workmen on the construction site of the Duomo; or the satisfied roar of the masses every time someone was burned at the stake below Palazzo Vecchio.

The Best of Florence

○ **The Best Hostel:** The **Hostel Archi Rossi** is likely the best hostel in Italy, so don't pass it up if you're backpacking in Florence. See p. 365.

○ **The Best Doable Hotel:** The proud owner of **Hotel Burchianti** treats all her guests like royalty and makes sure that you have enough caffeine in your system before you hit the town. See p. 370.

○ **The Best Gelateria:** They scoop out the gelato by the gallon at **Vivoli** daily. An afternoon spent in Santa Croce is nowhere near complete without a visit to this institution. Prepare yourself for the most delicious brain freeze ever. See p. 376.

○ **The Best Museum on a 5€ budget:** One of the few Florentine sites with an admission fee lower than 5€, **Santa Croce** is, of course, a church in the southeast part of the city; but it offers a collection of

frescoes and sculptures by some of the greats, including Giotto and Donatello, that outshines many a museum. You'll also find a who's who of Florence buried within the grounds of Santa Croce—Michelangelo and Galileo's mortal remains are permanent residents of the gorgeous church. See p. 384.

○ **The Best Dive Bar:** The tiny street of Via delle Seggiole is a little eerie, but that's what makes **Teatro Scribe** so charming. Revelers flock to the grungy watering hole for cheap beer when everything else closes at 2 or 3am. See p. 377.

○ **The Best Bling Bar:** Sunglasses are a must at **Capocaccia,** not for the intense Tuscan sun, but to shade your eyes from the blinding glare from the ridiculous jewelry worn by the clientele. Just strut around with a little attitude and you'll be fine. See p. 376.

Getting There & Getting Around

Getting into Town

BY AIR

There are no direct flights to Florence from the U.S. Nonstop flights from the States to Italy go to Rome or Milan. If your flight lands in Rome, the **Leonardo Express** train will take you from Fiumicino International Airport to the Roma Termini train station for 9.50€. From Rome's central station, trains leave almost every 30 minutes to Florence's Santa Maria Novella station (trip time: 1¹/₂–2¹/₂ hr., depending on the class of train). If you fly into Milan's Malpensa airport, catch the **Malpensa Shuttle** bus (4.50€; ☎ 02-5858-3185) into Milano Centrale train

station; from there, trains for Florence's Santa Maria Novella station depart every 30 minutes or so (trip time: 3–4 hr., depending on the class of train).

If you fly into other European cities, such as London, Paris, Amsterdam—or even Rome or Milan for that matter—you can catch a connecting flight into Florence's **Peretola-Amerigo Vespucci** domestic airport. When you arrive, for 1€, you can take bus no. 62 into the center of the city.

Another option is flying through Pisa's **Galileo Galilei** airport. Pisa is only an hour from Florence by train or bus. If you're flying out of Pisa, the Florence Air Terminal, at track

FLORENCE

no. 5 at Florence's Santa Maria Novella train station, offers a convenient setup where you can check your luggage and get your boarding pass, then take the train to Pisa (trip time: 1–2 hr.; check the daily schedules).

BY TRAIN

If you're traveling to Florence from within Italy, rail is by far the most efficient, hassle-free option. As you roll toward the city, from the north or the south, you'll pass wonderful little medieval hill towns and cypress-dotted farmland to put you in a Tuscan frame of mind. Florence is one of Italy's most train-friendly cities because its position in the middle of the country means that almost all trains travel through the city's main station, **Firenze-Santa Maria Novella** (not to be confused with the secondary station, Firenze-Campo di Marte). Santa Maria Novella (or S.M.N., as it's known to rail jockeys), is in the northwest part of the city center, and within walking distance of almost all hotels and sights. (It's also a fine example of fascist, or rationalist, 1930s architecture.) If you're heading into Florence by rail from other parts of Europe, you'll often have to disembark from your international train and hop on a national (Trenitalia) train in Bologna, Milan, Turin, or Venice.

Keep in mind that it's not at all unusual for Italian trains (especially the regional lines) to run a few minutes to an hour behind schedule. The exception is the EuroStar, which almost always runs on time—Mussolini would have been proud. While trains that arrive and depart perfectly on schedule are also quite common, it's a good idea to build an extra hour or two into your schedule to accommodate such potential setbacks.

For more information about the national train system, consult Trenitalia's extremely handy, multilingual website, **www.trenitalia. com**.

BY CAR

Florence is a few kilometers east of the A1 autostrada that runs vertically through much of Italy, from Naples in the south to Milan in the north. The A11 connects Florence to Lucca and all points west, and the Raccordo Firenze-Siena highway links Florence with Siena, 40km (25 miles) to the south, while the SS67 plugs Florence into the party-hearty coast of Romagna, to the northeast. Once you're in the area, try to ditch the wheels in a long-term parking facility on the outskirts of town. Driving into the center of Florence is a nightmare of epic proportions due to construction on the roads surrounding the old city. Parking is another issue entirely; expect to pay upwards of 15€ per day for private lots in the center, or risk getting your ride towed due to unintelligible parking signs.

How about driving a car *outside* the city? Well, that's another matter entirely, and one which we heartily endorse. Tuscany is one of the most beautiful and congenial places in Italy for road-tripping. With its sun-blanketed hills, the cypress-lined country roads, the endless places to stop and eat, it really is as wonderful as those coffee-table books would have you believe. If you're traveling alone or with one other person, consider renting the popular Smart car, mainland Europe's smaller and more cartoonish analogue to the MINI Cooper (they have those here, too). Two-seater Smarts are tiny, fuel-efficient, and shockingly chic. **Happy Rent,** at Borgo Ognissanti 153/r (southwest of Santa Maria Novella station; ☎ **055/2399696;** www.happyrent.com), will rent you a Smart for 75€ per day. Slightly more economical Fiat hatchbacks are available for 65€ per day.

BY BUS

In the wider streets around Santa Maria Novella train station, you'll find the scattered stalls where Lazzi and SITA coach buses gather to pick up passengers, wipe their sweaty windshields, and bitch about their

FLORENCE

aching axles (I told you those cobblestones were a pain). Bus travel in Italy is generally slower (but no less expensive) than train travel, but sometimes it's your only option, especially if you're coming into Florence from a smaller Tuscan hill town that doesn't have a train station. For more info about the myriad destinations accessible by bus, check posted schedules in the offices at the **Lazzi station** (www.lazzi.it) near Piazza Adua, or at the **SITA depot** (www.sitabus.it) on Via Santa Caterina da Siena (directly southwest of S.M.N.).

Getting Around

ON FOOT

You can easily cover the entire breadth of the compact city in a matter of hours on foot. Everything revolves around Piazza del Duomo. If you get lost, try to locate the Duomo by peeking between side streets and alleys. More often than not, you'll be able to backtrack to the Duomo and reacquaint yourself with the layout of the streets radiating from the center. Of course, this being Italy, street names change every few blocks, and street numbers are even more confusing: They don't really follow any sort of ordinal sequence, and furthermore, they're divided into rosso ("red," commercial addresses) and nero ("black," residential addresses), which explains the "r" or "n" you'll see after street numbers.

In any case, Florence's diabolical street plan will probably have you crumpling up that city map and utilizing your newfound knowledge of Italian curses, such as the ever-useful *"Ma che cazzo?!?"* ("WTF?"). For finding your way to restaurants and bars, you'll definitely need a good, highly detailed map (available at most newsstands). Otherwise, locals are helpful and proficient enough in English and hand signals to help you on your way.

Besides the Duomo, Florence's other useful navigation tool when you're on foot is the river Arno. The bridges that connect the northern and southern halves of the city serve as handy markers for the main streets of Florence. Going north from Ponte Vecchio will lead you to Via Calimala, Piazza della Repubblica, and the Duomo. Ponte Santa Trinità will bring you through the swank Via de' Tornabuoni area, and Ponte alle Grazie leads tourists north to Santa Croce and south to Via de' Renai (where you can visit the chic nightspots Negroni and Zoe).

BY MOTOR SCOOTER

You can't get more Italian than traveling by motor scooter. In Italian cities, a *motorino* is not only cool—it's as essential a tool in the human existence as the opposable thumb. You'll find that every block in Florence has at least a dozen *motorini* parked along, or on top of, the sidewalk. With murderous gas prices and claustrophobic streets, it's no wonder Florentines prefer Vespas to Escalades. Maneuvering through the crowded and busy historical center on the back of your own 50cc bike can be a thrill, but until you've got a few miles in dense traffic under your belt, stick to the wider, less-congested thoroughfares on the outskirts of town. If you decide to brave the throngs of tourists, prepare to have a trigger finger on the horn and one foot ready to steady yourself on the ground. **Due Ruote,** a division of Happy Rent (Borgo Ognissanti 153/r, southwest of Santa Maria Novella station; ☎ **055/2399696;** www.happyrent. com), has Piaggio Liberty 50cc (plenty of power, even for two riders) scooters for 40€ a day, with discounted rates for longer-term rentals and plenty of helmets for rent.

Note: You'll need an international driver's permit to drive a scooter in Italy. See "Getting Around" in the "Basics" chapter for more info.

BY BUS

The only form of public transit in Florence is the **ATAF** bus, which you might never use, unless you go to the hills (for Piazzale Michelangelo, take bus no. 12 or 13; for Fiesole, take bus no. 7; all leave from Piazza Santa Maria Novella). Tickets good for 60 minutes cost 1€ and can be purchased at any newsstand or *tabacchi* shop. If you plan on using the bus within a larger time frame, you can obtain a ticket valid for 3 hours for 1.80€. A 24-hour ticket is also available for 4.80€. Don't forget to validate the ticket once you board the bus at one of the yellow timestamping machines. If you get caught riding without a validated ticket, you're in for a heavy fine. If all the machines are broken, notify the bus driver. Smaller, electric buses can get you close to the *centro storico,* but are not necessary in the compact area. A bus map would be handy, but ATAF hasn't gotten around to printing one just yet. In the meantime, schematics and schedules of the various lines are online at **www.ataf.net**, or you can call their offices at ☎ 055/56502222.

BY TAXI

For the most part, you'll have no use for taxis, but if you're carrying heavy luggage and just want to get from the train station to your hotel in the Oltrarno without a hassle, taxis are handy indeed. The other situation in which you might want a cab is if you're going out to any of the nightspots in the outskirts. There are **taxi stands** in front of the train station and in Piazza Santa Maria Novella, Piazza della Repubblica, Piazza del Duomo, Piazza Santa Croce, Piazza San Marco, and Piazza di Santa Trinità. You can also **call** for a cab at ☎ **055/4242,** 055/4390, or 055/4798. When the operator picks up, give the street address of your location as clearly as possible, and if there's a cab available, a recorded voice will tell you the *sigla* (medallion number) of the taxi they're sending. It's usually a city or river name, followed by a number (for example, Arno 55).

BY BICYCLE

Bikes are perfect if you're not ready to tackle the noisy, gas-powered scooter. Bikes can get you in the even narrower back alleys and are a much cheaper option. You can rent a two-wheeler from **Geordie Chopin,** located in several areas of Florence (in Santa Croce, they're at Via Fiesolana 10/r, just north of Piazza G. Salvernini; ☎ **055/245013**). **Florence by Bike** (Via San Zanobi, 91/r, at Via delle Ruote; ☎ **055/488992**) is another bike-rental outfit, where city bikes go for 7.50€ for 5 hours, or 13€ per day.

FLORENCE

Florence Basics

Florentines don't have specific names for the different parts of the city center—they generally just divide it into the area around the **Duomo** (north of the Arno), and the **Oltrarno** (south of the river). To help you understand what sort of scene you might encounter if you wander in various directions within the heart of the old city, we've broken down the lay of the land into the following arbitrary neighborhood distinctions, based around principal monuments, piazzas, or churches. The longest distance you might cover in any one stretch, from Santa Maria Novella train station in the west to Santa Croce in the east, for instance, is a leisurely 30-minute walk.

SANTA MARIA NOVELLA (S.M.N.) For better or worse, most visitors' first taste of Florence is the neighborhood around the train station, in the northwest part of the city center, and it can get a little scummy with vagrants that ply Via Nazionale, making obscene comments at tourists. Some bright spots in the area include the church of Santa Maria Novella to the south, and its adjacent grassy piazza, a clean and relaxing spot to wait for a train. Around here, you'll have no trouble finding an economical place to sleep;

there are a ton of hotels within a 1-block radius to satisfy any budget.

THE DUOMO There is never a shortage of tour groups and other camera-toting pedestrians in the geographic center of Florence, about a 10-minute walk east of the train station. Busloads of visitors stream from the monumental cathedral, Santa Maria del Fiore, and its baptistery, on down to the Ponte Vecchio every day, and countless souvenir stores take advantage of this by bumping up prices on things such as film, maps, drinks, and other traveler necessities. Naturally, you'll also find most of Florence's high-end hotels clustered around the city's most famous landmark. Just to the southwest, Piazza della Repubblica is another large square—and not a particularly pretty one—with its fair share of cafes and buskers. For shoppers, the streets just south of the Duomo are packed with midrange stores of every kind.

PIAZZA DELLA SIGNORIA A few blocks southeast of the Duomo, this enormous L-shaped square around the crenellated and clock-towered Palazzo Vecchio has long been the civic heart of Florence; it's also where the city's avalanche of art really begins. A marble statue of Neptune, atop his fountain, can be found in the northwest corner of Piazza della Signoria. There, he crooks his neck and watches the exit doors of the Uffizi gallery spit out busloads of tourists like exhaust fumes. When night falls, summer crowds around Piazza della Signoria are often treated to open-air concerts near the entrance of the Uffizi. During these free shows, moving about is nearly impossible—you're better off hanging around the gelaterias and restaurants on the fringes of the square. For the best views, try visiting after midnight. When the crowds thin out, the Uffizi, the fountain of Neptune, and the Palazzo Vecchio are illuminated by floodlights, and the expansive "square" becomes a truly memorable sight.

SAN LORENZO Between the train station and the Duomo, this neighborhood was the Medicis' old stamping grounds, but today, it's most famous for its markets. Shopping here can be hectic but gratifying—the stalls of Mercato di San Lorenzo and Mercato Centrale are a raucous collection of leather vendors, Florentine stationery sellers, and produce hawkers. Watch your purse or wallet, as pickpockets love the cramped conditions and won't hesitate to snatch your euros. Sights worth checking out in this 'hood are the church of San Lorenzo and the attached Laurentian Library, an unusual architectural work by Michelangelo.

SAN MARCO Despite the long queues outside the Galleria dell'Accademia to see Michelangelo's *David*, the largely residential area of San Marco, north of the Duomo, remains relatively quiet. Everything and everyone seems more laid-back as they stroll through the cafe-lined Piazza San Marco. With the university a few blocks away, it's not surprising that you'll find Florence's more alternative stores and restaurants in San Marco. Also in the neighborhood is the magnificent porticoed Piazza Santissima Annunziata.

MTV Best SANTA CROCE The eastern end of the old city is home to funky boutiques and the church of Santa Croce. In the streets surrounding Piazza Santa Croce, you'll find workshops of leather artisans where leather hounds will find goods of impeccable quality and a selection far more varied than at the busy market stalls of San Lorenzo. Also in this vicinity is **Vivoli** (p. 376)—a visit to Florence is not complete until you sample its unparalleled gelato.

PIAZZA SANTA TRINITÀ The glitziest of stores, including the world headquarters of Ferragamo, grace Piazza Santa Trinità, north of Ponte Santa Trinità, one bridge west of Ponte Vecchio. Compared to its ever-popular cousin, Ponte Santa Trinità seems deserted,

Talk of the Town

Four ways to start a conversation with a local

Though friendly and helpful, Italians have a flair for making conversation that is reverential and deprecating at the same time.

1. **Stately Vespas versus Moto Guzzi crotch-rockets?** Is it better to ride through the streets with your hair blowing gently in the wind or tear across the cobblestones striking fear into the hearts of tourists?

2. **Italian food versus any other country's food?** Bad news: It's a very short conversation. Good news: It's usually followed by a great Italian meal.

3. **Skyscrapers versus Florentine architecture?** Rail against decorative ornamentation in favor of glass boxes and see if you can start a fight.

4. **Italian soccer versus American football?** "Ah, fooobaall, but yew Americans do not like fooootbaall. We Italians looove fooootbaall. Gracefuull and elegant. How do you say . . . beautiful."

but it provides one of the best perches in all of Florence from which to admire the Arno and Ponte Vecchio. Florentines and travelers with bulging wallets can be seen up and down the high-end retail corridor of Via Tornabuoni, toting bags with the designer boutique names (Prada, Pucci, Cavalli, and Tod's).

OLTRARNO The district "beyond the Arno" (on the southern side of the river) is the preferred hangout of Florence's more bohemian citizens. With the galleries of the Pitti Palace and the Boboli Gardens serving as the main attraction, the westernmost end is all that most tourists see of the Oltrarno. Cool lounges like Negroni and Zoe, east of Ponte Vecchio, keep Florence's south side throbbing after nightfall. You'll also find incredible inconspicuous hotels and restaurants hidden along streets like Borgo San Jacopo, home to the Cinghiale Bianco, a fantastic Tuscan osteria, and the luxurious Hotel Lungarno.

THE HILLS Rising to the north and east of the city are the stately green hills of Florence. A few cultural attractions thrive in the distance, but the fresh air and vistas are the real reasons people head for the higher ground. Florentines' preferred hilltop retreat is the town of **Fiesole,** a 25-minute ride on bus no. 7 from Piazza Santa Maria Novella. More centrally located, but still requiring a hike (or bus), Piazzale Michelangelo is a magnificent perch on the southeastern end of the Oltrarno.

Tourist Offices

Stock up on your basic maps and brochures at the train station branch of Florence's tourism board (Piazza della Stazione 4; ☎ 055/212245; Mon–Sat 8:30am–7pm, Sun 8:30am–1:30pm). For even more information, head toward the Duomo. The tourist office on Via Cavour, 1/r, just north of Via de' Gori (☎ 055/290832; www.firenzeturismo.it; Mon–Sat 8:30am–6:30pm, Sun 8:30am–1:30pm.) has an even more comprehensive collection of brochures and maps. But instead of getting the stuff for free, you'll have to pay a nominal fee for their goods and services.

YOUTH INFORMATION SERVICES Unfortunately, there's no physical office where visitors can chat up clerks behind a layer of Plexiglas. Give them a ring at ☎ 055/2347329, and for your first question, ask them why they haven't opened up an office.

Recommended Websites

Most of these homepages are in Italian; click on the British-flag icon for the English version of the site.

○ **www.ataf.net**: The official site of Florence's public transit authority is the only place to find detailed bus maps and schedules.

○ **www.comune.fi.it/inglese**: Florence's municipal website, with event listings and basic city info here.

○ **www.firenze.net**: Independent tourism portal with info on events, nightlife, and weather, plus accommodations booking service for Florence and Tuscany.

○ **www.firenzemusei.it**: Admission fees, hours of operation, reservation numbers, and other practical info about Florence's most important museums.

○ **www.firenzeturismo.it**: Official site of the Florence tourism board has links to art-historical information, visitor services, a comprehensive hotel and restaurant-finding tool, and much more.

○ **www.trenitalia.com**: Find train timetables, prices, and other info on the official website for Italy's national train system.

Culture Tips 101

LANGUAGE   For decades, the open-air Renaissance classroom that is Florence has hosted platoons of foreign students, so English is widely spoken in the historical center. In fact, Florence is perhaps the only place in Italy where you can walk into a bar, deliver your best *"una Coca-Cola, per favore,"* and they'll respond, in a perfect, bored-American accent, "Diet or regular?"

DRESS   Summer brings out the fashionistas. Men aren't at all shy when it comes to experimenting with colors. Dudes will don the clam diggers and linen shirts, but, like the women, accessories are the focal points.

Be it a pair of outrageous sneaks or neon belts, outfits aren't complete without the extra exclamation point. More casual dress involves T-shirts with asymmetrical prints and designer jeans. Women are a little edgier. Of course, their accessory of choice comes in the form of the big-label and big-lensed sunglasses. Dolce & Gabbana is the popular label among the 20-somethings for both eyewear and clothes.

DRINKING & DRUGS   While Florentines have seen far too many exchange students' away-from-home antics to be shocked by outrageous behavior anymore, it's never cool to be an obnoxious drunk in this refined and elegant city. Young Florentines definitely know how to party, but there are some ground rules: (1) no singing "Come On Eileen" on Ponte Vecchio at midnight, (2) no open containers unless you see other well-groomed locals doing it, and (3) no body shots off *David*'s toe!

While Italy's immaculately clad Caribinieri—Italy's royal police force—are notorious for looking the other way, they are fairly strict about public drug consumption. It's not something anyone wants to be stopped for because it is definitely, no-question-about-it illegal.

Recommended Books, Movies, & Music

BOOKS

No survey of Tuscan literature can start anywhere but with Dante Alghieri, the 14th-century poet whose *Divine Comedy*, also published separately as *Inferno, Purgatorio,* and *Paradiso,* was Italy's first great epic poem since antiquity and the first major work to be written in the local vernacular (in this case, Florentine) instead of Latin. Allen Mandelbaum's edition of *Inferno* (Sagebrush, 1999) has the Italian and English translation side by side. The next generation of Tuscan writers produced Giovanni Boccaccio, whose *Decameron*

(Penguin, 2003), a story of 100 tales told by young nobles fleeing the Black Death, is Italy's *Canterbury Tales.*

E. M. Forster's *A Room with a View* (Bantam, 1988), half of which takes place in Florence, and *Where Angels Fear to Tread* (Vintage, 1992), set in San Gimignano, are perfect tales of uptight middle-class Edwardian society in Britain and how it clashes with the brutal honesty and seductive magic of Italy.

Poet and professor Frances Mayes can make us all jealous with her best-selling *Under the Tuscan Sun* (Broadway, 1996) and its sequel *Bella Tuscany* (Broadway, 1999), which chronicle her experience of buying and renovating a Tuscan dream house outside Cortona, exploring her new neighborhood, and cooking in her new kitchen.

Recently, a few literary histories set in Florence have enjoyed wild success. Ross King's slim tome *Brunelleschi's Dome* (Walker, 2000) tells the fascinating story behind the building of Florence's Duomo.

MOVIES

Tuscany's countryside and hill towns have served as backdrops for everything from Kenneth Branagh's *Much Ado About Nothing* (you can stay in the villa where it was filmed), to 1999's *A Midsummer Night's Dream* and *Tea with Mussolini.* And, in *The English Patient,* Ralph Fiennes convalesces in a monastery outside Siena, and there are cameos by Montepulciano and Pienza.

The greatest talent to come out of Tuscany in the past few years is actor, director, writer, and comedian Roberto Begnini, creator of several slapstick mistaken-identity romps *(Johnny Stecchino, Il Mostro)* available with subtitles on the foreign film shelf of your favorite video store. Then, in 1998 this Prato-area native won three Oscars, including Best Foreign Film and Best Actor (only the second non-English-speaking actor to do so)—with *La Vita è Bella (Life Is Beautiful),* an unlikely yet successful tragicomic fable set partly in Arezzo of one Jewish father trying to protect his young son from the horrors of the Holocaust by pretending the concentration camp they've been sent off to is one big game.

MUSIC

Florence, like all of Italy, is known for its long history of folk and classical music. When it comes to popular music, though, American imports—including everything from rap to pop—tend to rule the charts.

Florence **Nuts & Bolts**

Cellphone Providers & Service Centers Several stores rent cellphones to tourists short-term. The best provider is **Campus Telecom** (Via de' Conti 22/r, near San Lorenzo; Mon–Sat 10am–10pm, Sun noon–9pm; ☎ 055/2776469; www.webpuccino.it). Visitors can use their services (via Vodafone or Wind). Incoming calls from the U.S. and Canada won't cost you a cent (not the case for the person calling you, unfortunately) and if you dial a number to either country, you'll pay .27€ for each minute.

Embassies & Consulates If you're aching for the sight of the red, white, and blue, look no farther than **the U.S. consulate** at Lungarno Vespucci 38 (200m/656 ft. west of Ponte Vespucci; ☎ 055/266951). It's open Monday to Friday from 9am to 12:30pm and, by appointment only, from 2 to 4:30pm. The **U.K. consulate** is at Lungarno Corsini 2 (☎ 055/284-133) and is open Monday to Friday from 9am to 12:30pm and 2:30 to 4:30pm. Citizens of other countries must go to Rome for their consulates (p. 797).

FLORENCE

Emergencies   In an emergency, call the Polizia at ☎ 113; for non-emergencies (like lost or stolen property), use ☎ 055/49771 or visit the main police station (*questura*) at Via Zara 2 (near San Lorenzo). You can also turn to Italy's Army police force, the Carabinieri (who wear red-striped trousers designed by Valentino), to report emergencies or other disturbances of the peace. Call the Carabinieri at ☎ 112 for emergencies only; for non-emergencies, ☎ 055/2061. Their station (*caserma*) is at Borgo Ognissanti 48 (west of Santa Maria Novella). If your pocket gets picked, turn to the multilingual tourist aid police at Via Pietrapiana 24/r (near Santa Croce; ☎ 055/203911). To report a fire, a gas leak, or a grandma stuck in an elevator, dial ☎ 115 for the Vigili del Fuoco (fire department).

For medical emergencies, call an ambulance at ☎ 118, or visit the *pronto soccorso* (emergency room, where you will not be charged for treatment, regardless of your insurance status) at the **Ospedale Santa Maria Nuova** (Piazza Santa Maria Nuova 1, just east of the Duomo; ☎ 055/27581). The Polizia Municipale, who handle dog bites and other petty crimes, are at ☎ 055/328333, and the Vigili Urbani, who write parking tickets and tow cars and are the bane of every Italian driver's existence, are at ☎ 055/32831.

Internet/Wireless Hot Spots   **InternetTrain** (www.internettrain.it), with its 15 locations throughout town, is the best place to check your e-mail, online train schedules, or the status of your fantasy baseball team. Walk a few blocks in any direction on a main thoroughfare and chances are you'll run into an InternetTrain. Purchase an access card that keeps track of your minutes (it's valid in any of the locations); rates run about 3€ an hour. They also sell drinks and snacks, making it a great rest stop for sightseers. The location on Via de' Benci, just south of Santa Croce (Via de' Benci 36/r; ☎ 055/2638555; Mon–Fri 9:30am–1am, Sat 10am–1am, Sun noon–1am), is one of the largest, with 30 PCs, and it's frequently full of students and/or young travelers. Other locations are at Borgo San Jacopo 30/r (just south of Ponte Vecchio); Via Zannoni 1/r 9 (near San Lorenzo); Piazza Stazione 14/38 (opposite the train station); and Via Porta Rossa 38/r (south of Piazza della Repubblica).

Laundry   Yeah, that isn't the Arno that reeks of 3-day-old prosciutto. Head to one of the branches of **Wash & Dry** to get your threads smelling a bit fresher. There are eight locations in Florence, two in the city center: Via del Sole 29/r (just south of Piazza Santa Maria Novella) and Via Ghibellina 143/r (near Santa Croce). Both are open daily from 8am to 10pm. One load of washing will run you 3.50€; another 3.50€ will get you 20 minutes in the dryer.

Luggage Storage   Blindly searching for hotels with a 40-pound pack on your back can lead to an embarrassing face-plant on the cobblestones. Luckily, the *deposito bagagli* (luggage storage counter) at Santa Maria Novella train station will help lighten your load. Whatever you don't need to bring while you're out and about can be stowed for 12 hours at 3€ per piece; if you need to keep your stuff there longer, each successive 12-hour period will cost you 2€ per piece.

Post Offices   Florence's main post office is just off Piazza Mercato Nuovo at Via Pellicceria 3 (☎ 055/211147; www.poste.it/en). Open Monday through Friday from 8:15am to 7pm and Saturday from 8:15am to 12:30pm, the post office sells nifty yellow boxes and any other packaging supplies you might need. There are a few forms to fill out for parcels going overseas, but for all the bad press Italian government agencies get, the national mail system is actually quite hassle-free nowadays, with an excellent delivery record.

If you have important documents to send or need to get souvenirs to relatives securely and quickly, and you don't want to chance it with Italian bureaucracy, go to **Mail Boxes Etc.,** and see what brown can do for you: Ship your stuff via UPS from the MBE branches at Lungarno Guicciardini 11/r (☎ 055/212002), Corso dei Tintori 39/r (☎ 055/2466660), and Via della Scala 13/r (☎ 055/268173).

See p. 798 in the Rome chapter for more mailing tips.

Restrooms   When you're out and about in Florence and nature calls, you should have no qualms about stopping in the nearest bar/cafe or restaurant and politely asking if you can use their *bagno*. This is standard practice throughout Italy—unlike in the U.S., Italian bathrooms are *not* for customers only. So, as long as you're polite and not brandishing hypodermic needles, you'll be pointed to the restroom, which is usually a not-very-clean stall and almost invariably *in fondo a destra* (in the back, to the right).

There are also public restrooms in the train station that charge a fee, but they're mostly used by folks who don't know to ask at restaurants and by junkies who got turned away at all the bars and restaurants.

Safety   By and large, Florence is a safe city. The only crime prevalent in the city center is pickpocketing. Keep your belongings close while you shop in the tightly packed market zones and in Santa Maria Novella train station. As with other big cities, avoid dimly lit alleyways, the lowest part of the riverbanks, and unpopulated parks at night.

Telephone Tips   There are public pay phones (*cabina*) at the train station, in major piazzas and bus terminals, and at certain coffee bars (look for the white-and-red phone sign out front or the sticker in the window).

Tipping   See p. 799 in the Rome chapter for tipping advice.

Sleeping

Florence has a ton of accommodations options for every budget and taste, but the city is also inundated almost year-round with tourists, trade-fair attendees, and gourmands, so it pays to book as far in advance as possible. Most of Florence's hotels are concentrated in the area north and just east of the train station, in Santa Maria Novella, and while the train station isn't the most romantic 'hood in town, it really is an easy walk from here to all the sights. During high season, your chances of finding a decent (and decently priced) place go down dramatically as the day wears on.

If you don't have any luck with any of the places listed here, you can call

Consorzio Firenze Albergo (**Florence Hotel Consortium;** ☎ 055/2707278; Mon–Fri 9am–1pm and 3–6pm). You can also do a search through their online database at **www.firenzealbergo.it**. There's also a hotel-reservations kiosk at the train station, staffed by young and usually friendly English-speakers.

See p. 368 on info on staying in an apartment or *agriturismo* (farm).

Hostel

MTV **Best** → **Hostel Archi Rossi** ★★★
Probably the best hostel in Italy is just 2 blocks from Santa Maria Novella station. At first glance, the graffitied walls give the

Florence

SLEEPING ■
Hotel Abaco **9**
Hostel Archi Rossi **5**
Hotel Burchianti **7**
Hotel California **30**
Hotel Caravaggio **3**
Hotel Domus Florentiae **8**
Hotel Galileo **4**
Hotel Giglio **26**
Hotel Lungarno **21**
Hotel Monna Lisa **37**
Hotel Porta Faenza **2**

EATING ◆
Accademia Restaurant **28**
Acqua al Due/La Via dell'Acqua **49**
Caffetteria Piansa **38**
D'Antico Noé **39**
Il Pizzaiuolo **41**
Il Vegetariano **25**
La Maremma **50**
Le Mossacce **40**
Nella **15**
Nerbone **13**
Osteria de' Benci **54**
Paoli **42**
Salumeria Verdi **55**
Trattoria Enzo e Piero **25**
Trattoria La Casalinga **22**
Vivoli **51**

Partying ★
Capocaccia **16**
Central Park **18**
Fiddler's Elbow **11**
The Friends Pub **20**
H2O2 **51**
Loonees **44**
The Lounge **10**
Meccanò **19**
Negroni and Zoe **56**
Red Garter **53**
Space Electronic **12**
Tabasco **45**
Teatro Scribe **48**
Yab Yum **14**

SIGHTSEEING ●
Bargello **47**
Battistero (Baptistery) **33**
Cappelle Medicee (Medici Chapels) **6**
Duomo (Cathedral of Santa Maria
   del Fiore) **34**
Galleria dell'Accademia
   (Academy Gallery) **29**
Galleire degli Uffizi (Uffizi Galleries) **46**
Museo Archeologico
   (Archeology Museum) **31**
Museo dell'Opera del Duomo
   (Duomo Museum) **35**
Orsanmichele **43**
Palazzo Pitti **24**
Piazza della Signoria **48**
Ponte Vecchio **17**
Santa Croce **52**
San Lorenzo and Laurentian Library **32**
Santa Maria Novella **1**

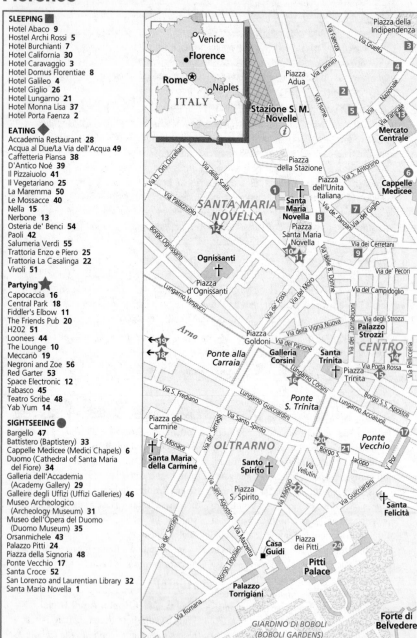

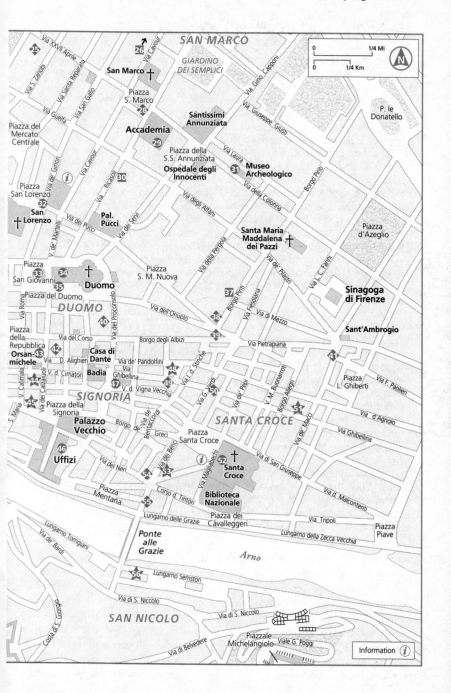

Staying in an Apartment or on a Farm

Each summer, thousands of visitors rent an old Tuscan farmhouse or "villa," a marketing term used to inspire romantic images, in reality guaranteeing no more than four walls and most of a roof.

Actually, finding your countryside Eden isn't that simple, and if you want to ensure a memorable experience, brace yourself for a lot of research and legwork. Occasionally you can go through the property owners themselves, but the vast majority of villas are rented out via agencies (see below).

One of the best agencies to call is **Renvillas.com** (formerly Rentals in Italy), 700 E. Main St., Ventura, CA 93001 (☎ 800/726-6702 or 805/641-1650; fax 805/641-1630; www.rentvillas.com). Its agents are very helpful in tracking down the perfect place to suit your needs. A United Kingdom agency—and one of the best all-around agents in Britain—is **International Chapters,** a division of Abercrombie & Kent, Sloane Square House, Holbein Place, London SW1W 8NS (☎ 08450/700-618; www.villa-rentals.com). Marjorie Shaw's **Insider's Italy,** 41 Schermerhorn St., Brooklyn, NY 11201 (☎ 718/855-3878; fax 718/855-3687; www.insidersitaly.com), is a good, small, upscale outfit run by a very personable agent. One of the most reasonably priced agencies is **Villas and Apartment Abroad, Ltd.,** 370 Lexington Ave., Suite 1401, New York, NY 10017 (☎ 212/897-5045; fax 212/897-5039; www.vaanyc.com).

Tuscany and Umbria are also at the forefront of the *agriturismo* movement in Italy, whereby a working farm or agricultural estate makes available accommodations for visitors who want to stay out in the countryside. *Agriturismi* are generally a crapshoot. They're only loosely regulated, and the price, quality, and types of accommodations can vary dramatically. Some are sumptuous apartments or suites with hotel-like amenities; others are a straw's width away from sleeping in the barn on a haystack. Most, though, are mini-apartments, often furnished from secondhand dealers and usually rented out with a minimum stay of 3 days or a week. Sometimes you're invited to eat big country dinners at the table with the family; other times you cook for yourself. Rates can vary from 15€ for two per day all the way up to 250€—as much as a board-rated four-star hotel in town.

Probably the most fantastic resource—because it is both user-friendly and has an English version—is **www.agriturismo.regione.toscana.it,** with databases of hundreds of farmstays, searchable both by text or by clickable map down to the locality level, with info about each property, a photo or two, and a direct link to each *agriturismo*'s own website.

impression that the hostel was once a squatters' haunt, but look more closely and you'll realize the inscriptions are notes left by previous guests. The rooms, which sleep from 4 to 10, coed or female-only, are extremely clean and spacious, with large closet-like lockers where you can throw your backpack or suitcase. Some rooms have private bathrooms, while others have a shared shower and toilet off the main hallway. The hostel also has a common dining room where fried eggs and bacon are served most mornings, and where movies in English are shown most nights. After a long day of art-gawking, pony up 3€ at the reception snack bar for a sizeable bottle of cold beer and head for the interior garden—furnished with Italianate carved stone benches and tables, plaster casts of the Venus de Milo, and ample greenery, it's an atmospheric spot where you can spend an evening socializing with fellow travelers, or just pre-load before hitting the bars. *Via Faenza 94/r (just north of Via Nazionale).* ☎ *055/290804. www.hostel archirossi.com. 21€ single bed in large dorm (10-person, coed), 22€ in medium dorm (8-person, female only), 23€ in small dorm (6-person, coed or female only), 24€ in small dorm (5-person, coed or female only), 25€ in small dorm (4-person, coed or female only); 30€ single room with shared bathroom; 75€ triple room with private bathroom. Amenities: Internet; laundry facilities; lockers; 11am–2:30pm room lockout; shared bathrooms (in some); TV (in common room); open-air garden/terrace.*

Cheap

→ **Hotel Abaco** ★★ I can't say enough about Bruno, the owner of this place. One look at him, with his Hawaiian shirt and shiny bald head, and all who enter the Abaco feel at ease. Bruno will see to it that you have everything you'll need. He'll do laundry for a reasonable price, and impart his vast knowledge of the town. Well laid-out rooms have old-world furnishings to match the Renaissance theme of the hotel, high wood-beam ceilings, and gilded-edge sofas. Further adding to the charm of the property, each room is named after a famous Italian artist (Caravaggio, Michelangelo, Leonardo, and so on) and, quite adorably, contains prints and color schemes fitting with the respective artist. Guests in a few rooms avail of the common lavatory in the hallway, but most have full private facilities; all are equipped with a private shower. *Via dei Banchi 1 (at Via dei Cerretani).* ☎ *055/2381919. www.abaco-hotel.it. 72€–82€ double, 85€–95€ with private bathroom; 95€–105€ triple, 110€–125€ with private bathroom, 135€–155€ quad with private bathroom.*

Rates include breakfast. Amenities: Internet; laundry service. In room: A/C, TV.

→ **Hotel California** ★ Hotel California offers quite a bit for its relatively low price tag. As with several other hotels in the center of Florence, many rooms have atmospheric little touches here and there—brick arches, frescoes, vaulted ceilings, partial views of the Duomo—that remind you that you're sleeping in the middle of the cradle of the Renaissance. Shower in your simple, spotless bathroom (a few rooms have Jacuzzi tubs), enjoy your buffet breakfast on the cozy terrace, and then get a head start on the *David*-seeking hordes at the nearby Accademia. *Via Ricasoli 30 (2 blocks north of the Duomo).* ☎ *055/282753. www.californiaflorence.it. 60€–120€ single, 75€–180€ double, 120€–243€ triple, 145€–300€ quad. Rates include breakfast. Amenities: Breakfast room. In room: A/C, TV, some bathrooms with Jacuzzi, safe.*

→ **Hotel Porta Faenza** ★ The combination of newer technologies and 18th-century decor is a little awkward in this government-rated three-star a few blocks from the train station. The keycard slots, "do not disturb" buttons at the door, and the talking elevator seem out of place in this otherwise charming and comfortable hotel. Decor is colorful and warm, and some rooms have restored wood-beam ceilings; all rooms have a full private bathroom. The pleasant staff is extremely knowledgeable and will even give you an abridged history of the building, which includes a noteworthy bit of archaeology near the Internet point: a medieval well. *Via Faenza 77 (a few blocks north of Via Nazionale).* ☎ *055/217975. www.hotelporta faenza.it. 60€–100€ single standard, 80€–150€ double standard, 100€–160€ triple standard, 110€–170€ quad. Rates include breakfast. Amenities: Bar; breakfast room; currency exchange; Internet port; laundry service. In room: A/C, TV, hair dryer, minibar, safe.*

FLORENCE

Doable

📺 Best → **Hotel Burchianti** ★★★
If you're lucky, you'll be greeted by the warm smile of Rela, the septuagenarian super-hostess. Rela maintains a gem of a hotel—one of Florence's best boutique properties—in an unassuming part of Via del Giglio. We recommend booking well in advance. Each room contains sumptuous baroque frescoes and stuccoed reliefs that are still being uncovered by the management—the former tenants of the building inexplicably whitewashed the gorgeous 17th-century wall decorations. Furnishings vary from room to room, but everything looks inviting, and is warmly lit. Security, for those concerned, is a non-issue—every guest needs to be buzzed in at the front gate, a painless process. *Via del Giglio 8 (off Via Panzani).* ☎ *055/212796. www.hotelburchianti. com. 90€–120€ single, 130€–170€ double, 160€–220€ triple, 150€–230€ suite, 170€–230€ studio. Amenities: Laundry service; travel desk. In room: A/C, TV, hair dryer, minibar, safe.*

→ **Hotel Caravaggio** ★ Across the street from Piazza Indipendenza, this hotel offers its guests the luxury of having quiet green space right outside its doors. Thanks to recent restorations, guest rooms are immaculate and comfortable. Unfortunately, the renovations were also heavy-handed in places, leaving the hotel a bit too modern-feeling, even though a few wonderful antique touches, like iron stoves, have been preserved. You could almost eat off the pristine, newly installed bathtubs. *Piazza Indipendenza 5 (just north of Via Guelfa).* ☎ *055/496310. www.firenzewelcomehotels. com. 70€–140€ single, 98€–220€ double, 120€–240€ superior double, 140€–250€ triple, 150€–300€ quad. Amenities: Bar (24 hr.); Internet. In room: A/C, TV, Internet, Jacuzzi (in some), minibar, safe.*

→ **Hotel Domus Florentiae** ★ As far as automatic doors go, the Domus has, quite possibly, the slowest sliding door I've ever seen. Once you finally get through the pregnant pause of the entryway, you'll be welcomed by an amicable staff and a bright, elegant reception. There are only 14 rooms, handsomely appointed with ocher- and rose-toned jacquard bedspreads and curtains, wide-plank wood floors, and pretty, understated light fixtures; each has a larger-than-average, clean bathroom. Despite its proximity to the street, the thick windows help ensure a quiet slumber. It's a definite upgrade from the Universo next door. Prices vary wildly from low to high season, so if you're coming in peak periods, the Domus Florentiae moves into "Splurge" territory. *Via degli Avelli 2 (Piazza Santa Maria Novella).* ☎ *055/2654645. www.domusflorentiahotel. com. 85€–180€ single, 95€–250€ standard double, 105€–270€ superior double. In room: A/C, TV, safe, hair dryer.*

→ **Hotel Galileo** ★ The throw rugs on the tiled villa floor and the sturdy dark-wood furnishings give the accommodations here a bucolic quality that you'd normally expect to find in an agricultural hill town outside of Florence. The 31 rooms, decorated in a refined Tuscan style, with warm colors and dark woods, have all the modern comforts you'll need, and the friendly staff will try to accommodate other requests you might have. *Via Nazionale 22/a (near Via Guelfa).* ☎ *055/496645. www.galileohotel.it. 80€–90€ single, 120€ double (single use), 130€–140€ double standard, 150€–170€ double superior, 175€–190€ triple (comes with bottle of red wine). Rates include buffet breakfast. Amenities: Bar; breakfast room; Internet point; travel desk. In room: A/C, TV, minibar, safe, hair dryer.*

→ **Hotel Giglio** ★ The only knock against Hotel Giglio is that it's about a 15-minute walk from the train station or the Duomo. On the plus side, it's close to the Accademia, and the streets surrounding it are especially quiet compared to centrally located hotels in Florence. If you don't mind walking the few extra blocks, Hotel Giglio is the perfect spot for a relaxing night's rest. Rooms are pristine and furnished nicely, with walls painted a rich buttercream hue, and bedding in muted green. The experienced staff, handpicked from well-respected hotels in Italy by the ever-hospitable manager Marco, are veritable fountains of Firenze knowledge. Furthermore, breakfasts are generous, and there's a 24-hour bar. *Via Cavour 85 (at Via Sant'Anna).* ☎ *055/486621. www.hotelgiglio. fi.it. 80€–125€ single, 90€–170€ double, 110€–195€ triple, 130€–220€ quad. Rates include breakfast. Amenities: Breakfast room; travel desk. In room: A/C, TV, Internet, safe.*

Splurge

→ **Hotel Lungarno** ★★★ This is where wealthy travelers book a room to get away from wealthy tourists. The difference between the two is that the former know where to blow their cash, whereas the latter haphazardly reserve a room at a big international chain five-star next to the Duomo. The Lungarno, the flagship of the Ferragamo family's exclusive Lungarno Hotels group, is literally "along the Arno," tucked away in a chic part of Oltrarno. There is no sign proclaiming its presence, nor is there a line of valets waiting to take your Benz. Instead, it sits quietly confident in its own luxurious splendor. The Lungarno incorporates entire archways and vaulted ceilings throughout its cavernous rooms, and throws in posh, contemporary furniture to balance new and old. The location provides guests with unparalleled views of Ponte Vecchio and the Arno. You can always come and have a drink or meal at the hotel's splendid riverside **Borgo San Jacopo** restaurant. *Borgo San Jacopo 14*

(between Ponte Vecchio and Ponte Santa Trinità). ☎ *055/27261. www.lungarnohotels. com. 220€ single, 330€ double (per person), 350€ double classic, 460€ double superior, 520€ double deluxe, 570€ executive, 720€– 1030€ junior suite, 1,380€–2,500€ presidential suite. Amenities: Bar; conference rooms; garage; limo service. In room: A/C, fax and modem line available, satellite TV.*

→ **Hotel Monna Lisa** ★★ The real *Mona Lisa* may be in Paris, but you'll get your fill of Leonardo's demure damsel (known as *La Gioconda* in Italy) at this luxury hotel a few blocks behind (east of) the Duomo. Originally a 13th-century convent, it was converted into a hotel in 1956. Random bits of art (mostly of the *Mona Lisa*) are sprinkled throughout the enormous property, but the most noteworthy is the *Rape of the Sabines* statuette. This miniature, rough version was the model that earned the sculptor Giambologna the commission for the real, full-size marble statue now found in Piazza della Signoria. Another work worth checking out is the painting of the *Mona Lisa* in the common area near the courtyard. Yup, that's a *canna*, or marijuana cigarette, in the madame's coy lips. Art aside, the hotel interior is decadent, with plush chairs, paintings gracing every wall, and high, wood-beam ceilings. The lush courtyard is the perfect place to enjoy your breakfast when the weather is pleasant. *Borgo Pinti 27 (off Via dell'Oriuolo).* ☎ *055/2479751. www. monnalisa.it. 110€–150€ single classic (shower only), 122€–180€ single superior, 140€–230€ double classic (single use), 155€–250€ double superior (single use), 182€–290€ double classic, 207€–350€ double superior, 235€–415€ triple, 270€–497€ quad, 280€–500€ junior suite, 410€–700€ suite. Rates include breakfast. Amenities: Bar; garden; health club; Internet point; solarium. In room: A/C, TV, minibar, safe.*

FLORENCE

Eating

Florentine cuisine takes full advantage of all the ingredients that thrive in the fields of Tuscany, and of the beasts that graze upon it. Menus are never without a good amount of olive oil, tomatoes, mushrooms, truffles, wild boar, and beef.

Once you've settled on a place to stuff your stomach, expect at least two or three courses to arrive at your table. Simple meals traditionally start off with an antipasto, or appetizer; the classic starter in Florence is *crostini,* toasted slices of country bread slathered with some kind of pâté, usually chicken liver (try it, it's quite tasty). After that gets your taste buds going, they'll get you started on the *primi,* or first courses, which are usually some kind of *ribollita* (stewy soup of cabbage, beans, and bread), risotto (rice dish with creamy sauce), or a pasta dish. Save some room for the main Tuscan event: the *secondi,* or meat-based courses. Florence's own *bistecca alla fiorentina* (1-in.-thick beef steak on the bone—mmm!!—meant to be shared by two diners). If you're a vegetarian or vegan, take advantage of the many vegetable-based soups and pastas and, because we're in Tuscany, beans, beans, and more beans!

As for *vino,* you are in Chianti country, so you should probably test Tuscany's most famous red at least once on its native turf. However, any restaurant's *vino della casa* (house red or white wine, brought out in ¼-, ½-, or 1-liter carafes—however you wish) is also made locally and usually very drinkable.

Hot Spots

→ **Accademia Restaurant** ★ CREATIVE FLORENTINE Hailing from Brooklyn, Gianni Aldo's wife has certainly influenced the way the native Florentine runs his restaurant. Many of the dishes in Accademia Restaurant marry traditional Tuscan fare with a Williamsburg twist with great gastronomic success. If you opt out of their four-dish, four-wine prix-fixe menu (35€), you can pick and choose from their a la carte creations. We emphatically recommend the ricotta-and-spinach-stuffed ravioli in a truffle sauce. *Piazza San Marco 7/r.* ☎ *055/ 217343. Lunch primi 6€, secondi 9€; dinner primi 7€, secondi 13€. Daily noon–3pm and 7–11pm.*

→ **Acqua al Due/La Via dell'Acqua** ★★ TUSCAN Show me someone who's studied in Florence in the past 10 years, and I'll show you someone who sings the praises of Acqua al Due. An institution favored by broke exchange program types, this homey trat near Santa Croce is famous for its *assaggio di primi,* a sampling of five different types of pasta or risotto that'll only set you back 8€. If the thought of five rounds of pasta has your carb-conscious soul quaking in its boots, there's also the *assaggio di insalate* (salad sampler). All in all, everything's pretty affordable, they're open late, and you're almost sure to find fellow young international folk with whom to strike up a conversation. Just be sure to make a reservation as they're required. La Via dell'Acqua, the new sister restaurant around the corner, is garnering praise for its comfier vibe. *Via della Vigna Vecchia 40/r (at Via dell'Acqua).* ☎ *055/ 284170. www.acquaal2.it. Primi 7–8€, secondi 8–17€. Daily 7:30pm–1am.*

→ **Nella** ★ FLORENTINE Most mornings start around 11am. Make up for it by indulging yourself at Nella, a small, homey trat between the Ponte Vecchio and Piazza Santa Trinità. Lunch is pretty much a locals' scene. Ask the gruff but energetic owner, Federico, to serve you the *gnocchetti rosé* (mini potato-pasta dumplings in a creamy tomato sauce) in all its messy glory. And then dig in to the pepper-crusted pork loin. The tangy cuts and the accompanying potatoes might be a hair salty for some tastes, but it's still mouthwatering. As Federico has his roots deeply entrenched in music, many visiting artists and musicians stop by Nella for lunch or dinner and a very tight relationship between Federico and the majority of his patrons is obvious. *Via delle Terme 19/r (near Via Pellicceria).* ☎ *055/218925. Lunch primi 6€, secondi 11€; dinner primi 8€, secondi 10€–16€. Daily noon–3pm and 7–10:30pm.*

Cheap

→**Il Vegetariano** ★ VEGETARIAN Florentine and Tuscan food are usually meat-heavy, so for greener alternatives, head for this casual spot, a 10-minute walk north of the Duomo. Il Vegetariano is one of few real restaurants in Florence where all meals are 100% vegetarian. Menus vary from day to day, but you'll find variations on typical local dishes with ingredients like squash, olives, sprouts, and bean curd replacing meat. Leave it to the health-food restaurant to have an alternative service system, too: First you order, then you pay, and then, when your food is ready, you pick up your plate from the server behind the counter. The prices are reasonable. *Via delle Ruote 3or (off Via Santa Reparata),* ☎ *055/475030. Primi 5€–6€, secondi 7.50€–8€. Tues–Fri 12:30–2:30pm, Tues–Sun 7:30pm–midnight. Closed 3 weeks in Aug and Dec 24–Jan 2.*

→**Le Mossacce** ★★ FLORENTINE Finding a restaurant that serves local cuisine that doesn't break the bank *and* is a block away from the Duomo is almost impossible. Le Mossacce is a trattoria small in stature, big on ambience, and easy on the wallet. Once you're seated, chipper waiters will take the time to explain all their dishes and specials-of-the-day. You can be polite, pretending to be interested, and wait until they're

finished, or you can just blurt out *"bistecca alla fiorentina"* the second they arrive. The gorgeous hunk of meat is grilled to perfection by masters. *Via del Proconsolo 55r (1 block south of the Duomo).* ☎ *055/294361. Primi 4.20€–4.70€, secondi 4.70€–14€. Mon–Fri noon–2:30pm and 7–9:30pm.*

→**Nerbone** ★ FLORENTINE/TUSCAN Head to this outpost at the Mercato Centrale and enjoy their *panino con bollito,* a boiled beef sandwich that's dipped in meat juices (Florentines call this *bagnato*). Writer Marchesa Bona Frescobaldi claims that this bagnato is "as much a symbol of Florence as is Michelangelo's *David"*—a bit of an exaggeration, but you get the point. The chefs proudly call their offerings "the food of the people," referring to such dishes as *trippa alla fiorentina* (tripe). The tripe is cooked in tomato sauce with a sprinkling of Parmesan. *Ribollita* is a hearty, slow-cooked stew made with old bread and vegetables (it's far more delicious than it sounds). Also try their chickpea or garbanzo soup and their pasta with Tuscan sausages and beans. Opened in 1872, this simple side-street stall has only five tables, which are always full. Don't despair; join the locals at the bar. *Mercato Centrale (entrance on Via dell'Ariento; ground floor stand no. 292).* ☎ *055/219949. Table reservations not accepted. Main courses 3.10€–8€. Mon–Fri 7am–2pm; Sat 7am–5pm. Closed 1 week at Christmas and 2 weeks in Aug (dates vary).*

→**Salumeria Verdi** SNACK/SANDWICH Stroll by Via Giuseppe Verdi and check out Salumeria Verdi. They always have specials in the afternoon for *primi piatti* (usually variations on lasagna) that will only set you back 3.80€. The serving size is also pretty decent for the price. *Via Giuseppe Verdi 36 (3 blocks south of Santa Croce). Via Verdi 36/r, near Santa Croce* ☎ *055/244517. Main courses 7€–16€. Mon–Sat 8:30am–3pm.*

FLORENCE

Doable

➔ **La Maremma** ★ TUSCAN La Maremma (named after Tuscany's cowboy country) is the place in Santa Croce to grab tasty Tuscan eats. Luca prepares an amazing *quaglia al ripieno Vermentino*. The stuffed quail, doused in the subtle Vermentino wine sauce, is tender and bursting with flavor. Before you dive into the main course though, start off with the traditional *crostini alla fiorentina:* toasted canapés with chicken liver pâté. Throw in the '60s soul hits of Al Green and Aretha Franklin with the sharp red-and-black decor, and you're left with a relaxing and satisfying Florentine dining experience. *Via Verdi 16/r (1 block north of Santa Croce).* ☎ *055/244615. www.ristorante lamaremma.it. Primi 6€–8€, secondi 10–15€. Thurs–Tues open for dinner.*

➔ **Osteria de' Benci** ★ TUSCAN Frequented by plenty of in-the-know locals, this trattoria offers reliably tasty cuisine and great value in a lively setting. Beyond traditional Tuscan plates *(ribollita, trippa alla fiorentina)*, you can also try more creative pastas, which change according to the season. One standout on the list of unusual *primi* is the "drunk spaghetti" *(spaghetti all'ubriacone)*, which is boiled in red wine and then tossed with garlic and *peperoncino* (red pepper). You might want to save your appetite and your euros for their fantastic desserts. *Via de' Benci 13/r (just south of Piazza Santa Croce).* ☎ *055/2344923. Primi 8€, secondi 10€–20€. Daily open for dinner.*

➔ **Trattoria Enzo e Piero** ★★ TUSCAN Tourists who come to Florence in late summer will miss out on this gem of a restaurant, which battens down its hatches for the best part of August. For three generations, the seafood-laden menu has been filling the stomachs of locals and foreigners. A true family business (Massimo runs it, his son is the chef, and his daughter is a hostess), the traditions also translate to the menu: Fish is

served only on Fridays and Saturdays. Plates like the *linguine argentario*, highlighted by cherry tomatoes, assorted seafood, garlic and chile, give your palate a pleasant kick. Still got room for dessert? Try Massimo's *nonna*'s cool, fluffy tiramisu. *Via Faenza 105/r (a few blocks north of the train station).* ☎ *055/214901. Primi 6€, secondi 7–14€. Mon–Sat noon–3pm and 7–11pm.*

➔ **Trattoria La Casalinga** ★ FLORENTINE The meals at "The Housewives Trattoria" are made up of simple but tasty local dishes, and portions are Hungry-Man-sized—this is the place to go when you want to spend less than 10€ *and* fill your stomach to the point of protrusion. The *ribollita* starter stew is robust and satisfying, preparing diners for an even bigger portion of *bollito misto*, a hodgepodge of boiled meats in a salty sauce. It sounds crude, but the flavors are potent and delicious. *Via Michelozzi 9/r (300m/984 ft. south of Ponte Santa Trinità, off Via Maggio).* ☎ *055/2679243. Primi 3.50€–4€, secondi 5€–10€. Mon–Sat noon–2:30pm and 7–10pm.*

Splurge

➔ **Antico Noé** ★★ TUSCAN The sandwich place next door gets much praise, but the tiny osteria of the same moniker deserves some recognition. At "Old Noah's Place," hidden in a somewhat dark alley, a balding beauty named Massimo creates dishes from the freshest ingredients available. I'm talking dude-comes-in-with-a-bushel-of-vegetables fresh. Watch him handpick enormous mushrooms on the side table and then trudge into the kitchen. The atmosphere alone is worth the price and is perfect for a cozy, romantic dinner. With fewer than eight tables and some scattered stools, the setting makes you feel like you're Massimo's personal guest. He'll hoarsely suggest the simple but exquisite pasta with mushrooms, doused only in olive oil and garlic, to start. Massimo serves smaller *filetti* (entrecôte) that he'll cook accompanied by

Gelato: Unmasked, Uncovered & Unfrozen

Gelato, very dense compared to ice cream, is actually less fattening because it's made with milk instead of the heavier, higher-calorie cream. Florentines will tell you that their city is the gelato capital of Italy, and the institution that other gelaterias model themselves after is **Vivoli** (p. 376). Some locals swear by **Badiani** (Viale dei Mille 20r), but it's a hike to the sports stadium. The best *melomero* (my favorite melon flavor, mixing cantaloupe and watermelon) can be found in the **Bottega del Gelato** (Via Por Santa Maria 33r), not far from Ponte Vecchio. Look for the neon sign on the left as you're heading north from the bridge.

Ordering the treat is half the fun. The protocol: First point to the size that you think you can handle, pay the clerk, and take your receipt. Don't limit yourself to a single flavor; even the smallest of cups deserves a variety of tastes. You can ask for as many taster spoons as you'd like and then give the receipt to the scooper point. The dollop of whipped cream *(panna)* on top is optional, but it's free, so why not go for it? Here are a few translations to get you started:

→ **Stracciatella:** Chocolate chip and cream.

→ **Bacio:** Chocolate hazelnut. A derivation of this, **variegato di Nutella,** features ribbons of the gooey topping in a cream gelato base.

→ **Nocciola:** Hazelnut.

→ **Mirtillo:** Wild blueberry.

→ **Frutti di Bosco:** Wild berries.

→ **Zuppa Inglese:** Italian sponge cake.

→ **Fior di Latte:** Just milk and sugar.

For a refreshing combination, give **agrumi** (citrus mix of lemon, lime, and orange) and **melone** (cantaloupe) a whirl. Craving something rich? Combine classic chocolate with **pistachio** (must be gray-green; the neon green variety is just an ultrasweet version that hides the natural taste of the pistachio).

FLORENCE

his favorite ingredient: mushrooms. In summer, cap off your delightful meal with an enormous slice of watermelon. *Volta di San Piero 6/r (just north of Piazza Santa Maria Maggiore).* ☎ *055/2340838. Primi 8€–10€, secondi 15€–20€. Mon–Sat 8am–midnight.*

→ **Paoli** ★ TUSCAN Generally, you'll want to avoid restaurants near the Duomo because, as with hotels, the closer you are to the Florentine centerpiece, the more you'll have to pay. Paoli supplies guests with food that almost warrants the higher price tag—the *entrecote di manzo arlecchino,* for instance. The "harlequin" beef is marinated in a delicious cognac cream sauce. Paoli has one of the most *suggestivo* (oft-used Italian

word for "evocative") settings in town, with tables under a 14th-century vaulted ceiling whose ribs and lunettes are covered with fading 18th-century frescoes. Reservations are recommended. *Via dei Tavolini 12/r (off Via dei Cerchi).* ☎ *055/216215. Primi 6€–12€, secondi 14€–18€. Wed–Mon noon–3pm and 7pm–midnight.*

Pizzeria

→ **Il Pizzaiuolo** ★★ NEAPOLITAN/PIZZA Despite their considerable skill in the kitchen, Florentines just can't make a decent pizza. It takes a Neapolitan to do that, so business has been booming ever since Naples-born Carmine opened this pizzeria.

Even with a reservation, you'll probably have to wait for a spot at a long, crowded, and noisy marble table. Save the great pizza for a main dish; start instead with a Neapolitan first course like *fusilli c'a ricotta* (homemade pasta spirals in creamy tomato-and-ricotta sauce). You'll have to make reservations if you want to have dinner; they're required. *Via de' Macci 113r (at the corner of Via Pietrapiana).* ☎ *055/241171. Pizza 4.50€–10€; primi 6.50€–13€; secondi 7.50€–13€. Mon–Sat 12:30–3pm and 7:30pm–midnight. Closed Aug.*

Cafes

→ **Caffetteria Piansa** SANDWICHES An interesting mix of jazz and late '80s pop entrance the tired masses that drop by this bar/sandwich shop. There's not a whole lot food-wise to fill the stomach, but the assortment of *panini*, desserts, and aperitifs make Caffetteria Piansa a perfect place to re-energize and rest. Listen for the Charlie Parker/ Bangles mash-ups. *Borgo Pinti 18/r (3 blocks east of the Duomo).* ☎ *055/2342362. Sandwiches 4€–6€. Mon–Sat noon–2pm.*

📺 Best → **Vivoli** ★★★ GELATERIA My theory as to how the majority of Florentines aren't morbidly obese lies in the tiny pink plastic shovel at Vivoli. If customers were supplied with anything bigger than a dollhouse teaspoon, the dense frozen treat would be inhaled and their measurements would suddenly read like the jersey numbers of defensive linemen. But go ahead: Buy a 1.50€ cup, fill it up with your favorite flavors and a dollop of whipped cream, and work it off by climbing the Duomo or just strolling north on Via Isola delle Stinche. While there are hundreds of gelato joints in Florence, none can touch the popularity and quality of Vivoli. *Via Isola delle Stinche 7/r (1 block west of Santa Croce).* ☎ *055/2392334. Tues–Sun 9am–1am. Gelato 2€. Closed Aug and Jan–Feb.*

Partying

Unlike other cities in Europe, the club scene in Florence isn't as crazy or beer-soaked as Berlin's or Amsterdam's, but it's still gobs of fun. Put on your sharpest duds and get your dancin' shoes on if you plan on meeting any locals. On any given weekend night, most of the 20-something crowd can be found inside one of the pulsating clubs.

To find the hot spots for the upcoming Saturday, you'll be wise to ask around the hipsterish stores on Via Nazionale. Storeowners and staff members are always happy to suggest various haunts to anyone strolling around their stores. While you check your e-mail in one of the Internet spots, check for flyers near the entrance. Almost every Internet point is full of flyers and ads for upcoming events. More often than not, these flyers will also give you free admission to whichever club it's advertising.

Bars & Lounges

📺 Best → **Capocaccia** ★★ Don your D&G shades, Zegna suit, and whatever hairstyle Beckham is sporting (either David or Victoria) and saunter around Capocaccia. This zoo of locals is a venerable breeding ground where every month is mating season. The crème of Florence society come here to show off their Louis Vuitton feathers while occasionally enjoying the prime location on the Arno. Even if the chi-chi scene isn't your kind of thing, it's still a fun time. The *aperitivo* (happy hour) buffet is generous—and free, as long as you buy a drink—and the scenery at sunset is unbeatable. *Lungarno Corsini 12–14 (between Ponte Santa Trinità and Ponte alla Carraia).* ☎ *055/210751. www. capocaccia.com. Tues–Sun noon–4pm (lunch) and 6pm–1am (aperitivo/dinner).*

➔ **The Lounge** ★★ This swank bar/restaurant, whose heavily designed interiors must have cost a small fortune, has quickly become a popular aperitivo and after-dinner drink spot with stylish 20- and 30-something Florentines. The restaurant, which serves sushi and small plates, as well as more elaborate, creative local cuisine, looks like what I imagine a Japanese hunting lodge would look like, with elongated silk divans, lacquered wood-backed chairs, and antlers mounted above the doorway. In the less formal lounge area, dining tables are casually interspersed with zebra-skin coffee tables and high-backed, white leather armchairs. Later at night, quaffers take to the Pink Room, a strikingly minimalist space suffused in a sensual fuchsia glow, with comfy white canvas banquettes, cushions and cocktail tables galore, and space-age ottomans where you can rest your feet. On warm nights, The Lounge has a well-furnished terrace, with sleek outdoor furniture, facing the piazza. *Piazza Santa Maria Novella 9/10/r.* ☎ *055/2645282. www.thelounge.it.*

➔ **Negroni and Zoe** ★ Both are in the Oltrarno, close to the river, and both draw the same type of crowd; in fact, color scheme and address are the only things that set these two happening lounges apart. From *aperitivo* (happy hour) till 1am, you'll find a diverse mix of revelers populating the smallish interior, ranging from students to older locals. Try to find a seat in the street-side terrace and enjoy the calm tree-lined park across the way. Evenings can get busy, but the quiet area and the proximity to the river make for a relaxing, yet fun night of cocktail-sipping. *Negroni: Via dei Renai 17 (between Ponte Vecchio and Ponte alle Grazie).* ☎ *055/243647. www.negronibar.com. Zoe: Via dei Renai 13/r (between Ponte Vecchio and Ponte alle Grazie).* ☎ *055/243111.*

MTV **Best** ➔ **Red Garter** ★ Relive the glory days of your college career on Via de'

Benci. Every Thursday, this divey bar draws a mostly American crowd, but Australians and Brits also partake in the beer pong tournament that starts at 10:30pm. Things can get rowdy pretty quickly and, as the sign near the entrance may suggest, management seems to have had problems in the past with the racket raised by patrons: AI CLIENTI CHE LASCIANO IL LOCALE CHIEDIAMO DI RISPETTARE LA QUIETE DEL VICINATO. Roughly translated: Keep it down while you're leaving. *Via de' Benci 33/r.* ☎ *055-234-4904. (2 blocks south of Santa Croce).*

MTV **Best** ➔ **Teatro Scribe** ★ Locals call this hole-in-the-wall near Santa Croce *teatrino* and with good reason. With not a whole lot of room to kick back and drink their ridiculously cheap beer, this "little theater" fills up to SRO fast. It's one of the few places open past 3am where house or techno isn't being blasted into your tired ears. Early in the evening, it can be difficult to find the entrance. Once they open their doors on the dark, borderline eerie street of Via delle Seggiole, just follow the crowd of young Florentines (or follow your ears to the music emanating from the bar's PA). *Via delle Seggiole 8/r (off Via Ghibellina).* ☎ *055/2345594.*

Pubs

➔ **Fiddler's Elbow** ★ Right on Piazza Santa Maria Novella, opposite the train station, this is probably Florence's most successful "Irish" pub, always packed with a lively crowd that's equal parts young Florentines, resident expats, and international students. Pints of Guinness, Harp, Strongbow cider, and others are 3.50€ until 9pm, 4.50€ after that. In warm weather, an improvised "beer garden" is set up on the piazza out front, and on some nights, there's a live Celtic band fiddling away. *Piazza Santa Maria Novella 7/r.* ☎ *055/215056.*

→ **The Friends Pub** ★ Looking for a simple place to chill and listen to good indie Brit-rock? Cross the Arno and look for The Friends Pub. The usual Harp, Kilkenny, and Guinness are on tap and bartender Alessandro has a mix of Oasis, Gorillaz, and the Zutons on constant rotation. Bartenders here are friendly and aren't shy about partying with patrons. Don't make the same mistake I did though: They *will* outdrink you if you dare challenge them. *Veni, vidi, vomiti:* I came, I saw, I puked. They're open daily from 11am to late night. *Borgo San Jacopo 51r (just southeast of Ponte Santa Trinità).* ☎ *055/294930.*

→ **Loonees** ★★ Every pint of beer in this immensely popular student joint, a few blocks south of Piazza della Repubblica, comes with a free shot. Need we say more? Inside, you'll find a fun-loving mix of locals and foreign college kids trying to hear each other over the live, or at least very loud, music that plays here every night. *Via Porta Rossa 16/r.* ☎ *055/2381290. Tues–Sun till late. Closed Aug.*

Clubs

→ **Central Park** Drink a ton of water before venturing to Central Park, the favorite dance club of local rich kids. Working your way through the five dance floors, combined with the 2km (1¼-mile) walk west of Santa Maria Novella just to get here, you'll be burning calories left and right. With the surrounding sport complexes (velodrome, hippodrome [horse racing track], and tennis club) to the north and Central Park in the south, Parco delle Cascine basically offers Florentines aerobic activities 24/7. Create your own triathlon of a 30km (19-mile) bike ride, a tennis match, and break-dance battles. *Via Fosso Macinante 2 (western outskirts—take a cab).* ☎ *055/353-505. Cover 8€ (free for students before 12:30am). Tues–Sat 11pm–3am.*

→ **H202** Tired of hearing the same hip-hop, R&B, and drum 'n' bass at the discos in Florence? H202, in addition to being a great place to check out concerts, walks the path less traveled and frequently pumps out funk, house, and Afro-beat. You'll still hear electronica once in a while (especially on the weekend) but selection is unique and more than danceable. Sundays feature live bands. On other days, head to the second floor, plop down on one of the comfy chairs, and enjoy some Fela Kuti. It's open only from October through May (Thurs–Tues 10pm–1am). *Via Ghibellina 47/r (near Santa Croce).* ☎ *055/243239.*

→ **Meccanò** Head-nodders need not apply here. Everyone who fills the four dance floors of Meccanò knows how to use the beats for all they're worth. It's a tough decision between **Central Park** and Meccanò, given that they're 200m (656 ft.) away from each other. Most partygoers hit Central Park first, and when it closes its doors at a geriatric 3am, they finish off at Meccanò. Cover can get a little steep, but promoters from both Yab (see below) and Meccanò collaborate to dish out flyers (at some Internet places) that'll get you in for free. Otherwise, it'll set you back a cool 20€. *Viale degli Olmi 1 (western outskirts—take a cab).* ☎ *055/31271. Cover 20€; free with flyer or with international student card.*

→ **Space Electronic** ★ This club holds the dubious distinction of being the place where one of our writers heard her first Backstreet Boys song, "Everybody," back in 1997—it was love at first manufactured pop hook. We checked back in with *Lo Space* in late 2005 and we're happy to report that nothing has changed. Some 8 years later, Space Electronic is still going strong, guided by the singular mission of bringing international college students and horny Florentines together in one cheesy, but quite fun, multifloor dance party. Downstairs, there's an American-style bar with karaoke; upstairs, a flying spaceship hovers over the laser-lit dance floor. If you're looking to score some cool points or are over 21, hit up Yab Yum instead. *Via Palazzuolo 37 (just south of Santa Maria Novella).* ☎ *055/293082. www.spaceelectronic.net. Cover 10€–15€; free with flyer or student ID.*

→ **Yab Yum** ★ Known simply as "Yab" these days, this ritzy locale on Via Sassetti provides a convenient spot for swingers to work up a sweat. Arrive at 9:30pm, tackle one of the shiny nouveau-industrial booths, and sit down to a fine dinner with a group of friends before downing your cocktails. Mondays are the nights in the summer for "YabSmoove" where hip-hop rules the PA. You can dole out 20€ to get in, or better yet, search some of the Internet points in Florence to find a flyer that'll get you in for free. R&B, soul, and funk are featured on other nights. You're handed a DrinkCard on the way in—it's marked every time you imbibe an alcoholic beverage, and you pay the cashier the cost of your drinks plus the cover charge on your way out of the club. Lose the card and pay the maximum amount. (As for the name, Yab stands for "you are beautiful," one of the most time-tested English pickup lines in all of Italy. *Via Sassetti 5 (just northwest of Mercato Nuovo).* ☎ *347/7248847 (cellphone). www.yab.it. Cover 8€–20€; free for international students, with 1-drink minimum.*

Gay Bars

ArciGay/Lesbica (aka Azione Gay e Lesbica), Italy's largest and oldest gay organization, has a center in Florence at Via Pisana, 32R

The Ultimate Concert Venue

Tenax ★★, on Via Pratese 46 (Peretola, northeastern outskirts; ☎ 055/308160; Tues–Sun 10pm–4am; cover 10€–20€; bus 29 or 30) is the ultimate concert venue in Florence. Everyone from the noise-pop rockers Jesus and Mary Chain to electronica's Tricky to the indie queen Ani DiFranco has stopped by this bar/club/concert hall in the outskirts near the airport. Despite covers as high as 20€ on Saturdays, Tenax is always full of local youths dancing up a storm. Check out their site at www.tenax.org and, if you're aching for a good old-fashioned "WTF?" click on "Philosophy" and then "Toilet Zone."

(☎ 055/220250; www.azionegayelesbica.it). It's open for visits from Monday to Friday 6 to 8pm.

Tabasco (Piazza Santa Cecilia, 3/r; ☎ 055/213000) is Florence's (and Italy's) oldest gay dance club, open daily 10:30pm to 3am, with a 10€ to 13€ cover. The crowd is mostly men in their 20s on up to their 40s. Florence's leading gay bar, **Crisco** (Via San Egidio, 43r; ☎ 055/2480580) is for men only, open Wednesday through Monday from 10:30pm to 3:30am and Friday and Saturday from 10:30pm to 5 or 6am. Cover is 9€ to 15€.

Performing Arts

If you're looking for English-language film, theater, and classical music, you won't have trouble finding things that interest you here, especially from June to September. The tourist offices (see "Florence Basics," above) have a ton of info on what's going on, as well as schedules for particular venues.

While most theaters feature American films, unless you know Italian, the dubbing makes it a little hard to understand. To the relief of cineplex-aholics, **Odeon Cinehall** (Piazza Strozzi; ☎ 055/214068) plays original-language films every Monday, and **Cinema Astro** (Piazza San Simone, near

Santa Croce; no phone) shows English-language films every other night.

The **Church of Orsanmichele** (Via Calzaiuoli; info ☎ 055/477805; box office at Via Faenza 139r; ☎ 055/210804), which plays host to the Florence Sinfonietta, is acoustically one of the best places to hear classical music—its Romanesque dome facilitates rich orchestral sounds.

Concerts of the **Regional Tuscan Orchestra** are often presented at Santo Stefano al Ponte Vecchio. Many other churches also have a regular schedule of free and low-cost concerts.

Teatro Comunale di Firenze (Corso Italia 16; ☎ 055/211158; box office Tues–Fri 10am–4:30pm, Sat 9am–1pm, and 1 hr. before curtain) is Florence's main theater, with both opera and ballet seasons running from September to December and a concert season from January to April. Tickets cost 21€ to 103€ for the opera, 12€ to 26€ for the ballet, and 18€ to 52€ for concerts.

Teatro della Pergola (Via della Pergola; ☎ 055/2479651; box office Tues–Sat 9:30am–1pm and 3:30–6:45pm, Sun 10am–noon; tickets 10€–23€) and **Teatro Verdi** (Via Ghibellina 99; ☎ 055/212320; box office Tues–Fri 10am–7pm, Sat 10am–1pm; tickets 5€–18€) also hold many theatrical and operatic performances. Stop by the theaters to obtain a program of the current offerings.

Sightseeing

They don't call Florence the world's greatest open-air art history classroom for nothing: There are a staggering number of museums, churches, and attractions in the Renaissance capital, so it might be smart to get your bearings and figure out your sightseeing plan of attack before you start hitting monuments and paying admission fees willy-nilly. Begin by visiting the tourist office, where helpful clerks will know exactly what events are taking place and which museums are closed for renovations or holidays. Otherwise, the staff members at your hotel or hostel are often quite knowledgeable about opening hours, discounted tickets, and other insider tourist info. Keep in mind that Monday—as in the rest of Italy—is most museums' closing day (that goes for the Uffizi, the Accademia, and the Pitti).

Festivals

January

Regatta on the Arno. The city of the Renaissance kicks off the new year with a boat race. Call ☎ 055-23-20 for details. January 1.

May & June

Maggio Musicale Fiorentino. The biggest festival in Florence presents an array of opera, dance, and classical music performances at the Teatro Comunale di Firenze, Teatro della Pergola, and other venues in the city. Buy tix at Biglietteria Teatro Comunale, Corso Italia 16 (☎ 055/211158; www.maggiofiorentino.com; May–June Tues–Fri 10am–4:30pm, Sat 9am–1pm). Throughout May and June.

Dissolvenze. A cultural and ethnic festival featuring live music, dance, and filma at Arena Estiva del Poggetto, Via M. Mercati 24b. Information at FLOG Centro Flog Tradizioni Popolari, Via Maestri del Lavoro 1 (☎ 055/4220300). Throughout June.

Festa di San Giovanni. The city goes wild with the celebration of Florence's patron saint. Parades and fireworks salute the angelic Saint John. Another feature of the festival is the final match of the Calcio Storico Fiorentino—an intense competition exhibiting the medieval version of soccer played in a sandlot with small goals. Set in

Piazza di Santa Croce, the spectator-filled bleachers become a rowdy foot-stomping exhibition of partisanship, chanting, and cheers. Purchase tickets, usually around 7.75€, at the box office on Via Faenza 139r (☎ **055/210804**). June 24.

June to September

Mondo Culto! This festival shows a series of "cult movies and incredible strange music." For information, call ☎ **0339/7263732** or go to www.mondoculto.com. Throughout June, July, August, and September.

Landmarks

➔**Piazza della Signoria** ★★★ A sublime example of show-stopping civic architecture, Piazza della Signoria is a jumble of imposing medieval government halls, monumental statuary, and fountains clustered around an L-shaped, flagstoned public square. The dominant and most theatrical feature on the piazza, by far, is **Palazzo Vecchio** ★★, built in the 13th century based on a design by Arnolfo di Cambio. With its facade of rough masonry, its teeth-like crenellations, and its 94m-high (308-ft.) clock tower thrusting upward like an angry craning canine neck. The "guard-dog" that is Palazzo Vecchio was built in a time of fierce feuding in Florence. On occasion, Florence found itself on defensive haunches, under attack by even bigger dogs, such as Milanese dukes and their powerful armies. Piazza della Signoria has long been the center of civic life in Florence: Parts of Palazzo Vecchio still function as city hall; and the open square itself has seen plenty of spectacular, and often violent, public demonstrations.

On the Loggia dei Lanzi (the arcaded platform on the southern side of the square), statues by some of the Renaissance's greatest sculptors—including Giambologna's marble *Rape of the Sabine Women* and Benvenuto Cellini's bad-ass bronze *Perseus*

with the Head of Medusa—lend even more drama to the stage of Piazza della Signoria. Most of the other statues are copies of originals now housed in museums around town: The oft-photographed *David* of Piazza della Signoria is a facsimile of Michelangelo's 1504 original, which is now in the Accademia. Most of the interior of the Palazzo Vecchio is open to the public; the monumental chambers where the Signoria (city council) used to meet are decked out with ridiculous amounts of fussy gold and over-the-top Renaissance frescoes. *Palazzo Vecchio: Piazza della Signoria.* ☎ *055/2768465. www.comune.firenze.it. Admission 6€. Sat–Wed 9am–7pm, Thurs 9am–2pm.*

➔**Ponte Vecchio** ★★ The legend of the German commander with a soft spot for bridges is well documented. The gist of it goes like this: In World War II, to slow American troops and their push north, Axis commanders destroyed bridges over strategic rivers in Italy. All of Florence's bridges were reduced to rubble, except for Ponte Vecchio ("old bridge"). So entranced by the beauty and history of the bridge was the Nazi commander that he decided to destroy the buildings at each end of the bridge rather than topple the structure entirely. Ponte Vecchio dates from the 13th century, when the shops and stalls built over the span were used by butchers and tanners, who used to soak animal hides in vats of urine as part of the leather-curing process. The Medici, who had to walk past the foul-smelling workshops every time they crossed the Arno (via the private walkway known as the Vasari Corridor, still preserved on the eastern edge of the bridge), were so disgusted by the perpetual stench on Ponte Vecchio that they kicked all the butchers and tanners out in 1593, freeing up real estate for more neutrally odored goldsmiths and silversmiths, who have been the bridge's sole tenants for 400 years. Be sure to walk over

Ponte Vecchio at least once at night, when all the jewelry shops are shuttered with their ancient-looking wooden doors and locks. *Via Por Santa Maria/Via Guicciardini. Bus: B or D.*

Churches

There are about a gazillion churches in Florence that you can visit; we've listed the most important ones (most of which charge an admission fee), but there are plenty of smaller churches that you can enter for free and see Renaissance masterpieces that have been hanging above the same altar for over 500 years.

➔ **Battistero (Baptistery)** ★★ With green and white marble striping, Florence's octagonal baptistery looks like a pretty gift box, and it would be even more visually impressive if it weren't dwarfed by its gigantic neighbor across the square—the Duomo. In any case, the baptistery's bronze doors are the real reason the building is swarmed like a honeycomb from dawn to dusk by tourist bees. The famous **east doors** ★★★ (facing the Duomo) have 10 scenes from the Old Testament and were cast in bronze and gilded by Lorenzo Ghiberti from 1425 to 1452. It makes you admire the vision and patience of Renaissance art patrons. Earlier in life, when he was 22, Ghiberti won a heated competition (against the likes of Donatello and Brunelleschi) to cast the baptistery's **north doors** ★★; the 28 gilded scenes from the New Testament were executed from 1403 to 1424.

Before Ghiberti came along, the baptistery only had one set of doors: The relief panels on the **south doors** were made by sculptor Andrea Pisano from 1330 to 1336. Come to the baptistery early in the morning on a clear day and start with Ghiberti's first set of doors. Everyone has a charged facial expression, and everyone is actively involved in their scenes. Now, walk around to the east doors: When the morning sun hits the gilding on Ghiberti's most famous doors, the Old Testament panels go stunningly, cinematically ablaze. Full of engaging background details, emotion and dynamism, the east doors look like still shots from some sweeping Biblical epic. Years after Ghiberti's death, Michelangelo was standing before these doors and someone asked his opinion. His response sums up Ghiberti's life accomplishment: "They are so beautiful that they would grace the entrance to Paradise." They've been called the Gates of Paradise ever since. Note that panels now mounted here are excellent copies; the originals are displayed in the Museo dell'Opera del Duomo. *Piazza San Giovanni.* ☎ *055/2302885. www.operaduomo.firenze.it. Admission 3€. Mon–Sat noon–6:30pm; Sun 8:30am–1:30pm.*

📺 Best ➔ **The Duomo (Santa Maria del Fiore)** ★★★ If at all possible, see the Duomo for the first time at night. There are few sights in Italy as breathtaking as the accidental glimpses you catch of its moonlit white, green, and red marble walls, down a deserted alley, from a few blocks away. These visual snippets that hint at the Duomo's majestic bulk are far more magical and impressive than any straight-on shot of the cathedral in broad daylight. Built from 1296 to 1466 and funded by the powerful Wool Merchants' Guild, the church is crowned by an impossibly large, terra-cotta-tile-clad cupola (dome). The dome dominates the skyline of Florence. More than just a grandiose monument, the cupola of the Duomo is an enduring marvel of engineering, whose ingenious construction methods were devised almost single-handedly by Filippo Brunelleschi. Florence's Duomo is all about the candy-striped and red-topped exterior.

If you do want to go inside, however, there are a number of ways to do so. For 6€, you can **climb the dome** ★★★ (463 steps) or Giotto's 14th-century **campanile (bell tower)** ★★ (414 steps) immediately adjacent. Both offer spectacular panorama of Florence's rooftops and the surrounding hills, but the dome ascent allows you an up-close-and-personal encounter with Brunelleschi's masonry techniques. The stairways for both the dome and the campanile are narrow and steep, not for the claustrophobic or faint-hearted. The interior of the Duomo itself is free to enter. (In high season, however, lines to get into the Duomo can take over an hour. In that case, you have our permission to skip it.) *Piazza del Duomo* ☎ *055/2302885. www.operaduomo.firenze.it. Church: Free admission. Mon–Wed and Fri 10am–5pm, Thurs 10am–3:30pm; 1st Sat of month 10am–3:30pm, other Sat 10am–4:45pm; Sun 1:30–4:30pm. Free tours every 40 min. daily 10:30am–noon and 3–4:20pm. Cupola: Admission 6€. Mon–Fri 8:30am–6:20pm; Sat 8:30am–5pm (1st Sat of month to 3:20pm). Campanile: Admission 6€. Daily 8:30am–6:50pm.*

→ **Cappelle Medicee (Medici Chapels)** ★★ Michelangelo-designed tombs for the Medici family in the **Sagrestia Nuova (New Sacristy)** are the big hoopla here; unfortunately, they should have been an even bigger hoopla, but Michelangelo never got to finish the tomb for Lorenzo de'Medici the Magnificent—for his tomb, the wise ruler of Florence, poet of note, and Mr. Moneybags behind much of the Renaissance only got a dinky marble slab and inscription. Furthermore, he has to share the unfinished tomb with his brother, Giuliano. (They did, however, get a lovely statue of the Virgin Mary by Michelangelo.) The vaulted spaces of the new sacristy are done up in harmonious tones of white *intonaco* (plaster) and dark grey *pietra serena*. On the left wall is Michelangelo's tomb of Lorenzo, Duke of Urbino (and Lorenzo the Magnificent's grandson). Below him, *Dawn* (female) and *Dusk* (male), a pair of Michelangelo's most famous sculptures (1524–31), languish over the elongated curves of the tomb. *Dawn* and

Dusk mirror the similarly fashioned and equally important *Day* (male) and *Night* (female) across the way (1526–33), on the tomb of Giuliano, Duke of Nemours. The two female figures, on the other hand, are startlingly ridiculous looking. If artists learn from what they observe in real life, it's pretty clear in *Dawn* and *Night* that Michelangelo wasn't getting much action from the Florentine ladies.

For a real 1808 turn in artistic style, or lack thereof, check out the **Cappella dei Principi (Chapel of the Princes).** Begun in 1604, this mausoleum has the dubious distinction of being one of the world's most gloriously god-awful memorials, dedicated to the Medici grand dukes—the clan got more and more inbred as the years passed, and the Medici princes buried here were some of Florence's most dysfunctional and arrogant tyrants. The domed chapel is an exercise in bad taste, like a centrifuge in which cut marbles and semiprecious stones have been splattered onto the walls and ceiling with no regard for composition or chromatic unity. For more than a century, ducal funds were poured into further cluttering the monstrosity. *Piazza Madonna degli Aldobrandini (behind San Lorenzo).* ☎ *055/2388602. Admission 6€. Daily 8:15am–5pm. Closed 1st, 3rd, and 5th Mon, and 2nd and 4th Sun of the month.*

→ **Orsanmichele** ★ The "Garden of St. Michael," a tall, blocky building halfway down Via dei Calzaiuoli, looks more like a Gothic warehouse than a church—which is because the 14th-century structure started out as a granary/grain market. After a miraculous image of the Madonna appeared on a column inside, however, the lower level was turned into a chapel. The city's merchant guilds commissioned such masters as Ghiberti, Donatello, Verrocchio, and Giambologna to cast or carve sculptures of the guilds' patron saints to set in the street-level tabernacles

FLORENCE

around the exterior. Across Via dell'Arte della Lana from Orsanmichele's main entrance is the 1308 Palazzo dell'Arte della Lana (Palace of the Wool Guild). This Gothic palace was home to medieval Florence's most powerful body, the Wool Merchants' Guild, which employed about a third of Florence in the 13th and 14th centuries. Up the stairs inside Palazzo dell'Arte della Lana, you can cross over the hanging walkway to the first floor (American second floor) of Orsanmichele. These are the old granary rooms, now housing a museum of the statues that once surrounded the exterior. A few are still undergoing restoration, but eight of the original sculptures are here, well labeled, including Donatello's marble *St. Mark* (1411–13); Ghiberti's bronze *St. John the Baptist* (1413–16), the first life-size bronze of the Renaissance; and Verrocchio's *Incredulity of St. Thomas* (1473–83). Actually getting into Orsanmichele is a game of Russian roulette—neither the museum nor the church pays much attention to their posted hours, which are largely dependent on the whims of fickle and limited staff. *Via dell'Arte della Lana 1 (at Via Calzaiuoli).* ☎ *055/284944. Free admission. Church: Random hours (though never open during riposo). Museum: Daily 9–9:45am, 10–10:45am, and 11–11:45am (plus Sat–Sun 1–1:45pm). Closed 1st and last Mon of the month.*

→ **San Lorenzo and Laurentian Library** ★★ It's surrounded by the loud stalls of the leather market, and its facade of rusticated masonry is unfinished: San Lorenzo hardly looks distinguished from the outside, but it's most likely the oldest church in Florence, founded in A.D. 393. San Lorenzo was the city's cathedral until the bishop's seat moved to Santa Reparata (later to become the Duomo) in the 7th century. More important, it was the Medici family's parish church, and as those famous bankers began to accumulate their vast fortune, they started a tradition of lavishing it on this church that lasted until the clan died out in the 18th century. (The Medici tombs, listed

separately below, have a separate entrance around the back of the church and have different hours.)

Find the entrance to the cloister to reach the stairwell to the right leading up to the **Biblioteca Laurenziana (Laurentian Library)** ★★, which can also be entered for free without going through (and paying for) the church (the separate entrance is just to the left of the church's main doors). Michelangelo designed this library in 1524 to house the Medici's manuscript collection, and it stands as one of the most brilliant works of Mannerist architecture. The Laurentian Library's real star feature, however, is Michelangelo's elegant, and totally original, *pietra serena* tripartite staircase: The central flight of stairs consists of broad, convex steps that seem to flow toward you like cooling lava, while the more rectilinear lateral stairs seem to possess the upward motion of an escalator. This actual library part, however—filled with intricately carved wood and handsomely illuminated manuscripts—was closed indefinitely in 1999 until "urgent maintenance" is completed. *Piazza San Lorenzo.* ☎ *055/216634. Church: Admission 2.50€. Mon–Sat 10am–5pm. Laurentian Library: Free admission. Mon–Sat 9am–1pm.*

MTV **Best** → **Santa Croce** ★★★ Of the dozens of churches you can visit in Florence, Santa Croce, in all its Gothic glory, really shouldn't be missed. The inventory of boldface name sepulchers here reads like an all-obituary *US Weekly* from Renaissance Florence. But tombs of the rich and famous are not the only attraction at Santa Croce: Its Gothic interior is wide and gaping, with huge pointed stone arches creating the aisles and an echoing nave trussed with wood beams, in all giving the architecture a wonderful barn-like feel.

On the right aisle is the first tomb of note, a mad contraption by Giorgio Vasari containing the bones of the most venerated of Renaissance masters, Michelangelo

ᴍᴛᴠ🖳 The University Scene

Though not as large as Bologna's or Rome's, Florence's large T-shirt-clad university population is unmistakably present, especially at Florence University–area haunts like **Cabiria Cafe** (Piazza Santo Spirito; ☎ 055/215732; Wed–Mon 11am–2am). Cabiria gets crowded with cheery, backpack-wearing students and student types who'd rather be chatting than studying. Piazza di Santo Spirito, the nighttime outdoor hangout point for stylish university kids, is best from Thursday through Saturday, when all the locales are open for business.

The city is also home to a seemingly endless list of foreign university programs (mostly American), and many centrally located hangouts are almost exclusively patronized by students from abroad. The city is especially rife with fine art schools—who wouldn't want to study painting in Michelangelo's hometown? Check out all the options at www.art-courses-italy.com.

Buonarroti, who died of a fever in Rome in 1564 at the ripe old age of 89.

Another eternal tenant of Santa Croce is one of the victims of the Inquisition, Galileo Galilei, whose excommunication from the Catholic church was lifted only in 1992, 350 years after his death. His 18th-century tomb, decorated appropriately with a heliocentric relief, lies near that of Lorenzo Ghiberti, the 15th-century sculptor who cast the famous bronze doors on the baptistery. Next comes a wall monument to Niccolò Machiavelli, the 16th-century Florentine statesman and author whose famous book *The Prince* is the ultimate how-to manual for a powerful Renaissance ruler. Beyond Machiavelli's cenotaph is a 19th-century funerary monument (with a real body this time): Here lie the remains of Gioacchino Rossini (1792–1868), composer of the *Barber of Seville* and the *William Tell Overture*. With all these tombs, plus Gaddi's stained-glass windows, Giotto's frescoed chapels, and Donatello's *Crucifix,* Santa Croce is one of the most art- and relic-packed churches in Italy. *Piazza Santa Croce.* ☎ *055/244619. Admission 4€. Mon–Sat 9:30am–5:30pm; Sun 1–5:30pm.*

→**Santa Maria Novella** ★ Santa Maria Novella is worthy of a quick look. Of all Florence's major churches, this home of the

Dominican order is the only one with an original facade that matches its era of greatest importance. The lower Romanesque half was started in the 14th century; in the 16th century, Leon Battista Alberti got out his protractor and finished the facade, adding a classically inspired Renaissance top that not only went seamlessly with the lower half but also created a Cartesian plane of perfect geometry. Inside, Giotto's recently restored *Crucifix* hangs in the center of the nave. Against the second pillar on the left of the nave is the pulpit from which Galileo was denounced for his heretical theory that the earth revolved around the sun. Just past the pulpit, on the left wall, is Masaccio's *Trinità* (ca. 1428), the first painting in the world to use perfect linear mathematical perspective. The transept is filled with spectacularly frescoed chapels. *Piazza Santa Maria Novella.* ☎ *055/282187. Admission 2.50€. Mon–Thurs and Sat 9:30am–5pm, Fri and Sun 1–5pm.*

Museums

→**Accademia** ★★ Definitely avoid coming here between noon and 3pm. Lines are not only around the block, but the location of the Accademia gives tourists no shelter from the afternoon sun. Once inside, however, you'll instantly forget about your

FLORENCE

scorched skin when you catch a glimpse of Michelangelo's *David,* with his slingshot coolly draped over his left shoulder and massive right hand holding on to a stone, just in case Goliath comes back for another ass-whooping. When you're finished gawking at the naked biblical hero, take the time to inspect Michelangelo's *Prisoners.* Also sprinkled around the museum are many works by Michelangelo's students—some are so skillful that they're often mistaken for products of the master chiseler himself. Fortunately, the museum's plaques will tell you who made what. *Via Ricasoli 58–60 (2 blocks north of the Duomo).* ☎ 055/2388609. *www.sbas.firenze.it/accademia. (Reserve tickets at* ☎ 055/294883; *www.firenzemusei.it.) Admission 6.50€ adults. Tues–Sun 8:15am– 6:50pm; last admission 30 min. before close. Closed Dec 25, Jan 1, and May 1. Bus: 1, 6, 7, 10, 11, 17, 25, 31, 32, 33, 67, 68, or 70.*

→ **Bargello** ★★ If the Uffizi and the Pitti have all of Florence's best paintings, the Museo Nazionale del Bargello has all the statues. In this imposing 13th-century palazzo, once home to prisons and torture chambers, the hits just keep on coming: The most famous piece here is probably Michelangelo's *Drunk Bacchus* (1497), an uncannily realistic depiction of the god. Earlier works include a bronze *David* (1440) by Donatello—the first free-standing nude sculpture since antiquity, which must have influenced Michelangelo—and some bronze panels of the *Sacrifice of Isaac* by Ghiberti and Brunelleschi. Don't miss the Bargello's Giambologna masterpieces: In *Mercury* (1564), one of the Dutch artist's best works, the fleet-footed messenger god truly looks as if he could take off and fly away at any moment. Finally, if you catch sight of a downward-gazing bronze bust that looks oddly familiar but you can't quite place it, it's probably Daniele da Volterra's portrait of Michelangelo; this depiction of the master is the most frequently reproduced image

of him. *Via del Proconsolo 4 (2 blocks south of the Duomo).* ☎ 055/2388606. *www.sbas. firenze.it/bargello. (Reservations:* ☎ 055/ 294883; *www.firenzemusei.it.) Admission 4€ adults. Daily 8:15am–1:50pm. Closed every other Mon and Sun of the month.*

→ **Museo Archeologico** ★ Florence's archaeological museum still manages to attract a handful of tourists even though the majority of visitors in town have eyes only for Michelangelo and Botticelli. It's their loss, for the Museo Archeologico houses a fascinating and not-too-overwhelming collection of Roman, Egyptian, and Etruscan artifacts—which will look positively exotic after all the Renaissance art in the rest of Florence. One of the most interesting and important pieces here is the ferocious 5th-century B.C. Etruscan bronze *Chimera. Via della Colonna 36 (a few blocks north of the Accademia).* ☎ 055/23575. *Admission 4€ adults. Mon 2–7pm; Tues and Thurs 8:30am– 7pm; Wed and Fri–Sun 8:30am–2pm.*

→ **Museo dell'Opera del Duomo (Duomo Works Museum)** ★ With fascinating wooden models of the original design for the Duomo, as well as some of the actual machinery that built the church, from the 13th to the 15th centuries, this is a must for aspiring engineers (and anyone else who habitually flips to the History Channel when nothing else is on TV). The rest of the museum is dedicated to preserving and showcasing masterpieces of art deemed too delicate or valuable to stay where they were originally intended—inside or on top of the Duomo itself. Among the museum's permanent works is one of Donatello's more morbidly fascinating sculptures, a late work in polychrome wood of *The Magdalene* (1453–55), emaciated and veritably dripping with penitence. Another important piece is Donatello's *Beardless Prophet,* with its drooping, aged face; and just in case you haven't had your fill of gloom, Brunelleschi's

The Uffizi: One of the World's Great Museums

The **Uffizi** ★ ★ ★ is the granddaddy of museums in Florence, and has as much to offer when it's closed as when it's open. My favorite perch at night is the courtyard of the Uffizi after 9pm. Surprisingly, there are very few people milling around and the Carabinieri rarely pass by on their routine patrols. It's impossible to remain unmoved when you're sitting on the steps (on the Arno side of the Uffizi), gazing at the statues of Dante, Michelangelo, and other Renaissance legends uniformly lit by the spotlights along the base of each bust. As for visiting the museum, give yourself at least a couple days to absorb the 40+ rooms within the gallery.

Remember that much like the Accademia and the Duomo, lines to enter the museum can get downright ridiculous—if you haven't reserved your ticket in advance, you can wait more than an hour. Also, if you arrive at the Uffizi later in the day, you risk having the museum close on you. Upon entering note that many of the paintings constantly get shuffled around and rooms are routinely closed off (they're still renovating from a 1993 terrorist bombing), so be sure to pick up a map at the information desk.

Most art museums house their masterpieces in two or three rooms, but the Uffizi draws no distinction between its works because, well, *every* work of art here is a masterpiece.

- **Michelangelo's *Holy Family:*** The moment you enter **Room 25**, all eyes fix on this lushly colored and detailed *tondo* (round painting), one of Michelangelo's earliest works. The attention given to the characters' limbs, their meticulously painted muscles, and the beautifully rich hues are unfathomable to the novice viewer, and a wonderful comparison for those who have seen, or will be seeing, Michelangelo's later frescoes at the Sistine Chapel in Rome.

- **Botticelli's *Birth of Venus* and *Primavera:*** In person, *Primavera* looks less like a 15th-century blacklight poster and more like a snapshot of stoned chicks doing their twirling dance at Lilith Fair, circa 1482. In **Room 10/14.**

- **Leonardo da Vinci's *Annunciation:*** **Room 15** contains da Vinci's depiction of the archangel Gabriel kneeling before the Virgin Mary—you've seen this on countless Christmas cards. Though some critics still don't believe that a young Leonardo painted this masterpiece, the consensus is that he completed it while an apprentice.

- **Caravaggio's *Medusa* and *Bacchus:*** Be sure to slow down once you reach the last corridor before the Uffizi's exit. Moved from the main galleries, Caravaggio's best works, from the 1590s, were placed in the first floor (named "The New Rooms").

The Uffizi is located at Piazzale degli Uffizi 6 (☎ **055/2388651**; www.polomuseale. firenze.it). Admission is 8.50€. It's open Tuesday through Sunday 8:15am to 6:50pm. For reservations, dial ☎ **055/294883** (booking charge of 3€, but *highly* recommended in high season; www.firenzemusei.it).

FLORENCE

death mask is also on display. *Piazza del Duomo 9.* ☎ *055/2302885. www.operaduomo. firenze.it. Admission 6€. Mon–Sat 9am–7:30pm, Sun 9am–2pm. Tickets sold until 30 min. before close. Bus: 6, 11, 14, 17, or 23.*

12 Hours in Florence

1. **Climb up the Duomo or Giotto's bell tower.** Maintain your balance, and you'll see stunning views of the ancient city.
2. **Eat gelato at Badiani or Vivoli (p. 376).**
3. **Chill on the steps at San Spirito and Piazza della Signorìa (con vino).** You'll never want to leave, unless you run out of wine.
4. **Browse the tombs in Santa Croce.**
5. **See *David* at the Accademia.** The dude is truly spellbinding—don't let the crowds bother you!
6. **Club at Yab Yum or Space Electronic.**
7. **Eat at Acqua al Due/La Via dell'Acqua.** For must-eat, cheap Italian soul food, these places can't be beat.
8. **Take a hike up Piazzale Michelangelo.** The super views of the Duomo, Santa Croce, and Ponte Vecchio will take you out of time.
9. **Visit the Botticelli room in the Uffizi.** Take a seat and salivate at how ahead of his time Botticelli was.
10. **Shop at San Lorenzo market.** Also flex your credit at the shops on Via Tournabuoni and near the Duomo and Palazzo Vecchio.

→ Palazzo Pitti ★★ The main tourist draw in the Oltrarno, by far, is the Palazzo Pitti and the relaxing greenery of the Boboli Gardens (p. 389) immediately adjacent. Apparently, with hopes of getting on *MTV Cribs*, Cosimo de' Medici's wife decided to upgrade the former home of banker Luca Pitti, thus creating the palace, which is now an enormous museum complex, housing the fabulous Medici collections of art, separated into the **Galleria Palatina, Galleria d'Arte Moderna, Galleria del Costume (Costume Gallery), Appartamenti Reali (Royal Apartments), Museo degli Argenti (Silver Museum)**, and the **Giardino Boboli.** Note that admission to the palace is free, but you'll have to pay to enter the most interesting galleries. What most people are heading for when they make their way to the Pitti is the Galleria Palatina. The majority of the paintings here are from High Renaissance artists—such as Raphael, Titian, Rubens, and the proto-baroque Caravaggio—skewing about 100 years later than the most famous works at the Uffizi, with more entertaining and light-hearted themes, for the most part. The large flagstoned space in front of the drive up to the palace in summer is often littered with sunbathers. *Piazza Pitti (Oltrarno): Admission for inclusive ticket for Galleria Palatina, Museo degli Argenti, Galleria d'Arte Moderna, and Giardino Boboli 11€. Galleria Palatina:* ☎ *055/2388614; reservations 055/294883. www.firenzemusei.it. Admission 6.50€ (with entrance to Royal Apartments), 1.55€ (without), 8€ after 4pm. Tues–Sun 8:15am–6:50pm. Giardino Boboli:* ☎ *055/2651816. Admission 4€. Daily Nov–Feb 8:15am–4:30pm, Mar 8:15am–5:30pm, Apr–May and Oct 8:15am–6:30pm, June–Sept 8:15am–7:30pm. Galleria d'Arte Moderna:* ☎ *055/2388601. Admission 5€. Daily 8:15am–1:50pm. Closed every other Mon and Sun of the month. Galleria del Costume:* ☎ *055/2388713. Admission 5€. Daily 8:15am–1:50pm. Closed every other Mon and Sun of the month. Museo degli Argenti (Silver Museum):* ☎ *055/2388709. Admission 4€. Daily Nov–Feb 8:15am–4:30pm, Mar 8:15am–5:30pm, Apr–May and Oct 8:15am–6:30pm, June–Sept 8:15am–7:30pm.*

Playing Outside

Dodging Vespas and standing in those museum queues not providing the exercise you're looking for? Head to **Parco delle Cascine**—a former game reserve of the Medici, on the western outskirts of town—and you'll find tennis courts, wooded jogging paths, and several pools. Tennis will set you back about 25€; for the same price, you can also hit around with a certified coach. To the west is the **Campo di Marte,** encircled by the Viale Manfredo Fanti. Plenty of soccer fields are available for foot-happy athletes, and you can catch locals here playing pickup games on the weekend. There's even a baseball diamond on the northeast corner if you can find enough people to field a team (okay, wishful thinking).

→**Boboli Gardens** ★★ The less sports-inclined can wander through Florence's "green lung" par excellence, attached to the back of the Pitti Palace in the Oltrarno section south of the river. For a 4€ admission fee, the former property of Luca Pitti, a 15th-century Florentine banker, can become your own playground. There are fountains, statues, grottoes, and secluded gardens perfect for spending a lazy Sunday afternoon. *Piazza Pitti.* ☎ *055/2651816. Admission 4€. Daily 8:15am to 1 hr. before sunset.*

→**Fiesole** ★★ Smart Florentines escape the heat and crowds of the city center by heading for the hills. A one-time Etruscan stronghold, the hilltop village of Fiesole is just over 2 miles northeast of the Duomo. Catch the bus from Piazza Santa Maria Novella, and in under 30 minutes, you can be breathing fresh air, enjoying a meal on restaurant-lined **Piazza Mino** (Fiesole's panoramic main square), or tromping through the **Teatro Romano** archaeological park (Via Portigiani 1; ☎ **055/59477;** daily 9am–sunset; Nov–Mar closed Tues) that spills down the hillside, including some fascinating ruins of a Roman theater and the well-preserved heating system of some Roman baths. *Bus: 7 (25-min. ride to main square, Piazza Mino).*

→**Piazzale Michelangelo** ★ This panoramic piazza high above the Oltrarno is the requisite park-and-make-out spot for young Florentine studs who manage to snag themselves a foreign female fling. By day, it's also a de rigueur stop for tour buses. The balustraded terrace offers a sweeping vista of the entire city, spread out in the valley below and backed by the sensual green hills of Fiesole beyond. The monument to Michelangelo in the center of the piazza is made up of bronze replicas of *David* and his sculptures from the Medici chapels. You can walk from the Oltrarno. (On foot, the most direct route here is from Ponte Vecchio to Via de' Bardi, which changes names to Via San Niccolò, then turn right at Porta San

Go La Fiorentina!

The main sports stadium, **Stadio Comunale Artemio Franchi,** plays host to the local soccer team, La Fiorentina. Their season—in Italy's premier Serie A league—runs from September through May. Fiorentina fans are a lively but nonviolent bunch, so if you're in town when they've got a **home game** ★★, you're in for a wonderful cultural spectacle. For tickets, show up at the stadium box office 3 hours before game time (Via Manfredi Fanti 4; ☎ 055/2625537), or check out www.acffiorentina.it. Good seats cost from 20€ to 45€; "tribune of honor" seats will set you back 140€. Women get a 30% discount on all but the most expensive tickets. Hit the stands out front before the game and pick up some purple scarves to show your support.

FLORENCE

Miniato onto Via del Monte alle Croci. Less direct and steeper, but with plenty of stunning views along the way, is the Ponte Vecchio-Costa dei Magnoli-Via di Belvedere-Via del Monte alle Croci route.) *Bus: 12 or 13 from Piazza Santa Maria Novella.*

Shopping

When you show up in Florence and realize that your khaki Ex-Officio pants with the zip-on legs ain't gonna cut it in this chic city, it doesn't take much time or money to get you outfitted *propah*—just head to the zoo of market stalls around San Lorenzo for fun and inexpensive, this-minute fashion accessories, T-shirts, jeans, and, of course, leather jackets (which are not the highest quality and can be a bit expensive).

Florence is perhaps the best shopping city in Italy—its layout, which is far more compact than Rome's or Milan's, means that you can cover a lot of retail territory in a single shopping-dedicated afternoon, even if you're just wandering around. If you want to approach credit card debt in a more targeted fashion, head for these key zones: Mass-market and mostly affordable chain stores are in the area immediately **south of the Duomo** (Via Roma, Via Calzaiuoli, Via del Corso); designer boutiques are scattered a bit everywhere, but mainly concentrated on and around **Via Tornabuoni**; smaller, funkier boutiques are on **Via de' Neri** in Santa Croce; and artisans still practice and sell their old-world crafts in the **Oltrarno.**

→ **Bartolucci** It's hard to miss Bartolucci in all its wooden glory on either of these streets and it's easy to be overwhelmed by the sheer amount of timber in this toy store. The Italian chain has two locations where you can get your niece or nephew a kitschy Florence snow globe. Two locations. *Via Condotta 12/r.* ☎ *055/211773. Borgo dei Greci, 11/a–r.* ☎ *055/2398596. www.bartolucci.com.*

→ **Bologna** ★★ Try as we might, we can never resist buying a pair of shoes or boots here when we're in town. Its location, on heavily touristed Piazza del Duomo, might make savvy shoppers think that they can dig deeper into Florence's backstreets and find better shoes, but this is not the case. Bologna does a brisk business, so if you want to try something on, you'll have to assert yourself to get a sales clerk's attention; once you do, they'll be your staunch, opinionated ally in choosing the best—hottest or most practical, let 'em know your needs—footwear to perfume your luggage with the aphrodisiac smell of Italian leather. With most pairs priced around 250€, Bologna's not cheap, but you're guaranteed several seasons' worth of "*where* did you get those

To Market

Florence boasts a ton of great markets, led by the profusely leathery-smelling **Mercato di San Lorenzo** (Piazza di San Lorenzo; daily 9am–7pm), which specializes in belts, wallets, jackets, bags, jewelry, and ties.

The bohemian **Mercato La Loggia** (Via dei Neri; Thurs–Sun 8am–7pm) has clothing, foreign handcrafted jewelry, and drums, while the market at **Sant'Ambrogio** (Piazza Ghiberti, open weekday mornings and some afternoons) is a pack rat's dream: Old books, light fixtures, postcards, and assorted household goods re hawked by the stall keepers. Remember, always bargain for a lower price when shopping at the markets. Many vendors will knock off 10% to 20% when they see you're interested (but not too interested).

boots?!?!" back home. *Piazza del Duomo 13/15/r.* ☎ *055/290545.*

→ **Coin** ★★ Gotta love Coin—this department store might not offer the coolest shopping bags for flaunting your purchases around town, but Florentines are faithful to its consistently strong selection of fashion accessories (better quality than what you'll find at the open-air market stalls) and housewares (good souvenirs for Mom and Dad). *Via dei Calzaiuoli, 56/r.* ☎ *055/280531. www.coin.it.*

→ **Data** ★ If you're seized by an overwhelming desire to hear the Rolling Stones' "Beast of Burden," make your way over to Data—the city's best resource for '60s and '70s rock, blues, and soul—and ask the clerk if he'll sell your pitiful soul a copy of *Some Girls. Via de' Neri 15/r (Santa Croce).* ☎ *055/287592.*

→ **e-vision** ★ A couple doors down from Ultra, ladies can find more elegant options at e-vision. Dresses and tops feature a remarkably Italian flair with flowing lines and asymmetric patterns. Clerks don't understand English well but try to help you as best they can. Fortunately, they understand the universal language of "MasterCard" and "Visa." *Via Nazionale 154.* ☎ *055/496300.*

→ **G'Art** ★ This local men's label has racks full of obscure, arty T-shirts that'll make a significant dent in your stash of euros. Layer it with one of their cleanly designed blazers and you're ready to impress. Pieces here are pricey, but compared to other, more established names found on Via Tornabuoni, that 250€ blazer looks like a steal. *Via dei Pecori 15/17r.* ☎ *055/289497. www.gart.it.*

→ **La Feltrinelli** Italy's equivalent of Barnes & Noble has several locations in Florence. Though there are heaps of used bookstores in Florence to scour for books in English, if you're looking for a particular Pynchon, minus the dog-eared pages, Feltrinelli's your best bet. *Via Cavour 12–20.* ☎ *055/219524. www.lafeltrinelli.it.*

→ **La Rinascente** Florence's other midrange department store beats Coin on just three counts: the cosmetics floor; the lingerie selection; and the rooftop cafe, which has splendid views over the Duomo, Palazzo Vecchio, and rosy rooftops. *Piazza della Repubblica 1.* ☎ *055/219113.*

→ **Old English Store** If you're aching for a cup of Earl Grey (the only reason I came to this place), Old English Store has everything, well, British. Bolts of tartan cloth (in case you forgot to buy some in Scotland), cans of authentic teas, and even chocolate and candies from the U.K. can be had here. It's also a fantastic place to just step out of the Florentine state of mind and inspect the tailored pants and ties. Once you've had your fill of all things British, get out of there, grab a gelato and enjoy Firenze! *Via Vecchietti 28/r.* ☎ *055/211983.*

→ **Peluso** ★ Peluso is like Payless, only oozing style. Designed like a condensed warehouse, the store offers women slides, pumps, boots, and flip-flops that'll match any outfit or bag. (The selection is awfully sparse for dudes.) Local artisans design most of the shoes, but prices remain extremely reasonable. Some pairs can be had for as low at 14€, which probably means you won't be walking miles in them, but you'll at least have the memories when they're worn out. There are two locations. *Via del Corso 1/11r.* ☎ *055/268283. Via del Corso 6/8r.* ☎ *055/282235.*

→ **Piccadilly Sound** ★ Head to San Marco if your CDs are getting tired and boring. The clerks' English may not be up to snuff, but throw out some names and he'll find it in no time. Most albums released before 2005 are reasonably priced (I found Zep's *Houses of the Holy* and Nick Drake's *Five Leaves Left* selling for 10€). New releases and recent albums can go as high as 20€. *Piazza San Marco 11.* ☎ *055/11220.*

FLORENCE

→ **Ultra** ★ Via Nazionale has a small stretch of edgy boutiques where you can stock up on the latest styles. Ultra is one such shop. Old-school Nikes, Carhartt gear, tons of G-Star, and footwear from Duffs give you an idea of the various stateside influences. Giovanni, the clerk, is always willing to help you find the right vintage T-shirt or pair of weathered jeans. If you're absolutely clueless about Florence's nightlife, ask Giovanni, who's well versed in the alternative world of Firenze. There are two locations. *Via Nazionale 118/r.* ☎ *055/216017. Via XXVII Aprile 37/r.* ☎ *055/489861.*

Road Trip

To be old and still considered cool by throngs of young 'uns is no easy accomplishment. Johnny Cash pulled it off. The '68 mustang definitely pulled it off. Mick Jagger . . . not so much. **Bologna** has all three icons beat, however, with an impressive 400 years on them and 400,000 groupies residing within its borders, thanks in part to the presence of the world's oldest university smack in the heart of the city. Walk along the miles of porticos and you'll quickly realize that Bologna is really a 22-year-old in a 700-year-old's body. The city's flavor, edgy and alternative, starkly contrasts the glamorous aura of Milan to its west and the classical gracefulness of Florence to its south.

I recommend visiting Bologna as a day trip—that should be enough time to take in the university scene and the city's major museum, the Museo Tattile di Pittura Antica e Moderna.

Getting into Town

The best way to travel to Bologna from Florence (or elsewhere in Italy) is by rail. It's about an hour-long ride, and costs 25€. Because of its geographic location, Bologna's **Central Station** (Piazza Medaglie d'Oro 2; ☎ **051-6302111**) is one of the busiest train stations in the country. The station sits at the city's northern edge and is a busy terminus for the ATC (the city bus system). Munich, Frankfurt, and Paris are some of the major hubs it's connected to—all three are reachable via overnight train. For more information about the national train system, consult Trenitalia's extremely handy, multilingual website, **www.trenitalia.com**. You might also try driving to Bologna—it's a relaxing ride. If you leave from Florence, or any point from the south, the A1 will take you within a few kilometers of Bologna.

General information for tourists is available by calling ☎ **051-246-541.** If you'd rather browse the brochures in person or chat with someone face to face, head to one of three **tourist offices.** The first is located in the train station on Piazza Medaglie d'Oro 2 (Mon–Sat 8am–8pm). There's another in the airport (Mon–Sat 8am–8pm, Sun 9am–3pm). The main tourist office is conveniently placed in the busy Piazza Maggiore 1 (daily 9am–8pm).

Sightseeing

Bologna's city center, shaped like an irregular pentagon, is wonderfully compact and easy to navigate. Most major streets and roads radiate from 🎬 **Best** **Piazza Maggiore,** with the busier *viales* surrounding the area and creating the city's unusual, five-sided shape. The northeast quadrant, where the university buildings and student population are concentrated, is noticeably livelier than other areas and chock-full of pubs for post-class binge drinking. The northwest, especially near **Piazza dei Martiri,** is where you'll find less-than-savory folk hanging around the fountain and discount stores. Head south towards Piazza Maggiore and the scene changes dramatically: Both the architecture and environment become much more

ᴍᴛᴠŲ The University Scene

Europe's oldest university, **Alma Matter Studiorum,** or the **University of Bologna** (www.unibo.it/Portale/default.htm), was founded here, and to this day it fills the city with intellectual intensity and a liberal attitude. You can e-mail the Foreign Exchange office (percorsiculturali@ammc.unibo.it) for info on programs.

Locals enjoy relaxing at the gorgeous botanical gardens maintained by the university at Via Irnerio 42 (☎ 051-351-299; Mon–Fri 8am–3pm, Sat 8am–1pm, closed holidays) in the northeast of the city. It's a sprawling 2,023 hectares (5,000 acres) and contains just as many species of plants and trees. Aside from being a green space to escape the city commotion, the gardens also feature three greenhouses and an area where various habitats are re-created.

Another great place to experience Bologna student life is along Via Zamboni, the heavily postered main drag of the university district, near Via delle Belle Arte and Via Zamboni. Here students mingle at all hours of the day and night, talking shop, making plans, dining in one of the cheap restaurants, or checking each other out.

aesthetically pleasing. The tourists who do decide to stop by Bologna usually concentrate on exploring everything south of and around Piazza Maggiore. In addition to the big museums and attractions, you'll also find more luxurious shopping in the south. The area is a great deal quieter and perfect for a relaxing post-dinner stroll. If you venture farther south and a bit to the east, you'll stumble upon the public gardens, just outside of the city center.

Ⓜ **Best** FREE → **Museo Tattile di Pittura Antica e Moderna** ★★ I can safely say that this is the only place where feeling up

the *Mona Lisa* is not only acceptable, but encouraged. In Bologna, the blind are given a chance to enjoy the same great pieces of art as everyone else. Famous pieces, such as the *Birth of Venus,* are created three-dimensionally so that people can actually touch the famed clamshell. Even if you're in possession of all your senses, the Tactile Museum is definitely worth your time. Booking in advance is recommended. *Via Castiglione 71.* ☎ *051-332-090. www.cavazza.it/arte/edmnv/comunic.en. htm. Free admission. Fri 9am–6pm; Sat 9am–1:30pm.*

FLORENCE

The French Riviera

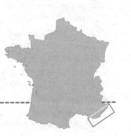

Even if you don't like beaches, go to the French Riviera. It's a cultural introduction to society. The socialist in you may argue that such wealth and ostentation is obscene: purple yachts, sports cars that cost more than some nation's education budgets, hotels that cater to hard bodies with perfect coifs and never-cracked nails. The capitalist in you can revel in the nonstop restaurants and places, from casinos to cafes, to part with your hard-earned cash. It is something to see and to embrace, if that's your thing. Otherwise, you can park yourself in a cafe or at the back of the beach to simply watch. Just remember to bring your sunglasses.

The *very* rich, *very* famous, and *very* hip come for the scene. And that is what is easiest to see, especially in the summer. Coco Chanel came to Cannes and became the first of the fashionable to boast a bronzed body. But authors and painters have sought these shores for decades, if not centuries. It may be the light, the winds that come off the Mediterranean, or the horizon. Usually, these things calm the soul; here it ramps people up for clubbing until dawn.

Don't expect Caribbean- or Greek-style beaches here. Many of the beaches are private, and most are pebbly. Think back to the old movies where the stars emerged from cabanas only to flop themselves down on folding chairs. Nice has no sand; Cannes, a little. Yet life revolves around the beachfront.

The hotels that line the sea are prohibitively expensive, and unless you're a trust-fund kid, you'll most likely appreciate the architecture from afar, although in St-Tropez, the best nightclub is attached to the Hotel Byblos. Big stars come here to mingle around the pool during the day, and to pre-game in their suites before going to the club until dawn. Trying to get in might be an adventure in itself.

The Best of the French Riviera

○ **The Best Cheap Meal:** Experience a real salad Niçoise at **Restaurant Voyageur Nissart.** The restaurant is right next to the train station, and the food is cheap and super-good. Nice is known for its fabulous cuisine, and this is authentic down-home cooking at its best. See p. 403.

○ **The Best Town to Call Home Base: Nice** is beautiful and relatively inexpensive compared to other Riviera hubs. The hostels here are filled with people you can connect with, and the town is situated so that day trips to Cannes, St-Tropez, and Monaco are pretty easy. And the nightlife ain't so bad here either. See p. 398.

○ **The Best Rock-Star Hotel:** In the famous words of Ferris Beuller, "If you have the means, I highly recommend" it. **Hôtel Byblos** is where the rich and famous people from all over go to mingle with their own kind. One of the hippest night clubs in St-Tropez is attached to the hotel. See p. 408.

○ **The Best Outdoor Activity:** Make the **beach** your epicenter for all things social and you won't be wanting. Meet people, pretend you're not working on your tan (bad for the skin, no!), and, no matter what your gender, check out the topless French chicks.

○ **The Best Casino:** This is one of the top casinos in the world. When you walk into the main room of the **Monte-Carlo Casino,** you may feel as if you're walking into a movie. Opulence with no excuses reigns here. And it *has* been re-created in many films. The front room has the slot machines and other games for most of us slobs. A more exclusive—and more expensive—room draws big-stakes gamblers with baccarat, roulette, and chemin de fer. See p. 416.

○ **The Best Hidden Museum:** On Promenade des Anglais in Nice, the 145-room **Hotel Negresco** is home to thousands of works of art. Dress well and the concierge might let you walk around the enormous rooms on the main floor; you'll see Renoir sculptures, portraits of the French kings, and a sculpture by Niki de St-Phalle. The ceiling in the Salon Royal was designed by Gustav Eiffel (who also constructed a famous tower in Paris). See p. 403.

French Riviera Basics

Festivals

Some of the celebrations along the French Riviera date from the Middle Ages, although most are recent innovations. So many worthy events could be listed below, from mushroom fests and fireworks competitions to the famous film festival (p. 414), but if we did that, this book would be twice the size. Check the calendars at the tourism offices for full lists.

February

▶ Best **Nice Carnaval.** The biggest festival of the year boasts parades, elaborate costumes, and endless festivities, including masked balls and fireworks. The theme for this decadent tradition over the past 122 years celebrates the excesses of society. Get a seat in the bleachers for 15€ to 25€ (free admission if you are in costume). Call ☎ 08-92-70-74-07 or go to www.nicecarnaval.com for more information. 10 days, usually in February.

THE FRENCH RIVIERA

Free & Easy

→ You must pay for some of the nicest oceanfront property. But all the destinations in this chapter—Cannes, Monaco, Nice, and St-Tropez—have free **beaches** that are perfectly good—as long as you don't mind the pebbles.

→ A few **museums** are free to the public on the first and third Thursday and Sunday of each month. They usually offer reduced rates for students during the rest of the week.

→ The **Changing of the Guard** at the Palais Princier (Prince's Palace) in Monaco is free. It takes place daily just before noon.

→ Off the coast of Cannes lie a few islands that are worth exploring, if you have extra time. The Ile Ste. Marguerite has an old Spanish fort that dates back to the 17th century. The **Museum of the Sea** there is free for students. (But you'll have to pay 10€ for the boat there and back.)

→ If you're here for **Carnaval,** don your costume. Revelers in disguise can get into the parades for free.

→ The **Fête du Musique** in June is all free. Music's in the air and everywhere!

May

Formula One Grand Prix. Monaco hosts what is probably the most-watched car-racing event in Europe. ☎ 93-15-26-00. Second week in May.

July

Nice Festival du Jazz. One of the many summer festivals, this weeklong gathering features hundreds of artists, over 70 concerts, and theme nights. It's one of the biggest jazz festivals in Europe and attracts over 45,000 visitors every year. Call ☎ 04-97-13-36-86 or go to www.nicejazzfest.com for more information. Eight days in mid-July.

Bastille Day. You can't escape the fireworks that go off to celebrate the storming of the Bastille in Paris many, many years ago. July 14.

Culture Tips 101

It's pretty rare to see someone openly smoking a joint on the street in Cannes, Nice, or Monaco. Monaco clubs don't see much drug use, at least not openly. Gay clubs tend to have more of a drug thing going on, usually some E. Keep in mind that the penalty for being caught is stiff. The French government cracked down on hash smoking about 15 years ago, and the penalty is jail time (like 7 years!). As for booze, the legal minimum drinking age is 16 (or younger if you're with your 'rents). You're pretty safe having a drink on the beach or on the streets of Vieux-Nice or Cannes, but it's just not done in Monaco. In general, the French like their wine as much as you do, and as long as you don't cause trouble, there shouldn't be a problem.

The French Riviera Nuts & Bolts

Business Hours Business hours here are erratic. Most banks are open Monday to Friday from 9:30am to 4:30pm. Many people do take a lunch break, and they post their hours on their doors. Museums often close 1 day a week (usually Tues), and they're

The French Riviera

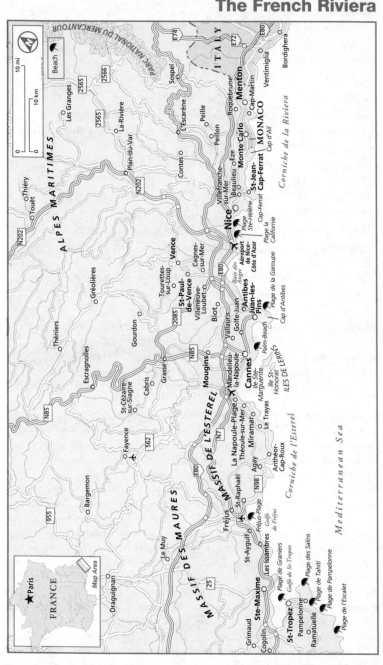

generally shut on national holidays. Usual hours are from 9:30am to 5pm. Most French museums are closed Sunday morning but open Sunday afternoon.

Cellphone Providers & Service Centers There are cellphone stores in Nice that sell all three major brands of phone.

Currency France uses euros, and the best way to access them is to use an ATM.

Embassies The embassies are all located in Paris (see "Paris Nuts & Bolts" on p. 699).

Emergencies Dial ☎ 17 for the police, ☎ 15 for an ambulance, ☎ 18 for the fire department. **Riviera Medical Services** (☎ 04-93-26-12-70) is an emergency service in English that locates English-speaking doctors.

Laundry Laundromats (*laverie* in French) are around the towns. Ask at the reception of your hotel for the closest public laundromat.

Post Office You'll find post offices in all three towns, but you can also buy stamps from *tabacs* (tobacco shops).

Safety There are pickpockets, so use common sense as you would in other areas.

Telephone The French use a **télécarte,** a phone debit card, which you can purchase at rail stations, post offices, and other places. Sold in two versions, it allows you to use either 50 or 120 charge units by inserting the card into the slot of most public phones. Depending on the type of card you buy, the cost is 7.45€ to 15€. If possible, avoid making calls from your hotel; some French establishments double or triple the charges.

Tipping All bills, as required by law, are supposed to say *service compris*, which means that the tip has been included. Tip 1€ to 1.50€ for every item of baggage the porter carries on arrival or departure. You're not obligated to tip the concierge, door-person, or anyone else—unless you use his or her services. In cafes, waiter service is usually included. Tip **taxi drivers** 10% to 15% of the amount of the meter.

Nice

As you're wandering from pub to pub in the old town of MTV Best **Nice** ★★★ , through the pedestrian streets where there is a bar on every block, you may start to think about how Nice is the very antithesis of Paris. While Paris may seem cold, rainy, and intimidating, Nice is warm and sunny, and everyone here seems to be on vacation.

As you walk into the next pub and order a pint you may think about what you expected from Nice: lounging on sandy beaches with champagne in hand. Were you disappointed when you realized that the beaches here are made of rocks, not sand, and that instead of going back thinner you feel you may have added a few "kilos" because of all the beer

and pasta? And is Nice seemingly less French than you imagined. I mean what's with all these pubs?

We're in France; we're expecting to sip wine in a bistro, not slog down a pint in a British pub. But that's Nice for ya. British culture has become a part of Nice's culture. Just look at the main boardwalk, the most important street in Nice. It's called Promenade des Anglais (English promenade), then it turns into quai des Etats Unis (USA St.). You may feel bombarded with English culture, but the fact that Nice is so international is one of the things that makes it so unique.

Nice has been attracting tourists since the 19th century when British, American, and

Nice

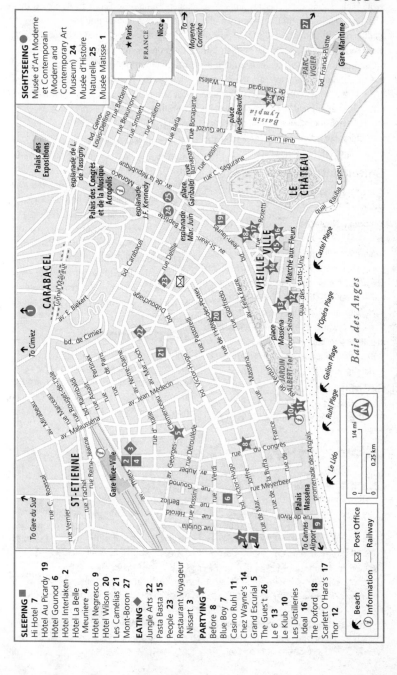

SIGHTSEEING ●
Musée d'Art Moderne
et Contemporain
(Modern and
Contemporary Art
Museum) **24**
Musée d'Histoire
Naturelle **25**
Musée Matisse **1**

SLEEPING ■
Hi Hotel **7**
Hôtel Au Picardy **19**
Hôtel Gounod **6**
Hôtel Interlaken **2**
Hôtel La Belle
Meunière **4**
Hôtel Negresco **9**
Hôtel Wilson **20**
Les Camélias **21**
Mont-Boron **27**

EATING ◆
Jungle Arts **22**
Pasta Basta **15**
People **23**
Restaurant Voyageur
Nissart **3**

PARTYING ★
Before **8**
Blue Boy **7**
Casino Ruhl **11**
Chez Wayne's **14**
Grand Escurial **5**
The Gues't **26**
Le 6 **13**
Le Klub **10**
Les Distilleries
Ideal **16**
The Oxford **18**
Scarlett O'Hara's **17**
Thor **12**

✷ Beach
☒ Post Office
ⓘ Information
— Railway

Russian aristocracy flocked to balmy Nice to avoid their ferocious northern winters. Nice was the first major tourist town on the Mediterranean, and today, it is the capital of the French Riviera and the biggest city between Genoa and Marseille. It used to be the most elite destination on the French Riviera, but in the last 30 years smaller towns like Cannes and St-Tropez have gained popularity with the world's billionaires and megastars. For young people, Nice reigns as the top spot on the French Riviera.

Getting into Town

GETTING THERE

By Air

Aéroport Nice-Côte d'Azure (☎ 08-20-42-33-33) is the international airport, about 30 minutes outside Nice. To go from the airport to the center of town, take city bus no. 98, which drops you off at the Gare Routière (4€) or take a shuttle (4.50€). Bus no. 99 goes back and forth between the train station and the airport every 20 minutes starting at 7:15am and ending at about 8:30pm (4€). A taxi will cost at least 25€ from the airport to the center of town.

By Train

You'll arrive at **Gare Nice-Ville** (av. Thiers; ☎ 08-92-35-35-35). The **tourist center** at the train station offers maps and info; it's open Monday to Saturday 8am to 6:30pm, and Sunday 8am to noon and 2 to 5:30pm. The tourist areas of Nice (all of the shopping, hotels, pubs, and museums) are between the train station and the water, which is only about a 10- to 15-minute walk away. Check out the **SNCF** (France's national train line) website (www.voyages-sncf.com).

By Bus

The main intercity bus station is **Gare Routière** (5 bd. Jean-Jaures; ☎ 04-93-85-61-81). The buses that come from other Riviera towns tend to be about the same prices as the trains or a little cheaper, but they also tend to be slower. Most people use the train because it is often more convenient. Some small towns don't have train stations (like St-Tropez), so you are obliged to take the bus to get there. (To get to St-Tropez, you have to change buses in St-Raphael. The total bus ride will be about 27€.)

GETTING AROUND

By Bus

You can walk almost everywhere in Nice, but city buses can offer respite for weary legs. The main city bus station is **Station Centrale** (10 av. Félix-Faure; ☎ 04-93-13-53-13) near

Internet Cafes

Email Café This is the only cybercafe in Vieux Nice. It has six computers with fast connections, printers, scanners, and a digital card reader to download all the photos you've been taking. In the cafe, look for the three ethernet terminals for laptops and Wi-Fi access. Just don't spill your crepe or salad fixings on your work. The charge is 4.50€ per hour, but you only pay for the minutes you use. *8 rue St-Vincent, Nice.* ☎ *04-93-62-68-86. cafe@wanadoo.fr. Daily 8:30am–7pm.*

3D. Com This Internet cafe is right next to the main port in Nice. It has a relaxed atmosphere with high-speed Internet, fax machines, printers, Web cams, and free candy. It also sells phone cards. It's 3€ an hour for the Internet. *37 bd. Stalingrad.* ☎ *04-97-00-01-61. www.3dcomm.xooit.net.*

Panini and Web This small Internet cafe, on Promenade des Anglais, is a great place to eat panini while your use the Web. *25 Promenade des Anglais.* ☎ *04-93-88-72-75. web.nice@wanadoo.fr.*

Talk of the Town

Three ways to start a conversation with a local

1. **What do you think about the American administration?** Love it or hate it, chat up your theories on the current U.S. government. The French go wild for political discourse.

2. **Can you teach me a few words of Niçois and Provençal?** These and other regional languages were spoken back in the day. Many older folk take pride in their local culture (although most of the young people can't speak the local languages).

3. **Do you think the schools should be privatized?** Try to get someone to talk to you about the French education system. It is very different than the American one (for example, college is pretty much free in France). Some French people can get very passionate about France's move towards privatization and a more "American" system of education.

place Masséna. To ride, you can buy a ticket on the bus for 1.30€ or a *carnet*, which gives you 14 rides for 16€.

By Scooter

The best place for scooter and bike rentals is **Cycles Arnaud** (5 rue François 1er; ☎ 04-93-87-88-55; Mon–Fri 9am–noon and 2–7pm). Bikes and mopeds rent for 15€ per day. You must have a driver's license. Or check out **Nicea Location Rent** by the train station (12 rue de Belgique; ☎ 04-93-16-10-30; www.nicealocationrent.com). Prices are comparable with Cycles Arnaud and they rent Rollerblades, too.

Nice Basics

ORIENTATION: NICE NEIGHBORHOODS

Think of the city shaped as a semicircle. The flat part of the semicircle is the beach and Promenade des Anglais. The top point of the semicircle is the train station. To the right is the port and just before that is Vieux Nice. Most of its major sites are tucked between the train station and the coast, so it's fairly simple to navigate. Restaurants and shopping are centralized in **Vieux Nice** (**Old Nice**, also called Vielle Ville on maps) on the eastern side of town, by the water. **Promenade des**

Anglais ★★ is the boardwalk that runs up and down the bay (Bai des Anges); as you continue east, the Promenade eventually turns into **quai des Etats Unis** at Vieux Nice where you will find restaurants, shops, and bars.

Three **tourist offices** are in Nice: at 5 Promenade des Anglais near place Masséna (☎ 04-92-14-46-46), at the airport (☎ 68-20-42-34-33), and at the train station (☎ 68-92-35-35-35). The offices help visitors with hotel reservations and also offer a book that lists all the hotels and prices in Nice (reservations: ☎ 08-92-70-74-07). Also, check out the city's helpful website at www.nicetourisme.com.

Sleeping

HOSTELS

→ **Hôtel La Belle Meuniere** This 200-year-old hotel near the train station attracts scores of backpackers in summer who gather at the hotel garden's picnic tables. The double is nice but often booked. *21 av. Durante, Nice.* ☎ *04-93-88-66-15. 15€–20€ dorm bed. 36€–55€ double with private bathroom. Rates include breakfast. Closed Dec and Jan. Amenities: Laundry (staff does it for you with minimum of 5.50€); towels and sheets.*

➜ **Les Camélias** This Hostel International (HI) hostel gets high ranking for its cleanliness and ideal location in the town center. Even though it has 136 beds, it's often booked in summer, so you should try to get a reservation before showing up. Make a reservation online, or arrive very early in the morning (by 8am). The hostel bar (as well as the fully equipped kitchen) serves as a great hangout to meet fellow travelers. *3 rue Spitalieri, Nice.* ☎ *04-93-62-15-54. www.hi hostels.com. 20€ dorm bed. HI membership required (2.90€ at hostel). Rates include breakfast. Amenities: Bar; bike storage; elevator; Internet (5€ hourly); kitchen; laundry facilities; lockers (1€ daily); lockout 11am–3pm; lounge; sheets included; wheelchair friendly.*

➜ **Mont-Boron** This other HI hostel is far from the town and has a 12:30am curfew, but the intimate atmosphere makes it worth the hike: Mont-Boron is tucked into a mountain near hiking trails, and there are exceptional views of Nice from the dorm rooms. Unfortunately, it's a 45-minute walk (at least) into town, and the nearest bus runs only from 6:50am to 8pm. *Route Forestière du Mont Alban, Nice.* ☎ *04-93-82-23-64. www. hihostels.com. Bus: 14. 16€ dorm bed. Rates include breakfast. HI membership required (2.90€ at hostel). Amenities: Bike storage; Internet; kitchen; laundry facilities (6€); lockers; lockout 10am–5pm.*

CHEAP

➜ **Hôtel Au Picardy** Across from the main bus station and next to Vieux Nice, this hotel is a 5-minute walk from museums and the beach. The cheapest hotel option in the area features rooms with either views of the busy street or the lovely interior courtyard. The rooms are simple and clean. *10 bd. Jean-Jaurès, Nice.* ☎ *04-93-85-75-51. 25€–32€ single; 24€–45€ double, depending on the size and bathroom (shared or private); 49€ triple. Amenities: TV (in common room).*

➜ **Hôtel Interlaken** You can't miss this striking pink hotel across from the train station. The Interlaken, founded in 1870, still has some of its original antique furniture. The high ceilings and enormous windows help offset the fact that rooms have no air-conditioning. Unexpected bonus: The beds sport cheetah-print spreads. *26 av. Durante, Nice.* ☎ *04-93-88-30-15. 45€ double with shared bathroom, 50€ with private bathroom; 70€ triple with private bathroom; 77€ quad with private bathroom. Breakfast 5€. In room: TV.*

➜ **Hôtel Wilson** This hotel takes up a floor of an apartment building (a few floors above a probation office). It's a basic place, cheap for Nice, and some rooms have balconies. Rooms with shared facilities are even cheaper. *39 rue de Hôtel des Postes, Nice.* ☎ *04-93-85-47-79. www.hotel-wilson-nice. com. Oct 15–Apr 14 26€–32€ single or double with sink, 35€–37€ with shower and TV, 40€–44€ with private bathroom and TV; Apr 15–Oct 14 34€–38€ single or double with sink, 40€–44€ with shower and TV, 45€–49€ with private bathroom and TV. Breakfast 5.50€. Extra person 10€. In room: TV.*

DOABLE

➜ **Hôtel Gounod** ★ Close to both the train station and the beach, the small, basic rooms have small but sufficient bathrooms with tubs or showers. Guests can swim in the pool, use the sauna, get snacks at the cafe/bar and play in the Jacuzzi at Hôtel Splendid next door. *3 rue Gounod, Nice.* ☎ *04-93-16-42-00. www.gounod-nice.com. 95€–135€ double, 130€–210€ suite. Closed Nov 20–Dec 20. Bus: 8. Amenities: Bar; gym; Internet; laundry and dry cleaning service; massage; nonsmoking rooms; pool. In room: TV, 24-hr. room service.*

SPLURGE

➜ **Hi Hotel** ★★ The Hi Hotel's modern conceptual design depends on bright colors, geometric shapes, and input from Philippe Starck. Rooms have nine different design concepts with names like "Digital," "Straight," "Up and Down," and "Techno Corner." The shower in one room, for example, was built inside a fuchsia-and-neon-green Plexiglas cubicle elevated on a platform. Amenities in some rooms include lava-rock bathtubs, sofas with built-in headsets, and even a beta fish in a bowl. A rooftop pool with lounge chairs has incredible views of Nice. Be prepared, though: Some rooms' bathrooms lack doors, and the food in the restaurant is displayed in Tupperware containers. *3 av. des Fleurs, Nice.* ☎ *04-97-07-26-26. www.hi hotel.net. 190€–375€ single, 210€–395€ double. Amenities: 24-hr. bar and snack bar; Internet; laundry and dry cleaning services; nonsmoking and limited mobility rooms; rooftop pool; spa; Wi-Fi. In room: A/C, TV, safe, 24-hr. room service.*

MTV Best → **Hotel Negresco** ★★★ This hotel is a work of art. The owner, Madam Augier lives on the top floor, and she has spent most of her life collecting now-priceless works of art to fill her hotel. Even if you can't stay here, go in and have a look at the lobby and its Louis XIV room with a life-size painting of the Sun King. The room is filled with antiques from the 17th century. In the Royal Salon you will find a stained-glass domed ceiling in the Belle Epoque style (designed by Gustav Eiffel), which naturally lights up the room's dozens of paintings and sculptures. The hotel has two restaurants, one gourmet and the other a brasserie that is designed to look like a carousel. The staff members dress in 17th-century outfits and are warm and welcoming to the guests. *37 Promenade des Anglais, Nice.* ☎ *04-93-88-35-68. www.hotel-negresco-nice.com. 250€–525€ double, 605€–830€ suite. Amenities: 2 restaurants; bar; fitness center; laundry and dry cleaning service; massage; nonsmoking rooms. In room: A/C, TV, room service.*

Eating

If you choose to go out for meals, go for a cheaper lunch, and then plan a picnic for dinner. Try to avoid hotel breakfasts if they charge for them; instead, go to the boulangerie around the corner and pay a couple euros for a copious amount of pastries. If you are a coffee drinker, drink your espresso at the counter; cafes charge extra if you sit at a table.

CHEAP

→ **Pasta Basta** ITALIAN This Italian restaurant in Vieux Nice serves gigantic portions of every kind of pizza, pasta, and salad imaginable. For the homemade pasta, you choose the shape, and then the sauce. It's a good idea to make a reservation. *18 rue de la Préfecture, Nice.* ☎ *04-93-80-03-57. Salads 3€–10€; pizzas 7€–10€; fixed-price menu 13€. Daily 7–11pm.*

MTV Best → **Restaurant Voyageur Nissart** ★ NIÇOISE The same family has been running this restaurant for three generations (since 1908), and they maintain its fantastic reputation by serving market-fresh Niçoise specialties. Lunch includes local delights like *farcis* (veggies stuffed with a meat mixture and topped with cheese), *daube Niçoise* (a local beef stew), ravioli, and, of course, the salad Niçoise. *19 rue Alsace Lorraine, Nice.* ☎ *04-93-82-19-60. www. voyageur-nissart.com. Lunch 8€–10€; dinner 13€–20€. Tues–Sun for lunch and dinner. Closed for part of Aug.*

DOABLE

→ **Jungle Arts** AFRICAN Jungle Arts has an African theme and serves ostrich and kangaroo in addition to beef and chicken. Check out the wild animal–print theme. *6 rue Lepante (at the intersection of rue Biscarra), Nice.* ☎ *04-93-92-00-18. Lunch fixed-price menu 11€; dinner fixed-price menu 20€. Mon–Sat 7pm–midnight.*

THE FRENCH RIVIERA

→**La Zucca Magica** ★ ITALIAN/ VEGETARIAN One of the best restaurants in Nice, it's fun, friendly, and unique. There is no menu; you just sit, and the waitstaff brings a five-course meal with the market-fresh dishes of the day. *4 bis quai Papacino (at the intersection of rue de Foresta), Nice.* ☎ *04-93-56-25-27. Lunch 17€; dinner 27€. Tues–Sat noon–2pm and 7–10pm.*

Partying

Riviera-style partying means starting early and saving enough cash to pay for a late-night cab back to your hotel. Most pubs and bars close at 2am (or 2:30) and the only nightclubs worth going to are at the port on the east side of town, which could be a 30-minute trek home if your hotel is near the train station. The clubs tend to keep people in until 5 or 6am.

BARS & CLUBS

→**Before** A very *branché* (popular) bar to hit between 6pm and midnight. The hip Niçoise come here after work to enjoy an *apéro* and snacks from 8 to 10pm (drinks 3.50€–8€). The bar starts to rock by 10pm, and the music switches from lounge to house, electro, funk, and disco. After, the Before people tend to migrate toward the pubs in Vieux Nice. *18 rue du Congrès, Nice.* ☎ *04-93-87-85-59.*

→**Chez Wayne's** The most popular pub in Nice is an Anglophone hangout with an international crowd and live music most nights. Expect live classic rock and pop music, crowded rooms, and beautiful drunk girls revealing their boobs to not only the barman but also the barman's camera (check the website!). The pub also serves Tex-Mex food at a pretty reasonable price. *15 rue de la Préfecture, Nice.* ☎ *04-93-13-46-99. www. waynes.fr.*

→**Grand Escurial** Whether its claims to being the biggest night club on the French Riviera are valid, this place can get packed on summer weekends. Not for you unless

How to Get In

If you want to party until the break of dawn with the beautiful people of Nice, you gotta get through the door first. Door policies can be strict, especially at clubs like The Gues't, and you need to dress in nightclub clothes to get in. If you are a boy or a group of boys and you aren't accompanied by a lady, company policy says you won't get in. Making reservations is the best way to ensure that you get through the door.

you like being surrounded by hundreds of sweaty bodies dancing to the latest pop, R&B, hip-hop, and house music. Its size also makes it look totally empty on weekdays or in the winter. *29 rue Alphonse Karr, Nice.* ☎ *04-93-82-37-66.*

→**The Gues't** This most exclusive bar in town is on the port. If you don't have a reservation and you aren't friends with the owner, don't expect to get in. The club turns away hundreds of people every night here. If you do get in, you will be ushered into the first room, which is filled with couches, low tables, and red dim lights. Everything is centered on a huge dance floor where the DJ spins music that makes you want to get up and dance. To sit at a table, you must buy a bottle of something (the cheapest is 110€). Alternatively, you can wander around the four rooms and get cocktails from the bar. The rooms seem like a series of underground caves (plans are afoot to open four more). *5 quai des 2 Emmanuel, Nice.* ☎ *04-93-56-83-83.*

→**Les Distilleries Ideal** Les Distilleries is a unique bar in Vieux Nice. The inside sports rusty machines that turn and crank to move pulleys and spin fans. It has a very 1920s industrial feel, with polished brass distillery vats and more rusty machines on the walls. The DJ spins music ranging from reggae to

The Gay Scene

Most of the town's nightclubs welcome Nice's large gay population—and gay tourists. A few hangouts include **Le Klub** (6 rue Halévy; ☎ **04-93-16-27-56;** 15€ cover), where you'll find high energy and a mostly under-35 crowd; **Le 6** (6 rue de la Terrasse; ☎ **04-93-62-66-64**), which has live singers nightly; and **Le Blue Boy** (9 rue Jean-Baptiste Spinetta; ☎ **04-93-44-68-24;** cover 10€), the oldest gay disco in the French Riviera, with two bars and two dance floors.

rock to jazz. *24 rue de la Préfecture, Nice.* ☎ *04-93-62-10-66.*

→ **O'Neill's Irish Pub** This should be a stop on your pub-crawl because students often come for the cheap beer. *40 rue Droite, Nice.* ☎ *04-93-80-06-75.*

→ **The Oxford** Come here for the more relaxed atmosphere and the live music. It's a small pub, and it's open until 5am. *4 rue Mascoïnat.* ☎ *04-94-92-24-54.*

→ **Thor** The unique surroundings—it's a pub built into a cellar, with stone walls and stone ceiling—draw a crowd that's young and beautiful. The pub is pretty small and fills up quickly on the nights that they play live music—usually rock and always entertaining. *32 cours Saleya, Nice.* ☎ *09-93-62-49-90.*

CASINOS

→ **Casino Ruhl** This twinkling haven attracts all types of gamblers. Its slots room boasts more than 300 slot machines (called *machines à sous*) and there's also a gaming room *(sale de jeux).* The slot machines are available from 10am until 4am daily, but if you want to get into a game, you'll have to wait until 8pm. To get into the game room, you have to pay 11€ for an all-day pass. It gets you access to roulette (French and English), blackjack, punto banco, and stud poker. Some rules may differ from American-style gambling, so ask before you lay down the chips. *1 Promenade des Anglais, Nice.* ☎ *04-97-03-12-22.*

Sightseeing

→ **Musée d'Art Moderne et Contemporain (Modern and Contemporary Art Museum)** This museum has a huge collection of avant-garde art from the '60s to today. The museum dramatically reveals the evolution of parallel arts movements in two countries: '60s American pop art and Nouveau Réalism in the French Riviera. You're either going to like it or hate it. The building is, um, very modern: It looks like a box with no windows. *Promenade des Arts. Nice.* ☎ *04-93-62-61-62. www.mamac-nice.org. Admission 4€; 2.50€ students. Free entrance on the 1st and 3rd Thurs of the month. Tues–Sun 10am–6pm. Closed most holidays. Bus: 3, 5, 6, 16, or 17 to Promenade des Arts; 7, 9, or 10 to Garibaldi; or 1 or 2 to Promenade des Arts/Garibaldi.*

→ **Musée d'histoire Naturelle (Barla)** This museum, founded in 1846, contains an enormous collection: almost a million specimens from the Mediterranean. The museum has a huge permanent collection of cephalopods (think giant squid, octopus, and

Museum Pass

If you plan to visit a lot of museums, consider purchasing the Museum Pass. A 7-day pass (6€) allows admission to all municipal museums in Nice. There is also a Riviera Museum Pass (1-day pass 10€, 3-day pass 17€, 7-day pass 27€), which will get you into 65 museums, monuments, and gardens throughout the French Riviera.

so on), and a good audiovisual tour with a Jules Verne theme. *60 bd. Risso, Nice.* ☎ *04-97-13-46-80. Free Admission. Daily 10am–6pm, except some public holidays.*

→ **Musée Matisse** ★★ Head to Cimiez, which is 5km (3 miles) out of town, to take in the gorgeous paintings of Henri Matisse, who died in Nice in 1954. There is a chronologically arranged series of paintings from 1890 to 1919 as well as a series of paintings from certain periods of his life, in addition to collages and prints. *154 av. Des Arènes-de-Cimiez.* ☎ *04-93-53-40-53. Admission 4€ adults; 2.50€ students. Wed–Mon 10am–6pm. Bus: 15 or 17 from place Masséna in Nice and get off in the Villa des Arènes-de-Cimiez.*

Playing Outside

📺 **Best** BEACHES The beaches—pebbly, not sandy—are a great place to hang out on a sunny day. There are free beaches and private beaches that cost 10€ to 15€ and usually include lounge chairs and umbrellas. Nude sunbathing is forbidden, but the women often go topless. Take bus no. 9, 10, 12, or 23.

HIKING Nice, with more than 300 hectares of gardens, has won the title of "city with the best gardens" for so long (over 10 years) that it's no longer allowed to compete. On the east side of town, the large hill has hiking trails with amazing views of Nice and the bay. You can take bus no. 14 up to the top and hike around. The last bus to get back is around 7pm, or hike about 1 hour to get back into town.

SCUBA DIVING **Centre International de Plongée de Nice** (2 ruelle des Moulins; ☎ **04-93-55-59-50** or 06-09-52-55-57). It is next to the old port between quai des Docks and bd Stalingrad). If it's your first time (a *baptême*), it will be about 30€. For experienced divers with diving licenses it will be about 35€ for a one-tank dive.

Shopping

The main shopping streets are rue Masséna, place Magenta, avenue Jean-Médecin, rue de Verdun, and rue Paradis. There are also a couple of flea markets: **Marché à la Brocante** (cours Saleya; Mon 8am–5pm) and **Les Puces de Nice** (place Robilante; Tues–Sat 9am–6pm). In Vieux Nice, you can find tons of shops with local specialties like soaps, perfumes (nearby town of Grasse is known for its perfumes), colorful Provençal fabrics, lavender, and, of course, herbs de Provence (a combination of local herbs used in cooking). Think: souvenirs.

St-Tropez

When French writer Guy Maupassant sang the praises of this small fishing village in his 1888 memoir "Sur L'Eau," he inspired a generation of artists and writers like Jean-Paul Sartre, Simone de Beauvoir, and Henri Matisse to vacation at **St-Tropez** ★★ at the beginning of the 20th century. They unintentionally set the trend that would be followed by such stars as Brigitte Bardot, Mick Jagger, and recently P. Diddy, Beyoncé, Bono, Cindy Crawford, Denzel Washington, and Mary-Kate and Ashley Olsen, just to name a lot. St-Tropez is a small fishing village turned expensive resort town. It is small, safe, and beautiful and it has become the meeting place for the world's elite for these reasons.

This village of 5,500 expands tenfold in the summer, due to the exclusive location, the stars, and those who are star searching. This has become known as Saint Trop, meaning "Saint too much" in French, because of the excesses that draws the crowds here. People come to St-Tropez to sleep late, go to a private beach in the afternoon, and then prepare for a night in expensive restaurants and even more expensive nightclubs.

This town is a hedonistic heaven like none other.

Getting into Town
GETTING THERE

Expect to shell out the cash, and here's why. There is no train station here, so you have to either rent a car or take a helicopter (750€), bus, boat, or taxi, all of which will cost an arm and a leg. The beaches are a few miles out of town on a road with no sidewalk, so don't even think about walking. There is a bus that goes to the beaches a few times a day but only during the summer. So, to get there, you need a car or a taxi and, bam, that just cost you another arm. Say you decide it may be cheaper to just rent a car for a few days. If you want to park in St-Tropez, that's going to cost you another leg. Then you haven't got a leg to stand on and you still haven't paid for a hotel or food. Good luck, as this city was designed to keep poor people out.

By Bus

The cheapest and slowest way is to come by bus. Go first to St. Raphael, which has a train station. Take the **Beltrame** bus (☎ 04-94-95-95-16; www.sva-beltrame.com; 17€) or the train (☎ 877/2TGVMED; www.raileurope.com) from Nice to St. Raphael. Once there, take the **Sodetrav** bus no. 104 (☎ 04-25-00-06-50; www.sodetrav.fr) to St-Tropez, which will cost about 9€ and should take 80 minutes. You could also take a shuttle from Nice (☎ 04-92-00-42-30; July–Sept 15 Tues–Sun, Sept 16–June Tues, Thurs, and Sun; 33€ one-way, 45€ same-day round-trip), which leaves at 9am and arrives at 11:30am. It then departs at 4:30pm and arrives back in Nice at 7pm.

You can also take a shuttle from Cannes (☎ 04-92-98-71-30; mid-July to mid-Sept daily, June and end of Sept on Tues, Thurs, and Sat–Sun; 15€ one-way, 32€ same-day round-trip), which leaves at 10am and gets to

Recommended Movies

You should check out the movie *And God Created Woman* (1956) starring Brigitte Bardot; it made St-Tropez what it is today. Because it was filmed here, it brought a great deal of attention to this little town.

St-Tropez at 11:30am. It departs St-Tropez at 4:30pm and returns to Cannes at 5:45pm.

GETTING AROUND
By Scooter

One of the best places to rent a scooter is **M.A.S.** (3 rue Quaranta; ☎ 04-94-97-00-60; www.location-mas.com) It rents bicycles (12€ for 24 hr.), scooters, and motorcycles (15€–55€ for 24 hr.). Some of the larger motorized scooters rented here require a valid driver's license (valid foreign licenses are acceptable). Others, depending on their size, require a minimum age, either 14 (with the consent of parents or guardians) or 18.

St-Tropez Basics

The tourist office overlooks the port at the intersection of quai Jean Jaures and rue V. Laugier (☎ 04-94-97-45-21; tourism@saint-tropez.st). There are various festivals and events throughout the summer such as boat races, car shows, and concerts. You can find out more info in the tourist office or at www.ot-saint-tropez.com.

There are numerous companies that will give **boat tours** for different prices depending on length of time and time of year. Try **Le Brigantin** (book with Victoria at the old port or by phone at ☎ 06-07-09-21-27; www.taxi-bateau.com) for a 1-hour tour of the gulf of St-Tropez with English commentary for only 8€.

You can check your Internet at **Kreatik Cafe** (19 av. Gal Leclerc; ☎ 04-94-97-40-61; www.kreatik.com).

THE FRENCH RIVIERA

Sleeping

DOABLE

➜**Hôtel Playa** Right next to the Vieux Port, Hôtel Playa is simple but bright and is considered to be one of the less expensive hotels in town, even though it is a government-rated three-star hotel. *57 rue Allard, St-Tropez.* ☎ *04-89-12-94-44. www.playahotel sttropez.com. Low season 90€–168€ double; tourist season (June 6–Sept 15) 121€–230€ double. Breakfast 10€. Amenities: Bar. In room: A/C, TV, hair dryer, safe.*

➜**Hôtel Sube** On the port, this hotel has nice seaside rooms with good views of all the yachts. The rooms are simple, the area is calm, and the bar, sophisticated. *15 quai de Suffren, St-Tropez.* ☎ *04-94-97-30-04. www. hotel-sube.com. 65€–90€ single, 115€–190€ double. Breakfast 10€. Closed Jan. Amenities: Cafe; bar. In room: A/C, TV.*

➜**Hôtel Les Palmiers** This hotel, just off place des Lices, is close to everything. It's a cozy place decorated with bright colors, probably the cheapest place to stay in town. *Bd. Vasserot, St-Tropez.* ☎ *04-94-97-01-61. www.hotel-les-palmiers.com. 65€–102€ small double with shower, 75€–124€ with shower or tub; 83€–134€ standard double with shower, 98€–147€ with tub; 136€–205€ large double with tub. Breakfast 10€. In room: A/C, TV.*

➜**Les Lauriers** This establishment is in the center of town next to place des Lices. It's a clean and classic hotel that is simply but tastefully decorated in Provençal colors. It is cheaper than most other hotels in town and it has A/C. *Rue du Temple, St-Tropez.* ☎ *04-94-97-04-88. Oct–Nov 70€–90€ double; 135€ suite. Apr–May 115€ double; 165€ suite. Breakfast 7€. Closed Dec–Mar. In room: A/C, tub/shower combo.*

SPLURGE

MTV **Best** ➜**Hôtel Byblos** ★ This mythic hotel was built to look and feel like a self-contained village, but it's a village full of wealthy people who like to party. Rich and famous people come to St-Tropez, but the richest and most famous of them come to Hôtel Byblos. One of the hottest nightclubs in town (see Les Caves du Roy in "Partying," below) is attached to the hotel, as are two exceptional restaurants (see Spoon Byblos in "Eating," below). Byblos is the rock-star hotel and has been since 1967. Famous people rent party suites to entertain before heading to the club downstairs. The hotel and bar are centered on a pool where you will find well-oiled lounging ladies during the day. *Av. Paul-Signac, St-Tropez.* ☎ *04-94-56-68-00. www. byblos.com. 305€–310€ single, 390€–830€ double, 725€–20,000€ suite. Breakfast buffet 25€. Amenities: 2 restaurants; 2 bars; gym; laundry and dry cleaning service; massage; nightclub; nonsmoking rooms; outdoor pool; spa; sauna; salon; Wi-Fi. In room: A/C, TV, hair dryer, safe.*

CAMPING

Your cheapest bet may be camping, although the campsites are out of town, and public transportation, even in the summer, is infrequent (and nonexistent in the winter). Most of the campsites open at the end of March or beginning of April and close sometime in the fall. For a complete list of campsites, go to the tourist office. **Kon Tiki** and **Toison d'Or** (Plage de Pampelonne, Ramatuelle; ☎ **04-94-55-96-96** or 04-94-79-83-54; www. riviera-villages.com) are two campsites on the Pampelonne beach in Ramatuelle (which is where you will find the best beaches of St-Tropez). You are far away from the town center, but this is where all the people go during the day. The campsite alone will cost you anywhere from 10€ to 50€ (if you are coming in the middle of the summer, count on spending 50€ with 5€–10€ extra per person). Though they are somewhat isolated, the campgrounds have everything you would need including a beach, tennis courts, volleyball courts, Ping-Pong, wine tasting, a gym, laundry facilities, bars and restaurants, and tons of stuff for kids. During the summer you can rent mobile homes starting from 30€ to 105€, which sleep at least three people and have their own bathroom. They also have beach houses facing the water. There is a bus four times a day leaving from the bus station (Gare routière) in St-Tropez, but only during the summer.

Eating

Like everything else in St-Tropez, the restaurants tend to be on the extremely overpriced side, though you can still find a good meal without breaking the bank. At place des Lices, there is a market some mornings and there are fast-food restaurants with pizza, salads, and shawarma. While in St-Tropez, you should try a *tarte tropizienne,* which is quintessential St-Tropez. It is an excess of good things: a big pastry-cream sandwich topped with more cream and powdered sugar.

There are so many good restaurants worth visiting if you have pockets full of cash, but the Spoon is worth pointing out.

MTV Best → **Spoon Byblos** ★★ INTERNATIONAL   This is one of the series of Spoon restaurants opened by famous chef Alain Ducasse. It has a wide range of international dishes ranging from lobster ravioli with a tomato-ginger syrup to tajines. *In the Hôtel Byblos, av. Paul-Signac, St-Tropez.* ☎ *04-94-56-68-00. www.spoonbyblos.com. Reservations required. Main courses 28€–40€. July–Aug daily 8pm–12:30am; otherwise daily 8–11pm. Closed mid-Oct to mid-Apr.*

Partying

NIGHTCLUBS

The nightclubs are open from about 11pm to 5am and, though the drinks are astronomically expensive, they don't charge a cover. If you want to sit at a table, you should count on spending a few hundred euros for a bottle of something. Getting into these clubs in the summer is not a piece of cake. The lines are long and the bouncers are selective (it's easier to get in if you are a girl or have one with you). You should definitely dress up as much as you can. These clubs are open every night in the summer and occasionally on the weekends during the rest of the year.

→ **Les Caves du Roy** They advertise that they are paparazzi free, which is one of the reasons that the stars come here. This club is a legend in St-Tropez. DJ Jack E spins eclectic dance music. If you are obscenely wealthy, Les Caves claims to offer the world's most expensive bottle of alcohol, an enormous 30,000€ bottle of Kristal. *In the Hôtel Byblos, av. Paul-Signac, St-Tropez.* ☎ *04-94-56-68-02. www.byblos.com.*

→ **Le VIP Room** The VIP Room is another club that gets crowded in the summer welcoming stars and normal people alike. It is a two-story club with a balcony on the second story where the *real* VIPs can look down at the dancing people below. *Résidence du Nouveau-Port, St-Tropez.* ☎ *04-94-97-14-70. www.viproom.fr.*

→ **Papagayo** This is one of the most famous clubs in St-Tropez. It is right next to the VIP on the port. Same story: hard to get into, dance music, and expensive drinks inside. The young and wealthy flock to this club in the summer. *Résidence du Nouveau-Port, St-Tropez.* ☎ *04-94-97-07-56 or 04-94-79-29-50.*

Playing Outside

HIKING   If you start from the Port in St-Tropez and you walk along the beach you can get to the beaches of **Pampelonne** in about 3¹⁄₂ hours. At Pampelonne about 35 businesses occupy a 4.8km (3-mile) stretch, located about 10km (6 miles) from St-Tropez. On your way, you will see other beautiful and more isolated beaches. Go to the tourist office at the port for a hiking map that also explains some of the plants in the area.

MTV Best   BEACHES ★★★   The beach is the top daytime attraction in St-Tropez. Look for the free beaches to the west of town (if you are looking at the water, they are to your left), the biggest of which is called **Plage de la Bouillabaisse.** The most popular and beautiful beaches are a few miles out of town along the bay of **Pampelonne;** many of these are private, but there's one in front of Nikki Beach that's good.

The most famous of the private beaches are **Nikki Beach, Club 55,** and **La Voile Rouge. Nikki** attracts a young, jet-set crowd. It's got sand but it isn't on the water. You have to leave the private area and walk through the public beach if you want to take a dip in the Mediterranean. But there's a pool and a bar and restaurant (a three-course meal is 70€), so you may not even need the sea. The DJ sets the mood with chilled-out lounge music until about 5pm,

and then the club music kicks in until about 8pm when people start going back to their hotels to prepare for a night on the town (route de L'Epi; ☎ 04-94-79-82-04; 20€ per person for a bed).

La Voile Rouge (route des Tamaris; ☎ 04-94-79-84-34) is like Nikki but with no pool. It's famed for champagne-spraying extravaganzas. Business tycoons and bronzed beauties alike come here to work on their tans and socialize with stars.

At **Le Club 55** (bd. Patch; ☎ 04-94-97-20-99), you get more of a relaxed, family atmosphere than at Nikki Beach or La Voile Rouge. The restaurant serves simple traditional local dishes, such as *panier de crudités;* it's about 50€ for a meal (not including wine). Lounge chairs cost 18€ a day.

Cannes

Cannes ★★★ is the city in France where the most conventions are held because of its mild climate, numerous hotels, and enormous convention center (which is also where they roll out the red carpet for the International Film Festival held here). You will be able to see fabulous yachts, sandy beaches, and topless bronzing beauties, and you'll find all the shopping you'd ever need. There are festivals year-round, and though Cannes is filled with glamour and gilt, you can actually afford a hotel. Cannes is similar to Nice but smaller and a little ritzier. In Cannes you won't really see the hordes of English-speaking tourists going on pub-crawls like you'll see in Nice, but the town does have some very elite nightclubs that are known throughout the French Riviera.

Getting into Town
GETTING THERE

Coming in by train is the most practical and economical way to get here. For info on the **trains** call ☎ 08-92-35-35-35 or go to

www.voyages-sncf.com. There is also a **bus, Rapid Côte Azure** (place de l'Hôtel de Ville, Cannes; ☎ 04-93-39-11-39), that leaves every 20 minutes for Nice and charges about 6€.

The closest international airport is in Nice (see "Nice," above, for details), which is about 30 minutes away by car. There are buses that shuttle between Cannes Gare Routière (place de l'Hôtel de Ville, Cannes; ☎ 04-93-45-20-08) and the airport every 40 minutes during the day.

GETTING AROUND

The **bus depot** is at place de l'Hôtel de Ville (☎ 04-93-39-18-71), and tickets for local buses are about 8€.

To rent a moped or a bike, call the **Bike/Moped Rental Alliance** (19 rue des Frères Pradignac; ☎ 04-93-38-62-62). It's open daily from 9am to 7pm. The cost varies depending on what kind of bike you choose and how long you want to cruise. **Mistral Location** (4 rue Georges Clemenceau; ☎ 04-93-39-33-60; www.mistral-location.

com) also rents bicycles (14€ per day), scooters (26€–58€ per day), and motorcycles (49€–55€ per day). Some of their scooters can be rented without licenses. The prices include unlimited mileage, helmet, insurance, and a lock. They also rent cars starting at 38€ per day.

Cannes Basics

Cannes is a pretty small town and it is easy to navigate. The train station is about a 5-minute walk from the beach. **La Croisette** ★★ is the promenade that lines the beach where you will find many super-expensive hotels and restaurants. Much of the beach is private, meaning reserved for people who pay for a lounge chair and umbrella, but there are still plenty of spots where you can relax for free on the beach. Between the train station and the beach is where you will find most of the action. As a general rule, the closer you get to the train station, the cheaper the hotel, and the closer you get to the beach, the more expensive the hotel.

The **tourist office** is located in the Palais des Festivals, esplanade Georges-Pompidou (☎ **04-93-45-20-08;** www.cannes.fr), right between the Vieux Port and La Croisette.

Sleeping

Cannes is one of those cities where you really need to ask yourself: What do I want in a hotel room? If you just want a bed and you have a budget, opt for some of the cheap, shady looking hotels near the train station. If you are going to go all out and you want to have a ritzy, schnazzy room for a few nights, head for the palaces on the Croisette.

HOSTELS

➜ **Chanteclair** Well located in the Forville neighborhood, steps away from the Vieux Port and the Palais des Festivals, this hostel is in a Provençal house. You must arrive before 9pm in the summer and 7pm in the winter. *12 rue Forville, Cannes.* ☎ *04-93-39-68-88. 2-night minimum stay. From the train*

station, keep right on rue Meynadier until Marché Forville, about 900m (2,953 ft.) down. 48€ single with shower only, 52€ with shower and toilet; 52€ double. Amenities: Luggage storage; Wi-Fi. In room: Linens and towels.

➜ **Le Chalit** This center-city hostel is a 5-minute walk from the train station and 10 minutes from la Croisette. The staff is friendly and the rooms are clean. The only drawback for some is a lights-out-at-midnight policy, even though there is no curfew. *27 av. Gallieni, Cannes.* ☎ *04-93-99-22-11. 2-night minimum stay. Closed Nov to mid-Dec. 20€–25€ dorm bed. Amenities: Kitchen (low season only); laundry (4€ for washing, dry clothes on the line outside); free lockers; lockout 10:30am–5pm. In room: Sheets (3€).*

➜ **Les Iris Hostel** Another hostel near the train station, this one boasts many amenities that hostels usually lack, but you'll have to make do without a kitchen. *77 bd. Carnot, Cannes.* ☎ *04-93-68-30-20. www.iris-solola.com. 20€ dorm bed. Amenities: Internet; free laundry facilities. In room: Free sheets.*

CHEAP

➜ **Azurene Royal Hôtel** The story here is the same as at the other budget hotels: Don't expect a lot. The benefit to this hotel is you can usually check your e-mail in the lobby for free and it's a block away from the beach. *28 rue Commandant André, Cannes.* ☎ *04-93-99-10-51. www.azurene-royal-hotel.com. 50€–70€ single, 60€–85€ double, 70€–100€ triple, 85€–120€ quad. Breakfast 5.50€. In room: A/C, TV, Internet (upon request).*

➜ **Hôtel le Florian** Another clean, basic hotel in a great location. The best deal is to rent out the apartment with kitchen for 1€ more than a double room (they don't rent it out July–Aug). Renovations made the rooms look fresher than many other area hotels. *8 rue Commandant André, Cannes.* ☎ *04-93-39-24-82. www.hotel-leflorian.com. 45€–62€ single, 48€–75€ double. Breakfast 5€. In room: A/C, TV, hair dryer, Internet, safe.*

Cannes

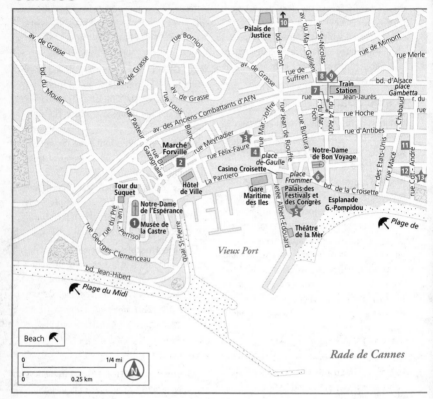

→ **Hôtel L'Estrel** This is a simple, but colorful government-rated two-star hotel near the train station. It is has a lot of natural light. *15 rue du 24 Aout, Cannes.* ☎ *04-93-38-82-82. www.hotellesterel.com. 40€–59€ single, 56€–79€ double. Breakfast 7.80€. Amenities: Wheelchair friendly; Wi-Fi. In room: A/C.*

→ **Hôtel PLM** The lobby is more inviting and newer than those of other budget hotels in the neighborhood near La Croisette and the train station, and the rooms are as basic as you can get, but they are clean and bright. The rooms with private bathrooms are small with either a tub or a shower. *3 rue Hoche, Cannes.* ☎ *04-93-38-31-19. www.hotel-plm. com. 42€–58€ single with shower, toilet, and*

TV; 49€–63€ double; 53€–68€ deluxe double with tub, toilet, and TV; 55€–69€ twin bed double. Breakfast 7€. Amenities: Elevator. In room: TV, Internet.

DOABLE

→ **Hôtel de Provence** Provençal colors and balconies overlooking the beautiful garden make this hotel a gem. The neighborhood is cute and quiet, yet it is still close to the train station and the beach. Breakfast in the summer is served in the garden. *9 rue Molière, Cannes.* ☎ *04-93-38-44-35. www.hotel-de-provence.com. 56€–72€ courtyard single, 82€–102€ double with garden-view terrace, 72€–92€ courtyard double. Breakfast 7.50€. Amenities: Bar. In room: A/C, TV, Internet.*

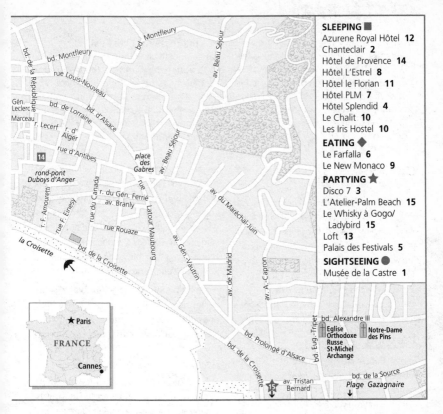

SLEEPING ■
Azurene Royal Hôtel **12**
Chanteclair **2**
Hôtel de Provence **14**
Hôtel L'Estrel **8**
Hôtel le Florian **11**
Hôtel PLM **7**
Hôtel Splendid **4**
Le Chalit **10**
Les Iris Hostel **10**

EATING ◆
Le Farfalla **6**
Le New Monaco **9**

PARTYING ★
Disco 7 **3**
L'Atelier-Palm Beach **15**
Le Whisky à Gogo/
  Ladybird **15**
Loft **13**
Palais des Festivals **5**

SIGHTSEEING ●
Musée de la Castre **1**

SPLURGE

➜**Hôtel Splendid** ★ The name explains it all: This hotel is simply splendid. It overlooks the small port and its many yachts. Next to La Croisette, the Palais des Festivals, and sandy beaches, the all-white turn-of-the-20th-century building has intricate architectural details on the facade and balconies. The lobby is simple and unpretentious; the rooms, elegant with modern amenities (like flatscreen TVs that look like mirrors when they are turned off). Most rooms have tubs. *4–6 rue Félix Faure, Cannes.* ☎ *04-97-06-22-22. www.splendid-hotel-cannes.fr. 112€–192€ single, 124€–254€ double, 202€–264€ suite. Rates include buffet breakfast. Amenities: Non-smoking and limited*

mobility rooms. In room: A/C, TV, hair dryer, Internet, limited room service, safe.

Eating

La Bouillabaisse is a traditional fish stew not to be missed—with local fish, potatoes, and veggies, served with toast and an aioli (a garlic mayonnaise). Most of the restaurants on the Vieux Port sell this.

➜**Le Farfalla** FRENCH/MEDITERANEAN This establishment has a nice atmosphere; electro-jazz music sets the mood for a relaxed meal in a trendy restaurant. The food is fresh and local and the waitstaff is friendly (when the place is not crowded). *Place A. Frommer, Cannes.* ☎ *04-93-68-53-81*

The Film Festival

Cannes is known throughout the world for its **International Film Festival,** which is held at the end of May in the Palais des Festivals on the Promenade de la Croisette. If you want to come to this event, you better plan your trip well in advance because the hotels fill up (and they usually bump up the price significantly). If you do come for the film festival, it is super-hard to get into the screenings, but you can wait outside the premieres with the paparazzi and try to get a picture of some of the world's biggest movie stars walking by on the red carpet. Go to www.festival-cannes.fr for more information.

or 04-93-68-93-00. *Main courses 10€–15€. Daily 11am–3pm and 7–11pm.*

→ **New Monaco** FRENCH/ITALIAN/PROVENÇAL The affordable food includes daily specials that often include homemade pasta or more traditional dishes such as rabbit with mustard sauce or grilled sardines. The place is intimate and cozy, with only 38 seats. *15 rue du 24 Aout, Cannes.* ☎ *04-93-38-37-76. Main courses 7€–14€; fixed-menu 14€–25€. Mon–Sat noon–3pm and 7–10pm.*

Partying

In the **Palais des Festivals** (Bât. G jetée Albert Edouard), the large brown convention center on La Croisette, there are enough activities to keep you busy for a night. Among them are the **Casino Barrière de Cannes Croisette,** where you can play French and English roulette, blackjack, stud poker, punto banco, and craps (10€ admission to the casino and you must have ID; ☎ **04-92-98-78-53**) and **Jimmy'z** (Thurs–Sat 11:30pm to whenever; ☎ **04-92-98-78-78**), which is the sister club of the one in Monaco with the same name.

→ **Disco 7** This is a fun and festive club filled with gays, heteros, transsexuals, and bisexuals. Anything goes!! The nightly drag shows are a hoot. *7 rue Rouguière, Cannes.* ☎ *04-93-39-10-36.*

→ **L'Atelier-Palm Beach** With a large terrace overlooking the water, this club attracts an older jet-set crowd. Drinks will be expensive and you may have to pay for a table with a view, but if you pre-game at the hotel and come here to just dance, you can spend a good night with a chic crowd and not blow a wad of cash. There is a casino in the building in case you get the urge. *Place Franklin Roosevelt, Cannes.* ☎ *04-97-06-36-90.*

→ **Le Whisky à Gogo/Ladybird** Two names identify this gathering place that draws the youngest of the town's partyers, masses of kids under 20. In its two stories, you'll hear mostly house music. *115 av. Lérins, Cannes.* ☎ *04-93-43-20-63.*

→ **Loft** The music mix here tends toward disco, Asian, house, and French. The crowds are mixed, too, with people in their 20s and 30s. It's above the restaurant, **Tantra,** which serves expensive gourmet meals (which means small, but tasty, portions). *13 rue du Monod, Cannes.* ☎ *04-93-39-40-39.*

Sightseeing

Cannes is a small town surrounded by hills. Atop one of the hills is Suquet Hill, the old town of Cannes. Here you will find the **Musée de la Castre** ★ in the Chateau de Castre, Le Suquet (☎ **04-93-38-55-26;** admission 2€.) It's open June to August, Tuesday to Sunday 10am to 1pm and 3 to 7pm; April to May and September, it's open from Tuesday to Sunday 10am to 1pm and 2 to 6pm; and October to March, you can visit between Tuesday and Sunday 10am to 1pm and 2 to 5pm. You'll find sculptures, paintings, pottery, and artifacts. It is the biggest museum in Cannes and really the only one worth going to. It is also in a very beautiful old part of town.

The **Iles de Lerin** are beautiful islands off the coast of Cannes. Boats leave regularly until 30 minutes before sunset. A round-trip costs about 10€. The islands consist of **Ile Ste-Marguerite,** where you will find a Spanish fort from the 17th century, and a **Musée de la Mer** (☎ 04-93-38-55-26; admission 3€ adults, free for students; Tues–Sun 10:30am–1:15pm and 2:15–4:45pm), where there are artifacts from Roman, Arab, and Ligurian civilizations. The other island is **Ile St. Honorat,** which is smaller (only a mile long) and contains a monastery that dates from the 5th century and medieval ruins. This island also has beautiful beaches.

Shopping

The main shopping street in Cannes—rue d'Antibes—runs right through the center of the town and parallel to the beach. Here you can find very high-fashion, expensive stuff

Where Is Everybody?

Most things in Cannes are closed on Sunday, including the shops, boutiques, and most of the grocery stores. Many restaurants will stay open and some of the main grocery stores will be open in the morning.

mixed with affordable stores. A **thrift shop** at 2 rue de Lerins sells used designer clothes. **FNAC** on rue Antibes (81 rue Antibes) has music and books and tickets to concerts and expositions.

Playing Outside

Best **BEACHES** The great outdoors in Cannes consists of the beach. Unlike Nice, Cannes has a sandy beach, which is one reason why it attracts so many tourists. As always, in the French Riviera, tops are not necessary, but bottoms are. And you better put on clothes once you're off the beach, Cannes is not one of those towns where you can walk around the city in your bikini.

THE FRENCH RIVIERA

Road Trip

Nice's central location means you can take lots of day trips, including one to **Monaco.** (Cimiez is also a good day trip just to see the Musée Matisse; see p. 406.)

Monaco is not in France. It's its own principality (this means that its headed by a prince; there is no king). The country gained and lost its independence from France until 1861 when it definitively became an independent principality. It is a small territory (195 hectares/482 acres) filled with foreigners. In 2000 (their last formal census), there were 32,020 inhabitants, 81% of whom were foreigners. Why so many foreigners? In 1869, a law declared that residents would going forward be exempt from land, personal, and residency taxes, and the tax on licenses for

trades and professions. The laws have changed very little; basically Monégasques don't pay taxes. The casinos and tourism (and various other economic activities) provide the government with all of the money that it could ever need. Many wealthy people claim Monaco as their primary residence but may not actually live here.

As a tourist, there is not a whole lot to do in Monaco beyond seeing the Prince's palace, the casino, and a few museums and beaches. We recommend a day trip.

Getting into Town

The easiest way to go is by **train** (☎ 08-92-35-35-35; www.sncf.fr). No border formalities exist when entering Monaco from mainland

France, but you should take your passport because you need it to get into all of the casinos.

Monaco is quite small and almost everything is accessible by walking. There are six city buses if you need them. Bus maps are available in the tourist office (see below).

Sightseeing

Most of the interesting spots for tourists are in Monte-Carlo and Monaco-Ville. The **tourist office** is located at 2A bd. Des Moulins (☎ **92 16 61 66;** www.visitmonaco.com).

🔺 Best ➜ **Monte-Carlo Casino** ★★
This is probably the most famous casino in the world. Built in 1878 by Charles Garnier, it has welcomed the richest risk takers in the world. You can walk outside in the gardens or have a drink in the cafe overlooking the parking lot where the nicest cars in the world pull up. The gaming rooms are lavishly decorated with enormous paintings, sumptuous fabrics, and super-high ceilings with exquisitely detailed molding, sculptures, and chandeliers. To go into the gaming rooms, you have to pay 10€ and you will have access to slot machines, French and English roulette, trente et quarante, chemin de fer, and punto banco. Some of the rooms are private; they cost an extra 20€ to get into and they require formal attire and big bets to enter. In the main gaming room, there is no dress code. The opening hours for the various games differ, but all games are open by 5:30pm. *Place du Casino, Monaco.* ☎ *92 16 21 21. www.casino-monte-carlo.com. Daily 24 hr.*

➜**Musée Océanographique et Aquarium**
★★ This spectacular museum boasts a huge aquarium, with an enormous (450 sq. m/4,844 sq. ft.) shark tank and other smaller aquariums. The location couldn't be better, overlooking the sea (stop in at the terrace restaurant). *Av. St-Martin, Monaco.* ☎ *93 15 36 00. www.oceano.mc. Admission 11€ adults; 6€ students. July–Aug daily 9:30am–7:30pm; Oct–Mar daily 10am–6pm; Apr–July daily 9:30am–7pm.*

➜**Palais Princier (Grands Appartements)/Prince's Palace (State Apartments)** ★ Don't miss the Palace tour, which provides audio tapes in English that guide you through the Italian-influenced architecture and exquisite salons. You will also be able to see the Throne Room, the Palatine Chapel, and the Courtyard of Honour. The ideal time to arrive is 11:55am to watch the 10-minute **Relève de la Garde (Changing of the Guard),** which happens everyday at the same time. *Place du Palais, Monaco.* ☎ *93 25 18 31. www.palais.mc. Daily June–Sept 9:30am–6pm; Oct 10am–5pm.*

FREE ➜**Plage de Larvotto** You can hang out with all the other peasants on the free beach, off of avenue Princesse-Grace (bus: 4 or 6). It is a beautiful, sand beach where you can laugh about how those tools at the nearby Monte-Carlo Beach club are paying 100€ a person for the same thing but with a chlorinated pool and a mattress.

Glasgow

For decades, Glasgow was seen as little more than Edinburgh's bastard cousin to the west. With the decline of the city's shipbuilding industry came years of relative poverty. Yet, the past 20 years have brought a renaissance, so much so that in 1990 the E.U. named Glasgow (pop. 586,000) a "European Capital of Culture." Though Edinburgh's city center is classically more beautiful (and more savvy with tourists), Glasgow is proud of its working-class roots.

And the city is not without charm. Walking through town is like taking a course in architecture, from the medieval center near the Cathedral of St. Kentigern to the Victorian homes of the wealthy tobacco barons to Charles Rennie Mackintosh's School of Art. The Tenement House museum shows off a different side of the city. Old and new coexist rather messily here, particularly in Merchant City, where traditional dark, Scottish pubs abut sleek, airy modern bars. And right next door is the famous Mackintosh-designed Willow Tea Room. And next to that, trendy boutiques that are beginning to be destination spots themselves.

Culture—high and low and edgy—is the theme in food, music, and art as well here. Glasgow's killer clubs, DJs, and international acts keep the nightlife jumping. If banging techno and smooth, lounge-y house doesn't light your wick, the city is cluttered with cool bars and restaurants that now serve the best food in Scotland. It won't be too hard to fight the temptation to just hang out with some of the friendliest locals you'll find anywhere on the continent.

The Best of Glasgow

○ **The Most Colorful Hotel:** From its bright walls to its sumptuously styled bedrooms, **The Brunswick Hotel** sports a veritable rainbow of colors. When you tire of admiring all the shades, head to nearby, hip Merchant City for great shopping and restaurants. See p. 426.

○ **The Best Cheap Meal:** Although **The Wee Curry Shop,** the child of the equally fantastic Mother India restaurant, is indeed tiny, the portions are anything but. In a city with lots of curry spots, this place has the best. Even better? A two-course lunch costs less than £6. See p. 429.

○ **The Best Pub:** Chances are, if you ask a Glaswegian which pub to visit, he'll tell you to have a drink at **The Horse Shoe Bar.** He'll probably invite himself along, too, but that's another story. This atmospheric pub, which claims to have the longest bar in the world, doesn't seem old and musty even though it opened in the early 20th century. Cocktails and food from the upstairs buffet are cheap and the patrons are chatty. See p. 432.

○ **The Best Museum:** Sir William Burrell, a fabulously wealthy industrialist, made his money in shipping and collected art over the course of his long life. More than 9,000 works of art are displayed at **The Burrell Collection,** including pieces by Rodin, Degas, and Cezanne, plus rooms of ceramics and furniture from across the globe. The manicured gardens and acres of wild countryside surrounding the Burrell are as beautiful as the artwork inside. See p. 435.

Getting There & Getting Around

Getting into Town

BY PLANE

The **Glasgow Airport** is at Abbotsinch (☎ 0141/887-1111), 16km (10 miles) west of the city via M8. You can use the regular Glasgow CityLink bus service to get to the city center. From bus stop no. 2, take bus no. 900 or 901 to the Buchanan Street Bus Station in the center of town. The ride takes about 20 minutes and costs £4. A taxi to the city center costs about £15. You can reach Edinburgh by taking a bus from Glasgow Airport to Queens Station and then changing to a bus for Edinburgh. The entire journey, including the change, should take about 2 hours, and costs £7 one-way or £12 round-trip.

There's a taxi stand right in front of the airport. It will cost you close to £20 to get into central Glasgow from the airport. Alternatively, call **Cab Fly** at ☎ 0141/848-4588 to pre-book a taxi before you get to Glasgow.

BY TRAIN

Headquarters for British Rail is at Glasgow's Central Station and Queen Street Station. For **National Rail Enquiries,** call ☎ 08457/484-950. The **Queen Street Station** serves the north and east of Scotland, with trains arriving from Edinburgh every 30 minutes during the day; the one-way trip between the two cities costs £8 and takes 50 minutes. You'll also be able to travel to such Highland destinations as Inverness and Fort William from here.

The **Central Station** serves southern Scotland, England, and Wales, with trains arriving from London's Euston and King's Cross stations (call ☎ 08457/484-950 in London for schedules) frequently throughout the day (trip time is about 5¹/₂ hr.).

BY BUS

The **Buchanan Street Bus Station** is 2 blocks north of the Queen Street Station on North Hanover Street (☎ 08706/082-608).

National Express runs daily coaches from London's Victoria Coach Station to Buchanan frequently throughout the day. Buses from London take 8 hours and 40 minutes to reach Glasgow, depending on the number of stops en route. **Scottish CityLink** (☎ **08705/505-050**) also has frequent bus service to and from Edinburgh, with a one-way ticket costing £3 to £5.

Contact **National Express Enquiries** at ☎ **0990/808-080** for more information.

Getting Around
BY PUBLIC TRANSPORTATION

Public transport is one of the most convenient ways of getting around Glasgow. The **Strathclyde Passenger Transport bus** offers discount tickets and a hop-on/hop-off service. The buses come in a variety of colors, the lighter ones (blue and yellow) tend to serve the Kelvin Central and Strathclyde rural areas, and the darker ones cover the urban zones. Fares are £2.50, but you must have exact change. A special round-trip bus ticket for £2.10 operates after 9:30am. Call ☎ **0141/423-6600** for schedules.

The **Glasgow subway**—also known as the Clockwork Orange, thanks to its brightly colored trains—links the city center to far-flung parts of the town. At peak times on weekdays and Saturdays, expect a train to call at your stop every 4 minutes. Day tickets on the public transport system are a far cry from London's extortionate travel cards—they cost £1.90 any time after 9:39am. Service is Monday to Saturday 6:30am to 10pm and Sunday 11am to 6pm.

The **Travel Centre** at St. Enoch Square (☎ **0870/608-2608**), 2 blocks from the Central Station, is open Monday to Saturday 6:30am to 9:30pm and Sunday 7am to 9:30pm. Here you can buy a £8 **Underground pass,** valid for a week's access to all the subway lines of Glasgow, as well as access to all the trains serving routes between Central Station

Touring Discounts

For only £4, you can buy a FirstDay Tourist Ticket that allows you to hop on and off buses and get discounts for some attractions. A pocket-size city map is also provided. The ticket is valid daily from 9:30am to midnight. It's available at tourist information centers, underground or bus stations, and at certain attractions. For more information, check www.seeglasgow.com.

and the southern suburbs, or a £7.80 **day-tripper card,** covering one adult and one child for a day. For details, call ☎ **0141/332-7133.**

Go to www.spt.co.uk for details on all types of public transport in Glasgow or call ☎ **0870/608-2608** for their **Traveline,** the public transport hot line.

BY TAXI

Taxis are the same excellent ones found in Edinburgh or London. You can hail them on the street or call **TOA Taxis** at ☎ **0141/429-7070.** Fares are displayed on a meter next to the driver. When a taxi is available on the street, a taxi sign on the roof is lit a bright yellow. Most taxi trips within the city cost £4 to £6. The taxi meter starts at £1.80 and increases by 20p every 61m (200 ft.), with an extra 10p assessed for each additional passenger after the first two. An 80p surcharge is imposed midnight to 6am. Tip at least 10% of the fare shown on the meter.

BY BICYCLE

There aren't many designated bicycle lanes in Glasgow, making it dangerous to traverse the city this way. If you want to risk your life by cycling in the city, there are definitely places that will take your money, like **West End Cycles** (16–18 Chancellor St.; ☎ **0141/357-1344;** £10–£15 daily rental plus deposit).

GLASGOW

ON FOOT

Glasgow is a fantastic city to explore on foot. There are some pedestrian precincts, notably Sauchiehall Street, Buchanan Street, and Argyle Street, with more proposed for the near future.

BY CAR

Glasgow is a fairly easy city to get around in on foot or on public transport. However, if you plan on exploring the surrounding countryside or even taking day trips to attractions slightly outside the city, like The Burrell Collection, it might be worth renting a car. Well-known outfits like **Enterprise** (135 Milton St.; ☎ 0141/331-4622), **Hertz** (138 Hydepark St.; ☎ 0141/248-7736), and **Avis** (70 Lancefield St.; ☎ 0870/608-6339) have locations in central Glasgow. Whatever you do, remember the cardinal rule for driving in the U.K.—keep left!

Glasgow Basics

Orientation: Glasgow Neighborhoods

Bigger and less concentrated than Edinburgh, Glasgow is easier to get around in, thanks to its grid of streets. Making things even easier, many attractions, from bars to museums, are within walking distance of each other, clustered in the city center and around the West End.

Within the city center, the architecturally stunning and slightly snooty Merchant City, near geographically central George Square, the bohemian School of Art, and most of Glasgow's nightclubs, offers plenty to amuse besides museums and the like. A circular subway line joins downtown to the West End, where the University of Glasgow sits in the middle of a groovy mecca for young folks. Quirky little shops, cafes, bars, and other hangs clutter Byres Road.

Tourist Offices

The local tourist office, the **Greater Glasgow and Clyde Valley Tourist Board** (☎ 0141/204-4400; subway: Buchanan St.), is located at 11 George Sq. and is central to shops, restaurants, and attractions. You'll find informative brochures, a small bookshop, a currency exchange office, and a hotel reservations desk. October to May, it's open Monday to Saturday 9am to 6pm; June to September hours are daily 9am to 6pm; August daily 9am to 8pm.

If you'd like to find out about Glasgow online, go to the official tourist site, **www.seeglasgow.com**; for Scotland as a whole, visit **www.visitscotland.com**, official site of the Scottish Tourist Board.

Recommended Websites

○ **www.travelbritain.org**: A very useful site for all of Great Britain. You can plan your trip, e-mail questions to the Tourist Authority, and order brochures.
○ **www.glasgowmuseums.com**: Provides exhaustive coverage of the many places to visit in the city and surrounding area.
○ **www.timeout.co.uk**: Has the latest round-up of who's playing in the city's clubs and concert halls.

Culture Tips 101

Unlike Edinburgh, which is generally pristine, areas of Glasgow are gritty and impoverished-looking. The Gorbals, once the city's most notorious slum, is now in the process of being demolished and gentrified but Govan, just west of central Glasgow, is still rather grimy. While the English call common folks "chavs," Glaswegians have their own name for lower class: "neds," thought to stand for Non Educated Delinquents. Hang around a local long enough and you'll hear them mentioned.

Connected to the city's poverty problem is some pretty heavy drinking. Glasgow locals

Talk of the Town

Three ways to start a conversation with a local

1. **Which Glasgow football team is the best?** Expect a 10-minute minimum lecture in response. The two teams are called the Rangers and the Celtic. Rangers are historically the Protestant team and the Celtic team is Catholic, which to this day gives fans of each side enough reason to beat each other up. You can spot a Rangers fan by his blue shirt—and he might be waving a Union Jack. A Celtic fan, on the other hand, could be carrying an Irish flag and will be wearing green. *Note:* Never join in the fight! The subway even has an info heading on its website: "Travel safely on football match days." Be forewarned.

2. **What makes Glasgow superior to Edinburgh?** Ditto the 10-minute lecture. Usually they'll tell you that Edinburgh natives are snobs, and that Glaswegians are the true Scots, as their city is less affected by expatriates and English culture. What's that you say? Edinburgh has the Festival? Well, you'll hear that Glasgow has the best live-music scene in the country, plus a more modern cultural vibe.

3. **What do you recommend I do in Glasgow?** Locals *love* chatting and are very opinionated about what you should do with your time.

are known for their ability to drink an awful lot. Whether they're tossing back "drams" of whiskey, or pints of lager, you'll find pubs packed with folks day and night.

Under-18s aren't supposed to drink, but the only places that ever seem to card are nightclubs. As with everywhere in the U.K., stiff penalties await anyone dumb enough to drink and drive. Recreational drugs are illegal, but they're around to some degree. The city has had its share of problems with hard drugs and has managed to clean up a bit.

Recommended Books, Movies & Music

BOOKS

Novels written about Glasgow tend to focus on the poverty experienced by the average Glaswegian in the last century. Some go back even further, such as *The Beggar's Benison* by George Mills, which takes place among the rapidly expanding slums of the 19th century. Jeff Torrington's Whitbread Prize–winning *Swing Hammer Swing!* is set in the 1960s and follows a writer for a week, documenting his problems living in the poor Gorbals district. Janice Galloway's *The Trick is to Keep Breathing* was short-listed for a Whitbread First Novel award. The novel about a depressed drama teacher living on Glasgow's outskirts and later inspired a song title by the Scottish band Garbage.

MOVIES

While Scotland's most famous film, *Trainspotting* (1996), was set in Edinburgh, most of it was filmed in Glasgow. When Renton and Sickboy debate Sean Connery movies and Renton shoots a dog with an air rifle, they're in Rouken Glen Park. The pub where Begbie throws a glass over the balcony and then starts a fight is the Crosslands on Queen Margaret Drive. Even the London hotel room at the end is actually the interior of the George Hotel on Buchanan Street. Glasgow is a favorite with film crews, as it has everything from gritty streets to pretty scenery. A more recent film to really use Glasgow's potential was 2004's *The Jacket*, starring Brit beauty Keira Knightley. Glasgow doubled as Iraq in a war sequence, and the Bangour Village Hospital stood in for a psychiatric unit supposedly in rural Vermont. Another surprise? Jet Li's martial arts flick *Unleashed* (2005) was filmed in the ancient city.

Other films to check out are Bill Forsyth's *Comfort and Joy* (1984), the true story of Italian immigrants fighting over the city's ice-cream market, and *Shallow Grave* (1994) a movie about housemates trying to dispose of a body—this film also happened to make Ewan McGregor famous. Ken Loach's critically lauded 1998 film *My Name is Joe* is set in the crumbling suburb of Ruchill. Actor Peter Mullan played Joe, and won Best Actor at

Cannes for his efforts. The most recent high-profile film to be made in Glasgow also starred Peter Mullan: *On A Clear Day* (2005).

MUSIC

Glasgow has experienced a music resurgence in the past few decades, firmly establishing itself as a vital part of the U.K. music scene. (Twenty years ago, Glasgow's best known musical export was Lulu of "you make me wanna *shout*" fame). Music notables from here include earnest post-rockers like Belle & Sebastian, Mogwai, Travis, Arab Strap, and the Beta Band. For the past few years, the Franz Ferdinand members have been the city's indie-rock darlings.

Glasgow Nuts & Bolts

Cellphone Providers & Service Centers If you need to purchase a SIM card for the duration of your stay, try the **Carphone Warehouse** (☎ 08701/680-223) in the busy shopping district of Buchanan Street. Also on Buchanan Street is the **o2 store,** which will sell you SIM cards for the popular o2 network (☎ 0141/248-2620). Right down the road is **The Orange Shop** (128 Buchanan St.; ☎ 0141/229-5290), which sells phones under the Orange network.

Currency The currency in Scotland is worth exactly the same as it is in England, and has the same name—pounds sterling. There are currency-exchange offices all over the city, such as at the tourist office in George Square. That failing, you can change your dollars to pounds at any bank. Banks are open Monday to Wednesday and Friday 9:30am to 4pm, Thursday 9:30am to 5:30pm, and Saturday 10am to 7pm.

Embassies All embassies are in London. See "Edinburgh Nuts & Bolts" (p. 339) for info on the U.S. consulate.

Emergencies Dial ☎ **999** from any phone for police, ambulance, and fire service. The Glasgow Royal Infirmary is your best bet for a local hospital (84 Castle St.; ☎ 0141/211-4000 for the switchboard). If you need a doctor at the last minute, call **BUPA Wellness Glasgow** (9 George Sq.; ☎ 0845/606-0325), the most centrally located doctors' surgery.

Internet/Wireless Hot Spots Thanks to the phone company BT, the city center of Glasgow is now a Wi-Fi Zone. Six "hot spots," located in pay phones, means you can access the Internet anywhere in the main business district. There are three **EasyInternetCafes** (www.easyinternetcafe.com) in Glasgow, owned by the easyJet Corporation and highly visible thanks to their huge orange signs. These can be found at 45 Kilmarnock Rd., 57–61 St. Vincent St., and 163 Trongate Shopping Centre. That failing, go to any Starbucks, predictably found at every street corner. There you can access the Internet with your laptop, although it's pricey (£5 for 1 hr., and £7.50 for 3 hr.).

Laundry   Very few laundromats are in the city center; most laundromats are found in residential areas outside of the tourist zones. Your best bet is to get your hotel to do your laundry for you, although this is hardly cheap. Hostels have amenities for you to do your own laundry. If you're desperate to do a wash, try these two places: **Euroclean** (15 North Canal Bank St.; ☎ 0141/353-3330) or **U.K. Laundry Services Ltd.** (1 Park Terrace; ☎ 0141/331-6443).

Luggage Storage   Your best bet, because it's so central, is **Buchanan Bus Station,** right in the center of town on Killermont Street. You can leave your luggage at a staffed facility at a charge of £4 per piece, or you can put your stuff in a locker, which costs between £5 and £7 per 24 hours. Call ☎ 0141/333-3708 if you have further questions.

Pharmacy   **Boots** (200 Sauchiehall St.; ☎ 0141/332-1925) sells everything from anti-histamines to condoms. It's open Monday to Wednesday, Friday, and Saturday 8:30am to 6pm, and Thursday 8:30am to 7pm.

Post Offices   The three most central post offices for your snail mail needs are located at the following addresses: 47 St. Vincent St. (☎ 0845/722-3344), 230 Springburn Way (☎ 0845/722-3344), and 30 Main St.(☎ 0845/722-3344).

Restrooms   If you need a restroom, go into a hotel, ask at a restaurant, or use one of the city's public toilets—found in stations and the like.

Safety   There are loads of CCTV—or Closed Circuit Television—cameras all over the city center of Glasgow. So, if something happens, chances are it'll be caught on tape. Crime is fairly rife in some areas of the city, mostly south of the river, so don't wander around in unfamiliar places alone or at night. Stick to the pedestrian streets and shopping areas of Buchanan Street, Sauchiehall Street, and Argyle Street when possible, and if you do find yourself in a rough area at night, call a taxi.

Telephone Tips   A reliable service for directory assistance is ☎ 118118, although it can be expensive. You can also visit them online at www.118118.com.

Tipping   Generally, Glasgow restaurants include a tip with the VAT charge. If not, use your discretion, but a 15% tip is the norm. Tip your taxi driver about £1 if he or she is especially friendly, and leave a few pounds for housekeeping if you stay in a nice hotel. Remember: It is *not* customary to tip at a British pub.

GLASGOW

Sleeping

Not as jam-packed with guesthouses as Edinburgh, Glasgow has its share of bed-and-breakfasts. This Scottish cottage industry competes with other accommodations varying in cost from ultracheap to extravagant. In addition to hostels and hotels, many of Glasgow's universities rent out dormitories when school is out.

Hostels

→ **Bluesky Hostel**   This hostel is small and cozy, and only for 18- to 35-year-olds—eliminating pesky, older, budget travelers. There are reportedly 50 bars, pubs, and clubs within a 5-minute walk from the hostel's central location in the Charing Cross

Glasgow

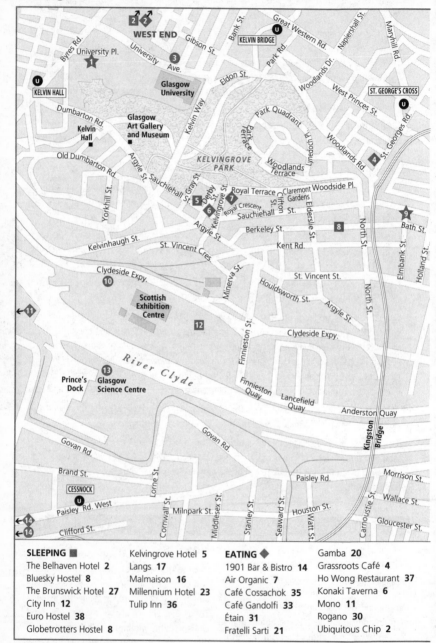

SLEEPING ■

The Belhaven Hotel **2**
Bluesky Hostel **8**
The Brunswick Hotel **27**
City Inn **12**
Euro Hostel **38**
Globetrotters Hostel **8**

Kelvingrove Hotel **5**
Langs **17**
Malmaison **16**
Millennium Hotel **23**
Tulip Inn **36**

EATING ◆

1901 Bar & Bistro **14**
Air Organic **7**
Café Cossachok **35**
Café Gandolfi **33**
Étain **31**
Fratelli Sarti **21**

Gamba **20**
Grassroots Café **4**
Ho Wong Restaurant **37**
Konaki Taverna **6**
Mono **11**
Rogano **30**
Ubiquitous Chip **2**

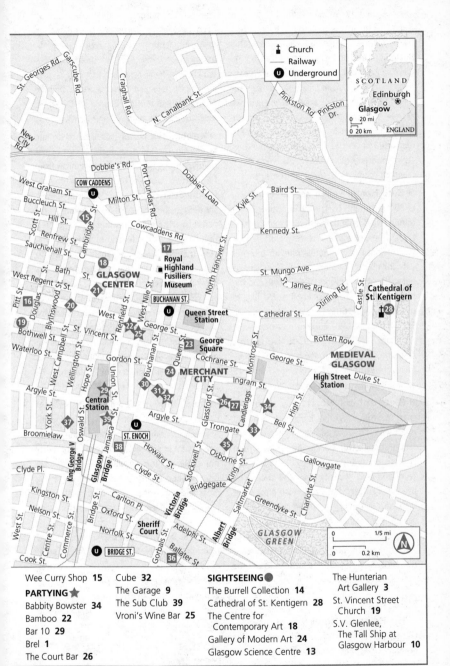

Church
Railway
U Underground

SCOTLAND
Edinburgh
Glasgow
0   20 mi
0 20 km   ENGLAND

St. Georges Rd.
Garscube Rd.
Craighall Rd.
N. Canalbank St.
Pinkston Rd. Pinkston Dr.
New City Rd.
Dobbie's Rd.
COW CADDENS U
West Graham St.
Buccleuch St.
Milton St.
Dobbie's Loan
Baird St.
Hill St.
Scott St.
Renfrew St.
Cambridge St.
Cowcaddens Rd.
Kyle St.
Kennedy St.
Sauchiehall St.
15
18
Bath St.
GLASGOW CENTER
17
Royal Highland Fusiliers Museum
St. Mungo Ave.
West Regent St.
Pitt St.
16
Douglas St.
Blythswood St.
20
21
West
West Nile St.
BUCHANAN ST. U
North Hanover St.
St. James Rd.
Stirling Rd.
Castle St.
Cathedral of St. Kentigern
19
Bothwell St.
St. Vincent St.
22
25
George St.
Queen Street Station
Cathedral St.
28
Waterloo St.
West Campbell St.
Wellington St.
Hope St.
Gordon St.
Renfield St.
Buchanan St.
Queen St.
23
George Square
Cochrane St.
Montrose St.
George St.
Rotten Row
MEDIEVAL GLASGOW
Argyle St.
Union St.
29
24
MERCHANT CITY
Ingram St.
High Street Station
Duke St.
York St.
37
Oswald St.
39
30
31 32
Glassford St.
Candleriggs
26 27
34
High St.
Bell St.
Central Station
ST. ENOCH U
Argyle St.
Trongate
33
Broomielaw
38
Howard St.
Stockwell St.
Osborne St.
35
Gallowgate
Clyde Pl.
King George V Bridge
Glasgow Bridge
Jamaica St.
Clyde St.
Bridgegate
King St.
Saltmarket
Charlotte St.
Greendyke St.
Kingston St.
Nelson St.
Bridge St.
Carlton Pl.
Oxford St.
Victoria Bridge
Albert Bridge
GLASGOW GREEN
West St.
Centre St.
Commerce St.
Norfolk St.
Sheriff Court
Adelphi St.
Gorbals St.
Ballater St.
0   1/5 mi
0 0.2 km
Cook St.
BRIDGE ST. U
36

Wee Curry Shop 15
PARTYING ★
Babbity Bowster 34
Bamboo 22
Bar 10 29
Brel 1
The Court Bar 26

Cube 32
The Garage 9
The Sub Club 39
Vroni's Wine Bar 25

SIGHTSEEING ●
The Burrell Collection 14
Cathedral of St. Kentigern 28
The Centre for Contemporary Art 18
Gallery of Modern Art 24
Glasgow Science Centre 13

The Hunterian Art Gallery 3
St. Vincent Street Church 19
S.V. Glenlee, The Tall Ship at Glasgow Harbour 10

GLASGOW

area of the city, so you won't be short of things to do at night. Bluesky even offers free breakfast and free Internet access. This hostel is entirely nonsmoking. *65 Berkeley St., Charing Cross.* ☎ *0141/221-1710. www.bluesky hostel.com. Low season £10 dorm, £10 room for 4 people, £13 twin room; high season £10 dorm, £12 room for 4 people, £15 twin room. Rates are per person per night and include breakfast. Rail station: Central or Queen St. Amenities: Complimentary tea and toast; kitchen; TV (in common room); Wi-Fi. In room: Free sheets.*

→ **Euro Hostel** Euro Hostel, part of a chain, is located right in central Glasgow, a 5-minute walk from the best shops and attractions. The atmosphere is very chill, with a game room and TV lounge plus an Internet cafe for checking your e-mails. The Osmosis bar is lively most nights of the week, and the hostel offers cut-rate deals if you'd like to use the nearby fitness center. *318 Clyde St.* ☎ *0141/222-2828. www.euro-hostels.co.uk. £14 dorm, £40 double. Rail station: Central. Amenities: Bar; game room; Internet; kitchen; laundry facilities; TV (in common room). In room: TV (in twin rooms), lockers, sheets.*

→ **Globetrotters Hostel** Just down the road from Bluesky, this independent hostel is known for its relaxed, friendly atmosphere and is popular with backpackers. The garden is great on sunny days. You'll find 24-hour reception and security. Oh, and their free breakfast is just what you'll want after a big night out. *56 Berkeley St.* ☎ *0141/204-5470. www.ukglobetrotters.com. From £12 dorm. Rates include breakfast. Rail station: Central or Queen St. Amenities: Bike rentals; garden; kitchen; lounge; meeting facilities; storage. In room: Shared bathrooms, sheets.*

Cheap

→ **The Belhaven Hotel** ★ The Belhaven is in the quiet, pretty West End opposite the Botanical Gardens. Small and romantic, it boasts a Jacuzzi and a lounge bar that serves light meals. Rooms are decorated in deep

maroons and purples, so they feel luxurious even though the prices are reasonable. *15 Belhaven Terrace.* ☎ *0141/339-3332. www. belhavenhotel.com. £35–£50 single, £55–£75 double, £75 twin, £75–£105 family, £85 premier (with 2-person Jacuzzi). Rates include breakfast. Rail station: Central or Queen St. Amenities: Bar. In room: TV, hair dryer.*

→ **Kelvingrove Hotel** This small, charming family-run hotel is right in the center of the relatively quiet West End, a stone's throw from Kelvingrove Park. The basic rooms contain all the necessities, plus the strongest power showers in the city. Breakfast is lovingly prepared by the staff, with whom you'll be on a first-name basis by the end of your stay: The very friendly Somerville family is willing to give advice on absolutely everything. This hotel is entirely nonsmoking. *944 Sauchiehall St.* ☎ *0141/339-5011. www.kelvingrove-hotel. co.uk. From £40 single (per person), from £25 double or twin (per person), from £25 triple or family room (per person). Rail station: Central or Queen St. Subway: Kelvin Hall. Amenities: Ironing facilities; laundry services. In room: TV, coffee/tea maker, hair dryer, Internet.*

→ **Tulip Inn** The Tulip Inn is one of Glasgow's larger hotels, with 114 well-appointed rooms. You'll find all the extras you'd want in a hotel, like free Wi-Fi and digital cable, all for a really great price. The Bibo bar and bistro serves a decent evening meal and stays open later than most of the city's pubs. There are often good package deals for rooms if you visit in the autumn or winter. *80 Ballater St.* ☎ *0141/429-4233. www. tulipinnglasgow.co.uk. £60–£90 double standard or executive room. Rail station: Central. Amenities: Restaurant; Wi-Fi. In room: TV w/pay movies, coffee/tea maker, hair dryer, iron/ironing board, trouser press, wheelchair friendly, Wi-Fi.*

Doable

MTV Best → **The Brunswick Hotel** ★★
In stylish, young Merchant City, this tiny

boutique hotel boasts cool decor. Each floor is painted in hues so bright, you'll feel like you're on the set of a reality show, about to enter a mirrored diary room and confess all. The rooms are small but well decorated, and great for couples—the sunken bed, moody colors, and close quarters scream sexy. The restaurant, Brutti Ma Buoni, serves tasty food to the sound of Euro music and will mix drinks 24 hours a day. The hotel is also close to the Italian Center's shopping. *106–108 Brunswick St.* ☎ *0141/552-0001. www.brunswickhotel. co.uk. £55 single, £65–£95 double, £395 3-bedroom penthouse. Rail station: Central or Queen St. Amenities: Bar/restaurant; laundry service; 24-hr. room service; wheelchair friendly. In room: TV, coffee/tea maker, hair dryer, Internet (in most).*

→ **City Inn** City Inn is part of a modern, stylish chain and is located slightly out of the city center on the waterside. However, the area is perfect for exploring some of the sites around Finnieston Quay, like the Science Center and the Tall Ship museum. The rooms are equipped with flatscreen TVs and DVD players and are very comfortable for the price range. Their City Café offers modern Continental cuisine with lots of vegetarian choices. *Finnieston Quay.* ☎ *0141/240-1002. www.cityinn.com. £99 double/twin. Rail station: Central or Queen St. Amenities: Restaurant; bar; health club. In room: A/C, TV/DVD, bathrobes, CD player, coffee/tea maker, hair dryer, newspaper (upon request), room service, trouser press.*

→ **Millennium Hotel** ★ This striking Victorian building couldn't be in a better location for shopping and sightseeing. The Modern Art gallery is literally a stone's throw away, as are the shops of Merchant City and all the tour buses. The climate control rooms are a major bonus during freezing Scottish autumns and winters, and each suite has Wi-Fi Internet access. The service here is also particularly good, considering the moderate prices. *George Sq.* ☎ *0141/332-6711. www.*

milleniumhotels.com. £175–£295 double, £210–£430 suite. Rail station: Queen St. Amenities: Restaurant; 2 bars; laundry service/dry cleaning; wheelchair friendly. In room: A/C, TV, hair dryer, safe.

Splurge

→ **Lang's** ★ Lang's is a large, trendy but rather impersonal boutique hotel located nearby many of the city's best shops and sights. You may feel as if you're sleeping in the house of a very *nouveau riche* neighbor—the one with a helipad on his roof. If it's raining and you don't feel like going out, there's always a PlayStation and a satellite TV to keep you entertained in your room. The bathroom is sizeable and stocked with sweet-smelling toiletries. The hotel's Oshi restaurant is cringingly ostentatious (think: waterfall and flaming statues) but serves good fusion food and a fabulous breakfast. This hotel is entirely nonsmoking. *2 Port Dundas Place.* ☎ *0141/333-1500. www.langs hotels.co.uk. £160 double. Rail station: Queen St. Amenities: 2 restaurants; 2 bars; massage; meeting facilities; spa; Wi-Fi. In room: TV, CD player, coffee/tea maker, hair dryer, iron/ ironing board, PlayStation, room service, Wi-Fi.*

🅼🆅 **Best** → **Malmaison** ★★ Malmaison is the city's most glamorous hotel, housed in a converted 19th-century Greek Orthodox Church. As soon as you walk in, you'll feel immersed in the drama of the whole place— the hallway's ornate staircase and striking chandelier create an atmosphere befitting an Oscar ceremony. You'll love the new Champagne Bar and Brasserie and the ultra-modern fitness room, called Gymtonic. The rooms are all individually decorated and include free Internet access. *278 West George St.* ☎ *0141/572-1000. www.malmaison-glasgow.com. £125 double, from £170 suite. Bus 11. Amenities: Restaurant; bar; health club; Internet; meeting facilities; Wi-Fi. In room: TV, CD player, laundry service, minibar, room service.*

Eating

Only a few decades ago, Scotland was renowned solely for its frankly terrifying national cuisine. Visitors balked at the idea of eating local delicacies such as haggis (see p. 344 for a full description). Breakfast in Scotland meant black pudding—although this sounds harmless enough, it's actually made entirely of animal blood. To add insult to injury, "neeps and tatties," or turnips and potatoes, would be served alongside every main meal.

Luckily, modern day Glasgow is experiencing a culinary revolution. The birthplace of celebrity chef Gordon Ramsay, the city has recently opened many internationally acclaimed dining spots, where you can expect to find more variety and less of a *Fear Factor* quotient. There isn't just one area to find a good restaurant; eateries are scattered around from the West End down to Merchant City. However, West Regent Street and West George Street have more than their fair share of above-average brasseries and cafes. Thanks to its diverse population, Glasgow boasts a wide array of ethnic restaurants that deserve attention, so try to have an Indian takeout or a Chinese dinner at least once.

Hot Spots

➔ **étain** ★ FRENCH French for "pewter," étain is a destination restaurant owned by Sir Terence Conran, the man responsible for many restaurants all over London. Despite the name, this place doesn't feel overly hip or shiny; service is great and it's obvious that attention has been paid to the details. The menu is decidedly French, although the ingredients used are Scottish, like venison and lamb. *2nd floor, Princes Sq., Buchanan St.* ☎ *0141/225-5639. www.conran-restaurants. co.uk. Main courses £20. Mon–Fri noon–2:30pm and 7–11pm; Sat 7–11pm; Sun noon–3pm. Rail station: Queen St.*

➔ **Gamba** ★★ SEAFOOD Glasgow's best-known and most-beloved restaurant deserves its reputation. The main staple here is seafood, and the menu boasts every ocean-dwelling creature you can imagine, from oysters and scallops to bream and lobster. If the prices deter you, try the pre-theater menu, which allows you to enjoy three of chef Derek Marshall's fantastic courses for only £18. *225a West George St.* ☎ *0141/572-0899. www.gamba. co.uk. Lunch £16–£19; a la carte £19–25; pre-theater £15–£18; graduation £25; pre-fixe (parties of 8 or more) £40. Mon–Sat noon–2:30pm and 5–10:30pm. Rail station: Central or Queen St.*

➔ **Russian Café-Gallery Cossachok** ★ RUSSIAN Café Cossachok is an art gallery–cum–restaurant–cum–live music venue on cool, artsy King Street. Run by the Atlas family, Cossachok bills itself as an authentic Russian restaurant. Accordingly, the menu is packed with traditional, heavy fare like borscht, blinis, and beef stroganoff. The atmosphere is lively and bohemian, making this place a hit with locals and tourists. *10 King St.* ☎ *0141/553-0733. Main courses £7–£14. Tues–Sat 11:30am–10:30pm; Sun 4pm–late. Subway: St. Enoch.*

➔ **Ubiquitous Chip** SCOTTISH Known simply as "the Chip," this restaurant has been credited with starting Scotland's cultural and culinary renaissance in the '70s. Scottish produce, such as Aberdeen Angus beef and wild rabbit, fill the menu. It's expensive, and many Glaswegians save up to hold their birthday parties here. If you can't handle the prices, try the brasserie upstairs, called Upstairs at the Chip. *12 Ashton Lane.* ☎ *0141/ 334-5007. www.ubiquitouschip.co.uk. Prix-fixe lunch £22; prix-fixe dinner £33. Mon–Sat noon–2:30pm and 5:30–11pm; Sun 12:30–3pm and 6:30–11pm. Subway: Hillhead.*

Cheap

→**Café Gandolfi** SCOTTISH/FRENCH Seamus MacInnes' cheap and cheerful cafe in Merchant City caters to food snobs living on a budget. Everything here is Scottish down to the furniture, which was created locally. The black pudding is renowned; but if the thought of eating blood turns your stomach, order the steak sandwich or some pasta instead. *64 Albion St.* ☎ *0141/552-6813. Main courses £8. Mon–Sat 9am–11:30pm; Sun noon–11:30pm. Subway: St. Enoch/Cannon St.*

→**Fratelli Sarti** ITALIAN Although this Italian cafe is a chain, the original joint on Wellington Street remains my favorite. Expect perfect pizza with a thin crust and heaping dishes of pasta with Italian sausage. The cafe is part delicatessen, so you can browse the shelves while waiting for your order. *133 Wellington St.* ☎ *0141/204-0440. www.sarti.co.uk. Main courses under £10. Mon–Thurs 8am–10:30pm; Fri–Sat 8am–11pm; Sun noon–10:30pm. Rail station: Central.*

→**Grassroots Café** ★ VEGETARIAN Grassroots is simply the best choice in Glasgow for vegetarians. The whole place screams granola, and you half expect to see barefoot hippies milling around. Try the organic beer to wash down some goat cheese risotto. The cafe is connected to a whole-food market if you're tempted to take some healthful food home to snack on. *93–97 St. Georges Rd.* ☎ *0141/333-0534. www.grassroots organic.com Main courses £7. Daily 10am–10pm. Subway: St. George's Cross.*

→**Konaki Taverna** GREEK The owners of what is arguably the city's best Greek restaurant hail from Crete, so the menu is slightly different from your average feta cheese and olives. If you're here on a Friday night, prepare to be entertained by some Greek plate-smashing—really! *920 Sauchiehall St.* ☎ *0141/342-4010. www.konakitaverna.com. 2-course lunch £6.85. Mon–Sat noon–2:30pm and 5–11pm; Sun 5–11pm. Subway: Partick.*

MTV **Best** →**The Wee Curry Shop** ★★
INDIAN Aptly named Wee (that's Scottish for "small"), this tiny place is an offshoot of the equally great Mother India restaurant. Though the space may be small, the portions are large and delicious. The menu may seem limited but each dish is prepared perfectly by the chefs in the open kitchen. You won't find a better *murgh aloo* (chicken breast on the bone with potatoes) for miles. *7 Buccleuch St.* ☎ *0141/353-0777. 2-course lunch under £6. Mon–Sat noon–2:30pm and 5:30–10:30pm. Subway: Cowcaddens.*

Doable

→**1901 Bar & Bistro** FRENCH If you're planning a day trip to The Burrell Collection, stop in for lunch at the nearby 1901. The decor is bleu-blanc-rouge in accordance with French fare such as steak frites. Portions are large—perfect if you've worked up an appetite walking around Pollok Park. The creamy mango cheesecake is a must-have for dessert. *1534 Pollokshaws Rd.* ☎ *0141/632-0161. Fixed-price dinner £16. Mon–Fri noon–2:30pm and 5–9:30pm; Sat–Sun noon–9:30pm. Rail station: Shawlands.*

→**Air Organic** ORGANIC FUSION Right in the heart of the West End is the reliable Air Organic, its menu filled with local fare like lamb and scallops served in a modern, minimalist setting. If you're dining *à deux*, order a Bento box to share for £12 to £17. *36 Kelvingrove St.* ☎ *0141/564-5200. Main courses £9–£18; fixed-price 2-course dinner (daily 5–7pm) £12; bento boxes £12–£17. Sun–Thurs noon–10pm; Fri–Sat noon–10:30pm. Subway: Hillhead.*

→**Mono** VEGAN Quite possibly the most PC place in all of Scotland, Mono is not only vegetarian but vegan, so don't expect to find meat or dairy. Order a delicious zucchini potato cake or a Thai stir fry. There's also an in-house music store and some free trade goods on offer. On weekends, local acoustic bands play here. *12 Kings Ct.* ☎ *0141/553-2400.*

GLASGOW

Main courses under £10. Mon–Sun noon–10pm. Subway: City Centre.

Splurge

→ **Ho Wong** ★ CHINESE This is the best Chinese restaurant in Glasgow by far. The menu features fresh seafood and various duck options, and you really can't go wrong with the five-course prix-fixe menu—it might seem pricey at £27 but wait till you see the mountains of food. *82 York St.* ☎ *0141/221-3550. www.ho-wong.com. Main courses £12–£35; a la carte £27–£28; seafood gourmet table (minimum 4 people) £42. Mon–Fri noon–2pm and 6pm–midnight; Sun 6pm–midnight. Rail station: Central.*

→ **Rogano** ★★ SEAFOOD The interior of this well-known seafood restaurant is modeled after the luxurious Queen Mary ocean liner, and you can expect the same sort of pomp and circumstance you'd get at sea. Nothing here is cheap and nothing is particularly light or healthful, but it's all wonderful. Favorite menu items include Moules Mariniere and Lobster Thermidor. An entree in the elegant main restaurant will set you back up to £35, but if you're in a rush, you can eat a sandwich at the bar for £12. If you want to make sure you get a chance to dine here, make reservations ahead of time. *11 Exchange Place.* ☎ *0141/248-4055. www.rogano.co.uk. Main courses £18–£34; fixed-price lunch £17. Restaurant daily noon–2:30pm and 6:30–10:30pm; cafe Mon–Thurs noon–11pm, Fri–Sat noon–midnight, Sun noon–11pm. Subway: Buchanan St.*

Cafes & Tearooms

The best-known tearoom in Glasgow is a tourist haven, so expect it to be crowded every afternoon during the summer months. **The Willow Tea Rooms** (two locations: 217 Sauchiehall St. [☎ **0141/332-0521**] and 97 Buchanan St. [☎ **0141/204-5242**]) opened in 1904 and were designed by the famed Charles Rennie Mackintosh, one of the city's most beloved sons. Cream tea and snacks are the staples at both the original location at 217 Sauchiehall St. and the newer version on Buchanan Street, but don't assume that the Willow is old-fashioned. Both locations have Wi-Fi Internet, so bring your laptop.

In the West End is the less crowded, rather bohemian **Tchai Ovna** (42 Otago Lane; ☎ **0141/357-4524**; www.tchaiovna.com), where you can order one of 80 teas and listen to live music or poetry in the evenings. If the mood strikes, order a shisha pipe or a hookah with flavored, scented tobacco, starting at £4.80. For a very hippie experience, try **Where the Monkey Sleeps** (182 West Regent St.; ☎ **0141/226-3406**), a combination cafe/gallery serving up cappuccinos and soup to students.

Coffee Houses

If you insist on going the chain route, you'll find Starbucks and outlets of British cafes like Caffé Nero and Costa Coffee all over Glasgow. I recommend checking out one of the city's independent cafes instead. **Banana Brothers** (192 St. Vincent St.; ☎ **0141/572-2072**) serves coffee from Vermont and fresh juice. Coffee

Late-Night Munchies

If you're hungry after a big night out, you'll find plenty of places open late on Sauchiehall Street. If you're craving Chinese for cheap, try **Canton Express** (407 Sauchiehall St; ☎ **0141/332-0145**). Farther afield, **Spice Gardens** serves Indian food (11–17 Clyde Place; ☎ **0141/429-4422**) until 4am nightly. For a big, greasy breakfast 24 hours a day, try **Insomnia Cafe,** a student favorite (38 Woodlands Rd.; ☎ **0141/564-1530**).

snobs should try the **Tinderbox Espresso Emporium** in the West End (189 Byres Rd.; ☎ **0141/339-3108**), where you can score really good cappuccino and also buy CDs and magazines.

Partying

Drinking establishments here fall into two basic categories: cool and conventional. Leaving the standard set for the old folks and teenage drinkers, Glasgow's young people prefer the style-conscious bars and pubs that dot the West End and Merchant City, many of which are so near to each other that pub-crawling means walking around the block.

Glasgow's fashion sense is "smart casual," excluding sneakers and wife-beaters—many venues openly discourage athletic gear or shabby streetwear. Clubs open later in the evening, staying open until 3am for the most part, and the few that stay open until 5am stop serving drinks at 3am. The crowds tend not to arrive before 11:30pm or midnight, preferring pre-club cocktails elsewhere to empty dance floors.

Buy a copy of *The List* magazine for a day-by-day listing of every imaginable event in the cities of Glasgow and Edinburgh. Alternatively, there's a *Going Out* guide published every Thursday in the *Glasgow Herald* newspaper.

Clubs

→ **Bamboo** For a more upmarket night, head to sleek, stylish Bamboo, with its cocktail lounge and R&B night known as Disco Badger. If you want to find all the best dressed, most attractive Glasgow Uni students on a Friday night, chances are they're here, sipping Liquid Cocaine (vodka, white wine, and Red Bull). *51a West Regent St.* ☎ *0141/332-1067. www.bamboo51.com. Cover £4–£8. Subway: Buchanan St.*

→ **The Garage** For a big, young crowd comprised mainly of uni students, try The Garage. There's a downstairs area playing the latest in Brit pop, but the biggest draw is the huge dance floor. Just be prepared to answer questions like, "What are you studying?" and expect to see girls go to the bathroom in groups of 10. No jeans or sneakers are allowed, so dress up. *490 Sauchiehall St.* ☎ *0131/332-1120. Cover £3–£5. Subway: Buchanan St.*

→ **The Sub Club** If you like house music, head for this ultracool spot beloved of artsy student types. The downside is that it takes itself rather seriously (two cases in point: high-tech website, nights with names like Kinky Afro). It can cost more than £10 to get in, but chances are the DJs like Layo, Bushwacka, and Paul Arnold will make it worth your while. *22 Jamaica St.* ☎ *0141/221-1177. www.subclub.co.uk. Cover £10–£12. Subway: St. Enoch.*

Bars & Lounges

Glasgow is packed with places to booze, both quaint old pubs and modern lounge bars. If you're a wine lover, try **Vroni's Wine Bar** (47 West Nile St.; ☎ **0141/221-4677**) in the city center. The place feels very French, with banquette seats and candles everywhere. The wine list is top-notch, and you can order by the glass or bottle, or try their house cocktail, the Vronitini: Drambuie, Chambord, and Butterscotch Schnapps. For a more conventional night of vodka tonics, try **Bar 10** (Mitchell Lane; ☎ **0141/572-1448**), with a cool decor and a good mix of people milling around. There are DJs on the weekends and bar food is served in the daylight hours. If you're bored by your friends, you can always use the Internet because Bar 10 provides Wi-Fi access.

In the boho West End, head for **Brel** (Ashton Lane; ☎ **0141/342-4966**), a Belgian bar housed in former stables. With Belgian beers and a French-leaning menu, Brel feels better suited for Brussels than Glasgow, but the theme isn't overwhelming. In Merchant City, try the **Babbity Bowster** (16–18 Blackfriars St.; ☎ 0141/552-7774). The food is consistently good and there's outside seating, in case you're visiting on a rare sunny day. Every Saturday you can listen to folk musicians jamming while you drink your pint.

Gay Bars

→**The Court Bar** This is the best gay bar in central Glasgow. The crowd gets visibly more male as the night wears on, but it's a popular place for both gays and lesbians to gather and chat. It does, however, rival your kitchen cupboard for size. *69 Hutcheson St.* ☎ *0141/552-2463 Rail station: Paisley Gilmour.*

→**Cube** ★ Scotland's 2005 nightclub of the year, Cube has two well-attended gay nights each week, Passionality on Mondays and FUN on Tuesdays. It's just a coincidence that this funky club is located on Queen Street! On other nights, Cube is just as packed with young Glaswegians dressed to the nines. If you're in town on a Sunday, check out their newest night, Cubana, with DJs spinning reggaeton, soca, and dancehall. *33–34 Queen St.* ☎ *0141/ 226-8990. www.cubeglasgow.co.uk. Cover £2–£8. Rail station: Argyle. Subway: St. Enoch.*

Pub-Crawls

Glasgow University students have perfected the art of the pub-crawl. However, their twist on the formula is known as the "Sub Crawl," in which they use the subway to get from pub to pub. Buy a Discovery Ticket—it offers unlimited travel all day for £1.70—and start at the Hillhead station. You can have a drink at **Curlers Bar** (260 Byres Rd.; ☎ **0141/334-1284;** subway: Hyndland), the nearest watering hole to the subway. From there, head to Kelvinhall and keep going in the same direction.

Here are a few favorite pubs:

📺 Best The Horse Shoe Bar ★ Hands down my favorite bar in Glasgow, The Horse Shoe has been around since the early 20th century, but the atmosphere is more cozy than musty. Before you're even finished ordering from the bar—it won't be hard to get a spot because it's the longest in the world—you're bound to rub elbows with some chatty locals. The upstairs buffet boasts cheap cocktails and food. *17 Drury Lane.* ☎ *0141/229-5711. Rail station: Central.*

Brunswick Cellar This cool, subterranean bar is candlelit and dim. Walk in and you'll be blinded until your eyes adjust. Dance music and TVs drone on in the background. The happy hour will probably keep you very happy—from 3 to 8pm. *239 Sauciehall St.* ☎ *0141/353-0131. Bus: 57.*

Budda Bar Another subterranean choice but with plush couches and pillows to cozy up in. Rock 'n' roll accompanies the conversation, mostly from 20- and 30-somethings (on Fri and Sat nights), who crowd in for a drink before heading upstairs to the bar's nightclub. Look for the big-bellied Buddha on the street. *142 St. Vincent St.* ☎ *0141/243-2212. Bus: 6, 8, or 16.*

Halt Bar Although it looks like every other bar, this one draws an odd assortment of patrons, from students who come for the all-day Happy Hour between 11am and 6pm (when pints are £1.50) to old guys, locals, who won't stop frequenting *their* bar, no matter how popular it becomes. Local bands jam here Friday and Saturday nights, there's football on the big-screen TV most days, and Sundays has become quiz night. *160 Woodlands Rd.* ☎ *0141/564-1527. Subway: Kelvinbridge.*

Live Music

The live-music scene in Glasgow is probably the best in the U.K. Famous bands have been discovered here: Consider, for instance, Oasis, who were signed after they were seen playing in local rock bar **King Tut's Wah-Wah Hut** (272a Vincent St.; ☎ 0141/221-5279; www.kingtuts.co.uk). You probably won't catch a megaband like Franz Ferdinand, but you'll be able to catch lesser-known local bands every night of the week at venues ranging from the tiny **Barfly** (260 Clyde St.; ☎ 0870/907-0999; www.barflyclub.com) to the big, beer-soaked **Barrowland Ballroom** (244 Gallowgate; ☎ 0141/552-4601; www. glasgow-barrowland.com).

Strange though it may seem, Glasgow natives love country and western music. Accordingly, famous country acts from the U.K. and U.S. play at the **Grand Ole Opry** (2–4 Govan Rd.; ☎ 0141/429-5396), where you can join in some line dancing and eat off a chuck wagon. **Nice 'n' Sleazy** (421 Sauchiehall St.; ☎ 0141/333-9637) is your best bet for live acts in an intimate setting because the basement bar only holds about 200 people.

Performing Arts

In the shadow of the Edinburgh International Festival, Glasgow's performing-arts scene is used to taking a back seat—even though the city boasts most of Scotland's major classical music, dance, and opera companies. In addition to the big companies and the annual visits by London's Royal Shakespeare Company, Glasgow has several small theaters and companies committed to innovative work. The center of the national film industry—which boomed following successes like *Trainspotting*—Glasgow is something of a cinematic hot spot. To find out what's hot, look in *The List* for reviews and schedules.

Performance Halls

The most prestigious performance space in Glasgow is the **Royal Concert Hall** (2 Sauchiehall St.; ☎ 0141/353-8000), arguably the center of the city's cultural action. As well as providing a space for renowned international acts like Ladysmith Black Mambazo, the RCH is home to the Royal Scottish National Orchestra. Visit www.grch. com for more details of schedules. For smaller venues, try the **City Halls and Old Fruitmarket** (Candleriggs, near Glasgow Cross; ☎ 0141/353-8000; www.glasgowcity halls.com), currently undergoing renovations. The Scottish Symphony Orchestra has played here for years. On Renfrew Street you can find the **Royal Scottish Academy of Music and Drama,** or RSAMD (100 Renfrew St.; ☎ 0141/332-8901; www.rsamd.ac.uk). Here you'll find performances of mainstream musicals like *Hello Dolly.*

Comedy Clubs

The city's most famous comedy club is a franchise of an Edinburgh establishment called **The Stand** (333 Woodlands Rd.; ☎ 0870/600-6055; www.thestand.co.uk; tickets usually only cost about £2–£3). If you want to see local amateurs, go on a Tuesday night. Another good comedy club is **The Vault,** a bit out of the city center (1110 Pollokshaws Rd.; ☎ 0141/649-0007; tickets about £7). Monday nights are free. Because it's part of a large chain, the acts at **Jongleurs Comedy Club** tend to be watered down compared with naughty performances at other clubs—but that doesn't necessarily mean they're less funny. It's in the UGC cinema building in the city center (7 Renfrew St.; ☎ 0870/011-1965).

GLASGOW

Sightseeing

There's absolutely loads to do in Glasgow, a city that caters to everyone from architecture fans to modern artists. Luckily, many of the main attractions are right in the city center, such as the Museum of Modern Art and the cathedral. The best way to see the entire city if you don't have much time is to take a **Glasgow City Tour** by bus. If nothing else, such a tour will help you decide where to devote more of your precious time. Tour buses leave from George Square; each ride costs £8.50. Go to www.scotguide.com for more information or call ☎ 0141/204-0444.

Make sure to check out the **Lighthouse** (11 Mitchell Lane; ☎ 0141/221-6362; www.the lighthouse.co.uk), a museum devoted to architecture and design. The views from the top of the tower are stunning, and should help you get your bearings in the city.

Festivals

January

Celtic Connections. This festival celebrates folk and traditional music and draws musicians from as far away as Basque country and North America and is staged primarily at the Royal Concert Hall. For tickets and details, call ☎ 0141/240-1111 or 0845/330-3501. Throughout January.

Robbie Burns Night. This night marks the celebration of Scotland's favorite son. Expect lots of toasting with whiskey. For details, call ☎ 01292/443-700 in Ayr, or ☎ 0131/473-3800 in Edinburgh (☎ 01387/253-862 in Dumfries). January 25.

March

Glasgow Comedy Festival. A newbie compared to Edinburgh's Fringe Festival, this fest attracts top comedians to Glasgow. Call ☎ 0141/564-1530 or go to www.glasgow comedyfestival.com. Last 2 weeks of March.

July

The International Jazz Festival. Jazz musicians from all over the world descend upon the city. Go to www.jazzfest.co.uk for more details. Throughout July.

MTV **Best** **In The Park** ★★. Held halfway between Glasgow and Edinburgh, this rock, dance, and world-music extravaganza in Balado, Kinross, lasts for 2 full days, drawing attendees from all across the U.K. Call ☎ 0141/339-8383 or visit www.tinthepark. com. Mid-July.

August

World Pipe Band Championships. Come to hear approximately 1,000 participants play bagpipes and strut around in kilts. Call ☎ 0141/204-4400. Mid-August.

September

Doors Open Days. In Edinburgh and Glasgow, buildings that are usually off limits to the public open their doors. Call ☎ 0141/248-1188 or go to www.doorsopendays. org.uk for dates.

October & November

Big Big World Festival. Here you'll see acts from Asia, Africa, and everywhere in between. Call ☎ 0141/221-0359 or go to www.soundsfine.co.uk for exact dates.

---

where to Find out what's on

Check out the tourist-friendly website **What's On Glasgow** at www.glasgow.gov.uk/en/Visitors/WhatsOn. Not only does the site have a handy calendar of events, but there's also information on regular activities and classes. Another good website full of comprehensive information on exhibitions is **www.myglasgow.org**. You can find out about gigs and concerts, or even singles and dating events.

MTV🅤 The University Scene

The city's main center of learning is **Glasgow University,** which sits atop a hill in an attractive area of town. The 500-year-old school has earned itself a solid reputation over the years. To find out more about it, visit www.gla.ac.uk. The other two large universities in the city are Glasgow Caledonian and Strathclyde.

Glasgow's students haunt the city's various clubs all nights of the week, although they have two student unions where they can buy cheap booze. Buzz over to **The Hive** (32 University Ave.), the top student nightclub in the city. For more info on Glasgow University student nights and the Hive, check out the Union website (www.guu.co.uk) or call ☎ **0141/339-8697.**

Glasgay! This is the U.K.'s largest multiarts festival for the LGBT community. It's lots of fun, so check out the film, theater, and visual arts on offer. Call ☎ **0141/552-7575** or go to www.glasgay.co.uk. Mid-October to mid-November.

December

Hogmanay. New Year's Eve is a huge deal in Scotland. Over 100,000 revelers take to the streets, and a lucky 25,000 are herded into George Square for fireworks to herald the New Year. Call ☎ **0131/473-3800** for more info. December 31.

Top Attractions

🅜🆅 (Best) (FREE) ➔ **The Burrell Collection** ★★★ A jewel of a museum, The Burrell Collection houses excellent exhibits along with the treasures of Sir William Burrell. In addition to the Greco-Roman artifacts and Degas paintings, the museum curates regular special exhibits. *Pollok Park, 2060 Pollokshaws Rd.* ☎ *0141/649-7151. Free admission. Mon–Sat 10am–5pm; Sun 11am–5pm. Bus: 45, 48, or 57.*

(FREE) ➔ **The Centre for Contemporary Art** The CCA doesn't charge fees because it's government-owned, and exhibits tend to be edgy and provocative, like the recent "In the Poem about Love You Don't Write the Word Love," showcasing art by the likes of Andy Warhol and Jean-Luc Godard, which makes a distinction between the literal and the visual.

There's a small theater that shows artsy and foreign films, and a space for hip-hop and drama classes. *350 Sauchiehall St;* ☎ *0141/332-3226. www.cca-glasgow.com. Tues–Fri 9am–10pm. Saturday 10am–10pm. Free admission. Subway: Cowcaddens or Buchanan.*

(FREE) ➔ **Gallery of Modern Art** If you love modern art you must visit the Gallery of Modern Art (GOMA), right in the heart of town in Royal Exchange Square. Some of the art on show is by the "new Glasgow boys" who became famous in the '80s, including Steven Campbell and Sir James Guthrie. The exhibits are usually small but well curated, so each piece is something to see. *Royal Exchange Sq.* ☎ *0141/229-1996. www.glasgowmuseums.com. Free admission. Mon–Sun 10am–5pm (Thurs till 8pm). Subway: Kelvinhall.*

➔ **Glasgow Science Centre** ★★This is Britain's most successful millennium project. On the banks of the River Clyde, it lies in the heart of the city, opposite the Scottish Exhibition and Conference Centre. Opened in 2001, the center is the focal point of Glasgow's drive to become one of Europe's major high-tech locations. In three landmark buildings, the center features the first titanium-clad structures in the United Kingdom, including Scotland's only Space Theatre. The complex also contains the only 360-degree rotating tower in the world. Other features include innovative laboratories, multimedia

GLASGOW

Arty Architecture

When you arrive in Glasgow, there are two names you'll hear over and over again: **Charles Rennie Mackintosh** and **Alexander "Greek" Thomson.** Their influence on the Victorian city has been massive, and you won't turn a corner without seeing their work. Mackintosh, a favorite son, died in 1928, so his buildings have a slightly pre–Art Nouveau feel. His architectural gifts to Glasgow include the Lighthouse museum building, the famous Willow Tea Rooms, and the Scotland Street School. Although Mackintosh remains better known, his precursor Alexander Thomson is generally esteemed as being more innovative. Thomson earned the nickname "Greek" because he brought Grecian design to Victorian Scotland in the mid–19th century. He was also a fan of Egyptian, Assyrian, and other Eastern motifs. To see some of his influence on the city, look no further than Eton Terrace in the West End, St. Vincent Street Church, Holmwood House, and the Grecian buildings that house the Center for Contemporary Art. Thomson died young, before he could travel to the exotic countries that influenced his work. However, a scholarship was set up in his name for young architects to study abroad. The second winner was a 22-year-old named Charles Rennie Mackintosh.

and science theaters, and interactive exhibits. The overall theme is that of documenting the challenges facing Scotland in the 21st century. *50 Pacific Quay.* ☎ *0141/420-5010. www.gsc.org.uk. Admission £6.95 adults, £4.95 students and seniors. Daily 10am–6pm. Subway: Buchan St. Station to Cessnock, from which there's a 10-min. walk.*

FREE → **The Hunterian Art Gallery** ★★
The Hunterian is a bit farther from the city center but it's definitely worth a visit. Housed at the university, this collection includes works by Rembrandt and Pisarro, and some by Scottish artists. Nearby is the Hunterian Museum, which devotes its space to a wide range of relics, from Viking-era plunder to the story of Capt. Cook's discovery of Australia. *22 Hillhead St.* ☎ *0141/330-5431. www.hunterian. gla.ac.uk. Free admission. Mon–Sat 9:30am– 5pm. Subway: Hillhead.*

Other Attractions

FREE → **Cathedral of St. Kentigern**
★★★ This cathedral, dating from the 13th century, is a must-see for history buffs and architecture fans. Some of the design elements are

from different time periods, like the Gothic lower church with its dramatic arches. Right across from the Cathedral is the Central Necropolis, a famous graveyard housing a statue of the reformer John Knox and burial place of Jewish settlers. ***Note:*** This place is also known as St. Mungo's after the founder of Glasgow. *Castle St.* ☎ *0141/552-6891. www. glasgowcathedral.org.uk. Free admission. Mon– Sat 9:30am–6pm; Sun 1–5pm. Rail station: Queen St.*

→ **Holmwood House** An Alexander "Greek" Thomson–designed building popular with visitors is Holmwood House, a masterpiece of Victorian architecture—complete with all the architect's famous ornamental decorations. It's operated by the National Trust, so you'll have to pay a few pounds for entrance, which goes toward the upkeep of this and other stately homes. *61–63 Netherlee Rd.* ☎ *0141/637-2129. www.nts.org.uk. Admission £5 adults, £4 students. Apr 1–Oct 31 Thurs–Mon 1–5pm. Subway: Catchart. Bus: 66 or 44.*

FREE → **St. Vincent Street Church** This is an impressive structure, designed by

12 Hours in Glasgow

1. **Take a double-decker bus tour.** This is the best way to see the city in a short time. Leave from George Square, get off the bus, and take a short stroll to **Royal Exchange Square.** Here you can check out the artwork at the **Gallery of Modern Art.**

2. **Have a look at the shops in pedestrian-friendly Buchanan Street.** Make sure to stop at the Buchanan Galleries in between all the window-shopping. Also pop into **Rogano,** a wonderful, if slightly expensive, place to have lunch and rest for a bit.

3. **Take the bus to The Burrell Collection.** This is the best art gallery in Glasgow. You won't regret the trip. Stroll around **Pollok Country Park,** surrounding the Burrell Collection, before you head back to the center of the city.

4. **Go see the Glasgow Cathedral.** Also check out the **Necropolis grave-yard** across the ravine.

5. **Relax at the famous Willow Tea Rooms.** Designed by beloved son Charles Rennie Mackintosh, the rooms are definitely worth at least a cup of tea.

6. **Dinnertime, followed by drinks.** Try **The Wee Curry Shop** for the best Indian meal around. Head to a traditional pub afterwards for a few pints before hitting the hay.

GLASGOW

Thomson and featuring exotic, Indian-looking designs. Look out for the decorative shellfish and plant motif—this is probably the only church with starfish and flowers all over its pillars. *265 St. Vincent St. No phone. www.greekthomsonchurch.com. Free admission. Sun service at 11am and 6pm. Subway: Buchanan.*

→ **S.V. Glenlee, the Tall Ship at Glasgow Harbour** While it's not really a building, there's a lot of history associated with the Tall Ship at Glasgow Harbour. Built in the 19th century, the *S.V. Glenlee* circumnavigated Cape Horn 15 times. You can explore it and take a look at the onboard exhibition about its history. *Stobcross Rd. ☎ 0141/222-2513. www.thetall ship.com. Admission £4.95. Mar–Oct daily 10am–5pm; Nov–Feb daily 11am–4pm. Rail station: Finnieston/Exhibition Centre.*

Playing Outside

GARDENS & PARKS Glaswegians aren't really health nuts, but the few that bother to exercise do so in the parks around town. One of the best parks in Glasgow is **Kelvingrove Park** in the West End. It's lush, green, and hilly and contains some eccentric little extras like the Gothic Stewart Memorial Fountain with signs of the Zodiac and the head of Thomas Carlyle emerging from a rock face over the Prince of Wales Bridge. If that doesn't totally relax you, pay a visit to the **Botanic Gardens,** home to a conservatory of exotic plants known as Kibble Palace. The gardens are a favorite with locals, who tend to picnic on the lawns instead of checking out the greenhouses.

For jogging near the city center, try **Glasgow Green** (780 Great Western Rd., near Hillhead underground station); the green also includes People's Palace, a museum dedicated to the history of ordinary Glaswegians. **Pollok Country Park,** to the south of the city center, surrounds The Burrell Collection and is worth a look around if you have an extra hour.

SPECTATOR SPORTS   Scotland's two biggest football teams, the Catholic Celtic and the Protestant Rangers, are long-time combatants. Competing not just for victory but for sectarian pride, the teams—and their fans—are fanatics. When they play, age-old religious rivalries erupt both at matches and in the streets, often resulting in injury and death. Such hooliganism is increasingly discouraged these days, and while lasting peace is nowhere in sight, the growing tranquillity has lured families back into attendance at local matches. The season lasts from August to May. Celtic plays at **Celtic Park** (18 Kerrydale St.; ☎ **0141/551-4308;** rail station: Bridgeton; tours offered Mon–Sun 11am, noon, 1:45, and 2:30pm; tour price £8.50; box office ☎ **0141/551-8653;** game tickets £22–£25) and the Rangers at **Ibrox Stadium** (150 Edmiston Dr.; ☎ **0870/600-1972;** rail station: Cardonald; tours offered Thurs–Fri 11am, 12:30, and 2:30pm; tour price £7; box office ☎ **0870/600-1993;** game tickets £20–£22). Home games usually sell out, so book in advance.

The city is home to one other much beloved sport: 📺 Best **curling** ★, which is much like bowling or bocce, except with the added difficulty of being played on ice. Curling is an official sport in the Winter Olympics. **The Lagoon Leisure Centre** (see later in this chapter) offers indoor facilities that include six curling lanes.

SPORTS COMPLEXES   The **Kelvin Hall International Sports Arena** is on Argyle Street (☎ **0141/357-2525;** www.glasgowclub. org; subway: Kelvin Hall), near the River Kelvin. It offers volleyball and basketball courts, as well as an indoor track. It's open daily from 9am to 10:30pm; you can use the weight room for £2.90 or the fully equipped gym for £4.20. This is also the country's major venue for national and international sports competitions. Check with the tourist office for any events scheduled for the time of your visit.

WATERSPORTS & ICE-SKATING   The **Lagoon Leisure Centre** (11 Christie St., Paisley; ☎ **0141/889-4000;** www.renfrew shireleisure.com) offers indoor facilities including a freeform pool with a wave machine, fountains, and flume. You'll also find sauna suites with sun beds, Jacuzzis, and a Finnish steam room in addition to the curling lanes, mentioned earlier. There are also bar and catering facilities. Call for schedules and pricing information.

Shopping

Glasgow is considered second only to London—10 times its size—for shopping, so it's not surprising that Glaswegians tend to be well dressed. A few years back, you would never expect to find a Versace store in a Scottish city. Since Glasgow's cultural renaissance in the '80s and '90s, designer garb is easy to find and little boutiques dot the city. But it has its share of places to buy cheap club clothes, too.

The best shopping is to be found on pedestrian Argyle Street, Sauchiehall Street, and Buchanan Street, but make sure to venture to Merchant City and the West End for some more eclectic finds.

The **Italian Center** will have little Prada numbers—or Gucci, or Versace, and so on (7 John St.; ☎ **0141/552-6099**). **Cruise** contains labels like Vivienne Westwood, Armani, and Prada. It's right in the Italian Center, where you'll also find the U.K.'s first Versace store and an Escada boutique. If your budget doesn't really stretch to Alexander McQueen, head down the street to **Cruise Jeans,** the boutique's more casual, streetwise sister, featuring brands like Fake London and Maharishi, who make the best pants for lounging (180 Ingram St.; ☎ 0141/552-99-89; Mon–Fri 10am–6pm, Sat 9am–6pm, Sun 1–5pm; subway: to Buchanan St.).

Fashion-conscious models and high schoolers know that **Topshop** (229–249 Buchanan St; ☎ 0141/332-4537) remains your best bet for an up-to-the-minute outfit that looks like it was stolen from Kate Moss's wardrobe or copied meticulously from the runway.

Princes Square (Buchanan St.; ☎ 0141/221-0324; www.princessquare.co.uk) is perhaps the most stylish of the city's few shopping malls, with upmarket chain stores as well as some cute cafes and bars. Once inside, look out for preppy cashmere at Lacoste, lotions and potions by Brit beauty guru Jo Malone, and upscale luxury and leather goods boutique Penhaligons. Bigger and more run-of-the-mill is **Buchanan Galleries** (220 Buchanan St; ☎ 0141/333-9898; www.buchanangalleries.co.uk), with a similar look to American malls. You'll find anything you need, from clothes and shoes at John Lewis and H&M to food at Sainsburys and toiletries at Boots.

For books, there's nowhere better than **Caledonia Books** (438 Great Western Rd.; ☎ 0141/334-9663; www.caledoniabooks.co.uk). It's a far cry from Borders, with antique and rare books and a philosophy of quality over quantity. If you absolutely must bring some souvenirs home for Mom, resist the urge to buy something cheesy and try the **National Trust for Scotland** shop at Hutcheson Hall (158 Ingram St.; ☎ 0141/552-8391; www.nts.org.uk). The building itself is old and beautiful, and you can pick up jewelry or ceramics made by contemporary Glaswegian artists. If you're searching for tunes, you'll find many good record shops in the city, the best of which is indie store **Avalanche** (34 Dundas St.; ☎ 0141/332-2099).

Vintage

Check out **Dr. Jives, a vintage boutique** in Merchant City (111 Candleriggs; ☎ 0141/552-5451). It used to be a skater store in the '80s but has evolved into the arbiter of hip style for Glasgow. For some *very* vintage looks, head to **Starry Starry Night** (Dowanside Lane; ☎ 0141/337-1837) in the West End. You can find clothes dating back to Victorian and Edwardian times—but keep in mind that people were tiny back then! Also stop in if you're into military chic because they sell authentic army gear too.

GLASGOW

The Greek Islands

After taking her LSATs, a very smart friend of mine flew to Athens and boarded the first ferry she could find to the islands. She didn't care where she went. She didn't care how long she'd be gone. She carried one bag.

The Greek Islands are extraordinary, and one group of them, the Cyclades, brings you right to the heart of island life. There's an amazing range here, from traditional towns to mega-nightspots. We can guide you to places that will satisfy both sides of this island wanderlust: the ancient ruins (some of the best archaeological sites in the world) and the let-your-hair-down clubs. And no matter your vantage point, the scenery will be breathtaking.

The Best of The Greek Islands

◦ **The Best Beach Vibe:** At **Kamari,** the water is clear, the surrounding cliffs (shall we say it once more) breathtaking, and the local hangout, Perissa, rocks at night with backpackers in barely-there bikinis and board shorts. See p. 452.

◦ **The Best Cheap Sleep:** Head straight to the beach for the island's hippest hostel, **Youth Hostel Anna,** if staying in the center of town isn't a priority. A backpacker's dream: no curfew, hot showers, sheets for 1€, a restaurant with discounts for hostel patrons, and a rockin' bar/nightclub. See p. 447.

◦ **The Best Hotel Atmosphere:** Hands down, the **Astra Apartments** are the best accommodations and have the most spectacular location in all of Santorini, with the friendliest—and probably coolest—staff, to boot. The hotel is a sprawling complex of whitewashed buildings which seem to tumble down the dramatic cliffs of Imerovigli. See p. 448.

◦ **The Best Fast Food: Lucky's** serves gyros to customers who come from across the globe and who might even claim they are the best in all of Greece. This tiny stand in Fira's main square also doles out a tzatziki that you could eat plain and great french fries, as well as other Greek standards like souvlaki. See p. 449.

◦ **The Best Seafood Meal:** For traditional Greek food with all the stages, try **The Octopus Tree.** The name refers to the octopuses hanging outside the restaurant to dry (and then to be used in the wonderful food inside). The menu is whatever was caught on the owners' fishing boat that day and includes *mezes* that may take hours to get through. See p. 458.

○ **The Best Splurge Meal:** What's in changes as readily as the tide here. **Interni** is the place of the moment for the chicest dinner and drinks on Mykonos. The open-air dining area mimics the whitewashed Cycladic buildings—and even the multilingual waitstaff is dressed in white. The Italian food plays second to the scene, and it is expensive, so be forewarned. See p. 463.

○ **The Best Nightlife Warm-Up:** People typically start their night in Mykonos at

Museum Hours Update

If you visit Greece during the summer, check to see when sites and museums are open. According to the tourist office, they should be open from 8am to 7:30pm, but some may close earlier in the day or even be closed 1 day a week.

Little Venice, an area along the water at the edge of town (also near the windmills). Here fashionistas can dip their pedicured toes into the water while

Island-Hopping by Boat

High winds and unpredictable weather mean that schedules change frequently and trips are often cancelled, making the service very unpredictable. The estimates for time are also variable and change depending on the weather.

REGULAR FERRIES **From Santorini,** ferries go to and from Piraeus at least twice daily; the trip is around 9 to 10 hours by car ferry on the Piraeus-Paros-Naxos-Ios-Santorini route. It's around 4 hours by catamaran on the Piraeus-Paros-Santorini route. In July and August, ferries connect several times a day with Ios (1–2 hr.), Naxos (3 hr.), Paros (2½ hr. by hydrofoil, 4 hr. by car ferry), and Mykonos (4–6 hr.).

From Ios, four daily ferries link Ios to Piraeus (7 hr.), Paros (2½ hr.), and Naxos (1¼ hr.). Daily ferries from Ios sail to Santorini (1 hr.) and Mykonos (4 hr.). Four ferries per week link Ios to Anafi (2 hr.) and two weekly to Syros (2¾ hr.).

From Mykonos, there are daily ferry connections to Andros, Paros, Syros, and Tinos; five to seven trips a week to Ios; four a week to Iraklion, Crete; and two a week to Ikaria, Samos, Skiathos, Skyros, and Thessaloniki.

FLYING DOLPHINS (HYDROFOILS) **Hellas Flying Dolphins** offers service from Piraeus (☎ **210/419-9100** or 210/419-9000; www.ferries.gr/hfd) in summer. On Mykonos or while on the mainland in Athens, your best bet for getting boat information is to check at individual agents, like Delia Travel (☎ **22890/22-490**). Three daily Flying Dolphins link Ios Island to Santorini (30 min.) and Naxos (50 min.). Two to three daily hydrofoils go from Ios to Paros (1½ hr.), Mykonos (2¾ hr.), and Tinos (3½ hr.).

CATAMARANS (HIGH-SPEED FERRIES) Daily Catamarans link Ios to Santorini (30 min.), Naxos (50 min.), Paros (1½ hr.), Syros (2¾ hr.), and Rafina (4 hr.). It's about 4 hours from Piraeus to Santorini.

FYI: It's possible to confirm ferry schedules by phone, but the following offices rarely answer. All the same, try **Athens GNTO** (☎ **210/327-1300** or 210/331-0562), the **Port Authority in Piraeus** (☎ **210/459-3223**), or the **Port Authority in Santorini** (☎ **22860/22-239**). The Piraeus Port Authority (☎ **210/422-6000**) has schedules.

swilling Appletinis and swaying to the latest Euro-track the DJs inside the clubs are spinning. People walk freely from bar to bar, holding drinks from wherever they picked them up. Club boundaries are so fuzzy that you may not notice when you leave one and enter another. See p. 463.

○ **The Best Bar:** The highlight of Fira's bar scene is **Tropical Bar.** A slew of hot, young tourists—mostly American, Brits, and Aussies—converge here for sunset cocktails, late-night dancing, and beers aplenty. See p. 450.

○ **The Best Sunset Views: Walk!** Hike the path from Fira to Imerovigli. Ia gets a lot of hype as the ultimate sunset destination, but the path offers even more dramatic views, with the whitewashed buildings of Ia in the distance and the caldera before you. See p. 452.

○ **The Best Camping:** Far Out boasts three swimming pools, tennis courts, water slides, a massive beach area, three bars, a restaurant . . . wait, did anyone plan on sleeping while here? They've got that covered too: "Roughing it" in a beach bungalow or tent isn't really that bad—the bungalows in **Far Out Club Camping** are equipped with beds, mirrors and desks, and have a thatched-roof, "Love Shack" appeal. See p. 455.

○ **The Best Side Trip:** A sacred island a mile away from Mykonos, **Delos** is home to some of the greatest archaeological treasures in Greece. The island, once considered the holiest sanctuary of all Greece, is dotted with artifacts—some more "ruined" than others, but all of them an amazing sight to see. See p. 463.

Santorini

Close your eyes and conjure up an image of a Greek island. If it's precipitous cliffs with whitewashed buildings and blue-domed churches that look as if they should tumble into the sea, you're thinking of the dramatic landscape of Santorini, whether you know it or not. The island has become the poster child for the Greek Islands. Crescent-shaped Santorini is actually the rim of a volcano; devastating earthquakes submerged the rest of the mountain thousands of years ago. Come to Santorini to savor the caldera views—with a cocktail at a local taverna, perhaps—and the glorious sunsets that burn into the sea each night.

This spectacular setting has drawn scores of American, British, and Australian expats to now call the island home. Then again, the draw could be the overwhelming warmth of the locals and the island's fascinating history, the divine restaurants—red, ripe tomatoes; fresh grilled fish; and savory tzatziki abound—or knowing that the party never seems to end at the island's discos and bars.

During July and August, the island swells to capacity with tourists and day visitors from the unending line of cruise ships that stop here, but the draw of the island's beauty far surpasses the inconvenience of moving along streets at the pace of molasses.

Getting There & Getting Around

GETTING INTO TOWN
By Plane

Olympic Airways (☎ **210/966-6666** or 210/936-9111; www.olympic-airways.gr) is Greece's main airline and offers daily flights between Athens and the Santorini airport at Monolithos. You can make connections to Mykonos five times a week. For more information and reservations, head to the Olympic office in Fira on Ayiou Athanassiou (☎ **22860/22-493**), just outside of town on the road to Kamari, or in Athens (☎ **08210/44-444** or 210/966-6666). Your other option is **Aegean Airlines** (☎ **210/998-2888** or 210/998-8300 in Athens), which has an office at the

The Cyclades

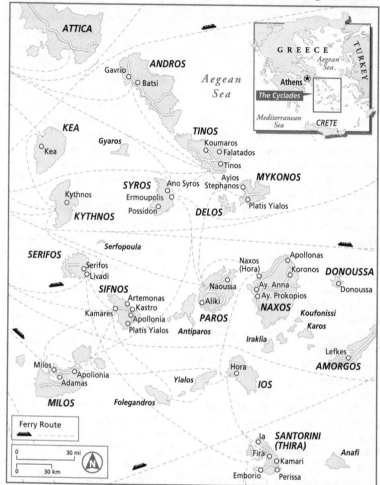

Ferry Route

0 — 30 mi
0 — 30 km

Monolithos airport (☎ 22860/28-500), and also offers several flights daily between Athens and Santorini.

A bus to Fira (3€) meets most flights; you'll find a schedule posted at the bus stop, next to the airport entrance. Taxis (☎ 22860/22-555 or 22860/23-95) are also available; a trip to Fira costs about 8€. Many hotels also offer transfer services to/from the airport; check with your hotel when booking.

By Boat

The cheapest and probably least convenient way to get to Santorini is via ferry (see p. 441 for more info). If you want to get there sooner, opt for a faster boat.

Most ferries will dock at the port of Athinios and a slew of buses meet each boat and head straight to Fira and the Fira bus station (2€ one-way). If you're heading to another part of the island, you can catch connecting buses from Fira. Taxis are also available from Athinios but will cost far more than the bus fare. Most travel agencies on the island sell ferry tickets. There is another, much smaller port, Skala, which sits beneath the cliffs of Fira. Because Skala is an exposed port and unsafe for larger boats, it's usually only frequented by small cruise ships, excursion boats, yachts, or private vessels. To get to Fira from here, you can take a cable car (3€) or a mule or donkey ride (3€). The mule ride sounds cooler than it is—exhausted donkeys bump along the steep cliffs to Fira passing by smelly mounds of donkey poo and the occasionally weary tourist trying to endure the 45-minute climb up to the town.

GETTING AROUND
By Bus

Santorini's bus service is incredibly reliable and convenient to use. The main bus stations is south of Fira's main square, and schedules are clearly posted here. Buses to various points of the island generally run every half-hour from 7 to 11pm during the high season (less frequently in the off season). Fares range from 1€ to 3€ and are collected by a conductor on board. Destinations include the tourist hub of Akrotiri, Athinios (the ferry pier), Ia, Kamari, Monolithos (the airport), Perissa, Perivolas Beach, Vlihada, and Vourvoulos. Excursion buses travel to major attractions; ask a travel agent for details (see below). If you travel by bus to Ia to watch the sunset, be forewarned that buses get absurdly crowded for the late-night return trips (10–11pm), and some passengers aren't even able to squeeze onto the last bus. Plan to depart Ia as early as possible so you don't get stuck paying a hefty taxi fare (15€).

By Car

It seems that everyone and his mom have some sort of "rental" agency on the island.

Your best bet for getting a car is to hit one of the island's travel agents. Granted, the local companies such as **Zeus** (☎ 22860/24-013) tend to offer lower prices, but the quality isn't always the best. Or try **Budget Rent-A-Car,** below the bus stop square in Fira (☎ 22860/22-900); a small car costs about 50€ a day, with unlimited mileage. You can often get cheaper prices if you reserve the car in advance through **Budget** in the United States (☎ 800/527-0700).

Parking rules are strictly enforced, and if you do park in a no-parking zone or in town, police remove your license tags and you will be responsible for retrieving them from the police station and paying a fine. While driving on the island isn't particularly scary or dangerous, it's not really necessary to have a car when buses and taxis provide ample and convenient service.

By Moped

Locals will beg and plead with you not to rent a moped, and they have a point. Sure it looks tempting to zip around the island with wind in your hair and caldera views below. But the roads are narrow, winding, and really treacherous. Local drivers tend to drive at top speed and take curves even faster; if you're not sure where you're going or what you're doing—and even if you think you do—you can get seriously hurt. In fact, the hospital often fills up in peak season with injured moped drivers. Not to mention that it's illegal unless you have a motorcycle license. A moped will cost about 20€ per day (less off season).

Safety First

Use caution when walking around Santorini, especially at night. Keep in mind that many drivers on the roads are newcomers to the island and may not know every twist and turn.

Santorini

By Taxi

The taxi station (which is really just a line of taxis near a taxi sign) in Fira is just south of the main square and pretty hard to miss. You or your hotel can also book a taxi ahead by phone (☎ **22860/22-555** or 22860/23-951). As with taxis everywhere, make sure to agree on a price before heading out, as most point-to-point trips have fixed prices. (The most popular routes include Fira to Ia for 15€, and Fira to Imeroviglio for 5€.) For a taxi outside Fira, you'll be charged a pickup fee of at least 1.50€. Because all bus service usually shuts down at midnight, it's a good idea to book a taxi in advance if you'll need it late at night. Taxis are seriously hard to come by after hours.

By Foot

Strolling through Fira and Ia is one of the highlights of being on this island, but walking to get farther afield isn't practical. One exception is the hike along the caldera rim between the two towns (see p. 452 for details). You will need to take a bus or taxi to get to most beaches and archaeological sites.

Santorini Basics

ORIENTATION: SANTORINI NEIGHBORHOODS

The volcanic island of Santorini is crescent shaped, with the interior of the crescent facing the caldera, or the volcano crater, and home to the island's two major towns, Fira and Ia, where most of the island's action takes place. The popular beach towns of **Kamari** and **Perissa** sit on the southeast of the island, at the back of the crescent. Also to the south, lies the **Red Beach** and the ancient ruins of **Akrotiri**, a major archaeological site and a popular tourist destination.

FIRA (THIRA) The island's main town of Fira is a spectacular maze of whitewashed buildings and streets perched along the crest of the caldera. Nearly every corner, every balcony, provides a stunning view of the water and the rest of the island curving around it. Here you will find the hub of all things: hotels, bars, clubs, shopping. As it's in the center of the crescent-shaped island and is also the island's transportation hub, try to get a hotel here, if you like that convenience.

IA Santorini's other major town is Ia, which is often thought to be the prettier of the two. Ia is more tranquil, but its location on the farthest point of the island is not as convenient to nightlife or sightseeing. Ia is best known for its spectacular sunsets and hordes of tourists who descend upon the town nightly for the event. Yes, the views are lovely, and yes it's worth seeing, but check out the choice views from nearby Imerovigli.

IMEROVIGLI Diminutive Imerovigli has some of the island's finest accommodations and incredible views of the caldera—far better panoramas than either Fira or Ia. The best sunset vista is here, where the looming rocky promontory, known as Skaros, juts into the sea, and Santorini's dramatic landscape sprawls before you.

TOURIST OFFICES

Though you won't find an official government tourist office, you will encounter a multitude of travel agencies that serve the same purpose. Check out **Best of Cyclades Travel** (☎ 22860/22-622) in Fira or **Kamari Tours,** 2 blocks south of the main square on the right (☎ 22860/31-390; kamaritours@san.forthnet.gr). Other agencies include **Joint Travel Service** (☎ 22860/24-900; fax 22860/24992; joint@otenet.gr), next to the Olympic Airways Office in Fira; **Nomikos Travel** (☎ 22860/23-660 or 22860/23-666), with offices in Fira, Karterados, and Perissa; and **Karvounis Tours** (☎ 22860/71-290; mkarvounis@otenet.gr), on the main street of Ia. These agencies can generally help you find accommodations, rent a car, get boat tickets, or book a tour. Bus tours to Akrotiri or Ancient Thira are about 25€, and it's about the same for a day-trip boat excursion to the islands of the caldera.

RECOMMENDED WEBSITES

○ **www.travel-to-santorini.com**: This is a good site for tourist information before you start your trip.

○ **www.santorini.com**: Another good source of general info.

○ **www.greektravel.com/greekislands/santorini/index.html**: An American expat has set himself up as the guru of Greek travel. Check out his opinions and see if you agree.

Santorini **Nuts & Bolts**

Banks Banks are generally open Monday to Friday from 8am to 2pm. The National Bank, with an ATM, is a block south from the main square on the right near the taxi station.

Embassies See "Athens Nuts & Bolts" (p. 106) for embassy info.

Emergencies The police station is located south of the main square near the post office in Fira (☎ 22860/22-649 or 22860/22-649). For medical emergencies, go to the health clinic (☎ 22860/22-237), which is on the southeast edge of Fira on Ayiou Athanassiou, below the bus station and the new Archaeological Museum.

Internet/Wireless Hot Spots　Many of the tourist offices offer Internet access for 3€ per hour. Also, try **P.C. Club**, on the main square in Fira, in the office of **Markozannes Tours** (☎ 22860/25-551).

Laundry　Head to **Penguin Laundry** (☎ 22860/22-168) at the edge of Fira on the road to Ia, just north of the main square. It's open daily 9am to 9pm. Wash and dry costs about 5.50€.

Post Office　The post office (☎ 22860/22-238), open Monday through Friday from 8am to 1pm, is south of the bus station.

Safety　The island is, for the most part, quite safe, though it's always smart to play it safe and not travel alone at night. Take precautions with your personal belongings, as theft is not unheard of—even here in paradise.

Telephone Tips　Pay phones accept phone cards, not coins, which can be purchased at kiosks or convenience stores in increments of 3€, 6€, 12€, and 24€.

Tipping　See "Athens Nuts & Bolts" on p. 106.

Sleeping

If you plan to visit Santorini during the high season, it's imperative to make reservations in advance—at lease 2 months beforehand, if possible; the island is fairly tiny and can reach maximum tourist capacity in the summer. When you arrive in the port, expect to see hawkers offering rooms. I wouldn't trust these offers entirely; the accommodations tend to be of lower quality and more remote than rooms offered in town. If you've got a couple extra euros to spare, spring for a hotel room on the caldera, or at least with caldera views. The whole point of Santorini is its caldera and cliffs!

Just a note: Often the accommodations rates vary every 2 months, so rather than note every detail, we've included a range that depends on the season.

HOSTELS

→ **Thira Youth Hostel** This is the island's backpacker hub—and home to about 200 beds. Though the accommodations are bare-bones—after all, this was a monastery at one time: dorm-style rooms, clean sheets and a blanket,

and a tiny, shared bathroom are about all there is to speak of—you'll be in the center of Fira, practically on top of the nightlife. No curfew here means the partying may be at your doorstep. Dorm rooms with up to 20 beds are available; there are some doubles and triples. During the summer months, management adds beds on the rooftop veranda. *Main road no. 12 (near Fira's main square).* ☎ *22860/22-387. 9€–13€ dorm. Closed Dec–Mar. Amenities: Shared bathrooms. In room: Sheets.*

MTV Best → **Youth Hostel Anna** ★ If staying in the center of Fira isn't a priority, enjoy the comforts of Youth Hostel Anna in Perissa village (near the beach). It is owned and operated by the kind-hearted couple Panos and Anna Fiorentis. The hostel's amenities make this a nice change from some bare-bones accommodations elsewhere; you'll find hot showers, cheap sheets, and a restaurant that gives discounts to hostel patrons. Anna and Panos like to help travelers find a good time, whatever the definition: The hostel staff sometimes organizes pub-crawls, biking expeditions, volleyball tournaments, sunset scooter tours, and bon-fires, and provides volcano-tour information. Check in before 11pm because reception closes then. Ask about free transfers from the port. *Entrance of Perissa.* ☎ *22860/ 82-182. www.envision2000.com/anna/index. html. 10€–15€ per person. Closed Nov–Mar. Amenities: Bar/nightclub; bike rental; Internet; kitchen; free laundry facilities; lug-gage storage; moped rentals; safes; shared bathrooms. In room: A/C, sheets (1€).*

➜**Youth Hostel Oia** ★ Though the location in Ia isn't as happening as lodging in Fira, the Youth Hostel Oia makes up for it with magnificent 86-bed accommodations in a former convent. The hostel features a well-maintained, often sunny courtyard, and the 4-, 6-, and 10-person dorm-style rooms (with metal bunk beds and beige curtains) are well ventilated with vaulted ceilings. You won't find a party atmosphere here, but you will enjoy clean bathrooms and a daily breakfast of coffee or tea, bread, butter, and jam served on a terrace with views to the sea. Don't bother trying to make reservations, though. Owner Manolis Karvounis accepts visitors on a first-come, first-served basis. *Near the bus stop in Ia.* ☎ *22860/71-465. mkarvounis@otenet.gr. 15€–20€ dorm. Rates include breakfast. Closed Nov–Mar. Amenities: Breakfast room, laundry facilities, shared bathrooms.*

CHEAP

➜**Artemis Village** Don't be swayed by the fact that it's not in the center of Fira; it's a 5-minute ride away. Artemis Village offers extraordinary accommodations and a free shuttle into Fira or the port for dirt-cheap room rates. Friendly owners Artemis Danasis and his lovely wife, Anna, offer guests access to a well-maintained swimming pool, and the rooms are a mere 91m (300 ft.) from the beach at Karterados. The hotel's 20 bright and airy rooms accommodate singles up to four persons. *Karterados Beach.* ☎ *22860/*

24-884. www.artemisvillage.com. 40€–70€ double. Amenities: Pool; 24-hr. reception. In room: A/C, TV, fridge.

➜**Santorini Camping** Die-hard campers can set up shop at Santorini Camping, located just a quick hop from the center of Fira. A variety of accommodations is available—from open-air areas where you can unpack and unwind with just your sleeping bag to two- and four-person tent rentals that include beds. A bamboo roof covers the sleeping bag area, and the tents include a lock, mattresses, mattress covers, and tiled floors. Sheets and pillows aren't available. The facilities are ideal for meeting and hanging out with other travelers. The campsite's pool and pool bar can get crowded as evening falls. *Fira.* ☎ *22860/22-944. www. santorinicamping.gr/english/index.htm. Site: 8.50€–21€. May 1–Oct 20. Amenities: Bar; Internet; kitchen; laundry facilities; lock; lug-gage lockers; pool w/bar; shared bathrooms; TV (in common room); wake-up service.*

➜**Theoxenia Hotel** The only downside to Theoxenia is that it doesn't sit on the edge of the caldera, though some rooms on the top floor do have caldera views. The plus side: Not sitting on the caldera means more reasonable rates. The Theoxenia has more pluses than that, though. Its nine rooms are minimally decorated, as is the custom on the island, with white linens and wrought-iron beds. You can try out the hot tub (for communal use), continental breakfast on the roof is included, and the hotel sits in downtown Fira amid all the action. *Fira.* ☎ *22860/22-740. www.greekhotel. com/cyclades/santorin/fira/theoxenia/home. htm. 80€–215€ double. Rates include break-fast. Amenities: Roof deck; hot tub. In room: AC, TV, minibar, phone, hair dryer, Internet.*

DOABLE

📺 Best ➜**Astra Apartments** ★★★
Hands down, these are the best accommodations in the most spectacular location in all of Santorini, with the friendliest—and probably

coolest—staff, to boot. Astra is known for its luxury accommodations, but what the hotel doesn't always advertise is its very affordable studios for up to three people. The hotel, a sprawling complex of whitewashed buildings that seem to tumble down the dramatic cliffs of Imerovigli, offers rooms with kitchenettes, and breakfast is served on your own private terrace or balcony. You'll definitely want to get some sun (bring sunscreen!) at the magnificent infinity pool overlooking the caldera and Skaros. And while you're there, order a Bloody Mary from Nanud, the pool bartender. Ask Sharon at the front desk for nightlife and sightseeing recommendations; she may well be Santorini's greatest asset. If you can, book a room during the last week of July; it will coincide with manager George's legendary annual birthday party. *Imerovigli.* ☎ *22860/24-850. www.astra.gr. 130€–640€. Amenities: Bar; laundry service; pool. In room: A/C, TV, hair dryer, in-room breakfast, kitchen, minibar.*

Eating

For a rundown on local food, see the Athens chapter. There are two things to watch out for here, though. First, beware of any restaurant with hawkers at the door; the food will inevitably be mediocre, and the pricing often higher for tourists. Second, if you're given a menu without prices (it happens), be sure to ask about cost before ordering anything, and this includes most fresh fish, which is priced per kilo.

Most island locals start dinner around 10pm. You won't find street vendors or even grocery stores in Fira or Ia, so if you're in need of cheap food, head to Lucky's (see below).

CHEAP

MTV **Best** → **Lucky's** ★ GYROS/TAKEOUT
For a gyro that could launch 1,000 ships, head straight to Lucky's—customers from across the globe will dreamily declare them the best gyros in all of Greece. This tiny gyro stand in Fira's main square serves a steady stream of visitors meat-packed gyros topped with an unreal tzatziki and french fries, as well as other Greek delights like souvlaki. *Main square in Fira. No phone. Gyros 1.50€.*

→ **Toast Club** GREEK FAST FOOD   This 24-hour hot spot sits right in the heart of Fira's main square, and dishes up good, cheap eats like souvlaki, burgers, salads, sandwiches, and even a decent pizza. Some items at the counter are already prepared, but they serve made-to-order items as well. We liked the "Toast Club Special, a calzone-like sandwich filled with gyro meat, feta, and gouda or a *peinirli,* a baguette stuffed with ham, cheese, and bacon. *Fira.* ☎ *22860/22-092. Main courses 5€.*

DOABLE

→ **Koukoumavlos** ★★ GREEK   Go for the view. The terrace overlooks the caldera. And the food is almost as great as the panorama. The menu changes often, with the seasons, and the chef tries out new dishes with ingredients not always used in Greece (mushrooms, for one). It's a creative take on Greek food that you'll find here: shrimp poached in retsina, for example, and for dessert, a yogurt panna cotta with pistachios, thyme honey, and sour cherry. *Fira (below the Atlantis Hotel). ☎ 22860/23-807. Main courses 18€–23€. Daily noon–3pm and 8pm–midnight.*

→ **Naoussa** TRADITIONAL GREEK   Diners can't help but warm up to Naoussa owner Kostas after he offers them a complimentary glass of local wine—given to help smooth over the wait most will have to endure at this popular restaurant. The dining area is upstairs, overlooking the busy pedestrian shopping streets of Fira, and the kitchen serves outstanding versions of typical Greek fare, like tzatziki, tomato *keftedes* (little meatballs), and *melintzana salata* (eggplant salad). *Fira.* ☎ *22860/24-869. Main courses 7€–15€.*

→**Taverna O Panos** SEAFOOD/GREEK If you visit the beaches at Karterados, stop by O Panos for a meal made from the freshest ingredients—all the vegetables are grown in the garden out back, and the seafood is caught fresh daily off the shore. Any of the grilled fish will be divine, and don't miss out on the fresh Greek salad. *Karterados Beach.* ☎ *22860/24-905.*

SPLURGE

→**Selene** ★★★ The undisputed best restaurant in Santorini is well worth the splurge, particularly if you're looking to do some romancing—the caldera views are stunning. And if the vista doesn't do it, the food should. Owners Evelyn and George Hatziyiannakis use only locally grown produce to highlight dishes such as sea urchin salad; pasta with shrimp, clams, mussels, and octopus baked in a clay pot; and grilled lamb in an egg-lemon sauce. Don't miss their acclaimed fava balls with caper sauce! Reservations are recommended. *Fira, between Atlantis and Aressana hotels.* ☎ *22860/22-249. www.selene.gr. Main courses 17€–25€. Mid-Apr to early Oct daily 7pm–midnight.*

Partying

After every last soul on the island has paid homage to the sunset—Santorini's nightly ritual—and nightlife begins to kick into high gear, people looking to party head to Fira's bars and tavernas to get their drink on. Being a tourist-filled island means that entrance into clubs isn't particularly difficult, and the dress code is as relaxed or sexy as you make it. Most of the places don't have specific addresses; just ask at your hotel or restaurant for info. Also, drinks can be expensive, around 10€ each.

The highlight of Fira's bar scene is MTV Best **Tropical Bar** (☎ 22860/23-089) and its manager Jeanne, likely Greece's most rockin' barkeep (if she digs you, she'll join you for a shot of tequila after her shift).

What the small, dark room with its smattering of wooden tables and benches lacks in decor makes up for in party atmosphere. From sunset cocktails to late-night tabletop dancing and beers aplenty, Tropical's never-ending party attracts a slew of young and hot American, British, and Australian tourists. If you can't get by without your pint of Guinness, or just the wild and crazy scene at an Irish pub, check out **Murphy's** (☎ 22860/22-492) which is easily recognized by the line of 20-somethings winding out the door waiting to get inside. Pretty much anything goes among the young crowd here (from raucous behavior to khakis and tees). Beers and shots are cheap, nightly specials abound, and dancing on the bar is commended. Looking for a more casual evening? For dimly lit atmosphere, progressive artwork, and chill jazz tunes, stop by **Kira Thira Jazz Bar** (☎ 22860/22-770) for a cocktail and conversation. Then, for a touch of sophistication, amble over to **Rastoni** (☎ 22860/24-248) for its yummy caipirinhas and romantic caldera views.

Once midnight rolls past, the partying kicks it up a notch as locals and tourists head in droves to the island's two biggest dance clubs. **Enigma** (☎ 22860/22-466) has the sexier atmosphere, with mod white decor, cavern-like rooms, and curving stone walls. Eventually, you'll hit the outdoor bar—don't forget to look up and check out the glass catwalk above you. Ladies, beware: People really can see the full Monty when you're standing up there in a skirt. DJs spin techno, trance, and hip-hop till the wee, wee hours of dawn. For a more tropical flavor, head to Santorini's other major disco, **Koo Club** (☎ 22860/22-025). Three outdoor bars complete with palm trees and director-style chairs lend a more casual atmosphere to the club, but the DJ still spins decent tunes and the place fills to capacity with a throbbing, dancing crowd each night.

Sightseeing

Most of the main sights in Santorini are easily accessible by bus, however, the island holds a wealth of interesting places to visit, from the oldest bakery in the Aegean, to an ancient monastery, and even the island's oldest Byzantine church (11th c.). To get a feel for the non-touristy side of the island, away from the throngs of maddening cruiseship crowds, check out **Thirak Tours** (☎ 22860/23-927; www.santorini-guide.info), owned and operated by the über-friendly and informative Joerg Neuschafer, who will customize island tours to include whatever may interest you—churches, secluded beaches, donkey rides, ruins, winery, lighthouse, local art gallery, and so on. You'll be driven in an air-conditioned van and chat with locals galore, seeing sights that most other American tourists will encounter. It's a splurge (prices can run up to 200€ for a small group) but split the cost among friends; it's well-worth every euro.

→ **Ancient Akrotiri** ★★★ The end-all, be-all of Santorini sights is allegedly Ancient Akrotiri, the ruins of a surprisingly advanced civilization that thrived on the island until about 1450 B.C. when the island's volcano erupted, burying the town under ash and lava and preserving it in the process. It's believed that the residents knew of the town's impending doom, as human remains were largely absent during the site's excavation, beginning in 1967. Scholars believe the residents fled to nearby Crete. Today, visitors can wander through a maze of streets and see the buildings—some two stories high—and plazas where this culture once flourished. The remnants of preserved wall paintings from the site can now be found at the Museum of Prehistoric Thira in Fira. Though the history of Akrotiri is fascinating, the ruins themselves aren't particularly captivating right now. A metal roof that covers and protects the site is under construction as of this writing,

leaving much of Akrotiri covered in scaffolding.

The scaffolding isn't segregated to one particular area of the ruins, so some structures are covered and others aren't. The covered parts are discernible through the scaffolding. It's just that—excuse my ignorance—everything looks, well, ruined. A lot of crumbling walls that once represented the homes, shops, and streets of the ancient people. Problem is: Today, they don't look like buildings, and it's difficult to differentiate one structure from the next. Walking through the entire site would take no longer than 30 to 45 minutes, if you don't dawdle. So, if you're interested in ancient cultures, it's worth the trip, but do call beforehand as the site is not always open when it should be. *Akrotiri.* ☎ *22860/81-366. Admission 6€. Tues–Sun 8:30am–3pm.*

→ **Ancient Thira** ★★ Situated between the beaches of Kamari and Perissa, on top of a steep hill, lie the ruins of Ancient Thira, a site that was originally inhabited in the 9th century B.C. by the Dorians. The crumbling remains of Roman and Byzantine structures also fill the site, which is traversed by a main street and numerous side streets that are open to explore. While walking through the site, take note of the two agoras (market areas), the theater, the Roman baths, and the Terrace of the Festivals, which offers sprawling views of the Santorini and the nearby islands. Ancient Thira can be reached by hiking from the beach at Kamari or by taxi. *Kamari.* ☎ *22860/31-366. Admission 4€. Daily 8am–2:30pm.*

→ **Boutari Winery** One of the islands most famous exports is its white wine, and Boutari is Santorini's largest winery—a must-see for vino lovers. The island's three varieties of grapes—Asirtiko, Aidami, and Athiri—are used to make the wines Nichteri, Kalliste, and Vin Santo (a sweet dessert wine). Admission includes a tour of the facilities and tasting of

That's the Ticket

If you plan to visit the ancient sites and the museums in Santorini, get the discounted 8€ ticket that's good for the Archaeological Museum, Ancient Akrotiri (if open), Prehistoric Thira, and Ancient Thira. Also, always call for hours before you go.

six wines and snacks. *Megalohori (1.6km/1 mile south of Akrotiri).* ☎ *22860/81-011. Admission 6€. Daily 10am–sunset.*

FREE → **Museum of Prehistoric Thira** ★★ Be sure to take a trip to this small but interesting museum that houses many of the frescoes taken from Akrotiri, as well as the remains of pots, jugs, small statues, jewelry, and even the only piece of gold (a re-creation of a bull) found at Akrotiri. If you can't make it to the ruins of Akrotiri, definitely plan a trip to this museum. *Fira (just past the bus station).* ☎ *22860/22-217. Free admission. Tues–Sun 8:30am–3pm.*

→ **Naval Museum** If you plan a trip to Ia for more than just a sunset viewing, check out this maritime museum which outlines the seafaring history of the island through a collection of photographs, naval equipment, ship models of ancient and new boats, and figureheads. The museum is housed in a restored mansion, which alone is worth the visit. *Ia.* ☎ *22860/71-156. Admission 2€. Wed–Mon 12:30–2pm and 5–8pm.*

Playing Outside

MTV **Best** **BEACHES** ★ Of course no trip to a Greek island is complete without lounging on the beach, and the most popular of Santorini's beaches are **Kamari** and **Perissa,** on the island's east coast—a half-hour bus ride from Fira. Kamari's black-sand and pebble beach is flanked by dramatic cliff walls and the beach town is quite developed, with restaurants and bars lining the beach's promenade. The beach at Perissa is similar, but often attracts a younger crowd, and beach bars like the Magic School Bus cater to young travelers looking to party while getting their tans. If you've taken the bus to Akrotiri, plan ahead and bring some beach gear, as the ruins are just a short hike away from the island's Red Beach. Tucked into a cliff, this dramatic respite really does have red sand, but beware—it gets uncomfortably crowded during July and August. And if you want white sand, head to Mykonos.

BOAT TOURS ★ Across the caldera, you'll notice the small islands of Thirassia, Palea Kameni, and Nea Kameni. Full-day boat tours offered by a variety of companies depart from the port at Fira (15€–25€) and make stops at the three somewhat unremarkable islands. A better option, if you have the money, is to charter a catamaran tour. **Blue Lagoon Cruises** (Vlihada Marina; ☎ 69442/41-162; www.santorinisailing.com), owned and operated by Ted Stathis and his wife, Dina, run half- and full-day tours around the island on a 12m (41-ft.) catamaran that include visits to hot springs, swimming, and a lunch extravaganza of fresh prawns, calamari, steak, and salads. A semi-private tour runs about 100€.

MTV **Best** **WALKING** ★ Hikers will love the challenging hikes the island offers, especially the path along the caldera from Fira to Ia, which passes through the small, charming towns of Firostephani and Imerovigli. The views along the path are stupendous, with vistas of the caldera's curve and the impossibly placed towns on the cliffside. The 10km (6-mile) walk takes at least 2 hours, and signs point the way. It's not at all recommended to make the walk after dark. Another great hike leads from Imerovigli to Skaros, the towering rock structure rising from the sea that was home to Santorini's governing offices. You'll find signs for the trail near the Blue Note

Taverna in Imerovigli; from there you'll cross a land bridge until you get to the promontory. The hike is only 1.6km (1 mile), but the path is steep, with precipitous dips and rocky terrain.

Shopping

Many jewelry stores fill the streets of Fira and Ia, and in between are countless stores that sell tourist trinkets from T-shirts to the worry beads you'll see locals twirling around their fingers to the ubiquitous blue-glass tokens that ward off the evil eye. If you're looking for souvenirs, try picking up some local sponges, purportedly caught off the coast, or some of the lovely local handicrafts such as embroidery, ceramics, or hand-knit sweaters. Don't waste your money buying the pumice stones; if you take a good look around you on the beach, you'll notice that pumice stones aplenty are naturally mixed in with the beach's stones and pebbles.

Ios

With a widespread reputation as the reigning "party central" of Greece's photogenic Cyclades islands, it's a safe bet that most travelers are shipping out to Ios looking for a good time. Because the overwhelming majority of visitors to the island are backpackers under the age of 30, what you'll experience on Ios is probably the most laid-back island paradise in the Greek Isles. Now, when I say laid-back, I'm talking only about prices and dress codes: Bars and clubs clustered in the center of Ios's teensy-weensy main town Chora stay rocking literally until dawn and beaches like the Far Out Beach Club have no shortage of hot-bodied young Aussies, Italians, Brits, and Americans looking for someone to help them slather on their Hawaiian Tropic. But those of you who aren't necessarily always the first in line for the beer bong needn't steer clear of the island because of its party hearty reputation. Among the wet T-shirt contests and the drink specials, there are other reasons for visiting, namely R&R rather than T&A.

Despite its ancient origins, Ios's major historical/cultural claim to fame is being the alleged site of the classical Greek poet Homer's grave. It's not hard to imagine Ios as the inspiration for works like the Iliad and the Odyssey—the majority of the land here likely looks exactly as it did 2,000 years ago. Outside the main town, which admittedly is congested with partyers and backpackers, there are very few Ios natives living here, and most of the island is uninhabited and downright primitive—dirt roads; cliffs descending into foamy, crashing waves; "virgin" beaches. If the rock-star lifestyle's not your game, it's easy to create your own Ios experience that isn't all booze and bikinis. Just a fair warning: It's easy to lose track of time here, and Ios's vibe is intoxicating, if not addicting, to say the least; just think of Homer's alluring Sirens—he had to get inspired somewhere, right? Most people who own the island's restaurants and hotels are non-Greeks who will gladly regale you with stories about how they "came here on a 2-week holiday X-number of years ago and just never left."

Getting There & Around

GETTING INTO TOWN

By Air

From Athens, take a ferry from Athens' port, Piraeus. Or check out **Olympic Airways'** links to the larger Cycladic islands of Naxos, Syros, Santorini, Mykonos, Paros, and Milos. You can take a ferry to Ios from any one of these islands.

By Boat

The central Cyclades—Paros, Naxos, Ios, and Santorini—are the most visited and have the best transportation links with the mainland (see p. 441 for details). Because Ios is quite a hike via the slow-moving ferries from Piraeus, I'd recommend paying a bit more for a high-speed boat such as a hydrofoil or a cat. In summer, there are daily hydrofoils between Mykonos, Naxos, Paros, and Syros. There are daily cats between Syros, Mykonos, Tinos, Paros, Naxos, Ios, and Santorini.

For detailed information on getting to the island, contact **Amirakadis Travel** (Port of Ios, 840 01; ☎ **22860/91-252**). They are the main contact point for all the ferry companies that service the island, and can tell you the most up-to-date information on fares and schedules.

Once your ferry pulls into the port area in Ios, there will be a small throng of people waiting to sell you a room or transport you to your already booked lodgings. I recommend having your reservation already made. Francesco's Hostel in Chora and the Far Out Beach Club in Mylopotas are the most popular places for backpackers, and they always have a big van waiting for their guests who have arrived. Most other hotels have transportation, too, but make sure you let them know what time you'll arrive to secure a ride. Otherwise, hop on a bus at the bus stop next to the port (there's an awning and a bench, as well as a big sign) for .50€, payable when you get on the bus, which can take you to Chora or Mylopotas.

GETTING AROUND
By Scooter

Renting a scooter is by far the most popular way to zip around Ios next to using the public bus system. Not only is it a great way to get from the port to Chora to Mylopotas, but it's also a great way to explore places that are off the beaten path—there are well over 30 beaches in Ios and it's quite possible to have one all to yourself for a day if you're willing to explore. Just be careful, and please, please, please don't drink and drive—motorbike accidents are not a rarity

on the island, proof that being a tourist doesn't mean you're invincible. One great rental place is **Vangelis Rent a Bike** in Chora (☎ **22860/91-919**). Scooters are 12€ a day, 15€ for 24 hours, and 74€ for a week. (*Remember:* Technically—that is, legally—you need an international drivers license for a motorcycle.)

On Foot

Happily, no cars or bikes are allowed inside the town of Chora, so you'll have to hoof it. The island's main attractions are well within walking distance—and the trek from Chora to Mylopotas can be a great way to recover from the previous night's festivities. Cars and motorbikes do zip up and down the road that connects the two areas, so avoid the walk after dark. During the day, though, lots of people trek the 2.9km (1³/₄ miles) downhill from the town to the beach.

Ios Basics

ORIENTATION: IOS NEIGHBORHOODS

Only three places on the island are populated with hotels and restaurants: the port, Chora (the main town), and Mylopotas Beach. A single bus system runs every 15 minutes to each of these places; fare is .50€. The port is home to a few quieter hotels and some restaurants that serve slightly overpriced food for visitors arriving from or waiting for the ferries. Chora, the island's main town, is up the hill from the port, and is where the island's nightlife scene rocks out 7 days a week. This is also where a lot of shops, hostels, and rooms are for rent. Mylopotas is the beach area where the always-busy Far Out Hotel and Camping resort is located—this is the main beach and where you'll also find a few restaurants and little shops selling sunglasses, cheap clothing, and beach towels. Generally speaking, days are spent beach-bumming at Mylopotas, nights are spent partying in Chora, and the port is for arrivals and departures.

Ios Nuts & Bolts

Currency Exchange There is only one ATM in Chora, at the edge of town closest to the main road. And one is in Mylopotas at the Far Out Beach Club.

Emergency All of the main offices for tourism, health, and safety are located in the main town of Chora—a really small area where everything is (but annoyingly, nothing has an address). Once you're in the town, it should be simple to find any place you need (ask if you need directions).

You can reach the police at ☎ 22860/91-222 or 92-222, the port police at ☎ 22860/91-264, and the health center at ☎ 22860/91-227.

Internet/Wireless Hot Spots Internet on the Greek islands is not exactly lightning fast—at any Internet kiosk you find, the amenities are likely to be spare and the connection is likely to be a bit dodgy. The best, most reliable one is at **Acteon Travel Agency;** it has locations at the port, Chora, and Mylopotas. Rates are about 1€ per 15 minutes. Call ☎ 22860/91-343 or log on to www.acteon.gr.

Safety Most crime is pretty petty. However, some issues do arise, naturally, especially during high season when many people are drunk—things like harassment, petty theft, and traffic accidents. Just use common sense and try to use the buddy system.

Websites The most informative English website for all things Ios is www.greeka.com/cyclades/ios. It contains information on restaurants, clubs, and hotels. For detailed clubbing information, check out www.iospartyisland.com. It lists just about all the party places on the island, and includes reviews from site visitors.

Sleeping

Despite being a small and remote Grecian island, because Ios relies so heavily on the tourist trade, the overall accommodations situation is quite good and standards are high even in low-budget places. Most visitors to Ios don't fall into the five-star luxury demographic anyway, and a lot of great options exist for people just looking for a clean place to lay their heads after a long day on the beach (and a long night in the bars). The accommodations market has become more commercial and organized in the past decade or so, with hugely successful businesses like Francesco's Hostel and Far Out Beach Club housing a majority of the island's revelers. Also, it's possible to find individuals renting out private rooms. To find out more, call the **Rooms-to-let Association** (☎ 22860/91-591) for a listing of independent room providers offering a homey, affordable alternative for staying on the island. Along with the places listed below, check out websites like www.iosgreece.com.

Note: Prices at hotels increase considerably during the high season from the end of July through September 1. From April to July, and for the month of September, lower prices apply.

CHEAP

MTV Best → **Far Out Club Camping** ★ Should you choose to stay outside of Chora, the Far Out resort reigns supreme as the hub for accommodations and partying outside of the main town. What Francesco's is to Chora, Far Out is to Mylopotas. Located smack on the beach, Far Out boasts three swimming pools, tennis courts, water slides, a massive beach area, three bars, and a restaurant. For sleeping, Far Out owns two midrange hotels, one directly on the beach, and one on the hill between Chora and Mylopotas, as well as a vast and ridiculously popular camping resort area on the beach in Mylopotas. "Roughing it" in a beach bungalow or tent isn't really that bad—the bungalows are equipped with beds, mirrors, and desks, and have a thatched-roof "Love Shack" appeal. Shared bathrooms have toilets, sinks, and showers—but don't forget to bring your own toilet paper, just one minor annoying aspect to an otherwise pretty user-friendly camping experience. *Mylopotas Beach.* ☎ *22860/91-468. www.faroutclub.com. 8€–18€ bungalows, 5€–11€ bed tents, 4€–8.50€ camping, 4.50€–10€ tent rental. Amenities: Restaurant; bars; 3 pools; tennis courts.*

➜ **Francesco's** Without doubt, one of the best backpacker accommodations in Chora, and the proprietor Francesco, who oversees five clean, affordable hotels in town, happily assumes the title of "Godfather of accommodations in Ios." He's a native Greek and a true character on Ios—buy him a drink and try to get him to tell you a story or two. Island visitors seem to make their way to Francesco's at some point during their stay on Ios, whether they have a room here or not. The hotel's bar is a prime jumping-off point to get the night started with other like-minded travelers, and the breakfast terrace with its striking views of the harbor is a prime location to dish about the previous night's debauchery over big plates of eggs, bacon, and toast. You'll find a young, easy-going staff, and mostly college-aged Aussie, Canadian, and British backpackers. Rooms here are sparsely furnished—pretty much just beds with sheets—but they have air-conditioning, many have TVs, and they are cleaned daily. A welcome drink when you check in helps you get into the reigning party atmosphere at Francesco's. *Chora.* ☎ *22860/91-223. www.francescos.net. 20€–25€ single, 25€–30€ double, 36€–45€ triple, 48€–60€*

quad. *Amenities: 24-hr. access; Internet/fax cafe. In room: A/C, TV (in some).*

DOABLE

➜ **Brother's Hotel** For a quieter, less party-central place to head home to at night's end, the Brother's Hotel near the port is a cozy choice. Popular with families and young couples, each room at the Brother's Hotel is minimally decorated with wooden furniture and white curtains and sheets, and private bathroom—some rooms have private balconies. Breakfast is served by the mother of the hotel's owner Nicky, and his lovely British wife is always happy to dish about her experiences and offer recommendations on the island. *Kambos (near the port).* ☎ *22860/91-508. 35€–60€ double (depending on season). Rates do not include breakfast. Amenities: Restaurant; bar; Internet in lobby; lockers. In room: A/C, minifridge, TV (in some).*

➜ **Far Out Hotel** Much like the older, slightly more refined brother of the Far Out family who still likes to party (like the ex-frat guy who still chugs beer, only now it's at upscale bars and not a domestic brew), the Far Out Hotel sits on the hill above Mylopotas Beach and is a bit more removed from the partying ground zero where the Camping and Village are. It's quieter here, but definitely not boring: Young couples drink daiquiris by day at the pool bar (by the very nice pool!) and at night join other revelers at the clubs in Chora. The accommodations are a little more luxe than the beach bungalow's thatched roofs: Each room has a private balcony, amenities, and heck, even toilet paper. *Mylopotas Beach.* ☎ *22860/91-446. www.faroutclub.com. 30€–60€ single, 35€–80€ double, 50€–100€ triple. Amenities: Breakfast room; Internet; minivan service; pool; pool bar. In room: A/C, TV, minibar, radio.*

SPLURGE

➜ **Levantes Luxury Resort and Suites** For well-heeled travelers who want to avoid the "see-and-be-seen" vibe of isles like Mykonos, Ios's upscale hotels are a new favorite destination, namely the brand-new Levantes hotel (eight rooms, seven suites). Perched on cliffs overlooking Mylopotas Beach, rooms are so hooked up with amenities you may find it hard to leave once you set down your bags. Each individually decorated room features artists (replicas) such as Frida Kahlo and Georgia O'Keeffe, includes a private bathroom with Jacuzzi, and has a choice of with or without a private pool. The prices are high for Ios, but service and amenities like this would cost double on Mykonos or Santorini. *Mylopotas.* ☎ *22860/92-588. www.levantes.gr. 67€–144€ double, 101€–209€ suite, 140€–350€ executive suite. Amenities: Restaurant, breakfast hall; Jacuzzi; pool; pool bar; safe. In room: A/C, TV, minibar, minifridge, pool (in some rooms).*

Eating

Ios isn't the center of the world for fine dining, but it's no slouch when it comes to options for a fun, filling food experience that won't totally clean out your pocketbook. Most restaurants fall into the same price category—affordable, but not dirt cheap—and options for cuisine range from traditional Greek to unexpected far-flung offerings of Thai, Chinese, and even Mexican. If you're not looking for a sit-down deal and just want to grab something to tide you over before hitting the beach, you're in luck—cheap gyro and souvlaki stands abound in Chora and Mylopotas.

All of the following, with the exception of the Octopus Tree, are closed during the winter season, from about November through March.

➔ **Ali Baba's** INTERNATIONAL Proof that a name can be deceiving—here you can get everything from Middle Eastern dishes to Chinese lo mein to a seriously hearty rack of barbecue ribs. The owner may defy your expectations, as well; a good-natured, British, big teddy bear of a guy, Cookie Davies ensures

that Ali Baba's is more than just another restaurant in Ios—it's a hangout. Come here for movie nights, an Internet cafe, and live music along with the eclectic menu. Try the restaurant's fresh juices and iced coffees during the brunch hours, or head in for a more serious drink after dark, when live rock-music provides a great alternative hangout if you've had enough of the thumping club scene. *Chora.* ☎ *22860/91-558. Main courses 9€–18€. Daily 11am–3pm and 6pm–late.*

➔ **Harmony** MEXICAN The view overlooking Mylopotas Beach isn't Harmony's only draw. The restaurant makes every effort to ensure that the backpacker/college student types who come for dinner feel at home. The ground floor serves huge mixed drinks (literally in buckets) to those waiting for a table in an area equipped with hammocks and guitar-playing surfer types. Started by Norwegian husband-and-wife team Geir and Liz Orjan, who were backpackers in Ios themselves 15 or so years ago, the restaurant's staff gives off a big old summer-camp vibe. Make sure to try the "Backpacker's Corona" (the cheap local beer, Mythos, with a slice of lime) or a margarita, and the fresh guacamole. There's live acoustic music on most nights—mostly staff members (and sometimes even Geir) on their nights off, strumming covers of Pearl Jam, The Beatles, and Lisa Loeb. *Beginning of Mylopotas Beach.* ☎ *22860/91-613. Main courses 10€–17€. Daily noon–late.*

➔ **Lord Byron's Taverna** GREEK/MIDDLE EASTERN A perennial favorite among visitors to Ios, Lord Byron's offers up traditional Greek fare like tzatziki dips and a dizzying array of native goat cheeses, along with an occasional global touch, like baba ghanouj. Decorated in a funky, shabby-chic style and filled with owner Molly's personal knick-knacks and old family photos, Lord Byron's is like heading to your hippest aunt's house for dinner and drinks. A bit more expensive than other options on the island, but by no means a splurge. *Chora.* ☎ *22860/92-125. Dinner with drinks 22€–28€. Daily noon–3pm and 6pm–late.*

MTV **Best** ➜ **The Octopus Tree** ★ GREEK For a dining experience oozing with Greek tradition, head to the Octopus Tree—a favorite of locals and visitors—where the teenage daughter of the owners, Lizzy and Apostolis Karras, waits all the tables, and the menu is what Apostolis and his father caught on their fishing boat that day. The restaurant is named for the way the restaurant prepares their famous octopus dishes (they dry out the octopus by hanging it on the tree in front of the restaurant), and dinner is a night-long event in itself. *Mezes,* or "tastes," of a variety of Greek specialties are served over the course of a few hours. Definitely a place to try things you never thought you would (like octopus and the traditional Greek liquor, ouzo) and get into the relaxed pace of island life. *The port.* ☎ *22860/ 91-572. Mezes and drinks 20€–25€. Daily 9:30am–late.*

Partying

For many visitors to Ios, the lodging and dining accommodations are really just means to an end: getting it started, Black Eyed Peas style, on the party scene. But if you're not the most seasoned clubgoer around, don't be intimidated. A good-natured atmosphere pulsates through all the clubs and bars in the main town of Chora, and everyone who's out really just wants to have fun, so no Prada shoes or flashy jewelry is required. Bikinis, wife-beaters, and flip-flops are more than enough to get you through the door at any one of these places—in fact, you'll wanna steer clear of the whole stiletto thing because navigating those cobblestone walkways after a few ouzos can be positively dangerous.

Aside from different kinds of music spun by the DJs, pretty much all of the clubs in Ios

are similar in terms of clientele, and there are really no ultratrendy or ultralame nightspots. All the bars listed are in Chora and are open nightly during the summer from 11:30pm till early in the morning (6 and 7am closing times are not unheard of).

➜ **Astra Bar** For a fresh alternative to the typical, surefire get-drunk-quick-and-cheap rum and Cokes, Astra Bar serves, hands down, the best cocktails on Ios. The experienced (and superhot) bartenders whip up drinks with names like "Green Destiny" from only top-shelf liquor and freshly squeezed juices while the DJ spins smooth funk and house music. A great place to head around 11pm to kick off the night, Astra is located on its building's second story where you can plop yourself down among the cushy pillows around the window seats, perfect for watching the streets fill up with revelers. *Chora.* ☎ *22860/92-183.*

➜ **Barmacy** A more laid-back feeling rules over Barmacy, where the DJ spins a relatively mellow mix of jazz, funk, Latin, and disco beats. Groovy, moody decor—think disco balls and psychedelic artwork—and tasty (but strong!) cocktails like the "Orgasm" keep people coming in for a chill experience. *Chora.* ☎ *22860/92-034.*

➜ **Bull Dog** The only bar on Ios that caters more to a Greek crowd or to people who want a more authentic local experience, the Bull Dog plays mostly Greek classic and pop tunes. The owner, George, a legendary native Greek on the island who also owns the more typically tourist-centric Red Bull and Slammer bars, goes for a more sophisticated vibe with the Bull Dog—but that doesn't mean he won't sit down and talk with you over an ouzo or two poured by one of his gorgeous bartenders. *Chora. No phone.*

➜ **Shooters Bar** Rocking and rowdy, with girls dancing on the bars and specials alerting that if you "buy seven drinks, you get a free T-shirt!" Shooters is a place where everyone lets loose and parties in "what happens in Ios, stays in Ios" style. American Top 40 hits pulsate through the DJ's speakers, and you might swear you're back at your college's craziest local dance club instead of on an island in Greece. Their special cocktail, the "Flaming Lamborghini," is seriously wild stuff. *Chora.* ☎ *22860/91-131.*

Sightseeing

MANGANARI BEACH ★   A quieter, cleaner, more hidden gem of a beach than the rocking Mylopotas, Manganari can only be reached by boats or buses that leave twice a day from the port. The trip is worth it though: Swimming in water of swimming pool–like clarity and lying on the white sand at the beach feels like the ultimate island paradise. I recommend taking the boat if you don't have problems with seasickness—it's the only way to get such a unique perspective of the uninhabited parts of Ios's perimeter. Boats and buses both leave from the port at 11am and 1pm and return at 6pm—round-trip tickets for either cost 6€, and you buy them as you get on the bus or the boat.

CHURCHES   Among the all-white buildings that dot the island are some 300 churches (legend has it that there is one for every day of the year, each dedicated to that day's patron saint). Though there isn't really much to see at any of these, as they are basic structures with

only a cross or two adorning the outside and flowerbeds maintained by dedicated locals, they are often located at the tops of hills offering amazing panoramic views of the island—great for photo ops. The largest of these structures is the Cathedral of Ios, which overlooks the town of Chora, painted in the traditional Cycladic white color.

HOMER'S GRAVE   Legend has it that the famous blind poet, who penned classics like the Iliad and the Odyssey, died and was buried in Ios because it was his mother's hometown. Actual historical details are shaky at best, but it's pretty much the only claim to fame Ios has aside from its gorgeous beaches and nightlife. The only way to get to the little gravesite (just a grave marker in the middle of nowhere, really) in Plakoto on the north part of the island is by renting a car or a motorbike. Not a must-see, but a decently cool way to kill a few hours and see the really rural parts of the island.

Shopping

As far as shopping goes, most agriculture and production is limited. Most inhabitants of the island are completely centered on little other than tourism. There are a bunch of goats on Ios, however, and the island is somewhat known for its goat cheeses—a local specialty is called *xinotiri*—as well as its golden honey. At any little market in Chora you can pick up some of the local favorites.

Mykonos

Guys: Pad your wallets. Girls: Pad your bras. In the judgmental, beautiful people–filled world of Cycladean nightlife, it's not what you know, but who you know. And who you air kiss. And how you look. And most of all, how much you spend. Remember that Mykonos is Greece's answer to Manhattan's summer getaways in the Hamptons; so it's all about schmoozing, scheming, and looking fabulous while you're at it.

The most chic, upscale, and scenester-oriented of all Greece's Cycladic islands, Mykonos is a favorite vacation destination for Greek, Italian, and international celebrities and trust-fund babies—Paris Hilton, Madonna, and P. Diddy sightings are not uncommon additions to the scenery of white-washed buildings and sapphire blue seas. The designer-clad visitors to Mykonos also include a huge population of impeccably coiffed gay men and the supermodels who love them. My first night on the island, when I asked a well-heeled Greek tourist if Mykonos was "pretty gay-friendly" she laughed, "Darling, I think the term I would use is '*straight*-friendly.' It's their party here—we're just crashing it."

The natural result of the hotter-than-hot status of Mykonos? Higher-than-high prices. Dropping 10€ on a cocktail is de rigueur. It's possible to have fun here on a smaller budget, but the island definitely doesn't court the pennypinching backpacker crowd—and even in places where younger, more laid-back people congregate, there's a feeling of tension and buzz that comes from being in such a trendy place as Mykonos. This is a place for beautiful people to show up, dress up, and hook up.

Getting There & Getting Around

GETTING INTO TOWN
By Plane

Reservations in summer are hard to come by for the 35-minute flights from Athens to the itsy-bitsy airport here, so book early. **Mykonos Airport** is at ☎ 22890/223-27.

Olympic Airways (☎ 210/966-6666 or 210/936-9111; www.olympic-airways.gr) has several flights daily (once daily in off season) to Mykonos's small airport from Athens, and one flight daily from Mykonos to Iraklion (Crete) and Santorini. Also, **Aegean Airlines** (☎ 210/998-8300 or 210/998-2888; www.aegeanair.com) has service to Mykonos daily in summer.

By Boat

From Piraeus, **Ventouris Lines** (☎ 210/482-5815 or 210/482-8001; www.ventouris.gr) has departures at least once daily, usually at 8am, with a second on summer afternoons (about 6 hr.). See the box on p. 441.

GETTING AROUND

No cars are allowed in the streets of the main town of **Hora** (also called **Mykonos Town**), as it's been decreed an architectural

landmark, so the only way to get around town is to walk. There is a very busy road that wraps around Hora along which many of the town's larger hotels are found and where cars and motorbikes are permitted.

By Bus

Mykonos has a great bus system; the buses run frequently and on schedule. Fares are priced according to distance, and a ticket costs about .50€ to 3.50€ There are two bus stations in Hora: one near the Archaeological Museum and a larger one near the Olympic Airways office—they are all clearly marked by signs and will be pretty obvious by the big buses parked there. Check at the tourist office to see which station the bus you want leaves from or look for one of the schedules sometimes available in hotels. Bus information is available from the **KTEL office** (☎ 22890/23-360; www.bus-service-crete-ktel.com).

By Car & Moped

Rental cars are available for around 70€ per day, including insurance, in high season; most agencies can be found near one of the two bus stops in town and require that the renter be 25 years old. More convenient may be renting a moped or scooter—there are a bunch of moped rental shops around the bus station near the Olympic Airways office in Hora. Expect to pay about 15€ to 30€ a day. Be careful: Roads on the island can be tricky to navigate and are often populated with less-than-sober drivers after dark. Laws about parking in town or in no-parking zones are apparently pretty strict, and tourists don't get breaks from the police. And you'll need an international motorcycle driver's license—officially.

Renting a car/scooter on Mykonos is an expensive but worthwhile proposition. Try **Kosmos** (near the ferry port; ☎ 22890/240-13; www.kosmos-carrental.com). The cheapest car you'll find in high season is around 18€ per day, and scooters are usually around 12€ per day.

By Taxi

Taxis are always waiting at the port when ferries arrive—just hail one. To get a taxi in Hora, walk to Taxi (Mavro) Square, near the statue, and join the line. You can also call **Mykonos Radio Taxi** at ☎ 22890/22-400. For late hours and out-of-town service, call **Central Taxi Station** at ☎ 22890/23-700.

Mykonos Nuts & Bolts

Currency Exchange   The **National Bank of Greece** (Othos Akti Kambani; ☎ 22890/229-32; Mon–Thurs 8am–2pm and 6–8pm, Fri 8am–1:30pm, Sat–Sun 10am–1pm) is the money changer of choice. You'll find ATMs at multiple locations in Hora.

Emergency & Health   For the police, dial ☎ 22890/227-16. If you need to summon an ambulance, dial ☎ 166. Mykonos Hospital (Ano Mera; ☎ 22890/239-94; daily 9am–1pm and 5–10pm) has a 24-hour help line with a message stating which doctor is on duty. The **Medical Center** (Agiou Ioannou; ☎ 22890/242-11; daily 8:30am–midnight) is in Mykonos Town and has better hours.

Internet   Using the Internet is expensive on Mykonos. The **Mykonos Cyber Café** (26 M. Axioti, on the road between the south bus station and the windmills; ☎ 22890/27-684), is usually open daily from 9am to 10pm and charges 15€ per hour or 4€ for 15 minutes.

Sleeping

There is no shortage of hotels on the island, but options for a traveler on a budget? Not so much. There is a huge contingent of upscale resorts busting their buns to top each other in terms of luxury and service—and the loaded clientele they attract is happy to spend the money on having a personal tanned and toned pool boy on hand to fetch mojitos and magazines. Overall, the island just doesn't cater to young travelers on a shoestring budget—you've gotta look hard and shop around for a good deal, especially during the high season in July and August. The **Mykonos Tourist Office** is near the boats to Delos and can help with lodgings; call ☎ 22890/239-90 for hours and other info.

The off season (spring and fall) has more favorable rates and is less crazy. Often, many small hotels, restaurants, and shops close in winter, especially if business is slow.

CHEAP

➔ **Paradise Beach Cabins and Camping** Paradise Beach is a center for beautiful young people—a scene of partying and total hedonism, day and night. The most welcoming beach spot for those who may not be wearing Dior sunglasses or a La Perla bikini, these accommodations at the beach are priced in a more down-to-earth realm than most of Mykonos. The beach cabins are spare—a couple of beds and bare walls—but there are lockable doors, linens, and electricity in each one and some larger ones also have private bathrooms. The camping facilities are a bit less private, and are more like roughing it—but if you're on a tight budget and plan on spending most of your snoozing time on the beach during the day, they're not a bad option. You've got to bring your own tent, or rent one of theirs. If you have valuables, make sure you use a safe, which is available near the check-in area. *Paradise Beach (4.5km/2³/₄ miles from Mykonos town, a bus ride from Hora).* ☎ *22890/22-852. www.paradise-greece.com. 25€ cabins, 17€ bed tents, 9€ camping. Amenities: Safe. In room: Linens.*

DOABLE

➔ **Hotel Madalena** A tasteful, simple, moderately priced hotel in Mykonos Town, Madalena offers clean rooms with bare walls, solid-colored bedspreads, and wooden furnishings—a simple place for guests to sleep and keep their luggage while they spend most of their time beach-bumming and cocktail-swilling. The hotel also has a pool and a bar, and huge bonus: Each room has its own small private balcony with great views of Hora and the Aegean Sea. *Hora.* ☎ *22890/22-954. www.madalena-mykonos.com. 69€–122€ single, 81€–127€ double, 97€–152€ double studio or triple, 115€–163€ triple studio or family room for 4 people (depending on season). Amenities: Bar; pool. In room: A/C, fridge, kitchen utensils, radio, safe.*

➔ **Rochari Hotel** Along with its "new baby sister," the Little Rochari Hotel, the Rochari is the best bet for a relatively moderate price right in town on the peripheral road around Hora. Run by the original owner's daughter, Stavroula, the Rochari offers privacy and simple rooms with white linens and private bathrooms. Stavroula and her husband make sure each guest has the best experience on the island, personally arranging everything from ferry tickets to restaurant recommendations and reservations upon request. Quite popular with both gay and straight young couples. Ask for a room with a balcony—the view of Mykonos and the water at sunset is absolutely breathtaking. The pool and pool bar area is a quiet place where many guests spend their early afternoons after brunch, mellowing out before nightlife. The Little Rochari across the street is a few dollars cheaper, but has all the same accommodations and services—it was pretty much built to deal with the large number of reservations overflowing at the Rochari. *Hora.* ☎ *22890/23-107. www.rochari.com. 50€–90€ single, 78€–155€ double, 98€–191€ triple, 130€–250€ suite. Rates include buffet*

breakfast. Amenities: Pool, pool bar. In room: AC, TV, hair dryer, minifridge, safe.

SPLURGE

➔ **Belvedere Hotel** ★ Long regarded as the undisputed best hotel in Mykonos, the sublime Belvedere Hotel upholds its reputation among an influx of new luxury hotels on the island. You can work out away from the heat, check your e-mail, and dine at sushi haven, Nobu. Downstairs you'll find Matsuhisa Cellar—a state-of-the-art, 5000-bottle wine cellar with a small tasting room. In any season, splurge on a massage. Off season, the extras are more along the lines of a free Jeep for the day if you stay 4 nights, or a fifth night free. *Hora.* ☎ *22890/25-122. www.belvederehotel.com. 155€–295€ standard single or double, 210€–375€ superior single or double, 186€–450€ triple, 240€–457€ suite. Rates include American buffet breakfast. Amenities: 2 restaurants; bar; fitness center; Jacuzzi; pool; sauna. In room: A/C, TV, hair dryer, Internet, minibar.*

Eating

By now, you probably get the message that Mykonos is pricey and sceney—and chowing down is no exception to the Mykonian rule. So we haven't picked any "Hot Spots" (the whole island is a hot spot). As in other parts of Greece, if you're on a tight budget, seek out the little gyro and kebab shacks.

CHEAP

➔ **Piccolo** DELI A Mykonian favorite since its opening in the 1980s, Joseph Salahas serves up made-to-order sandwiches from some of the best fresh bread and high-quality meats and cheeses you're liable to find in the whole country. There is also a great selection of homemade pastries—try local classics like *melopita*, or honey pie. No seating here, though—Piccolo is straight-up deli-style service: a display case, a counter, and a strip of floor where you wait in line.

Hora. ☎ *22890/22-208. Sandwiches 3€.*
Mon–Sat 9am–6pm.

DOABLE

→ **Sesame Kitchen** GREEK/CONTINENTAL
A haven for health nuts (or just those who
want to look good on the birthday-suit
friendly beaches of Mykonos), Sesame Kitchen
has a great offering of nutritious, delicious,
and often vegetarian fare at relatively good
prices. This restaurant is cozy (read: small) so
be prepared to wait for a table—the wait is
well worth it, though, as the servers are
knowledgeable about the cuisine and the food
is excellent. Try the veggie moussaka—a traditional Greek dish without the traditional beef.
Hora. ☎ *22890/24-710. Main courses 7€–12€.*
Daily 7pm–12:30am.

SPLURGE

📺 Best → **Interni** ★ ITALIAN At
press time, this was the chicest place to go
for dinner and drinks on Mykonos. In the
same vein as the whitewashed buildings of
the Cyclades, the entire dining area of this
modern, luxurious open-air restaurant is
draped in white—as are the model-esque,
breezily multilingual waitstaff. The food here
is Italian, and super-expensive—but it's
really just an afterthought to the scene. If
you have the extra dough, it is all worth it for
the service and the setting. *Hora.* ☎ *22890/
26-333. Main courses 28€–38€. Daily 8:30pm–
2am. Drinks served till 3am.*

Partying

The central nightlife scene starts in the area
near the windmills, along the water at the
edge of town, called 📺 Best **Little Venice.**
It's a more refined pub-crawl, with mixed
drinks and bars instead of beer and pubs.

After getting amped up in Little Venice,
the scene heats up in Hora's Manto Square.
There are three main clubs here: **Pierro's**
(☎ **22890/22-177**), the island's most popular
gay disco; **Icarus** (☎ **22890/22-718**); and

Manto's (no phone). All of these places are
pretty interchangeable, to tell the truth—
throbbing disco/techno/euro music; expensive
drinks; beautiful, immaculately groomed gay
men. This is a pretty liberal scene—lots of gay
action and just overall showing of skin and
sexiness. Don't forget your cash—the non-
negotiable (no matter how cute you are) cover
charge for each place is around 14€. These
places start to die down around 2am; everyone
follows the great-smelling guys to the **Yacht
Club** back in Hora—a dance club/bar place
that stays rocking the best electronic music for
the mostly gay crowd until as early as 8am.

Sightseeing

Mykonos is known mostly for its beautiful
beaches, beautiful people, and windmills.
Most of the island's "sightseeing" can be
done right on the beach or from a high point
on the hotel balcony—the water here is bluer
than blue, the people are tanned and toned,
and the pristine white buildings are a perfect
complement to the gorgeous nightly sunsets.
As far as culture/museum stuff goes, this
place is a dead zone—but you'll have no
shortage of photo ops here on the island.

📺 Best **DELOS** ★★★ A sacred island
located a mile away from Mykonos, Delos is
home to some of the greatest archaeological
treasures in Greece. The entire island is
covered in architectural artifacts—some
more "ruined" than others, but all of them an
amazing sight to see. Boats to Delos
leave from the dock in town near the
Paraportiannis church. Round-trips cost 4€.
Grab a map for a couple of euros when you
get to the island: Guided tours are pricey and
aren't really worth it. Boats depart Tuesday
through Sunday from 9am to 2:30pm (about
four times a day). Admission is 4€; bring cash
because they don't accept credit cards.

Follow the windmills (near the water, next
to Little Venice) to the site of the **Tria
Pigadia (Three Wells)** ★. Local legend says

that if a virgin drinks from all three she is sure to find a husband . . . hey, whatever. Don't actually try to drink the water, though—it's not exactly Poland Spring.

There are a few museum options to check out, if you've got a free afternoon or an interest in the stuff. For exports from the aforementioned Delos, head to the **Archaeological Museum** (☎ 22890/22-325; www.culture.gr) near the harbor—it's open Monday and Wednesday to Saturday 9am to 3:30pm, Sunday and holidays 10am to 3pm. Admission is 3€ and is free on Sunday. The **Museum of Folklore** (☎ 22890/25-591) has local crafts and artwork and is open Monday to Saturday 4 to 8pm; admission is free. Bring a euro for admission and you can check out the model ships and indulge all your Gilligan, Ginger, and Mary Ann dreams at the **Nautical Museum of the Aegean** (☎ 22890/22-700) on Enoplon Dinameon Street. It's open daily 10:30am to 1pm and 7 to 9pm.

Playing Outside

📺 Best BEACHES Lots of great beaches to choose from here! For a debaucherous party at pretty much any time of the afternoon and well into the night, head to the south of the island's Paradise and Super Paradise Beaches. Both beaches are not for the modest or faint of heart—Paradise was home of the island's first official nude beach (although, officially nudist or not, *nobody* at Mykonian beaches will blink an eye at the removal of a bikini top). These are attached to the low-budget camping grounds, so are most popular with the young backpacker set. Also on the south coast is Platis Yialos, Psarou, and Ornos—all more family-oriented

beaches if you're looking for less of the "Singled Out" episode scene. You can reach all the south coast beaches by bus from the bus station in town—they leave around every 15 to 20 minutes during the summer months.

For an even quieter beach experience, head to the undeveloped, "virgin" north coast beaches—buses don't head in that direction, but you can get there if you rent a car or scooter. The reason they're less popular than those on the south coast is because they're also much windier. Two beaches that are reasonably sheltered from the wind are **Panormos** and **Ayios Sostis**. Remember that these are undeveloped beaches—so if you've gotten used to the full service of the south coast beaches (beach umbrellas, bars, and so on) you might be in for a shock, as these places are definitely BYO, well, everything.

DIVING A super-popular sport in Mykonos is diving—as the island's waters are one of the few areas in the Aegean where the sport hasn't been forbidden to safeguard against the potential robbing of deep sea treasures. Your best bet is heading under the sea in the month of September—the water temperature hovers around 75°F (24°C) and visibility is high. You've got to be certified to participate in guided dives right off the bat—but if it's your first time, you can sign up for introductory classes and snorkeling is also available. Head to **Mykonos Diving Center** (☎ 22890/24-808; www.dive.gr) at Psarou Beach; it offers 5-day PADI certification courses in English for about 500€ (including equipment). Dives for certified divers begin at around 50€, and 60€ classes and dives are available for beginners. Similar programs are available from **Dive Adventures** (☎ 22890/26-539; www.dive mykonos.gr) on Paradise Beach.

Ibiza

Those who appreciate the finer cultural nuances of traveling abroad should not visit Ibiza in the summer. Most points of interest involve gin, strobe lights, and at least some sounds of the tide. The clubs and beaches are why everyone's here. But if you like to dance, look good, feel good, and ride excess like a bareback horse, Ibiza will knock your socks off. Its sunny, beautiful beaches and good-natured locals appear wholesome by day. When the sun goes down, though, this island emerges as a wild thing, hard-partying and looking for almost-scary fun. It's a mix of festive, colorful, theatrical elements—plus the relentless thumping of music that seems to never stop, until morning, that is. That's what Ibiza is like every day from the middle of July until the end of August. So, if you want to go to Ibiza, go now, because it might kill you (or your career, or your sanity) when you're older. This is the biggest damn Slip 'N Slide of a party you ever saw.

This small island was once best known for its beautiful beaches and the small artisan communities that grew from a European hippie invasion in the early and mid-1970s. Ibiza still holds true to this character for 9 months of the year (and year-round in the inland villages). In the past decade, however, Ibiza has become a giant, fire-breathing Godzilla of a party. Each summer, this island rears its head, thumps it chest, and emits a terrifying war cry in the form of electronic music from the world's greatest DJs. Ibiza is one of the epicenters of modern disco/rave culture, and savvy Europeans and Aussies seek the sounds that came out of this island in the late '80s like some people seek Dead tapes from the early '70s. Young Europeans know this little island as *the* place for summer holiday. You'll find a lot of Americans and Brits now, too, and also Germans, Italians, and Spanish, but in fewer numbers.

Even at its worst, Ibiza is fascinating to watch: boorish tourists who refuse to speak anything other than English to the locals, who put up with their antics for 3 months every summer so that they can live in peace during the other 9 months of the year. At its best, though, Ibiza is a beautiful, almost spiritual, and very tolerant place. The gay community is so well established here that it practically merits its own section.

People-watching is free, but everything else here will hurt. A week's worth of nightlife will cost you as much as a new Hyundai. Getting into clubs can cost up to 60€, and most hotels double (and sometimes triple!) their prices in July and August.

The Best of Ibiza

- ○ **The Best Beaches:** Pack the sunblock, if nothing else, before you seek out **Las Salinas Beach,** a nudist beach 11km (7 miles) from Ibiza Town; **Cala Xarraca Beach**, up on the north coast; or any of the more unspoiled beaches in **Formentera,** a tiny island 16km (10 miles) south of Ibiza. See p. 477.
- ○ **The Best Excuse for Imbibing:** The **Disco Bus** is cheap and probably more reliable than finding a sober friend to drive you home. It runs during the season from every major club to every major hotel on the island. See p. 467
- ○ **The Best Place to Watch the Sunset:** Check out **Café Mambo** in San Antonio (p. 474).

- ○ **The Best Party Calisthenics:** Warm up on the beach at **Bora Bora** (p. 473). Get your full workout across the street at **Space** (p. 476), and then cool down at **Bora Bora** again.
- ○ **The Best Traditional Party:** Renaissance at **Pachá** (p. 475) is still pretty wild.
- ○ **The Best Sea-View Walk:** Spend a couple of hours strolling the area around **D'Alt Villa,** the Old Fortress (p. 468), with its beautiful views out over the water.
- ○ **The Best Place to Lay those Weary Bones: Casa de Huespedes Vara de Rey** is an eye in the storm of Ibiza. The couple who run this hostel use an artist's touch to make each of the 10 rooms a calm and serene nest away from home. See p. 470.

Getting There & Getting Around

Getting into Town

BY AIR

Iberia and Air Europa fly into **Es Codolar International Airport** (☎ **971/809-000**), which is 5.5km (3½ miles) southwest of Ibiza Town, just above the southern coast. Buses leave from the airport and drop passengers at the Bus Stop Bar in about 15 minutes. Service runs hourly 7:30am to 10:30pm and costs around 1.20€.

BY BOAT

Trasmediterránea (Andenes de Puerto Estación Marítimo; ☎ **971/454-645**), operates a **ferry service** from Barcelona four times a week; a one-way ticket costs 50€. One boat per day arrives daily from Valencia (70€ one-way). From Palma, there are four ferries per week, Tuesday to Friday; a one-way ride runs 69€. Boats from Barcelona, Valencia, and Palma de Mallorca leave all day long. If you arrive by boat, you'll be dropped off right in the middle of it all.

Getting Around

BY BUS

The only public transportation is the bus system. Buses leave Ibiza Town from the **Bus Stop Bar** on Isidoro Macabich (no phone), which is open daily from 9am to 11pm; you'll pay 1.80€ or less per fare. The service here is slow. Sometimes the woman behind the counter will just close up shop for 20 minutes while she chats with her friend behind the bar, regardless of the number of people in line. You can always buy a ticket from the actual bus driver, which is recommended because there are four different bus companies in Ibiza and it's easy to get confused. Getting back into Ibiza Town is always easy because the buses are the biggest, loudest things around. Missing one would be like missing a marching band in your backyard.

The ⁅TV⁆ ⁅Best⁆ **Disco Bus** (☎ 971/192-456) is what it's all about here. The fare is around 1.75€ or 2€, and the destinations are every major club and hotel on the island.

The Disco Bus hits each location once per hour and runs (like everything else) mid-May through end of September. See www.ibizanight.com to learn more about the Disco Bus and lots of other club-related info.

BY TAXI

Cabs are available and recommended for club-hopping if you have the extra cash to spare (☎ 971/307-000). It's more expensive than it should be, but you won't be ripped off any more than you are anywhere else on the island. Here, .50€ or so is plenty for a tip. Like most of the natives here, the cabbies are mellow and safe people.

BY BIKE & MOPED

Valentín Car & Bike (Av. Bmé. Vte. Ramón 19; ☎ 971/310-822; Mon–Fri 9am–1pm and 3:30–7:30pm, Sat 9am–noon and 6–7pm) rents motorbikes for 25€ to 30€ per day. You pay gas. It has everything from old Vespas to spanking-new 250cc Yamahas. **Bravo Rent a Car,** Avenida de Santa Eulária (☎ 971/313-901; daily 9am–1pm and 4–8:30pm) brings in new cars and bikes each year. In both places, helmets are required for anything bigger than 50cc.

ON FOOT

Once in Ibiza, the town, plan to walk everywhere. The city is compact and easily covered by foot. You really only need to take a bus to get out of town.

Ibiza Basics

Orientation: Ibiza Neighborhoods

San Antonio is on the west coast, and **Ibiza Town** is on the east. San Antonio is a nightmarish combination of suburban shopping mall, soccer riot, and frat party, where the youngest and most terrible of the tourists come to party. Except for the Café Mambo (p. 474), it should be avoided at all costs. But a mere half-hour bus ride away, on the other half of the island—and the opposite end of the spectrum—is Ibiza Town, the focal point of the island. Unless otherwise stated, all recommended venues are located here.

Ibiza Town is on the southern end of the island's eastern coast and lies to the south and west of the Marina. A small and unremarkable portion of Ibiza Town does curve around to the north of the Marina, but you won't be spending any time there. The **Sa**

Penya neighborhood is where the action is—action like you may never have seen before. Dozens of bars, restaurants, street vendors, drag queens, and nationalities converge here and get warmed up for the nightly sacrifice to the club gods. During the day, you can find good fashion shopping, pubs, and groceries here. The beginning of Sa Penya is marked by Plaça d'Antoni Riquer and the street that runs through it, parallel to the Marina, which is called Calle de Lluís Tur i Palau to the west of the Plaça, and Passeig des Moll to the east.

Calle de La Virgen is the most famous of the streets here; it is a long, narrow street that runs parallel to the Marina, from the eastern tip of the city to the equally busy Calle de Pou, which begins right at the Marina and runs north to south. Sa Penya continues south for about 8 misshapen blocks before it runs into the foot of the elevated Old Fortress.

📺 **Best** **D'Alt Villa (Old Fortress)** ★ is the one touristy thing you should make time for, if nothing else. Ibiza Town more or less ends at the southern point of the Old Fortress. Paseo de Vara de Rey is the other major landmark in Ibiza Town—several hostels, the tourism office (below), a travel agency, and a few good shops and restaurants are all on this street. Paseo de Vara de Rey is 3 blocks to the west of D'Alt Villa and runs northeast to southwest. Everything that we've mentioned here can be walked between in 20 minutes or less.

Other villages worthy of a day or half-day trip for some rural relaxation are **Santa Gertrudis** (to the northwest of Ibiza Town, in the very middle of the island, about 30 min. by bus), **Santa Eularia** (to the east of Ibiza Town, on the coast, 20 min. by bus), and **San Rafael** (directly between Ibiza Town and San Antonio). The clubs Privilege and Amnesia (see "Clubs," below) are both just outside of Ibiza Town. No point on the island of Ibiza is much more than an hour from Ibiza Town by bus, or 90 minutes by scooter. **Playa d'en Bossa** is a mere 15-minute bus ride south of Ibiza Town. This is one of the most crowded and commercial beaches on the island, but Space (see "Clubs," below) and Bora Bora (p. 473) are here.

Ibiza is ridiculously small. The villages are even smaller. Venues that aren't in Ibiza Town or San Antonio simply have the village listed for the address because all of the stores, bars, and such are located on one central street. Basic maps and road signs work just fine if you're going to scooter it between beaches and villages, and the buses go to all villages we have named and many beaches. And the clubs themselves (also reachable by bus) are landmarks that every cab driver and local knows. You'd have to work really hard to get lost on this island.

Tourist Offices

Go to the tourist office on Vara de Rey 13 (☎ **971/301-900**) for info; it's open Monday to Friday 9am to 1pm and 5 to 8pm, and Saturday 10:30am to 1:30pm. A second, smaller tourist office is right across from where the boats let you off. They won't make hotel reservations for you. *Tip:* Call hotels and make your reservations long before you get here.

Recommended Websites & Magazines

- ○ *DJ Mag Ibiza:* Gives you the most info on clubs, bars, restaurants, beaches, and markets in the least amount of words, along with short interviews from the big DJs.
- ○ *Ministry in Ibiza:* This is like the *Maxim* of this island: funny articles written by a staff that jumps into the whole Ibiza scene headfirst.
- ○ *Party San:* You can pick it up at the Sunset Café (p. 474).
- ○ *7:* Another party mag we like.
- ○ **www.ibizanight.com**: Gives you basic info on the clubs but is more useful for its

detailed info on the Disco Bus (see "By Bus," above), restaurants, and—most importantly—reservation information (make your reservations early!). The site is in English and Spanish.

Culture Tips 101

The official language of the Balearic Islands is Catalán, the language of Barcelona. But, you'll often be able to speak English (and German).

One quick way to lose money here is by handing it over to José Law when he pulls you over for swerving around on your rented scooter. El Hombre isn't really out to get you, but let's face it: If your island were invaded each summer by 2 million hallucinating British Gen X-ers, you, too, would want to try to control things at least a little bit. Road blocks with breath tests are the

Rules of the Game

Despite their abundance, drugs (including marijuana) are illegal in Ibiza. However, in traditional Spanish fashion, people *usually* don't get busted unless they get violent. The standard Spanish chill factor applies here as well, but the locals have become less patient with the rowdy English-speaking tourists in recent years, so if you do get in a bind, don't go shooting your mouth off. Also be forewarned that most people get a good searching when traveling from Ibiza to another country.

newest attempt to keep you and your wasted friends out of harm's way. Take our advice: Use a cab at night.

Ibiza **Nuts & Bolts**

IBIZA

Currency   You will get the best exchange rate at an ATM. Although there aren't many of them right in Sa Penya, there are several scattered all around the Paseo de Vara de Rey, particularly at the southwestern end.

Embassies   For embassy info, see "Madrid Nuts & Bolts" on p. 591.

Emergencies   For emergencies, call ☎ **092.** The Red Cross 24-hour ambulance service is at ☎ **971/390-303** or 971/191-009.

Pharmacies   The pharmacy on **Paseo de Vara de Rey** has condoms *(preservativos)*. It's open Monday through Saturday 9am to 1:30pm and 5 to 9pm, Sunday from 5 to 9pm. The one in D'Alt Villa is open 24 hours for you and your horny/nauseous/sunburned friends.

Telephone Tips   The city code is **971.** For the operator, dial ☎ **1003**; the international operator is at ☎ **1005.** Note that recent changes in Spain's phone system now require that all local calls be dialed with the 971 prefix.

Sleeping

The thing about Ibiza: People usually don't just pass through. This is their destination. People come to this island for a wild vacation and expect to pay for it. But the prices aren't too, too crazy—it's simply finding a room here that's a big pain. Save yourself a huge headache and make a reservation for a room before you arrive on the island. A little planning ahead will get you a sweet little room at Vara de Rey or something with a view at the Hotel Montesol.

Cheap

→ **Pension La Peña** This pension seems to have the cheapest rooms in Ibiza Town. The common bathrooms are of questionable character, but many of the rooms (though small and bare) have a beautiful view of the sea. The 10 doubles and 3 single rooms are rented out almost exclusively to gay guys who want to be near the action that makes the Calle de la Virgen famous. *Calle de la Virgen 76.* ☎ *971/190-240. 15€–25€ single, 25€–35€ double. Amenities: Shared bathrooms.*

→ **Sol y Briso** A relatively reasonable price makes this another option. *Avinguda B.V. 15.* ☎ *971/310-818. 18€ single, 30€ double. Amenities: Shared bathrooms.*

Doable

📺 Best → **Casa de Huespedes Vara de Rey ★** The young couple that runs this hostel is beautiful to look at and fun to talk with. Their artists' touch makes every room a calm and serene haven from Ibiza's madness. Call ahead, as many guests have been returning for years. Already a great place to make new friends because there are only 10 rooms here, Vara de Rey only got more irie when the rooftop terrace was completed in the summer of 2000. Great, great people and beautifully painted rooms. *Paseo de Vara de Rey 7.* ☎ *971/301-376. www.hibiza.com. 27€–45€ single, 48€–80€ double. Amenities: Rooftop terrace, shared bathrooms.*

→ **Hotel Montesol** This place has been the hotel in Ibiza Town since 1934. Private bathrooms, phones, air-conditioning, and TVs make this place worth the extra bucks. All rooms have great views either of the harbor, old city, or quaint Paseo de Vara de Rey.

Big rooms and spacious closets, plus bathtubs! The sophisticated bar here is more fashionable in the off season. *Northeastern end of Paseo de Vara de Rey 2.* ☎ *971/310-161. www.hotelmontesol.com. 40€–60€ single, 65€–106€ double. Amenities: Bar. In room: A/C, TV.*

→ **Hostal Parque** Of the 29 rooms here, many have a pleasant view of the park and plaza below, but what's most interesting for tourists is that your neighbors will most likely be Spanish. *Plaza del Parque 4, just south of Paseo Vara de Rey.* ☎ *971/301-358. www.hostalparque.com. 35€–50€ single with shared bathroom, 45€–70€ with private bathroom; 50€–80€ double with shared bathroom, 55€–100€ with private bathroom; 75€–135€ triple with private bathroom. Amenities: TV (in common room). In room: A/C, TV, hair dryer (in some rooms).*

Splurge

→ **Tagomago Aparthotel** Spanish coeds jam this place and they have *come to party!* Bright modern rooms with a full kitchen (save cash by cooking!), living room, balcony (view of harbor), and TV. If you're smooth, you'll be able to get extra folks on the floor—the staff doesn't really pay attention to who's coming and going. Also, the single beds are big and can comfortably fit two people. The hotel has cafeteria/snack bar and currency exchange, and will help you to rent cars and bikes. Just a 1-minute walk to Pachá and 5 minutes to El Divino and a few paces away from mini-golf, paddle tennis, and real tennis. *Paseo Marítimo (opposite side of the harbor from Sa Penya, a 5-min. cab ride from there).* ☎ *971/316-550. www.ibiza-online. com/hoteltagomago/index_e.html. 31€–55€ single, 50€–100€ double. Amenities: A/C; cafeteria; darts; Internet kiosk; pool table; pool; TV (in common room).*

Ibiza

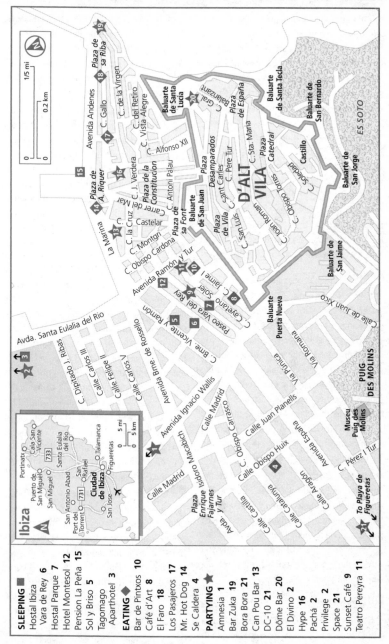

SLEEPING 🟦
Hostal Ibiza .... Vara de Rey **6**
Hostal Parque **7**
Hotel Montesol **12**
Pension La Peña **15**
Sol y Briso **5**
Tagomago Aparthotel **3**

EATING ◆
Bar de Pintxos **10**
Café d'Art **8**
El Faro **18**
Los Pasajeros **17**
Mr. Hot Dog **14**
Se Caldera **4**

PARTYING ⭐
Amnesia **1**
Bar Zuka **19**
Bora Bora **21**
Can Pou Bar **13**
DC-10 **21**
Dôme Bar **20**
El Divino **2**
Hype **16**
Pachá **2**
Privilege **2**
Space **21**
Sunset Café **9**
Teatro Pereyra **11**

Eating

Try to eat at least one decent meal a day. It will help you go the distance at night. It's sad to note that all-night food in Ibiza is only a little more common than an acoustic Happy Mondays song. Although some of the clubs sometimes have a guy in the parking lot selling pretzels and bottled water for a price that would usually get you a case of wine, you really can't count on it. Your best bet is to buy food at a local market (they're everywhere) during the day and stow it away in your hotel room for when you come back at night. Think smart and buy in advance: You'll probably want something salty and a little protein, and I'm a big believer in buying bananas and oranges for those highs and lows (respectively). And some bottled water!

Cheap

→**Los Pasajeros** CLASSIC SPANISH You'll never pass for a local in Ibiza, but if you want to eat where they do, check out this trendy second floor *cantina*, where you get a full meal for the price of a bottle of water in Pachá. The clientele is more on the gay side, like everything else here, and the food is delicious, classic Spanish fare. Owner Maria keeps the place lively and the prices accessible. *Vicente Soler 6, 1st floor. No phone. Main courses 4€–8€. Sun–Fri 1–5pm and 8pm–midnight; Sat 8pm–midnight.*

→**Mr. Hot Dog** FAST FOOD We like the fair price and good food here. Mr. Hot Dog will serve you a big-ass yummy cheeseburger for 5€. The French bread and chicken breast is also recommended. Their terrace seating is right in the middle of it all, providing you with some great people-watching. *At the Marina. Daily 9:30am–4:30am.*

Doable

→**Bar de Pintxos** CAFE/TAPAS This is a small outdoor cafe away from the hoopla in the harbor, right next to the old city. The

staff is pleasant and the food is classic Basque tapas. *Conde de Rosellón 1. ☎ 971/399-559. Pinchos fríos (small uncooked things like salmon on yummy bread) 1.20€–3.60€; calamari 6.20€. Daily 11:30am–3:30pm and 8pm–2:30am.*

→**Café d'Art** CAFE/TAPAS This small cafe has nothing to do with art, but the old country store sells all kinds of semi-gourmet meats, cheeses, fresh bread, wine, and ready-made tapas. Perfect stuff for a picnic at a quiet beach of your choice, or you can sit outside at the base of the old city and eat at one of the cafe tables. *Cayetano Soler 9. ☎ 971/302-972. Mon–Sat 10am–9pm.*

Splurge

→**El Faro** SPANISH/SEAFOOD Very touristy, very ritzy. Kings, presidents, rock-'n'-roll stars, and famous athletes have been eating here regularly for 20 years. Choose from the living fish and lobsters for your dinner. Like Se Caldera, you can pay up to 35€ for paella here, but unlike Se Caldera, the atmosphere here is downright swank. The restaurant is right in front of the water and a little distance from the Sa Penya hoopla a few blocks down. Reservations should be made. The owner's name is Mercedes, which totally makes sense. *Plaza Sa Riba 1. ☎ 971/313-233. www.elfaro-ibiza. com. May–Oct daily 6am–4am.*

📺 **Best** →**Se Caldera** ★ SEAFOOD The restaurant of choice for locals (even other restaurant owners) of Ibiza Town. Run by the same native Ibizenco couple for 15 years now: The husband cooks, and the wife runs the show. All the food is "down-home," specializing in fresher-than-fresh fish. The menú del día costs up to a whopping 14€, but includes spectacular main dishes like fresh salmon. Located a little away from the port (about a 10-min. walk), so you won't see the sunset or hear the tide with your meal, but you will be treated right and get a great look at the locals in action. *Obispo Padre Huix 19.*

☎ *971/306-416. Menú del día 11€–14€, main courses 14€–22€. Sun–Fri 1–5pm and 8pm–midnight; Sat 8pm–midnight.*

Partying

Bars

As you would expect with a Spanish island, Ibiza has a bar for every occasion. Some are for cool beachside drinks, others are for hot late-night action, but the bulk of the bars you'll encounter in Ibiza Town are meant to operate like giant cannons that will blast your wasted ass into the disco stratosphere. Keep your chin up, strap on your crash helmet, and head on down to the crowded international big-top mayhem that is the Sa Penya district. It's your job to get there at about 11pm or midnight and to be ready to perform death-defying stunts of fashion and consumption.

Among the extreme clothing, you may notice a fair number of attractive and seemingly coked-up folks who—despite all of their talking—are rather stationary. It's their job to get you into their bar. Here's how it usually goes: A sexy and fast-talking hawker approaches you and says "Hey there, mate. How about tickets for Amnesia tonight?" Be sure that you know where you want to go ahead of time because they will always try and sell you on the less-attractive events first (such as a foam party [p. 475] instead of a hot dance scene that ends with live sex on stage). So having already done your homework, you say, "How about tickets for Pachá?" What usually happens next is that you'll agree to go in for a drink. Yes, that's right; if you agree to a couple of (relatively) cheap whiskey-and-Cokes, you'll get a big discount or even free admission! What a great system! Make sure that you get your tickets inside the bar; scalpers have been known to sell fakes on the street. As so many of the 20-something party people here already know, looking sexy and freaky will

get you what you want because the clubs want beautiful people!

→ **Bar Zuka** The candles, old tile floor, and beautifully painted walls add to the more-refined-less-hectic vibe (until they break out the tequila later at night). Regular attendance by some of England's biggest DJs. Less queeny and painted-up than the rest of Calle de la Virgen. Bring cash 'cause they don't take credit cards. *Calle de la Virgen 75. No phone.*

MTV Best → **Bora Bora** ★ When the MTV beach parties grow up, they want to be Bora Bora. Drink, dance, and chill while coming down from nearby Space (or while gearing up for it, depending on your schedule and stamina). Along with the party people, there are many unaware beachgoers here who have a dim realization that they are not in the same state as everyone else at the bar. This is a very mellow, very appropriate, very Ibiza way to end a disco marathon: 2€ for a beer and usually around 500 people. Open

IBIZA

Wired

You're a serious addict if you're wasting your time, money, and mind in front of a computer screen in Ibiza when you could be wasting those same things on the beach or at a club. If you need that fix, though, log on at **Centro Internet Eivissa** (Av. Ignacio Wallis 39 Bajos; ☎ **971/ 318-161;** www.centrointerneteivissa. com; Mon–Sat 10am–11pm, Sun 5–11pm). Along with 14 PCs, scanners and color printers are also available if you need them, you geek.

Hanging Out

You'll have no trouble finding the cool kids on this island, friends. Ibiza is one big party, but go to the beaches if you want to really hang out, especially because all of them are topless and many are nude (see "Playing Outside," below). Kids don't mass on the plazas or squares here. With all the beautiful, long stretches of sand around, why would they?

Ibiza's best hangout, however, is difficult to find. Not only are these fabled **full-moon parties** hard to suss out, you also have to accept that they're only going to happen once a month. When they do go down, there will be no flyers, and the Germans and the English won't be able to help, but if you make friends with just a few locals, they'll be able to tell you the day and location of one of the island's best events. Drum circles, booze, bonfires, and more on secluded black-sand beaches that are beautiful enough to make you cry.

Calle de Santa Agnes, in San Antonio, is probably the last place you want to hang out, unless you're 16, belligerent, and culturally void: The scene here is vomiting and groping in the streets: 100% rude, 100% lame.

all the time—really. *Playa d'en Bossa, across the street from Space. No phone.*

MTV Best → **Café Mambo** ★ In San Antonio, but nobody's perfect. Listen to mellow ambient music, have a drink, and watch a magnificent sunset over the water from the terrace (a must-see while in Ibiza). The rabid British party monkeys that swarm San Antonio do show up later on, but it's fun to slip slowly from the mellow sunset to that

high-energy fiesta while getting sauced on gin and tonics. Including the surrounding beach, max capacity is about 2,000 people. Around 7€ for a drink. *End of Av. de Vara de Rey, in San Antonio. No phone.*

→ **Can Pou Bar** Has been a local favorite for over 80 years, except that the customers back then were all fishermen, not club and clothing store owners. There are a few terrace tables and the inside is comfy. It doesn't cram people in here for the extra buck as so many other places do. Coffee, juice, small sandwiches, and breakfasts are served. Walls are lined with beautiful artwork that reflects the local temperament. Right on the Marina between Sa Penya and Paseo de Vara de Rey, this is usually the place where you'll get the cheapest club tickets. *Corner of Lluis Tur i Palau and Montgri.* ☎ *971/310-875.*

→ **Hype** What's in a name? This is only one of the very many bars that operate in this way in the Sa Penya district. Drink your way to cheap disco and watch the show pass by from the terrace seating. *Calle d'Emile Pou 11A. No phone.*

→ **Sunset Café** You'll find food here in addition to alcohol. The chicken sandwiches are tasty, and the fresh juice and "breakfast salads" (garden salads with a lot of fruit) for 4.50€ are nothing short of miraculous after a night of partying. Good house music with its own DJ from 9pm till 1am. Be sure to say hi to Patrick, the friendly German owner, and whichever hottest-woman-ever happens to be behind the bar with him. Sitting on their pleasant plaza right off the Paseo de Vara de Rey is a great getaway from Ibiza Town nonsense. *Plaza del Parque 3.* ☎ *971/394-446.*

Live Music

Live music? Yeah, right. Only the most popular DJs on earth spin here on a nightly basis. Save for a handful of German and Dutch expats who live inland, there's not much of a

Good Clean Fun

Amnesia and one or two other clubs host the infamous *espuma* (foam) parties that you've seen on E!, full of scantily clad hotties splashing around and getting it on in over-the-head bubbly goodness. Well, color me soaking wet with soap in my eye! Who thought that being buried alive in foam was going to be a good time? Listen. If you're gonna do a foam party, do it right because—no joke—you'll wind up gagging, getting felt up (which might be what you're lookin' for), and slipping and cracking your head in 2m (6 ft.) of the stuff. Being prepared, though, can make a foam party a lot more fun. The foam pros show up with backpacks containing goggles, bathing suits, beach sandals or old sneakers, and a towel. They gear up before the foam comes to town (it rains down like one of the 10 Plagues, like the fury of God himself, in terrifyingly enormous quantities), and make sure that they're a good 9m (30 ft.) from the center of the dance floor.

live-music scene on this island. If middle-aged Germans covering the Eagles and the Dead is your thing, though, be sure to rush on over to **Teatro Pereyra** (corner of Calle Conde Rosellón and Calle Aníbal; no phone; 7am–4am daily). The good times get rolling at 11:30pm. Despite everything, they do get points for being open 21 hours a day and for having an enormous and beautiful bar. The big round tables can seat about six stools, and capacity is about 300 European preps. Lord knows why they came to Ibiza.

Clubs

→ **Amnesia** If Pachá is the Sean Connery of clubs, Amnesia, which was full of hippies and liquid acid in the early '80s, is more like Mick Jagger: past its prime and blissfully unaware of it. Yes, it's as big as an airplane hangar. Yes, it has a retractable roof. Yes, it has trees and drag queens and several rooms and dancers and balconies, but big deal—where's the love? Best nights: Godskitchen on Tuesday and Cream on Thursday. *A 2-min. walk south of San Rafael, which is 15 min. by bus or 10 min. by cab from Ibiza Town.* ☎ 971/198-041. www.amnesia.es.

→ **DC-10** The best place to be on a Monday morning—that is, of course, if you have the rest of the week to recover. This new classic hosts CircoLoco, a wild, wild, sunglasses-mandatory kind of party. Located next to the airport under the shadow of a DC-10; legend has it that this was a local music bar before becoming Ibiza's favorite takeoff runway for after-hours astronauts. *Se Salinas 10.* ☎ 971/198-086. www.circoloco.com.

→ **El Divino** Beautiful (almost opulent) and often semi-exclusive. You can get here by taking the boat that leaves every half-hour from the Marina. You can't miss it; it's the one with the flashing lights and the big sign that says "El Divino." The best areas of the enormous and ornate deck on the water are usually roped off for the many VIPs that attend this club. One of the main events, Miss MoneyPenny, is basically prom night for a lot of English drag queens. Hed Kandi is on Saturdays. Another night, be prepared to wear your latex and leather and bring a whip because you're gonna git your freak on tonight! Be prepared for wild costumes, excessive groping, and shagging in the bathrooms. Straight out of a movie—or hell, if you're a Puritan. *On the Paseo Marítimo at the Puerto de Ibiza Nueva, across the harbor from Ibiza Town.* ☎ 971/318-338. www.eldivino-ibiza.com.

MTV **Best** → **Pachá** ★ Open since 1975, this is the original Ibiza disco and is considered to be one of the finest nightclubs on planet Earth. Like Sean Connery or your

IBIZA

club scene

Because they're the big business here, all of the clubs adhere to the same high prices and late schedule. Here's the lowdown (exceptions are noted in the club descriptions):

→ Clubs run from the middle of May until the end of September and are open from midnight till 6 or 8am daily. Prime time is from around 3:30 to 5:30am.

→ Cover is between 40€ and 60€! Discount tickets are easy to come by, though, and bring the price down to 20€ to 35€ (see "Bars," above, to learn more). Little bottles of water are around 6€ and drinks are 10€ to 15€. All of the clubs take at least Visa and MasterCard. They want your money, in any form.

→ None of the clubs is exclusive at the front door. Instead, they have exclusive rooms within.

→ Each club holds between 5,000 (Pachá) and 10,000 (Privilege) people at once! They all have smaller rooms tucked away here and there (especially Pachá), so don't get put off if you don't like the feel of the main room.

→ The crowds are between 19 and 30 years old. Despite the fashion blitzkrieg here, there are also thousands of preps and dorks and family men running around this island. These folks are more likely to not make it past the bar scene at Sa Penya, though.

favorite M.I.L.F., Pachá has aged with elegance over the years and hosts a more noticeable contingent of 30- and 40-year-olds (although they are very far from the majority). Pachá is *muy fashion,* as they say here, and the most international (read: not ²/₃ English and German) of the clubs. The go-go girls are fly and the dance floor gets hot and grimy (the way you like it, baby), but the drag queens and freak-outs that keep the other clubs churning are usually not here (so don't dress out for Pachá—dress *up*). Famous people stop by all the time. You can even come here in winter as it's open year-round. *Av. 8 de Agosto, on the Paseo Marítimo, a 20-min. walk southwest of Ibiza Town.* ☎ *971/310-959. www.pacha.com.*

→ **Privilege** This place is midgets and strobe lights and 10-foot drag queens on stilts, people shagging on stage (really!), fire-eaters, and an enormous swimming pool, and music, and Lord knows what else running around all over the place. And you have to pay money for toilet paper! Privilege tends to be more gay than other clubs, particularly for Manumission (Mon), which is also its best event. *A 10-min. walk north of San Rafael (15 min. by bus, 10 min. by cab from Ibiza Town).* ☎ *971/198-160. www.privilegeibiza.com.*

[MTV] [Best] → **Space** ★ Even on Sunday, this place is still insane and happy from the night before. Whoop! This x-tensive club doesn't even open till the others close, so pretty much the whole island congregates here around 8am. A big open-air room with a semi-translucent tarp for the ceiling gives the whole club a sitting-under-a-shady-tree kind of feel. Space ties with Pachá as our favorite club. Best event: Home, starting Sunday at 8am (the regular hours are 8am–6pm—how wild is that?). *Playa d'en Bossa.* ☎ *971/314-078. www.space-ibiza.es.*

Gay Bars

Gay life here is hard to miss, so we'll just point out that a lot of mostly gay bars are on the Calle de la Virgen and Calle Mayor in Ibiza town.

➜**Dôme Bar** Check this place out the for some of the trendiest and queeniest times on the island. *Calle Alfonso XII 3. No phone.*

➜**Es Cavellet Beach** It's 95% gay, 100% nude. Expect bad techno music, a whole lot of drugs, and a lot of naked gay men (and some women). Straight girls sometimes stop by for a bit of sightseeing and weird fantasizing. *15-min. bus ride south of Ibiza Town, close to the southernmost tip of the island.*

Performing Arts

All the performance on this island takes place in the clubs: live sex acts, striptease, midgets, stilt freaks, fire-eaters, drag queens, go-go girls, aliens, latex—and then there's all the freaks who pay to get in. Just what goes on in the bathrooms during Manumission at Privilege (p. 476) is more "performance" than most people will need in a lifetime.

Playing Outside

MTV Best **BEACHES** ★★★ The Ibiza tourist office claims that this tiny island has about 56 beaches! If you really want to explore, head to the tourist office (p. 468) and pick up the free *IBIZA: Playas a la Carta.* This catalog describes each of the beaches and tells you how to get there, too.

To get away from the tourist hype that envelops the beaches closer to Ibiza Town, try **Las Salinas Beach** (about 11km/7 miles south of Ibiza Town; follow the signs for the airport), a full-on nudist beach that's less than 15 minutes from Ibiza Town by scooter. The attractive crowds here tend to be a little older (as in over 21), more local, and with more money. This beach is the height of cool in Ibiza.

You'll miss **Cala Xarraca Beach** unless you're looking for the restaurant of the same name. It makes sense, though, because the restaurant is the only thing here besides a few beautiful houses. The super-cool, topless beach is more tiny pebbles and shells than sand. Surrounded by rocky cliffs, the water is very clear with tints of blue and doesn't get deep for quite a while. Bring goggles and a snorkel for collecting stones in the water. **Paddle boats** are rented by the restaurant.

Boy Meets Girl?

Yeah, more like boy meets boy on this island. Or girl meets boy dressed like girl, or boy meets girl who looks like a boy dressing as a girl, or . . . whatever. Ibiza is not a place for the shy. The whole point of this island is that you can do whatever you want, baby. Do it loud, do it bright, do it in spandex, and do it topless—you can rest when you get home. When the summer rolls around, the local hippie types will often refer to "the colors returning," referring to the bright clothes, jewelry, and smiles that come to this island each summer. So make sure you play up the part! The gay nightlife here is not a separate entity; it's all swirled together. Our best advice: Be safe (no matter who you end up with), because Lord knows you'll have opportunities here. The one thing we don't recommend is buying too many drinks, especially at as much as 16€ a pop.

Modification

There are dozens of tattoo shops on the island, but the one that stands above the others is **Inkadelic,** Plaza Constitución 10 (no phone). Its owner, Neil, has a cool studio with objects brought from his trips all over the world. He offers a good variety of tats, from your average dragon to some very cool Japanese designs, but otherwise getting scratched in Ibiza can be tricky. That Mitsubishi symbol probably seemed like a good idea at 9am on a Saturday morning when you were still going from the night before, but the significance will be hard to explain later on when you return home and are trying to get a job that does not involve checking IDs.

The tiny island of **Formentera** is about 10 miles south of Ibiza and features dreamy and unspoiled stretches of white sand that seem to go on forever. Its three beaches, Illetes, Levant, and Es Pujols, all outdo anything on Ibiza; they're prettier and the crowds are cooler. Only 5,000 people are permanent residents on this island, and although that number jumps to 20,000 in the summer, this place is still more chill than a penguin on ice. Boats leave Ibiza Town at least once an hour from 7:45am to 10:30pm. You'll get to Formentera in about 30 minutes and will pay about 34€ round-trip. Contact **Balearia Lines** (Calle Aragón 71; ☎ 971/ 310-711; central reservations: 902/160-180; daily 7:30am–6:30pm, later in summer) for more info.

SCUBA DIVING   Ibiza has some of the best diving in the Mediterranean. Some people come here specifically for the clear waters and the unique marine life and mysterious shipwrecks that can be found beneath the surface. For a beautiful adventure, contact **Ibiza Diving** (Puerto Deportivo in the village of Santa Eulária; ☎ 971/332-949; www. ibiza-diving.com; daily 9:30am–1pm and 2–6pm) or **Figueral** (Playa de Es Figueral, a 45-min. bus ride north of Ibiza Town, on the northeastern coast; ☎ 971/335-079; daily 9am–2pm and 4–6:30pm). Instructors at both places speak English.

HORSEBACK RIDING   This is a scenic, memorable experience. The **Centro Ecuestre Easy Rider** (Camí del Sol d'en Serra, Cala Llonga, outside Santa Eulalia des Riu; ☎ 971/ 339-192) offers a 2-hour coastal ride with scenic dips inland.

Shopping

Between the influence of the hippies and the already artistic leanings of the native Ibizan culture, there's plenty of artistry, beautiful pottery, clothes, and jewelry on the island. I'd set aside some money for gifts.

→ **Hippy Market** This is what the locals call a fun outdoor market. The biggest and best of them takes place in Es Canar (northeast of Santa Eulária). Unlike many other outdoor markets, this one has some truly beautiful stuff: great hats and sarongs for the beach, all sorts of handmade wind chimes, instruments, ceramics, fans, and also the requisite T-shirts, bowls, and watches. The market at Es Canar is in the middle of a hippie village and has been running since the early '70s. Get here by bus (1€) or by scooter (30 min. maximum). It's easy to spend a few hours among the nearly 400 booths here, so give yourself some time. The bright woodcarvings of Paulo Viheira capture the warm and creative essence of non-disco Ibiza. Although he does have his own studio in Santa Eulária, you'll have an easier time tracking him down here.

Prices range from about 16€ for something the size of a dinner plate to nearly 238€ for enormous carvings that you could windsurf on. Highly recommended, and easy to find. Ask any of the friendly workers at the market. *In Es Canar (northeast of Santa Eulária, a 20-min. bus ride from Ibiza Town). Apr–Oct Wed 9:30am–7pm.*

→ **Holala!** "Unique clothing for unique people." In sticking to this creed, it has taken used clothing and brought it into the world of high fashion. Written up in nearly every fashion magazine you can think of (including *Elle, Vogue,* and *Cosmopolitan*), this trend-setting place always has something cooking. It sells everything from old kimonos and military surplus to modern clothing like Dickies and Adidas. But bring your wallet—those old 501s don't sell for cheap. *Plaza de Mercado Viejo 12.* ☎ *971/316-537.*

→ **Libro Azul** This bookstore and gallery space hosts one or two readings and art expos every month. The art here leans toward the enormous, as in sculptures as big as a fridge. The books, many of them second-hand, lean toward the New Age and are in German, English, Spanish, and Catalan. *Village of Santa Gertrudis.* ☎ *971/197-454.*

→ **Mapa Mundi** It's all about the shoes, which are totally unique, not too costly, and make a great gift for Mom, Sis, girlfriends, or yourself. The dresses here are beautiful, but out of the range of most travelers (they begin at 150€). If Indiana Jones and Stevie Nicks opened a store together, it might look like this place. Beautiful, flowy dresses in an old-world setting with maps, old travel trunks, and beautiful tribal-looking jewelry. *Plaza de Vila 13, at the base of the Fortress.* ☎ *971/391-685.*

IBIZA

Interlaken

Yes, intrepid travelers: There was life for your wanderlusting forefathers before the trusty guidance of E!'s "Wild On," STA Travel, and the *MTV Guide to Europe*. Legend has it, for instance, that tourism to Interlaken (pop. 21,000) began over 300 years ago, when out-of-towner Margrave Frederic Albert of Brandenburg made the treacherous trek up the town's highest mountain peak, the Jungfrau, just for kicks. One look at this town—dubbed for its location between two lakes, Thun and Brienz—and you'll see why it's been a traveler's playground since 1690. The scenery is breathtaking. In one glance, you can take in those ice-blue lakes and some of the finest views of the Swiss Alps, including the stunning, craggy peak of the Jungfraujoch, home to the highest railway station in Europe, at 3,400m (11,333 ft.).

Interlaken is postcard-ready Switzerland: horse-drawn carriages; cog railways; snow-capped mountains; shops filled with lace and chocolate; and, of course, cheese, cheese, and more cheese. But unlike some Swiss resorts, 36-sq.-km (14-sq.-mile) Interlaken doesn't just cater to monied travelers' Heidi fantasies; its unparalleled geographic features have made it a year-round mecca for the extreme-sports crowd. (Hiking trails are everywhere, and gondolas or trains connect many, so you can wander for as long or as short a time as you please.) Ascot-wearing baby boomers and the nipped and tucked women who love them share the little town with scruffy Fanta-chugging backpackers jonesing for their next adrenaline rush, and it's a surprisingly peaceful setup. You'll take from this town whatever you fancy—be it Cartier diamonds, canyon-jumping adventures, or a breath of truly delicious mountain air.

The Best of Interlaken

○ **Best Hostel:** The place to be is **Balmer's Herberge.** Rooms are clean, and the social scene thrives, both indoors (the hostel's Metro Bar) and out (the open-air garden has a sweet happy hour). An extensive activities desk can help arrange adventure sports year-round—paragliding, white-water rafting, glacier-skiing, and more. See p. 483.

○ **Best Cheap Eats: Brasserie 17** (at Happy Inn Interlaken Hostel) serves excellent chicken wings, blares top 40 music, and comes pretty close to the college-town atmosphere you might be trying to escape. If not, the wise-guy bartenders, huge portions of food, and varied beer menu make this a good choice. We recommend the sample-size fondue. See p. 485.

○ **Best Activity:** Nature is the museum here. Instead of singling out one sport, the best idea here is to get out and do something, anything, or everything outdoors, whether it's paragliding, river-rafting, climbing, or hiking. You can even golf, play tennis, and go horseback riding.

○ **Best Sidetrip:** The train trip to the top of the **Jungfraujoch** is as essential in one's life list as a trek to the top of Kilimanjaro or a trip to Angel Falls. Only it's much easier to get here! The engineering to get you to the top (to the highest train station in Europe) is a marvel unto itself. Once there, you can dine at of the many cafes and restaurants, or bring some snacks of your own and just enjoy the view. See p. 488.

○ **Best Show:** Head to the tiny town of **Kleine Scheidegg** for some day hiking and if you're lucky, you may hear a rumbling unlike any other (you'll know it when you hear it). Look up and into the not-so-distant mountains. You may see an avalanche, as extraordinary as any monument you might see elsewhere in Europe. See p. 488.

Getting There & Getting Around

Getting into Town

BY TRAIN

Interlaken doesn't have an airport, so you'll arrive by train or car. The Swiss rail system—as efficient and punctual as its reputation—feeds into two train stations: Interlaken Ost (East) and Interlaken West. West is closest to the city center. Several trains arrive daily from Zurich (a 2-hr. trip) and from Bern (40 min.). Train service also connects Geneva with Interlaken (2¹/₂ hr.). For additional rail information, call ☎ 090/030-03-00.

BuY This Pass—Before You Arrive

A transportation pass for the Bernese Oberland (this mountainous region of Switzerland) is available from the Swiss Rail System, but you have to buy it at least 1 week before you arrive. It's a train ticket that pays for most railroads, all mountain trains, cable cars, chairlifts, and steamers on Lakes Thun and Brienz and on most postal-bus lines in the area. The ticket also gets you 25% off the cost of the Kleine-Scheidegg-Eigergletscher-Jungfraujoch railway and the Mürren-Schilthorn aerial cable line. It's valid for 7 days and costs 195F in second class (233F in first class); you'll travel free for 3 days and pay a reduced fare for the final 4 days. Or you can opt for a 15-day pass. Call ☎ **800/794-7795** for details, or check the Web at www.myswissalps.com/regionalrailpasses.asp for more information.

INTERLAKEN

The Taxman Giveth

As a visitor in Interlaken, you pay a resort tax on your hostel or hotel room. This pays for your **visitor's card,** which you should get from your hostel or hotel and will be good for the duration of your stay for discounts and freebies throughout the city in restaurants, stores, and for tours. Don't forget to ask about it!

BY CAR

If you're driving from Bern, head south on N6 to Spiez, and then continue east on N8 to Interlaken.

Getting Around

Once in town, grab a taxi only if you're loaded down with luggage (it will be expensive). Otherwise, just hoof it. There is a bus system, but it's really only for getting to the outskirts of Interlaken or to neighboring towns. The bus station is at Areckstrasse 6 (☎ 033/828-88-28).

Interlaken Basics

Tourist Office

The **Tourism Organization Interlaken** is in the Hotel Metropole (Höheweg 37; ☎ 033/826-53-00). The office offers maps, brochures, and information about side trips and tours. It's open in July and August, Monday through Friday from 8am to noon and 1:30 to 6:30pm; Saturday from 8am to 5pm; and Sunday from 5 to 7pm. The rest of the year, it's open Monday through Friday from 8am to noon and 2 to 6pm, and Saturday from 8am to noon.

Recommended Website

○ www.interlakentourism.ch: This site offers specific tips for visiting Interlaken in all seasons, as well as up-to-date weather and event information for the town.

Recommended Books & Movies

This is the stamping ground of many writers, who come to gawk at the extreme beauty of nature here. It's also become a place location scouts love for movies (see p. 490 about the James Bond movies filmed here). *The Eiger Sanction* (book and movie), a great genre thriller, also makes great use of the landscape here. And Sherlock Holmes aficionados might recognize this setting (p. 489).

Interlaken Nuts & Bolts

Currency   The official currency in Interlaken is the **Swiss franc (F).** The tourist office is a good place to change money and traveler's checks, as are banks. ATMs are easy to find—a great 24-hour one is at the bank adjacent to the Interlaken West train station. **Banks** are open Monday to Friday from 9am to 1pm and 2 to 4:30 or 5pm.

Emergencies & Safety   Interlaken is extremely safe—crime is practically nonexistent. Still, exercise caution as you would in any city. For the police, dial ☎ 117, for firefighters dial ☎ 118, for general emergencies dial ☎ 112. For medical assistance, go to **Interlaken Hospital** (Weissenaustrasse 27; ☎ 33/826-26-26). For a doctor during business hours or on weekend duty (from Fri at 8pm to Mon at 8am), call ☎ 033/823-23-23.

Internet/Wireless Hot Spots   Internet is heartbreakingly expensive. Hostels usually have the best deals, relatively—but you'll still end up paying around 2F for 8 to 10 minutes. My favorites were **Backpackers Villa Sonnenhof** (Alpenstrasse 16; ☎ 033/826-71-71; www.villa.ch; daily 8am–11pm) and **Daniel's Internet Café** (Hauptstrasse 19, Matten; ☎ 033/822-01-75; daily 9am–10pm).

Language   Many people speak English here, although the first language is Swiss German. This Swiss dialect is so different from what's spoken in Germany that even some Germans have a hard time understanding it.

Laundry   You can find a laundromat at the Villa Sonnenhof Hostel (Alpenstrasse 16; ☎ 033/826-71-71; www.villa.ch).

Luggage Storage   Lockers are available at the Interlaken West train station on the Bahnhofstrasse.

Pharmacies   A pharmacy is called an *apotheke* in German. Regular pharmacy hours are Monday to Saturday 9am to 6pm (some close earlier on Sat). You can find one on the Höheweg, Interlaken's main street.

Post Office   The main post office is on the main Bahnhofstrasse, about a block east of the train station (☎ 033/224-89-50). It's open Monday to Friday from 8am to noon and 1:45 to 6pm, and on Saturday from 8:30 to 11am.

Telephone Tips   The area code for Interlaken is **033.** You need to dial this area code both from inside Interlaken and from elsewhere in Switzerland.

Sleeping

Didn't the Swiss, like, *invent* hospitality? If not, they've definitely come to do it really well. The standards for Swiss hotels and hostels are practically unparalleled—chances are that in Switzerland, even if you're staying in the cheapest hostel you can find, your breakfast will be hearty and your sheets clean and crisp. Interlaken has grown to cater both sides of the tourism coin—the cash-loaded ski bunnies as well as the cash-strapped backpackers—so a great selection of hotels and hostels is loaded into this little town.

FYI: Most hotels and hostels have two very different rates—the more expensive for the high season (May 15–Sept 30) and a cheaper low-season rate for the rest of the year.

Hostels

→ **Backpacker's Villa Sonnenhof Youth Hostel** New amenities and a quieter, family feel describe this hostel, which opened in 1998. The prices are a bit higher than other hostels in Interlaken, but you get what you pay for—free Wi-Fi Internet access, clean and quiet rooms, and really kind service. Not a party central like Balmer's, but if you want a guaranteed good night's sleep, this is the cheapest way to get it. *16 Alpenstrasse.* ☎ *033/826-71-71. www.villa.ch. 29F–33F dorm, 70F–77F single, 44F–48F double, 39F–43F triple, 34F–38F quad (rates are per person per night). Rates include breakfast. Amenities: Shared bathrooms; game room; kitchen; free entry to mini-golf, public pools, spas, and gyms; free use of local buses. In room: Locker, sheets, towels.*

MTV Best →**Balmer's Herberge** ★ Hands down, Interlaken's mainstay for backpackers and young people. Clean beds; friendly, in-the-know staff; and the most banging bar in the city (the Metro Bar,

Interlaken

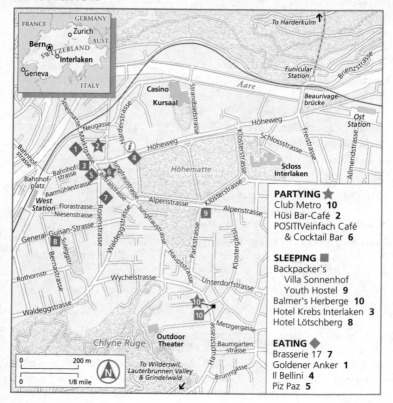

PARTYING ⭐
Club Metro **10**
Hüsi Bar-Café **2**
POSITIVeinfach Café
& Cocktail Bar **6**

SLEEPING ◼
Backpacker's
Villa Sonnenhof
Youth Hostel **9**
Balmer's Herberge **10**
Hotel Krebs Interlaken **3**
Hotel Lötschberg **8**

EATING ◆
Brasserie 17 **7**
Goldener Anker **1**
Il Bellini **4**
Piz Paz **5**

underneath the hostel) make Balmer's the primo destination for meeting other travelers. There are tents available that are even cheaper than the rooms, and they really aren't as bad as you might think, but if you really want a decent night's sleep, splurge for at least a dorm bed. Balmer's is smack in the middle of the younger, extreme sports-heavy Matten area, and even has its own activities office where you can book everything from skydiving to white-water rafting through a reputable adventure company. There's also an open-air garden with a bar open during the summer for happy hour, and a restaurant that serves decent, cheap bar food like burgers and fries. *Hauptstrasse 23–33.* ☎ *033/822-19-61. www. balmers.ch. 24F–26F tent, 24F–27F dorm, 30F–* *35F double, 27F–31F triple/quad (rates are per person per night). Rates include breakfast. Amenities: Bar; Internet; laundry services. In room: Shared bathrooms, sheets, towels.*

Doable

→ **Hotel Lötschberg** A simple, family-run hotel in a key location—the center of town and only 3 minutes' walk from the train station. Rooms are colorful, high-ceilinged, spacious, and sunny; the building is a sprawling Swiss villa dating back to the turn of the 20th century. Swiss hospitality exudes from the hotel owners, husband-and-wife team Susi and Fritz Hutmacher. If you can, try to book a room in Susi's Guesthouse across the street—it's cheaper and has the same high standards as the hotel. The hotel is entirely nonsmoking. *General Guisanstrasse 31. ☎ 033/822-25-45. www.lotschberg.ch. 92F–155F hotel double, 72F–125F guesthouse double. Rates include breakfast. Amenities: Bike rental; Internet; laundry facilities; TV (in common room). In room: TV, alarm clock (on request), hair dryer (on request).*

Splurge

→**Hotel Krebs Interlaken** This government-rated four-star lodging still manages to have a homey bed-and-breakfast feel. The lobby has a game room, fireplace, and small library, and the hotel's restaurant is a first-class place to sit and watch the action on Interlaken's main street, the Bahnhofstrasse. If you can, ask for a room on one of the top floors facing the Bahnhofstrasse—there are spectacular views of the Jungfrau from here, but the rooms are snatched up quickly by those in the know. The hotel also has its own tourism expert, a sweet Swiss gent who can hook you up with all kinds of tickets and deals. *Bahnhofstrasse 4. ☎ 033/822-71-61. 150F–250F standard single or double. Rates include full breakfast. Closed Nov–Apr. Amenities: Restaurant; bar; game room; library. In room: A/C, TV, minibar, radio.*

Eating

The incredible views and unprecedented hospitality come at a price. You won't get ripped off here—it's just that in an area as tourist-dependent as this, no one's getting away with a free lunch. And many of the best food is in the pricier hotels.

I fill up on fast food from the supermarket. For groceries, head to one of the many **COOP** stores in town—the biggest one is right across the street from the Interlaken East train station. It's a fully stocked, reasonably priced store that also carries toiletries and some cheaper clothing (see www.coop.ch for hours and more details).

Cheap

MTV (Best) →**Brasserie 17** ★ INTERNATIONAL/BAR FOOD This might feel a lot like the most popular bar/restaurant in your local college town—complete with excellent chicken wings, loud Top 40 and rock music, and wise-ass bartenders and waiters. The Brasserie offers excellent food in huge portions for (relatively) cheap, along with 20 different beers. It serves a daily special for 15F and a vegetarian option for 12F. Try anything with the Swiss cheese—especially their sample-sized fondue. Chat up the waitstaff; a lot of them are Americans and Aussies working for the cash to spend on extreme sports, so they know the ins and outs of being a backpacker in Interlaken. *At Happy Inn Interlaken Hostel, Rosenstrasse 17. ☎ 033/822-32-25. www.happy-inn.com.*

Doable

→**Goldener Anker** SWISS With classic Swiss food (stews, noodles, and cheese), in a classic Swiss environment (wood paneling and plaid, plaid, plaid), this place is a favorite for hearty meals among 20-something travelers and workers, who come to the Anker to have a beer or two and shoot some pool. Live music on Thursdays: It's hit or miss. Sometimes the bands are decent; sometimes they're really quite bad. If you try the macaroni and cheese (this is the serious Swiss-cheese stuff), I guarantee you'll never look at Kraft the same way again. *Marktgasse 57. ☎ 033/822-16-72. www.anker.ch. Appetizers 8F–10F; main courses 23F–37F; vegetarian menu 17F–28F. Mon–Sat 4pm–1:30am.*

→**Piz Paz** ITALIAN The pizza and pasta dishes at this Italian restaurant in the center of town are slightly generic, but they're big and definitely tasty. A good place to fill up on carbs and relax in the romantic, candlelit vibe. It has an inviting atmosphere with really fun, friendly waitstaff. If you're not up for a huge pasta meal, save a few bucks by ordering a smaller portion, which shaves 3F off of the price. *Bahnhofstrasse 1.* ☎ *033/822-25-33. Pasta 12F–20F; pizza 13F–20F. Tues–Sun noon–2pm and 6–11pm.*

Splurge

→ **Il Bellini** ★★ FRENCH One of Interlaken's best hotels, the Metropole, is home to one of its best restaurants. The name is deceptive—this is not an Italian restaurant, *c'est français, bébé,* with a lot of seriously fancified Swiss dishes, too. Much of the

menu's fish comes straight from the kitchen's massive tank, the menu's prime beef is from Bernese Oberland's cows, and even the homemade sorbets are flavored from the herb garden on the hotel's rooftop. Don't miss the opportunity to try some of Switzerland's wines. With more than 300 kinds available on the mind-boggling list, you're sure to find one you like. The view of the entire town from the Metropole's top floor is just one more reason the price tag is worth it. *Hoheweg 37.* ☎ *033/828-66-66. Fixed-price menu 67F–89F without wine, 99F–129F with wine. Daily 11:30am–2pm and 6:30pm–midnight.*

Partying

You might think the adrenaline-sports crowd would add a little vodka to their sugar-free Red Bulls and paint the town red as soon as the sun goes down. Alas, the geography tends to tucker people out and/or they're athletes who take their bodies seriously. As a result, the nightlife and bar scene in Interlaken is, more often than not, downright quiet. There's no shortage of people, however, looking to chill and have a beer and a chat while resting their muscles for tomorrow morning's canyon-jumping or parasailing excursion.

📺 Best → **Club Metro** ★ A party can be found daily here, below the Balmer's Herberge Hostel. Top 40, rap, and R&B thump over the crowds, and the mostly American, Canadian, and Aussie folks throw back Heinekens and swap stories about their travels. A fun time, but because it's the most popular hot spot in town, it gets pretty packed—so leave your jacket in your room. Head there to have a good time, but guys shouldn't expect a hookup: The girl-to-guy ratio is seriously uneven. *Hauptstrasse 23.* ☎ *033/822-19-61. www.balmers.ch.*

→ **Hüsi Bar-Cafè** Interlaken's hipster, international crowd heads to Hüsi. The name means "little house," and it pretty much says it all. The mix of friendly locals and tourists helps make the place cozy. Beer runs from 3F to 44F (the 44F is for the 5-liter portion) and long drinks (big old cocktails, like gin and tonic) are 10F. They also serve coffees, teas, and pizzas—perfect for snacking over a game of darts or while striking up a conversation. Definitely chill. *Postgasse 3.* ☎ *033/822-33-34. www.huesi.ch.*

→ **POSITIVeinfach Café & Cocktail Bar** A dressed-up, hotshot crowd can be found at this cafe/bar, where DJs spin smooth electronic-jazz fusion at tastefully subdued volumes for its Gucci loafer–clad clientele. Popular with local young professionals and visitors from within Switzerland and the environs—it feels a lot more Euro than some of the other American- and Aussie-dominated bars. The cocktails are pricier, but with a little luck and flirtation, you might get someone with a Swiss bank account to buy you at least one or two, right? *Centralstrasse 11.* ☎ *033/823/40–44. www.positiv-einfach.ch.*

Sightseeing & Playing Outside

The large green **Höheweg** ★★ area in the center of town covers 14 hectares (35 acres) between the two train stations. Once the property of Augustinian monks, it was turned into a park in the 19th century. Walking along the bench-lined **Höhenpromenade,** you'll get a fabulous view of the snow-covered Jungfrau Mountain. You might also get up close and personal with flushed parasailers—most of them land in the center of the park. During the summer, this entire area is literally blooming with flowers, and diners crowd the area's many street cafes.

The quick trip across the Aare River to see the **Unterseen church** is more for the view than the church itself, unless you like Gothic towers. Built in 1280 by Berthold von Eschenbach, its tower dates to the 15th century. If you stand in just the right spot, this place is great for a photo op—the tower, framed by the Monch and the Jungfrau, is one of the most beautiful sights in the Bernese Oberland.

Adventure Sports

During the winter, skiing, snowboarding, and glacier hiking reign supreme here. You can get great deals on snow sports because Interlaken's high season is actually in the summer, unlike the other, higher altitude resorts in the Alps.

Summer is when Interlaken flourishes, though. Favorite sports are bungee jumping, kayaking, canyoning, parasailing, and white-water rafting. Extreme adventure sports and adventure sport–booking companies have long been a huge draw for Interlaken, but as a few high-profile accidents in recent years have proven, just because it's popular doesn't mean it's without serious bodily risk. Even experienced adventure clubs, who plan group excursions with knowledgeable leaders and well-tested equipment, acknowledge the dangers involved in their outings. You should always use common sense, especially when choosing a company. Ask questions, lots of them. Make sure you feel you know what you're getting into, and don't just go with the lowest price.

The most experienced groups usually have certification marked by an italic s, meaning it's been labeled a member of Safety in Adventure. The below mentioned groups all have the Safety in Adventure label.

- For everything from bungee jumping to canyoning to kayaking and much more, **Outdoor Interlaken** (☎ 033/826-77-19; www.outdoor-interlaken.ch) is your place.
- The paragliding experts are at **Paragliding Interlaken** (☎ 033/823-82-33; www.paragliding-interlaken.ch).
- Watersports are the specialty at **Swissraft** (☎ 033/823-02-10; www.swissraft.ch).
- **Alpin Raft** (☎ 033/823-41-00; www.alpinraft.ch) is another leader in outdoor adventures, with daily scheduled activities from skydiving to horse trekking.

Shopping

Everything in Switzerland, and especially Interlaken, is pricey. I'd only recommend picking up novelty items, like Swiss Army knives or a Swiss-made watch, that have some sort of sentimental value by actually coming from Switzerland. One of the best touristy shops is **Heimatwerk Interlaken** (Hoheweg 115; ☎ 033/823-16-53); it stocks only things made in Switzerland.

Other stores are all along the main road, the Hoheweg, and you can find the likes of Benetton and higher-end boutiques selling Gucci and Burberry.

For sports equipment, check out **Intersport** (Postgasse 16; ☎ **033/822-06-61**).

Most **stores** are open Monday to Saturday from 9 or 10am to 6 or 7pm; some stay open on Friday to 8 or 9pm.

Road Trips

Side trips are a must for a trip to Interlaken—the Swiss train system is easy to use and well run, and Interlaken is perfectly situated as a jumping-off point to many places worth seeing.

Jungfraujoch

A train trip to the top of the [iV] [Best] **Jungfraujoch** ★★★, a glacier-covered mountain summit that is the pride and joy of the entire area, is a must for any visitor to Interlaken—it never disappoints. The ride through massively cut rock to the chilly top brings you to the a place that only hikers usually get to experience. It's the highest altitude train station in Europe (at 3,400m/11,333 ft.). A round-trip, scenic tour during the summer months (June 6–Aug 28) costs 150F. The trip involves taking a series of trains to reach the uppermost station, but your Eurail pass won't help you out here—it's run by an independent railway station. A Swiss Card that you can get at your hotel or any train station, however, knocks the price down to 96F. Departures are usually daily at 8am from the East station in Interlaken; expect to return around 4pm. To check times, contact the sales office of **Jungfrau Railways** (Höheweg 37; ☎ **033/828-71-11** or 033/828-72-33; www.jungfraubahn.ch).

Make sure you have clear weather for your trip; it's a bummer to pay that much money and have views obscured by fog or clouds. On a nice day though, the trip is well worth it. The view includes the **Mönch** mountain summit, the steep **Eiger** wall, and the **Jungfrau**, which was named for the Augustinian nuns who lived in medieval Interlaken (Jungfrau means "virgin").

You'll come into the tiny town of [iV] [Best] **Kleine Scheidegg** ★★ and switch trains there for the final ascent to the Jungfraujoch.

Once you're up at the top, there's a mini-world with cafes, restaurants, and even a post office. These places obviously have a captive audience, and are mostly kitschy, overpriced, and not very good. Bring some snacks of your own and just enjoy the view. It's fun to watch hikers returning from glacial explorations while you're cozy inside sipping tea. Make sure you bring your sunglasses—the sun gets intense—and be careful as you get used to the higher altitude—it can make you dizzy and short of breath being so high above sea level.

Meiringen

The resort town of **Meiringen** ★ lies about 13km (8 miles) from Brienz and can be easily visited on a day trip from Interlaken. Several trains headed to Meiringen stop daily at Interlaken's two railway stations. Travel time each way is about 50 minutes. And yes—Meiringen is famous for its meringue, a dessert that was invented here. Try one at any of a few local bakeries—one of the more famous is **Tea Room Luthi** (Versandbäckerei; ☎ **33/971-10-62;** www.frutal.ch). According to legend, the dessert was created when Napoleon visited the town and the local chef in charge of the welcoming banquet had a lot of leftover egg whites. In a rush, he whipped up the puffy mounds and served them to a very impressed Napoleon—and voilà, a dessert was born.

If you want to work off all that creamy deliciousness, try a hike—Meiringen is home

The Murder of Sherlock Holmes

In 1891, the English writer Sir Arthur Conan Doyle, creator of the most famous fictional detective, Sherlock Holmes, acted too hastily in killing off his hero. In a story entitled *The Final Problem*, after a battle with Professor Moriarty (called "The Napoleon of Crime"), Holmes and the fiendish villain were sent plunging to their deaths into Reichenbach Falls at Meiringen.

Although the Sherlock Holmes stories had proven successful, Conan Doyle apparently decided that he'd had enough of Sherlock's sleuthing. His rather outraged public disagreed, so Conan Doyle was forced to call back his detective from the dead, and Holmes went on to solve at least 60 more crimes.

At the upper part of the cog railway station that takes you up the mountain for the best, closest view of the spot where the water rushes down the mountain, you can find Sherlock Holmes history and even stick your face into a wooden cutout of the detective—come on, you know you want to.

The wonder of the falls is reason enough to visit the site, but Holmes devotees wanted more, so in May 1991 the town leaders opened a **Sherlock Holmes Museum** (Bahnhofstrasse 26; ☎ 033/971-42-21; www.sherlockholmes.ch) in an old, Anglican church at Meiringen. There, you can visit a re-creation of Sherlock Holmes's sitting room at 221B Baker St., in London, with exhibits donated by fans from around the world. The museum is open May through September, Tuesday to Sunday from 1:30 to 6pm, and October to April, Wednesday to Sunday 4:30 to 6pm. Admission is 4F. The cog railway leaves its station from the base of the mountain every 15 minutes daily from 8:15 to 11:45am and from 1 to 6pm mid-May to mid-September (8F). For more info, call ☎ **033/971-40-48.**

to more than 298km (185 miles) of hiking trails through unspoiled natural settings appropriate for every activity level. You can explore these on your own: The trails are very clearly marked and mapped out, and you can pick up information at the helpful **tourist office** situated opposite the train station (☎ 033/972-50-50; www.meiringen hasliberg.ch; July–Aug Mon–Fri 8am–6pm, Sat 8am–noon and 4–6pm).

Grindelwald

If you're feeling really ambitious, you can head out to **Grindelwald** ★★★, a small town that is a 27km (17-mile) hike from Interlaken and one of the greatest walks in the Jungfrau region. Along the way you can absorb the stunning panoramas of the Eiger massif, with its massive gray rock walks. Bus stops along the way can take you back to

Grindelwald, if you get tuckered out. The walk takes from 6½ to 9 hours.

Lake Thun

Lake Thun (Thunersee) ★★, about 27km (17 miles) south of Bern, was once connected to Lake Brienz (Brienzersee) and there is a frequent rail service to and from Interlaken, every 20 minutes on weekdays. Lake Thun is 21km (13 miles) long and 3.2km (2 miles) wide, and known as the "Riviera of the Bernese Oberland" for its status as a bourgeois playground and its convenience for summer watersports such as waterskiing and yachting. The area around the lake and in the resort town of Thun is home to golf courses, tennis courts, horse stables, and the like.

On a clear, warm day, a lake tour across the Thun is a great afternoon option—the

On the Trail of James Bond

Near Mürren, a village high above the Lauterbrunnen Valley, and about 30km (19 miles) south of Interlaken, rises the Schilthorn, which is famous for its 360-degree view of its neighboring mountains—and its appearance in *On Her Majesty's Secret Service,* a classic Bond thriller. You may recognize the aerial cableway and the steep slopes that in reality serve as the start of the world's longest downhill ski race.

From October 1968 to April 1969, volunteers transformed the Schilthorn into the film's "Piz Gloria." A landing pad for helicopters was constructed that was also used as a curling rink in the film and now serves as a sun terrace. Today, you can take a 20-minute cable-car ride to the top that leaves every 30 minutes from Mürren and costs 94F round-trip. For details, call ☎ **033/826-00-07.**

views of the Jungfrau (4,158m/13,642 ft.), the Mönch (4,099m/13,448 ft.), and the Eiger (3,970m/13,025 ft.) mountains are unparalleled.

A fleet of ships with a total capacity of 6,720 passengers operates on **Lake Thun** daily from April to October. A 4-hour voyage from Interlaken West to Beatenbucht, Spiez, Overhofen, Thun, and back costs 60F in first class, a little less in second class, and the boats have restaurants and bars. Your Eurail pass is valid on these boats. Similar tours are also available across Lake Brienz, but the views of the mountains aren't as good—so save your money for the Thun cruise.

Istanbul

I stanbul is the world's only city to sprawl across two continents, and its mix of traditions makes it one of the culturally richest cities in the world. Once the capital of the Christian world and then the capital of the Muslim world and the Ottoman Empire, today it's a city juggling polarities. The population is predominantly Muslim, but the government is secular; First-World attractions sit side by side with grinding poverty; and traditional values co-exist with blossoming liberal attitudes.

Istanbul started taking off as a tourist destination in the 1960s, when European hippies flocked here to sample the Silk Road way of life, and a carefree sensibility still lingers on in many of the city's quarters. Its population of around 8 million people in the city proper makes it one of the largest cities in Europe, however, and its tourist infrastructure has definitely matured over the years to keep up with this growing population. Turkey's recent push to become part of the European Union has only cemented Istanbul's status as one of the most vibrant places in Europe. The city is filled with romantic winding streets and monumental mosques and minarets, but it also boasts nightclubs, cutting-edge art galleries, and painfully cool restaurants.

The Best of Istanbul

○ **The Best Cheap Sleep:** Stay at **Bauhaus Guesthouse,** and you're guaranteed not only an inexpensive place to crash but also a chance to pick up a hottie at the bustling bar—it's hands down the best place to meet fellow travelers in the city. See p. 499.

○ **The Best Splurge Restaurant:** Housed in the penthouse of a 19th-century apartment, **360˚ Istanbul** truly lives up to the claims made by its name. The walls of the restaurant are made of clean, clear glass, which provides an unbeatable view of the city. The best part is that the food here is as good as the views. See p. 505.

○ **The Best Museum: Topkapı Palace** has room after room of spectacular treasures. Not surprising because this is where the Sultan's sinful duo of the Harem and the Treasury were once kept. See p. 510.

○ **The Best Place to Shout to be Heard:** The **Grand Bazaar** is pushy and crowded, but it's also a great time. If you're willing to haggle, you might just leave with a bargain. See p. 514.

○ **The Best Place to Park your Helicopter: Reina** simply oozes glitz, so dress up if you come here. Special allowances will be made if you are a world-famous model or if you pull up in a helicopter. See p. 506.

Getting There & Getting Around

Getting into Town

BY AIR

Flights to Istanbul originate from most airports all over the world; if not, connections are available from most major international airports. In addition, flights within Turkey are a steal—flying between Istanbul and the other major outposts within the country rarely costs more than 300TRY. Another plus? The **Atatürk International Airport** (aka Istanbul International; www.dhmiata.gov.tr) has free wireless Internet to help you kill time if you need to.

The best, cheapest way to get to the city center from the airport is by taxi. A taxi into Sultanahmet should cost around 15TRY and a ride into Taksim around 22TRY, depending on traffic and whether or not you travel the scenic route. Alternatively, **Havaş** operates a shuttle bus every 30 minutes from just outside the airport exit to both the Aksaray and Taksim neighborhoods. The fare is about 3TRY and the ride takes approximately 30 minutes, but it's still a short taxi from the drop-off point to your hotel.

BY TRAIN

If you're traveling throughout Turkey, I recommend busing unless you're taking the night train from Istanbul to Ankara. Although the bus is faster by about 3 to 4 hours, skyrocketing bus fares might make it worth your while to take the train instead. Visit www.tcdd.gov.tr for schedules and fare information.

Sirkeci Station (☎ 0212/527-0050) on the city's European side has been serving train passengers arriving into (and departing from) Istanbul from European cities for over a century, and has served as a model for railway stations throughout central Europe. A tram stop is immediately outside the station entrance, or you can grab a taxi there.

Haydarpaşa Station (☎ 0216/336-0475) in Kadikoy on the Asian side is the end of the line for trains arriving from Anatolia and elsewhere in the East; there's a ferry landing just outside the station with service throughout Turkey.

BY SEA

Years ago, the most efficient way to traverse the terrain between the Bosporus and the rest of the world was to travel by boat. Nowadays, it's one of the slowest—partially because a still-simmering grudge between the Greeks and the Turks demands that travelers submit all sorts of paperwork. Still, traveling by boat is a great way to go if you are touring the Mediterranean and don't mind allotting extra time for the visa checkers.

Long-distance ferries or the faster seabuses provide transportation to the Princes' Islands (from Eminönü and Kabataş) and to points along the southern coast of the Marmara Sea. If you're interested in traveling by car to cities along the Marmara region (that is, Bursa, Çanakkale, and points south), the easiest and quickest way is to take a car ferry or seabus from Yenikapı to Yalova (then drive to Bursa, a 50-min. trip) or from Yenikapı to Bandırma (then drive to Çanakkale or İzmir, a trip of about 1³/₄ hr.).

For information on fares and schedules for the seabuses, contact **Istanbul City Ferry Lines** (Şehir Hatları Vapurları; ☎ 0212/244-4233). For seabuses, consult the **Istanbul Deniz Otobüsleri** website (in Turkish and English) at **www.ido.com.tr**, or in Istanbul, call the automated information line at ☎ 0212/516-1212. You can also contact the port offices directly: Bostancı (☎ 0216/362-0444), Kabataş (☎ 0212/249-1558), Kadıköy (☎ 0212/336-8819), Karaköy (☎ 0212/251-6144), and Yenikapı (☎ 0212/517-7137).

Getting Around

BY CAR

Driving is not for the faint of heart. If you are set on driving, remember to check out your rental car *very carefully* before driving it. Some of the more reputable rental agencies are: **Avis** (☎ 800/230-4898; www.avis.com), **Budget** (☎ 800/527-0700; www.budget.com), and **National Car Rental** (☎ 800/227-7368; www.nationalcar.com). The rates are pretty much the same at all three, and they all have stands at the airport.

BY BUS

Municipal buses are a cheap way to get around, but you'll have to plan on about 40% more time on the bus than what you figure it would take by car. The city's modern green buses are for commuters with debit tokens only, while the used-up old orange buses are for everybody else. Tickets can be purchased from the cashier on board, and aren't usually more that 4TRY per hour of travel. Ticket sellers can also be found in the yellow canopied stalls with the bus symbol or in the blue canopied stalls throughout the city.

One of the most useful bus routes is the no. 14, which runs between Taksim and Sultanahmet about every 35 minutes, except on Sunday. The bus stop in Sultanahmet is located on Sultanahmet Park, across form the tourist info office.

Major bus companies include **Ulusoy** (☎ 0212/249-4373), **Varan** (☎ 0212/251-7474), and **Nevtur** (☎ 0212/658-1213).

BY DOLMUŞ

A dolmuş is essentially a minivan with passenger seats. The main dolmuş stands are located in Taksim, Sirkeci, and Aksaray, and connect to points all over the city. Dolmuşes are often more direct than metropolitan buses and cheaper than taxis, cutting down on time and leaving more money in your pocket. When boarding, tell the driver your destination, and ask how much it will be *("ne kadar?")*. For shorter distances, 1€ should cover it.

BY TRAMWAY

For visitors staying in Sultanahmet, the tram can be your best friend, connecting the Egyptian Spice Bazaar (stop: Eminönü) and the buses of Eminönü with Sirkeci Train Station (stop: Sirkeci), Sultanahmet (stop: Sultanahmet), and the Grand Bazaar (stop: Çemberlitaş or Beyazit) for .75TRY per ride. Token *(jeton)* booths are located at the entrance to the turnstiles, or if they're still using the antiquated paper ticket, simply drop it in the slot next to the booth.

Another tramway makes the walk along Istiklal Caddesi shorter, connecting Taksim and Tünel just when your feet are ready to fall off. This aboveground streetcar costs .25TRY, and makes stops in front of the Hüseyn Ağa Camii, at Galatasaray High School/Flower-Fish Market, and in Beyoğlu at Nutru Sokak (in front of the Turkiye Iş Merkezi). Visit www.iett.gov.tr for hours and other info.

BY METRO

The Turkish underground is surprisingly quick and relatively cheap. More akin to an underground funicular, the subway known as Tünel connects the neighborhood of the same name at the end of Istiklal Caddesi with Karaköy and the Galata Bridge for about 10TRY. Tünel trains run Monday through Saturday from 7am to 9pm and Sundays from 7:30am to 9pm. From Karaköy you can catch a bus going to Eminönü on the other side, or walk the span of this scenic bridge to connect with the tramway (or simply wander around the back streets of Eminönü and Sirkeci).

There's a relatively new railway connecting Taksim with its northern suburbs. Because there's *always* traffic on these roads, hopping on the Metro will not only save money, but also time. The Metro runs from Taksim to Levent (Akmerkez is only a short cab ride away), making stops in Osmanbey (walking distance to Nişantaşı), Şişli/Meçidiyeköy (commercial center), and Gayrettepe (more commerce). The Metro is open from around 6:30am until midnight and costs about 1.30TRY per ride. Visit www.iett.gov.tr for more info.

BY TAXI

Taxis are so plentiful in Istanbul that cabbies are more likely to hail you than vice versa. Avoid taxis that congregate around the main tourist spots like Topkapı Palace, Ayasofya, and at the cruise-ship landing in Karaköy—these are the ones adept at confusing tourists with the number of zeros on banknotes. Better to have your hotel call a cab for you. When you're out and about, simply pop into the nearest hotel and have the receptionist call a taxi for you. A taxi from Sultanahmet to Taksim will cost anywhere from 5TRY to 7TRY, depending on traffic, while nighttime rates are slightly higher.

Istanbul Basics

Orientation: Istanbul Neighborhoods

Istanbul's varying neighborhoods have one thing in common: They're all completely different. Crossing from one to another can feel like you're visiting different cities. The city's layout is dictated by two bodies of water, the Sea of Marmara and the Black Sea, which are connected by the Bosporus. European Istanbul, to the west, is further partitioned by the natural harbor known as Halic, or the Golden Horn. *Note:* Addresses in Turkey name the major thoroughfare followed by a logical walk-through of the smaller avenues until you get to the actual street address.

EURO SIDE

EMINÖNÜ   Mainly known for being the home of the **Egyptian Spice Bazaar,** Eminönü sits right at the Golden Horn in the Old City. Ships came and deposited their goods here hundreds of years ago, and the neighborhood remains a vibrant market area. This 'hood's streets are narrow and winding, so it's best explored on foot.

SIRKECI   For lack of a better analogy, Sirkeci, which extends eastward of Eminönü to the streets around the train station, is the Istanbul equivalent of Compton. It's chock-full of fun things such as electronics stores, caloric mountains of fast food, dodgy book-stores, and the tourist favorite—prostitutes. There is little benefit to staying in Sirkeci, except that the main attractions of Sultanahmet are only a few minutes' walk away.

SULTANAHMET   You can't walk more than 1 block before seeing some ancient piece of history, lodged between baklava vendors, in this hood. Unfortunately, the area's touristy sites also attract shark-like salesmen who tout everything from handbags to leather to pipes. In addition to avoiding these predatory vendors, it's best to avoid Sultanahmet at night; the entire neighborhood seems to go on lockdown when it's dark.

FATIH   In addition to being a good distance from most of the city's major sights, shopping, and food, Fatih is the most religious neighborhood in town. It also lacks hotels or hostels, so a journey here isn't necessary unless you have some special reason to come.

BEYOĞLU A monstrous neighborhood, Beyoğlu technically includes **Karaköy (Galata)**, **Tünel**, and **Taksim**, smaller neighborhoods that some claim peaked a century ago. Others say it's making a comeback: Parts have been revamped and the area now includes parks, five-star hotels, and trendy boutiques. Depending on where you go, though, Beyoğlu still retains some of the old-world charm (and sprinkling of sketchiness) that made it a stop for the wealthy patrons of the Orient Express so many years ago.

KARAKÖY (GALATA) Located right off the Galata Bridge (which, unless you have a death wish, you should avoid crossing on foot), Karaköy is home to what may actually be the oldest part of present-day Istanbul. There are several attractions here that tourists commonly overlook, such as some less famous architectural monuments. You'll also find more electronic stores, along with the hookers who seem to accompany them.

TAKSIM Centered around an enormous bronze statue of Atatürk (the father of the Turkish Republic), Taksim has a little something for everyone. Every type of person comes here, from severe, gray-clad businessmen to harlequinesque transvestites. When the sun rises, Taksim is a trendy, high-status area, crowded with designer stores and coffee shops where patrons can smoke *nargilah* pipes. At night, Taksim launches into full-scale bacchanalia—restaurants morph into clubs, gallons and gallons of the Turkish spirit *raki* are consumed, and good citizens turn bad for at least a few hours. However, the night also brings out the dregs of Turkish society: Thieves and creepy people in general seem to view Taksim as their prowling ground, so be careful.

BEŞIKTAŞ Rife with greenery, wide lanes, and palatial sultanic homes, Beşiktaş is where

wealthy tourists stop if they are staying at one of the exclusive hotels nearby and where the rest of us go if we are just passing by.

MTV Best **ORTAKÖY** What happens when a little fishermen's suburb catches the eye of rich, pretty people? Find out in Ortaköy. What used to be the cute, quaint home of fishermen has been transformed into one of those rare places that are so ostentatiously fashionable that it just might turn full circle and wind up as quaint as ever. The bill from a fish lunch will show what really lies beneath the cobblestone exterior, however. Ortaköy is also home to the two most exclusive clubs in the city: **Reina** and **Sortie.**

LEVANT Mostly a financial district at the very end of the tram line, Levant exceeds the expectation that the outskirts of the city must be the dirtiest, dingiest places in the entire area. Levant promotes their high-rise apartment buildings and hotels and urges mall-rats to come taste the mega-malls, such as **Akmerkaz.** Within a 10-minute subway ride to Taksim, or a 20-minute cab ride to almost anywhere in the city, it's a good place to stay as well as shop.

ASIA SIDE

The Asia side is a quiet and predominantly upper-class residential area interspersed with a smattering of notable mosques and synagogues. Here are two highlights:

BAĞDAT CADDESI This fashion-conscious area centers around the street Bağdat Caddesi—a wonderful place to go pick up some high-quality duds. A few bargain stores can be found, too.

ÇAMLİCA Çamlıca Hill is more of a park than a neighborhood—it's that leafy. During the summer, the tea house here is a lovely place to sit down and contemplate life—and take in great views of the city. You'll need to get here by taxi or car, as it's not possible to walk here.

Istanbul, aka Constantinople

A Short History of a City

Originally named Byzantium, Istanbul became a major shipping point when it was founded in 667 B.C. It gained international recognition when the Church split and Byzantium (renamed Constantinople, after Constantine, the first Roman emperor to convert to Christianity) became the capital of the Eastern Roman Empire in A.D. 330. Constantinople remained the seat of the Eastern Orthodox Church for roughly another 1,000 years, when Mehmet the Conqueror took the city, renamed it Istanbul, and made it the seat of a new Ottoman Empire. For centuries, the Ottoman Empire was the most powerful in the world—until the sultans became overconfident. By the end of the 18th century, the Ottoman Empire was faltering, and after World War I Turkey lost a good deal of its European and Asian provinces. The sultan was thrown from power 5 years after the war's end, which led to the formation of the Republic of Turkey in 1923. Atatürk, the new leader, effectively modernized the country by separating mosque and state, drawing up a new alphabet and language, and making every person in the Republic equal. He also moved the capital from Istanbul to Ankara.

Tourist Offices

Istanbul's tourist offices are best for having simple questions answered and getting free maps of the city because these places are generally staffed by people who don't speak English very well. Offices are located in most of the city's tourist neighborhoods. A few follow: **Sultanahmet Meydani** (☎ 0212/518-1802), **Hilton Taksim** (☎ 0212/233-0592), **Beyazit Meydani** (near the Grand Bazaar; ☎ 0212/522-4902), and at the **Karaköy Seaport** (☎ 0212/249-5776).

Recommended Websites

- ○ **www.istanbul.com**: Tons of info, photos, and other fun stuff about Istanbul.
- ○ **www.istanbulcityguide.com**: Another great place to get the inside scoop on Istanbul.

Culture Tips 101

All over town, men and women clutch their cancer sticks. Smoking restrictions, although on the rise, are very minimal. By law, you can't drink in public places, including parks.

You have to be 18 to buy alcohol or smokes, but enforcement of these laws is not so strict. As long as you have your little brown bag to cover your container, and you keep to yourself, it's unlikely you'll be disturbed. Just be reasonable: Don't start doing shots in a mosque courtyard. And all recreational drugs are illegal. You will land in jail if you're caught.

Recommended Books, Movies & Music

Before visiting Istanbul, you should read up enough to get a grasp, however tenuous, on the goings-on in the area in the last 2,000 years. Check out *A Traveller's History of Turkey* by Richard Stoneman, a great, portable overview of the country's history. *Istanbul Intrigues/a True-Life Casablanca* by Barry Rubin provides for a spot of fast-paced adventure and is a true (albeit dramatized) story about life in Istanbul. If you prefer dime-store romance, try Dora Levy Mossaenen's *Harem*, which offers a lurid look at concubine life. Lastly, Orhan Pamuk's *Istanbul: Memories and the City* (2005) offers a poetic overview of the city, told from the point of

Talk of the Town

Three ways to start a conversation with a local

Most people you talk to want to find out what you know and to show off their own culture at its best. Here are a few topics to get you started:

1. **What are your thoughts on *Midnight Express*?** Most locals think that this movie was deeply flawed, and will be happy to shed light on its errors.

2. **How about a *raki*?** Anyone will be impressed that you know about this hard-core drink, let alone that you're willing to try it.

3. **So what soccer team do you think will win this year?** Soccer is a *huge* sport here, and folks should jump at the chance to chat about it.

view of an author who had criminal charges brought against him in 2005 for criticizing the Istanbul government.

In terms of movies, you can't miss *Midnight Express,* a classic movie about drug smuggling set in Istanbul. Another classic, but far less controversial, is *Topkapı,* a fun heist-adventure story. For a more recent flick, rent anything by director Fatih Akin. I particularly like *Head On* (2004), which explores issues of arranged marriage and ethnicity within the Turkish community in Germany.

In addition, Akin's *Crossing the Bridge: The Sound of Istanbul* (2005) offers a good introduction to Turkey's myriad musical sounds, from modern electronic tunes to Arabesque (a combination of Turkish folk and Middle Eastern music) songs. The performances and interviews read like a who's who of the Turkish music scene; highlights include the rapper Ceza and Sezen Aksu (a Western-style pop singer who made it big in the 1980s).

Istanbul Nuts & Bolts

Cellphone Providers & Service Centers   The main cellphone carrier in Turkey is **TurkCell** (www.turkcell.com.tr) and once you purchase a SIM card at one of their branches, you can get refills at various city supermarkets (yes, really). TurkCell also sells and rents cellphones—they have a shop in Beyoğlu at İstikal Cad 51, Beyoğlu (☎ **0212/ 2510883**).

Currency   The Turkish currency has evened off since the massive inflation that occurred in 2002 and the conversion from the Turkish lira to the New Turkish lira in 2005. See the "Basics" chapter for conversion rates.

ATM machines can be found at all the main tourist centers and most, if not all, are open 24 hours. A **Citibank** is at Istanbul Caddesi (34/3 Fisekhane Caddesi; ☎ **0212/660- 5052**). It's open from Monday through Friday from 8:30am to 4:30pm. Or simply look for the dark blue "Yapi Kredi" 24-hour stands throughout town. A word to the wise: Some banks are not open on Sunday, so be sure you have enough cash to tide you over.

Embassies   The **Australian Embassy** is located at 58 Tepecik Yolu, Etiler (☎ **0212/ 257-7050**); the **Canadian Embassy** is at 107/3 Buyukdere Caddesi, Gayrettepe (☎ **0212/ 251-9838**). If you're from the U.K. and find you need some help, you can go to the **U.K.**

Embassy at 34 Mesrutiyet Caddesi, Tpebasi (☎ 0212/293-7540); and if you're from the U.S., get to Istineye Mahellesi, Kaplicalar Mevkii 2 (☎ 0212/335-9000) to see someone at the **U.S. Embassy.**

Emergencies   For the fire department, dial ☎ 110; for a medical emergency, dial ☎ 112; if you need the police, call ☎ 155.

Internet/Wireless Hot Spots   Internet cafes have been spreading throughout the city for the past few years, so you're bound to stumble upon 1 or 10. One of the best places to check e-mail and have a hot cup o' joe is **Gloria Jeans,** which is not, defying all logic, a store in which to buy blue jeans. Instead, it's a bit like Istanbul's version of Starbucks, with locations in all major shopping areas (Istiklal Caddesi and Akmerkaz, to name a couple). It provides free Wi-Fi to customers. Most major hotels also often have dial-up or Wi-Fi, and those that don't usually have an office area (basically a luxury computer lab) that you can use. You will usually have to pay, but it'll cost the same as Internet cafes on the street.

Laundry   The cheapest place to soak your duds is **Star Laundry** (Yeni Akbiyik Caddesi 18, Sultanahmet; ☎ 0212/638-2302). It charges only 2TRY for a kilo of laundry, and you won't have to worry about separating your white and colors because the attendant will do it for you.

Luggage Storage   A luggage storage area at the airport (☎ 0212/663-0793) charges from 9TRY per day. Most hotels will hold your bags if you are staying there, of course.

Pharmacies   If you need a pill fill, call ☎ 0212/6336-9964 to find the nearest pharmacy.

Post Offices   All post offices (called PTTs) sell stamps and most exchange currency. You can usually also buy phone cards. The post offices in the city's most touristy areas are generally open from 8am to midnight, which is good considering that you may need a whole day to wade through the lines. All post offices can be recognized by their distinctive yellow sign.

Restrooms   While most of the restrooms in this rapidly modernizing country are just what you would get at home—think gleaming porcelain and paper towels—this ancient city still has some more uncivilized lavatories. Generally speaking, the "Turkish Hole," literally, a hole in the ground, is no longer in production. Museums are a good bet if you need to go, but there are also tons of pay toilets throughout the city that charge only a nominal fee.

Safety   Istanbul's covered bazaars and Sultanahmet neighborhoods are prime spots for pickpockets, but you should be okay if you take common-sense precautions like keeping your handbag zipped tight. Also, don't leave valuables in your hotel room, unless it's in the room's safe.

Tipping   There are more people in Turkey who expect tips than in some other parts of the world. The following people generally receive tips, but if someone outside of this list is especially helpful, feel free to be generous: bellhop (1TRY–2TRY per bag), waiter (10% of check), cab driver (depending if he was fast, talkative, and/or not cheating, 4TRY, though it isn't expected), masseur (depending on the massage, 4TRY–5TRY; check ahead to see if tip is included in the *hammam* price).

Sleeping

Where you stay in Istanbul really depends on what you wish to accomplish while you are in town. If historical attractions and being a healthy, sober tourist take precedence, your best bet is **Sultanahmet.** The downside to staying here is that you'll have to deal with carpet-sellers and early morning mosque calls. If late nights fueled by drinking is more your style, check out the **Taksim** area. The catch to staying there is that the hotels and hostels are usually more expensive than those in Sultanahmet.

Note that Istanbul has special-class "hotels," or rooms in converted houses that usually go for about the same as a two-star establishment elsewhere. Ask at a tourist office for details.

Hostels

Best → **Bahaus Guesthouse** ★★
Despite the age restriction placed on patrons (you must be 15–50), this hostel deservedly earned the right to wear the reigning 2005 World Hostel crown via Hostels.com. You can choose between coed or single-sex dorms. Each day you are given a choice among breakfast, barbecue, or moonlit dinner on the rooftop terrace. The bar usually begins swinging at around 11pm. The location is excellent because it is housed far enough away from the ringing bells of carpet-sellers but it is still close enough to the sights. *Akbıyık Caddesi, 11 Bayramfirin Sokak, Sultanahmet. ☎ 0212/638-6534. 14TRY dorm, 30TRY double with private bathroom. Rates include breakfast. Tram: Cankurtaran. Amenities: Restaurant; bar; bike rentals; Internet; laundry facilities; library; lockers; luggage storage; shared bathrooms (in some rooms); TV (in common room). In room: Ceiling fans, Wi-Fi.*

→ **Chillout Hostel Café** ★ This is the only hostel in Beyoğlu. The Chillout Hostel Cafe is clean, friendly, and chock-full of backpacking party-people. That's because it's smack in the middle of the Taksim/Beyoğlu nightlife scene. In addition, it's a very healthy walk from the attractions of Sultanahmet. The breakfast is made up of mediocre Turkish food (cheese, vegetables, yogurt, and so on), but most evenings, the hostel throws a spontaneous barbecue party for guests. *Balyoz Sok. 17–19 İstiklal Caddesi, Asmalimescid Mah, Beyoğlu. ☎ 0212/249-4784. www.chillouthc.com. 15TRY dorm, 20TRY double. Rates include breakfast. Metro: Aksaray. Amenities: Cafe; Internet (with a fee); lockers; sheets; shared bathrooms.*

Hotels

→ **Cordial House Hotel** This comes across as a skeezy motel that you would find in a daytime soap opera, but don't get me wrong— it's still a good place to stay. The decor is drab, but the place is clean; the breakfast consists solely of croissants, black coffee, and some fruit, but what more could you expect at these prices? Try to book online because the prices tend to be about 20% cheaper. Want more money-saving perks for staying here? You get a discount at the **Çemberlitaş Hamamı,** only a few short blocks away, and discounted door-to-door taxi service. *Divanyolu Caddesi Peykhane Sokak 29, Sultanahmet. ☎ 0212/518-0576. www.cordialhouse.com. 8€ dorm, 36€ 4-person family room. See website for other room rates. Rates include breakfast. Tram: Çemberlitaş. Amenities: Educational activities; Internet (for a fee); laundry services; luggage storage; safe; shared bathrooms (in some rooms); tourist information center; TV (satellite and cable, in common room); Wi-Fi (free for hotel guests).*

Doable

→ **Hanedan Hotel** ★★ "Hanedan," which means "dynasty" in Turkish, is a charming little hotel with 10 rooms, organized according to the 10 different ancient civilizations that existed in or around Turkey. The

Istanbul

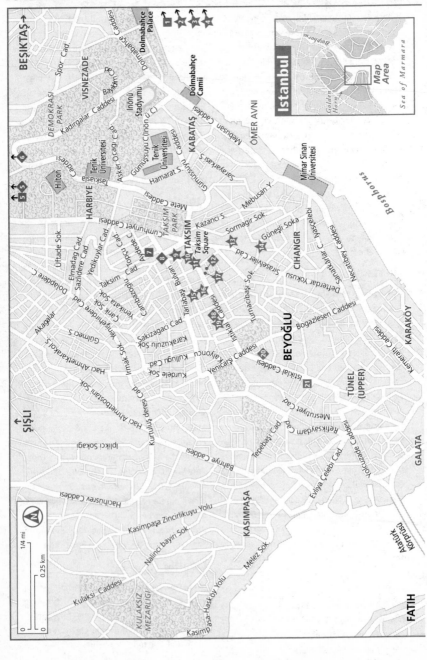

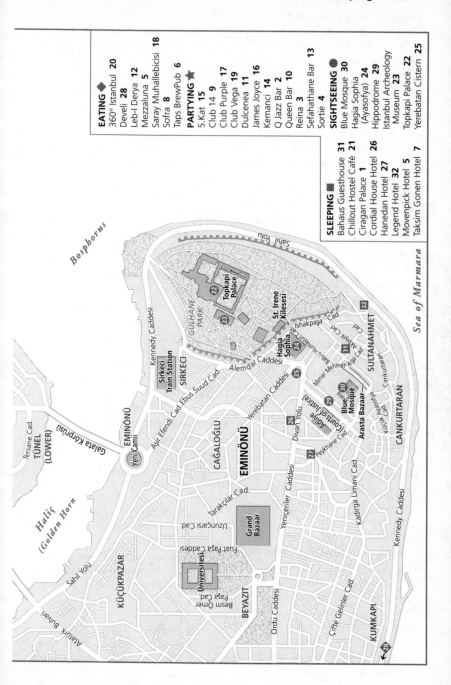

EATING ◆
360° Istanbul 20
Develi 28
Leb-I Derya 12
Mezzaluna 5
Saray Muhallebicisi 18
Sofra 8
Taps BrewPub 6

PARTYING ★
5.Kat 15
Club 14 9
Club Purple 17
Club Vega 19
Dulcenea 11
James Joyce 16
Kemanci 14
Q Jazz Bar 2
Queen Bar 10
Reina 3
Sefahathane Bar 13
Sortie 4

SIGHTSEEING ●
Blue Mosque 30
Hagia Sophia
(Ayasofya) 24
Hippodrome 29
Istanbul Archeology
Museum 23
Topkapi Palace 22
Yerebatan Cistern 25

SLEEPING ■
Bahaus Guesthouse 31
Chillout Hostel Café 21
Ciragan Palace 1
Cordial House Hotel 26
Hanedan Hotel 27
Legend Hotel 32
Movenpick Hotel 5
Taksim Gonen Hotel 7

hotel is rife with wall hangings and frescoes, and has a cobblestone terrace on the roof (where the complimentary breakfast buffet is served). The rooms have clean, white sheets and large windows. The Hanedan is known for its efficient service; they will arrange airport transfers and city tours with a guide upon request. With all this, it still manages to stay economy-priced. *Akbiyik Caddesi, 3 Adliye Sok, Sultanahmet.* ☎ *0212/516-4869. www.hanedan hotel.com. Nov 1–Apr 1 25€– 35€ single, 35€–45€ double, 45€–55€ triple, 55€–65€ family room; Apr 1–Nov 1 and Dec 20–Jan 5 35€ single, 55€ double, 65€ triple, 75€ family room. Rates include breakfast. Discount for cash payment. Tram: Sultanahmet Sq. Amenities: Breakfast terrace. In room: A/C, hair dryer, safe.*

➔ **Legend Hotel** Though it's small and has only around 40 beds, the Legend is loaded with satellite TV, free breakfast, and views of Sultanahmet. The quality of the rooms really depends on where the room is. In addition, this place is across the street from the Blue Mosque and a block from both the Hagia Sophia and the Grand Bazaar. *Peykhane Caddesi 16, Sultanahmet.* ☎ *0212/518-3348. www. hotellegend.com. From 87TRY double; call for other rates. Rates include breakfast. Discount for cash payment. Tram: Sultanahmet Sq. Amenities: Restaurant; 2 bars; car rental; concierge; currency exchange; fax/photocopy services; Internet; iron/ironing board (on request); laundry services; room service; Wi-Fi (free for guests). In room: A/C, TV (satellite), hair dryer, minibar, safe.*

➔ **Taksim Gönen Hotel** The Taksim Gönen Hotel (TGH) is full of luxury but unfortunately, it's of the unremarkable sort. The rooms are reasonably sized with yellow, brown, and white tones and marble bathrooms, but there are very few memorable effects. The location of the TGH is perfect, though: It's a 5-minute walk to the center of Taksim Square, Istiklal Caddesi, and the subway stop. An added plus is that the staff here is multilingual. *15 Aydede Caddesi, Taksim.* ☎ *0212/297-2200. www.taksimgonen hotel.com. Jan 1–Mar 31 60€ single, 80€ double; Apr 1–Dec 1 80€ single, 100€ double (Internet rates, rates are higher if you call or walk in; call for holiday rates). Rates include breakfast, taxes, and free airport-arrival transfer (must schedule ahead; 3-night minimum). Metro: Taksim. Tram: Sultanahmet Sq. Amenities: Restaurant; bar; dry cleaning/ laundry services. In room: A/C, TV (satellite), hair dryer, minibar, radio, safe.*

Splurge

➔ **Çirağan Palace** ★★★ If you're in the habit of living like a sultan, come to the Çirağan (pronounced "chee-*ran*") Palace, a converted summer home of one of the last Ottoman sultans. The guest list here says it all: The Kennedys, pretty much every royal who has existed since the 1950s, and myriad rock stars and movie stars. They probably never guessed that they were sleeping in a cleaned-up trash dump. Now, rotten fruit has been replaced with thick rugs, fancy bathrooms, and high ceilings. Ask for river views; otherwise, you'll face a noisy (albeit very green) street. Even if you can't spring for a room, stop in and walk through what is considered the most exclusive hotel in Istanbul. *Çirağan Caddesi 84, Beşiktaş.* ☎ *800/426-3135. www.ciraganpalace.com. 390€–962€ hotel rooms (depending on view and room type), 1,035€–4,871€ hotel suites (depending on suite type), 2,030€–16,237€ palace suites (depending on view, floor, and suite type). Rates include (a really good) breakfast. Metro: Taksim. Tram: Kabataş. Amenities: 4 restaurants; bar; copy center; health club; Jacuzzi; laundry services; massage; 2 pools; putting green; sauna; shopping arcade; solarium; Turkish bath; Wi-Fi. In room: A/C, TV, bathrobe/ slippers, hair dryer, Internet, minibar, newspaper (upon request), safe, scale, umbrella (upon request).*

➜ **Mövenpick Hotel** ★★ Built to cater to business travelers, the Mövenpick is the perfect den for those who love the city but want an excuse to get away from it, too. Located in the Levant neighborhood, the hotel is a 30-second walk from the subway station, and only a 25TRY cab ride to the farthest reaches of Istanbul. As if this wasn't good enough, the Mövenpick also manages to dazzle its guests with an underground spa, and a breakfast that includes custom-made omelets and sugar pastries. *Buyukdere Caddesi, 4 Levant.* ☎ *0212/319-2929. www.moevenpick-hotels. com/hotels/HKISTYY. 230€ single, 280€ double, 320€ suite . Rates include breakfast. Metro: Levant. Amenities: 2 restaurants; 2 bars; health club (with vitamin bar); Jacuzzi; jogging track; massage; 2 pools; sauna; snack bar (gourmet pastries); wheelchair friendly; whirlpool. In room: A/C, TV (cable), bathrobe, electrical adapters, hair dryer, Internet, minibar, safe, Web TV.*

Eating

Thanks to its unique location at the crossroads between three continents, Turkey's cuisine has become one of the most exciting in the world. You'll see a wide range of dishes. There's an emphasis on lamb, beef, and chicken in the interior of the country, but as you head towards the coast, the sea takes precedence. Many of the same spices and cooking methods are the same throughout the country, though; for instance, eggplant is often a main ingredient. Even if you dislike the purple vegetable, give it a chance—the Turks have many ways of preparing it, so you might find yourself surprised.

Another staple of Turkish cuisine is the appetizer round, or *mezes,* consisting of many plates of salads, spreads, sauces, and flatbread to put it all on. Mezes include a soft white cheese made from cow's and goat's milk, melon (in season), eggplant purée, and *ekmek*—very small toasted pieces of traditional Turkish bread. Baklava is the signature sweet—don't leave without trying one. Turkish delight runs a close second; otherwise known as *lekum,* this sweet candy is made of cornstarch, nuts, syrup, and an endless variety of flavorings to form a treat that takes some getting used to.

Kebaps is a national dish whose stature rivals that of pasta in Italy. Kebap, simply put, means "roasted" and denotes an entire class of meats cooked using various methods;

any type you try will make for a filling, cheap meal. Another popular street food is *kofte,* Turkey's answer to the hamburger (flat or round little meatballs served with slices of tomato and green chiles).

Turkish citizens also love their grains and vegetables. You'll come across tons of street stands selling corn on the cob, *kumpir* (a big, stuffed potato), and last, but definitely not least, *simit,* a hot, crunchy bagel-type delicacy covered in sesame seeds.

Hot Spots

➜ **Sofra** ★ TURKISH   Having made a name for itself in London, this British-based chain of Turkish restaurants waited for the right climate to open a branch on native soil. It may have been the exposure to the tastes of foreign palates that elevates traditional recipes to a more creative level: The *imam bayildi* (stuffed eggplant) comes chopped in cubes along with some unexpectedly tasty chickpeas; cinnamon sticks appear as a garnish. Other uncommon items are the *midya tava* (fried breaded mussels) and *sucuk izgara* (mild sausage). Warm weather invites diners to the spectacular roof terrace, which enjoys views of Taksim from underneath the hotel's neon sign. But even when sequestered indoors, the decor of snazzy glass plates, red textured walls, and wrought iron keeps it from feeling claustrophobic. *Tarlabasi Bulv*

ISTANBUL

36, Beyoğlu (inside the Cartoon Hotel). ☎ *0212/238-5201. Reservations required. Main courses 7TRY–10TRY. Daily noon–3pm and 7–11pm. Metro: Taksim.*

Cheap

→**Develi** ★★ KEBAPS Develi's success has translated into a blossoming of sister locations around the country, and Develi remains consistent and fabulous. For their regional specialties, they follow outstanding recipes from the Gaziantep region of southeastern Turkey—this translates roughly as "blisteringly spicy." Adventurous eaters should order the *çig köfte*, beefy meatballs combined with every spice in the book, rolled up into flat little meatballs served raw in a soothing lettuce leaf. Other notable menu items include the *muhamara*, a delectable purée of bread, nuts, and chickpeas; the *findik lahmacun*, a thin-crust pizza made Turkish-style with chopped lamb; or the lamb sausage and pistachio *kebap*. Leave room for the *künefe*, a warm slab of baklava pastry oozing cheese, dipped in syrup, and covered with crushed pistachio nuts. The rooftop terrace is stupendous in the summer, and there's a non-smoking room for indoor wintry evenings. *Balıkpazarı. Gümüşyüzük Sok. 7, Samatya.* ☎ *0212/529-0833. Reservations required. Dress smart. Main courses 5TRY–10TRY. Daily noon–midnight. From the Koca Mustafapaşa Train Station, look for the sign for Develi Otopark on the right; follow the sign and look for the fish market and the restaurant.*

→**Saray Muhallebicisi** TURKISH Although this historic restaurant (it's been around since 1935), is a small chain now, eating here doesn't feel touristy. Translated as "Rose-Water Pudding Palace," Saray Muhallebicisi serves a variety of delightful traditional Turkish sweets ranging from the namesake *muhallebicisi*, a mountain of different *baklava*, and *tulumba* (thick honey in sweet dough) to *tavukgögsü*, a sweet rice pudding made with chicken (for the daring diner).

The restaurant also serves main courses, but try to save your appetite for the desserts. Go with a group so you can sample more of the confections. *102 Istiklal Caddesi, Taksim.* ☎ *0212/534-1384. www.saraymuhallebicisi.com (in Turkish only). Meal and 2 desserts 8TRY–10TRY. Daily 24 hr. Metro: Taksim.*

Doable

→**Mezzaluna** ★ ITALIAN Widely considered to be the best Italian restaurant in Istanbul, Mezzaluna lives up to its reputation, serving steaming, flavorful plates of pasta and thin, crusty pizzas made with delicious toppings. The atmosphere is relaxed yet formal enough to feel "posh," tastefully decorated with waxing and waning moons. It can get busy, so call and make reservations. *Abdi Ipekçi Caddesi 38/1, Maçka, Nisantasi.* ☎ *0212/231-3142. Main course 13TRY–20TRY. Daily noon–11:30pm. Metro: Taksim.*

→**Taps Restaurant and Brewery** AMERICAN I was lucky. I came on a brewing day and had a warm beer. Taps is the only brewery in Istanbul, and they don't do anything halfway: The entire brewing process is visible to restaurant patrons. Beer is used in everything from chicken to onion rings. Taps seems to have taken a page out of the '50s American diner scene to create their restaurant, which has a heavy emphasis on green and brown, and boasts furniture created almost exclusively from polished wood and pleather. Even if you go for nothing other than a warm glass of beer, Taps is a great choice. Call ahead to find out their brewing days. *Sokak, 5 Tesvikiye, Nisantasi.* ☎ *0212/296-2020. www.tapsistanbul.com. Main courses 10TRY–20TRY. Mon–Fri 11:30am–12:30am; Sat–Sun 11:30am–2:30am. Metro: Taksim.*

Splurge

→**Leb-I Derya** ★★ TURKISH The best of Turkey can be found at this chic, quaint rooftop resto-bar. Serving the finest examples of Turkish cuisine, Leb-I Derya has made a name for itself among the Turkish rich and the traveling foreigner alike. Boasting views that were unmatched until 360° came along, Leb-I Derya still remains a favorite venue for those seeking escape and a taste of Turkey. It's open for breakfast, lunch, and dinner. The saffron chicken is a great choice. *Kumbaracı Yokuşu, Kumbaracı Işhani 115/7, Beyoğlu Tünel, Taksim.* ☎ *0212/293-4989. www.lebiderya. com. Main courses 30TRY–35TRY. Mon–Fri 9:30am–10pm; Sat–Sun 9am–9:30pm. Metro: Taksim.*

Best → **360° Istanbul** ★★★ CONTINENTAL Super-trendy with a super view, 360° is an excellent place to experience Istanbul at its wealthiest and most beautiful.

In the penthouse of a 19th-century apartment, 360° has walls of clean, clear glass, providing a view of the city, which alone makes it worth coming here. Fortunately, the food passes the test, though if the restaurant was a hair less posh, the names of their dishes would be laughably trashy. However, here it just seems ahead of the crowd: Order the "Bollywood Pizza" (pizza with tandoori chicken and caramelized onions) or the "Death by Chocolate: Part II" for an experience in fine dining. *Istiklal Caddesi, Misir Apt. 309, Beyoğlu.* ☎ *0212/251-1042. www.360 istanbul.com. Main courses 35TRY–40TRY. Mon–Fri noon–4pm and 6pm–1am; Sat–Sun 6pm–3am. Metro: Taksim.*

Partying

Many Westerners may think that Turkey, as an Islamic country, would have the usual prohibitions: no alcohol, no tight and/or revealing clothing, and an anti-homosexual sentiment (more on this later). This view could not be farther from the truth. When Atatürk founded the Republic of Turkey, he envisioned a modern, secular society with a clear line between mosque and state. Yes, there *are* thousands of mosques across the city, but there just may be more bars and nightclubs.

Like most cities in Europe, the night in Istanbul starts late. Dinner is usually at around 9pm, with a stop at bars afterwards, and drunken dancing only kicks into high gear around 1 to 2am.

Just Say No

All drugs will land you in prison. Even though young Turkish elite have been known to scorn the rules at times, you should not attempt to do the same. See "Culture Tips 101," above, for more info.

The traditional Turkish spirit is called *raki*—sometimes called "lion's milk" by the Turks, although this isn't a literal translation. If you order one, you will receive two glasses: both clear. One is water, the other is *raki*; you must mix them to produce a milky colored drink. Then, suck it down.

As for clothing, most young Turks have decided that they can and will wear the most current fashions, regardless of how revealing they may be. Don't worry about showing too much skin, you will probably be more clothed than many of the other guests.

Clubs

→ **Kemanci** A three-floor paradise for dancing fools, the always-packed Kemanci plays a variety of music to suit most tastes. Floor 1 plays popular worldwide hits, complete with the people who love them (read: girls with tight jeans and halter tops, and prepster guys who come to pick them up); Floor 2 has Turkish hits from the last 5 to 10 years; Floor 3 blasts hard-rock/heavy-metal music spanning the past 3 decades (lots of piercings, eyeshadow, and black clothing).

ISTANBUL

Sýraselviler Caddesi 69, Taksim. ☎ *0212/251-2723. Metro: Taksim.*

MTV Best → **Reina** ★★★ Arguably the best club in Turkey, Reina is in a constant battle with Sortie to lay claim to being the hottest, most beautiful, and most celebrity-packed club in Istanbul. It is an amazingly good time—if you can get in. Pull out all the stops to party at this venue: Yes, I am talking about anything with a designer label. You will also need to spend money: Drinks are 7TRY to 10TRY each. If you haven't got the clothing, go early to eat at one of the eight multicultural restaurants inside and then just walk down the stairs to the club. You'll hobnob with the crème de la crème of Turkish society, listen to a playlist of Turkish pop and remixed American music, and also see one of the most amazing sights in the world: the bridge that links Europe to Asia. *Muallim Naci Caddesi 44, Ortaköy.* ☎ *0212/259-5919. www.reina.tr. Cover 40TRY. Take the rail to the Taksim stop and either take a cab from there or walk past the Hilton, make a left at the mosque and continue to the club. Metro: Taksim. Tram: Kabataş.*

MTV Best → **Sortie** ★★ As hip as Reina, but possibly harder to get into. In the ongoing "club war" between Reina and this place, youth, wealth, and beauty are valued above all else; Sortie completely pulled out of the running for a few months, totally changed everything about the club, made it harder to get into, and re-opened in June 2005. It is once again neck-and-neck with Reina for the hip crown. If you somehow finagle your way past the discriminating bouncers, you'll find inside a waterfront paradise populated by about 400 men who hold 99% of Turkey's wealth, their friends, and their legions of Barbie-look-alike "daughters." The music here is also almost the same as it is in Reina. Once you are in, everyone is friendly because you're all part of the same ironclad clique. But again, you must stick to the dress code: Unless it costs more than most computers,

don't wear it. *Kuruçesme Caddesi 57, Ortaköy.* ☎ *0212/293-4110. Cover 50TRY (includes 2 drinks). Metro: Taksim. Tram: Kabataş.*

Bars & Lounges

→ **Dulcenea** This little emporium houses anything the intellectual could want (well, except Fri–Sat). Opening at 10am, Dulcinea starts out as a cafe and then turns into a restaurant for the lunch and dinner crowd. At 10pm, the bar opens. On Friday and Saturday nights, the space is handed over to amateur DJs who turn the bar into a "club experience." On these nights, the bar is packed with young people who love trance and techno but don't want to pay for the more expensive, exclusive clubs that play that type of music. *Istiklal Caddesi, Meşelik Caddesi 20, Beyoğlu.* ☎ *0212/245-1071. www.dulcinea.org. Metro: Taksim.*

→ **5.Kat** A casual bar/club/restaurant, 5.Kat caters to a liberal, bohemian type of crowd, attracting artists, writers, and actors from across Istanbul. You may not even notice them, though, with the stunning 5.Kat (meaning fifth floor) view, which takes in the modern high-rises of Istanbul and the primeval beauty of the Bosporus and Golden Horn. The restaurant here is equally stunning: Meals are cooked (in the bohemian spirit) by one of Turkey's famous theater actresses, Yasemin Alkaya. *Siraselviler Caddesi, Soğanci Sokak 7, Taksim.* ☎ *212/293-3774. Metro: Taksim.*

→ **James Joyce** Though it's named for the famous Irish author, I would wager that few of the people who drink here have actually heard of the man. Like every other Irish bar the world over (except for those in Ireland), James Joyce seems to think that serving barrels of Guinness, lots of wood and brass, and some pictures depicting Irish history (I think they were of the potato famine) make for an Irish bar. But despite being completely inauthentic, James Joyce still guarantees a very good time, with packed crowds of American and English expats swilling beers (6TRY each) and imported drinks (10TRY) in the relaxed space. *Zambak Sokak 6, Istiklal Caddesi, Beyoğlu.* ☎ *0212/244-0241. Metro: Taksim.*

→ **Q Jazz Bar** Alcohol flows like water in the hallowed halls of the opulent Çirağan Palace (p. 502)—but so will your cash. This bar inside the famous hotel is undoubtedly beautiful, with a decor that can best be described as glitzy. There are rarely empty seats, so come early unless you want to contend with the rich Turks who will tell you off with snobby, broken English competing for a table. During the summer, Q hosts barbecues where you can view the Bosporus is its full glory; during the winter, the scene moves indoors and underground. *Çirağan Palace, Beşiktaş.* ☎ *0212/236-2121. Cover 15TRY; free for hotel guests. Metro: Taksim. Tram: Kabataş.*

→ **Sefahathane Bar** An odd exercise in crosscultural nightlife, Sefahathane Bar attracts artists, students, emo kids, rockers, and general malcontents, but it won't let the differences get in the way of having a good time and meeting other people. The big draw? A gigantic video screen in the back, which plays some of the strangest movies I have ever seen. One regular screening is for *The Man Who Saved the World,* a Turkish cult classic that includes scenes taken directly from the *Star Wars* series. I wasn't there for a screening, but the other patrons spoke glowingly about it. *Istiklal Caddesi, Atlas Pasaji 209, Taksim.* ☎ *251/22-45. Metro: Taksim.*

Gay Nightlife

Simply put, Istanbul has a rollicking gay scene. Maybe it's a remnant left over from Ottoman times when homosexuality was just another part of life, but while other Islamic countries have tried to repress the scene, Turkey just lets loose. The transsexual community is thriving here and most of the city's gay bars have drag shows at some point during the week.

Istiklal Caddesi, the street that runs from the Taksim subway station all the way to the chic Tünel area, is the main place to go out to bars and the city's more moderately priced clubs. During the day, it is a designer street crammed with name-brand stores. At night, it becomes a haven for the young, and is also ground zero of the Istanbul gay scene. On that note, a word of advice for all of the young men reading this: Don't walk around here at night by yourself if you don't want attention. You *will* get strange men coming up and coming on to you, and often they do not respond to a simple no.

→ **Club 14** You never know what you'll hear next at this Taksim club, and rarely is a playlist repeated. Why? Because the music in the club is played off an FM radio station 2019. It can sometimes feel like a high school dance with alcohol, due to the complete lack of frills, but the lively atmosphere, friendly staff, and a young crowd keeps this club hopping well into the morning. *Abdulhakhamit Caddesi 14, Belediye Dukkanlari, Taksim.* ☎ *0212/256-2121. Metro: Taksim.*

→ **Club Purple** This place fulfills a real need for an upscale gay club in the city, with some very skilled bartenders. The DJ changes nightly, and the crowd is eclectic, in a wealthy sort of way. Customers here are not exclusively gay; some couples and single women come here to avoid the catcalls and harassment prevalent at the city's other bars. *Istiklal Caddesi, Mis Sokak 20, Beyoğlu.* ☎ *0212/245-8933. Cover charge (weekends only) 10TRY. Metro: Taksim.*

→ **Club Vega** ★ With drinks this cheap, it's a wonder that they keep the white decor here so spotless. Club Vega makes generous use of mirrors to give the feel of a much larger space. Use them to your advantage to discreetly scan the crowd as you buy a drink, starting at 5TRY for beer on tap; fancy drinks of the coconutshell variety generally do not rise above

ISTANBUL

10TRY. *İstiklal Caddesi, Sadri Alişik Sokak 19, Beyoğlu.* ☎ *0212/251-8925. Metro: Taksim.*

➜ **Queen Bar** Billing itself as the "only exclusively gay" gay bar in Istanbul (a label that is not entirely true), Queen Bar does try its darnedest to cater to upscale patrons who come in search of a flaming good time. Wednesday nights are "show nights," although rarely will you know what the show will be until the very moment it starts. The drinks are about the same as at any of the other bars in the area (5TRY–15TRY) but because the owner has been in the business for well over a decade, you can expect fun at every turn. *İstiklal Caddesi, Zambak Sokak 23. Taksim.* ☎ *0212/249-2397. www.queenbar.net. Metro: Taksim.*

Performing Arts

To get the scoop on what's happening in town, check out the English/Turkish monthly *Istanbul Kültür Sanat Haritası* (Istanbul Map of Culture and Arts), which covers new exhibitions, movies, books, and galleries. If you want to know what the latest local and global fuss is, get a copy of *Turkish Daily News* (www.turkishdailynews.com), written in crisp British English.

When you need a hit of opera, ballet, or classical music, head to Beyoğlu, to **AKM** (Taksim Sq.; ☎ **0212/251-56-00**). The quality of events in this modern opera house is excellent and ticket prices are absurdly low—they start at 5TRY. The open space in front of AKM is also the number-one trysting spot in the city. For movie theaters head to Istiklal Caddesi to see a made-in-Burbank release.

During the summer, AKM hosts the International Film and Music festivals. See "Festivals," below, for more info.

Sightseeing

History is not something to sit back and look at here; it's a living part of everything you see and do. On an ordinary bus ride, you'll pass Roman arches, spectacular Ottoman mosques still used for prayer, and 1,000-year-old fountains that children still drink from. Unless otherwise stated, all the places below (except Kariye Museum and Galata Tower) are around Sultanahmet Square, and within easy walking distance from each other.

Festivals

April

International Istanbul Film Festival. The best and brightest come out to play in this film festival (at Istiklal Caddesi 146, Beyoğlu) that celebrates the Turkish silver screen. Call ☎ **0212/334-0724** for more info. Early April.

June & July

International Istanbul Music Festival. Music performances representing the worlds of opera, jazz, classical music, and ballet are held at various locations around the city. For schedules, dates, and tickets, contact the Istanbul Foundation for Culture and Arts (☎ **0212/293-3133**; www.istfest.org). Throughout June and July.

October

International Arts Biennale. The Istanbul Foundation for Culture and Arts (see above for phone and website) puts on this major visual-arts event organized around a current political or philosophical theme. Artists are selected from over 45 countries, and displays are exhibited in venues like the Yerebatan Cistern. Third week in October.

Cumhuriyet Bayrami (Republic Day). This event celebrates the proclamation of the Republic of Turkey in 1923. Parades, public speeches, and firework displays are just a few of the organized events. October 29.

Top Attractions

FREE → **Blue Mosque** ★★ Impossible! This is what everyone told the man who built this fantastic structure, which looks like it would be more at home in the lost city of Atlantis than in modern day Istanbul. Built between 1609 and 1617 by Sultan Ahmet I, the Blue Mosque inspires people. The completion of the Blue Mosque meant drama. Look at the top of the mosque; you can count six minarets rising gracefully up into the sky. Faux pas, Sultan Ahmet I! The Ka'aba in Mecca also had six minarets at the time, and many took this as a sign that Ahmet was equating the holiness of Istanbul with that of Mecca. Fortunately, a solution presented itself: They built a seventh spire on the Ka'aba.

The word "blue" is used to describe the mosque because most of the decoration was created with either blue or sea-green Iznik tiles. Originally, the mosque was covered with them, but some fell off with age, others were damaged, and still others were sold. Dress conservatively while visiting the mosque; women and men will be given a blue sheet to cover up with (girls, you need to conceal your hair completely). Try to avoid visiting during prayer time; if you hear the call to prayer, wait an hour and then go. *Sultanahmet. Free admission. Daily 9am–6pm. Tram: Sultanahmet.*

MTV Best → **Hagia Sophia (Ayasofya)** ★★ Built by Constantine in A.D. 537, this was considered the hugest church ever until the 16th century. About 500 years after the church was completed, the crusaders stripped the church of all of its valuable relics, including the altar. What damage they did not cause was later wrought by a series of earthquakes, which caused the dome to collapse several times. When the Turks took control, they converted the structure into a mosque and reinforced it in 1453, effectively erasing all iconic images (the Koran forbids human images). Please keep in mind that although the Ayasofya is currently a museum, it started out as a religious building and remained one for over 1,500 years. That means no hot pants. *Sultanahmet.* ☎ *212/522-1750. Admission 18TRY. Tues–Sun 9:30am–4:30pm. Tram: Sultanahmet.*

FREE → **Hippodrome** ★ You can't help but pass through the Hippodrome on your way to the Ayasofya or the Blue Mosque—you just may not know that you are walking through it. The second largest hippodrome in the entire world (after the Circus Maximus in Rome), it was built in A.D. 203 for some fun weekend activities like chariot racing, boxing, and wrestling (Six Flags wasn't around yet, I guess). Dignitaries brought their own personal touches to the arena, as you'll see if you take the time to look at the three obelisks that stand in the center. The **Egyptian Obelisk** was erected at around 1500 B.C. by the Egyptian Pharaoh Tuthmosis III. Made from pink granite, the obelisk stood 27m (89 ft.) high, but was broken when it was brought to Constantinople in A.D. 390 (apparently it didn't go with the sand). The Emperor Constantine built the **Constantine Column** in the 4th century. It stands 32m (105 ft.) high and was originally covered with shiny brass, but in A.D. 1204 the brass was melted down for coins. The oldest of the columns is the **Serpentine Column.** Built in the mid-400s B.C., it was donated to the Oracle at Delphi after the Greek city-states won their war against the Persians. The names of the 31 city-states are carved into this 5m (16-ft.) column, which at one time featured three golden snakes. Two of the snake heads have been found; one resides in the **Istanbul Archaeology Museum** and the other in the British Museum. *At Meydanı (Horse Plaza), Sultanahmet. Free admission. Daily 24 hr.*

→ **Yerebatan Cistern** A deliciously creepy escape from the summer heat, the Yerebatan Cistern was constructed by Emperor Justinian in the 5th century because he was worried that the city might experience drought. By transporting water from all over the empire (well, from the Black Sea mostly), this water cistern functioned right up until the Turks invaded and the water was diverted to the Topkapı Palace Gardens (located a block away) instead. Eventually, probably because they had so much going on (collapse of the empire, and so on), the sultans stopped using this source, and it wasn't used again until 1987 when city officials decided to reopen it. The collected dirt and grime has been swept aside to reveal a mysterious space complete with bridge-like walkways, high columns (salvaged from Greek and Roman ruins), and some pretty dim lighting. At the far end of the walkway here, you'll find two mysterious Medusa heads—archaeologists haven't yet determined their origins. *Yerebatan Caddesi (diagonal from St. Sophia), Sultanahmet.* ☎ *0212/522-1259. Admission 11TRY. Wed–Mon 9am–5pm. Tram: Sultanahmet.*

Museums

→ **Atatürk Museum** Mustafa Kemal lived in this house for a year while he was staying in Istanbul before the War of Independence, and because he is considered one of the greatest of the Turks (hence the moniker, Atatürk, which means "Father of the Turks") they converted the house into a museum dedicated to him. Inside you will find a range of artifacts from Atatürk's life, including baby pictures, clothing, writings, painting and other personal belongings. It's a small museum and it's usually pretty empty, so you shouldn't have a problem navigating it at your own pace. *Halaskargazi Caddesi, Sisli.* ☎ *0212/236-4844. Tues–Sun 8:30am–noon and 1–5pm. Metro: Fatih.*

→ **Istanbul Archaeology Museum** Built at the end of the 19th century by the Turkish architect Valluary and supported by the famous Turkish painter Osman Hamdi Bey (like the subway stop), this museum was not used until 1917. Now it houses a very old, very impressive collection of ancient Greek, Roman, Anatolian, Babylonian, Sumerian, Assyrian, and Egyptian artifacts—in other words, the artifacts of all Semitic peoples that have existed for the last 6,000 years. One of the most interesting exhibits is the collection of sarcophagi: One on display is said to have been Alexander the Great's, whose burial site has never been found. *Topkapı Palace (to the right of and behind St. Irene).* ☎ *0212/520-7740. Tues–Sun 9:30am–4:30pm. Tram: Sultanahmet.*

Ⓜ️ **Best** → **Topkapı Palace** ★★★ If you haven't noticed it by now, the sultans liked to live it up in ways that even the most bling-happy rapper couldn't fathom. Still need proof? The Topkapı Palace should convince you of the sultans' decadence. The sprawling palace grounds could easily contain a small town, which is essentially what the palace was. Just 1 of the 20 elegant buildings here is around 10 times the size of the average home. Then there are the extras: Delicate carvings and careful filigree on the walls and ceilings attest to the craftsmanship of the sultans' artisans, as do the vibrantly colored sultans' garments that are arrayed in glass cases. And the jeweled memorabilia—from the Topkapı dagger to the Spoonmaker's Diamond, the fifth-largest diamond in the world—rivals the Smithsonian's coffers in the sheer weight of precious stones on display. You'll also be able to view a range of artifacts that most people have only read about in the Old Testament, New Testament, or the Koran, such as a Staff of Moses (debatably real, but not as strange as the finger/toenails of Mohammed or pieces of Christian saints on display).

If you're feeling promiscuous after viewing so much glitz, the **Harem** is a short walk away, and at only 12TRY, you get a much better deal than the previous inhabitants, who gave up their lives to enter this enclave. If all of this mesmerizing opulence has instead made you hungry, treat yourself to lunch at

12 Hours in Istanbul

Hanging out in Istanbul without spending money is a tricky business, indeed. But it can be done, provided you like the outdoors and you like to walk. My personal favorite place to hang out is the **Ortaköy** neighborhood in the mid-to late afternoon. No cars, worn black cobblestones, and many trees join together to form an extremely pleasant place. If you can't find anything to do, just start walking. Istanbul is full of lovely little parks, unrecognized statues, and other random things of interest. Strolling around the city's alleyways or through the little handicrafts markets is a particularly excellent way to pass the time.

1. **Walk the Istiklal Caddesi.** Stroll along this pedestrian street from Taksim and take in the neo-Gothic churches, cafes, consulates, cinemas, and gaggles of people.

2. **Go back in time.** Archaic, Hellenistic, Roman, Byzantine, Ottoman—pretty much all the cultures that made this city find their place in **the Istanbul Archaeology Museum.**

3. **Take a merry ferry.** Cross to the other side (Asia side) just for the hell of it. Act incognito: Have some tea and *simit* (a type of sesame bagel) and pretend you're a local.

4. **Go to the Aganigi Naganigi.** During the day, the Sirkeci area by the train station is one of the busiest spots in the world. Walk over to the Spice Bazaar and take a whiff.

5. **Experience the quintessential Bosporus.** Take a walk or jog on the Europe side of the Bosporus shore, from Remelihisar northward. Buy some fish and some bread on the shore to finish you off.

6. **See the Galata Tower.** One of the best views of the city. Pay tribute to the guy (Ahmet) who glided with giant wings from the top of this tower to the Asia side. As a reward for his scientific and courageous achievement, he was jailed by the sultan. The tower is at Sisane (☎ **0212/245-1160;** daily 9am–1am).

7. **Shop till you drop.** Haggle the rest of your afternoon away at one of the city's many markets.

8. **Take sides in the club war.** Cap off your day with a night at either **Reina** or **Sofia** (see "Clubs," above). Decide for yourself which place deserves to lay claim to being the hottest nightclub in town. If you'd prefer less of a scene, head to the much cheaper, but still cool, **Kemanci.**

the **Topkapı Restaurant,** where you can either eat at the cafeteria with the peons, or feel like royalty at the raised restaurant. *Sultanahmet, entrance at the end of Babuhumayun Caddesi, behind the Ayasofya.* ☎ *0212/512-0480. Admission to the palace 14TRY; separate admission for both the Treasury and the Harem 12TRY each. Wed–Mon 9am–5pm (Harem closes at 4pm). Tram: Sultanahmet.*

The University Scene

Istanbul University, one of the oldest universities in Europe (it was founded in 1453), sprawls over five campuses. The main campus is in Eminönü (Universitesi Center Campus; ☎ **0212/440-0000**). Seeking out local students around here shouldn't be a problem, due to the sweet-natured local addiction to coffee houses. One such place in Beyoğlu, **K.V.** (Tünel Gecidi 10; ☎ 0212/251-43-38; daily 9am–9pm), is full of ornamental distractions: a sphere glowing with cosmic light in one corner, purple old-lady shoes in another. Sit here for hours and suck in that Turco-European air. Another option is **Hisar** (bus: 40 from Taskim to Rumelihisar), a sidewalk overlooking a small pier; the under-35 crowd

that gathers here is mostly affiliated with the American-style Bogazici University up the hill, so language isn't going to be a problem.

If you are interested in mastering a little Turkish during a summer visit, you can enroll in language classes at **The Language Center** (Bogazici University; tlcp@boun.edu.tr; www. boun.edu.tr/special/web.html). Classes run about 3,700TRY for a short semester.

Playing Outside

Istanbul is not the most active of cities—unless you count wandering around its steep hills as exercise. Hardy outdoor types looking for a hard-core adventure tour may want to check out **Atölye Mountaineering & Climbing** in Ortaköy (Muallim Naci Caddesi 65–67; ☎ 0212/236-0595; www.atolye.org). The club features a climbing wall in the shop along with a professional-grade wall in the cafe next door (daily 9am–11pm; about .40TRY per hour). The club also hosts rock-climbing and mountaineering activities. **Bird-watchers** should also take note: As the crossroads for multiple continents, Turkey is an ideal laboratory of migrating species. For more information, contact the **Natural Wildlife Protection Association** (Doğal Hayatı Koruma Demeği; P.K. 18 Bebek/ Istanbul; ☎ 0212/279-0139).

To say that **soccer** is a popular sport in Turkey is to miss the point entirely. Soccer is

closer to a religious experience; club rivalries are waged with an intensity comparable to the holy wars. The three main soccer clubs in Istanbul are **Fenerbahçe, Beşiktaş,** and **Galatasaray,** the last of which owns its own private island club in the middle of the Bosporus. Main matches are played from late August to May on Friday, Saturday, and Sunday nights at 7pm. (A few late-summer matches are played at 8pm.) Tickets are available at the stadium the day of a match, but for more popular matches, they're a bit harder to come by, and you'll have to contact the ball club directly for advance tickets. Home matches are played every other week at **Inönü Stadium,** above Dolmabahçe Palace, for Beşiktaş; at **Alisami Yen,** in Mecidiyeköy, for Galatasaray; and at **Fenerbahçe Stadium,** near Kadıköy on the Asia side, for Fenerbahçe.

Shopping

Istanbul is one of those cities that has everything: If you want it and can pay for it, you can get it. The city is most known for its expensive jewelry, soft leathers, and, of course, rugs. Just be prepared to haggle. **A hint on haggling:** Decide on a price you feel is appropriate, deduct 20%, and use that as your starting price. Stay at that price until the vendor looks disgusted and turns away, and then sigh and go up to your price minus

10%. With your "renewed" interest the dealer should go lower. If he finds a price and starts sticking to it, shake your head sadly and start to walk away. When he shouts at you with a new, lower price, come back and tell him you can go no higher than your desired price. If he doesn't give it to you, go to the stall next door—they are bound to have it.

The hours for modern high-rise shopping centers are usually 10am to 9pm, and unlike the bazaars and markets, stores open and

Taking a Hammam

The Turkish bath, or *hammam,* is one of the best things that the Ottomans gave the world. The mechanics are simple: A circular chamber with a domed roof is heated from under the floor, while water is constantly splashed in to make the room steamy. There are marble fountains on the sides of the chamber that spew cool, clear water, and at some *hammams,* you might use the same white copper instruments (for rinsing) from hundreds of years ago. On arrival, you are given a choice: You can just chill at the bath, get a massage, get a rubdown, or do all three. I recommend all three. Just be sure to keep yourself hydrated.

Cağaloğlu Hamamı This is the oldest working *hammam* in the city and, with 3 centuries under its belt, it's still going strong. Still, it's definitely lacking some important things—there isn't a credit card machine, the prices are somewhat higher than some of the other *hammams* in town, and the massages and/or rubdowns are less than impressive. Good thing the baths are housed where they are, under a giant, latticed dome that really showcases the stars. There is a bar and cafe/restaurant on the premises. *Cağaloğlu, Sultanahmet.* ☎ *0212/ 522-2424. info@cagalogluhamami.com.tr. 19TRY bath, massage, and scrub. Daily 8am–10pm (men only 8–10pm).*

Çemberlitaş Hamamı ★★ One of the few *hammams* in the city that takes Visa, the Çemberlitaş is located a stone's throw away from the Grand Bazaar, Yerebatan Cistern, and other assorted sights. The massage here is amazing, and the glove-rubdown made my skin glow. Even better are the prices; services here are better than the other places reviewed. *Vezirhan Caddesi 8, Çemberlitaş, Sultanahmet.* ☎ *0212/522-7974. www.cemberlitashamami.com.tr. 32TRY bath, massage, and scrub. Daily 6am–midnight.*

ISTANBUL

close at these times. Markets open considerably earlier (around 6am) to make allowances for the people who need to buy breakfast supplies, and they usually wind down at around 7pm.

Shopping Malls & Markets

➔ **Akmerkez Shopping Center** A massive, ostentatious show of capitalism at its best (or worst?), the Akmerkez is a mall that everyone cannot help but love. Winding circles, shiny-floored alleys, and layers and layers of fashionable designer wear form this behemoth shopping center. Housed in the neighborhood of Etiler, the Akmerkez Shopping Center is not just known in Turkey. It has been named the best mall in Europe, and if you go, you will likely see why. It's easy to get lost amid all the shops: Keep your eyes on the mall maps, and if you lose sight of those, check with one of the English-speaking staff members. *Nispetiye cad. Ulus–Etiler.* ☎ *0212/ 282-0170. www.akmerkez.com.tr.*

➔ **Cevahir Shopping Center** The Cevahir Shopping Center, called CSC by those in the know, opened on October 15, 2005, as the second-biggest mall in the entire world (at 39,019 sq. m./420,000 sq. ft.). Even the clock on the ceiling is the largest in the world. Complete with an IMAX theater and a roller-coaster, not to mention 280 stores and a two-floor food-and-beverage court, this hulking giant took a long 16 years to build. After spending a few hours walking the boulevards, though, you may wonder whether those 16 years were really worth it. Size isn't

Carpet Bagging

If you are looking for a carpet or *kilim*, *do not* try to buy one in the Grand Bazaar. The salesmen here often sell carpets that are not even made in Turkey for prices that would bankrupt a sultan. Also, do your research so that if you see something that you like, you'll know how much it should cost. There are a wide variety of carpets available, made with many different types of threads, patterns, and weaves. If you can learn to discern between the different pieces from different parts of the country, you'll get a better carpet.

everything, after all, especially when a place is as soulless as this. *Büyükdere Caddesi 22.* ☎ *0212/233-1191.*

→ **Egyptian Spice Bazaar** ★ Yes, it is as fancifully exotic as it sounds. This is one part of Istanbul that has withstood the test of time. Located on the sea at the Golden Horn, the Spice Bazaar was once the first place merchants would go to unload their wares from across the globe. Now, the exact same thing happens, just with better technology. Sold by weight, the spices found here are fresh and often rare. Kind of like a sister to the Grand Bazaar, the Egyptian Spice Bazaar is the place

to go for food-related purchases. It's easy to wander through the Spice Bazaar for hours on end, spending change on the succulent baklava and other scrumptious goodies on hand. The only advice I have for you is to go hungry, and bring a lot of change (and an open mind). *Mısır Çarşısı in Eminönü. Mon–Sat afternoons.*

MTV Best → **Grand Bazaar** ★★ Sure, it looks like your run-of-the-mill covered market, but in reality it is so much more. The Grand Bazaar is like a world in and of itself, where the kaleidoscope of products makes heads spin. If you want it, you can find it here. A word to the wise, though: You only have two options within these walls. You can either pay exorbitant amounts of money for something that is sold all across the city, or you can haggle to get what you want. Also remember that most of the things on sale at the Bazaar are fakes—such as the carpets, "authentic" antiquities (which are illegal to take out of the country, anyway), and the omnipresent designer bags. *Best entrances through the Beyazit Gate (across from the Beyazit stop on the tramway along Divanyolu) and the Nurosmaniye Gate (from the Çemberlitaş tramway stop on Divanyolu, follow Verizhani Caddesi to the arched entrance to the mosque grounds, which lead to the bazaar). Maps of the bazaar are available at newsstands. Mon–Sat 8:30am–7pm.*

Road Trip

Okay, so it isn't technically a day trip. You'll want to stay more than a day in Bodrum so that the 4 hours it takes to get here are worth it. Sunshine; loads of tan, attractive Turks; and a raging nightlife—**Bodrum** claims to be home to the largest discothèque in the entire world, **Halikarnas**—make this a summer hot spot. It's virtually dead in wintertime, though.

There are many ways to get to this outpost on the Sea of Marmara. **Turkish Air** (☎ 0252/

536-6597) flies here in the summer just about every hour for under 200TRY. You can drive, but due to the unstable road situation (treacherous cliffs), I wouldn't advise it. There are also buses (around 30TRY); **Pamukkale** (☎ 0252/315-1369) is one bus company that runs the length of the area, but I recommend you fly. It's only around a half-hour flight, and the other 3½ hours saved can be spent on the beach.

ᴍᴛᴠᵁ Summer School in Bodrum

So the sun, sea, and tsunamis of umbrella-ed alcoholic drinks just aren't doing it for you? Feel the need to enrich your life? Bodrum offers a rich selection of courses for all types. Aura feeling cloudy? Take the 7-day **yoga/meditation** class, which should center you in no time. And it'll only cost you about 1,000TRY for accommodations, breakfast, and four dinners (www.yoga turkey.co.uk).

Can't stop thinking about swimming? Take a 4-day **PADI dive course** instead! Check out www.padi.com to choose from the 11 dive shops in Bodrum.

If those classes still won't quell the Lara Croft/Indiana Jones in you, **The Bodrum Museum of Underwater Archaeology** occasionally offers courses on archaeology. Contact them for more info at ☎ 0252/316-2516, or visit www.bodrum-museum.com.

Sleeping

CHEAP

➔ **Hotel Gulec** The cheapest room in town is not necessarily the dirtiest. This place is very basic, from the simple breakfast to the spartan rooms. There is a monstrous garden in back, and the pool at the nearby Delphi Hotel is open to Hotel Gulec guests. *Uc Kuyular Caddesi 18/A.* ☎ *0252/316-5222. 30TRY double, 740TRY suite. Rates include breakfast. Amenities: Bar; TV (in common room).*

SPLURGE

➔ **Marmara Bodrum** Yes, it's expensive, but how can you not love the New Age bathroom doors (yes, they are clear, but magic happens when you lock them) and the sleekly designed rooms that combine classical white with shiny black and bamboo? The panorama from the windows gives guests insight into the tiny white stucco homes on the oceanfront and the vendors who love to tout their fish and meats. The Jacuzzi and pool are awash with beautiful, rich Turks, and the *hammam* inside is warm and classic. The staff here is superbly professional. *Yocusbasi Mevii, PK 199.* ☎ *0252/313-8130. www.bodrumhotels.com/themarmara/index.htm. 490TRY double. Rates include breakfast. Amenities: Restaurant; bar; business center; concierge;* health club; Internet; Jacuzzi; laundry and dry cleaning services; lounge; pool; room service; salon; sauna; shock showers; spa; squash court; tennis court, Turkish bath. In room: A/C, TV, balcony or terrace, Internet, minibar, safe.

Partying

➔ **Halikarnas** ★ Even if it isn't the biggest nightclub in the world, it definitely qualifies as one of the most extravagant. Built to hold 5,500 people, Halikarnas boasts three monstrous pillars that would not be out of place in one of the Seven Wonders of the World (one of which sits quite close). Famous pop stars perform regularly, and the club sponsors theme nights a few times a week (Foam Party, Free Beer Night, Ladies Night) attracting scantily clad people of all ages to bask in the laser show that happens around midnight. Better hope you get here between April and October 'cause it's closed for the remainder of the year. *Cumhuriyet Caddesi 178.* ☎ *0525/313-8000. Cover 20TRY.*

➔ **Havana** ★★★ Possibly one of my favorite clubs in the entire world, Havana is ultraexclusive, ultraexpensive, and ultrapacked. You'll have to break out the designer duds for this one, kids, and when you go, you need to act as entitled as possible. The bouncer will probably tell you that there is a private party;

just speak really fast and make up some story about how important you are (favorite of mine: Mexican soap star). The club is literally on the beach, and if you can tear yourself away from the young, pulsating crowd, the sea and the sand are just a short stroll away. The drinks are around 10TRY and lean toward the tropical and gem-hued. *Be warned:* The ride to get here is kind of long (30 min. from Bodrum). *Gölköy Yali Mevkii, Göltürkbükü.* ☎ *0252/357-8250. Cover charge varies by event.*

Sightseeing

→ **Maki Beach** The daytime equivalent of nightlife is at Maki Beach, a hotel and beach. Pronounced "*mu*-kee," the beach dominates the daytime social scene with its white beaches, long lounge chairs, and a bar that challenges the Marmara Sea in sheer liquid weight. This is the ultimate place to see and be seen by the social elite of Turkey and vacationing tourists who know Turkey well enough to realize that Maki Beach is way more worthwhile than the sunken-ship expeditions occurring just off Bodrum's shore. Break out your little swimsuits and Vespa goggles if you want to blend in. *Kelesharimi Caddesi Mimoza S. 10.*

→ **Mausoleum of Halicarnassus** This structure really makes you appreciate the fine workmanship that went into building a burial chamber for a king. It also makes you value the steps taken by previous civilizations to preserve the structure . . . Wait, what? Only the foundations are left? Cross another of the Seven Wonders of the World off the checklist. Still, the foundations alone should make you appreciate the size of the place, and the pictures on display will show you what the mausoleum looked like before it was "looted"—think statues of kings and queens and golden chariots. *Turgut Reis Cad., up the hill off Hamamı Sokagı.* ☎ *0252/316-1219. Admission 3TRY. Tues–Sun 8am–noon and 1–5pm.*

→ **St. Peter Castle** This castle was built in 1406 by the knights of St. John using the stones from the Mausoleum of Halicarnassus, which can still be seen (they are the shiny greenish ones integrated into the fortress). Much of the original art was taken from the mausoleum, including some friezes depicting battles between the Greeks and the Amazons (now in a British museum). The castle now houses a museum for underwater artifacts discovered off the coast, appropriately called the **Bodrum Underwater Archaeology Museum.** One of the highlights of the museum is the sarcophagus of Queen Ada and the oldest known shipwreck in the world. *St. Peter's Castle, Bodrum center.* ☎ *0252/315-2516. Admission 10TRY. Tues–Sun 8:30am–noon and 1–5:30pm.*

Lisbon

Though Lisbon is not usually on backpackers' radars, it should be—this brilliant city is truly the best of Europe rolled into one compact, fascinating city. The broad, tree-lined Avenida da Liberdade, with its marvelous mosaic walkways and rows of high-end shops, is reminiscent of Paris's Champs-Elysées; the bougainvillea-draped wrought-iron balconies throughout the Alfama district bring to mind Barcelona, and the view from Bairro Alto over Lisbon's clusters of red-tiled roofs and twisting streets conjures up images of Rome.

To get to the heart of Lisbon and the Portuguese sensibility, it's important to understand *fado*, traditional Portuguese music marked by sentiments of longing and heartbreak, sung by women in plaintive, woeful melodies. Like *fado*, Lisbon is all about soul. But Lisbon is not overwhelmed by centuries-old tradition. Modernity lurks around many corners, most notably in areas renovated to celebrate Expo '98, which commemorated the 500th anniversary of Vasco da Gama's exploration of India. In Parque das Nações, you'll find the world's second-largest aquarium and a slew of modern shops, restaurants, and apartment buildings. Lisbon also lays claim to a gritty but decidedly hip mystique, which is most tangibly seen along the twisting cobblestone streets of the graffiti-filled Bairro Alto district. And there's nothing musty about Lisbon's nightlife. When the sun slides down beyond the Tagus River, bars and clubs heat up to a frenetic pace that doesn't slow down till dawn, easily rivaling the bar and club scene in any other major city.

The Best of Lisbon

○ **The Best Cheap Sleep:** The **Lisbon Lounge Hostel** has to be one of Europe's funkiest hostels, tucked into one of Lisbon's main hubs. The decor is unusually hip: Think mod kitchen appliances, *Jetsons*-like light fixtures and furniture, IKEA-esque bathroom fixtures—the works. The irresistible lounge offers a warm vibe for hanging out and meeting other travelers. See p. 524.

○ **The Best Budget Meal:** Catch some local flavor and an amazing meal at **Bom Apetite,** a small, no frills restaurant. You'll be met with family-style dining, friendly and efficient staff members (who are more than happy to help interpret the menu through sign language), and enormous portions of traditional meat or seafood dishes and yummy veggies—all for amazingly low prices. See p. 528.

○ **The Best Place to Look Smart:** Situated in the heart of Baixa-Chiado—one of Lisbon's central hangouts—is the city's most famous cafe, **Café A Brasileira do Chiado.** Stopping here for a cup of tea or a coffee is somewhat of a tradition in Lisbon, and has been ever since the poet Fernando Pessoa made it his haunt in the 1920s. See p. 529.

○ **The Best Collection of Kitsch:** The city's best place to meet up with friends before heading out elsewhere is **Pavilhão Chinês Bar.** You'll be greeted by a huge collection of knickknacks and baubles set amidst a vintage Victorian decor, punctuated by a crowd of friendly locals. See p. 531.

○ **The Best Slice of Local Culture:** Spend a night listening to *fado* (fate), the magnificent art that melds poetry (often about love or jealousy) and singing into a soulful, sorrowful blend. But don't go if you're suffering from a breakup. Think a Portuguese version of Beck's *Sea Change* album on downers, and you'll get an idea of the sound. See p. 532.

Getting There & Getting Around

Getting into Town

BY PLANE

All foreign and domestic flights land at Lisbon's **Aeroporto de Lisboa** (☎ 21/ 841-35-00; www.ana.pt), about 6.4km (4 miles) from the center of the city. You can find an **AERO-BUS** that runs between the airport and the **Cais do Sodré train station** every 20 minutes from 7am to 9pm. Tickets cost 2.45€, and it makes 10 stops, including Praça dos Restauradores and Praça do Comércio—two of the city's hubs. There's no charge for luggage. Taxis are generally inexpensive and a good option for travelers hoping to head straight to their hotel. There is a line of taxis by the sidewalk in front of the airport, or call **Radiotaxi** at ☎ 21/793-27-56.

On average, taxi fare from the airport to central Lisbon is 10€. Each piece of luggage is 1.50€ extra.

BY TRAIN

Most international rail passengers arrive at the main train terminal, **Estação da Santa Apolónia,** Avenida Infante Dom Henrique, near the Alfama district. Two daily trains make the 10-hour trip from Madrid to Lisbon. National rail lines from northern and eastern Portugal also use this station.

Another hub for long-distance and suburban trains is **Gare de Oriente** at Expo Urbe, which serves Porto, Sintra, the Beiras, Minho and the Douro, among other places. It's at the Estação do Rossio, between Praça dos Restauradores and Praça de Dom Pedro IV.

Talk of the Town

Four ways to start a conversation with a local

So you want to talk to a local. How? Here are a few surefire conversation starters to get the chatty ball rolling with the Lisboans.

1. **What's your take on the many renovations since Expo '98 was held here,** like the Oceanario aquarium, or the influx of trendy discos and restaurants? While most folks dig the changes, some argue that they're bringing an influx of noisy, unwanted tourists. Discuss.

2. **War or peace?** Every young Euro worth his salt gets plenty riled up when the topic of the war in Iraq gets brought up. Ask them their opinion on Portugal's laissez-faire attitude toward the current conflict, and the country's avoidance of military conflict during World War II—which earned them a nod from Brazil, who offered the city a towering statue of Jesus in recognition of their peace-loving ways.

3. **Beer versus port wine—which does the young, hip set prefer?** Heck, it's Portugal, land of the wine, home of the port, which *should* they prefer? Is the culture of port wine a dying trend?

4. **What's the best local beach?** Folks in this town are *very* opinionated when it comes to the finest sands and bluest waters. But take heed if they dare tell you to head to Estoril—there's no way you're going to a tourist trap.

The **Estação do Cais do Sodré,** just beyond the south end of Rua Alecrim, east of Praça do Comércio, handles trains to Cascais and Estoril on the Costa do Sol.

If you want to head to the Algarve and Alentejo, catch a ferry at Sul e Sueste, next to the Praça do Comércio. It goes across the Tagus to the suburb of Barreiro, where you can catch the trains that go south. For all rail information, call ☎ **808/208-208** daily between 7am and 11pm or visit www.cp.pt.

BY BUS

Buses from all over Portugal arrive at the **Rodoviária da Arco do Cego** (☎ **21/358-14-81;** www.rede-expressos.pt). If your hotel is in Estoril or Cascais, you can take bus no. 1, which goes on to the Cais do Sodré. At least six buses a day leave for Lagos, a gateway to the Algarve, and nine buses head north every day to Porto. There are 14 daily buses to Coimbra, the university city to the north.

Getting Around

Lisbon's hilly terrain, sprawling neighborhoods, and narrow and awkwardly sized streets make it the perfect place to take full advantage of public transportation, including the subways, buses, and taxis. Forgo all thoughts of walking long distances or—heaven forbid—renting a car. Of course, walking within the different districts isn't a problem, but finding transportation is essential if you want to get across the city.

BY PUBLIC TRANSPORTATION

CARRIS **CARRIS** (☎ **21/361-30-30;** www. carris.pt) is the sole operator of Lisbon's funiculars, trains, subways, and buses. If you're in town for a few days, it makes sense to purchase a *bilhete de assinatura turístico* (tourist ticket), good for 4 days of unlimited travel across the entire network for 9.95€. For shorter or longer stays, a 1-day pass costs 2.75€; 7-day passes cost 14€. Passes can be bought at CARRIS booths (daily 9am–5pm), in most Metro stations, and in network train stations.

METRO Lisbon's Metro is incredibly convenient, reliable, and safe; stations can be recognized by their giant M signs and are generally quite clean. A single ticket costs .70€; 10 tickets at one time cost 6.50€. Service runs daily from 6:30am to 1am; keep an eye on the clock if you're planning to be out late in the Bairro Alto, as you'll need a taxi to get back. For more information, call ☎ 21/355-84-57 or visit www.metrolisboa.pt.

BUS & TRAM Hopping onto a bus or tram is the cheapest way to get around Lisbon, though it's not always as convenient as the Metro. The *eléctricos* (cable cars) make the steep run up to the Bairro Alto and can be picked up on the Avenida da Liberdade. The city's eléctricos offer an unusual way to get in some sightseeing and get off your feet. Check out the no. 28, which cuts through some of the city's more interesting neighborhoods. Note that the double-decker buses used in the city actually come from London, and tend to get quite crowded during rush hour.

The base fare on a bus or eléctrico is 1€ if you buy the ticket from the driver, but the system is actually divided into zones numbered one through five. The fare you pay depends on how many zones you traverse. Buses and eléctricos run daily from 6am to 1am. Schedules for the tram and bus routes can be found at the foot of the Santa Justa Elevator, on Rua Aurea, or you can call ☎ 21/361-30-00 or visit www.carris.pt for info.

ELECTRIC TRAIN If you are heading to one of the nearby beaches or towns, you might want to hop aboard one of the modern electric trains that connect Lisbon with towns all along the so-called Portuguese Riviera. You can pick up the train at the Cais do Sodré Station in Lisbon and head up the

coast all the way to Cascais. A one-way ticket from Lisbon to Cascais, Estoril, or Sintra ranges from 1.25€ to 2.50€ per person. Call ☎ 21/261-30-00 or visit www.carris.pt for info.

FUNICULARS Lisbon has a trio of **funiculars** (☎ 21/261-30-00; www.carris.pt): the Glória, which goes from Praça dos Restauradores to Rua São Pedro de Alcântara; the Bica, from the Calçada do Combro to Rua do Boavista; and the Lavra, from the eastern side of Avenida da Liberdade to Campo Martires da Pátria. A one-way ticket on any of these costs 1€.

BY TAXI

Luckily for travelers on a budget who still like life's little conveniences, taxis in Lisbon are quite inexpensive; trips within the city rarely cost much more than 5€. The basic fare is 1.80€ for the first 153m (502 ft.), .05€ for each extra 162m (531 ft.), plus an evening surcharge of 20% from 10pm to 6am. It's common to tip about 20% of the fare. If your driver speaks no English, it's helpful to write down the name of your hotel so that you don't get taken for a ride (it does happen). For a **Radio Taxi,** call ☎ 21/811-90-00.

BY CAR

Though I don't recommended driving here—locals are wild on the roads and parking is a nightmare—you will find most well-known car-rental companies in Lisbon. There are kiosks at the airport and offices in the center, including **Avis** (Av. Praia da Vitória 12C; ☎ 21/354-15-60; daily 8am–7pm) and **Hertz** (Av. Severiano Falcão 7 2685–378 Prior Velho; ☎ 21/942-63-00; Mon–Fri 8:30am–6:30pm, Sat 9am–6:30pm). There's also a **Budget** (Rue Castillo 167B; ☎ 21/386-05-16; daily 9am–7pm).

ON FOOT

When exploring areas like the Alfama or Bairro Alto, it's easy do so on foot, but to reach some of Lisbon's environs, such as

Belém, you'll need to depend on public transportation. For the most part, Lisbon is very pedestrian-friendly and the neighborhoods are compact.

Lisbon Basics

Orientation: Lisbon Neighborhoods

BAIXA   In Baixa, you'll find Lisbon's business district, which consists of a lot of banks, but also some good shopping streets. To get your bearings, note that the main street of Baixa, heading south, separates Praça do Comércio from the Rossio. You'll also find an arch leading from the square to Rua Augusta, a street lined with clothing stores. When you're ready to buy some bling, head to **Rua da Prata (Street of Silver)** and **Rua Aurea,** formerly called Rua do Oro (Street of Gold) because it's a hotbed of jewelry stores, silversmiths, and goldsmiths.

CHIADO   Chiado is a bustling shopping district located on one of Lisbon's hills. You'll find some of the city's fanciest shops here, such as Vista Alegre, a well-known china shop.

MTV Best   BAIRRO ALTO   Nestled high above the city and accessible by Lisbon's famed cable cars is the Bairro Alto (Upper City) district. Locals rave about the charm of the Alto's narrow, winding streets, but be warned that it's a bit dirty and graffiti-covered. Take note, though: As night falls, the Bairro Alto comes alive as Lisbon's party central. All those shuttered, spray-painted storefronts light up around 9pm, and play host to a rockin' bar scene.

THE ALFAMA   The oldest district in Lisbon, the Alfama was the Moorish section of the capital, as evidenced by its narrow streets and tall whitewashed buildings. Today, you'll find much of the traditional, old-school way of life here, thanks to the abundance of fishermen and *varinas* (fishwives). That big castle overlooking the Alfama is **Castelo São Jorge (St. George's Castle),** which was eventually used by the Romans. Though it should be safe by day, be careful of muggers in parts of the Alfama at night.

BELÉM   When you're ready to see the sights, head straight to Belém for some of the country's greatest monuments and museums. Two of the country's main attractions are here: the **Mosteiro dos Jerónimos,** an enormous structure erected in the 16th century and said to house the tomb of Vasco de Gama, and the **Museu Nacional dos Coches,** the National Coach Museum. Equally interesting are some of the neighborhood's monuments, many of which were built during Portugal's Age of Discovery and pay tribute to the explorers who helped discover the New World.

CACILHAS   On the south side of the Tagus River, which cuts through the city, Cacilhas is home to many factories and some good seafood restaurants. Cross over by bridge or take a ferryboat from Praça do Comércio.

Two enormous bridges span the Tagus. The **Ponte do 25 de Abril,** a 2.4km-long (1¹/₂-mile) bridge has an enormous statue of Jesus with arms outstretched to the heavens standing guard high up on the left bank. The statue was a gift from Brazil to Portugal in appreciation for Portugal not getting involved in World War II.

Lisbon's greatest architectural achievement is the 16km (10-mile) **Ponte Vasco da Gama** (the longest suspension bridge in Europe), which opened in 1998, just in time for Expo '98.

Tourist Offices

Lisbon's primary **tourist office** is at the Palácio da Foz, Praça dos Restauradores (☎ 21/346-63-07; Metro: Restauradores), at

LISBON

the Baixa end of Avenida da Liberdade; it's open daily from 9am to 8pm.

Recommended Websites

○ **www.portugal.org**: General information about tourism and attractions.

○ **www.portugal-info.net**: A great source of info about hotels, food, entertainment, sporting events, and nightlife.

○ **www.atl-turismolisboa.pt**: The official tourism website, with comprehensive information on the region.

Culture Tips 101

People move to Lisbon from all over the world—mainly Brazil, Asia, and Africa—which greatly influences how the locals stuff themselves, what kind of music they groove to, and how they like to party. Travelers from all over the world also come to Lisbon. You tend to see more Europeans and Australians than people from the U.S., but they're all equally welcome. Because there's so much American and British media and music imported to Lisbon, most folks under 35 speak English, and lots speak Spanish or French. Some might even tell you they prefer to speak English or French.

Most folks here have slugged down at least one Super Bock beer by the legal minimum drinking age of 16. They'll even carry beer around in the streets in transit to another bar. Drugs in Lisbon are mostly visible in the Bairro Alto and at clubs. Hash is often treated as if it were a cigarette, quickly rolled with tobacco and casually smoked in and outside certain bars and clubs. It's illegal here, even in personal-use quantities. Most everyone young is talking about, and waiting for, legalization, but don't exhale yet.

Recommended Books, Movies & Music

Portugal has bred many fine and creative minds, including a winner of the Nobel Prize for Literature. To get into a Portuguese state of mind—and beware, it can be a dismal one—check out the novel *Blindness* (1999), by Jose Saramago (said winner of the Nobel). For something a bit cheerier and trendier, pick up *The Last Kabbalist of Lisboa* (2000), by Richard Zimler. Written in 1999, this murder mystery follows the lives of 16th-century Jewish mystics living in Portugal.

If you are ready to commit to a *fado* CD purchase, check out Amália Rodrigues' *Art of Amalia* (1998) or her *Essential Collection* (2005). Rodrigues, who died in 1999, is considered one of the country's legendary *fado* singers. She was so beloved by her native fans that they declared 3 days of national mourning after her death.

Portugal isn't exactly a cinematic hot spot, but if you feel you must rent a flick with some Portuguese flavor, check out the 1997 flick *Inês de Portugal,* and you'll get a bonus history lesson. The movie details the steamy 14th-century love affair of Pedro I of Portugal and Inês de Castro, a maidservant, which cruelly ended when Inês was murdered by Pedro's father. Pedro avenged his lover's death, ultimately forcing the nobility to accept Inês posthumously as his wife and queen of Portugal.

Lisbon **Nuts & Bolts**

Cellphone Providers & Service Centers   You can purchase a local phone from the offices of one of the city's main cell providers: **Vodafone** (Parque das Nações, Comunicações Pessoais, Avenida Dom João II; ☎ **21/091-50-00**; www.vodafone.pt) and **Optimus** (Edificio Green Park, Av. das Combatentes 43–13; ☎ **21/723-36-00**). Subscription packages range from 15€ to 25€. Otherwise, you can purchase pre-paid SIM cards at convenience stores around Lisbon; these cards give you a local phone number and come with a preset amount of calling time.

Currency   There are currency-exchange booths at Santa Apolónia station and at the airport, both open 24 hours a day. The post office (see below) will exchange money as well. ATMs offer the best exchange rates, however, and they pepper the streets of the central Baixa district,. They're found less frequently in other parts of the city.

Emergencies   To call the police or an ambulance, call ☎ 112. In case of fire, call ☎ 21/342-22-22. In case of a medical emergency, ask at your hotel or call your embassy and ask the staff there to recommend an English-speaking physician. Or try the **British Hospital** (Rua Saraiva de Carvalho 49; ☎ 21/394-31-00), where the telephone operator, staff, and doctors speak English.

Embassies   The **United States Embassy** is at Avenida das Forças Armadas (☎ 21/727-33-00). It's open Monday to Friday 8am to 5pm. The **Embassy of Canada** is at Av. da Liberdade 200, EDIT Victoria, 4th Floor (☎ 21/316-46-00). It's open Monday to Friday 9am to noon and 2 to 4pm (July–Aug Fri till 1pm). The **Embassy of the United Kingdom** (Rua São Bernardo 33; ☎ 21/392-40-00) is open Monday through Friday 9 to 11:30am and 3 to 4:30pm. The **Embassy of the Republic of Ireland** (Rua de Imprensa à Estrêla 1; ☎ 21/392-94-40) is open Monday through Friday from 9:30am to 12:30pm and from 2:30 to 4:30pm. **Australians** and **New Zealanders** should go to the British Embassy (see above).

Internet/Wireless Hot Spots   Can't live without checking your e-mail? Head to **Cyber.bica** (Duques de Bragança 7; ☎ 21/322-50-04), in the Chiado district. It's open Monday to Friday 11am to midnight. If the terminals there are clogged, check out **Lisboa Welcome Center** (Praça do Comércio, second floor; ☎ 21/031-28-10). It's open daily 9am to 8pm.

Laundry   You'll find a self-service laundromat at **Lavatax** (Rua Francisco Sanches 65A; ☎ 21/812-33-92).

Luggage Storage   Store your bags at the **Estação da Santa Apolónia** (☎ 21/888-40-25), near the Alfama. Lockers cost 3€ for up to 48 hours; call for pickup and drop-off hours. Another alternative is to ask at your hotel or hostel if they'll store your luggage; many offer this service.

Pharmacies   **Farmácia Vall** (Av. Visconde Valmor 60B; ☎ 21/797-30-43) is centrally located and well stocked.

Post Offices   The main post office, Correio Geral, in Lisbon is at Praça do Restauradores (☎ 21/323-89-71); it receives visitor mail but you'll need a passport to pick it up. Hours are Monday to Friday 8am to 10pm, and Saturday and Sunday 9am to 6pm.

Restrooms   When you gotta go, your best bet might be to scurry into a restaurant or bar—most places won't force you to buy something to use the toilets. Otherwise, train stations have bathrooms, but you'll most likely have to pay .50€.

Safety   Lisbon isn't the safest of cities, particularly late at night in districts like the Alfama or Bairro Alto. It's not uncommon to hear tourists say they've been held up at knifepoint. Use plenty of common sense and do not walk around at night or in abandoned

LISBON

areas alone. By day, beware of crowded areas because pickpockets tend to lurk there and prey on tourists. Keep your purse and wallet in your reach at all times.

Telephone Tips When using public pay phones, you can use a *cartão telefônico* (calling card), which can be bought at newspaper stands, tobacco shops, or post offices for 5€ or 10€. Most local numbers will cost either .20€ or .50€.

Tipping It's common practice to leave a 10% to 15% tip at restaurants when you've received good service. At the bar of a cafe, 5% is acceptable. When buying drinks at a bar, it is customary to leave a .50€ tip or slightly less, depending on the type of establishment.

Sleeping

Lisbon's reputation for reasonably priced accommodations holds true, but luxury accommodations are becoming more common. The city is home to a growing number of *pousadas,* which are luxury, traditional hotels set in unique locations (from monuments to secluded country homes).

Lisbon is home to numerous guesthouses, called *pensãos,* which offer very basic accommodations at very low prices. Often bathrooms in these pensions are shared, but some rooms feature sinks with running water. If you do want to book a room at a pensâo, keep in mind that they fill up quickly during the summer and it's a good idea to book in advance.

When you first arrive, you may be approached by owners offering to take you to their pensâo—they're pretty honest and safe, but use your good judgment. As far as cheap central pensions go, your best bet is to stay in the Baixa. It's easy to get anywhere from here, and it's a short walk from the train station. There are some good ones in Alfama, and though it looks closer on the map to the station, the hills make it actually quite a haul. Don't be tempted by the hip Bairro Alto if you're on a budget—rooms ain't cheap, the facilities can be filthy, and you may run into some shady characters. Toward the Avenida da Liberdade are some lux hotels.

Hostels

→ **Lazy Crow & Co. Guesthouse** You'll get your socializing game on at the Lazy Crow, which caters to young backpackers. A welcome drink is offered at check-in—along with a sniff from the cat-in-residence, Lolita, and that's just the beginning. A large lounge room and back garden area are popular hangouts for travelers looking to meet new friends, and the hostel organizes bar-crawls, wine tastings, barbecues, and movie nights to add to the party atmosphere. Mixed dorms for four, six, or eight people are available; linens and towels are included, as is breakfast—bonus! The Crow also offers free Internet, no lockout, no curfew, and fully equipped kitchen and laundry facilities. *Tv. Santa Quiteria 12.* ☎ *21/390-90-20. www. lisbonlazycrow.com. 17€ dorm. Rates include breakfast. 2-night minimum. Metro: Rato. Amenities: Bar; breakfast room; bike rental; Internet; kitchen; laundry; movies; planned activities; shared bathrooms; sheets; telephone (in common room); TV (in common room); Wi-Fi.*

📺 **Best** → **Lisbon Lounge Hostel** ★★ Smack dab in Lisbon's main hub, the Lisbon Lounge is one of Europe's coolest hostels. The decor is super-futuristic, from the mod kitchen appliances to the *Jetsons*-like light fixtures and furniture to the IKEA-esque bathroom fixtures. The immaculate rooms

Lisbon

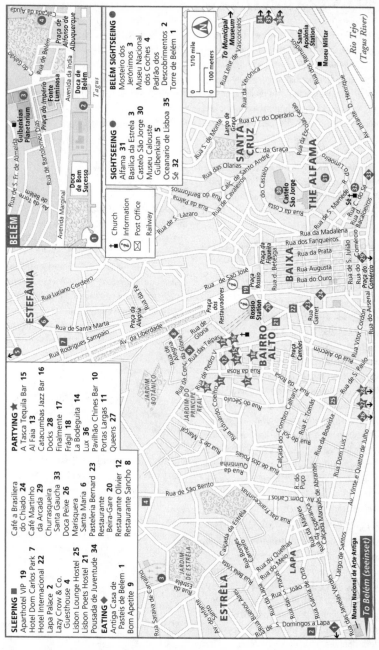

SLEEPING ■
Aparthotel VIP **19**
Hotel Dom Carlos Park **7**
Hotel Internacional **22**
Lapa Palace **2**
Lazy Crow & Co.
   Guesthouse **4**
Lisbon Lounge Hostel **25**
Lisbon Poets Hostel **21**
Pousada de Juventude **34**

EATING ◆
Antiga Casa de
   Pastéis de Belém **1**
Bom Apetite **9**
Café a Brasileira
   do Chiado **24**
Café Martinho
   da Arcada **29**
Churrasqueira
   Santa Gaúcha **33**
Doca Peixe **26**
Marisquera
   Santa Maria **6**
Pastelería Bernard **23**
Restaurante
   Beira-Gare **20**
Restaurante Olivier **12**
Restaurante Sancho **8**

PARTYING ★
A Tasca Tequila Bar **15**
Al Faia **13**
Catacumbas Jazz Bar **16**
Docks **28**
Finalmente **17**
Frágil **18**
La Bodeguita **14**
Lux **36**
Pavilhão Chinês Bar **11**
Portas Largas **10**
Queens **27**

BELÉM SIGHTSEEING ●
Mosteiro dos
   Jerónimos **3**
Museu Nacional
   dos Coches **4**
Padrão dos
   Descobrimentos **2**
Torre de Belém **1**

SIGHTSEEING ●
Alfama **31**
Basílica da Estrela **3**
Castelo São Jorge **30**
Museu Calouste
   Gulbenkian **5**
Oceanário de Lisboa **35**
Sé **32**

+ Church
(i) Information
✉ Post Office
— Railway

are sparsely decorated, but if all you need is a bed, you're in luck. Sheets are clean; pillows are fluffy. Four mixed dorms offer four- or six-person rooms. The two bathrooms have three showers and three toilets, though each room has its own sink with hot running water. An added bonus? The friendly lounge and bar area make it easy to meet other visitors. An open kitchen, laundry services, and Internet access seal the deal—try to stay here at all costs. *Rua de São Paulo 111, 2nd floor.* ☎ *21/346-20-61. www.lisbonlounge hostel.com. 18€ dorm, 20€ per person double. Metro: Cais do Sodré. Amenities: Bar; Internet; kitchen; laundry facilities; shared bathrooms; sheets; telephone (in common area); TV (in common area).*

➜ **Lisbon Poets Hostel** ★ Amid Lisbon's most happening neighborhoods—Bairro Alto, Chiado, and Rossio—the Poets Hostel is in a 17th-century home that has been upgraded with modern appliances. A cozy sitting area features traditional Portuguese tiles, beanbag chairs, and lots of books to exchange. Guests also have access to an immaculate kitchen, laundry, and minibar. The hostel offers 30 twin (bunk) beds in shared rooms, two double bedrooms, and four shared bathrooms. You'll be grateful there's no curfew; solo travelers shouldn't have a problem meeting up with other backpackers in the inviting lounge. *Rua do Duque 41.* ☎ *21/346-10-58. www.lisbonpoetshostel.com. 18€–20€ dorm, 40€ double. Breakfast 3€. Metro: Rossio or Baixa-Chiado. Amenities: Bar; breakfast room; kitchen; Internet; laundry facilities; library; shared bathrooms. In room: Lockers.*

➜ **Pousada da Juventude/Parque Das Nações** No sign advertises this hostel. Instead, look for the sign reading INSTITUTO PORTUGUES DA JUVENTUDE to know you've arrived. It's far from Lisbon's center, though some travelers appreciate the proximity to its Oriente train station. The 92-bed pousada offers doubles and four-person dorms, but beware—you'll only be issued one key for each dorm, so unless you're traveling in a group, it's not the most convenient. Juventude hosts many backpackers, but the scene does not scream party—no alcohol is allowed on the premises, and school groups on trips often stay here. You must be a member of Hostelling International (HI) to book a room. *Via de Moscavide L 47–101.* ☎ *21/892-08-90. http://juventude.gov.pt. 11€–13€ dorm, 30€–37€ double. Rates include breakfast. Metro: Oriente. Amenities: Lockout (noon–6pm); shared bathrooms; sheets.*

Cheap

➜ **Aparthotel VIP Eden** ★ You'll really think you entered the VIP lifestyle at Eden. The hotel's 75 suites and 59 two-bedroom apartments are fully equipped with comfy beds, private bathrooms, Internet access, desks, and full kitchens. Its Art Deco–style facade is somewhat reminiscent of Miami Beach, and a swimming pool, solarium, and rooftop bar with city views all cement the fact that Eden is just that: paradise. *Praça dos Restauradores 24.* ☎ *21/321-66-00. www.viphotels.com. 79€–89€ double, 99€–129€ 4-person apt. Metro: Rossio. Amenities: Bar; business facilities; car rental; Internet; laundry service; pool; room service; solarium; wheelchair friendly. In room: A/C, TV, hair dryer, kitchenette, safe.*

➜ **Hotel Internacional** If you happen to visit Lisbon during the sweltering summer months, you will thank the gods of hospitality that Hotel Internacional has air-conditioning. In fact, if you've spent the past few weeks roughing it in hostels and want to upgrade just a notch, you will appreciate this hotel's conveniences, such as private bathrooms in all rooms, Internet access, and praise be, a bar! To boot, it's in the Rossio's main square, which means you are steps away from, well, everything the city has to offer. *Rua da Betesga 3.* ☎ *21/324-09-90. www.hotel-internacional.*

com. 50€–75€ single, 60€–90€ double, 85€–120€ triple. Metro: Rossio. Amenities: Bar; elevator; Internet; laundry facilities; free shuttle to airport; TV (in common room); wheelchair friendly. In room: A/C, hair dryer.

Doable

→ **Dom Carlos Park** This hotel was renovated in 2005, and rooms are exceptionally well appointed, with large comfortable beds, full-length mirrors, deep-hued wood furnishings, cable TV, video-on-demand, and high-speed Internet. The atmosphere is a bit staid—it feels very much like a business traveler's hotel—but its comforts appeal to backpackers and other travelers, too. A large breakfast room is converted during the afternoon into a reading lounge and library, and in the early evening it is again transformed into a bar with make-it-yourself cocktails. The hotel is in the heart of the city's hopping Marques de Pombal square. Av. Duque de Loulé 121. ☎ 21/317-35-75. www.domcarlospark.com. 77€–210€ single, 91€–275€ double. Metro: Marques de Pombal. Amenities: Bar; breakfast room; fax (in common area); laundry service; high-speed Internet; library; telephone (in common area); travel information desk; TV (in common area); wheelchair friendly. In room: A/C, cable TV, hair dryer, safe, video-on-demand.

Splurge

→ **Lapa Palace** ★★ Favored by Sting, Madonna, Sir Paul McCartney, and do-gooder Bono, Lapa Palace is Lisbon's most coveted high-end accommodations. Staff members here claim Lapa's guest list is so exclusive that many of its visitors book two rooms—one for themselves, and one for their bodyguards. Housed in a 17th-century palace, every inch of this hotel is opulent. Here you can soak in your marble tub, sip port on your private Juliet balcony, and thank the doormen for opening every door you go through. Or you can simply gawk at the rich fabrics and hand-carved furniture carefully designed to re-create 17th-century decor. If staying here would kill your budget, you can get a peek at the good life at the hotel's Rio Tejo bar. Rua do Pau de Bandeira 4. ☎ 21/394-94-94. www.lapapalace.com. From 325€–725€ double, from 650€–2500€ suite. The hotel isn't near a metro, so you'll need to get a taxi. Amenities: Restaurant; bar; breakfast room; car rental; cooking school; fax (in common area); health club; Internet; laundry service; massage; pool; salon; sauna; wheelchair friendly. In room: A/C, TV, fridge, hair dryer, Internet, safe.

LISBON

Eating

Lisbon is a fish-lover's paradise. The freshest meals in town tend to include seafood. The most popular food is bacalhau, codfish that's been salted and dried and finally soaked before being made into dozens of mouthwatering dishes. Also popular are sardines, which are enormous compared to their U.S. counterparts, and not de-boned—get ready to work for your dinner! Another typical dish is caldo verde, a cabbage and potato soup usually made with some meat or sausage. When it's time to order drinks, keep in mind that

Portugal is well known for its wines, in particular the vinho verde, or green wine, which isn't green at all, but light, fruity, and somewhat bubbly. Your sweet tooth will be satisfied with a pastéis de nata de Belém, traditional puff pastries—almost like a tart—filled with custard.

Your cheapest bet for a meal in Lisbon is to hit up one of the many pastelerias, or fast-food restaurants, that dot the city streets. You'll appreciate the range of inexpensive offerings, from pastries to little sandwiches filled with ham and cheese or something similar. You'll find many near the Baixa-Chiado area. **Pasteleria Bernard** (Rua Garrett 104; ☎ 21/347-31-33) is one of the best; sandwiches here will run you anywhere from 1.50€ to 2.50€.

Lisboans tend to eat much later than most American, Canadian, and British visitors, although not as late as their Spanish neighbors. Some restaurants stay open very late.

Hot Spots

→ **Cafe Martinho da Arcada** CAFE/TEAROOM   Sure, Café A Brasileira do Chiado gets all the hype as Lisbon's most famous cafe, having been the former hangout of famed poet Fernando Pessoa. Truth is (according to the waitstaff here), Pessoa spent even more time at Martinho, which also claims to be Lisbon's oldest cafe (established 1782) and to have one of the city's best people-watching perches (right on the Praça do Comércio). While the interior has maintained some of its 18th-century charms like tiny, old-fashioned bistro tables, the place to sit is at one of the outdoor tables. *Praça do Comércio 3.* ☎ *21/886-62-13. Snacks 1.50€–15€. Mon–Sat 8am–11pm. Metro: Baixa-Chiado.*

🎬 **Best** → **Restaurante Olivier** ★★ PORTUGUESE/FRENCH   Reservations are a must at the Bairro Alto's hottest restaurant, and you'll actually have to knock on the white front door to gain entry to the limited space. With black-painted wood walls and a beamed ceiling, black and red chairs, and startling white tablecloths, the decor is an ideal mix of cozy and trendy. The French-Portuguese owner, Olivier, specializes in Mediterranean cuisine, and his wine selection is among Lisbon's most interesting. A prix-fixe menu (30€) includes delicacies like bull carpaccio, game sausage with grouse egg, and foie gras in balsamic vinegar sauce. *Rua do Teixeira 35.* ☎ *21/343-14-05. Prix-fixe menu 30€. Mon–Sat 8pm–1am. Tram: 28.*

Cheap

🎬 **Best** → **Bom Apetite** ★★ PORTUGUESE   Catch some local flavor and an amazing meal at this small, no-frills restaurant. Tucked inconspicuously off the Avenue de Liberdade, Bom Apetite offers family-style dining, a friendly and efficient staff (who are more than happy to help interpret the menu through sign language), and enormous portions of traditional meat or seafood dishes and yummy veggies all for amazingly low prices. Try the chicken stew—it is served in what can only be described as a cauldron. *Travessa da Gloria 20.* ☎ *21/346-01-01. Main courses 7€–12€. Mon–Sat 5–11:30pm. Metro: Avenida.*

→ **Churrasqueira Gaúcha** ARGENTINE   If dining in seafood-rich Portugal has left you feeling all fished out, head to Gaúcha for a protein overdose straight from the cow. *Churrasqueiras* serve up heaping quantities of various grilled meats, and this place lives up to that bargain. Gaúcha's large portions of beef, lamb, and pork won't disappoint. Located near Praça do Comércio, 1 block from the river. *Rua dos Bacalhoeiros 26C–D.* ☎ *21/887-06-09. Main courses 5€–12€. Mon–Sat 9am–midnight. Metro: Baixa Chiado.*

→ **Restaurante Beira-Gare** PORTUGUESE   Don't be thrown off by this restaurant's proximity to the Rossio train station; this quick-service restaurant serves up a surprisingly extensive menu, and offers traditional Portuguese options like *caldo verde* and *leitao assado* (roasted pork). Sit down and relax, even though the cramped tables and the sterile, diner-like decor are less than inspiring: The joint is more casual cafeteria than well-heeled eating establishment. *Rua 1 de Dezembro 116.* ☎ *21/442-42-48. Main courses 10€. Mon–Sat 6am–midnight. Metro: Rossio.*

Doable

→ **Marisqueira Santa Maria** PORTUGUESE   As you enter this restaurant and beer hall, take a look at the night's specials. They're hanging in the window—an enormous, artistically arranged display of the day's catch. Brightly lit, with long rows of family-style tables, and often, a soccer game blaring on the television, it's not exactly cozy. But the food is great; start with the *sopa alentejana,* a simple broth seasoned with garlic, and follow that with the seafood salad in vinegar. If you're tired of fish, try the *medalhões de vitela,* or veal medallions. *Travessa do Enviado de Inglaterra 1.* ☎ *21/352-56-38. Main courses 12€–17€. Daily 9am–midnight. Metro: Cais de Sodre.*

➜**Restaurante Sancho** ★★ POR-TUGUESE   Cross your fingers that Gonçalo is your waiter (ask for his section when you call to make reservations, which are recommended), as he will make a wonderful dining experience even better with his insider tips on attractions and nightlife. This restaurant oozes old-fashioned charm, with stucco and wood-paneled walls, ceilings crossed with thick wooden beams, and many wrought-iron candelabras. Start with the grilled shrimp in oil and garlic, and then dive into the mixed shellfish platter, or for meat-lovers, the *steak au poivre.* Finish off with a mixed cheese plate, in particular the *queijo da serra* (cheese from the hills), a mix of artisan cheeses well known throughout Portugal. Beware the shots of *ginginha,* a brandy-like liquor made from a pickled berry—which Gonçalo may try to push on you once you've warmed up with some *vinho verde. Travessa da Gloria 14.* ☎ *21/345-97-80. www.restaurante sancho.com. Main courses 10€–15€. Mon–Sat noon–3pm and 7–10:30pm. Metro: Avenida or Restauradores.*

Splurge

➜**Doca Peixe** ★ SEAFOOD   This outstanding seafood restaurant, which translates as "Fish Dock," sits in the midst of the Doca de Santo Amaro, a trendy hub of waterfront bars and restaurants almost under the Ponte do 25 de Abril. Aim for an outdoor seat, under umbrellas and alongside the Tagus River. A variety of fish can be prepared grilled or, my favorite, baked in salt. If you're feeling adventurous, spring for the cod cooked with clams and coriander. Just be sure to ask for the price per kilo because the fish can get quite expensive, and try to make reservations because it's popular with both locals and natives. *Doca de Santo Amaro, Armazém 14.* ☎ *21/397-35-65. www.docapeixe. com. Main courses 14€–40€. Tues–Sun noon–3pm and 9:30pm–1am. Bus: 15 or 38.*

Cafes & Tearooms

➜**Antiga Casa de Pastéis de Belém** CAFE   This cafe is the best and most famous maker of Lisbon's traditional *pastéis,* and it draws tourists and locals who gather in droves to sit under the tile roof and savor these delightful pastries. The little tarts can also be bought by the box for takeout. *Rua de Belém 84.* ☎ *21/363-74-23. www.pasteisdebelem.pt. Pastéis 2€–4€. Daily 8am–11:30pm. Commuter train to Cascais from Cais do Sodré; get off at Belém.*

Ⓜ Ⓑ**Best** ➜**Café A Brasileira do Chiado** ★★★ CAFE   Stopping into this dimly lit hideaway, in the heart of Baixa-Chiado, for a cup of tea or a coffee is somewhat of a tradition in Lisbon, and has been ever since the poet Fernando Pessoa made it his haunt in the '20s. Since then, the cafe has played its role as literati central, attracting a seemingly intellectual crowd in a prime locale with outdoor seating. The beautiful Art Nouveau decor remains intact, though it's a bit faded. *Rua Garrett 120–122.* ☎ *21/346-95-41. Daily 9am–2am. Snacks and drinks 1€–5€. Metro: Baixa-Chiado.*

Partying

When the sun sets and young Lisboans come out to party—and oh, do they ever party—the place to be is Bairro Alto. This neighborhood's narrow streets are choked with bars and the drunken revelry that inevitably follows mass consumption of alcohol makes it a crowded and rowdy area. You'll stumble upon any number of bars while wandering the area, but the choicest ones are on Rua da Atalaia, Rua do Diário Notícias, and the Rua do Norte, where every doorway seems to lead into a bar or tiny club. After you've warmed up in the Bairro, head to one of the clubs and bars on the waterfront at the Doca de Santo Amaro. After 1am, this area turns into a late-night hub. Attire at bars is casual, but don't expect to get into clubs wearing jeans, sandals, or sneakers. And drink your energy drinks if you need to; the party in Lisbon lasts till dawn.

Bars & Lounges

→ **A Tasca Tequila Bar** Though partying usually gets started around 9pm or so in Lisbon bars, A Tasca is the exception. When the doors open at 6pm, drinkers from around the globe descend on what could easily be mistaken for one of Cancun's wildest Mexican bars. As salsa and meringue music thumps away, the bar fills up quickly with people taking advantage of the drink and shot specials (1€–4€) and the party tends to pour out of the bar's doors and into the street until the wee hours of the morning. *Travessa da Queimada 13–15.* ☎ *21/343-34-31. Tram to Bairro Alto.*

→ **Al Faia** Drop by Al Faia for a port tasting; at only 1€ a cup, it really can't be beat, and you can't leave the home of port without sampling the goods, can you? This tiny bar/wine shop only holds a few tables in a tiny back room. Don't be offended if the proprietor ignores you at your table; head to the front counter to order and he'll be happy to

serve you. Small snacks are also on the menu, if you're interested in a plate of cheese or some olives. *Travessa da Queimada 22.* ☎ *21/346-12-32. Tram: to Bairro Alto.*

→ **Catacumbas Jazz Bar** You can't help feeling like a cooler person after visiting Catacumbas. This renowned jazz bar doesn't attract many tourists, yet it's a jazz aficionado's paradise. The decor is dark and dingy, but warmed up by posters of Miles Davis and Dizzy Gillespie. It's the perfect setting for hunkering down with a glass of red house wine and grooving to some live old-school blues. Patrons are welcome to tickle the ivories on the house piano during the week, and alternating Thursdays feature live blues or jazz performances. *Travessa Água da Flor 43.* ☎ *21/346-39-69. Tram: to Bairro Alto.*

→ **La Bodeguita** Viva Che! No, seriously, this bar is all about Che Guevara. Somehow the red walls, hand-painted Che portraits, and mess of communism-inspired graffiti is too amusing to pass by. The scene is, as you might have guessed, laid-back, with some chill rock music playing and a lot of cigarette smoke filling the air, thanks to the disaffected young folks sitting around the bar denouncing "The Man." The mojito specials are really something—3€!—and beers run as cheap as 1.25€. As the night rolls on, don't be surprised to find the bartenders leading the

---

Hanging Out

Wanna chill out before the bar-fueled revelry begins? Make like a local and head to the cafe-filled streets of the **Baixa-Chiado** and grab a coffee or ice cream. This open space acts as the common meeting point for packs of teens and 20-somethings trying to iron out late-night party plans.

crowd in a Cuban dance routine. *Travessa da Queimada 17.* ☎ *21/343-13-57. Metro: Rossio.*

📺 Best → **Pavilhão Chinês Bar** ★★ You may not find a more fascinating bar in all of Europe. Just don't expect to glide right in; you have to ring a doorbell and be granted admittance (no one gets turned away). Upon entering, you'll be overwhelmed by a mishmash of kitsch, from GI figurines to dolls. This place is liveliest earlier in the evening because most locals meet here before clubbing. *Rua Dom Pedro V 89.* ☎ *21/ 342-47-29. Metro: Rato.*

→ **Portas Largas** While carousing around the Bairro, a stop at Portas Largas is almost mandatory. This large bar is open-air in the warm weather, with tiny wooden tables and free peanuts for the beer-swilling patrons. Sure, it's a dive, but it never hurts to get down and dirty with a drink now and again. *Rua da Atalaia 105.* ☎ *21/346-63-79. Metro: Baixa Chiado. Tram: 28.*

Gay Bars & Clubs

You'll find a majority of Lisbon's gay- and lesbian-friendly bars in the Bairro Alto, most located on the Praça Luis de Camões and Travessa da Queimada. Check out www. portugalgay.pt for a rundown of the ever-changing events listings in the city's various venues. A few of the clubs in the Santo Amaro docks, like Queen's (see listing below), are notorious for their hot gay and lesbian clientele.

→ **Finalmente** One of Lisbon's most popular gay clubs lets you groove to Culture Club, Madonna, and the requisite techno beats. Though this Bairro Alto club attracts a mostly male crowd, the lesbian scene really heats up on weekends. You'll find plenty of opportunity for mingling and meeting at the club's bar, and then you can take your new honey onto the tightly packed dance floor. Try to catch one of the funkadelic, twice-weekly

drag shows while you're there (call for schedules). *Rua de Palmeira 38.* ☎ *21/347-99-23. Cover 5€–10€. Bus: 100.*

→ **Frágil** This is one of Lisbon's most fashionable gay nightspots. Though a fair number of heteros hang here on weeknights, come Saturday and Sunday this is where the boys are (and some girls). Frágil is a victim of its tiny size, though—its small bar and miniature dance floor get uncomfortably packed as the night wears into the wee hours. Though not a "club," per se—there's no cover and the dress is casual—the dance floor fills up with oodles of buff guys. *Rua da Italia 126.* ☎ *21/346-95-78. Cover 8€–10€. Metro: Chiado.*

→ **Queens** You'll find all the pretty boys of Lisbon hitting the dance floor at Queens, an industrial-style warehouse by the waterfront. While most clubs see a variety of sexual persuasions, Queens definitely caters to a gay clientele, and is a much larger venue than other local clubs on the gay circuit. *Rua Cintura do Porto de Lisboa, Armazém (Warehouse) 8, Naves A–B.* ☎ *21/395-58-70. Cover 10€. Tram: 14 or 15.*

Nightclubs

→ **Dock's** This waterfront club plays up the seafaring theme and still manages to be hip. The crowd is slightly older, but gets up and shakes its groove thing all the same on a spacious dance floor surrounded by amphitheater-like balconies, perfect for watching the action on the floor below. You'll hear a variety of music rather than obvious house and techno—everything from '80s tunes to Brazilian dance music. If you arrive early enough and the place is empty, you might not have to pay a cover; otherwise, expect to shell out 15€. *Rua da Cintura do Porto de Lisboa 226.* ☎ *21/395-08-56. Cover 15€. Tram: 15.*

→ **Lux** Locals love to brag that John Malkovich is part-owner of Lisbon's hottest nightclub. Knowing that the arbiter of weird has a hand in this joint comes as no surprise

Fado

I've said it before, but it bears repeating: The true musical soul of Portugal lies with traditional MTV Best *fado*. You'll encounter many *fado* restaurants in the Bairro Alto, and to be fair, a newcomer to the art wouldn't know between mediocre or great. Still, prices at these places are generally prix fixe for a meal and performance, and can run pretty high. You'll be guaranteed a quality show at **O Faia** (Rua da Barracca 54/56; ☎ **21/342-67-42**; www.ofaia.com), one of Lisbon's oldest and most reputable *fado* restaurants, around since 1947. Ask to meet Pedro Ramos, the current proprietor and son of the club's owner, as he'll regale you with tales of the club's name: You'll hear four performers over the course of many hours and get tons of food. Entrees run from 22€ to 29€, and the cover (which includes appetizers of olives, sausages, mackerel, and bread) is another 7€. Suck up the splurge—the experience is unforgettable.

once you see the decor that includes a chandelier made from metal wires and tampons, and a giant Alice in Wonderland-esque chair. The club is a two-story series of interconnected rooms, with a lot of mod white furnishings. You'll find dance floors on both levels with international DJs spinning house and techno. The party kicks in around 3am and can last until 7am. *Av. Infante Don Henrique, Armazen (Warehouse) A, Cais da Pedra a Sta. Apolónia.* ☎ *21/882-08-90. Bus: 9, 39, or 46.*

Performing Arts

Check out the town's must-see museums and churches. Embrace Portugal's intriguing cultural offerings; visit an edgy visual art showcase, or attend a performance. To find out what's going on and when, check out the arts and leisure section of the newspaper, *Publico,* available at all newsstands.

FREE → **Centro Cultural de Belém** Whether it's live music or an offbeat art exhibit that floats your culture boat, you'll more than likely find it at the Centro Cultural—part gallery, part music venue, part convention center. Though locals first despised the pink-marble-and-granite behemoth when it was built in 1991, today they seem to grudgingly accept it. Check out the funky jewelry, furniture, and other odds and ends, including a purple, pony-shaped chair in the Museu do Design galleries, which are broken into categories: Luxury, Pop, and Cool. Widely publicized and ever-changing events are also held here regularly, from concerts to film festivals. Schedules and events vary. *Praça do Império.* ☎ *21/361-24-00. Admission to center free; varies for temporary exhibitions and concerts. Daily 10am–7pm. Tram: 15 to Belém.*

FREE → **EuroArte** This ultracontemporary showcase is a hipster's dream come true, filled with avant-garde, untraditional works by some of Portugal's and Spain's up-and-coming young artists, as well as aspiring artists from across the European Union. This is a venue where starving artists dream of holding exhibits in because it's über-prestigious in the contemporary European art community. At any given time, you're likely to stumble upon cutting-edge acrylics, drawings, engravings, and the occasional mixed media. *Rua Rodrigo de Fonseca 107.* ☎ *21/385-40-69. Free admission. Mon–Sat 10am–noon and 2–7pm. Metro: Marquês de Pombal.*

→ **São Jorge Movie Theater** Even Lisbon has its rainy days. Should you have the urge to catch a flick, English-language or otherwise, check out this charming old three-screen theater across from the Praça dos Restauradores tourist office. You'll mostly catch big, blockbuster hits and popular comedies that premiered a few months back in the U.S. But no matter, the movies are most often shown with subtitles, rather than dubbed, and there's popcorn and beer for sale. *Avenida da Liberdade 174.* ☎ *21/242-25-23. Tickets around 5€. Box office daily 1–10pm. Metro: Restauradores.*

→**Teatro da Trinidade** If you don't have the patience to sit through a performance in a foreign language even if it's performed in the country's most famous theater, but you *really* want to see a show, you'll be grateful for this theater's occasional English-language performances. The theater often hosts international plays and theater groups, some performing in English. *Largo da Trinidade 7A.* ☎ *21/342-00-00. Tickets 15€–60€. Box office Mon–Sat 2–8pm; performance days 2pm to 1 hour before show. Metro: Baixa-Chiado.*

→**Teatro Nacional de São Carlos** This 18th-century theater near the Museu do Chiado in the Bairro Alto is the city's mecca for international opera performers, as well as for the country's own symphony, the Orquestra Sinfonica Portuguesa. The opera season lasts from December to mid-June, while the symphony plays from December to July. Ballet companies from around the world also grace the stage here, performing from September to July. *Rua Serpa Pinto 9.* ☎ *21/325-30-45. Tickets 5€–60€ (no discounts apply). Box office Mon–Fri 1–7pm; performance days 1pm to 30 min. before show. Tram: 6, 28, or 28B. Bus: 46.*

Sightseeing

A fantastic way to see the city's major attractions without wearing yourself out trying to find them is to take a bus tour. While a number of agencies run bus tours, we recommend **Carristur** (☎ **96/629-85-58**; www.carris.pt), which operates four different routes through Lisbon, hitting sights like the Alfama, the monuments in Belém, and churches and museums.

The double-decker buses are open-air, and each person is given headphones to listen to an interesting and informative recorded guide. Pick up the bus at Praça do Comércio. Tickets cost 14€ to 17€.

Another touristy but fun excursion: Take a ride on the **Elevador de Santa Justa** (Rua do Ouro 1100; ☎ **21/342-79-44**; daily 8am–9pm; round-trip ticket 2€; Metro: Baixa-Chiado)—the big, unmistakable metal tower smack dab in the middle of the Baixa. Turns out this elevator on steroids was designed by a student of Gustav Eiffel, and built in 1901 to lift people up the steep Chiado without them having to climb steep steps. Once you get off the elevator at the top, you'll be met with sweeping 360-degree views of the city—a darn good photo op.

Get Carded

The **Lisboa Card** will hook you up with unlimited free city transportation and free entrance to around 25 different museums and attractions, and discounted entrance to numerous others. The card can be purchased at tourist offices, train stations, and travel agencies; for adults, a 1-day pass costs 14€, a 2-day pass costs 23€, and a 3-day pass costs 28€.

Festivals

You'll be sorely disappointed to learn Lisbon shuts down tighter than a clam on these days: New Year's Day and Universal Brotherhood

Day (Jan 1); Carnaval (early Mar—dates vary); Good Friday (Mar or Apr—dates vary); Easter (Mar or Apr—dates vary); Liberty Day, anniversary of the revolution (Apr 25); Labor Day (May 1); Corpus Christi (June—dates vary); Portugal Day (June 10); Feast of the Assumption (Aug 15); Proclamation of the Republic (Oct 5); All Saints' Day (Nov 1); Restoration of Independence (Dec 1); Feast of the Immaculate Conception (Dec 8); and Christmas Day (Dec 25). The Feast Day of St. Anthony (June 13) is a public holiday in Lisbon, and the Feast Day of St. John the Baptist (June 24) is a public holiday in Porto. Two of the best festivals to check out follow:

June

Festas dos Santos Populares. The party starts June 13 and 14, as feasts and parades spring up around the city to honor the city's patron saint, St. Anthony. Expect to see large groups of singers and musicians trouncing along Avenida da Liberdade. Join them in the wine-drinking and sardine-snarfing. On June 23 and 24, the locals celebrate the feast of St. John the Baptist by lighting bonfires and jumping over the flames in a rowdy display of religious fervor. The final celebration takes place on June 29 for the feast of St. Peter. Check out the Lisbon tourist office (☎ 21/346-63-07; www.egeac.pt) for more information on specific locations, as venues vary. June 13 to 29.

July

Colete Encarnado (Red Waistcoat). Ah, the old running-of-the-bulls phenomenon. Taking a cue from the famous feria in Pamplona, Spain, this festival showcases bulls running through narrow streets, topped off with bullfights, Fandango dancing, and a rodeo-like competition. On Vila Franca de Xira, north of Lisbon on the river Tagus; for more information, call ☎ 24/333-03-30. First or second Sunday in July.

Top Attractions

FREE → **Alfama** ★★ The Alfama was the only quarter in Lisbon to survive mostly unscathed after the devastating 1755 earthquake, and the area's narrow twisting streets, stairways, and alleys are perfect for aimless exploring. The area is filled with local color: You'll come across street markets with colorful produce and fishmongers. Try to make your way to the **Largo das Portas do Sol** for a superb photo op. This balcony faces the sea, and gives a sweeping view of the town.

FREE → **Basilica da Estrela** Tucked into the Bairro Alto, across from the Jardim da Estrela, this domed basilica makes its mark on the city skyline with a dominating set of belfries. Construction on the basilica wrapped up in 1796, after Dona Maria I promised God that if she had a male heir, she'd go to any lengths to show her gratitude. She eventually did have a son, and in thanks built this striking church. *Praça da Estrela.* ☎ *21/396-09-15. Free admission. Daily 7:30am–1pm and 3–8pm. Tram: 28.*

Best FREE → **Castelo de São Jorge** ★★ You can't miss this enormous castle looming over the city, but it's worth a closer visit while you're in the Alfama. The castle has survived a turbulent history. Erected in the 5th century A.D. by the Visigoths, it was taken over by the Saracens in the 8th century, and was later occupied and enlarged by the Moors in the 9th century. The castle's name is a reference to the Anglo-Portuguese pact believed to have been enacted in the 14th century—George is England's patron saint. Take a stroll around the castle gardens and grounds, and be sure to climb to the top of the castle, as its perch above the city offers some of the finest views in Lisbon. *Rua da Costa do Castelo.* ☎ *21/ 887-72-44. www.egeac.pt. Free admission. Apr– Sept daily 9am–9pm; Oct–Mar daily 9am– 6pm. Tram: 12 or 28.*

→ **Mosteiro dos Jerónimos** After the explorer Vasco da Gama's journey to India in 1502, the Mosteiro was built as a sign of gratitude; today it houses da Gama's tomb. The building features a Manueline-style architecture, native to Portugal, with evidence of Moorish and Gothic effects, as well. Check out the chapel Ingreja de Santa Maria, built by

Henry the Navigator to honor St. Mary. The church is known for its intricate stone carvings and its two-story cloisters, and for housing the tombs of other notable Portuguese figures. *Praça do Império.* ☎ *21/362-00-34. Free admission to church; cloisters 4.50€ adults, 2.25€ ages 15–25. May–Sept Tues–Sun 10am–6pm; Oct–Apr Tues–Sun 10am–5pm. Tram: 15. Bus: 27, 28, 29, 43, or 49.*

➜ **Oceanario de Lisboa** ★★ At what's billed as the second-largest aquarium in the world, you'll be able to explore four of the world's oceans. Housed in a striking glass-and-stone building, the Oceanario was constructed in anticipation for Expo '98, and is the centerpiece of the Parque das Nações (Park of Nations). The main exhibit is a 1.3-million-gallon tank that shows how the four different ecosystems representing the world's oceans differ. You'll encounter sharks, manta rays, crabs, and sea horses. You'll also find plants and animals native to those regions above "sea level." Interactive exhibits featuring soundscapes and even smells abound, aiming to teach visitors about the underwater world. *Esplanada d. Carlos I.* ☎ *21/891-70-02. Admission 9€ adults, 4.60€ students. Summer daily 10am–7pm; winter daily 10am–6pm. Metro: Estação do Oriente.*

➜ **Padrão dos Descobrimentos** Designed to look like the bow of a ship, the Monument to the Discoveries proudly overlooks the Tagus River, paying homage to numerous Portuguese explorers like Vasco da Gama and Henry the Navigator. Look closely at the carved figures and you'll see mapmakers, navigators, and monks represented. Also be sure to check out the marble map of the world marked with the dates of discoveries set into the ground in front of the monument. *Praça da Boa Esperança, Av. de Brasília.* ☎ *21/303-19-50. Admission 1.90€. July–Aug Tues–Sun 9:30am–9pm; Sept–June Tues–Sun 9:30am–5pm. Tram: 15, or walk from the monastery along the waterfront.*

➜ **Sé (Cathedral)** This cathedral was Lisbon's first church, designated as such after 12th-century crusaders captured the city. Inside the Gothic-style structure is believed to be the bath where St. Anthony was christened. Try to check out the cloister and the sacristy, though you will need a guide to see the relics, paintings, iron grille, and other treasures inside. *Largo da Sé.* ☎ *21/886-67-52. Tues–Sat 9am–7pm; Sun–Mon 9am–5pm. Free admission to cathedral admission; cloister 1.50€. Tram: 28.*

➜ **Torre de Belém (Tower of Belém)** ★ Images of Lisbon's famous tower can be found all across Portugal. It's a point of national pride. Built in the early 16th century, the four-sided tower marked by Moorish-style balconies is one of two major monuments honoring the country's Age of Discovery, when Portugal's navy was at its finest and explorers reached new worlds. *Praça do Império, Av. de Brasília.* ☎ *21/362-00-34. Admission 3€ adults, 1.50€ students. Oct–Apr Tues–Sun 10am–5pm, May–Sept 10am–6:30pm. Tram: 15, or walk from the monastery along the waterfront.*

Museums

➜ **Museu Calouste Gulbenkian** Touted as having one of the finest private art collections in the world, the Gulbenkian exists thanks to the philanthropist Calouste Gulbenkian (a native Brit who chose to live in Portugal), who left his art to the country when he died in 1955. The museum is in a sprawling estate house and includes a number of Renaissance tapestries, medieval illuminated manuscripts, French Impressionist paintings, and artwork by Rembrandt, Rubens, Renoir, and Cassatt. *Av. de Berna 45.* ☎ *21/782-30-00. www.museu.gulbenkian.pt. Admission 3€, free for students and on Sun. Tues–Sun 10am–6pm. Metro: Sebastião.*

➜ **Museu Nacional dos Coches (National Coach Museum)** For reasons I can't quite fathom, this museum is Lisbon's

12 Hours In Lisbon

1. **Sample pastries at a cafe in the Baixa-Chiado, near the bustling Metro stop.**

2. **Get lost in the charming Alfama district.** Allow yourself to absorb the charm and magic of this medieval quarter.

3. **Bask in the sun by Praça do Comércio.** Watch endless streams of tourists stroll by.

4. **Exercise your credit card along the Avenida de Liberdade.** Or simply do some mean window-shopping at the designer boutiques on this street.

5. **Hit the bars of the Bairro Alto.** Order a happy-hour Super Bock beer and chat up the omnipresent hipsters mingling by the bar.

6. **Play hide-and-seek in the battlements of the Castelo de São Jorge.** You can climb the reconstructed towers and run among the ramparts of this 12th-century citadel.

7. **Taste some port at Al Faia wine bar in the Bairro Alto.**

8. **Make your way to a _fado_ club to get a real flavor for the soul of this city.**

9. **Hit the discos along the Doca de Santo Amaro marina.** Shimmy the night away to international DJs spinning groovy beats, until the sun rises over the Tagus.

most visited attraction. In a former 18-century riding academy, the museum is attached to the Belém Royal Palace. The opulent, gold-gilded 17th- and 19th-century coaches are on display in the center of the horse ring. *Praça de Afonso de Albuquerque.* ☎ *21/ 361-08-50. Admission 3€. 1.50€ students 14–25. Tues–Sun 10am–5:30pm. Tram: 15. Bus: 14, 27, 28, 29, 43, 49, or 51.*

The University Scene

Though it's home to some 58 universities (most of them quite small), Lisbon's college scene is not centralized. **Universidade de Lisboa** (Cidade Universitaria 1649–004; ☎ **21/796-76-24;** www.ul.pt; Metro: Cidade Universitaria) is the city's main university with 5,800 students, but it's way out in the northern reaches of the city. Other than the student residences and the requisite cheap and thrill-less cafes, there's not much to be found in the Cidade neighborhood. Instead, students head into bar-filled hubs like the **Bairro Alto** or the club-laden **Doca de Santo Amaro** to drink and hang with friends. Because these areas are so far from the university, travelers won't really get a strong sense of a university culture in the heart of Lisbon.

Playing Outside

BEACHES It seems every visitor to Portugal strives to hit the beaches in the nearby towns of **Estoril** and **Cascais,** but locals will tell you to bypass those crowded, polluted shores for the glorious sands and clean, sapphire waters of **Caparica,** south of the city on the northwestern tip of the Setúbal Peninsula. Caparica is a 12-mile stretch of sand divided into 20 different beaches that grow increasingly isolated and wild the farther south you travel. The beaches and grass-covered dunes are set against a dramatic, rocky backdrop. Don't get too excited when you learn there's a nude beach—think very old men playing paddle ball. To get there, take the Metro to P. Espanha, and then take bus no. 153 to Caparica (the bus station is right outside the Metro stop). A round-trip ticket is 2.80€. When you arrive at the main town Caparica, hop aboard the narrow-gauge train (tickets are for either one zone or two zones; spring for the 3.80€ for the two zones—the beaches are more remote) to reach the beaches down the coast. The beaches along the coast are free, though most have beach clubs; a chair and umbrella run 7.50€.

If you still insist on heading to Estoril or Cascais, take the electric train from the Cais do Sodré station (Metro: Cais do Sodré) to either town. Trains run every 20 minutes, and it's a half-hour trip. Tickets cost 1.40€.

BIKE RENTAL   Lisbon's lack of bike paths make it one of the least bike-friendly cities in Portugal; however, if you head to Expo '98, the site of the Oceanario, you'll find a better bike scene with the option to rent and ride bikes along the Tagus River. For a super-cheap rental, stop by **Tejo Bike** (Parque das Nações, Rossio dos Olivais and Sony Plaza, next to the Jumbotron; ☎ 21/891-93-33). It's open daily in summer from 10am to 8pm; winter hours are 10am to 6pm. Bike rental ranges from 2€ to 7€ per hour.

FUTBOL   That's *soccer* to all you Anglos out there. If you can't keep your feet still and you need to run off some steam, or at least watch other people run off steam, indulge in a peek at the Portuguese national pastime, either by joining a pickup game in **Parque Eduardo VII** (Praça Marquês de Pombal; ☎ 21/388-22-78; daily Apr–Sept 9am–6pm, Oct–Mar 9am–5pm; Metro: Marquês de Pombal), or better yet catching a game featuring one of the city's two main teams,

Sporting and Benfica. From late August until the following June, games featuring either team, as well as the end-of-season Cup Final, can be seen at the 50,000-seat **Estado Nacional-Jamor** (Complexo Desportivo do Jamor, Praça da Maratona 1495; ☎ 21/419-72-12; Tues–Sun 8am–8pm; tickets 5€–30€; train: to Algés from Cais do Sodré; bus: 76 to Faculdade de Motoricidade Humana). It's possible to buy tickets at the stadium on the day of the event, but a safer bet is to buy them in advance from the tourist booth in the Praça do Restauradores.

GARDENS & PARKS   Take a stroll through **Jardim Zoológico de Lisboa** (Estada de Benfica 58; ☎ 21/723-29-00; www.zoolisboa. pt; admission 11€; Apr to mid-Oct daily 10am–8pm, mid-Oct to Mar daily 10am–6pm; Metro: Jardim Zoológico or Sete Rios), a sprawling 26-hectare (64-acre) park, once you've had your fill of the city's monuments and museums. You'll commune with all types of nature,

No Bull

In Portugal, unlike Spain, the bull isn't killed during a bloody and pro-longed event in the bullfighting ring. Still, the bullfights in Lisbon aren't exactly a walk in the park, and some of the bull's blood is drawn when it is stabbed with spears in the neck. If you think you're up for it, though, you're in for a cultural phenomenon. Bullfighting is a spectacle, acted out by richly dressed *cavaleiros* (horse-men) who charge at the bull, and other men who actually hand-wrestle with the bull. You can catch a bull-fight most Thursdays from June through September at **Praça de Touros de Lisboa** (Campo Pequeno; ☎ 21/793-21-43; Metro: Campo Pequeno).The bullfighting season runs from Easter until mid-July; call for exact hours.

including some 2,000 animals, in the Park of Laranjeiras. You can stay to watch twice-daily animal shows featuring either birds or reptiles, or rest your feet on a cable-car ride as you gaze at the zoo's free range areas for larger animals.

GOLF Lisbon's environs, especially the area around the Estoril coast, are well-known for their high-quality greens. There are approximately nine top-notch courses nearby, but the most convenient is at **Lisbon Sports Club** (Casal da Carregueira, Belas; ☎ 21/431-00-77; daily 8am–7pm; greens fees 47€, 57€ on weekends), an 18-hole, par-69 course reached by a 20-minute car/taxi ride. Founded in 1922 by Brits, the golf club is the second oldest in Portugal.

SKATEBOARDING You won't find any rentals here, but if you brought your board, or just want to hang with some like-minded, old-school skate rats, head on over to the Doca de Santo Amaro, in Belém (tram: 15), where kids skate, smoke cigarettes, and just hang out along the sprawling pavement.

Shopping

Portuguese artisans are probably best known for the ubiquitous blue-and-white glazed tiles that seem to cover every imaginable building wall in town, as well as porcelain and pottery products, embroideries from the Madeira region, hand-woven baskets, fado music, and gold jewelry. A central hub for shopping for bric-a-brac to bring home to the fam is in the Baixa district. Stroll along the Rua Augusta and Rua Aurea as well as the aptly named Rua da Prata (Street of Silver), and you'll come across many goldsmiths and jewelers. Head to Rua Garrett in the Chiado for finer-quality stores.

Monday to Friday, most stores open between 9 and 10am, close at noon for lunch, reopen at 2pm, and close for the day at 7pm. Some shopkeepers take lunch from 1 to 3pm, so check before making the trip. On Saturday, many stores only stay open to 1pm, and most stores are closed entirely on Sunday. Exceptions to this norm are noted in the reviews below.

➔ **Agência 117** ★ Though the wares here are mostly affordable, you'll want to empty your bank account so that you can buy all the vintage, hip-hop, retro-inspired gear in this ultratrendy shop. There's a bar and also an on-site hairstylist and a makeup artist. *Rua do Norte 117.* ☎ *21/346-12-70. Metro: Baixa-Chiado.*

➔ **Diesel Lisboa** The clothes are always styling, in particular those dead-sexy jeans and tees, and as an added bonus the show has catchy music thumping throughout its two floors of fashion. *Praça Luís Camões 30.* ☎ *21/342-19-80. Metro: Baixa-Chiado.*

➔ **Livraria Bertrand** If you prefer sharp-minded political dialog to go with your book purchases, head to Lisbon's oldest bookstore (opened in 1732), which gained notoriety for drawing customers keen on debating politics and literature alike. You'll find a decent selection of English-language books, magazines, travel guides, and maps of Lisbon. *Rua Garrett 73–75.* ☎ *21/346-86-46. Metro: Baixa-Chiado.*

➔ **Livraria Britanica** Chances are, you'll need something to read for the long train ride out of Portugal, and you'll probably want it in English. Britanica offers the city's best selection of English-language books, and you'll find selections ranging from Dan Brown to Dante. *Rua Luís Fernandes 14–16.* ☎ *21/342-84-72. Metro: Rato.*

➔ **Raveman Records** Don't be fooled by the name—it's not all glow sticks and pacifiers at this vinyl-junky heaven. Head to Raveman for acid, punk, house, techno, trance, and psychedelic tunes, as well as CDs, DJ equipment, and staff recommendations on local after-hours parties in the 'hood. *Travessa da Quiemada 33.* ☎ *21/347-11-70. Tram: 28 to Bairro Alto.*

→**Valentim de Carvalho** Can't get enough of those woeful *fado* singers? You'll find all the traditional Portuguese lamenters, both old and new, on the shelves here. Look for the names Amalia Rodriguez, Nuno Câmara Pereira, Carlos Ducarmo, and Carlos Paredes. The store is also a veritable supermarket for international music ranging in genre from rock to folk to punk to house. *Rua Ventu du Jesus Caraças 17.* ☎ *21/324-97-50. Metro: Baixa-Chiado.*

Markets

When hunger strikes, unless you're into dumpster diving (and hopefully, you're opposed), you're gonna have to spend some euros—but it doesn't have to be a lot. Consider grabbing some dirt-cheap fruits, meats, cheeses, and bread from the sprawling **Mercado da Ribeira** (Av. 24 de Julho; ☎ **21/346-29-66;** Metro: Cais de Sodré; Mon–Sat 6am–2pm) and head to the lovely **Parque Eduardo VII** (Praça Marques de Pombal; ☎ **21/388-22-78;** daily Apr–Sept 9am–6pm, Oct–Mar 9am–5pm; Metro: Marques de Pombal) to munch on your goodies and sit along the hillside, enjoying its winding mosaic paths, shady trees, neatly trimmed gardens, and pond.

The big market of **Ribeira Nova** is as close as you can get to the heart of Lisbon. Behind the Cais do Sodré train station, an enormous roof shelters a collection of stalls offering the produce used in Lisbon's fine restaurants. Some of the freshly plucked produce arrives by donkey, some by truck, and some balanced on the heads of Lisboan women in the Mediterranean fashion. At the market, women festively clad in voluminous skirts and calico aprons preside over the mounds of vegetables, fruit, and fish. On cue, the vendors begin howling about the value of their wares, stopping only to pose for an occasional snapshot.

If high-end fashion doesn't fit your budget, sniff around for some vintage and thrift duds at the **Feira de Ladra (Thieves' Market),** a flea market held every Tuesday and Saturday morning from 7am until late afternoon. For the best offerings of tie-dyed tees and other casual duds, plan to arrive as early as humanly possible. It's on Campo de Santa Clara, behind the Igreja São Vicente de For, a 5-minute walk from the waterfront in the Alfama district.

LISBON

Road Trip

One of Portugal's gems, the spellbinding town of **Sintra** sits on a hillside surrounded by lush vegetation and has captured the souls of its visitors for ages, inspiring Lord Byron to call it "a glorious Eden." The perfect day trip from Lisbon, Sintra is marked by magnificent castles and even more stunning views of the surrounding countryside from its high perch.

Getting into Town

Head to Lisbon's Estação Sete Rios, where trains depart every 15 minutes. It's a 45-minute ride—so there's no need to stay overnight—and costs 1.40€. Once you arrive, you'll have to take a taxi to the sights or hike up a steep hill to the palace.

Sintra Basics

You'll find the **tourist offices** in the train station (☎ **21/924-16-23;** daily June–Sept 9am–8pm, Oct–May 9am–7pm) and at Praça da República 23 (☎ **21/923-11-57;** daily June–Sept 9am–8pm, Oct–May 9am–7pm), where you can pick up maps and get more detailed information from the English-speaking staff.

Eating

When you get hungry, head for the Avenida Heliodoro or the Rua João de Deus, where many restaurants are clustered. If you're looking for a quick snack to get you by, head over to the **Lojo do Vinho** (Praça da República 3; ☎ 21/924-44-10; daily 9am–10:30pm), a wine bar and shop on the main square that offers a smattering of tables where patrons can enjoy light bites like sausages, cheese, or olives. For something more substantial, head to **Alcobaça** (Rua das Padarias 7–11; ☎ 21/923-16-51) in the town center, where you'll be sated with a traditional Portuguese meal. You can't go wrong with the *bacalhau,* or any seafood served *bulhão pato* (with garlic sauce).

Sightseeing

You'll want to head straight to the **Palácio Nacional de Sintra** (Largo da Rainha Dona Amélia; ☎ 21/910-68-40; admission 3€ adults, 1.50€ ages 14–25). This exquisite palace was once the summer home of Moorish sultans, and boasts a varied architecture with elements that are Gothic, Moorish, and Manueline. Be sure to admire the paintings and tapestries, and don't miss the lavish Room of the Mermaids.

Next head to the **Palácio Nacional de Pena** (Estrada de Pena; ☎ 21/910-53-40; admission 6€, students 4€; June–Sept daily 10am–5:30pm, Oct–May daily 10am–4pm) where you'll find fabulous vistas and a well-preserved decor from the reign of Queen Amelia in the early 20th century, and a shrub-filled park. Finally check out the UNESCO World Heritage Site, **Quintas de Regaleiga** (Rua Visconde de Monserrate; ☎ 21/910-66-50; admission 5€; June–Sept daily 10am–8pm, Oct and Feb–May daily 10am–6:30pm, Nov–Jan daily 10am–5:30pm), a manor house with turrets that provides fabulous photo ops of the breathtaking environs. The house is filled with interesting antiques and artifacts, and there's even a park to stroll through on the property.

London

London, once the capital of a vast empire and now the arbiter of cool for modern Europe, may straddle the past and the present better than any other city on earth. Nowhere else could Shakespeare's tiny, thatched Globe Theatre sit comfortably down the river from the hulking metal structure of the London Eye, the world's most extreme Ferris wheel. As much a global capital as New York or Tokyo, London easily holds its own on the fashion frontier, churns out some of the hottest music, makes its mark in the art world, and has recently built a reputation for fine cuisine. London (pop. 7.5 million) has embraced the 21st century, yet Great Britain's capital retains some of its old "charm." As a visitor, you'll have to learn to obey anachronistic drinking laws and to deal with some pubs shutting at 11pm. And while you can have the time of your life in London, you'll want to remember to mind your Ps and Qs. The city may have spawned hell raisers like Sid Vicious, but the influence of the Queen still seeps into most sensibilities. All Londoners—from MPs to hackney cab drivers—are as proud of their British sense of decorum as they are their city's many attractions.

Flirt with London instead of cramming in all spots along the tourist trail. If you try to see all the big sights in one visit, you'll come away with your prejudices reinforced against stiff upper-lipped British bulldogs—and you won't meet a soul who isn't a fellow tourist. Wander the streets. Get lost. Start, maybe, by exploring Soho, which has long ago morphed from a sleazy area into London's playground of fancy clubs and restaurants and its hottest gay scene. Leave behind stereotypes of neighborhoods like Chelsea—these days you'll find posh older families hanging out there, not swinging rockers—and Notting Hill—you will *not* encounter Hugh Grant types around every corner. For the most up-and-coming areas, go east to Shoreditch, home to the city's really struggling artists; south to Brixton, a hood far more West Indian than white-guys-with-dreadlocks Notting Hill; and north, to areas like Islington, a hotbed of creative, but mostly gainfully employed, 20-somethings. Just remember that this city ain't cheap, so keep an eye on what you spend even in these fringier hoods.

The Best of London

○ **The Best Hotel for Insomniacs:** You may not get a lot of sleep at **Wake Up! London** because guests here tend to stay up chatting and blasting loud music, but don't say the name didn't warn you. See p. 560.

○ **The Best Diner Food:** The fare at **Automat** is decidedly more upscale than at your average greasy spoon, but there's no denying that it's comfort food. Best of all, you can order cocktails to accompany your mac 'n' cheese or Mississippi mud pie. See p. 562.

○ **The Best Curry in a Hurry:** The **Angel Curry Centre** in Islington is a great place for a cheap, quick curry fix. Even better, the BYOB policy means you'll have that much more money left over at the end of the meal. See p. 562.

○ **The Best Club:** Housed on multiple levels and packed on weekend nights with sweaty music lovers, **Fabric** is the crème de la crème of clubs. Make sure you down some vodka Red Bulls before hitting the dance floor(s) because you'll be dancing for hours to the latest drum 'n' bass. See p. 566.

○ **The Best Bar to Keep Secret:** Ssshhh. You'll need to make reservations if you're not a member of **Milk and Honey**'s secret society. The hush-hush nature of this place ensures that the clientele stays as cool as the bar itself—the game room alone is worth a visit. See p. 567.

○ **The Best Place to Discover Your Inner Artist:** In what was once a disused power station south of the Thames, the **Tate Modern** displays major international artwork from Fauvism onward. Expect to find significant works by Pollock, Rothko, and Warhol, among others. Check the website for special exhibitions and don't forget to stop at the eclectic gallery shop for Paint-It-Yourself kits. See p. 576.

○ **The Best Crash Course in British History:** In a city filled with must-see attractions, **Westminster Abbey** truly can't be missed. Writers Chaucer, Dickens, Hardy, and Kipling, and monarchs such as Queen Elizabeth I, are buried here, so it's hard to leave without learning something about the country's storied history. See. p. 572.

○ **The Best One-Stop Shop:** Forget touristy Harrods and overpriced Harvey Nichols. The ultimate department store for Londoners in the know is **Selfridges,** off Oxford Street. This is a shopper's paradise, selling everything from sour candy to Stella McCartney duds. See p. 579.

○ **The Best Vintage Duds:** Original street clothes from the '50s, '60s, and '70s make **Pop Boutique** a destination in its own right. The prices are reasonable, and there's no VAT (value-added tax) on used clothing. See p. 579.

Talk of the Town

Four ways to start a conversation with a local

1. **Where's the best place to get a pint?** *Everyone* has a favorite pub, from college-age guys to little old ladies.

2. **What are your thoughts on Brit music?** Gone are the days of Brit-pop boy bands and Cool Britannia. Instead, weepy moaners like Keane and James Blunt rule the airwaves. Do Londoners long for the days when foul-mouthed Oasis topped the charts, or are the clean-living good boys of Coldplay here to stay?

3. **Do you feel safe on the Tube?** Ever since the terrorist attacks of July 7, 2005, Londoners have changed the way they see their beloved Underground—arguably the cleanest, best-organized city subway system on earth.

4. **Are you counting the seconds until the 2012 Olympics?** The city petitioned hard to win the honor of hosting the Olympics—so hard that some locals wonder whether the money spent to win the hosting honor was worth it.

Getting There & Getting Around

Getting into Town

BY AIR

London boasts five airports and numerous train stations. If you're flying from America or Canada, chances are you'll arrive at **Gatwick** (www.gatwickairport.com) or **Heathrow** (www.heathrowairport.com). If you're traveling from other locales, you might fly into the slightly less convenient **Luton** (www.london-luton.com), **Stanstead** (www.baa.co.uk), or **City Airport** (www.londoncityairport.com) airports. Balance your needs; sometimes the airports farther out have cheaper flights.

From Heathrow, the **Underground** is the best option for getting into town. There are two airport Tube stations on the Piccadilly line: one for terminals 1, 2, and 3, and one for Terminal 4. The journey into central London takes 40 to 50 minutes. Heathrow is in zone 6 and therefore is not covered by most travel cards. One-way fares to or from zone 1 are £3.80 for adults.

Another option is the **Heathrow Express** (☎ 0845/600-1515; www.heathrowexpress.com), a luxury nonstop rail service to and from Paddington Station. It takes 15 minutes from terminals 1, 2, and 3, and 20 to 25 minutes from Terminal 5. Standard-class one-way tickets costs £14. **National Express** (☎ 08705/747777 for info, 08705/808080 for bookings; www.gobycoach.com) runs two airport bus services and accepts online bookings.

The **Airbus** leaves twice an hour from just outside every Heathrow terminal and goes to 23 stops in central London. One-way tickets cost £8 for adults. The **Hotel Hoppa** runs between each terminal and the main Heathrow hotels from 5:30am to 11:30pm. One-way tickets cost £2.50. **Black taxis** are always available at Heathrow. The approximate fare to London is £45, which is a good-value, door-to-door cost if you can fill the cab with the maximum five passengers and still have room for luggage. The taxi desk numbers are **Terminal 3** at ☎ 020/8745-4655, and **Terminal 4** at ☎ 020/8745-7302.

From Gatwick, there are four ways of making the 25-mile trek into London. The most popular is the **Gatwick Express** train, which takes around 30 minutes to reach Victoria, and costs £11 one-way. The station is below

London

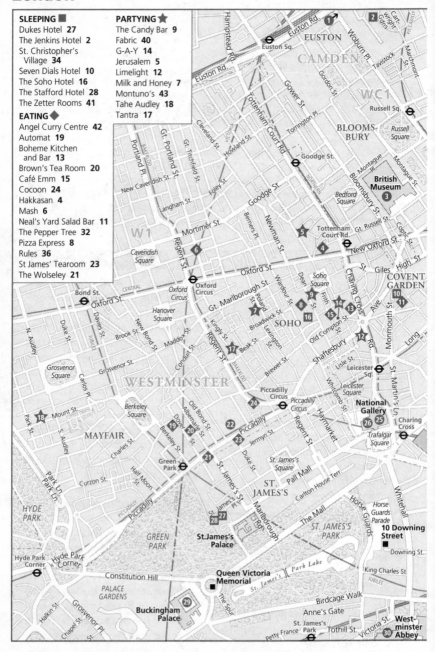

SLEEPING ■
Dukes Hotel **27**
The Jenkins Hotel **2**
St. Christopher's
Village **34**
Seven Dials Hotel **10**
The Soho Hotel **16**
The Stafford Hotel **28**
The Zetter Rooms **41**

EATING ◆
Angel Curry Centre **42**
Automat **19**
Boheme Kitchen
and Bar **13**
Brown's Tea Room **20**
Café Emm **15**
Cocoon **24**
Hakkasan **4**
Mash **6**
Neal's Yard Salad Bar **11**
The Pepper Tree **32**
Pizza Express **8**
Rules **36**
St James' Tearoom **23**
The Wolseley **21**

PARTYING ★
The Candy Bar **9**
Fabric **40**
G-A-Y **14**
Jerusalem **5**
Limelight **12**
Milk and Honey **7**
Montuno's **43**
Tahe Audley **18**
Tantra **17**

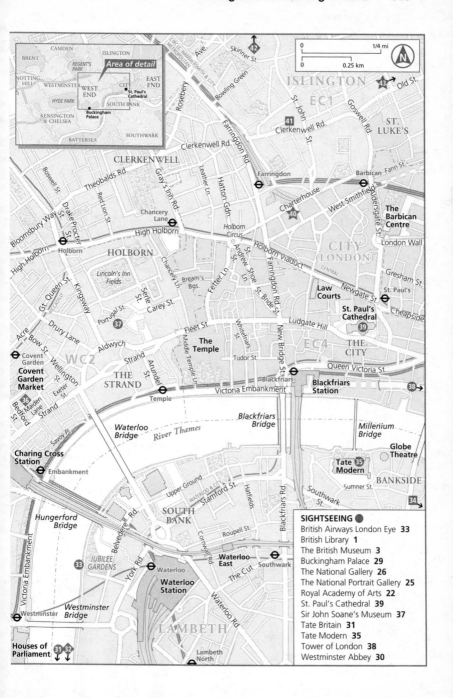

SIGHTSEEING ●

British Airways London Eye 33
British Library 1
The British Museum 3
Buckingham Palace 29
The National Gallery 26
The National Portrait Gallery 25
Royal Academy of Arts 22
St. Paul's Cathedral 39
Sir John Soane's Museum 37
Tate Britain 31
Tate Modern 35
Tower of London 38
Westminster Abbey 30

West London

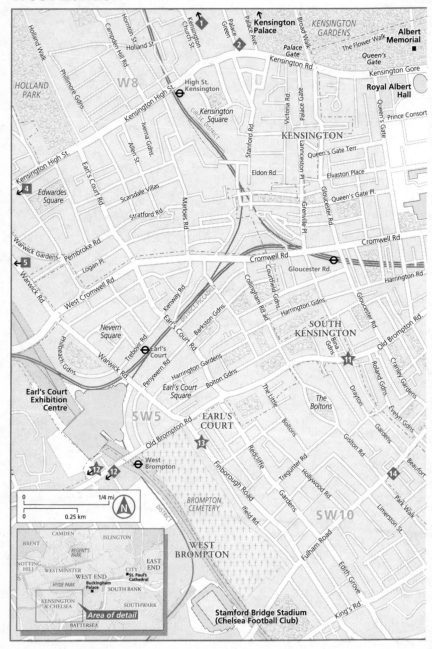

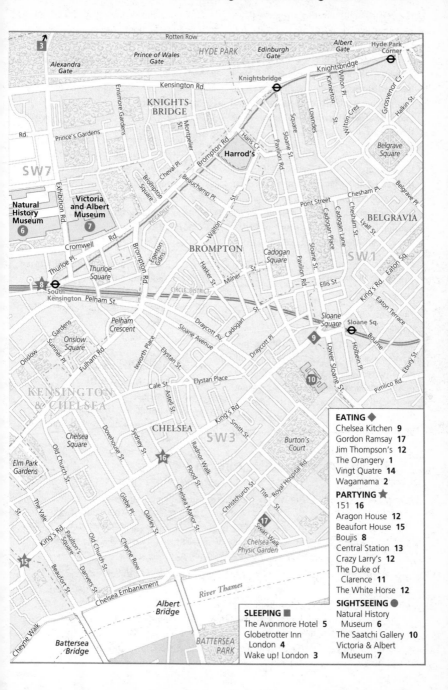

EATING ◆
Chelsea Kitchen **9**
Gordon Ramsay **17**
Jim Thompson's **12**
The Orangery **1**
Vingt Quatre **14**
Wagamama **2**

PARTYING ★
151 **16**
Aragon House **12**
Beaufort House **15**
Boujis **8**
Central Station **13**
Crazy Larry's **12**
The Duke of
   Clarence **11**
The White Horse **12**

SIGHTSEEING ●
Natural History
   Museum **6**
The Saatchi Gallery **10**
Victoria & Albert
   Museum **7**

SLEEPING ■
The Avonmore Hotel **5**
Globetrotter Inn
   London **4**
Wake up! London **3**

the airport, and trains depart every 15 minutes from 6:50am to 10:50pm. The slightly cheaper option is **South Central Trains,** which charges £8.20 one-way and takes 35 to 45 minutes, depending on how often it stops between Victoria station and the airport. For information on both, call **National Rail Enquiries** (☎ 08457/484950), or pre-book through www.thetrainline.com.

BY TRAIN

If you're coming from France, Belgium, or the Netherlands, you can take the **Eurostar** (www.eurostar.com) straight into Waterloo International train station, the main railway hub for London. Tube stops are located at every train station in London, including Waterloo.

Getting Around

BY CAR

The most obvious tip about driving in London also happens to be the most important: Look before you cross because they drive on the left here. Because London traffic is horrendous at all hours of the day, renting any sort of vehicle is not recommended. It makes more sense to hop on a bus or Tube rather than sit in a queue breathing carbon monoxide. If you must rent a car to drive outside the city, your best bet is Enterprise, Europcar, or one of the other large agencies. Rent from an airport or from Waterloo train station. **Enterprise** is at 466 Edgware Rd. (☎ 020/7723-4800), and **Europcar** is at 12 Semley Place, near Victoria (☎ 020/7259-1600).

BY TRAIN

If you plan on traveling throughout the United Kingdom, consider buying a **BritRail Classic Pass.** This allows unlimited rail travel anywhere during a set time period; prices vary. You must purchase passes on the phone or online directly from BritRail (☎ 866/BRITRAIL; www.britrail.net).

BY TUBE

London is justifiably proud of its efficient and clean Underground system. However, the Tube bombings on July 7, 2005, shook Londoners, some of whom have sworn off the subway system in favor of increasingly crowded buses. You can find Tube maps, bus schedules, and anything else you might need to get around on the **Transport for London** website at **www.tfl.gov.uk/tfl**.

The London Underground operates on a system of six fare zones. These radiate out in concentric rings from the central zone 1,

Talk the Talk: Local Jargon

Drop the following bizarre words into conversations, and you just may achieve cool Londoner status. Some words are derived from Cockney rhyming slang; for more info, check out www.cockneyrhymingslang.co.uk to learn more.

→ **Yob/Yobbo:** Hooligan. Often affiliated with football fandom and a love of lager.

→ **Fag:** Cigarette. No, we can't explain this either.

→ **Bog/Loo:** Toilet. Not especially polite, but more used than "bathroom."

→ **Chav:** British equivalent of white trash, or someone with more money than taste. Think Posh Spice and head-to-toe Burberry.

→ **Offie:** Off-License liquor store. Where to buy a bottle of vodka when everywhere else is shut.

→ **Naff:** There is no American equivalent to this word. Think cheesy and uncool, like doilies on sofas.

which is where visitors spend most of their time. Zone 1 covers an area from the Tower in the east to Notting Hill in the west, and from Waterloo in the south to Baker Street, Euston, and King's Cross in the north. You will need a zone 2 ticket, though, for a trip to Camden, Hampstead, and Greenwich. The city's buses used to share the same zone system but **London Transport (LT)** has simplified the bus system: Now, for ticket-buying purposes, there's just zone 1, and then the rest of London; there are four fare zones for bus passes, though.

Single (one-way) tickets within zone 1 on the Underground cost £1.60 for adults; simply double that for a return (round-trip) fare. The price of a book of 10 single tickets, a **Carnet,** is £12, two-thirds that of the same number bought individually. Adult bus fares are £1 within central London zone 1, 70p outside zone 1, and £1.50 on night buses.

BY BUS

Night buses are in operation far later than the Underground, so if you find yourself broke after a night out, it makes sense to take a bus rather than a taxi home. Just keep in mind that they can be slow.

You buy single-trip bus tickets on the bus itself. On older buses, a conductor comes around, but most new buses are now driver-only, so you pay when you board. In either case, proffering a note bigger than £5, unless you're only expecting small change, is likely to produce some very strong language, particularly from the notoriously eccentric conductors. If inspectors find you without a ticket, the on-the-spot fine is £5.

BY BIKE

The **London Bicycle Company** offers rental bicycles and also organizes comprehensive tours of the city for decent prices—£3 per hour or £16 for the whole day. They'll also provide maps and advice on routes. See www.londonbicycle.com for details or call ☎ **020/7928-6838.** The shop is located at Gabriels Wharf, right by Blackfriars Tube.

BY TAXI

Black cabs carry up to five people and can make sound economic sense for group jaunts. All the drivers are licensed and have to pass a test called The Knowledge first, so they know London very well. Look for the yellow FOR HIRE sign lit up on the roof and wave wildly. Before you get in, tell the driver where you want to go. Except in the West End, many drivers go home at midnight. You can order a black cab but you'll have to pay an extra charge for the time it takes the taxi to get to you—up to £3.80. These two companies dispatch cabs around the clock: **Dial a Cab (☎ 020/7253-5000)** and **Radio Taxis (☎ 020/7272-0272).** The average cost of a taxi ride is said to be £8—but that means daytime, within central London, and with no unusual traffic jams. The minimum charge is £1.40, and the meter goes up in increments of 20p.

Minicabs are generally cheaper than black cabs, but drivers don't have to have a special license, and some won't know their way around any better than you do. Technically, they must operate from a sidewalk office or through phone bookings, and are not allowed to cruise for fares. But some do, of course, particularly at main railway stations and late at night in the West End. With minicabs there are none of the guarantees you get with a black cab. Minicabs don't have meters. Always negotiate the fare with the office, and confirm it with the driver. Most firms are open round-the-clock, and you can pre-book for later, or for the next morning if you've got an early start. They tend to be locally based, so ask your hotel or B&B to recommend a reputable one. **Addison Lee (☎ 020/7387-8888)** operates citywide.

LONDON

Travelcard

Anyone planning to use public transport should check out the range of passes that are available for all public transportation: the Underground, buses, and the Docklands Light Railway. These make travel cheaper, and also get you **a third off most boat trips** through Thames River Services (www.londontransport.co.ul/river).

→ **One-Day Travelcards** can be used for unlimited trips after 9:30am Monday to Friday, and all day on Saturday, Sunday, and holidays, and on N-prefixed night buses. Adults traveling within zones 1 and 2 pay £4.10 off-peak and £5.10 peak. The **One-Day LT Card** is available for all zones at peak travel times for £8 per adult.

→ **Weekend Travelcards** are valid for 1 weekend, or any 2 consecutive days if Monday is a national holiday, and on night buses. These cost £6.10 for adults in zone 1 and 2.

→ **One-Week Travelcards** are good for any number of trips, any hour of the day, and on night buses. The card for zone 1 costs adults £17.

→ **Bus passes,** valid for travel only on London Transport buses, are available for all zones for 1 day at £2 per adult, for 1 week at £17.

You can buy all these, as well as monthly and yearly passes, at Tube stations, tobacconists, and newsagents with a **Pass Agent** sticker in their window.

ON FOOT

Many of London's most famous attractions are within walking distance of each other. For example, you can get from the West End's theater district to the shops of Oxford Street in about 10 minutes on foot. Whatever you do, don't look at the Tube map as any indication of distance, as the interconnected colored lines bear no relation to what is aboveground.

If you want to go on an organized tour, join a walking tour of London. The best one is **Tour London**'s. It encompasses every major sight from Parliament to the Tower to Buckingham Palace, and includes a double-decker bus ride. Go to **www.tourlondon.com** for more information and call ☎ 020/8531-8243 to find out where the tour commences.

London Basics

Orientation: London Neighborhoods

The best way to orient yourself within London is to think of the city as beginning at Chelsea, on the north bank of the Thames, and stretching north through Kensington to Hampstead, then east and south to Tower Bridge.

Trafalgar Square is considered the center of this area. If you stand here facing the National Gallery you'll be facing **Piccadilly Circus**—the hub of tourist London—and the many streets that make up the restaurant and bar-laden **SoHo area.**

South from Trafalgar Square is **Whitehall,** home to nearly all the British government buildings, including the home of the prime minister. Farther south are the Houses of Parliament and Westminster Abbey. Southwest from Trafalgar is **The Mall,** lined with parks and mansions that lead to Buckingham Palace. Farther south you'll find the wealthy neighborhood of **Knightsbridge,** and beyond that almost as pricey, edgier **Chelsea** 'hood and King's Road, a fancy shopping district.

West from Trafalgar are Regent Street and Piccadilly, and beyond that the elegant shops of **Mayfair.** Continuing in that direction, you'll hit **Hyde Park,** one of the biggest parks in the world.

Charing Cross Road runs north from Trafalgar Square, past Leicester Square. This is London's theater district. The road then funnels into St. Giles Circus, beyond which is **Bloomsbury,** home of the University of London and the British Museum. Northwest of the square is **Covent Garden,** known for its Royal Opera House, and a major shopping and eating district.

If you follow The Strand eastward from Trafalgar Square, you'll hit **Fleet Street,** once the largest concentration of newspaper offices in the world. Temple Bar stands where The Strand becomes Fleet Street, and here is where you officially enter the city of London. At the far eastern edge of the city rises the Tower of London.

Following is a more in-depth breakdown of the city's 'hoods:

KNIGHTSBRIDGE   Posh Knightsbridge is very wealthy and very fashionable in a way that is both solid establishment and gossip-column glitz. At **Harrods,** the main attraction in Knightsbridge, green-liveried doormen turn people away for having grubby or inappropriate clothing. Knightsbridge Barracks, on the edge of the park, is where the Household Cavalry lives—they're the ones you see in the Changing of the Guard.

BELGRAVIA   Belgravia reached the peak of its prestige in the reign of Queen Victoria, but for the nouveau riche and for those aristocrats whose forebears didn't blow all the family heirlooms, it's still a very fashionable

address. The Duke of Westminster, who owns vast tracts of Belgravia and Chelsea, lives at Eaton Square. Architecture buffs will love the town houses, especially in the area's centerpiece, Belgrave Square. Budget travelers can hover on the verge of a smart address at the B&Bs in Ebury Street, though that is really Victoria.

CHELSEA   The action really starts at Sloane Square, with Gilbert Ledward's Venus fountain at its center, and moves east down that dangerously captivating shopping heaven, the **King's Road.** Some large chain stores moved in a few years ago, but it's still more chic than cheap, and retains a funky fashionable feel begun in the 1960s by Mary Quant, who started the miniskirt revolution, and built on by that doyenne of tarty punk, Vivienne Westwood. Chelsea has always been a favorite of writers and artists, including Oscar Wilde, Henry James, and Thomas Carlyle, whose home you can visit. Residents today include aging rock stars (Mick Jagger), aging politicians (Margaret Thatcher), wealthy young Euromigrant families, and former "Sloane Rangers" of the 1980s. Temporary residents won't find many cheap places to stay, but there are a handful of good values and a mix of cheap pop-in eats and restaurants with excellent set meals.

KENSINGTON   The late Princess Diana lived here, and it's still home to a gang of family members. You can visit the palace (but not the royals, who inhabit their own wing). There are a couple of great bathless budget sleeps just off Kensington Church Street, which is lined with by-appointment-only antiques shops.

South Kensington is best known as the home of London's major museums, which stand along Cromwell Road: **the Natural History Museum, Victoria & Albert Museum,** and the **Science Museum.** They're all built on land bought with the proceeds of Prince Albert's Great Exhibition of 1851. He gave his name to two spectacular landmarks here: The **Royal Albert Hall,** where the famous Promenade concerts are held every year, and the Albert Memorial, commissioned by his grief-stricken wife Queen Victoria and completed with garish Victorian splendor in 1872. South Ken, as it's often called, is stuffed to the gunwales with surprisingly good-value B&Bs and self-catering accommodations.

EARL'S COURT   This neighborhood has gone through many incarnations. Between the wars, it was regarded as a staid residential district full of genteel ladies. It then became a haven for poor newcomers to Britain and young Brits buying an affordable first apartment, and it was London's first gay enclave—there are still plenty of gay bars here. There are whole streets of budget hotels that really are dives, and whole streets of lovely Victorian terraces. Things are changing overall, and an upmarket sensibility is creeping in. You can see it on the main street, Earl's Court Road, where the smarter cafe chains are starting to join the late-night fast-food joints. The huge Earl's Court Exhibition Centre brings in a lot of convention-size business.

To the south of Earl's Court is **Fulham,** centered around the Tube stop **Parson's Green,** a residential area filled with some notable pubs and restaurants.

NOTTING HILL   Notting Hill is in the process of becoming a victim of its own hype. When house prices began to rise in the mid-1990s, the press climbed on the bandwagon and hip media, music, and fashion types moved in to what had been a decent and sometimes grotty neighborhood. The popular film *Notting Hill* provided a final rocket-blast to the real-estate boom. Bye-bye boho scruffiness; hello Starbucks. Visitors flock here in hordes to visit the great **Portobello Market.** And there are good-value sleeps on this winding street. **Holland Park,** the next stop west, is a chi-chi residential neighborhood for fat wallets only.

Budget travelers can stay at the youth hostel located in the middle of the park.

PADDINGTON & BAYSWATER   Since 1836, Paddington has been the terminus for trains coming into London from the west and southwest. The presence of the station eventually transformed the area's once-genteel Georgian and Victorian terraces into scruffy sleeps for people just passing through. The area is about to enjoy a massive redevelopment around the canal basin. But there are still good B&B deals to be had here, just west of the West End.

Bayswater is a generalization rather than a definable area, arising from Bayswater Road, the main road running across the top of Hyde Park. Walk 5 minutes from Paddington, and you'll come to it. The buzziest bit is **Queensway,** a street of cheap ethnic restaurants, often tacky shops, and an ice-skating rink, with the old Whiteley's department store, now a shopping mall, at the northern end. That is also where Westbourne Grove starts, an increasingly funky street that links up with Notting Hill.

MAYFAIR   Bounded by Piccadilly, Hyde Park, Oxford Street, and Regent Street, Mayfair is filled with luxury hotels and grand shops. The Georgian town houses are beautiful, but many of them are offices now. Grosvenor (*grove*-nur) Square is nicknamed "Little America" because it's home to the U.S. Embassy. You must visit **Shepherd Market,** a tiny, rather raffish village of pubs and popular eateries: Sofra Bistro is a good and very reasonable Turkish restaurant. The old market was shut down for "fornication and lewdness," among other things, but upmarket prostitutes reputedly still cater to loose-trousered politicians in the vicinity.

MARYLEBONE   Most visitors head to Marylebone (*mar*-lee-bone) to explore Madame Tussaud's waxworks or trudge up Baker Street in the fantasy footsteps of

Sherlock Holmes. Generally, this is an anonymous area, with most of the action in a strip running just north of Oxford Street. St. Christopher's Place is a pretty pedestrian street with some reasonable restaurants and unreasonable boutiques close to Bond Street Tube. Marylebone High Street now has a gaggle of posh shops.

ST. JAMES'S Often called "Royal London," St. James's basks in its associations with everybody from the "merrie monarch," Charles II, to Elizabeth II, who lives at its most famous address, Buckingham Palace. English gentlemen retreat to their St. James's clubs. St. James's starts at Piccadilly Circus and going southwest, incorporates **Pall Mall, The Mall, St. James's Park,** and **Green Park.** Budget travelers must day-trip here to sample the lingering pomp and pompousness. Cheap eats are hard to find, except close to Piccadilly Circus, but the parks are prime picnic territory. You can get the necessities, or stop for tea, at the world's most luxurious grocery store, **Fortnum & Mason.**

SOHO Few cities have their strip joints and red-lights right next to fancy restaurants, thriving media companies, and a traditional fruit-and-veg market (Berwick St.). The council is enforcing ever more stringent controls on the sex trade by buying flats used as unlicensed brothels and selling them to charities that in turn develop social housing. Of all London's neighborhoods, Soho's narrow streets are the most densely thronged, especially on weekends.

Soho's boundaries are Regent Street; Oxford Street (a mecca for mass-market shopping); Charing Cross Road, which is stuffed with bookshops; and the theater-lined Shaftesbury Avenue. Urban streetwear stores are finally starting to push back the tide of tourist schlock on Carnaby Street. In the middle of Soho, Old Compton Street is the heart of gay London, with scores of gay bars,

pubs, and cafes. Cross Shaftesbury Avenue and you come to Chinatown, which is small, yet authentic, and packed with excellent restaurants.

PICCADILLY CIRCUS & LEICESTER SQUARE
Neon-lit Piccadilly Circus is packed with crowds morning, noon, and way past midnight, grazing on fast food, gawking at the bright lights, and shopping at the megastores. Though there's a fast-food flavor to the area, you'll find great set menus at Marco Pierre White's Criterion. Teeny-bopper delights abound at the Trocadero, where floor after floor is filled with video games and noisy attractions kids love. **Leicester** (*Jes*-ter) **Square** is wall-to-wall neon, too. Once a swish address, it changed forever when the Victorians opened four giant entertainment halls, which today are megacinemas. At one end you'll find the half-price tickets booth, an essential stop for theater-lovers. It's tacky, but fun. Keep a tight hold on your wallet, as pickpockets cruise for careless tourists. Both Piccadilly Circus and Leicester Square are hubs for London's West End theater scene.

BLOOMSBURY Northeast of Piccadilly Circus, beyond Soho, is Bloomsbury, the academic heart of London. Much of the University of London, as well as several other colleges, is based here. It's quite a staid neighborhood, but writers such as Virginia Woolf, who lived here, have fanned its reputation. Russell Square is the area's main hub, and the streets around it are crammed with excellent-value B&Bs. Most visitors come to see the treasures in the **British Museum,** and there are a few really good and good-value restaurants in the area.

Nearby is **Fitzrovia,** bounded by Great Portland Street, Oxford Street, and Gower Street (lots of B&Bs there). Goodge Street is the main Tube stop and the village-like heart, with many shops and restaurants. It was the stamping ground of Ezra Pound, Wyndham

Lewis, and George Orwell. Broadcasting House, in Portland Place, is an area landmark. It's the old BBC HQ and you can get inside if you get tickets to a radio show.

HOLBORN   This is the heart of legal London, where the ancient Inns of Court and Royal Courts of Justice lie. Dickens was a solicitor's clerk here when he was 14 and used the experience to good effect in *Little Dorrit.* Once you're off the traffic-laden High Holborn, time rolls back. This is too business-like to be a hotel zone.

COVENT GARDEN & THE STRAND   The fruit-and-flower market moved to an unromantic modern shed south of the river in 1970, and Professor Henry Higgins would find today's young women in Covent Garden far too fashionable for Eliza Doolittle–style experiments. This is a very fashion-oriented neighborhood, with more shopping and general razzle-dazzle than Soho, and certainly more tourists. It's quite pricey, too. The restored market hall is in the middle of a big pedestrian piazza and filled with little boutiques. The character of Covent Garden owes a lot to its long theatrical history, which is why there are so many great pre-theater deals at the restaurants.

The **Strand** is a winding thoroughfare lined with theaters and hotels. **Trafalgar Square** is a visitor must-see all by itself. Nelson's Column—the triumphal memorial to England's victory over Napoleon in 1805—stands in the center, and the **National Gallery,** with the **National Portrait Gallery** just behind it, demarcates the northern side.

WESTMINSTER   Edward the Confessor launched Westminster's rise to political power when he moved out of London to build his royal palace there in the 11th century. Dominated by the **Houses of Parliament** and Gothic **Westminster Abbey,** Westminster runs along the Thames east of St. James's Park. Whitehall, which has long been synonymous with the

armies of civil servants who really wield the power, is the main thoroughfare from Trafalgar Square to Parliament Square. Visit **Churchill's Cabinet War Rooms,** and then peer through the gates guarding **Downing Street.**

Westminster also takes in **Victoria,** a strange area that is both businessy and, because it's dominated by the station, full of cheap (and sometimes nasty) hotels. The classiest ones are in Ebury Street on the fringes of Belgravia. Art lovers come here to visit Tate Britain.

THE CITY   The City is where London began. Now it's one of the world's leading financial centers. The Bank of England (or the Old Lady of Threadneedle St.), the London Stock Exchange, and Lloyds of London are all located here. Much of the City was destroyed in the Great Fire of London, the Blitz, and later in the 1990s with some help from the IRA. Nowadays, it's a patchwork of the ancient and the very modern. You'll see some of the most god-awful modern architecture here, alongside such treasures as **St. Paul's Cathedral.** The **Museum of London** is home to 2,000 years of history and St. Paul's draws plenty of tourists, but the biggest draw in this neck of the woods is the **Tower of London,** which should be at the top of every visitor's must-see list.

CLERKENWELL   Clerkenwell evolved into a muck-filled 18th-century cattle yard, home to cheap gin distilleries. In the 1870s, it became the center of the new socialist movement: John Stuart Mill's London Patriotic Club was in Clerkenwell, as was William Morris's socialist press later in the 1890s. Lenin lived here while he edited *Iskra.* Neither West End nor City proper, its fortunes dwindled, but they're on the up and up again today as old commercial buildings turn into chic lofts and new restaurants open. Art galleries and shops run by small designers line Clerkenwell Green. Gritty working life goes on as meat lorries rumble into Smithfield Market. Still, this is one of the city's top neighborhoods when it comes to nightlife.

DOCKLANDS Since the London Docklands Development Corporation was set up in 1981, billions of pounds have gone into the most ambitious regeneration scheme of its kind in Europe. **Canary Wharf** is the focal point of this new river city, which runs east from Tower Bridge. Canary Wharf's 244m (800-ft.) tower is in the center of a covered piazza filled with shops. New skyscrapers are sprouting up around it now, and guesstimates say 60,000 new workers will be needed over the next few years.

To see this area you might want to take a trip on the Docklands Light Railway (DLR). Up on elevated rails, it snakes past historic buildings, grotty empty spaces, and 21st-century shrines to big business. Or take the Jubilee Line: Canary Wharf station is one of the most striking of all the high-design stops on the new extension.

THE EAST END This collection of boroughs, east of the City, has long been one of the poorest areas of London. Now, though, it's hoped that the construction of a big Channel Tunnel rail interchange at Stratford will drag development eastward. The Huguenots, fleeing religious persecution in France during the 16th century, were the first of successive waves of immigrants right up to the large Bengali population today. Yet it's also home to the ultimate Londoner, the Cockney born within the sound of Bow Bells. This referred to the bells of St. Mary-le-Bow church, which rang the city curfew until the 19th century. Close to the docks, the East End was bombed to smithereens during the Blitz. Nudging Clerkenwell on the western edge is **Hoxton,** the hottest hotbed of Young British artists and the entrepreneurs who know how to hype them.

Shoreditch, the newest kid on the block, is East London's capital of cool. The artists of Shoreditch are thought to be more genuine than their West London counterparts, and the scarcity of residential space here means later drinking. This area is home to **Spitalfields** (p. 580), one of the city's best markets.

SOUTH BANK This is a loose definition, devised by Londoners on the north bank of the Thames, to define the only bit south of the river they're really interested in. As more and more redevelopment takes place, the definition widens. The core is the **South Bank Centre,** the largest cultural complex in Europe and now planning a big expansion and redevelopment. It houses the National Theatre, Royal Festival Hall, Hayward Gallery, and the National Film Theatre, as well as several restaurants. Upriver, facing the Houses of Parliament, is the landmark giant Ferris wheel, the British Airways London Eye. Beside it is County Hall, once home to the Greater London Council, now part upscale Marriott hotel and part budget Travel Inn, with the London Aquarium in the basement and the new Saatchi Gallery and Dali Universe upstairs. Go downriver (east), and you come to Tate Modern and the new Millennium Bridge, linking **Bankside** with St. Paul's and the City. With Shakespeare's Globe Theatre only a stone's throw away, this is a really exciting neighborhood.

Still farther east, you come to London Bridge and **Southwark.** Known as the outlaw borough, it was the city's medieval hot spot for prostitutes, theaters, drinking dens, and crime. There's a feast of history to revisit in this once run-down area that is now starting to revive in a big way. Next to Tower Bridge is the brand-new (opened in 2002) glass-walled London City Hall, HQ for the London mayor and the Assembly.

Far out in southwest South London, **Brixton** has a justifiably dodgy reputation but it's worth a trip for its tons of great bars and restaurants.

LONDON

ISLINGTON Islington has always had a hint of raffishness, but today it's the center of all things hip. The Almeida theatre, which has attracted such illustrious names as Ralph Fiennes, Kevin Spacey, and Rachel Weisz, has its home here. Visitors should head for the antiques market at Camden Passage, to look even if they can't afford to buy. This is also a not-to-miss neighborhood when it comes to bars and restaurants.

CAMDEN The Victorian slums that grew up around the canal have now been transformed into a gentrified, if still patchily seedy, neighborhood, first attracting artists such as Lucien Freud and Frank Auerbach, and later the burgeoning indie music industry. The biggest draw, and it is very big, is **Camden Market.** This is a whole village of offbeat streets, covered areas, and old buildings, specializing in everything from New Age crystals to artsy-craftsy bits and bobs. Note that, these days, the wares seem pretty stuck in the 1990s.

HAMPSTEAD & HIGHGATE People who live in Hampstead live in Hampstead, not in London. This delightful village-style almost-burb northwest of Regent's Park has its own 324-hectare (800-acre) patch of countryside, Hampstead Heath. Everybody from Sigmund Freud to D. H. Lawrence to Anna Pavlova to John Le Carré has lived here. Hampstead makes a delightful day trip and isn't that far by Tube.

Highgate is on the northeastern edge of Hampstead Heath, and almost as villagey. It's worth a visit, if only to go to the famous Highgate Cemetery where Karl Marx and George Eliot are buried. There are marvelous and morbid Victorian mausoleums.

Tourist Offices

Upon arriving, hit the Britain and **London Visitor Centre** (**www.visitbritian.com**). The staff is multilingual and the office provides last-minute accommodations, transport, tours, plus a bureau de change and theater and entertainment tickets. It's located at 1 Regent St. and is open Monday to Friday 9:30am to 5pm and Saturday and Sunday 10am to 4pm; the nearest Tube is Piccadilly Circus. Alternatively, there are London Visitor Centres at major gateways to the city; in Heathrow Terminals 1, 2, and 3; in the Victoria Station Forecourt; and in the Waterloo International Terminal.

Recommended Websites

○ **www.londontown.com** and **www.view london.com**: Information on attractions, events, restaurants, and more. The latter is good for getting yourself on club guest lists.

○ **www.visitlondon.com**: This official website for London contains great deals on hotel rooms among other helpful items.

○ **www.thisislondon.com**: A website for the *Evening Standard* newspaper, this is also a goldmine of information on the latest happenings, with constantly updated offers for tickets.

○ **www.itchylondon.co.uk**: Besides providing reviews of seemingly every restaurant in the city, this offers forums for exchanging ideas and job boards.

○ **www.gingerbeer.com**: For info about the LGBT community. "Ginger beer" is Cockney slang for "queer."

Culture Tips 101

Londoners are quite set in their ways even though their city is at the forefront of all things cool. You'll notice, for instance, that locals reserve Sundays for reading the papers, eating a lavish roast, and watching sports on the telly—particularly football, cricket, or Formula One motor racing.

Although England's legal minimum drinking age is 18, the only aspect of the liquor law that's strictly enforced regards drunk driving. As for recreational drugs, they're all illegal.

Hash is commonplace because it's relatively cheap, and hard drugs are around, but most partygoers can easily avoid them.

Recommended Books, Movies & Music

BOOKS

Chronologically, start with Chaucer's bawdy portrait of medieval London, his *Canterbury Tales*. Follow with Shakespeare and Ben Jonson. Pepys and Evelyn are wonderful friends with whom to explore 17th-century London. For the 18th century, take Fielding, Swift, and Defoe. Anything by Dickens or Thackeray will unlock Victorian London for you. The period from the turn of the 20th century to the 1940s is best captured in the works of Virginia Woolf, Henry Green, Graham Greene, Evelyn Waugh, P. G. Wodehouse, and Elizabeth Bowen.

Some of my favorite contemporary London authors are Muriel Spark, Iris Murdoch, Angus Wilson, V. S. Naipaul, Martin Amis, Ian McEwan, Jeanette Winterson, Graham Swift, Anita Brookner, Kazuo Ishiguro, Hanif Kureishi, and Zadie Smith—though this is just scratching the surface. Harry Potter notwithstanding, one of London's most famous recent literary creations is Bridget Jones, the single girl with a diary in Helen Fielding's best-selling novel of the same name. If you'd prefer a decidedly more masculine take on London singletons, check out any of Nick Hornby's books—*High Fidelity* is especially good.

Make sure you pick up a *London A–Z* guidebook—it's invaluable, with street maps of every conceivable area. All Londoners worth their salt have one (call it the "A to Zed").

MOVIES

With its beautiful architecture and wide open green spaces, London is a cinematographer's dream. Watch Julie Andrews enchant the children of 17 Cherry Tree Lane in the musical *Mary Poppins*. *My Fair Lady* fans will recognize Covent Garden as the location of several scenes in that 1964 musical.

More recent films that use London as a backdrop include Guy Ritchie's gangster films, though *Lock, Stock and Two Smoking Barrels* is the best. No guide to London is complete without a mention of *Notting Hill* and *Bridget Jones' Diary* and its sequel (set all over London). Head for the Church of St. Bartholemew's the Great in Spitalfields to see where much of *Shakespeare in Love* was made.

Don't just restrict your preview pleasures to London-specific movies, though. Think of the following as British Culture 101. Start with the 1997 hit *The Full Monty*. Then add *Secrets and Lies*, *Naked*, *Trainspotting*, *Four Weddings and a Funeral*, *The Crying Game*, *Mona Lisa*, *My Beautiful Laundrette*, *Educating Rita*, and *A Clockwork Orange*. Oh, and follow up with the full Merchant Ivory backlist and any of the Harry Potter films.

MUSIC

Add anything by the following artists to your playlist for some only-in-London sounds: The Beatles, The Rolling Stones, The Kinks, The Sex Pistols, The Clash, Coldplay, Blur, Oasis, MIA, Lady Sovereign (or any grime music). These are just the biggies, though. Check out *NME*, available on newsstands throughout London, for the latest on London's thriving music scene.

London Nuts & Bolts

Cellphone Providers & Service Centers The best-known and most reliable cellphone providers are **BT Cellnet** (☎ 099/0214000), **Vodafone** (☎ 083/1191), **One2One** (☎ 095/8121121), and **Orange** (☎ 097/1100150). Your cellphone will probably switch over to one of these networks automatically when you arrive in London if you use GSM service. If not, you can buy a SIM card relatively cheaply through any of the above carriers.

Currency   There are bureaux de change—or currency exchange bureaus—all over London, for example in railway stations and airports and on main shopping or tourist streets. It's cheapest to simply withdraw money from a bank ATM, though—you'll stumble upon countless ones throughout the city.

Embassies   This list will help you out if you lose your passport or have some other emergency. The **Australia** High Commission is at Australia House, Strand, WC2 (☎ 020/7379-4334; www.australia.org.uk), and is open Monday to Friday from 9am to 5pm (Tube: Holborn or Temple). The **Canada** High Commission is at 38 Grosvenor St., W1 (☎ 020/7258-6600; www.dfait-maeci.gc.ca), and is open Monday to Friday from 8am to 11am (Tube: Bond St.). The **New Zealand** High Commission is at **New Zealand House,** Haymarket, SW1 (☎ 020/7930-8422; www.newzealandhc.org.uk), and is open Monday to Friday from 10am to noon, and 2 to 4pm (Tube: Piccadilly Circus). The **United States** Embassy is at 24 Grosvenor Sq., W1 (☎ 020/7499-9000; www.usembassy.org.uk), and is open for walk-in inquiries 8:30am to 12:30pm and 2 to 5pm (to 5:30pm for phone calls; Tube: Marble Arch or Bond St.).

Emergencies   Dial **999** from any phone in an emergency for the police, ambulance, and fire service. If you need a doctor right away, call **Doctorcall** at ☎ 020/7291-6666. A physician will come to you, and you can pay with cash or a credit card.

Internet/Wireless Hot Spots   The owner of easyJet has opened 17 **EasyInternet cafes** all over London, in areas ranging from residential Fulham to touristy Piccadilly Circus. Go to www.easyinternetcafe.com/map for information on each cafe. Most of them are attached to an actual coffee shop so you can eat and drink while you surf. London is also attempting to get with the program when it comes to wireless Internet—or Wi-Fi, as it's called. Currently, the most reliable places to get Wi-Fi for your laptop are at Starbucks cafes, which you'll predictably find everywhere. At £7.50 for 3 hours, it's very expensive.

Note: Journey to London's fringier neighborhoods, like Bayswater, to find the city's cheapest Internet cafes, which are often tucked inside ethnic restaurants.

Laundry   The coolest new service to hit London is **The Big Laundry (www.thebig laundry.com)**. All you have to do is fill in an online form or call them at ☎ 020/8442-0450, and they'll pick up your laundry, wash it, and dry it for you, and drop it back off. Or, try these places: **Westing House Laundromat** (East Dulwich Rd.; ☎ 020/7639-4743 Tube: Southwark); and **The Laundromat & Dry Cleaning Centre** (28 Golborne Rd.; ☎ 020/8960-2908; Tube: Westbourne Park).

Luggage Storage   ABC Storage (www.abcselfstorage.co.uk) has three convenient locations in London. Their Southwark location is particularly good if you're backpacking and don't have too much to store. All locations feature lockers that are 1 sq. m (11. sq. ft.) for £35 per 4 weeks, or 1.5 sq. m. (16 sq. ft.) for £45. This works out to as £8.75 to £11 per week. Otherwise, all major railway stations and airports have storage lockers, although they're more expensive.

Post Offices Call ☏ **034/5223344** to find the one nearest you. The one with the longest operating hours is in Trafalgar Square, open Monday to Saturday from 8:30am to 6:00pm.

Restrooms If you're dying to go and can't find one, go to a hotel lobby.

Safety You'll feel particularly safe in London thanks to the sheer amount of CCTV—or Closed Circuit Television—cameras everywhere, from street corners to buses. Obviously the safety tips your mom taught you at age 5 still apply here—don't take candy from strangers, look both ways when crossing the street, and so on. Watch out for pickpockets on the Tube and in crowded, touristy areas like Leicester Square.

Telephone Tips A reliable service for Directory Assistance is ☏ **118118**, although it can be expensive. You can also visit them online at www.118118.com. Some telephone booths in London now have Internet access.

Tipping Generally, London restaurants include a tip with the VAT (value-added tax) charge. If not, use your discretion, but a 15% tip is the norm. Tip your taxi driver if he or she is especially friendly, and leave a few pounds for housekeeping. *Remember:* It is *not* customary to tip at a British pub.

Sleeping

London has a deserved reputation as one of the most expensive cities in the world when it comes to hotels, but deals can be had. Keep in mind that it often pays to leave the city center when looking for accommodations—you'll find a ton of cheap hotels in Earl's Court and Paddington. Also consider staying at one of the city's legions of B&Bs. Some are great, but you have to be careful or you'll be stuck in a depressing room with a prefab bathroom no larger than what you'd find on an airplane. Some can be really pleasant, though.

The following reliable services will recommend and arrange a B&B room for you: **London Bed & Breakfast Association** (☏ **800/852-2632** in the U.S.; fax 020/8749-7084, or 619/531-1686 from the U.S.) and **The London Bed and Breakfast Agency Limited** (☏ **020/7586-2768**; fax 020/7586-6567; www.londonbb.com). The latter is another reputable agency that can provide inexpensive accommodations in selected private homes for £22 to £44 per person per night, based on double occupancy (although some accommodations will cost a lot more).

Increasingly popular alternatives to hotels are **serviced apartments,** which offer space, flexibility (to eat out or cook a meal), and relative value for the money. (Prices can end up as little as £50 per person per night for five-star options.) A good-value, chain name in this field is the Europe-wide **Citadines Apart'hotels** (☏ **0800/376-3898** within U.K.; www.citadines.com). Also check out www.london4rent.com, which specializes in high-end properties but includes cheaper options.

Hostels

→**Globetrotter Inn London** ★ The Globetrotter in Hammersmith (far west London) tops many lists of London hostels because it's one of the city's cleanest and most modern. Unlike many hostel staff members who seem to have just arrived in the country themselves, the desk clerks here are knowledgeable, friendly, and clued-in. The dorm rooms—all shared, with communal bathrooms—are a bit more comfortable than most, with a privacy curtain around each bed. Check out the bar for drinks specials and, if you're sick of the Tube, ask about hiring a bicycle. *Ashlar Court, W6.* ☎ *020/8746-3112. www.globetrotterinns.com. £17 dorm, £42. double. Tube: Stamford Brook. Amenities: Bar; breakfast room; bike rentals; gym; laundry; Internet; shared bathrooms; supermarket; travel desk; TV and films (in common room).*

→**St. Christopher's Village** While slightly out of the way in Southwark, St. Christopher's Village is ideal for any cash-conscious traveler. This hostel is known for its *Animal House* atmosphere, mostly due to the raucous bar next door, fittingly called Belushi's, and a rooftop sauna and hot tub. The dorm accommodations with shared rooms and bathrooms are run-of-the-mill, but the vibe here is clean and safe. On Fridays, the staff provides a free tour of London. *165 Borough High St., SE1* ☎ *020/7407-1856. www.st-christophers.co.uk. £15 dorm. Tube: London Bridge. Amenities: Bar; breakfast room; hot tub; Internet; laundry; sauna; shared bathrooms; sheets; travel desk; TV (in common room).*

MTV Best →**Wake Up! London** ★ As hostels go, this is one of the city's best. Relive your freshman year of college by sleeping in a dorm and making a packet of Ramen noodles (available for purchase) at this lively but impersonal hostel. The entire place is utility-chic, attracting young Australians and Euros with body piercings and quibbles about Internet cards. It's charming if you like metal bunk beds and techno music throbbing through the walls. Guests seem like seasoned hostel-stayers, mingling easily and smoking on the stoop. Make sure to grab your two-for-one drink tickets for cocktails at the in-house bar at check in. *1 Queens Gardens, W23.* ☎ *020/7262-4471. www.wakeuplondon.co.uk. £20 dorm, £30–£40 single. Tube: Paddington. Amenities: Bar; Internet; linens; shared bathrooms; travel desk; TV (in common room); Wi-Fi. In room, Hair dryer (in some), lockers (in dorms), some shared bathrooms.*

Cheap

→**The Avonmore Hotel** ★★ This comfortable B&B is situated in the residential area of West Kensington, only a 3-minute walk from the Tube. The Avonmore is perfect for safety-conscious travelers because the street is quiet and there is a code on the door to ensure that only guests gain access. Each room contains a large fridge of must-haves like sodas and peanuts. The owner Margaret is very friendly and knows the city well; she and her knowledgeable staff will assist with directions and will find you a cab. This is the best all-round B&B in London and is justifiably popular with all sorts of travelers—book ahead. *66 Avonmore Rd., W14.* ☎ *020/7603-4296. www.avonmorehotel.co.uk. £60–£110 double. Rates include breakfast. Tube: West Kensington. Amenities: Bar; breakfast room; shared bathrooms (in 2 rooms). In room: TV, hair dryer, fridge, minibar.*

→**The Jenkins Hotel** Don't expect trendy or hip here—in fact, the Jenkins is defiantly small but friendly, with staff members who go out of their way to help. The rooms are comfortable if drab, featuring cool pod-like bathrooms similar to what you'd find on an airplane. The minibar makes a welcome change, selling Perrier for 75p as opposed to the usual £3. The location is perfect for history buffs, with the British Library, British Museum, and UCL right next door. Oxford Street, with its mammoth shops, is only 10 minutes away, but you wouldn't know it—the hotel is set in a quiet, leafy residential zone with similar small hotels nearby. You'll also find a comfier bed here than in some pricier joints. *45 Cartwright Gardens, WC1H.* ☎ *020/7387-2067. www.jenkinshotel.demon. co.uk. £52–£72 single, £85 double. Tube: Russell Sq. Amenities: Breakfast room; garden; kitchen; shared bathrooms (in most); tennis courts. In room: TV, fridge, hair dryer, minibar, safe.*

→**Seven Dials Hotel** This tiny Covent Garden B&B has just 10 rooms, so book in advance. The enviable location is the real attraction here—the Seven Dials is an easy walk to most central London hot spots like the West End, with its museums and musicals. The rooms, while small, contain the necessities and are well maintained. The staff is always willing to dish out advice with your continental breakfast. *7 Monmouth St., WC2.* ☎ *020/7681-0791. £85 double. Rates include breakfast. Tube: Covent Garden. Amenities: Breakfast room; shared bathrooms (in cheaper rooms). In room: TV, hair dryer.*

Doable

→**Dukes Hotel** Tucked away at the end of a gorgeous tree-covered driveway, Dukes is a hidden gem. The rooms aren't trendy and could use a design overhaul to attract a younger market, but contain the usual amenities and are very comfortable. An on-site health club/gym and handy jogging maps of local parks make this the perfect hotel for health-conscious travelers. It boasts a great location for both theater-lovers and movie buffs—Leicester Square and Piccadilly Circus are a mere few minutes' walk away. *St. James's Place, SW1.* ☎ *020/7491-4840. www. dukeshotel.co.uk. £235 double. Tube: Green Park. Amenities: Restaurant; bar; dry cleaning; gym; laundry service; sauna/spa; travel desk. In room: Cable TV, fridge, Internet, minibar, VCRs (in some).*

→**The Zetter Rooms** ★★ This funky boutique hotel in trendy Clerkenwell has all the perks of a larger luxury hotel but with far lower prices. Each room has been lovingly decorated with futuristic flair—Judy Jetson would be at home here. Expect all the newest extras, like high-speed Internet and an interactive TV. For slightly more money, you can stay in a rooftop studio with unparalleled views and a little balcony where you can have drinks in the summer. Special touches like hot-water bottles with knitted covers add some kitsch to the Zetter, already a favorite with celebrities. *86–88 Clerkenwell*

Rd., EC1. ☎ *020/7324-4444. www.thezetter. com. £140 double. Tube: Farringdon. Amenities: Restaurant; bar; travel desk. In room: A/C, broadband TV, digital music library, Internet.*

Splurge

→**41** ★★ If money's no object, check into the Executive King suite—two floors of mod, hip, fabulous black-and-white decor mixed with animal prints and stripes. The retractable roof with its skylight and topiary headboard is worth the price of the room. Everything works by remote control. Soak in the huge Jacuzzi while watching a flatscreen TV. This hotel has it all, including iPod speakers to turn your room into a party suite. *41 Buckingham Palace Rd., SW1.* ☎ *020/7300-0041. www.41hotel.com. £295 double. Rates include breakfast. Tube: Victoria. Amenities: Restaurant; bars; breakfast room; gym with sauna and swimming pool; spa services. In room: A/C, TV, DVD library, fax, iPod dock, Jacuzzi in suites.*

→**The Soho Hotel** ★★ This upmarket boutique spot tucked away in hip, gay Soho adds chic glamour to an otherwise quiet street. Each room contains a big fluffy bed, a flatscreen TV with a DVD player, and unique decor such as patterned mannequins. This place is obviously for the young, savvy traveler. If you can pry yourself away from your achingly cool room, head onto your balcony—perfect for people-watching over the busy Soho streets. *4 Richmond Mews, W1.* ☎ *020/7559-3000. www.firmdale.com. £235 double. Tube: Covent Garden. Amenities:. Bar/restaurant; film rooms; gym; room service; spa. In room: A/C, TV with DVD player.*

→**The Stafford Hotel** ★ Stay in well-appointed rooms in Queen Anne's converted stables, known as the Carriage House, with a split door and all. The beautiful interior design gives the feeling of a classy country hotel, and the glorious, flower-covered courtyard is lovely. The interior bar is known for its flawless martinis and is frequented by

LONDON

celebs. The Stafford is ideal for easy access to the whole West End. *St. James's Place, SW1* ☎ *020/7493-0111. www.thestaffordhotel.co.uk.*

£250 double. Tube: Green Park. Amenities: Bar/restaurant; room service; Wi-Fi. In room: A/C, TV, safe.

Eating

If you've seen the film *Snatch,* you may remember the memorable lines uttered by Dennis Farina, playing Cousin Avi: "London. You know: fish, chips, cup of tea, bad food." Fortunately, there's more to London cuisine than that now. Many of the city's restaurants have won a coveted Michelin star, and some are owned by celebrity chefs like Gordon Ramsay of *Hell's Kitchen* fame. Of course, you'll still find "chippies"—or fish and chip shops—on most corners, along with greasy kebab joints.

Cousin Avi was, however, right about one thing. Britons love their tea, so you'll find the national drink on every menu. Another omnipresent but delicious drink you'll see Londoners downing? Pimms. It's booze, but its ingredients are top secret, and have been for years. In the summer, big jugs of Pimms mixed with lemonade, cucumber, and fresh fruit are shared in pub beer gardens.

When in doubt, go with curry. Countless Indian restaurants are scattered around London. Indian food is so beloved here that one of England's football anthems is entitled "Vindaloo" after a favorite dish.

Hot Spots

MTV Best → **Automat** ★ AMERICAN Billed as an "American brasserie," Automat serves top-notch comfort food and the best desserts around. For lunch, try the creamy macaroni-and-cheese or soft-shell crab. Leave room for some Mississippi Mud pie and order one of their classic American cocktails, like a Manhattan or Cosmopolitan. *33 Dover St., W1.* ☎ *020/7499-3033. www. automat-london.com. Main courses £18. Mon–Fri noon–midnight; Sat–Sun 11am–midnight. Tube: Green Park.*

MTV Best → **Cocoon** ★ ASIAN This hip eatery is the place to see and be seen in the city, and a favorite for pre-clubbing. The decor is supposed to evoke the life cycle of a butterfly. Pretentious, yes, but also pretty. Their signature Asian-inspired dishes include wasabi prawns and jungle curry with mixed seafood. Food is shared family-style. *65 Regent St., W1.* ☎ *020/7494-7600. Main courses £16. Mon–Fri Noon–3:00pm and 5:30pm–1am; Sat 5:30pm–1am; Sun 5:30pm–11pm. Tube: Regent St.*

→ **Hakkasan** ★★ CHINESE This Michelin-starred Chinese restaurant is still trendy. The food is always perfect, with inventive dishes like roasted silver cod with champagne and Chinese honey. The prices, however, might bring tears to your eyes. Also come prepared to shout over the music, which is cranked up to create a party-like atmosphere. *8 Hanway Place, W1.* ☎ *020/7927-7000. Main courses £30–£100. Mon–Fri noon–3pm and 6–11:30pm; Sat–Sun noon–5pm and 6pm–midnight (Wed–Sat till 12:30am). Tube: Tottenham Court Rd.*

Cheap

MTV Best → **Angel Curry Centre** ★ INDIAN The Angel Curry Centre is smack dab in the middle of Islington, one of London's trendiest areas, so expect this Indian restaurant to get crowded. A BYOB policy and tasty food like tandoori chicken and numerous vegetarian options simply add to the popularity. *5 Chapel Market, N1.* ☎ *020/ 7837-5727. Main courses £7. Sun–Thurs noon–2pm and 6pm–midnight; Fri–Sat noon–2pm and 6pm–12:30am. Tube: Angel.*

→ **Café Emm** MODERN Right in the heart of Soho, this friendly cafe serves up huge portions for less than £6 a plate. Try the falafel or Cajun chicken with a bottle of Rioja; you won't be disappointed. *17 Frith St., W1.* ☎ *020/7437-0723. Main courses £6. Mon–Thurs noon–3pm and 5:30–10:30pm; Fri noon–3pm and 5:30pm–12:30am; Sat 5pm–12:30am; Sun 5pm–10:30pm. Tube: Leicester Sq.*

➔**Chelsea Kitchen** ENGLISH Very cheap, old, and defiantly untrendy, the Chelsea Kitchen serves consistent fare in an enviable King's Road location. This place hasn't changed since the '60s. Staples include fish and chips and chicken curry. *98 King's Rd., SW3.* ☎ *0871/3328713 Main courses £8. Mon–Sat 8am–11:30pm; Sun 9am–11:30pm. Tube: Sloane Sq.*

➔**The Pepper Tree** THAI Where else can you find delicious traditional Thai fare for under £5 a dish? Start with barbecue prawns, and then sample some pork curry, all in a bustling atmosphere. In leafy and lovely Clapham Common, in far south London. It's about a 30-minute Tube ride from central London. *19 Clapham Common.* ☎ *020/7622-1758. Main courses £6. Mon noon–3pm and 6–10:30pm; Tues–Fri noon–3pm and 6–11pm; Sat noon–11pm; Sun noon–10:30pm. Tube: Clapham Common.*

➔**Pizza Express** ITALIAN Yes, Pizza Express is a chain. No, it's absolutely nothing like Pizza Hut, so don't be put off by its name or the ubiquity of its neon-blue signs throughout central London. The best branch of this pizza franchise is undoubtedly on King's Road. *The Pheasantry, 152 Kings Rd., SW3.* ☎ *020/7351-5031. www.pizzaexpress.co.uk. Main courses £7. Mon–Sat 11:30am–midnight; Sun 11am–11:30pm. Tube: Sloane Sq.*

➔**Wagamama** ✦ ASIAN This chain was recently voted "London's Most Popular Restaurant" by Zagat, and for good reason. You can get delicious, fresh noodles with any topping you like for a few pounds at any of 50 Wagamama outlets in central London.

The atmosphere is cafeteria style—diners share long tables with one another. Try the *yaki soba*—stir-fried chicken and prawns with soba noodles and pickled ginger. My favorite location is the one in Kensington. *26a Kensington High St., W8* ☎ *020/7376-1717. www.wagamama.com. Main courses £8. Mon–Sat 11:30am–9pm; Sun 12:30pm–9pm. Tube: High St. Kensington.*

Doable

➔**Boheme Kitchen and Bar** FRENCH In the heart of the Soho 'hood is this cool French brasserie with modern furniture and hangover-curing Sunday brunches. Try the goat cheese and caramelized onion tart—yum. *19 Old Compton St., W1.* ☎ *020/7734-5656. www.bohemekitchen.co.uk. Main courses £10. Mon–Sat 11am–1am; Sun noon–midnight. Tube: Covent Garden.*

➔**Jim Thompson's** THAI There are always a few people sitting at the picnic tables outside this pan-Asian joint on King's Road. The food here is terrific, as is the atmosphere. Feel free to chat up the bar staff (they're super-friendly). *617 King's Rd., SW6* ☎ *020/7731-0999. Main courses £12. Mon–Sat 11am–midnight; Sun noon–11:30pm. Tube: Fulham Broadway.*

➔**Mash** ENGLISH Mash is very popular with the after-work crowd. It's a super-stylized restaurant, bar, and brewery in one. It's great for groups, so bring your friends and order one of Mash's beers and some swordfish steak. *19–21 Great Portland St., W1* ☎ *020/7637-5555. Main courses £11. Mon–Sat 6–11pm. Tube: Oxford Circus.*

➔**Neal's Yard Salad Bar** VEGETARIAN Get a meal for £10 and up in this oasis of calm amidst the tourist hell of Covent Garden. Expect to dine next to hippy student types. Neal's Yard Salad Bar serves fresh organic food. Try the heavenly Brazilian cheese bread, a customer favorite. Vegans and vegetarians will find tasty pizzas to meet

LONDON

their specifications. *2 Neal's Yard, WC2.* ☎ *020/7836-3233. Main courses £10. Mon–Sat 11:30am–7pm. Tube: Covent Garden.*

➜ **Vingt-Quatre** ★★ MODERN   This modern brasserie wins accolades for its delicious light meals and for its operating hours—24 hours a day, 365 days a year. If you fancy a bowl of pasta or corn-fed chicken and mash after a night of drinking, this is the place to go. The menu is small, but the quality of the food makes up for it. *325 Fulham Rd., SW10.* ☎ *020/7376-7224. Main courses £14. Daily 24 hr. Tube: Fulham Broadway.*

Splurge

➜ **Gordon Ramsay** ★★ EUROPEAN   This first restaurant from *Hell's Kitchen* nightmare chef Gordon Ramsay is one of only three restaurants in the U.K. to have three coveted Michelin stars. It's also consistently been voted onto top 10 lists worldwide. Definitely make reservations, as this is as exclusive as it gets. Go for lunch and order the delectable lobster consommé with the sweet, delicate *millefeuille* to follow. *68 Royal Hospital Rd., SW3.* ☎ *020/7352-4441. www.gordonramsay. com. Main courses £30. Daily noon–2:30pm and 6:30–11pm. Tube: Sloane Sq.*

➜ **Rules** ★ TRADITIONAL BRITISH   This ultra-British restaurant has been around for 200 years and seems likely to survive another 200. But despite the hammy quaintness, Rules is a very modern restaurant operation. It markets the house specialty, "feathered and furred game," as healthy, free range, additive-free, and low in fat. The fixed-price midafternoon meal is a splurge, but it's still a great deal because you can select two courses from anything on the menu. The food is delicious: traditional yet innovative, until you get to the puddings (desserts), which are a mix of nursery and dinner-dance classics. The wine list is pricey, but Rules does have three brown ales, so try one of those instead. Reservations are

essential. *35 Maiden Lane, WC2.* ☎ *020/7836-5314. Main courses £17–£23; weekday fixed-price menu (served 3–5pm) £20. Mon–Sat noon–11:15pm; Sun noon–10:15pm. Tube: Charing Cross or Covent Garden.*

➜ **The Wolseley** EUROPEAN   Expect to see a celeb or five at dinner here, in the wealthy Green Park area of Mayfair. This French-style brasserie serves expensive dishes like Chateaubriand for two with béarnaise sauce and pommes pont-neuf. Still, if Parisian cuisine doesn't strike your fancy, the Wolseley serves a mean roast beef and Yorkshire pudding. Don't forget to dress for the occasion. *160 Piccadilly, W1.* ☎ *020/7499-6996. www.thewolseley.com. Main courses £17. Tube: Green Park.*

Cafes & Tearooms

➜ **Brown's Tea Room** ★★ Sipping tea at Brown's is the ultimate, quintessential London experience. Eat a scone with thick clotted cream and enjoy the endless cups of tea in the hotel's oak-paneled drawing room. Word to the wise: Call for dress code info. *Brown's Hotel, 33–34 Albermarle St., W1* ☎ *020/7518-4108. Tea and snacks £28. Sat–Sun 3–6pm. Tube: Green Park.*

➜ **The Orangery** This cafe is a bit on the pricey side, but it's worth it. The location is beautiful, romantic, and centrally located, right in the leafy Kensington Gardens. *Kensington Palace, W8.* ☎ *020/7376-0239. Tea and snacks £14. Daily 10am–6pm (Nov–Feb to 5pm); tea served from 3pm. Tube: High St. Kensington.*

➜ **St. James's Tearoom** Located inside the Fortnum & Mason food emporium, St. James's Tearoom opened in the 18th century. If you're feeling rich, order a champagne tea. *Fortnum & Mason, 181 Piccadilly, W1.* ☎ *020/7734-8040. Tea & snacks £22. Tues–Sat tea 3–5:30pm; Sun noon–5pm; Mon 10am–5pm. Tube: Piccadilly Circus.*

Coffee Houses

There are three chains of coffee houses competing for preeminence in London: the ubiquitous Starbucks, Café Nero, and Costa Coffee. All three can be found just about anywhere, often in close proximity to each other. However, there are plenty of London coffee houses that aren't part of franchises. Try **Raison D'Etre** (18 Bute St.; ☎ 020/7584-5008; Tube: South Kensington), where there is very good coffee and also first-class cakes

and sandwiches. **Bar Italia** (22 Frith St.; ☎ 020/7437-4520; Tube: Leicester Sq.) in Soho is somewhat of an institution. It serves some of the best cappuccinos in the city. Check out the website at www.baritalia soho.co.uk. Late night coffee-lovers should try **La Brasserie** (272 Brompton Rd.; ☎ 020/7581-3089; Tube: South Kensington) on Brompton Road, which is open until 11pm daily.

Partying

London was the birthplace of the Swinging '60s and *the* place to go in the '90s to take E and dance like a fool at one of its huge rave clubs. Those eras have thankfully passed, but London is still a party city at heart. Although antiquarian liquor laws have recently been relaxed, many pubs still close at the way-too-civilized hour of 11pm. However, there are an increasing number of bars open late and clubs will never fail to stay open until the wee hours, often till about 3am.

At all costs, avoid the cheesy clubs in the Leicester Square area—it's where London suburbanites go to try to have a good time. You'll find better clubs in the King's Cross and Clerkenwell neighborhoods, which will most likely be filled with university students, not tourists. If you have a special type of music in mind, resources like those listed in the "Recommended Websites" section have information about every kind of club for every taste in tunes. Weekend nights are still the best nights to go out, but some clubs are best midweek, like Boujis on Tuesdays.

As far as pubs go, they're a dime a dozen. Avoid those that boast an affiliation with a chain or franchise on their signs, like Wetherspoons. They have no character.

A word to the wise: The legal minimum drinking age here may be 18, but that won't stop bouncers from bouncing you if you don't bring ID. Also, appropriate club wear depends

on the club. For Fabric, anything from a boiler suit to a minidress will work. For small boutique clubs like Boujis, the chicer the better: That means blazers and Prada loafers for the boys, and whatever was in this month's *Vogue* for the girls. At teenybopper clubs like Crazy Larry's, jeans are fine, as is anything picked up at Top Shop (p. 580). One more tip for going out in London: If you think your vodka and Coke tastes weak, it's because English measures, at 25ml, are far smaller than, say, American portions of liquor.

Clubs

→**151** A favorite with the public-school set (that's boarding school to non-Brits), who refer to the King's Road as "the KR" because they spend so much time there. You'll find plenty of rich young things quaffing champagne and dancing to cheesy pop music. This small club is one of those places where you'll always have fun even though its name might provoke rolled eyes from older Londoners. *151 King's Rd., SW3.* ☎ *087/1332-3202. Cover £10. Tube: Sloane Sq.*

📺 Best →**Boujis** ★ Hollywood A-listers, hot young aristocracy, famous models . . . you'll find them all rubbing elbows at this boutique club in pricey South Ken. While the venue is small and the decor is nothing spectacular, the hipper-than-thou crowd and the good music is what has made Boujis the only place to go on a Saturday night. Or a Tuesday. It's "members only," so make friends with the right person or call to get on the guest list. *43 Thurloe St., SW7.* ☎ *020/7584-2000. www.boujis.com. Cover varies. Tube: South Kensington.*

→ **Crazy Larry's** Okay, so the dance floor is tiny compared to the seating area, and there are far too many polo shirts with the collars up, but the '80s dance music makes up for it. Larry's is a King's Road establishment and a guaranteed good night out, especially if you're under 20. Watch out for sleazy older guys here. *533 King's Rd., SW10.* ☎ *087/ 1332-3327. Cover £10. Tube: Sloane Sq.*

MTV **Best** → **Fabric** ★★ The 15 Victorian brick arches of this minimalist super-club (capacity 2,500) used to be the old cold-storage area for Smithfield meat market. There are three rooms, various bars, a roof terrace, and chill-out rooms. A hi-tech sound system pumps the beat from some of the city's best house, garage, techno, and drum 'n' bass up through the main dance floor. One grumble: Fabric is notorious for its mile-long lines, both to get in and for the unisex bathrooms. Open Friday 10pm to 5am and Saturday 10pm to 7am. *77a Charterhouse St., EC1* ☎ *020/ 7336-8898. www.fabriclondon.com. Cover £12–£15. Tube: Barbican or Farringdon.*

→ **Limelight** Right in the center of Soho and housed in a converted church, meaning the acoustics are fantastic. This is a club purely for dancing, with two huge dance floors on different levels and a variety of music, from techno to hip-hop. The downstairs area can get rather sweaty. *136 Shaftesbury Ave., W1.* ☎ *087/1332-6614. Cover varies. Tube: Leicester Sq.*

→ **Tantra** This place emanates cool as soon as you walk in, with a transparent dance floor under which models in lingerie writhe provocatively. Think an MTV video come to life. The crowd is somewhat pretentious—you'll spot lots of nouveau riche celebs drinking expensive cocktails—and the door

staffers have been known to be rude, but it's worth a gander. *62 Kingly St., W1* ☎ *087/ 1075-1754. Cover £20. Tube: Oxford Circus.*

Bars & Lounges

MTV **Best** → **Aragon House** ★★ See how the other half drink in this smart Fulham pub, known for its "posh totty": well-heeled 20-something, ex–boarding school student patrons. Owned by a former student of Sherborne Boys'—where Coldplay's Chris Martin honed his piano skills—Aragon House lures a seething pack of good-looking blue-bloods on Thursday and Friday nights. Stop in for a G&T (slang for the pervasive gin and tonics) mixed by an improbably attractive staff, but be sure to get there before 8pm if you want a table in the pretty beer garden out back. *247 New King's Rd., SW6.* ☎ *020/ 7731-7313. Tube: Parsons Green.*

→ **Beaufort House** Relax on a leather sofa and watch the beautiful people walk by at this sleek, comfortable pub, filled to the rafters on Friday nights with 20-something party-lovers screaming to be heard and drinking the house white wine by the bottle. It's also a good stop for an afternoon pint while leafing through the papers. *354 King's Rd., SW3.* ☎ *087/1223-5734. Tube: Sloane Sq.*

→ **The Bricklayers Arms** ★ Much frequented by artists and excellent for weekend breakfasts. Do not dress up! The look is deconstructed to the point of apocalyptic. *63 Charlotte Rd., EC2.* ☎ *020/7739-5245. Tube: Old St.*

→ **The Duke of Clarence** Bright and airy with sofas and lots of windows, the Clarence serves tasty gastropub food, with particularly juicy burgers. The space is big by London standards, with a long wooden wraparound bar and lots of good-size tables—a great spot to enjoy not being crowded for a change. The extensive wine list has "it" wines from Australia and Chile. *148 Old Brompton Rd., N1* ☎ *020/7373-1284. Tube: Gloucester Rd.*

Pub-Crawls

There are so many pubs in London that a concise listing of pub-crawls is nearly impossible. Thankfully, Aidan's London Pub Crawls website tests possible pub-crawls in areas from Southwark to Mayfair. The site (www.alpc.co.uk) includes descriptions of each pub, maps, and even the precise time taken for each crawl.

→ **Jerusalem** Dank, dark, and subterranean, Jerusalem is not your typical quaint pub. Thankfully, the clientele is also very different. Set in an underground dungeon just far enough away from the Tottenham Court Road shoppers, Jerusalem offers cocktails as well as a satisfying if unimaginative bar menu. Share a long wooden table with other drinkers in this unabashedly cool lair, or snag a table in the back for some one-on-one privacy. *33–34 Rathbone Place, W1.* ☎ *087/1332-5652. Cover £5 after 10pm. Tube: Tottenham Court Rd.*

MTV **Best** → **Milk and Honey** ★★ This tiny Soho establishment has been accused of snobbery due to its lengthy list of rules by which customers must abide, including Rule #1: "No name dropping; no star f***ing." However, the drinks and the game room here remain a powerful draw. *61 Poland St., W1.* ☎ *070/00ML-KHNJ. Tube: Leicester Sq.*

→ **Montuno's** In the center of the happening Shoreditch neighborhood is this old-fashioned jazz bar, modeled in Art Deco style after New Orleans–style speakeasies. Order bourbon and listen to the live music, a medley of jazz, plus funk, soul, and blues. *138 Shoreditch High St., E1* ☎ *087/1223-5319. Tube: Liverpool St.*

→ **Tahe Audley** This is the place to go to pick up a rich pinstriped city boy or a pretty socialite. In the heart of wealthy Mayfair, this pleasant pub is best in the summer, when you can nurse a Pimms outside on the picnic tables. Year-round, it's the type of place where you can happily spend a whole afternoon, enjoying the particularly good pub grub without feeling rushed. *41 Mount St., W1.* ☎ *020/7499-1843. Tube: Green Park.*

→ **The White Horse** This popular pub overlooks pretty Parson's Green and boasts a large outdoor beer garden where summer barbecues abound. The clientele is decidedly upper-class—the pub earns its nickname, the Sloaney Pony, from its patrons. Ignore the crowd and dig into the delicious food and tons of beers on tap. *1–3 Parson's Green, SW6.* ☎ *020/7736-2115. www.whitehorsesw6.com. Tube: Parson's Green.*

Live Music

Wembley Stadium was long the venue for huge rock concerts in the capital, but now that it's closed, nearby **Wembley Arena** (Elvin House; Tube: Wembley Park) hosts popular teenybopper acts like Take That and Brit-pop act McFly. Go to www.whatsonwembley.com to see a schedule of performers.

For a smaller venue, check out the **100 Club** (100 Oxford St.; ☎ **020/7638-0933;** www.the100club.co.uk; Tube: Oxford Circus) in the West End. It's a venerable dive, with rock and jazz, blues, and R&B live bands or music, depending on the night. Two more venues to keep in mind are **Brixton Academy** (211 Stockwell Rd.; ☎ **020/7721-2000;** Tube: Brixton) and **Sheperds Bush Empire** (Sheperds Bush Green; ☎ **020/7721-2000;** Tube: Sheperds Bush). Tickets to both are £10 to £25.

The website www.aloud.com is an excellent source of info on concerts in the city.

Gay Bars

→ **The Candy Bar** This is the U.K.'s first lesbian bar, and it's open 7 days a week with a license for female strippers. Don't get the wrong idea, though: This place isn't seedy in the slightest, and it caters to everyone from butch to lipstick. There are two floors, although the dance floor downstairs is only really packed on the weekends. *4 Carlisle St., W1.* ☎ *020/7494-4041. Cover £5 after 9pm. Tube: Tottenham Court Rd.*

➜ **Central Station** A different sort of pub—a laid-back crowd comes here for the cabaret, sports bar, roof terrace, and cruising at the basement's club nights (Mon and Thurs, men only). Open Monday to Wednesday 5pm to 2am, Thursday 5pm to 3am, Friday 5pm to 4am, Saturday noon to 4am, and Sunday 11am to midnight. Happy hour is Monday to Friday from 5 to 9pm. *37 Wharfedale Rd., N1.* ☎ *020/7278-3294. Cover £5. Tube: King's Cross.*

➜ **G-A-Y** With its three floors, plasma screens featuring music videos, and wall-to-wall men (and women too!), G-A-Y is without a doubt the premier gay club in London. The downstairs bar caters to lesbians, and is cutely titled "Girls Go Down." Drinks aren't too expensive, and you'll get your money's worth. *30 Old Compton St., WC2* ☎ *087/1223-7807. Tube: Leicester Sq..*

Late-Night Bites

The best place for eating after midnight in London is undoubtedly **Vingt-Quatre** (p. 564). Vingt-Quatre is French for 24, which is how many hours per day the Fulham brasserie is open. If you've been clubbing in the West End, stop for food at **Market Place** (4 Market Place; ☎ **020/7636-9671;** Tube: Oxford Circus), where the menu is advertised as "Latin street food." It's pretty good for the price. You can't sit down in the tiny **Brick Lane Beigel Bake** (159 Brick Lane; ☎ **020/7729-0616;** Tube: Bethnal Green) in lively Shoreditch, but you can get any sort of bagel and topping you'd like at bargain-basement prices, 24 hours a day. In Soho? Try the largely gay **Old Compton Café** (34 Old Compton St.; ☎ **020/7439-3309;** Tube: Leicester Sq.) for a full English breakfast at 2am. For Chinese food at all hours, try **1997** (19 Wardour St.; ☎ **020/7734-3868;** Tube: Piccadilly Circus), named for the year Hong Kong was handed back to the Chinese.

Performing Arts

Performance Halls

The most famous performance hall in London is the 📺 **Best** **Royal Albert Hall** (Kensington Gore; Tube: South Kensington) home to the annual BBC Proms concert, numerous awards shows, and charity performances. To see what's on and buy tickets, go to www.royalalberthall.com or call ☎ **020/7589-8212.** Another well-known space is the **Barbican** (Silk St.; Tube: Barbican), venue for the London Symphony Orchestra. Contemporary musicians also play the Barbican regularly. Go to www.barbican.co.uk or call ☎ **020/7638-8891** for info.

Theaters

Ticket prices at London's 40 or so West End theaters range from £10 to £35. That's a bargain compared to Broadway and many other theatrical venues in the U.S. There are two fantastic websites for finding out all the theater gossip. The half-price ticket booth in Leicester Square, **www.officiallondontheatre.co.uk** is run by the Society of London Theatres. Listings include summary, cast, times, prices, and the date a show is guaranteed to run until. For pretty good reviews of West End shows, surf **www.whatsonstage.com**.

➜ **Donmar Warehouse** Sam Mendes, who directed the Oscar-winning film *American Beauty*, was only 24 when he took over the Donmar, now one of the hippest and most highly rated theaters in London. Under his artistic direction, this Covent Garden stage produces a huge range of old and new shows, including performances by visiting companies and a cabaret season, Divas at the Donmar. The box office is open from 10am to 8pm, but phone booking is round-the-clock. The 20 standing tickets go on sale once there's a full house. *41 Earlham St., WC2.* ☎ *020/7369-1732. www.donmar-warehouse. com. Tickets usually £15–£25, but vary for each show; standing tickets £5. Box office 10am–8pm. Tube: Covent Garden.*

→**The King's Head** London's oldest pub-theater produces new writing and neglected classics, some of which have gone on to the West End and Broadway. It also trains up to 12 young directors each year. Come for a pint before you see the tiny stage where Hugh Grant and Gary Oldman started their careers. In addition to evening shows, they often stage plays at 1pm for the lunchtime crowd. *115 Upper St., N1* ☎ *020/7226-1916. www.the kingshead.com. Tickets £8.50–£18. Box office Mon–Sat 10am–8pm; Sun 10am–4pm. Tube: Angel, Highbury, or Islington.*

→**Royal National Theatre** The core repertory company and ever-changing guest stars perform in three auditoriums in this huge theater complex on the South Bank. The large open-stage **Olivier,** the traditional proscenium of the **Lyttelton Theatre,** and the smaller, studio-style **Cottesloe** put on dozens of productions a year: reworked classics, cutting-edge premieres, musicals, and shows for young people. There's always a lot going on in addition to the productions. **Platforms** are talks and readings by hot names in the performing arts. They take place at lunchtimes in the Terrace Café and on stage in the early evening. Tickets are practically given away at £3.50, or £2.50 for students. From the end of June through August, the Theatre Square and the National's terraces are abuzz with **Watch This Space,** a free alfresco festival of music, mime, street theater, acrobats, and magic from all over the world. There's something going on every day but Sunday, mostly in the early evening. Try and make it one Saturday

for a Waterloo Sunset spectacular (10:15pm). For events info, call ☎ **020/7452-3327.**

The 1-hour **backstage tour** provides a fascinating glimpse into day-to-day theatrical life. Tours take place Monday through Saturday at 10:15am, 12:30pm (12:15 on Olivier matinee days), and 5:30pm, and cost £5, or £4.25 students and seniors. It's a good idea to reserve in advance because there are only 30 places on each tour. *South Bank, SE1.* ☎ *020/7452-3400 or 020/7452-3000 for the box office. www.nt-online.org. Tickets £10–£32; all tickets unsold 2 hr. before performance in the Olivier and Lyttleton theaters £15; student standby (45 min. before curtain at all 3 theaters) may also be available for £8. Box office Mon–Sat 10am–8pm. Tube: Waterloo or Embankment (cross over Hungerford Bridge). River services: Festival Pier.*

→**Shakespeare's Globe Theatre** Academics and historians will always chew over the authenticity of the reconstructed theater and the re-staged drama. Critics will sniff at crowd-pleasing performances and the theme park atmosphere. But a night out at the Globe is a really fun experience. The replica stands on the site of Shakespeare's original amphitheater, which burned down in 1613. Constructed from the same materials as the original, four tiers of banked benches encircle the stage where the company performs the Bard's great works as their predecessors would have done in his day. The Elizabethan set shuns lighting and scenery. There are no cushions on the wooden bench seats or protection from the elements, hence the summer-only season.

Call to find out about the huge range of workshops (stage fighting, voice work, and so on), lectures, staged readings, and Walkshops—guided tours of the historical sights of Southwark and a quick look round the Globe. Most take place on weekends, others on weekday evenings. Usually £5 to £13, tickets are free one mid-June weekend to celebrate the birthday of the man with the vision to rebuild the Globe, Sam Wanamaker.

LONDON

Stage Call

Time Out magazine is the bible for all sorts of goings on around the capital, from restaurants to everything in between, but particularly comes in handy for theater listings. Pick up a copy at any newsstand or bookshop and take a look at the many listings. For tickets to West End musicals and other plays, queue up at the ticket booth on the southernmost side of Leicester Square. You'll get the best deals on remaining seats, often just an hour or two before the curtain goes up.

The season runs from the end of April through September; booking starts in mid-February. *21 New Globe Walk, SE1.* ☎ *020/7401-9919. www.shakespeares-globe.org. Tickets £8–£30; £5 yard-standing tickets. Box office Mon–Sat 10am–6pm. Tube: Mansion House and St. Paul's (cross over Millennium Bridge), Southwark. River services: Bankside Pier.*

Comedy Clubs

The **Comedy Store** in St. James is legendary, and plays host to the top comedians in the world. Call ☎ **020/7344-0234** for details and tickets (Haymarket House, 1a Oxendon St.; prices vary according to live acts; Tube: Piccadilly Circus). **Banana Cabaret** (77 Bedford Hill; cover £12–£15; Tube: Balham) is slightly farther afield, south of the river in Balham, but admission is only about £10 on the weekend. Call ☎ **020/8673-1756** for information. At the **Canal Café Theater** (Delemere Terrace; prices vary according to live acts; Tube: Warwick Ave.), in Little Venice, expect shows every night of the week, although some nights are reserved for drama. Call ☎ **020/7289-6054** for show details. The **Comedy Café** (66 Rivington St.; cover £5–£15; Tube: Old St.) in trendy Shoreditch is known for its excellent lineups, and is one of the few venues that was actually built as a comedy club. Phone ☎ **020/7739-5706** or visit www.comedycafe.fsnet.co.uk to learn more.

Sightseeing

There's so much to see and do in London that the best way to get quickly acquainted with the city's landmarks is on a double-decker bus tour. Try to find one with a live tour guide rather than earphones, and definitely sit on top. One of the best companies is **Big Bus Tours** (www.bigbustours.com; buses run 8am–5pm; adults £18), where your ticket is valid for 48 hours in case you can't handle a whole day of sights at once. The tours leave from Green Park, right by the Tube stop, and you can get on and off at your leisure. The bus tour will help you get your bearings. And what are some of the best sights to see? Certainly look around Westminster Abbey, the Houses of Parliament, the Tower of London, Shakespeare's Globe, the London Eye, and London's numerous art galleries,

including the two Tates. If the bus tour is too expensive, just buy a day Travelcard and take a regular double-decker bus to see London as the locals do.

Festivals

There's always some sort of festival going on in London, and there are daily events that attract lots of visitors. Below are the major highlights; the website **www.visitlondon.com** has an excellent month-by-month "Events Diary" with more extensive listings.

February

Shrove Tuesday. Known as Mardi Gras in France and in the U.S., Londoners commemorate the holiday with pancake races and parties. Visit www.alternativearts.co.uk for info on one favorite Shrove event—the

Free & Easy

- The **art galleries and museums** listed under "Museums & Art Galleries" below are for the most part free, although you will probably have to pay to see special exhibitions.

- Other free art galleries include **The Courtauld Institute** (Somerset House; ☎ 020/7848-2526; www.courtauld.ac.uk), the **Britart Showroom** (60–62 Commercial St.; ☎ 020/7033-4321; www.britart.com), the **Camden Arts Centre** (Arkwright Rd.; www.camdenartscentre.com; ☎ 020/7472-5500), and the **Whitechapel Art Gallery** (80–82 Whitechapel High St.; ☎ 020/7522-7888; www.whitechapel.org), among many others

- All over London, you'll find **"Pay What You Can" cinema nights and theater performances.** These won't be the newest or most polished films and plays, but they're often in cool venues like old churches. Check cafe and university bulletin boards throughout the city for info.

- There are free **comedy nights** on Mondays at the Theatre Royal (Theatre Royal Stratford East, Gerry Raffles Sq.; ☎ 020/8534-0310).

- If you don't want to shell out a ton of money to tour the Tower of London, you can visit **All Hallows** and its crypt in **Tower Hill** for free. It's located right next to the Tower of London; call ☎ 020/7481-2928 for info.

- Other historical adventures you can embark upon without opening your wallet include the "Holocaust Exhibition" at the **Imperial War Museum** (Lambeth Rd.; ☎ 020/7416-5000) and the "Milestones of Flight" exhibition, exploring 100 years of airplanes, at the **Royal Air Force Museum** (Grahame Park Way; ☎ 020/8205-2266) in Hendon, north of the city.

For more freebies, and to get more info on the above, check out the very comprehensive www.londonfreelist.com.

Great Spitalfields Pancake Race. The Tuesday before Ash Wednesday.

March

Oxford/Cambridge Boat Race. This massive race on the Thames takes off from the Putney Bridge. It's watched by about 400 million people worldwide on television, though most Londoners watch at the pub, not by the river. Call ☎ 020/7611-3500 or visit www.theboatrace.com for info. Late March or early April.

May

FA Cup Final. The climax of the football season. Visit www.thefa.com. Mid-May.

Chelsea Flower Show. Held at the Royal Hospital in Chelsea. Visit www.rhs.org.uk or buy tickets online at www.kethprowse.co.uk. Late May.

June

📺 Best **Wimbledon.** The entire nation is gripped by Wimbledon fever when the world's premier tennis tournament is held at the All England Lawn Tennis Club, usually over the last weekend in June into July. The games are always exciting but one thing's for certain—Tim Henman will disappoint. Late June to early July.

Spitalfields Festival Fringe. This ragtag of contemporary art events, exhibitions, theater, and more takes place around the Spitalfields/"Banglatown" area of east London, held in tandem with the Spitalfields

Festival of classical and contemporary music. See www.alternativearts.co.uk. All month.

July

Pride London. The annual Gay Pride parade is usually held on one of the first days in July. For more information, visit www.prideinthepark.com. First Saturday in July.

Rise. A free anti-racism, pro-diversity, open-air music festival, formerly known as Respect. Past acts have included De La Soul and Public Enemy. It's held in a different London park every year. See www.rise festival.org. Mid-July.

August

Proms. The annual BBC Sir Henry Wood Promenade Concerts (www.bbc.co.uk/proms/pitp). Held from mid-July to mid-September, but really pick up steam in August.

Notting Hill Carnival. This colorful street parade celebrates Caribbean culture in London. The procession route is along Great Western Road, Chepstow Road, Westbourne Grove, and Ladbroke Grove. Check www.mynottinghill.co.uk for info. Usually the last Sunday and Monday of August.

September

The Brick Lane Festival. Celebrates London's Bangladeshi community with music and stalls along Brick Lane. See www.bricklanefestival.com. Second Sunday of September.

Open House. Allows access to around 500 architecturally significant buildings normally closed to the public. See www.london openhouse.org. Two days in mid- to late September.

October

Trafalgar Weekend/Trafalgar Day Parade. To glimpse a very British celebration, check this out in Trafalgar Square (of course). This holiday commemorates Admiral Nelson, who led the British navy against Napoleon's navy and defeated them at the Battle of Trafalgar. See www.sea-cadets.org. Sunday nearest October 21.

Diwali. The 5-day Hindu and Sikh Festival of Lights celebrates the victory of good over evil. It's celebrated in Trafalgar Square with Bollywood and other traditional dance performances. See www.london.gov.uk/mayor/diwali. Dates vary during October and November.

November

Guy Fawkes Night. Every British child knows the saying "Remember, remember the 5th of November"—the date when a Catholic man called Guy Fawkes was found in a cellar underneath the Houses of Parliament with barrels of gunpowder in what was known as the Catholic Gunpowder Plot. He was later executed, and this night bizarrely remembers the event with bonfires, on top of which burns a "guy," or a model of the man himself. Visit www.timeout.com/London for locations. November 5 or the nearest Friday or Saturday night.

Historic Buildings

▧ Best → **Westminster Abbey** ★★★
This self-proclaimed "House of God" and "House of Kings" is a must-see for any visitor. Poet's Corner, while often crowded with tourists, is worth a look—it contains the tombs of Chaucer, England's first poet, and more modern writers like Dickens, Hardy, and Kipling. *Dean's Yard, SW1.* ☎ *020/7654-4847. www.westminster-abbey.org. Admission £10 adults. Mon–Fri 9:30am–3:45pm; Sat 9:30am–1:45pm. Tube: St. James's Park.*

→ **St. Paul's Cathedral** ★★ Built in the late 17th century after its predecessor was destroyed in the Great Fire of London in 1666, St. Paul's has had an interior face-lift in the last 100 years or so, after famous moaner Queen Victoria declared it dingy. St. Paul's hosted one of the most widely watched weddings of all time—Prince Charles to Lady

12 Hours in London

1. **Get your bearings by taking a bus tour.** Alternatively, hop on a regular double-decker bus and see where it takes you.

2. **Head to the Tate Modern.** There's no better museum in all of London.

3. **Ride on the British Airways London Eye.**

4. **Tour the Tower of London.** Have a look at the Crown Jewels.

5. **Eat at Wagamama.** These are the cheapest and tastiest noodles around.

6. **Take the Tube to Oxford Street.** Visit Selfridges and Top Shop. The former is the best department store in London, and the latter is the world's largest fashion store. Try not to blow your inheritance.

7. **Walk up Tottenham Court Road.** You'll eventually get to the British Museum and British Library in academic Bloomsbury.

8. **Stop for a drink at a local pub.** Earn extra points if it is dark, dingy, and smoky—this is the London the tourists don't really see.

9. **Take the Tube to Piccadilly Circus.** Wander around the most crowded, touristy bit of London, and thank yourself for having avoided it for the better part of a day.

10. **Head to the King's Road.** Young Londoners come here en masse to hang out at the pubs and clubs. You won't be disappointed.

11. **Go to Vingt-Quatre.** The 24-hour bistro is a stone's throw from the King's Road.

LONDON

Diana Spencer. *Cannon St.* ☎ *020/7246-8348.* *www.stpauls.co.uk. Admission £8 adults. Mon–Sat 8:30am–4pm. Tube: St. Paul's.*

→**Tower of London** Okay, so it costs an extortionate amount of money to tour the famous Tower, built by William the Conqueror and the place where two of Henry VIII's wives breathed their last breath. However, if your parents are paying for your trip, seeing the **crown jewels** is worth the price of admission. *Be warned:* The one attempt to steal the gems in 1671 ended in tears, although the perp, Colonel Blood, was eventually pardoned, much to the chagrin of most of the King's court. *Tower Hill, EC3.* ☎ *087/0756-6060. www.toweroflondontour. com. Admission £15 adults. Tues–Sat 9am– 6pm; Sun–Mon 10am–6pm. Tube: Tower Hill.*

→**Buckingham Palace** During August and September when the Queen and her

brood make their annual trip to Scotland, the Palace's 19 staterooms are open to visitors. In the lavishly decorated rooms are paintings by the likes of Poussin and Rembrandt, and exhibitions like the late Queen Mother's wardrobe. See p. 575 for info on the **Changing of the Guard.** *Buckingham Palace Rd.* ☎ *020/7766-7300. www.royal.gov.uk. Admission £14 adults. Daily 9:30am–6:30pm. Tube: Victoria.*

→**British Airways London Eye** The view from the top of the Eye—which resembles a huge Ferris wheel with viewing "pods"—is breathtaking—on a clear day, you can see all the way to Windsor Castle, some 25 miles away. While the wheel may seem to turn slowly from the ground, don't worry—each trip takes only half an hour. It makes sense to buy a ticket online or over the phone so you can beat the obnoxiously long queues in the summer months. *South Bank, SE1.* ☎ *087/ 0990-8883. www.londoneye.com. Admission £13 adults. Daily 9:30am–10pm. Tube: Waterloo.*

Museums & Art Galleries

FREE ➜ **British Library** ★★ If you love English literature, make it a point to visit the British Library, housed in a new building in St. Pancras designed by Colin St. John Wilson and opened in 1998. The library has three exhibition spaces. The **John Ritblat Gallery** displays the permanent collection of treasures brought from the library's old home, the British Museum: the *Magna Carta*, Shakespeare's first folio, the handwritten manuscript of Charlotte Brontë's *Jane Eyre*, and dozens of others. What's most amazing, though, are the interactive exhibits that allow you to flip through an illuminated manuscript, such as Leonardo da Vinci's *Notebooks*. A second gallery is used for temporary exhibitions, and the third (The Workshop of Words, Sounds & Images) traces the history of book production from the earliest written documents to the current digital revolution—and there are regular free book-craft demonstrations. Also in the busy events schedule are free Monday lunchtime talks and Friday lunchtime author visits and discussions. *96 Euston Rd., NW1.* ☎ *020/7412-7332. www.bl.uk. Free admission. Galleries and public areas Mon and Wed–Fri 9:30am–6pm; Tues 9:30am–8pm; Sat 9:30am– 5pm; Sun 11am–5pm. Public-area-tour tickets: £6 adults; £4.50 seniors and students. Public- area tours: Mon, Wed, and Fri 3pm; Sat 10:30am and 3pm. Reading-room-tour tickets: £7 adults; £5.50 seniors and students. Reading-room tours: Tues 6:30pm; Sun 11:30am and 3pm. Tube: Euston or King's Cross.*

MTV Best FREE ➜ **The British Museum** ★★ The British Museum contains an impressive collection of historical artifacts, from Roman and Greek relics to Asian and Pacific idols. There are $2\frac{1}{2}$ miles of galleries, so you'll need to weed out what

really interests you and make a plan of attack. If you only have time or interest for "the greatest hits," pop in to see the much fought-over **Parthenon Sculptures** formerly known as the Elgin Marbles. The Egyptian antiquities are also a must—they include **mummies,** sarcophagi, and the **Rosetta Stone.** It would also be a shame not to take in a bit of local history, like the leathery remains of garrotted **Lindow Man,** or the glittering Anglo-Saxon silver and gold of the **Sutton Hoo treasure.** Then wander into the new **Sainsbury African Galleries,** a modern imaginative exhibition a far cry from the dusty trophy rooms of empire days. *Great Russell St.* ☎ *020/7323-8000. www.thebritish museum.ac.uk. Admission to permanent collections is free. Sat–Wed 10am–5:30pm; Thurs–Fri 10am–8:30pm. Tube: Russell Sq.*

FREE ➜ **The National Gallery** In the heart of tourist London sits the impressive National Gallery building, which houses more than 2,300 Western European pieces dating from 1250 to 1900. The Gallery contains some of the country's all-time favorite masterpieces, such as *The Fighting Temeraire* by Turner, which was voted "Greatest Painting in Britain" by the public. Nothing is too edgy here, but there are always exciting exhibitions if you're willing to shell out some cash. *Trafalgar Sq.* ☎ *020/7747-2885. www.national gallery.org.uk. Free admission. Daily 10am– 6pm. Tube: Leicester Sq.*

FREE ➜ **Natural History Museum** Right next to the Victoria & Albert Museum sits the Natural History Museum, known for its kid-friendly atmosphere and amazing exhibitions. The architecture is as impressive as the mammoth skeletons. *Cromwell Rd.* ☎ *020/7942-5000. www.nhm.ac.uk. Free admission. Mon–Sat 10am–5:50pm; Sun 11am–5:50pm. Tube: South Kensington.*

FREE ➜ **The National Portrait Gallery** The National Portrait Gallery is the most comprehensive of its kind in the world, featuring

Changing of the Guard

Looking more like toy soldiers than honed fighting machines, these men some-how do their duty, oblivious to kids pulling silly faces and the clicking of holiday snaps. The **Changing of the Guard** takes place at **Buckingham Palace** daily from April through August at 11:15am, and on alternate days September through March; at **St. James's Palace,** St. James's St., W1 (Tube: Green Park) at 11:15am, same dates; and at **Horse Guards** (Apr–Sept daily 10am–6:30pm; Oct–Mar daily 9:30am–6pm; Tube: Charing Cross).

Appropriately, it's the Household Cavalry that mounts the guard at Horse Guards. The soldiers ride across town every day from Knightsbridge Barracks, on the edge of Hyde Park, in their shiny breastplates and plumed helmets. The smartest men at the morning inspection get the plum position, on horse-back in the sentry boxes, and get to go home at 4pm. Those on foot have to stay until 8pm.

Note: Very bad weather and state events disrupt the schedules.

likenesses of every famous Brit from royalty to television personalities. Recent acquisitions include portraits of Alexander McQueen and writer Zadie Smith. The NPG puts on free lectures and events, on a huge range of topics, on Tuesday and Thursday lunchtimes and weekend afternoons. Thursday evening lectures mostly start at 7pm (free to £3). On Friday at 6:30pm, there are free musical events. *St. Martin's Place, WC2.* ☎ *020/7306-0055. www.npg.org.uk. Free admission. Daily 10am–6pm. Tube: Leicester Sq.*

FREE → **Royal Academy of Arts** The RA collection focuses on British artists working from the 18th century to present. Highlights include works by Gainsborough and David Hockney. Exhibitions here are always well curated but cost more than average for entrance. *Burlington House, Piccadilly, W1.* ☎ *020/7300-8000. www.royalacademy. org.uk. Free admission. Sat–Thurs 10am–6pm; Fri 10am–10pm. Tube: Piccadilly Circus.*

→ **The Saatchi Gallery** The Saatchi Gallery provides a forum for contemporary artists, many of them not-so-young YBAs (young British artists) like Damien Hirst. Super-collector Charles Saatchi presides over this vast collection of pieces that probably wouldn't find a home elsewhere. County

Hall is close to other attractions like the British Airways' London Eye. *County Hall, Southbank, SE1.* ☎ *020/7928-8195. www. saatchi-gallery.co.uk. Admission £9 adults; £6.75 students. Sun–Thurs 10am–8pm; Fri–Sat 10am–10pm. Tube: Waterloo.*

MTV Best FREE → **Sir John Soane's Museum** ★ The distinguished architect Sir John Soane died in 1837, leaving provisions in his will to ensure that his house was preserved as a museum so that "amateurs and students" could view great art for free. To this day the Soane museum is a favorite with Londoners and visitors alike, with sculpture, furniture, and paintings by the likes of Hogarth and Canaletto adorning the walls. The Soane is popular for school visits, but if you go on a Saturday you can explore the museum without crowds of children. *13 Lincoln's Inn Fields, WC2.* ☎ *020/7440-4263. www.soane.org. Free admission. Tues–Sat 10am–5pm. Tube: Holborn.*

FREE → **Tate Britain** ★ The oldest works at this London institution date to about 1500, and the most recent include paintings by contemporary artists like Lucien Freud. The great J. M. W Turner, Britain's favorite landscape painter, gets his own collection. Each year, Turner Prize finalists are exhibited at

LONDON

ᴍᴛᴠ 🆅 University Scene

London's university scene centers around UCL—**University College London** (Gower St.; ☎ 020/7679-2000; www.ucl.ac.uk; Tube: Euston Sq.), the city's largest and best-known institute of higher learning. The campus is located in Bloomsbury, long a seat of academia. In the early part of the 20th century, the Bloomsbury Group, including economist John Maynard Keynes, historian Lytton Strachey, and doomed novelist Virginia Woolf, met periodically to pick each other's brains. Today, Bloomsbury is home not only to the UCL campus but also to the British Museum and the British Library, making the area the place to be for academics of all sorts. Students tend to live in housing provided by the university or in their own cheap flats nearby. While many first-years choose to drink at the cheap Student Union bar, older, savvier UCL students go out on nearby Tottenham Court Road, to bars like **Jerusalem** (p. 567).

ther universities in and around London include City University, University of Westminster, University of Greenwich, Kingston University, and the 20 colleges of the University of London, of which UCL and other famous colleges like King's and Goldsmith's are a part.

To really get a sense of student life in London, though, why not try staying in one of the city's dorms? The London School of Economics rents out its residence halls in the summer (mid-Aug to late Sept), the most convenient and best of which is the **High Holborn Residence**, in nearby Covent Garden (178 High Holborn, WC1; ☎ 020/7107-5737; www.lse.ac.uk/collections/vacations; £49–£70 twin).

the Tate Britain, putting it on the cutting edge of London's art scene. There is a handy Tate to Tate riverboat service, taking you from the Tate Britain to the Tate Modern. *Millbank, SW1. ☎ 020/7887-8000. www.tate.org.uk. Daily 10am–5:50pm. Tube: Pimlico.*

ᴍᴛᴠ Best FREE →Tate Modern ★★★

London's wildly popular cathedral of modern art occupies the defunct Bankside Power Station on the South Bank of the Thames opposite St. Paul's Cathedral. Except for a two-story glass addition on the roof, the vast bunker-like facade looks much as it ever did, right down to the London grime. Then you enter the building, down a ramp into the huge old turbine hall, left empty, and three floors of ultraplain white galleries. The work is arranged thematically rather than chronologically: **Landscape/Matter/Environment, Still Life/Object/Real Life, History/Memory/Society,** and **Nude/Action/Body.** In some rooms, paintings are next to

sculptures next to installations. Others are devoted to a single artist—like the marvelous Joseph Beuys sculptures. The display concept is certainly challenging, but the themes often seem spurious, lacking the quirky spirit of a mixed private collection where one person's taste is the guide.

Set aside half a day for your visit. Free guided tours start daily at 10:30, 11:30am, 2:30, and 3:30pm, each focusing on one of the four themes. *Bankside, SE1. ☎ 020/7887-8000 or 020/7887-8888 for events. www.tate.org.uk. Admission for permanent collections is free; temporary exhibitions £5.50–£8.50. Sun–Thurs 10am–6pm; Fri–Sat 10am–10pm; galleries open at 10:15am. Closed Dec 24–26. Tube: Southwark, Mansion House, or St. Paul's (cross over Millennium Bridge). River services: Bankside Pier.*

FREE →Victoria & Albert Museum ★

The V&A is the world's foremost design museum, containing ceramics, furniture, fashion, glass, jewelry, metalwork, photographs, sculpture, textiles, and paintings from as far back 3,000 years ago. The best part of a visit here is that you can touch all the stuff: Many exhibits are interactive.

Cromwell Rd. ☎ *020/7942-2000. www.vam. ac.uk. Free admission. Mon–Tues and Thurs– Sun 10am–5:45 pm; Wed 10am–10pm. Tube: South Kensington.*

Playing Outside

If you come to London any time around the holiday season, you'll have to spend a few hours doing as Londoners do and hit the ice rinks. Nothing will fill you with Christmas/Hanukkah/Kwanzaa spirit like an evening **ice-skating** outside 📺 **Best** **Somerset House** (Strand; ☎ **020/7845-4600;** www.somerset-house.org.uk; £9.50 adults), an absolutely stunning 18th-century building housing the Courtauld Institute of Art. Not content with thousands of delicate fairy lights and a Christmas tree the size of a bus? Check out the Ice Café and the huge **Ice Wall** ★ instead. Yes, you read that correctly—there's a 8m (26-ft.) Ice Wall at Somerset House, which you can climb using crampons, ice picks, and ropes. It costs about £40 and is open from late November to the end of January.

If you're here during the summer, when you might be lucky to get 3 or 4 days in a row without rain, you'll discover that the city lends itself to outdoor concerts and festivals thanks to its acres and acres of open spaces. In 2006, the second annual **Wireless Festival** (www.wirelessfestival.co.uk) will take place in Hyde Park, where live music, markets, and shows will attract crowds for 4 days in June. In 2005 there were acts as diverse as druggie tabloid king Pete Doherty and fun dance band Basement Jaxx, so expect a stellar lineup. The **Sprite Urban Games** (www.spriteurbangames.com) are held yearly in July and feature extreme sports like skating and BMX. Other than death-defying acts, the festival features tons of stalls and activities for visitors.

Gardens & Parks

The most famous London park is undoubtedly 📺 **Best** **Hyde Park** (Kensington; Tube: Hyde Park Corner), which was first acquired by royalty in 1536 by Henry VIII for hunting. At the northeast end of Hyde Park is **Speakers Corner,** a cradle of free speech, where eccentrics spout their views for all to hear. The Serpentine boating lake in the middle of Hyde Park has pedal boats for rent. **Kensington Gardens** (Kensington; Tube: to Lancaster Gate) is another beautiful royal park, now famous as the site of the Diana, Princess of Wales Memorial playground and fountain. Other Royal Parks located in central London include **Regent's Park** (Camden/Chalk Farm; Tube: to Regent's Park), **St. James's Park** (Westminster; Tube: St. James's Park), and **Green Park** (Mayfair; Tube: Green Park).

While London isn't known as a particularly fitness-conscious city, what with all the pints of lager consumed daily, there are some beautiful places to jog. Many hotels will provide jogging maps, but if not, simply head to Hyde Park and follow the footpath.

Jolly Good Darts

You'll find dart boards at pubs all over town (along with the odd pool table or two), but two of my favorite spots to hit the bull's-eye are **The Queen Adelaide** (412 Uxbridge Rd., Sheperds Bush; ☎ **020/8746-4931)** and the **Park Hotel** (220 Park Lane, Tottenham; ☎ **020/8808-3391).**

The Lowdown on Wimbledon

....

For the first 8 days of the famous Wimbledon ★★ (Tube: Southfields) tennis tournament, around 500 seats for each show court are sold on match day. People camp out on the pavement to get them; depending on the court and the day, prices range from £24 to £79. For a chance at advance tickets, send a SASE and International Reply coupon to All England Lawn Tennis & Croquet Club, P.O. Box 98, Wimbledon SW19 5AE, between August and December. For information, call ☎ 020/8971-2473 (not during the tournament).

Spectator Sports

The British national sports are cricket and football. Both sports are played weekends in Regent's Park by teams of varying levels of seriousness: Football's played in fall and winter; cricket starts in late spring.

FOOTBALL   London has three clubs in the elite Premier League. Catch the **Spurs** (Tottenham Hotspurs) at White Hart Lane, or **Arsenal** (Avenell Rd., Highbury; ☎ 020/7704-4000; www.arsenal.co.uk; Tube: Arsenal; season runs Aug–May) or **Chelsea** (Stamford Bridge, Fulham Rd.; ☎ 020/7385-5545; www.chelseafc.co.uk; Tube: Fulham Broadway) at their respective grounds. Tickets cost from £8 to £30 for all three clubs, and more for Premiership games. The **FA (Football Association) Cup Final** is fought at **Wembley Stadium** (Empire Way, Wembley Middlesex; ☎ 020/8902-0902; www.wembleynationalstadium.co.uk; Tube: Wembley Park), as is the Rugby League (as opposed to the Union) Silk Cut Trophy. Because you'll never get tickets to either, go see another match at this 70,000-seater.

CRICKET   You can watch amateur cricket games in Regent's Park, or in Holland Park, where there's a designated Cricket Lawn with adjacent tearoom. Professional cricket is played at **Lords** (St. John's Wood Rd.; ☎ 020/7432-1066; www.lords.org/mcc/welcome.asp; Tube: St. John's Wood) the hallowed turf of British cricket since 1811, and the **Oval** (Kennington Oval; ☎ 020/7582-6660; Tube: Oval).

Shopping

London is a haven for shopaholics, filled with decadent department stores like Harrods and eclectic boutiques like those found on Carnaby Street. Nothing in London is a bargain!

Smaller London shops tend to open at about 9:30 or 10am and close at 5:30 or 6pm Monday to Saturday; larger stores often stay open at least an hour or two more. On Sundays, shops are generally now open for up to 6 hours, usually 11am to 5pm.

➜ **Ad Hoc** Ad Hoc is tiny but always packed with everyone from teenagers searching for an outfit for Saturday night to housewives looking for a fancy dress. This little boutique is chock-full of the trendiest clothes but is better known for its accessories, from delicate Indian slippers to chunky '80s legwarmers. Great for one-of-a-kind gifts. *153 King's Rd.* ☎ *020/7376-8829. Tube: Sloane Sq.*

➜ **Fortnum & Mason** London's most famous and fabulous food emporium, dating from the 18th century. The produce is so beautifully wrapped you won't want to eat it. The shop is right in touristy Piccadilly and is a welcome respite from the hordes—stop in for some tea before you head back into the fray. *181 Piccadilly.* ☎ *020/7734-8040.*

www.fortnumandmason.com. Tube: Piccadilly Circus.

→**Hamley's** Arguably the greatest toy store on earth and certainly worth a visit. You'll find 7 floors of toys, a very helpful staff, and children throwing tantrums left and right. If you value your life, don't go within a month of Christmas unless you enjoy seeing weeping mothers fighting tooth and nail over the last "it" game. Not an exaggeration. 188 Regent St. ☎ 087/0333-2455. www.hamleys.com. Tube: Oxford Circus.

→**Harrods** ★★ The most famous shop in London and possibly in the world, Harrods is a shrine to all things gilded, tacky, and wonderfully indulgent. Billionaire owner Mohammed Al Fayed's staff will find you anything your heart desires, from a new private jet to some alligator meat for a dinner party. If you're a few pounds short of an airplane, just cruise into the Knightsbridge shop and check out the world-renowned Food Hall and the rooms of designer duds. Just don't wear ripped clothes or old sweats or the snooty doormen won't let you in. 87–135 Brompton Rd. ☎ 020/7730-1234. www.harrods.com. Tube: Knightsbridge.

→**Hatchard's** The city's oldest bookshop is frequented by royals and known for attention to detail and personal service. It's a tad snobbish, but you'll find any book you're looking for. Authors love Hatchard's as much as customers; recent celeb writers stopping by for readings and signings have included Manolo Blahnik and Nick Hornby. 187 Piccadilly. ☎ 020/7494-1313. www.hatchards.co.uk. Tube: Piccadilly Circus.

→**Liberty of London** This quaint department store still retains its Victorian charm. Liberty only stocks clothes by the most cutting-edge designers like Dries Van Noten and Ozwald Boateng, although the store is best known for its own line of original, imaginative fabrics. The Beauty Hall is an uncluttered haven, lovingly filled with expensive brands such as Perricone and devoid of perfume sprayers. Regent St. ☎ 020/7734-1234. www.liberty.co.uk. Tube: Oxford Circus.

📺 **Best** →**Pop Boutique** ★★ This is the best vintage shop in London, with a collection of clothes spanning the decades. From hippy '60s dresses to new wave '80s tights, you'll find all the vintage duds you'll need at this stylish warehouse, tucked away in Covent Garden. 6 Monmouth St., WC2. ☎ 020/7497-5262. Mon–Sat 11am–7pm. Tube: Covent Garden.

→**Salvatian Army** Because this charity shop is located on posh Oxford Street, it reaps the benefits of vintage designer clothes and shoe donations. You'll also find a slew of 1970s skirts, dresses, and bags—some priced as low as £7.50. 9 Princes St., W1. ☎ 020/7495-3958. Tube: to Oxford Circus.

📺 **Best** →**Selfridges** ★★ Chicago salesman Harry Selfridge opened this store in 1909, stunning Londoners with his marble halls and sheer variety of goods. An opulent revamp, just completed, is stunning them again. The ground-floor perfumery and cosmetics department is the biggest in Europe. Upstairs is crammed with covetable designer fashions and home accessories. And Miss Selfridge is several shops within a shop within a shop. It has its own teen-queen label—which you can also find in a chain of outlets around the country—and hosts high street names, including Oasis and Warehouse, alongside some funky young designers. Selfridges also boasts one of London's finest food halls, and the biggest choice of restaurants and cafes of all the department stores. 400 Oxford St. ☎ 020/7629-1234. www.selfridges.co.uk. Tube: Bond St. or Marble Arch.

→**Sounds of the Universe** This airy basement shop started out selling a substantial selection of hip-hop, dance, and reggae tunes but has broadened to hawk Latin, disco, and punk albums too. 7 Broadwick St., W1. ☎ 020/7494-2004. Tube: to Tottenham Court Rd.

carnaby Street

This winding side street made a name for itself in the Swinging Sixties with its hip boutiques, and it has enjoyed a recent renaissance. There are 140 shops, including hipper-than-thou European names like Miss Sixty, but Carnaby Street (www.carnaby.co.uk; Tube: Oxford Circus) is better for quirky little vendors like Deal Real and Phonica, selling vinyl records, and The Face, with its vintage mod clothing.

➔ **Steinberg and Tolkien** This King's Road boutique is stuffed to the rafters with vintage couture, from 1960s Pucci shift dresses to Valentino gowns from the decadent 1980s. If you look carefully, you'll see name tags describing famous ex-owners of each colorful piece, like a particularly hideous purple suit labeled "once owned by Elton John." The top floor is dedicated to accessories, like immaculate lace gloves and garish Chanel logo bags from years gone by. *193 King's Rd.* ☎ *020/7376-3660. Tube: Sloane Sq.*

➔ **Top Shop** ★★ This is the flagship store for Britain's preeminent high-street label. Big-name designers like Hussein Chalayan have contributed lines to Top Shop, and the chain has earned a deserved reputation for stylish jeans and contemporary wear for reasonable prices. While most of the clothes aren't the best quality, Top Shop is ahead of all the trends. Note to males: Top Man is upstairs, providing a welcome respite from the glitter and glitz below. *216 Oxford St.* ☎ *020/7636-7700. www.topshop.com. Tube: Oxford Circus.*

Markets

➔ **Brick Lane Market** Also known as Curry Mile, this is London's center of Bangladeshi culture—as well as home to the best selection of tandoori (Indian) and Bengali restaurants. You'll find a market specializing in leather but carrying everything from treasure to trash. The market is open Sunday morning till about 2pm. *Brick Lane, E1. Tube: Aldgate East.*

➔ **Camden Market** Located in north London at Camden Lock, this market has grown in size year by year and is now open 7 days a week from around 10am to 6pm, although the busiest time to shop is Sunday. Stalls sell everything from African art to body piercings, for every price range. You can also expect to find all sorts of delicious ethnic food sold by shouting vendors. Camden is fun for a few hours, but really saw its heyday in the '90s, when neon club wear was all the rage. The clothes sold here today seem dated. *Camden High Rd. and Chalk Farm Rd. Tube: Camden Town.*

➔ **Petticoat Lane** Established over 400 years ago by the Huguenots who came over from France to sell lace petticoats to prudish Victorians, Petticoat Lane thrives all week, growing in size on Sundays from 9am to 2pm and selling clothes, watches, toys, and more. Food stalls serve up traditional Jewish fare, among other ethnicities. Petticoat Lane is reachable by Tube—the station is at the top of the sprawling market street. *Middlesex St., E1. Tube: Aldgate East.*

(MTV) (Best) ➔ **Portobello Road** ★★ Several markets in one, from the 2,000 antiques dealers of the Notting Hill end, past the fruit-and-veg traders, to the trendy stalls of vintage stuff under the Westway, and on into the junk of Goldborne Road. It's London's best flea market, or at least most famous. The antiques area is open Saturday 7am to 5:30pm; everything else is open Monday to Saturday 9am to 5pm; (closes at 1pm Thurs). *Portobello Rd., W11–W10. Tube: Ladbroke Grove or Notting Hill Gate.*

➔ **Spitalfields** ★ Located in the shadow of Christ Church in Shoreditch, Spitalfields has experienced growing popularity thanks to the emergence of boho fashion. What Covent

Garden was like before it became a tourist haven, Spitalfields is today. It sells organic food, new clothes by young designers, and even vintage cars. Go on a Sunday between 10am and 4:30pm and eat at Meson Los Barilles, a Spanish tapas cafe popular with local artists. *65 Brushfield St., E1.* ☎ *020/ 7247-8556. www.oldspitalfieldsmarket.com. Daily 10am–7pm; market stalls weekdays 10am–3pm and Sun 9:30am–5pm. Tube: Liverpool St.*

Road Trip

Only a couple of hours from central London, **Bath** makes a perfect location for a day trip or a weekend respite from the city. It's simply beautiful—you can imagine a Jane Austen character strolling up its cobbled, leafy streets, and nothing much has changed in the last century. The city is historic, with numerous museums and attractions to visit, plus it's lots of fun, with great shopping and tons of bars.

Bath Basics

The easiest way to reach Bath is by train from London Paddington or London Waterloo for £29 round-trip, although you can rent a car easily, too. For train timetables, go to www.nationalrail.co.uk or call ☎ **084/5748-4950.** There are buses to Bath from London Victoria bus station daily; the journey takes approximately 2 hours and 45 minutes and costs £15. For information on the city of Bath, go to www.visitbath.co.uk, the official site. Other good, comprehensive sites include www.cityofbathco.uk and www. thisisbath.com, in association with the *Bath Chronicle* newspaper.

Sleeping

Bath has all sorts of accommodations ranging from cozy B&Bs to luxury hotels. In central Bath, try the boutique **Queensberry Hotel** (Russel St.; ☎ **012/2544-7928;** www. thequeensberry.co.uk; £110 double) on Russel Street, which is rather expensive but has a great in-house restaurant called the Olive Tree. Slightly cheaper and also central is the **Kennard Hotel** (11 Henrietta St.; ☎ **012/2531-0472;** www.kennard.co.uk; £98

double), a Georgian town house restored with all modern conveniences and stylish decor. Cheaper still and perfect for larger numbers of people is the **Royal Hotel,** near the train station (Manvers St.; ☎ **012/2546-3134;** www.royalhotelbath.co.uk; £80 double). For bed-and-breakfast accommodations, there are a lot of good places to choose from. **Apsley House Hotel** (Newbridge Hill; ☎ **012/2533-6966;** £70 double) is family run and just a mile from the city center. It has very grand bedrooms and lots of print accolades. Similarly luxurious and only a few minutes' walk from central Bath, with epic views, is the **Oldfields Hotel** (102 Wells Rd.; ☎ **012/2531-7984;** www. oldfields.co.uk; £65 double). The prices are pretty good for the standard of accommodations. **Dorian House** (1 Upper Oldfield Park Rd.; ☎ **012/2542-6336;** www.dorianhouse. co.uk; £65–£140 double) has spectacular views of the Royal Crescent and decorations with a musical flavor because owner Tim Hugh is the principal cellist with the London Symphony Orchestra. You can also book a restorative massage here.

Eating

There are lots of choices for eating out in Bath, whether you're looking for five-star cuisine or a sandwich. For consistently good French food, try **Beaujolais,** just a few minutes' walk from the main shopping area on Milsom Street. If you want to sit outside, try **Café du Globe,** a Moroccan-owned restaurant with some delicious *mezze,* couscous, and lamb *tagine.* It's on North Parade, a few meters from the Abbey. The **Bath Priory Restaurant** has a coveted Michelin star—it's expensive, but if you fancy quail salad, clam risotto, or foie gras in a beautiful garden setting, this is the place to come. For cheaper noshes, try the **Green Street Seafood Café,** on Green Street. The fish soup is above par and you can get sandwiches to take away and eat in the sun. For desserts, try **Scoffs** in Kingsmead Square. The cake is to die for, so don't go if you're on a diet. For a classic English fry-up at any time of day, head to **PJ Peppers** on George Street. The cappuccino is pretty good, too.

Partying

The closest thing to a super-club in Bath is **Babylon** (Kingston Rd.; ☎ 012/2546-5002; cover £3–£6), packed with sweaty teenagers till closing time at 2am on weekends. The music is consistently good, and this is the first club a local will recommend to you. Another fun club in Bath is **The Fez Club** (6 Bladdud Building, The Paragon; ☎ 012/2544-4162; cover £5). Granted, the Moroccan theme is somewhat overdone, but this place makes up for it with their very comfortable bed-like chairs. **Moles** (14 George St.; ☎ 012/2540-4455; cover £5) is popular with students for its live music, particularly local acts. You can dress down and not feel guilty. It's also open till 4am on weekends.

There's no shortage of pubs and bars in Bath. **The Boater** (9 Argyle St.; ☎ 012/2546-4211) is right on the river and has a pretty beer garden. It gets really crowded when the Bath rugby team's playing a match. **Adventure Café** (5 Princes Buildings, George St.; ☎ 012/2546-2038) is a real favorite with locals, for good reason. Its atmosphere is reminiscent of a Parisian brasserie and the cocktails are delicious. The **Central Wine Bar** (10 Upper Borough Walls; ☎ 012/2533-3939) is cool without being pretentious, with a huge selection of beers on tap and a top wine list. Go early, as it closes at 11pm. The

Garricks Head (St John's Place; ☎ 012/2531-8368) is slightly more pretentious and popular with the gay crowd. It's also right next to the theater, making it perfect for post-play boozing. **Pulp Bar** (38 Monmouth St.; ☎ 012/2546-6411) is enduringly popular and has a really long cocktail list and a trendy clientele. It's pricey, but you're guaranteed a fun night out.

Exploring Bath

Bath is just over 161km (100 miles) from London but it couldn't be more different, with its hot springs, Roman Baths, vast Abbey, and gorgeous houses reminiscent of Georgian crescents. Definitely check out the baths the Romans built around Britain's only hot spring (Abbey Church Yard; ☎ 012/2547-7785; www.romanbaths.co.uk; admission £10; daily 9:30am–5:30pm; closed Dec 25–26). It's still working, so you can choose to peek at the water's source while walking around the extensive ruins and ancient pavements.

The Jane Austen center (40 Gay St., Queen Sq.; ☎ 012/2544-3000; www.janeausten.co.uk; admission £5.95 adult, £4.50 student; daily 10am–5:30pm in summer; check website for other times) is definitely also worth a visit. This museum pays homage to the city's most famous resident with costumed tour guides and a Regency-style tea shop.

If you want to see exactly how people lived in the late 18th century, visit **No. 1 Royal Crescent** (1 Royal Crescent; ☎ 012/2542-8126; www.bath-preservation-trust.org.uk/museums/no1; admission £4; Tues–Sun 10:30am–5pm; varied hours from late Oct to late Nov), a World Heritage house restored and decorated as it was hundreds of years ago. The best museum in Bath is the **Holburne** (Great Pulteney St.; ☎ 012/2546-6669; www.bath.ac.uk/holburne; admission £4.50; Tues–Sat 10am–5pm, Sun 11am–5pm, open on Bank Holiday Mon), which houses paintings by Stubbs and Gainsborough among others, plus a fabulous collection of silver and

Going to Glastonbury

The Somerset town of **Glastonbury** is these days synonymous with a summer music festival—and that's about it. However, there's a lot more to this town than a few days of Coldplay every year. The area is steeped in history, particularly relating to spirituality. It's believed to be the birthplace of the Christian Church in England but attracts visitors of many other faiths due to the purported power of the White and Red Springs. You can't turn a corner in Glastonbury without finding a shop dedicated to the occult or a tarot card reader. Worth a visit is the **Glastonbury Tor**, mainly to see the eccentric folks who climb this ancient hill to commune with Gwyn Ap Nudd, King of the Fairies. The Tor is rumored to be part of the landscape of King Arthur's Avalon. Other attractions worth your time are **Glastonbury Abbey, the Abbey Visitors' Center,** and the **Rural Life Museum** on Chilkwell Street, which will give you a sense of domestic life in Victorian Somerset. However, just walking down the high street is an attraction in itself, with its bizarre collection of arty little shops, old-fashioned cafes, and tourist traps. If you plan on staying the night, try **Glastonbury Backpackers** (4 Market Place; ☎ 01458/833353; www.glastonburybackpackers.com), an upmarket hostel with bright, colorful rooms for budget prices. You'll find every facility you'll need, from Internet access to a bar, and a dorm room will only set you back £12 (it costs £30 for a double room). For more information on the town of Glastonbury plus information on where to eat and sleep, go to www.glastonbury.co.uk.

Of course, you might want to journey to Glastonbury to check out the 3 days of music—the Glastonbury festival is the largest performing arts festival in the world. Around 150,000 people attended in 2005 to catch acts like Basement Jaxx and New Order. Info is posted at www.glastonburyfestivals.com.

Glastonbury is definitely not easy to reach, but with a little planning you'll be there within a couple hours of leaving London. The nearest train station is Castle Cary, in Somerset, from where you can take the bus. However, this service is sporadic. You're better off taking a train from London (or anywhere else) to Bristol—they leave every half-hour—and taking a bus to Glastonbury from there. For more information and schedules, check out the National Rail website at www.nationalrail.co.uk or call ☎ 084/5748-4950.

furniture. Entry fees in Bath are far less than those in London, so your wallet will thank you. Go to www.visitbath.co.uk for more information and directions to all these sites.

Shopping

Bath is known for its chic independent boutiques, which sell fabulously expensive wares to rich ladies-who-lunch from the surrounding countryside. It's also a city for the young, so expect some shops for college-age clotheshorses. **Square** (5 Shires Yard, Milsom St.; ☎ 012/2531-5172) is a favorite

with fashionistas from miles around. You'll find clothes by Brit designers like Stella McCartney and Alexander McQueen, plus a range of jeans by Joie. Accessories for men and women are by the likes of Burberry, Miu Miu, and Maharishi. The threads are not cheap by any stretch of the imagination, but you'll find something hot to wear for a night out. For men's clothes, try **John Anthony** (28 High St.; ☎ 012/2542-4066), for cutting-edge designers like Paul Smith. On Abbey Green is the **Tricker's** shoe store for men, which proudly holds the royal warrant from Prince Charles—meaning it has his endorsement (9 Abbey Green; ☎ 012/2546-3353). **Jolly's** (13 Milsom St.; ☎ 087/0160-7224) is part of the excellent House of Fraser chain of department stores; you'll find anything you need here. For more on the huge variety of great shops in Bath, check out www.bath shopping.co.uk.

Madrid

Folks in Madrid toss down little cups of coffee like muscle cars guzzle gas, smoke cigarettes like it was their last day on earth, eat nothing but fried foods, and drink till—at (the very) least—3am. This town is one of the true world-class capitals of late, late-night fun. In fact, there are more bars and pubs here than in the other western European capitals combined. On most nights, seemingly the whole city is drinking and dancing at an untold number of venues until the sun comes up. The actual experience of a weekend in Madrid is kind of like a 72-hour (don't forget about Sun) bungee jump: Just give into the gravity and know that somehow you'll bounce back by Monday morning.

With all these vices, you would think that the average resident of this sprawling capital would have Homer Simpson's body and Keith Richards' face, but, remarkably, it isn't so. The locals are thin, healthy, and happy, smoking and drinking until a ripe old age. How do they do it? Well, if you ask a group of Madrileños, they'll tell you that their health is the result of *una vida más tranquila,* a more easygoing way of life. "Enjoy yourself here," they'll tell you, "nobody wants problems."

Not surprisingly, the sunny inhabitants of this city are tolerant of all sorts. Still, young global travelers wandering in flocks are sometimes perceived here as odd birds: swooping down with baseball hats and big running shoes, demanding Internet access and Rollerblades. Madrileños are also happy to know that visitors are interested in learning more about their language and culture. It's only in the last 20 years or so (since the end of Franco's reign) that Spain has emerged as a significant First World nation. This means that the country has opened itself up to Hollywood,

Levi's, and nearly every fast-food chain that America has spawned. The result is that younger people listen to Eminem, they have cellphones, and they rave. Still, even though young people are more likely than their parents to speak English, this ain't Holland or Sweden, *amigo.*

With so much going on, it's hard to figure out what you're gonna do in the next 5 minutes, much less the next few days. Don't freak out; just get your hands on the all-knowing, all-powerful Buddha of nightlife, *Guía del Ocio.* This weekly magazine has everything, man: live music, movies, performing arts, bars, clubs, and more. Buy it for 1€ at any kiosk, and kneel down and worship (or read). Other good sources of info are the flyers and employees at hipster and club clothing stores (such as those on Calle Fuencarral) and also the millions of posters around town.

Also Madrileños like to get close—really close. At first it's a little frightening when people keep putting their cheerful faces right up to yours when they're speaking, but try and stifle the urge to shove the natives back. If you look around, you'll see that Spanish guys often have a hand on their buddy's shoulders and that many women walk arm in arm with their good friends. Spanish closeness, of course, also has its own etiquette. Although men simply shake hands when meeting for the first time, women kiss each other—and men—on both cheeks when first introduced. Does this imply some lovin' later on? Absolutely not. The tradition of *dos besos* (two kisses) is as old as the culture itself, and you'll seem cold and standoffish if you don't give out dos besos to a woman to whom you've been introduced.

The Best of Madrid

○ **The Best Hostel (Ever): Cat's Hostel** has got the art of the youth hostel down to a T. Great location, beautiful building, a bar, and a pre-going-out club to hook up before you even set your foot out the door. See p. 593.

○ **The Best Restaurant to Try New Spanish Cuisine:** That is, without spending your entire trip's budget on one meal. **Finos y Finas** offers a very modern and creative Spanish menu at a price that won't reduce your shopping list. See p. 600.

○ **The Best Lunch Special:** This Spanish cultural advantage (aka *menú del día*) is best experienced at **La Austríaca.** The sassy family that runs it will not let you go until you clean your plate, not that you'll need any incentive. See p. 600.

○ **The Best Museum to Get Your Art History Together:** Of the three biggies, the collection at **Thyssen-Bornemisza Museum** is the one that reflects almost every period in the history of art, from El Greco to de Kooning. See p. 607.

○ **The Best Bar to Feel the Spirit of Flamenco without Seeing Any Show:** **Candela** is dark, gritty, and dangerous (not really, not anymore), the polar opposite of your average tourist flamenco show, but its walls breathe the spirit of all the big guys that perform at the exclusive backroom "cave." If you manage to get in, please tell us how. See p. 605.

Getting There & Getting Around

Getting There

BY PLANE

Barajas International Airport is about 13km (8 miles) northeast of the city. You can find everything any major airport offers: ATMs, tourist office (on Terminal 2), post office, and, of course, shops and bars. Walking from one terminal to the other is better than taking the bus and is facilitated by the hundreds of meters of automated walkways. All major airlines are to be found here.

The best way to get in and out of the airport is the Metro service (1.25€ one-way) that runs directly from the airport via line 8 and takes less than 15 minutes to the commercial center of the city, though you'll probably have to connect to a different line and carry your luggage up a few flights of stairs in some stations, to get to the old part of town. Also, on your way out, you can check your bags at the Nuevos Ministerios station at the beginning of your line 8 ride. A bus (1.25€ per ride; ☎ 91-408-6810), runs about every 15 minutes from terminals 1, 2, and 3 to Plaza de Colón (2.50€), and it takes about 30 min.; you can switch to the Metro or a taxi from there. A taxi to the center will set you back around 18€. The information number for the airport is ☎ 90-235-3570 (www.aena.es; Metro: Aeropuerto).

BY BUS

Estación Sur de Autobuses (Calle de Méndez Alvaro s/n; ☎ 91-468-4200; Metro: Méndez Alvaro) is the bus station. If your trip is not too long and you are trying to save some money, the bus can be a good option. Most buses to the south and other parts of

MADRID

Talk of the Town

Four ways to start a conversation with a local

1. **Bullfighting: Cruel and unusual or merely unusual?** If you want to check it out first, go to the Plaza Monumental de Toros de las Ventas (Metro: Ventas) for listings. Seats in the sun cost less.

2. **Madrid or Barcelona?** Madrileños love to diss their counterparts up in Barcelona. They'll tell you that the folks in Barcelona are *más cerrados* (closed minded), *separatistas* (separatists), and *más europeos* (more European, less Spanish). The Congress recently passed a law *(estatut)* giving Cataluña an unprecedented level of financial autonomy causing a boycott of Catalan products in the rest of Spain.

3. **Want a smoke?** The recent smoking ban in public places, although not fully enforced, is sure causing some stir. All you have to do is ask for a cigarette or ask someone to turn it off and you are bound for some discussion.

4. **Hash versus marijuana?** Now that some residents grow MJ on their balconies, the quarrel is more alive than ever.

the country depart from here and the ones that don't, usually have offices in it. **AutoRes** (www.auto-res.net) and **Alsa** (www.alsa.es) are some of the companies serving the south of Spain and neighboring provinces.

BY TRAIN

Both of Madrid's major train stations are adorned with easy-to-read signs that will direct you to the Metro, but you should take the "cercanías" commuter train if you're going from station to station—it's much faster than the Metro. For times and fares contact **Renfe** (☎ 90-224-0202; www.renfe.es).

Estación Puerta de Atocha (Glorieta del Emperador Carlos V) is more central—also older, prettier, and bigger. It's steps away from the museum triangle and hub for most of your national connections in Spain. Spain's pride, the lightning fast AVE train joins Seville and Madrid in $2^{1}/_{2}$ hours every day, or you can take an extra hour and save some money on the Talgo (www.talgo.com).

Estación de Chamartín (Agustín de Foxá s/n; ☎ 91-323-2121; Metro: Chamartín) is the arriving and departing point for most international and a few, northbound national trains. For the night, get on the Metro and get off at Tribunal, Antón Martín, Sol, or Gran Vía to put yourself in the center of town.

Getting Around

BY CAR

Madrid is not ideal for driving. Gas is expensive and hard to find in the city, parking is scarce, and the roads are crammed and disorienting. For a cycle or scooter, call **Motoalquiler** (☎ 91-542-0657).

BY PUBLIC TRANSPORTATION

It all boils down to the Metro (subway) and the EMT (buses). Both use the same tickets, but the Metro is infinitely easier to use. Plus, it's (usually) fast, safe, and clean. Buy your 10-trip MetroBus pass in the subways stations at booths or automated machines for only 5.80€ or pay 1€ for each single ride. Metro system *planos* (maps) are located at the ticket windows. The subways are closed from 2am till 6am.

BY TAXI

Taxis are fairly easy to find and relatively cheap. When you flag down a taxi, the meter should register 1.35€; for every kilometer thereafter, the fare increases by .65€. A supplement is charged for trips to the railway station or the bullring, as well as on Sundays and holidays. *Warning:* Make sure the meter is turned on when you get into the taxi. Otherwise, some drivers assess the cost of the ride, and their assessment, you can be sure, will involve creative mathematics. Also, there are unmetered taxis that hire out for the day or afternoon. They are legitimate, but some drivers operate as gypsy cabs. Because they're not metered, they can charge high rates. They are easy to avoid—always take either a black taxi with horizontal red bands or a white one with diagonal red bands. If you take a taxi outside the city limits, the driver is entitled to charge you twice the rate shown on the meter. To call a taxi, dial ☎ 91-447-5180. If you're having a hard time finding one, you can always call **Radio Taxi** (☎ 91-405-5500) or **Tele Taxi** (☎ 91-371-2131; www.tele-taxi.es).

BY BICYCLE

Madrid is a great size city for riding a bike. You can probably go all around the center neighborhoods in 1 day, but, you have to be really into pedaling up and down the many hills and dealing with a pretty crazy mass of drivers. Because people from Madrid are not much into any exercise—other than dancing—there aren't many bike paths or racks. But if you are a bike activist, or just want to enjoy a Sunday ride around El Retiro, check out **Bike Spain** (Carmen 17, 2; ☎ 91-522-3899; www.bikespain.info). They charge 15€ a day or 75€ a week.

ON FOOT

Choose an area a day and you won't even have to worry about the subway. Walking around is the best way to see everything the city has to offer and discover those things that you can only find by bumping into: the street vendors, the dealers, the street ladies on calle Montera, the punk kids and Rastafarians. In general, be very careful with cars; they don't necessarily respect pedestrians. And be particularly mindful with traffic lights. The moment the red dude starts blinking, you better run for your life; it will leave you barely enough time to make it to the opposite sidewalk.

Madrid Basics

Orientation: Madrid Neighborhoods

Puerta del Sol is the geographic center of Madrid and because many big arteries converge here, you'll find yourself visiting it more than you would like to. The neighborhood names and borders are not very clear, but they tend to be defined by the area surrounding a Metro stop of the same name. Try to find the Dibuk guides to the neighborhoods (www.eldibuk.com) at trendy stores and restaurants, which contain maps with hot spots for each area.

SOL   The very center of downtown Madrid. Most buses and the busiest Metro lines converge here, as do the thousands of travelers who come to gawk at the impressive Plaza Mayor. Good shopping (at El Calle de Preciados) and good drinking (at bar haven Plaza Santa Ana) are also in this general area. The Puerta del Sol, which used to be located at the east limit of the city and is now the center, is sort of Madrid's Time Square on New Year's Eve as thousands of people embark on the arduous task of eating one white grape with each of the first 12 bells of the New Year.

EL PRADO   This is the ultimate cultural neighborhood, former home of many great Spanish writers. The impressive heritage is still alive in the magnificent Fuente de la Cibeles and the city's three main cultural attractions: El Prado, Reina Sofía, and Thyssen-Bornemisza. Madrid's three world-class museums are simply too good to miss.

They are very close to each other and not far from the other attraction in this neighborhood: Parque del Buen Retiro, Madrid's green lung and great for outdoor fun or people-watching on Sunday.

LA LATINA   One of the oldest neighborhoods in Madrid, this former working-class area is turning into Madrid's newest hot spot thanks to a combination of bars and restaurants and a new wave of entertainment-industry people choosing it as their home base. House of the massive Feria del Rastro on Sundays—that's when the 'hood comes to life, and the best day to stroll around the jam-packed tapas bars and try to spot local film and TV celebrities.

LAVAPIES   Madrid's most picturesque and multicultural neighborhood has been turning into a center for underground arts and culture. In its hundreds of bars and restaurants you are likely to find Manu Chao and his type, the anti-corporate citizens of the world. Also find here some of the most authentic and grimy flamenco bars in town.

MALASANA   The heart, together with Chueca, of the *movida madrileña* in the '80s is now full of artists and musicians, along with the associated poetry readings, great coffee houses, vegetarian restaurants, and most significant drinking holes. The famed, funky, and fabulous Calle Fuencarral begins in this neighborhood and continues right out to the Gran Vía Metro stops.

CHUECA   West of Calle de Fuencarral is the epicenter of Madrid's gay and lesbian

MADRID

communities. This groovy neighborhood has great cafes and shopping by day and perhaps some of the wildest bar scenes in Madrid by night. Also home to Madrid's most pompous modernist building, Sociedad General de Autores y Editores.

ASTURIAS This neighborhood is where you will find Madrid's most grandiose buildings, from the times where kings and royalty were more than just a smiling face on the cover of *Hello* magazine. Around the Opera Metro station, you'll find the Palacio Real, Plaza de Oriente, and Plaza de la Villa, among other landmarks.

SALAMANCA & RUBEN DARIO The *pijo* part of town, a modern neighborhood with straight streets and brand-name designer stores. Some very interesting museums, like the Museo Arqueológico and Museo Sorolla, are in this area. Also at the border, and boy does it mark a border, is Plaza Colón, Madrid's skater cathedral.

Tourist Offices

A good place to pass by at the beginning of your visit is the tourist office at Barajas airport (☎ **91-305-8656;** Mon–Sat 8am–8pm, Sun 9am–2pm). Here you can pick up a map and some free English magazines like *In Madrid* and *What's On.* The offices at both train stations have the same opening hours, and if you need another map, you can get it at the central office at Plaza Mayor 27 (☎ **90-210-0007** or 91-588-1636; www. esmadrid.com; daily 9:30am–8:30pm).

Recommended Websites

○ **www.esmadrid.com**: Official website of the city; available in many languages.
○ **www.guiadelocio.com/madrid**: The Web version of the entertainment bible in Spanish.
○ **www.webmadrid.com**: A good English-language travel guide to the city.

○ **www.madridman.com**: An American-in-Spain's website. Very detailed, but a little too much advertising.
○ **www.madaboutmadrid.com**: A blog-style website in English.

Culture Tips 101

The legal minimum drinking age in Madrid is 18, but the police certainly don't enforce that law with the same vigor as they can in some places. Although all other drugs are illegal, many people in the city smoke porros. Porros are tobacco rolled together with hash or marijuana, and it's pretty much the only way that Spaniards get high.

Hash, or *chocolate*, is legal to possess in small amounts for personal use only (a half-gram or less). Smoking tobacco and drinking on the streets or in parks is fine with the law—usually, and as long as you're cool and in control. Laws—and interpretations of the law—change quickly. So always remember that using drugs overseas can lead to jail, a fine, and/or deportation.

Recommended Books, Movies & Music
BOOKS

The most famous Spanish novel is *Don Quixote* by Miguel de Cervantes; some people read it in Spanish and say that, even if it takes a lifetime, it's worth it. Ernest Hemingway completed many novels on or in Spain, none more notable than *The Sun Also Rises* (1926) and *For Whom the Bell Tolls* (1940).

Elizabeth Nash's highly individual *Madrid* (A Cultural Literary Companion) is a more personal view of the city; it's in Signal Books' "Cities of the Imagination" series. If you want the lowdown on the monuments and historical background of Castile, check out Alistair Boyd's *Companion Guide to Madrid and Central Spain* (Collins). A succinct and offbeat intro to the capital's surrounding towns and villages is provided by Peter Stone's *Madrid Escapes* (Santana Books).

Top 10 Local Favorites

Johann, the hottest Spain MTV veejay, originally from Holland but living in Madrid for years offers this as his top 10.

- **St. Andrews:** An old hunter's hall filled with widows and people over 50 with a freak element.
- **José Alfredo:** A cocktail lounge.
- **Vía Láctea:** Rock-'n'-roll and vintage-soul bar.
- **Nasti:** Indie music club.
- **Parnaso:** Decadent bar with loads of antiques.
- **Plaza Colón:** Madrid's skate spot. Now more restricted by police.
- **La Latina:** One of Madrid's oldest neighborhoods, full of bars and restaurants, good for hanging out on Sundays afternoons. Lots of ladies mingling around.
- **El Cisne Azul:** A tapas bar specializing in mushrooms and flower salads. Succulent.
- **Le Garage:** Dingy, sleazy karaoke bar that turns into an electro/rock club on Thursdays.
- **La Viuda de Vacas:** Spanish restaurant in La Latina.

MOVIES

Pedro Almodóvar and Madrid are almost synonyms; watching a retrospective of his movies is like watching a historical documentary of Madrid, only a lot more fun. All except for his last few movies take place here. *El día de la Bestia,* by Santiago Segura, is a completely wacked-out version of Madrid, in a hysterical science-fiction story of the son of Satan descending upon Spain's capital and the quest of a Basque priest, a heavy metal fan, and friends to stop him.

MUSIC

Joaquín Sabina is sort of the Bob Dylan of Madrid. His light rock songs are as Madrileños as you can get and if you understand Spanish, the lyrics in *Malas Compañías* will give you a tour of Madrid that no travel guide ever could, except maybe this one.

Madrid Nuts & Bolts

Cellphone Providers & Service Centers   The main cellphone providers in Spain are Amena, Movistar, and Vodafone. You can find them all over the city on main drags. To buy a new cellphone, get a line, or service, check out **The Phone House** (Malasaña branch: Fuencarral 66; ☎ 91-701-4690; www.phonehouse.es; Sat–Thurs 11am–9pm; Metro: Gran Vía).

Crisis Centers   For help with substance abuse, call the Dirección sobre Drogas (Recoletos 22; ☎ 91-822-6121). For sexual abuse or harassment, call the general emergency number: ☎ 112.

Currency   As anywhere else, if you have an ATM card, use it. Banks are open weekdays from 8:30am to 2pm. And finally, if you are really inclined to supporting the Spanish economy in the form of ridiculous exchange rates and fees, there are plenty of exchange booths in or around Puerta del Sol and Plaza Mayor. For your traveler's checks, visit **American Express** at Plaza de las Cortes 2 (☎ 91-572-0320; Metro: Banco de España).

Embassies   If you are in need of some good metal detection and X-ray action, say "hi" to Uncle Sam at the **U.S. Embassy** at Serrano 75 (☎ 91-58—2200; www.embusa.es; Mon—Fri 9am—6pm). The **Canadian Embassy** is at Núñez de Balboa 35 (☎ 91/423—3250; Mon—Thurs 8:30am—5:30pm, Fri 8:30am—2:30pm). For the **U.K. Embassy,** go to Calle Fernando el Santo 16 (☎ 91/319-0200; Mon—Fri 9am—1:30pm and 3—6pm). The **Australian Embassy** is at Plaza Diego de Ordas 3, Edificio Sana Engracia 120 (☎ 91/441—6025; Mon—Thurs 8:30am—5pm, Fri 8:30am—2:15pm).

Emergencies   In an emergency, call ☎ 112. The two main hospitals in Madrid are **Ciudad Sanitaria la Paz** (Paseo de la Castellana 261; ☎ 91-727-7000; Metro: Begoña) and **Hospital General Gregorio Marañón** (Doctor Esquerdo 46; ☎ 91-586-8000; Metro: Ibiza or O'Donnell). **Unidad Médica Anglo-Americana** (Conde de Arandá 1; ☎ 91-435-1823; Metro: Retiro) is not a hospital but a private outpatient clinic offering the services of various specialists. This is not an emergency clinic, but someone on staff is available daily from 9am to 8pm.

Internet/Wireless Hot Spots   There are Internet cafes all over town, often with kids playing Web games. The little-higher-than-average prices at **Bbigg** (Mayor 1; www.bbigg. com; 24 hr.; Metro: Sol) guarantee no waiting in line at this Internet franchise, where you can scan, fax, Xerox, print, and e-mail that picture in the Plaza Mayor to anyone who could bear to see it. It costs 2.20€ per hour and 5€ for 3 hours. If checking your e-mail is more of a pretext to meet new people, go to **Natura Gran Vía** (Gran Vía 16; ☎ 91-521-7573; daily 8am—2am; 1€ per hour), a ground-floor bar and restaurant with coin-operated computers in the basement.

Laundry   If you are in Malasaña, check **Wash Wash.** This creatively named laundromat will do your dirty work for 9.25€ per 6.5kg (14-lb.) load. Service is usually overnight.

Luggage Storage   Go to Atocha or Chamartín train stations and you can park your bags in a *consigna* for 3€ a day.

Pharmacies   For a late-night pharmacy, look in the daily newspaper under "Farmacias de Guardia." Most drugstores close at 8pm. Or go to any pharmacy, which, even if closed, often posts a list of nearby pharmacies that are open late that day. One of the most central is **Farmacia Gayoso** (Arenal 2; ☎ 91-521-2860; Metro: Puerta del Sol). It's open Monday through Saturday from 9:30am to 9:30pm.

Post Offices   Send one of those postcards with the fabric flamenco dresses from your local post office or the main one, at **Palacio de Comunicaciones** (Plaza Cibeles; ☎ 91-396-2443; www.correos.es; Mon—Sat 8:30am—9:30pm).

Restrooms   Some public restrooms are available, including those in the Parque de Retiro and on Plaza de Oriente across from the Palacio Real. Otherwise, you can always go into a bar or *tasca,* but you should order something. The major department stores, such as Galerías Preciados and El Corte Inglés, have good, clean restrooms.

Safety   Economic stability has brought Madrid to a state of safeness comparable to most European cities. However, with the increase of tourism there's also been an increase in pickpocketing. Just use your common sense. Avoid the less populated areas of Lavapies at night; some streets near Puerta del Sol, where the professionals of the night offer their services, are probably not the best place to stop and ask for directions.

Telephone Tips   To call the operator, dial ☎ **1009;** you'll get an international operator by dialing ☎ **1008.** All pay phones in Spain can use *tarjetas telefónicas* (phone cards), which can be bought at tobacco stores and *estancos.* Remember to take your card out of the phone after your call!

Tipping   Waiters here get paid decent wages so tipping is 10% or less. Only foreigners tip at bars, and you don't tip the masseuse. Cabbies are sometimes tipped .50€.

Sleeping

Don't sweat trying to find a hostel in the "right" area. Madrid's a big city, but it's physically squished. The various zones are surprisingly close together, and if you're centrally located you'll never have to walk for more than 20 minutes to get to your destination (5 or 10 is usually more like it). The Metro will obviously make any trip a lot shorter. The most common type of accommodations are the *hostales,* usually old buildings converted into guesthouses, most often found in Chueca and Malasaña. Use common sense; if the lobby of the building smells like urine and there's trash everywhere, go to a different one. Also, most hostels in Madrid keep their main doors locked and buzz their tenants in. Although annoying and inconvenient, it's true that your backpack is a lot safer this way. So, even though most hostels will tell you that they don't have a curfew, be patient when you are ringing the bell to be let in at 6am!

Hostels

➔ **Barbieri International Hostel** With not as much personality as Cat's (see below), this hostel inside a typical Madrid building will make you feel like you're back at your dorm, minus the lava lamp. The mixed or single-sex rooms are small but they have only two, four, or eight beds. The pastel-colored, parquet-floored common spaces are IKEA cozy with big multicolored couches and furniture. There's a fully equipped kitchen, a computer with Internet access, lockers in most rooms, and a safe in reception. The ambience is as friendly as it can get, and the bathrooms are sparkly clean most of the time. However, the best feature, besides the lowest prices this side of the western equator, is the location; it's in the center of the fun-filled Chueca 'hood. *Barbieri 15, 2nd floor.* ☎ *91-531-0258. www.barbierihostel.com. 15€–16€ dorm. Rates include breakfast and linens. Metro: Chueca or Gran Vía. Amenities: Kitchen; Internet (in common area); shared bathrooms (single sex); travel desk; TV (in common area). In room: Locker (in most).*

📺 **Best** ➔ **Cat's Hostel** ★ Walking into this 18th-century Andalusian-style palace makes me wish I were 20 and single again. Aside from the sultan-worthy tile and glasswork and a fountain maintained from the original building, this place is a backpacker's dream. The dorms sleep between 6 and 14 people (a little crowded, but who's sleeping anyway?) and they are either single-sex or coed. There are coin-operated washers and dryers on both floors. A cool bar by the entrance is probably one of Madrid's better pickup spots, topped, or rather bottomed, by the underground "cave," with DJs, live music, and computers with free Internet access, which opens from 7pm to midnight, so that you can start your night by

Madrid

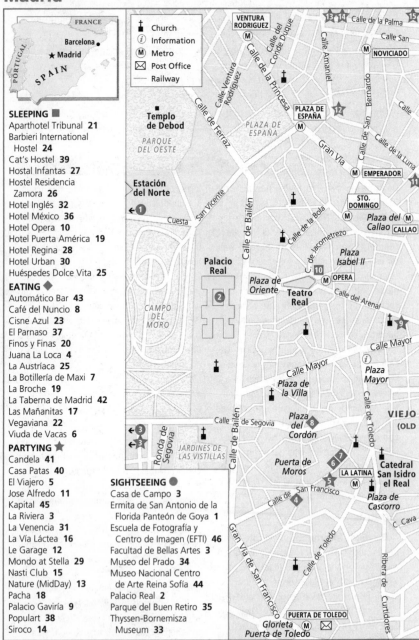

SLEEPING ■
Aparthotel Tribunal **21**
Barbieri International
  Hostel **24**
Cat's Hostel **39**
Hostal Infantas **27**
Hostel Residencia
  Zamora **26**
Hotel Inglés **32**
Hotel México **36**
Hotel Opera **10**
Hotel Puerta América **19**
Hotel Regina **28**
Hotel Urban **30**
Huéspedes Dolce Vita **25**

EATING ◆
Automático Bar **43**
Café del Nuncio **8**
Cisne Azul **23**
El Parnaso **37**
Finos y Finas **20**
Juana La Loca **4**
La Austríaca **25**
La Botillería de Maxi **7**
La Broche **19**
La Taberna de Madrid **42**
Las Mañanitas **17**
Vegaviana **22**
Viuda de Vacas **6**

PARTYING ★
Candela **41**
Casa Patas **40**
El Viajero **5**
Jose Alfredo **11**
Kapital **45**
La Riviera **3**
La Venencia **31**
La Vía Láctea **16**
Le Garage **12**
Mondo at Stella **29**
Nasti Club **15**
Nature (MidDay) **13**
Pacha **18**
Palacio Gaviría **9**
Populart **38**
Siroco **14**

SIGHTSEEING ●
Casa de Campo **3**
Ermita de San Antonio de la
  Florida Panteón de Goya **1**
Escuela de Fotografía y
  Centro de Imagen (EFTI) **46**
Facultad de Bellas Artes **3**
Museo del Prado **34**
Museo Nacional Centro
  de Arte Reina Sofía **44**
Palacio Real **2**
Parque del Buen Retiro **35**
Thyssen-Bornemisza
  Museum **33**

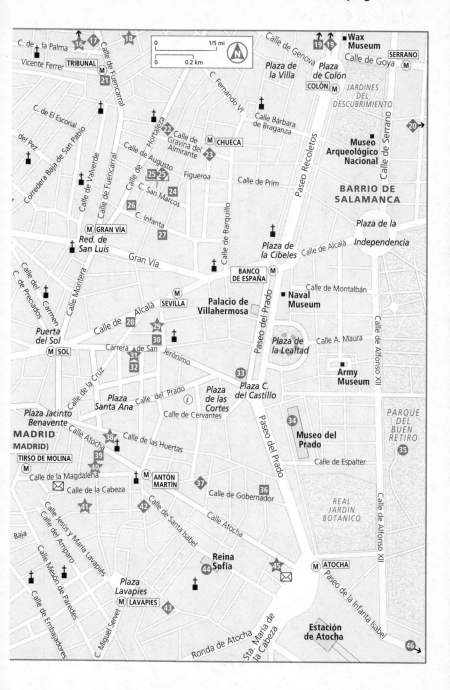

Madrid Metro

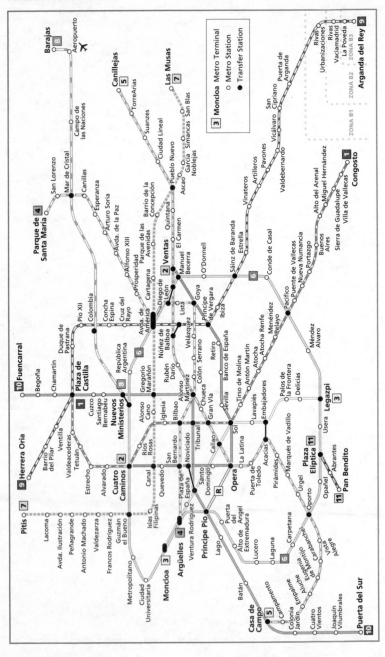

meeting people and drinking 2€ pitchers of beer. Breakfast, sheets, towels, private lockers, and a great location are included in a price that seems too good to be European. *Cañizares 6.* ☎ *91-369-2807. www.cats hostel.com. 17€ dorm. Metro: Antón Martín or Sol. Amenities: Internet; shared bathrooms; sheets; TV. In room: A/C.*

Cheap

→**Aparthotel Tribunal** This apartment-style hotel is a great option if you are a vegetarian, organic food freak, or just prefer to cook your own meals without sharing. There's a big, sober reception with a lobby-like area by the elevators. Each fully furnished one- or two-bedroom apartment has a kitchenette with utensils, a small fridge, and a big '60s modern couch; some have a view to Fuencarral. The walls' colors are a little dim—ambience is not exactly exuding from every ochre surface—but the Malasaña neighborhood has plenty to make up for it. English is spoken fluently and families fit right in; you can add a third bed for 20€. *San Vicente Ferrer 1 (corner of Fuencarral).* ☎ *91-522-1455. www.aparthotel-tribunal.com. 50€ single, 80€ double. Metro: Tribunal. Amenities: Elevator; en suite kitchenette; laundry service; shared bathrooms; TV. In room: A/C, hair dyer, safe.*

→**Hostal Infantas** Enter this classic Madrid building to a dark and massive lobby, walk up the majestic wooden stairs, and ring the bell on apartment 1I. Inside you'll find a quiet and safe little hostel featuring seven rooms with showers and sinks (shared toilets), some with full bathroom including bathtub. Most rooms have balconies, a night table, a closet and desk, and are very clean. The modern 20th-century Formica furniture has that kind of interesting-without-trying charm, the common areas have new parquet floors, and the shared bathrooms are as clean as only your grandmother could keep

them. *Infantas 30, 1st Izquierda.* ☎ *91-521-0673. 30€ double with shared bathroom, 40€ with private bathroom. Metro: Gran Vía, Banco, or Chueca. Amenities: A/C; TV.*

→**Hostel Residencia Zamora** Renovated only a few years ago, and all the rooms now have private bathroom, television, heat, and air-conditioning. Really nice patterned hardwood floors, too. Because the rooms overlook the Plaza Vázquez de Mella, all the rooms are bright as well as quiet. If you don't have a reservation and are worried about getting stranded, check out this hostel first because there are several others in the same building. Convenient to Gran Vía, Sol, and Calle de Fuencarral. *Plaza Vázquez de Mella 1, 4th floor.* ☎ *91-521-7031. 36€ single, 45€ double. In room: A/C, TV. Metro: Gran Vía.*

→**Hotel México** Ready for a Mexican Deco break in the museum area? Hotel Mexico feels a little past its time of splendor, but its sober, simple homage to Mexican culture makes it a good option for a quiet night of rest. The bright marble lobby has comfy couches and is very welcoming. The rooms are furnished with reproductions of famous Mexican paintings all over and all have clean white private bathrooms. The windows don't have much of a view, but the mattresses are firm and the sheets are soft. Have breakfast at the cute little dining room with a wooden bar. *Gobernador 24.* ☎ *91-429-2500. www.hotel mexico.es. Single 55€, double 65€–70€, double with extra bed 75€. Metro: Antón Martín. Amenities: Wi-Fi. In room: A/C, TV, safe.*

→**Huéspedes Dolce Vita** Out of the hundreds of *hostales* that you can find in single floors of buildings around Malasaña and Chueca, Dolce Vita may be one of the most fun, if not comfortable. Right out of an Almodóvar movie, you may get a room with three blue plastic stars on top of your bed as night lamps; a bathroom with yellow, orange, and white striped walls; or a hot-pink shower curtain. Try to get a room with a

MADRID

balcony, it may be noisier, but the other ones can be a little dark. The furniture is cheap, but it exudes in personality what it lacks in sturdiness. All rooms have a tenement house–style shower and sink; some even have a full bathroom. They offer a 3€ breakfast, but the windowless "dining" room is not the hotel's best feature; better to go downstairs and have a *chocolate con churros* in a bar served by your neighborhood drag queen. *San Bartolomé 4, 3rd floor.* ☎ *91-522-4018. www.hospedajedolcevita. com. 25€ single with shared bathroom, 35€ with private bathroom; 40€ double with shared bathroom, 55€ with private bathroom. Metro: Chueca or Gran Vía. Amenities: Internet; laundry service; shared bathrooms. In room: TV, ceiling fans, sink.*

Doable

→ **Hotel Inglés** This hotel goes next to the definition of "classic Madrid" in the dictionary. More than 150 years old, its walls breathe history. Unfortunately the decoration has been recently renovated to adhere to the boring-average-hotel E.U. standards but that also includes the average, spotless rooms and friendly, 24-hour English-speaking staff. The great thing about it is the location, 1 block from Puerta del Sol and within walking distance of every neighborhood that matters. There are 58 rooms; the ones in the front are brighter and louder than the ones in the back. Moreover, if you want to burn all that cerveza off, you can always use the gym. *Echegaray 8.* ☎ *91-429-6551. 75€ single, 95€ double. Metro: Sol. Amenities: Cafeteria; bar; elevator; health club; laundry service. In room: A/C (in some), TV, hair dryer (in some), safe.*

→ **Hotel Opera** A modern classic in the middle of the Asturias neighborhood, this hotel is quite woody: parquet floors, paneled walls, and classy dark furniture. You can hang out in the six conference rooms, the requisite marble lobby, a cafe with a lovely marble bar, an English bar out of a Sherlock Holmes story, or a huge restaurant with a grand piano. The rooms have comfy beds. The ones with terraces have views of old Madrid that are worth the whole price of the stay itself—especially in low season, when they offer great deals. The quirkiest feature of this hotel: The dinner served by the staff of "singing" Broadway-style waiters. *Cuesta de Santo Domingo 2.* ☎ *91-541-2800. www. hotelopera.com. 65€–110€ single, 75€–140€ double. Metro: Opera. Amenities: Restaurant; bar; laundry service. In room: A/C, TV, hair dryer, Internet, safe.*

→ **Hotel Regina** Check out this midprice swank hotel with a lot of bang for the buck. A bright and modern lobby with comfy couches and reception area welcomes hordes of American tourists yearning for comfort a la Marriott. There's a modern street-level cafeteria, a classic dining room, a conference room, and a beautiful brick-wall bodega-style winery. The 180 rooms are plush and spacious with huge beds, modern wooden furniture, and dark marble bathrooms with double sinks and hair dryers. Try to get the *buhardilla* (attic) rooms with cute slanted ceilings with thick wooden beams and great views of the city. They'll also pick you up and drop you off at the airport. *Alcalá 19.* ☎ *91-521-4725. www.hotelreginamadrid.com. Single 120€, double 150€, triple 180€. Metro: Sevilla. Amenities: Restaurant; cafeteria; laundry service; wheelchair friendly. In room: A/C, TV, hair dryer, Internet, safe.*

Splurge

→ **Hotel Puerta América** If you care about interior design, check this place out. Don't be fooled by the facade. Twenty celeb architects and designers (such as Isozaki, Norman Foster, Zaha Hadid, and Ron Arad) took on the design of one full floor each, plus the common spaces and even the garage, creating 12 different auteur hotels in one. You walk into this huge hotel through a tiny electric door hidden in the wall and the staff will take you on a tour in a glass elevator to pick your favorite world. Some of the creations include a room made out of Corian (mix of resin and marble) in one piece; a full Feng Shui room, including Inoki wood bathtubs from Japan; some with round beds and projectors instead of TVs; leather walls, you name it. The rooms aren't too big and the location isn't the best, but the list of amenities makes up for everything. All of this doesn't come cheap. *Av. de América 41.* ☎ *91-744-5400. www.hotelpuertamerica.com. From 220€ single and double. Metro: Cartagena. Amenities: Restaurant; coffee bar; health club; laundry service; pool; room service; safe; wheelchair friendly; Wi-Fi. In room: A/C, TV, Internet, safe.*

→ **Hotel Urban** A great exercise in modern luxury, the urban hotel's motto seems to be the contrast of the old and the new. Built in 2005, with a flashy decor worthy of any New York superstar hotel, you'll find antique Buddhist and Egyptian artifacts, including some in your room, with its oak floors and walls. An internal glass elevator takes you from the supercool lobby with C-shaped leather couches to the rooftop pool, where you can swim while looking at the city or have a drink at the outdoor bar, open also to the public. The rooms are big and slick, with all the amenities you can imagine. *Carrera de San Jerónimo 34.* ☎ *91-787-7770. www.derby hotels.com. From 180€ standard room. Amenities: Restaurant; fitness center; laundry service; pool; wheelchair friendly. In room: A/C, TV, hair dryer, Internet, 24-hr. room service, safe.*

Eating

Spanish people talk about food as much as Americans talk about cars. It's not uncommon to overhear conversations that go over which type of Ibérico is better or what kind of cheese goes better with pears. In the last couple of years, Spanish cuisine has seen a new renaissance, from the hand of superstar chefs like Ferrán Adriá, in Barcelona. Madrid is a big part of this movement, and that, added to the huge increase in immigration and the subsequent opening of more ethnic restaurants, shows up in an increased variety and quality of eating options, although at higher prices.

For budget eating, in general, your options are (1) something that came from a pig, (2) a Spanish tortilla (a tasty, thick, omelet kind of thing made of eggs and potatoes), or (3) fast food (like everywhere). Alternatively, take three steps in any direction and walk into the nearest pub! Nearly all bars and cafeterias are open from about 7am till 2am and serve tapas (small sandwiches or portions of food) like tortillas, calamari, olives, or something with bacon. In the afternoon, usually from around 1 to 4pm, the larger of these cafeterias will serve *el menu del día* (about 8€–12€), which consists of bread, an appetizer (usually a vegetable), two main plates (usually pasta, soup, or a meat dish), dessert, and a drink (beer, water, or wine). Other inexpensive options are the *alimentación* stores (a Spanish convenience store), outdoor markets, and even supermarkets. Día is a particularly low-cost chain with several locations. A handful of restaurants at Plaza Emperador Carlos V/Ronda de Atocha (Metro: Atocha) stay open for 24 hours on the weekends, but other than that, you will have to settle for a 7-Eleven or the Spanish equivalent, VIPS, after you've sampled the local *chocolate* and are red-eyed and starving. Also remember that you can drink in any restaurant in Spain; even Burger King and KFC serve beer!

MADRID

Hot Spots

MTV Best →**Automático** ★★TAPAS In the competition for best tapas bar, not many can challenge this '60s mod Lavapiés classic, which also houses one of the most popular terrazas. In the winter, the slick sounds of jazz and blues fit with the even smoother *croquetas, migas,* dates with bacon, and a bunch of homemade pâtés. On weekend mornings you'll find the leftover party animals from the night before; in the afternoon, Madrileños tired of bargaining at El Rastro come here for well-deserved wine and deliciousness. *Argumosa 17.* ☎ *91-530-9921. Tapas/aciones 1.50€–8€. Mon–Fri 6pm–1:30am; Sat–Sun noon–1:30am. Metro: Lavapiés.*

MTV Best →**Finos y Finas** ★ CREATIVE SPANISH You don't have to be a royal (although some members of the royal family have been spotted here) to enjoy the nueva cocina. At this modern spot in the Salamanca neighborhood, you can find out what all the buzz is about without spending a week's wages for it. The clientele can be on the *pijo* side, but once you read the menu you won't care about anything but the food. Executive chef/owner Luis Barrutia travels all over the country looking for the best ingredients for his creative Spanish dishes. Mouthwatering creations like *salmorejo* (a traditional tomato mousse of sorts) with herring caviar and cockles, the best Ibérico you'll ever get, and a won-ton ravioli that seems to encompass all of Spain in a tiny square: mushrooms, ham, Manchego, and truffle. They also have a tasting menu that takes you on a culinary journey of a different in-season region of Spain for 32€ including coffee and dessert. *Espartinas 6.* ☎ *91-575-9069. Main courses 14€–20€. Tues–Sat 12:30–4pm and 8–11pm; Sun 12:30–4pm. Metro: Goya, Velázquez, or Príncipe de Vergara.*

→**Juana La Loca** TAPAS Aptly named, this nouveau tapas bar can get pretty crazy, especially on Sundays and particularly if you were hoping to sit down. But if you don't mind being elbow to elbow with super-trendy film and entertainment business Madrileños, you'll be rewarded by some of the most creative and delicious tapas in town. The old tavern style of large dark wooden tables and the purple tile walls give it an old/modern feel that matches the cuisine perfectly. The tapas vary every day, but if you're lucky, you'll be able to try the light and exquisite pumpkin won-ton, or the mushroom risotto. Be smart and go during the week to enjoy their value meal *(menú* that is to McDonald's what champagne is to Coca-Cola. *Puerta de Moros 4.* ☎ *91-364-0525. Tapas 6.50€–9.20€. Tues–Sun noon–1:30am. Closed Aug. Metro: La Latina.*

Cheap

MTV Best →**La Austríaca** ★ SPANISH This homey, hole-in-the-wall type restaurant gets packed during lunch hours by a mix of Spanish office workers who are in the know and the trendy young artists from Malasaña. Family business at its core, Juan, Antonio, Mary, and Chus have been feeding Madrid for 52 years and will make sure that you finish your plate. They make *lentejas* like no one else in the city. Hopefully, they'll have them when you go there, if not, try the *marmitaco,* or their delicious *tartas* that give this place the reputation for having the best *menú del día* in town. Sit at the bar or in one of the communal tables and experience lunch Madrid-style, while you take a break from shopping at calle Fuencarral. *San Onofre 3.* ☎ *91-531-3174. Menú del día 8€. Daily 8am–4pm. Metro: Gran Vía.*

→**La Botillería de Maxi** MADRILEÑO Yes, the Spanish like their animals, and this is a good place to find them. This La Latina favorite bursts with people on weekends (be ready for a long wait on Sun) aching to taste the typical examples of *cocina Madrileña* accompanied by a very decent wine list. Have a drink at the busy bar before sitting in the salon, surrounded by cookie-jars with beans, cooking utensils hanging on the brick walls, and vintage ceiling fans cooling you from above. The service, once you're seated, is surprisingly quick for Spanish standards. Be adventurous and try the specialties (*rabo de toro, callos a la Madrileña,* or *cocido Madrileño*) without asking what's in them, and stay away from the hummus and other lesser- quality Middle Eastern tapas; this is not for vegetarians. *Cava Alta 4.* ☎ *91-365-1249. Main courses 7.50€–17€. Tues–Fri 12:30–4pm and 8:30pm–midnight, Sat–Sun 12:30–6pm. Closed Aug. Metro: La Latina.*

➜ **La Taberna de Madrid** TAPAS   Much like the neighborhood, the crowd populating this lively and typical Lavapiés tapas bar is a mix of recent immigrants, bohemian South American intellectuals and hip underground artists. What brings them all together? Mojitos as quintessential as only Fidel could make them and a menu of creative not-your-average tapas (the tuna carpaccio alone is worth the trip) at your average tapas prices. The walls feature detailed ironwork and antiques, and the big tables are ready for you to bring all your new friends. *San Simón 3.* ☎ *91-539-8980. www.latabernademadrid. com. Tapas 2.40€. Daily 11am–12:30am. Metro: Lavapiés.*

➜ **Vegaviana** VEGETARIAN   Being a vegetarian in Madrid is not easy; you bump into some sort of dead animal product every two steps and your options are usually tortillas or lentils, if you're lucky. Fortunately, a few new places crop up like Vegaviana, a quiet and very cozy restaurant where you can take a break from flesh and the loud noises of neighboring Chueca. Try the succulent vegetarian paella or tasty whole-wheat pizzas at one of their many small tables served with Zen-like manners. *Pelayo 35.* ☎ *91-308-0381. www.accua.com/vegaviana. Main courses 7€–9€. Tues–Sat 1:30–4pm and 9–11:30pm. Metro: Chueca.*

Doable

➜ **Cisne Azul** TAPAS   Vegetarians arise! Carnivores sharpen your teeth! If the mouthwatering effect of a menu could be measured, this unassuming, tiny bar with a few tables would rank very high. The pale blue walls and '70s bar are cute, but it's not for the decor that you'll come here. Every day, chef-owner Julián Pulido Vega brings from the country the most exquisite products shown in the crates by one of the walls. With 14 types of mushrooms, zucchini flowers, duck foie gras, and the delicious lamb ribs and cold cuts, this makes this place an irresistible temptation for the average Joe and connoisseurs alike. The ration-style servings are very simply made; it's all about the natural flavor of the fresh products. Try to come with a group of people so that you can try it all! *Gravina 19.* ☎ *91-521-3799. Main courses 9€–18€. Daily 1–5pm and 8–2am. Metro: Chueca.*

➜ **Las Mañanitas** TORTILLERIA   If you're feeling a little New World, and want to take a break from the old one, try this lively *tortillería* in the middle of busy Fuencarral. Despite the common language, many Mexican restaurants in Spain are, well, crappy. Las Mañanitas, however, is *muy bueno.* The maize-colored floor tiles, mariachi music, and simple (but comfortable) furniture—along with great nachos, quesadillas, and margaritas—will make you happy to be there. Try their special *guisos* (stews) and you'll feel like you never left L.A. *Fuencarral 82.* ☎ *91-522-4589. Main courses 9€–17€. Mon–Fri 1:30–4pm and 9–11:30pm; Sat 9–11:30pm. Metro: Bilbao or Tribunal.*

➜ **Viuda de Vacas** CASTILIAN   It doesn't get more Castilian than this old taverna housed in a 17th-century building in trendy La Latina. Its ornate tile walls have seen more history than many museums and so have the Cánovas, who have been running this place for three generations. Talk about following footsteps. Sit at the zinc bar or at one of the little wooden tables and enjoy the best Spanish traditional food, including, of course, all sorts of animal parts, like the infamous bull's tail, which is pretty good, if you can forget about what you're actually eating. Come early or make reservations unless you want to wait hours among 30-something Madrid hipsters. *Cava Alta 23.* ☎ *91-366-5847. Main courses 9.50€–19€. Mon–Wed and Fri–Sat 1:30–4:30pm and 9:30pm–midnight; Sun 1:30–4:30pm. Closed last 2 weeks of Sept. Metro: La Latina.*

Splurge

➔**La Broche** CATALAN   This place has gained a quick reputation as one of the most creative restaurants in Madrid and possibly in Spain. Opened in 1997 by superstar-chef Sergi Arola, it is a necessary stop for food connoisseurs wanting to experience the best of the Costa Brava region cuisine. The wait-staff is young and fast, an oddity around here, and the nouveau Mediterranean dishes are served in small portions, allowing you to try more variety without fear of indigestion. The menu changes periodically, but see if you can get the confit potatoes with tomato and aioli or the outer-worldly mushroom carpaccio with fresh pasta and pignoli vinaigrette, mmmhh. Pull out your credit card, close your eyes, and open your mouth. *Miguel Angel 29.* ☎ *91-399-3437. Main courses 30€. Mon–Fri 1:30–3:30pm and 9–11:30pm. Closed Aug. Metro: Gregorio Marañón.*

Cafes & Tearooms

➔**Café del Nuncio** CAFE   Get your caffeine fix at this traditional Spanish cafe in an old La Latina house in two levels. The hip 30-something crowd incessantly sips coffee after coffee while they engage in all sorts of discussions, mostly about food. The red and dark-brown wood panels and classic marble bar make it a perfect place for spending those couple of hours between lunch and dinner. *Segovia 9.* ☎ *91-366-0853. Daily noon–2am. Metro: La Latina.*

➔**El Parnaso** CAFE   Parnaso was the mount of the poets, but this Huertas cafe has little to do with poetry. All sorts of decorative antiques and furniture surround the bar. The seats in the back are not the most comfortable but possess the charm of the old. It's a great place to go with that special someone and confess your love without having to yell over the din. Order one of their sumptuous banana, coconut, or chocolate *batidos*, with or without alcohol, and you'll also get a dreamy Arab pastry that will give you more conversation material. *Moratín 25.* ☎ *91-420-1975. Metro: Antón Martín.*

Partying

Live Music

Yeah, the Spanish dance their flamenco, they fight their bulls, and they have their Goyas and Dalís, but they don't do rock 'n' roll very well. It's usually uninspired, unoriginal, high school–level musicianship. The blues scene doesn't bring much more to the table—many of the acts have an American front man and a barely acceptable local backing group. But the jazz scene is a lot better, and reggae, salsa, and other world beat–style bands usually have it together. And, of course, big-name tours stop in Madrid often. The Rolling Stones, Depeche Mode, and Method Man are just a few of the big acts that have recently played in football stadiums or venues around Madrid.

As always, consult the entertainment bible, *Guía del Ocio* (and the thousands of posters around the city) to see who's playing and where. For the most part, the clubs here open at about 9:30pm, the live music starts between 10 and 11pm and ends at around 2am, and—in the traditional Madrid style—

the clubs remain open till 6am with a DJ. Keep in mind, though, that the Spanish invented arriving fashionably late. Midnight is when things are hottest for live music in this town. You can also skip the live music and just swing by around 3am for the DJ session. These clubs also do not accept plastic unless noted otherwise.

If you're still hell-bent on seeing some Spanish rock 'n' roll, check out the spots recommended below.

Nightclubs

→ **Kapital** So, you like deep house but not enough to listen to it for hours; you can try some salsa steps, but after a while, everyone can tell you're bluffing. Head to this dance supermarket, a seven-story megaclub with options for every taste. Discover each floor and pick the one you like the most, browsing between hip-hop, techno, Latin, and pretty much everything that you can shake your tail to. If you thought you would never be able to listen to Eminem, Moby, and Celia Cruz at the same venue, think again; everything goes in Madrid. *Atocha 125.* ☎ *91-420-2906. Metro: Atocha.*

→ **Le Garage** What makes a city's nightlife above average are those unusual parties that you can't find anywhere else. Le Garage takes place in a Chinese karaoke located inside a parking lot on Thursday nights. After singing your guts off, you can dance your butt off to the best electro and techno this side of the English Channel, compliments of David Kano, from Spanish electronic wonders Cycle. The ambience is something out of Manchester in the '90s with the cool and the beautiful mingling together and keeping Madrid's night real and unique. *Plaza de los Mostenses (in the parking lot). No phone. Metro: Plaza de España.*

→ **Mondo at Stella** Walking into Mondo you'll understand why Madrid is one of the world capitals of partying. Dance the night away under a universe of mirror balls, to the electronic music mixed by guest foreign DJs. Its two dance floors, a couple of bars, and all the music you can handle make this an obliged stop for laid-back, hard-partying Madrileños. That's right, the tourist quotient here is surprisingly low, so come meet your nightlife guides and maybe something else. *Arlabán 7.* ☎ *91-531-6378. Metro: Sevilla.*

→ **Nature (MidDay)** Nature (pronounced "nah-*too*-reh") is absolutely worth a visit, especially on Thursdays. Unlike the normal club scene, this place is laid-back and dreddy, with a very open, hole-in-the-wall atmosphere, and DJs spinning mostly house and the occasional (relatively good) techno. The metallic decor and low, red lighting makes it seem like Han Solo might show up later on. Little TVs show Japanese anime; wear your old T-shirts, sunglasses, and comfortable sneakers. *Amaniel 13 (Covarrubias at Luchana). Metro: Bilbao.*

→ **Pacha** The Madrid branch of this megaclub signature franchise is housed in a beautiful theater built in 1930, that won many architecture prizes before becoming Madrid's dance cathedral in the '80s. You will find the biggest international names behind the turntables; the hottest locals, if a little on the *pijo* side; and, of course, you and a bunch of other tourists that come attracted by the synonym of loud, mm-ch, mm-ch nonstop fun that Pacha's two cherries symbol has come to represent (although some say they are actually the dilated pupils that characterize its patrons). Bounce your way in for an all-night extravaganza or visit "Pacha Light," their early evening session for those who keep going, and going, and going. *Barceló 11.* ☎ *91-447-0128. www.pacha-madrid.com. Metro: Tribunal.*

→ **Palacio Gaviría** How do you turn a beautiful 19th-century Renaissance palace into a giant cheese ball? Just fill it up with

Tapeo

Like its cousins, the pub-crawls, the tapeo starts in one bar and advances to another. Tapas are the appetizers that go with the drinks. In Madrid, they're served everywhere. Simple examples are toasted almonds or slices of ham or cheese; more elaborate are potato omelets, herbed snails, stuffed peppers, peppery *pulpo* (octopus), *anguilla* (eel), *cangrego* (crabmeat salad), and even bull testicles.

lights, a huge sound system, half-naked studs and babes, do a different thematic night every day of the week, and get as many tourists as possible to come. Actually, if you do want to meet fellow foreigners in an all-you-can-dance environment, this is probably your best bet. The majestic stairs and beautiful paintings make it almost worth the entrance fee, and on Thursdays, the International Exchange Party is like a U.N. convention on X. They also have reggaeton, Brazilian, and Latin nights with four dance floors and 13 different rooms to practice the international language of love. *Arenal 9.* ☎ *91-526-6069. www.palaciogaviria.com. Cover 9€–15€. Metro: Sol.*

Bars & Lounges

Madrileños call their nightlife *la marcha* (the march) because they typically prefer to have a single drink in a bar before moving on to the next (and the next, and the next). So, trying to sum up Madrid's bar scene by describing only a few bars is like trying to tell someone about a beach by showing them only a few grains of sand. Add to the nearly limitless possibilities the fact that there are thousands of people in the streets and the bars don't close until 3am. Use the following bars as highlights and *marcha* your butt off—it's the only way to get the full effect. All of these bars have a similar

prime time of around 1am on the weekends. The only exception is El Viajero, which usually sees action by 11 at night.

→**El Viajero** A great bar and restaurant in the very cool La Latina district of Madrid. Get an aerial view of this artist's community while eating on the third-floor terrace or relax on the second floor, which is lit almost entirely by candles—both are potentially very romantic. A little more expensive than average, but so worth it. *Plaza de la Cebada 11.* ☎ *91-366-9064. Metro: La Latina.*

→**José Alfredo** If you had to define the quintessential cocktail bar for a police sketch artist, the end result would probably look a lot like José Alfredo. The couches are big and comfy in dark, earthy tones; the lights are dim; and there are lots of mirrors where the young and fabulous patrons can look at themselves and each other in all their trend-setting glory. The lounge music is barely audible for the place is always packed with thirsty patrons enjoying excellent cocktails while getting ready to start the nightlife. Try to get there early and score a table with couches, and you're very likely to make some new friends. It's like buying a convertible to pick up girls, only much cheaper. *Silva 22. No phone. Metro: Noviciado.*

→**La Venencia** WINE BAR The old bottles lining the walls of this ancient sherry bar have more dust on them than my Rick Astley tapes. The dozen different types of sherry are stored in dark, wooden barrels behind the bar and served directly to your glass. Sample different kinds of this Jerez province specialty, accompanied by great cold cuts and juicy olives brought straight from Andalusia. The ancient bartender will write up your bill with chalk on the bar and trust that you won't erase it. Don't miss this authentic sample of Madrid's pre-Franco past. *Echegaray 7.* ☎ *91-429-7313. Daily 1–3:30pm and 7pm–1:30am. Metro Sol.*

→**La Vía Láctea** The milky way of this bar is composed of old posters of big rock 'n' roll stars, many of whom probably had a go at the pool table or a drink at one of the two bars. One of the main scenes during the movida, in the '80s, this bar is now considered an authentic classic by the makeup girls and glam boys that populate it. There's a little area with couches in the front, a tiny DJ cabin, and,

besides the pool table, a couple of booths that have probably seen more action than a Jet Li movie. Good rock 'n' roll blasts on the speakers, and funky bartenders with multicolored hair pour a good selection of drinks. *Velarde 18.* ☎ *91-446-7581. Metro: Tribunal.*

Performing Arts

Performance Halls & Stadium Shows
ROCK & POP

➜**La Riviera** This venue features most not-stadium-worthy international acts like Jack Johnson, Black Eyed Peas, or Simple Plan in a interesting space with Art Deco interiors and outdoor summer concerts. Afterwards it doubles as a club with good DJs and fun until the early morning. *Paseo Bajo de la Virgen.* ☎ *91-365-2415. Metro: Príncipe Pío.*

➜**Nasti Club** Nasti is everything an indie music venue should be: small red doors covered in graffiti; a very simple, smoky, dark, black-and-white hall; and tons of hipsters hanging out. Add to that a good amount of grime and dirt and musical acts that go from guitar/bass/drums garage bands to crazed-out paint-covered electro-punk performance combos and you got yourself a great exponent of the Madrid underground. Formerly known as Maravillas, it is a stepping-stone for many soon-to-be-bigger acts, the difference being that many of these rising stars aren't from Spain. Local bands play at floor level and bigger foreign ones get a small stage. If you're lucky enough you may catch shows like Peaches or Kula Shaker, which, in a 300-people venue, have a lot more flava. *San Vicente Ferrer 35.* ☎ *91-521-7605. Metro: Tribunal.*

➜**Siroco** This venue is small, dark, and loud—the way a rock club should be. The upper floor adds some space, but the stage—

and most of the action—is crammed into the basement. The 18- to 30-year-old clientele is dressed in 1976 AC/DC (Back In) Black, the preferred attire of Spain's rock 'n' rollers. This is a very popular venue on weekends, and a lot of times it's better to arrive after 1am to skip the live shows and enjoy the awesome DJs that spin hip-hop, breaks, and funky styles. *San Dimas 3.* ☎ *91-593-3070. www.siroco.es. Cover varies, depending on the act. Metro: San Bernardo.*

JAZZ & BLUES

➜**Populart** The place for Madrid's lukewarm blues. But its small stage is also graced by "live music of all types," including swing, salsa, reggae, and flamenco. Decorated with old horns and photos of American blues and jazz heavyweights, this midsize bar attracts a mix of 25- to 40-year-old yuppie types and college-age Spanish artists and musicians (many of whom can speak a little English). Upcoming acts are listed by the entrance. Because it's a smaller venue here, you'll want to get a good seat by showing up on time (more or less), usually about 10pm. *Huertas 22.* ☎ *91-429-8407. Metro: Sevilla or Antón Martín.*

FLAMENCO

🔲 **Best** ➜**Candela** ★ This is flamenco at its darkest. A grimy, dirty place that was closed a couple of times for heroin, the drug of choice among *cantaores.* Now they're trying to stay clean, but the faces are still the same. The walls feature beautiful flamenco posters and photos of the biggest luminaries in the art, which used to, and still do, play at the back room, *la cueva*. Unfortunately, not everybody can get in and, unless you come with somebody who knows somebody, your chances as a guiri are pretty slim. The local fauna and ambience at the bar still make it worth a visit or two. *Olmo 2.* ☎ *91-467-3382. Daily 10pm–close. Metro: Antón Martín.*

➜ **Casa Patas** Some say that you can't see the real-deal flamenco in a heartless slab of stone like Madrid, but this *tablao* sure comes close. Skilled and heart-wrenching classical guitar will impress you even before the dancers come out. The locals come here, and they all know that the delicious meals are definitely secondary when compared to the show. Entrance is expensive (but very worth it). *Cañizares 10.* ☎ *91-369-0496. Restaurant daily noon–5pm and 8pm–3am; show times Mon–Thurs 10:30pm, Fri–Sat midnight. Cover 30€. Metro: Tirso de Molina or Antón Martín.*

Sightseeing

You can also feed those few remaining brain cells with world-class museums and historical buildings, and/or get some sun and exercise at one of the nature-filled parks.

Festivals

Madrid has a bunch of festivals that correspond with Christian holidays, including the Entierro de la Sardina, in which a sardine is placed in a small casket, paraded about Madrid, and then buried at Paseo de la Florida (on Ash Wednesday). However, the best festivals take place in the summertime, particularly in May.

May

San Isidro Festival. This is the time when Madrid is at its very best. San Isidro is the patron saint of the city, and man, do they love him. There are kids in costumes, a tremendous amount of hoopla (including live music, carnival food, street markets, dance performances, and more), and drinking and dancing in the streets (particularly in the Las Vistillas neighborhood). The local tourist offices and the *Guía del Ocio* will have all the info. Third week of May.

Dos de Mayo. This celebration in the Plaza Dos de Mayo in Malasaña is great, especially if you've got at least one tattoo or more than two earrings. The holiday commemorates Madrid's rebellion against Napoleon's occupation of Spain, but the only people who bother to celebrate are those who live in the plaza of the same name. It's a neighborhood party kind of thing (with food, bands, and so on), but what a neighborhood! May 2.

Historic Buildings

FREE ➜ **Ermita de San Antonio de la Florida Panteón de Goya** Goya painted the ceiling of this church shortly before his death. Although considered his finest moment, it is, after all, only one moment. Unless Goya is your god, if your time is limited, best stick to the museums downtown. *Paseo de la Florida 5.* ☎ *91-542-0722. Tues–Fri 10am–2pm and 4–8pm; Sat–Sun 10am–2pm. Free admission. Metro: Príncipe Pío.*

➜ **Palacio Real** ★★ Real? Royal? No matter how you spell it, it means splendor and opulence on a level you never thought possible. The nifty clocks alone make it worth a visit, but the official tour can make it all seem big, beautiful, and boring. *Plaza de Oriente, Bailén 2.* ☎ *91-454-8800. www.patrimonionacional.es. Admission 9€ (includes a guided tour). Mon–Sat 9:30am–5pm; Sun and holidays 9am–2pm. Metro: Opera.*

Museums & Art Galleries

Madrid's art museums are awesome, and they're half-off if you have a Spanish student card (anything from a foreign school—particularly if it doesn't have a date on it—usually won't fly). But even at full price, most venues are only about 6€. The following days are free for all museums: May 18 (International Day of Museums), October 12 (Fiesta Nacional de España), and December 6 (Día de Constitución Española). If you're walking everywhere, you may want to do the three biggies (Prado, Reina Sofía, Thyssen) together because they form a surprisingly small triangle with each other. The Palacio Real and the Museo de la Real Academia de Bellas Artes de San Fernando are also relatively close to each other. The other museums listed here are a little farther out and may not be worth your time if you don't have a lot of it. It depends on how much of an art-fiend you really are.

MTV Best → **Museo del Prado** ★★★
Miss the enormous collection of medieval and Renaissance work in this top-notch museum, and your parents will never send

you anywhere again. Miss the moody Goyas and trippy Boschs, and you only cheat yourself. *Palacio de Villanueva, Paseo del Prado.* ☎ *91-330-2900. museoprado.mcu.es. Admission 6€. Tues–Sun 9am–8pm. Metro: Banco de España or Atocha.*

→ **Museo Nacional Centro de Arte Reina Sofía** ★ With a whole lot of Picasso, Dalí, and Miró, it's like a modern-art supermarket. Price check on the Guernica at register 6. *Santa Isabel 52.* ☎ *91-774-1000. museo reinasofia.mcu.es. Admission 3€; free Sat after 2:30pm and Sun all day. Mon and Wed–Sat 10am–9pm; Sun 10am–2:30pm. Metro: Atocha.*

MTV Best → **Thyssen-Bornemisza Museum** ★★★ If you were going to be stranded on a desert island for the rest of your life, which museum would you want with you? Well, the Thyssen would make good company because it's got a little bit of everything: from Renaissance to realism and

MADRID

12 Hours in Madrid

1. **Stroll down Calle de Fuencarral.** Start at the McDonald's on Gran Vía (for Pete's sake, don't go in!), cross the street, and you'll pass stores selling everything from wristwatches and Walkmans to pornography, but the street quickly transforms itself into a hipster's wet dream.

2. **Enjoy a small cup of good coffee at La Glorieta de Bilbao.** Sit at the sidewalk tables of Café Comercial.

3. **Shop the Plaza de España.** Come here for a dose of modern—and decidedly un-hip—Madrid consumer culture.

4. **Climb up to El Templo de Debod.** The Egyptian artifacts here were given to Spain and other countries in exchange for financial assistance in the building of Egypt's Aswan Dam. You can pay to go into the small museum at the top of the hill, but you'll have just as much fun taking in the view of the city below, including Palacio Real and its gardens.

5. **Take a ride on Madrid's Teleférico.** Climb into one of the cable cars and relax. Go to the cafetería and have a drink.

6. **Go the Prado.** Enough said.

7. **If you're here on a weekend, go to the Rastro Sunday Market.** This is the city's best flea market.

8. **Enjoy a night of flamenco.**

cubism to pop art. *Palacio de Villahermosa, Paseo del Prado 8.* ☎ *91-369-0151. Admission 6€. Tues–Sun 10am–7pm. Metro: Banco de España.*

Gardens & Parks

➜**Casa de Campo** ★ This eastside park is a lot wilder than Retiro and it's great for riding your bike and feeling a little closer to nature. Its 1,200 hectares (2,965 acres) used to be the king's hunting grounds until it was opened to the public in the '30s. It houses a Zoo-Aquarium and an amusement park. Getting there is the most fun; you have to catch the *teleférico* (cable railway). It's open 24 hours but you don't want to be caught there after dark, when it becomes Madrid's

"green" red zone. ☎ *91-479-6002. Metro: Lago or Bátan.*

➜**Parque de Retiro** ★ The locals enjoy running and in-line skating through this enormous park with its tall trees, peaceful lawns, and ornate fountains. It becomes a real spectacle on the weekends when the streets swell up with families, musicians, performers, and vendors. A great attraction here are the rowboats that you can rent for use in the huge man-made pond (it's a small lake, really) located in the center of the park (4€ for 45 min.; 10:30am–dusk). Although the parks in Madrid are fun, they're not a place to be at night if you are alone. *May–Sept 7am–midnight; Oct–Apr 7am–10pm. Metro: Retiro.*

Playing Outside

Of course, the easiest place to go running is the huge city park, **El Retiro** (Metro: Retiro). The only problem is that you might be running from pickpockets and panhandlers as much as for your health. The Calle de Moyano is the best entrance for running and in-line skating because it is far from all of the pond-related hype that goes down in the central part of the park. The high altitude of the **Parque Juan Carlos I** (daily 9am–11:30pm; Metro: Campo de las Naciones) and its removal from the city makes it worth the half-hour Metro ride from downtown. A weird mix of nature and huge modern statues and bridges gives the park a post apocalyptic, *Planet of the Apes* vibe that is somehow very calming. Without a doubt, this is Madrid's best location for biking, running, Rollerblading, skateboarding, kite flying, Frisbee throwing, and day-tripping. You might even enjoy the *espectáculos* on Thursday through Sunday nights at 10:30pm; they include music, fireworks, and synchronized fountains. As with most things, consult the *Guía del Ocio* for specific times and prices. *FYI:* Parque Juan Carlos I is completely safe for single women during the day. Nobody hangs out here unless they've come for one of the specific activities listed above. The weirdness/sliminess factor is zero.

Shopping

Shopping in Madrid is as much fun as anything else. If you are looking for young, high-fashion designers, head to Chueca and particularly the streets Almirante, Prim, and Monasterio. If your Louis Vuitton purse got snatched, replace it in Salamanca, around Serrano Street, which looks like a spread-out Barney's. For urban wear and funky designers, there's nothing like Fuencarral Street, and there's even a street that specializes in shoes: Augusto Figueroa, former residence of Imelda Marcos.

➔ **Casa Del Libro** This huge, corporate-feeling mega-bookstore will have any book that you could ever want, especially maps and dictionaries. They have some titles in English, too. You can sit and read for as long as you want without anyone bothering you. *Maestro Victoria 3.* ☎ *91-521-4898. www.casa dellibro.com. Metro: Opera.*

➔ **Centro Comercial Barceló** This three-story mall is not far from the one in Fuencarral, but it couldn't be more different. Instead of hipsters in their 20s, you'll find oldsters in their 60s, and instead of wide-legged pants and nose rings, there's hams, booze, and sewing shops. Come for the produce and the excellent tapas at the bar. *Barceló (corner of Mejía Lequerica). No phone. Metro: Tribunal.*

➔ **Chemical Tattoo** Want a new piercing or tat? Get it here, together with a sauna or massage, and get rid of the tension that you get from having your privates perforated. *Augusto Figueroa 11.* ☎ *91-532-3500. www. chemicaltattoo.com. Metro: Tribunal or Gran Vía.*

➔ **El Rastro** The infamous outdoor market is a seething concoction of bootlegged T-shirts, questionable antiques, and won't-find-anywhere gifts for friends back home. It's one of the most fun things you'll see in Madrid. There are some true artisans mixed in with the homeless people selling a few rusty nuts and bolts, and there are also plenty of bars where you can have a bite to eat and maybe a small *caña* of beer. Watch your pockets here, and try to check out the scene on Sundays before noon; the place becomes unbearably crowded by 12:30pm. *Various streets. Metro: La Latina or Tirso de Molina.*

➔ **Manuel Contreras II, Luthier** Manuel Contreras comes from a family that's been making fine instruments for over 40 years, and though not cheap, you can get a much better price for his guitars here than back home. *Calle Mayor 80.* ☎ *91-542-2201. www. manuelcontreras.com. Metro: Opera or Sol.*

➔ **Mercado Fuencarral** This three-story-high mall is a must-see for those who wanna get with it in Madrid. This throbbing core of coolness features nearly 50 stores that sell clothes, jewelry, smoking equipment, music,

MADRID

MSL (Madrileño as a Second Language)

Here's a little glossary to the most common slang terms used in this guide and in the streets of Madrid.

→ **Guiri:** What's a *guiri*? Well, you are. *Guiri* is Spanish slang for anyone who is foreign—and doesn't necessarily understand the finer points of Spanish culture. The word doesn't have bad connotations; really, it's just what they call you and your baseball hat–wearing friends.

→ **Pijo:** *Pijos* are a subgroup of Spain's youth. It usually means those Prada-wearing fake-tan boys and girls from rich families. They have a reputation for being snobby, pretentious, and conservative. The word is used also as an adjective, to describe a place with those characteristics.

→ **Terrazas:** This isn't a rooftop terrace, but rather a sidewalk cafe.

→ **Gatos:** A *gato* is actually pretty much the opposite of *guiri:* The Spanish word for "cat" is the nickname adopted by people from Madrid—for their nighttime habits, rather than for their gracefulness.

→ **Movida:** This is the "movement" that made Madrid what it is today. After 30 years of Franco's dictatorship, Madrileños found themselves in the '80s with more freedom that they could handle and experimented with everything they could. The *movida* spawned Almodóvar, Sabina, Antonio Banderas, and many Spanish clubs.

and other (sub)culturally relevant items. Also has a (sometimes free) movie theater and two bars (one of them with Internet and a hairstylist, each of them named a variation of Fuencarral). *Fuencarral 45.* ☎ *91-521-5985. Metro: Tribunal, Gran Vía, or Chueca.*

→**Triburbana** Get all the Volcom, Etnies, and Suspect you can handle at this small but powerful skate shop on two levels. The music is loud, the staff knows their stuff, and they have a hip-hop store around the corner where they also sell graffiti supplies. *San Felipe Neri 1.* ☎ *91-542-9433. Metro: Sol or Opera.*

Milan

People who tell you that Milan is one of the ugliest cities in Italy and isn't worth a visit are on the one hand right, and on the other hand wrong. There are uglier cities in Italy (Pescara and Livorno are tied for the most hideous) but, no, it's not exactly Venice either. And as far as world-famous art and architecture, Milan is certainly not Florence or Rome. However, it does happen to be the third-largest city in the country, and in many respects, it's the most important.

Just the sheer number of media, fashion, and finance firms based here should give you a clue that *something* is going on. Milan is one of the top places to work in Italy and certainly the best place to party. Forget pounding Peronis on some sad, marble fountain and watching small-town kids gawk back at you—this is where Madonna comes to get into the groove, and she has some 40-plus years of nightlife under her bustier.

Milan's nightclubs are the liveliest in Italy and the shopping is possibly the best in the world. The *aperitivo,* or happy hour, is unbeatable anywhere else; the two soccer teams (A.C. Milan and Inter) are regular winners (next only to Torino's Juventus in the standings); and, yes, there is at least some art to check out. Leonardo da Vinci's *Last Supper* is a must-see on any trip to Europe. Nearby Bergamo is also busting with precious paintings and palaces.

Meanwhile, the design scene in Milan—think contemporary art meets chairs and can openers—will change your whole outlook about kitchenware.

For those who came to see Old Europe, and snap photos of the same tired monuments, you might give this place a skip, or at least after a shot of the Duomo and La Scala. For those who want to see the future, and have a blast in a cosmopolitan, European city, you have come to the right place. And note, the gorgeous shores of Lake Como start just 40 minutes to the north of this city.

The Best of Milan

○ **The Best Cheap Meal:** Pizza is always the cheapest way to go, and pizzerias are absolutely everywhere in Milan. So how about a variation on the theme? The *panzerotto* is the stuffed-dough snack that inspired Hot Pockets. And **Luini Panzerotti** is a classic place for them. For only 3€, you can get a quick, filling lunch. See p. 620.

○ **The Best Pub:** Especially during the *aperitivo* hour, college students and yuppies disguised as such spill out of **Bar Magenta** into the outdoor seating and nearby alleyways. Soak up that pint with Magenta's legendary sandwiches crafted by old men and an even older, hand-cranked meat slicer. See p. 622.

○ **The Best Club:** This fashion-frenzied metropolis is swimming in dance floors and turntables, and the granddaddy of them all is the **Hollywood.** Other spots may have a more interesting clientele and fresher sounds these days, but nobody tops this Corso Como mainstay for eye-candy potential. See p. 623.

○ **The Best Budget Shopping:** You probably won't be buying much in the "golden triangle" around Via Manzoni. A better bet is to scour the shops around **Via Torino.** Funky, lower-priced gems are hiding there amid some otherwise cheesy gear. See p. 628.

Getting There & Getting Around

Getting into Town

BY AIR

If you're flying to Milan directly from North America, you will end up at **Malpensa,** the farther of the two airports from the town center. The **Malpensa Express** train (9€ one-way) connects the main terminal (Terminal 1) with Cadorna Station, not far from the Duomo. It runs every half-hour and the trip takes about 40 minutes. Other buses are just as frequent, and cheaper (5.50€), but the trip is at least 20 minutes longer, and even then you run the risk of hitting hella traffic in the city's northern suburbs. Taxis are a luxury at 75€ or so.

It's much easier to get to the city center from **Linate** airport, but you'll likely only have that choice if you're flying from elsewhere in Europe, as it handles only Alitalia and other European carriers. Downtown buses leave from right in front of the terminal every 10 minutes and require a regular bus ticket, which costs 1€. For a taxi to downtown, expect to shell out about 20€. For both Malpensa and Linate airport information, get online and check out **www.sea-aeroportimilano.it**.

Finally, there is **Bergamo's Orio al Serio** airport, which handles traffic from mostly charters and European budget airlines such as Ryanair and easyJet. You can take one of the hourly buses from the terminal to Milan's Garibaldi Station for 6.70€. That's usually the best bet, although another option is to take a bus to Bergamo's train station (1€ and

10 min. away) and from there a train into Milan (3€–4€ depending on the arrival station in Milan, which is about 1 hr. away).

BY TRAIN

The main rail station for arrivals is Mussolini's mammoth **Stazione Centrale** (Piazza Duca d'Aosta; ☎ 892021), where you'll find the National Railways information office open daily 7am to 9pm.

In general, you can save some money by taking an Intercity train instead of a Eurostar if you have a little more time to spare. For example, Venice is 2³/₄ hours (21€) away on the Eurostar, versus 3 hours (19€) on the Intercity. Rome is 4¹/₂ hours (47€) on the Eurostar and 6 hours (41€) on the Intercity. The price difference to Florence is the most dramatic, and it's only about an hour longer; it's 2³/₄ hours (29€) on the Eurostar and only 3²/₃ hours (18€) on the Intercity.

BY CAR

Moving around by car is almost never a good idea here. You can get anywhere worth going by train, and finding parking in Milan is unpleasant. Don't even try to drive around the crowded, confusing main tourist areas of Milan.

Getting Around

BY SUBWAY

Milan has three **subway** lines: MM1 (red), MM2 (green), and MM3 (yellow). Subways, buses, and trams require the same tickets: 1€ for a single ride, good for 75 minutes. Other options include a 24-hour pass (3€), a 2-day pass (5.50€), a weekly pass (17€ for the first one, 9€ for a renewal), and a monthly pass (38€, 30€ for a renewal). Weekly and monthly passes are most useful for people who go to work on a daily basis. For those who prefer to take it 1 day at a time, a better option might be the *carnet* of 10 tickets (9.20€.)

To find information and schedules for Milan's forms of public transport, call ☎ **800-808180,** or visit www.atm-mi.it (click the link in the upper-right-hand corner for the English version).

BY TRAM

Trams are far and away the best way to get around Milan. The old light fixtures, rumbling wheels, and ancient wooden benches are so cool, in fact, that the City of San Francisco has been buying up Milan's old trams and running them along the tracks of Market Street and the Embarcadero. Gradually, however, Milan is amassing a fleet of newer trams, all of which are quieter and air-conditioned but a little shorter on charm.

There are dozens of **tram** lines, each important in their own way, but the most important ones to remember are the 29 and the 30, which curve around the city's inner ring road, from the Repubblica Metro stop all the way around to the Navigli, and the 3 and the 14, which run from the Duomo south along Via Torino and also end up near the Navigli. Those are key tram lines because they bring you to places that are a far walk from the subway, whereas the other neighborhoods are fairly well connected.

BY BUS

The honor system of ticketing (you will only need to present it if an official climbs aboard the bus or tram and checks) is so tempting that you may decide to try your luck. Be warned that you are risking a 100€ fine and significant public shame.

Once you stamp your ticket, it is valid for 75 minutes; you may want to use it right afterward to hop a bus or tram. Unfortunately you have to stamp a fresh ticket every time you get on the subway.

BY TAXI

Finding a taxi is fairly easy in Milan, as long as there isn't a subway strike or heavy rain. Look for the white cars with thin red stripes: If the taxi light is lit, you're in business. Cab meters start at 3.10€, and add a nighttime

MILAN

Milan

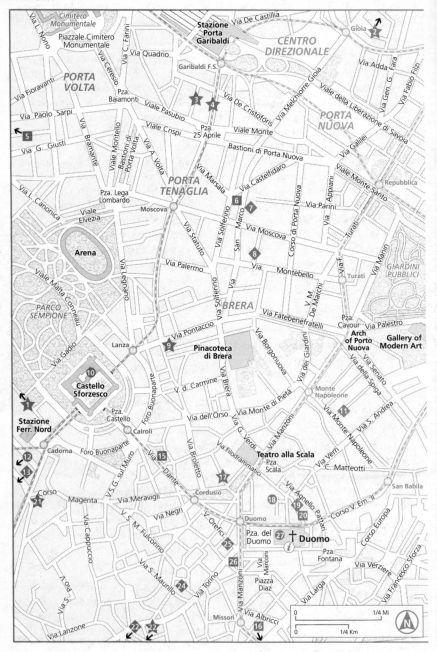

Cimitero
Monumentale
Piazzale Cimitero
Monumentale
Stazione
Porta
Garibaldi
Via De Castillia
Gioia
CENTRO
DIREZIONALE
Via L. Nono
Via C. Farini
Via Quadrio
Garibaldi F.S.
Via Adda
Via Gen. G. Fara
Via Fabio Filzi
PORTA
VOLTA
Pza.
Baiamonti
Viale Pasubio
Via De Cristoforis
Via Melchiorre Gioia
Viale della Liberazione di Savoia
PORTA
NUOVA
Via Fioravanti
Via Ceresio
3
Via Paolo Sarpi
Viale Crispi
Pza.
25 Aprile
Viale Monte
Via Galilei
5
Via G. Giusti
Via Bramante
Viale Montello
Bastioni di Porta Volta
Via A. Volta
Bastioni di Porta Nuova
Via Monte Santo
Repubblica
Via L. Canonica
Pza. Lega
Lombardo
PORTA
TENAGLIA
Via Marsala
Via Castelfidaro
6
Viale Monte Santo
Viale
Elvezia
Moscova
7
Via Appiani
Via Parini
Via F. Turati
Arena
Via Statuto
Via Solferino
Via San Marco
Via Moscova
Corso di Porta Nuova
8
Via Palermo
Via
Montebello
Turati
GIARDINI
PUBBLICI
Viale Malta Conneau
PARCO
SEMPIONE
Via Legnano
Via Solferino
BRERA
Y. M.
De Marchi
Via Fatebenefratelli
Pza.
Cavour
Via Palestro
Via Pontaccio
9
Pinacoteca
di Brera
Via Borgonuova
Via dei Giardini
Arch
of Porto
Nuova
Gallery of
Modern Art
Lanza
Via Gadio
10
Castello
Sforzesco
V. d. Carmine
Via Brera
Via Monte di Pietà
Monte
Napoleone
Via della Spiga
Via Senato
1
Pza.
Castello
Foro Buonaparte
Via dell'Orso
Via G. Verdi
Via Manzoni
11
Via Monte Napoleone
Via S. Andrea
Stazione
Ferr. Nord
Cairoli
Via Broletto
Teatro alla Scala
Via Verri
Cadorna
Foro Buonaparte
Via Dante
15
Via Filodrammatici
Pza.
Scala
C. Matteotti
12
13
V.S.G. sul Muro
17
18
Corso V. Em. II
San Babila
Corso
Magenta
Via Meravigli
Cordusio
19
20
21
V. S. M. Fulcorno
Via Negri
V. Orefici
Duomo
27
Duomo
Corso Europa
Via Cappuccio
23
Pza. del
Duomo
Pza.
Fontana
Via Larga
Via A. Orti
26
Via Marconi
Piazza
Diaz
Via Verziere
Via Francesco Sforza
Via S. Maurilio
24
Via Torino
Via Manzoni
Missori
22
27
16
Missori
Via Albricci
Via Lanzone

0   1/4 Mi
0   1/4 Km
N

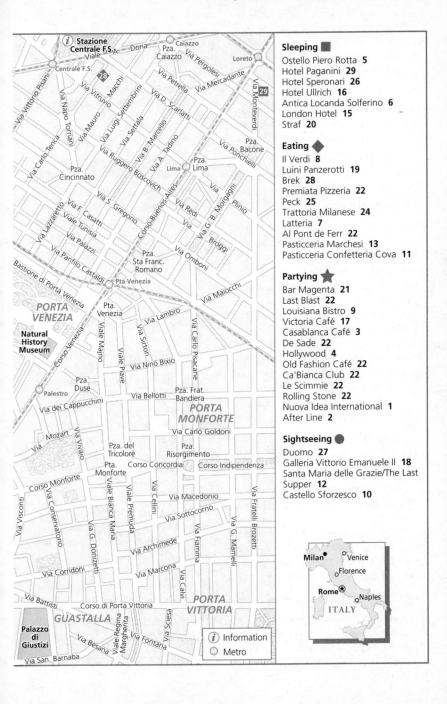

Sleeping ■
Ostello Piero Rotta **5**
Hotel Paganini **29**
Hotel Speronari **26**
Hotel Ullrich **16**
Antica Locanda Solferino **6**
London Hotel **15**
Straf **20**

Eating ◆
Il Verdi **8**
Luini Panzerotti **19**
Brek **28**
Premiata Pizzeria **22**
Peck **25**
Trattoria Milanese **24**
Latteria **7**
Al Pont de Ferr **22**
Pasticceria Marchesi **13**
Pasticceria Confetteria Cova **11**

Partying ★
Bar Magenta **21**
Last Blast **22**
Louisiana Bistro **9**
Victoria Café **17**
Casablanca Café **3**
De Sade **22**
Hollywood **4**
Old Fashion Café **22**
Ca'Bianca Club **22**
Le Scimmie **22**
Rolling Stone **22**
Nuova Idea International **1**
After Line **2**

Sightseeing ●
Duomo **27**
Galleria Vittorio Emanuele II **18**
Santa Maria delle Grazie/The Last
Supper **12**
Castello Sforzesco **10**

surcharge of 3.10€ and a Sunday surcharge of 1.55€. Expect to shell out up to 15€ for a typical ride across town. Two taxi numbers to call (speaking in Italian, of course) are ☎ **02-4040** and 02-8585.

ON FOOT

During one subway strike, when all the cabs were taken, I ended up walking from one end of Milan to the other. It took about an hour and 15 minutes, and that was literally walking across the entire city. Subway stops, for the most part, will get you within 15 minutes of where you want to go. Just remember to wear comfortable shoes because cobblestones, rough patches in the sidewalk, and tram tracks can make the going a little rough at times.

Milan Basics

Orientation: Milan's Neighborhoods

Milan is set up as a classic medieval city, with a cathedral and a fortress (the Castello Sforzesco) at its epicenter, and concentric rings around it that once hosted defensive walls. Each of the gates in the walls, in turn, were named after the city or region toward which that road led. So you have **Porta Venezia** in the northeast, **Porta Romana** in the south, and **Porta Genova** and **Porta Ticinese** (toward the Ticino River) in the southwest. Everything inside these gates can roughly be termed the *centro storico.* The ring roads *(circonvallazione)* that connect them are the most useful in the city.

Tourist Offices

Facing the Duomo, the **tourist office** is just to your right in a boxy, Soviet-looking building on the same square (Via Marconi 1; ☎ **02-72524301;** www.milanoinfotourist. com). It's open 9am to 1pm and 2 to 6pm. There are a number of free brochures to pick up, as well as *Hello Milano,* which has a great listing of local events. Expect to stand in a brief line to speak with someone.

Recommended Websites

○ **www.hellomilano.it**: This site can answer almost any question you have—in English—about hotels, nightlife, events and tourist sights, and has good maps of the city.

○ **www.easymilano.it**: This is the online version of Milan's expat community magazine, most useful for classified ads for long-term and short-term apartment rentals.

○ **www.mymi.it**: The hippest online venue for news on dining, clubbing, art shows, and fitness centers; in Italian only.

○ **www.anteospaziocinema.it**: Feel like a movie? Click on the "Sound & Motion" tab for a list of English-language films playing in Milan.

Culture Tips 101

There's no minimum legal age for purchase or consumption of alcohol here—rather, you're completely at the mercy of the shopkeeper and the barkeep. As long as you're not acting like a drunken fool, you shouldn't have a problem securing drinks. Drinking is usually concentrated in *locali* (bars, cafes, and other going-out places), not on the streets. While you can bring a bottle of wine outside on the Piazza del Duomo, it's not a common thing—the general anti-intimacy of Milan's traffic-heavy streets kinda takes the allure out of it. Milan does have a local pot-smoking street scene in Parco Sempione (though pot is illegal here), where scores of bongo-playing hippies hang out.

Recommended Books, Movies & Music

See p. 795 in the Rome chapter on for recommendations on Italian books and movies.

Milan Nuts & Bolts

Cellphone Providers & Service Centers   There's a Vodafone store at P. Le Cadorna -Box Triennale (☎ 02/8900413; www.190.it) where you can buy an Italian SIM card or get your phone serviced.

Currency   Banks are everywhere. Just look for the BANCOMAT signs. Note that ATMs in Milan can remind you of old-school Christmas-tree lights: One goes out and they all go out, due to connection failures that usually last a few hours. Many bancomats still go offline at midnight.

Embassies   The **U.S. Consulate** is at Via Principe Amadeo 2/10 (☎ 02-290351); it's open Monday through Friday 9 to 11am and 2 to 4pm (Metro: Turati). The **Canadian Consulate,** at Via Pisani 19 (☎ 02-67581), is open Monday to Thursday 8:30am to 12:30pm and 1:15 to 5:30pm (Metro: F.S. Centrale or Repubblica). The **British Consulate,** at Via San Paolo 7 (☎ 02-23001), is open Monday to Friday 9:15am to 12:15pm and 2:30 to 4:30pm (Metro: Duomo). The **Australian Consulate,** at Via Borgogna 2 (☎ 02-777041), is open Monday to Thursday 9am to noon and 2 to 4pm (Metro: San Babila).

Emergencies   For immediate help, call the Carabinieri at ☎ 112, or the police at ☎ 113. (There is also an English-speaking staff at ☎ 02-863701.)

For **medical emergencies,** call the *pronto soccorso,* or ambulance, at ☎ 118. If you can make to the hospital on your own, the most central of all is **Ospedale Fatebenefratelli** (Corso Porta Nuova 23; ☎ 02-63631; Metro: Turati) in the Brera area, or else **Ospedale Maggiore** (Via Francesco Sforza 28; ☎ 02-55031; Metro: Missori; some people on staff speak English). For non-emergencies, English-speaking patients might find it more helpful to visit the **American International Medical Center** (Via Mercalli 11; ☎ 02-58319808; Metro: Missori).

Internet/Wireless Hot Spots   There are several sleek and flashy Internet spots around Milan run by big corporations such as Mondadori and Telecom Italia, but for the best deal, look for the international telephone centers run by, and catering to, immigrants. There is at least one in every neighborhood. There are fewer terminals, but you will pay about half the price a larger place charges. Below are a few of the more popular, bigger venues. Prices range from 4€ to 6€ per hour.

→   **Grœzianet** (Piazza Duca d'Aosta 14, next to central train station; ☎ 02-6700543)

→   **Mondadori Multicenter** (Via Marghera 28, near the Duomo; ☎ 02-48047311)

→   **Internet Enjoy** (Alzaia Naviglio Pavese 2, on the Naviglio Pavese canal; ☎ 02-8357225)

→   **Phone@point** (Via Vigevano 20, near *The Last Supper;* ☎ 02-58307274)

Laundry   A convenient spot to have your clothes washed is **Minola,** south of the Duomo at Via San Vito 5 (follow Via Torino from the Piazza del Duomo for about 5 blocks where it intersects with Via San Vito; ☎ 02-58111271; Metro: Missori). The staff will do your laundry (wash and dry) for 10€ per 5 kilograms (11 lb.) and dry cleaning for 12€ per 5 kilograms (11 lb.). It's open Monday to Friday from 8am to 6pm and Saturday from 8am to noon.

Luggage Storage Drop off your heavy gear at the **Stazione Centrale**. The luggage room is open daily from 5am to 4am; the fee is 2.60€ per piece of baggage for each 12-hour period. Note that luggage storage rooms in Italian train stations are sometimes closed in Italy when terrorist threats are perceived as high.

Post Offices There's no such thing as a quick stop at the post office but getting there late morning midweek may help your chances of avoiding the rush. There are dozens of offices spread out around the city, but the **main branch** is just outside the Cordusio Metro on Via Cordusio 4 (☎ **02-72482126**). It's open Monday to Saturday 8am to 7pm.

Restrooms Doubtlessly, the best place to answer nature's call is in a bar. To make a *bella figura,* order a cup of coffee and then look for the signs.

Safety Milan is a pretty safe place as far as violent crime is concerned. Even pick-pockets are rarer here than in Rome. That said, it is never a good idea for a woman to walk through a park alone late at night. Parco Sempione is particularly dubious, as it is rife with seedy characters. The central train station and the adjacent neighborhood around the Caiazzo Metro are also not the best places to take a late-night stroll.

Tipping See p. 799 in the Rome chapter for tipping advice.

Sleeping

You need to budget to spend the night in Milan. *Nothing* is cheap. Hotels start at a rock-bottom price of 60€ per double and rocket upward from there. But there are a few reasonable options, listed below. In a pinch, you can also inquire with the **hotel booking kiosk** in the Stazione Centrale (main train station)—they act as a clearinghouse for unsold rooms in cheerless government-rated three-stars near the train station. It won't be the most romantic room in town, but you can get a double with a private bathroom, mini-bar, slippers, and *cuffia doccia* (shower cap) for about 70€ a night.

Hostel

→ **Ostello Piero Rotta** Milan has one youth hostel and it is nowhere near the city center. It is out by the stadium, in the San Siro neighborhood, and unless you've come specifically to see a game and then leave, there's little reason to stay here. There's no doubt that this is the cheapest option, but with dorm beds with shared bathrooms at 19€ a head, you and a friend might want to

pitch in a few extra euros for a cheap double downtown. *Via Salmoiraghi 1.* ☎ *02-39267095 or 02-33000191. www.ostellionline.org. 20€ dorm bed. Rates include breakfast. Closed Dec 23–Jan 13. Metro: QT8. Bus: 90, 91, or 68. Amenities: Breakfast room; Internet; laundry facilities; shared bathrooms; TV (in common room).*

Cheap

→ **Hotel Paganini** Occupying an old house off the north end of Corso Buenos Aires, the stamping grounds for some rather lonely looking women on the street corners after 9pm, the Paganini appears to be a dismal option as you are buzzed in and walk up to the front desk. Still, the management goes to great lengths to keep this a clean, no-nonsense budget hotel: The guest rooms are large and bright, with high ceilings, solid beds, and banal modular furnishings of varying ages. The best rooms are in the rear, overlooking a huge private garden. There is much to be said for this location: If shopping is on your agenda, the nearby Corso Buenos Aires is one of the city's bargain-fashion meccas. *Via Paganini 6.* ☎ *02-2047443. 65€ double. Metro: Loreto. Tram: 33, 55, 56, 90, 91, or 93. Amenities: Concierge; shared bathrooms. In room: Hair dryer.*

→ **Hotel Speronari** ★ This is a real find, a budget hotel in a deluxe location, tucked into a tiny pedestrian side street between Via Torino and Via Mazzini. The staff is earnest, and the rooms are basic but done well: cool tile floors, functional furnishings, working cot springs, and fuzzy towels in the bathrooms. Even those without a full bathroom have a sink and bidet, and all, save a few of those with shared bathrooms, have TVs. Rooms on the third and fourth floors are brighter, and those on the courtyard are a tad quieter than rooms facing the street. *Via Speronari 4.* ☎ *02-86461125. hotelsperonari@ inwind.it. 73€ double with shared bathroom, 93€–104€ with private bathroom; 98€ triple with shared bathroom, 140€ with private bathroom; 155€ quad with private bathroom. Metro: Duomo or Missori. Tram: 1, 2, 3, 4, 12, 14, 15, 19, 20, 24, or 27. Amenities: Shared bathrooms (in some). In room: TV, fans.*

→ **Hotel Ullrich** ★ A 10-minute walk south of the Duomo, this attractive *pensione* offers a lot of comfort in addition to its good location. The management is friendly, and rooms are furnished with pleasant modern pieces and decent beds. Each has a tiny washroom with sink and bidet but no toilet; large, spanking-clean bathrooms are accessible from the hallway. Rooms on the street side open to small balconies, but are noisier than those overlooking the *cortile* (courtyard). The Ullrich books up quickly, so be sure to call ahead. *Corso Italia 6.* ☎ *02-86450156 or 02-804535. 70€–75€ double, 90€–100€ triple. Metro: Duomo. Tram: 15, 24, 65, or 94. Amenities: Breakfast room; laundry facilities; shared bathrooms.*

Doable

→ **Antica Locanda Solferino** ★★★ If this charming old hotel in the arty Brera neighborhood hadn't been discovered long ago by members of the fashion world and film stars (this was Marcello Mastroianni's preferred Milan hostelry), you would consider it a find. The rooms have more character than they do modern comforts, but, to the loyal guests, the eclectic smattering of country antiques and Art Nouveau pieces more than compensate for the absence of minibars. Nor do the repeat customers seem to mind that some of the bathrooms are miniscule (though modern), or that there is no lobby or breakfast room (coffee and rolls are delivered to your room). So be it—this is a delightful place to stay in one of Milan's most enticing neighborhoods, and reception manager Gerardo Vitolo is very friendly. *Via Castelfidardo.* ☎ *02-6570129 or 02-6592706. www.anticalocandasolferino.it. 130€–200€ double, 170€–220€ apt, 40€ extra bed. Rates include breakfast (served in room). Closed 2–3 weeks in mid-Aug. Metro: Moscova or Repubblica. Tram/bus: 11, 29, 30, 33, 41, 43, or 94. Amenities: Laundry service; room service. In room: TV, hair dryer, safe.*

→ **London Hotel** ★ The London sticks to its old-fashioned ways. The big fireplace and cozy green velvet furniture in the lobby say a lot about the comfort level and friendly atmosphere that bring many guests back time after time. Just beyond the lobby, there's a bar where beverages are available almost around the clock; guests can purchase cappuccino or a continental breakfast in the morning. Upstairs, the rooms look like they haven't been redecorated in a number of decades, but they're roomy and bright, and the heavy old furnishings lend a charm very much in keeping with the ambience of the hotel. Rooms on the first floor tend to be the largest, and they get smaller as you go

MILAN

up. Guests receive a 10% discount at the trattoria next door, the Opera Prima. *Via Rovello 3.* ☎ *02-72020166. www.hotellondonmilano. com. 100€–150€ double. 8€ continental breakfast. Closed Aug and Christmas. Metro: Cordusio. Tram/bus: 1, 2, 3, 4, 12, 14, 18, 19, 20, 24, or 27. Amenities: Bar; concierge; dry cleaning; laundry service; room service (limited). In room: A/C, TV, hair dryer, Internet.*

Splurge

→**Straf** ★★ Hidden behind a 2-century-old facade, this hotel is close to La Scala and the deluxe shopping street, Via Montenapoleone. The landmark Duomo lies outside your door. Its burnished brass and black stone create a minimalist aura for the jet set who check in. Stylish and comfortable, bedrooms are elegant. The special rooms are five units equipped for chromotherapy and aromatherapy, with Japanese auto-massage chaise longues. Even the less grand accommodations will still make you feel fashionable. *San Raffaele 3.* ☎ *02-805081. www.straf.it. 257€– 325€ double (15% discount often available for Internet bookings). Metro: Duomo. Amenities: Restaurant; bar; business services; car rental; dry cleaning; health club; laundry service; massage; nonsmoking rooms; 24-hr. room service; wheelchair friendly. In room: A/C, TV, hair dryer, Internet, minibar, safe.*

Eating

The Milanese are that rare breed of Italian who appreciate a quick meal. Lunch is generally a sandwich or salad on the run. Dinner, on the other hand, is time to relax. The area is famous for its veal cutlet *(cotoletta milanese)*, its filling *cassouela* stew, and, of course, *risotto milanese.* One other peculiarity of Milanese restaurants, besides their strangely efficient service, is that very few of them offer outdoor seating. Expect a cozy indoor atmosphere, sometimes with a funky modern decor. Oh, and it's not going to be cheap. That is, unless you can forgo a real "meal." The generous buffet spreads offered at aperitivo hour—usually a mix of carbs, cheeses, and cured meats—provide plenty of calories, and they're free as long as you buy something to drink.

Hot Spots

→**Il Verdi** ★ PASTA/VEGETARIAN This trendy but cozy restaurant earned the distinction of spawning the city's first yuppie scene in the '90s. Some things have changed since then: The menu is still healthy and the clientele relatively young, but now there is something for all tastes. The most popular dish seems to have remained the risotto with pears drizzled with balsamic vinegar, though the salads are perhaps the best in the city, especially those with crabmeat and avocados. The wine selection is also very good. *Piazza Mirabello 5.* ☎ *02-6590979 Primi 10€–14€; salads from 9€. Mon–Sat 12:30– 2:15pm and 7:30pm–midnight. Metro: Turati.*

[MTV] Best →**Luini Panzerotti** ★ SNACKS A Milan mainstay since 1948, it's so good they've even opened a branch in London. At this stand-up counter near the Galleria, you'll have to elbow your way through a throng of well-dressed patrons to purchase the house specialty: *panzerotto,* a stuffed pocket of pizza crust. You'll also find many different kinds of panini here. *Via S. Radegonda 16.* ☎ *02-86461917. www.luini.it. Panzerotto 2.50€. Mon 10am–3pm; Tues–Sat 10am–8pm. Closed Aug. Metro: Duomo.*

Cheap

→**Brek** CAFETERIA No, it's not Milanese. Yes, it's a chain cafeteria. But if you want to eat cheaply and well, this is the place. Pastas and risotto are made fresh; pork, veal, and chicken are roasted to order; and the large selection of cheeses would put many a formal restaurant to shame. Excellent wines and many kinds of beer are also available. Behind-the-counter service is friendly and helpful. *Via Lepetit 20.* ☎ *02-6705149. www. brek.it. Primi and pizza 3€–6€; secondi 3.50€–7€. Mon–Sat 11:30am–3pm and 6:30–10:30pm. Metro: Stazione Centrale.*

➔**Peck** ★ DELI   Milan's most famous food emporium offers a wonderful selection of roast veal, risottos, porchetta, salads, aspics, cheeses, pastries, and other fare from its exquisite larder in this natty snack bar around the corner from its shop. Stay, and you will eat at a stand-up bar where, especially around lunchtime, it can be hard to find elbowroom. This shouldn't discourage you, though. *Via Spadari 9.* ☎ *02-8023161. www.peck.it. Primi 3.50€–8€; secondi 9€–13€. Mon–Sat 7:30am–9pm. Closed Jan 1–10 and July 1–20. Metro: Duomo.*

➔**Premiata Pizzeria** PIZZA/PAN-ITALIAN The most popular pizzeria in the Navigli stays packed from early dinnertime until the barhopping crowd stops by for late-night munchies. The restaurant rambles back forever, exposed copper pipes tracing across the ceilings. Shaded outdoor terraces are set with long, raucous tables. Seating is communal and service hurried, but the wood oven pizzas are excellent. There's a long menu of pastas, meat courses, or platters of cheese or *salumi* built for two. *Via Alzaia Naviglio Grande 2.* ☎ *02-89400648. Pizzas 4.50€–12€. Wed–Mon noon–2:30pm; daily 7:30–11:30pm. Metro: Porta Genova.*

Doable

📺 Best ➔**La Trattoria Milanese** ★★ MILANESE   Don't be fooled by the boring, touristy-sounding name. Tucked into a narrow lane in one of the oldest sections of Milan, just west of the Duomo, this is a Milanese institution. In the three-beamed dining room, local families and other patrons share the long, crowded tables. The *risotto alla Milanese* with saffron and beef marrow

is excellent, as is a minestrone that's served hot in the winter and at room temperature in the summer. The *cotolette alla Milanese,* breaded and fried in butter, is cooked to perfection. If you want to try their twin specialties without pigging out, the dish listed as *risotto e osso buco* buys you a half portion each for just 18€. Make reservations—if you just show up, you won't get in. *Via Santa Marta 11.* ☎ *02-86451991. Primi 7€–10€; secondi 6€–18€; menù turistico_30€ without wine. Wed–Mon noon–3pm and 7pm–1am. Metro: Cardusio.*

➔**Latteria** MILANESE   In the La Brera neighborhood, this delicious, homemade fare includes minestrone and other vegetable soups, and risotto. The menu changes daily, and the friendly staff, including owners Arturo and Maria, won't mind explaining the different dishes. The place is tiny, and doesn't take bookings, so if you want to get one of the popular tables, arrive when it opens or wait until 8:30pm or later. *Via San Marco 24.* ☎ *02-6597653. Primi 9€–10€; secondi 7€–13€. Mon–Fri 12:30–2:30pm and 7:30–10pm. Metro: Moscova.*

Splurge

➔**Al Pont de Ferr** ★ PAN-ITALIAN   This is one of the more culinarily respectable of the dozens of restaurants around the Navigli, with tables set out on the flagstones overlooking the canal (regulars know to bring tiny cans of bug spray to battle the mosquitoes in summer). The *paste e fagioli* is livened up with bits of sausage, and the ricotta-stuffed ravioli inventively sauced with a pesto of *rucola* (arugula) and veggies. For a second course, try the *tocchetti di coniglio* (oven-roasted rabbit with potatoes), *porchetta* (pork stuffed with spices), or the vegetable couscous—or just sack the whole idea of a secondo and order up a *tavolozza* selection of excellent cheeses. There's a surprisingly good selection of half-bottles of wine, but most full bottles start at 15€. *Ripa di*

MILAN

Porta Ticinese 55 (on the Naviglio Grande). ☎ *02-89406277. Primi 6€–11€; secondi 14€–19€. Mon–Sat 12:30–2:30pm and 8pm–1am. Tram: 3, 15, 29, 30, or 59.*

Cafes & Tearooms

There are hundreds of coffee bars around Milan, and all serve a stand-up cup of espresso, but for something more Audrey Hepburn–esque, try one of two refined pastry shops. The first is **Pasticceria Marchesi** (Via Santa Maria alla Porta 13; ☎ **02-862770**; Metro: Cardusio), a distinguished pastry shop with an adjoining wood-paneled tearoom. It's open Tuesday to Sunday 8am to 8pm. **Cova** (Via Montenapoleone 8; ☎ **02-6000578**; Metro: Montenapoleone), smack in the Golden Triangle, is in its third century of refined surroundings near the similarly atmospheric Museo Poldi-Pezzoli. It's open Tuesday to Sunday 8am to 8pm.

Partying

If any place in Italy knows how to rage, it is Milan, though in a city obsessed with keeping up appearances, the temptation to down that extra shot and start grinding on a bar counter is met with pause. In general, Italians frown on drunkenness. The Milanese are no different. Yet these are the people who invented the *aperitivo:* the 6 o'clock martini or *negroni* that paves the way for dinner.

After dinner, the next decision is where to go out at night. There are bars and clubs spread out over the city, but the five areas with the most action are Corso Como, Porta Romana, Porta Ticinese, the Navigli canal neighborhood, and most famously, Brera. In general, Corso Como draws the fashion crowd, Porta Ticinese the design crowd, Porta Romana is more local-oriented, while Brera and the Navigli are the bread-and-butter of Milan partying. If you don't feel like getting dressed up and just want to put back a few beers at long wooden tables, go to the Navigli. Also remember that locals don't hit clubs till 11pm or midnight and don't pack it in till sunrise.

Pubs & Bars

MTV **Best** →**Bar Magenta** ★ Locals have begun calling this place the Piccadilly of Milan, either for its publike atmosphere or the fact that it is a favorite among the English-speaking community. Despite the pints of Guinness and American-style cocktails, this is definitely not an "expat bar." It is a Milanese legend, and the first stop for any scarf-wearing *tifoso* headed toward San Siro for a soccer game. With expert meat-slicers and an endless supply of *cotolette milanese* on hand, the Magenta also gets my vote for best late-night sandwich in town. Expect Motown, rock, and R&B classics on the speakers. *Via Carducci 13.* ☎ *02-8053808. Metro: Cordusio or S. Ambrogio.*

→**Last Blast** One of dozens of beer-happy pubs to choose from on the Naviglio Pavese canal, Last Blast is unique because it has good, live music. The tables are usually packed in front of singer/guitarist Roberto Santoro, who, every night, covers the gamut from U2 to Patti Smith to Italy's answer to Bob Dylan, Fabrizio de Andre. *Via Acanio Sforza 15.* ☎ *02-58105685. Metro: Porta Genova.*

MTV **Best** →**Louisiana Bistro** ★ MTV Generation, welcome home. A former Brera bordello turned party central brings in models in casual wear with its videos on the tube, great tunes on the turntables, and all the burgers and fries you can eat. There's nothing Italian about the place at all (the owner is from New Mexico), but that seems to be what the clientele likes best. *Via Fiori Chiari 17.* ☎ *02-86465315. Metro: Lanza.*

→**Victoria Café** This is classic Milan: Liberty-style decor, a killer cocktail, friendly bartenders, and a swarming *aperitivo* hour packed with people who work for a living. If you're in the Duomo area and looking for a good place for a drink before venturing farther afield for the night, this is the place. *Via Clerici 1.* ☎ *02-8053598. Metro: Duomo.*

Clubs & Lounges

→ **Casablanca Café** If you get through the door, get to the back room immediately, in the Moroccan-style tent. Pretty much commercial stuff here, nothing too cutting edge, but a chill night out for the late-20s/early-30s set. *Corso Como 14.* ☎ *02-62690186. Closed Aug. Cover 10€–15€ (includes 1 drink). Metro: Garibaldi.*

→ **De Sade** You never know what you're going to turn up at this spot. Music varies from night to night, and so does the clientele. *Via Piazzi 4.* ☎ *02-6888898. Closed June–Aug. Cover 16€–20€ (includes 1 drink). Metro: Porta Genova.*

MTV Best → **Hollywood** ★ Hollywood is like Disneyland: touristy, childish, but something that even the stars never outgrow. The celebs usually show up on Sunday night, Friday is student night, and Wednesday—"pervert" night—seems to draw the largest crowd. It is definitely a sexy night and not to be missed. *Corso Como 15.* ☎ *02-6598996. Cover 15€–20€ (includes 1 drink). Metro: Garibaldi or Moscova.*

→ **Old Fashion Café** The Old Fashion is tucked away inside Parco Sempione and is a nice hideaway from the too-cool-for-school fashionista crowd. This is how the rest of the city lives—in fact, it's so down-to-earth you may even hear a little Neil Diamond. Wednesday nights foreigners get in for free (bring some ID) while Mondays and Saturdays are slightly more upscale. Sunday brunch is also pretty good. *Viale E Alemagna 6.* ☎ *02-8056231. Cover 8€–20€. Metro: Cadorna. Tram: 1 or 27.*

Live Music

The **Ca'Bianca Club** (Via Lodovico il Moro 117; ☎ 02-89125777; Metro: Bisceglie) offers live music and dancing on Wednesday night, from folk music to cabaret to Dixieland jazz. This is a private club, but no one at the door will prevent nonmembers from entering. The show, whatever it might be, begins at 10:30pm (closed Sun and Aug). Cover is 16€ for the show and the first drink, or 45€ to 80€ for dinner.

At **Le Scimmie** (Via Ascanio Sforza 49; ☎ 02-89402874; bus: 59), bands play everything from funk to blues to creative jazz. They also serve food. Doors open nightly around 8pm, and music is presented 10pm to around 3am.

Rolling Stone (Corso XXII Marzo 32; ☎ 02-733172; tram: 4 or 20) features head-banging rock bands. It's open every night, usually 10:30pm to 4am, but things don't get going until at least midnight; it's closed in August. Cover ranges from 10€ to 30€.

Gay Nightlife

Nuova Idea International ★★ (Via de Castillia 30; ☎ 02-69007859; Metro: Garibaldi), is the largest, oldest, and most fun gay disco in Italy, very much tied to Milan's urban bustle. It prides itself on mimicking the large all-gay discos of northern Europe, and it draws young and not-so-young men. There is a large video screen and occasional live entertainment. It is open Tuesday and Sunday 9:30pm to 1:30am, Thursday and Friday 10:30pm to 3am, and Saturday 10pm to 4am. Cover is 8€ on Tuesday and Thursday, 11€ on Friday, 18€ on Saturday, and 10€ on Sunday.

Straights flock to **After Line** (Via Sammartini 25; ☎ 02-6692130; Metro: Stazione Centrale), but the club enjoys even more popularity among Milan's gay community. Many nights are devoted to themes. Strong drinks and recorded music fill the night air, and the place is very cruisy. It's open daily 9pm to 3am.

MILAN

Performing Arts

The most complete list of cultural events appears in the large Milan newspaper, the left-wing *La Repubblica.* Try for a Thursday edition, which usually has the best listings.

The world's most famous opera house is **La Scala** ★★★, located on Piazza della Scala (Metro: Duomo). La Scala is fully restored, with a technologically advanced stage and a splendid auditorium. Critics have raved about the new acoustics. There are now three moveable stages and 200 added seats. Tickets are hard to come by and should be arranged as far in advance as possible. Ranging in cost from 10€ to 170€, tickets can be purchased at **Biglietteria Centrale,** in the Galleria Vittorio Emanuele, on the corner of Piazza della Scala (☎ **02-72003744;** daily noon–6pm; Metro: Duomo). For more information, search out www.teatroallascala.org.

Other operas are staged at the modern 2,500-seat, newly constructed auditorium, **Teatro degli Arcimboldi** (Zona Bicocca, Viale dell'Innovazione; ☎ **02/72003744;** www.teatroarcimboldi.com; Metro: Precotto, then bus no. 162), on the northern outskirts of Milan. It lies alongside a university campus and dreary housing developments. Because the new opera house is difficult to reach by public transportation, the theater operates shuttle buses departing from the Piazza Duomo between 6:45 and 7pm on the nights of performances. Tickets cost 20€ to 155€. The opera house is closed in midsummer (late July and all of Aug). The new season begins every year on December 7.

Sightseeing

Festivals

June & July

National and International Dance Festival. At this monthlong festival, major artists put on various dance performances. For info and reservations, contact Comune di Trezzo sull'Adda—Ufficio Cultura (☎ **02-90987052;** www.comune.trezzosulladda.mi. it). Mid-June to mid-July.

Milan International Film Festival. Not as big as Venice's festival, this movie fest still brings together a respectable number of stars and filmmakers from all over the world. Call ☎ **02-6597732** or go to www. miff.it for more info. Early June.

December

La Scala Opera Season. At the most famous opera house of them all, the Teatro alla Scala, the season opens on the feast day of Milan's patron St. Ambrogio and runs about 7 months. Call ☎ **02-860787** or 02-860775 for the box office, or ☎ **02-72003744** for the information line (www. teatroallascala.org). December 7 to July.

Top Attractions

FREE →**Castello Sforzesco** Though it's been clumsily restored many times, most recently at the end of the 19th century, this fortresslike castle continues to evoke Milan's two most powerful medieval and Renaissance families, the Visconti and the Sforza. The Visconti built the castle in the 14th century and the Sforza, who married into the Visconti clan and eclipsed them in power, reconstructed it in 1450. The castle houses a series of small museums known collectively as the Civici Musei Castello Sforzesco, which includes prehistoric finds from Lombardy, and the last work of 89-year-old Michelangelo, his unfinished *Rondanini Pietà. Piazza Castello.* ☎ *02-62083940. Free admission. Tues–Sun 9:30am–5:30pm. Metro: Cairoli, Cadorna, or Lanza.*

12 Hours in Milan

1. **Get lost in the Duomo.** The most impressive church in Italy—maybe in the world.

2. **See *The Last Supper*.** As long as it lasts, it will remain one of the world's greatest artistic treasures.

3. **Barhop on the Navigli canals.** So many happy-hour deals, so little time. Start early, end late, stumble home.

4. **Splurge on something designer.** In this fashion mecca, buy one thing Gucci, Prada, Versace, Armani, Krizia, or Dolce & Gabbana.

5. **Chill out in Le Scimmie.**

6. **Go to a soccer game.** There's nothing better than watching the best in the world at their sport in the middle of 60,000 chanting lunatics.

7. **Attend the opera at La Scala.** You are completely thrust into a time warp. Standing-room-only tickets are available for some shows.

8. **Eat some risotto.** No other Milanese food compares for price, taste, and variety. Il Verde has some of the city's best.

→ **Duomo** This is the fourth-largest church in the world with 135 marble spires, a stunning triangular facade, and 3,400-some statues that you can see up close and personal by climbing the stairs to the roof—one of the must-do's on your Milan checklist. It's also a great place to overlook the city and even the Alps on a clear day. You are joined high above Milan by the spire-top gold statue of *Madonnina* (the little Madonna), the city's beloved protectress. Don't expect anything too ornate on the inside, although it is a great place to come for some peace. *Piazza del Duomo.* ☎ *02-860358 or 02/86463456. Duomo: Free admission; daily 6:50am–7pm. Roof: Admission 3.50€, 5€ with elevator; daily 7am–7pm. Crypt: Admission 1.55€; daily 9am–noon and 2:30–6pm. Museum: Admission 6€ adults; combination ticket for museum and elevator to roof 7€; Tues–Sun 9:30am–12:30pm and 3–6pm. Metro: Duomo.*

FREE → **Galleria Vittorio Emanuele II** Milan's elegant late-19th-century version of a mall is this wonderful steel-and-glass-covered, cross-shaped arcade. The designer of this urban marvel, Giuseppe Mengoni, didn't live to see the Milanese embrace his creation: He tripped and fell from a girder a few days before the Galleria opened in 1878. *Just off Piazza del Duomo and Piazza della Scala.* ☎ *06-460272. Free admission. Mon–Sat 10am–11pm, Sun 10am–8pm. Metro: Duomo.*

→ **Santa Maria delle Grazie/*The Last Supper*** ★★ As famous as the painting (called *Cenacolo*, or "little supper," in Italian) is today, da Vinci's masterpiece was in a sorry state for a long time. The church was a Dominican convent when the fresco was commissioned. The monks cooked their meals behind the now-famous wall, and the artwork had to be touched up over and over again. To make matters worse, Allied bombing during World War II tore off the room's roof, leaving the fresco exposed to the elements for 3 years. It remains amazingly powerful and emotional nonetheless. Only 25 people are allowed to view the fresco at one time, and they must pass through a series of devices that remove pollutants from clothing. Accordingly, lines are long and tickets usually sell out days in advance. *Piazza Santa Maria delle Grazie.* ☎ *02-89421146. Admission*

Lake Como & Bellagio

The hype is true and the cameras don't lie: Lake Como is drop-dead gorgeous. Imposing mountains—the foothills of the Alps—cascade down to the lakeshore, where palm trees flourish on waterfront promenades. All along the lake—but especially on the western shore of the Como branch—are private villas so precious and dreamy that they seem to come out of a model train set.

High season on the lake runs June to September, when the seaside villages are booked to capacity, and boats filled with holiday-makers zip up and down the lake, hoping to catch sight of George Clooney. The vast lake, whose three slender basins meet in **Bellagio** ★★★, is almost melancholy the rest of the year, but the jaw-dropping beauty is always there. Bellagio is lovely but it's an older demographic—that is, you won't be partying much—and most hotels are expensive. For a more affordable Lake Como experience, the towns on the western shore, from **Tremezzo** to **Menaggio,** have some budget-friendly hotels, but the view ain't as good as it is from Bellagio. The city of **Como** is also a good base.

Trains arrive daily at Como from Milan every hour. The trip takes 40 minutes, and a one-way fare is 5.85€. The main station, **Stazione San Giovanni** (Piazzale San Gottardo; ☎ 0147/888088), is at the end of Viale Gallio, a 15-minute walk from the center (Piazza Cavour). **Bus service** connecting the major towns along the lake is offered by **SPT,** located at Piazza Matteotti (☎ 031-2769911). A one-way fare from Como to Bellagio is 2.60€ (bus: 30). Travel time depends on the traffic.

Once at the foot of the lake, the best way to get around is by boat, but keep in mind that the last boats usually leave in the evening. One-way transit from

---

6.50€ plus a booking fee of 1€. Tues–Sun 8am–7:30pm (may close at 1:45pm in winter). Metro: Cadorna or Conciliazione.

The University Scene

Students from Milan have a greater sense of purpose than those coming from other, poorer Italian towns. You won't see hordes of moped-riding students with brightly colored Invicta backpacks lounging or chatting for

hours in the streets or in the neighborhood bars. Here, 20-something daytime culture is shaped by university classes and steady jobs. At night, kids hang out in the Ticinese, Navigli, or Garibaldi districts with friends. The **University of Milan** is one of the largest in Italy, with about 60,000 students (☎ 39/02503111; www.unimi.it). Student info can be found on the student affairs site (www.studentistatale.it/portale/Kids), but it's in Italian.

Playing Outside

Parks & Gardens

Milan has two major parks: **Parco Sempione** and the **Giardini Pubblici (Public Gardens).** The Public Gardens (Metro: Palestro) are often filled on the weekend with strollers, pony rides, and puppet shows. It is a beautiful park and an excellent place for a picnic, if slightly crowded. Parco Sempione (Metro:

Cordusio or Cadorna) on the other hand, is much larger, not quite as charismatic.

If you want to try an uninterrupted, full-side soccer game, head to **Parco Forlanini,** next to the Linate airport. There's not much in the way of amenities, but if you're looking for expanses of green on a hot, summer day, you'll find it here.

Como to Colico, at the northern end of the lake, takes 4 hours by **ferry** and 90 minutes by **hydrofoil** (see contact information below), and includes stops at each of the towns en route. Transit each way costs 8€ to 12€, depending on which boat you take. One-way transit between Como and Bellagio takes 2 hours by ferry and 45 minutes by hydrofoil, and costs 6.20€ to 9.20€ per person. There's no service from Como between October and Easter.

From Como, boats stop first at Bellagio: by ferry 2 hours; by hydrofoil 35 to 45 minutes. They continue on to Menaggio: by ferry another 15 minutes; by hydrofoil, another 5 minutes. About half the boats then stop in Varenna as well (plus there are about 2 dozen short-haul ferries each from Bellagio and Menaggio to Varenna): by ferry another 10 minutes; by hydrofoil, another 5 minutes. You can also get day passes good for just the central lake or for the whole lake.

Schedules vary with the season, but from Easter through September a ferry or hydrofoil makes the trip from Como to Bellagio and other towns along the lake at least hourly. Contact **Navigazione Lago di Como** (☎ 800/551801 or 031/579211, www.navigazionelaghi.it); the office is in Como on Lungo Iario Trieste.

The **Cavalcalario Club** (Loc. Gallasco 1, Bellagio; ☎ 031-984814; cell 339-538138; www.bellagio-mountains.it) runs mountain bike treks, horseback rides through panoramic mountain passes, kayak excursions around the lake, canyoning (a combination of hiking, swimming, rappelling, and, well, jumping up and down a river gorge), and tandem paragliding lasting anywhere from an hour or 2 to 3 days, starting around 35€.

Spectator Sports

Milan's two soccer teams, **Inter** (www. inter.it) and **A.C. Milan** (www.acmilan.com) share a stadium, in the San Siro neighborhood, known officially as Stadio Giuseppe Meazza, but usually referred to simply as San Siro. The stadium itself is worth a visit, as it was rebuilt for the 1990 World Cup and is a beautiful example of Milanese architecture.

○ For A.C. Milan home games, go to **Milan Point** (Via San Gottardo 2, entrance in piazza XXIV Maggio; ☎ 02-89422711;

Metro: Porta Genova; tram: 29). It's open 10am to 7:30pm Monday through Saturday. Bring cash because credit cards are not accepted.

○ For Inter home games, go to **Ticket One** inside the Spazio Oberdan complex (Viale Vittorio Veneto 2; ☎ 02-2953 6577; www.ticketone.it; Metro: Porta Venezia). It's open from 10am to 10pm Tuesday through Sunday. You can use a credit card if you purchase your tickets online, but if you pay at the gate, you'll have to bring cash.

Shopping

People don't come to Milan to sightsee. They come to shop. The internationally renowned "Golden Triangle" of Via Manzoni, Via Montenapoleone, and Via della Spiga is the

place for those looking to pick up the top names at top prices.

The best time for the savvy shopper to visit Milan is for the **January sales** (mid-Jan

MILAN

Top Designer Fashions on the cheap

If you're not in the income bracket to shop at Prada or outfit yourself in Armani, you *can* purchase designer "seconds" or last season's fashions—all at heavily discounted prices.

The wares of designer hotshots are best showcased at **Il Salvagente** (Via Bronzetti 16; ☎ 02-76110328; Metro: San Babila), a legendary shop where you'll find people fighting each other for slashed prices on Alberta Ferretti, Marni, Armani, Prada, and others. At sales times (usually from early Jan into early Feb and once more in late June and July), prices are often cut by an astonishing 30% to 70%. Of course, you must shop wisely, as returns are forbidden. Expect some clothing to have been worn on the runways (now *that's* a talking point). Not all garments are in A-1 condition.

Another outlet, **Biffi** (Corso Genova 6; ☎ 02-8311601; Metro: San Ambrogio), is one of Milan's oldest and most trendsetting boutiques, with discounts galore. The fashion range is cutting edge and avant-garde.

MILAN

to Feb). Most shops open at 9am, unless they're very chic, and then they're not likely to open until 10:30am. They remain open, for the most part, until 1pm and they reopen between 3:30 and 7:30pm.

MTV Best Corso Buenos Aires has some more sensible yet unique options sandwiched between the big retailers like Benetton, Zara, and Stefanel. The same is true around the **Duomo** and **San Babila,** which also houses names like Guess, Diesel, H&M, and the Italian department store where Giorgio Armani started off his career as a store window designer, **La Rinascente** (Piazza del Duomo; ☎ 02-88521; Metro: Duomo), which bills itself as Italy's largest fashion department store. In addition to clothing, the basement carries a wide variety of giftware, including handwork from all regions of Italy. There's a ground-floor information desk, and on the seventh floor are a bank, a travel agency, a hairdresser, an Estée Lauder Skincare Center, a coffee bar, and the Brunch and Bistro restaurants.

For a funkier take-home get-up, check out the pink boas and flame-embroidered jeans on **MTV Best Via Torino** ★★. Even farther south from the Duomo, **Viale Papiniano** hosts a clothing market every Saturday, where you can dig through the piles of socks and underwear to get to some low-priced (as in: "they fell off a truck") gear by names like Versace and Dolce & Gabbana.

Moreover, Milan is the capital of design, as in kitchenware, lighting, and furniture. Art buffs will go gaga in Milan's hip home-gadget boutiques that make Ikea look like an antiques fair. The stores are found all over the city, but especially in the neighborhoods Porta Romana, Porta Ticinese, and Brera.

The Porta Ticinese area has probably the coolest stores, with stuff you can afford and aren't likely to find in the States. Most of the stores listed in the box above are found in that neighborhood, which is just south of the Duomo at the end of Via Torino.

Munich

Munich, for all intents and purposes, is like that girl next door in high school who was valedictorian, star tennis player, and of course, prom queen, although with one slight surprise: Underneath that picture-perfect, fairy-tale prom dress, tucked into her garter, is a flask. Munich earns its reputation as one of the drinking capitals of the world but, like that girl next door, it manages to retain its elegance. Much of Munich's low skyline—its enchanting city center—looks like it came straight out of a sweet Brothers Grimm story.

Museums here range from the artistically comprehensive (Alte, Neue, and Moderne Pinakotheks) to the downright kooky (ZAM's Easter bunny exhibit, for example). You can work off that impending beer belly by traipsing through miles of unique galleries and exhibits. If that's not enough, you can pretend to be a boisterous Bavarian ruler by visiting the pimped-out Residenz or nearby Neuschwanstein, an astonishing 19th-century white castle. It's this captivating city's offbeat museums, unique parks, and fairy-tale atmosphere that will leave visitors feeling most buzzed.

The Best of Munich

○ **The Best Cheap Sleep:** The only downside to **Wombat's Hostel** is that it has exploited the poor furry beast's name. Other than that, the hostel is *the* place to crash in Munich with tons of cool people, comfy beds, and clean bathrooms, all just 2 minutes away from Hauptbahnhof. Roll out of bed, shower, down a couple of aspirin for your hangover, and you'll still have time to catch that 8am train to Berlin. See p. 636.

○ **The Best Club for Your 100-Year-Old Grandma:** She'll be the life of the party in the easygoing disco at **Atomik Café,** where her old-school moves will floor dancers on the 1920s themed night. See p. 645.

○ **The Best Beer Hall:** It's touristy, loud, and full of patrons downing ridiculously large containers of beer. In other words, **Hofbräuhaus** is the ultimate beer hall in Munich. See p. 644.

○ **The Best Nightspot for Celebrity Hobnobbing:** Boogie down with Boris Becker! It doesn't matter if you don't know your forehand from a stagehand, **P1** is a super-glitzy club that draws the biggest German celebrities on a nightly basis. Don your froufrou gear and strut past the velvet rope for a fun and pricey evening. See p. 646.

○ **The Best Quirky Museum:** Where else can you admire chamber pots en masse than **ZAM?** If you think that gallery stinks, there are seven other unique exhibits, such as the bunny museum or the perfume container collection. Few places in the world can match the quirkiness of ZAM. See p. 650.

○ **The Best Museum For a Short Attention Span:** What was I talking about? Buttons, levers, lights, giant gears, and a full-size aircraft all help make **Deutsches Museum** a delight for children

and adults alike. Parents bring their kids here and college kids pretend to be high schoolers on a field trip, just to enjoy the gizmos and gadgets in this amusement park–cum–museum. See p. 648.

○ **The Best U-Bahn Line:** Get on the **U6** at the historic Sendlinger Tor on the south side of Altstadt and go one stop to Marienplatz. Once you've had enough of the Glockenspiel show and the tourist crowds there, catch the U-Bahn up to Odeonsplatz, where you'll get more culture than a month-old bottle of spoiled beer. Don't expect the three Pinakotheks to appear immediately as you exit the station—it's a short 5-minute walk from the Odeonsplatz stop. Once you've had your art fix, backtrack to the Odeonsplatz stop and continue north on the U6 until you reach the Universität stop. Here you can impress a college cutie with your new-found knowledge of Flemish art and invite her to coffee in one of the relaxing cafes in Münchner Freiheit. Riding high on caffeine, take the U6 one more time to get to the smoothly designed Frottmaning stop. There you can cap the day off by watching the Allianz Arena morph into a psychedelic porcelain stadium in the night sky.

Getting There & Getting Around

Getting into Town

BY AIR

The **Munich International Airport,** officially called the Franz-Joseph-Strauss International Airport (☎ **089/97-42-13-13;** www.munich-airport.de/EN), receives flights from many North American hubs as well as most major cities in Europe. It's located 29km (18 miles) northeast of the city.

Budget airlines like RyanAir (flies through Freidrichschafen, located a few kilometers from Munich) and easyJet enable travelers to scoot around western Europe for less than

30€ a flight, provided you reserve at least a month in advance. You might want to take advantage of the cheap air travel for international flights within Europe; otherwise, travel throughout Germany is best done on the railways.

S-Bahn (☎ **089/414-243-44**) trains connect the airport with the Hauptbahnhof (main railroad station) in downtown Munich. Departures are every 20 minutes for the 40-minute trip. The fare is 9€; Eurailpass holders ride free. A taxi into the center costs about 50€ to 60€. Airport buses, such as those operated by Lufthansa, also run between the airport and the center.

BY TRAIN

From its main rail station of **Hauptbahnhof,** you can easily reach almost any major European city: Prague to the east, Berlin and Paris to the north, and Florence and Rome to the south. It's a beautiful station: The unique GRUNDIG sign at the end of the tracks anchors the simple and functional modern-industrial look of the station, making it worth a photo or two before you board your train. There are also gads of facilities for any needs a traveler may have: a bank, hotel, restaurant, Internet cafe, tons of food vendors, amazingly clean bathroom facilities (bring some euro change for access), car parking, and access to both the U-Bahn and S-Bahn.

From Berlin (about 7 hr.) and Frankfurt (4 hr.) alone, there are more than 20 daily trains going to and from Hauptbahnhof. Overnight trains also arrive and depart from Florence, Bologna, and Prague. Chances are you won't be traveling enough to take advantage of the BahnCard, a discounted pass that will give riders more miles on the track. Students can get a reasonable discount on this card, but make sure you'll use it before you purchase one. Check www.bahn.de for schedules and ticket prices or call ☎ **0800/150-7090** for information.

Getting Around

BY BUS

For small jaunts in Bavaria, you can depend on a regular four-wheeled coach to get you where you want to go. The bus is a viable option for destinations within a 50km (31-mile) radius, but if you travel any farther, you'll be awfully uncomfortable as the bus navigates the winding roads that thread through the Bavarian forest. Couple that with the high-speed Autobahn and anyone not accustomed to the faster paced highways might be on edge for most of their journey.

For peace of mind and a fatter wallet, stick to trains for small trips and RyanAir or EasyJet for international travel.

Hauptbahnhof, in addition to being the rail station, is where most buses pick up their passengers. For other departures and arrivals, head to the nearby Deutsche Touring Terminal (Arnulfstrasse 3, a 5-min. walk from Hauptbahnhof). For more information about bus schedules and fares, call **Deutsche Touring GmbH** (☎ **089/323-040**).

BY CAR

Munich's clean, smooth asphalt roads are just begging you to test out some marvels of German automotive engineering, but you're better off admiring locals whizzing by in Beemers than renting one yourself. Rental-car rates are extremely expensive and better deals can be found outside of Germany. Parking fees aren't much better; you can expect to pay roughly 30€ per night in one of the city's parking lots. If you decide to swallow the ludicrous rates and rent a car, use caution when weaving through the streets. Drivers here are rather aggressive (think: urban Autobahn). Stay on your toes and don't be bashful about using those blinkers and horns.

BY U-BAHN & S-BAHN

Scooting around Munich via public transport is a cinch. Rather than getting ripped off by a cabbie, opt for one of several forms of cheap, public transportation: U-Bahn, S-Bahn, bus, or tram. More often than not, you'll find yourself using the U-Bahn or S-Bahn exclusively. The lines are reasonably simple, and the stops usually occur in busy, frequently visited areas. The U-Bahn covers everything within the city limits with its old-fashioned trains, while the more modern cars of the S-Bahn extend their trips to the surrounding neighborhoods of Munich.

MUNICH

Purchasing a ticket involves determining your destination's zone. From the city center to the farthest reaches of the S-Bahn, there are four zones (only one stop, Munich International Airport, actually reaches the fourth zone). If you only travel within one zone, a single-ride ticket will cost 2.20€.

A great option for travelers staying in Munich for 3 days or longer is the **Munich Welcome Card.** Available at the airport, the tourist offices in Marienplatz and Hauptbahnhof, and in hotels, the card entitles you to limitless travel on any form of public transportation in Munich. Flash the card in certain museums and attractions and you'll receive a discount on admission fees. See p. 649 for more info. Another option for multiple U-Bahn or S-Bahn trips is the **streifenkarte (strip ticket).** These come with 10 total strips and cost 10€. To travel through one zone, you'll have to burn two strips. Two zones are four strips, three zones are six strips, and the full four zones will take eight strips off your ticket. If you only plan on going as far as two stops on the U-Bahn or S-Bahn (or four stops on the tram or bus), it's considered a "short trip" and only one strip needs to be validated. As long as you're traveling in one constant direction, you'll be able to use the validated strips even if you interrupt your trip by getting off at a particular stop (1 hr. for a short trip, 3 hr. for one zone, and 4 hr. for two zones or more). If you cross through the same zone twice in one trip, you'll have to pay for that zone twice.

Note: Eurail passes are valid for travel on the state-run S-Bahn.

ON FOOT

While much of Aldstadt is manageable by foot, it's difficult to cover all of Munich's attractions without using the U-Bahn or S-Bahn. For instance, though it's not impossible to walk from Hauptbahnhof to the Englischer Gartens, it'll take an inordinate amount of time. With that in mind, certain streets and areas like Leopoldstrasse, Aldstadt, and aximillianstrasse are best explored via leisurely strolls. Just use caution when crossing the streets. It might be second nature to scoff at crosswalks and to jaywalk, but the police don't take such infractions lightly. You'll notice that nearly every pedestrian patiently waits for the light on the crosswalk to change. Avoid the crosswalks or jump the gun on the light and the police will tag you with a sizeable fine.

Munich Basics

Orientation: Munich Neighborhoods

Here are a few places that you'll frequently visit during your trip to Munich:

ALDSTADT This is the "old city" where Munich is at its most quaint. It's anchored by the historic plaza Marienplatz, where you'll be treated to an entire Glockenspiel performance at 11am and noon, with an encore at 5pm. The rest of present-day Munich grew from the medieval center, but many of the landmarks still exist in Aldstadt, such as the Rathaus (town hall) in the aforementioned Marienplatz and the palatial Residenz. It's also one of the minihubs for the U-Bahn where connections to two of the north-south lines are made.

MAXIMILLIANSTRASSE Bring on the bling! Every high-class store imaginable has a branch on this ultrachic boulevard. While you might not be able to afford the hotels or restaurants here, it's worth checking out. Your ears will be inundated with the sound of cash registers ringing up purchases for wealthy clientele and the haughty laughs of diners enjoying their caviar and Cristal.

OLYMPIAPARK West of Schwabing sits the old grounds of the 1972 Olympics. You

Talk of the Town

Four ways to start a conversation with a local

1. **How about raising a glass to Munich?** Hit up any beer hall, or bar for that matter, turn to your buzzed neighbor and let out a hearty "Prost!" It's the German equivalent of "Cheers!" and it'll set off a chain reaction of clinking glasses and smiles. It bears repeating that beer is an essential part of life in Munich.

2. **Dude, can I, like, borrow your board?** The Englischer Gartens (Munich's huge public park) has plenty of schmoozing opportunities, but unless you want to flirt with a topless 80-year-old in the nude section of the beach, you're better off settling near the "endless wave." There you'll find a younger, much better-looking crowd, and you can laugh at poor, inexperienced surfers trying to tackle the small artificial wave. Think you have the chops to tame the pipe? Some surfers and body boarders are more than willing to inflate their self-confidence by seeing someone crash and burn—that someone being you.

3. **So, what exactly is that puppet doing?** Most people flock to Marienplatz to stare at the Glockenspiel not knowing what the copper figures are doing. Before you make your way to the crowded square, arm yourself with a good dose of Glockenspiel history.

4. **Who's got the keys to my bimma?** Chances are they won't get the '90's pop reference, but given the fact that the BMW museum and the Autobahn are in the immediate vicinity, you might be able to strike up a conversation about their wonderful example of German engineering.

probably weren't even born back then, but you might have heard of the terrorist attack that took place there more than 30 years ago. Eleven Israeli athletes ended up dead, and it took Munich quite a while to recover from the incident. Fast-forward to today and Olympiapark is now the site of outdoor concerts. The newly constructed Allianz Arena also now welcomes hundreds of thousands of soccer fans.

SCHWABING   Follow Leopoldstrasse north through this area and you'll get a great feel for what makes Schwabing a trendy and laid-back neighborhood. The main avenue is lined with chill cafes and cool boutiques. The nearby university ensures there's no shortage of youthful energy, and the presence of the enormous Englischer Garten gives the wired masses a place to burn that joie de vivre.

Tourist Offices

Even the most clueless of visitors can find help in one of two conveniently placed tourist offices. The first one you'll run into is located around the block from Hauptbahnhof on Bahnhofplatz 2 (☎ 089/2-33-03-00; www.muenchen-tourist.de; Mon–Sat 9am–8pm), whereas the other is smack dab in the middle of Marienplatz in Neuen Rathaus (Mon–Fri 10am–8pm). In either office, you can stock up on brochures, get your bearings with a city map, and buy U-Bahn tickets or passes.

Recommended Websites

○ **www.muenchen-tourist.de/englisch/ index_e.htm**: Munich's official tourism site.

○ **www.munich-airport.de/EN**: Airport information.

○ **www.mvv-muenchen.de**: Public transportation information.

○ **www.oktoberfest.de/en/index.php**: Everything you need to know about Oktoberfest.

Recommended Books, Movies & Music

Bertolt Brecht was born in Bavaria and spent many of his early years in Munich. The playwright was best known for his creations on stage, but his poetry is among the greatest ever written by any German. If you want to pull a Cyrano on a college cutie in Café AnDerUni, scan his verses in *Bertolt Brecht: Poems 1913–1956* on your flight or train ride. Feeling like delving even further into the German experience? Try out any of the works by Thomas Mann (1875–1955). A long-term Munich resident, Mann is today heralded as one of Germany's most celebrated writers. *Death in Venice* (1925) and *The Magic Mountain* (1927) are two of his most famous works.

For a searing take on the 1972 Munich Olympics terrorist kidnappings and their aftermath, rent Steven Spielberg's *Munich* (2005).

While Munich is known for churning out classical musicians like Richard Strauss, there is one band in particular that belts out pretty damn good rock. Notwist, originally a metal/punk band, formed in Munich in the late '80s and spent a good chunk of their infancy as a band there. As the '90s came and went, Notwist slowly became a respected indie group. Their album *Neon Golden* shows that Munich can produce rockers that are almost as talented as the classical legends that also called the city home.

Culture Tips 101

Thankfully, the Germanic language spawned the dialect that we now call American English so most Münchners understand our bastardization of the Queen's English. While basic phrases are recognizable, certain concepts are not. So ask for help from storeowners or flirt with the cutie in the Englischer Garten without using unnecessary exaggerations or clichés. Be direct and clear and you'll be rewarded with smile or, if you're truly a smooth operator, a beer garden date. Fashion decisions in Munich are equally simple. Locals dress rather conservatively and even the alternative youth don't stray far from conformity. Save the studded leather vest for Berlin and opt for a slightly preppy look instead.

The legal minimum drinking age in Munich is 18, or 16 if you're accompanied by the 'rents. Some places that score big with teeny-boppers actually do check IDs, so bring your passport with you if your boyish/girlish charms leave any doubt that you're of age. Drinking is allowed anywhere in the city: No one will bother you if you grab a seat on the grass and crack open a cold one, but it's not something regularly done here. Marijuana and hash are legal—sort of. It's legal to carry around a small amount (just enough for personal consumption), but it's illegal to sell it on the street. Münchners tend to spark up *die tuete* (the joint) outdoors, in the fresh air of parks, or in alleys next to bars. Lighting a fat doobie after a nice meal at a restaurant is not very cool at all.

Munich Nuts & Bolts

Cellphone Providers & Service Centers   There's one company whose logo you'll be awfully familiar with by the time you leave the city: **T-Mobile.** The communications giant not only sponsors the biggest sports team in the region (their name is emblazoned on the jerseys of FC Bayern München), but it also has quite a stranglehold on the wireless communications market in Germany. You'll have no trouble finding a T-Mobile store anywhere in the city center, but visit www.t-mobile-international.com if you want info on specific locations.

Currency Munich is an extremely expensive city and banks take advantage of the need for instant cash by conveniently throwing countless ATMs in tourist-laden areas. You'll have no problem finding a **Deutsche Bank** anywhere in Munich. The financial powerhouse has branches placed almost a bratwurst's throw from each other. If you're fresh off your flight and have a wad of cash to exchange, you can get some euros at Hauptbahnhof train station (the exchange windows are open daily 6am–11:30pm).

Embassies All major embassies are unfortunately located in Berlin. Check the Berlin chapter for detailed info, but if you somehow lose your passport or run into other problems, call the **U.S. consulate** in Munich at Koningstrasse 5 (☎ 089/28-880), or the **U.K. consulate** at Burkleinstrasse 10 (☎ 089/21-10-90).

Emergencies If you're in need of an ambulance, dial ☎ 112. If the ambulance accidentally catches fire, call the same number (☎ 112) for the fire department. If someone stole your cellphone while you were calling the fire department, report them and any other crime to the police at ☎ 110. If all three occur, call me for a hug; you've had a rough day.

If your medical situation doesn't necessitate an emergency visit, but still needs some attention, you can find some relief at **Notfallpraxis** (Elisenstrasse 3; ☎ 089/551-771). They'll be able to help you with any dental or medical problems you may have any day of the week (Mon–Tues and Thurs 7–11pm; Wed and Fri 2–11pm; Sat–Sun 8am–11pm).

Internet/Wireless Hot Spots Catch up on e-mails or check out online train schedules in the 24-hour **Munich Internet Service Center** (Tal 31; ☎ 089/207-027-37; www.misc24.de; 2€ for 1 hr.). In addition to the 20-plus PCs, there's a bicycle rental desk and a separate smoking room with 10 additional terminals. If you're about to board your train and somehow need to send an important e-mail before you leave, look for the **Times Square Bistro** (Bayerstrasse 10a, adjacent to Hauptbahnhof; ☎ 089/51-262-600) on the southeast end of Hauptbahnhof. It's part restaurant, part bar, part Internet cafe, and a 100% rip-off. A few minutes will cost you a ludicrous .50€ for 5 minutes, so you're better off heading to MISC for your computing needs.

Laundromats Most lederhosen is dry-clean only, so drop off your leather trousers and the rest of your Oktoberfest gear to get them fresh and spiffy at **SB Wasch Center** (Lindworm 124; ☎ 089/767-586-21).

Luggage Storage For temporary luggage storage, Hauptbahnhof train station is replete with lockers of various sizes. Drop off your bags here and, if you've just arrived, scout out some hotels in the area without the added weight. Otherwise, if you're on your way out, run back to Hofbräuhaus for one last liter.

Post Offices The main post office is across from the Hauptbahnhof in Bahnhofplatz (☎ 089/599-0870; Mon–Fri 7am–8pm, Sat 9am–4pm, Sun 10am–3pm).

MUNICH

Restrooms What goes in, must go out. Given that Munich takes in more beer than most cities, the massive amounts of liquid have to end up somewhere. There are public restrooms scattered around the city, mainly in U-Bahn/S-Bahn stations and in Hauptbahnhof, but you'll have to bring some change to use their facilities. These restrooms are run by a chain called "McClean" (www.mcclean-group.com). Most are equipped with toilets and urinals, but some have showers where travelers can wash up in relatively sanitary conditions. The use of a toilet costs 1.10€, urinal usage is .60€, and showers will set you back a cool 7€.

Safety Luckily, most of Munich's streets are relatively safe, even at night. You can walk home after a long night of partying without worrying about getting mugged, but that doesn't mean you should let your guard down. This applies in the daytime because pickpockets target tourist areas. Keep your belongings close to you in the congested Marienplatz. If you decide to spend some time in Olympiapark or the Englischer Garten, keep an eye on your possessions. Take extra care if you decide to join the saggy masses in some nude sunbathing: It's a long walk to the closest clothing store.

Tipping See p. 152 in the Berlin chapter for tipping info.

Youth Information A Youth Info Service Office is at Jugend Information Zentrum München (Paul-Heysestrasse 22; ☎ **089/51-41-06-60;** www.jiz-muenchen.de).

Sleeping

For most of the year, finding a bed is a painless affair. During Oktoberfest, you'll have to book a room almost a year in advance. Reservation pains aside, rooms for the most part are simple and functional, and of typical German interior design. Hotels near Schwabing, Aldstadt, and Hauptbahnhof are among the priciest, but nothing compares to the luxury accommodations found on Maximillianstrasse.

Hostels

🅃🅥 Best → Wombat's Hostel ★★
Anyone under 30 should stay at Wombat's, even if they can afford the priciest hotel in the city. The owners have tried their damnedest to make this one of the best hostels in the world, and for the most part, they've succeeded. To start off, the staff members are wonderfully chill and laid-back. Freebies, like a drink coupon for the hostel's bar (the womBar; daily 6pm–2am), certainly help. Another plus is that the crowd is young and vibrant, not old and creepy. When the masses come home from Atomic Café or Nachtwerk, you're sure to find a few unconscious folks who couldn't quite make it to their rooms crashing on one of the couches in the pimped-out courtyard.

Speaking of the rooms, each is stocked with clean, comfortable, wooden Ikea furnishings. Luckily, the bunk beds are strong, and your Rubenesque roommate's climb to the top bunk won't disturb your sleep. Finally, the vending machines in the reception will have everything that you need to finish your night: Wombat T-shirts, towels, toothpaste/toothbrushes, and Wombat condoms. To top it all off, the hostel is a 5-minute walk to Hauptbahnhof train station. Do your social life and wallet a favor and book your bed here ASAP. *Senefelderstrasse 1.* ☎ *089/59-98-9180. www.wombats.at. 16€–25€ single bed. Breakfast 4€. U-Bahn: Hauptbahnhof. Amenities: Bar; breakfast room; Internet (20 min. for 1€); laundry; shared bathrooms.*

MUNICH

Cheap

➜**Hotel Alcron** You'd never guess from the unassuming and tiny entrance that a hotel exists on Ledererstrasse. Richard, the owner, doesn't seem worried about the lack of advertising because the interior should be enough to motivate loyal guests to book a room on their next visit to Munich. Ascend the few floors by a wide, spiral, wooden staircase. It gives the Alcron a creaky, antique authenticity. Most rooms continue the theme with hefty, dark-wood bed frames and period furniture. Only doubles feature the beautiful furnishings now, but the single rooms should be renovated soon. *Ledererstrasse 13.* ☎ *089/22-835-11. www.hotel-alcron.de. 60€–70€ single, 80€–95€ double, 95€–105€ triple. Rates include breakfast. U-Bahn: Sendlinger-Tor. Amenities: Breakfast room; TV (in common room). In room: TV.*

➜**Hotel Am Markt** If there's any hotel in Munich that needs an extreme makeover, the Hotel Am Markt is the prime candidate. The dark-wood interior probably hasn't been renovated since the 1950s. The bare furnishings and walls scream *Leave It to Beaver* and the lampshades are aged and burnt to the point of dulling the light. Once they get a new coat of paint and a few new chairs, though, the Am Markt can be great place to crash. It's literally within the confines of the Viktualienmarkt and is neighbor to a couple of popular watering holes. *Heiliggeiststrasse 6.* ☎ *089/22-50-14. www.hotelinmunich.de. 38€ single with shared bathroom, 66€ with private bathroom; 66€–68€ double with shared bathroom, 87€–92€ with private bathroom; 99€ triple with shared bathroom, 123€ with private bathroom. U-Bahn: Marienplatz. Amenities: Lounge. In room: TV.*

➜**Hotel Atlanta** ★ The Atlanta is a steal. Rooms are rather spacious, beds have super-soft mattresses, and the wood furniture, offset by matching hardwood floors and sizeable windows, makes for a bright and relaxing environment. Also appealing are the numerous stores lining the block, including everything from affordable German clothing chains to small bookstores to little souvenir shops. The only downside to Hotel Atlanta is that while all rooms have showers, some don't offer a toilet. Instead, a communal water-closet is placed on each floor for those lacking the john. *Sendlingerstrasse 58.* ☎ *089/26-36-05. www.hotel-atlanta.de. 30€–80€ single with shared bathroom, 50€–100€ with private bathroom; 70€–120€ double with shared bathroom, 75€–125€ with private bathroom. Rates include breakfast. U-Bahn: Marienplatz. Amenities: Breakfast room; shared bathroom in some rooms. In room: TV/radio.*

➜**Hotel Europaischer Hof** The overnight train to Munich can leave your sleeping patterns all out of whack. Luckily, you can stumble out of Hauptbahnhof, onto Bayerstrasse, and into this nearby hotel. The setup is a little spartan, but the mattresses are plush enough to right your circadian rhythms. As with many budget hotels in Germany, there's no air-conditioning. Here, though, if the nights somehow reach 32° C (90° F; they rarely do) you can rent an oscillating fan from the front desk for 1.50€ a day. *Bayerstrasse 31.* ☎ *089/55-15-10. www.heh.de. 70€–120€ single, 90€–150€ double. U-Bahn: Hauptbahnhof. Amenities: Internet; (13€ per day). In room: TV, safe.*

➜**Hotel Jedermann** ★★ Don't be deceived by the map. It looks like Hotel Jedermann is a couple of blocks away from Hauptbahnhof, but it's actually a little farther. The "trek" is worth it, though. I arrived here after a grueling overnight train ride from Bologna, and the staff members quickly set me up with a room to grab a hot shower, and they then led me to their breakfast room. The accommodations in the Jedermann might be no-frills and simple, but the breakfast more than makes up for it. The various cereals, yogurts, meats, cheeses, juices, and fruits are a perfect cure to a post-Oktoberfest hangover (the main area of the

Munich

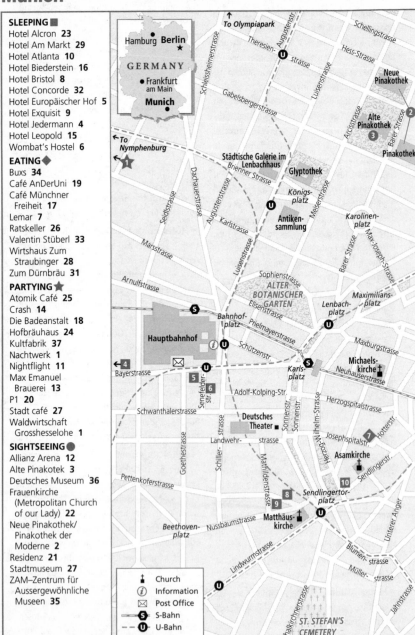

SLEEPING ■
Hotel Alcron **23**
Hotel Am Markt **29**
Hotel Atlanta **10**
Hotel Biederstein **16**
Hotel Bristol **8**
Hotel Concorde **32**
Hotel Europäischer Hof **5**
Hotel Exquisit **9**
Hotel Jedermann **4**
Hotel Leopold **15**
Wombat's Hostel **6**

EATING ◆
Buxs **34**
Café AnDerUni **19**
Café Münchner
  Freiheit **17**
Lemar **7**
Ratskeller **26**
Valentin Stüberl **33**
Wirtshaus Zum
  Straubinger **28**
Zum Dürnbräu **31**

PARTYING ★
Atomik Café **25**
Crash **14**
Die Badeanstalt **18**
Hofbräuhaus **24**
Kultfabrik **37**
Nachtwerk **1**
Nightflight **11**
Max Emanuel
  Brauerei **13**
P1 **20**
Stadt café **27**
Waldwirtschaft
  Grosshesselohe **1**

SIGHTSEEING ●
Allianz Arena **12**
Alte Pinakotek **3**
Deutsches Museum **36**
Frauenkirche
  (Metropolitan Church
  of our Lady) **22**
Neue Pinakothek/
  Pinakothek der
  Moderne **2**
Residenz **21**
Stadtmuseum **27**
ZAM–Zentrum für
  Aussergewöhnliche
  Museen **35**

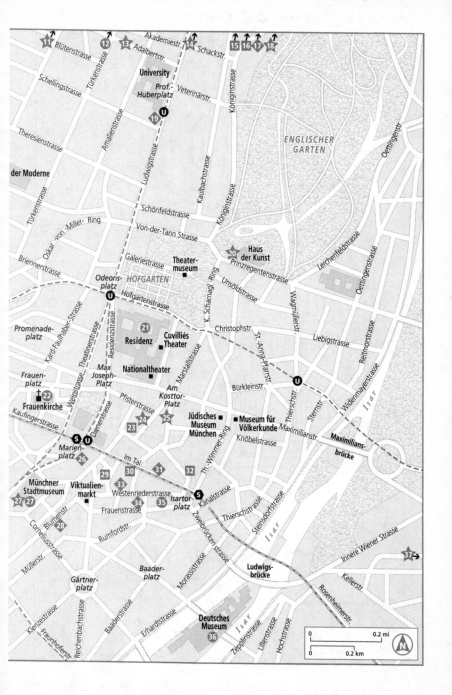

Munich U-Bahn & S-Bahn

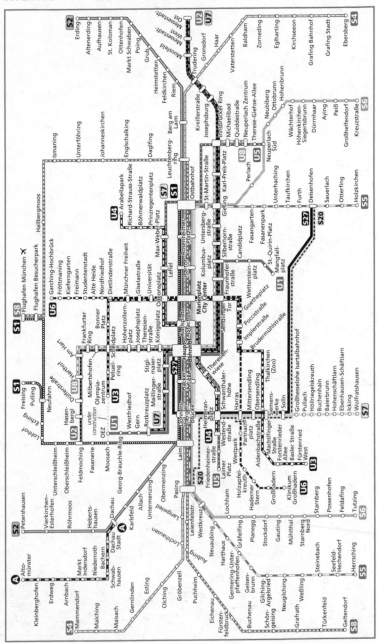

fall festival actually takes place a few blocks from the Jedermann). *Bayerstrasse 95.* ☎ *089/54-32-40. www.hotel-jedermann.de. 49€–99€ single with private bathroom, 34€–49€ with shared bathroom, 67€–149€ double with private bathroom, 57€–86€ with private shower/shared bathroom, 49€–74€ with shared bathroom. Rates include breakfast. U-Bahn: Hauptbahnhof. Amenities: Bar; Internet. In room: A/C, TV, hair dryer, safe.*

Doable

→**Hotel Biederstein** ★ During Oktoberfest, beer-chugging fiends can get rather rowdy. To escape the raucous scene in central Munich, you can find some peace west of the Englischer Garten. Hotel Biederstein is a popular place for couples or solo travelers looking for a quiet night's sleep. It's on a residential, tree-lined street, and you'll have to walk a few minutes to reach the closest U-Bahn station. *Keferstrasse 18.* ☎ *089/389-997-0. www.hotelbiederstein.de. 89€–104€ single, 102€–158€ double, 157€–190€ apt. Breakfast 9€ per person. U-Bahn: Münchner Freiheit. Amenities: Breakfast room. In room: TV, balcony, minibar.*

→**Hotel Bristol** Although the rooms are ultrasimple and small, you'll have no trouble falling asleep in Hotel Bristol. The rates are tough to beat in the pricey region of central Munich and each guest has access to their own balcony, a nice perk for someone expecting barebones accommodations. There's a free Internet point as well, but in proportion to the rooms it's in a small phone-booth like alcove. Even though there's nothing spectacular about the Bristol, they do just enough to make it worth the 100€ to spend a night there. *Pettenkoferstrasse 2.* ☎ *089/599-93-902. www.bristol-muc.com. 75€–100€ single, 85€–125€ double. Rates include breakfast. U-Bahn: Sendlinger. Amenities: Breakfast room. In room: TV, balcony, Internet, minibar.*

→**Hotel Concorde** I'm assuming the management of the Concorde is in a strange state of denial. It's advertised everywhere else as a three-star hotel (and rightly so) but the metal sign on the front still has four of those suckers welded to its name. The interior is a throwback to the '80s with aqua and white splashed gratuitously on the walls of the tiny guest rooms. The chrome-tubing furniture and particle-board bed frames (with slightly uncomfortable mattresses) also add to the *Miami Vice* feel of the hotel. Fortunately, the staff members are incredibly friendly, and they take extra steps to make you happy. *Herrnstrasse 38–40.* ☎ *089/22-45-15. www.goldentulip.de/ticoncorde. 98€ single, 128€ double, 159€ triple, 154€ suite. U-Bahn: Marienplatz. S-Bahn: Isartor. Amenities: Laundry service; safe. In room: TV, hair dryer, Internet, minibar.*

→**Hotel Leopold** ★ Hidden behind a grotesque structure from the '80s is a small cottage-like building housing Hotel Leopold's reception. It's situated quite a distance up Leopoldstrasse, but it's worth the hike or U-Bahn ride. Jokey staff members make the stay here feel like a weekend with your favorite aunts and uncles. Also, facilities will help you forget that you're 20 minutes from downtown Munich: sauna, fitness room, and a gorgeous courtyard. *Leopoldstrasse 119.* ☎ *089/36-70-61. 99€–128€ double, 128€–159€ suite. Rates include breakfast. U-Bahn: Münchner Freiheit. Amenities: Breakfast room; fitness room; sauna (8€ per use). In room: TV, hair dryer, minibar.*

Splurge

→**Hotel Exquisit** ★★ Walk down Pettenkoferstrasse and it'll be hard to miss the pink-and-maroon building on the right. The gigantic Pop-Tart is actually Hotel Exquisit. Compared to other nearby hotels, the setup of Exquisit is noticeably more sophisticated. If you can shell out a few extra euros, you'll find that the double rooms are more spacious and feature a balcony facing the small attractive garden in the center of the hotel. For those looking to get a little toasted, there's a solarium and sauna on the premises. Thankfully, there are working timers in the tanning beds so you don't end up looking like the exterior of Exquisit. *Pettenkoferstrasse 3. ☎ 089/55-199-00. www.* *hotel-exquisit.com. 125€–195€ single, 160€– 235€ double, 215€–295€ suite. Rates include breakfast. U-Bahn: Sendlinger Tor. Amenities: Breakfast room; bar; laundry service; sauna; solarium. In room: TV, Internet, hair dryer, minibar, safe.*

Eating

Welcome to the land of sausages, sauerkraut, schnitzel, and roast pork. These things can get awfully expensive pretty quickly, so get ready for some meals at the city's ubiquitous *Döner kebab* stands if you want to save cash. A *Döner kebab* is turkey or lamb meat shaved off a rotating spit and shoved into a pita with lettuce, tomato, and onion—it's perfect for when you've worked up a mean appetite after a long night of clubbing and drinking. Vendors are found every couple of blocks and a serving is rarely more than 3€. I just wish they were as easy on the stomach as they are on the wallet. (After eating one, make sure you take the bottom bunk in the hostel for your roommate's sake).

Hot Spots

→ **Café Münchner Freiheit** ★ CAFE During the summer months, a little part of Miami can be found in the flamingo pink confines of Café Münchner Freiheit. You can have a satisfying lunch inside, but you're better off enjoying it alfresco if the sun is out. The large outdoor seating area is usually packed with locals downing mugs of coffee and fluffy pastries, but the waitstaff can bring you something more substantial if you've skipped breakfast. *Münchner Freiheit 20. ☎ 089/22-00-79-90. www.muenchner-freiheit.de. 2€– 5€ for snacks. Daily 6:30am–10pm. U-Bahn: Münchner Freiheit.*

→ **Ratskeller** BAVARIAN Tourists can work up a mean appetite after they exhaust their cameras on Marienplatz. Most of them usually end up in the huge tourist draw of the Ratskeller. The restaurant has plenty of intimate booths where you can cozy up with a significant other or with a significant liter of beer. Either way, their menus feature the best of Bavarian cuisine: sausage, schnitzel, and more sausage. Thankfully, a cartoony icon on the menu accompanies the dish names to help you decipher which animal you'll be digesting. Oddly enough, the poor pig icon looks a little scared; the pork schnitzel must be a crowd favorite. *Marienplatz 8. ☎ 089/21-99-89-0. Main course 11€–20€. Daily 10am–midnight. U-Bahn/ S-Bahn: Marienplatz.*

Cheap

→ **Buxs** VEGETARIAN All the sausage and wieners in Munich can bring the wurst out of anyone. (In my case, that means my sense of humor.) But sauerkraut and sausages can do a number on a foreign stomach, and you'll need to take a break once in a while. Viktualienmarkt, home to Buxs, will have everything you need to purge all that processed meat from your system. The fringes of the famous market are lined with several vegetarian restaurants in addition to Buxs. You can pick cafeteria-style (pay by the gram) and choose from the various salads, quiches, and soups. Once you've loaded your tray, pay the cashier at the end and enjoy your roughage. *Frauenstrasse 9. ☎ 089/ 29-19-55-0. Main course 2€ per 100 grams. Mon–Fri 11am–6:45pm. Sat 11am–3pm. U-Bahn: Marienplatz.*

Doable

→ **Lemar** AFGHANI If you're in an exotic mood (and don't consider schnitzel with a sprig of parsley exotic), you'll be happy to know that a place like Lemar exists in Munich. A relatively young restaurant, Lemar is decked out with Eastern influenced couches and low tables rather than traditional decor. Foodwise, the Sabsi Tschalau and its fresh spinach will have you pining for seconds. *Brünnstrasse 4.* ☎ *089/269-49-454. Main courses 9€–13€. Mon–Sun 6pm–1am. U-Bahn: Sendlinger Tor.*

→**Valentin Stüberl** GERMAN The outdoor dining area of Valentin Stüberl almost overlaps with the dining areas of neighboring restaurants, so eating outside can get a little noisy. You can choose to sit inside, but every inch of the walls are covered with antler horns and other hunted beasts. Despite the very intimidating and very dead animals watching you while you eat, you'll still enjoy their traditional Wiener schnitzel (a delightful veal schnitzel with pan-fried potatoes and salad). *Dreifaltigkeitsplatz 2.* ☎ *089/22-69-50. www.valentinstueberl.de. Main courses 9.50€–16€. Mon–Sat 10am–11pm. U-Bahn: Marienplatz. S-Bahn: Isartor.*

→**Wirtshaus Zum Straubinger** ★ BAVARIAN The tables here are constantly packed and always shared, so before you take advantage of the beer garden, plop down next to your new Bavarian buddy and get something substantial to sop up the alcohol. The waiters will suggest the *lauwarmer schweinsbraten mit frischern meerrettich, bauernbrot, kresse und meersalz.* The name and the dish itself is a mouthful: It's a lukewarm German roast pork served with a creamy sauce, bread, and sprouts. *Blumenstrasse 5.* ☎ *089/232-3830. www.zumstraubinger.de.*

Main courses 7€–15€. Daily 10am–1am. U-Bahn: Marienplatz.

Splurge

→**Zum Dürnbräu** ★★ BAVARIAN Zum Dürnbräu isn't a bad place to have your first dining experience in Munich, though it's on the pricey side. Lederhosen-clad waiters and waitresses will sit you down at one of the long communal wooden tables and will be happy to explain the dishes on their menu. Give them a breather and go straight for the *schweine-filet vom grill* (grilled pork filet with mushrooms), or if you're in a particularly sausagey mood, give the *wurstl brotzeit* a try. *Dürnbräu 2.* ☎ *089/222-195. Main courses 9€–24€. Daily 9am–11:30pm. U-Bahn: Marienplatz.*

Cafes

→**Café AnDerUni** College classes can get awfully stressful, and university students in Munich have a few places where they can kick back and unwind between mind-numbing lectures. Café AnDerUni is one of their favorite haunts. The fare is tasty sandwiches, espressos, and beer and cocktails for bleary-eyed crammers. When the weather is pleasant, the prime seats are near the entrance, inside a glass greenhouse-like enclosure. Chilly? Head indoors, grab a seat in one of the rickety bar chairs, and catch a Bayern München match or an F1 race with their national racing hero, Mr. Schumacher, on the big screen. *Ludwigstrasse 24.* ☎ *089/289-866-00. www.cadu.de. Snacks and sandwiches 2€–10€. Daily 8am–1am. U-Bahn: Universität.*

Partying

Munich might be considered Berlin's little brother when it comes to bars and clubs, but this sibling can hold its own. The city proudly inhales more beer per capita than any city in the world (roughly 280 liters each year), so it's not surprising that there are loads of

kooky bars and watering holes. To find out what's going on and when, check out the stores on Leopoldstrasse (Schwabing). The storeowners and clerks within the boutiques are great sources on what's hot at night. You'll also find a ton of flyers and cards to clubs that, if you bring them along, will give you either a discount or free admission.

Once you've decided where to go, you'll be left with two fashion options: Dress to impress or dress like a mess. For the latter, you don't want to wear your tattered duds, but rather feel free to wear anything from jeans and a T-shirt to a silk Italian shirt and wool pants. Beer halls and most bars don't care what you're wearing. On the other extreme, glitzy clubs and high-class bars require the finest in contemporary couture. You'll usually know these places simply by their obnoxious or ridiculous names, but if you're unsure, ask the front desk of your hotel. If they don't recommend wearing a Zegna suit, you're safe to wear whatever you wish.

Expect to pay anywhere from 4€ in a low-key club to upwards of 10€ to 15€ in a place like Nachtwerk. It's only pricey considering the fact that many of the clubs close between 2 and 3am. Yet if you've downed some Red Bull, and you're itching to dance the morning away, you're not without options. While the majority of places close relatively early, there are a couple of places sprinkled around town where the music stops just in time for brunch.

Bars & Lounges

➔ **Crash** Beer by the liter not your thing? Crash serves up more reasonably sized beers to a decent crowd of students, old hippies, and has-been rock groupies. The music here is meat-and-potatoes rock 'n' roll, a true rarity in a city ruled by the bassy boom-boom-chicka of Euro-techno. *Ainmillerstrasse 10.* ☎ *089/39-16-40. www.c-r-a-s-h.de. U-Bahn: Giselastrasse.*

➔ **Stadt Café** If previous nights have left you dehydrated and spent, Stadt Café can be a nice respite from the usual Munich offerings. Folks don't come here to get trashed or to listen to ridiculously loud music. Rather, you can enjoy your respectable half-liter glass of Spaten while chatting up local intellectuals, catch up on current events with one of their newspapers, or simply pre-game for the night's festivities with some friends. Whether you choose the plush couches in the corner, a seat at the bar, or a table in the middle, you'll have plenty of opportunities to kick back with food and nonalcoholic drinks, too. *St. Jacobs-Platz 1 (Stadtmuseum).* ☎ *089/26-69-49. U-Bahn: Sendlinger Tor.*

Beer Halls

📺 Best ➔ **Hofbräuhaus** ★★ Whether you're an 80-year-old on an excursion with your Bingo group or an eager senior in college looking to get completely smashed, you'll somehow find your way to the liter-mugs of Hofbräuhaus. The cavernous landmark serves some great dishes to accompany your beverage, but they're mere appetizers when you look at the amount of brew that the Hofbräuhaus serves day in and day out. To complete the touristy ambience, there's an oompah band that pumps out wicked accordion solos, which drunken revelers can teeter to in their lederhosen. While you knock back your mug, check out some of the paintings on the ceilings. The interior decorators after World War II must have been über-lazy: You'll notice the swastika shapes were simply painted more colorfully or given some bizarre pattern. *Am Platzl 9.* ☎ *089/22-16-76. www.hofbraeuhaus.de. S-Bahn: Isartor.*

➔ **Max Emanuel Brauerei** Stuff your gullet with weissewurst and wash it down with an enormous mug of Lowenbrau at this beer hall, housed in a former brewery that churned out suds for the very same beer company. Today, locals use the facilities to down the wonderful alcohol with their peers. This place also has a decent food selection in case you want to postpone the impending drunkenness. *Adalbertstrasse 33.* ☎ *089/271-5158. Cover 7€ Wed. 8€ Fri–Sat. U-Bahn: Universität.*

➜**Waldwirtschaft Grosshesselohe** If you are nowhere near the Englischer Garten, there's a great alternative for outdoor beer guzzling to be found at Waldwirtschaft Grosshesselohe. It's way over on the west side of the city, so hop on the S-Bahn and get off at Isartal Bahnhof. There's plenty of space for everyone, and the speakers pump a variety of old-school songs ranging from Dixieland to slinky jazz. *George-Kalb-Strasse 3.* ☎ *089/749-94030. S-Bahn: Isartal Bahnhof.*

Clubs

📺 Best ➜**Atomik Café** ★★★ Stumble out of Hauptbanhof station and round the corner to Neuturmstrasse. If you're in the mood for some tasty music, the retro digs of Atomik Café will serve many different tastes. Most nights have themes or live acts, though if you're aching for something a little offbeat, you might want to give their 1920s night a whirl. Old, big-band tunes scratch through the P.A. while Munich's youth submit to catchy melodies with fantastically spasmodic flapper moves. Their unabashed appreciation for a forgotten era is refreshing and a hoot to watch. On other nights, the extremely laid-back and approachable patrons enjoy cutting-edge indie rock and alternative music while relaxing on their retro love seats or while leaning on the bar and flirting with possible mates. *Neuturmstrasse 5.* ☎ *089/228-30-54. www.atomic.de. Cover 4€. S-Bahn: Isartor.*

➜**Die Badeanstalt** This is the place where, quite literally, you can dance in a pool of sweat. Constructed on the former site of an aquatic center, Die Badeanstalt's dance floor sits on the bottom of a drained pool, accessible by a wide staircase rather than a slippery metal ladder. If you'd rather go the Hasselhoff route and play lifeguard while grooming your wonderfully ample chest hair, there are lounge chairs on the surrounding balcony (aka "poolside"). Local DJ's spinning house, electronica, and drum 'n' bass provide the melodies. Once in a while, Münchners are treated to celebrity guests like Paul Van Dyk and Carl Cox. *Leopoldstrasse 250.* ☎ *089/358-94-923. www. badeanstalt.net. Cover 8€–15€. U-Bahn: Milbertshofen.*

➜**Kultfabrik** Indecisive partyers should avoid Kultfabrik at all costs. It's not one particular club; rather it's a buffet of 21 bars and dancehalls organized on a complex on Grafingerstrasse. The entire spectrum of danceable music is covered from Irish songs in The Temple Bar to tabla-dance and trance in Natraj Temple. More traditional clubbing tunes can be heard with Matador's R&B and hip-hop, Octagon's electronica and techno, as well as the oddly named Titty Twister with straight up rock 'n' roll. If the clubs and bars aren't enough, there are attractions that make the complex worth a visit even in the daytime. Bamboo Beach, during the summer months, is a little oasis of beach volleyball and margaritas where you can while away the day. *Grafingerstrasse 6. www. kultfabrik.info (contains an extremely useful map and links to all the bars/clubs). Cover varies. U-Bahn/S-Bahn: Ostbahnhof.*

➜**Nachtwerk** ★★ After P1, this is Munich's most popular disco-hall. There are several separate dance areas, but you'll find most locals slinking around to edgier rock with the occasional electronica and acid jazz tune thrown in. Underage Münchners particularly enjoy Nachtwerk because it offers two exclusive under-18 areas where they can party-hardy without feeling out of place. *Landsbergerstrasse 185.* ☎ *089/578-38-00. Cover 6€–10€. U-Bahn: Westendstrasse.*

➜**Nightflight** Losing your luggage can be a huge bummer, so why not kill some time while they track down your bags in the nearby Nightflight? It's the only club in Germany that calls the main airport home. Spacey lights and heaps of fantastic house music make the awkward commute worth it. Naturally, locals regard the gimmicky club as

MUNICH

a tourist trap and you'll find that the hip Munich masses usually flock to Nachtwerk or P1. Don't mind them, though; it's still worth a visit, and you are, after all, a tourist. Gimmicky can equal "Gobs of Fun." *Wartungsallee 9.* ☎ *089/97-59-79-99. Cover 8€–10€. S-Bahn: Flughafen.*

MTV Best ➔ **P1** ★★★ Check your humility at the door and waltz into the posh surroundings of P1. The crème-de-la-crème of Munich love to dally at the swank bar and, when the mood suits them, they mosey onto the massive dance floor and sway just enough to barely break a sweat. If you can get past the ludicrous cover and the persnickety bouncers (overwhelm them with bling and attitude and you're a shoo-in), you'll likely run into German celebrities, both local and international. Glitz and glamour aside, P1 can be an extremely fun night if you have the cash to burn and the entourage to boot. Although there's no cover, you might want to try and slip the bouncer a 20€ note to get past the insanely long line outside. *Prinzregenstrasse 1.* ☎ *089/211-11-40. www.p1-club.de. U-Bahn: Prinzregentenplatz.*

Gay Nightlife

While Munich's nightlife pales in comparison to Berlin's, the LGBT community can breathe a sigh of relief because Munich is home to a few outstanding gay bars and clubs, mostly within the area bordered by the Viktualienmarkt and Gartnerplatz. Here are a couple worth checking out:

➔ **Old Mrs. Henderson** Homosexuality isn't a requisite to get into Old Mrs. Henderson, and outnumbered straight partyers shouldn't worry. The cabaret shows here pander to both crowds and anyone who passes through its doors is guaranteed an entertaining night. While the weekends are home to the younger, foot-happy clubbing type, Thursdays and Sundays feature the cross-dressing antics of Old Mrs. Henderson's cabaret performances. *Rumfordstrasse 2.* ☎ *089/263-469. Cover 8€ for cabaret, Fri–Sat 5€ for club. U-Bahn: Frauenhoferstrasse.*

➔ **Oschen Garten** If you remembered to pack your leather gimp-suit, this is the place to show it off; Oschen Garten is one of the best S&M joints in town. Due to its size, especially from Thursday to Saturday, men will usually find themselves cramped in a sea of fetish wear. While that might be a negative for some bars, it actually might be Oschen Garten's best selling point. *Mullerstrasse 47.* ☎ *089/266-446. U-Bahn: Sendlinger Tor.*

Performing Arts

To find out what's happening in the Bavarian capital, go to the tourist office just outside the Hauptbahnhof and request a copy of *Monatsprogramm* (a monthly program guide; 1.50€). It contains a complete cultural guide, telling you not only what's being presented—from concerts to opera, from special exhibits to museum hours—but also how to purchase tickets. You can purchase most tickets to cultural, entertainment, or sporting events through **München Tickets** (☎ 089/54-81-81-81).

Theaters & Concert Halls

Besides the venues listed below, it's worth checking out the following: **The Bavarian State Opera** (☎ **089/2185-1920;** tickets 15€–130€; U-Bahn/S-Bahn: Marienplatz), **Munich Studio Theater** (☎ **089/230-721-328;** tickets 10€–40€; U-Bahn/S-Bahn: Marienplatz), and **Deutsches Theater** (☎ **089/55-23-44-44;** tickets 16€–44€; U-Bahn/S-Bahn: Karlsplatz/Stachus).

➔ **Altes Residenztheater (Cuvillies Theater)** The Residenz, an enormous palace that houses a number of Munich's performing venues (p. 649), isn't just another photo op for tourists. Nestled inside it is the rococo Cuvillies Theater, home to some of Munich's premier performances. The Bavarian State Opera and the Bayerisches Staatsschauspiel use the limited space to delight the eyes and ears of anyone willing to pay the hefty ticket prices. *Residenzstrasse 1.* ☎ *089/218-51940. Opera tickets 18€–150€; play tickets 15€–60€. U-Bahn: Odeonsplatz.*

➜**Münchner Philharmoniker (Munich Philharmonic Orchestra)** The acoustics in all five halls here have felt the reverberation of classical music since the late 1800s, and they still sound as glorious, I imagine, as they did back in the day. In addition to the music halls, there's a conservatory and municipal library in the building. Philharmonic performances start in mid September and run until July. *Rosenheimerstrasse 5.* ☎ *089/480-880. www.muenchnerphilharmoniker.de. Tickets 10€–51€. S-Bahn: Rosenheimerplatz.*

Sightseeing

Marienplatz is the perfect place to start your tour of Munich; the tourist office here will have the usual sightseeing tools (maps, brochures, and such) on hand, but they'll also have bulletin boards teeming with event announcements and festivals in the area.

Festivals

February

Fasching. The city's second most popular festival after Oktoberfest. Although this event normally spans a few weeks, the streets of Munich really hit full Fasching-swing around the first Tuesday of February; the city's usually quiet and peaceful avenues are invaded by costume-wearing Münchners celebrating their version of Mardi Gras. Revelers congregate along closed-off Viktualienmarkt and beads are replaced with doughnuts. Legend has it that the pagans had to choose a "king" to rule their tribe for a year, and they did so by placing a coin in a pastry that would be distributed with other pastries to the "candidates"—the lucky recipient of the currency would be dubbed king. After his "term" of a year, he was sacrificed. Throughout February and March, depending on the dates of the Lenten season.

June & July

Filmfest München. A few months before the beer taps start flowing, 8 days are set aside in June and July to showcase international films. In addition to screenings of German and European movies and American indie flicks, there are award shows, workshops, and other celluloid-related events that add to the red-carpet glitz. Late June.

Christopher Street Day. The big day for the estimated 100,000 gay men and lesbians who live in the city attracts people from across Bavaria. This fun-filled parade, with its outrageous costumes, is one of the largest such events in Europe. It is named after the street in New York's Greenwich Village that was the site of the 1960s Stonewall Riots, said to have launched the Gay Liberation Movement. July 15.

September & October

Oktoberfest. Most travelers to Munich come to participate in this festival, the biggest and greatest excuse for drinking around. Most activities are centered around Theresienwiese, where local breweries sponsor gigantic tents that can hold up to 6,000 beer drinkers. Contact the **Munich Tourist Bureau** (☎ **089/23396500;** www.muenchen-tourist.de) for particulars, or just

MUNICH

Free & Easy

→ Hidden under Munich's hefty price tags are some finds that will please even the most frugal of travelers. The best deal in town is Munich's art museum, the **Alte Pinakothek.** In previous years, art lovers could visit on Sundays and not pay a single euro to enjoy the pieces within the museum. Fairly recently, the museum started charging a very affordable 1€. Of course, the downside is that it gets crowded every Sunday. Expect to enjoy that Peter Paul Rubens painting in close quarters.

→ The best free thing in Munich happens to also be the largest thing in the city, in terms of acreage. **The Englischer Garten** offers a ridiculous number of activities for visitors young or old, active or lazy, and clothed or bucknaked. See "Playing Outdoors" for everything that Munich's biggest park has to offer.

show up. It lasts from the middle of September to the first Sunday in October.

Top Attractions

→**Alte Pinakothek** ★★ A single euro won't get you far in the expensive stores and attractions of Munich, but it's a different story on Barerstrasse on Sundays. It's a steal considering that the museum houses an ungodly amount of masterpieces. Legendary artists such as Dürer, Rembrandt, and van Dyck all are represented among Alte Pinakothek's 900 paintings. The most striking works, though, come from the brush of Peter Paul Rubens. Hours should fly by in Room 8, home to Rubens' paintings, such as *Der Hollensturz der Verdammten* (*The Fall of the Damned*), which are disturbing and delightful all at once. *Barerstrasse 27.* ☎ *089/238-050-216. Admission 5€, 3.50€ students; reduced 1€ admission Sun. Tues–Sun 10am–5pm (Tues till 8pm). U-Bahn: Theresienstrasse.*

MTV Best →**Deutsches Museum** ★★ The only thing I remember when I first visited Munich as a 9-year-old were the ridiculously fun, interactive displays in the Deutches Museum. Fifteen years later, not much has changed: The place still rules. Even those with an incredibly short attention span

will have a field day banging buttons, yanking levers, and looking through microscopes. No other technological museum in the world can compete with this museum's sheer number of gizmos, gadgets, and machinery. Anything with a mechanical or electrical pulse created in the last 300 years can probably be found here, either as a replica or as a Plexiglas-enclosed original. Motor heads, on the other hand, might be annoyed to find that the automobile exhibition has been removed from the museum. Due to the popularity and increasing size of the car collection, a separate mini-museum dedicated to the gas-guzzling beasts is currently being constructed and should be completed by the time this goes to print. *Museumsinsel 1.* ☎ *089/217-91. www.deutsches-museum.de. Admission 7.50€ adults, 3€ students. Daily 9am–5pm. Closed on major holidays. U-Bahn: Fraunhoferstrasse. S-Bahn: Isartor.*

FREE →**Frauenkirche (Metropolitan Church of Our Lady)** World War II ravaged much of Munich's skyline and the Metropolitan Church of Our Lady was one of the hardest-hit buildings in the city. The cathedral was renovated after the war but now lacks many of the intricate designs it once had. Though a shell of the old church, it does posses a minimalist beauty. Outside the

That's the Ticket

If you plan on visiting the Alte Pinakothek, Neue Pinakothek, or Pinakothek der Moderne, it might be worth investing in a combination ticket. For 12€, 8€ for students, you can gain admission to all the museums—just be sure to plan your visit on a day when they're all open. (Not on Sun, though, because the Alte Pinakothek *is* only 1€ then.) Anyone staying in the city for more than 3 days should invest in a **Welcome Card.** The transportation pass entitles the holder to unlimited travel on the U-Bahn and S-Bahn. When you're not zooming around on Munich's smooth public transportation system, you can even use the card for discounts at numerous museums, shops, and restaurants. A single-person card for the inner core of Munich is 6.50€ for 1 day or 16€ for 3 days. For 28€, you can buy a 3-day card for the total area of Greater Munich, including the lakes of Starnbergersee and Ammersee and the Dachau concentration camp. The Munich Welcome Card is available at the Munich tourist office branches located at the Hauptbahnhof (Munich's main rail station) and the Neues Rathaus (Town Hall), at the tourist information center of the Munich International Airport, at the MVG transportation service centers located at Marienplatz and Poccistrasse 1–3, and at several other sites.

church is an amazing round fountain with bronze lily pads, surrounded by a series of amphitheater-like steps where locals like to congregate and relax. *Frauenplatz 1.* ☎ *089/290-0820. Free admission. Sat–Thurs 7am–7pm; Fri 7am–6pm. U-Bahn/S-Bahn: Marienplatz.*

➔ **Neue Pinakothek/Pinakothek der Moderne** Though not as impressive as the Alte Pinakothek, the neighboring Neue and Moderne Pinakotheks are worth a visit as well. The former contains works from 18th- and 19th-century artists ranging from van Gogh to Manet. Pinakothek der Moderne showcases contemporary legends like Kadinsky and Warhol. *Neue Pinakothek: Barerstrasse 29.* ☎ *089/238-051-95. Admission 6€ adults, 3.50€ students, 1€ on Sun. Wed–Mon 10am–5pm (Thurs till 10pm). Pinakothek der Moderne: Barerstrasse 40.* ☎ *089/238-053-60. Admission 9€ adults, 5€ students, 1€ on Sun. Fri–Sun and Wed 10am–5pm, Thurs 10am–8pm. U-Bahn: Theresienstrasse.*

➔ **Residenz** Much has changed since this palace's beginnings as a plush home for

Bavarian rulers. World War II destroyed much of the palace, but it has since been renovated and is back to its beautiful self. Nowadays, it's separated into several galleries, including the Residenz Museum and the Schatzkammer (Treasury Museum) as well as being home to the Alte Residenztheater where operas and concerts take place during the summer. Check out some paintings, drool over some bling, and listen to sopranos belt out a tune or two all within the premises of perhaps the most breathtaking building in Munich. *Max-Joseph-Platz 3.* ☎ *089/290-671. Admission for combination ticket Residenz Museum and the Schatzkammer 9€ adults, 4.50€ students; single ticket for either Residenz Museum or Schatzkammer 6€ adults, 3€ students. Daily 9am–4pm. U-Bahn: Odeonsplatz.*

➔ **Stadtmuseum** Anyone interested in Munich's past and artists' representations of the city should visit the Stadtmuseum. You'll find collections of film, wooden models, musical instruments, and various exhibitions that display moments and scenes from Munich's lush history. It sounds awfully dry, but the curators at the Stadtmuseum do a

12 Hours in Munich

1. **Wander the paths of Viktualien Market.** The best time to visit Munich's famed market is in the early morning. Around 8am, the tourist rush has yet to invade the stalls and the smells of vendors preparing their wares will wake you up in no time.

2. **Catch a show at Marienplatz.** The Glockenspiel show occurs twice a day in Marienplatz: once at 11am and then again at 5pm. Because the "play" takes place a few stories above everyone's heads, there's no prime seat in the joint.

3. **Do lunch at the Ratskeller.** Despite its popularity and possible over-hyping, it's worth visiting the Ratskeller. It can get pretty busy in the evenings, so lunch is your best bet for scoring an intimate booth.

4. **Take in the Deutches Museum.** Few science museums in the world can match the Deutches Museum in terms of breadth and interactivity. Come here during the weekday and you'll have to wade through the sea of school children filling the halls. My advice is to just let loose and act like an 8-year-old again.

5. **See how the other half lives on Maximillianstrasse.** Even if you can't afford the plastic shopping bags they give their customers, it's a great opportunity to do some major window-shopping.

6. **Relax in the Englischer Garten.** Once you find yourself within the confines of this beautiful green space, it's hard to comprehend why some Münchners ever leave the city premises. You can take your turn at surfing, biking, sun-bathing, or simply sitting under a tree and reading.

7. **Close out your evening with a session at Hofbräuhaus.** Grab your dinner and your liter of booze in one shot at this expansive hall, which happens to be one of the world's most famous beer halls. You can certainly come here alone, but it's much more enjoyable with a group of people.

great job setting up each display to make it pretty interesting, even to completely sober visitors. If you're still bored, check out the movies that the film museum pulls out at 6 and 9pm. *St. Jacobs-Platz 1.* ☎ *089/23-32-23-70. Admission 4€ adults, 2€ students; free on Sun. Tues–Sun 10am–6pm. U-Bahn/S-Bahn: Marienplatz.*

📺 **Best** → **ZAM–Zentrum für Auber-gewöhnliche Museen** ★★★ With a name like "Center for Extraordinary Museums," it's tough to ignore this amusingly kitschy complex. There are eight different galleries to choose from, but the Easter Bunny Museum and the Museum of Scent are among the most popular. Neither, unfortunately, can compare to the Bourdalou (Chamber Pot) Museum. You can literally piss your time away here. *Westenriederstrasse 41.* ☎ *089/290-41-21. Admission 4€ adults, 3€ students. Daily 10am–6pm. U-Bahn: Marienplatz. S-Bahn: Isartorplatz.*

The University Scene

The area just north of Aldstadt, on the wide Ludwigstrasse, is prime real estate for Munich's cache of college students. The nearby university, the **Ludwig-Maximilians-University of Munich,** is the center of a vibrant area where cafes are rife with intellectuals chatting about anything from Hegel and Kant to global warming. Farther up, as Ludwigstrasse turns into Leopoldstrasse, the stores and restaurants also reflect the youthful demographic by oozing style and energy: Racks in clothing stores have noticeably edgier threads, and menus in street-side cafes offer more adventurous food.

Luckily the student population in Munich, tends to be friendly and extremely approachable. See for yourself at a favorite university hangout, the **Café AnDerUni** (p. 643).

Playing Outside

BIKING Munich is chock-full of bike paths. Most major streets have bike lanes, and the city's many parks and gardens offer hours of riding. You can rent bikes at **Mike's Bike Tour,** Hochbruckenstrasse (☎ **089/ 255-43-987;** www.mikesbiketours.com) for 12€ to 18€ for the day.

PARKS & GARDENS City parks are ideal for kickin' off your shoes, strolling through the grass, watching nude sunbathers, and surfing. Correction: City parks in *Munich* are ideal for those activities. Off to the northeast, near Schwabing, the **Englischer Garten** is a 20-hectare (49-acre) swath of green where Münchners flock to escape the stresses of city life. The park is as quirky as Munich itself. For example, certain areas permit sunbathers to bronze their entire birthday suits. Unfortunately, the only folks ready and willing to bare all are mostly esteemed members of the elderly community. I highly recommend walking briskly by the tanners unless you want an eyeful of wrinkles and varicose veins.

In the summer months, don't forget to visit the **Chinesischer Turm** beer garden in Englischer Garten. The Chinesischer Turm is the pagoda-like structure in the center of the park and it houses one of the most popular beer gardens in the city. Hofbräuhaus may be the place to be in the colder months, but Chinesischer Turm is where you'll find beer guzzlers when the mercury rises.

SKIING When the mercury drops in the winter months, cross-country skiers can use

specially made paths in Englischer Garten for their grueling sport. Luckily, they don't have to worry about stray nude grandpas wandering through their trails.

SPECTATOR SPORTS All sports in Europe take a backseat to the foot-happy game of soccer. In Germany, in particular, the game is a religion of sorts; most locals are parishioners of FC Bayern München. A smaller sect of fans pledge allegiance to the less popular and less successful squad of TSV 1860. Either way, both parties go to church in the **Allianz Arena.** The stadium is worth a visit in the evening hours. During the day, the structure looks like a porcelain bowl with a strange diamond pattern. As it gets darker, the shell begins to emit a glow, shimmering and alternating between the team colors of FC Bayern München and TSV 1860. It sounds like a bad LSD trip, but the skin of the stadium is able to give off a cool aura without any external lights. For info, contact the **Soccer League Association** at ☎ **089/69-93-10.** To get tickets for any event, call ☎ **089/54-81-81-81.**

SURFING You're better off admiring the surfer dudes and surfer chicks at the endless wave along the **Isar River.** A result of a redirected canal, the tricky wave constantly rushes in the same crescent shape. While any boarder would kill to have such predictability, the wave is tough to manage and only a few skilled surfers can extend their rides past a minute.

SWIMMING & BOATING When the sun starts to beat down, there are a few places

MUNICH

where you can enjoy the sea breeze or take a dip. Englischer Garten provides **rowboats** throughout the park's lakes; you can rent one near the Kleinhesseloher See, or you can travel to Olympiapark's Olympiasee and use their rowboats. **Olympiapark** is also home to the **Olympia-Schwimmhalle** (☎ 089/306-722-90; U-Bahn: Olympiazentrum), which has a competition-size pool that anyone can use for the nominal fee of 3.50€.

Shopping

So you have the urge to splurge but you have no idea where to blow your trust fund. It's okay, it happens to every spoiled kid, but we're here to help. Hop into your limo and cruise down **Maximillianstrasse.** There you'll find ritzy stores that'll give your platinum American Express a workout.

The rest of us can enjoy the shops in the center of Altstadt near the tourist magnet of **Marienplatz.** Amid the souvenir stands and cheesy restaurants are a number of places where you can give your own plastic some exercise. Pick up a Bayern München jersey, a couple of novels, some new duds for your night at P1, and then call it a day by watching the figurines on the Glockenspiel do their thing.

Let your belly do some shopping for a change in the **Viktualienmarkt** ★★ (U-Bahn or S-Bahn: Marienplatz). Locals love to gather here to grab some weissewurst and purchase produce. Vendors sell all sorts of food, such as cheeses, fresh bread, fruits and vegetables, and different meats and sausages. It's an all-out assault on your olfactory system but also a great place to burn a roll of film or two. Shoppers show up daily around 8am; by 5pm only the hardiest of merchants remain in place, and by early evening the kiosks are locked up tight.

Most stores are open Monday to Friday 9am to 6pm and Saturday 9am to 2pm; exceptions are noted in the reviews that follow.

➜ **Peter Stücken** ★ Picturing your friend in a pair of tight lederhosen might be worth a chuckle, but those short-shorts can get really expensive. Buy them something that they'll actually like at Peter Stücken. There are two other locations that sell postcards and stationery, but the branch on Rosental has shelves of quirky toys and doodads designed by German artists, which make for unique souvenirs that can't be found outside of the country. Some of the pieces are a bit unwieldy, like the larger-than-life boar's head in the corner, but the smaller desk pieces and unique gadgets are perfect for getting on your boss's good side. *Rosental 9.* ☎ *089/24-21-3787. U-Bahn or S-Bahn: Marienplatz.*

➜ **Rag Republic** Much like the target audience of the Lifetime channel, most of Rag Republic's customers are women or metrosexual men. A quarter of their outfits are designed for males, while the rest of the store panders to females. Pick out one of their uniquely designed and colorful slinky dresses or pair one of their artsy T-shirts with a rugged-chic blazer. Be careful when trying on clothes in the backroom—the large cactus is just waiting for unsuspecting customers to bump into it. On the plus side, it'll give your holey jeans a spiffy, worn-in look. *Feilitzschstrasse 3.* ☎ *089/38-89-88-80. U-Bahn: Münchner Freiheit.*

➜ **Robot** Leopoldstrasse is lined with trendy boutiques and hip shoe stores, but few have owners like Gunther at Robot. The hip, graying shopkeeper stocks his racks with fauxvintage rock shirts, g-star jeans, Stüssy gear, classic kicks from Vans, and punk belts to get you prepared for the Berlin leg of your trip. While you scan the threads in Robot, chat up

Gunther and his younger sidekick, Matt, for some nightlife information. *Leopoldstrasse 69.* ☎ *089/34-36-32. U-Bahn: Münchner Freiheit.*

➔**Soma Store** ★★ Threads here are as chic today as they would've been 40 years ago. Offbeat color combinations with traditional materials create a vibrant, urbane, and earth-toned look that'll turn more than a few heads in Marienplatz. *Rumfordstrasse 2.* ☎ *089/260-194-69. www.soma-store.de. U-Bahn or S-Bahn: Marienplatz.*

➔**Texxt** Who are you trying to impress with that hefty copy of *War and Peace?* Trade in Tolstoy for Shatner in Texxt. That's not a typo—the little bookstore on Sendlingerstrasse has a disproportionate number of novels penned by the Captain of the Enterprise. The bulk of used English texts in the store include trashy novels with names like *Foetal Attraction.* Worried that

the Pulitzer Prize–winning *A Mother's Gift* (co-authored by Britney and Lynne Spears) is sold out? You'll probably find copies swimming around the bins, though you'll have to fish among the tons of novels adapted from straight-to-DVD movies. *Sendlingerstrasse 24.* ☎ *089/26-94-95-03. texxt@web.de. U-Bahn: Sendlinger Tor.*

➔**Words'Worth** Texxt might satisfy your romantic-novel craving, but for something with a little more substance, Words'Worth has a large selection of English books, ranging from the classics to contemporary fiction to travel guides. If you want to flex your gray matter, you can flirt with the university students that frequent the bookstore. There's nothing sexier than a man/woman who can wax intelligent about Schopenhauer. *Schellingstrasse 21.* ☎ *280/91-41. www.words worth.de. U-Bahn: Universität.*

Road Trips

Dachau Concentration Camp

Dachau, one of the most infamous Holocaust concentration camps, sits half an hour outside Munich as a stark reminder of what occurred here more than 50 years ago. While it may not be an enjoyable visit, it's a visit that everyone should make. Tours of the camp are available and will leave an indelible effect when you think of the more than 206,000 prisoners who suffered here. You can reach the concentration camp by taking the S2 S-Bahn train to Dachau. From there, bus nos. 724 and 726 will shuttle you to the entrance. Admission is free, and a short documentary is available for visitors from 11:30am to 3:30pm. The camp is open Tuesday to Sunday from 9am to 5pm; call ☎ **08131/ 66-99-70** or visit www.Kz-gedenkstaette-dachau.de for more information.

Neuschwanstein Castle

While Munich's architecture is picturesque, it pales in comparison to the castles of

Bavaria. Neuschwanstein Castle is the most-visited castle in the region, for good reason. Built in the middle of dense evergreens and surrounded by mountains, Neuschwanstein is an absolutely breathtaking building that rivals any castle your imagination cooked up as a child. You can join a tour group for around 50€, but I recommend taking a train up (a Bayern ticket costs 17€; www.rail europe.com) and hiking near the Alpsee Lake by yourself. Information about the castle can be found at **Kurverwaltung** (Rathaus, Münchnerstrasse 2, in Schwangau; ☎ **08362/ 93-85-23;** www.neuschwanstein.de; Mon–Fri 8am–5pm, Sat 9am–noon).

Weihenstephan Brewery, Freising

One of the oldest breweries in the world lies just 40 minutes north of Munich and is a great lesson in beer creation—if you come on the right day. Hop on the S1 and get off at the terminus of Freising (two strips on your strip card). Make sure you're on the right half of the train; some trains in Neufahrm drop off the tail end and the front three cars head to Freising, while the rest of the train is led to the airport. Once in Freising, put your ego on hold and ask the locals for some help to the brewery, or you're bound to get a massive migraine. (Signs to Weihenstephan are sometimes vague, pointing to a fork in the road or leading to the Weihenstephan School.) Once you find the brewery, locating the entrance is another small adventure. (It's a nondescript door on the opposite side of the beer garden.)

Before heading to Freising, you must call the brewery (☎ **08161-5360;** www.brauerei-weihenstephan.de) to find out when they give free tours of the complex. The days vary every week and usually run 8 or 10 times a month. If you arrive on a nontour day, you won't be able to explore the brewery. In that case, find the beer garden and down a much-needed pale ale.

Naples, Capri & the Amalfi Coast

The sun-kissed Mediterranean coastline that stretches from Naples to Amalfi is one of the most stimulating, soul-stirring places on Earth. With its southern boisterousness, over-the-top natural beauty, and fresh gastronomic bounty, Campania—the region which encompasses Naples, Capri, and the Amalfi Coast—in many ways epitomizes the idea of Italy as romance novel. On Ischia and the Amalfi Coast, waves lap at pink stucco buildings while fishing boats bob in the harbor. In Naples and Sorrento, people talk across the street as they hang clothes on laundry lines outside their third-floor windows. Throughout the region, sexy women and men aren't shy about getting in your business, and we like it.

However, Campania is not a completely blissful summer fling. It doesn't take long to realize that the region has an unpleasant side, which you'll encounter on the dirtier streets of Naples or when you ride the Circumvesuviana train past the blight of impoverished coastal suburbs like Torre Annunziata. Don't avert your eyes. Get some perspective on what life is like for a lot of people here. The real Campania is grittiness mixed with overwhelming splendor. Wash it all down with a few glasses of Lacryma Christi (a local wine made from grapes grown on the slopes of Vesuvius) and a few slices of fresh peach, whose color perfectly matches the amber glow of that gorgeous sunset over the water.

The Best of Campania

○ **The Best Food:** Campania is the only place in the world where you can get real, fresh, honest-to-goodness **mozzarella di bufala campana DOP.**

○ **The Best Way to Travel Back in Time:** Stepping through the gates of **Pompeii** is like entering a time machine that shoots you back about 2,000 years. The once-prosperous ancient Roman town was buried when Mt. Vesuvius erupted in 79 A.D. and is eerily well preserved today. See p. 670.

○ **The Best Museum:** The halls of the **Museo Archeologico Nazionale** in Naples are where all the best stuff from the excavations at Pompeii ended up. Browse stupendous mosaics, emotionally charged marble sculptures, and everyday kitchen utensils, and be sure to reserve a guided visit to the Gabinetto Segreto, where they stashed all the ancient porn (figurines, frescoes, and phalluses galore) they uncovered at the site. See p. 668.

○ **The Best Excursion:** On Capri, the 2-hour **full-island boat tour** (12€) with Gruppo Motoscafisti is an exhilarating way to see the most beautiful island in the Mediterranean Sea. En route, the clumsy rowboat detour into the spectacular **Blue Grotto** is an absolute must. See p. 677.

Naples

Getting into Town

BY AIR

Naples' airport is **Aeroporto Capodichino** (Via Umberto Maddalena; ☎ 081-7896259), 6km (4 miles) north of the city, but a 30-minute ride through traffic-congested streets. To get into the city, take the **Alibus** (3€), which runs about every half-hour and stops at Napoli Centrale–Piazza Garibaldi train station (the stop is in front of McDonald's; turn right when exiting the station) and in Piazza Municipio, near the port of Molo Beverello. If you prefer a taxi, make sure the driver gives you the flat airport-to-city rate (it generally runs from 20€) and does not use the meter.

BY TRAIN

Naples' train station is **Napoli Centrale** (sometimes abbreviated as **NA C.LE;** www.napolipiazzagaribaldi.it) in Piazza Garibaldi. Trenitalia (FS) trains connect Naples to other Italian cities such as Rome, Florence, Milan, and Venice. **Circumvesuviana** trains are regional subway-like trains connecting Naples with Campania destinations such as Sorrento and Pompeii, and depart from the lower level of the train station. Rail passes are not valid on Circumvesuviana trains. Although the city center is close by, the area around the train station is pretty seedy, so you might not want to hang around, especially at night. Luckily, Piazza Garibaldi has plenty of buses and taxis to whisk you away from the squalor. Inside the station itself, there are travel agents with whom you can book your ferry and hydrofoil tickets to Capri and Ischia, to spare you the potential hassle of having to do so at the hectic ticket offices at the port. **365 Travel Agency** (☎ 081-267125) is open daily from 8am to 9pm. **Wasteels** (☎ 081-201071) is open daily from 7am to 9pm.

BY BUS

SITA buses (connecting Naples to regional destinations such as Pompeii and Sorrento) depart from Piazza Garibaldi, in front of the train station. Alternately, if you're staying near the harbor or transferring from the ferry, you can also catch the bus from the SITA station by the port: The bus terminal is in the big red building at the end of the long parking lot next to the port.

BY FERRY

The main port of Naples is called **Molo Beverello.** Several ferry companies operate here, running ferries and hydrofoils to Sorrento, Capri, Ischia, and the Amalfi Coast.

How to Survive Neapolitan Traffic

Never *ever* get behind the wheel in Naples. Even getting in a vehicle with a local driver can be a harrowing experience. You will, however, inevitably be confronted with this traffic nightmare when attempting to cross the street. Stepping off the curb at first will seem like a death wish, but it is quite simple if you follow one basic rule: Just go. Don't step into the middle of the freeway or in front of speeding vehicles, but generally cars and scooters will swerve around you. If in doubt, watch a local and then follow suit.

To get to the port, take any bus to Piazza Municipio and then walk down to the waterfront. The city's secondary port is called **Mergellina,** a few kilometers up the coast in a much nicer neighborhood. From Mergellina, there are hydrofoils to Capri and Ischia.

Getting Around

BY BUS

Local orange **ANM** buses (*autobuses*) are often slow and crowded, although special circular lines (marked with an R) can be handy as they service most tourist sites and all intersect at Piazza Municipio, near the port. Other useful lines are the C16 (Mergellina–Vomero), C21 (Mergellina–Posillipo), C25 (Piazza Amedeo–Piazza Municipio), C27 (Piazza Amedeo–Via Manzoni–Posillipo), and 140 (Castel dell'Ovo–Mergellina–Posillipo). The night buses are notoriously unreliable and unsafe, and so should be avoided—if you're traveling more than a few blocks at night, and especially if you're alone, it's best to be safe and take a taxi. Purchase bus tickets (1€) from *tabacchi*, newsstands, and transport information booths. For more information,

call the **ANM information line** (☎ 800-639525; www.anm.it).

BY METRO

Naples' **subway** system is a good way to travel for longer distances on the outskirts of the *centro storico* and farther inland—the Metro has very few stops near the waterfront. From the train station, you can catch Metropolitana Line 2 from platform 4, on the lower level. Elsewhere in Naples, Metropolitana stations are marked with a red M. Useful stops for tourists include Piazza Cavour (for the northern half of the *centro storico*), Montesanto (for the southern part of the *centro storico* and shopping on Via Toledo and the market of Via Pignasecca), Piazza Amedeo (for Chiaia), and Mergellina (for the hydrofoil port). The same tickets that are used on the bus are also used on the Metropolitana; purchase them at *tabacchi*, newsstands, and transport information booths.

BY FUNICULAR

These three super-slanted railways connect the lower parts of Naples to the Vomero district above, offering great views of the city along the way. The **Funicolare di Chiaia** departs from just east of Piazza Amedeo to Vomero (south of Piazza Vanvitelli and adjacent to the Villa Floridiana Park). The **Funicolare Centrale** is a much longer line leading from the southern end of Via Toledo up to the Vomero (southeast of Piazza Vanvitelli). Finally, the **Funicolare di Montesanto,** farther north, was closed for restoration at press time. Use regular bus tickets (1€), which can be purchased at *tabacchi*, newsstands, and transport information booths.

BY TAXI

Neapolitan taxi drivers are well known for ripping off tourists, so insist on the driver using the meter (except for airport service, when they must abide by a set rate). There are taxi stations near major transport hubs and attractions, or you can call one of the following radio taxi dispatchers: **Taxivagando** (☎ 800-403040), **La Cometa** (☎ 081-5513422), or **La Sibilla** (☎ 081-5510964).

ON FOOT

Although Naples as a whole is quite spread out—along the waterfront and up the hills—its main attractions are close to each other and easy to get to on foot.

Naples Basics

ORIENTATION: NAPLES NEIGHBORHOODS

One key to staying oriented in the city is to keep in mind that, while the Mediterranean seacoast is more or less north-south in most of Italy, Naples's shoreline actually faces south, due to its position on the crescent-shaped bay of Naples, which runs from Cape Misenum in the west to the Sorrentine peninsula in the east.

STAZIONE CENTRALE The area around the train station, especially the part to the east, has an abundance of budget accommodations, ethnic restaurants, and street vendors hawking everything from sunglasses to fresh produce. Unfortunately this is also the area that has given Naples its bad rap for seediness and sketchiness: It's dirty, smelly, unsafe, and full of folks you'd hate to meet in a dark alley.

THE WATERFRONT Unfortunately, Naples has yet to take advantage of its huge stretch of coastal land—the seaside area that runs adjacent to the center of town is essentially an industrial area and parking lot, with the port, Molo Beverello, at the eastern end, near the Castello Nuovo. If you venture a little further down the coast, however, you'll find Mergellina, which has a bit more life and atmosphere to it, although it's constantly packed by cruise groups. There are numerous good seafood restaurants by the water.

CENTRO STORICO Called Spaccanapoli by the locals, this is the historical heart of the city. Wander through its maze of streets and you'll discover cheap restaurants and tiny shops, as well as churches and monuments, political buildings, and the university.

PLEBISCITO Stretching inland from the enormous rounded colonnade of Piazza Plebiscito, this neighborhood encompasses two sections: Straight ahead from the piazza, you'll find the posh shopping street Via Toledo and its adjacent shopping mall Galleria Umberto I—probably the most ornately decorated shopping mall you'll ever find; to the west is the Quartieri Spagnoli (Spanish Quarters), a warren of narrow streets where you'll find cramped street-level apartments, restaurants, more shops, and vendors hawking virtually anything you can imagine.

THE VOMERO & POSILLIPO Just to the west of the city center, these are residential areas that sit high above the rest of Naples. The air is fresher and the views are splendid. Vomero is the livelier of the two—its centerpiece, cafe-filled Piazza Vanvitelli, is a popular evening hangout for young locals. The real stunner, however, is Posillipo: Sitting on the verdant, finger-like cliffs that bend toward the sea, dotted with gorgeous private villas, this is Naples at its snobbiest.

MERGELLINA Situated far from the center, this residential neighborhood lies near Naples' pleasant marina. It's chock-full of restaurants and cafes.

CHIAIA This neighborhood is centered around the public park, Villa Communale. The shore area here is loaded with upscale shopping and clubs.

TOURIST OFFICES

The main **EPT Tourist Office** (Piazza dei Martiri 58; ☎ 081-4107211; www.inaples.it) is open Monday through Friday 9am to 2pm, with a telephone information line available

Talk of the Town

Three ways to start a conversation with a local

1. **Want to talk politics?** Most locals love discussing anything but Italian issues, which no one seems willing to discuss other than to say that every politician in Italy is corrupt.
2. **What's your favorite soccer team?** Try to feel out what team they're for before you make any keen observations about the season.
3. **Parla inglese?** Give speaking Italian a shot. It's not like you can learn the language in a single conversation, but you can pick up some funny phrases that you won't find in books, such as a special saying for "good luck."

from 8:30am to 3:30pm. There is also a branch office in Stazione Centrale (☎ 081-268779), which is open Monday to Saturday 8:30am to 8pm and Sunday 8am to 2pm.

There is also a helpful **OTC** tourist office (☎ 081-2525711) in Palazzo Reale, next to the entrance to the Galleria Umberto I shopping mall. It's open daily 9am to 3pm.

Whichever tourist office you visit, be sure to pick up a free map and the indispensable tourist publication, *Qui Napoli,* which gives detailed information on the month's events, as well as a good rundown of the city's attractions, restaurants, and accommodations.

Recommended Websites

○ **www.inaples.it**: The official website of the tourist office, with information on attractions, accommodations, transport, and so on. You can also get the online version of the *Qui Napoli* magazine.

○ **www.naplesnews.com**: Get the Naples daily news in English here.

○ **www.napoli.com**: The *Around Napoli* website provides information on sights and attractions as well as the history and culture of the city.

Culture Tips 101

Naples' southern, seaside location gives it a culture different than what you will find in other Italian cities. It is a port city, so it attracts all walks of life from all regions of the world. It is the first stop for many immigrants from less-developed countries looking for a better life and it's the first major city that the northerners hit on their way to the sunny beaches of Capri and the Amalfi Coast. This mix of people has influenced the culture, architecture, and even language: Many speak Napolitano here, a dialect of Italian.

While there are probably drugs in Naples and the Amalfi Coast's nightclubs, the rules here are the same as anywhere: If you use them and get caught, you'll get busted. Rules are more lax as far as drinking is concerned—though tourists probably drink more wine than the locals do.

Recommended Books, Movies & Music

Several Italian authors have written movingly of the harsh and beautiful rural life of southern Italy. Most famous perhaps is Carlo Levi's *Christ Stopped at Eboli* (2000), about the author's sojourn in a small village where he was exiled during the fascist period. Among the many travel writers who wrote on this region, one of the first is also one of the best: Johan Wolfgang von Goethe's *Italian Journey* (1816). Goethe writes about a trip up to Mt. Vesuvius during an eruption, among other things. See p. 795 in the Rome chapter for more recommended books, movies, and music for Italy.

Naples **Nuts & Bolts**

Cellphone Providers & Service Centers There's a **Vodafone** store at Via Scarlatti (☎ 081/5586395 140).

Currency There is an American Express branch at **Every Tours** (Piazza Municipio 5; ☎ 081-5518564).

Embassies The **U.S. Consulate** is at Piazza della Repubblica (☎ 081-5838111; Metro: Mergellina; tram: 1). It's open Monday to Friday 8am to 1pm and 2 to 5pm. The **U.K. Consulate** is at Via Dei Mille 40 (☎ 081-4238911; Metro: Amedeon). It's open Monday to Friday from 8am to 1pm and 2 to 4pm. Citizens of **Canada, Australia,** and **New Zealand** will have to go to the embassies or consulates in Rome (p. 797).

Emergencies If you have an emergency, dial ☎ 113 to reach the police, and for medical emergencies, dial ☎ 118. If you need medical attention but it is not an emergency, ask for the closest Guarda Medica Permanente.

Internet/Wireless Hot Spots **Internetbar** can be found at Piazza Bellini 74 (☎ 081-295237; Metro: Piazza Cavour; bus: Piazza Dante). It's open Monday to Saturday 9am to 1am, and Sunday 6pm to 1am.

Laundry Self-service laundromats are rare in Naples; your best bet is a *tintoria* (dry cleaner). One central location is **Lavanderia Tintoria** at Via San Tommaso d'Aquino 43 (☎ 081/5511895).

Luggage Storage You can leave your bags for the day at Napoli Centrale (p. 656). There are no lockers, but there is a luggage storage area which is closed at night. This is the most reliable way to store your luggage in Naples.

Post Offices There are many post offices in town, but one of the most central is at Piazza Matteotti Giacomo 2 (☎ 081-5511456).

Restrooms Public bathrooms are basically nonexistent. Your best bet is to use those in bars and cafes (you might have to buy at least a coffee to use one).

Safety There is less and less crime every year in Naples, but you still have to be careful. High unemployment here has led to a lot of petty crime. Be aware of your surroundings on public transportation especially if it is really crowded. Often, on the small streets, a couple on a scooter will ride by and try to grab your purse. Make sure your purse has thick straps that would be hard to cut (leather is good). Keep your money and valuables out of pockets that would be easy for people to get to. Be extra careful here.

Tipping In hotels, the service charge of 15% to 19% is automatically added to your bill. In restaurants, 15% is usually added to your bill to cover charges. Taxi drivers get at least 15% of the fare.

Sleeping

One good thing about the reluctance of tourists to visit Naples is that you can usually find a place to stay without a problem. Naples has some excellent hostels. There are also numerous budget hotels in the area near the train station (which is rather seedy).

If the places below are booked, try the **Promhotel** booth at the train station (☎ 081-266-908; Mon–Sat 9:30am–1pm

Naples

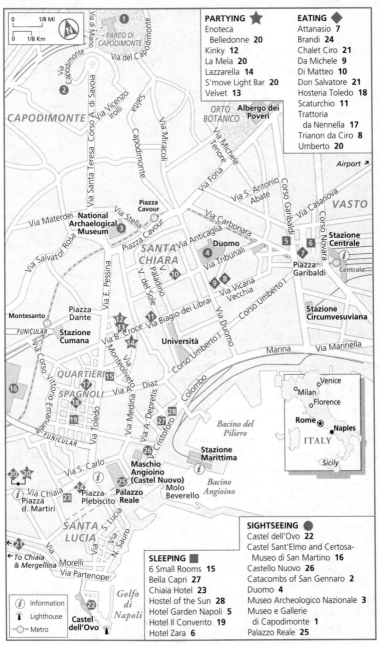

PARTYING ⭐
Enoteca
Belledonne **20**
Kinky **12**
La Mela **20**
Lazzarella **14**
S'move Light Bar **20**
Velvet **13**

EATING ◆
Attanasio **7**
Brandi **24**
Chalet Ciro **21**
Da Michele **9**
Di Matteo **10**
Don Salvatore **21**
Hosteria Toledo **18**
Scaturchio **11**
Trattoria
da Nennella **17**
Trianon da Ciro **8**
Umberto **20**

SLEEPING ■
6 Small Rooms **15**
Bella Capri **27**
Chiaia Hotel **23**
Hostel of the Sun **28**
Hotel Garden Napoli **5**
Hotel Il Convento **19**
Hotel Zara **6**

SIGHTSEEING ●
Castel dell'Ovo **22**
Castel Sant'Elmo and Certosa-
  Museo di San Martino **16**
Castello Nuovo **26**
Catacombs of San Gennaro **2**
Duomo **4**
Museo Archeologico Nazionale **3**
Museo e Gallerie
  di Capodimonte **1**
Palazzo Reale **25**

ⓘ Information
🕯 Lighthouse
—◉— Metro

and 3:30–7pm, Sun 9:30am–1pm) or the **365 travel agency** (in the train station; ☎ **081-267-125**; daily 8am–9pm).

HOSTELS

→ **Bella Capri** ★★ Because this place is across the street from the Hostel of the Sun (see below), guests are often sent here when the other is full, and although it lacks the atmosphere of its neighbor, the staff members are just as friendly and helpful. In addition to the dorms, there are also private rooms available. *Via Melisurgo 4 (off Via Depretis), on the waterfront.* ☎ *081-5529494. www.bellacapri.it. 20€–22€ dorm; 45€–50€ single with shared bathroom, 57€–69€ with private bathroom; 50€–60€ double with shared bathroom, 66€–80€ with private bathroom; 66€–84€ triple with shared bathroom, 80€–100€ with private bathroom; 80€–96€ quad with shared bathroom, 90€–110€ with private bathroom. Rates include breakfast. Bus: R2. Amenities: Kitchen; Internet; laundry facilities; TV. In room: A/C.*

🅼 **Best** → **Hostel of the Sun** ★★★ Hands down the best budget accommodations in Naples, and perhaps in all Campania. Helpful, bubbly staff members go out of their way to ensure that guests have a great time and make an effort to get to know everyone who stays there. There's a friendly, sociable atmosphere. Rooms are decently sized and bathrooms are clean. *Via Melisurgo 15, 7th floor (off Via Depretis), on the waterfront.* ☎ *081-420-6393. www.hostelnapoli.com. High season: 20€ dorm, 45€ single, 55€ double or 70€ with private bathroom, 80€ triple or 90€ with private bathroom, 90€ quad or 100€ with private bathroom; low season: 18€ dorm, 40€ single, 50€ double or 60€ with private bathroom, 70€ triple or 80€ with private bathroom, 80€ quad or 90€ with private bathroom. Rates include breakfast. Bus: R2. Amenities: DVD collection; Internet; kitchen; laundry facilities; shared bathrooms; TV (in common room).*

→ **6 Small Rooms** ★★ A sociable place run by a friendly Australian, with a kitchen, TV, and a large video collection. Rooms are small (hence the name) but bright and clean and some come with a small terrace. Reservations are not taken until the night before your arrival. *Via Diodato Lioy 18 (near Piazza Carità), Via Toledo, Centro Storico.* ☎ *081-7901378. www.at6smallrooms.com. 18€ dorm, 50€ double, 75€ triple, 100€ quad. Rates include breakfast. Metro: Piazza Cavour. Amenities: Kitchen; shared bathrooms; TV in common room; videos.*

CHEAP

→ **Hotel Zara** ★ In a non-sketchy area near the train station, this is a good budget option if you're arriving late or leaving early. Rooms are pretty bare and some are cramped, but all are clean and recently renovated. The two young owners love to dole out advice to guests. *Via Firenze 81 (at Via Torino), Piazza Garibaldi, Stazione Centrale.* ☎ *081-287125. www.hotelzara.it. 40€–45€ single with shared bathroom, 55€–65€ double with private bathroom, 75€–90€ triple with private bathroom. Bus/Metro: Piazza Garibaldi. Amenities: Bar; Internet; library; TV room.*

DOABLE

→ **Hotel Garden Napoli** A nicer option near the train station—if you can ignore the traffic congestion and seediness of nearby Piazza Garibaldi. Rooms are large and airy, with a terrace in some, although there isn't much to look out on. *Corso Garibaldi 92, Piazza Garibaldi, Stazione Centrale.* ☎ *081-284826. www.hotelgardenapoli.it. 65€–122€ single, 83€–148€ double, 100€–192€ triple. Rates include breakfast. Bus/Metro: Piazza Garibaldi. Amenities: TV. In room: Internet.*

→ **Hotel Il Convento** ★★ You can stay in the heart of the action in the Spanish Quarter, in a 17th-century palazzo. The owners say the hotel has been restored to resemble its original form, but it actually looks more like an

18th-century cottage inside, with small, cozy alcoves and dark wooden furniture. Rooms are nicely furnished with comfortable beds and welcoming decor. And although they are a bit cramped, rooms are also clean and bright. Most bathrooms also have bathtubs. *Via Speranzella 137A (near Piazza Carità), Quartieri Spagnoli, Centro Storico.* ☎ *081-403977. www.hotelilconvento.it. 68€–145€ single, 83€–180€ double, 115€–230€ junior suite. Rates include breakfast. Off-season discounts available. Bus: R1, R3, or R4. Amenities: Bar; concierge; room service; laundry service. In room: A/C, TV, minibar, dataport, hair dryer, safe.*

SPLURGE

➜ **Chiaia Hotel** ★★ Stay in the heart of the action on happening Via Chiaia, around the corner from Piazza Plebiscito; look for the banner hanging above the entrance and buzz to enter the gates. Housed in a beautifully restored palazzo, rooms may be small but are bright and spotless, with heavenly comfortable beds. Staff members are a bit weary of those who don't exude richness, but can be helpful if questioned for advice. *Via Chiaia 216 (near Piazza Plebiscito), Plebiscito.* ☎ *081-415555. www.hotelchiaia.it. From 95€ single, from 150€ double. Rates include breakfast. Bus: R2 or R3. Amenities: Cafe; room service. In room: A/C, TV, hair dryer, Jacuzzi (in some), minibar, safe.*

Eating

Naples is where pizza was invented, and it's still the best place in the world to eat it. Locals fiercely defend this culinary reputation. Even the cheap slices from the takeout stands are outstanding, though they are nothing compared to what you'll get in some of the restaurants that have been producing pizza pies for decades. If you tire of pizza, never fear. Being a coastal city, Naples also has delicious seafood, as well as delectable classic pasta dishes that are heavy on the tomatoes, garlic, and olive oil.

HOT SPOTS

➜ **Chalet Ciro** ★★ GELATO This hugely popular and delightfully retro spot is immersed in tropical greenery along the marina drive/parking lot of Mergellina harbor. Stop in at Ciro's indoor/outdoor counter for a cone or cup of gelato (regarded by many as the best in Naples), a refreshing *macedonia* (fresh mixed-fruit cup), or a jolt of espresso. To-go orders start at 2€, but you'll pay double for the privilege of eating your treat at the outside tables. *Via Francesco Carracciolo, Mergellina, on the waterfront.* ☎ *081-669928. www.chaletciro.it. Thurs–Tues 7am–2am. Metro: Mergellina. Bus: C24 or R3.*

CHEAP

➜ **Trattoria da Nennella** ★★★ NEAPOLITAN If you're looking for an authentic dining experience, you won't find a better place than this little restaurant in the Spanish Quarter. A wonderful family-run establishment where you can experience Neapolitans at their best: Customers shout orders to busy waiters who then pass food from the busy kitchen over the heads of other customers. Other diners include working class locals as well as big men in suits and dark glasses. Come with an appetite, as the daily menu includes two hefty courses. There's often a line-up, no matter what time you arrive: Give your name at the door to be added to the waiting list. *Vico Lungo Teatro Nuovo 103 (off Via Toledo), Plebiscito.* ☎ *081-14338. Set-price menu 7€. Daily 11am–3pm and 7–11pm. Bus: C25 or R2.*

DOABLE

➜ **Hosteria Toledo** ★ NEAPOLITAN The alleys of the Spanish Quarter are filled with little restaurants serving satisfying local specialties; this is one of the best for quality, atmosphere, and price. This cozy restaurant offers a variety of local dishes, but the seafood entrees are the best: For a culinary

Best Pizza in Naples

Try the **stands near the train station** ★★★. If you don't mind navigating the seedy, trash-strewn alleys around the train station, you'll find what is regarded by most true Neapolitans as the best pizza in the city. Greasy, drippy, piping-hot slices are available to go for about 1.50€. Just keep an eye on your wallet as you scarf it down!

MTV Best Brandi ★★ Serving piping-hot pies since 1780, Brandi is a more upscale place to sample some of the best pizza in Naples. It's even rumored that the pizza margherita (the kind with mozzarella and tomatoes) was invented here. Dine on the tiny terrace out front or in the cozy upstairs dining room. The entire place fills up minutes after opening, so a reservation is a good idea. *Salita S. Anna di Palazzo 1 (off Via Chiaia), on the waterfront.* ☎ *081-416928. Primi 5.30€–9.50€, secondi 6.50€–11.80€, pizza 3.70€–26€. Daily 12:30–3pm and 7:30pm–midnight. Bus: C25 or R2.*

Di Matteo ★ Walking along Via dei Tribunali, it's very easy to mistake this little place for just another takeout joint. The atmosphere may be lacking, but the pizzas are cheap, huge, and delicious—this is the best place to fill your belly on a tight budget. *Via dei Tribunali 94 (at Vico Gigante), Centro Storico.* ☎ *081-455262. Pizzas 3€–5€. Mon–Sat 9am–midnight. Metro: Piazza Dante. Bus R1 or R2.*

Da Michele One of Neapolitans' favorite pizzerias, this super-authentic joint in Spaccanapoli only has two choices on its menu: pizza margherita and pizza marinara (without mozzarella). It's not exploding with flavor, but it's incredibly fresh and satisfying. *Via Sersale 1, Centro Storico.* ☎ *081-5539204. Pizzas from 3€. Mon–Sat 10am–10pm. Closed 2 weeks in Aug. Bus: R2.*

Trianon da Ciro ★ Across the street from Da Michele, Trianon is where locals come when the lines are too long at Da Michele. *Via Pietro Colletta 46, Centro Storico.* ☎ *081-5539426. Daily 1–10pm for lunch and dinner. Pizza from 4€. Bus: R2.*

adventure, try the cuttlefish or octopus. *Vico Giardinetto 78A (off Via Toledo), Plebiscito.* ☎ *081-421257. Primi 5€–9.50€; secondi 6.50€–14€. Daily 7:30pm–midnight. Bus: C25 or R2.*

→**Umberto** ★ SEAFOOD In Chiaia, this family-run trattoria has been serving seafood and pasta dishes in a peaceful garden-like setting for 90 years. Try the gloriously flavorful *tubettoni treddeta*, which is pasta tossed with baby octopus, clams, and cherry tomatoes (9.50€). They also bake a mean pizza here. *Via Alabardieri 30 (near Piazza dei Martiri), Chiaia.* ☎ *081-418555. www.umberto.*

it. *Salads 5.50€–8.50€; primi 5.50€–9.50€; secondi (both meat and fish) 5€–14€; pizza 3.20€–8.50€. Daily noon–4pm and 7pm–midnight. Bus: C25.*

SPLURGE

→**Don Salvatore** ★ SEAFOOD One of the few places in Naples where you can actually dine beside the sea, although you'll have to make the trek out to Mergellina to do so. At this busy place, packed with locals on the weekend, you can dine in a converted boat shed on some truly fine seafood, including pastas, calamari, and fish right out of the bay. *Via Mergellina 5, on the waterfront.*

☎ *081-681817. Primi 6€–10€; seconði 10€– 21€. Thurs–Tues noon–4pm and 7:30pm–midnight. Bus: C24 or R3.*

COFFEE, PASTRY & GELATO SHOPS

When it comes to a strong culinary tradition, Naples doesn't stop at pizza and seafood— oh, no. The city is also home to some pastry and gelato shops that are so kick-ass, locals will make pilgrimages across town, just to satisfy their sweet tooth. And for the caffeine-sensitive, you should know that Neapolitan coffee is known for its palpitation-inducing strength. **Caffè Gambrinus,** the most well-known cafe/tearoom in Naples, is gorgeous but frequented by a stuffy, older set. Instead, just follow a local to a down-to-earth neighborhood bar.

[MTV] [Best] → **Attanasio** ★★★ PASTRIES If the area around the train station has one redeeming quality, it's this outstanding little pastry shop, where they make the best *sfogliatelle* on Earth. (*Sfogliatelle* are the Neapolitan version of *millefeuille*—triangles of layered puff pastry, filled with delicious ricotta.) They're best fresh out of the oven. *Vico Ferrovia 2/3, Piazza Garibaldi, Stazione Centrale.* ☎ *081-285675. Tues–Sun 9am–8pm. Closeð July. Bus/Metro: Piazza Garibaldi (main train station).*

→ **Scaturchio** ★★ PASTRIES This picture-perfect, old-guard pastry shop, right in the heart of Spaccanapoli, is a city institution. You'll get better *sfogliatelle* at Attanasio, but Scaturchio's *babà al rhum* (traditional Neapolitan eggy cake, soaked in rum) is good here. Their *zeppole* (fritters dusted with sugar and cinnamon) aren't bad, either. *Piazza San Domenico Maggiore 19, Piazza Cavour, Centro Storico.* ☎ *081-5516944. www.scaturchio.it. Metro: Museo or Piazza Cavour. Bus: R2.*

Partying

Naples is unexpectedly serene at night; perhaps that's what happens after a heavy dinner of pizza and pasta. In the summer, what action there is takes place outside: Take a walk along the waterfront or down Via Toledo, and then head to one of the piazzas in the city center where you can either pay high prices to sit in one of the bars lining the piazza or follow the local example and spend a few euros on a beer from a street vendor and chill in the piazza. The most popular piazzas, especially with a young crowd, are **Piazza Santa Maria La Nova** (north of the port at Piazza Municipio) and **Piazza San Domenico** and **Piazza Bellini** in the *centro storico.* For something a little more exciting, and in cooler weather, Naples is home to numerous bars and posh clubs. Here, style is key, as is enough cash to pay exorbitant cover charges (usually more than 10€).

BARS & PUBS

→ **Enoteca Belledonne** ★★ A bit inland from Chiaia's pretty greenbelt, this is a hot and unpretentious spot for an *aperitivo* (7:30–9pm), with budget-friendly wines by the glass. Belly up to the bar with the after-work crowd of tanned (and surprisingly friendly) Neapolitan yuppies who look like they've come straight from a Nautica photo shoot. Open daily 6pm to midnight. *Vico Belledonne a Chiaia 18 (off Via Ferrigni), Chiaia.* ☎ *081-403162. Closeð Aug. Bus: C25 or R3.*

→ **Kinky** ★★ A cafe in the early evening and laid-back bar at night, popular with young trendsetters. If you've had a long day, spend a mellow night relaxing here. Also a good place to stop by for a last drink at the end of a crazy night, as it's open late (5pm–4am). *Via Cisterna dell'Olio 21 (off Via D. Capitelli, near Piazza Gesù Nuovo), Centro Storico.* ☎ *081-5521571. Bus: R1 or R4.*

→ **Lazzarella** ★ A small trendy bar with high stools and stainless-steel decor, and quiet enough to have a deep conversation over coffee or to hit on a local over cocktails. Also a great place to satisfy late-night munchies, as they serve the usual Italian snacks as well as hot dogs and hamburgers. *Calata Trinità 7/8 (off Piazza Gesù Nuovo), Centro Storico.* ☎ *081-551005. Bus: R1 or R4.*

NIGHTCLUBS

➜ **La Mela** ★ One of Naples' most exclusive clubs. Don't even bother trying to get in unless you're dressed to kill, and even then you'll probably have to suck up to the bouncers. Inside, you'll find the city's beautiful people, all trying to outdo each other in style and moves on the dance floor as they groove to live DJ beats. Open Thursday to Sunday noon to 4am. *Via dei Mille 40 (off Via Nisco).* ☎ *081-410270. Bus: C25 or R3.*

➜ **S'move Light Bar** ★★ Perfect for shaking off that pizza you just scarfed down at dinner, crowded and friendly S'move is the best place to bust a move in the Chiaia district. It's done up in a vaguely Moroccan theme and spread out over three floors with interconnecting lounge, dance floor, and bar areas. The ground floor gets the most traffic, while the downstairs level is mellower, with more cushy chairs to crash in. Upstairs, the loft-style attic is frequented by young VIPs. Open daily 8pm to 4am; it's closed in July and August. *Vico dei Sospiri 10A (off Via Ferrigni), Chiaia.* ☎ *081-7645813. www.smovelab.net. Bus: C25 or R3.*

➜ **Velvet** ★★ One of the only clubs where you'll be let in the door in jeans and a T-shirt, this small, casual spot was a popular underground club in the 1980s and today cranks out electronica. Live shows are also occasionally held here. *Via Cisterna dell'Olio 11 (off Via Domenico Capitelli, near Piazza Gesù Nuovo), Centro Storico.* ☎ *339-6700234 (cellphone). www.velvetnapoli.it. Bus: R1 or R4.*

Performing Arts

If you want to catch some classical music, try the **Centro di Musica Antica Pieta dei Turchini** (Via Santa Caterina da Siena 28; ☎ **081-402395;** www.turchini.it). Ticket prices vary depending on the performance. You can get discounts with the Artecard (see "Campania Artecard: Museums & Bus Fare!" below).

Sightseeing

EXPLORING NAPLES

Allow yourself at least a couple of days in the city, as that's how long it will take to begin to appreciate its craziness (and not just feel overwhelmed by it).

Festivals

April & May

Maggio dei Monumenti (May of Monuments). An annual festival highlighting Naples' rich cultural heritage, with numerous performances, shows, sporting events, and fairs taking place on the weekends, and free entry into many of the city's museums and monuments, which often hold special exhibitions. Check out **www.maggiomonumenti.com** for more information. Throughout April and May.

September

San Gennaro Festival. The annual celebration of the patron saint of Naples and his miraculous vials of blood, which are said to liquefy on this day every year. Crowds of Neapolitans wait for the vials to be revealed by the presiding cardinal, and breathe a collective sigh of relief when their contents are revealed in liquid form—if the blood fails to

---

where the Boys Are

Most gay nightlife in Naples is centered in Posillipo, where you'll find **Tongue** (Via Alessandro Manzoni 207; ☎ **081-7690800**). It has a mixed crowd that dances to techno music. It is open only on weekends 9pm to 3am and charges a cover of 15€.

liquefy, it's a sign of imminent catastrophe. September 19.

Pizzafest. A festival dedicated to—what else—pizza! The best pizzerias in the city and around Campania converge for this festival, competing for awards. Performances and music also celebrate this beloved pie. Go to **www.pizzafest.info** for more info. Mid-September.

HISTORIC BUILDINGS

→ **Castel dell'Ovo** ★ Built on the waterfront on Megaris Island, the "Castle of the Egg" gets its name from the legend of the enchanted egg supposedly buried beneath the building which protects the small island from calamities; skeptics say the name actually just refers to the island's egg-like shape. While the interior of the castle is only open during special exhibits, it's worth a visit even just to walk along the exterior edge for the gorgeous views of the bay—from here, you can see Vesuvius and the Amalfi Coast on a clear day. Outside the castle walls, restaurants and cafes fill cobblestone streets.

Borgo Marinari (off Via Partenope), on the waterfront, Royal Naples. ☎ *081-2400055. Admission varies depending on exhibition. Mon–Sat 8:30am–7pm; Sun 8:30am–2pm. Bus: C24, C25, C28, or R3. Tram: 1.*

→ **Castello Nuovo** ★★ Naples' 13th-century "new castle" (also known as the Maschio Angioino, or Angevin Stronghold) is more interesting than the older, more picturesque Castel dell'Ovo. Inside, you can visit the dungeons where the Anjou monarchs kept their prisoners; according to tradition, the Fossa del Coccodrillo is where prisoners were eaten alive by crocodiles lurking in the ditch (now covered with a grate). There are also bones galore—in the glass-covered tombs of the Angevin barons and in the glass-covered cemetery lying underneath the interior courtyard. From the castle's upper ramparts, there are, once again, gorgeous views of the city and bay. *Piazza Municipio, on the waterfront.* ☎ *081-420-1241. Admission 5€. Mon–Sat 9am–7pm; Apr–May also Sun 9am–2pm. Bus: R2 or R3. Tram: 1.*

Campania Artecard: Museums & Bus Fare!

If you plan on visiting museums and historic sites here, the Campania Artecard gives you a lot of bang for your buck, especially if you're under 26. Purchase the card at the airport, train station, port, participating museums, or online at **www.campaniartecard.it**. There are three types of cards:

→ The **Napoli and Campi Flegrei card** will buy 3 days of local transportation (including unlimited rides on public transportation, a trip on the Alibus airport shuttle, and a return trip on the MM1 line of the Metro del Mare ferry), free admission to two sites, and half-price admission to the rest (and free admission to all sites for those under 26). The card costs 13€ for adults over 25; 8€ for those 18 to 25.

→ The **3-Day All-Site + Transport card** is the best deal for most travelers, giving you free admission to a wider range of sites, including Pompeii, and transport on the regional network of city buses and metros, the Circumvesuviana train (for Pompeii and Sorrento), and even local buses on Capri and Ischia. Adults pay 25€; those 18 to 25 pay 18€.

→ The **7-day All-Site card** includes free admission to all sites for a week, but unlike the 3-day card, transportation is *not* covered: Adults over 25 pay 28€; those 18 to 25 pay 21€.

➔**Castel Sant'Elmo and Certosa-Museo di San Martino** ★★ Naples is full of fine vistas and great views; but **Castel Sant'Elmo,** perched high on the hill, ups the ante and offers visitors a truly breathtaking **panorama** ★★★. Take the elevator to the roof, where the six-pointed-star-shaped battlements offer stunning 360-degree views of the city, Vesuvius, and all that gorgeous water in the bay. Built in 1329 during the reign of Roberto of Anjou, and later enlarged when it became a fortress, Castel Sant'Elmo occasionally hosts temporary exhibitions during which you can take a walk through the dark halls of the castle. Next door, you'll find the **Certosa** (charterhouse) and **Museo Nazionale di San Martino,** housed in a 14th-century monastery and displaying historical artifacts such as carriages and ship replicas, and historic documents, as well as a large collection of *presepi* (crèches, or nativity-scene dioramas). *Castle: Via Tito Angelini 20, Vomero.* ☎ *081-5784030. Admission 2€. Tues–Sat 8:30am–6:30pm. Museum: Largo San Martino 5.* ☎ *081-5781769. Admission 6€. Tues–Sat 8:30am–7:30pm; Sun 9am–7:30pm. Funicular: Centrale.*

FREE ➔**Duomo** Dedicated to the Madonna Assunta, construction began on Naples' Duomo in the 13th century, and was finished in the 14th century, although with renovations and additions to the Gothic facade, they were still hammering away in the early 20th century. Inside, treasures and artwork have piled on since the 14th century: The **Chapel of San Gennaro** houses the vials of the saint's blood that are said to miraculously liquefy three times a year. *Via del Duomo 147 (at Via Tribunali), Centro Storico.* ☎ *081-449097. www.duomodinapoli.it. Free admission. Daily 8am–12:30pm and 4:30–7pm; holidays 8am–1:30pm and 5–7pm. Bus: C25 or R2.*

➔**Palazzo Reale** ★★ A huge palace dominating the area adjacent to Piazza Plebiscito, it was built in the late 16th century for the expected visit of the new King Philip III who never ended up making it to Naples. It was later taken up by the Bourbons, descendants of the Spanish royal family. Facing Piazza Plebiscito, statues of former Neapolitan rulers line the exterior wall of the palace. Enter the complex around the corner on Via Chiaia, where you can wander the exterior grounds for free; here, you'll find piazzettas with fountains and statues, and a small garden whose shade and quietness provide a welcome respite from the bustling city outside. If you purchase a ticket, you'll be allowed into the interior. The royal apartments contain original furnishings, as well as numerous works of art from the period. You'll also find the colossal library originally created by the Bourbons, which now houses over a million books. *Piazza del Plebiscito 1, waterfront, Royal Naples.* ☎ *081-400547. Admission 4€; E.U. students 2€. Thurs–Tues 9am–7pm. Bus: R2 or R3.*

MUSEUMS & ART GALLERIES

➔**Catacombs of San Gennaro** ★ Pay homage to the remains of San Gennaro, patron saint of Naples, whose bones were transferred to this underground cemetery in the 5th century. Well-preserved frescoes line the walls near his tomb. The subterranean alleys of Naples are also interesting to explore, though not for the claustrophobic. To explore the catacombs and alleys, you must enter on a guided tour, offered several times in the first half of the day. *Via Capodimonte 13, Capodimonte, north of city center.* ☎ *081-741101. Admission 5€. Tours: Tues–Sun hourly 9am–noon. Bus: R4.*

MTV Best ➔**Museo Archeologico Nazionale** ★★★ If you have time for only one museum in Naples, this is the one to see. Touted as the oldest and most important archaeological museum in Europe, it contains wonderful finds from Pompeii and Herculaneum, the ancient Roman towns that were remarkably preserved when Mt.

12 Hours in Naples

1. **Eat a pizza.**
2. **If it's daytime, get a motorbike.** Look around for a mountain, ride to the top, and get a view of the whole city.
3. **Eat gelato, and lots of it.**
4. **Go to the Museo Archeologico Nazionale.** Feel your mind expand by just being there.
5. **Go to Campo de' Fiori at night.** Ask one of the strolling musicians to play you a bawdy love song.
6. **Make like Audrey Hepburn.** Eat a chocolate bread and drink coffee while checking out the display windows of all the outlandishly expensive clothing stores.
7. **Hang out at a cafe.** Drink espresso, try to decipher the newspaper, or listen to a soccer match on the radio.

Vesuvius exploded in the 1st century A.D. and covered everything in a thick deposit of ash, pumice, and volcanic mud. On the first floor, you'll find **paintings** ★, **household instruments and tools** ★★, and religious objects from Pompeii, as well as **gladiators' weapons and armor** ★★ found at the amphitheater. On the mezzanine, there are some outstanding **mosaics** ★★ recovered from Pompeii, including the impressive *Alexander Fighting the Persians* mosaic, from the House of the Faun. Also on the mezzanine, adjacent to the mosaic rooms, is the **Gabinetto Segreto (Secret Cabinet)** ★★, with some highly erotic objects and artworks also found at Pompeii. (The Gabinetto Segreto can only be visited with a guided tour, normally offered every hour—call or inquire at the ticket booth when you arrive.) The ground floor is home to a mind-boggling collection of Greek and Roman sculpture, including the powerful *Farnese Hercules* ★★★ (3rd century B.C.), whose downcast gaze and hulking, fatigued figure is one of the finest examples of emotive, Hellenistic sculpture in the world. Also here, the 3rd-century B.C. *Farnese Bull* ★★★ is an enormous marble group—the largest single sculpture that has survived from antiquity.

The museum's collection goes on and on with priceless Mediterranean antiquities. *Piazza Museo 19 (off Via Pessina), Centro Storico.* ☎ *081-440166. www.archeona.arti. beniculturali.it. Admission 6.50€ adults; 3.75€ adults 18–25. Wed–Mon 9am–7:30pm. Metro: Cavour or Museo. Bus: 47, C5, or E1.*

→ **Museo e Gallerie di Capodimonte** ★★
This massive museum, housed in an 18th-century palace originally constructed as a royal hunting residence, is the most important art gallery in Naples, and home to the impressive Farnese collection of painting, on the first floor. Assembled from all the major schools of Italian and European painting, the collection includes pieces by Botticelli, Giovanni, Bellini, and Caravaggio. Also on the first floor are the royal apartments, with furnishings and decorations from the 18th to 19th century. These rooms are beautifully decorated with wealth befitting royalty. The second floor houses a collection of 13th- to 18th-century Neapolitan art that was rescued from various monasteries facing persecution in the 19th century. To fully appreciate all of the masterpieces in Capodimonte, give yourself at least a couple of hours. *Via Miano 2 (off Corso Amedeo di Savoia), Capodimonte,*

Pompeii: What Happened When Vesuvius Went Off

On the morning of August 24, A.D. 79, Mt. Vesuvius blew its top big-time. So powerful was the pyroclastic eruption that a column of ash and gas spewed as high as 33km (21 miles) above the crater. When it came back down, the shower of pumice darkened the midday sky and a cloud of volcanic gas descended on the prosperous Roman town of 📺 **Best** **Pompeii** ★★★, sealing the entire town and its 20,000 inhabitants in over 7m (23 ft.) of ash.

Today Pompeii is an incredible witness to both Roman life at the start of the first millennium, as well as the destructive havoc that a volcanic explosion can cause. Pompeii is on par with such archaeological sites as Cambodia's Angkor Wat and China's Great Wall. The city is astonishingly intact, and you can spend several wide-eyed hours wandering through streets, houses, baths, theaters, government buildings, and market areas that look and feel much as they would have 1,900 years ago. The amazing thing is that, with a few keys to understanding the ruins, you can totally picture yourself living here. It feels eerily familiar.

Pompeii is an easy day trip from Naples. Give yourself at least 3 hours in Pompeii, and more if you can spare it. Bring a hat and water, as there isn't much shade, and it gets mighty hot from May to September.

Pompeii is actually divided into two sections: a modern town and the old town (the *scavi,* or excavations). There's not much of interest in modern Pompeii—except for the FS Train Station and a few mediocre shops and restaurants—so spend your time in the old town. The main **tourist office** is in modern Pompeii at Via Sacra 1 (☎ **081-8507255;** www.pompeiturismo.it; Mon–Fri 8am–8:30pm, Sat 8am–2pm).

north of city center. ☎ 081-7499111. Admission 7.50€ adults; 3.75€ E.U. citizens 18–24. Audioguide 4€. Thurs–Tues 8:30am–7:30pm. Bus: R4.

THE UNIVERSITY SCENE

The **University of Naples** (☎ 081/2531111; www.unina.it) is centered around Corso Umberto I, and the social center of Naples for tourists and locals alike is Galleria Umberto I. You'll find Naples' students in the city's outdoor piazzas, where most of them seem to congregate with their posses, their cellphones, and their scooters. There's a naval school right on the marina, so you'll find plenty of wannabe sailors hanging out here as well.

Playing Outside

Don't come to Naples expecting stretches of sand. There is one word to describe the beaches here: disappointing. While the city has miles of coastline, there are no actual beaches. As testimony to this lack of development of what could be a prime stretch of waterfront, the old steelworks at Bagnoli, west of Mergellina, was closed down decades ago and has yet to be dismantled! That being said, when it gets hot, locals are content to grab a boulder on the rocky shore, and spend the day swimming in the water and lazing about near the seaside. It ain't exactly Mediterranean luxury, but it'll cool you down.

Try the area to the west of Castel dell'Ovo or the shoreline in Mergellina.

FREE ➔ **Camaldoli Park** ★ One of the better reasons to visit the residential district of Vomero, this park sits on a hill at the highest point in Naples, offering sweeping views of the chaotic city below, the bay, and even as far as Sorrento on a clear day. Originally a 16th-century hermitage of Camaldolian monks. Spend an afternoon relaxing in the cool woods of the park, or walking along its rocky expanse. If you're lucky, you may spot lizards, bats, turtledoves, and quails. *Via Sant'Ignazio di Loyola, Vomero. Free admission. Daily 7am to 1 hr. before sunset.*

FREE ➔ **Parco della Floridiana** ★ Also in Vomero, and much easier to reach than the Camaldoli, this is local residents' favorite spot to stroll along green paths, or take the kids to the playground, which makes for some fun observing of Neapolitan family life. Because you're in hilly Vomero, there are good views over the bay from the southern edge of the park. *Via Cimarosa 77, Vomero.* ☎ *081-5781776. Daily 8:30am to 1 hr before sunset. Bus: E4 or V1. Funicular: Chiaia or Centrale.*

Shopping

Bargains galore exist in Naples: This is the home of designer knockoffs. Watch out for vendors looking to cheat tourists, and don't expect quality. And never, ever purchase electronic items off the street.

For high-end shopping, **Via Toledo** is the main shopping street in Naples, and is a fun place to walk and window-shop. A stop in **Galleria Umberto I** ★ is a must: Even if you can't afford a single item in any of these stores, you have to check out this incredible shopping mall, featuring a beautiful domed ceiling and gorgeous marble architecture—Mall of America, eat your heart out!

Finally, if you really want to see Naples at its most traditional, a shopping experience not to be missed is the stretch of market stalls along **Via Pignasecca** ★★ (just west of Via Toledo and north of Piazza Carità). Here, you'll find a bazaar where fishmongers, perfume sellers, kitchenware boutiques, salami vendors, and lingerie shops draw the community daily, creating wonderful local color. (Most shops and vendors are open only 8am–1pm.)

NAPLES, CAPRI & THE AMALFI COAST

Capri

If your idea of an island getaway is that tropical cliche of palm trees and endless sandy beaches—the sort of scene depicted on Capri Sun foil juice packs—well, the first thing to know is that the real **Capri** ★★★, Italy's jewel of the Mediterranean, is not that kind of island. Capri, like most of Italy's celebrated islands, is a drama queen with strong features, proud bearing, and classical training. Maybe you've seen it in pictures, but Capri's lush beauty—lemon trees, bougainvillea, and umbrella pines flourishing on hillsides, limestone cliffs plunging thousands of feet down to the sea—will absolutely floor you once you see it in person. In a country

with no shortage of splendid sights and settings, Capri is still thrilling, even by Italian standards.

Capri is beautiful year-round, but for some, it's just too damn crowded in the high season, when the heat and hordes of daytrippers make it harder to enjoy the island's many delights (but when Capri's nightlife is at its peak). Come in the mild shoulder-season months (late Apr to early June, or late Sept to Oct, when it's often warm enough still for swimming), and stay for a night or two, and you'll have a less expensive, more comfortable, and probably more enjoyable experience. Finally, do us all a favor and learn how to pronounce the name: It's *cah*-pree, not cah-*pree*.

Capri Basics

ORIENTATION: CAPRI

Capri is shaped more or less like an Oscar-night dress, 7km (4¹/₄ miles) long from east to west, and barely 3km (1³/₄ miles) wide at its thickest section (the "hem" of the gown) from north to south. The eastern end of the island is the bust of the gown, where you'll find Capri town (160m/525 ft. above sea level), the famed Piazzetta, and most of the hotels, restaurants, shopping, and action in general. Pretty much everything on the eastern end of the island can and must be explored on foot. The "interior" of Capri town is a mostly level, residential warren of narrow, bougainvillea-filled lanes where local children leave their trikes and smudge-faced doll babies parked against whitewashed walls. If you feel like working off those three gelatos you had yesterday, there are several really cool hikes you can take from Capri town, which range in difficulty from mellow to strenuous.

The longer, western end of the island is considered by most to be the "real" Capri. It's quieter, more agricultural, and home to the sleepy, higher-altitude village of Anacapri (299m/981 ft. above sea level); Monte Solaro; and the Blue Grotto.

TOURIST OFFICE

There are three branches of the **Azienda Autonoma Cura Soggiorno e Turismo (AACST) Isola di Capri** tourist office. In Capri town, there's an office on the Piazzetta (☎ 081-8370686); in Marina Grande, it's along the port near the funicular station (☎ 081-8370634). In Anacapri, the office is at Via G. Orlandi 59. The official site of the AACST (**www.capritourism.com**), is packed with all the practical information you could possibly need about everything from accommodations to outdoor activities.

Getting Around

BY FUNICULAR

Once you've disembarked from your ferry or hydrofoil at Marina Grande, your next transportation experience on Capri is the funicular railway, which connects the port with the center of Capri town. *Note:* If you're not traveling with too many heavy bags, just bring your luggage aboard; otherwise, you'll have to take a taxi (about 10€) from the port to the town above. Funicular tickets are 1.30€ for one-way; 2.10€ for 60 minutes (1 funicular ride plus 1 bus ride with transfer); 6.70€ for 1 day (limit of 2 funicular rides, plus unlimited bus rides). Tickets for Capri's funicular and buses are plasticized "souvenir" cards, which require a deposit of 1€. Most visitors forget (or choose not) to turn them in at the end of their stay to reclaim the deposit, so the town of Capri makes an extra 1€ in taxes off almost everyone who sets foot here.

BY BUS

Capri's fleet of orange **buses** is handy when you need to travel between Capri town and Anacapri, to the beach at Marina Piccola, or to the Blue Grotto by the overland route and not by boat. The bus also links Marina Grande with Capri town, but the funicular is a much faster and cooler way to climb the hill. The bus terminus of Capri town is located at Piazza Ungheria, just north of the funicular station and the Piazzetta. *Note:* Buses are packed in high season. Buses to and from Capri town are run by **SIPPIC** (☎ 081-8370420); **Staiano** (☎ 081-8372422) operates the bus routes out of Anacapri, 1.30€ one-way; 2.10€ for 60 minutes (two rides or transfers); 6.70€ for 1 day of unlimited bus rides (but only two funicular rides).

BY TAXI

Capri's signature taxis are convertible four-door, seven-seater sedans (some are *Dolce*

Vita–ish '50s cabriolets), which look totally gargantuan after all the shrunken Fiats and Smart cars you will have grown accustomed to seeing in Italy. Most budget travelers never use the taxis of Capri, as the fares run a steep 10€ for even short trips. After a long day of hiking up and down the island's rugged terrain, however, that taxi stand at the beach of Marina Piccola starts to look mighty tempting. All hotels and restaurants should call taxis for you, but if you want to call one yourself, do so by dialing the **Cooperativa Taxi di Capri (Co.Ta.Ca.)** at ☎ **081-8376657.**

ON FOOT

The narrow lanes of Capri town can only be navigated on foot (and by golf-carty vehicles that hotels use to lug guests' suitcases up from the port). A few hundred meters from the Piazzetta, where the whitewashed houses of Capri town give way to lemon and olive groves, paths lead to some of the island's most spectacular (and non-strenuous) hikes. The easiest beach access, if you're walking, is at Marina Piccola, down the hairpin path of Via Krupp, which starts below the Certosa. (Via Krupp is technically closed due to rock-slide dangers. Locals often sneak past the gate.) The road from Capri town to Anacapri (4km/2^1/$_2$ miles away) is a narrow cliff-hugger, riddled with crosses and memorials—better not to do this one on foot. If you're feeling really hard-core, you can go down to Marina Grande and then hike up the ancient Scala Fenicia stairs to the edge of Anacapri. In Anacapri town itself, everything's fairly level and easy to reach on foot.

Sleeping

Most guidebooks shepherd budget-oriented travelers to the sleepy hamlet of Anacapri, instead of Capri town. We beg to differ: While Anacapri certainly has more budget options (and we do love Villa Eva, below), it's an older-demographic scene with little in the

way of nightlife. (So, if you're partying in Capri town and have to get to your Anacapri hotel late at night, you'll have to fork over at least 20€ in cab fare.) Whatever you do, try not to stay in the overdeveloped port area of Marina Grande (where the ferries and hydro-foils arrive).

In Capri town proper, Via Roma and Via Marina Piccola (the roads leading down toward the beach on the south side of the island) are home to a number of Capri's more affordable one- and two-stars, but it's about a 15-minute uphill hike from here to the center of things. If you can splurge on lodging, panoramic Via Tragara (on the high eastern border of Capri town) is home to a whole slew of boutiquey government-rated three- and four-stars (only one, Punta Tragara, is listed here), many with intimate, chalet-style accommodations and lovely swimming pools overlooking the bay at Marina Piccola.

CHEAP

➔ **Da Giorgio** ★ About 100m (328 ft.) down the road to the west of the funicular station is the government-rated one-star Da Giorgio, yet another testament to the civilized nature of the Caprese people: Even budget hotels on this island are tasteful and well kept. Rooms are bright and contemporary, with furniture painted the color of sea foam; a few rooms have small terraces with a chair and table overlooking the Bay of Naples—a fine touch indeed in this price range. Its only slightly out-of-the-way location, away from the most picturesque part of Capri town, is the only strike against it. *Via Roma 34, Capri.* ☎ *081-8375777. www.dagiorgiocapri.com. 85€–120€ double. Amenities: Restaurant. In room: TV.*

➔ **Hotel La Tosca** ★★ For price, comfort, and location, this is the best deal on the island. In the heart of Capri town, on a narrow lane just a 5-minute walk from the *Piazzetta*, La Tosca is as classy as government-rated one-stars get in Italy. Rooms are simple but cool, relaxing, and immaculate; best of all, the communal terrace (where breakfast is served, and where you can bring your own food and drink any time of day you please) has wonderful views over whitewashed rooftops to the Faraglioni. Owner/manager Ettore jaunts off on the hydrofoil many days for business in Naples, but he's always helpful in suggesting scenic walks or arranging island boat tours for hotel guests. Needless to say, with rates as low as these, La Tosca fills up quickly, so be sure to book well ahead. *Via Birago 5, Capri.* ☎ *081-8370989. www.latoscahotel.com. 63€–125€ double. Rates include breakfast. Amenities: Bar; breakfast terrace; library/ lounge. In room: A/C.*

→ **Villa Eva** ★★ Our token Anacapri entry, this is a fabulous place to stay if you'd like a little more room and a few more comforts, and you don't mind being a cab or bus ride away from the buzz of Capri town. With its lush garden setting and spacious, cottagey rooms—and oh, did we mention the lovely swimming pool with poolside bar?—Villa Eva will make you think you've died and gone to budget-traveler heaven. With five- to eight-person apartments that start at 35€ per person, it's one of Capri's most affordable places to crash, and it doesn't even skimp on style or service-oriented staff. *Via la Fabbrica 8, Anacapri.* ☎ *081-8371549. www.villaeva.com. 35€–45€ per person apt for 5–8 people with private bathroom, 90€–100€ double, 110€– 140€ triple, 140€–180€ quad. Amenities: Snack bar; swimming pool. In room: A/C, Internet.*

DOABLE

→ **Villa Krupp** ★★ This longtime favorite was the villa where early-20th-century Russian revolutionaries Gorky and Lenin stayed when on Capri. Surrounded by shady trees, it offers panoramic views of the sea and the Gardens of Augustus from its terraces. At this family-run place, the front parlor is all glass with views of the seaside and

semitropical plants set near Hong Kong chairs, intermixed with painted Venetian-style pieces. Rooms are comfortable and vary in size, with spacious bathrooms. *Via Matteotti 12, Capri.* ☎ *081-8370362. 110€– 140€ double. Amenities: A/C, hair dryer.*

Eating

In Capri, as in the rest of Campania, get ready to indulge in plenty of tomatoes and mozzarella—this is the home of the caprese salad, after all—and some of the most amazing seafood you'll have in your life. However, the island is also fraught with plenty of tourist traps that serve mediocre food. Eating all meals out can get pricey, and it's also a bit inconvenient because you're likely to be out and about during lunch. Grab a sandwich with fresh prosciutto and mozzarella from any of the small delis in town. Note that a lot of Capri's restaurants have curtailed hours in the low and shoulder seasons (Apr–May and Sept–Oct), and many close down for the winter entirely.

HOT SPOTS

→ **Bar Funicolare** CAFE   Stop by this cafe next to the funicular station, around the corner from the Piazzetta, to have your morning cappuccino and *cornetto* (croissant-like pastry) with the likes of Capri's harbormaster and other swarthy, marina-bound locals. *Piazza Diaz, Capri.* ☎ *0818370363. Daily 5:30–10:30pm.*

CHEAP

→ **Da Giorgio** ★★ CAPRESE   In the hotel of the same name, this is a favorite for island habitués who love its reasonable, traditional fare—linguine with *frutti di mare, pappardelle* with shrimp, and all kinds of grilled fish. The panoramic dining room overlooks the Bay of Naples, where all the seafood is caught daily. Everything at the restaurant is served on hand-painted "Da Giorgio" ceramic plates. *Via Roma 34, Capri.* ☎ *081-8375777. Primi*

8€–12€; secondi 10€–15€. Daily noon–3pm and 7–11pm.

➔ **Il Solitario** ★ CAPRESE A delightful little eatery in quiet Anacapri, "the hermit" is another insiders' favorite that will feed you dependable local fare (like ravioli Caprese, with ricotta and mozzarella, topped with tomato sauce) for far less than comparable restaurants in Capri town. Come for lunch before or after a trip to Monte Solaro, and enjoy the shade of the peaceful back garden. Via G. Orlandi 96, Anacapri. ☎ 081-8371382. Primi 7€–9€; secondi 9€–12€. Daily noon–3pm and 7:30–11:30pm.

SPLURGE

➔ **Villa Verde** ★★ ITALIAN With a cozy indoor dining area and a lovely, enclosed garden patio, this fashionable trattoria down an alley near Anema e Core (see below) has awesome homemade pasta with seafood as well as other local specialties. Villa Verde can even stay in the "doable" category if you eschew the more elaborate lobster recipes and stick to pizza. Vico Sella Orta 6, Capri. ☎ 081-8377024. www.villaverde-capri.com. Primi 12€–20€; secondi 18€–30€. Apr–Oct daily noon–4pm and 7pm–2am; Nov–Mar Tues–Sun noon–4pm and 7–11pm.

Partying

If you come to Capri in the peak summer months, you'll find plenty to do on the island at night. From casual wine bars to seaside dance floors, modern discothèques to raucous live-music taverns, there's something for everyone's taste and budget. Come to the island in the less-crowded months, and you'll find half those venues either closed for the season or depressingly deserted. When all else fails, head for the Piazzetta. No matter the time of year, you can always pull up a chair at one of the intimate cafe tables here, sip some prosecco before dinner or some limoncello after, and be in the company of plenty of others, from celebrities to

marina hands, engaging in that time-honored southern Italian tradition: scoping each other out. As in Naples, covers here are pricey—sometimes as much as 20€.

BARS

➔ **Bar Quisi** ★★ On the terrace of the Grand Hotel Quisisana, this elegant bar attracts a swinging scene of younger-generation jet-setters who've decided the Piazzetta has become, well, too *popular*. Nevertheless, the Quisi itself is quite well attended, especially during the *aperitivo* hour—from 6 to 9pm, come here to nibble on the free happy-hour buffet and clink glasses with Ferrari scions and their entourages. Hey, you never know who you're gonna run into on Capri. Via Camerelle 2, Capri. ☎ 081-8370788. www.quisi.it.

➔ **Bar Tiberio** ★ Of the four cafes on the Piazzetta, this is generally the youngest and friendliest, offering a bit more than the others in the way of bar snacks. If you can't snag a table here, don't stress—angle for a front-row spot at Gran Caffe, Bar Caso, or Piccolo Bar, all within 4.5m (15 ft.) of each other. It's open Thursday to Tuesday from 6am to 2am (sometimes 4am). Piazza Umberto I, Capri. ☎ 081-8370268.

➔ **Hotel La Palma** ★ The bar at this government-rated four-star hotel on the chi-chi shopping street of Via Vittorio Emanuele is recommended as an *aperitivo* spot. La Palma has a more subdued atmosphere than the Bar Quisi (above), but its roof-garden setting, amid thick, imported tropical vegetation, is a sultry spot once you've found your island honey for the night. There's also a restaurant here, the Relais La Palma, which does excellent, if pricey, Mediterranean fare. Via Vittorio Emanuele 39, Capri. ☎ 081-8370133. www.lapalma-capri.com.

➔ **Pulalli** ★ Inside the clock tower next to the Piazzetta, Pulalli was once an inn that accommodated new arrivals from the port below; it has since been transformed into a smart little wine bar that also serves small plates from early evening through the wee hours. There's a laid-back vibe and the view of the white lights strung loosely over the Piazzetta is rather magical. Closed Tuesdays. *Piazza Umberto I, Capri.* ☎ *081-8374108.*

NIGHTCLUBS

→**Anema e Core** ★★ Sooner or later, all the jet-setters end up at Capri's most venerable nightlife institution, where entertainment is not provided by slick DJs spinning house music, and partying isn't done under low lights. Anema e Core is a folksy theater-in-the-round where Guido Lembo, local minstrel and "undisputed ruler of Capri," is "capable of transforming inhibited politicians into caterwauling crooners," according to his own PR. Of course, how much fun you have depends a bit on the crowd in attendance that night (it can often be an older, B-list set), but toss back a few cocktails and hey . . . Open May through September daily; in April and October, Saturday and Sunday only. *Via Sella Orta 39/e, Capri.* ☎ *081-8376461. www.anemaecore.com. Cover 20€–25€.*

→**Number Two** ★ One of the few proper discothèques on the island, this is where you go when you actually feeling like dressing up and having a bona fide organized night out. However, it's usually pretty crowded with foreigners and visiting Italians, thanks in large part to the fact that the club lets it be known that Naomi Campbell is a regular here when she's on Capri. *Via Camerelle 1, Capri.* ☎ *081-8377078.*

→**O Guarracino** ★ This rustic underground joint actually used to be an olive press, and there must be some oil left over in the place because the men here sure have a lot of grease in their hair. Still, it's an animated watering hole with a mixed crowd where you can knock back a beer or five while live Neapolitan music is played. It's

not as wild 'n' crazy as Anema e Core, and it's also not as expensive to get in—there's no cover. *Via Castello 7, Capri.* ☎ *081-8370514.*

Sightseeing

Most of the sights worth seeing in Capri are natural attractions—scenic hikes, boat trips, and beaches—which are listed in "Playing Outside," below. But Capri wouldn't be Italian if it didn't have its requisite number of cultural heritage sites, too. There's a rather impressive archaeological site with ruins of an imperial Roman villa, a Carthusian monastery, and even an adorably hokey "Capri in Miniature" attraction.

FREE →**Certosa di San Giacomo** ★ With its stuccoed arches and vaults half-collapsed in ruins, Capri's 14th-century Charterhouse of St. James has a gutted look that is somewhat reminiscent of The Alamo. The building complex, on the southern slopes of Capri town, started out as a monastery for the Carthusian brotherhood of monks, who were forever quarrelling with the Capresi over grazing and hunting rights on the island. When, in the 17th century, a plague broke out among the islanders, the monks stayed disease-free by quarantining themselves within the walls of the Certosa, instead of helping the sick of Capri town. In true Neapolitan fashion, the incensed townspeople dumped the infected corpses of their plague victims over the walls and into the cloisters. The Certosa was also sacked and torched by pirates in 1553. By 1808, when Napoleon had subjected Capri to French rule, the Certosa became a prison. Today, it's a museum, school, and altogether pleasant place, with some fabulous views—what else is new? this is Capri—from its towers. *Viale Certosa, Capri.* ☎ *081-8376218. Free admission. Tues–Sun 9am–2pm.*

→**Villa Jovis** ★★ One of the bigger freak shows ever to assume the imperial throne, Tiberius ruled Rome from 14 to 37 A.D. and in that time built no fewer than 12 villas on Capri, each dedicated to one of the gods. Of the original dozen, only three remain in any recognizable state, and Villa Jovis (dedicated to Jove, or Jupiter) was the most sumptuous in its day, and today is the best preserved—which is not to say it's perfectly intact. You'll need to use your imagination to picture the bygone lavishness of the place: Most of the villa's masonry and brick walls are reduced to rubble, and whatever marble was recovered from the site is now in museums or private collections. Still, the most impressive thing about the Villa Jovis is its lonely position on the high eastern end of the island, where, just beyond the archaeological site, gray limestone cliffs plunge 354m (1,161 ft.) down to the sea. *Tiberio (only accessible by a 45-min. walk from the Piazzetta, up a steady, but not strenuous inclining path), Capri.* ☎ *081-8370634. www.villajovis.it. Admission 2€. Daily 9am to 1 hr. before sunset.*

Visiting the Blue Grotto

Capri's most famous natural wonder is the 📺 Best **Blue Grotto (Grotta Azzurra)** ★★★, a cave whose water glows an otherworldly, incandescent blue due to unique refraction of the sun's rays. Everyone who lands on Capri should visit the grotto, and indeed most do so. Getting there, however, is a minor odyssey, so there are a few things you should know before embarking. First, acquaint yourself with the grotto's convoluted system of admission fees: You have to pay to get to the cove area outside the grotto, which is either 8.50€ for the Blue Grotto–only shuttle service from Marina Grande, or 12€ for the full-island circumnavigation trip (which we highly recommend); *then* you have to pay another 4.50€ per person to the guy in the dinghy who will row you and a few other passengers into the grotto itself; and finally, you have to pay a 4€ "monument" fee which ostensibly goes to the Capri heritage department and is used for the "upkeep" of the Blue Grotto. Whatever. It's totally worth it.

Next, be aware that getting to the Blue Grotto also requires agility. Once you've arrived at the rowboat staging area outside the grotto entrance, you have to clamber awkwardly from your motorboat, over the open sea, to the dinghy, almost surely sustaining bruises and maybe even flashing your fellow passengers in the process. When you and your rowboat-mates are about to enter the grotto, your captain will abruptly ask you to lie all the way down (more likely, he'll just manhandle you into position with a few meaningful grunts). This is necessary so that when he yanks you, via overhead chain, through the 1m-high (3-ft.) hole that is the entrance to the grotto, nobody gets decapitated. Once inside, you'll be treated not only to the truly magical quality of the silvery-blue light reflecting off the sea bottom, but to a chorus of pirate songs as the *capresi* boatmen, in voices soft to booming, harmonious to off-key, join in for a memorable seafaring serenade.

The Grotto is at its least crowded after 3pm, but even during peak hours, it can be fun watching all the action as the rowboat guys jockey for passengers, bumping up against each other and shouting at each other in colorful dialect.

Swimming into the Blue Grotto is really only feasible after the boat traffic has called it a day (5pm or so), but it's a hairy endeavor that only experienced swimmers should attempt. Swells of any size tend to slap against the rock wall where the grotto entrance is located, so if you're not careful, you could get seriously clocked in the head, and there's no lifeguard on duty.

Playing Outside

BOAT TOURS AROUND THE ISLAND

If the trip to the Blue Grotto seems like a rip-off, the lovely 2-hour 📺 Best **boat trips** around Capri, offered by **Gruppo Motoscafisti Capri**, are an incredible bargain at 12€ per person. (When you get to the Blue Grotto, you still have to pay another 8.50€.) Cruise in a snappy and stylish traditional wooden launch while your handsome, charming old salt of a captain expertly navigates Capri's rugged coast and dramatic rock formations, guiding you in and out of tiny grottoes, and regales you with tales of how Roman emperor Tiberius used to throw his prisoners off a cliff on the northeast corner of the island. The boats accommodate about 25 people, and even when they're full (July–Aug), everyone has a good view. The tours leave from Marina Grande (☎ **081-8377714** or 081/837-5646; www.motoscafisti capri.com).

THE MONTE SOLARO CHAIRLIFT

It makes some sketchy squeaks and groans, but what the hell, this single **chairlift** ★★ in Anacapri (Via Caposcuro 10, Anacapri; ☎ **081-8371428**; one-way 4.50€, round-trip 6€; Mar–Oct 9:30am to 1 hr. before sunset, Nov–Feb 10:30am–3pm) takes you on a 12-minute ride from Anacapri town, over villagers' backyards and lemon groves, with views over the western end of the island to the sea, up to Capri's highest point, 589m-high (1,932 ft.) Monte Solaro. If you're feeling frisky, you can take the chairlift up and walk back down the hill (about 1 hr.), or vice versa.

BEACHES

What passes for a "beach" in Capri is a rocky, bumpy, and above all, dinky stretch of terrain that meets the sea. Try as you might, you will not find any traditional expanses of sand on the island. Many bathers (especially those more interested in sunning than swimming) opt for the luxury and stunning views of their hotel pools, but for those who want a good, old-fashioned dip in the Med, there is some glorious 📺 Best **swimming** to be done in the crystalline, deep emerald waters off Capri's shoals. If you're planning a longer outing, bring a sandwich from an *alimentari* in town; otherwise, you're stuck with the pricey, often mediocre food at beach club restaurants.

→ **Bagni Nettuno** ★ One of the nicer, full-service bathing clubs on the island, it's also the only place from which it's possible to swim into the Blue Grotto. Note that swimming into the grotto, while permitted after 5pm, when the tourist boats have all left, is a bit hairy, even in calm seas. See the box (p. 677) for advice. *Località Grotta Azzurra, Anacapri.* ☎ *081-8371362, www.nettuno-capri. com. Bus: Grotta Azzurra.*

→ **Bagni Tiberio** Set below the remains of one of the Emperor Tiberius's Capri villas (he had 12 total), this is one of few bathing establishments on the north side of the island, which gets shady quite early. In front of the beach, a steady traffic of motorboats shuttling between Marina Grande and the Blue Grotto means that the water is not as still and crystalline here as on other parts of the island. *Via Palazzo a Mare 41, Marina Grande.* ☎ *081-8370703. Bus: Bagni Tiberio. Motorboat: from Marina Grande (7€–8.50€ round-trip).*

→ **La Fontelina** ★ This "beach" is hardly more than a few flattish rocks near the water, but you can go for a swim here with the Faraglioni (the huge rocks off Capri's south coast) towering overhead. Just watch out for passing motorboat traffic. *Località Faraglioni, Capri.* ☎ *081-8370845. Steep 15-min. walk from the end of Via Tragara, or access by motorboat from Marina Grande (10€ round-trip).*

→ **Marina Piccola** ★ This is the no-brainer swimming destination for most who visit

Capri. There are a few "beach clubs" (with restaurants and a few other facilities) here, but you can also just plop your towel down in the pebbly, free-access zone around the rock outcropping known as the Scoglio delle Sirene (Mermaids' Reef). Swim out about 15m (50 ft.) for seemingly bottomless, green-blue sea—the color and clarity of the water is astonishing. Be sure to take in the gorgeous view back toward Capri's southern coast and the Faraglioni. *Capri. Bus: Marina Piccola; or 20-min. walk down Via Krupp (technically closed, but those in the know just hop over the barricades).*

Shopping

You'll find a microcosm of the international fashion world on Via Camerelle and Via Vittorio Emanuele—from Gucci to Pucci, the big designer names are all here.

Capri is also home to a number of home-grown specialties that make great souvenirs. For deluxe perfumes made right on the island, head for **Carthusia** (Viale Parco Augusto 2, Capri; ☎ **081-8370368;** www. carthusia.com). Design your own sandals and have them handmade on the spot at **Canfora** (Via Camerelle, Capri; ☎ **081-8370487;** www.canfora.com). Feed your addiction for lemony after-dinner drinks at **Limoncello di Capri** (Via Listrieri 25/a, Capri; ☎ **081-8373059;** www.limoncello. com). All the shops stay open late—the better to trap inebriated tourists who've had too much limoncello on the Piazzetta

The Amalfi Coast

Centuries ago, sirens crooned off the shores of the **Amalfi Coast** ★★ to lure Odysseus into the sea with their song. Today not that much has changed. This part of southern Italy still tempts travelers—but with good wine, good food, and good times rather than some magic ditty. Forget about educational trips to the museum or guided tours that go on and on—in most of these little towns, it's all about doing as little as possible for as long as you want. A typical Amalfi Coast regimen entails lazing the morning away on the beach or a boat, venturing inland for an afternoon espresso on a cobblestone piazza, and relishing a leisurely dinner of fresh octopus followed by lemon profiteroles, washed down with bottles of local wine. Morning will arrive before you know it, when you're partying under the stars in smoky outdoor discos.

The best time to tour the islands and small towns of the Amalfi Coast is April through October. Otherwise, you'll find that many hotels, restaurants, and shops will be closed. Crowds are heaviest in July and August, when Italians are on monthlong vacations.

A great itinerary for the Amalfi Coast would be to start at Naples and take a hydrofoil (45 min.) to Ischia or Capri. Come back to Naples, and hop on a 2-hour bus ride to Amalfi for an afternoon or a day. From Amalfi you can catch a local bus to Ravello, a short 15 minutes away. After a few days in this quiet haven, you'll be ready to move on to the livelier Sorrento. From Sorrento, you could easily take a ferry (45 min.) out for another visit to Capri or Ischia. However, you might want to stay overnight in Sorrento while visiting these pricey isles. Each of these towns can be covered in a day easily.

Amalfi: A Tiny Gem

Amalfi ★ is great for several reasons: It's small enough that you can see everything and still have time for the beach; it's unpretentious and affordable; it has managed to retain its charm despite being a tourist magnet; and it's just so darn picturesque. Arriving in town by ferry, guests are greeted by views of the beach and the Duomo rising in the heart of the city. Amalfi also makes a good base for exploring other, more expensive, towns along the Amalfi Coast.

GETTING INTO TOWN

BY FERRY   This is the part of the country where taking a ferry or hydrofoil is sometimes the most efficient (or only) way to get where you're going. Between hydrofoils (*aliscafi*), high-speed ferries (*navi veloci*), and slow ferries (*traghetti*), there are dozens of daily crossings between mainland Italy (the ports of Naples and Sorrento) and Capri and Ischia, as well as up and down the Amalfi Coast.

Advance booking isn't necessary, which makes a last-minute decision to visit the islands easy from a transportation standpoint. Capri is closer to Sorrento (14km/8³/₄ miles), but Naples (30km/18¹/₂ miles from Capri) is often a better jumping-off point because it's easier to reach from other parts of Italy. Ischia is a bit closer to Naples (34 km/21 miles), but it makes sense to sail to Ischia from Sorrento (about 40km/25 miles away) if you're already based in the south. A few boats connect Capri and Ischia (roughly 42km/26 miles apart) daily.

Call or visit the websites for up-to-date timetables, fares, and general information.

○ **Alilauro:** ☎ 081-991888; www.alilauro.it
○ **Caremar:** ☎ 199-123199 (toll-free); www.caremar.it
○ **Medmar:** ☎ 081-3334111; www.medmargroup.it
○ **NLG** (Navigazione Libera del Golfo): ☎ 081-5520763; www.navlib.it
○ **SNAV:** ☎ 081-4285555; www.snav.it

BY BUS   **SITA** (☎ **199-730749**) runs buses between Sorrento and Amalfi (about 2 hr.; 2.40€), stopping in Positano along the way. The bus can be a bit of a nightmare as the road between Positano and Amalfi is winding and narrow; thus, getting between the two towns takes forever and is a test of anyone's nerves. Buses arrive in Piazza Flavio Gioia, in front of the harbor. To get here from Naples, take the Circumvesuviana train to Sorrento (no rail passes), and then catch the SITA bus from there. Buy bus tickets at the *tabacchi* across the street from the piazza.

GETTING AROUND

From Piazza Flavio Gioia, head straight up away from the water and through the archway, which will take you into Piazza Duomo. Via Lorenzo d'Amalfi runs straight up from there.

TOURIST OFFICE

Amalfi's **AAST Tourist Office** is at Corso delle Repubbliche Marinara 27 (☎ **089/871107;** www.amalfitouristoffice.it; Mon–Sat 8:30am–1:30pm and 3–5pm, although sometimes they decide to close early for apparently no reason).

SLEEPING

➜ **A' Scalinatella** ★★ While Amalfi itself is lacking in dorm beds, nearby Atrani is home to this popular hostel. Dorm beds are provided in clean, bright rooms, and private rooms are available in several other buildings around town. The hostel organizes day trips for its guests. *Piazza Umberto I no. 6.* ☎ *089/871492. www.hostelscalinatella.com. 18€–21€ dorm; 45€–60€ double with shared bathroom, 50€–83€ with private bathroom. To get here, see directions below for getting to Atrani. Once at Atrani, walk through the arch behind the beach and look for signs just beyond the piazza. Amenities: Internet; kitchen; laundry facilities; shared bathrooms.*

➜ **Hotel Lidomare** ★ In a quiet small piazza just up from Piazza Duomo and run by a friendly staff, this hotel is worthy of your euros only if you can wrangle one of the rooms with a terrace overlooking the sea: These are large, bright, and have a Jacuzzi shower or tub. Cheaper rooms are a bit worn down and mildewy. *Via Piccolomini 9 (look for signs in top left corner of Piazza Duomo and walk up the stairs).* ☎ *089/871332.*

The Amalfi Coast

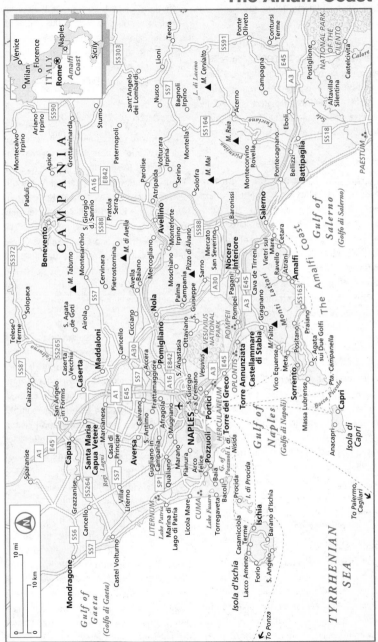

www.lidomare.it. 50€–55€ *single,* 99€–120€ *double. Rates include breakfast. In room: TV, A/C, minibar.*

EATING

→ **Il Tari** ★ ITALIAN/SEAFOOD   There's no terrace here, but there are plenty of large windows for watching the evening crowd stroll by. The seafood pizza here is especially tasty (8.50€). *Via P. Capuano 9.* ☎ *089/871832. Primi 6.50€–13€; secondi 6€–20€; pizza 4€–8.50€. Cover 1.50€. Thurs–Tues 11:30am–3pm and 7–10:30pm.*

MTV Best → **Osteria da Luisella Enoteca** ★★ AMALFITAN/SEAFOOD   Here you'll find upscale dining at affordable prices, with a friendly, professional staff. The vegetables, fish, cheese, and olive oil are all locally produced. Try the mouthwatering house specialties: braised tuna with soy sauce (12€) and sea bass with green pepper (14€). *Piazza Umberto, Atrani.* ☎ *089/871087. www.osteriadaluisella.it. Primi 8€–12€; secondi 10€–18€. Cover 2€. Thurs–Tues noon–3pm and 7–11pm.*

PARTYING

Amalfi doesn't have a whole lot going on in the evenings. Most people stroll along Via Lorenzo d'Amalfi or hang out in Piazza Duomo. For a more lively scene, head over to Atrani where a backpacker crowd fills the bars in Piazza Umberto. Try **Bar Directo** ★ (Piazza Umberto I no. 1; ☎ **089/874231**), which has a huge terrace occupying a large section of the piazza, or its more lively neighbor, **La Risacca** ★ (Piazza Umberto I no. 2; ☎ **089/871087**).

SIGHTSEEING

Amalfi is very small, and easily explored in a few hours, leaving the rest of the day for lounging on the beach. Cafe-lined Piazza Duomo is the center of the action, with tourists milling about the stairs of the **Duomo** (Piazza del Duomo; ☎ **089/871059**; July–Sept daily 9am–9pm, closes earlier in

the winter) and the fountain in the center. From here, Via Lorenzo d'Amalfi is the main street in town, filled with restaurants and souvenir shops. Narrow alleyways leading off of this street allow you to explore a quieter side of Amalfi, and often lead up to piazzettas with stunning views over the town and sea.

Sorrento

Overrun with tourists and on the expensive side, Sorrento is nonetheless worthy of at least a stop for the day if just for its utter beauty: The town sits perched up on the cliff ledges of the peninsula that marks the southern tip of the Bay of Naples. On a clear day (which is typical of the region), you can see Naples, Vesuvius, and Capri from here. The town acts as a convenient transit point between Naples and the Amalfi Coast and seems to attract mainly geriatric tour groups and jet-setting yuppies.

GETTING INTO TOWN

BY TRAIN **Circumvesuviana** trains (☎ **800/053939**; www.vesuviana.it) run frequently between Naples and Sorrento (about 1 hr.; 3.20€), stopping at Pompeii in between (30 min.; 1.80€). Rail passes are not valid on these trains. The train station sits just to the south of Corso Italia, to the east of the town center. Purchase tickets at the train station office.

BY BUS **SITA** buses (p. 680) connect Sorrento with Amalfi (2.40€) via Positano (1.30€), leaving nearly every hour from just below the train station.

BY FERRY   Ferries run from **Marina Piccola,** down the steps and toward the water from Piazza Tasso. In the summer, there are frequent connections to Capri (from 5.80€) and Naples (from 4.50€), and Amalfi (7€), as well as daily connections to Ischia (15€) and Positano (7€). For more information about ferry and hydrofoil travel in the region, see "Getting There: By Ferry," earlier in this chapter.

GETTING AROUND

ON FOOT   Sorrento is small enough to navigate on foot. From the train and bus station, walk down the stairs and head down the street straight ahead to Corso Italia, the main street. From there, turn left and walk to Piazza Tasso, and then either continue on Corso Italia, or turn right on any of the side streets from there to get to the old city. From the port at Marina Piccola, walk toward the town and then up the stairs to Piazza Tasso. (The stairs from Marina Piccola to Piazza Tasso, and vice versa, are not feasible if you have luggage; instead, take the bus.)

BY BUS   Public buses are orange (as opposed to the blue or green SITA interregional buses), and cost 1€ for a 60-minute ticket. Line B runs between Piazza Tasso and Marina Piccola. Line D runs between Piazza Tasso and Marina Grande (the larger port where cruise ships and fishing boats dock).

TOURIST OFFICE

The **AAS Tourist Information Office** is at Lungomare de Maio 35 (☎ **081-8074033;** www.sorrentotourism.com; Mon–Sat 8:45am–6:15pm, closed holidays). To get here, head through Piazza Sant'Antonino to Via Luigi de Maio and enter into the compound on the right. As well as a poor-quality map, the tourist office has copies of the indispensable transportation schedule, which lists departure times for the Circumvesuviana train between Sorrento and Naples, the SITA bus schedule between Sorrento and the Amalfi Coast, and a list of ferry departures between Sorrento and Capri, Naples, Ischia, Positano, and Amalfi.

The online Sorrento Information Guide, **www.sorrentoinfo.com**, provides a directory of hotels and restaurants, as well as general information on the city and its attractions, and valuable reviews of all these by other visitors. The official website of the Sorrento Tourist Office, **www.sorrentotourism.com**, contains information on transport, accommodations, restaurants, and sites, as well as a handy map section.

SLEEPING

Sorrento has some incredible accommodations options: Imagine waking up in a Mediterranean-style suite and stepping out onto your balcony to admire the view of the bay and the town below. If you can afford the splurge, check out the fancy hotels lined along Via del Capo. For those with more realistic budgets, there are more moderately priced places to stay, though finding budget accommodations can be difficult during peak season as the options are few and so tend to get grabbed quickly.

➡**Hotel Sorrento City** ★★ One of several hotels on busy Corso Italia, this is one of the few here that won't break the bank. Rooms are tiny but pretty, with tiled floors, silky bedspreads, and lush curtains. Some also have balconies large enough to sit on. *Corso Italia 221 (near Via degli Aranci), Sorrento.* ☎ *081-8772210; www.italyby.com/hotelcity/index.html. 115€ double, 140€ triple, 165€ quad. Rates include breakfast. In room: A/C, TV, safe.*

➡**La Sirene** ★ This is the sole hostel in Sorrento, and by far the most affordable place to stay. Conveniently located on a noisy street near the train station, rooms with up to 10 dorm beds are bright with clean bathrooms, and some also have balconies, although there's not much to see. The hostel also runs a cozy cafe and bar next door, with a 10% discount for hostel guests. *Via degli Aranci 160, Sorrento.* ☎ *081-072925; www.hostel.it. 16€–20€ dorm; 50€ double with bunk bed, 60€ with double bed. Rates include breakfast. Amenities: Cafe; bar; Internet; TV room.*

EATING

Sorrento has no shortage of restaurants, but being a touristy town, most are geared toward this crowd—which explains the number of establishments designed to imitate a British pub. Sorrento's Italian restaurants offer the usual fare of pasta, pizza, and panini. For the best authentic seafood and great views, head to Marina Grande.

➜ Bagni Sanna Restaurant and Snack Bar ★★ SEAFOOD

This is the best of the restaurants that line Marina Grande's shore. Walk down the wooden pier to the casual, airy restaurant where diners graze on fresh seafood dishes and then retire to the end of the pier, where sun beds and a swimming area are provided for customers. What more could you ask for? As this is probably the best place in the city to swim, it's worth the price of a snack to be able to use the bathing facilities. *Marina Grande. Primi 6€–9€; secondi 6€–10€. Daily 11:30am–midnight.*

➜ Taverna dell'800 ★ PUB

An old-school British pub in old-school Sorrento, but probably one of the only places in Italy where you'll be able to satisfy a craving for fish and chips. They also serve a mean burger here. The pub is a busy place in the evenings, particularly with British tourists. *Via Accademia 29 (at Via Tasso).* ☎ *081-8785970. Snacks (burgers, fries, and such) from 3€; fish entrees 6€–14€; meat entrees 6€–15€; pizza 4€–6€. Tues–Sun noon–3pm and 6pm–2am.*

PARTYING

Sorrento's nightlife centers on Piazza Tasso and Corso Italia, where crowds come to stroll and people-watch in the evenings. For those looking to nurse a pint while watching sports, Sorrento offers several British pubs where you can do so, although you'll find nary an Italian in sight. Both locals and tourists of various ages fill the clubs in the city, partying until the early hours of the morning.

➜ Chaplin's Pub/The English Inn ★

Sorrento's obsession with the English pub is evident at these two spots across the street from each other. Both are about as British as they come, with a brass bar spanning the

length of the pub, Guinness flowing on tap, and crowds absorbed in the football (translation: "soccer") match. Chaplin's attracts an older crowd of football fans, while those at the larger English Inn seem to prefer conversation and a bit of dancing. *Chaplin's Pub: Corso Italia 18.* ☎ *081-8072551. The English Inn: Corso Italia 56.* ☎ *081-8074357.*

➜ Fauno Bar

Sprawling across an entire side of Piazza Tasso, tourists flock here for the atmosphere and views. Even if you're not up for the pricey dinner served here, Fauno is worthy of a stop for a drink on its massive terrace. Fauno also turns up the beats on the dance floor, and it's a riot watching aging yuppies attempt to get their groove on. Skip the touristy musical show offered in the adjacent theatre in the evening. *Piazza Tasso.* ☎ *081-8781021. www.faunonotte.it.*

➜ Matilda Club ★★

A gigantic place down the stairs behind Piazza Tasso (look for the signs), with six floors offering anything and everything you could want in a club: a restaurant, pub, Internet cafe, disco, and comfy room for chilling out. Karaoke runs from 9pm to midnight, at which point the music begins to pound and crowds pack the dance floor of the disco. *Piazza Tasso.* ☎ *081-8773236.*

SIGHTSEEING

Sorrento is a yuppie tourist's paradise, with swank shopping boulevards and a charming and easily accessible old town, as well as a slew of fancy hotels with immaculate views of the bay.

The center of the action in Sorrento is **Piazza Tasso,** a busy square jam-packed with restaurants, traffic, and tourists. **Corso Italia,** the main street, runs through the piazza, and is full of swank shops and pedestrian shoppers, making it a nice place for a stroll. From here, continue on to **Via Capo,** home to the fancy hotels and great views of the bay and its coastline. To escape the chaos, wander through Sorrento's old town.

Unfortunately, Sorrento is seriously lacking in beaches—the few that are here are privately owned by the upscale hotels. Your best bet for swimming is off a pier at Marina Grande (see below). Just don't go skinny-dipping: We did this one late night, several years back, and the locals called the Carabinieri on us. Not our proudest moment as American students, to be sure.

The Old Town

Running in between Corso Italia and the waterfront, Sorrento's **old town** ★ is a maze of cobblestone streets that provide a welcome relief from the overwhelming traffic of Corso Italia, but not from the hordes of tourist groups that run rampant in the city. The most happening streets of the old town are Via Sant'Antonino and Via Giuliani, filled with restaurants and souvenir shops. In between, you'll find quieter alleyways with historic buildings, shops catering to locals, and a few restaurants. For a bit of culture, step in the ornate Church of Sant'Antonino, a 17th-century building dedicated to the patron saint of Sorrento. It's located at Piazza Sant'Antonino and admission is free.

Marina Grande

A short but pleasant walk from the center of town, the small fishing village of **Marina Grande** ★★ is a quiet oasis in Sorrento and much less touristy than the old town. This is one of the only places around here where you can actually lay on a beach chair and take a dip in the sea, although you'll have to do so from the pier, as there is no actual beach. It's also the best place in town to come for a seafood meal; several restaurants line the waterfront. To get here: Follow Via Marina Grande from Piazza della Vittoria and then head down the steps to enter the village. Alternately, you can take the Line D bus from Piazza Tasso.

Ischia

A short hop on the hydrofoil from Naples, **Ischia** ★★★ (pronounced "*ees*-kee-ya') has become the new *it* vacation destination for continental Europe's yuppie crowd. Most common among the tourist crowd are middle-aged Germans, who come here to subject themselves to various age-defying treatments involving Ischia's thermal waters—and then bake themselves under the hot Mediterranean sun. But if you can manage to break away from busy Ischia Porto, the main town, to one of the other settlements on the island, you'll discover a more laid-back, and breathtakingly beautiful island with friendly people, great beaches (much better than Capri's), and enough hiking to satisfy any fitness buff's craving. Give Ischia Porto a try, and then escape the dirty looks of the Prada-clad moneybags for Forio, Sant'Angelo, and the other towns along the coast. While Ischia is forever compared with Capri, its more striking—and more cliché—sister to the south, Ischia stands on its own as a wonderful, low-key getaway.

ISCHIA BASICS

Orientation: Ischia

The island is known for its [MV] [Best] **sandy beaches,** health spas (which utilize hot springs for hydromassage and mud baths), and vineyards producing the red and white Monte Epomeo, the red and white Ischia, and the white Biancolella. The largest community is at **Ischia Porto** on the eastern coast, a circular town seated in the crater of the extinct Monte Epomeo, which functions as the island's main port of call. The liveliest town is **Forio** on the western coast, with its many bars along tree-lined streets. The other major communities are **Lacco Ameno** and **Casamicciola Terme,** on the north shore, and **Serrara Fontana** and **Barano d'Ischia,** inland and to the south.

Tourist Office & Website

Ischia's **tourist office** (Industriali del Turismo dell'Isola d'Ischia) is in Ischia Porto at Via Alfredo De Luca 153 (☎ **081-3334820;** www.ischiaonline.it/tourism; Mon–Fri 9am–

Heading Inland to Ravello

Who says you have to be on the water to be the most impressive town on the Amalfi Coast? Set back from the sea, 6km (4 miles) from Amalfi and over 335m (1,099 ft.) high in the hills, 📺 Best Ravello ★★★ is the bald eagle of the Amalfi Coast. It's favored by an older, quieter set (as well as some famous writers, like Gore Vidal), but it's so spectacular that everyone who visits the Amalfi Coast should come here for a half-day side trip. To get to Ravello, take a bus from Amalfi's Piazza Flavio Gioia; buses run about every hour, and fare is 1.20€ one-way—a small price to pay when you see what it takes to get a multiple-axle vehicle up the hair-pinned road to Ravello!

In town, the first major attraction you'll see from the bus stop is the **Villa Rufolo** ★ (Piazza Duomo; ☎ 089-857657; admission 4€; daily 9am–6pm, Apr–Sept until midnight), with its Moorish-inspired architecture and terraced gardens offering sneak-peek views of the coastline below. A 10-minute hike from Villa Rufolo, up the narrow and stepped (but not particularly steep) Via Santa Chiara, is the **Villa Cimbrone** ★★ (Via Santa Chiara 26; ☎ 089-857459; admission 3€; daily 9am–sunset)—absolutely not to be missed if you're going to make the trek to Ravello. The villa's buildings, which the attendant will be keen to usher you toward, are fine and all, but the real star here is the **panoramic garden terrace** ★★★. From the white marble parapet, punctuated by evocatively "ruined" busts of Greek and Roman sculpture, the view over the coast, through the mist that so often hangs in the air here, is quite simply one of the most stunning vistas we've ever seen.

After you've worked up an appetite on the walk to and from Villa Cimbrone, retreat to **Cumpa' Cosimo** (Via Roma 44–46; ☎ 089-857156) for lunch. Locals and celebs alike pack its tables for the best home cooking in town, including fried-fish platters from the sea below, and vegetable and meat dishes in keeping with Ravello's more inland, hillside position. Open daily for lunch and dinner.

1pm and 4–6pm). The website provids a searchable accommodations database, interactive map, events listings, and general information about the island of Ischia.

GETTING INTO TOWN & AROUND

Ischia's bus company **SEPSA** (☎ 081-991808; www.sepsa.it) runs a convenient transport system between the island's towns. There are three main lines: **CS** runs clockwise around the island, **CD** runs counterclockwise, and the **no. 1** runs between Ischia Porto and Sant'Angelo. Purchase a 90-minute ticket (1.20€) or 24-hour ticket (4€) from ticket booths or *tabacchi*, and be sure to validate it once on board.

Ischia's towns are small enough to be easily navigated on foot, though overpriced taxis (with a minimum fare of 10€) offer transport within and between towns.

SLEEPING

→ **Hotel Poggio Del Sole** ★★ One of three properties in Forio run by the friendly 20-something Colella brothers, this hotel offers basic rooms with clean bathrooms, and many with balconies with great views of the harbor. Mamma Tina runs the restaurant downstairs (see below), and the small swimming pool is open in the summer. When you arrive, give them a call, and they'll come pick you up. *Via Baiola 193.* ☎ *081-987756. www.hotelpoggiodelsole.it. 32€–52€ single,*

64€–104€ double. Breakfast 3€. Amenities: Restaurant; pool. In room: A/C, TV, hair dryer, minibar, safe.

➜ **Ostello Il Gabbiano (HI)** As is typical of Hostelling International properties, Il Gabbiano is a large building with a sterile environment inconveniently located south of Forio. That being said, it is also, by far, the cheapest place to stay on the island, even if you factor in the bus fare. The beach is also close by. S.S. Forio-Panza 162. ☎ 081-909422. 13€ dorm. Rates include breakfast. Amenities: Garden; pool; shared bathrooms.

EATING

Dine on traditional Ischian cuisine such as seafood dishes and rabbit in Ischia Porto's restaurants—check out the side streets off Corso Vittoria Colonna for less touristy restaurants. For the cheapest eats, hit the beach in Forio.

➜ **Bar Diana** ★ ISCHIAN/ITALIAN   Yes, it is usually filled with German tourists, but this is also probably the most affordable place to eat on Ischia Porto's main street. The owner, a dead-ringer for Luigi of Super Mario Bros. fame, likes to explain each item on the menu to diners in order to help them choose. Corso Vittoria Colonna 178/180, Ischia Porto. ☎ 081-991024. Bruschetta 4.50€; pizza around 5€. Daily 7am–1am.

➜ **Sirena** ★★ ISCHIAN/SEAFOOD   A small trattoria on Corso Vittoria Colonna, popular with both locals and tourists who come to sample traditional Ischian cuisine in a cozy environment. If you have no qualms about eating a cute bunny, try the Ischian rabbit, raised traditionally in burrows underground. Corso Vittoria Colonna 9, Ischia Porto. No phone. Primi 4.50€–9.50€; secondi 6€–15€; pizza 3.10€–6€. Daily 11am–3pm and 6–11pm.

PARTYING

Nightlife centers on Ischia Porto. Most people stroll down Corso Vittoria Colonna in the evening after dinner, window-shopping along the stores that stay open late due to the extra-long afternoon siesta. Both Ischia Porto and Forio have a few spots where both locals and tourists indulge in alcohol-imbibed pleasures, though on an off night (that is, during the week and in the winter) these places are deserted.

MTV Best ➜ **Hot Springs Party** ★★ For something a little different that's both fun and relaxing, the Ring Hostel and its associated hotel often have hot-springs party nights: For 10€ you get an hour of unlimited drinking at the hotel's restaurant and transport south to Sorgeto hot springs—utter heaven at night when the water is lit solely by moonlight—where the natural pools of steaming water buttress the sea, so you can easily cool off in the Mediterranean when things get too steamy in the hot water. For information, contact the Ring Hostel. Forio. ☎ 081-987546. www.ringhostel.com. Event price 10€.

➜ **New Valentino** ★ Ischia's most established, and most popular, disco. Open only on the weekends (there wouldn't be much of a point in opening during the week), it's definitely the place to be, if you can stand being surrounded by groping couples on the dance floor. For something a bit tamer, stop in at the Ecstasy piano bar next door. It's open Friday to Sunday from 11pm to 5am. Corso Vittoria Colonna 97, Porto Ischia. ☎ 081-992653.

SIGHTSEEING
Exploring Ischia Porto

The harbor doesn't have much to it besides a few restaurants and travel agencies. Corso Vittoria Colonna is a nice place to stroll and window-shop trendy boutiques and vendors selling cheap knockoffs, and there is an abundance of street-side cafes from which you can watch the tourists stroll by. To reach Ischia Porto's beach, walk 1 block down any of the side streets off of Corso Vittoria Colonna.

➔**The Aragonese Castle of Ischia** ★★
Perched upon an island linked to the mainland by a stone bridge, this ancient castle was initially constructed as a fort by the Greeks in the 5th century B.C., and then later overtaken by a string of other conquerors ranging from the Romans to the Normans to the Arabs. Be sure to visit the Casa del Sole, housing an excellent modern painting exhibition, and the Nun's Cemetery, where dead bodies used to be put on benches where their body fluids were drained as they decomposed, while fellow nuns watched as a meditation on the uselessness of the body. For something a little less morbid, walk along the Path of the Sun, which gives access to enchanting views of the sea. *Ischia Ponte.* ☎ *081-991959. Admission 10€. Daily 9:30am until sunset. Bus: 7 from Ischia Porto; or walk down Corso Vittoria Colonna about 20 min. to the very end.*

Exploring Forio

On the west coast of Ischia, Forio is a small town with a wonderfully laid-back vibe, lacking the pretentiousness of Ischia Porto. With that in mind, Forio is a great place to base your stay on Ischia, or spend a relaxing day in. Buses and ferries drop off passengers on the main street that runs along the waterfront. From here, walk up the street next to the Captain Morgan booth to reach the old town and its labyrinth of winding alleys. Forio is home to possibly the nicest stretch of public beach on the island: **Chiaia Beach** ★, next to the harbor, is a long stretch of clean sandy beach lined with casual restaurants.

TAKING THE WATERS

You don't have to spend a fortune staying in one of the posh hotels on Ischia in order to enjoy the island's thermal spas. **Poseidon** ★ (located south of Forio; ☎ **081-908711;** www.giardiniposeidon.it) is pampering heaven! Entry (full-day 27€; half-day [after 1pm] 22€) includes access to 22 thermal pools of varying temperatures, the sauna and garden, and to a large stretch of beach where you'll be provided with a complimentary chair and umbrella, and also includes a hydromassage. And if this isn't enough, various healing treatments using thermal waters are also available.

Paris

People think of the City of Lights as a place for lovers, and, in fact, getting to know Paris can be as intoxicating as a good love affair. Sometimes, strolling down a broad boulevard under the chestnut trees and blue sky, sun glinting off the cafe tabletops, you could swear that Paris is embracing you. But then you find yourself backed against the window of a drafty, overpriced brasserie, coldly ignored, waiting to be charged tourist rates for a cheese sandwich, and you suspect Paris might've been stringing you along the whole time. And you think, was I ever in? Was I even close?

Being in, or *branché* (literally, "plugged in"), is what Paris is all about. A joint can be dead and dull, but still keep its rep if the right people are there, if it's branché. Most young Parisians will affect total ignorance about what spot is or is not branché, but in fact they're in constant anxiety over not being branché. Those who are, in fact, in, won't even use the word; they may say that a scene is trendy or say nothing about it at all.

So, if you want to be in with the in crowd, it's essential—more so than in any other place in Europe—that you meet a few French natives. And where can you find such people? Ménilmontant (it's partly in the 11th arrondissement, partly in the 20th) and Batignolles (17th arrondissement) are where the wild things are these days. Talk to locals at any bar or nightclub in these 'hoods, and the oft-misunderstood French culture might begin to make sense. Though Parisians work hard to preserve their distinctive heritage, their seeming aversion to outside influence often hides an underlying intrigue with other cultures. The young especially are more apt to break out into English, either to go on about the latest 50 Cent album or to inform you that they're vehemently opposed to an Americanized McParis.

Today, not only is Paris transforming with the influx of immigrant populations from Africa, the Arab world, Asia, and eastern Europe—creating both excitement and political tension—but the European Union (E.U.), the Chunnel, and the juggernaut of globilization has made Parisians generally more open and friendlier than they've ever been. The mythology and even the history of Paris may be steeped in its literary and artistic past, but its contemporary culture has never been fresher.

The Best of Paris

○ **The Best-Located Value Hotel:** The coziest hotel in Paris is the **Hôtel du Champs de Mars.** From the warm welcome you will get from the owner to the inviting pastel bedspread that complements the color of the walls, this place is all about the details. I couldn't recommend it more. See p. 704.

○ **The Best Cheap Meal:** You'll find little falafel joints all over town, and it'd be a shame to pass up a chance to sample the French version of fast food. **Maoz,** where you can load your falafel with toppings from a self-serve bar, is one of the city's best. See p. 709.

○ **The Best Café:** Le Fumoir is, hands down, the city's best place to grab a *café* and soak in a decidedly French atmosphere. The bar also serves tasty cocktails, making this a prime happy-hour spot for locals. See p. 710.

○ **The Best Bar: Sanz Sans** helped revitalize the now hopping 11th arrondissement back in the 1990s. It remains one of the area's best bars, with a DJ who spins the latest dance music until dawn and plenty of lavishly decorated nooks for lounging and sipping decently priced cocktails. See p. 714.

○ **The Best Tourist Trap:** Yes, you will wait in long lines until you are herded into an elevator with other tourists. But you'll feel even more foolish if you leave Paris without a picture in front of the **Tour Eiffel.** For the best picture of you with the Eiffel tower, try Trocadéro. See p. 722.

○ **The Best Museum:** If you're too crushed for time to take in the **Louvre,** head to the inside-out building that is the **Centre Pompidou,** which houses some of the best and worst modern art in the world. It has the largest collection of modern and contemporary art in Europe, with works by legendary artists such as Picasso, Dalí, Kandinsky, Matisse, Magritte, and Warhol on permanent display. See p. 723.

○ **The Best One-Stop Shopping:** Paris's **outdoor food markets** are full of cheap picnic supplies, so they're perfect pit stops if you're trying to save money. Depending on the day and market, you'll see that the entire neighborhood turns out to do shopping and have coffee or a glass of wine. See p. 729 for a list of the city's best markets.

○ **The Best Beach Party:** Visit Paris from mid-July to mid-August, and you'll be able to take part in a 3.2km-long (2-mile) beach party, called **Paris Plage.** About 2,000 tons of sand are shipped in to create a man-made beach along the Right Bank for sun-starved city dwellers. UNESCO recently added 12km (7¹/₂ miles) of Paris riverbank to their list of World Heritage Sites, and for good reason. Even without the man-made beach's many bonuses—including music sets and sports from Tai Chi to beach volleyball—the setting is lovely. See p. 722.

○ **The Best Way to See Paris If You're Sober:** Strap on some Rollerblades, and whiz past all those average backpackers. There are free in-line skating runs at place Raoul every Friday night at 10pm, so you might leave Paris a winner. See p. 726.

Getting There & Getting Around

Getting into Town

BY AIR

If you are flying into Paris, you'll most likely arrive at **Charles de Gaulle Roissy** airport (☎ 01-48-62-22-80). The best way to get into town is to take the **RER,** which is like a mix between a train and a subway, with many stops in downtown Paris. Simply follow the signs for the RER or Métro in the airport to the station, where you can buy a ticket to the center of town (7.50€). The train takes 30 to 45 minutes and it stops at some major stops downtown where you can transfer to other Métro stations.

Another option, the **Roissybus** (☎ 01-48-04-18-24), departs from a point near the corner of the rue Scribe and place de l'Opéra every 15 minutes from 5:45am to 11pm. The cost for the 50-minute ride is 8€.

Taxis from Roissy into the city run about 40€ on the meter. At night (8pm–7am) fares are about 40% higher. Long queues of both taxis and passengers form outside each of the airport's terminals in a surprisingly orderly fashion.

There are a few other airports in Paris (Orly, Roissy, and Beauvais), which are used more rarely. **Beauvais** (www.aeroport beauvais.com), outside the city, is the base for a bunch of budget airlines that offer cheap flights to cities in France and England. A shuttle will cost 28€ to 55€ one-way.

BY TRAIN

There are six major train stations in Paris: **Gare d'Austerlitz,** 55 quai d'Austerlitz, 13e (serving the southwest, with trains from the

Loire Valley, the Bordeaux country, and the Pyrenees); **Gare de l'Est,** place du 11 Novembre 1918, 10e (serving the east, with trains from Strasbourg, Nancy, Reims, and beyond to Zurich, Basel, Luxembourg, and Austria); **Gare de Lyon,** 20 bd. Diderot, 12e (serving the southeast with trains from the Côte d'Azur and Provence to Geneva, Lausanne, and Italy); **Gare Montparnasse,** 17 bd. Vaugirard, 15e (serving the west, with trains from Brittany); **Gare du Nord,** 18 rue de Dunkerque, 15e (serving the north, with trains from Holland, Denmark, Belgium, and Germany); and **Gare St-Lazare,** 13 rue d'Amsterdam, 8e (serving the northwest, with trains from Normandy).

Go to **www.voyages-sncf.com** to get ticket prices and schedules.

UNDER THE CHANNEL

One of the great engineering feats of our time, the $15-billion Channel Tunnel (Chunnel) opened in 1994, and the **Eurostar Express** now has daily service from London to both Paris and Brussels. The 50km (31-mile) journey takes 35 minutes, though the actual time spent in the Chunnel is only 19 minutes. Stores selling duty-free goods, restaurants, service stations, and bilingual staffs are available to travelers on both sides of the Channel.

Eurostar tickets are available through **Rail Europe** (☎ 877-272-RAIL; www.raileurope. com). In the U.K., make reservations for **Eurostar** at ☎ 0870-530-0003; in the United States, call ☎ 800-EUROSTAR. Chunnel train traffic is roughly competitive with air travel, if you calculate door-to-door

PARIS

travel time. Trains leave from London's Waterloo Station and arrive in Paris at the Gare du Nord.

The tunnel also accommodates passenger cars, charter buses, taxis, and motorcycles, transporting them under the Channel from Folkestone, England, to Calais, France. It operates 24 hours a day, running every 15 minutes during peak travel times and at least once an hour at night. You can buy tickets at the tollbooth at the tunnel's entrance. With **Le Shuttle** (☎ 0870-535-3535; www.euro tunnel.com), gone are the days of weather-related delays, seasickness, and advance reservations.

Before they board Le Shuttle, motorists stop at a tollbooth and pass through British and French immigration at the same time. Then they drive onto a 1km-long ($1/2$ mile) train and travel through the tunnel. During the ride, motorists stay in air-conditioned carriages, remaining inside their cars or stepping outside to stretch their legs. When the trip is completed, they simply drive off. Total travel time is about an hour. Once on French soil, British drivers must remember to drive on the right-hand side of the road.

BY BUS

Bus travel to Paris is available from London and many other cities on the continent. In the early 1990s, the French government established strong incentives for long-haul buses

not to drive into the center of Paris, so the arrival/departure point for Europe's largest bus operator, **Eurolines France,** is a 35-minute Métro ride from central Paris, at the terminus of Métro line 3 (Gallieni), in the eastern suburb of Bagnolet. **Eurolines France** is at 28 av. du Général-de-Gaulle, 93541 Bagnolet (☎ 01-49-72-51-58). The price of a round-trip ticket between Paris and London (a 7-hr. trip) is 55€ to 72€ for passengers 26 and up, and 55€ to 65€ for passengers under 26.

Getting Around

BY FOOT

The best way to see Paris is to hoof it around town—walking will let you absorb the city's atmosphere slowly, as it's meant to be.

BY METRO

The **Métro** is the Paris subway system. You can buy a ticket from a machine in the subway station or from a ticket window. To get through the turnstiles to the Métro, put your ticket in the slot, then take the ticket with you on the train; you'll need it to get out of the Métro. Mean-spirited *controleurs* dressed in uniform can stop you at any time on the Métro or in the station and ask to see your ticket; if it's bona fide, you'll be fined. A Métro ticket costs 1.40€ and a package of 10 is 11€. Don't worry that Paris is divided into Métro zones; you don't need to understand the zones unless you are planning

---

Paris Visite

If you plan to ride the Métro a lot, the **Paris Visite** pass may be worthwhile. You get unlimited rides for 1 to 5 days depending on the price (8.35€ for 1 day, 14€ for 2 days, 18€ for 3 days, and 27€ for 5 days, all for zones one to three only, which do not include Disneyland, the airport, or Versailles).

Most economical, for anyone who arrives in Paris early in the week, is a **Carte Orange.** Sold at large Métro stations, it allows 1 week of unlimited Métro or bus transit within central Paris for 14€. It's valid from any Monday to the following Sunday, and sold only on Mondays, Tuesdays, and Wednesdays. You'll have to submit a passport-size photo.

to travel outside of Paris to places like Versailles or the airport. The Métro is open from 5:20am to 1:20am, so get ready to cab it home from a late night at the bar. Go to **www.ratp.fr** for info on the French subway, and check out the map on the inside front cover of this book.

BY BUS

Bus travel is much slower than the subway. Most buses run from 7am to 8:30pm (a few run until 12:30am, and 10 operate during the early morning hours). Service is limited on Sundays and holidays. Bus and Métro fares are the same and you can use the same carnet tickets on both. At certain stops, signs list the destinations and numbers of the buses serving that point. Destinations are usually listed north to south and east to west. Most stops along the way are also posted on the sides of the buses. To catch a bus, wait in line at the bus stop. Signal the driver to stop the bus and board.

Most bus rides (including any that begin and end within Paris's 20 arrondissements and nearby suburbs) require one ticket. For bus travel to some of the more distant suburbs, an additional ticket might be required. If you intend to use the buses a lot, pick up a **RATP bus map** at its offices at place de la Madeleine, 8e (Métro: Madeleine); or 54 quai de la Rapée, 12e (Métro: Gare de Lyon); or at any tourist office. For details on bus and Métro routes, call ☎ **08-92-68-77-14.**

BY TAXI

There are taxi stands all over Paris; be warned that at around 2am when the Métro closes, lines get pretty long. You can book cabs in advance with **Taxis Bleus** (☎ **01-49-36-10-10;** www.taxis-bleus.com),

Alpha Taxi (☎ **01-45-85-85-85**), or **Taxi G7** (☎ **01-47-39-47-39;** www.taxisg7.fr).

BY BICYCLE

You can rent bikes from a number of places in town. *Maison Roue Libre* rents bicycles for about 9€ to 14€ for 1 day and 20€ for 5 weekdays in a few locations in Paris, near Hôtel de Ville (av. Victoria) and in the park (bois de Vincennes) in front of the château (esplanade du château) and at porte d'Auteuil/Gare Routière RATP. They also have two central offices at Les Halles (1 passage Mondétour; ☎ **08-10-44-15-34;** Mentétour is at the intersection of rue Ramuteau and rue Mondétour; Métro: Châtelet Les Halles) and 37 bd. Bourdon (☎ **01-44-54-19-29;** www.ratp.fr or www.rouelibre.fr; Métro: Bastille).

BY CAR

To rent a car in Paris, you must have an international driver's license. To rent scooters and motorcycles with engines smaller than 50cc, you don't need a driver's license at all. See the "Basics" chapter for more info.

You can choose from one of Paris's countless car-rental companies, including **Hertz, Budget,** and **Europecar** (www.auto-reservation-plus.com). **Freescoot** (www.freescoot.com) rents bicycles, motorcycles, and scooters. They have two locations: one at 114 bd. Voltaire (☎ **01-44-93-04-03;** Métro: Voltaire) and the other at 63 quai de la Tournelle (☎ **01-44-07-06-72;** Métro: Jusseau). **Motorail** (190 rue de Bercy Gare de Lyon; ☎ **01-43-07-08-09;** www.motorail.fr; Métro: Gare de Lyon) rents scooters, motorcycles, and bicycles with all the necessary equipment (helmets, gloves, jackets).

Paris Basics

Orientation: Paris Neighborhoods

To orient yourself in Paris, remember that the Seine River (which runs east to west) cuts the city in half. The north section is called **Rive Droit** and the south section is called **Rive Gauche.** The city is also divided into neighborhoods called *arrondissements.*

The 1st arrondissement contains the Louvre and the Jardins des Tuileries. From here, the arrondissements continue in a clockwise spiral. Most of the action for tourists is in the center of town near the Seine and in Montmartre. Things get less expensive and somewhat shadier the farther you get from the center of town. As a frame of reference, think that the 1st is the **Louvre,** the 4th is the MTV Best **Marais,** the 5th is the **Latin Quarter,** the 6th is **St-Germain,** 7th is the **Eiffel Tower,** the 8th is **Champs Elysées** and **Arc de Triomphe,** the 11th is the **Oberkampf,** and the 18th is **Montmartre.** These are the most important neighborhoods to see.

1ST ARRONDISSEMENT (LOUVRE) The biggest attractions here are the **Louvre** and **Les Halles,** a huge shopping mall built on the site of an old marketplace. In Les Halles you can find all sorts of shops, many of which are very reasonably priced. Hotels in this 'hood are expensive and shopping in the little boutiques will cost you, but have a walk around if you've got time to kill post–*Mona Lisa.*

2ND ARRONDISSEMENT (LA BOURSE) Home to the **Bourse** (stock exchange), this Right Bank district lies between the Grands Boulevards and rue Etienne-Marcel. From Monday to Friday, brokers play the market until it's time to break for lunch, when the movers and shakers of French capitalism channel their hysteria into the area restaurants. Much of the eastern end of the arrondissement (Le Sentier) is devoted to

wholesale outlets of the Paris garment district, where thousands of garments are sold (usually in bulk) to buyers from clothing stores throughout Europe.

3RD ARRONDISSEMENT (MARAIS) Most of Paris's gay and Jewish populations call the Marais home, and a stroll down one of the small streets will afford you views of many kosher delis and gay bars. Two of the chief attractions are the **Musée Picasso,** a kind of pirate's ransom of painting and sculpture the Picasso estate had to turn over to the French government in lieu of the artist's astronomical death duties, and the **Musée Carnavalet,** which brings to life the history of Paris from prehistoric times to the present.

4TH ARRONDISSEMENT (ILE DE LA CITE/ ILE ST-LOUIS & BEAUBOURG) This neighborhood includes the Seine's islands (Ile de la Cité and Ile St-Louis) where you will find **Notre-Dame** and **Ste-Chapelle** (both on Ile de la Cité) and the **Hôtel de Ville** on rue de Rivoli. Come nightfall, the large concentration of bars makes it a hot destination. Shopping is abundant on **rue de Rivoli.** The 4th is also home to the freshly renovated **Centre Pompidou,** one of the top attractions in France.

5TH ARRONDISSEMENT (QUARTIER LATIN) Known as the Quartier Latin because of its student district and famous Sorbonne (where Latin once ruled as the 12th-century language of choice), the 5th arrondissement can be a rocking good time. The 5th also has the **Panthéon,** built by Louis XV after he recovered from gout and wanted to do something nice for Ste-Geneviève, Paris's patron saint. It's the resting place of Rousseau, Gambetta, Zola, Braille, Hugo, Voltaire, and Jean Moulin, the World War II Resistance leader whom the Gestapo tortured to death.

6TH ARRONDISSEMENT (ST-GERMAIN) Just across the boulevard St-Michel, lies the neighborhood of St-Germain in the 6th arrondissement with its ultraexclusive shops—it's way out of the price range of most tourists. The 6th also takes in the **Jardin du Luxembourg,** a 24-hectare (59-acre) playground where Isadora Duncan went dancing in the predawn hours and a destitute Ernest Hemingway went looking for pigeons for lunch. Really.

Best 7TH ARRONDISSEMENT (EIFFEL TOWER/MUSEE D'ORSAY) Paris's most famous symbol, **the Eiffel Tower,** dominates Paris and especially the 7th, a Left Bank district of residences and offices. The tower is one of the most recognizable landmarks in the world, despite the fact that many Parisians (especially its nearest neighbors) hated it when it was unveiled in 1889. Many of Paris's most imposing monuments are in the 7th, like the **Hôtel des Invalides,** which contains Napoleon's Tomb and the Musée de l'Armée, and the **Musée d'Orsay,** the world's premier showcase of 19th-century French art and culture, housed in the old Gare d'Orsay. But there's much hidden charm here as well. **Rue du Bac** was home to the swashbuckling heroes of Dumas's *The Three Musketeers* and to James McNeill Whistler, who moved to no. 110 after selling *Mother.* Auguste Rodin lived at what's now the **Musée Rodin,** 77 rue de Varenne, until his death in 1917.

8TH ARRONDISSEMENT (CHAMPS-ELYSEES/MADELEINE) Grab your walking shoes for a jaunt into the 8th. The endless **Champs Elysées** leads from the **place de la Concorde** to the **Arch de Triumph.** The **Egyptian Obelisk** rising from the place de la Concorde is the oldest man-made object in Paris (it was carved around 1200 B.C. and given to France by the viceroy of Egypt in 1829).

9TH ARRONDISSEMENT (OPERA GARNIER/PIGALLE) From the Quartier de l'Opéra to the strip joints of Pigalle (the infamous "Pig Alley" of World War II GIs), the 9th endures,

even if fashion prefers other addresses. The building at 17 bd. de la Madeleine was where Marie Duplessis, who gained fame as the heroine Marguerite Gautier in Alexandre Dumas the younger's *La Dame aux camellias,* died. (Greta Garbo played her in the film *Camille.*) **Place Pigalle** has nightclubs but is no longer home to cafe La Nouvelle Athènes, where Degas, Pissarro, and Manet used to meet. Other attractions include the **Folies-Bergère,** where cancan dancers have been high-kicking since 1868. It is the rococo **Opéra Garnier** (home of the *Phantom*) that made the 9th the last hurrah of Second Empire opulence. Renoir hated it, but generations later, Chagall did the ceilings. Pavlova danced *Swan Lake* here, and Nijinsky took the night off to go cruising.

10TH ARRONDISSEMENT (GARE DU NORD/GARE DE L'EST) The **Gare du Nord** and **Gare de l'Est,** along with porno houses and dreary commercial zones, make the 10th one of the least desirable arrondissements for living, dining, or sightseeing.

11TH ARRONDISSEMENT (BASTILLE, OBERKAMPF) For many years, this quarter seemed to sink lower and lower into decay, overcrowded by working-class immigrants from the far reaches of the former Empire. The opening of the **Opéra Bastille,** however, has given the 11th new hope and new life. The facility, called the "people's opera house," stands on the landmark place de la Bastille, where on July 14, 1789, 633 Parisians stormed the fortress and seized the ammunition depot, as the French Revolution swept across the city. Over the years, the prison held Voltaire, the Marquis de Sade, and the mysterious "Man in the Iron Mask." The area between the Marais, Ménilmontant, and République is now a "blue-collar chic" 'hood, as the *artistes* of Paris have been driven from the costlier sections of the Marais and can now be found walking the gritty sidewalks of rue Oberkampf. Hip

Parisians in search of a more cutting-edge experience live and work here, among the decaying 19th-century apartments and the 1960s public housing with graffiti-splattered walls.

12TH ARRONDISSEMENT (BOIS DE VIN-CENNES/GARE DE LYON) The 12th, once a depressing urban wasteland, has been singled out for budgetary resuscitation and is beginning to sport new housing, shops, gardens, and restaurants. Many will occupy the site of the former Reuilly rail tracks.

13TH ARRONDISSEMENT (GARE D'AUSTER-LITZ) Centered on the grimy **Gare d'Austerlitz,** the 13th might have its devotees, but we've yet to meet one. British travelers who flitted in and out of the train station were among the first of the district's foreign visitors and wrote the 13th off as a dreary working-class counterpart of London's East End. The 13th is also home to Paris's **Chinatown,** stretching for 13 square blocks around the Tolbiac Métro stop.

14TH ARRONDISSEMENT (MONTPARNASSE) The northern end of this large arrondissement is devoted to **Montparnasse,** home of the "lost generation" and stamping ground of Stein, Toklas, Hemingway, and other American expats of the 1920s. After World War II, it ceased to be the center of intellectual life, but the memory lingers in its cafes. One of the monuments that sets the tone of the neighborhood is **Rodin's statue of Balzac** at the junction of boulevards Montparnasse and Raspail. At this corner are some of the world's most famous **literary cafes,** including La Rotonde, Le Select, La Dôme, and La Coupole.

15TH ARRONDISSEMENT (GARE MONT-PARNASSE/INSTITUT PASTEUR) This is a mostly residential district beginning at **Gare Montparnasse** and stretching to the Seine. In size and population, it's the largest quarter of Paris but draws few tourists and has few attractions, except for the **Parc des Expositions,** the **Cimetière**

du Montparnasse, and the **Institut Pasteur.** In the early 20th century, many artists—like Chagall, Léger, and Modigliani—lived here in a shared atelier known as "The Beehive."

16TH ARRONDISSEMENT (TROCADERO/BOIS DE BOULOGNE) Originally the village of Passy, where Benjamin Franklin lived during most of his time in Paris, this district is still reminiscent of Proust's world. Highlights include the **Bois de Boulogne;** the **Jardin du Trocadéro;** the **Maison de Balzac;** the **Musée Guimet** (famous for its Asian collections); and the **Cimetière de Passy,** resting place of Manet, Talleyrand, Giraudoux, and Debussy. The arrondissement also has the best vantage point to view the Eiffel Tower: **place du Trocadéro.**

17TH ARRONDISSEMENT (PARC MONCEAU/PLACE CLICHY) Flanking the northern periphery of Paris, the 17th incorporates neighborhoods of bourgeois respectability (in its west end) and less affluent neighborhoods in its east end.

18TH ARRONDISSEMENT (MONTMARTRE) Montmartre oozes old-school Parisian vibes (think *Moulin Rouge*). The neighborhood is built on a hill and crowned by the glorious **Sacré Coeur.** Though the church overlooks all of Montmartre, it doesn't stop the area from being a pretty sinful place. With numerous strip clubs and peep shows in the neighborhood, some say this place is godforsaken. Note that Pigalle is where most of the city's strip clubs and peep shows and prostitutes are. You will find the Moulin Rouge on boulevard de Clichy.

Tourist Offices

At the Office de Tourism you will find all the info you need on Paris. They can even help book hotels. Their website is excellent and essential for planning your trip to Paris (☎ **08-92-68-30-00;** www.parisinfo.com). They have eight welcome centers in most of the tourist districts but some are not open all year:

○ **Pyramids:** 25 rue des Pyramids. Métro: Pyramids. Open daily 9am to 7pm.

○ **Opéra:** 11 rue Scribe. Métro: Opéra. Open Monday to Saturday 9am to 6:30pm.

○ **Gare de Lyon:** 20 bd. Diderot. Métro: Gare de Lyon. Open Monday to Saturday 8am to 6pm.

○ **Tour Eiffel:** Between the East and North Pillars. Métro: Ecole Militaire. Open daily from March 25 to October 31 11am to 6:40pm.

○ **Gare du Nord:** 18 rue de Dunkerque. (Paris-Welcome kiosk beneath the glass roof in the Ile-de-France Zone.) Métro: Gare du Nord. Open daily 8am to 6pm.

○ **Montmartre:** 21 place de Tertre. Métro: Abbesses. Open daily 10 am to 7pm.

○ **Carrousel du Louvre:** 99 rue de Rivoli. Métro: Palais Royal-Musée du Louvre. Open daily 10am to 6pm.

Recommended Websites

○ **www.bparis.com**: Offers a fun, chatty perspective on the great city from an expat's point of view.

○ **www.parisdigest.com**: Provides helpful visitor information on hotels, museums, activities, restaurants, monuments, and parks.

○ **www.parisfranceguide.com**: *The* place to visit for nightlife listings for theater and live music.

Culture Tips 101

If you don't speak French at all, don't worry; most Parisians speak some English, but you should still make an effort to learn some rudimentary phrases like *pardon* (excuse me), *s'il vous plaît* (please), and *merci* (thank you). If you are trying to pronounce a word you don't know, the general rule of thumb is to not pronounce the last few letters. As if that's not hard enough, there's also slang. *Verlan* is one of many types of French slang,

in which speakers generally cut the word in half and put the second half before the first half. For example, *vas-y* (pronounced "vah-zee"), which means go on, is changed to *ziva*.

Since the 1970s, when North Africans were imported to work in the mines and heavy industry, this group has occupied a special place in French society. North African couscous and the *tagines* of delicious stewed meats seasoned with vegetables and raisins have become accepted standards of the Parisian diet, but the same acceptance cannot exactly be said of the North Africans themselves. They are French without being French, and have borne the brunt of the French paranoia about national and cultural identity. The 2005 racial riots captured some of the picture.

Drugs are a big part of the poverty problem here. Walk certain streets of Paris, like the quays bordering the Seine and the area surrounding Pont Neuf, and you're bound to have a North African kid try to sell you some hash, but don't be suckered. High unemployment has pushed a lot of North African teenagers toward selling drugs (or pretending they have drugs to sell) and created a lot of resentment from many native-born French against all North Africans, even those who actually do hold respectable jobs.

There is no enforced legal minimum drinking age in France, but neither are there great drunks; people consume moderately and get drunk with great composure. It's only tourists you'll hear shouting "Yahoo!" while under the influence. In most public parks, like the Champ de Mars, you'll find kids sneaking a toke, though busts are rare.

Recommended Books, Movies & Music

BOOKS

A few of the masterpieces of the 19th century are *Madame Bovary* (Bantam, 1982), by Gustave Flaubert, in which the carefully wrought characters, setting, and plot attest to Flaubert's genius in presenting the

PARIS

tragedy of Emma Bovary; Victor Hugo's *Les Misérables* (Signet, 1987), a classic tale of social oppression and human courage set in the era of Napoleon I; and *Selected Stories* (Kessinger, 2005), by the master of short stories, Guy de Maupassant.

For an American's take on the City of Lights, try Henry James's *The Ambassadors* (Penguin, 1987) and *The American* (Penguin, 1981). Representing a very different era are *A Moveable Feast* (Scribner, 1996), Ernest Hemingway's recollections of Paris during the 1920s, and *The Autobiography of Alice B. Toklas* (Vintage, 1990), by Gertrude Stein, which is her account of 30 years in Paris. Also from the same era is *Tropic of Cancer* (Grove, 1987), the semi-autobiographical story of Henry Miller's years in Paris.

For a decidedly more serious take on the country, dip into some French philosophy. Anything by Parisian-born Jean-Paul Sartre will give you a sense of French existentialism. Or pick up *The Stranger* (Vintage, 1999) by Albert Camus, a story of a man who waits to be executed for murder.

If you want a more contemporary (and lighter) read, try *Me Talk Pretty One Day* (Back Bay Books, 2001), by David Sedaris. He sums up French culture, as told from the viewpoint of an American tourist, in a remarkably hilarious way. Or check out *Paris to the Moon* (Random House, 2001), by Adam Gopnik, an engaging tale about an American living in Paris.

Of course, you'll run into mentions of *The Da Vinci Code* (Anchor, 2006) during your travels. Both the movie and the book were panned by most reviewers. Still, it's fun to read about or view the places you'll be visiting, and the Louvre is featured predominantly in both.

Talk of the Town

Five ways to start a conversation with a local

Here are some conversation starters that should help you bridge the language gap:

1. **What's your favorite American movie?** The French don't only love Clint Eastwood, they love Westerns you've never heard of, Marilyn as a serious comedienne, and Hitchcock, and probably know far, far more than you about, say, Ernst Lubitsch. Just skip the whole Jerry Lewis thing.

2. **Do you prefer freedom fries or french fries?** Any Parisian worth his or her salt has an opinion on the Iraq war and France's decision not to get involved in it.

3. **What are your thoughts about the racial tension in Paris?** Simmering tensions between North African Arabs and native French people escalated into the race riots of November 2005, and anti-Semitism is reportedly on the rise. Any conversation about racial conflict should also address how your home country handles this problem, of course.

4. **Yea or nay to globalization?** Most young Parisians are probably against the imminent decline of all things French and the rise of all things American, like multinationals and fast food. This will bring the conversation around to . . .

5. **Where were you during the jobs bill crisis?** Thousands of Parisian students went on strike in early 2006 to protest a law that would have given employers free reign to fire workers under 26 within the first 2 years of work. Most young people will have a *lot* to say on this subject.

MOVIES

Definitely check out some movies by New Wave directors like François Truffaut and Jean-Luc Godard before coming to Paris. Don't expect action-packed adventures, but you will glimpse wonderful scenes shot in Paris that will give you an idea of how the city looked in the '50s and '60s.

More recent must-sees include the French flick *Amelie,* which was mostly shot in the picturesque Montmartre district, and American films like *French Kiss* or *Before Sunrise* or *Before Sunset*—all of these will surely put you in a romantic mood. If suspense films are more your style, *Ronin* is an action movie with thrilling car chase scenes throughout the streets of Paris, and *Cache* is a psychological thriller set in Paris.

For biting social commentary, rent *Le Placard* with Gérard Depardieu, Daniel Auteuil, and Thierry Lhermitte, a funny movie that deals with the issue of homosexuality in French society. *La Haine* was made in 1995 but foreshadows the 2005 riots in the Parisian ghettos.

MUSIC

Listen to some classic Edith Piaf—a French torch singer who found fame in the 1940s—and you'll be instantly transported to the streets of Paris. It'll be hard to avoid hearing her most famous song, "La Vie en Rose," while you're in the City of Lights. Often thought of as the French Elvis Presley, Johnny Halladay has remained one of the country's top performers since the 1960s. He's probably best known outside of France for his film roles, though, such as in 2003's *The Man on the Train*. Serge Gainsbourg, a French poet, singer/songwriter, actor, and director, has achieved similar success across the arts. He started out singing *ye-ye pop* (light French pop music) but branched out to produce a number of highly influential concept albums.

Today, France's biggest exports are electro-pop bands like Daft Punk and Air, and French rap, which has come a long way since the '80s when MC Solaar ruled the charts—current bands like NTM boast uncompromisingly sharp rhymes and tight beats.

PARIS

Paris Nuts & Bolts

Cellphone Providers & Service Centers   The main cellphone providers in France are **France Telecom** (www.francetelecom.com), **SFR** (www.sfr.fe), and **Orange** (www.orange.com). Orange has a pay-as-you go plan called "Idée nomade" which may be your best bet if you are traveling in France for a while. With this plan, you can buy time in most cellphone shops and tobacco stores (called *un tabac,* pronounced "tah-bah"). There are about a million cellphone stores in Paris so you shouldn't have any trouble finding one—check the websites mentioned here for details.

Currency   For the best exchange rates, cash traveler's checks at foreign-exchange offices or banks, rather than at your hotel or in a shop. Still, your best bet is to use your ATM to directly withdraw euros. Banks in Paris are generally open Monday to Friday from 9am to 4:30pm. There's a **Citibank** at 125 av. des Champs Elysées (☎ **01-49-05-49-05;** www.citibank.fr).

Embassies   The **Embassy of the United States,** at 2 av. Gabriel, 8e (☎ **01-43-12-47-08;** Métro: Concorde), is open Monday through Friday from 9am to 6pm. Passports are issued at its consulate at 2 rue St-Florentin (☎ **01-43-12-22-22;** Métro: Concorde). The **Embassy of Canada** is at 35 av. Montaigne, 8e (☎ **01-44-43-29-00;**

Métro: Franklin-D.-Roosevelt or Alma-Marceau), open Monday through Friday from 9am to noon and 2 to 5pm. The **Embassy of the United Kingdom** is at 35 rue Faubourg St-Honoré, 8e (☎ 01-44-51-31-00; Métro: Concorde or Madeleine), open Monday through Friday from 9:30am to 1pm and 2:30 to 5pm. The consulate is at 18 bis rue d'Anjou, 8e (☎ 01-44-51-31-02; Métro: Concorde or Madeleine), open Monday through Friday from 9am to noon and 2 to 5pm. The **Embassy of Australia** is at 4 rue Jean-Rey, 15e (☎ 01-40-59-33-00; Métro: Bir-Hakeim), open Monday through Friday from 9:15am to noon and 2:30 to 4:30pm. The **Embassy of New Zealand** is at 7 ter rue Léonard-de-Vinci, 16e (☎ 01-45-00-24-11; Métro: Victor Hugo), open Monday through Friday from 9am to 1pm and 2:30 to 6pm.

Emergencies To call an ambulance dial ☎ 15. To call the fire department, dial ☎ 17. To speak with a doctor, dial ☎ 01-47-07-77-77.

Internet/Wireless Hot Spots Paris has tons of Internet cafes, but these are the best:

➔ **@Z Net** (14 rue Descartes; ☎ 01-43-25-32-18; Métro: Cardinal Lemoine or Maubert-Mutualité) costs 3€ for 1 hour of Internet access. It's open Monday to Thursday 11am to midnight and Friday from 11am to 7pm. Sunday and holidays its hours are from 1pm to midnight. The items available are printer, Web cam, CD burners, scanners, fax, and a copy machine.

➔ **Cyber world C@fé** provides Internet service for the discounted price of 5.50€ an hour for students and unemployed people (how very socialist). They also offer scanners, Web cams, printers, fax machines, and photocopiers (20 rue de l'Exposition; ☎ 01-53-59-96-54; www.cyberworld-cafe.com; Métro: Ecole Militaire). It's open Monday to Saturday from noon to 10pm and Sunday and holidays from noon until 8pm.

➔ **@bbessesxv3.com** offers 1 hour for 3€, and also has a fax machine, printer, scanner, and photocopier (22 rue Houdon; ☎ 01-42-23-07-05; www.tatoolagoon.com/sites/abbessesxv3; Métro: Abbesses or Pigalle). It's open daily 7am to 7pm.

➔ **Cyber** has slightly cheaper rates than other cybercafes in the area with 1 hour of Internet for 3€. They also have a fax machine, scanner, and printer (30 Grenier St-Lazare; ☎ 01-42-77-12-21; Métro: Etienne Marcel). Open daily noon to midnight.

Luggage Storage At Paris's major train stations you'll find a left-luggage office, which charges around 7€ to 8.50€ to store a bag for 24 hours. There are also *consigne automatiques,* which are computerized locker systems that allow you to store bags for up to 72 hours, costing anywhere from 3€ to 6.50€. Many of these are currently not in operation for fear of terrorist threats. You can also ask at your hotel or hostel—most places do offer luggage storage for guests.

Laundry Throughout Paris, you'll find *laverie libres,* or self-service laundries, dotting the streets. These cost about 3.50€ per load, and about .40€ to .80€ for 5 to 10 minutes of drying time. If you're near the Louvre, check out **Laverie Libre Service** (7 rue Jean Jacques Rousseau, 1er; daily 7:30am–10pm; Métro: Louvre-Rivoli). In the Latin Quarter, try the location at 215 rue St-Jacques, 5e (daily 7am–10pm; Métro: Luxembourg).

Post Office When you're ready to ail those postcards, head to the main **Bureau de Poste** (52 rue du Louvre; ☎ 01-40-28-76-00; Métro: Louvre-Rivoli), which is open 24 hours a day. For a small fee, you can receive mail at this post as well; just bring your passport to do so.

Safety   Paris is a fairly safe city, and the main thing you need to be aware of is pickpocketing, especially at the hands of child thieves. Pickpockets are particularly prevalent around major tourist hubs such as the Louvre, Eiffel Tower, Montmartre, Notre Dame, and on the Métro.

If someone comes up to you and asks if you speak English, always say no. If you say yes, gypsy women or children will often put some piece of paper or book in front of you with words written in English. While you are reading about how this poor person has no job and needs money, they cut your purse strap or pick your pockets.

Don't leave an MP3 player or cellphone charging in a hostel unless you are in the room. Don't keep them out on the tables in sidewalk cafes either.

Tipping   After a meal, 5% to 10% is expected, though the tip is often included (it may say *service compris* on the bill or menu). If so, your waiter has no incentive to be nice or quick. One thing to note is that after your meal the waiter often won't bring your bill until you ask for it *(l'addition, s'il vous plaît)*. It's preferred to let customers relax and digest their meal rather than rushing them to free up a table.

Sleeping

Paris is supposed to be the most-visited city in the world, so it's not surprising that the city is well equipped for tourists. All the hotels in Paris are government rated with a star system (zero to four stars), which is often based on arbitrary criteria. For example, you'll see a lot of nice two-star hotels whose small lobby lost them a star. The best way to really evaluate a hotel is to ask to see a room before staying. A hotel without stars usually means that you have to share a toilet and shower with the other guests on your floor.

The 5th and 6th arrondissements are the best places to stay because you can find reasonably priced hotels, and you'll be close to lots of tourist attractions, bars, and restaurants. These are also probably the safest parts of town for tourists. The 4th arrondissement runs a close second because it has copious bars and it's within walking distance of pretty much everything in Paris. The 7th arrondissement is ideal for someone who wants to sleep, not to party—nightlife is virtually nonexistent here. Many hotels in this neighborhood have Eiffel Tower views. The

18th and 19th arrondissements boast many hostels and hotels, but it can get shady at night because lots of strip clubs are in the area. Still, the hostels here fill up with a young, international crowd so you're bound to meet travelers to hang with.

Hostels

→**Centre International BVJ Paris-Louvre** ★ This 200-bed hostel with modern amenities is run by the Bureau des Voyages de la Jeunesse. Rooms are far and away cleaner than the average hostel, and you can't beat the location close to the Louvre. If you're in a Left Bank state of mind, there's another location on 44 rue des Bernardins, 1er. *20 rue Jean-Jacques Rousseau, 1er. ☎ 01/53-00-90-90; bvj@wanadoo.fr. 25€ per person. Rates include breakfast. Métro: Louvre-Rivoli. Amenities: Breakfast room; shared bathrooms.*

→**Le Village Hostel** The best things about Le Village are its common spaces, such as the fully equipped kitchen and bar/lounge,

Paris Sleeping & Eating

SLEEPING ◼

Centre International BVJ
  Paris-Louvre **13**
Hôtel Axial Beaubourg **20**
Hôtel Bonséjour **1**
Hôtel Britannique **18**
Hôtel Burgundy **3**

Hôtel du Champs de Mars **5**
Hôtel Du Commerce **30**
Hôtel La Tour Eiffel **4**
Hotel Langlois **10**
Hôtel Royal Fromentin **7**
Hôtel Stella **25**
Hôtel St. Jacques **35**

Le Village Hostel **8**
L'Hôtel **24**
Woodstock Hostel **11**
Young and Happy
  Hostel **31**

EATING ◆

Berthillion **27**
Breakfast in America
  (B.I.A.) **28**
Café Delmas **32**
Café Very **12**
Chez Lena & Mimile **34**

Curieux Spaghetti Bar **21**
Jenny **15**
L'As du Fallafel **22**
Le Café Charbon **16**
Les Enfants de
  la Cuisine **19**
Le Fumoir **17**

Le Grenier de
  Notre-Dame **29**
Le Paname **9**
Le Tire Bouchon **6**
Le Vigneron **33**
Les Deux Magots **23**
Mandala Ray **2**

Maoz **26**
Stohrer **14**

where you'll be sure to meet fellow English-speaking travelers. They also have a good location and everything is fairly clean. The downside? Management kicks you out during the day for cleaning but, hey, at least there's no curfew. The dorm rooms contain bunk beds with thin sheetless mattresses; be prepared to rent or bring your own. Some rooms have amazing Sacre-Couer views. The maximum stay is 1 week. *20 rue d'Orsel, 18e. ☎ 01-42-64-22-02. www.villagehostel.fr. 20€–25€ dorm bed (room for 3–8 people), 25€–27€ double. Métro: Anvers. Amenities: Bar; lounge; Internet; kitchen; 11am–4pm lockout; shared bathrooms; sheets (2.50€); telephone (in common room); towel (1€).*

→**Woodstock Hostel** ★ You'll party like a rock star until bedtime. The bar in the hostel teems with foreigners, but the party ends at 2am when the bar closes and the curfew takes effect. This clean hostel has a kitchen, common spaces to meet people, and bunk beds with thick mattresses, but the benefits end there. The 2am curfew can be a pain if you're into partying outside of the hostel, and they kick you out between 11am and 3pm for cleaning. Alcohol from the outside isn't allowed, so if you do party in the hostel bar, be prepared to buy semi-pricey booze. *48 rue Rodier, 18e. ☎ 01-48-78-87-76. www.woodstock. fr. 21€ dorm bed, 24€ per person for bunk-bed room. Prices decrease by 3€ Oct–Mar. Rates include breakfast. Métro Anvers. Amenities: Breakfast room; curfew (2am); Internet; kitchen; 11am–3pm lockout; luggage storage; shared bathrooms; sheets; telephone (in common room); towels.*

→**Young and Happy Hostel** This hostel has a friendly vibe and a great location in the Latin Quarter, which makes up for a slightly downtrodden decor. The rooms contain four beds maximum and there is a common area and a bar with cheap beer where you can chat up other backpackers. *80 rue Mouffetard, 5e. ☎ 01-47-07-47-07. www.youngandhappy.fr.*

21€–26€ dorm bed. Rates include breakfast. Métro: Place Monge. Amenities: Breakfast room; bar; 2am curfew; Internet; kitchen; luggage storage; shared bathrooms.

Cheap

→**Hôtel Bonséjour** ★ The best deal in Montmartre, this hotel is located near the Sacre-Coeur and many restaurants and bars. You won't find any frills, but if you're looking for a cheap, clean room with a bed, this place is for you. Rooms have no toilets (one toilet per floor and there are about five rooms per floor) and almost all have a shower. Showerless rooms have a sink and access to a shower for 2€. Some rooms have balconies with a view on the quiet rue Burq. *11 rue Burq, 18e. ☎ 01-42-54-22-53. 25€–30€ single; 36€ double, 42€–46€ with shower; 49€ triple, 57€ with shower. Métro: Abbeses or Blanche. Amenities: Shared bathrooms (in some).*

[MTV] Best →Hôtel du Champs de Mars ★★ This adorable hotel is a family run place and the owners Françoise and Stéphane Gourdal will treat you like honored guests at their impeccably decorated home. Every room is decorated differently but they are all clean, cozy, and colorful. Each room has its own color scheme usually featuring bright pastels with rich fabric and tasteful paintings. Most of the bathrooms have tub/shower combinations. *7 rue du Champs de Mars, 7e. ☎ 01-45-51-52-30. www.hotel-du-champ-de-mars.com. 79€ single or double, 84€ 2 twin beds, 100€ triple. Breakfast available for 6.50€. Métro: La Motte-Picquent Grenelle. Amenities: Wheelchair friendly. In room: TV (satellite), safe.*

→**Hôtel Du Commerce** This budget hotel boasts the sort of small frills that make the difference to a weary backpacker. The decor is pretty much nonexistent or jarring (I mean, who paints a room orange?), and the walls are thin. But the free Internet access and printer in the lobby, microwave, fridge, plates, cutlery, and TV in the lounge can cause a tired traveler to weep tears of joy. You can get a shower and toilet if you want to pay 20€ extra. *14 rue de la Montagne Ste-Geneviève, 5e.* ☎ *01-43-54-89-69. www. commerce-paris-hotel.com. 29€ single with shared bathroom; 39€ double with shared bathroom; 49€ with private shower; 59€ triple with private bathroom; 89€ quad with private shower. All prices increase by 10€ Mar–June and Sept–Dec. Métro: Maubert-Mutualité. Amenities: Fridge (in common room); Internet; microwave (in common room); shared bathrooms (in some); TV (in common room).*

→ **Hôtel La Tour Eiffel** This hotel has rooms overlooking a small street, the Eiffel Tower, or the garden of the Romanian Embassy, and is slightly cheaper than some of the other hotels in the area. The rooms are basic with sparse furniture and minimalist, yet tasteful, decoration. *17 rue de l'Exposition, 7e.* ☎ *01-47-05-14-75. www.hotel-toureiffel.com. 55€–70€ single, 65€–85€ double, 75€–95€ double with twin beds. Breakfast available for 6€. Métro: École Militaire. Amenities: Breakfast room; wheelchair friendly; Wi-Fi. In room: TV.*

→ **Hôtel Stella** ★ Step into the lobby of Hôtel Stella, and you might think you've entered your grandma's living room. The furniture is mismatched and a TV rattles on somewhere in the background; basically, the no-nonsense owner treats the place like her home (because it is). The building dates back to the French Revolution and though they have remodeled since, it still has the rustic charm of high ceilings and exposed structural beams. The hotel is smack dab in the middle of the 16th arrondissement, close to tourist attractions like the Arc de Triomphe. *41 rue Monsieur Le Prince, 16e.* ☎ *01-40-51-00-25. site.voila.fr/hotel-stella. 45€ single; 55€ double; 75€ triple; 85€ quad. Métro: Odéon or Luxembourg. Amenities: TV (in common room).*

Doable

→ **Hôtel Britannique** ★ The Hôtel Britannique is the best value and has the absolute best location if you want to stay in the 1st arrondissement: next to the Seine, a short walk from the Marais, the Louvre, Notre-Dame, and the Latin district. An international, English-speaking staff will greet you; rooms and hallways are accented with deep red highlights; walls are decorated with copies of Turner paintings. There are 39 cozy rooms that have been recently renovated. *20 av. Victoria, 1er.* ☎ *01-42-33-74-59. www.hotel-britannique.fr. 139€ single, 168€ double, 219€ triple, 247€–288€ junior suite. Breakfast available for 13€. Métro: Châtelet. Amenities: Breakfast room; elevator; laundry service; room service; wheelchair friendly; Wi-Fi. In room: A/C, flatscreen TV, dataport, hair dryer, minibar, safe.*

→ **Hôtel Langlois** ★★ Converted from an 1870 bank, the Hôtel Langlois is worth the extra cash it now takes to stay here. The spacious bedrooms sport downright cinematic decor—which is probably why Ted Demme chose to shoot his 2001 remake of *Charade* here. *63 rue St-Lazare, 9e.* ☎ *01-48-74-78-24. www.hotel-langlois.com. 84€–94€ single, 94€–104 double. Métro: La Chapelle. Amenities: Breakfast room; Internet. In room: A/C, TV, hair dryer.*

→ **Hôtel Royal Fromentin** ★ This former cabaret hall boasts a decadent atmosphere that still appeals to artists—Blondie and Nirvana have stayed here. Many of the spacious rooms, richly decorated in traditional French style, feature views of the Sacre-Coeur. *11 rue Fromentin, 9e.* ☎ *01/48-74-85-93. www.paris-hotel-royalfromentin.com. 69€–130€ single, 79€–155€ double. Rates include breakfast. Métro: Opéra. Amenities: Breakfast room; bar; elevator; laundry service; room service. In room: TV, hair dryer.*

PARIS

➔**Hôtel St. Jacques** The best value in the Latin Quarter, the Hôtel St. Jacques is perfect for small budgets. Despite the affordable price, it maintains the standards of classic French comfort—check out the marble lobby and Impressionist art that hangs in the rooms and hallways. Murals decorate the room walls and room no. 30 has a view of Sacre-Coeur. *35 rue des Ecoles, 5e.* ☎ *01-44-07-45-45. www. paris-hotel-stjacques.com. 55€–85€ single, 95€–124€ double, 152€ triple. Breakfast available for 8.50€. Métro: Maubert-Mutualité. Amenities: Internet; luggage storage; safe; tourist desk. In room: TV (satellite), hair dryer, Internet, safe, scale.*

Splurge

➔**Hôtel Axial Beaubourg** ★★ In the heart of the Marais, within walking distance of the Centre Pompidou, the Louvre, and Notre-Dame, this hotel attracts legions of young fashionistas. The sleek interior design uses colors, textures, fabrics, and light to convey coziness. This hotel has definitely gone the extra mile to make guests feel comfortable. The owners are renovating the building next door to add 17 rooms, a bar, and an exercise room (a rare luxury for Parisian hotels). The staff is nice yet discreet. Small details are appreciated, such as the soundproof windows that open onto a busy street and the comfortable fabrics on the beds. *11 rue du Temple, 3e.* ☎ *01-42-72-72-22. www.axialbeaubourg.com. 112€ single with shower, 130€ with tub; 160€–210€ double. Breakfast available for 11€. Métro: Hôtel-de-Ville. Amenities: Breakfast room; laundry service; lounge; room service. In room: A/C, TV, dataport, hair dryer, minibar, safe.*

➔**Hôtel Burgundy** ★ Relatively inexpensive compared to the palatial hotels nearby, the Hôtel Burgundy dates back to 1857 and proudly touts that Charles Baudelaire wrote poetry while he was staying here in the 1860s. It has a spacious lobby and restaurant where you can have a continental buffet breakfast for 16€, complemented by spacious rooms, a bar, and a restaurant. *8 rue Duphot, 1er.* ☎ *01-42-60-34-12. www.burgundy hotel.com. 173€–203€ single, 173€–213€ double, 183€–213€ double or twin (2 people), 238€–268€ triple (3 people), 208€–238€ superior room (1–2 people). Breakfast available for 16€. Métro: Madeleine. Amenities: Breakfast room; limited room service; wheelchair friendly. In room: TV, dataport, hair dryer, minibar.*

MTV Best ➔**L'Hôtel** ★★★ One of the most luxurious and romantic small hotels in St-Germain, this place sits on a quiet street right next to the Seine and all of the action of the Marais and Latin district. One of this hotel's claims to fame is that Oscar Wilde died here (in room 16), but this hotel has more to brag about than that. It only has 20 rooms, but each of them is decorated with care and attention. Celebrities like Johnny Depp appreciate the elegant yet discreet charm and the homey feel. Each room is decorated with luxurious fabric wall-coverings and beds that are inviting enough to dive into. The bathrooms are small but stocked with Hermès toiletries. One of the highlights of the hotel is their private spa in the basement, which you can reserve for 1-hour intervals. You have exclusive access to a *hammam* (steam room) and a saltwater pool free of charge. *13 rue des Beaux-Arts, 6e.* ☎ *01-44-41-99-00. www.l-hotel.com. Low season: 255€–350€ double (depending on view), 240€ deluxe room and suite, 540€ junior suite, 640€ apt; high season: 280€–370€ double (depending on view), 640€ deluxe room and suite, 640€ junior suite, 740€ apt. Breakfast available for 17€. Métro: St-Germain-des-Prés. Amenities: Restaurant; bar; hammam; laundry service; room service; spa; swimming pool; Wi-Fi. In room: TV, dataport, minibar, robe, safe, slippers.*

Eating

Once you arrive in Paris, you'll find that the word "French," although used frequently, isn't very helpful in describing cuisine. "French" covers such a broad scope that it doesn't prepare you for the offerings of the specialty chefs. Even the Parisians themselves might ask, "What *type* of French cooking?" Sometimes a chef will include regional specialties, classic dishes, and even modern cuisine all on one menu. In that case, such a restaurant is truly "French." Other chefs prefer a more narrow focus and feature the cooking of one region or one style—classic or modern. Still others prefer to strike a middle ground between classic and modern; they're called "creative."

You'll also find hundreds of bistros, brasseries, and cafes. In modern times their designations and roles have become almost meaningless. Traditionally, a **bistro** was a small restaurant, often with Mom at the cash register and Pop in the kitchen. Menus are most often handwritten or mimeographed, and the selection of dishes tends to be small. They can be chic and elegant, sometimes heavily Mediterranean, and often dispensing gutsy fare, including the *pot-au-feu* (beef simmered with vegetables) the chef's grandmother prepared for him as a kid.

French for "brewery," most **brasseries** have an Alsatian connection, and that means lots of beer, although Alsatian wines are also featured. They are almost always brightly lit and open 24 hours. Both snacks and full meals are available. The Alsatian establishments serve sauerkraut with an array of pork products.

The **cafe** is a French institution. Not just places for an aperitif, a café au lait, or a croissant, many serve rib-sticking fare as well, certainly entrecôte with french fries but often classics like *blanquette de veau* (veal in white sauce).

Parisian restaurants can be pricey, but that won't matter if you're open to sampling the city's cheap but great **street food** here. The cheapest options are at the snack stands selling shwarma, falafels, and crepes. The **5th arrondissement,** between boulevard St-Michel and rue St-Jacques, is the best place in the city for cheap one-stop eating. This street is home to hundreds of restaurants featuring every type of food imaginable, though it has a number of creperies. You'll find men standing in front of the restaurants trying to lure tourists inside, and most offer a *menu* with options for an appetizer, main course, and dessert. Most will set

Nice Day for a Picnic

You can't beat buying grub from a grocery store, patisserie, or boulangerie and picnicking if you're looking for a cheap meal in Paris. The Pont des Arts is my favorite picnic spot in the city. This pedestrian bridge has unforgettable views of Ile de la Cité and the top of the Eiffel tower, and it fills up with couples and groups of friends sharing elaborate picnics and copious amounts of wine. Montmartre is another unbeatable location—you can picnic on the steps of the Sacre-Coeur with a view of all of Paris.

E.D. (☎ 01-42-51-73-91) is the city's cheapest grocery store, with a very limited but sufficient selection. You'll find locations at 37 rue Lacépède (Métro: Place Monge) and 31 rue d'Orsel (Métro: Anvers). They're open from 9am to 8pm.

Of course, the steps of the Eiffel Tower also lend themselves to a picnic. One cheap grocery store close to the tower is **Leader Price** (43 rue Cler), at the corner of Cler and rue Champ de Mars.

you back about 15€. It's still possible to find a meal under 5€, but don't count on gourmet French food. Rue Mouffetard (Métro: Place Monge, censier Daubenton, or Les Gobelins) is another street to hit in the Quartier Latin. The vibe here is generally mellower than around St-Michel. In **Marais,** the center of Paris's Jewish community, you'll find the requisite delis with bagels but also some of the best falafel and shwarma spots. One of the places you have to go if you are in **Montmartre** is place du Tertre—it's a hot spot for French restaurants.

Hot Spots

→**Curieux Spaghetti Bar** ★★ ITALIAN Before you even walk in, you can tell that this place is *branché* (hip). Simply follow the jets of steam billowing from above the door, and you'll enter a restaurant that feels more like a bar than a restaurant—with colorful lighting, young gay waiters, upbeat house music, and closely set tables. Mostly gay, 25- to 35-year-old men comprise the crowd. The fashionable waiters may be cute, but they aren't fast with the food. The restaurant, obviously, specializes in spaghetti. Choose from eight sauces to top your enormous portions of spaghetti. At night, people hang out around the bar, which is lit by chandeliers made from tools used to measure amounts of spaghetti. This place is definitely a Marais experience. *14 rue St-Merri, 3e* ☎ *01-42-72-75-97. www.curieuxspag.com. Main courses 8€–11€. Sun–Wed noon–2am (happy hour 6–8pm with 2-for-1 drinks and Thurs–Sat noon–4am). Métro: Hôtel-de-Ville.*

→**Le Café Charbon** FRENCH This is one of the oldest restaurants/bars in the area, as evidenced by the architecture and interior design: The high ceilings, enormous mirrors, and glass entrance date to the early 1900s. Try coming here at night for an illicit (at least in America) absinthe or a beer. The French food is nothing to write home about but, despite this, it gets packed with French students and trendsters around 10 or 11pm. *109 rue Oberkampf, 11e.* ☎ *01-43-57-55-13. Main courses 10€–20€. Mon–Thurs 9am–2am; Fri–Sun 9am–2am. Métro: Parmentier.*

📺 Best →**Mandala Ray** ★ ASIAN FUSION Part of a small chain of super-expensive, chic, exclusive restaurants (think big plate with a big price but a tiny amount of food), Mandala Ray is renowned as a place to see and be seen. Count on paying at least 50€ per person (not including drinks) for haute fusion cuisine with an Asian and South American influence. You can find risotto and sushi on the menu, for example. This super-chic restaurant also has a very exclusive lounge and nightclub. *32–34 rue Marbeuf, 8e.* ☎ *01-56-88-36-36. www.manray.fr. Main courses 26€–37€. Sun–Thurs 7pm–2am, Fri–Sat 7pm–5am (for the club). Métro: Champs Elysées.*

Cheap

→**Café Very** CREPES/SANDWICHES This cafe in the Tuileries serves tasty open-face sandwiches and crepes under the chestnut trees or in the woodsy interior. *Jardin des Tuileries, 1er.* ☎ *01-47-03-94-84. Main courses from 4€. Daily lunch–10:30pm. Métro: Concorde or Tuileries.*

→**L'As du Fallafel** KOSHER MIDDLE-EASTERN Get your falafel and shwarma (what the L'As du Fallafel calls "cocktails of meat"; as in "you really don't know what's in it, but it's good") fix at the mecca of Parisian falafel restaurants. Family-run, L'As has been dishing up falafel for 27 years. Everything here is kosher, and the falafels are all vegan. You can get the falafel and shwarma to go, or for slightly more you can eat inside the restaurant. Larger entrees, wine, and beer are also served. *34 rue des Rosiers, 3e.* ☎ *01-48-87-63-30. Falafel 4€; shwarma 6€. Sun–Thurs noon–midnight, Fri noon–6pm, closed Jewish holidays. Métro: St-Paul.*

➜**Les Enfants de la Cuisine** CONTINEN-TAL/LUNCH   This informal restaurant offers sandwiches and salads with tables inside or on the sidewalk. The food is simple but tasty and the restaurant is minutes away from Centre Pompidou, which ensures that you will see plenty of tourists recharging between museum exhibits. *12 bd. de Sébastapol, 4e.* ☎ *01-42-74-26-56. www.les enfantsdelacuisine.com. Lunch main courses 7.50€. Daily 10am–6pm. Métro: Châtelet.*

[MTV] (Best) ➜**Maoz** ★★ FALAFEL   If you are on a really tight budget, and you want a cheap but filling meal, hit up this falafel restaurant and its limited but excellent menu. Maoz primarily serves takeout falafel (fried balls of chickpeas in a pita) and french fries for a mere 4€. Grab a falafel, load it with toppings, and picnic in front of the nearby Notre-Dame (unless you somehow snag one of the few seats). Veggie-lovers, take note: Maoz is vegan. *8 rue Xavier Privas, 4e.* ☎ *01-43-26-36-00. www.maozveg.com. Main courses 4€. Mon–Thurs 11am–1am; Fri–Sat 11am–2am; Sun 11am–midnight. Métro: St-Michel.*

Doable

➜**Breakfast in America (B.I.A.)** AMERI-CAN DINER   I'm kind of embarrassed to mention this place because Paris is a place to sample French, not American, cuisine. But if you must sate that craving for a milkshake, you'll find all the basics here, from burgers and hot dogs to, yes, milkshakes. *17 rue des Écoles, 5e.* ☎ *01-43-54-50-28. www.breakfast-in-america.com. Main courses 6.50€–11€. Daily 8:30am–10:30pm. Métro: Cardinal Lemoine or Jussieu.*

➜**Café Delmas** ★ NOUVELLE FRENCH Indecisive readers, take note: This place is divided into two parts, a creperie where savory and sugary crepes are made, and a cafe/bar with a more extensive menu. The restaurant serves average-priced, French-inspired international cuisine, and the decor on both sides is modern with lots of white, purple, and silver. The crowd tends to be young, and on the weekends they have a DJ. *2 place de la Contrescarpe, 5e.* ☎ *01-43-26-51-26. Daily 8am–2am. Happy hour 6–9pm. Main courses 12€–23€. Métro: Place Monge or Cardinal Lemoine.*

➜**Jenny** ALSATIAN   One of the city's most famous and popular Alsatian restaurants was established in 1930 by members of the Jenny family, who commissioned one of the noteworthy craftsmen of the era, Spindler, to create marquetry panels for the sheathing of the walls. Today, little has changed since its inauguration, except for the fact that the clientele is a lot more contemporary-looking than in the old days. Up to 220 diners can fit into this nostalgia-laden setting, where Alsatian *Gemütlichkeit* prevails. An ongoing specialty is the *choucroute* (sauerkraut) *de chez Jenny,* which is piled high with sausages, tender pork knuckles, and slices of ham. Any of these taste wonderful accompanied by one of the Alsatian wines (especially Rieslings) that fill the wine list. *39 bd. du Temple, 3e.* ☎ *01-44-54-39-00. Reservations recommended. Main courses 17€–28€; prix-fixe menu 17€–24€. Daily noon–midnight. Métro: République.*

➜**Le Grenier de Notre-Dame** VEGETAR-IAN/VEGAN   Ironically, this vegetarian restaurant is located on rue de la Bûcherie ("road of the butcher"). Opened in 1978, it's been serving up veggies to a mostly foreign crowd ever since. They offer macrobiotic, organic, and vegan options, but if you are vegan, specify when you order (the word for vegan is *vegitalian* and not "vegetarian," which is the same in French as English). Expect vegan goodies like Seitan and Polenta. *18 rue de la Bûcherie, 5e.* ☎ *01-43-39-98-29. 3-course dinner menu 18€. Summer daily noon–11:30pm; winter daily noon–2:30pm and 6–11pm. Métro: Maubert-Mutualité.*

➜**Le Paname** BOURGUIGNONNE/SAVOY-ARDE (FRENCH)   Paname is another word

PARIS

for Paris, but the food here hails from Bourguignonne (east of Paris) and Savoy (in the French Alps). Dine here to experience *raclettes*, or tableside grills. Put your cheese on small dishes under the grill, pour the melted cheese over potatoes and ham, and voilà: Dinner is served. Get ready for a heavy meal, but fear not, salads accompany most dinners. *4 rue des Trois Frères, 18e.* ☎ *01-42-59-05-08. Main courses 12€–22€. Fri–Mon 10:30am–3pm and 6pm–midnight; Tues–Wed 6pm–midnight. Métro: Abbesses.*

➜**Le Tire Bouchon** CREPERIE   Set amidst dozens of other restaurants and bars, Le Tire stands out because it doubles as a piano bar by night. *9 Rue Norvins, 18e.* ☎ *01-42-55-12-35. Crepe prix-fixe menu 10€–14€. Mon–Sat 7:45–9:45pm; Tues–Fri noon–2pm and 7:45–9:45pm. Closed Aug and around Christmas. Métro: Abbesses.*

➜ **Le Vigneron** SOUTHWESTERN FRENCH If you are looking for a light dinner, this restaurant is not for you. The southwest of France is known for extraordinary cuisine and this restaurant offers a selection of typical, and very filling, southwestern French dishes such as cassoulet, duck cooked every way imaginable, and some vegetarian options. The restaurant is dark and rustic— perfect for a candlelit dinner. You can get a three-course, gourmet meal for only 13€ (you have to be an early bird, though; after 8pm the prices increase). *18–20 rue du Pot de Fer, 5e.* ☎ *01-47-17-29-99. Main courses 13€–26€. Daily noon–midnight. Métro: Place Monge.*

Splurge

➜**Chez Lena & Mimile** FRENCH SEMI-GASTRONOMIQUE   This restaurant is more expensive than the nearby restaurants on rue Mouffetard, but if you want a gourmet meal and can spare 35€ per person, consider that the 35€ includes an appetizer, main course, dessert, wine, and a coffee to top it

all off. While not the best bargain in town, you'll at least get your fill of romance because Chez overlooks a calm small square and little fountain. You'll also be treated to dishes like fowl with a curry basil Thai sauce, spiced pork with honey, or even guinea fowl with a lemon sauce served with fresh pasta. *Bon appétit! 32 rue Tournefort, 5e.* ☎ *01-47-07-72-47. Fixed-price lunch 18€; dinner main courses 35€. Daily noon–2:30pm and 7–10:30pm. Métro: Place Monge.*

Cafes & Sweets

➜**Berthillon** ★★ ICE CREAM   One of the world's most famous ice-cream shops since it opened in 1954, Berthillon dishes out decadently good ice-cream cones, filled with flavors made from real fruit, to a mix of tourists and locals. Stop at the terrace if you want to spy on the boats floating down the Ile St-Louis. *31 rue St-Louis-en-l'Ile, 4e.* ☎ *01-43-54-31-61. www.berthillon-glacier.fr. Wed–Sun 10am–8pm. Métro: Pont-Marie.*

➜**Les Deux Magots** CAFE   This legendary hangout (Sartre and de Beauvoir once sipped coffee here) for the sophisticated residents of St-Germain-des-Prés becomes a tourist favorite in summer. *6 place St-Germain-des-Prés, 6e.* ☎ *01-45-48-55-25. Daily 7:30am–1:30am. Métro: St-Germain-des-Prés.*

📺 Best ➜ **Le Fumoir** ★★ CAFE/BAR An intriguing mix of hip Parisians and Euro-lounger types comes to linger over coffee or eat relatively good food in a setting of book-lined walls that recall the great cafes of Mitteleuropa, French colonial Indochina, and the American '30s. *Place du Louvre, 6 rue de l'Amiral-Coligny, 1er.* ☎ *01-42-92-00-24. Daily noon–2am. Métro: Louvre.*

➜**Stohrer** ★ CAFE/DESSERTS   Opened in 1730 by Louis XV's personal chef, Stohrer survives as one of Paris's oldest pastry shops for good reason—the goods here are indeed sweet. Come for some of the city's best croissants and tortes, and to admire the pretty murals by Paul Baudry, who designed the foyer at the Palais Garner. *51 rue Montorgueil, 2e.* ☎ *0- 42-33-38- 20. Métro: Étienne-Marcel.*

Partying

No matter what you fancy, the Paris nightlife scene has it covered. Some of the world's poshest clubs lurk on this city's streets—of course, as a backpacker, you might not have the funds or wardrobe to get in—but really, who needs 'em? Plenty of bars and nightclubs will welcome scruffy (or reasonably coiffed) North American travelers. Pick up a copy of *Pariscope,* available in newspaper shops, to get the scoop on clubs and bars in town. Also keep your eye out for the ubiquitous flyers floating around bars and cafes advertising the next big party. Parisians will usually go out to party after dinner (and they eat late here), so expect bars to get lively around 11pm and clubs to fill up around midnight or 1am.

In general, the French dress up, so don't even think about sporting sweatpants or wife beaters while in town. The situation is even more extreme at clubs. Most clubs have dress codes (some stricter than others) and the bouncers at the door are trained to choose the hottest clientele. If you're not it, you won't get in. Sandals or tennis shoes are generally no-no's, and jeans are often forbidden. Black pants and collared shirts are standard for guys for the posh clubs. Girls just need some sexy, upscale clothing, but for more exclusive clubs, you'll really need to dress up.

The 11th arrondissement, along the gritty sidewalks of the rue Oberkampf, is the place where young trendsters flock. It's slightly far away from the center of town and you'll probably need to take a cab home, but it's worth it if you want to hang like a French student. Even more up and coming than the Oberkampf is the bar quarter of **rue St-Mauer** in the 11th arrondissement, concentrated on tiny rue Ste-Marthe close to the Belleville Métro stop. A mix of ethnic bars and eateries, ranging from Brazilian bars like **Coisas do Brasil** (rue Ste-Marthe 14; no phone), to African spots like the **Algerian Chez Mama** (216 rue St-Mauer; no phone) dot this very hot strip.

The Marais, in the 4th arrondissement, and the Beauborg in the 10th arrondissement, are notoriously popular with gay males. The 18th arrondissement (home to the Moulin Rouge) is the ultimate spot for evening action—as in strip clubs and sex shops. Don't wander here if you're a girl alone, thinking that you'll run into a crooning Ewan McGregor.

Bars

→ **The Fifth Bar** This Irish-American dive bar draws an international crowd, mostly students who cue up at the pool table or watch NFL and rugby on TVs. Don't try to practice your French with the barmaid; here you'll meet some Anglos or Anglophones who've come to drink and hang out (as opposed to French bars, where they go to hang out and drink). With pints at 4€ and cocktails at 5€ during happy hour (from 5–10pm) you can get properly sauced without breaking the bank. It occasionally features organized theme nights, such as singalong diva nights with American music. *62 rue Mouffetard, 5e.* ☎ *01-43-37-09-09. Métro: Place Monge.*

→ **La Petit Fer à Cheval** This small bar/cafe's outdoor seating area is great for enjoying an afternoon aperitif during the summer or beer at the cozy bar in the winter. Not much at La Petit seems to have changed since before World War II, which lends it an old-fashioned and typically French air. The

Paris Partying & Sightseeing

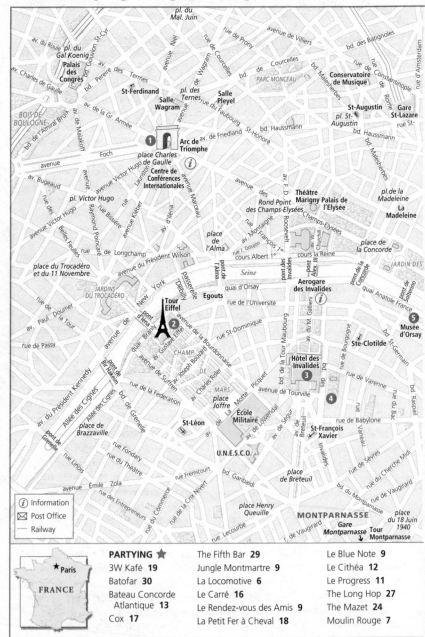

PARTYING ⭐

3W Kafé **19**
Batofar **30**
Bateau Concorde
 Atlantique **13**
Cox **17**

The Fifth Bar **29**
Jungle Montmartre **9**
La Locomotive **6**
Le Carré **16**
Le Rendez-vous des Amis **9**
La Petit Fer à Cheval **18**

Le Blue Note **9**
Le Cithéa **12**
Le Progress **11**
The Long Hop **27**
The Mazet **24**
Moulin Rouge **7**

O'Sullivan's **8**	**SIGHTSEEING** ●	Centre Pompidou–	Musée Rodin **4**
Raid Bar **15**	Arc de Triomphe **1**	Musée national d'Art	Musée d'Orsay **5**
Sanz Sans **23**	Basilique du	moderne **15**	Musée du Louvre **14**
Wax **22**	Sacré-Coeur **10**	Cimetière du	Musée National du Moyen
	Cathedrale de	Père Lachaise **21**	Age Thermes de Cluny **26**
	Notre Dame **25**	Eiffel Tower **2**	Musée Picasso **20**
	Catacombes de Paris **28**	Hôtel des Invalides **3**	

crowd is more hetero than in other neighborhood bars and the lack of blasting house music makes it a quiet place to chill out with a drink. *30 rue Vieille du Temple, 4e.* ☎ *01-42-72-47-47. www.cafeine.com. Métro: St-Paul.*

→ **Le Cithéa** ★★ Housed in an old movie theater, this bar features music ranging from jazz and reggae to afro, rock, and electro. More a small bar with a dance floor than a nightclub, the ambience tends to alter with the music playing. Because it's open until 5:30am, people head here when other bars on Oberkampf have closed. Prices are average, but if you want to sit down with your drink, you may have to pay an extra 2€. *114 rue Oberkampf, 11e.* ☎ *01-40-21-70-95. Cover 5€ (weekends only); varies if live music is scheduled. Métro: Ménilmontant.*

→ **Le Progress** This is a chill neighborhood restaurant/bar with a friendly staff serving traditional French cuisine that is open daily for lunch. After lunchtime is over, though, it morphs into a bar that attracts everyone from foreign tourists to neighborhood regulars. Chessboards are available for people who want to relax with a drink and a game. Drinks are priced fairly; cocktails start at about 7€ and a pitcher of wine goes for 10€. *7 rue des 3 Frères, 18e.* ☎ *01-42-64-07-37. Daily noon–2am (lunch served only until 4pm). Métro: Place-de-Abbesses.*

→ **The Long Hop** Stretch out with a cheap pint on the Long Hop's huge terrace and admire the views of Notre-Dame, an ideal spot to end your day in the Latin Quarter. They have an international, college-aged crowd clearly drawn in by the 5€ pints and cocktails. Every night has a theme: Tuesdays ladies drink for half-price, Wednesdays there's half-price cocktails, Thursdays mean students pay only 4.50€ for drinks, and weekends lay claim to DJs. They're open in the summer from 4pm to 2am and from 6pm to 2am in the winter. *25–27 rue Frédéric Sauton, 5e.* ☎ *01-43-29-40-54. www.long-hop.com. Métro: Maubert-Mutualité.*

→ **The Mazet** This British pub has been around for 50 years, made famous by the legend that Jim Morrison drank here 2 hours before he died. Local lore also claims that the pub is named after a famous doctor who prescribed beer to cure yellow fever. This St-Germain version of a dive bar features a huge selection of cocktails at 5€ and pints at 6€—cheap, considering it's in one of the most expensive *quartiers* in town. Though a British pub, the barman is French as are the majority of patrons. In summer the weekend crowd can get good and rowdy. *61 rue St-André-des-Arts, 6e.* ☎ *01-43-25-57-50. Métro: Odéon or St-Michel.*

→ **Sanz Sans** ★★ Come to Sanz Sans, where you'll see a bar lit by cymbals (yup, like the kind you play), relax, order a drink, and check out the crowd. Now go into the next room (which, I should mention, is covered in red velvet with Louis XVI–style furniture in cheetah patterns). A gold picture frame on the wall shows a live video projection of the people hanging out at the bar. Yes, everyone in the bar now knows that you just checked out the bar. The relaxed ambience of this place is great for meeting people, and the luxurious fabrics covering almost everything in sight make you feel oh-so-regal. They serve dinner with international fusion cuisine (entrees cost about 10€–16€), but the real reason to come here is to drink. Sanz Sans is open Sunday from 6pm to 2am and Monday 9pm to 2am; for the revelers who like to start their weekends early, Tuesday through Saturday they're open 9pm to 5am. *49 rue du Faubourg St-Antoine, 11e.* ☎ *01-44-75-78-78. Métro: Bastille.*

→ **Wax** The decorations at Wax scream 1970s—bright orange is omnipresent, as are cool, retro egg-shaped chairs. A DJ plays a variety of music, depending on the night.

Cocktails are about 9€—pretty normal for Paris. On weekends it's a good idea to reserve a table in advance. This bar is popular with the young French trendsters and students. *15 rue Daval, 11e.* ☎ *01-40-21-16-16. Métro: Bastille.*

Live Music

→**Jungle Montmartre** ★ At this Senegalese bar/restaurant that morphs into a music venue by night, performances range from afro-electro beat to reggae and traditional African music. Cocktails are 3€ to 6€ (one of their specialties is the ginger rum for 3€). Meals are also served in the upper section for about 13€ for an entree. They're open daily from 11am to 2am. *32 rue Gabrielle, 18e.* ☎ *01-46-06-75-69. Métro: Abbesses.*

[MTV] [Best] →**Le Blue Note** ★★ This eclectic bar with live music is on "the other side" of Montmartre. Tourists, restaurants, and shops pack much of Sacre-Coeur, but the East side is significantly less touristy and Le Blue Note is one of the only late-night joints on the street. It specializes in Brazilian jazz and jam sessions (totally hot in France right now) and features Brazilian dance music on the weekends. Cover is free, but you're pretty much obliged to order a drink: 5€ for beer and 10€ for cocktails. It's open every day except Christmas from 9:30pm to 2am. *14 rue Muller, 18e.* ☎ *01-42-54-69-76. www.leblue noteparis.com. Métro: Chateau Rouge.*

Nightclubs

→**Bateau Concorde Atlantique** ★ You don't need to break out the Armani and Gucci gear to get into this club across from the Jardin des Tuileries. The bouncer will let you in as long as you look presentable. The party boat has three levels, and the top has views of the Musée d'Orsay and the Louvre. They serve food from 7pm to 1am at about 10€ for an appetizer and 15€ for a main course. The food is served on the top deck, which becomes a lounge for people who don't like to ('cause they can't) dance. The dancing is on the lowest level, which boasts a club atmosphere with cheaper drinks (3€-8€ for a cocktail). They play disco, house, R&B, pop, and general electro. The crowd here is really eclectic and varies depending on the day of the week. If you get there before 10pm, you can bypass the 10€-to-15€ cover charge. Open until about 5am. *South side of the river between Pont de la Concorde and Passerelle Solferino bridges.* ☎ *01-47-70-01-48. Métro: Assemblée Nationale.*

→**Batofar** Take the Métro to get to this nightclub —situated on a red boat on the Seine—and a cab to get home. It's worth the euros and will spare you a helluva walk. Hundreds of concerts are performed here yearly and the venue caters to an eclectic blend of sounds, including techno and house, alternative, punk, reggae, rap, rock, emo, and anything else that you could imagine. Small-time artists from across the globe come to perform at this intimate setting with two bars and a big dance floor. *11 quai François Muriac, 13e.* ☎ *01-53-60-17-30. Métro: Bibliothèque François Mitterand or Quai de la Gare.*

→**La Locomotive** Partying at this Parisian nightclub adjacent to the Moulin Rouge has become a tradition for many visitors. Each floor cranks out different music and atmosphere, ranging from house/techno and rap to '70s and '80s music to metal electro and even Goth. La Locomotive draws a young, international crowd, so as long as you're not dressed like a slob, it's not that hard to get in. Drinks run about 4€ to 10€. *90 bd. de Clichy, 18e.* ☎ *01-53-41-88-89. Cover weekdays 14€ (includes 1 drink); Fri–Sat 5€ before midnight, 10€ after midnight. Métro: Blanche.*

→**Le Rendez-vous des Amis** If the world music and friendly local clientele aren't a draw, at least head over here to check out the happy-hour drink specials: 2€ drinks from 8 to 10pm. They're open daily

6:30pm to 2am. Thursday nights feature live music. *23 rue Gabrielle, 18e (corner of Gabrielle and Rue Drevet).* ☎ *01-46-06-01-60. Métro: Abbesses.*

➜ **O'Sullivan's** ★ This pub/nightclub, next to the Moulin Rouge, has two main parts: a pub at the entrance where you can relax with a beer and a huge dance floor that has a tendency to get wild late-night. It's not that hard to get into (don't worry if you're living out of a backpack; just shower and don your best T-shirt—you'll be fine). Like any club, if it's a slow night, you risk having a drink in a calm pub, but on a good night you risk dancing on the bar because the dance floor has reached capacity. Open until 5am. *92 bd. de Clichy, 18e.* ☎ *01-42-52-24-94. Cover 10€ after midnight on weekends. Métro: Blanche.*

Gay Nightlife

Note: Gay bars for men and women tend to be segregated in Paris, and there's an abundance of bars for gay men and just a handful of lesbian bars.

➜ **Cox** Does the name give away the fact that this cafe/bar is popular with gay men? Cox is the place to go to pick up a date—not where you would go *with* your date. You will find men of all ages here (though some are on the older side). The bar has few tables and most people seem to congregate around the tall tables around the periphery. The bar seems like it was designed more for checking someone out than approaching them. *15 rue des Archives, 4e.* ☎ *01-42-72-08-00. www.coxbar.com. Métro: Hôtel-de-Ville.*

➜ **Le Carré** Though frequented by high-class gay men, this bar is accessible to all, and though it's always crowded, it's never out of control. Attractive waiters serve drinks to attractive men at the outdoor tables. The inside has high ceilings and huge floor-to-ceiling windows, and it is very tastefully decorated. It's open 10pm to 4am. *18 rue du Temple, 4e.* ☎ *01-44-59-38-57. Métro: Hôtel-de-Ville.*

➜ **Raid Bar** This gay, newly renovated bar in the heart of the Marais advertises a hot shower show. Need I say more? Okay, I will. They have two DJs a night and a shower booth with nude dancers nightly. They're open from 9pm to 5:30am in the summer with a happy hour from 9pm to 10pm. *21 rue du Temple, 4e. No phone. www.raidbar.com. Métro: Hôtel-de-Ville.*

➜ **3W Kafé** This lesbian bar's name stands for "woman with woman," but all kinds hang out here. You can come to chat up gals, or simply to relax; you can belly up to the bar and chat with the friendly barmaid or barman or you can choose a table. The inside of the bar is basic, with less attention to design than the other nearby bars. Open daily from 6pm to 2am. *8 rue des Écouffes, 4e.* ☎ *01-48-87-39-26. Métro: St-Paul.*

Performing Arts

Announcements of shows, concerts, and operas are plastered on kiosks all over town. You'll find listings in the weekly *Pariscope,* an entertainment guide with a section in English, or the English-language bimonthly *Boulevard.* Performances start later in Paris than in London or New York—from 8 to 9pm—and Parisians tend to dine after the theater. You may not want to do the same because many of the less expensive restaurants close as early as 9pm.

There are many ticket agencies in Paris, most near the Right Bank hotels. *Avoid them if possible.* You can buy the cheapest tickets at the box office of the theater or at discount agencies that sell tickets of up to 50% off. One is the **Kiosque Théâtre,** 15 place de la Madeleine, 8e (no phone; Métro: Madeleine), offering leftover tickets for about half-price on the performance day. Tickets for evening shows are sold Tuesday to Friday from 12:30 to 8pm and Saturday from 2 to 8pm. Tickets for matinees are sold Saturday from 12:30 to 2pm and Sunday from 12:30 to 4pm. Other branches are in the basement of the Châtelet—Les Halles Métro station and in front of Gare Montparnasse.

Students with ID can often get last-minute tickets by applying at the box office an hour before curtain time.

Art Galleries

Art galleries abound in Paris, and if you're lucky you'll happen upon an exposition opening where you can mingle with the Parisian artsy crowd while munching on free snacks and beverages. The 4th arrondissement is the base for many of the city's galleries. **Galerie Pierre-Marie Vitoux** is a well-known space that features paintings and sculptures from contemporary artists (3 rue d'Ormesson, place Ste-Catherine, 4e; ☎ 01-48-04-81-00; Métro: St-Paul). The **Art Symbol** gallery in the heart of the Marais (24 place des Vosges, 4e; ☎ 01-40-27-05-75; Métro: Place-de-la-Bastille or Chemin-Vert) specializes in figurative contemporary art. **Galerie Baudoin Lebon** (38 rue Sainte Croix la Bretonnerie, 4e; ☎ 01-42-72-09-10; Métro: Hôtel-de-Ville or Rambuteau) rotates different expositions of international contemporary art.

The 6th arrondissement is also home to many contemporary art galleries, including **Galerie Aittouares** (2 rue des Beaux-Arts; ☎ 01-40-51-87-46; Métro: St-Germain-des-Prés) and the **St-Père** (19 rue St-Pères, 6e; ☎ 01-55-04-89-10; Métro: St-Germain-des-Prés), which exhibits a wide variety of modern art.

Opera

If you want a classy night out on the town, try one of the two major opera houses in Paris. Both feature operas, plays, and ballets. If you plan to go, buy your tickets as far in advance as possible (try 3 months). Tickets range from 20€ to 130€ depending on what you are seeing and where you want to sit. The two main opera houses are at **Opéra Bastille** at place de la Bastille (120 rue Lyon, 12e; ☎ 01-40-01-17-89; Métro: Bastille) and the **Palais Garnier** at place de l'Opéra (8 rue Scribe; ☎ 01-40-01-17-89; Métro: Opéra).

Theater

You'll be hard-pressed to find a play in English in Paris. If that doesn't deter you, check out some of these theaters for upcoming plays and dance performances: **Théâtre de la Ville** has two show houses, and tickets range from 12€ to 23€. The first location is at Théâtre de la Ville 2 (place du Châtelet 4e, Métro: Châtelet) and the second location is at les Abbesses (31 rue des Abbesses, 18e; Métro: Abbesses). Call ahead or check their website for more information (☎ 01-42-74-22-77; www.theatredelaville-paris.com). The **Théâtre des Champs-Elysées** is a spectacular theater where you can see operas, ballets, orchestras, and plays. From its beautiful exterior to its lavish interior—you sit in red velvet armchairs with gold fringe—this place screams class. The tickets run from 7€ to 130€ depending on the performance and the seating (15 av. Montaigne, 8e; ☎ 01-49-52-50-50; www.theatrechampselysees.fr; Métro: Alma-Marceau or Franklin-Roosevelt).

Cabarets & Performance Halls

→**The Moulin Rouge** Though a trip to the Moulin Rouge is a bit trite, touristy, and expensive, it still makes for a pretty cool Parisian experience. This cabaret opened up in 1889, at a time in Paris when social barriers collapsed and social taboos loosened. The show here has changed a lot since the cancan dances of the 1800s. The Las Vegas–like revue features more than 100 artists, including 60

PARIS

female dancers donning skimpy costumes of feathers, sequins, and rhinestones. The cabaret experience includes eating a gourmet dinner as you watch the dancers strut their stuff. Dress code prohibits wearing shorts, and jackets and ties are appreciated. You are required to arrive 30 minutes before the show or dinner starts, but plan on coming super-early to get a good table. There are three fixed menus with three courses for 140€ to 170€. Dinner starts at 7pm, followed by the show at 9pm (show not included in dinner price). The show is 97€ at 9pm and 87€ at 11pm. *82 bd. de Clichy, 18e.* ☎ *01-53-09-82-82. Métro: Blanche.*

→ **Villa d'Este** This club proudly touts that it once booked Amalia Rodrigues, Portugal's leading *fadista* (singer of traditional Portuguese music), and French chanteuse Juliette Greco. Nowadays, you're more likely to hear French singer François de Guelte or other top talent from Europe and America. It's also likely that you'll hear some of the greatest hits of beloved French performers like Piaf, Aznavour, Brassens, and Brel. There is a cover (including first drink) of 30€; for dinner (including wine) and a show, the price is 42€–115€. *4 rue Arsène-Houssaye, 8e.* ☎ *01-42-56-14-65. Métro: Charles-de-Gaulle–Etoile.*

Sightseeing

You could spend your whole life going to museums in Paris and still not see all the offerings. Conveniently, many of the city's incredible museums are within walking distance of each other, which helps expedite the viewing process. Still, direct Métros service most major sights.

Tours

Seeing Paris by boat offers a not-to-be-missed vantage point of the city—with sweeping vistas of the riverbanks and great views of Notre-Dame. **Bateaux Parisians,** a boat with glass windows and roof, leaves from the Eiffel Tower for an hour-long guided tour (9.50€ for adults; leaves every 30 min. Apr–Sept 10am–10:30pm, hourly Oct–Mar 10am–10pm). The company also offers dinner cruises on the Seine. It's located on the bank right in front of the Eiffel Tower on quai Branly. Take the Bir-Hakeim or Trocadéro Métro.

The **Batobus** (☎ 08-25-05-01-01; http://batobus.com) tour is a hop-on/hop-off boat tour around Paris on the Seine, letting tourists stop at eight of Paris's monuments (Eiffel Tower, Musée d'Orsay, St-Germain-des-Prés,

Notre-Dame, Jardin des Plantes, Hôtel de Ville, Louvre, and Champs Elysées). Pick up the boat on the bank of the river at the aforementioned sights every 15 to 30 minutes. It's open April 22 to September 30 from 10am to 10pm, March 18 to April 21 and October 1 to November 2 from 10am to 7pm, and February 5 to March 17 and November 3 to January 2 from 10:30am to 4:30pm. A 1-day pass is 11€, and they give discounts for students with student ID cards.

If you'd rather see Paris by land, try a guided organized bike tour with **Fat Tire Bike** tours (24 rue Edgar Faure, 75015 Paris; ☎ 01-56-68-10-54; www.fattirebiketours paris.com). They offer tours during the day (22€–24€) and night (26€ to 28€). The tours are easy rides and stop at all the big monuments for pictures. The night tour includes a boat ride with free wine. Check out their website for specific meeting times and places.

For Paris's cheapest bus tours, take the **no. 95 bus** that goes by the Opéra, Louvre, Palais Royal, St-Germain-de-Prés, and Montparnasse, or the **no. 69 bus,** that starts at the Eiffel Tower and ends at Père-Lachaise cemetery. See p. 693 for bus info.

Free & Easy

→ On the first Sunday of each month, **museums** are generally free. See listings below for specifics. Many museums are also free for people under 18; discounts are often offered for people between 18 and 25 with a valid student ID.

→ If you plan to hit mad amounts of museums and monuments, it's probably worth it to buy a **museum pass.** They're sold in most museums, and at major monuments and major Métro stations. This pass gets you in free to permanent collections and you get to bypass many long entrance lines. The passes are valid at most museums and monuments; a 1-day pass is 18€, a 3-day pass is 36€, and a 5-day pass is 54€. For more information, contact **InterMusées** (☎ 01-44-61-96-60).

→ You can take in a free half-hour **haute couture fashion show** at the **Galeries Lafayette,** every Friday at 3pm. You must reserve a seat by calling ☎ 33-1-42-82-30-25.

Festivals

For more details and exact dates for festivals and events in Paris, go to www.parisinfo.com.

January & February

Fashion Week. New collections and countless parties are on the agenda at fashion week. The event in the Porte de Versailles convention facilities is geared to professionals, but for the merely fashion-conscious, the rules are usually bent. For details, call ☎ 01-44-94-70-00 or visit www.pret paris.com. A second fashion week takes place in early September. End of January into February.

March to May

Foire du Trône. A mammoth amusement park that its fans call France's largest country fair, the Foire du Trône (Bois de Vincennes, 12e) originated in A.D. 957. This high-tech continuation of the tradition has a Ferris wheel, carousels, and fire-eaters that call to mind a Gallic Coney Island. Call ☎ 01-46-27-52-29 for details. End of March to end of May.

June

Fete de la Musique. This celebration of the summer solstice is the only day on which noise laws don't apply in Paris. Musicians and wannabes pour into the streets, where you can make music with anything, even if it means banging two garbage cans together. Musical parties pop up in virtually all open spaces, with more organized concerts at place de la Bastille and place de la Republique. For details, call ☎ 01-40-03-94-70 or visit www. fetedelamusique.culture.fr. Mid-June.

Gay Pride Parade. You'll find the world's largest gay parade proudly marching through the streets of Paris in late June. Expect flamboyant floats and costumes and music and festivities. There are many events held during the same week throughout the town, particularly in the Marais. Call or fax ☎ 01-53-01-47-01 or visit www.inter-lgbt.org.

July

Bastille Day. France's equivalent to the 4th of July commemorates the storming of the Bastille. Festivities include military parades with marching Frenchmen and tanks, and tons of fireworks. July 14.

Tour de France. This is Europe's most visible, highly contested, and televised bicycle race. Crews of wind tunnel–tested athletes speed along an itinerary tracing the six sides of the French "hexagon," detouring deep into the Massif Central and the Swiss Alps. For details, call ☎ 01-41-33-15-00 or visit www.letour.fr. Throughout July.

PARIS

August

MTV Best **Rock en Seine** ★★. An annual rock fest in the riverside parkland nearby the Boulogne–Pont-de-St-Cloud Métro station will host its third year of concerts in 2005. Approximately 48,000 people showed up in 2004 to see acts by bands like the White Stripes and the Chemical Brothers. Tickets for 2005 ran 65€ for 2 nights and 39€ for 1. Visit www.rockenseine.com for info. Late August.

September

Rendez-Vous Electroniques Festival. A highlight of this 10-day-long electronic festival featuring techno concerts and art expositions is the **Paris Techno Parade** ★. Visit www.techopol.net for details. Early September.

November

Beaujoulais Nouveau. November is a traditionally calm month for France—except for the release day of this special type of wine that is best sipped when it is young. Every year there are various specials and festivities in bars and restaurants revolving around this festive wine. Connoisseurs compare it with previous years' harvests and the non-connoisseurs just sip it down and refill all night long. Third Thursday in November.

December

Fete de St-Sylvestre (New Year's Eve). This holiday is most boisterously celebrated in the Latin Quarter around the Sorbonne. At midnight, the city explodes. Strangers kiss strangers, and boulevard St-Michel and the Champs-Elysées become virtual pedestrian malls. December 31.

Attractions & Monuments

→**Arc de Triomphe** ★ The largest triumphal arch in the world (who knew there was more than one?), the Arc de Triomphe is 49m (161ft.) high and 44m (144ft.) wide. The French consider this one of the most important monuments in Paris because it represents some of France's accomplishments, as opposed to, say, the Eiffel Tower which was made for tourists. The Arch was commissioned by Napoleon in 1806 to commemorate the victories of the Grand Armée. It was finished in 1836 under the rule of King Louis-Philippe, and 4 years later, Napoleon's coffin passed under the finished Arch on its way to Invalides. Since then, it has become the site of many state funerals and it is also where you will find the tomb and eternal flame of the Unknown Soldier. The arch is covered with sculptures depicting war and peace and is engraved with the names of hundreds of generals who fought in the Napoleonic battles (the names that are underlined are those who died in battle).

You can go into the Arc de Triomphe, but don't try to cross the street to get there. This is one of the busiest intersections in Paris, so it's much safer to take the underground passage. Once in the arch, you can climb the stairs or take an elevator to the top, where there is a great view of Paris (taking in the nearby Champs Elysées) and an exhibition about the Arc's history. *Place Charles de Gaulle-Etoile, 8e.* ☎ *01-55-37-73-77. www. monum.fr. Admission 4.50€–7€. Daily Apr–Sept 10am–11pm; Oct–Mar 10am–10:30pm. Métro: Charles-de-Gaulle–Etoile.*

→**Catacombes de Paris** In the 18th century, the Paris government realized that the city's cemeteries were not only disgustingly dirty, but that they were also unhygienic and taking up a lot of room. So, in 1785, the government decided to move over 6 million graves to a series of former limestone quarries underneath Paris. Today, you can visit 1.7km (1 mile) of the total 300km (186 miles) of paths making up the catacombs. The grossest part is that the bones are on display, and some are even artistically arranged in patterns or shapes. This is a great way to learn about the gory history of Paris, though: During the period of political instability

following the French Revolution, the commu-
nards hid out in the narrow bone-filled tunnels of the catacombs; the catacombs also
served as the headquarters for the German
Air Force during World War II; and during the
1960s and 1970s, hippies came here to host
underground concerts and poetry readings.
1 av. du colonel Roi-Tanguy, 14e. ☎ *01-43-22-
47-63. Admission: 2.60€–5€. Tues–Sun 10am–
5pm. Métro: Denfert-Rocherreau.*

➜ **Cimetière du Père-Lachaise** ★ Of the
roughly 70,000 people who are buried here,
in perhaps the world's most famous grave-
yard, the most famous are Oscar Wilde,
Molière, Proust, Balzac, Edith Piaf, Gertrude
Stein, and Jim Morrison. Some of the tombs
are elaborate works of art—many families
tried to outdo each other by building
increasingly more ostentatious graves. *16 rue
de Repos, 20e.* ☎ *01-55-25-82-10. www.pere-
lachaise.com. Mon–Fri 8am–6pm; Sat 8:30am–
6pm; Sun 9am–6pm (Nov to early Mar closes
at 5:30pm). Métro: Philippe-August, Gambetta,
or Père-Lachaise.*

➜ **Hôtel des Invalides/Napoleon's Tomb**
★★ In 1670, the Sun King decided to build
this "hotel" to house disabled soldiers. It
wasn't an entirely benevolent gesture considering the men had been injured, crippled,
or blinded while fighting his battles. When
the building was finally completed (Louis XIV
had long been dead), a gilded dome by Jules
Hardouin-Mansart crowned it and its corridors stretched for miles. The best way to
approach the Invalides is by crossing over
the Right Bank via the early-1900s Pont
Alexander-III and entering the cobblestone
forecourt, where a display of massive cannons makes a formidable welcome.

To accommodate **Napoleon's Tomb,** the
architect Visconti had to redesign the church's
high altar in 1842. First buried on St. Helena,
Napoleon's remains were exhumed and
brought to Paris in 1840 on the orders of Louis-
Philippe, who demanded the English return the
emperor to French soil. The remains were

locked inside six coffins in this tomb made of
red Finnish porphyry, with a green granite
base. Surrounding it are a dozen Amazon-like
figures representing Napoleon's victories.
Almost lampooning the smallness of the man,
everything is done on a gargantuan scale. In
his coronation robes, the statue of Napoleon
stands 2.5m (8¼ ft.) high. The grave of the
"King of Rome," his son by second wife Marie-
Louise, lies at his feet. Surrounding Napoleon's
Tomb are those of his brother Joseph
Bonaparte; the great Vauban, who built many
of France's fortifications; World War I Allied
commander Foch; and the vicomte de
Turenne, the republic's first grenadier (actually, only his heart is entombed here). *Place
des Invalides, 7e.* ☎ *01-44-42-37-72. www.
invalides.org. Admission to Musée de l'Armée,
Napoleon's Tomb, and Musée des Plans-Reliefs
7€ adults, 5€ students. Daily Oct–Mar 10am–
5pm; Apr–May and Sept 10am–6pm; June–Aug
10am–7pm. Closed Jan 1, May 1, Nov 1, and
Dec 25. Métro: Latour-Maubourg, Varenne, or
Invalides.*

➜ **La Basilique du Sacre-Coeur de
Montmartre** ★ A huge white church built in
the Romano-Byzantine style, Sacre-Coeur was
constructed between 1876 and 1910 in order to
lure tourists and churchgoers to the ill-
frequented hill on which it rests. This plan
didn't work at first because cabarets like the
Moulin Rouge attracted a more party-loving
crowd to the area. Today, the church—at 100m
(328 ft.) long and 50m (164 ft.) wide and
crowned by an 83m-high (272 ft.) dome—is an
attraction in its own right. It's worth the trip,
if only for the great view of all of Paris; though
the church is closed at night, it looks
most beautiful when it's lit up. *Place St-Pierre,
18e.* ☎ *01-53-41-89-00. www.sacre-coeur-mont
martre.com. Admission: Free to basilica; 5€
dome and crypt. Basilica daily 6am–11pm;
dome and crypt 9am–6pm. Métro: Abbesses;
take elevator to surface and follow signs to
Sacre-Coeur.*

PARIS

MTV **Best** → **Notre-Dame** ★★★ Probably the most famous church in all of France, Notre-Dame is located smack dab in the center of Paris on the Ile de la Cité. Construction on it started in 1163 and lasted until the 14th century. Before entering, take a walk around the rear of the cathedral and check out its fine flying buttresses (that's right, I said buttress—that's a fancy way of saying the external side supports). Once inside, take some time to admire the stained-glass windows. The most famous, the rose window, is on the wall right above the front door above the enormous organ. If you have time, climb the towers to get an up-close look at the gargoyles made famous by Victor Hugo's *Hunchback of Notre-Dame* (this book's popularity actually saved the cathedral from getting torn down in the 19th c.). *6 place du parvis Notre-Dame, 4e.* ☎ *01-42-34-56-10. www.cathedraledeparis.com. Free admission to cathedral; towers 4.10€–6.10€, treasury 1€–3€. Cathedral daily 8am–6:45 pm; towers and crypt daily Apr–Sept 9:30am–6pm. Oct–Mar 10am–5:15pm; museum Sat–Sun 2–5pm; treasury Mon–Sat 9:30–6pm, Sun 2–6pm. Métro: Cité or St-Michel.*

MTV **Best** → **The Seine** ★★★ This is the essential Paris experience. Even if you're broke, out of luck, or out of love, you can wander the banks of the Seine and feel good about the world. In the summer, the city dumps sand in a long swath along the river and out come volleyball nets, lounge chairs, food vendors, and more. Years ago, when the Seine was more polluted, it would never have attracted such a following. Now, even UNESCO has joined the bandwagon and added over 10km (6¼ miles) of the riverbank to its World Heritage Site list.

MTV **Best** → **Tour Eiffel** ★★★ One of the most famous monuments in the world, this

PARIS

12 Hours in Paris

1. **See a museum.** I'd avoid the Louvre because you need *at least* a couple of hours to explore it properly. Instead, head to the Musée d'Orsay or the Centre Pompidou.

2. **Take a hike.** Walk down the Voie Triumphale from the **Arc de Triomphe** through **place de la Concorde** and the **Tuileries Garden.**

3. **Take a boat tour.** Take a relaxed boat trip along the Seine—you'll float past the city's major monuments (Notre-Dame and the Eiffel Tower for example).

4. **See Notre-Dame.** If you have time in the afternoon, you should stop by Notre-Dame. If you're pressed for time, don't worry about trying to climb up the towers—just observing this building from up close is amazing.

5. **Hang out at a sidewalk cafe in the Latin District.** After your boat tour, go to the Latin District and find a sidewalk cafe, where you can tuck into a Parisian meal and accomplish some serious people-watching.

6. **Check out a marché.** Wander through one of the city's open-air markets and, if you haven't already eaten to the point of exploding, just try to resist snacking.

7. **Go for ice cream.** If you somehow resisted snacking at the market, head to **Berthillon** for the city's best ice cream.

8. **Wander while you wait for the day to end.** Amble through and explore the **Marais** and, specifically, place des Voges, at sunset, when the galleries cast long shadows over the court.

wrought iron structure stands 317m (1,040 ft.) high. It was built by Gustave-Alexandre Eiffel (the same engineer who designed the framework for the Statue of Liberty in New York) in 1889 for the Universal Exhibition in Paris. This structure is an engineering masterpiece because it weighs 7,000 tons but it exerts the same amount of pressure on the ground as an average-size person does sitting in a chair. The view is fantastic from all of the levels but from the top, you can see up to 65km (40 miles) away on a clear day. On each level there are attractions such as exhibitions, a bar, and a restaurant. *Champs de Mars, 7e.* ☎ *01-44-11-23-23. www.tour-eiffel.fr. Admission: 1st landing 3.70€, 2nd landing 7€, 3rd landing 10€; stairs to 2nd landing 3.20€. Daily May–Sept 9:30–11pm; June–Aug 9am–midnight (fall–winter, stairs open till 6:30pm). Métro: Trocadéro, École-Militaire, or Bir-Hakeim. RER: Champs de Mars or Tour Eiffel.*

Museums

MTV **Best** →**Centre Pompidou** ★★ Another must-see for Paris. This building sticks out like a sore thumb amidst the city's more classic buildings and churches. It literally looks as if it was made inside out, with colorful pipes and ducts lining the outside of the building. This monstrosity holds the largest collection of modern and contemporary art in Europe with legendary artists such as Picasso, Dalí, Kandinsky, Matisse, Magritte, and Warhol on permanent display. It's in the heart of the Marais and a 5-minute walk from Les Halles, so there'll be no shortage of places to shop or eat after you've finished gawking. *Place Georges Pompidou, 4e.* ☎ *01-44-78-12-33. www.centrepompidou.fr. Admission 3.50€–10€ (depends on discount and exhibitions). Wed–Mon 11am–9pm. Métro: Rambuteau or Hôtel-de-Ville.*

MTV **Best** →**Musée du Louvre** ★★★ The most famous museum in France and possibly in the world, the Louvre was originally built in the 12th century as a royal fortress

and palace for Philip II. The grand building contains paintings, sculptures, and graphic art from the Middle Ages and Greek, Etruscan, Roman, Oriental, and Egyptian antiquities. It houses the famous *Mona Lisa* (called *La Joconde* in French), *Venus de Milo,* and *Winged Victory,* but these are just a few of the roughly 30,000 works that are on display. You simply can't see everything, so the best thing to do is figure out what you want to see before you get in; you can decide in the line, which might take an extremely long time. One way to avoid the line is to buy tickets in advance; see the number that follows. *99 rue de Rivoli, 1e.* ☎ *01-40-20-53-70. Order tickets in advance at* ☎ *08-92-68-46-94, and then pick them up at any FNAC store. www.louvre.fr. Admission 8.50€. Mon and Thurs 9am–6pm; Wed and Fri 9am–9:45pm. Free on 1st Sun of the month. Parts of museum close at 5:30pm. Admission 7€–5€. Métro: Palais-Royal or Louvre-Rivoli.*

MTV **Best** →**Musée d'Orsay** ★★★ This is one of the top museums in the world, so bank on there being a long line. It'll be worth the wait. Manet, Monet, Cézanne, van Gogh, Degas, Whistler, Renoir, Delacroix, Matisse, and Gauguin are just a few of the big names you'll see here. Even the building itself is an attraction; it used to be a beautiful, neoclassical train station and the inside of the museum preserves the original grandiose architecture. *1 rue de la Légion d'Honneur, 7e.* ☎ *01-40-49-48-84. www.musee-orsay.fr. Admission 7.50€ adults over 24, 5.50€ adults 18–24. Tues–Wed and Fri–Sat 10am–6pm; Thurs 10am–9:45pm (June 23–Sept 28 9am–6pm); Sun 9am–6pm. Métro: Musée-d'Orsay or Solférino.*

→**Musée National du Moyen Age Thermes de Cluny** You really have to be into medieval art to like this museum, but I recommend coming here simply to glimpse one of the only buildings in Paris that uses medieval architecture. In the 15th century, a

ᴹᵀᵛ◉ The University Scene

The 5th arrondissement is the closest that you'll get to a student district in Paris. Here you'll find Paris's most well-known universities, including the Sorbonne (www.sorbone.fr) branch of the University of Paris. You may have heard that the main **College de Sorbonne** campus, centered on 47 rue des Ecoles, has a long-standing reputation for excellent culinary classes. If getting into the Zen of chopping for an entire semester isn't an option, you can still learn to cook at 30-minute classes hosted by **L'Atelier des Chefs** (10 rue de Penthièvre, 8e; ☎ 01-53-30-05-82; www.atelierdeschefs.com). For about 25€, you'll learn to prepare a Sorbonne-quality meal—*and* you get to eat it.

Bars and cafes overflow with students in this 'hood, but this is also a very touristy part of town, so you may meet more fellow travelers than real Parisian students. If you want to go where the French students hang out, check out **rue Oberkampf.** If you insist on staying put in the Sorbonne area, the prime spots to spark up a conversation are either place de la Sorbonne—on the square itself or in one of its many cigarette-smoke-clogged cafes—or immediately inside the Sorbonne (Sorbonne III and IV; Métro: Cluny–La-Sorbonne), in the courtyard. Or head to **Le Reflet** (6 rue Champollion, 5e; ☎ 01/43-29-97-27; Métro: Cluny–La-Sorbonne; daily 10am–2am), a cramped little room opposite an art house theater of the same name. It's still one of the best places in Paris to work on your novel, have an espresso, maybe a little tempeh salad, flirt with the waitstaff, and meet the coolest and most low-key members of the university student set.

wealthy abbot built the building you see today on top of Roman baths. In 1833, Cluny was rented to Alexandre du Sommerard who filled it with medieval artwork. When he died in 1842, the building and the collection transferred to the government's control and it was made into a museum. Most people come to see the famous *The Lady and the Unicorn Tapestries,* an allegory of the five senses. *6 place Paul-Painléve. ☎ 01-53-73-78-00. www.musee-moyenage.fr. Admission: 4.50€–6.50€ (reduced price those under 25). Wed–Mon 9:15–5:45pm. Métro: Cluny, La Sorbonne, or St-Michel.*

→ **Musée National Picasso** ★ This museum guides you through the stages of Picasso's life, as seen through his art. It holds hundreds of paintings, sculptures, collages, bas-reliefs, and ceramics along with thousands of sketches and engravings by the artist who rocked the modern art world. The emphasis is on his Minotaur, ceramic, and cubist stages but there is also a rare 1901 self-portrait which illustrates his classical training in painting. *In Hôtel Salé, 5 rue de Thorigny, 3e. ☎ 01-42-71-25-21. www.musee-picasso.fr. Admission 6.70€ adults over 25, 5.20€ adults 18–25 and seniors. Wed–Mon Apr–Sept 9:30am–6pm; Oct–Mar 9:30am–5:30pm. Métro: St-Paul, Chemin-Vert, or Filles-du-Calvaire.*

→ **Musée Rodin** ★★ Rodin's sumptuous figures seem to glow with life at this museum, built from a beautiful mansion/hotel from the 1700s where Rodin lived. Spectacular gardens are attached to the building, where you can see such famous sculptures as *The Thinker* and *The Burghers of Calais. 75bis/77 rue de Varenne. 7e. ☎ 01-44-18-61-10. www.musee-rodin.fr. Admission 5€ adults over 25, 3€ adults 18–25. Tues–Sun Oct–Mar 9:30am–4:45pm; Apr–Sept 9:30am–5:45pm. Garden 1€. Métro: Varenne.*

Playing Outside

The problem with playing outside in Paris is that it rains more often than not. If you're blessed with sun during your trip, you should take a walking tour. Start at the Arc de Triomphe and follow the Champs Elysées down to place de la Concorde. Continue onto the Louvre via the Jardins des Tuileries, then walk along rue de Rivoli and check out some shops, after which you should continue on to Notre-Dame. Cross the bridge onto the Rive Gauche and walk around the Quartier Latin and St-Germain. Then take a Métro either to the Eiffel Tower or Montmartre to soak in the sunset.

If you're visiting after 2007, you might be lucky enough to take advantage of two permanent swimming pools that are slated to open along the Seine.

Gardens & Parks

BOIS DE BOULOGNE

One of the most spectacular parks in Europe is the **Bois de Boulogne,** Porte Dauphine, 16e (☎ **01-40-67-90-82;** Métro: Les-Sablons, Porte-Maillot, or Porte-Dauphine),

Parkour It

Parkour is an urban sport that involves running, jumping, and vaulting over city streets, walls, and just about any other inanimate object. It's been around since the 1980s, when it was invented in the Paris suburbs, but it's really started taking off here recently because of the film *District B13* (2006 English release). The last weekend of each month, parkour training sessions are held at the Dame du Lac monument in Lisses (RER: Evry Courcouronnes; bus: 59 to Dame du Lac), for about 7€. Check out www.parkour.net for details.

often called the "main lung" of Paris. You can traverse it by horse-drawn carriage or car, though I recommend walking so that you don't miss its hidden pathways.

Note, however, that when the French say *parc,* they might mean something very different from what you expect. They mean, "Aren't the sycamores lovely?" and most definitely, "Keep off the grass." This is not the best place to run and toss a Frisbee, and you might be put off by the featureless paths. Bois de Boulogne is open daily from 9am to dusk, charging 1.50€ for adults over 26 and .75€ for folks 7 to 26.

JARDIN DU LUXEMBOURG

The 🎵 Best **Jardin du Luxembourg** has always been associated with artists, though children, students, and tourists predominate nowadays. Hemingway used to catch pigeons here. Watteau came this way, as did Verlaine. Balzac didn't like the gardens at all. In 1905, Gertrude Stein would cross them to catch the Batignolles/Clichy/Odéon omnibus, pulled by three grey mares, to meet Picasso in his studio at Montmartre, where he painted her portrait.

Marie de Médicis, the wife of Henri IV, ordered the **Palais du Luxembourg** built on this site in 1612, shortly after she was widowed. Alas, the queen didn't get to enjoy the palace, as her son, Louis XIII, forced her into exile when he discovered she was plotting to overthrow him. She died in poverty in Cologne. You can visit the palace only on the first Sunday of each month at 10:30am, for 8€. However, you must call ☎ **01-42-34-23-62** to make a reservation.

You don't really come to the Luxembourg to visit the palace, though; the gardens are the real attraction. For the most part, they're in the classic French tradition: well groomed and formally laid out, the trees planted in patterns. Urns and statuary on pedestals—one honoring Paris's patroness, Ste-Geneviève, with pigtails reaching to her thighs—encircle a central water basin. Another memorial is dedicated to Stendhal. Kids can sail a toy boat, ride a pony, or attend an occasional Grand Guignol puppet show. And you can play *boules* (lawn bowling) with a group of elderly men who wear black berets and have Gauloises dangling from their mouths.

JARDIN DES TUILERIES

The spectacular statue-studded **Jardin des Tuileries** ★, bordering place de la Concorde, 1er (☎ **01-40-20-90-43**; Métro: Tuileries or Concorde), is as much a part of Paris as the Seine. Louise XIV's gardener, and planner of the Versailles grounds, designed the gardens. The park is the epitome of orderly French design—even the paths are arrow straight.

Friday Night Roll

The 📺 **Best** **Paris Roller Rando** takes over the city on Friday nights, "rando" being short for *randonnée,* meaning tour or excursion. The starting time is around 10pm at the place de l'Italia (also the name of the Métro stop). Roller folk from Paris and throughout Ile-de-France amass here to begin the 3-hour weekly journey through the city on Rollerblades. Every Friday three motorcycle policemen lead the way with dome lights flashing, signaling moving cars to get out of the way. First-aid wagons follow the "rollers." On an average night in Paris, some 20,000 rollers show up. Many visitors like to stay up late that night to watch these "mad, mad Parisians" in all their crazed "rollermania." Check with **Pari Roller** (62 rue Dulong, 17e; ☎ **01-43-36-89-81;** www.pari-roller.com) or **Roller Club de France** (37 bd. Bourdon, 4e; ☎ **01-44-54-94-41;** www.nomadeshop.com) for details.

Parc André Citroen & Parc de Bercy

Different beasts entirely from the well-manicured parks mentioned above, Parc André Citroen and Parc de Bercy are newly green spaces created from industrial spaces. **Parc André Citroen** on the Left Bank used to be a car plant, but assembly line layoffs opened up the 23 hectares (57 acres) of land for an inventive, decidedly modern park—complete with computerized fountains, waterfalls, and sensory gardens dotted with black tulips. DJs play here in the summer, but if the music fails to move you, you can also take a ride on the world's largest tethered balloon, the Eutelstat. Call ☎ **01/44-26-20-00** for details. The entrance to Parc André Citroen is at rue Balard, 15e.

Parc de Bercy transformed a former docking sight off the Seine, famous for its wine warehouses, into a 13-hectare (32-acre) public park, adjoined by Bercy Village—a complex of shops, a concert hall, and a Frank Gehry–designed exhibition center that houses the Cinemathèque Française—the largest collection of film archives in the world. The park is at rue de Bercy, 12e.

Both parks are open Monday to Friday at 8am and 9am Saturday and Sunday. Closing times vary.

Jogging & Walking

If you're a jogger or walker, there's nothing like the quays along the 📺 **Best** **Seine** (p. 722); you may have to stop occasionally for tourists or traffic, but the views you'll soak in during your workout will be worth the interruptions. Otherwise, the cobblestone banks of the Canal St-Martin and Basin de la Vilette are uninterrupted and traffic-free.

Rock Climbing

If you are a diehard *grimpeur* or *grimpeuse* (that's rock climber in French), have no fear: Paris has indoor 📺 **Best** **rock-climbing** gyms and you can climb Fontainebleau nearby if you have your own gear. Gyms are slightly different in France than what you might expect; they usually include a bar where people smoke cigarettes and drink coffee and beer before or after climbing. The rating system of climbs is different as well—gyms usually have color-coded routes with colors corresponding to the difficulty. *Antre Bloc* is one of the city's best gyms, with enormous walls, a friendly staff, and a standard gym attached with exercise equipment. It's at 5–7 rue Henri Barbusse (☎ **01-47-26-52-44;** Métro: Villejuif or Leo Lagrange).

Basketball, Soccer & Handball

If you want to practice your b-ball, head to **Jardin du Luxembourg** (p. 725) in the 6th arrondissement or **Square St-Eloi** in the 12th arrondissement (rue du colonel Rozanoff; Métro: Montgallet).

Small public squares with soccer, basketball, and handball courts are also in the 11th arrondissement (40 rue Emile Lepeu; Métro: Caronne), the 4th arrondissement (Jardin de St-Paul, 9 rue Charlemagne; Métro: St-Paul), and the 10th arrondissement (247 rue la Fayette; Métro: Louis-Blanc).

Shopping

You'll *love* Paris if shopping is your thing. As the city that invented the department store, popularized haute couture by such powerhouses as Chanel and Givenchy, and crafted Cartier bling, it's not surprising that Paris is overflowing with shopping areas, from fashion boutiques to souvenir shops. The most expensive shopping area is the 1st arrondissement. The **Champs Elysées** here is lined with everything from perfume and cosmetic shops to a Virgin Megastore. **Rue St-Honoré** is where you will find the most outrageously expensive fashion boutiques, with the latest Parisian fashions. Nearby **place Vendome** and **rue de la Paix** are where you should go if you want to look at jewelry from Cartier, Tiffany's, and other similar jewelry stores.

In the Marais, hit 📺 **Best** **rue de Rivoli** for both pricey and affordable fashion boutiques and **rue Montorgueil** for vintage finds. **Les Halles** is also right nearby (Métro: Les-Halles), which used to be a huge market place but is now a mall where you can find everything from sports equipment to fashion stores. The 6th arrondissement is one of the most famous shopping areas in Paris, particularly the **rue du Bac** that stretches from the 6th to the 7th—it's only for the truly wealthy and glamorous. The city's big department

stores—including Au Printemps and Galeries Lafayette—are all in the 9th arrondissement, lining the Boulevard Haussman.

Usual shop hours are Monday to Saturday from 10am to 7pm, but hours vary, and Monday mornings don't run at full throttle. Small shops sometimes close for a 2-hour lunch break and some may not even open at all until after lunch on Monday. Thursday is the best day for late-night shopping, with stores open until 9 or 10pm. Sunday shopping is limited to tourist areas and flea markets, though there's growing demand for full-scale Sunday hours. The big department stores are now open on the five Sundays before Christmas.

➜ **Au Printemps** Take a look at the facade of this store for a reminder of the Gilded Age. Inside, the merchandise is divided into housewares **(Printemps Maison),** women's fashion **(Printemps de la Mode),** and men's clothes **(Le Printemps de l'Homme).** It's better than Galeries Lafayette for women's and children's fashion. Although visitors feel more pampered in Galeries Lafayette, Au Printemps's customer service is dazzling, putting all major department stores in Paris to shame. Check out the magnificent stained-glass dome, through

Best Buys

A discount of 20% to 30% makes perfume and beauty products a great buy. Duty-free shops abound in Paris and are always less expensive than the ones at the airports. For bargain cosmetics, try out French dime-store and drugstore brands like **Bourjois** (made in the Chanel factories), **Lierac,** and **Galenic. Vichy,** famous for its water, has a skin-care and makeup line. The newest retail trend in Paris is the *parapharmacie,* a type of discount drugstore loaded with inexpensive brands, health cures, beauty regimes, and diet plans. These usually offer a 20% discount.

Sure, you can buy couture or *prêt-à-porter* (ready-to-wear), but French teens and trendsetters have their own stores where the latest looks are affordable. Even the dime stores in Paris sell designer copies and hotshot styles. In the stalls in front of the department stores on boulevard Haussmann, you'll find some of the latest accessories, guaranteed for a week's worth of small talk once you get home.

which turquoise light cascades into the sixth-floor **Café Flo,** where you can have a coffee or a full meal. Interpreters at the Welcome Service in Printemps de la Mode will help you find what you're looking for, claim your VAT refund, and so on. Au Printemps also has a tourist discount card, offering a flat 10% discount. Immediately adjacent to the store and under the same management, but with its own phone and storefront, is **Citadium** (56 rue Caumartin, 9e; ☎ 01-55-31-74-00), which specializes in sporting equipment and clothing for men, women, and children. Open Monday to Wednesday and Friday to Saturday 9:35am to 7pm; Thursday 9:35am to

9pm. *64 bd. Haussmann, 9e.* ☎ *01-42-82-50-00. Métro: Havre-Caumartin. RER: Auber or Haussmann–St-Lazare.*

→**Come On Eileen** ★ Judging from the name, the owners of this three-story vintage warehouse are Dexy's Midnight Runners fans. Thankfully, their musical taste doesn't extend to the fashions on sale, which range from cowgirl duds to 1960s to 1970s flowery dresses. *16–18 rue des Taillandiers, 11e.* ☎ *01/43-38-12-11. Mon–Fri 11:30am–8:30pm, Sun 4–8pm. Métro: Ledru-Rollin.*

→**Fauchon** ★★ At place de la Madeleine stands one of the city's most popular sights—not the church, but Fauchon, a hyper-upscale, mega-delicatessen that thrives within a city famous for its finicky eaters. It's divided into three divisions that include an *épicerie* (for jams, crackers, pastas, and exotic canned goods); a patissierie (for breads, pastries, and chocolates); and a *traiteur* (for cheeses, terrines, pâtés, caviar, and fruits). Prices are steep, but the inventories—at least to serious foodies—are fascinating. At some (but not all) of the counters, you'll indicate to attendants what you want from behind glass display cases, and get an electronic ticket, which you'll carry to a *caisse* (cash register). Surrender your tickets, pay the tally, and then return to the counter to pick up your groceries. In other cases, you simply load up your shopping basket with whatever you want and pay for your purchases at a cash register, just as you would at any grocery store.

On the same premises, Fauchon has a restaurant, **Brasserie Fauchon,** and a tea salon, which showcases the pastry-making talents of its chefs. Among the many offerings is a *Paris-Brest,* a ring in the shape of a bicycle wheel that's loaded with pastry cream, almond praline, butter cream, and hazelnut paste capped with almonds. Open Monday to Saturday 9:30am to 7pm. *26–30*

Market Watch

Paris's outdoor markets are a great place to get fresh fruits and veggies. There are markets in every neighborhood square most mornings until about 1 or 2pm. Often, you can't choose the fruit or veggies yourself; some vendors in the markets don't even want you to touch the produce. Ask before selecting anything.

Below is info on a few of the city's best outdoor markets, but there are daily markets in every arrondissement. Ask at your hotel or hostel for the closest market. Also, **www.parisinfo.com** lists all the markets in Paris on their "Daily life" page off the "Practical Paris" tab.

Marché Couvert St-Germain, a market with fresh produce, is located at 4/8 rue Lobineau (Métro: Mabillon). It's open from Tuesday to Saturday from 8:30am to 1pm and 4 to 7:30pm; also on Sunday from 8:30am to 1pm.

Marché des Enfants Rouge is a farmer's market in northern Marais where you can get fixings for an ample picnic lunch for about 6.50€—there's a good wine selection, too. Open Tuesday to Sunday from 9am to the afternoon.

Marché Couvert Monge, another outdoor market in the Marais, sells both food and clothing. It's located at place Monge (Métro: Place Monge). It is open from Tuesday to Saturday 8:30am to 1pm and 4 to 7:30pm. On Sunday, it is open from 8:30am to 2pm.

Marché des Batignolles is an organic food market near the Champs Elysées and the Louvre, which takes place every Saturday from 9am to 2pm. It's located at Terre-plein boulevard des Batignolles (Métro: Rome).

Best **Marché aux Puces St-Ouen de Clignancourt** ★★★ is not to be missed. Made up of more than a dozen flea markets, in a complex of 2,500 to 3,000 open stalls and shops on the northern fringe of the city, the market begins with stalls of cheap clothing along avenue de la Porte de Clignancourt. As you proceed, various streets will tempt you. Hold on until you get to rue des Rosiers, and then turn left. Vintage French postcards, old buttons, and bistro ware are affordable. Each market has its own personality and an aura of Parisian glamour you can't find elsewhere.

Vendors start bringing out their offerings around 9am and start taking them in around 6pm, but hours are flexible depending on weather and crowds. Monday is traditionally the best day for bargain seekers because the market is more sparsely attended and the merchants are more eager to sell.

place de la Madeleine, 8e. ☎ 01-47-42-60-11. Métro: Madeleine.

➜**FNAC** This chain store has multiple locations in town where you can buy CDs, books, techie equipment, and tickets to concerts or museums, and special exhibits. Opéra: 24 bd. Italiens. ☎ 08-92-68-36-22. Forum des Halles: 1 rue Peirre Lescot (☎ 01-44-08-18-00). Champs Elysées: 74 av. Champs Elysées. http://fnac.com. Métro: Les-Halles.

➜**Galerie de la Java** A flea market on three levels, with live jazz in the evening. 105 rue du Faubourg-du-Temple, 10e. ☎ 01-42-02-20-52. 1st weekend of the month (Fri–Sun) 10am–10pm. Varied admission charged. Métro: République.

➜**Galleries Lafayette** ★★ Europe's largest department store, and the most famous store in Paris, sells almost everything you could possibly imagine, from perfume to socks to gourmet foods. There are also daily fashion shows at the Salon Opéra section of the store; info on these is available at the welcome desk on the ground floor. This place is one of the most expensive stores in Paris, so don't come here looking for a bargain. It's worth a visit just to look at the ornate building itself, which is protected as a historic monument. It's open Monday through Saturday from 9:30am to 6:45pm (till 9pm on Thursday). *40 bd. Haussmann, 9e.* ☎ *01-42-82-34-56. Métro: Chausée-d'Antin.*

➜ **Marais Plus** A treasure trove of reasonably priced unusual gifts, toys, T-shirts, posters, and greeting cards. Also has a tea salon with scrumptious desserts. *20 rue des Francs-Bourgeois, 3e.* ☎ *01-48-87-01. Métro: St-Paul.*

➜ **Shakespeare & Company** If you've run out of English-language books, head to this conveniently located bookstore overlooking Notre-Dame. Famed for publishing Henry Miller's *Tropic of Cancer,* this charming store is practically overflowing with books—tomes are piled from floor to ceiling over two floors. The staff is friendly and fluent in English, and will help you find anything from rare old classics to the latest *New York Times* best seller. Open daily noon to midnight. *37 rue de la Bûcherie.* ☎ *01-43-25-40-93. http:// shakespeareco.org. Métro: St-Michel.*

Road Trips

Versailles

GETTING THERE

To get to Versailles catch the **RER** line C at the Gare d'Austerlitz, St-Michel, Musée d'Orsay, Invalides, Ponte de l'Alma, Champ de Mars, or Javel stop and take it to the Versailles Rive Gauche station, from which there's a shuttle bus to the château. Priced at 5.20€ round-trip, the transit takes 35 to 40 minutes; Eurailpass holders travel free on the RER, but they'll need to show their Eurailpass at the kiosk near any RER entrance to receive a ticket that will open the turnstile leading onto the RER platforms.

An alternate method of reaching Versailles from central Paris involves regular **SNCF trains,** which make frequent runs from two railway stations (Gare St-Lazare and Gare Montparnasse) to Versailles. Trains departing from Gare St-Lazare arrive at the Versailles Rive Droite railway station; trains departing from Gare Montparnasse arrive at Versailles Chantiers. Both stations lie within a 10-minute walk from the château, and we highly recommend the walk as a means of orienting yourself with the town, its geography, its scale, and its architecture. If you can't or don't want to walk, you can take bus B, bus H, or (in midsummer) a shuttle bus marked CHATEAU from any of the three stations directly to the château for a fee of 2.50€ each way per person. Again, this time because of the vagaries of each of the bus schedules, we highly recommend the walk. Directions to the château are clearly signposted from each of the three railway stations.

As a last resort—and frankly, we do not recommend it—you can use a combination of **Métro** and **city bus.** Travel to the Pont de Sèvres stop by Métro, then transfer to bus no. 171 for a westward trek that'll take 35 to 60 minutes, depending on traffic. The bus will cost you three Métro tickets and deposit you near the château gates.

If you have a **car,** take N-10, following the signs to Versailles, and then proceed along avenue de Général-Leclerc. Park on place d'Armes in front of the château.

You can easily see Versailles in a day—leaving early in the morning and returning to Paris by dinnertime.

TOURIST OFFICE

Three main avenues radiate from place d'Armes in front of the palace. The **tourist office** is on one of them, at 2 bis av. de Paris (☎ **01-39-24-88-88**).

EXPLORING VERSAILLES

Versailles started out small—as the hunting pavilion for Louis XIII—but grew increasingly grander as Louis's descendants added on wings and gardens, and filled it with breathtaking art. A tour of the massive estate is a half-day event, but certainly merits the time. Much of the original art and furniture has been restored and put into place as it was during Louis's rule. After walking around for a few hours, you'll get a good idea of the ostentatious luxury the French kings demanded.

The most famous room at Versailles is the 71m-long (233-ft.) **Hall of Mirrors** ★★★, built to link the north and south *appartements* (apartments). Begun in 1678 by Mansart in the Louis XIV style, it was decorated by Le Brun and his team with 17 large arched windows matched by corresponding beveled mirrors in simulated arcades, plus amazing chandeliers and gilded lamp bearers. The vaulted ceiling is covered with paintings in classic allegorical style depicting key episodes (some of them lavishly embellished) from the life and career of Louis XIV. On June 28, 1919, the treaty ending World War I was signed in this corridor. Ironically, the German Empire was also proclaimed here in 1871.

The estate (☎ **01-30-83-77-77**; www. chateauversailles.fr) is open Tuesday through Sunday from March 26 to October 31 from 9am to 6:30pm. The rest of the year, it's open until 5:30pm. It's closed some French holidays. Admission prices depend on what you want to see; I recommend paying the extra 15€ to 20€ to see the royal apartments.

Giverny

GETTING THERE

Take a train leaving from St-Lazare going to Vernon. In Vernon, take the bus no. 240 to Giverny, 5km (3 miles) away.

EXPLORING GIVERNY

If you're a Claude Monet fan, hop a train to Giverny and visit the **Claude Monet Foundation,** the house where the artist lived and painted. You'll feel as if you're inside one of his paintings, with the colorful garden outside and shockingly bright blue and yellow decor inside. It's located at 84 rue Claude Monet (☎ **02-32-51-28-21;** www. fondation-monet.com). Admission is 4€ to 5.50€. It's open Tuesday through Sunday from 9:30am to 6pm. It's closed on Mondays and from November 1 to March 31.

Also stop by the **Musée d'Art Américain Giverny,** near Monet's house (about 91m/300 ft. away). It showcases the American-born Impressionists who were influenced by Monet and lived at Giverny. Expect to see John Singer Sargent and William Metcalf, for example. It's at 99 rue Claude Monet (☎ **02-32-51-94-65**). Admission is 5.50€, but free admission is offered the first Sunday of every month. It's open daily April through November from 10am–6pm.

Prague

P rague is known as one of the last great Old European capitals left essentially untouched by the devastation of World War II, but this little city of 1.2 million also happens to be an international mecca for hedonism. It's apparent that strange heavenly forces are at work as you survey the Gothic arches of Old Town through a beery haze (or, for you truly brave hedonists, an absinthe blur) while getting completely lost on a pub-crawl. Perfectly preserved spires, angels, baroque onion-dome cathedrals, and Renaissance graffiti are your backdrop as you mix with ever-morphing Czechs at their favorite pubs—generally the grimiest and cheapest of the many beer halls in the pedestrianized medieval center around Old Town Square.

Since the 1989 revolution, Prague has been so massively made over and infused with Western investment that about the only signs of the old ways are the smoked-meat shops, trams, and frozen-in-time pubs. Of course, the idea of counter service hasn't fully penetrated yet, and feminism seems not to have caught on. Still, consumer fever is in full force, and the youngest generation, who barely remember pre-1989 life here, are busy exploring life's more meaningful pursuits—namely drinking, drugs, and dancing (all of which are fully tolerated, though officially a drug crackdown is growing in force, so it doesn't pay to be carrying). When in Prague, never forget: Ideologies may come and go, but sharing a good half-liter of Budvar with some newfound friends is to be treasured forever.

The Best of Prague

❍ **The Best Hotel for Rocking Out:** The **Hotel Aria** is a music-themed, luxurious hotel, in the heart of Malá Strana and has everything you'll need to nurse your inner rock star, including a library of CDs, DVDs, and books about music and a full-time musicologist on staff. See p. 747.

❍ **The Best Hotel for Serving Time:** You won't feel like a prisoner at the **Pension Unitas,** which was used as a secret police station during the communist era. Comfy mattresses, arty decor, and a decent breakfast make this place decidedly posher than the average prison. See p. 746.

❍ **The Most Unforgettable Dining Experience:** It's all about the view at **Kampa Park,** where you can dine in the shadow of Prague's most famous bridge during the high season. The good food, including seafood and barbecue favorites, simply seals the deal. See p. 747.

❍ **The Best Dawn or Dusk Stroll:** At dawn, the 6-centuries-old **Charles Bridge** is even more beautiful without crowds. Or go at dusk when the odd play of light turns the bridge and city panorama into something completely different than in the morning. See p. 760.

❍ **The Best Stamping Grounds:** The downhill jaunt from **Prague Castle,** through Malá Strana (Lesser Town), and across Charles Bridge to **Old Town Square,** constitutes a day trip in itself. The journey recalls the route taken by the carriages of the Bohemian kings; today it's lined with quirky galleries, shops, and cafes.

❍ **The Best Slow Ride:** Anyone can see Prague by land, but to get a truly unique perspective on the city, the **Vltava River**'s where it's at. The low-angle and low-stress vantage point of a rowboat you pilot yourself will let you take in many of the city's most striking architectural landmarks. See p. 764.

Getting There & Getting Around

Getting into Town

BY AIR

All flights to Prague arrive into the newly rebuilt **Ruzyně Airport** (☎ 220-113-314; www.csl.cz), which is 19km (12 miles) west of the city center. At the airport, you'll find currency exchange offices Travelex, Acron, or AVE (daily 7am–9pm), telephones, and several car-rental offices.

In addition to standard carriers, one of Europe's most popular low-cost airlines, **easyJet** (☎ 0871/244-2366; www.easyjet. com; London daily 8am–8pm), offers flights to Prague from London's Stansted and Gatwick airports, and also from Bristol, Newcastle, Basel, and Dortmund.

Plenty of registered taxis operated by **AAA Radiotaxi** (☎ 14014 or 222-333-222; www.aaa.radiotaxi.cz) line up in front of Ruzyně Airport. The fare to nám Republiky in the center of town is 440Kč and a ride to the city center takes about 20 minutes.

CEDAZ (☎ 220-114-296; www.aas.cz/ cedaz) operates an airport shuttle bus to náměstí Republiky in central Prague and from that point you can take the metro (see below for info) to all of Prague's train stations. It leaves the airport daily every 30 minutes from 6am to 9pm and stops near the náměstí Republiky metro station (metro line: B) for 90Kč (trip time: 30 min.). You can also take **city bus no. 119** from the airport to the Dejvická metro station (metro line: A) for 20Kč (trip time: 30 min.).

PRAGUE

BY TRAIN

Check out the selection of travel passes on www.raileurope.com or www.eurail.com. You'll find some good deals on train travel, but you still can't beat the best air fares offered by easyJet.

Passengers traveling to Prague by train typically pull into one of two central stations: Hlavní nádraží (Main Station) or Nádraží Holešovice (Holešovice Station). Both are on line C of the metro system and offer a number of services, including money exchange, a post office, and a luggage-storage area.

At both terminals you'll find **AVE Ltd.** (☎ 251-551-011), an accommodations agency that arranges beds in hostels as well as rooms in hotels and apartments. It's open daily from 6am to 11pm. If you arrive without room reservations, this agency is definitely worth a visit.

Hlavní nádraží (Wilsonova třída; ☎ 224-614-071) is the grander and more popular station, but it's also seedier. Built in 1909, this once-beautiful four-story Art Nouveau structure was one of the city's beloved architectural gems before it was connected to a darkly modern dispatch hall in the mid-1970s. It has been neglected for years, but the city has plans for a massive reconstruction of the station's building complex and its surroundings. The station includes a **Prague Information Service** (☎ 12444; www.pis.cz). See "Tourist Offices," below, for more info.

Also useful is the **ČD center** (☎ 840-112-113; www.cd.cz), run by Czech Railways. It provides domestic and international train information as well as currency exchange and accommodations services. It is open daily 7 to 11am, 11:30am to 2pm, and 2:30 to 5:45pm. The information window is open 3:15am to 12:40am (the train station is closed 1–3am).

After you leave the modern terminal hall, a 5-minute walk to the left puts you at the top of Wenceslas Square and 15 minutes by foot to Old Town Square. Metro line C connects the station easily to the other two subway lines and the rest of the city. Metro trains depart from the lower level, and tickets, costing 14Kč to 20Kč, are available from the newsstand near the metro entrance. *Note:* Gouging taxi drivers line up outside the station and are plentiful throughout the day and night but are not recommended.

Nádraží Holešovice (Partyzánská at Vrbenského; ☎ 224-615-865), Prague's second train station, is usually the terminus for trains from Berlin and other points north. Although it's not as centrally located as the main station, its more manageable size and location at the end of metro line C makes it almost as convenient.

Prague contains two smaller train stations. **Masaryk Station** (Hybernská ulice; ☎ 221-111-122) is primarily for travelers arriving on trains originating from other Bohemian cities or from Brno or Bratislava. Situated about 10 minutes by foot from the main train station, Masaryk is near Staré Město, just a stone's throw from náměstí Republiky metro station. **Smíchov Station** (Nádražní ulice at Rozkošného; ☎ 224-617-686) is the terminus for commuter trains from western and southern Bohemia, though an occasional international train pulls in here. The station contains a 24-hour baggage check and is serviced by metro line B.

BY BUS

The **Central Bus Station—Florenc** (Křižíkova 4–6; ☎ 900-144-444 for timetable

Beware the Taxi Driver

Most of Prague's taxi drivers will take advantage of you; getting an honestly metered ride from the airport is close to impossible. The fare from the airport to Hlavní nádraží (the main train station) should be no more than about 500Kč.

info), is a few blocks north of the main train station. Most local and long-distance buses arrive here. The adjacent Florenc metro station is on both lines B and C. Florenc station is relatively small and doesn't have many visitor services. Even smaller depots are at **Želiv-ského** (metro line: A), **Smíchovské nádraží** (metro line: B), and **Nádraží Holešovice** (metro line: C).

Getting Around

BY FOOT

The city's countless nooks and crannies are probably best explored by foot. I'm hard-pressed to think of another world capital where there is so much in such a compact area.

BY CAR

Driving in Prague isn't worth the money or effort. The roads are frustrating and slow, and parking is minimal and expensive. However, a car is a plus if you want to explore other parts of the Czech Republic. Try **Europcar Czech Rent a Car** (Pařížská 28; ☎ **224-811-290;** www.europcar.cz), or at Ruzyně Airport (☎ **235-364-531**). There's also a **Hertz** (Karlovo nám. 28; ☎ **222-231-010;** www.hertz.cz). **Budget** is at Ruzyně Airport (☎ **220-113-253;** www.budget.cz) and in the Hotel Inter-Continental (náměstí Curieových; ☎ **222-319-595**).

Local car-rental companies sometimes offer lower rates than the big international firms. Compare **CS Czechocar** (Kongresové centrum [Congress Center]; ☎ **261-222-079** or 261-222-143; www.czechocar.cz; metro: line C to Vyšehrad), or at Ruzyně Airport (☎ **220-113-454**); or try **SeccoCar** (Přístavní 39; ☎ **220-800-647;** www.seccocar.cz).

PUBLIC TRANSPORTATION

Prague's public transport network is a vast system of subways, trams, and buses. You can ride a maximum of five stations on the metro (not including the station of validation) or 20 minutes on a tram or bus, without transfers (on the metro you can transfer from lines A,

B, and C within 30 min.), for 14Kč. This is usually enough for trips in the historical districts. Rides of more than five stops on the metro, or longer tram or bus rides, with unlimited transfers for up to 75 minutes (90 min. Sat–Sun, public holidays, and Mon–Fri after 10pm) after your ticket is validated, cost 20Kč.

You can buy tickets from coin-operated orange machines in metro stations or at most newsstands. Hold on to your ticket (which you must validate at the orange or yellow stamp clocks in each tram or bus when you get on board or at the entrance to the metro) during your ride—you'll need it to prove you've paid if a ticket collector asks. If you're caught without a valid ticket, you have to pay a 400Kč fine to a ticket controller on the spot.

Warning: Oversize luggage (larger than carry-on size) requires a single-trip ticket for each piece. You may be fined 50Kč for not having tickets for your luggage.

Metro trains operate daily from 5am to midnight and run every 3 to 8 minutes. The most convenient stations are Můstek, at the foot of Václavské náměstí (Wenceslas Sq.); Staroměstská, for Old Town Square and Charles Bridge; and Malostranská, serving Malá Strana and the Castle District.

Electric **tram lines** run practically everywhere. You never have to hail trams; they make every stop. The most popular, **no. 22** and **no. 23,** run past top sights such as the National Theater and Prague Castle. Regular bus and tram service stops at midnight, after which selected routes run reduced schedules, usually only once per hour. If you miss a night connection, expect a long wait for the next bus.

BY BIKE

Though there are no special bike lanes in the city center, and smooth streets are unheard of, Prague is a good city to bike in when the crowds are thin. Car traffic is limited in the city center, and this area's small, winding streets seem especially suited to two-wheeled

PRAGUE

Talk of the Town

Four ways to start a conversation with a local

You'll encounter an initial shyness among Czechs, but if you give them their space, speak softly, and don't go on about what a bargain everything is, you'll have a dozen new friends by the end of the third round of Staropramen half-liters. Remember that their monthly wage, even in the wild free-market days of megamalls and techno parties sponsored by Lucky Strike, barely covers the rent in some shared apartment out in the boonies.

1. **So, which beer do you prefer?** Budvar, Prazdroj, Kozel, Radegast, or Krušovice? Prague natives love their beer, so this question is likely to start a long conversation.

2. **How 'bout that Jágr?** Jaromír is the Olympic gold–winning Czech hockey god and NHL all-star, but, of course, you knew that.

3. **Did you know that the Bond movie** Casino Royale **was shot in Prague?** After you're done talking about 007, you might ask if Miloš Forman shot any films here recently.

4. **You mean you like Aneta Langerová?** She's considered the Czech Alanis Morissette and is the first Czech Pop Idol, so be prepared to be serenaded with a power ballad or two in response.

vehicles. Surprisingly, few people take advantage of this opportunity; cyclists are largely limited to the few foreigners who have imported their own bikes. The city's ubiquitous cobblestones make mountain bikes the natural choice. Check with your hotel about a rental, or try **Dodosport** (Na Zderaze 5; ☎ 272-769-387).

BY TAXI

If you must go by taxi, call reputable companies with English-speaking dispatchers: **AAA Radiotaxi** (☎ 14014 or 222-333-222; www.aaataxi.cz), **ProfiTaxi** (☎ 844-700-800; www.profitaxi.cz), or **SEDOP** (☎ 271-722-222; www.sedop.cz). Demand a receipt for the fare before you start, as it'll keep them a little more honest.

Prague Basics

Orientation: Prague Neighborhoods

Prague was originally developed as four adjacent self-governing boroughs, plus a walled Jewish ghetto. Central Prague's neighborhoods have maintained their individual identities along with their medieval street plans.

HRADČANY   The Castle District dominates the hilltop above Malá Strana. Here you'll find not only the fortress that remains the presidential palace and national seat of power but also the Loreto Church, Strahov Monastery,

and the main national art gallery at the archbishop's palace. You can take a scenic walk down the hill via Nerudova or through the lush Petřín Hill gardens.

MALÁ STRANA (LESSER TOWN)   Prague's storybook Lesser Town was founded in 1257 by Germanic merchants who set up shop at the base of the castle. Nestled between the bastion and the river Vltava, Malá Strana is laced with narrow, winding lanes boasting palaces and red-roofed town houses. The parliament and government and several embassies reside in palaces here. **Kampa Park,** on the riverbank, just south of Charles Bridge, forms the southeastern edge of Lesser Town, and the riverside **Liechtenstein Palace** on the park's northern edge was used as the U.S. Embassy in the Tom Cruise version of *Mission: Impossible* (the real U.S. Embassy is a few blocks away). **Nerudova** is the steep, shop-lined alley leading from the town square to the castle. Alternate castle routes for the strong of heart are the New Castle Stairs (Nové zámecké schody), 1 block north of Nerudova, and the Old Castle Stairs (Staré zámecké schody), just northwest from the Malostranská metro station. Tram no. 22 or 23 will take you up the hill if you don't want to make the heart-pounding hike.

🖍 Best **STARÉ MĚSTO (OLD TOWN)** Staré Město was chartered in 1234, as Prague became a stop on important trade routes. Its meandering streets, radiating from Staroměstské náměstí (Old Town Sq.), are still big visitor draws. Old Town is compact, bordered by the Vltava on the north and west and Revoluční and Národní streets on the east and south. You should be able to wander safely without having to worry about straying into danger. Once here, stick to the cobblestone streets and don't cross any bridges, any streets containing tram tracks, or any rivers, and you'll know that you're still in Old Town. You'll stumble across beautiful **baroque and Renaissance architecture** and find some wonderful restaurants, shops, bars, cafes, and pubs.

JOSEFOV Prague's Jewish ghetto, entirely within Staré Město, was surrounded by a wall before almost being completely destroyed to make way for more modern 19th-century structures. The **Old-New Synagogue** is in the geographical center of Josefov, and the surrounding streets are wonderful for strolling. Prague is one of Europe's great historic Jewish cities, and exploring this remarkable area will make it clear why.

NOVÉ MĚSTO (NEW TOWN) Draped like a crescent around Staré Město, Nové Město is where you'll find **Václavské náměstí (Wenceslas Sq.),** the **National Theater,** and the central business district. When it was founded by Charles IV in 1348, Nové Město was Europe's largest wholly planned municipal development. The street layout has remained largely unchanged, but many of Nové Město's structures were razed in the late 19th century and replaced with the offices and apartment buildings you see today. New Town lacks the classical allure of Old Town and Malá Strana, but if you venture beyond Wenceslas Square into Vinohrady, you'll find restaurants, interesting shops, and a part of Prague that feels more like a normal city instead of a tourist attraction.

While violent crime is still relatively rare, you should take caution here at night, especially around Wenceslas Square and nearby Perlová Street, where prostitutes and drug dealers ply their trades.

Tourist Offices

The **Prague Information Service (PIS;** at the City Hall, Staroměstské náměstí 1; ☎ **12-444;** fax 222-220-700; www.pis.cz or www. prague-info.cz), near Wenceslas Square, provides tips and tickets for upcoming cultural events and tours. It can also help you find a room. From April to October, it's open Monday to Friday from 9am to 7pm and Saturday and Sunday from 9am to 6pm. During the rest of the year, it's open Monday to Friday from 9am to 6pm and Saturday and Sunday from 9am to 5pm. There is another PIS office inside the main train station.

For those arriving by train or air, **AVE Travel** (☎ **251-091-111;** www.avetravel.cz) can arrange accommodations or transfers inside these terminals. It has outlets at the airport, open daily from 7am to 10pm; at the main train station, Hlavní nádraží, open daily from 6am to 11pm; and at the north train station, Nádraží Holešovice, open daily from 7am to 9pm.

Čedok (Na Příkopě 18; ☎ **800-112-112** or 224-197-111; fax 224-216-324; www.cedok.cz) was once the state travel bureau and is now a privatized agency. Its entrenched position still gives it decent access to tickets and information about domestic events, and the staff can book rail and bus tickets and hotel rooms. Čedok accepts major credit cards and is open Monday to Friday from 9am to 7pm; Saturday 9:30am to 1pm.

Avoid kiosks that look like information points but are really ticket touts for tours and concerts. Also, asking for directions from a Czech on the street will often be more useful than the surly response you'll probably get from the person staffing the kiosk.

Recommended Websites

○ **www.e-travel.cz**: If you want to arrange accommodations before you come, this Prague-based site offers handy English websites. Once in the city, you can find E-travel.cz near the National Theater at Ostrovní 7; or call their 24-hour call center (☎ **224-990-990**; fax 224-990-999).

○ **www.prague-info.cz**: Award-winning, comprehensive site covering history, attractions, and events.

○ **www.praguepost.com**: All the week's news and entertainment listings, plus comprehensive restaurant reviews, tips on residency, and events calendar.

○ **www.radio.cz**: Transcripts of daily newscasts in English, plus loads of archives on all questions societal.

○ **www.ticketpro.cz**: Full schedule of all performances of the National Theatre, ballet, opera, and major symphonies, as well as rock concerts, DJ shows, or sport events and about the only way to order tickets for them in advance from abroad.

○ **www.alive.cz**: Information about discounts for ISIC and IYTC card holders visiting the Czech Republic.

○ **www.seznam.cz**: Snappy Czech-language search engine.

Culture Tips 101

Since the Velvet Revolution, Praguers have been obsessed with style. Many people—especially the novobohatí (nouveau riche)—rushed out to buy the flashiest Mercedes or BMWs they could find with the quick money gained from the restitution of communist-seized property. While the average annual income per person is still just around $9,000, the trappings of conspicuous consumption are evident throughout Prague, from the designer boutiques in the city center to the newly developed luxury suburbs with split-level ranch homes and tailored lawns. Women's fashion has had the most stunning revolution: The blur of loud polyester minidresses that used to dominate the streets has been replaced by the latest looks from Europe's catwalks.

Prague's avant-garde community used to thrive in secret while mocking communism, but it now has to face the realities of capitalism, such as rising rents and stiff competition. Many have had to find more mainstream work to survive. But if you look hard enough, you still might find an exhibition, a dance recital, or an experimental performance that's surprising, shocking, and satisfying.

In the evening, you can find a typical Bohemian playing cards with friends at the neighborhood *hospoda* or *pivnice* (beer hall) or debating at a *kavárna* (cafe). Most likely, though, the typical Czech will be parked in front of the TV, as the country maintains one of the highest per-capita nightly viewing audiences in Europe. Pop literature has also overwhelmed the classics since the Velvet Revolution, with scandal sheets surging in newspaper sales and pulp-fiction romances ruling the bookshops.

There's no real legal age minimum for drinking here (as long as you can see over the table), and IDs are never required.

People are allowed to drink what they choose anywhere they like, but in practice only foreign college kids ever drink on the street because everyone else prefers to do it in a pub or cafe. As throughout Europe, atmosphere and the ritual of going to the pub are just as important as what you're drinking. Besides, beer from a bottle is always inferior to beer freshly tapped, and this isn't a country with a strong wine tradition of any kind.

All recreational drugs are illegal but you may see some in circulation. Enforcement used to be spotty, but Parliament was finally forced by the explosion in drug trafficking to act and, in all their wisdom, gave the police complete powers of discretion in enforcing new zero-tolerance laws. Which means a cop can throw someone in jail for having so much as a joint or a tab of E, and then let said person rot in a stinking cell for a month or more before even coming up with formal charges. Not cool at all.

Recommended Books, Movies & Music

BOOKS

Any discussion of Czech literature with visiting foreigners usually begins with Milan Kundera. Reviled among many Czechs who didn't emigrate, Kundera creates a visceral, personal sense of the world he chose to leave in the 1970s for the freedom of Paris. In *The Unbearable Lightness of Being*, the anguish over escaping the Soviet-occupied Prague he loves tears the libidinous protagonist Dr. Tomáš in the same way the love for his wife and the lust for his lover does. Kundera's biting satire of Stalinist purges in the 1950s *The Joke*, however, is regarded by Czech critics as his best work.

Jaroslav Hašek wrote the Czech harbinger to *Forrest Gump* in *The Good Soldier švejk*, a post–World War I satire about a simpleton soldier who wreaks havoc in the Austro-Hungarian army during the war.

Bohumil Hrabal, author of the *Czech Everyman* and maybe the country's all-time favorite, died in early 1997 when he fell (so they said officially) out of a fifth-story window while trying to feed pigeons. His death was eerily similar to the fate of a character in one of his stories. He had two internationally acclaimed hits: *Closely Watched Trains* (also translated as *Closely Observed Trains*, on which the Menzel film was based), and *I Served the King of England*. When then-President Bill Clinton visited Prague in 1994, he asked to have a beer with Hrabal in the author's favorite Old Town haunt, the pub U Zlatého tygra (At the Golden Tiger).

No reading list would be complete without reference to Franz Kafka, Prague's most famous novelist, who wrote his originals in his native German. *The Collected Novels of Franz Kafka*, which includes *The Castle* and *The Trial*, binds his most popular works into a single volume.

Finally, for an epic intellectual tour of the long, colorful, and often tragic history of the city, try the 1997 release of *Prague in Black and Gold* by native son and Yale literature professor Peter Demetz.

MOVIES

While Czech literature and music have carved their places in classical culture, the country's films and their directors have collected the widest praise in the mid- to late 20th century. Cunning, melancholy views of Bohemian life (before the Soviets moved in for a few decades) were captured by some of the finest filmmakers in the era known as the "Czech New Wave" of the 1960s.

Directors Jiří Menzel and Miloš Forman were in the vanguard. An easy-to-find example of this period's work (with English subtitles) is Menzel's Oscar-winning *Closely Watched Trains*, a snapshot of the odd routine at a rural Czech train station. Forman made a number of celebrated Czech films before he emigrated to the big budgets of

Hollywood and first shocked Americans with *Hair*. He then directed the Oscar-winning *One Flew Over the Cuckoo's Nest* and *Amadeus*, along with *The People vs. Larry Flynt*.

A new Czech wave began in the '90s. The father-and-son team of Zdeněk and Jan Svěrák won the Best Foreign Film Oscar in 1997 for *Kolja*, the bittersweet tale of an abandoned Russian boy grudgingly adopted by an aging Czech bachelor on the cusp of the 1989 revolution. After a previous Oscar nomination for the 1992 *Elementary School (Obecná škola)*, the 30-something director Jan and his actor father are making an industry out of golden reflections about Czech life.

Prague has also become a popular location for major motion pictures, in spite of itself. Producer/actor Tom Cruise and director Brian De Palma chose it for the stunning night shots around Charles Bridge in the early scenes of *Mission: Impossible*. *Immortal Beloved*, a story of Beethoven, made use of Prague's timeless streets (shooting around the graffiti). Still, the film about Prague probably most familiar to American audiences is *The Unbearable Lightness of Being*, based on the book by émigré author Milan Kundera.

MUSIC

Prague may not be the next Seattle (or Omaha or whatever) but it does attract all the serious underground bands you'd expect in a famed capital of Bohemian living. The Velvet Revolution had its roots in the underground rock clubs that kept the braver Czech sonic youth tuned in to something more than the monotones of the Party during the gray 1970s and 1980s period known as Normalization. The communists' persecution of the garage band Plastic People of the Universe, motivated playwright Vaclav Havel and his friends to keep the human rights heat on the Politburo. While some of the wannabe bands playing Prague today lack the political edge of the pre-revolution days, some have kept their Slavic passion—highlights include the no-holds-barred horns of Laura a jetji tyfri (Laura and her Tigers) and the acerbic pounding of Psi vojaci (Dog Soldiers).

Prague is also a well-known folk (of the polka and bluegrass variety) and jazz spot (see info on the annual Jazz Festival on p. 760), and local heroes include the legendary (in this town, anyway) Iva Bittova, an avant-garde violinist with a manic art-rock following. Just remember that Mozart and Dvořák lived here, too—the city has a storied classical music history.

Prague **Nuts & Bolts**

Cellphone Providers & Service Centers   T-Mobile has branches throughout the city; call ☎ **603/603-603** or visit www.t-mobile.cz for info.

Currency   Even though the Czech Republic is now a member state of the European Union, it has not accepted the euro as its currency, yet. That may take another 5 to 10 years. You'll find that some Prague hotels and restaurants list prices in euros anyway. At this writing, 1€ buys 30Kč.

Komerční banka has three convenient Praha 1 locations with ATMs that accept Visa, MasterCard, and American Express: Na Příkopě 33, Spálená 51, and Václavské nám. 42 (central switchboard for all branches: ☎ **800-111-055;** www.kb.cz). The exchange offices are open Monday to Friday from 8am to 5pm, but the ATMs are accessible 24 hours. **Živnostenská banka** (Na Příkope 20; ☎ **224-121-111;** www.ziba.cz), has an exchange office open Monday to Friday from 10am to 9pm and Saturday from 3 to 7pm.

Embassies   The **U.S. Embassy** (Tržiště 15; ☎ 257-530-663) is open Monday to Friday from 8am to 4:30pm. The **Canadian Embassy** (Muchova 6; ☎ 272-101-800) is open Monday to Friday from 8:30am to 12:30pm and 1:30 to 4:30pm. The **U.K. Embassy** (Thunovská 14; ☎ 257-402-111) is open Monday to Friday from 8:30am to 12:30pm and 1:30 to 5pm. You can visit the **Australian Honorary Consul** (Klimentská 10; ☎ 296-578-350) Monday to Friday from 9am to 1pm and 2 to 5pm. The **Irish Embassy** (Tržiště 13; ☎ 257-530-061) is open Monday to Friday from 9am to 1pm and 2 to 5pm. Visits to the **New Zealand Honorary Consul** (Dykova 19; ☎ 222-514-672) are by appointment.

Emergencies   Dial the **European Emergency Number** ☎ 112 or you can reach Prague's police at ☎ 158 and fire services by dialing ☎ 150 from any phone. To call an ambulance, dial ☎ 155.

If you need a doctor or dentist and your condition isn't life-threatening, you can visit the **Polyclinic at Národní** (Národní 9; ☎ 222-075-120) during walk-in hours from 8am to 5pm; for emergency medical aid, call ☎ 777-942-270. You'll be asked to show proof of insurance or to pay upfront. The **Medicover Clinic** (Vyšehradská 35; ☎ 224-921-884) provides EKGs, diagnostics, ophthalmology, house calls, and referrals to specialists. Normal walk-in hours are Monday to Saturday from 7am to 7pm.

For **emergency medical aid,** call the **Foreigners' Medical Clinic** (Na Homolce Hospital, Roentgenova 2; ☎ 257-272-146, or 257-272-191 after hours).

Internet/Wireless Hot Spots   See "The Hottest Hot Spots" on p. 746.

Laundry   **Laundry Kings** (Dejvická 16; ☎ 233-343-743) was Prague's first American-style, coin-operated, self-service laundromat. Each small load costs about 70Kč. An attendant can do your wash for 180Kč in the same day. Laundry Kings is open Monday to Friday from 7am to 10pm and Saturday and Sunday from 8am to 10pm. **Laundryland** (Londýnská 71; ☎ 222-516-692) offers dry cleaning as well as laundry service and charges about the same as Laundry Kings. Located 2 blocks from the Náměstí Míru metro station and close to the I. P. Pavlova metro station, it's open daily from 8am to 10pm.

Luggage Storage   The **Ruzyně Airport Luggage Storage Office** never closes and charges 60Kč per item per day. Left-luggage offices are also available at the main train stations, **Hlavní nádraží** and **Nádraží Holešovice.** Both charge 30Kč per bag per day and are technically open 24 hours, but if your train is departing late at night, check to make sure someone will be around. Luggage lockers are available in all of Prague's train stations, but they're not secure and should be avoided.

Post Offices   Post offices are plentiful and are normally open Monday to Friday from 8am to 6pm. Mailboxes are orange and are usually attached to the sides of buildings. If you're sending mail overseas, make sure it's marked "Par Avion" so it doesn't go by surface. If you mail your letters at a post office, the clerk will add this stamp for you. Mail can take up to 10 days to reach its destination.

The **Main Post Office** (Hlavní pošta; Jindřišská 14; ☎ 221-131-111), a few steps from Václavské náměstí, is open 24 hours. You can receive mail, marked "Poste Restante" and addressed to you, care of this post office. If you carry an American Express card or Amex traveler's checks, you would be wiser to receive mail care of **American Express** (Václavské nám. 56, Wenceslas Sq.; ☎ 222-800-237).

Pharmacies   The most centrally located *lékárna* (pharmacy) is at Václavské nám. 8 (☎ 224-227-532); it's open Monday to Friday from 8am to 6pm. The nearest emergency (24-hr.) pharmacy is at Palackého 5 (☎ 224-946-982). If you're in Praha 2, there's an emergency pharmacy on Belgická 37 (☎ 222-519-731).

Restrooms   You'll find plenty of public restrooms throughout the city. Toilets are located in every metro station and are staffed by cleaning personnel who usually charge users 5Kč and dispense a precious few sheets of toilet paper.

Be aware, though—even though restrooms at the city's train stations are staffed, you need to get your toilet paper by yourself from a dispenser situated on the wall before you actually enter the restroom. The charge here is 6 Kč.

Restaurants and pubs around all the major sights are usually kind to non-patrons who wish to use their facilities. Around the castle and elsewhere, public toilets are clearly marked with the letters wc. For comfort and cleanliness, try lobby-level lavatories in Prague's better-known hotels or the new restrooms in the Municipal House (Obecní dům), the Art Nouveau palace next to the Powder Tower in Old Town.

Safety   In Prague's center you'll feel generally safer than in most Western cities, but always take common-sense precautions. Be aware of your immediate surroundings. Don't walk alone at night around Wenceslas Square—one of the main areas for prostitution and where a lot of unexplainable loitering takes place. All visitors should be watchful of pickpockets in heavily touristed areas, especially on Charles Bridge, in Old Town Square, and in front of the main train station. Be especially wary on crowded buses, trams, and trains. Don't keep your wallet in a back pocket and don't flash a lot of cash or jewelry. Riding the metro or trams at night should feel just as safe as during the day.

Telephone Tips   For **directory inquiries** regarding phone numbers within the Czech Republic, dial ☎ 1180. For information about services and rates abroad, call ☎ 1181.

There are two kinds of **pay phones** in normal use. The first accepts coins and the other operates exclusively with a phone card, available from post offices and newsagents in denominations ranging from 50Kč to 500Kč. The minimum cost of a local call is 4Kč. If you're calling the States, you'd better get a phone card with plenty of points, as calls run about 20Kč per minute; calls to the United Kingdom cost 15Kč per minute.

Even if you're not calling person-to-person, collect calls are charged with the hotel fees, making them pricey. Charging a long-distance call to your phone credit card from a public telephone is often the most economical way to phone home.

Tipping   Rules for tipping aren't as strict in the Czech Republic as they are elsewhere in Europe. At most restaurants and pubs, locals just round the bill up to the nearest few koruny. When you're presented with good service at tablecloth places, a 10% tip is proper. Washroom and cloakroom attendants usually expect a couple of koruny, and porters at airports and train stations usually receive 25Kč per bag. Taxi drivers should get about 10%, unless they've already ripped you off, in which case they should get a referral to the police. Check restaurant menus to see if service is included before you leave a tip.

PRAGUE

Sleeping

Prague's accommodations have expanded so much in the past 5 or so years that it's relatively easy to find a comfortable bed here these days. You'll have your pick of small hotels and pensions, which are cheaper than the Hilton-style hotels in town, but more expensive than western B&Bs. Or you can go the hostel route—which tend to be cheap, relatively clean, and comfortable (though not very private because many of them are converted classrooms during July–Aug school vacations).

One of the cheaper areas to stay in town is Vinohrady, just above Wencelas Square and part of New Town. Accommodations in hotels in Hradcany, Malá Strana, and Old Town tend to be the priciest. If you need help finding a place, a great source for self-contained apartments and rooms is the incredibly patient **Stop City** (Vinohradská 24; ☎/fax **222-521-252**; www.stopcity.com; daily 10am–9pm; metro: line A to Náměstí Míru) in New Town; the info desk at Prague's main train station (p. 734); or **Čedok** (p. 738). Any kindly looking old folk approaching you with Polaroids of rooms are usually fine also, though you may feel badly stumbling through their door at 4am.

Hostels

The good news for backpackers is that there's an ongoing explosion of hostel options in Střáleckýostrov, in Old Town, and in Malá Strana, where you'd be lucky to find a hotel room at all in peak season.

→**Travellers' Hostels** ★ This is one of the best hostels in the city center. A flagship in the local Traveller's group of hostels, it's just a few blocks off Old Town Square and a few floors above the wildest dance club in town, the Roxy. The rooms are clean, with high ceilings and comfortable beds. There's a total of 90 beds—which can be expanded from singles to sextets—on two floors. *Dlouhá 33 (other locations as well; inquire at desk).* ☎ *224-826-662. www.travellers.cz. 550Kč per person double, 400Kč per person triple, 370Kč per person quad, 280Kč per person dorm. Rates include breakfast. Metro: line B to Náměstí Republiky. Amenities: Bar; breakfast room; Internet; kitchen; laundry; safe; shared bathrooms (some rooms w/private showers); travel desk; TV (in common room).*

→**Welcome Hostel Strahov** Situated across from the giant Strahov Stadium on the biggest hill overlooking the castle and city below, this complex of dormitories was built to house competitors for socialist *Spartakiáda* exercise festivals that were held before the fall of communism. Today, these concrete high-rises serve as student dormitories and are a popular choice for backpackers from all over the world. Most rooms are doubles, not one has a private bathroom, and all are open 24 hours. Expect nothing much more than a bed and a place to throw your things in a pretty but small single or double room, but it's clean, cozy, and the price is right. *Building 3, Vaníčkova 5, on Strahov Hill.* ☎ *224-320-202. www.hostels.com. 300Kč–400Kč per person double. Metro: line A to Dejvická, then bus no. 143 or 217 to "Koleje Strahov" stop. Amenities: Internet; kitchen; linen; travel desk.*

Cheap

→**The Clown & Bard** ★ Party-loving shoestring travelers from all over come here because they're hip to its location right in the center of pub-heaven, Žižkov, where most rooms are in overpriced hotels and not much different than what you get here. In fact, one of the friendliest of these pubs is in the lobby, where chess games, blues jams, and notes-comparing go on nightly into the wee hours. There is a drop-off laundry, a safe, currency exchange, and summer barbecues, but no breakfast, and you should try to arrive by 7pm. *Bořivojova 102.* ☎ *222-716-453.*

Prague

SLEEPING ■
Archibald U Karlova Mostu **9**
The Clown and Bard **20**
Hotel Aria **7**
Hotel Sax **6**
Hotel Sieber **19**
Pension Unitas/
  Art Prison Hostel **32**
Travellers' Hostel **52**
Welcome Hostel Strahov **12**

EATING ◆
Bohemia Bagel **46**
Cafe Slavia **28**
Caffrey's Irish Bar **45**
Country Life **38**
Dahab **50**
Dobrá cajovna **26**
Hergetova Cihelna **3**
Kampa Park **4**
Kavárna Medúza **15**
Kavárna Obecní d*m **49**
Pálffy Palác **2**
Pizzeria Rugantino **44**
U Modré kachnicky **11**

PARTYING ★
AghaRTA **40**
Aqua Club 2000 **22**
Chateau **47**
Club Stella **18**
Duplex **39**
Érra Café **33**
Friends **31**
Jáma **24**
Klub Lávka **34**
Lucerna Music Bar **25**
Malostranská Beseda **5**
Marquis de Sade **48**
Mecca **54**
Palác Akropolis **21**
Radost/FX **17**
Rock Café **27**
Roxy **51**
Sauna Marco **16**
Tingl Tangl **29**
U Malého Glena **8**
U medvěd* **30**
U Staré paní **36**
U Vystřeleného oka **21**
Železně dvere **37**

SIGHTSEEING ●
Bertramka (W.A. Mozart
  Museum) **13**
Charles Bridge **35**
Church of St. Nicholas **42**
Jewish Museum **43**
Kampa Museum–
  Sovovy mlýny **10**
National Museum **23**
Old Town Hall &
  Astronomical Clock **41**
Prague Castle **1**
Veletrzní Palace–
  National Gallery
  Collection of Modern and
  Contemporary Art **53**
Vysehrad **14**

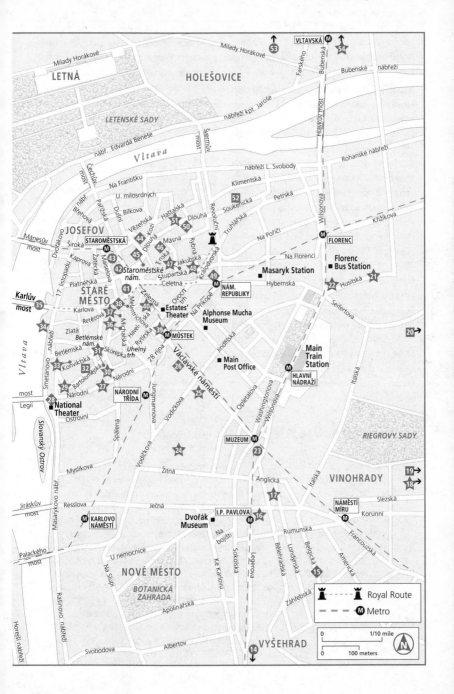

www.clownandbard.com. 250Kč dorm bed, 350Kč per person 6-person apt. 450Kč per person double. Metro: line A to Jiřího z Poděbrad. Amenities: Bar; laundry; safe; shared bathrooms (for most rooms); travel desk.

MTV **Best** →**Pension Unitas/Art Prison Hostel** ★★ With a quirky history and an unbeatable location, the Unitas is great value for the money. On a side street between Old Town Square and the National Theater stands this former convent, which was conveniently seized for use as secret police holding cells under the communists. One of their most frequent guests, before the place was turned into a post-revolution pension, was none other than the pesky dissident and soon-to-be-president Václav Havel. Once the bizarre allure of staying in Havel's former abode wears off, you realize that this is a pretty good attempt at providing decent accommodations at a good price. The rooms range from doubles to quads, with comfy mattresses and clean linen provided. A recent rebranding of the complex added some funky wall murals to give it the added subtitle of being an Art Prison Hostel. The complimentary breakfast of cold cuts, rolls, and cheese is fresh and

plentiful. The joint bathrooms are clean enough to pass. If you feel you are becoming a bit too bohemian from too many backpacking days on the road, there is even a well-equipped laundry room. *Bartolomějská 9. ☎ 224-221-802. www.unitas.cz. 1,200Kč–2,000Kč pension double, 980Kč–1,700Kč hostel double. Rates include breakfast. Metro: line B to Národní třída. Amenities: Breakfast room; laundry; linens; safe; shared bathrooms; TV (in common room).*

Doable

→**Hotel Sax** This is a rare find in Malá Strana: a clean, reasonable, and well-run option just blocks from the district's main square. The rooms are standard with clean bathrooms and the service outstanding (for Prague), but the setting, amid narrow cobbled lanes, is the showstopper. *Jánský vršek 3. ☎ 257-531-268. www.hotelsax.cz. 3,700Kč single, 4,400Kč double. Rates include breakfast. Tram: 12, 22, or 23 to Malostranské náměstí. Amenities: Bar; Internet; laundry; travel desk; TV (in common room). In room: TV.*

→**Hotel Sieber** It's no boutique hotel, but it's solid, courteous, and reasonable. You can

The Hottest Hot Spots

Prague is one serious cyber city, with Internet cafes popping up like mushrooms after the rain—and some highly accomplished hackers who pride themselves on the pirated software they've scored, often on the day it ships. **Internet Café Spika** (Dlážděná 4; ☎ 224-211-521; http://netcafe.spika.cz; daily 8am–midnight; metro: line B to Náměstí Republiky) offers a quiet atmosphere of unpretentious browsing, plus MS Office, games, and color printing and copying, all within a cool I-beamed Art Nouveau space with tile mosaics and a spy balcony. Surf here for 20Kč per 15 minutes weekdays, 16Kč on weekends. A great place to surf the Internet for 1.50Kč per minute and have a good cup of coffee to boot is **Globe Bookstore and Coffeehouse** (p. 757). Also offering Internet connections for 1.80Kč per minute is **Bohemia Bagel** (p. 748). Check your e-mail and surf at the very centrally located Internet cafe **Inetpoint.cz** (Jungmannova 32; ☎ 296-245-962). It's open daily 10am to 10pm, and the connection charge is 25Kč per 15 minutes. Another place to get on the Internet is **Cyber Cafe-Jáma** at V jámě 7 (☎ 224-222-383).

choose from 1 of the 20 pretty spacious rooms with clean bathrooms. What makes this place a good choice is the exceptionally helpful and polite staff. It takes 10 minutes by metro from the city center, but then you are only a 5-minute walk from Vinohrady's shops and Žižkov's pubs. Because it's technically a business hotel, it offers big summer discounts and it's not listed with many traditional booking agencies, so it's a good spot to look into when the official word is "there's not a room free in Prague." *Slezská 55.* ☎ *226-201-910. hotel-sieber@prague-holiday.cz. 2,952Kč single, 3,570Kč double. Metro: line A to Jiřího z Poděbrad. Amenities: Restaurant; bar; laundry; travel desk; wheelchair friendly. In room: A/C, TV, hair dryer, Internet, minibar, safe.*

Splurge

→**Archibald U Karlova Mostu** With only 26 rooms, this enchanting, renovated Renaissance-era inn on Vltava Island fills up fast. Ask for a river view (the higher the better) and you might just land a raftered garret space with Old Town glowing outside your window just across the Charles Bridge. Basic breakfast is included, via the classy on-site patio pub, and discounts in the off-season are significant. *Na Kampě 15.* ☎ *257-531-430.*

www.archibald.cz. 5,600Kč double, 7,000Kč apt. Tram: 12, 22, or 23 to Malostranské náměstí. Amenities: Restaurant; bar; Internet. In room: TV, hair dryer, minibar, safe.

MTV **Best** →**Hotel Aria** ★★★ Feel like rocking out at the club *and* at your hotel? Then the Hotel Aria is the place for you. This music-themed hotel lies in the heart of Malá Strana, just around the corner from the St. Nicholas Cathedral. Each of its four floors is tastefully decorated by Versace designers to evoke a different genre of music, famous composers, and musicians. There is an impressive library of CDs and DVDs as well as books about music off the lobby and a full-time resident musicologist available to help you choose a concert in the city. The Aria will delight any romantic soul with its luxurious, but cozy rooms, and the extensive list of amenities, which includes a roof terrace garden with spectacular views of Malá Strana. *Tržiště 9.* ☎ *225-334-111. www.aria hotel.net. 8,010Kč double. Rates include breakfast. Metro: line A to Malostranská, then tram no. 12, 22, 23 to Malostranské náměstí. Amenities: Restaurant; bar; 24-hr. business center; courtesy car from the airport; exercise room; room service. In room: A/C, TV, DVD/CD player, hair dryer, Internet, PC, minibar, safe.*

PRAGUE

Eating

Prague restaurants have a well-earned reputation for two things: heavy, lumpy peasant food and surly service. Fortunately, things are looking up: A whole crew of places is setting new standards, both in international cuisine and in modernized Czech food. The schnitzels and goulashes of neighboring Germany and Hungary are still on menus here, but they're served with a twist on the regular spices and sauces. Vegetarians can find solace in the national dishes of dumplings and cabbage.

Just remember that Czech restaurants close early. Some won't take food orders

after 8pm. Even in spots with good service, the tradition is a 2- or 3-hour spread, so don't plan to do anything when you're going out for a good dinner. Also, it always pays to double-check the bill—some less progressive restaurants still try to scam customers by charging absurd amounts for table snacks that were never requested.

Hot Spots

MTV **Best** →**Kampa Park** ★★ CONTINENTAL/SEAFOOD A modern, airy, stone-terraced spot that sits right on the Vltava River in the shadow of Charles Bridge, Kampa

Park makes for the best waterside dining in the city. A Scandinavian staff lends some solid creds, evident in the tasty yet simple seafood dishes like fresh salmon, and the indoor bar is a major networking scene. *Na Kampě 8b.* ☎ *296-826-102. www.kampagroup.com. Main courses 345Kč–795Kč. Daily 11:30am–1am. Metro: line A to Malostranská.*

→ **Kavárna Medúza** ★ CAFE FARE Musty, but hip. The decor here might scream "attic," but its comfortable mix of visitors and students makes it one of the most happening scenes in town. Big is also in here: The cappuccino comes in bowls, not cups. In addition to standard cafe fare, the Medúza offers some very tasty garlic bread. *Belgická 17.* ☎ *222-515-107. Cappuccino 25Kč; pastries/light meals 39Kč–95Kč. Mon–Fri 10am–1am; Sat–Sun noon–1am. Metro: line A to náměstí Míru.*

→ **U Modré kachničky** ★ CZECH Stay at the "Blue Duckling," a hot spot located a few blocks upstream on a quiet cobbled street in Malá Strana, long enough and you might just see every movie star filming in Prague walk discreetly through the door. In other words, this place is happening. Its charming upstairs gallery has the feel of a famous artist's country home, which perfectly complements the menu—heavy on wild game like roast rabbit. Your roast boar will be served under fantastical murals painted by the owners, who've also sought out the best Czech wines to go with it. *Nebovidská 6.* ☎ *257-320-308. www.umodrekachnicky.cz. Main courses 290Kč–690Kč. Daily noon–4pm and 6:30–11:30pm. Tram: 12, 18, 22, or 23 to Hellichova.*

Cheap

→ **Bohemia Bagel** BAGELS/SANDWICHES This was the city's first source of the Yiddish wonder bread. It's complemented with a serious assortment of coffees and fresh-baked muffins and brownies. All the hip, non-suit expats you'd expect gather here day and night, and the bulletin board always features info on the latest happenings. The egg-and-salsa bagel's always a good bet. *Újezd 16.* ☎ *257-310-694. www.bohemiabagel.cz. Main courses 150Kč. Daily 7am–midnight (Sat–Sun from 8am). Tram: 12, 22, or 23 to Újezd. Second location at Masná 2.* ☎ *224-812-560. Metro: line B to náměstí Republiky.*

→ **Country Life** VEGETARIAN Here you'll find all the young Czech intellectuals who denounce meat and favor the sometimes-pasty vegetarian concoctions this joint sells, cafeteria-style, for almost nothing. It's a friggin' madhouse at lunch, probably because it's the fastest and cheapest spot in Old Town—watch out for scuffles at the do-it-yourself salad bar. The lumpy, arty wooden seating is, shall we say, interesting. *Melantrichova 15.* ☎ *224-213-366. Main courses 75Kč. Sun–Thurs 9am–3pm and 6–8:30pm, Fri 9am–6pm. Metro: line A or B to Můstek.*

Doable

→ **Caffrey's Irish Bar** IRISH Even though this place opens onto Old Town Square, it's neither cheesy nor a rip-off. Amazing. Instead, it's a rollicking, plank-floored gathering point for well-heeled expats drawn in by the satellite sports coverage and phenomenal steaks in Guinness sauce. The traditional Irish fry, complete with black-and-white pudding, is a much-sworn-by morning hangover cure. *Staroměstské nám 10.* ☎ *224-828-031. www.caffreys.cz. Main courses 200Kč–500Kč. Daily 10am–2am. Metro: line A to Staroměstská.*

→ **Pálffy palác** INTERNATIONAL A candlelit, parquet-floored baroque dining room is run by one of the city's most charming hosts, Roman Řezníček, the man behind **Mecca** (p. 752). The outdoor balcony is blissfully breezy in the warmer months, so don't miss it. Try the homemade ravioli, followed by a baked banana. *Valdštejnská 14.* ☎ *257-530-522. www.palffy.cz. Main courses 390Kč–788Kč. Daily 11am–midnight daily. Tram: 12, 22, or 23 to Malostranské náměstí.*

➔**Pizzeria Rugantino** PIZZA Young and old alike come here for generous iceberg salads and the best selection of individual pizzas in Prague. The wood-fired stoves and handmade dough result in a crisp and delicate crust, no matter what type of pizza you order. My favorite was the Diablo with fresh garlic bits and very hot chiles, which goes nicely with a salad and a pull of Krušovice beer. *Dušní 4.* ☎ *222-318-172. Individual pizzas 100Kč–250Kč. Mon–Sat 11am–11pm, Sun 5–11pm. Metro: line A to Staroměstská.*

Splurge

➔**Hergetova Cihelna** ★★INTERNATIONAL/ CZECH You'll pay a bit more to dine at Hergetova, one of Prague's best restaurants, but it'll be worth it. Housed in a converted brick factory dating from the 18th century, this place sports a remodeled interior that is divided into a restaurant, cocktail bar, cafe, and music lounge. From the large summer terrace overlooking the river you can experience one of the most exciting and unforgettable views of the river and Charles Bridge. The food is excellent; I liked the homemade Czech potato soup with forest mushrooms and garlic called *bramboračka. Cihelná 2b.* ☎ *296-826-103. www.kampagroup.com. Main courses 215Kč–695Kč. Daily 11:30am–1am. Metro: line A to Malostranská.*

Cafe & Tearooms

Maybe it's backlash against the prevailing beer culture, but a lot of young Czechs love tea. A few of the more extreme radicals among them have established a counterculture of tearooms that look like they were transplanted whole from Tibet or Sumatra. Being in one of these places, where black-robed servers are bidden by little brass bells, can be a little disorienting when you're expecting the stone cathedrals of old Prague.

➔**Dahab** CAFE/MIDDLE EASTERN/TEAROOM This tearoom was founded by Prague's king of tea, Luboš Rychvalský, who introduced Prague to Eastern and Arabic tea cultures soon after the 1989 revolution. Dahab (meaning "gold" or "oasis" in Arabic) provides a New Age alternative to the clatter of the *kavárny.* The soothing atmosphere is perfect for relaxing quietly over a cup of tea or coffee. You can choose from about 20 sorts of tea and more than 10 kinds of coffee. Arabic soups, hummus, tahini, couscous, pita bread, and tempting sweets are also on the menu. *Dlouhá 33, at Rybná.* ☎ *224-827-375.*

Cafe Society

In their heyday in the late 19th and early 20th centuries, Prague's elegant *kavárny* (cafes) rivaled Vienna's as places to be seen and perhaps have a carefree afternoon chat. But the Bohemian intellectuals, much like the Parisian Left Bank philosophers of the 1920s, laid claim to many of the local cafes, turning them into smoky parlors for pondering and debating the anxieties of the day.

Today, most of Prague's cafes have lost the indigenous charm of the Jazz Age or, strangely enough, the communist era. During the Cold War, the venerable MTV Best Café Slavia ★★ (Národní at Smetanovo nábřeží; ☎ 224-218-493), across from the National Theatre, became a de facto clubhouse in which dissidents passed the time, often within listening range of the not-so-secret police. It's here that Václav Havel and the arts community often gathered to keep a flicker of the Civic Society alive. New Bohemian haunts have popped up. One of these is actually not so new: **Kavárna Obecní dům** (náměstí Republiky 5; ☎ 222-002-763) is an older cafe that has been returned to its pristine splendor. Cafe life may return to Prague yet again.

PRAGUE

www.dahab.cz. Main courses 125Kč–329Kč. Daily noon–1am. Metro: line B to náměstí Republiky.

→ **Dobrá čajovna** CAFE/TEAROOM   On the walk toward the National Museum on the right side of Wenceslas Square, there is an island of serenity in the courtyard at no. 14. Inside the Dobrá čajovna (Good Tearoom), a pungent bouquet of herb teas, throw pillows, and sitar music welcomes visitors to this very understated Bohemian corner. The extensive tea menu includes green Japanese tea for 55Kč a cup. *Václavské nám. 14.* ☎ *224-231-480. 40Kč–120Kč for a pot of tea. Mon–Fri 10am–9:30pm; Sat–Sun 2pm–9:30pm. Metro: line A or B to Můstek.*

Partying

You won't find a bunch of stylish mixed-drink bars here, Czech wine is famously bad, and pubs tend to be unapologetically smoky, fly-specked, and uncomfortable. Wait! Even if dive bars aren't your thing (which some people might see as a serious character flaw), hold on—you do have a few positives on your side: First, there's Czech beer (see "Beer 101" on p. 751 for more on that). Second, you'll share bench seating at the pubs with anyone who has space, so it's the perfect environment for gathering new drinking buddies. Third—and most important—whatever else might be lacking is completely made up for by absinthe, the wondrous blue-green worm-wood extract that is still banned in much of western Europe as a madness-inducing poison for degenerates (see "The Truth about Absinthe" on p. 752). Most pubs do serve food, but unless otherwise stated, you're better off eating elsewhere.

Things don't really get started at Prague's clubs until after 11pm. A good source on the latest club spaces, raves, and parties is *Think* (www.think.cz), a free monthly usually found at **Radost/FX** (see below). While you're there, check out the bulletin board, which is sometimes even better. **U Malého Glena** (p. 755) is also a nightlife nerve center that carries *Think* and sports its own bulletin board. Also try the **Czech Techno** site (www.techno.cz/party).

Club gear is fine if you've got it, but nobody really cares if you go in with sneakers and jeans, even at glammy RadostFX. For those with the bucks, Quicksilver and mile-high shoes are it. For those making do, which is most of us, special dispensations are allowed. For instance, Radost/FX will devote a night to the glam crowd, who get fully decked out in tight designer stuff, and then they'll hold a Tuesday Soul Night, at which anybody in a sweatshirt and jeans will feel welcome. About the only place where you may feel noticeably underdressed in Prague is at the opera or symphony, but even there the balconies are filled with young music lovers without the budget for a tux or evening gown.

Bars

→ **Chateau** Any conversation at this busy and fun place must be shouted. Just a block from the Marquis, this hell-red bar is all about contact sports: You'll have to shove through a seriously cruising crowd to reach the bar, grabbing whatever comes your way. *Jakubská 2.* ☎ *222-316-328. Metro: line B to náměstí Republiky.*

→ **Érra Café** ★ Another basement-level mecca of style. It's got a classy, gay-friendly atmosphere, with gold-framed mirrors, a house soundtrack, Op-Art seating, and a fire-place. Best chicken-garlic-sesame sandwich in town, too. *Konviktská 11.* ☎ *224-233-427. Metro: line B to Národní třída.*

→ **Jáma** Arguably your best option near Wenceslas Square, Jáma is hopping with a more yuppified expat crowd reliving its

Beer 101

With a brewing tradition spanning over 500 years, beer is the center of the drinking universe here. Plus, it's cheap and, even better, it's good. Preferred beers are the bitter Pilsner Urquell; the more mellow Budvar; the delicious Gambrinus, Radegast, and Krušovice; the up-and-coming Bernard; and Starobrno brewery's Červený Drak, a Moravian award-winner. Beers can be ordered dark (tmavé), light (světlé), or mixed (řezané), but are always preceded by the toast "Na zdraví" (to your health) and sometimes a clunk on the table for emphasis. (Always look whomever you're clinking mugs with straight in the eye if you want to get any respect in the beer world here.)

college bar days amid rock posters, Mexican food, and spontaneous drink specials. Sunday movie nights, a video rental counter, and *The Prague Revue*, a literary semiannual put out by the owners, further set this place apart. *V jámě 7.* ☎ *242-222-383. www.jamapub.cz. Metro: line A or B to Můstek.*

➔ **Marquis de Sade** A place to pick up dancing (or whatever) partners before heading down the street to **Roxy** (p. 753), where everybody who's anybody comes to meet up with friends and down an obligatory absinthe shot. It's a big, well-worn pub space for making plans of attack and fueling up on decent pizza (before the kitchen closes at 11pm, anyway). Despite the name, the action is pretty traditional—there's no latex or whips lying around. *Templová 8.* ☎ *224-817-505. Metro: line B to náměstí Republiky.*

➔ **U Medvídků** A pub/bar serving up South Bohemian Budvar beer, great slabs of pork in brandy or beer sauce, dumplings, and an atmosphere loved by everyone from Czech students to American novelist wannabes.

With 700 years of experience in this location, it's no big shock that this place does what it does so well. Don't sit anywhere near the hay wagon on a Friday or Saturday night—that's when the appallingly bad folk band, in their kitschy "traditional" costumes, moves into it and jams for all they're worth—which ain't much. *Na Perštýně 7.* ☎ *224-211-916. www.umedvidku.cz. Metro: line B to Národní třída.*

➔ **U Vystřelenýho oka** This spot serves up cheap Czech beer in a classically run-down Žižkov pub environ, with a beer terrace outside; occasional loud, drunk bands; and surreal decor by a member of the Prague underground band Už Jsme Doma. The name of this place literally means "At the Shot-Out Eye"—ask anyone here about its deeper meaning. *U božích bojovníků 3.* ☎ *222-540-465. Metro: line B or C to Florenc, then bus no. 133 or 207 to Jeronýmova.*

MTV **Best** ➔ **Železné dveře** ★ ★ This is the hottest bar in Old Town, with a big fish tank and a coat of gold fleck paint on the walls of a cavernous cellar bar, plus occasional sushi snacks. The cool mix of veteran expats and hip Czechs who are part of the expat scene (teachers, folks who work in expat bars, writers for expat publications) will soon make you forget that anything's missing. The young, mixed crowd definitely has some money to spend, but is a long, long way from yuppie. *Michalská 19.* ☎ *224-216-869. Metro: line A or B to Můstek.*

Clubs

Where else in the world but Prague can you dance in a crumbling underground former cinema like the Roxy, then stop off for the herbal wonder liqueur Becherovka in a Romanesque stone cellar? The center of this Gothic city hasn't changed much since medieval days, and clubbing is probably the best way to get into that ancient vibe. Be prepared for cramped and smoky downtown club spaces, thanks in part to their underground—

PRAGUE

The Truth about Absinthe

Yes, the blue-green demon in the bottle is still illegal in most of the West, perhaps understandably, because so many Paris artists and writers used it as a cheap ticket to cuckoo-ville during the '20s. But the wormwood extract's no-nonsense punch is a thrill to be savored, and one you'll probably survive if you take it with a modicum of moderation. Don't just down it, though: The time-honored ritual is to take a spoonful of sugar, soak it in the stuff, set it alight until it caramelizes, then stir it back into the glass. For God's sake put it out first, though, or the whole thing will become a little hunka-hunka-burnin' love in your glass. Having proven yourself an old hand at Bohemian indulgence, you may then lift your glass, make firm eye contact with your partners in crime, and say, without a trace of irony, "Na zdraví" (to your health). The effects aren't subtle—in fact, if you're short of cash you can achieve roughly the same sensation by whacking yourself over the head with a plank and spinning in a circle till you drop. Nevertheless, the makers of absinthe assure customers that the current version is 5 proof milder than the stuff that sent all those Parisians to the nuthouse back in the day. All of 5 proof, huh?

literally—nature. Prague is full of spooky subterranean spaces because the original town was buried in the 12th century and the current one was built on top of it to provide a high-water haven during Vltava River floods. Landlords here are still highly suspicious of clubs, which further fuels the need to be creative in finding space: hence all the strange alternative spaces like out-of-business factories that open and close as clubs every summer. Below are some less transient options.

→ **Duplex** Prague's most blatantly commercial music and partyers can be found here, above Wenceslas Square. With loads of glass, steel, incredible views, at least it's pure in its aim to be Prague's glitziest meat market. It's also got full sit-down dinner service and an outdoor terrace that's a trip, especially for late-morning coffee. *Václavské nám. 21.* ☎ *224-232-319. www.duplex.cz. Cover 100Kč. Metro: line A or B to Můstek. Tram: to Národní třída.*

→ **Klub Lávka** Here you can take advantage of the riverside outdoor seating during warmer months. Lávka's black-light and Day Glo dance area, where techno-dance tunes pound, stands in contrast to the terrace,

which provides quiet respite. *Novotného lávka 1.* ☎ *221-082-278. www.lavka.cz. Metro: line A to Staroměstská.*

→ **Mecca** The hottest thing going, with packed monthly shows by funky house-master DJ Loutka, hilarious transvestite fashion nights, "model nights" (read: wannabe nights), and a respectable bar and restaurant running till 11pm. It may not be underground, exactly, but it is in a former factory and definitely worth the cab ride out to the inconvenient Holešovice district. A more mature (but still giddy) international crowd digs this break from the hard-edged techno scene. *U Průhonu 3.* ☎ *283-870-522. www.mecca.cz. Tram: 12, 25, or 54 to Dělnická.*

🆀 Best → **Radost/FX** ★★ In New Town, the Radost is much more glam, with a much less anarchistic, much more expat crowd than Roxy, but it also has its act much more together: regular Thursday gay nights, soul on Tuesdays, beach parties in summer—sometimes with trucked-in sand—and the all-night vegetarian cafe, gallery, and lounge upstairs. *Bělehradská 120.* ☎ *224-254-776. www.radostfx.cz. Metro: line C to I. P. Pavlova.*

City of Love

Take a dark, winding cobbled street. Add moonlight, mist, a gargoyle or two, and cheap, sublime alcoholic beverages. Throw in the natural freedom and exuberance you feel when abroad, especially in a once-forbidden city still caught between now and then. If none of this can inspire you to make that foolish, rash move you always repress back home, maybe you should consider a life in the clergy. But for anyone who's not above a bit of bleary sin, Prague is what you'd call romantic. And don't think Czechs don't feel it, too. Modern sexual mores here are noticeably freer than in most Western cities. Feminism, if it means pay equity, might not be altogether rejected by a Prague woman, but if it means foregoing a single male overture, or heading out on a Friday night looking less than stunning, it's going to be a tough sell. Pouting to get your way is much more the style here, and PDAs are rampant, particularly on the metro. The severe apartment crunch in Prague is probably a factor, as it eliminates more private options. A bigger factor, affecting the whole romance mind-set, is that the Czech Republic still has not experienced serious levels of some Western social ills like AIDS. Then again, there's an old Bohemian saying that Slavs just have warm hearts. And after you live through one winter here, you may just see for yourself how body heat can be a lifesaver.

→**Roxy** ★★ Old Town's best overall club is one of the spookiest around, with potholes in the dance floor still marking where the seats were once bolted into this once-glamorous movie palace beneath the streets. As in most Prague clubs, it leans heavily toward house and techno, booking a lot of hot Berlin, Amsterdam, and London DJs, but you'll hear just about anything here. The tearoom—an intact slice of Morocco with harem-like pillow seating, hookahs, and mint tea—that used to be located off the main floor, has moved next door (check it out, it's really great), and a chill-out space has been inserted in its place. Young (and we mean young) club kids and 20-something Czechs who are into the electronic music scene crowd the place all night, but don't expect to make any great conversation here—the volume is incredible, and most people are really here to dance, not talk. *Dlouhá 33.* ☎ *224-826-296. www.roxy.cz. Cover 50Kč–250Kč. Metro: line B to náměstí Republiky.*

Gay Bars & Clubs

Gay culture in Prague is growing but is still in the finding-its-feet stage. A hub of gay pubs and clubs is located in the working-class Žižkov district, while cross-dressing "travesty shows" both here and in Old Town have become a regular feature of nightlife. Outdoor cruising happens, appropriately, around the enormously phallic Metronome sculpture in Letná Park, visible from anywhere along the Old Town riverbank. Bars are obviously the indoor places for pickups, though these days, increasing numbers of bars are more dedicated to providing a comfortable (or over-the-top) atmosphere instead of just being meat markets. A bunch have put up an exclusive front, but don't be intimidated—they're really pussycats if you just grin your way in.

Amigo (www.amigo.cz) is a hip monthly guide with comprehensive events listings, in Czech, but it's fairly decipherable. It's available at most newsstands. Gayguide.net (www.gayguide.net) has updated info on every bar, cruise, gay-run accommodations, and hot line in the city.

→**Aqua Club 2000** ★★ Here's the original champ of the genre, with shows Monday,

Wednesday, Friday, and Saturday in a large, industrial-looking Žižkov building hidden away behind blazing neon. It also features saunas and upstairs rooms for, well, you know. *Husitská 7.* ☎ *222-540-241. Metro: line B or C to Florenc, then bus no. 135 or night bus no. 504.*

➔ **Club Stella** There's nothing dingy about this romantically lit cafe-bar. And despite the get-it-on lighting, this place is mainly for jovial hanging out, especially on the patio in summer. *Lužická 10.* ☎ *224-257-869. Tram: 4, 22, or 34, or night tram no. 57 to Jana Masaryka.*

➔ **Friends** ★ One of the classier bars in Old Town, with a mellow atmosphere best summed up by the placard next to the door that welcomes "folks of every walk of life as long as they are open-minded." They've also added weekly dance parties, but keep in mind that this is a bar—don't expect any sirens or smoke machines. If you like '60s dance music, though, this is the place to be. *Bartolomějská 11.* ☎ *224-236-772. Metro: line B or night tram no. 51, 54, 57, or 58 to Národní třída.*

➔ **Sauna Marco** With a steam room, Jacuzzi, bar, and video cabins, this is a popular spot close to the clubs listed above, located on the edge of Žižkov. *Lublaňská 17.* ☎ *224-262-833. Cover 195Kč. Metro: line C to I. P. Pavlova, then tram no. 4, 6, 11, 16, or 22, or night tram no. 51, 56, or 57.*

➔ **Tingl Tangl** Hidden in a courtyard on a tiny street leading away from the front of the **National Theater** (p. 755), Tingl Tangl is always a riot and welcoming to all orientations. The current reigning queen of drag shows has nightly low-budget extravaganzas that go well beyond cheesy, and a loyal audience that eats them up. The heavily mirrored basement bar accented in fire-engine red just proves you never know what's going on beneath the cobblestones of Old Town. *Karoliny Světlé 12.* ☎ *242-238-278. Metro: line B or night tram no. 51, 54, 57, or 58 to Národní třída.*

Live Music

➔ **AghaRTA** Here is where the younger jazz talents play, many of them recorded on the club's own label and available on CDs sold in the entryway. It's hip, tiny, packed with jazz buffs both Czech and foreign, and just a short walk from Wenceslas Square and Old Town Square. *Železná 16.* ☎ *222-211-275. www.agharta.cz. Cover 80Kč. Metro: line A or B to Můstek.*

➔ **Lucerna Music Bar** Right on Wenceslas Square, Lucerna is super-convenient and has a great, tattered, hastily remodeled, 1920s-club atmosphere. Neither the idols of Czech rock who play here nor their crowds seem to mind the awful acoustics. *Vodičkova 36.* ☎ *224-217-108. www.musicbar.cz. Cover 80Kč–150Kč. Metro: line A to Můstek.*

➔ **Malostranská Beseda** Across the river in Malá Strana, this spot is not much more than a battered bar, but has solid live music creds as the Home of Cheap Shows. A whole crew of mostly Czech local rockers and blues folks rule the stage. *Malostranské nám. 21.* ☎ *257-535-092. Cover 80Kč. Tram: 12, 22, 23 to Malostranské náměstí.*

➔ **Palác Akropolis** This place books local artists plus a host of international acts, presenting them with great acoustics and lighting in its small basement theater. Slink around the labyrinth of connecting bars (four in all) to become part of the mob of students, graphic designers, local musicians, and artists from the underground scene doing the post-show-hangout thing. It's definitely worth the short ride into the Žižkov district. *Kubelíkova 27.* ☎ *296-330-911. www.palacakropolis.cz. Metro: line A to Jiřího z Poděbrad.*

➔ **Rock Café** The best Old Town live-rock alternative to the mostly DJ-ruled **Roxy** (p. 753), the Rock Cafe favors a bizarre lineup of Czech cover bands who "revive" everyone from Sade to the Stones by way of Janis Joplin and ABBA. The impersonal, sound-sucking hall doesn't seem to affect performance quality either way, and the big guys spilling beer on their Rutgers sweatshirts don't seem bothered by it. *Národní 20.* ☎ *224-933-947. Cover 80Kč. Metro: line B to Národní.*

➜ **U Malého Glena** This American-run bar/club is technically a jazz hole, but it's the major force in town for attracting new talents of all genres. There's a Sunday night jam, and the hottest names in local straight-up jazz play throughout the week. The basement music hall is so small you'll have to stand in the doorway if you don't arrive early. If you start to freak, take a breather in the jumping-yet-less-cramped pub on the floor above. *Karmelitská 23.* ☎ *257-531-717. www.malyglen.cz. Cover 70Kč. Tram: 12, 22, 23 to Malostranské náměstí.*

Performing Arts

Any city as eerie and entrancing as Prague is bound to have an interesting visual arts movement. Still, artists in Prague, as in many former Soviet satellites, are searching for identity. Films, exhibitions, and fashions, like the Czechs, tend more toward the subtle and ironic than in your face. In addition, having had free development of the arts cut off for 50 years is bound to have lingering effects on a country—especially one as small as this one. But there are bright spots: Follow the happenings and track the openings in the pages of *Umělec (Artist)* or *Atelier*, both of which have sections in English and can be found at Galerie Jiří Švestka, or in *The Prague Post.*

Events rarely sell out far in advance, except for major nights during the Prague Spring Music Festival or a staging of *Don Giovanni* in the high season. To secure tickets before arriving, contact the travel bureau **Čedok** in Prague (p. 738). You can also contact the Prague ticket agency **Ticketpro** (Prague Tourist Center, Rytířská 12; ☎ 296-333-333; www.ticketpro.cz). This largest computerized ticket service sells seats online to most events around town. You can purchase tickets on the Web and pay when you arrive.

Once in Prague, you can get tickets for most classical performances at the box office in the modern Nová scéna annex to the **National Theater** (Národní třída 2; ☎ 224-901-448; www.nd.cz). You can purchase tickets either at theater box offices or from any one of the dozens of ticket agencies. The largest handle most of the entertainment offerings and include a service charge. Ask how much this is before buying, as sometimes rates are hiked substantially. Large, centrally located agencies are **Prague Tourist Center** (Rytířská 12; ☎ 296-333-333; daily 9am–8pm) and **Bohemia Ticket** (Na Příkopě 16; ☎ 224-215-031; www. bohemiaticket.cz; Mon–Fri 10am–7pm, Sat 10am–5pm, Sun 10am–3pm).

Visual Arts

➜ **The French Institute** This gallery has consistently excellent photo and painting exhibits whose openings are a must. It's also equipped with a fine patio cafe where you'll meet all the Francophiles you care to. The free screenings of Godard and the like in the downstairs theater aren't bad, either. *Štěpánská 35.* ☎ *221-401-011. Mon–Fri 8:30am–7pm. Metro: line A or C to Muzeum.*

➜ **Galerie MXM** This gallery specializes in a group of 30 or so Czechs whose work you'll never see at the National Gallery—and who don't mind that fact at all. Some of them have done prank billboards on the main Czech freeway, others work in comic-strip form, and still others try anything irreverent they can think up. *Nosticova 6.* ☎ *257-311-198. Tues–Sun 11:30am–6pm. Tram: 12, 22, or 23 to Malostranské náměstí.*

→ **Jiří Švestka Galerie** Respected curator Jiří Švestka operates this New Town space, showing work from the likes of Dan Graham and ex-President Havel's decorator, Bořek Šípek. It hosts some of the most spontaneous and provocative art to be seen here, both local and international. *Biskupský dvůr.* ☎ 222-311-092. *www.jirisvestka.com. Tues–Fri noon–6pm; Sat 11am–6pm. Metro: line B or C to Florenc.*

→ **Prague House of Photography** Photography has a long, well-developed tradition in Czech art, dating back to Josef Sudek and František Drtikol. Shows here range from Russian silver-plate experiments to personal documents by rising new talents. *Václavské náměstí 31.* ☎ 222-243-229. *Daily 11am–6pm. Metro: line A to Můstek.*

→ **Velryba** This New Town's place combines gallery space and caffeine; you just have to wander to the back room and down the spiral staircase to find it. It's predictably full of "outsider art," some of which may well require a stiff gin from the upstairs bar to really get the hang of it. *Opatovická 24.* ☎ 224-912-391. *Daily 11am–midnight. Metro: line B to Národní třída.*

Performing Arts

As the old saying goes, to be Czech is to be a musician—and judging by the number of string-pickers and horn-blowers you see here, it appears to be true. Chamber music, symphonies, and opera divas perform nightly in the city's top halls: the National Theatre, the State Opera, the Estates' Theatre, and the Rudolfinum, all within a 15-minute walk of each other. It's not all powdered wigs, though. Remember, Prague has always been on the cutting edge of music: The original musical bad boy, Mozart, hung out here, holed up at a friend's with lots of drugs and willing women (and you thought Keith Moon invented the concept). Book concert tickets most easily through **Ticketpro** (at Prague

Tourist Center, Rytířská 12; ☎ **296-333-333;** daily 9am–8pm).

→ **Archa Theater** This theater sets the example for progressive booking in Prague with everyone from Siouxie and Budgie to the DV8 Physical Theater, all in a black box with prime acoustics and lighting. Archa brings in avant-garde talents as diverse as Min Tanaka and Brian Eno (yeah, he's still cutting-edge). Bonus: You can reserve tickets online. *Na Poříčí 26.* ☎ 221-716-333. *www.archa theatre.cz. Music and concerts 120Kč–490Kč; theater and dance 65Kč–120Kč. Metro: line B or C to Florenc.*

→ **Czech Philharmonic Orchestra at Rudolfinum** Named for Prince Rudolf, the beautifully restored Rudolfinum has been one of the city's premier concert venues since it opened in the 19th century. The Rudolfinum's Small Hall mostly presents chamber concerts, while the larger, more celebrated Dvořák Hall is home to the Czech Philharmonic. Though the acoustics aren't faultless, the grandeur of the hall makes a concert experience here worthwhile. *Alšovo nábřeží 12.* ☎ 227-059-352. *www.rudolfinum. cz. Prices vary. Metro: line A to Staroměstská.*

→ **Estates Theatre** The Estates is where Mozart himself conducted the premiere of *Don Giovanni* in 1787, and it's still going strong with a repertoire that, not surprisingly, favors Amadeus, but also includes top Prague ballet and modern dance performances. *Ovocný trh 1.* ☎ 224-215-001. *www.nd.cz. Opera 900Kč–1,050Kč; ballet 550Kč–700Kč. Box office Mon–Fri 10am–6pm; Sat–Sun 10am–12:30pm and 3–6pm. Metro: line A or B to Můstek.*

→ **National Theatre** A symbol of Czech culture stages its own stalwart operas—often different versions of the same piece going on at the State Opera, so don't let them play you. This is a classic 19th-century opera house, ringed with box seats and known for colorful—if not defining—productions. *Národní travída 2. ☎ 224-901-448. www.nd.cz. Opera 700Kč–950Kč; ballet 600Kč–800Kč. Box office daily 10am–6pm. Tram: 6, 9, 18, 22, or 23 to Národní Divadlo.*

➔ **Prague State Opera House** A lush 19th-century wedding cake of a performance hall, the State Opera House is also a slice of unadulterated Old Europe, where you can catch a stirring Verdi aria for about the price of a movie back home. Located southeast of Old Town. *Wilsonova 4. ☎ 296/117-111. www. opera.cz. 400 Kč–1,200Kč opera, 200 Kč–550Kč ballet. Box office Mon–Fri 10am–5:30pm; Sat–Sun 10am–noon and 1–5:30pm. Metro: line A or C to Muzeum.*

➔ **Prague Symphony Orchestra in the Municipal House** Named for the popular composer and fervent Czech nationalist Bedřich Smetana (1824–84), Smetana Hall is in one of the world's most distinctive Art Nouveau buildings, the Municipal House (Obecní dům). Since its 1997 reopening after the building's painstaking reconstruction, the ornate and purely exhilarating hall has hosted a series of top-notch events. *In the Municipal House, náměstí Republiky 5. ☎ 222-002-336. www.fok.cz. Prices vary. Metro: line B to náměstí Republiky.*

Movie Theaters

Unlike neighboring Germany, which has made dubbing so commonplace that it has become the scourge of the industry, foreign films are generally screened here in their original language, with Czech subtitles. Now, better Czech films are also being screened for visitors with English subtitles. Unlike the pre-revolution days, when hardly a decent Western film could be seen, the cinemas *(kinos)* are filled with most first-run films from Hollywood and the independents within a few weeks after their general release.

Many cinemas are on or near Václavské náměstí (Wenceslas Sq.). Tickets cost 80Kč to 180Kč. Most screenings have reserved seats, and many popular films sell out in advance, so choose your places early. Check the *Prague Post* for listings, or for a more accurate list, look at the billboards outside **Kino Lucerna,** Vodičkova 36, near Wenceslas Square (☎ 224-216-972; metro: line A or B to Můstek).

A new complex of cinemas is at the shopping gallery **Palác Flóra,** Vinohradská 149 (☎ 255-742-021; www.cinemacity.cz). Here, at the **IMAX,** you can visit the virtual world if you get a ticket (160Kč) for one of the 3-D movie shows offered at the screening. On the programs of eight other cinemas are the newest films in English. At the centrally located shopping and cultural center **Slovanský Dům** (Na Příkopě 9/11; ☎ 221-451-214; www.palacecinemas.cz), you also can enjoy the latest releases at their **Palace Cinemas.** The same chain opened its **Multiplex** at the brand-new shopping center **Nový Smíchov** (Plzeňská 8; ☎ 257-181-212; www.palacecinemas.cz).

Bookstores

➔ **Big Ben Bookshop** At the far side of the courtyard behind Týn Church near Old Town Square, Big Ben is a good place to find that commemorative or educational book on Prague in English. There are also city tours to take home on videocassette and a wealth of maps to guide you into the hinterlands. *Malá Štupartská 5. ☎ 224-826-565. www.bigben bookshop.com. Metro: line A or B to Můstek.*

➔ **Globe Bookstore and Coffeehouse** ★ The undisputed international heart of Prague's literary scene, the Globe boasts a cafe that everyone from Allen Ginsberg to

Lit Life

Prague's literary scene has been endlessly built up as the modern equivalent of Paris in the '20s—but who the hell could live up to that? Unfair expectations aside, there is a genuinely nurturing atmosphere for writers here, who inherit a long literary tradition of Praguers from Rilke to Kafka. The Globe Bookstore and Coffeehouse is at the center of things, with connections to annual PEN club events and promising new ventures like the Prague School of Poetics.

Anthologies, small presses like Twisted Spoon, and literary journals like *Trafika, Optimism,* and *The Prague Revue* offer more outlets for mad scribblers than you'll find in any other capital of the former East Bloc.

Radost/FX (p. 752) continues to host its infamous reading nights, Sundays at 7pm, nowadays held in the space-age basement disco, which is eerily quiet at that time of week. It's all very low-key and the perfect opportunity to approach a scruffy expat scribbler, buy him/her a drink, and glean all there is to know about boho life here. Don't expect to see Czechs, though, unless you look in the vegetarian cafe upstairs.

Andrei Codrescu has paid their respects to. They stock thousands of major works in paperback, plus translations of Czech works you'll never find elsewhere, and serve a Sunday brunch that's an institution in itself. Plus, their bulletin board is an expat nerve center—all in a setting that's as cozy as it gets. *Note:* At press time, this place was up for sale. Let's hope it stays around. *Pštrossova 6.* ☎ *224-934-203. www.globebookstore.cz. Metro: line B to Národní třída.*

→ **Literární kavárna G plus G** You'll certainly meet Czech literary sorts here, even if you only talk to the barman. Chances are he's one of the former dissidents who set up this cafe/small press, which is the country's sole publisher of books in English on Romany issues. Regular readings (not always in Czech) and acoustic music nights are scheduled here, and they stock all kinds of esoteric journals you can flip through on the comfy seating in the back room. *Čerchovská 4. No phone. Metro: line A to Jiřího z Poděbrad.*

Sightseeing

While classical music and the Czech Republic's unmatched beer are among some of the better reasons to visit Prague, you won't really get to know the city until you simply stroll its winding cobblestone streets and soak in the unique atmosphere. Exquisite examples from the history of European architecture—from Romanesque to Renaissance, from baroque to Art Nouveau to cubist—are crammed next to one another on twisting narrow streets. Seen from Charles Bridge, this jumble of architecture thrusts from the hills and hugs the riverbanks, with little of the 20th century's own excesses obscuring the grandeur from the past

millennium. The most revered areas remain relatively free of the blindingly electric Technicolor world—however, splotches of graffiti and seemingly constant reconstruction often taint the mood.

While Prague's leaders have been slow to tap into the city's true potential as a primary European tourist destination, there have been some marked improvements in recent years. Buildings within the city center, the walking zone Na Příkopě and Václavské náměstí, have undergone the most notable changes and renovations.

Hanging Out

Islands in the Vltava River are prime hangouts during spring and fall for Praguers of all ages. One of the best spots for catching a sundown with a cold brew in hand is Slovanský ostrov (across a footbridge from Masarykovo nábřeží), just upstream of the **National Theater** (p. 755). This Vltava River island is the only one with its own palace, fronted and backed by green lawns, winding paths, shade trees, and folks out for a relaxing stroll. Another is Kampa (in the Malá Strana district, just downstream from the bridge called most Legií) with a big meadow of grass and shade trees much favored by hippie drummers in town for summer rock fests.

Festivals

The best way to stay on top of the festival schedule, which is revised throughout the year, is to tap into the **Prague Information Service (PIS)** website at www.pis.cz or www. prague-info.cz.

March

Days of European Film. Cinema directors and actors from all corners of Europe, both quirky and big-budget, old and new, come to Prague with just one premise uniting them: to watch festival movies. Call ☎ 224-234-875 for info. Throughout March.

Febiofest. This is one of the largest non-competitive film festivals in central Europe. ☎ 221-101-111. www.febiofest.cz. March 23 to 31.

May

Prague Spring Festival ★★. The grandest of Prague's dozens of music festivals, dating back to the post–World War II days and attracting such global lights as the orchestras of the Met and the BBC. ☎ 257-312-547. www.festival.cz. May 11 to June 3.

June

Tanec Praha. Biggie modern dance festival that attracts the likes of the Martha Graham Dance Company as well as avant-garde talents from all over Europe. ☎ 224-817-886. www.tanecpha.cz. Throughout June.

PRAGUE

Free & Easy

→ Head to the **Old Town Square** (metro: line A to Staroměstská) to get inspired by the Jan Hus statues, Bohemia's greatest heretic and martyr to religious reform, and watch the world go by all day.

→ On **Slovanský ostrov** island, you can score a rowboat for 60Kč for an hour, grab a table at the floating pub for the 25Kč price of a beer, or claim a bench for nothing and just sit under the shade trees with a good book, watching the Vltava River flow by.

→ The private galleries all along **Národní třída** also make for free and stylish shelters (and even the national galleries will set you back a mere 70Kč in exchange for an afternoon of resplendent art and reverie).

→ If you're still cash poor at the end of the night, head to the **Charles Bridge** for a late night romp: "Peace, Love, Spare Change" describes the scene, as musicians, street performers, and flower people come out late at night to become one with the bridge. Why not join them?

September

Prague Autumn. The second-string classical music event of the year has nothing to apologize for with a past that has included illustrious fiddlers and stunning symphonies that jam at Prague's finest halls. ☎ 222-540-484. www.pragueautumn.cz. September 12 to October 1.

October

International Jazz Festival. Springhill, Sugar Blue, and Arnowitt were guests at this celebration of jazz music in recent years. ☎ 224-235-267. www.jazzfestivalpraha.cz. Late October.

December

Saint Nicholas' Day. On this holiday, Prague is overrun by men in white cotton beards, accompanied by angels and devils, who go about asking little children how they've behaved this year and offering lumps of coal to those whose stories don't jibe. December 5.

Major Sights

Thanks to the fortunes of war over the centuries, which miraculously spared Prague from destruction time and again, the whole freakin' city center is a museum, topped by an intact 1,000-year-old castle straight out of your favorite bedtime story. Prague Castle and the Old Jewish Cemetery are the big must-sees, the latter being a ghostly tumble of tombstones on a tiny Old Town plot in the old Jewish Quarter.

Best ➜ **Prague Castle** ★★★ The huge hilltop complex on Hradčany, encompasses dozens of houses, towers, churches, courtyards, and monuments. A visit to the castle can easily take an entire day or more, depending on how thoroughly you explore it. Still, you can see the top sights—St. Vitus Cathedral, the Royal Palace, St. George's Basilica, the Powder Tower, and Golden Lane—in the space of a morning or an afternoon. *Hradčanské nám.* ☎ 224-373-368.

www.hrad.cz. Combination ticket for all above 350Kč adults, 175Kč students without guide; 440Kč adults, 265Kč students with English-speaking guide. Ticket is valid for 2 days. Apr–Oct daily 9am–5pm (Nov–Mar till 4pm). Metro: line A Malostranská, then tram no. 22 or 23.

➜ **Jewish Museum** An incredible collection of Judaica, which, along with the neighboring synagogues and the Old Jewish Cemetery, make up the heart of the Jewish Quarter tour. Even more incredibly, the museum treasures were assembled by Hitler, who intended it to be an exhibit on an extinct race. *U Starého hřbitova; the entrance is from Široká 3.* ☎ 222-317-191. *www.jewishmuseum.cz. Admission 300Kč adults, 200Kč students. Apr–Oct Sun–Fri 9am–6pm; Nov–Mar Sun–Fri 9am–4:30pm. Metro: line A to Staroměstská.*

Best **FREE** ➜ **Charles Bridge** ★★ Prague's most celebrated structure, the Charles Bridge links Prague Castle to Staré Město. For most of its 600 years, the 510m-long (1,700-ft.) span has been a pedestrian promenade, though for centuries walkers had to share the concourse with horse-drawn vehicles and trolleys. Today, the bridge is filled with folks walking among artists and busking musicians. The best times to stroll across the bridge are early morning and around sunset, when the crowds have thinned and the shadows are more mysterious. *Karlův most. Free admission. Daily 24 hr. Metro: line A to Staroměstská.*

➜ **Church of St. Nicholas** This church is one of the best examples of high baroque north of the Alps. However, K. I. Dienzenhofer's 1711 design didn't have the massive dome that now dominates the Lesser Town skyline below Prague Castle. Dienzenhofer's son, Kryštof, added the 78m-high (260-ft.) dome during additional work completed in 1752. Smog has played havoc with the exterior, yet the gilded interior is stunning. Gold-capped marble-veneered columns frame altars packed with statuary and frescoes. A

ᴹ ᵀ ᵛ 🎓 The University Scene

Founded in the 1300s, the **University of Prague** (also called Charles University) is one of the oldest in Europe and it has a long history of famous professors and students to show for it—Jan Hus and Albert Einstein once taught here. Drop by the main info building (Celetná 13; ☎ 224/491-850; www.cuni.cz/iis) for info on the international exchange program.

If you'd rather mingle with students off campus, collegiate elbow rubbing is inevitable if you drop by **Jo's Bar** (Malostranské náměstí 7; ☎ 290-011-612; tram: 12, 22, or 23; night tram: 57 to Malostranské náměstí) during the daylight hours. This was once the only place in Prague for foreigners jonesing for nachos and free coffee refills. The quiet back room, done up in ochre and whatever someone didn't need when they moved, is a natural conversation pit.

Café Konvikt (Bartolomějská 11; ☎ 224-232-427; Mon–Fri 9am–1am, Sat–Sun noon–1am; metro: line B to Národní třída), just off the main drag that encircles Old Town, is where young Czech loafers head to peruse magazines and get their caffeine fixes. This place is also more chat-friendly by day, with big pools of sunlight streaming in, friendly service, and mismatched junk-shop tables and chairs.

Káva Káva Káva (Národní třída 37; ☎ 224-228-862; metro: line B to Národní třída), hidden in a courtyard just off gallery-heavy Národní, is a quiet patio cafe that's a magnet for local creatives who are serious coffee junkies, with a global bean selection, a dozen teas, and massive carrot cake slices.

About the only 24-hour pub in the vicinity of Old Town is **U Kotvy** (Spálená 11; ☎ 224-930-768; metro: line A or B to Můstek, all-night tram to Lazarská crossroads on Spálená). Hopefully it won't be raining when you go—the beer garden out back is much nicer than the smoky front room, which is perpetually filled with pasty-faced alcoholic zombie locals (read: students).

giant statue of the church's namesake looks down from the high altar. *Malostranské nám. 1* ☎ *257-534-215. www.psalterium.cz. Admission 50Kč adults, 25Kč students; concerts 390Kč. Daily 9am–5pm; till 4pm in winter season; concerts are usually held at 5pm. Metro: line A to Malostranská.*

→**Old Town Hall** ★ Crowds congregate in front of Old Town Hall's astronomical clock *(orloj)* to watch the glockenspiel spectacle that occurs hourly from 8am to 8pm. Built in 1410, the clock has long been an important symbol of Prague. It's not possible to determine the time of day from this timepiece; you have to look at the clock on the very top of Old Town Hall's tower for that. This astronomical clock, with all its hands and markings, is meant to mark the phases of the moon,

the equinoxes, the seasons, the days, and numerous Christian holidays. When the clock strikes the hour, a kind of politically incorrect medieval morality play begins. Two doors slide open and the statues of the 12 apostles glide by, while the 15th-century conception of the "evils" of life—a Death skeleton, a preening Vanity, a corrupt Turk, and an acquisitive figure of Greed—shake and dance below. *Staroměstské nám.* ☎ *724-508-584. www.pis.cz. Admission to tower 50Kč adults; 40Kč students, children under 10, and seniors. Mar–Oct Mon 11am–6pm, Tues–Sun 9am–6pm; Nov–Feb Mon 11am–5pm, Tues–Sun 9am–5pm. Metro: line A to Staroměstská.*

FREE →**Vyšehrad** An open-air park and assembly of ruins that mark the original seat of the pagan Bohemian royals (one of which was

PRAGUE

Libuše, famous for chucking ex-lovers into the Vltava River below), this national cemetery lies within an ancient citadel on the east side of the Vltava. It's the final resting place of some 600 honored Czechs, including composers Antonín Dvořák and Bedřich Smetana and Art Nouveau painter Alfons Mucha. The complex of churches and gardens is a pleasant getaway from the city crush. *Soběslavova 1.* ☎ *241-410-348. www.praha-vysehrad.cz. Free admission. Daily 24 hr. Tram: 3 or 16 from Karlovo náměstí to Výtoň south of New Town.*

Museums

→ **Bertramka (W. A. Mozart Museum)** Mozart loved Prague, and when he visited, he often stayed at this villa owned by the Dušek family. Now a museum, it contains displays of his written work and his harpsichord. There's also a lock of Mozart's hair, encased in a cube of glass. Much of the Bertramka villa was destroyed by fire in the 1870s, but Mozart's rooms, where he finished composing the opera *Don Giovanni,* were miraculously left untouched. Chamber concerts are often held here, usually starting at 5pm. *Mozartova 169.* ☎ *257-318-461. www.bertramka.cz. Admission 110Kč adults, 80Kč students; concert tickets 350Kč adults, 250Kč students. Apr–Oct daily 9am–6pm; Nov–Mar 9:30am–4pm. Tram: 4, 6, 7, 9, 10, 14, or 16 from Anděl metro station.*

→ **Museum Kampa–Sovovy mlýny** This building on Kampa island served for most of its history, due to the location, as a mill. Throughout the centuries it was struck by floods, fires, and destructive wars. The premises underwent several transformations and reconstructions. In September 2003, the Sovovy mlýny was opened as a museum of modern art by Czech-born American Meda Mládková and her foundation. She has been collecting works of Czech and central European artists since the 1950s. Her dream came true when she presented the permanent exhibition of František Kupka's drawings and Otto Gutfreund's sculptures. *U Sovových mlýnů*

503/2. ☎ *257-286-147. www.museumkampa.cz. Admission 120Kč adults, 60Kč students. Daily 10am–6pm. Metro: line A to Malostranská.*

→ **National Museum** The National Museum, dominating upper Václavské náměstí, looks so much like an important government building that it even fooled the Soviet soldiers, who fired on it during their 1968 invasion, thinking it was the seat of government. If you look closely on the columns, you can still see shell marks. This grandiose statement of nationalist purpose opened in 1893, as the national revival gained momentum. The exterior is rimmed with names of the great and good of the homeland (albeit with several foreign guests such as astronomer Johannes Kepler). Inside the grand hall on the first floor is the lapidarium with statues depicting the most important figures in Czech history, including the Father of the Republic, Tomáš Masaryk. Also on the first floor is an exhaustive collection of minerals, rocks, and meteorites from the Czech and Slovak republics. *Václavské nám. 68.* ☎ *224-497-111. www.nm.cz. Admission 100Kč adults, 50Kč students; free for everyone 1st Mon of the month. May–Sept daily 10am–6pm; Oct–Apr daily 9am–5pm; closed 1st Tues of the month. Metro: line A or C to Muzeum.*

→ **Veletržní Palace-National Gallery Collection of Modern and Contemporary Art** This 1925 constructivist palace, built for trade fairs, was remodeled and reopened in December 1995 to hold the bulk of the National Gallery's collection of 20th-century works by Czech and other European artists. Three atrium-lit concourses provide a comfortable setting for some catchy and kitschy Czech sculpture and multimedia works. Alas, the best cubist works from Braque and Picasso, Rodin bronzes, and many other primarily French pieces have been relegated to the second floor. Other displays are devoted to peculiar works by Czech artists that demonstrate how creativity flowed even

12 Hours in Prague

1. **Make a noon visit to U medvídků.** Faced with the excruciating choice of which two or three pubs to hit out of the hundreds of good ones in Prague, you could do worse than this place. Central, cheap, with blissful South Bohemian Budvar brew, needed for christening any fast crawl through this city (p. 751).

2. **Take in the view at Café Slavia.** Just up Národní, once the literary heart of this literary town (though now overmodernized, to be sure), this is a fine spot for a Becherovka and castle/Vltava River view (p. 749).

3. **Chill at Kampa Park.** This open green space, just across the bridge from Café Slavia, is always good for spotting a neo-hippie drum jam (p. 737).

4. **Tour Prague Castle.** Experience Gothic wonder in Saint Vitus' Cathedral, followed by a trip out to the castle's overlooked northside garden, where you wind down the amazing maze of paths, fountains, and frescoes back to Malá Strana proper (p. 760)

5. **Splurge at Kampa Park (the restaurant).** If you're willing to spend a bit of cash, you can't miss primo seafood by the water's edge while gazing across at Old Town spires. See p. 747.

6. **Cross Charles Bridge.** Taking you back to Old Town, this beauty is an absolute must, and offers more neo-hippie guitar riffs.

7. **Hit another two or three pubs.** Choose any pub in Old Town and you can't really go wrong while you wait for the next stop to heat up.

8. **Get some glitzy disco action and veggie food at Radost/FX, an all-in-one emporium.** If you survive both, and still wake up in time for brunch, get it at the next stop.

9. **Grab a nourishing meal of latte, eggs, hash browns, and muffins at Globe Bookstore and Coffeehouse.** On your way out, purchase a fine translation of Czech lit so you can begin reading up on all the over-whelming reasons to come back now that you've got real time to spend. See p. 757.

PRAGUE

under the weight of the Iron Curtain. The first floor features temporary exhibits from traveling shows. *Veletržní at Dukelských hrdinů 47.* ☎ *224-301-111. www.ngprague.cz. Admission 250Kč adults, 120Kč students for 4 floors of the palace; 200Kč adults, 100Kč students for 3 floors; 150Kč adults, 70Kč students for 2 floors; 100Kč adults, 50Kč students for 1 floor. Tues–Sun 10am–6pm. Metro: line C to Vltavská. Tram: 17.*

Playing Outside

Prague may just be the unhealthiest city in the world. It boasts the highest per-capita beer consumption globally, and if it's not in the top 10 for filterless cigarettes, there's been a serious miscalculation. Smoking is seen as the only reasonable defense against the disgusting air quality, the argument being that the lungs need "toughening up." Sunshine is so fleeting that Czechs tend to burn themselves deep brown when it appears, or give up on the sun entirely and go through life with a pasty "pub tan." Worry is a favorite national pastime, second only to scarfing down fried pork with mayonnaise.

Perhaps because of the above, a growing number of young Czechs are forswearing beer completely (those rebels!) and spending every other evening at the gym. Prague does have some large and lovely parks good for running or blading, namely Letná and Stromovka, but you still see a lot more dog-walkers than runners—so watch where you plant that Air Jordan.

One beauty that balances Prague's pollution is the [MTV Best] **Vltava River,** which manages such grace as it cuts between baroque facades in Old Town and Malá Strana that you forget all about what might be lurking beneath the surface. Rent an old rowboat from **Lávka** (Novotného lávka 1; ☎ 221-082-299; www.lavka.cz; 50Kč an hour; daily 10am–6pm daily in good weather; metro: line A to Staroměstská) and glide away. Just head through the 24-hour bar and club (p. 752) to the boat launch beneath the deck out back.

If that somehow just doesn't burn your carbs, by all means hit Letná to pick up a pair of inline skates at **SKALA SPORT** (Čechova 3; www.skalasport.wz.cz; inline skates 150Kč per day; Mon–Fri 10am–8pm, Sat 10am–4pm, Sun 10am–2pm; tram: 1, 8, 25, or 26) and cruise the paths under the shade trees, then reward yourself with one of the best views of Old Town from the giant ticking Metronome sculpture.

Stromovka Park (Výstaviště exhibition grounds; tram: 5, 12, or 25 to Výstaviště) is a flatter stretch of woods that used to be the personal hunting grounds of the mad Emperor Rudolf II. It now makes for pretty running scenery. Unlike their American counterparts, these parks almost never have muggings.

To join the pack at bench pressing, try the fitness center and swimming pool at **Hotel Axa** (Na Poříčí 40; ☎ 222-323-967; 1Kč per minute; Mon–Fri 6–9am, noon–1pm, and 5–10pm; Sat–Sun 9am–9pm; metro: line B to náměstí Republiky).

For a far more typical Prague sporting experience, try pub bowling at **Kuželky** (Na Bělidle 25; no phone; 280Kč per hour for four players; daily 4pm–2am; metro: line B to Anděl). It's out of the way in the Smíchov district, but these bowling simulators are a trip. They also have darts, and the brews flow cheaply here. Hopefully, you'll never even break a sweat.

Shopping

Shopping in Prague is an experience that has traumatized more than a few, including veteran travelers. Most shop clerks here have proven themselves to be amazingly resilient to the tenets of capitalism and have managed to hold onto their jobs without compromising their rudeness or laziness one iota. The pre–Velvet Revolution idea that a customer is an annoyance still seems to hold sway in most of the city's stores.

One change for the better is that you can finally find just about anything you need here, including such once-impossible-to-get goods as vintage vinyl, trash fashion, and cool tunes, plus the traditional wonder fruits of the Havelská Street open market.

Shops in the center of town keep fairly long hours. Most are open Monday to Friday from about 9am to 6pm and Saturday from 9am to 1pm, but sometimes later. Malls, supermarkets, and bigger shops open on Sundays,too.

→ **Bontonland Megastore** The hottest names in Czech radio, from Lucie Bílá to Kabát, can be found at the bottom of Wenceslas Square. This store's three levels of rock, jazz, classical, and videos contain every significant and insignificant Czech recording imaginable, including some amazing deals on the local Supraphon classics label. *Václavské nám. 1.* ☎ *224-473-080. www.bontonland.cz. Metro: line A or B to Můstek.*

➜ **Fashion Gallery** ★ This is a place to catch the latest creations of Prague's top fashion designers, led by Helena Fejková, who has joined forces with a handful of others to open this glassed-in perch overlooking the 1920s-era Lucerna pasáž, a former shopping arcade glory of the First Republic on upper Wenceslas Square. Mousse and java are served to bored boyfriends and sugar daddies while their model girlfriends run rampant. *Štěpánská 61.* ☎ *224-211-514. www. helenafejkova.cz. Metro: line A or B to Můstek.*

➜ **Gigasport** With row upon row of clothes and equipment, Gigasport is Prague's mega–sporting goods retailer. However, the prices aren't much better than what you'd find abroad, and the company's overzealous security staff forces you to park all your belongings in cubbyholes (they'll help you to get the correct change, though). *Palác Myslbek, Na Příkopě 19.* ☎ *224-233-552. www. gigasport-cr.cz. Metro: line A or B to Můstek.*

➜ **Maximum Underground** It doesn't just stock all the vinyl jungle and breakbeat you can shake a deck at; they also carry second-hand leathers, pullovers, and pants. If the

---

Modification

What better souvenir of Prague is there than a nice Radegast beer logo tattooed on your chest? The tattoo studio inside **Maximum Underground** (see above) is certainly up to the task, and it can also provide any piercings you may need. It's a definite favorite among the pomo crowd, with a list of satisfied customers that includes as many Czechs as foreigners.

---

tracks you crave aren't here, they're certainly at the **Radost/FX** music shop (p. 752). *Jilská 22.* ☎ *604-873-558 (cell). www.maximum.cz. Metro: line A or B to Můstek.*

➜ **Mystic SK8s** The city's best selection of skateboards and snowboards is available at this conveniently located store. Baggy trousers and cool accessories are also on display. *Štěpánská 31.* ☎ *222-232-027. Metro: line A or C to Muzeum.*

➜ **Taiza** Since Osmany Laffita, a Cuban wizard of fashion, opened his first boutique in Prague in 1999, he has also established his name in Paris and New York. He sticks to his motto, "Be unique, be desired, and stay elegant!" and is celebrating a huge success. He is the personal designer for former first lady Mrs. Havel, and is very popular among Czech actresses. *At Millennium Plaza, V Celnici 10.* ☎ *257-315-487. www.taiza.com. Metro: line B to náměstí Republiky.*

Bazaars & Markets

Perhaps the proudest of all Czech traditions is haggling over potatoes. Large numbers of Bohemian housewives have been known to go as far as Poland to buy them for a few hellers (a few hundredths of a crown) less than their local grocer charges. You only have to go as far as **Havelský Trh (Havel's Market).** In the heart of the Old Town, you'll find killer deals on mountain honey, fresh strawberries, and blueberries on any midsummer morning. By afternoon, the trade has usually changed to handmade wooden toys, bad art, and linens. For true junk, you'll need to hit the bazaar or *vetešnictví,* as secondhand shops are known here.

➜ **Art Deco Galerie** This dandy store sells the trappings of Prague's golden age and is filled with colored perfume bottles and clothing from the 1920s and 1930s. Furniture and household items include Art Deco clocks and lamps. *Michalská 21.* ☎ *224-223-076. Metro: line A or B to Můstek.*

➔ **Bazaar P&J-P.Truhlář** At this bazaar, you'll find everything from discarded portraits of first working-class President Klement Gottwald to a nice hefty *džbán* (beer jug) for your mantelpiece. It's located in Vinohrady (away from the center and not overpriced!). *Anny Letenské.* ☎ *224-250-172. Metro: line A to náměstí Míru.*

Shopping Malls

➔ **Obchodní Centrum Nový Smíchov** This modern mall built on the defunct site of one of the city's most famous factories is Prague's new temple to post-communist consumption. In just a few-minutes metro ride from Old Town or Malá Strana, you can leave all the city's history behind and shop till you drop (with many things still much cheaper than you would find in western Europe or the U.S.). The mighty Tatra Smíchov heavy machine plant once stood in this old workers' neighborhood, and the front wall of the factory has been incorporated into the facade of the mall. Here, the French retail hypermarket Carrefour now draws Czechs in the thousands. On the three levels of surrounding concourses, international jeans shops stand shoulder to shoulder with fashion and cosmetic boutiques like **Zara, Marella,** and **Body Basics.** Sport shops include **Quicksilver** with all skateboarding must-haves. Entertainment offerings include a multiplex cinema screening international films dubbed or subtitled in Czech, plus arcade games, billiards, cafes, fast food, and full menu restaurants. *Plzeňská 8.* ☎ *251-511-151. www.novysmichovoc.cz. Metro: line B to Anděl.*

Road Trip

If you have time for only one day trip, consider making it 📺 Best **Český Krumlov,** 96 miles (155km) south of Prague. One of Bohemia's prettiest towns, Krumlov is a living gallery of elegant Renaissance-era buildings housing charming cafes, pubs, restaurants, shops, and galleries. In 1992, UNESCO named Český Krumlov a World Heritage Site for its historic importance and physical beauty.

Bustling since medieval times, the town is still exquisitely beautiful after centuries of embellishment. In 1302, the Rožmberk family inherited the castle and used it as their main residence for nearly 300 years. Looking out from the Lazebnický bridge, with the waters of the Vltava below snaking past the castle's gray stone, you'll feel that time has stopped. At night, with the castle lit up, the view becomes even more dramatic.

Avoiding the Crowds

Consider yourself warned: Word has spread about Český Krumlov. The summer high season can be unbearable, as thousands of visitors blanket its medieval streets. If possible, try to visit in the off season—we suggest autumn to take advantage of the colorful surrounding hills—when the crowds recede, the prices decrease, and the town's charm can really shine.

For more details about the town go to **www.ckrumlov.cz.**

Getting into Town

The only way to reach Český Krumlov **by train** from Prague is via České Budějovice, a slow ride that deposits you at a station relatively far from the town center (trip time: $3^2/_5$–$4^1/_5$ hr.). Seven trains leave daily from Prague's Hlavní nádraží, and the fare is 224Kč. For timetables, go to **www.jizdnirady.cz.**

By car from Prague, it's a 2-hour drive down Highway 3 through Tábor and České Budějovice.

Tourist Office

On the main square, in a renovated Renaissance building, the **Infocentrum** (náměstí Svornosti 2, Český Krumlov; ☎ **380-704-621**) offers a complete array of services from booking accommodations to ticket reservations for events, as well as a phone and fax service. It's open daily 9am to 6pm (Apr–May and Oct), 9am to 7am (June and Sept), 9am to 8pm (July–Aug), and 9am to 5pm (Nov–Mar). For more information about Český Krumlov visit its well-organized website (**www.ckrumlov.cz**), which features a very cool interactive map of the city.

Top Attractions & Special Moments

Bring a good pair of walking shoes and be prepared to wear them out. Český Krumlov not only lends itself to hours of strolling, but its hills and alleyways demand it. No cars, thank goodness, are allowed in the historic town, and the cobblestones keep most other vehicles at bay. The town is split into two parts—the Inner town and Latrán, which houses the city's famous castle. They're best tackled separately, so you won't have to crisscross the bridges several times.

Seeing the Cesk; Krumlov Chateau

Reputedly the second-largest castle in Bohemia (after Prague Castle), the Český Krumlov Château was constructed in the 13th century as part of a private estate. Throughout the ages, it has passed to a variety of private owners, including the Rožmberk family, Bohemia's largest landholders, and the Schwarzenbergs, the Bohemian equivalent of *Dynasty*'s Carrington family. Perched high atop a rocky hill, the château is open from April to October only, exclusively by guided tours.

Follow the path at the entrance for the long climb up to the castle and you'll be greeted by a round 12th-century tower—painstakingly renovated—with a Renaissance balcony. You'll pass over the moat, now occupied by two brown bears. Beyond it is the **Dolní Hrad (Lower Castle)** and then the **Horní Hrad (Upper Castle)**. There are 2 guided tours. The first tour begins in the rococo **Chapel of St. George,** and continues through the portrait-packed **Renaissance Rooms,** and the **Schwarzenberg Baroque Suite,** outfitted with ornate furnishings that include Flemish wall tapestries, European paintings, and also the extravagant 17th-century **Golden Carriage.** The second tour includes the **Schwarzenberg portrait gallery** as well as their 19th-century suite. Tours last 1 hour and depart frequently. Most are in Czech or German, however. If you want an English-language tour, arrange it ahead of time (☎ **380-704-721;** www.ckrumlov.cz). The guided tours cost 160Kč adults and 80Kč students for Tour I; 140Kč adults and 70Kč students for Tour II. The tickets are sold separately. The castle hours are from Tuesday to Sunday: June to August 9am to 6pm; April, May, September, and October 9am to 5pm (no Tour II in Apr). The last entrance is 1 hour before closing.

Tip: Once past the main castle building, you can see one of the more stunning views of Český Krumlov from **Most Na Plášti,** a walkway that doubles as a belvedere over the Inner Town. Even farther up the hill lies the castle's riding school and gardens.

PRAGUE

Begin at the **Okresní Muzeum (Regional Museum;** ☎ 380-711-674**)** at the top of Horní ulice and to the right of the Main Square. Once a Jesuit seminary, the three-story museum now contains artifacts and displays relating to Český Krumlov's 1,000-year history. The highlight of this mass of folk art, clothing, furniture, and statues is a giant model of the town that offers a bird's-eye view of the buildings. Admission is 50Kč, and it's open daily 10am to 5pm (May–June and Sept), 10am to 6pm (July–Aug); from Tuesday to Friday 9am to 4pm and Saturday through Sunday from 1 to 4pm (Apr and Oct–Dec).

Across the street is the **Hotel Růže (Rose),** which was once a Jesuit student house. Built in the late 16th century, the hotel and the prelature next to it show the development of architecture in the city—Gothic, Renaissance, and rococo influences are all present. Continue down the street to the impressive late Gothic **St. Vitus Cathedral.** Be sure to climb the church tower, which offers one of the most spectacular views of both the Inner Town and the castle across the river.

As you continue down the street, you'll come to **náměstí Svornosti.** For such an impressive town, the main square is a little disappointing, with few buildings of any character. The **Radnice (Town Hall),** at náměstí Svornosti 1, is one of the few exceptions. Its Gothic arcades and Renaissance vault inside are exceptionally beautiful in this otherwise run-down area. From the square, streets fan out in all directions. Take some time just to wander through them.

One of Český Krumlov's most famous residents was Austrian-born 20th-century artist Egon Schiele. He was a bit of an eccentric who, on more than one occasion, raised the ire of the town's residents (many were distraught with his use of their young women as his nude models); his stay was cut short when residents' patience ran out. But the town readopted the artist in 1993, setting up the **Egon Schiele Foundation** and

the **Egon Schiele Centrum** in Inner Town (Široká 70–72, Český Krumlov; ☎ 380-704-011). The center documents his life and work, housing a permanent selection of his paintings as well as exhibitions of other 20th-century artists. Admission is 180Kč adults, 105Kč students. It's open daily from 10am to 6pm.

For a different perspective on what the town looks like, take the stairs from the **Městské divadlo (Town Theater)** on Horní ulice down to the riverfront and rent a boat from **Maleček boat rentals** (Rooseveltova 28; ☎ 380-712-508; www.malecek.cz) for 400Kč per half-hour. Always willing to lend his advice, the affable Pepa Maleček will tell you what to watch out for and where the best fishing is (no matter how many times you say that you don't want to fish!).

Sleeping & Eating

Hotels are sprouting up, or are getting a "new" old look; PENSION and ZIMMER FREI signs line Horní and Rooseveltova streets and offer some of the best values in town. For a comprehensive list of area hotels and help with bookings, call or write the Infocentrum listed above.

We recommend **Hotel Konvice** (Horní ul. 144; ☎ 380-711-611) as a good-value choice. If you can get a room with a view out the back, take it immediately. Rooms themselves are small but clean and comfortable, with nice parquet floors and well-appointed bathrooms. As you overlook the river and the castle on the opposite bank, you'll wonder why people would stay anywhere else. Rates are 1,500Kč to 1,800Kč for a double; 1,800Kč to 2,700Kč for a suite. Breakfast is included. The hotel has a restaurant and a terrace, and each room has a TV.

If you like more ancient ambience, book yourself in **Pension Ve Věži (In the Tower;** Pivovarská 28, Český Krumlov; ☎ 380-711-742; www.ckrumlov.cz/pensionvevezi). This renovated medieval tower, just a 5-minute walk from the castle, is one of the most magnificent places to stay in town. It's not the accommodations themselves that are so grand (none has a bathroom and all are sparsely decorated) but the unique building. Rates are 1,200Kč for a double; 1,800Kč for a quad. The rates include breakfast. The hotel has a bar; two rooms share bathrooms with showers. Each room has its own minibar.

Also convenient is one of the best hostels in the city center, the **Travellers' Hostel** (Soukenická 43; ☎ **380-711-345;** www. travellers.cz). This tastefully renovated building from the 13th century offers clean rooms with private or shared facilities for very competitive prices. A double costs 340Kčý a four-bed apartment is 450Kč per person. Breakfast is also included.

For a typical Czech dining experience visit **Hospoda Na louži** (Kájovská 66; ☎ **380-711-280**), which offers diners good value for their money. The large wooden tables encourage you to get to know your neighbors in this Inner Town pub, located in a 15th-century house near the main square. The atmosphere is fun and the food is above average. If no table is available, stand and have a drink; the seating turnover is pretty fast, and the staff is accommodating. Main courses cost 58Kč to 158Kč. They're open Monday to Saturday 10am to 11pm and Sunday 10am to 10pm.

Located in the former cooling room of the local Eggenberg Brewery near the castle, **Restaurant Eggenberg** (Latrán 27; ☎ **380-711-761**), is one of the few big beer halls in town, with some of the freshest drafts anywhere. Traditional meat-and-dumplings-style Czech food is augmented by vegetarian dishes. Main courses cost 80Kč to 195Kč.

PRAGUE

Reykjavík

Visiting Iceland is like embarking on a trip to another planet. The island is left-over lava from an underwater volcano that erupted thousands of years ago, and the land is essentially dark red, moss-covered soil dotted with craters. Steam from geysers and hot springs emerges in puffs across the landscape, and the smell of sulfur lurks persistently. Cross the Arctic Circle in the north and you've entered the Land of the Midnight Sun, home to the spectacular Northern Lights and a summer sun that lingers above the horizon so long that night turns into day.

But geography's not the only thing that makes the country unusual. Iceland is one of the most prosperous nations on earth, with both the longest life expectancy and the highest standard of living—all this with extensive social welfare programs. It's the only member of NATO with neither an army nor a navy. The population is almost 100% literate and reads more books per capita than anyone else on the planet. And did I mention that Iceland elected the world's first woman president? They did: a whopping four times in a row.

And then there's the Icelandic people (all 300,000 of 'em): descended from the Vikings and speaking a language (Icelandic) that has barely changed over the past few thousand years. Icelanders are surprisingly friendly, trendy, and modern (think of the musician, Björk, and Reykjavík's notoriously wild pub-crawls). A short flight away from several northern European capitals, Iceland is an escape from the some-times overwhelming tourist crowds in the rest of the continent. Not to mention, it's an outdoors person's dream: from pony-trekking to skiing. You may wish you hadn't booked your return ticket.

The Best of Reykjavík

○ **The Best Cheap Meal:** Late-night hot dogs from **Bæjarins Bestu** come loaded with various toppings. The fried onions are particularly good. See p. 778.

○ **The Best Organic Cafe: Kaffi Hljomalind** in the center of town is totally unpretentious with a laid-back vibe and delicious organic eats such as pasta dishes and pies. The crowd mainly consists of New Age hippie types, mothers with young children, and serious-looking intellectuals. See p. 779.

○ **The Best Drink Specials:** In a city where you may be reduced to buying duty free at the airport just to save money on your buzz, the three-for-one early-bird deals at **Café Cozy** are justifiably popular. See p. 780.

○ **The Best Outdoor Activity:** Despite having to don a silly, big, red suit to keep warm, you can't do better than **whale-watching.** Three-hour tours start at 3,700ISK. Visit the tour companies at Aegisgarder harbor for details. See p. 784.

○ **The Best Way to Warm Up:** For a truly surreal experience, take a dip in the **Blue Lagoon** (www.bluelagoon.is). It's out of

Where Are the Trees?

When Iceland's settlers first arrived in the 9th century, they wrote of a land covered with trees. But over centuries, most of the forest was chopped down for timber and firewood, and volcanic eruptions and grazing sheep prevented new trees from taking root. Today, Iceland is attempting to reverse this trend, and the country now plants more trees per capita than any other: about 16 trees per inhabitant per year. Due to the harsh climate, the hardy dwarf spruce is usually the tree of choice; resulting in the common joke that goes, "What do you do if you get lost in an Icelandic forest?" Answer: "Stand up."

the way and expensive (day tours start at around 3,300ISK) but definitely worth the effort. See p. 786.

Getting There & Getting Around

Getting into Town

BY AIR

Flights land in **Keflavik Airport,** about 50km (31 miles) from Reykjavík. (*Tip:* Before leaving the airport, consider whether you plan on doing any drinking while in Iceland and, if so, stock up on affordable alcohol in the duty-free shop; prices in the city are appalling.) To get into Reykjavík from the airport, take the **Flybus** (www.re.is) from outside the terminal. The fare is 1,150ISK, and the bus stops at the BSI bus terminal, major hotels, and the youth hostel. If the Flybus doesn't stop near your hotel, you'll probably want to pay for a taxi from the bus terminal (see below).

BY TAXI

Taxis will cost you here. But Reykjavík is small enough that nearly all the fun stuff is within walking distance, so the only time you might want to consider taking a taxi is if you are dropped off at the BSI bus terminal upon your arrival in town. From there, a taxi into town will cost around 750ISK. To call a cab, try **BSR Taxis** (☎ 354/561-0000) or **Hreyfill-Bæjarleiir** (☎ 354/588-5522).

Getting Around

BY CAR

Take special care when driving in Iceland: roads are often rough and narrow, and weather conditions can make driving especially hazardous. Several car-rental agencies have locations both in town and at Keflavik airport. Rates vary considerably but start at around 4,300ISK per day. If you're flush, rent a four-wheel drive to make the rough ride a bit more fun. **ALP Car Rental** (Vatnsmýrarvegur 10; ☎ 354/562-6060; www.alp.is) near the BSI terminal, and **Atlantis Car Rental** (Grensásvegur 14; ☎ **354/588-0000**; www.atlantisiceland.com) have them. Other rentals include **AVIS Car Rental** (Knarrarvogi 2; ☎ 354/591-4000; www.avis.is), **Budget Car Rental** (Malarhöfði 2; ☎ 354/567-8300; www.budget.is), and **Hertz Car Rental** (Flugvallarvegur; ☎ 354/505-0600; www.hertz.is). Be forewarned: Driving and drinking don't mix, especially in as small a place as Iceland.

BY BUS

You probably won't need to take the bus to explore Reykjavík. The efficient buses run every 20 to 30 minutes. Schedule and route information is available at the main bus hub in Lækjartorg or at the tourist office. The fare is 220ISK for adults, or you can buy a block of nine tickets from 1,500ISK. Also consider purchasing a **Reykjavík Tourist Card** (p. 782). Be sure to ask for a transfer if you will be changing buses.

Reykjavík Excursions, BSI Bus Terminal (☎ **354/562-1011**; www.re.is) offers a 2$^1/_2$- to 3-hour bus tour of the city for 3,100ISK.

BY BICYCLE

Reykjavík is a bike-friendly city with lots of bike paths. You can ride on sidewalks and footpaths. **Borngarhjol (The City Bicycle;** ☎ **354/551-5653;** www.rent-a-bike) rents bikes at Hverfisgata 50. Prices run 1,550ISK for a half-day and 1,770ISK for a full day. For a guided bike tour, try one of the easy 3-hour options run by **Blue Biking** (Stekkjarhvammur 60; ☎ **354/565-2089;** www.simnet.is/bluebiking). Sure, you can take the regular city tour, but why not go for the volcano and lava tour.

ON FOOT

This is the best way to get around, so long as the weather holds out. You can pick up a **City Walks map** at the tourist information center on Adalstræti 2.

Reykjavík Basics

Orientation: Reykjavík Neighborhoods

Reykjavík is small and easy to navigate. The main part of the city is bordered by Hringraut to the south, Snorrbraut to the east, Sæbraut to the north along the water, and Tjarnargata to the west. The main street, running east to west across the city, is Laugavegur, a hub lined with shops, cafes, restaurants, and bars. The town's action swirls around this central area. Lots of restaurants and cafes, as well as most of the clubs and bars, can be found around Austurstræti, Hafnarstræti, and their side streets.

Tourist Offices

Grapevine Information, downstairs at Laugavegur 11 (no phone; www.grapevine.is)

is a great little place where the friendly staff provides information on Reykjavík culture and nightlife, with an emphasis on the local music scene. You can pick up Icelandic music and literature here. Hours are Monday to Saturday, noon to 10pm.

The main tourist information office is at Adalstræti 2. They offer a ton of brochures and helpful information; the **City Center Booking Service** in the same building (☎ **354/562-1818;** www.visitreykjavik.is) can book tours, accommodations, and car rentals. Hours are daily from 8:30am to 7pm in the summer; shorter hours the rest of the year. There is also a small branch of the office in the arrivals hall at the airport.

The travel agency **Iceland Visitor** (Lækjargata 2; ☎ **354/511-2442;** www.iceland

Talk of the Town

Four ways to start a conversation with a local

1. **What about those stories about Icelandic genetics?** A private company was granted the exclusive right to construct a database with access to every Icelander's health records. The people on the island, whose ancestors settled here 1,000 years ago, voted it in, but there's a debate on what the potential abuses might be. Check out www.decode.is for the latest developments on how genetic sampling of this very pure population is affecting the development of new drugs.

2. **How crazy do you get in the winter?** It might not be the politest way to strike up a conversation, but you could get an earful.

3. **Why is everyone so gorgeous here?** One common theory begins: "Well, the Vikings stole all of the beautiful women from Europe and brought them to Iceland . . ." It's best to agree; obvious flattery rarely fails.

4. **Should the U.S. military stay in Iceland even though the Cold War ended years ago?** Enough said.

visitor.com) books tours and accommodations and offers visitors helpful travel advice. Their hours are 9am to 10pm June to August and 10am to 6pm the rest of the year. Note that at press time they were at the address above, but they will be moving.

Recommended Websites

○ **www.whatson.is**: This is a good place to find out anything and everything you'll need to know about Reykjavík, from info on accommodations, restaurants, museums, and transportation to a handy events calendar.

○ **www.icetourist.is**: This site has good detailed practical information on traveling to Iceland.

○ **www.visitorsguide.is**: This is the online version of a publication with the same name; both have info on restaurants, attractions, and nightlife.

○ **www.visitreykjavik.is**: Reykjavík's tourist information center can be reached online here.

○ **www.icelandreview.com**: This online English-language magazine has features, news, and arts and entertainment listings.

○ **www.coupons.is**: This site provides coupons for restaurants, accommodations, and travel services in Iceland.

Culture Tips 101

The legal minimum drinking age is 20, but some clubs impose a 22-and-over rule on certain nights. Drinking on the street is not allowed, but this rule is frequently broken once the bars and clubs let out early on a weekend morning.

Illegal drug laws are strict here, both at Customs and in the city. Drug use is well hidden from the public eye in Reykjavík. Just a few years ago, some of the clubs had a reputation for being rife with drugs. But the word on the street is that drug use is down here as a result of increased enforcement and also simply because it's going out of style. The locals also stress that you may be hassled at Customs if you look suspicious and/or your flight originated in naughty Amsterdam. Travelers flying through Iceland from Europe to North America should note that a stamp in your passport from Amsterdam (or anywhere in the Netherlands) is a red flag for Customs officials.

Recommended Books, Movies & Music

BOOKS

Halldor Laxness, a Nobel Prize—winning author, wrote many novels about his native country. *Independent People* shows a few islanders as clearly as an anthropological study, while *The Atom Station* (1983) confronts the U.S. military base on the island.

Jon Kraukauer became famous writing about the tragedies on Mt. Everest, but his work is just as good when examining Iceland, especially when paired with the underexposed and excellent writings of David Roberts in their book *Iceland: Land of the Sagas* (reprint edition, 1998). Before Mark Kurlansky wrote *Salt,* he researched and wrote *Cod,* which takes his readers to many places, including Iceland.

To really dig deep while here, turn to the 12th- to 13th-century sagas, epic poems of battle, exploration, and mythology.

MUSIC

Anything by Björk, especially *Debut.* Also check out the Sugarcubes, Björk's band before she went solo and Sigur Rós, Iceland's version of Pink Floyd, complete with epic songs to match this land's penchant for sagas. The rap-rock band Quarashi is good as is the trio Múm, an electronica group that uses analogue and digital technologies with warm melodies and vocals. Reykjavík's music scene is a nursery of musicians who take chances and sometimes come out on top.

MOVIES

While horror hit *Hostel* (2005) didn't take place in Iceland, the character of drunken sex-maniac, Oli, caused director Eli Roth to ask the president of Iceland for an official pardon for making Icelanders look bad. Roth also formally apologized to the Icelandic minister of culture, for any damage the movie might do to Iceland's reputation. *Gargandi snilld* (2005) is a slight but entertaining documentary about many of the well-known bands to have come out of Iceland in recent years. Big surprise: Globetrotting 007 traveled to Iceland in 2002's *Die Another Day.* And in *No Such Thing* (2001) directed by Hal Hartley, a journalist travels to Iceland to track down her boyfriend only to be drawn into a strange friendship with a allegorical, murderous monster. Most of this film was shot on location.

Reykjavík Nuts & Bolts

Cellphone Providers & Service Centers   Iceland's three GSM operators, Iceland Telecom, Islandssimi, and TAL, cover most of the country, including all towns and villages with more than 200 inhabitants. All three sell prepaid GSM phone cards and offer GSM/GPRS services. Prepaid cards are available at gas stations around the country from 50ISK. GSM phones may be rented from **Iceland Telecom** (Ármúli 27; ☎ **354/800-7000;** www.simi.is). For those traveling in Iceland's more remote areas, ask Iceland Telecom about their NMT long-range mobile service.

Currency   The Icelandic monetary unit is the Icelandic króna. All Icelandic banks provide foreign exchange and are generally open weekdays from 9:15am to 4pm.

Embassies   The embassy of **Canada** is at Túngata 14 (☎ **354/575-6500**), the **U.K.** embassy is at Laufásvegur 31 (☎ **354/550-5100**) and **U.S.** citizens should head to Laufásvegur 21 (☎ **354/562-9100**).

Emergencies   In an emergency, dial ☎ 112. For non-emergency police, dial ☎ 569-9000. The **National University Hospital** is on Fossvogur (☎ 354/543-2000). For dental emergencies, call ☎ 354/575-0505.

Internet/Wireless Hot Spots   Wireless Internet is available virtually (ha) everywhere in the city. The tourist information center (Adalstræti 2; ☎ 354/562-1818; www.visitreykjavik.is; Mon–Fri 9am–6pm, Sat–Sun 9am–2pm), has an Internet cafe upstairs. Buy a card at the main desk downstairs. A half-hour is 350ISK; an hour is 500ISK. The time on the card is valid for 1 year.

Laundromats   Try **Laundry Service** (Vesturgata 12; ☎ 354/562-6820).

Luggage Storage   Available at the **BSI** bus terminal (☎ 354/591-1000) at a charge of 500ISK per day. Hours are daily 7:30am to 10pm.

Pharmacies   Pharmacies are called *Apóteks*. They are found throughout the city and are open during normal business hours; some are open at night as well. **Lyfja** (Lágmúli 7; ☎ 354/533-2300) is open daily 9am to midnight.

Passports & Visas   To enter Iceland, you need to have a passport valid at least 3 months beyond your intended stay. Most people are not required to have a visa.

Post Offices   The Central Post Office is on Posthusstraeti (at the corner of Austursraeti; ☎ 354/580-1101). Hours are Monday to Friday from 9am to 4:30pm. A postcard to Europe costs 60ISK; to North America, 90ISK.

Restrooms   You'll find public, coin-op toilets on the street.

Safety   Reykjavík is generally a safe city, and Iceland enjoys a very low crime rate. That being said, it's always a good idea to be aware of your surroundings, avoid dodgy-looking folks, and look both ways before crossing the street.

Telephone Tips   Pay phones are few and far between in Reykjavík. If you can find one, you can pay with a phone card (available at post offices) or coins. The country code for Iceland is **354**. Local phone numbers are seven digits.

Tipping   In general, Icelanders only tip at more upscale restaurants and only if the service warrants it.

Sleeping

In Reykjavík, accommodations generally come three ways. First up, sleeping bag palaces, usually dorm-style setups with no sheets or blankets provided. Second are the guesthouses, like B&Bs: small, cozy places where someone takes the time to make you feel at home. Finally, there are the hotels, which are significantly more expensive yet often not worth the splurge. You can also find combos: for instance, a guesthouse that has sleeping bag rooms.

Note: In general, seasons are May 1 to September 30 for summer rates and October 1 through April 30 for winter rates.

Hostels

→ **Reykjavík City Hostel (HI)** A bit out of the way, and with the usual sterile, homogeneous environment common to most HIs, City Hostel makes its name with its proximity to Laugarsavegur thermal pool, perfect for warming up at the start or end of the day.

Sundlaugavegur 34. ☎ *354/553-8110. www. hostel.is. From 1,700ISK dorm bed, 6,800ISK double, 9,400ISK triple. Amenities: Internet; kitchen; laundry facilities; library; sauna; TV (in common room). Bus: 14.*

→ **Salvation Army Guesthouse** Definitely a no-frills place: The rooms are small, have a distinctly unpleasant smell, and you may have to wait to share one of the few bathrooms. And because it is a Salvation Army establishment, you have the added evangelical and shelter-like atmosphere; there are always some "interesting-looking" (that is, sketchy) folk hanging around the common area. The only real reason to stay here is if you insist on being within stumbling distance of the main bars. *Kirkjustraeti 2.* ☎ *354/561-3203. www.guesthouse.is. May–Sept 2,500ISK dorm bed, 5,500ISK single, 8,000ISK double, 10,500ISK triple; Oct–Apr 2,000ISK dorm bed, 5,000ISK single, 7,500ISK double, 9,800ISK triple. Rates include breakfast for private rooms; dorm room breakfast 700ISK. Amenities: Kitchen.*

Cheap

→ **Butterfly Guesthouse** This bright, cozy guesthouse is in a quiet area just a few minutes from the city center. Run by a couple who strives to give the place a homey feel by allowing guests free access to the kitchen, computer, and backyard. The rooms are small but clean with a shared bathroom, and there are also two apartments with a kitchenette and private bathroom. *Ránargata 8a.* ☎ *354/894-1864. www.kvasir.is/butterfly. Late May to Aug 31 6,400ISK single; 8,600ISK double, 9,400ISK with private bathroom; 13,900ISK family room (4 people) with private bathroom; 16,900ISK apt (4 people). Closed in winter. Amenities: Internet; kitchen; laundry.*

Doable

→ **Domus Guesthouse** Housed in what was formerly the Norwegian Embassy and

then became home to Iceland's top youth choir, rooms here are clean and nicely decorated, especially those on the top floor, which are spacious, have hand-carved furniture, and local art on the walls. The shared bathrooms are clean and numerous, and the staff is extremely accommodating; the owner often chats with guests at breakfast. More upscale rooms and apartments are also available through the guesthouse at their satellite locations. *Hverfisgata 45.* ☎ *354/561-1200. www.domusguesthouse.is. June 1–Sept 31 2,900ISK dorm bed, 9,500ISK single, 11,300ISK double, 15,200ISK triple; Oct 1–May 30 1,900ISK dorm bed, 5,900ISK single, 7,900ISK double, 10,800ISK triple. Rates include breakfast; dorm room breakfast 900ISK. Amenities: Kitchen.*

→ **Flóki Inn** Friendly owners have been making tourists feel at home in Reykjavík's oldest guesthouse for 40 years. In a quiet area a few minutes from the city center you'll find rooms that are large and bright and come with minifridges and clean shared bathrooms. *Flókagata 1.* ☎ *354/552-1155. www. innsoficeland.is/iceland_accommodation. html. May–Sept 7,500ISK single, 9,900ISK double; Oct–Apr 5,500ISK single, 6,900ISK double. Rates include breakfast. Amenities: Kitchen. In room: TV.*

Splurge

→ **Center Hotel Skaldbreið** This hotel has a great central location right on bustling Laugavegur. Rooms have private bathrooms, but are a bit small. *Laugavegur 16.* ☎ *354/595-8510. www.centerhotels.is. May–Sept 14,900ISK–19,900ISK single, 19,900ISK–23,900ISK double; Oct–Apr 9,000ISK–11,300ISK single, 11,300ISK–13,500ISK double. Rates include breakfast. Amenities: Laundry. In room: TV, Internet.*

→ **Hótel Leifur Eiríksson** More impressive from the outside with its upscale-looking building and a bit pretentious on the

Reykjavík

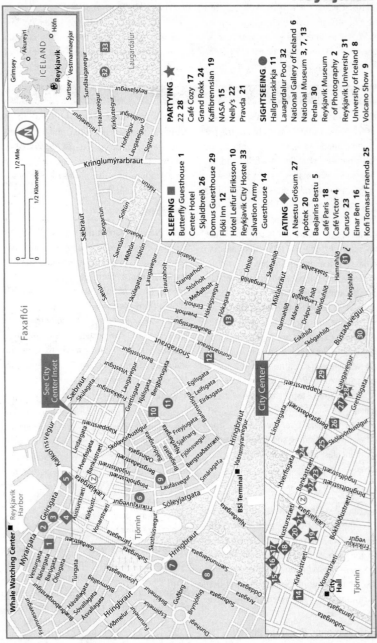

PARTYING ★
22 **28**
Café Cozy **17**
Grand Rokk **24**
Kaffibrennslan **19**
NASA **15**
Nelly's **22**
Pravda **21**

SIGHTSEEING ●
Hallgrímskirkja **11**
Lauagrdalur Pool **32**
National Gallery of Iceland **6**
National Museum 3, 7, **13**
Perlan **30**
Reykjavik Museum
  of Photography **2**
Reykjavik University **31**
University of Iceland **8**
Volcano Show **9**

SLEEPING ■
Butterfly Guesthouse **1**
Center Hotel
Skjaldbreið **26**
Domus Guesthouse **29**
Flóki Inn **12**
Hótel Leifur Eiríksson **10**
Reykjavik City Hostel **33**
Salvation Army
  Guesthouse **14**

EATING ◆
A Naestu Grösum **27**
Apótek **20**
Baejarins Bestu **5**
Café Paris **18**
Café Victor **4**
Caruso **23**
Einar Ben **16**
Kofi Tomasar Fraenda **25**

inside with staff members who think their hotel is classier than it actually is, Hótel Leifur Eiríksson is nonetheless perfectly situated a few minutes from the city center and across the street from majestic Hallgrims Church. All rooms have a private bathroom. *Skolavorousigur 45. ☎ 354/562-0800. www. hotelleifur.is. May–Sept 13,400ISK single, 16,400ISK double, 3,000ISK extra bed; Oct–Apr 8,300ISK single, 10,400ISK double, 2,500ISK extra bed. Rates include breakfast. Amenities: Room service. In room: TV.*

Eating

Iceland's traditional food reflects the limited preserving possibilities available in the past and the limited choice in such a cold, barren landscape. *Harfiskur,* which is dried cod, sort of like fish jerky, makes a great snack when hiking (if you can bear the smell). For lunch, try a sandwich on rye bread with either *hangikjöt* (smoked lamb) or smoked salmon, with a side of marinated herring, and perhaps some *skyr* (a yogurt-like dairy product) for dessert. Icelanders are big on using up each and every part of their animals, making for interesting "delicacies" such as singed sheep heads, blood-and-liver pudding, and ram testicles, to name a few. When eating out, be sure to sample one of Iceland's more appetizing delicacies, such as free-range lamb, whale meat, or puffin, a bird that looks like part parrot, part penguin and makes its annual migratory stop near Reykjavík each summer.

If you're hungry after hours, you won't have a problem finding something to satisfy your munchies. Most places are open until the wee hours.

Cheap

🎵 **Best** → **Bæjarins Bestu** ★ TAKE-OUT The best hot-dog stand in town, especially since it's open super late, which makes for a good snack on the way to or from a bar. Make sure to ask for one with everything—the ketchup, mustard, remoulade, and fried and raw onion. *Tryggvagata 101. No phone. Open until 3am.*

→ **Kofi Tomasar Fraenda** BISTRO This funky little basement-level place has cozy couches and tables that are usually lit by candles. It serves coffee, tea, and light meals until late. *Laugavegur 2. ☎ 354/551-1855. Snacks 390ISK–700ISK, sandwiches around 600ISK. Mon–Thurs 10am–1am; Fri–Sat 10am–5:30am; Sun 11am–5:30am.*

Doable

→ **Á Næstu Grösum** ★★ VEGETARIAN Reykjavík's premier vegetarian restaurant has been serving organic fare for more than 25 years. It has a warm atmosphere and an engrossing view of Laugavegur. You can choose from standards like lasagna, tortillas, pizza, salad, and soup, in addition to two daily specials. The portions are substantial. *Laugavegur 20b. ☎ 354/552-8410. www. anaestugrosum.is. Full meal 1,000ISK–1,300ISK. Mon–Sat 11:30am–10pm; Sun 5–10pm.*

→ **Cafe Victor** BISTRO/BAR A hopping restaurant that morphs into a popular bar later in the evening. It's as good for a meal as it is for a pre-pub-crawl cocktail (yikes!). Take a seat by the window and watch the locals skateboard in the square across the street. *Hafnarstræti 1. ☎ 354/561-9555. www. cafevictor.is. Burgers and sandwiches from 900ISK; main courses 1,250ISK–2,650ISK. Sun–Thurs 11am–1am; Fri–Sat 11am–5:30am.*

→ **Caruso** ITALIAN/SEAFOOD This large restaurant serves pasta and pizza as well as Icelandic fare such as lamb and seafood. Try the *pasta di mare* or catch of the day, such as fresh salmon or cod. On the weekends, dine to the sounds of the live band playing both Icelandic and international music. *Þingholtsstræti 1. ☎ 354/562-7335. Entrees*

1,700ISK–3,500ISK. Mon–Sat 11:30am–11pm; Sun 5:30–11pm.

→ **Viking Village** VIKING Offers as true a Viking feast as you'll get without going back in time—they'd like you to think. Guests are served in a traditionally decorated environment, where performers also entertain. Order the Viking dinner, which includes appetizer, lamb, and skyr for dessert, as well as a shot of Viking schnapps served in a lamb's horn. It's a memorable, if slightly cheesy, experience. Strandgata 55. Hafnarfjördur. ☎ 354/565-1213. www.fjorukrain.is/fjorukrain/en. Viking dinner, including drinks, soup, entree, and dessert; 5,600ISK; Main courses 1,800ISK–3,200ISK. Bus: 140.

Splurge

→ **Apótek** ★★ ECLECTIC This pharmacy-cum-restaurant is one of the hottest spots in town. A young, trendy, and well-dressed crowd comes to eat and then stays to mingle over drinks. You might feel underdressed in jeans. One of the most creative and diverse menus anywhere, with seafood, sushi, and a variety of meat dishes, as well as a simpler lunch menu of soups, sandwiches, and pizza. Austurstræti 16. ☎ 354/480-1390. www.veitingar.is. Lunch 480ISK–1,390ISK; dinner 2,480ISK–4,690ISK. Mon–Sat 11:30am–1am; Sun 4pm–1am (kitchen closes at 10:30pm, Fri at 11:30pm).

→ **Einar Ben** SEAFOOD Not a huge menu, but reasonably priced considering the location and ambience. From the dining room upstairs, you can watch the action in the square below. The set menus are especially affordable, and the early special is a great treat after a long day. Veltusundi 1. ☎ 354/511-5090. www.einarben.is. Early-bird special (before 7:30pm) 2750ISK–3250ISK; main courses 2,800ISK–4,900ISK. Mon–Fri 6–10pm; Sat–Sun 6–11pm.

Cafes & Tearooms

→ **Cafe Paris** CAFE Enclosed by floor-to-ceiling glass windows, this cozy cafe is a great place to people-watch. Stop in for a hot drink, a light meal, or something sweet. Austurstræti 14. ☎ 354/551-1020. www.cafe paris.is. Sandwiches and light meals 350ISK–890ISK. Mon–Thurs 8am–midnight; Fri 8am–1am; Sat 10am–1am; Sun 10am–midnight.

📺 **Best** → **Kaffi Hljomalind** ★★ CAFE In an old house right on the main strip, Kaffi Hljomalind serves organic drinks, scrumptious baked goods, and light meals. There is also a good used-book collection for browsing or purchase, and (occasionally) live music. Laugavegur 21. ☎ 354/517-1980. Drinks from 160ISK, baked goods around 200ISK, light meals around 650ISK. Mon–Fri 9am–11pm; Sat–Sun 11am–11pm.

REYKJAVIK

Partying

Reykjavík is notorious for its nightlife: These folks live close to the Arctic Circle, and they party heartier for it. Hordes of young people pack the streets on the weekend, hopping from bar to bar until the sun comes up (assuming it set in the first place). While the legal minimum drinking age is technically 20 years old, some very young-looking people are usually part of the crowd, so anyone under age probably won't be hassled (see "Culture Tips 101" on p. 773 for the legal details).

Yes, Björk is Iceland's biggest export, but the Reykjavík music scene goes far beyond this swan-dress-wearing chanteuse. The city has a very of-the-moment live music scene, and it's generally possible to find something going on every night. For suggestions, stop in at the Grapevine Information office (see "Tourist Offices," above). This is also the best place to find out the coolest places to party. Or, you can just join a runtur (pub-crawl) as you see a crowd moving from bar to bar.

Things generally don't get started until 11pm or midnight, and then the partying carries on through the night. Bars don't usually have a cover charge or dress code, but at some of the clubs, you may wish you'd ditched the jeans.

Nightclubs

→ **Nelly's** This casual place—one of the few spots in town you can feel comfortable wearing jeans and a sweatshirt—is where people usually go to end the night. However, cheap beer (from 600ISK) makes Nelly's an affordable stop any time of the evening. Things have a tendency to get a little wild. It's open Sunday to Thursday noon to 1am, and stays open late (until 6am) on Friday and Saturday. Þingholtsstræti 2. ☎ 354/561-1250.

📺 **Best** →**Pravda** ★ Probably Reykjavík's hippest spot, where local yuppies-in-training come to see and be seen. Definitely dress up: You won't even be allowed through the door in jeans. Pravda is open Sunday to Thursday from 11:30pm to 1am, but stays open until 3am on Friday and Saturday. Austurstræti 22. www.pravda.is.

→ **Rex** A trendy club with a swank interior. Chandeliers gently illuminate rooms filled with velvet couches and pillows. Generally an older (that is, mid-20s and up), posh crowd. It's open only on Friday and Saturday nights from 9pm to 4 am. Austurstræti 9. ☎ 354/552-5599. www.rex.is.

Bars & Lounges

→ **22** Originally a gay bar, these days 22 attracts a general alternative crowd. Dine on the first floor, have a drink at the casual second-level bar area, and dance your heart out on the top floor. Live DJs on the weekend, and occasional live gigs. Hours are Sunday through Thursday from 11am to 1am, until 5:30am on Friday and Saturday. Laugaveger 22. ☎ 354/511-5522.

📺 **Best** →**Café Cozy** ★ I'd describe this little place as lively rather than cozy. It's technically the sole gay bar in town, though the crowd—which often packs Café Cozy by 11pm—is an eclectic mix of tourists, students, and even ancient locals who purport to be Santa Claus. It serves what are probably the cheapest drinks in town: Before 11pm three beers or shots can be had for 1,000ISK. Open Monday to Friday 10am to 1am and Saturday and Sunday 8am to 6am. Austursurstræti 3. ☎ 354/511-1033.

→ **Grand Rokk** A casual place with decent beer prices, this is the place to go for an introduction to Reykjavík's local music scene; local bands play to packed crowds most nights of the week. Smiðjustigur 6. ☎ 354/551-5522. www.grandrokk.is.

→ **Kaffibrennslan** A cafe/restaurant by day, trendy bar by night—with a large selection of beer. A good place to come for a drink at the beginning or end of the night, but staying any longer may leave your wallet significantly lighter. Look for the London Underground sign. Its hours are Monday through Thursday from 9am to 1am, Friday until 3am, Saturday from 11am to 3am, and Sunday from noon to 1am. Posthusstræti 9. ☎ 354/561-3600. www.brennslan.is.

→ **NASA** Opened in 2001, NASA quickly became the largest venue for live music—from hard-core rock to jazz. Weekends bring in the bigger names; weekdays are a little less hot. Call for hours and schedule. Austurvöllur Sq. ☎ 354/511-1313. www.nasa.is.

→ **Stúdentakjallarinn** This was once the University of Iceland's pub, a mostly student affair. But in the last few years, new owners have transformed the place, now serve Mediterranean food, and call in a number of good musicians. So students still come but so do other, more grownup types. Hringbraut. ☎ 354/511-0905. www.studentakjallarinn.hi.is.

Gay Bars

It may be cold, but city folk warm up to gay life here. It's not as hopping as many other places in Europe, but Iceland's even got its own Gay and Lesbian Film Festival. Your best options at night are **Café Cozy** (see above) and the open house on Monday, Thursday, and Saturday evenings at the **Gay Community Center** (Samtökin 78; ☎ 354/552-7878; www.samtokin78.is). The "heart of Iceland's leather scene," **MSC Iceland** (Bankastræti 11; ☎ **354/ 562-1280;** www.msc.is) opens Saturday nights only, starting at 11pm. For more on gay nightlife, visit www.gayice.is.

Performing Arts

All those winter hours, all that time to contemplate—it's not surprising that Reykjavík has a thriving arts scene.

➔ **City Theatre** This repertory theater puts on at least seven large productions per season, plus smaller events. These include new Icelandic drama, contemporary writing, and classics. *Listabraut 3.* ☎ *354/568-8000 (box office and information). http://borgarleikhus. is. Season typically runs May–Sept only, but call to check for winter shows. Tickets 3.000ISK–5.000ISK.*

➔ **Icelandic Dance Company** Also at the City Theater, the Iceland Dance Company prides itself on developing, creating, and nurturing contemporary dance and choreography. It focuses on collaborating with other artistic sectors, especially music. *Listabraut 3.* ☎ *354/ 588-0900 or* ☎ *354/568-8000 (box office). www.id.is. Box office: Mon–Tues 10am–6pm, Wed–Fri 10am–8pm, Sat–Sun noon–8pm.*

➔ **Icelandic Opera** The world's northernmost opera house aims to build up and strengthen a professional basis for Icelandic singers. In coming years, most of the biggest productions will be well-known operas, but lesser-known works will also be featured. *Ingólfsstræti.* ☎ *354/511-4200 (box office and information). www.opera.is. Box office: Mon–Fri 2–6pm, Sat–Sun 1–6pm weekends.*

➔ **Laugardalshöll** This is not the place to see anything operatic unless there's a revival of The Who's *Tommy*. This large concert hall is the place to be for international stars. It's not as roomy as a giant stadium, but after all, this is Iceland. *Engjavegi 8.* ☎ *354/553–8990. www.laugardalsholl.is.*

➔ **National Theatre** With three stages, the National Theatre is able to open between 10 and 14 new pieces per season, a mix of Icelandic and foreign writers both classic and modern. *Hverfisgötu 101.* ☎ *354/551-1200 (box office and information). www.leikhusid.is.*

Sightseeing

Reykjavík's main appeal is its gorgeous natural surroundings, and most visitors come to spend time outside. However, some excellent museums and a few attractions in town warrant a visit.

For an overview (literally) of Reykjavík, go to either **Perlan** (☎ **354/562-0200;** www.perlan.is), a freaky, silver-domed building that supplies the city with water and has amazing views from the walkway at the top, or **Hallgrímskirkja** (☎ **354/510-1000;** www.hallgrimskirkja.is), Iceland's tallest church, also with wonderful city views.

And to learn more about the volcanic power pulsing just below the surface of this hunk of living rock, see the **Volcano Show** (at the Red Rock Cinema, Hellusund 6A; ☎ **354/845-9548**). Shows are daily yearround, with more shows during July in August, and some are in English.

That's the Ticket

If you plan to visit several museums and galleries, the **Reykjavík Tourist Card** is a good purchase. It gives free admission to most museums and galleries, as well as free public transportation, free access to all of the city's thermal and swimming pools, and free Internet access at the tourist information center. Cards cost as follows: 1,200ISK for 24 hours, 1,700ISK for 48 hours, and 2,200ISK for 72 hours. Pick one up at the tourist information center, the BSI Bus terminal, and various museums in the city.

Festivals

February

Winter Lights Festival. During this festival all of Reykjavík is lit up, a gorgeous sight. For more info, go to www.visitreykjavik.is. Late February.

June

The Festival of the Sea. This festival, held on the wharf by Reykjavík Harbour, highlights the sea in Icelandic culture. For more info, go to www.visitreykjavik.is. First weekend in June.

August

Reykjavík Gay Pride Festival. Several days featuring performances, displays, and events that celebrate Iceland's gay population. The highlight of the 4-day event is the parade, attracting over 50,000 people. For more info, call ☎ 354/862-2868 or go to www.this.is/gaypride. Mid-August.

September & October

Reykjavík Dance Festival. Choreographers from all over the world present dance performances each evening of this 4-day festival. For more info, go to www.dancefestival.is. Early September.

Reykjavík Jazz Festival. Jazz artists play to crowds who pack Reykjavík's bars and theaters. Last year's festival featured artists from Denmark, Norway, Japan, and America, as well as local Icelandic acts. For more info, call ☎ 354/862-1402 or go to www.reykjavikjazz.com. Late September to early October.

Free & Easy

While I've never agreed that the best things in life are free (hello, cable TV? shopping?) you can find a few freebies in Iceland worth checking out:

→ The **Reykjavík Museum of Photography** (☎ 354/563-1790; www.ljosmyndasafnreykjavikur.is) is the only independent photography museum in Iceland and has free admission every day.

→ Take advantage and wander on foot over to **Hallgrímskirkja,** Iceland's tallest church. (Climbing the tower will cost you, however.)

→ The **Reykjavík Art Museum** is free on Monday and the **National Museum** is free on Wednesday.

→ Drinks are pricey in Iceland, so do what the locals do and **drink at home,** and then go out for a late night on the town. Most bars and clubs don't impose a cover charge.

→ Buy a **Reykjavík Tourist Card,** and think of it as paying admission to a few museums and galleries, and getting free public transportation, Internet access, and access to the city's thermal pools in return.

12 Hours in Reykjavík

1. **Check out some city views.** Head to **Perlan's** 360-degree walkway or up the 75m-high (246-ft.) steeple of **Hallgrímskirkja** to get a bird's-eye view of the city.

2. **Take a hike.** The best way to see Reykjavík is on foot. A walking map (available at the tourist center) can guide you to the city center's best hidden parks, historic sights, and public art. Don't miss a stroll down **Laugavegur**, the best shopping street.

3. **Get educated.** Visit the **National Museum** for a brief tour through Icelandic history.

4. **Watch for whales.** Take an afternoon whale-watching tour.

5. **Warm up.** Head to the eastern part of the city to bask in the Laudardalslavg thermal pool.

6. **Rest up.** End the day with a hot drink at **Kaffibrennslan** or **Café Cozy** and relax before heading out for a crazy night on the town.

7. **Listen up (or drink up).** Check out the live music scene at **Grand Rokk** or join a *runtur.* Or do both.

Reykjavík International Film Festival. Going into its third year, the festival features independent films, human rights-focused flicks, and cult classics as well as film-related seminars, lectures, and workshops. For more info, call ☎ 354/552-2555 or go to www.filmfest.is. Late September to early October.

Iceland Airwaves. This international music festival is sponsored by Iceland's airline. For more info, call ☎ 354/552-0380 or go to www.icelandairwaves.com. Mid-October.

Museums & Art Galleries

→ **National Museum** ★ Ever wondered exactly how Icelanders ended up on this tiny island, and how they managed not only to survive but to become one of the wealthiest (per-capita) nations in Europe? Answers to these questions, and many others, are provided by the exhibitions in this museum. This is a great overview of Icelandic history from A.D. 800 to the present, with easy-to-follow displays, interactive videos, and creative symbolic portrayals (such as the use of an old instant photo booth to symbolize Iceland's

modernization). Also be sure to take a peek into the **National Gallery of Photography,** behind the gift shop. *Suourgata 41.* ☎ *354/ 530-2200. www.natmus.is. Admission 600ISK adults, 300ISK students and seniors; free on Wed. May 1–Sept 15 daily 10am–5pm; Sept 16–Apr 30 Tues–Sun 11am–5pm (until 9pm the 1st Thurs of the month).*

→ **Reykjavík Art Museum** Visiting this museum is a bit of a process, as it is actually divided into three sections, each in a different part of the city. Unless you have a strong interest in Icelandic art, it may be best to just choose the most appealing section and skip the others. **Hafnarhús** (Tryggvagata 17; ☎ 354/590-1200) is the largest section and houses various temporary art exhibits, as well as a permanent exhibition from the Erró collection. **Ásmundarsafn** (Sigtún; ☎ 354/ 553-2155) is a sculpture museum featuring the works of Ásmundur Sveinsoon, a pioneer Icelandic sculptor. Finally, **Kjarvalsstadir** (Flokagata; ☎ 354/517-1290) houses paintings by Jóhannes S. Kjarval, a famous Icelandic painter, as well as other temporary exhibitions. *www.artmuseum.is. Admission to*

*all museums 500ISK adults (free on Mon).
Daily May–Sept 10am–4pm, Oct–Apr 1–4pm.*

FREE →**Reykjavík Museum of Photography** For something a little different and
also more contemporary, check out this small
museum located in the same building as the
city library. Exhibits change regularly, but all
focus on prominent Icelandic photographers,
as well as works from abroad. *Tryggvatan 15.
☎ 354/563-1790. www.ljosmyndasafnreykjavik
ur.is. Free admission. Mon–Fri noon–7pm,
Sat–Sun 1–5pm.*

Playing Outside

HIKING ★ Good hiking in or near Reykjavík
includes the **Heidmork Nature Reserve** and
Mount Esja (914m/2,999 ft.), across the bay
from Reykjavík. You can enjoy a leisurely walk
on **Oskjuhlid Hill** near the Reykjavík airport
or in the **Ellidaardalur Valley** east of the
city. There are also coastal walks. Check with
the tourist office for maps.

HORSE-TREKKING ★ Another great way
to see the country is by Icelandic horse.
Ishestar Riding Tours (Sölaskeid 26;
☎ 354/555-7000; www.ishestar.is) has a
great range of enticements from 4-hour lava
tours with lunch to multiday treks. The short,
shaggy, docile Icelandic horses are all
descended from the stock the Vikings introduced in the 900s. They have a special gait,
lost in all other breeds, that allows a rider to
stay level with no bouncing in the saddle,
even over rough terrain. All tours include
pickup from your accommodations in
Reykjavík, and some include driving as well.

SKIING You've got two options near
Reykjavík, **Blafjoll** (☎ 354/570-7711; www.
skidasvaedi.is) and **Skálafell** (☎ 354/570-
7711; www.skidasvaedi.is). The season runs
from November to April, but when there's
not a lot of snow, you'll need to head elsewhere in Iceland.

THERMAL POOLS ★★ A great way to
warm up in Reykjavík is to make like the
locals and head to one of the city's many
thermal pools; utter heaven on a cold day.
The most popular one is **Laugardalslaug
Pool** (Sunlavgarvegur 105, near a youth
hostel; ☎ 354/553-4039) with a water slide,
whirlpool, and steam bath, plus both hot and
cold pools that are surprisingly clean for
public pools. The price for adults is 250ISK.
You can get a good soaking from Monday to
Friday 6:50am to 9:30pm and Saturday and
Sunday from 8am to 8pm.

📺 Best WHALE-WATCHING ★★★ A
definite must while in Reykjavík! Several
tour companies in town run whale-watching
tours. Tours usually last between 2 to 3
hours, and operators guarantee sightings or
else the next trip is free, but that is hardly
ever necessary: On my trip we saw more
than 30 whales! Don't expect big killer
whales, though; most of the year, the smaller
minke whales are most common. In the summer months, tours also make a stop at
Puffin Island, where the migratory puffin (a
cute critter that looks like a cross between a
penguin and a parrot) takes a break on its
way south.

→**Elding Whale Watching** This is the
cheapest of the whale-watching tour companies. Book online or visit them in person.
*Aegisgarder Harbour. ☎ 354/555-3565. www.
elding.is. Tours 3,700ISK adults; pickup from
hotel 500ISK adults. June–Aug tours daily at
9am, and 1 and 5pm. Ask about night tours
and fishing trips.*

→**The Whale Watching Center** The other
main whale-watching outfit, offering pretty
much the same quality service as Elding, at a
slightly higher fee. Price includes admission
to a small exhibition and information center

on whales and seabirds. *Aegisgardur Harbour.* ☎ *354/533-2660. www.whalewatching.is. Tours 3,800ISK adults; pick-up charge 500ISK. Tours* *Apr–May and Sept 9am and 1pm; June–Aug 9am, and 1 and 5pm; Oct at 1pm.*

Shopping

Laugavegur is the main shopping street in Reykjavík, where you will find designer clothes along with secondhand shops and several music shops in between the cafes and restaurants. Skolavoroustigur, off of Laugavegur, is also a good shopping street with similar types of stores.

Iceland is known for its woolen products, such as sweaters, mitts, and hats, and though expensive, they're tempting if you're freezing your buns off in winter. Souvenir shops around Austurstræti and Posthustræti sell woolen sweaters, gloves, and hats.

Road Trips

Several tour companies run excursions to the **Golden Circle** (see below) and the **Blue Lagoon** (see below), as well as other Iceland destinations. Trips can be booked through them directly, or at the tourist information office in Reykjavík.

Reykjavík Excursions (☎ **354/562-1011;** www.re.is) is one of the most popular companies, offering a variety of non-challenging tours where you'll simply be shuttled on and off a tour bus at the sites. For a Golden Circle tour, the cost is 6,800ISK; a Blue Lagoon tour will run 3,900ISK. You'll pick up your tour at the main office in the BSI Bus Terminal (open 24 hr.).

Iceland Excursions (main office: Höfòatún 12; ☎ **354/540-1313;** www.icelandexcursions. is) has the usual tours of the Golden Circle and Blue Lagoon, as well as a variety of more adventurous options, such as scuba diving and dog sledding. To take their Golden Circle tour, the cost is slightly less at 6,200ISK, and their Blue Lagoon tour is only 3,300ISK.

Destination Iceland (Lagmuli 4; ☎ **354/ 585-4270;** www.dice.is) also offers a variety of creative tours such as river rafting and ATV riding. A tour of the Golden Circle sites runs 6,800ISK and Blue Lagoon is 5,800ISK (includes a trip to Rekjanes peninsula).

The Golden Circle

The most popular day trip from Reykjavík, the **Golden Circle** ★, as some smart PR person has dubbed this, is actually three major sites (though some tour companies stop at several other minor sites, too). First on the itinerary is **Gullfoss waterfall,** a stunning flow of water that cascades over two cliffs, set along a beautiful plain. If you plan on getting close to the falls, it's a good idea to don rain gear. On sunny days, the river is haloed with a rainbow. On the trail heading toward the main viewing area, you'll see a rock carving of Iceland's first environmentalist, a headstrong farmer's daughter who worked to preserve the falls.

Next is a stop at **Geyser National Park,** where you may wonder what all the fuss is about until you find yourself standing 3m (10 ft.) from a hole in the ground that's shooting boiling water and steam straight up into the air: quite the unforgettable spectacle. The site's **museum** is also worth a visit: Through interactive exhibits, the geological principles behind the natural eruptions and explosions ubiquitous to Iceland are explained.

Finally, the tour stops at **Þingvellir,** the site of the world's oldest parliament. From A.D. 930 to the end of the 18th century, all important decisions on the island were discussed and decided here. (The area also lays claim to hosting other important activities, such as tossing adulterous women into the neighboring stream). Þingvellir is also where the North American and European tectonic plates meet (you won't be able to feel them moving apart at a rate of 2 centimeters/$^3/_4$ in. per year), which has created a stunning valley in the process.

The Blue Lagoon

Swimming in the steamy phosphorescent waters (which look as if they glow in the dark) of the ⓜ Best **Blue Lagoon** ★★★ (☎ **354/420-8800;** www.bluelagoon.is), surrounded by the lava fields of Iceland, is truly an otherworldly experience. While soaking in the lagoon, be sure to give yourself a silica mud facial. For extra pampering, step into the sauna or steam room. You will leave here feeling utterly relaxed and—more importantly—utterly warm. You can take the public bus from the BSI terminal here, but when combined with the entrance fee it's not much cheaper than going with a tour company, which will pick you up and drop you off wherever you're staying. It is also possible to stop over at the lagoon on your way to or from the airport.

Rome

Rome is tough to sum up in words, but when Italians talk about Rome, the word they use over and over is *fascino*. *Fascino* is a noun—derived from the Latin verb "to bind"—that doesn't translate perfectly into English, but it's a sort of cross between fascination, captivation, charm, and wonder—something that transcends beauty and inexplicably tugs at your heart.

First of all, Rome is the most visually impressive city in the world—it's an AK-47 of art and architecture that never stops firing ruins, fountains, churches, sculptures, frescoes, or spectacular green vistas into your sightlines. The Eternal City has been around for 2,800 years, after all, and you'd better believe she has a lot to show for it. That the splendors of Rome are all a bit rough around the edges only adds to the romance. Anyone with an ounce of nostalgia for the days of chariot races and gladiators will reel before the ruins of imperial Rome. The churches and fountains of Renaissance and baroque Rome amaze and delight all with their sheer scale, inventiveness, and richness of material. Between the postcard sights, modern Roman life is played out on cobblestone piazzas and narrow alleys. Beautiful women flash by on Vespas, and gorgeous men pause to smoke a cigarette and read the newspaper, both aware of their place in the urban tableau. Coffee, food, and wine are at every turn, and the low-attitude bars and restaurants of Rome will welcome you.

Rome is sublime, but for many who travel here, it's not love at first sight. Beyond the glories of ancient Rome and the treasures of the Renaissance and baroque, Rome is still a metropolis of 3 million. The traffic, chaos, and grit that go along with being a big city are enough to turn off plenty of people who whisk through Rome, stopping only to snap pictures at the obligatory sights, and then board a train out of town. As hectic as it seems on the surface, the soul of the city is laid-back (some might even say lazy)—the Romans don't particularly like how stressful their city can be, so they take measures to offset it. You should, too. Go for an *aperitivo* at an outdoor cafe before dinner, and spend a long time at the table once you get to your restaurant. Make an effort to adopt a Roman rhythm during your days here, and you'll get much more out of your visit than you would if you spent every last waking minute trying to tick off must-see monuments. The Vatican isn't going anywhere anytime soon, so if you miss the Sistine Chapel this time around, you can always come back. Most people do.

The Best of Rome

○ **The Best Cheap Hotel:** The **Albergo Sole al Biscione,** near Campo de' Fiori, is where I stayed when I was a student, and it's still where I choose to stay today. It's not fancy, but it overflows with Roman charm—interior rooms have shutters that open onto a multilevel courtyard with pink stucco walls, plants, and faux antique statuary. Hang out on the terrace, catch up on postcards, and soak up the rays of the Roman *sole.* See p. 802.

○ **The Best Pizzeria:** For overall fun and food quality, I head for loud and lively **La Montecarlo** (p. 810) when I'm in Rome. As for the best-tasting pies in town, that prize goes to **Dar Poeta** (p. 810) in Trastevere—also a lot of fun, but expect a wait!

○ **The Best Place to Party:** Every night, from 6:30pm on, the indoor-outdoor wine bars and pubs on **Campo de' Fiori** (p. 813) fill up with young local and international revelers. The American bars on the Campo offer drink specials every night, and the Italian enotecas have

glasses of wine that start at 1.55€. If clubs are more your scene, head for **Testaccio** (p. 817), where Via Galvani, Via di Monte Testaccio, and Via Zabaglia are packed to the gills with lounges and discos for all musical tastes and sexual orientations.

○ **The Best Example of Mad Engineering:** With its 43m-wide (141-ft.) hemispherical dome of poured concrete, the astonishing, 1,900-year-old **Pantheon** (temple to all the gods) is the best preserved ancient building in all the European, Asian, and African lands that used to make up the Roman Empire. See p. 822.

○ **The Best Street:** A few kilometers south of the Colosseum, the old **Appian Way** offers a welcome glimpse of the rustic Rome that lies just outside the chaos of the *centro.* Visit the catacombs, breathe the rural air of ancient farmland mixed with the scent of pine trees, and tread the 2,300-year-old basalt flagstones of the "Queen of Roads." See p. 821.

Getting There & Getting Around

Getting into Town

BY AIR

Most flights to Rome land in **Leonardo da Vinci International Airport** (☎ 06/65951), 30km (18¹/₂ miles) from the city center, though some charter flights land at **Ciampino Airport** (☎ 06/794-941). The website for both airports, www.adr.it, provides all kinds of practical information including flight schedules, ground transportation options, and duty-free shopping opportunities.

From Leonardo da Vinci, the easiest way to get into town is by taxi (it's also the cheapest option if you're in a group). Official, metered taxis have the SPQR city emblem on their doors and must wait in a queue on the airport drive directly outside the terminal. Anyone offering you a "taxi" inside the terminal is an illegal tout who will probably end up charging you a good deal more than what an official cab will cost. The metered fare from Fiumicino to most destinations in central Rome should be around 40€, with a small supplement for each large piece of luggage (although some drivers waive this fee).

If you're by yourself, taking the train into town is a much cheaper option. From the arrivals hall, follow the bilingual signs to the Railway Station, or FS. The most popular line with tourists is the **Leonardo Express,** which is a nonstop train to Rome's main train station, Roma-Termini, on the eastern end of the city center. The trip takes 31 minutes and costs 9.50€, with trains departing every 20 minutes from 6:30am to 11:30pm. The other line, the **FM1** to **Fara Sabina** or **Orte,** is a nicer, double-decker train used mostly by commuters and other locals. This train has a flat fee of 5€ and departs every 20 minutes from 6am to 11:30pm, making stops at several suburbs on its way toward the city center; in town, it stops at several of the city's secondary train stations but not Roma-Termini.

If you've arrived in Rome without accommodations lined up (which we do not recommend), the **Hotel Reservation** office (at Fiumicino, just outside the customs area; ☎ 06/699-1000) is open daily 7am to 10pm.

If you've flown into Ciampino, the easiest way to get into town is with the coach service run by **Terravision** (☎ 06/7949-4572; www.terravision.it), whose schedule coincides with all RyanAir, easyJet, and such arrivals. The bus drops you off on Via Marsala, on the north side of Termini train station. Tickets cost 8€ and can be purchased from the Terravision desk or from uniformed staff inside the arrivals hall at Ciampino.

Public transportation from Ciampino to central Rome is a two-part deal: First, take a blue **COTRAL** bus (1€) to Anagnina Metro station, and then take **Metro Line A** (another 1€) from Anagnina to Termini or wherever you happen to be headed. (For more information about areas served by the Metro, see "Getting Around," below.)

BY TRAIN

If you're traveling to Rome from within mainland Italy, rail is the most economical, and efficient option. Rome's principal train station, **Roma-Termini,** is a busy rail hub through which most of Italy's main train lines pass. There are also daily direct trains to Roma-Termini from Paris, Munich, and Vienna. Termini's location, on the less-than-gorgeous eastern end of town, makes for an unfortunate introduction to the city.

Keep in mind that it's not unusual for Italian trains (especially the regional lines) to run a few minutes to an hour behind schedule. The exception to this is the EuroStar, which almost always runs on time.

That's the Ticket

European rail passes are good for second-class travel on Italian InterCity (IC) trains as well as the sluggish regionale (R) and diretto (D) trains, but if you want to travel on Italy's express service, the EuroStar (ES), you'll have to pay a supplement—consult the literature that comes with your pass for more details. Note also that all EuroStar tickets must be booked at least 24 hours in advance, which gets you an assigned seat.

For more information about the national train system, consult Trenitalia's extremely handy, multilingual website (**www.trenitalia. com**).

BY CAR

Rome can be reached quite easily via the autostrada (toll expressway; with green signs) or strade statali (SS; slower state highways with blue signs), from any direction in Italy. Like spokes on a wheel, the 12 ancient *vie consolari* (consular roads) lead out from the city at every compass point.

Whether you're coming into Rome from the autostrada or the state highways, exit where you see the ROMA CENTRO signs. Once you're on city streets, always keep your eyes peeled for the white, bull's-eye centro signs and drive slowly—if you miss a turn, it can be murder trying to pick up the trail again. After a few kilometers of inching closer to the centro, you really need to start thinking about ditching that car because you won't find a place to park it in the old city. Furthermore, you won't be allowed to drive your car into the old city due to heavy restrictions on non-resident traffic.

On the south side of Termini, the **ES** lot (Via Giolitti 267; ☎ 06/4470-4073) charges 13€ for 24 hours. You'll also find a few large parking structures in the Via Veneto area (a bit west of Termini): The underground **ParkSì** lot (Villa Borghese, Viale del Galoppatoio; ☎ 06/ 322-5934) charges 15€ per day; nearby, **Parking Ludovisi** (Via Ludovisi 60, off Via Veneto; ☎ 06/474-0632) charges 18€ per day.

BY BUS

There's really no reason to take a bus to Rome, as every Italian city is connected to Rome by train, which is always more comfortable, faster, and more affordable. If, for some reason, you do get on some kind of national or international coach to Rome, it'll most likely drop you off at Tiburtina train station, on the eastern outskirts. From here, take Metro Line B toward the center (in the direction of Laurentina) or bus no. 492.

Regional bus service is operated by **COTRAL** (☎ 06/0437-31006; www.cotral spa.it); in the city, COTRAL terminals are outside several Metro stations. From Lepanto Metro station (Line A), near the Vatican, there are buses to the Etruscan necropolis of **Cerveteri** and the castle and low-key beach at **Santa Marinella;** from Cornelia Metro station (Line A), you can catch a bus to the beach resort of **Fregene.** From Ponte Mammolo Metro station (Line B), you can take a bus to **Tivoli** (Hadrian's Villa and Villa d'Este), and from Laurentina Metro station (Line B), there are buses south to chic beach destinations like **Sabaudia** and **San Felice Circeo,** both of which are impossible to reach by train.

Getting Around

BY MOTOR SCOOTER

Rome is the ultimate *motorino* (motor scooter) city. Renting a Vespa or other model scooter while in town is an activity I cannot recommend highly enough. While most distances in the tourist center are easily covered on foot, a motorino gives you near-instant access to farther-flung sights.

Rental outfits provide helmets (which you are required by law to wear), chain locks (always a good idea, unless you're just stopping for a few minutes somewhere), and insurance (leave the documents in the compartment beneath the seat—you'll need to show them in the unlikely event you have a run-in with the police).

My favorite motorino rental agency in Rome is **Roma Rent** (Vicolo dei Bovari 7a; ☎ 06/689-6555), near Campo de' Fiori. Rates for a 50cc scooter start at 35€ a day (9am–7pm); and 42€ per 24-hour period.

BY PUBLIC TRANSPORTATION

Buses, trams, and the Metropolitana subway (aka the Metro) are run by ATAC. If your hotel is not in the heart of town, you'll be utilizing public transportation quite a bit, so get familiar with how it works. First of all, bear in mind that Rome is not London, New York, or Paris, where efficient underground systems get you within blocks of everywhere you want to go. Instead, Rome is a bus town, with a few handy and scenic tram lines thrown into the mix. Yes, Rome does have a subway, but it's a dinky two-line system, and getting in and out of the stations—especially Termini—can be unpleasant and time-consuming, so wherever possible, we recommend you **take the bus or tram instead of the Metro.** In general, the stations along Metro Line B are less of a hassle than on Line A. Check out the ATAC website, www.atac.roma.it, for info.

BY TAXI

Taxis come in handy when you have to get from the train station to your hotel with a lot of luggage and when you find yourself not wanting to deal with the bus at the end of a long day of sightseeing. You'll also need taxis to get to and from any of the nightlife spots outside the centro. A few taxi rules to keep in mind: You can't hail a cab on the street. By law, free cabs must proceed to the nearest taxi stand and pick up new fares there.

There are taxi stands on three sides of Termini station; in front of the Colosseum Metro station; at Piazza Venezia; the Spanish Steps; Piazza del Popolo; the Pantheon; Largo Argentina; Palazzo Madama (on Corso Rinascimento, just east of Piazza Navona); at Piazza San Pietro (Vatican City); in Piazza Risorgimento, near the Vatican Museums; and off Piazza G.G. Belli in Trastevere. You can also call for a cab (in Italian or very clear, elementary English) at ☎ 06/3570, 06/4994, 06/6645, 06/5551, or 06/4157. The company at 06/3570 has the widest network of cabs, so call them first.

BY BICYCLE

Bicycling in Rome is only advisable if you're sticking to the parks; or on Sundays, when there's hardly any traffic in the centro storico; or if you're on a guided bike tour, such as that offered by **Enjoy Rome** (Via Marghera 8/a; ☎ 06/445-1843). Otherwise, biking in Rome is a harrowing affair involving bumpy cobblestones, swarms of Vespas, and careening buses.

BY CAR

There are a number of great little day trips you can take from Rome, some of which are most conveniently reached by car. If you're traveling alone or with one other person, consider renting the popular Smart car, mainland Europe's smaller and more cartoonish analogue to the MINI Cooper (they have those here, too). Two-seater Smarts are tiny, fuel-efficient, and shockingly chic. On the south side of Termini station, **Happy Rent** (Via Farini 3, at Via Cavour; ☎ 06/481-8185; www.happyrent.com), will rent you a Smart for 75€ for 24 hours. A slightly more economical option, Fiat hatchbacks are available for 50€ from 9am to 7pm. All the other major players, like **Avis** (www.avis.com) and **Hertz** (www.hertz.com), have offices at Fiumicino airport (Avis: ☎ 06/6501-1531; Hertz: ☎ 06/6501-1553) and Termini station at Via Giolitti 34 (Avis: ☎ 06/481-4373; Hertz: ☎ 06/474-0389).

Rome Basics

Most of the sights you'll want to see in Rome are within a rather compact swath of land that doesn't have a name that anyone agrees on but stretches somewhat amorphously from the Vatican in the west to Termini station in the east, and from Piazza del Popolo and Villa Borghese in the north to the archaeological park of the Baths of Caracalla in the south. The five major roads in this zone—Via del Corso, Via Nazionale, Via dei Fori Imperiali, Via del Teatro di Marcello, and Corso Vittorio Emanuele—converge at Piazza Venezia, the busy traffic roundabout at the geographic center of Rome.

Orientation: Rome Neighborhoods

CENTRO STORICO Despite the name, and the fact that it's one of the most artistically rich square miles in the world, this isn't actually the most touristy part of Rome (though it's up there). Nestled within the eastern curve of the Tiber's C-shaped bend, and crudely severed by the fascist-era Corso Vittorio Emanuele, the centro storico is a picturesque network of crooked, uneven cobblestone streets and ochre-washed palazzi that occasionally open up to magnificent public spaces like Piazza Navona or awesome ancient monuments like the Pantheon. Many of the backstreets here are slightly unkempt, which is an appealing contrast to the well-groomed blocks of the Tridente (Spanish Steps) area to the northeast. Every other business in the centro storico is a down-to-earth bar or neighborhood trattoria, although there are plenty of chic boutiques and more upscale bars, and restaurants have joined the fray in recent years. The area around Campo de' Fiori, with its daytime produce market and evening "meat market," is more rough-and-ready than the more gentrified Piazza Navona and Pantheon areas. East of Via Arenula is the old Jewish Ghetto, which is a quieter, more residential zone where you can sample Roman Jewish cuisine. The centro storico is also the best place in town to get in on Rome's infectious, easygoing nightlife: The casual alfresco bars around Campo de' Fiori and the streets west of Piazza Navona are humming with young locals 7 days a week.

SPANISH STEPS (AKA THE TRIDENTE) This is the high-rent slice of the centro, home to the vast, sun-drenched squares of Piazza del Popolo and Piazza di Spagna (the Spanish Steps), and between them, all the designer boutiques you could possibly imagine. The southwestern part of the Tridente is essentially an extension of the centro storico, with wonderful dog-legging alleys that feel like a time warp to the 16th century. The area south of Via del Tritone is hopelessly tourist-infested, thanks to the presence of the magnificent Trevi Fountain. The Tridente is not particularly strong on dining or partying options; the best bets are on the west side of Via del Corso, on the cafe-filled Piazza San Lorenzo in Lucina, and especially at the trendy 'Gusto conglomerate of bars and restaurants on Piazza Augusto Imperatore.

TRASTEVERE Derived from the Latin *trans tiberim* ("across the Tiber"), this is the pocket of old Rome that lies south of the Vatican on the western side of the river's S-shaped curve. It has the same ochre-washed, ivy-covered walls and cobblestone streets as the centro storico but fewer large piazzas and almost no famous monuments, as well as an independent, community atmosphere that gives it extra charm. Piazza Santa Maria in Trastevere is the heart of Trastevere; from here to Piazza Trilussa (Ponte Sisto) is the most picturesque section, with tons of places to eat and drink heartily—in fact, Trastevere gets almost too crowded in the evenings! West of busy Viale Trastevere is the quieter, more workaday part of Trastevere. Although it has plenty of modern influences, Trastevere is still the place in Rome where you can come and feel like you're in a different era—especially by day, when old men haul around carts of fruit, and when you can peek in the open doors of old-world workshops where carpenters craft table legs by hand and marble workers restore ancient-looking sculptures. The tree-lined ridge to the west of low-lying Trastevere is the Gianicolo (Janiculum Hill), de rigueur for its panoramic views back over the centro. Beyond lies the enormous Villa Pamphilj, the city's largest public park, great for hiking, picnicking, and relaxing with real Romans.

ANCIENT ROME, MONTI & THE CELIO South and east of busy Piazza Venezia, you'll find a mix of phenomenally impressive ancient ruins, gorgeous green hills, and cozy medieval streets (in the Monti district, north of Via dei Fori Imperiali). Between Via dei Fori Imperiali and Via del Circo Massimo is the monumental archaeological zone where you'll no doubt spend several hours climbing over fallen columns in the Forum, over crumbling brick walls on the Palatine, or up the stairs of the vomitoria at the Colosseum. Make sure you return at night, when the glories of ancient Rome are spectacularly floodlit. Monti straddles either side of ugly Via Cavour and is home to the best expat-frequented pubs in Rome. The Celio, which is the hill directly south of the Colosseum, has a grid of streets with some lively eateries (including Isidoro, our favorite pasta-sampling joint) and a few pubs; the rest of the Celio is occupied by rustic ancient churches and the lovely "green lung" of Villa Celimontana park.

TERMINI & ESQUILINO The area around the train station is a popular place to crash because it's home to (a) about 75% of the city's hotels, and (b) almost all of the budget sleeps. Trouble is, it's downright seedy (where drunk vagrants far outnumber other Romans). We strongly suggest you pay a little extra to be closer to the heart of things, which means heading west from the station. There are almost no authentic places to eat. (You'll find curry and shawarma purveyors galore, however.)

VIA VENETO & THE QUIRINALE The wide, slalom curve of tree-lined Via Veneto descends from the Villa Borghese park to the traffic and public transportation hub of Piazza Barberini. In the 1950s and 1960s, fabulous Hollywood types partied at the Art Nouveau cafes here, and their decadent lifestyle inspired Federico Fellini's classic film *La Dolce Vita*. Roman showbiz has-beens and the wealthy tourists who check into the luxury hotels here are desperately trying to hang on to some of that glamorous mystique, but for the most part, Via Veneto is beautiful but vapid. The Quirinale hill, just south of here, is mostly government buildings, with several interesting baroque churches, but little in the way of eating or drinking until you reach the western edge, which leads down to the Trevi Fountain.

THE VATICAN & THE PRATI The western side of Ponte Vittorio Emanuele, right across the river from the centro storico, marks the beginning of Via della Conciliazione, the bombastic fascist-era boulevard that leads straight to Piazza San Pietro. St. Peter's is the only part of the Vatican that greets the city with open arms; the rest of the papal state is a recluse within fortresslike 16th-century brick walls. The only other major monument on this side of the river is Castel Sant'Angelo. Between Castel Sant'Angelo and the Vatican is the medieval Borgo district, a small lattice of streets with some cute, if touristy, bars and restaurants. North of here begins the Prati district, where many upper-middle-class Romans who can't deal with the nonsense of the historical center choose to live. Prati has wider streets, block after block of repetitive 19th-century *palazzi*, and all the good shops and services that you'd expect in

ROME

a more well-to-do residential area. Via Cola di Rienzo is the main commercial drag, with department stores and smaller fashion boutiques, a supermarket, and some of the city's best delis. There are also a number of reasonably priced accommodations options in Prati and some excellent live-music venues. Restaurants and pubs aren't the first thing that come to mind when you think of Prati.

ROMA NORD: PARIOLI & FLAMINIO Venture north of Piazza del Popolo, and boldly go where no tourists (or at least very few) have gone before. Tram no. 2 plies the Via Flaminia from Piazzale Flaminio almost as far as the ancient Ponte Milvio. Along the way, there are several refreshingly modern cultural attractions to visit, including the new 21st-century art space, MAXXI, and the much-hyped Auditorium, an impressive new center for the performing arts. A bit downriver, on the west side of the Tiber, is the Stadio Olimpico, where you can (and absolutely should) catch a Roma or Lazio soccer game if they're in town. Moving eastward, onto the rolling hills north of Villa Borghese, you'll find Rome's most prestigious residential area, Parioli, a rare pocket of town where SUVs outnumber Fiat hatchbacks and Smarts. The main street, Viale Parioli—referred to by some as "the new Via Veneto"—has some very chic boutiques and restaurants.

Tourist Offices & Information

The **visitor center** of the Rome APT (Azienda di Promozione Turistica di Roma; www.romaturismo.com) is at Via Parigi 5 (off Piazza della Repubblica; ☎ **06/488-991**), and is open Monday to Saturday 9am to 7pm. The APT also has a desk at Fiumicino airport, Terminal B, open daily from 8am to 7pm. You can also get information from the APT's **call center** (☎ **06/8205-9127**), in operation every day from 9am to 7pm.

Throughout the city center, there are also **green kiosks,** run by the APT, where you can

get brochures and maps, and ask touristy questions. You'll find kiosks at Termini station, Castel Sant'Angelo, Via dei Fori Imperiali, Piazza Cinque Lune (near Piazza Navona), Largo Goldoni, Via Minghetti (near the Trevi Fountain), Via dell'Olmata (near Santa Maria Maggiore), and in Trastevere at Piazza Sonnino. The illustrated city map published by the tourist board is compact and quite good, so be sure to pick one up when you visit one of their offices.

For a more personal touch, stop in at **Enjoy Rome** (Via Marghera 8/a, a few blocks north of Termini; ☎ **06/445-1843;** www.enjoyrome.com), where a staff of friendly Italians and native English speakers will give you free maps and pamphlets and answer questions. They're open Monday to Friday from 8:30am to 6:30pm, and Saturday from 8:30am to 2pm. Enjoy Rome also runs fantastic walking tours, a seasonal bike tour, and bus tours to the catacombs and Pompeii.

Recommended Websites

Most of these homepages are in Italian; click on the British flag icon to bring up the English version of the site.

◯ **www.romaturismo.com**: The official website of the Roman tourist board is bright, clean, and user-friendly. There are comprehensive accommodations listings, sightseeing and transportation info, events calendar, as well as suggested itineraries for 48-hour or 96-hour stays. Coolest of all is the "Brochures" feature, which allows you to download some substantial (and informative) full-color booklets and pamphlets (in PDF format) about the Colosseum, the Appian Way, the fountains of Rome, and more.

◯ **www.vatican.va**: In addition to putting more archived papal speeches at your fingertips than you ever thought possible, the official website of the Holy See provides practical information and an abridged virtual tour of the Vatican Museums. To skip straight to the Vatican Museums info, go to **http://mv.vatican.va/3_EN/pages/MV_Home.html**.

Culture Tips 101

Most Romans speak very little English, but staff members at restaurants and bars in the centro are fluent enough to handle food and drink orders. Nevertheless, you should treat your time in Rome as a chance to master a few key words and phrases in the most fun, musical, and romantic language in the world.

Roman dress is casual but pulled-together year-round. Jeans, not khakis, should be the foundation of your travel wardrobe while in Rome. This is a cosmopolitan city, so there are no modesty concerns when it comes to dress, but shorts (and especially short shorts or miniskirts), worn anywhere but the beach or in your hotel room, are just plain bad taste in Rome. The other important thing to keep in mind is that Romans are very strict about what they wear in what season. Even though it never really gets that cold, and there are warm and sunny days in October and March, you'll never see locals bust out open-toed shoes between the end of September and mid-May. It's also a good idea to leave any expensive jewelry at home because of pickpockets.

The city is remarkably tolerant of alcoholic excess, but there's a big difference between the way Romans drink and the way many tourists do. Some Romans can be out all night and only have a few drinks; others will have more; but this is not a binge-drinking culture, so you'll rarely see Romans getting loud, obnoxious, or belligerent. You should follow course, and for heaven's sake, do not join one of the many pub-crawls that are pitched at the international backpacker set. Open containers are technically allowed everywhere, but should only be brought to piazzas (such as Campo de' Fiori or Piazza Trilussa), where other (non-derelict) locals are doing it, too.

Recommended Books, Movies & Music

Below are some of the best Roman-inspired books, movies, and music.

BOOKS

From the Colosseum to Michelangelo, T. W. Potter provides one of the best accounts of the art and architecture of Rome in *Roman Italy*, which is also illustrated. Another good book on the same subject is *Roman Art and Architecture*, by Mortimer Wheeler.

The Sistine Chapel: A Glorious Restoration, by Michael Hirst and others, uses nearly 300 color photographs to illustrate the lengthy and painstaking restoration of Michelangelo's 16th-century frescoes in the Vatican.

For some wildly entertaining books on ancient Rome, detailing its most flamboyant personalities and excesses, read *I, Claudius* and *Claudius the God*, both by Robert Graves. In 1998, the Modern Library placed *I, Claudius* at number 14 on its list of the 100 finest English-language novels published this century.

Many other writers have tried to capture the peculiar nature of Italy. Notable works include Italo Calvino's *The Baron in the Trees*, Umberto Eco's *The Name of the Rose*, Giuseppe di Lampedusa's *The Leopard*, Susan Sontag's *The Volcano Lover*, and Mark Helprin's under-appreciated masterwork, *A Soldier of the Great War*.

MOVIES

Go to a video store before you travel: Anything by Michelangelo Antonioni, Bernando Bertolluci, Frederico Fellini (especially *8½* and *La Dolce Vita*—the latter has a memorable Trevi Fountain romping scene), Vittoria da Sica's *Umberto D.* or *The Bicycle Thief*, and *Big Deal on Madonna Street* by Mario Monicelli are all good places to start.

One of my favorite Italian movies is *Roman Holiday* (1953), the Gregory Peck/

Talk of the Town

Three ways to start a conversation with a local

1. **What's your favorite Roman movie?** Go educate yourself at a video store before you chat. Once you've boned up on Fellini and DeSica and Antonioni (to name just the oldies), you'll be ready to start a passionate discussion about Italian cinema.

2. **Why *is* everyone so beautiful here?** This works as a pickup line, but it's also a good way to start a conversation about Italian culture.

3. **Why are things so damn expensive?** Attempt to get an acceptable answer (good luck).

Audrey Hepburn romance that is said to have caused a surge in tourism to Rome. Another hugely popular film of the same era is *Spartacus* (1960), the Oscar-winning Kirk Douglas movie about a slave revolt in ancient Rome.

MUSIC

Italy has produced many fine composers, but Giuseppe Verdi was the unquestioned operatic master of the 19th century. Verdi, son of an innkeeper, wrote exquisite melodies, and his musicianship was unsurpassed. He achieved success early on with his third opera, *Nabucco*, a huge hit, then turned out *Rigiletto, Il Trovatore, Un Ballo in Maschera*, and *Aïda*—works that remain popular today. Puccini came along a bit later, and his lyrical *La Bohème, Tosca*, and *Madama Butterfly* continue to please crowds.

Download these essential Eternal City tunes before your trip.

◌ **Er Piotta, "Supercafone":** "Er Piotta" is Roman dialect for "Fitty Bucks" (well, close enough), and his supercatchy, quasi-

hip-hop tune from 1999 is a tongue-in-cheek celebration of the stereotypical Roman "guido" who thinks he's God's gift to women.

◌ **Lando Fiorini, "La Società dei Magnaccioni":** A true Roman classic, "The Big Eaters' Club" is a table-slapping ode to gluttony and sloth.

◌ **Flaminio Maphia, "Ragazze Acidelle":** From local hip-hop duo G-Max and Rude MC, this is a more obscure but catchy number that rails against snobby Roman chicks.

◌ **Antonello Venditti, "Roma Roma Roma" and "Grazie Roma":** The former is the song everyone at the stadium sings at the start of A.S. Roma soccer games. The latter is the one you sing at the end of the game when Roma wins.

◌ **Renato Zero, "Cercami (Live at the Stadio Olimpico)":** Renato is a skinny, aging, melodramatic Italian rocker, and "Look for Me" is his overproduced, Andrew Lloyd Webber–style power ballad.

Rome Nuts & Bolts

Currency Cash machines (called *bancomat* in Italy) are everywhere in this well-touristed town, but you probably won't need to carry around a ton of euros while you're in Rome because credit and debit cards are accepted almost everywhere.

There's a branch of **Citibank** at Via Abruzzi 2 (☎ 06-42156502; Metro: Barberini). It's open Monday to Friday from 8:30am to 1:30pm and 2:30 to 4pm.

Embassies & Consulates   Most embassies and consulates are open Monday to Friday from 9am to noon; call for exact hours, and to find out exactly what documents you should bring with you to expedite your appointment.

→   **Embassy and Consulate of the United States:** Via Veneto 119A/121. ☎ **06/46741.** Metro: Barberini. Bus: 52, 53, 63, 95, 116, or 630.

→   **Embassy of Canada:** Via Zara 30, off Corso Trieste, northeastern suburbs. ☎ **06/ 445-981.** Bus: 36 or 60.

→   **Embassy of the United Kingdom:** Via XX Settembre 80, at Porta Pia. ☎ **06/4220- 0001.** Bus: 36, 60, or 62.

→   **Embassy of Australia:** Via Alessandria 215, off Corso Trieste, northeastern suburbs. ☎ **06/852-721.** Bus: 36 or 60.

→   **Embassy of New Zealand:** Via Zara 28, off Corso Trieste, northeastern suburbs. ☎ **06/440-2928.** Bus: 36 or 60.

Emergencies   In an emergency, call the polizia at ☎ **113;** for non-emergencies (like lost or stolen property), use ☎ **06/46861,** or visit the main police station (*questura*) at Via di San Vitale 15 (at Via Genova, north of Via Nazionale). You can also turn to Italy's Army police force, the Carabinieri (who wear red-striped trousers designed by Valentino), to report emergencies or other disturbances of the peace. Call the Carabinieri at ☎ **112** for emergencies only; for non-emergencies, ☎ **06/6758-2800.** Their central station (*caserma*) is at Via Cesare Battisti 6 (Piazza Venezia). If your pocket gets picked, turn to the multilingual tourist aid helpline at ☎ **06/422-371.** The polizia municipale, who handle dog bites and other petty crimes, are at ☎ **06/6769-4700,** and the vigili urbani, who write parking tickets and tow cars and are regarded as general *rompipalle* (pains-in-the-ass) by every Italian driver, are at Via della Consolazione 4 (on the south side of the Forum, off Vico Jugario; ☎ **06/67691**). To report a fire, a gas leak, or a grandma stuck in an elevator, dial ☎ **115** for the vigili del fuoco (fire department).

For medical emergencies, call an ambulance at ☎ **118,** or visit the *pronto soccorso* (emergency room, where you will not be charged for treatment, regardless of your insurance status) at the nearest hospital: **Fatebenefratelli** (on Tiber Island; ☎ **06/6821- 0828**), **Santo Spirito** (Lungotevere in Sassia 1, near the Vatican; ☎ **06/68351**), **San Giacomo** (Via Canova 29, near Piazza del Popolo; ☎ **06/36261**), or **San Giovanni** (Via dell'Amba Aradam 8, south of the Colosseum; ☎ **06/77051**).

Internet/Wireless Hot Spots   In addition to the Internet cafes listed below, you can often get online at pubs with a large expat clientele, and most hostels and budget hotels have an Internet terminal set up in the lobby, which guests can use for free or for a nominal fee. And there's a new federal law you need to remember—bring your ID when you need to use a public terminal.

Easy Internet (Piazza Barberini 2–16) is open daily 8am to 2am. There are 250 PCs and a Subway sandwich shop inside. Rates are from 3€ an hour. **Internet Train/Verba** (Via delle Fratte di Trastevere 44/b, off Viale Trastevere; ☎ **06/583-4033**) is open daily from 9am to 9pm. They have 15 PCs, and everyone there is so friendly. Sent many an

ROME

MTV chapter from here—threw the ole laptop on the motorino and plugged 'er in!! Rates are from 4€ per hour. **The NetGate** (Piazza di Firenze 25, near the Pantheon; ☎ **06/ 689-3445**) has 25 PCs.

Laundry   **Onda Blu** has two locations south of Termini, at Via Principe Amedeo 70/b and Via Lamarmora 12; both are open daily 8am to 10pm. **Wash&Dry** is in Trastevere at Via della Pelliccia 35 (at Piazza de' Renzi) and near Piazza Navona at Via della Chiesa Nuova 15/16; both are open daily from 8am to 10pm. At either Onda Blu or Wash&Dry, 3.50€ will get you one load washed, another 3.50€ will get you 20 minutes in the dryer.

Alternatively, seek out the local *tintoria* (full-service laundry/dry cleaning) where they'll wash, dry, and fold your load for a bit more than it would cost to do it yourself, but at least you won't be wasting valuable Rome time hauling dirty laundry across town and waiting for the spin cycle to be over.

Luggage Storage   The luggage storage *(deposito bagagli)* service at Termini Station (on the underground concourse, on the Via Giolitti side, near track 24; ☎ **06/4782-5543;** daily 6am–midnight) will store your stuff for 3.80€ per piece for the first 5 hours. Each successive hour (6–12 hr.) is .60€ per piece per hour. After 12 hours, the hourly rate goes all the way down to .20€ per piece.

Post Offices   When you're in the Vatican area, you can also send your postcards home via the **Poste Vaticane (Vatican mail).** Postage rates are the same as with the Italian mail, and Vatican stamps are as artistic as anything you'll find on the walls of the Sistine Chapel. The Vatican mail has a reputation for being faster and more reliable than the Italian mail—all outgoing mail is blessed by a special postal priest. The only drawback is that you can only mail your postcards and letters from the Vatican. It's located next to the info office in St. Peter's Square and is open Monday to Friday from 8:30am to 7pm and Saturday from 8:30am to 6pm.

There are several branches of the **Poste Italiane (Italian post office)** throughout Rome: Look for the yellow and blue PT signs.

Restrooms   You should have no qualms about stopping in the nearest bar/cafe or restaurant and politely asking the management if you can use their *bagno*.

Safety   Rome is probably the safest large city you'll ever encounter. Walking around at night in any of the central neighborhoods should be a nonissue; the only crime, usually in crowded tourist areas, at the train station, or on public transportation is pickpocketing. Gypsies, or *rom*, are a problem in Rome. On buses, Metro trains, or anywhere there are crowds and tourists (busy piazzas, museum lines, and so on), you should always be vigilant about your bags, money, and other valuables. This is also true of any cafe or restaurant with outside seating or any especially busy bar or pizzeria where a pickpocket could easily walk in and out unnoticed.

At night and on Sundays, the area around the Termini train station fills up with unsavory types; it can be unpleasant navigating your way through these hordes of derelicts. Everything else is common sense: Stay out of unpopulated parks at night; and beware of strangers (especially non-Italians) who are too friendly, as this can lead to a variety of bizarre and costly scams involving nightclubs, champagne tabs, and leather jackets.

Tipping In Rome, as in the rest of Italy, there are no hard and fast rules about tipping, but at the very least, all Romans tip the *barista* at their local coffee bar. You'll make a *bella figura* (good impression) and usually get faster service if you leave an extra 10 to 20 *centesimi* on the counter when you're having a *caffè* or cappuccino. For good service at restaurants, feel free to add a few euros (in cash only) to the bill as gratuity—it may be less than 10%, but it's plenty in this culture—but feel free, too, to withhold the extra change if service has been crappy. If you take a cab, round the fare up to the next whole euro amount: If the fare is 8.30€, give the driver 9€. If you're taking a cab to or from the airport, give the driver exactly 5€ as gratuity.

Sleeping

If you don't plan ahead, it can be very tough to find a desirable, cheap place to stay in Rome. "Cheap" is relative, and even with advance booking, you should expect to spend more on lodging here than anywhere else in Italy. Most of Rome's cheap hotels are on the seedy streets near Termini, but we only recommend a few because better options are out there.

Location is a huge key to enjoying your time in Rome, and you're generally much better off seeking lodging that's central, even if it means paying a premium for it. In the heart of the centro storico, **ℳ Best** **Campo de' Fiori** and **Piazza Navona** are the best all-around zones for eating and drinking, with streetlife that doesn't stop from sunrise to the wee hours, and you'll be able to walk pretty much everywhere. Another great area for charm and vitality is **Monti,** the medieval neighborhood just north of Ancient Rome. For posh surroundings but relatively quiet nightlife, head for the **Spanish Steps,** which is also convenient to most monuments. For an old-fashioned village-y feel by day and energetic vibe by night, stay in **Trastevere,** but it's a bit more removed from the sights. The **Vatican** area has some great value accommodations in more modern buildings, but you're in for a bus ride or a decent hike to get to most sights and the action of the centro storico.

Hostels

ℳ Best → **The Beehive** ★★ If you have to crash in the train station area, by all means, get a bed at this self-styled "hotel and art space" run by a friendly American couple who gave up their Los Angeles careers 8 years ago and came to Rome to open a hostel. If you didn't think hostels could get in on the whole "lifestyle" design game, guess again. Steve and Linda have poured a ton of taste and creativity into making their budget inn a cool place. Furnishings are modern and soothing, with vintage surf-inspired fabrics in the rooms and stylish, contemporary light fixtures casting a flattering glow throughout. There's also a small lounge, as well as an outdoor "living room" where you can chill, eat, or drink amid fig and lemon trees, vines, and herbs. (Note that the Beehive is a very chill hostel—so if you're intent on doing the obnoxious pub-crawl thing, you should stay elsewhere.) The Beehive's one dorm room has four bunk beds; each of the eight beds is equipped with its own adjustable reading light. The other rooms at the Beehive are private rooms, which can be booked as doubles or triples. While there's no A/C, all rooms have ceiling fans and screens for keeping the mosquitoes out in summer. The hotel is entirely nonsmoking. *Via Marghera 8.* ☎ *06/4470-4553. www.the-beehive.com.* 20€–22€

ROME

Rome

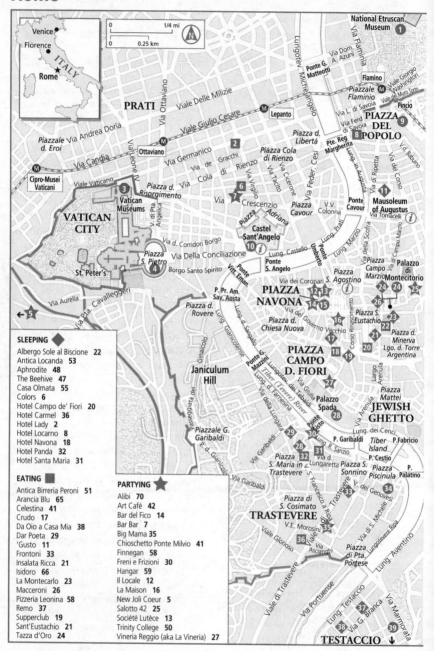

National Etruscan Museum 1

Venice
Florence
ITALY
Rome

PRATI

Lungotev. Michelangelo
Ponte G. Matteotti
Via Dom. A. Azuni
Via Flaminia
Flaminio
Flamino
Piazzale Flaminio
Viale Giorgio Washington
Viale del Muro Torto
Via Ottaviano
Viale Delle Milizie
Pincio
Lepanto
Via L. di Savoia
Via Ferd. di Savoia
Viale Giulio Cesare
Piazza d. Libertà
PIAZZA DEL POPOLO 9
Piazzale Via Andrea Doria d. Eroi
Via Candia
Viale Leone IV
Ottaviano
Via Germanico
Via de Gracchi
Rienzo
Piazza Cola di Rienzo
Pte. Reg. Margherita
Lung. in Augusta
8
V.d. Babuino
Via del Corso
Via di Ripetta
Ottaviano
Cipro-Musei Vaticani
Viale Vaticano
Piazza d. Risorgimento
Via Cola di
Via Virgilio
Via Tacito
Via Cicerone
Via Feder. Cesi
6
7
Crescenzio
Piazza Cavour
Ponte Cavour
V.V. Colonna
Mausoleum of Augustus 11
Via Tomacelli
VATICAN CITY
V. di Pta. Angelica
Vatican Museums
3
Via d. Corridori Borgo
Piazza Adriana
Castel Sant'Angelo
10
Lung. Castello
Lung. Marzio
Lung. Prati
Via della Scrofa
Via di Campo Marzio
Palazzo di Montecitorio
St. Peter's
Piazza S. Pietro
4
Via Della Conciliazione
Borgo Santo Spirito
Ponte Vitt. Eman.
Ponte S. Angelo
Ponte Umberto
Via dei Coronari
Piazza S. Agostino
Via di Campo Marzio
24
24
25
Via Aurelia
Via Pta. Cavalleggeri
P. Pr. Am. Sav. Aosta
Piazza d. Rovere
Lung. Gianicolense
Ponte Vitt. Eman.
PIAZZA NAVONA
12 13
14 15
Via del Governo Vecchio
Piazza S. Agostino
Corso Rinascimento
Piazza S. Eustachio
23
26
Palazzo di
5
Piazza d. Chiesa Nuova
16
17
22
21
20
Piazza S. Minerva
Lgo. d. Torre Argentina
Janiculum Hill
Lung. Sangallo
Ponte G. Mazzini
Lungotev. dei Fiorentini
Tiber (Tevere) River
18
19
PIAZZA CAMPO D. FIORI
27
Largo Arenula
Via Giulia
Via d. Farnesina
Lung. d. Farnesina
Palazzo Spada
28
Piazza Mattei
JEWISH GHETTO
Passeggiata del Gianicolo
Piazzale G. Garibaldi
P.le d. Gianicolo
Via Garibaldi
Via della Lungara
Ponte Sisto
Via Arenula
29
30
28
31
32
P. Garibaldi
Lung. R. Sanzio
Lung. dei Cenci
Tiber Island
P.Fabricio
Via d. Lungaretta
Piazza S. Sonnino
P. Cestio
Piazza S. Piscinula
P. Palatino
Piazza S. Maria in Trastevere
Via Garibaldi
33
34
Via Francesco a Ripa
Piazza di S. Cosimato
TRASTEVERE
V.E. Morosini
V. del Genovesi
35
Viale di Trastevere
Viale Glorioso
36
Via Asclanghi
Piazza di Pta. Portese
Lungotevere Ripa
Via di S. Michele
Via Portuense
Lung. Testaccio
Via G. Branca
Via Marmorata
Lung. Aventino
37
38
39
TESTACCIO ↓

SLEEPING ◆

Albergo Sole al Biscione 22
Antica Locanda 53
Aphrodite 48
The Beehive 47
Casa Olmata 55
Colors 6
Hotel Campo de' Fiori 20
Hotel Carmel 36
Hotel Lady 2
Hotel Locarno 8
Hotel Navona 18
Hotel Panda 32
Hotel Santa Maria 31

EATING ■

Antica Birreria Peroni 51
Arancia Blu 65
Celestina 41
Crudo 17
Da Oio a Casa Mia 38
Dar Poeta 29
'Gusto 11
Frontoni 33
Insalata Ricca 21
Isidoro 66
La Montecarlo 23
Macceroni 26
Pizzeria Leonina 58
Remo 37
Supperclub 19
Sant'Eustachio 21
Tazza d'Oro 24

PARTYING ★

Alibi 70
Art Café 42
Bar del Fico 14
Bar Bar 7
Big Mama 35
Chioschetto Ponte Milvio 41
Finnegan 58
Freni e Frizioni 30
Hangar 59
Il Locale 12
La Maison 16
New Joli Coeur 5
Salotto 42 25
Société Lutèce 13
Trinity College 50
Vineria Reggio (aka La Vineria) 27

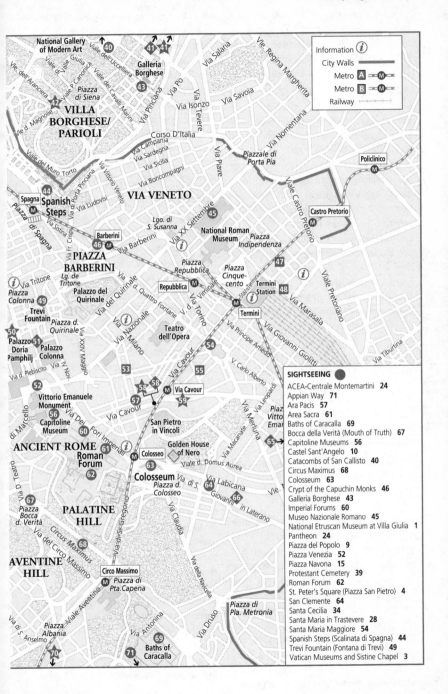

National Gallery
of Modern Art **40**

Galleria
Borghese

43

Viale dell'Uccelliera

Viale P. Canonica

Viale dei Cavalli Marini

Via dell'Arancera

Viale di Valle Giulia

41 41

Via Salaria

Vle. Regina Margherita

Via Po

Via Pinciana

Via Savoia

Via Isonzo

Via Tevere

47

*Piazza
di Siena*

**VILLA
BORGHESE/
PARIOLI**

Vle. d. Magnolie

Viale del Muro Torto

Corso D'Italia

Via Campania

Via Sardegna

Via Sicilia

Via Boncompagni

Via Pinciana

Via Vittorio Veneto

Via Nomentana

*Piazzale di
Porta Pia*

Policlinico Ⓜ

Viale Castro Pretorio

Castro Pretorio Ⓜ

Spagna Ⓜ **44**
**Spanish
Steps**

Piazza
di Spagna

Via di Porta Pinciana

Via Ludovisi

VIA VENETO

Lgo. di
S. Susanna

45

Via XX Settembre

**National Roman
Museum** *Piazza
Indipendenza*

Via Fr. Crispi

Via Sistina

Barberini Ⓜ

46 Via Barberini

**PIAZZA
BARBERINI**

Lg. de
Tritone

Via del Quirinale

Via d. Quattro Fontane

*Piazza
Repubblica*

*Piazza
Cinque-
cento*

**Termini
Station**

47

Viale Pretoriano

ⓘ

Ⓜ **Barberini**

Via Tritone

*Piazza
Colonna* **49**

**Trevi
Fountain**

**Palazzo del
Quirinale**

Via Nazionale

*Piazza d.
Quirinale*

Republica Ⓜ

Via d. Viminale

Via d. Torino

Ⓜ **Termini**

48

Via Marsala

Via Tiburtina

50
Palazzo 51
**Doria Palazzo
Pamphilj Colonna**

Via d. Plebiscito

Via XXIV Maggio

Via IV Nov.

Via Milano

53

*Teatro
dell'Opera*

54

Via Cavour

Via Principe Amedeo

Via Giovanni Giolitti

52

**Vittorio Emanuele
Monument**

56

**Capitoline
Museum 60**

Via Dei Fori Imperiali

Via Cavour

55

58 58 **Via Cavour** Ⓜ

57 59

**San Pietro
in Vincoli**

Via Macante

Piaz
Vitto
Eman

Via Carlo Alberto

Via Merluna

Via Leopardi

65

ANCIENT ROME
**Roman
Forum**

61 ⓘ

Ⓜ **Colosseo**

**Golden House
of Nero**

Viale d. Domus Aurea

Via Labicana

66 in Lateran

62

63

Colosseum Via di S.

*Piazza d.
Colosseo*

64

Via Giovanni

Via di Marcello

di Teatro

67
*Piazza
Bocca
d. Verità*

**PALATINE
HILL**

Via dis. Gregorio

Via Claudia

**AVENTINE
HILL**

Via del Circo Massimo

Circus Massimo

68

Circo Massimo Ⓜ

*Piazza di
Pta.Capena*

Via della Navicella

Via di S. Anselmo

*Piazza
Albania*

70

Viale Aventino

Via Antonina

*Piazza di
Pla. Metronia*

Via Druso

69
**Baths of
Caracalla**

71

Information ⓘ

City Walls ▬▬▬

Metro Ⓐ ═Ⓜ═

Metro Ⓑ ═Ⓜ═

Railway ┼─┼─┼

SIGHTSEEING ⬤

ACEA-Centrale Montemartini **24**
Appian Way **71**
Ara Pacis **57**
Area Sacra **61**
Baths of Caracalla **69**
Bocca della Verità (Mouth of Truth) **67**
Capitoline Museums **56**
Castel Sant'Angelo **10**
Catacombs of San Callisto **40**
Circus Maximus **68**
Colosseum **63**
Crypt of the Capuchin Monks **46**
Galleria Borghese **43**
Imperial Forums **60**
Museo Nazionale Romano **45**
National Etruscan Museum at Villa Giulia **1**
Pantheon **24**
Piazza del Popolo **9**
Piazza Venezia **52**
Piazza Navona **15**
Protestant Cemetery **39**
Roman Forum **62**
St. Peter's Square (Piazza San Pietro) **4**
San Clemente **64**
Santa Cecilia **34**
Santa Maria in Trastevere **28**
Santa Maria Maggiore **54**
Spanish Steps (Scalinata di Spagna) **44**
Trevi Fountain (Fontana di Trevi) **49**
Vatican Museums and Sistine Chapel **3**

ROME

dorm bed, 70€–75€ double, 25€ extra bed. Metro: Termini. Amenities: Cafe; concierge; gift shop; Internet; language classes; massage; Wi-Fi; yoga. In room: Ceiling fans, hair dryer (on request), Internet, iron (on request), Wi-Fi.

→**Casa Olmata** ★ One of the better budget accommodations options in the south-of-Termini zone. Just off Piazza Santa Maria Maggiore, in one of the few pockets of charm near Rome's main train station, this is a great setup with friendly service and rooms ranging from economical private doubles to six-person (mixed) dorms. The neighborhood is clean and safe, full of pubs and pizzerias frequented by other backpackers and resident expats. Fiddler's Elbow Irish pub is right next door. Guests at Casa Olmata have access to the building's fantastic rooftop terrace, with 360-degree views over the heart of the city. The hostel also sponsors a "Spaghetti Party" for its guests every other night—optional, but it can be a great way to meet and exchange travel tips with other young people from all over the world. Via dell'Olmata 36. ☎ 06/483-019. www.casaolmata.com. 20€–22€ dorm, 54€–58€ double, 75€ triple, 92€–120€ quad. Rates vary in high season. Metro: Termini or Cavour. Bus: 75. Amenities: Breakfast room; Internet; kitchen; linens. In room: TV.

→**Colors** ★★ I worked for the owners of this hotel/hostel, Pierluigi and Fulvia, for 5 years. They love Rome with all their hearts, and they'll do everything in their power to make sure you have a great time in their beloved city. Furthermore, they know backpackers better than you know yourself and will anticipate your every need. In short, they rock. Intimate and lovingly kept, their hotel has private rooms (some with private bathroom, some with shared bathroom) and dorm rooms, all of which are painted in bright, tasteful colors like tangerine and lime. Colors attracts a lot of young, independent travelers, and you can hang out with fellow guests in the fully equipped,

eat-in kitchen or on the terrace outside. One of Rome's best takeout delis, Franchi, is 2 blocks away. While Colors doesn't formally serve breakfast, they do stock the kitchen with Corn Flakes, coffee, tea, and jam. Colors is also affiliated with excellent walking tours. Via Boezio 31, at Via Terenzio. ☎ 06/687-4030. www.colorshotel.com. 25€ dorm, 90€–120€ double. Metro: Ottaviano. Bus: 23, 81, 87, 271, or 492. Amenities: Kitchen; shared bathrooms (in some rooms); sheets. In room: A/C.

Cheap

[M̄V̄ Best] →**Albergo Sole al Biscione** ★★ I can't even begin to tell you how much I love this place. I lived at this peach-walled hotel, a block from Campo de' Fiori, when I was a student, and it's still where I stay whenever I travel to Rome. Dating from the 15th century, the Sole is the oldest hotel in the city, with four floors that wrap around a multilevel interior garden where you can drink wine and write postcards. The rooms that overlook the courtyard garden are the best, so definitely request a camera sul giardino at the time of booking—you can open your shutters and take in all the romance of the surrounding ochre-washed walls, faux antique statuary, and greenery, and hear the church bells from Sant'Andrea della Valle several times daily. The cheaper rooms have a sink only (toilets and showers are down the hall and shared by very few other guests), but I actually prefer them to the cramped rooms with full private bathrooms, which put beds and toilets too close for comfort. The hotel is a popular choice for university groups, so there are usually a bunch of students running around or studying in their rooms with their doors open. At night, all the bars and restaurants of Campo de' Fiori are a minute away. Via del Biscione 76, at Piazza del Paradiso. ☎ 06/6880-6873. www.soalbiscione.it. 65€ single with shared bathroom, 85€ with private

Rome Metropolitana

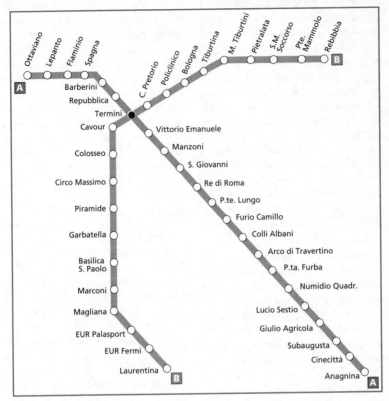

bathroom; 95€ double with shared bathroom, 110€–150€ with private bathroom. Bus: 30, 40, 46, 62, 64, 70, 87, 116, 492, or 571. Tram: 8. Amenities: Garden; shared bathrooms (in some rooms). In room: TV, fan.

→ **Aphrodite** ★ As you walk into the soothing reception area of this hotel, you might wonder, is the Aphrodite a hotel or a day spa? Opened in 2003, this place is an amazing oasis of tranquillity right across the street from the grime and chaos of Termini station. Modern rooms feature spotless wide-plank wood floors; bland furniture in light, calming tones; and boldly painted canvases above the beds. The quality of the bathrooms, considering the price, is also remarkable: Sinks have luxurious polished travertine counters, and the walls are done

up in colorful mosaics. The California-style rooftop terrace has redwood chaises, benches, tables, white canvas umbrellas, and boxes of geraniums. Via Marsala 90, at Via Milazzo. ☎ 06/491-096. www.accommodation inrome.com. 90€–120€ double, 90€–150€ triple, 110€–130€ quad. Metro: Termini. In room: A/C, TV, minibar, safe.

→ **Hotel Carmel** Of the few hotels in Trastevere, the Carmel is one of the best deals. The 20th-century building where the Carmel is located might not be the atmospheric 16th-century palazzo of your Roman dreams, but it's actually a good example of the kind of digs that most real Romans call home. This location is not the most charming part of Trastevere, but it's lively and plenty safe: A 5-minute downhill walk puts you in the thick of all the restaurants and village-y atmosphere of the neighborhood. The singles, doubles, and triples are decorated with richly colored bedspreads with stripes and florals that clash with Oriental throw rugs, which, in turn, clash with black-and-white checkerboard floor tiles. There's a roof garden with vines trained over a metal pergola and a bird's-eye view of the surrounding neighborhood. Surprise feature: The hotel also has a deal with a kosher kitchen. *Via Goffredo Mameli 11 (extension of Via Morosini, north of Viale Trastevere).* ☎ *06/580-9921. www.hotelcarmel.it. 85€ single, 90€–100€ double, 140€ triple. Tram: 8. Bus: 75, 780, or H. Amenities: Cafe; fitness center; garden. In room: A/C, TV, fridge, safe.*

➔**Hotel Lady** ★★ Oh, she's a lady, all right. This hotel is surprisingly elegant for such a low price. Ceilings with big, dark exposed wood beams and iron curtain rods create an old-world feel; and warm, parlor-style light fixtures and knotty pine doors and armoires give it a cozy, cabin-in-the-woods vibe. The rooms aren't exactly big, but they work. The cheapest rooms have a sink only; some have a shower; only a few doubles (the most expensive) have full bathrooms. There's an extra charge for A/C, and breakfast isn't included. Nearby is one of the better mainstream shopping streets in Rome, with plenty of coffee bars where you can grab your cappuccino. *Via Germanico 198 (near Via Fabio Massimo).* ☎ *06/324-2112. www.hotelladyroma.it. 50€–90€ single, 70€–150€ double, 90€–145€ triple. Metro: Ottaviano or Lepanto. Bus: 70 or 81. Amenities: Internet; shared bathrooms (in some rooms); shuttle service to airport. In room: A/C (for a fee), TV.*

➔**Hotel Panda** ★ It's no secret that this *pensione* on lively Via della Croce is the best value hotel in the Spanish Steps area, and its 20 rooms get booked up quickly. Rooms are spare, but not without a bit of old-fashioned charm, like characteristic Roman *cotto* (terra-cotta) floor tiles and exposed beam ceilings with light-colored wood. The cheaper singles and doubles do not have a private bathroom; the triples are with full private bathroom only. The en suite bathrooms tend to be cramped, however. Right outside your doorstep, there are several great cafes and wine bars. *Via della Croce 35, at Via Belsiana.* ☎ *06/678-0179. www.hotelpanda.it. 45€–68€ single, 65€–98€ double, 124€–130€ triple. Metro: Spagna. Amenities: Internet; shared bathrooms (in some rooms). In room: A/C.*

Doable

➔**Antica Locanda** ★★ A fantastic find in medieval Monti, the Antica Locanda is especially suited for couples not only because of its romantic decor, but because almost all rooms here are "matrimonial" doubles (not twin beds). Each of the 13 rooms is named for a different artist or composer: The Puccini is a cozy lair with a wrought-iron bedstead, buttercream walls, exposed beam ceiling, and Oriental rugs on the handsome terra-cotta tile floor. The Rossini is homey and elegant, like the guest room in your favorite relative's house, with a blue floral coverlet, brass bedstead, and dark-wood floors. Loveliest of all is the Mascagni Suite, which starts at a reasonable 155€ in the low season. Breakfast is served in the roof garden in warm weather. In the bohemian neighborhood, you'll find a number of excellent places to eat and drink. *Via del Boschetto 84 (at Via Panisperna).* ☎ *06/484-894. www.antica-locanda.com. 130€–210€ double, 155€–250€ Mascagni suite. Rates include breakfast. Metro: Cavour. Bus: 40, 64, 70, or 75. Amenities: 2 restaurants; garden. In room: A/C, TV, hair dryer, minibar.*

➔**Hotel Campo de' Fiori** ★ In an ivy-smothered building in the prime Campo de'

Fiori zone, this government-rated two-star is just a shade more comfy than the nearby Sole, Smeraldo, and Pomezia hotels, but priced about 50€ higher. Room decor—and comfort level—are all over the place in the hotel's 28 rooms, running the gamut from grandma's-house baby-blue florals in bright and spacious top-floor rooms to cramped and dark, cabin-y doubles with tiny private bathrooms. All guests have access to the hotel's panoramic roof terrace, with great views of the dome of Sant'Andrea della Valle. Continental breakfast is included in the room rate and served in a classy subterranean dining room. There's no lift. If the hotel's rooms are all booked, ask about the 15 short-term apartments they also rent. *Via del Biscione 6, off Campo de' Fiori.* ☎ *06/6880-6865. www.hotelcampodefiori.com. 150€–180€ double, 190€–220€ triple, 210€–250€ quad. Rates include breakfast. Bus: 30, 40, 46, 64, 70, 87, 116, 492, or 571. Amenities: Breakfast room; terrace.*

→ **Hotel Navona** ★★ It's hard to believe this wonderfully lived-in, historic inn between Piazza Navona and the Pantheon is only a one-star hotel. From the elegant entryway to the spacious and well-lit, tastefully decorated rooms, it's also hard to believe that the Australian family that runs the place has kept prices so low. The Navona is continuously being restored, but with careful attention to preserving its antique character, so rooms get more comfortable every year, with soft lighting and relaxing green bedding, while cozy period touches, like exposed beam ceilings, remain intact. The Romantic poets Keats and Shelley were once boarders on the upper floors, and there are ancient ruins in the basement. If you can score a room here, you'll definitely want to come back. All rooms have a private bathroom and A/C, but there's a 15€-per-day charge for it. *Via dei Sediari 8, off Corso Rinascimento.* ☎ *06/686-4203. www.hotelnavona.com. 90€–110€ single, 125€–140€ double, 160€–185€*

triple. *Bus: 30, 40, 46, 62, 64, 70, 87, 116, 492, or 571. Amenities: Breakfast room. In room: A/C.*

→ **Hotel Santa Maria** ★★ Hidden off a tiny alley in the very best part of Trastevere, the Santa Maria is quite a surprising treat to behold. It's a one-story property, with rooms arranged almost motel-like, on porticoed halls around a lovely courtyard with orange trees. The rooms, which range from singles to bilevel suites, aren't exactly palatial, but they're fresh and comfy, with simple oak furniture, *cotto* tile floors, and sunny bedspreads, and the suites are a good-value option if you're traveling in a group. Don't plan to have a loud night in your room—the romantic Santa Maria is a quiet hotel—but this incredibly nightlife-friendly location means you can hit the surrounding bars and eateries and have an easy commute back to your bed. In additional to its orange trees, the central garden has tables and chairs where an ample breakfast is served in warm weather; otherwise, you eat breakfast in a converted artisan's workshop. This is an absolute treasure in a hotel-starved neighborhood. *Vicolo del Piede 2, between Piazza Santa Maria in Trastevere and Via della Pelliccia.* ☎ *06/589-4626. www.htlsantamaria. com. 135€–165€ single, 155€–210€ double, 200€–250€ triple, 250€–320€ 4-person suite, 350€–450€ 6-person suite. Bus: 23, 271, or 280. Tram: 8. Amenities: Bikes for rent; Internet. In room: A/C, TV, hair dryer, minibar, safe.*

Splurge

🎵 **Best** → **Hotel Locarno** ★★ Sashay back in time to the glamorous 1920s at this fabulously stylish, understatedly hip hotel near Piazza del Popolo. The exterior of the hotel gives no indication of how wonderful this place is. The "deluxe" double rooms and suites in the east wing of the building are where you want to be: These are the *Great Gatsby* rooms, the breathtaking period pieces with original Art Nouveau furniture,

ROME

walls washed in sumptuously fading colors, and high, intricately coffered ceilings. The dark and cramped standard and "superior" doubles in the main building are not nearly as interesting (some are frankly depressing). All guests have access to a small, attractive patio in the back. Overall, the nostalgic, romantic atmosphere of the Locarno has made it a favorite with visiting filmmakers, poets, and other artistic types. *Via della Penna 22, off Via Ripetta.* ☎ *06/361-0841. www.hotellocarno.com. 140€ single, 210€– 310€ double, 450€–650€ suite. Metro: Flaminio. Amenities: Breakfast courtyard. In room: A/C, TV, minibar, safe.*

Eating

Rome's casual, high-quality dining scene is one of the city's most attractive qualities. All over town, you can just walk in and have an amazing meal with free-flowing wine in a fun, authentic place for less than 15€ per person. While finding and paying for *hotels* in Rome might stress you (and your wallet) out, the good news is, eating and drinking in Rome won't—the trick is to steer clear of restaurants that are right on the main squares, as they tend to be way-overpriced tourist traps.

Roman cuisine is traditional and simple. You won't find a whole lot of variety, but you will find time-tested, intensely flavorful and satisfying pastas; a selection of grilled or roast pork, beef, or seafood dishes; and a variety of tasty vegetable side dishes *(contorni)*. If you're looking for poultry, you're in the wrong town. Start your meal off with a bruschetta (pronounced "broo-*skeh*-tah")— toasted bread with garlic and whatever else smeared on top, and end it with whatever *dolce fatto in casa* (homemade dessert) they're offering. *Panna cotta* (cooked cream), tiramisu, *crème caramel,* or a simple *macedonia* (fresh fruit cup, with lemon juice squeezed on top) are all widely available.

As for drinks, the standard combo is vino (of course!) and *acqua minerale* (mineral water): You can request *liscia* (still), *frizzante* (sparkling), or, locals' favorite compromise, *Ferrarelle* (this is a brand name but is also understood to mean water with just a touch of fizz). All but the simplest restaurants have some kind of wine list, but the *vino della casa* (house wine) is what you'll be ordering most of the time. If you like cocktails with your dinner, too bad; it's simply not done in Rome. Note that very few Roman restaurants have a bar area where you can just come and have a drink either before or totally separate from your meal.

In general, the best areas for down-home Roman cooking and lively atmosphere are the backstreets of the centro storico, Monti, and Trastevere. For a young, social atmosphere and really cheap tab, sit-down pizzerias are your best bet. If you manage to befriend any locals, the weekend-night out-of-town meal, at a rustic osteria in one of the countless hill towns around Rome, is a favorite pastime of fun-loving types and a classic experience you'll not soon forget.

Hot Spots

➔ **'Gusto** ★★ ITALIAN The 'Gusto gourmet triumvirate occupies an imposing, fascist-era building on the northern side of Piazza Augusto Imperatore. 'Gusto itself is a modern restaurant and pizzeria (two different dining rooms with two different menus and festivity levels) in a buzzy, soaring space slightly reminiscent of high school wood shop, with blocky, unfinished wooden tables, white butcher-block-paper table liners, and industrial-looking ducts overhead. Black-clad staff is friendly (and much better looking than most customers), and there's a ton to choose from on the reasonably priced pizzeria

when in Rome, Breakfast as the Romans Do

The majority of Italian hotels throw in some kind of continental breakfast involving stale croissants, weak coffee, and—randomly—cheese, but you can and should get a much better, more authentic Roman breakfast at the nearest coffee bar, which are everywhere in Rome—just look for the words "bar" or "caffetteria." A typical *colazione* is taken standing up at your neighborhood bar and consists of cappuccino and a pastry from the bar's glass counter. Your drink and pastry should cost a whopping 2€, but you'll pay about double that if you sit down (Italians don't). If you like OJ in the morning, all Roman bars will squeeze you a fresh orange *spremuta* for about 2€. Until you become a regular, it's a good idea to pay first (there's usually a separate cashier), and always lay down a .10€ to .20€ tip on the counter when you place your order with the barista.

menu; the restaurant menu is more expensive and eclectic (the atmosphere is also more uptight). For either, it's a good idea to make reservations. *Piazza Augusto Imperatore 9, off Via Ripetta.* ☎ *06/322-6273. www.gusto.it. Pizzeria: pizza from 7€. Restaurant: primi from 9€; secondi from 14€. Daily 12:45–3pm and 7:45pm–midnight. Metro: Flaminio or Spagna. Bus: 913.*

→ **Macceroni** ★ ITALIAN   There's nothing too flashy about the restaurant itself, but this is a favorite of stylish young locals who work in TV, film, or finance, who come here for dinner in huge groups before laying siege to the equally hip and laid-back bars and clubs of the centro. The fare at Maccheroni is simple but perfectly executed, and reasonably priced, considering how frequently we use the term "heavenly" to describe it. The pasta *alla gricia* (with *pecorino Romano* cheese, black pepper, and pancetta) is a heavenly plate of steaming goodness. A long list of secondi includes a heavenly and oh-so-tender *tagliata di manzo con rughetta* (grilled beef strips on a bed of arugula) and good, old-fashioned *polpettine al sugo* (meatballs in red sauce). One of the more perfect spots in the centro storico for getting a little drunk (hello, the house wine is 3€ a liter!!), eating great food, and being in the company of some of the chicer citizens of Rome. *Via delle Coppelle 44, at Via degli Spagnoli.* ☎ *06/6830-7895. Primi 8€–14€; secondi 10–15€. Daily noon–3pm and 8pm–midnight. Bus: 30, 40, 46, 62, 64, 70, 81, 87, 116, 492, 571, or 628. Tram: 8.*

MTV Best → **Supper Club** ★★ GLOBAL For a transporting experience into modern Euro-fabulousness, check out this über-trendy spinoff of the original joint in Amsterdam. Its white interiors strike quite a contrast with its location, near the 1,900-year-old Pantheon, but just like the ancient Romans, here you eat lying down, get a massage, are served by half-naked waiters, and listen to great music (only nowadays of the chill-out variety; no lyre-strumming). Dinner is prix-fixe and actually delicious for such a themed place—expect several courses of creative, Mediterranean- and Asian-inspired dishes that are light, flavorful, and relatively easy to eat in a reclining position. After dinner, Supperclub is like a Habitrail for hipsters, with long, narrow tunnels that terminate in various play areas—dining rooms with broad white sofas, cage-like bars, or swank dance floors (but no hamster wheel, darn it all). Note that reservations should be made several days in advance for dinner; if they're booked, you can always come by around 11:30pm, when it morphs into a nightclub. *Via de' Nari 14, at Via Monterone.* ☎ *06/6880-7207. www.supperclub.com. Prixe-fixe*

ROME

dinner 75€ not including drinks. Hours vary, so call ahead.

Cheap

→**Antica Birreria Peroni** ★★★ ITALIAN/ MEATS Despite its location on the heavily trafficked tourist route between ancient Rome and the Trevi Fountain, this hugely popular lunch and dinner spot remains a locals' favorite. Sure, plenty of tourists end up here, too, but the overriding mood is fun, boisterous, and authentically Roman—though there are plenty of hearty dishes here that can pass as American comfort food (good to know when you're hung over). As the name suggests, beer is the drink of choice, so ask for a pitcher as soon as you sit down, or else you'll piss off your waiter. With such a loving attitude toward drinking, it should come as no surprise that the cuisine ain't fancy—the restaurant's claim to fame is an elusive sausage known as The Kilometer, strictly for the hard-core meat-eater. *Via San Marcello 19, off Piazza Santi Apostoli.* ☎ *06/ 679-5310. www.anticabirreriaperoni.com. Primi from 5€; secondi from 8€. Sun–Thurs noon– midnight; Fri–Sat noon–12:30am.*

→**Arancia Blu** ★ VEGETARIAN Gourmets and health freaks can meet each other

---

I Scream for Gelaterias

When it comes to settling on a gelato place, make sure you're getting the good stuff. Almost all gelaterias will advertise *produzione propria* ("made in-house") or *artigianale* ("homemade") even if they're not, so it always pays to do the **banana gelato color test:** If their banana flavor is a muddy, brownish beige (the color of a very ripe banana), it's all natural, and you're good to go. If it's too yellow, it means there are probably artificial colors and other weird chemicals present in all the other flavors at that gelateria, so move on! (One final grammatical point: If you're getting a cup or cone of ice cream, it's *un gelato,* not *gelati*).

Da Quinto ★ GELATO/SMOOTHIES Truth be told, the gelato at this hole in the wall west of Piazza Navona ain't that great—too icy, and kind of flavorless— but their enormous fruit smoothies are amazing. *Via di Tor Millina 15, at Via dell'Anima.* ☎ *06/686-5657. No credit cards. Daily 10am–1am. Closed Jan. Bus: 30, 40, 46, 62, 64, 70, 81, 87, 492, 571, or 628.*

Giolitti ★★ GELATO A de rigueur stop on the tourism shuffle through the *centro storico,* this Roman institution (pronounced "joe-*leet*-tee") is the city's oldest combination *gelateria-pasticceria* and is packed with locals and tourists alike. Some of their better flavors (among about 100 choices) are After Eight (mint chocolate chip), *fiordilatte* (a simple, exquisite sweet cream), and *lampone* (raspberry). *Via degli Uffici del Vicario 40, near Via di Campo Marzio.* ☎ *06/679-4206. www.giolitti.it. No credit cards. Daily 8am–2am. Bus: 62, 85, 95, 116, 175, or 492.*

Pellacchia ★ GELATO Gelaterias abound in the Vatican area, but traditionalists in the know come to Pellacchia, an intimate, old-fashioned combo coffee bar/gelateria right on the shopping strip of Via Cola di Rienzo. Not only is their gelato some of the best in the neighborhood, but staff is super-friendly and will let you try flavors before you place your final order. *Via Cola di Rienzo 103, at Piazza Cola di Rienzo.* ☎ *06/321-0807. No credit cards. Tues–Sun 10am–10pm (midnight in summer). Metro: Lepanto. Bus: 81 or 280.*

halfway at this hip spot in the ugly but lively San Lorenzo university district. The "Blue Orange" disproves the theorem that haute vegetarian food must, by definition, consist of at least 50% soy, and have weird texture and a flavor that only ruminants really enjoy. This is Italy, after all, so even though there's no meat at Arancia Blu, you'll find dishes—including awesome handmade ravioli—made with enough amazing vegetables, garlic, and olive oil to satisfy even the hungriest appetite. (I'm a huge carnivore, and I enjoy this place.) A few plates are safe for vegans, but most feature eggs or cheese in some form or another. The room is a very handsome take on textbook trattoria decor, with hundreds of bottles of wine lining one wall, dark-wood tables and chairs, terra-cotta tile floors, and subtle lighting. Taking advantage of an Italian tax loophole, Arancia Blu is technically not a ristorante but a social club, which explains the (free) membership card you have to fill out before dining. *Via dei Latini 65, at Via dei Sabelli.* ☎ *06/445-4105. Main courses 7€–10€. Daily 8pm–midnight. Bus: 71 or 492. Tram: 3 or 19.*

→ **Frontoni** ★ DELI   I have cured many a hangover (or tried to) with the marvelous pizza-bread sandwiches of Frontoni. You pick the size of pizza bread you want, and you can get as many fillings as you want—mortadella, mozzarella, salmon, basil, sun-dried tomatoes, roasted eggplant, all manner of condiments—and the white-haired men who work behind the counter will sing the names of the ingredients as they lovingly assemble your sandwich. Just be sure they slather it with plenty of olive oil and salt it generously—*mmm mmm!* Grab one of Frontoni's creations and head up to the Gianicolo, where you can plop down in the grass with your picnic and enjoy a glorious view. Besides the sandwiches, Frontoni has hot and cold plates also suitable for takeout. *Viale Trastevere 52, at Via San Francesco a Ripa.* ☎ *06/581-2436. www. frontoni.it. Sandwiches priced by ingredients*

and size, about 3.50€–5€. Mon–Sat 10am–11pm; Sun 5–11pm. Bus: 75, 780 or H. Tram: 8.

→ **Insalata Ricca** SALADS   When you can't bear the thought of one more pasta or pizza carb-fest, breathe easy and make your way to this wildly popular lunch and dinner spot, where the menu features dozens of meal-sized salads. (The name means "rich salad," and that's exactly what you get.) The lettuce is strictly—you guessed it—romaine, but the toppings run from surf to turf to garden patch to dairy farm, with crab meat, *bresaola* (cured beef), artichoke hearts, and fresh *mozzarella di bufala* among the ingredients. Salad-phobes (you know who you are) can also have a fine time here, as there are also plenty of pasta and meat dishes to choose from. Don't let the crowds throw you off—there's a huge inside seating area in addition to all the tables outside, so seats tend to become available pretty quickly. The success of the Insalata Ricca idea has spawned the opening of several other branches around town, none of which holds a candle to the flagship here, a few blocks from Campo de' Fiori. *Largo dei Chiavari 85, at Corso Vittorio Emanuele II.* ☎ *06/6880-3656. www.linsalata ricca.it. Salads from 7€. Daily for lunch and dinner. Bus: 30, 40, 46, 62, 64, 70, 81, 87, 116, 492, 571, or 628. Tram: 8.*

Doable

→ **Celestina** ★★ ROMAN   When Italian TV personalities, soccer stars, and other celebs you wouldn't recognize want a good traditional meal (in an environment where they're sure to get publicity), they come to this down-to-earth joint/hot spot in the posh Parioli neighborhood. For how varied the menu is, Celestina really does a good job on all of it: Among traditional meat- and veggie-based pastas, meat and fish secondi, and even some truly outstanding pizzas, you can't go wrong no matter what you order. While Celestina stays pretty attitude-free despite its continuous celeb clientele, make no

Pizza Party

The cheapest way to fill your stomach in Rome is with pizza. (No, it's not just an American myth—they really do eat a lot of pizza in Italy.) Roman pizzas are thin-crusted and priced anywhere from 4€ for a basic margherita to 8€ for pizzas with more gourmet toppings, like *mozzarella di bufala* and *funghi porcini*. In Rome, as in the rest of Italy, pizzas come in one size only (about 36 centimeters/14 in. in diameter) and are not meant to be shared. The Roman pizzeria is its own category of restaurant, with a young clientele and energetic vibe, and is usually open for dinner only; those that are open at lunch are probably tourist traps and should be avoided. Throughout the day, you can hit up your local *pizza al taglio* (by-the-slice) place for a cheap and delicious snack.

⭐ Best **Dar Poeta** ★★★ One of the most popular pizzas here, the *campagnola* (with fresh cherry tomatoes, *mozzarella di bufala,* and basil), tends to sell out as the night wears on, so try to order it early. Dar Poeta's Naples-style crust is already thicker than most Roman pies, but you can get extra-thick crust for 1€ more by ordering *doppio impasto*. Reservations taken for 7:30 to 8:30pm seatings only. *Vicolo del Bologna 45, near Via della Scala.* ☎ *06/588-0516. Pizzas from 6€. Daily 8pm–1am. Bus: 23, 271, or 280.*

⭐ Best **La Montecarlo** ★★★ If I'm traveling through Rome and only have 1 night for dinner, this is where I'm coming, with all my friends, for bruschetta, pizza, wine, and limoncello—that's how much I love this place. Loud, lively, and super-friendly, La Montecarlo really does feel like a party—there's always an energetic crowd of 20- and 30-somethings waiting for a table, but host extraordinaire Carlo will seat you in a flash if you stride confidently to the front of the line and pretend to be a regular. The pizza is thin-crusted, piping hot, and slightly misshapen, with toppings unevenly distributed—just how we like it. It's

mistake, you should not show up here looking like a schlep. Rock some hot jeans and a funky accessory or two, and the paparazzi who stop by nightly might even mistake you for visiting Hollywood royalty. *Viale Parioli 184, near Piazzale della Rimembranza.* ☎ *06/807-8242. Primi 8€–12€; secondi 10–16€; pizza from 6€. Daily 8pm–midnight. Bus: 52 or 53.*

➜ **Da Oio a Casa Mia** ★ ROMAN Just up the street from Testaccio's monumental (defunct) slaughterhouse, this paper-tablecloth trat keeps it real with no-nonsense *cucina romana* (read: they do a mean fried esophagus and have no time for squeamish tourists). Oio also prepares Roman classics that *don't* involve calf brains, but vegetarians will not find much to order beyond

bread and wine. (With the high volume of animal parts sloshing around in the kitchen, I wouldn't trust them to prepare a fully meat-free anything, even if they advertised such a dish on the menu.) In warm weather, there are a few outdoor tables on the sidewalk of Via Galvani; in cooler months, it's the spit-and-sawdust wood-paneled dining room, which suits this hearty fare perfectly. *Via Galvani 43–45, at Via Mastro Giorgio.* ☎ *06/578-2680. Primi 6€–8€; secondi 8€–12€. Daily 1pm–1am. Bus: 23, 30, 75, or 280. Tram: 3.*

➜ **Isidoro** ★★ PASTA From the outside, this looks like just another traditional Roman osteria, and it does have a full menu, but Isidoro is all about the kick-ass pasta sampling menu. Order the *assaggini misti,* get your partitioned, school-cafeteria type almost tourist-free, and for how busy it gets, service is ridiculously fast but you'll never feel rushed. *Vicolo Savelli 11, at Corso Vittorio Emanuele II.* ☎ *06/686-1877. www.sevoinapizzadillo.net. Pizzas from 5€. Tues–Sun for lunch and dinner. Bus: 40, 64, or 571.*

Pizzeria Leonina ★★ Without a doubt, the best pizza al taglio between the Colosseum and Termini station, and among the best in the entire city. At the lunchtime rush, locals crowd around the cases of freshly made, rectangular pizzas topped with dozens of different combinations of cheeses, vegetables, and meats. Indicate how much you want, and the workers will cut it and reheat it in the oven for a few minutes. There are even dessert pizzas with apples and cinnamon, Nutella, or ricotta and honey. *Via Leonina 84.* ☎ *06/482-7744. Pizza sold by weight and ingredients, usually 1€–3€ for a medium-size slice. Daily 7–11pm. Metro: Cavour.*

Remo ★ If you tell a local you're going to get a pizza in Testaccio—the neighborhood most famous for its slaughterhouse (which was closed in the 1970s) and Monte Testaccio, a 35m-high (115-ft.) pile of broken ancient Roman bottles—it goes without saying that you're going to Remo. The pizza here is classic, thin-crusted Roman, with your standard array of simple earthy toppings (such as fresh local veggies, prosciutto, or the tomato-and-mozzarella standard margherita) and dirt-cheap. Clientele is almost strictly regulars who live within 4 blocks of here, so you might be gawked at for the outsider tourist you are, but in a friendly way. The no-frills dining room consists of just a few rickety tables, so expect to wait at least 15 minutes for a table. *Piazza Santa Maria Liberatrice 44, at Via R. Gessi.* ☎ *06/574-6270. Pizzas from 4€. Mon–Sat 7pm–1am. Closed Aug. Bus: 23, 30, 75, 95, 170, 271, or 280. Tram: 3.*

plate in position, and then let the games begin. New batches of pasta emerge from the kitchen every 8 minutes or so—penne with walnut-nutmeg-cream sauce, gnocchi with gorgonzola, tagliolini with mushrooms and asparagus . . . the hits just keep on coming, so see how many rounds you last until you are KO'd by the carbs. (On some nights, you can also specify the *assaggini misti di pasta al pesce*, in which all the pastas are seafood based.) Our pro tip: Go easy on the water, as that will unnecessarily fill your stomach at a place like this; do order a flask of wine, as it will give you the courage to go more rounds than you would if you were sober. (By now, you've gathered that Isidoro will blow your Atkins/South Beach/whatever diet out of the water, but you're in Italy, damn it!—work it

off by doing a few laps around the Colosseum, just down the street, after dinner.) *Via di San Giovanni in Laterano 59a, 61, 63, near Via dei Querceti.* ☎ *06/700-8266. Assaggini misti, from 8€. Daily 8pm–midnight. Metro: Colosseo. Bus: 60, 85, 87, 117, 175, 271, or 571. Tram: 3.*

Splurge

➜ **Crudo** ★★ FUSION/RAW Opened in 2004, stylish Crudo brings a bit of the New York or London scene to a tiny cobblestone alley near Campo de' Fiori. Perhaps it takes its name and eponymous ethos ("raw") a bit too seriously, staunchly refusing to cook anything, but the striking space—a vast garage-like salon, with unfinished cement walls and floors, 1960s furniture upholstered in white and red leather, and a huge mural of a snarling wolf—is always packed with Roman 20- and 30-something scenesters having an *aperidinner* (that is, stopping in for a drink, and then noshing on enough oysters, sushi, and carpaccio to call it a meal). The food can be outstanding; it can also be just plain weird (such as unidentifiable and seemingly unnecessary sauces), but it's always beautifully presented and impeccably fresh—and of course, it gives Romans an excuse to throw around the word *wasabi*, an asset for trendiness in this image-conscious town. *Via degli Specchi 6, at Via Monte di Farina.* ☎ *06/683-8989. www.crudoroma.it. Small plates from 7€. Daily 12:30pm–2am. Closed for lunch Sun and dinner Mon. Bus: 23, 30, 40, 46, 62, 64, 70, 81, 87, 116, 271, 280, 492, or 571. Tram: 8.*

Cafes

→**Sant'Eustachio** ★★ COFFEE Sant' Eustachio's is by far the most celebrated espresso in the city, so if you're a coffee snob, you'd better make a pilgrimage to this classy little spot just west of the Pantheon. Look for the blue neon sign opposite the church (Sant'Eustachio) with the tape-recorded bells, and get in line. Your first stop is the cashier on the right, where everyone in front of you will be ordering *un grancaffè, per favore.* The grancaffè is Sant'Eustachio's specialty—it's a larger, creamier, and more expensive version of an espresso shot, but before you get peer-pressured into ordering one, know that you can get a regular caffè normale (espresso) or

cappuccino here, too, and they're just as good. Take your receipt to the Art Deco bar on the left, greet the *baristi,* say what you're having (they won't act like they're listening, but they are), and plunk down your .20€ tip on the zinc counter. All Sant'Eustachio drinks are served pre-sweetened unless you request otherwise, so if you don't like sugar in your coffee, specify *amaro* (bitter) or *senza zucchero* (without sugar) with the barista. *Piazza Sant'Eustachio 82, at Piazza dei Caprettari.* ☎ *06/656-1309. Coffee and snacks 2€. Daily 8:30am–1am. Bus: 40, 46, 62, 64, 70, 87, 116, 492, 571, or 628.*

→**Tazza d'Oro** ★ COFFEE Facing the Pantheon, on the northeast corner of Piazza della Rotonda, this is a big and atmospheric coffee bar, with burlap sacks of roasted espresso beans that fill the entire square with a powerful coffee aroma (although the grease stench from McDonald's, a few doors down, can be stiff competition). There's always a long line at the single cashier, but it moves quickly. The baristi are a bit surly, but these guys are lifers who know a thing or two about pulling coffee drinks. In summer, do not miss a chance to cool down and jolt up with their *granita di caffè,* a petite, clear plastic cup filled with crushed frozen espresso, interspersed with layers of full-fat whipped cream. It's the best 1.30€ you'll ever spend, I swear. *Via degli Orfani 84, at Piazza della Rotonda.* ☎ *06/678-9292. Coffee and snacks 2€. Mon–Sat 8am–8pm. Bus: 30, 40, 46, 62, 64, 70, 87, 116, 492, or 571.*

Partying

Club snobs dismiss Rome as a provincial place to party. Let them thumb their noses: If partying means having fun, not stressing about what you're doing or where you're going, drinking cheaply, and being able to change courses quickly, Rome is in fact one of the best places to party in the world. (But if

you're looking for cutting-edge DJs and über-sophisticated lounges, well, not so much.)

Because dinner is still a sacrosanct event around which an evening is built, nightlife in Rome has a definite rhythm to it; there's the aperitivo before your meal, the after-dinner drinks, and the nightclubs. Only at Rome's

Mating Ground

The evening scene at MTV Best **Campo de' Fiori**—produce and fish market by day, pickup central and playa's piazza by night—is like an Animal Planet documentary on Roman mating habits. This is by far the most happening square in Rome, though not the most cutting edge, and a perfectly contained (and traffic-free) world of bars, cafes, and restaurants that locals migrate to every single night. By 6:30pm, gaggles of young Romans have filled the chairs at the alfresco bars for an aperitivo. Some stay for dinner, but most eat elsewhere, so there's a bit of a lull from 8 to 10pm or so. After dinner, the crowds return and the Campo swells once again into one big outdoor party around 1:30 or 2am.

In general, you'll find a younger, more anything-goes scene in the northern half of the square, and a quieter, more middle-aged scene in the southern half. Some of our recommendations:

→ **Vineria Reggio:** Popular with young and old and cheap-cheap-cheap, "La Vineria" is the most democratic spot on the square. See full listing below.

→ **Taverna del Campo:** Similar to its next-door neighbor, the Vineria, but with some occasional unnecessary attitude, this is especially recommended on Sunday afternoons, when many of the other bars are closed. At Piazza Campo de' Fiori 16 (☎ 06/687-4402).

→ **I Giganti:** Loud music thumps inside, while pods of barstools and high tables on the cobblestones outside make for a more pubby atmosphere. The "in" spot for Romans 18 to 25 (which, in American years, is more like 14–21). At Piazza Campo de' Fiori 26 (☎ 06/687-4182).

→ **Il Nolano:** There's a mellower vibe and older demographic at this *bottiglieria* (a bar that takes its wine seriously). View the action from its old-school wooden cinema chairs. At Piazza Campo de' Fiori 11 (☎ 06/687-9344).

ROME

Irish-style pubs can you sit and drink from 5pm till close without looking like a loser. Most bars are open until 2 or 3am, and with the exception of Monday, which is slow throughout Italy, there are tons of people out every night of the week.

Because so many of the best bars and pubs are right in the heart of the centro storico (and within a 5-min. walk of each other), you don't need to worry too much about making a plan. Just start at one place and see where the night takes you. If you get a hankering for club-going, beware: It gets spendy in a hurry. In addition to the cab fare it'll take to get to most of Rome's discos, all the clubs charge a cover of 10€ to 20€, and drinks are usually 7€ to 10€.

The weekly events guide, **Roma C'è** (available at newsstands) is the best single resource for concerts and club events. It's in Italian, but with common words like "house" and "underground," you'll get the gist.

While Roman nights don't demand formal attire, khakis and flip-flops are a no-no unless you're going to one of the city's mostly expatriate Irish pubs. On the flipside, don't overcompensate by hitting the town in a black suit or a hussy outfit with big hair and too much makeup—no one will talk to you if they think you're part of the Russian mafia.

Bars & Lounges

→**Bar Bar** With a dark, cascading entrance that feels like a rabbit hole, and a long and winding bar full of psychedelic '60s colors and design elements, Bar Bar is like an updated and trendy version of Wonderland itself. This is a pretty fun place, with a steady flow of all the pop music you know by heart, and a sociable and hip crowd of 20-somethings who are usually only too willing to strike up a conversation with the fish-out-of-water Americano. Sunday nights are extremely popular for the free aperitivo buffet you get with your drink purchase. *Via Ovidio 17.* ☎ *06/6830-8435. Cover 5€–10€ Fri–Sat. Bus: 23, 81, 87, or 492.*

➜ **Bar del Fico** ★ "Il Fico" is as hallowed an institution in Rome as the Catholic church, but to lay eyes on it during the day, you'd never know: It just looks like a regular cafe, albeit one with a huge fig tree *(fico)* growing out of the cobblestones out front. At night, this is the bar where all the cool people end up when no other evening plans materialize. *Piazza del Fico 26.* ☎ *06/686-5205. Bus: 30, 70, 81, 87, 492, or 628.*

➜ **Chioschetto Ponte Milvio** ★★ It takes the best part of an hour to get here from the centro, and decor consists of little more than a gravelly expanse on the side of the road, some plastic tables and chairs, and a bar inside a shack, but this is no ironic boondocks *boîte.* This totally alfresco "kiosk" is where the young and beautiful people of affluent *Roma Nord* come for a drink when they don't feel like dressing up and dealing with the hassle of parking their Range Rovers and BMWs in the centro storico. In decent weather, you'll find huge, easygoing crowds here, sipping mojitos, beer, or even coffee. Immediately adjacent is the pedestrianized and rather atmospheric Ponte Milvio, where lots of Chioschetto patrons sneak off for make-out sessions. *Piazzale Ponte Milvio 44, at Lungotevere Maresciallo Diaz.* ☎ *06/333-3461. Bus: 32 from Piazza Risorgimento (Vatican area), 53 from Piazza San Silvestro (Via del Corso), then cross Ponte Milvio. Tram: 2 from Piazzale Flaminio, then cross Ponte Milvio.*

➜ **Finnegan** ★ Finnegan is the only Irish-owned and -managed Irish pub in Rome! Apart from natives of the Emerald Isle, clientele is big on beefy Kiwis, Scots, Aussies, and South Americans (and those Romans who strive to be them). Finnegan has a way of making everyone feel at home. For sports fans, the pub shows all English football games. *Via Leonina 66 (off Via dei Serpenti).* ☎ *06/474-7026. www.finneganpub.com. Metro: Cavour. Bus: 75.*

➜ **Trinity College** Ahhh, good ol' Trinity College. No young person's first stay in Rome is complete without a trip to this old standby, where the American university program coeds are naive and the Roman boys are horny (and as an added bonus, they also tend to be of the hot, water polo–playing variety). The bartenders think they're Tom Cruise in *Cocktail,* so you might as well order something elaborate like a strawberry *caipiroska* because even draft beers are subjected to a longwinded glass-flipping routine before they're served. It's always a party *al Trinity,* and the music—a high-energy mix of the greatest hits of right now—helps to drive that point home. *Via del Collegio Romano 6 (off Via del Corso).* ☎ *06/678-6472. Bus: 40, 46, 62, 64, 85, 95, 116, or 492.*

➜ **Vineria Reggio (aka La Vineria)** ★★★ An old Roman saying goes, "when the Colosseum falls, so too shall Rome." To hell with that—it's when the Vineria falls that Rome may well cease to exist. This unassuming wine bar on the west side of Campo de' Fiori is an integral part of the true Roman experience. Zero pretense despite a fairly fashionable clientele, quick and friendly service, tables on the piazza and a cozy indoor bar, and glasses of wine that start at 1.50€—what more could you ask? Start off with a toast of *prosecco,* and then have a glass of Falanghina—Roman superstition says that this local white wine brings a fun night to all who drink it. *Piazza Campo de'*

The Hot Spots: Coolest Bars & Clubs

Freni e Frizioni ★★ Ever since the popes reconsecrated pagan temples as Christian churches, the Romans have been very into reclaiming and reusing spaces for a completely different function. In the case of this new bar, "Brakes and Clutches," it's a former automotive repair garage that's been converted into a super-happening nightspot. Throngs of good-looking young locals meet here nightly for a great aperitivo buffet, interesting cocktails, and a friendly atmosphere. *Via del Politeama 4–6, off Piazza Trilussa and Lungotevere Raffaello Sanzio.* ☎ *06/5833-4210. Bus: 23, 280, 780, or H. Tram: 8.*

⓶ Best Salotto 42 ★★★ When you want to pretend you're cooler and more worldly than you really are, prepare some remarks about the latest exhibitions at the Venice Biennale, and head to this 3-year-old "book bar" opposite the ruins of Hadrian's Temple. On Saturday and Sunday, a fantastic international buffet brunch is served. *Piazza di Pietra 42.* ☎ *06/678-5804. www.salotto42.it. Bus: 40, 46, 62, 64, 85, 95, 116, or 492.*

⓶ Best Société Lutèce ★★ Definitely the coolest bar to open in Rome in a while, this spin-off of the Torino's ultrachic Brasserie Société Lutèce is well-hidden from the average tourist, on a cobblestone and ochre-washed corner only 5 minutes from Piazza Navona. The vibe makes everyone feel at home, and they haven't overdone it with the design: Exposed brick walls are painted white, and you sit on red velvet banquettes at small wooden tables, creating an atmosphere of pared-down French chic. There's an aperitivo buffet as well as an all-night menu of small plates to accompany the Hemingway-ish classic cocktails. *Piazza Montevecchio 17 (off Via dei Coronari).* ☎ *06/6830-1472. Bus: 30, 70, 81, 87, 492, or 628.*

ROME

Fiori 15. ☎ *06/6880-3268. Bus: 30, 40, 46, 62, 64, 70, 81, 87, 116, 492, 571, or 628. Tram: 8.*

Live Music

➔ **Big Mama** ★★★ Descend the stairs into this subterranean rock, blues, and soul joint and you're immediately greeted by the reassuring stink of old cigarette smoke and beer. In fact, Big Mama is the closest thing Rome has to a honky-tonk, with a surprisingly sophisticated, mixed crowd that really knows its music. I've come here tired, hungover, and heartbroken, and always left at the end of the night feeling like life is beautiful again. Everyone who gets booked here is unbelievably talented. The absolute best act you can catch here is called Più Bestial Che Blues, a Sam Cooke/Prince/Rolling Stones/Carole King/and such harmonica-playing cover band fronted by Davide Gentili. The

club is small, with big piers that block the view of the stage from some side tables, so if you want a good view of the show, call and book a table at least a day in advance. Concerts are held almost every night from September to May. Doors open at 9pm, shows start at 10:30pm, and the club closes at 1:30am. *Vicolo di San Francesco a Ripa 18 (at Via San Francesco a Ripa).* ☎ *06/581-2551. www.bigmama.it. Cover (monthly pass) 8€. Bus: 23, 271, 280, 780, or H.*

➔ **Il Locale** ★★ Feel like an insider as you watch relatively unknown Roman or Anglo bands take to the stage of this intimate, energetic rock venue on a tiny cobblestone alley near Piazza Navona. Whether or not the "talent" puts on a great show, the socializing between sets, and especially after the performance, is a ton of fun. Typical of small

Late-Night Munchies

La Base Slightly reminiscent of Bob's Big Boy, with loads of American kitsch all over the walls, this place is as much a Roman institution as the Colosseum or the Sistine Chapel. If you want a plate of penne at 4:30am, there's only one option: La Base. (And at that hour, you'll hardly notice that it's pretty disgusting. *Via Cavour 274. ☎ 06/474-0659. Daily 8pm–5am. Bus: 75 or 84.*

music clubs, there's a diverse, cool, and unpretentious crowd that keeps drinking and dancing to music on the stereo until Roman ordinance laws force them to call it a night. *Vicolo del Fico 3. ☎ 06/687-9075. Cover 5€–10€. Bus: 30, 40, 46, 62, 64, 70, 87, 116, 492, 571, or 628.*

Nightclubs

→ **Art Café** ★ For the average Roman, vacationing in Sardinia is the ultimate in aspirational luxury. No wonder, then, that the city's 20- and 30-somethings love the 1980s glamour of the Art Café, which looks and feels exactly like one of the mega-ferries that sail from Rome to Sardinia, except that it's in the Villa Borghese's subterranean mall/parking lot. In summer, it transfers out of its dated underground environs and into Piazza di Siena in the Villa Borghese park directly above, which is lined with umbrella pines and gorgeous lighting—quite fabulous, really. *Viale del Galoppatoio 33 (at the top of Via Veneto, in Villa Borghese). ☎ 06/3600-6578. Cover 15€–20€; early arrivals and women can sometimes get in free. Metro: Spagna. Bus: 52, 53, 95, or 116.*

→ **La Maison** ★ The exclusive Roman club that isn't really that exclusive . . . The *bella gente* of Rome who still have their original boobs and faces come to La Maison. Lucky

for you, it's right in the heart of the centro storico, and there's usually little problem getting in, as long as you dress the part (doesn't have to be fancy, just chic). On nights when big international celebs are here (like the time Naomi Campbell and Usher came to party here after the MTV Europe VMAs), it's a bit more of a challenge getting past the bouncer. The club isn't huge, but its plush decor (velvet couches, ornate chandeliers, and dark red walls) gives it a classy look that offsets the pure bacchanalia that takes place here every night. Sunday nights get started a bit earlier, and the resident DJ Flavia Lazzarini creates a laid-back vibe with her ethno-house sets. *Vicolo dei Granari 3, off Via del Teatro Pace, near Via dell'Anima. ☎ 06/683-3312. Cover 10€–20€; can be free if you are female and pretend to know someone. Bus: 30, 40, 46, 62, 64, 70, 87, 116, 492, 571, or 628.*

Gay Nightlife

For more info about gay and lesbian nightlife, check out the website for the **Circolo di Cultura Omosessuale Mario Mieli** (center for GLBT culture; www.mariomieli.org), which is affiliated with **Muccassina** (www.muccassina.com), the city's most venerable gay disco night, held Fridays at **Qube** (Via di Portonaccio 212; ☎ **06/541-3985** or 06/438-5445; tram: 5) in the southeastern suburb of Portonaccio.

→ **Alibi** ★★ Not only the best gay disco in Rome, but one of the best, period, on the Monte Testaccio strip (in a field of 20 or so, that ain't bad). It's cruisy, with a clientele of queens, muscle men, and straight-acting gays preening for each other on the club's multiple levels. Best of all is the roof terrace, which becomes the third dance floor in summer, against the rustic slopes and sycamore trees of Monte Testaccio. *Via di Monte Testaccio 39. ☎ 06/574-3448. Cover 10€. Metro: Piramide. Bus: 23, 75, 95, 175, or 280.*

In Da Club: Nightlife in Testaccio & Ostiense

The overwhelming majority of Rome's dance clubs are in the districts of
MTV Best **Testaccio and Ostiense,** just south of the center. Testaccio, where the
streets Via di Monte Testaccio and Via Galvani skirt a rustic "mountain" made of
pottery (this is where ancient Romans tossed all their used jugs), is the easier
option because it's well connected to the center by bus and Metro. Farther
south of Testaccio is Ostiense (specifically the area around Via Libetta); more of
a pain to reach by public transport, but its clubs tend to be slightly more
sophisticated but not by much.

In **Testaccio,** I like to hit up **Metaverso** (Via di Monte Testaccio 38/a; ☎ 06/
574-4712; www.metaverso.com) for the sheer variety of offerings. Wednesday
night is Reggae Night; on alternate Friday nights, DJs Pol Gee and Bob Corsi
spin a blender of all kinds of musical genres and some nights feature live musical acts. Come on Saturdays at 4pm for the hip-hop open mic event. A few
doors down, the '80s child in me is also a sucker for **ZooBar** (Via di Monte
Testaccio 22; ☎ 339/272-7995 [cell]; www.zoobar.roma.it), where The Clash,
Depeche Mode, and New Order are on heavy rotation most nights. To reach
Testaccio, take Metro B to Piramide, or bus no. 23, 75, 95, 170, or 280 to Via
Marmorata, or tram no. 3 to Via Marmorata.

In **Ostiense, Goa** (Via Libetta 13; ☎ 06/574-8277) has been doing the nebu-
lous Indian/African/Asian ethno house thing for a while, but it's still very popular
with the caftan-wearing, just-got-back-from-a-yoga-retreat-but-I'm-still-smok-
ing-and-drinking set. For some good old-fashioned *discoteca* fare (commercial
music), I've never been bored at **Saponeria** (Via degli Argonauti 20; ☎ 06/574-
6999), popular with Roman jocks and their cute-as-a-button female cohorts.
To reach Ostiense, take Metro B to Garbatella, and then it's a 10-minute walk
around the block; or take Metro B to Piramide and then hop on bus no. 23
south (in the direction of Pincherle) to Via Ostiense/Via Garbatella (Via Libetta is
off to the east).

➜ **Hangar** ★ Having survived since 1984, the
Hangar is a landmark on the gay nightlife
scene and a good place to socialize, and get
the lay of the land for gays in Rome. Women
are welcome any night except Monday, when
the club features videos and entertainment
for men. The busiest nights are Saturday,
Sunday, and Monday, when as many as 500
people cram inside. It's closed for 3 weeks in
August; call ahead for exact dates. *Via in Selci
69.* ☎ *06/488-1397. No cover, but there's a 7€
"membership fee." Metro: Cavour. Bus: 75.*

➜ **New Joli Coeur** ★ Just for lesbians, this
bar/lounge/disco is only open on Saturdays
or for special parties or theme evenings. The
space is divided into three rooms: one for
board and video games (how social!), one for
live music and cabaret, and one for dancing.
Via Sirte 5, off Viale Eritrea. ☎ *06/574-3448.
Cover 10€. Bus: 38, 80, or 86.*

Performing Arts

MUSIC   **Parco della Musica** ★ (Viale de
Coubertin; ☎ **06/802-411**) is the largest
concert facility in Europe, an ultramodern,
almost sci-fi building constructed in 2002 by
Renzo Piano. It offers 40,000 sq. m (430,600
sq. ft.) of garden and three separate concert

halls, plus one massive open-air theater. The best time to attend is summer, when concerts are often staged outside. Tickets and prices depend on the event. The auditorium can be reached by taking bus no. 53, 217, 231, or 910.

Teatro Olimpico (Piazza Gentile da Fabriano 17; ☎ **06/326-5991**; Metro: Flaminio) hosts a wide range of performances, from pop to chamber music to foreign orchestras. *Note:* The theater box office is open daily from 11am to 7pm.

Check the daily papers for **free church concerts** given around town, especially near Easter and Christmas.

Violin concertos, African vocalists, Brazilian jazz artists . . . there's a bit of everything at **Auditorium,** a cool new, Renzo Piano–designed center for the arts. Though much of the calendar is dedicated to classical or New Age stuff, there are also film screenings (with cast and directors sometimes present), and the summer season tends to bring in more recognized international names from the world of pop and rock to Auditorium's outdoor amphitheater. It's located at Viale Pietro di Coubertin, off Via Flaminia (☎ **06/8024-1281;** www.auditorium.com; bus: M, 53, 217, 910; tram: 2). Ticket prices vary.

OPERA   If you're in the capital for the opera season, usually from late December to June, you might want to attend the historic **Teatro dell'Opera** (Piazza Beniamino Gigli 1, off Via Nazionale; ☎ **06/4816-0255;** Metro: Repubblica). Nothing is presented in July and August. Call ahead or ask your concierge before you go. Tickets are 9€ to 130€.

DANCE   Performances of the Rome Opera Ballet are given at the **Teatro dell'Opera** (see previous entry). The regular repertoire of classical ballet is supplemented by performances of internationally acclaimed guest artists.

Sightseeing

In the cobblestone alleys of Rome's centro storico, baroque churches, fountains, and theatrical piazzas lurk around every corner. Rome is so rich in art and architecture that the entire centro has been declared a UNESCO World Heritage Site. Owing to its almost 3,000-year history, the cityscape is a fascinating mix of ancient, medieval, Renaissance, baroque, neoclassical, and fascist sights.

The other very cool thing about Rome is that you can see all the most impressive and "important" sights for about 20€.

Festivals

There are tons of events all over town every night during the summer; check the weekly listings guide, *Roma C'è* (at newsstands), or the festival's website, www.estateromana.it, for details. Some of our favorites for all-around fun and fabulousness:

June to August

Cornetto Free Music Festival ★. Italy's biggest packaged ice-cream brand, Algida, sponsors a huge free concert in Rome every summer. In 2005, Duran Duran, Beck, Velvet, and James Blunt played Rome. The concert has taken place at Piazza San Giovanni, the Circus Maximus, and in the Villa Borghese. Best of all, they give out a Cornetto to all who show up. www.cornetto algida.com. Various dates throughout the summer.

Jazz & Image ★★★. It doesn't matter if you like jazz: (a) Half the acts that play this festival aren't really jazz, and (b) the park where this takes place, the Villa Celimontana, above the Colosseum, is such a gorgeous place to pass an evening that you won't care what kind of music is on. Now miniature versions of some of Rome's hottest restaurants are set up around the festival, serving food

The Stuff You Need to See

The average first-time visitor in Rome stays for about 2½ days, which is a travesty. However, if you plan your days carefully, you can still see a lot. Another helpful feature of Rome is that most of the monuments are perfectly visible (and often more impressive) all night long. If you're staying in Rome for 1 day, hit the blockbuster sights, but realize that you're not getting the full picture. There's more to Rome than crazy traffic and hordes of tourists at the Colosseum! If you have a few days in the city, see the iconic attractions—just spend more time there and learn something—and mix it up with some of the less-famous, equally fascinating sights that make Rome so special.

➜ **You must:** Colosseum, Roman Forum, Capitoline Hill, Pantheon, St. Peter's Basilica, Vatican Museums, and Sistine Chapel

➜ **You really should:** Piazza Navona, Trevi Fountain, Castel Sant'Angelo, Appian Way, backstreets of the centro storico or Trastevere, Pincio or Gianicolo (for a view)

➜ **Nice, but overrated:** Spanish Steps, Mouth of Truth, Michelangelo's *Moses*

➜ **Under the radar but off the charts:** Galleria Borghese, Crypt of the Capuchin Monks, the Foro Italico

and plenty of drinks to concertgoers. Piazza della Navicella. ☎ **06/589-7807.** www.villacelimontanajazz.com. End of August.

Baths of Caracalla ★★★. The ruins of the city's best-preserved ancient Roman baths are turned into a venue for full-scale symphony and opera performances. The towering walls and umbrella pines are spectacularly floodlit—as long as you live, you'll be hard-pressed to find a more dramatic, powerful, or monumental setting for high *cultcha*. For opera, visit the Teatro dell'Opera's website, **www.operaroma.it**. For the symphony, see the Accademia di Santa Cecilia's site, **www.santacecilia.it**. To get to the Baths of Caracalla, take Metro Line B to Circo Massimo, or bus no. 18 to Viale delle Terme di Caracalla. Throughout July and August.

Tours

Not all tours are created equal. Bus tours are overpriced and have unintelligible guides—stick to walking tours. When it comes to picking a guide, steer clear of Italians (even if they're English-speaking): Because their

cultural bar is so much higher when it comes to art and architecture, they tend to assume you already know the basics.

There are dozens of walking tour companies that employ local expats, who focus on educating you while they entertain you. **Enjoy Rome** (Via Marghera 8a; ☎ **0604451843;** www.enjoyrome.com) offers walking tours of Rome costing 21€ for those 26 and over, or 15€ for those under 26. Three tours a week of Trastevere and the Jewish Ghetto are featured, a service provided by no other tour company in Rome.

See the "Catacombs of St. Domitilla below" for info on catacomb tours.

Ancient Ruins & Monuments

Most of Rome's major ancient sights are in the archaeological areas that spread out south of Piazza Venezia. A few other biggies, like the Pantheon, are nestled among other buildings in more modern parts of the city. A good place to start is at the Colosseum, which is accessed by Metro Line B (Colosseo stop); bus no. 60, 75, 85, 87, 175, 271, or 571; and tram no. 3.

Free & Easy

→ **Pincio** ★★ Above the landmark Piazza del Popolo, this terraced and lushly planted hillside is the most romantic place for a twilight walk. The stone parapets at the western edge of the Villa Borghese look out over the terra-cotta rooftops and domes of the centro storico to the Vatican. It's an amazing view. *Piazzale Napoleone. Metro: Flaminio. Bus: 117 or 119.*

→ **Gianicolo** ★★ Romans' other favorite lookout and make-out point is the Janiculum Hill, a tree-lined ridge above Trastevere. Depending on where you stand along the Gianicolo, the view takes in different parts of the city. *Passeggiata del Gianicolo. Accessible on foot from Trastevere; turn right up the hill at the top of Via Garibaldi. Bus: 115 or 870.*

→ **Vittoriano** ★★ As much as we love to hate this behemoth of white marble on the south side of Piazza Venezia, nothing beats the upper terraces of the Vittoriano for a bird's-eye view of the most famous monuments of Rome. Here, you're right in the middle of everything, so you'll have great views of the Pantheon, St. Peter's, the Roman Forum, the Colosseum, and the Palatine. *Piazza Venezia. Bus: 30, 40, 62, 64, 70, 85, 87, 95, 170, 175, 271, 492, or 571.*

→ **MTV Best Capitoline Hill** ★★★ It doesn't get much more sublime than the vertiginous view over the Roman Forum from the railings on the south side of the Campidoglio. *See p. 832 for more info.*

MTV Best →Colosseum ★★★ As barbaric as they were spectacular, gladiator and wild-animal fights—known as "games" to the blood-and-guts-loving ancient Roman masses—were held in this famous arena for more than 4 centuries. The Colosseum is by far the mightiest surviving monument of imperial Rome, even though it's only half intact.

A visit inside the Colosseum is a memorable experience you won't regret. Via the original stone stairways, you can climb as high as the middle ring, which is about 25m (80 ft). above the ground, and walk all the way around. The arena itself lost its original wooden floor long ago, but there's a modern wooden catwalk that allows you to tread on the same level as gladiator and animal did, and peer down to the subterranean level, where you can make out the vestiges of 32 elevator shafts. Take Metro Line B to "Colosseo" and emerge from the underground station to see the enormous, 15-story northern wall of the amphitheater looming before you.

Note: In high season, the lines to get into the Colosseum can be long. When they are, head down the street to the entrance of the Palatine Hill, on Via di San Gregorio. Buy your ticket there (there's usually no line), as the ticket for the Palatine is the same one that gets you into the Colosseum. *Piazza del Colosseo.* ☎ *06/700-4261. Admission 8€ (ticket also good for admission at the Palatine Hill); 10€ when there are special exhibitions inside the Colosseum. Daily 9am to 1 hr. before sunset. Closed Jan 1, May 1, and Dec 25. Metro: Colosseo. Bus: 60, 75, 85, 87, 117, or 175. Tram: 3.*

→ **Imperial Forums** ★★★ The dictator Julius Caesar and the emperors Augustus, Nerva, and Trajan all sponsored the construction of monumental fora (the proper plural of "forum") that would bear their names. Collectively, these public spaces are known as the Imperial Fora (in Italian, Fori Imperiali) and cover an area of nearly 3 sq.

ROME

km (1¹/₄ sq. miles). Because there's now a six-lane, heavily trafficked boulevard that runs roughshod over large sections of them, the Fori Imperiali can be difficult to understand. As you try to make sense of the sites, just keep in mind that they were all interconnected, and together with the Roman Forum, they were used for the same "downtown" purpose: social gathering (political or informal), shopping, and worshipping the pagan gods.

The ruins of the Imperial Fora, which were excavated in the 1920s and 1930s, lie well below street level. Only one of the areas, the **Forum of Trajan,** is regularly open to the public; the other areas **(Forum of Caesar, Forum of Augustus, Forum of Nerva)** are usually closed, but it doesn't matter—they're all easily visible (for free) from the pedestrianized viewing platforms along either side of Via dei Fori Imperiali. *Note:* The main hall of Trajan's Markets was temporarily closed as this guide went to press, but much of the exterior is still open to the public. *Via IV Novembre 94, at Via Magnanapoli.* ☎ *06/679-0048. Admission 3.20€. Apr–Oct Tues–Sun 9am–6pm; Nov–Mar 9am–4pm; last admission 1 hr. before closing. Bus: 40, 60, 64, 70, 75, or 170.*

📺 Best ➙ **Roman Forum** ★★ The vast ruin-filled pit at the center of Rome's archaeological zone is hardly the most well-preserved of the city's ancient monuments, but there is no place more important to the history of the Roman Republic and Empire than the Roman Forum. Highlights include the **Curia** built by Julius Caesar, the main seat of the Roman Senate (pop inside to see the 3rd-c. marble inlay floor); the **Basilica of Maxentiu;** the **Temple of Antoninus Pius and Faustina;** and the **Arch of Titus,** on which one relief depicts the carrying off of treasures from Jerusalem's temple. *Via dei Fori Imperiali.* ☎ *06-39967600. Free admission to Forum; Palatine Hill 8€ ($9.20); ticket includes admission to Colosseum.*

Apr–Sept daily 9am–7pm; Oct–Mar daily 9am–4:30pm. Last admission 1 hr. before closing. Closed holidays. Metro: Colosseo. Bus: 3, 8, 75, 85, 87, 117, or 186.

FREE ➙ **Circus Maximus** ★★ Once the entertainment capital of the Empire, Rome's old chariot race track is little more than a valley—the size of six football fields laid end on end—of half-dead grass today. Still, the Circo Massimo is a must-see, for its legendary place in Roman history, and for the powerful views of the Palatine Hill, just northeast of here.

Hike up to the top of the southeastern bank, sit down and take in the view across the valley of the track to the brick ruins of the Palatine Hill. *Via del Circo Massimo. No phone. Free admission. Metro: Circo Massimo. Daily 24 hr. Bus: 60, 75, 175, or 628. Tram: 3.*

➙ **Baths of Caracalla** ★★ Occupying a grassy, tree-filled space 400m (1,312 ft.) long and 330m (1,083 ft.) wide, the towering brick ruins of this imperial bath complex make for a wonderful oasis of peace and quiet today, but this was quite the happening hangout in ancient times. While extensive and atmospheric, the ruins here are not well marked, so prepare to use your imagination; even if you don't feel like doing a thorough tour, the 5€ admission is well worth it for the green and tranquil surroundings. There are fallen granite columns, shaded by umbrella pines, in the back garden area that make for perfect lounging and napping on a summer day. *Viale delle Terme di Caracalla 52.* ☎ *06/575-8626. Admission 5€. Tues–Sun 9am–sunset; Mon 9am–2pm. Closed Jan 1, May 1, and Dec 25. Metro: Circo Massimo. Bus: 60, 75, 118, 175, or 628. Tram: 3.*

OTHER ATTRACTIONS

📺 Best FREE ➙ **Appian Way** ★★★ Few places in Rome transport you to ancient times as well as the Via Appia Antica, whose black basalt cobblestones, still bearing the wheel ruts of ancient cart traffic, run south

ROME

of the city from Porta San Sebastiano. A few miles from the city walls, a rustic, agrarian landscape opens up on either side of the 4th-century B.C. highway; the scenery is scattered with imposing or modest remains of ancient tombs and villas, and shepherds drive flocks of sheep from pasture to pasture, right across the "Queen of Roads." For information, contact Parco Regionale Dell'Appia Antica. *Via Appia Antica 42.* ☎ *06/512-6314. www.parcoappiaantica.org. Admission 5€. Apr–Oct Thurs–Tues 8:30am–noon and 2:30–5:30pm (Nov–Mar till 5pm). Closed Feb. Bus: 118.*

FREE → **Area Sacra** ★ This sunken area right in the middle of a busy intersection contains the ruins of four Republican-era temples and a colony of several hundred cats. Archaeologists could tell that these were temples, but they weren't sure to whom they were dedicated. They still don't know, so the temples are known by the letters A, B (the round one), C, and D. Stand on the eastern wall for the best view, and then walk around to the northwest corner of the square (near Café Brek), and look down. You'll see some stone gutters left over from a *vespasiano* (ancient Roman slang for a pay toilet).

The Area Sacra's other claim to fame is that there is one large gray stone block here (on the western edge of the excavations) from the *Curia Pompei,* the senate house where Julius Caesar was stabbed on the Ides of March in 44 B.C. (The actual site of the assassination is buried beneath the no. 8 tram terminus here.) The lower part of the ruins is accessible by appointment only, so call ahead. *Largo di Torre Argentina.* ☎ *06/6710-3819. Free admission. Daily 24 hr. Bus: 30, 40, 46, 62, 64, 70, 87, 492, or 571. Tram: 8.*

📺 Best FREE → **Pantheon** ★★★ Surrounded by Renaissance palazzi 1,400 years its junior, the ancient Pantheon (temple of all the gods) holds its own in the heart of the centro storico. It's the best-preserved Roman building anywhere in Europe, Asia Minor, or North Africa—what used to be the Roman Empire. The structure of the Pantheon, which was built from A.D. 118 to 125 under the emperor Hadrian, is a perfectly hemispherical, poured cement dome, sitting on top of a hollow cylindrical masonry base. It continues to flabbergast modern engineers and cement workers, who can't quite figure out (1) how the Romans had the technology to build it in the first place, 1,900 years ago, and (2) that it's still here.

Inside is where jaws really start to drop. Crossing the threshold—through the immense, original 2nd-century A.D. **bronze doors**—your eyes are drawn up to the underside of the dome. Free of decoration, except for the elegantly telescoping coffers (square recesses) that also serve to lighten the load of the masonry, the gray **dome** measures 43m (141 ft.) in diameter, and 43m (141 ft.) in total height; that is, if you spun the dome around upside down inside the Pantheon, you'd have a perfect sphere. There is nothing like this design in the world. At the center of the dome is a 9m-wide (30-ft.) opening called the **oculus (eye).** The oculus lets the rain in, and if you want a magical experience, come to the Pantheon during one of Rome's more angry thunderstorms, or better yet, a hailstorm.

The most famous permanent resident is the Renaissance painter Raphael. The fancier tombs here, with honor guards and fresh flowers daily, belong to the 19th-century Savoy monarchs: King Vittorio Emanuele II (first king of unified Italy); his wife, Queen Margherita (she of the pizza); and their son, King Umberto I. *Piazza della Rotonda.* ☎ *06/6830-0230. Free admission. Mon–Sun 9am–7pm; public holidays 9am–1pm. Closed Jan 1, May 1, and Dec 25. Bus: 30, 40, 62, 64, 70, 87, 116, 492, or 571.*

📺 Best → **Catacombs of San Callisto** ★★ Twelve miles and four levels of hand-dug tunnels make up the underground network of Rome's largest catacombs, home to the tombs of a half-million Christians, buried here from the 1st to the 4th centuries A.D. Deep within the complex, a labyrinth of 10m-high (33 ft.) tunnels, with walls that are perforated up to the ceiling with *loculi* (tomb niches), is especially impressive (and uncannily reminiscent of college library stacks). This is the only catacomb where you can see bones; the rest have emptied their tombs to rebury the remains in ossuaries on the inaccessible lower levels.

Note: The best way to view the catacombs is via an underground tour. The best are provided by **Itinera** (☎ **06-27800785**) and **LUPA** (☎ **06-5741974**), both run by trained archaeologists. *Via Appia Antica 110–126 (at Via Ardeatina).* ☎ *06/5130-1580. www. catacombe.roma.it. Admission: 5€. Thurs–Tues 8:30am–noon and 2:30–5:30pm (Oct–Mar till 5pm). Closed Feb. Bus: 118.*

Monuments & Public Spaces

→**Ara Pacis** ★★ The sacrificial altar inside this new glass-concrete-and-travertine museum is only about 12 by 11m (39 by 36 ft.), but the Ara Pacis is a very big deal for the quality of the 2,000-year-old sculpture on it and for the fact that it even exists today. Back in 13 B.C., upon returning from the newly pacified provinces of Gaul (France) and Spain, the emperor Augustus promised to build an "Altar of Peace" (Ara Pacis) in Rome. It was dedicated 4 years later, on January 30, 9 B.C. The finest sculptors of the day were hired to decorate the marble screens that surrounded the central altar with scenes from mythology and real life. The most striking thing about the sculptures here—which are considered by most scholars to be the finest surviving examples of Roman art—are the exquisitely rendered portraits of the imperial family and entourage. They're so highly detailed, with such careful attention paid to individual hairstyles and drapes and folds of togas that they look like marble photographs. *Lungotevere in Augusta, at Piazza Augusto Imperatore.* ☎ *06-57250410. www.arapacisaugustae.it. Admission 5€. Tues–Sat 9am–9pm; Sun 9am–1pm. Bus: 70, 81, 186, or 628.*

FREE →**Bocca della Verità (Mouth of Truth)** ★ What is actually kind of a cool ancient relic is now just a dumb tourist trap, but if you're in the vicinity you might as well line up and get your picture taken. According to popular legend, the Mouth of Truth was an ancient sewer cover whose surface was sculpted in the shape of a face. The mouth itself is a hole that goes all the way through to the other side of the huge marble disk. At some point in the medieval period, the sewer cover was set up against the side of a building and became known as a lie detector. When they suspected their partners of cheating, men would bring their wives or mistresses to the Mouth of Truth and ask them if they'd been faithful; the suspect had to answer while placing her hand inside the hole in the mouth. Meanwhile, the inquisitor (who believed to know the awful truth already) would have hired a goon to stand behind the marble disk and chop off the woman's hand if she said "yes." Nowadays, there's just a continuous stream of tourists eager to snap that dorky photo of themselves sticking their hand in the old sewer cover. *In the front porch of the Church of Santa Maria in Cosmedin. Piazza della Bocca della Verità 18.* ☎ *06/678-1419. Free admission. Daily 9am–1pm and 2:30–6pm (till 5pm in winter). Bus: 30 or 170.*

→**Castel Sant'Angelo** ★★★ Presiding over the western bank of the Tiber like a big ol' medium-rare hamburger of history. It began as the mausoleum of the emperor Hadrian (d. A.D. 138), which explains its squat, cylindrical shape. In ancient times, the mausoleum was ringed with opulent statuary, and a mound of earth sat on top of it, planted with cypress trees. In the 13th century, the popes decided to appropriate the fortress for their own use and built themselves lavish apartments on the upper level. You'll get a commanding view of the centro storico and the river below from the castle's highest point. Castel Sant'Angelo is one of the more magnificent monuments to see by night. The bridge leading up to the castle, Ponte Sant'Angelo, is lined with fabulous marble statues of swooning angels. *Lungotevere Castello.* ☎ *06/687-5036. Admission 5€. Tues–Sun 9am–7pm. Closed public holidays. Bus: 23, 40, 46, 62, 64, 271, 280, or 571.*

FREE → **Piazza del Popolo** ★★ A massive, 4,000-year-old pink granite Egyptian obelisk with hieroglyphics presides over this grand, newly pedestrianized expanse at the top of the Tridente. At no. 12, on the north side of the piazza, the church of **Santa Maria del Popolo** ★ (☎ **06/361-0836;** Mon–Sat 7am–noon and 4–7pm; Sun 8am–2pm and 4:30–7:30pm; free admission) is a trove of art treasures, including two fine paintings by Caravaggio; to the south, the facades of seemingly twin churches make for pretty pictures. Romans and tourists alike bask in the late afternoon sun that floods this vast, traffic-free oval space. The two cafes on either side of the square, Canova and Rosati, are touristy but lovely. *No phone. Free admission. Metro: Flaminio. Bus: 117 or 119.*

FREE → **Piazza Navona** ★★★ Rome's grandest baroque square is the stage for an architectural smack-down between Francesco Borromini and Gianlorenzo Bernini. Weighing in on the western side of the oblong piazza is Borromini's **Sant'Agnese in Agone** (1653–57; closed Mon), a small church whose proud bearing is enhanced by its telescoping bell towers, oversized dome, and concave facade. Bernini's action-packed, obelisk-crowned **Fountain of the Four Rivers** (1651) is a feisty competitor, with four reclining figures representing the Danube, Plata, Ganges, and Nile.

Piazza Navona got its shape, and its name, from the ancient **Stadium of Domitian,** ruins of which still exist below the ground here (visible from the outside of the north side of the piazza). The square is at its best before 10am, when the tourist hordes and trinket sellers start to descend. Cafes and restaurants abound, but you'll never find locals dining here. Instead, head for one of the popular bars or restaurants in the action-packed nightlife area to the west of the piazza. *Piazza Navona. Free admission. Bus: 30 Express, 40, 62, 64, 70, 81, 87, 492, or 628.*

FREE → **Piazza Venezia** ★ This is the most central point of old Rome, the heart where major traffic arteries Via del Corso, Via Nazionale, Via dei Fori Imperiali, Via del Teatro di Marcello, and Via del Plebiscito meet, carrying a continuous, fluid exchange of *motorini,* buses, and cars over the bumpy cobblestones. By far the most prominent feature of Piazza Venezia is the 19th-century **Vittoriano** (Monument to Vittorio Emanuele II, the first king of unified Italy), which looms like a monumental exercise in bad taste at the southern side of the square. This garish heap of white marble is festooned with so much gaudy sculptural detail that it has been nicknamed the "wedding cake" by disparaging locals. The Vittoriano is open daily from 10am to 6pm; admission is free, and there's an outdoor snack bar, Caffè Italia, halfway up the monument on the left (east) side. The **view** ★★★ from the very top is the best comprehensive panorama of central Rome.

There's a museum inside Palazzo Venezia, but don't expect access to Mussolini's old war room or anything: Most of the fascist-era offices in the palace are closed to the public. Instead, what you're allowed to see is a mostly disappointing collection of decorative arts from the 14th to 17th centuries, and the occasional temporary exhibition. For the most part, the museum's a snooze. *Piazza Venezia Museum: Admission 4€. Tues–Sat*

9am–7:30pm. Bus: 30, 40, 62, 64, 70, 85, 87, 95, 170, 175, 492, or 571.

→ **Protestant Cemetery** ★★ One of the most peaceful and unexpected sights in Rome is the Cimitero Acattolico (non-Catholic cemetery), separated from the furious traffic of Piazzale Ostiense by a tall, ancient brick wall. This green, slightly unkempt haven is the final resting place of the Romantic poets John Keats and Percy Bysshe Shelley, and the founder of the Italian Communist Party, Antonio Gramsci. At the grave of William Wetmore Story, a 19th-century American sculptor who lived in Rome for many years, a marble angel—his own work—slumps in grief over the tombstone. It's one of the most moving funerary monuments in the world. *Via Caio Cestio 6, near Piazzale Ostiense.* ☎ *06/574-1900.* 1€ *donation expected. Tues–Sun 9am–6pm (Oct–Mar till 5pm); last admission 30 min. before closing. Metro: Piramide. Bus: 23, 30, 60, or 95. Tram: 3.*

FREE → **Spanish Steps (Scalinata di Spagna)** ★★ Fortunately, the sweeping beauty of the Scalinata di Spagna transcends the sometimes ugly crowds of tourists that populate the square day and night. The climb to the high terrace covers 12 curving flights of steps of varying width, but the view from the top, where you can finally look away from your feet, is exhilarating. Come between 2 and 6am, and you'll enjoy that rarest of Roman treats—having the fabulous stage of the Spanish Steps to yourself.

In summer, the Roman fashion commission puts on a sadistic fashion show here, in which models are forced to walk down the bumpy, slippery steps (in stilettos) as if they're on a runway! Rome's highest-end shopping is also located right in this vicinity, Via Condotti being the main road that leads straight to credit-card debt. *Piazza di Spagna. No phone. Free admission. Metro: Spagna. Bus: 117 or 119.*

FREE → **Trevi Fountain (Fontana di Trevi)** ★★★ An ingeniously sculpted travertine base of faux boulders and "fallen" building cornices gives rise to a dynamic pageant of mythological figures, over which thousands of gallons of water per minute thunder to the inviting, swimming-pool-blue basin below. In spite of the tourist swarms, Nicola Salvi's fountain (1732–62) is a monumental feast for the eyes that never fails to delight—and to surprise, given its location in such a tiny, hidden piazza. Tradition says that if you want to come back to Rome, you should throw a coin into the Trevi Fountain. There's even a prescribed coin-pitching choreography: With your back to the fountain, take a coin in your right hand and throw it over your left shoulder (crossing your heart . . . awww).

For the best Trevi experience, come between 2 and 7am. It's 100% safe (there are police here around the clock making sure no one goes for a swim), and you can recline on the travertine slabs and bliss out to the roar of the water. *Fontana di Trevi. No phone. Bus: 52, 53, 62, 95, 116, 175, or 492.*

The Vatican

As the headquarters of the Catholic Church and the world's smallest, richest city-state, the Vatican has plenty of intrigue—10,000-plus visitors each day. What you'll do at the Vatican is see its incredible legacies of art and architecture—in the Vatican Museums, the Sistine Chapel, and St. Peter's Basilica and Square.

FREE → **St. Peter's Square (Piazza San Pietro)** ★★★ Designed from 1656 to 1667 by Bernini to mimic a human embrace, this sweeping quadruple colonnade of 300 travertine piers is the gateway to the largest church in the world and one of the most recognizable images of the Vatican. In the center of the grand square stands an Egyptian obelisk that once served as a turning post in the Circus of Caligula, where St. Peter was martyred in A.D. 64. Along the south wall of the square are official Vatican souvenir and bookshops and a branch of the Vatican post office. On Sundays and Catholic holidays, Mass is celebrated in the square, and the pope often appears at his window in the Apostolic Palace (above the northern arm of the colonnade) to bless the faithful.

MTV Best FREE → St. Peter's Basilica (Basilica di San Pietro) ★★★ Confession (how appropriate!): I lived in Rome for a year before I bothered to go inside St. Peter's. I caught glimpses of it every day and thought to myself, yeah, it's big and important, but with that same image of the dome plastered all over every postcard rack in town, it seemed like a pompous cliché I didn't need to experience up close. Then, one day, I went inside St. Peter's and literally lost my breath when I took that first step over the threshold.

St. Peter's was built from 1506 to 1626, in the shape of a Latin cross, over the basilica that the emperor Constantine had dedicated to St. Peter in the 4th century A.D. At 211m (692 ft.) in length, St. Peter's is the longest, and overall largest, church in Christendom, with an area of 23,000 sq. m (247,570 sq. ft.) and capacity for 60,000 people during Vatican conferences or important masses. It's also the tallest building in Rome, with Michelangelo's dome crowning the skyline like a 136m-tall (446-ft.) papal tiara.

Once you've entered the basilica, walk to the central nave and take some time to soak it all in. Every square inch of the basilica's interior is covered with marble, bronze, or gold. Altarpieces that look like paintings are actually mosaics, made up of thousands of tiny chips of colored stone. Before you walk toward the main dome, turn back toward the way you came in: In the first chapel on the right is **Michelangelo's *Pietà*** ★★★, which he sculpted in 1499, at the age of 24. Second

only in fame to his *David* (at the Accademia in Florence), the *Pietà* depicts Mary cradling the limp body of Jesus in her lap. Unfortunately, the *Pietà* is behind a heavy pane of bullet-proof glass—in 1972, when it was unprotected, a hammer-wielding madman attacked the *Pietà* and broke off part of Christ's foot.

The four-legged creature that crouches under the dome of St. Peter's is Gianlorenzo Bernini's splendid ***baldacchino*** ★★★. This fantastically over-the-top baroque canopy was cast in the mid–17th century from bronze that Pope Urban VIII stole from the porch of the Pantheon. Under the baldacchino is the papal altar, where only the pope may celebrate Mass; straight beneath that, about 10m (33 ft.) down, is the site of **St. Peter's tomb,** accessible only by pre-arranged tours of the excavations *(scavi)* of the necropolis of St. Peter's.

Underneath the basilica (accessible by stairs in the piers that support the dome; free admission) are the **Vatican grottoes,** where the tombs of dozens of popes, including the **tomb of Pope John Paul II,** are. To climb the **dome** ★★ of St. Peter's, exit the basilica to the left and follow the signs to the cupola. *Note:* The dome of St. Peter's is not the absolute best place for a comprehensive view of Rome. It's the highest point in the city, but it's so far west of everything that you can't really get a good look at the monuments you'd recognize (such as the Colosseum), although you do get a great view of St. Peter's Square. Keep in mind that the lines are shortest right after the dome opens (8–9:30am) and right before it closes (Apr–Oct 5:30pm; Nov–Mar 4:30pm). *Piazza San Pietro.* ☎ *06/6988-4466 or 06/6988-4866. www.stpetersbasilica.org. Free admission to basilica and grottoes (crypt); dome 4€–5€. Daily 7am–7pm; grottoes 7am–6pm (Oct–Mar till 5pm); dome 8am–6pm (Oct–Mar till 5pm). Metro: Ottaviano. Bus: 23, 40, 46, 62, or 64. Tram: 19.*

VATICAN MUSEUMS & THE SISTINE CHAPEL

The 📺 Best **Vatican Museums,** the richest museum in the world, is enthralling in its quantity and quality, aggravating in its utter lack of explanatory signage. As a rule, the important stuff is where the crowds are, but try to resist the riptide of tour groups that washes headlong toward the Sistine Chapel because you'll miss a ton of fabulous art along the way. The museum guidebook—or, better yet, the CD-ROM audioguide—can make your meander through these masterpiece-packed halls vastly more meaningful. For the best understanding of the Sistine Chapel, consider a guided tour. Near the entrance of the museums, there's a bag-check, but don't leave anything here unless you absolutely have to—you'll probably be exiting the museums by way of the Sistine Chapel, and coming all the way back to the entrance to pick up your stuff is a serious detour. If you rent an audioguide, however, you'll have to come all the way back to return it and collect your ID, which you have to leave as collateral.

The Highlights of the Vatican Museums

Near the entrance of the museums is the Vatican **Pinacoteca (picture gallery).** In addition to the standard Italian lineup of Holy Family triptychs, the Pinacoteca is home to Raphael's *Transfiguration* (1520, his last painting), in Room 8; Leonardo's enigmatic *St. Jerome* (1482), in Room 9; and Caravaggio's eerie, green-fleshed *Deposition* (1604), in Room 12. Then cross the courtyard and head up the stairs to the Pio-Clementine Museums of classical statuary. One of the highlights in the **Octagonal Courtyard** is the exquisite marble *Apollo Belvedere* ★★ (a 2nd-c. A.D. copy of a 5th-c. B.C. original), a paragon of classical composure and ideal, unruffled beauty. In radical stylistic contrast, the terribly dramatic, 1st-century-A.D. *Laocoön* ★★★.

In the indoor gallery just beyond the Octagonal Courtyard, you'll find the expressive, though fragmentary, *Belvedere Torso* ★ (1st c. B.C.), which inspired Michelangelo's rendering of Christ in the *Last Judgment,* in the Sistine Chapel. The next major room is the Sala Rotonda (Round Room), where there is a fantastically preserved 1st-century-B.C. bronze statue of *Hercules* ★.

Upstairs, the **Etruscan Museum** ★ is well worth checking out—if it's open—for its knockout gold breastplates and pins from a 2,500-year-old tomb. The next room you hit is the **Gallery of the Tapestries,** which is dark and not very exciting unless you are into 16th- and 17th-century tapestries. From here, the Vatican Museums morph into fresco heaven. The 32 brightly colored frescoes in the **Gallery of the Maps** ★ are a wonderfully detailed, frame-by-frame cartographical record of 16th-century Italy. After the Gallery of the Maps, you are funneled into the Sala Sobieski. Keep going. In the **Sala di Costantino (Hall of Constantine)** ★, pink-tinged frescoes by Giulio Romano (1522–25) are a tribute to Christianity's triumph over paganism.

In the famed **Stanze di Raffaello (Raphael Rooms)** ★★ (1506–17), exquisite frescoes like *The School of Athens* ★★★ (in the Stanza della Segnatura) and *The Liberation of St. Peter* ★★ (in the Stanza di Eliodoro) display the harmony of color and balance of composition that were the hallmark of High Renaissance classicism and Raphael's mastery as a painter. After the Raphael Rooms, keep to the left for the direct route to the Sistine Chapel.

📺 Best → **The Sistine Chapel** ★★★ Michelangelo's spectacular frescoes—covering more than 1,000 sq. m. (10,764 sq. ft.) in all—very much live up to the hype, and after the thorough wipe-down they received in the 1980s and 1990s, they're more eye-popping than ever. On the ceiling (1508–12),

ROME

Michelangelo's stories of creation, Adam and Eve, and Noah are told in nine frames, surrounded by faux architectural elements and medallions. Michelangelo's *Last Judgment* (1535–41) is on the altar wall. In all, Michelangelo spent about 9 years in this room, permanently ruining his eyesight and screwing up his back beyond repair.

The lateral walls (the first part of the chapel to be decorated) are covered with 15th-century frescoes of the **life of Moses** and the **life of Christ,** including celebrated works by early-Renaissance masters Luca Signorelli, Sandro Botticelli, and Perugino, but not Michelangelo. On the altar wall, the swirling *Last Judgment* (1535–41) is much more fire-and-brimstone than his earlier work on the ceiling, reflecting the anger and disappointment of Michelangelo's later years. *Tip:* You can exit the Vatican Museums via the right rear door (the one marked GROUPS WITH GUIDE ONLY) of the Sistine Chapel to go straight to St. Peter's. Exit the chapel via the left door *only* if you have rented a Vatican Museums audioguide, which must be returned at the museum entrance. *Città del Vaticano.* ☎ *06/6988-3333. www.vatican.va. Admission 12€ adults, 8€ students; free (and ridiculously crowded) on last Sun of month. Mar–Oct and from Christmas to Epiphany Sun (early Jan) Mon–Fri 8:45am–4:45pm, Sat 8:45am–2:45pm (till 4:45pm on holiday weekends); Nov–Feb Mon–Sat 8:45am–1:45pm (Sat till 4:45pm during holiday weekends); last Sun of month 8:45am–1:45pm. (For the exact schedule, which changes slightly from year to year, check the museums' website.) Last admission is 1½ hr. before closing. Closed all national and religious holidays (except Easter week). Metro: Ottaviano.*

Museums & Galleries

→ **ACEA–Centrale Montemartini** ★★
Major cool points are scored at this unique museum. The blackish-blue, heavy-metal innards—industrial pipes, primitive turbines, gigantic bolts, and defunct machines—of this decommissioned electricity plant—make an unexpected but totally sexy backdrop to white marble statues of gods and goddesses, the leftovers from the Capitoline Museums' vast collection of ancient sculpture. Because the Capitoline Museums' cache of sculpture is so immense, even the 400 or so "second-tier" works of art displayed here are masterpieces. Above the Sala Caldaie (Boiler Room), there's a nice cafe/bookshop where you can hang out, overlooking the century-old furnaces and ancient torsos of Apollo. *Via Ostiense 106, near Piazza del GazoMetro.* ☎ *06/574-8030. www.centralemontemartini. org. Admission 4.50€. Tues–Sun 9:30am–7pm. Metro: Piramide. Bus: 23 or 271.*

→ **Capitoline Museums** ★★★ Atop ancient Rome's citadel hill, the Campidoglio, the Michelangelo-designed halls of the Capitoline Museums, are home to some of the most important sculptures in the world. In terms of sheer quantity, the collection is second only to the Vatican Museums, but in terms of personality, the Capitoline wins hands down. Start your visit in the Palazzo Nuovo. In the courtyard, you'll find the reclining statue of **Marforio,** believed to be a river god. Behind a protective glass wall to the right is the star piece of the entire museum, the nearly perfectly preserved bronze **equestrian statue of Marcus Aurelius** ★★ (ca. A.D. 180). Unfortunately, the glass prohibits a great view of the work.

Inside the Palazzo Nuovo, the **Dying Gaul** ★★ (Gaul = Frenchman) is one of the more celebrated marble sculptures in the collection. In the **Hall of Emperors** ★ (also in the Palazzo Nuovo), you'll meet with the unnervingly lifelike stares of several centuries' worth of imperial busts. In Roman art, portraiture tended to be realistic (as opposed to idealistic), so the faces are intensely communicative and personal—if a guy had a bulbous nose in real life, it was depicted as such in art; if he had big ears (as Claudius did), that was shown, too.

In the courtyard, you'll discover the photogenic fragments of the **colossal statue of** *Constantine* ★. The rest of the Palazzo dei Conservatori is a pinacoteca that has a number of fine works by Caravaggio, Titian, Tintoretto, and Guido Reni. Do not leave the Capitoline Museums without going downstairs to the ponderous tufa corridors of the **tabularium** ★★. This was the ancient Roman archive hall (78 B.C.) and today it sits underneath Palazzo Senatorio (the bell-towered building on Piazza Campidoglio), the modern-day city hall. *Piazza del Campidoglio.* ☎ *06/6710-2071. www.museicapitolini.org. Admission 7.80€. Tues–Sun 9am–7pm; public holidays 9am–1pm. Closed Jan 1, May 1, and Dec 25. Bus: 30, 40, 46, 62, 64, 70, 87, 170, or H.*

➔ **Galleria Borghese** ★★★ Immensely entertaining and mercifully manageable in size, the collection at this 17th-century garden estate is museum perfection. Ancient Roman **mosaics** ★★ in the entrance salon depict gory scenes between gladiators and wild animals (dripping guts is a recurrent theme). In Room 1, Canova's risqué *Pauline Bonaparte* ★ (1805–08) lies, topless, on an inviting marble divan. Bernini's staggeringly skillful sculptures of *David* ★★, *Apollo and Daphne* ★★★, and *Rape of Persephone* ★★ (1621–24), in Rooms 2 to 4, are so emotionally charged as to elicit sympathy, and so realistically rendered that their subjects seem to be breathing.

The paintings by Caravaggio in Room 8 range in tone from luscious (*Boy with a Basket of Fruit*, 1594) to disconcerting (*Sick Bacchus* ★★, a self-portrait, 1593) to strident and grisly (*David and Goliath* ★, 1610). Renaissance masterpieces like Raphael's *Deposition* (1507) and Titian's *Sacred and Profane Love* ★★ (1514) hang casually upstairs in the pinacoteca, as well as a bit of 16th-century soft porn in Correggio's

Danäe ★★ (1531). The museum's strict reservations policy keeps crowds to a blessed minimum; be sure to book at least a few days in advance. *Villa Borghese. Piazzale Scipione Borghese 5, near Via Pinciana.* ☎ *06/32810. www.galleriaborghese.it. Admission 8.50€. Tues–Sun 9am–7pm. Closed public holidays. Reservations required; try to book 1 week in advance. Bus: 52, 53, 116, or 910 to Via Pinciana. Tram: 3 or 19 to Viale delle Belle Arti.*

➔ **Museo Nazionale Romano** ★ This bright and airy palazzo right across the street from Termini has an embarrassment of ancient riches, including Roman paintings, mosaics, statues, and inscriptions. Frescoes teeming with delightful animal and vegetable motifs, rescued from the bedrooms and dining rooms of Roman villas, are the highlight here, and totally unique among Rome's museums. The National Roman Museum's mind-boggling collection of Etruscan and Roman artifacts, including stone inscriptions, vase fragments, everyday tools, marble busts, frescoes, and mosaics, is so vast, it's housed in four separate buildings: Palazzo Massimo alle Terme (Largo di Villa Peretti 1; Metro: Termini); Palazzo Altemps (Piazza San Apollinare 44; bus: to Piazza Navona); Baths of Diocletian (Viale Enrico de Nicola 79; Metro: Repubblica); and Crypta Balbi (Via delle Botteghe Oscure 31; bus: to Largo Argentina). ☎ *06/3996-7700. www. roma2000.it/munaro.html. Admission 6€. Tues–Sun 9am–7pm.*

➔ **National Etruscan Museum at Villa Giulia** ★ One of Rome's lovelier and more undervisited museums, Pope Julius III's gorgeous Mannerist villa houses priceless Etruscan artifacts, including intricate gold jewelry and a charming his-and-hers sarcophagus, from the civilization that ruled Italy before the Romans. Near the end of the itinerary that the museum has set for visitors to follow, look for the cases of jewelry, where pins and necklaces are decorated with miniscule animals rendered in tiny granules of gold—that this level of intricate detail was possible 2,500 years ago, and that it still exists, is astonishing. *Piazzale di Villa Giulia 9, at Viale delle Belle Arti.* ☎ *06/322-6571. Admission 4€. Tues–Sat 9am–7pm; Sun 9am–1pm. Bus: 52, 490, or 495. Tram: 2, 3, or 19.*

Churches

Rome is a minefield of churches. Duck into any of Rome's countless houses of God, and you're likely to stumble upon a painting by Caravaggio, a sculpture by Bernini, ancient mosaics, or, best of all, a saint's decaying body part! All of Rome's churches are free to enter (though some charge you a few euros to visit a subterranean level), so take advantage of their cool interiors in summer. Below are the best.

→**Crypt of the Capuchin Monks** ★★★ Macabre yet oddly pleasing, this must-see church crypt is decorated with the dismantled skeletons of thousands of monks. Attached to the church of Santa Maria della Concezione. *Via Veneto 27, at Via San Nicola da Tolentino.* ☎ *06/4882-748. 1€ donation expected. Daily 7am–noon and 3:45–7:30pm; crypt Fri–Wed 9am–noon and 3–6pm. Metro: Barberini. Bus: 52, 53, 62, 80, 95, 116, 175, or 492.*

12 Hours in Rome

This is an ambitious itinerary. Everything on this tour is free except for the Vatican Museums, Sistine Chapel, and the sights in number 7, below.

1. **You must see the Colosseum, the Roman Forum, the Capitoline Hill, and the Pantheon.** You need to see the Pantheon during the day because it's closed at night.

2. **From the Pantheon, head west to Piazza Navona.** Get lunch at one of the lively, less-touristy trattorias on the side streets west of Piazza Navona.

3. **After lunch, hightail it over to the Vatican Museums.** Last entry is at 3:20pm. You won't have time to see much, so zip through the galleries of ancient art and head straight for the **Sistine Chapel.** Exit the Sistine Chapel via the door that leads directly to **St. Peter's Basilica.**

4. **Take a break.** Head back to your hotel, freshen up, and hit **Campo de' Fiori** around 7pm for an **aperitivo** with all the young locals who party there every night.

5. **Eat dinner somewhere in the vicinity.** Then walk over to **Castel Sant'Angelo** to see how magnificent it (and its bridge) looks under the floodlights.

6. **Use your last energy to see the Piazza del Popolo and the Spanish Steps.** These are at their liveliest and prettiest at night. If you're still trucking late-night, go to the Trevi Fountain. It's at its most spectacular after 1am, when all the tourists have finally gone home.

7. **See the Galleria Borghese, the Crypt of the Capuchin Monks, and the Foro Italico.** These are great under-the-radar choices, if you have time to fit them in or have been to Rome before.

➔**San Clemente** ★ This "lasagna of churches" is the best place in Rome to understand the city's archaeological evolution. The ground-level chapels aren't particularly exciting (even though they're about 800 years old); what's so fascinating about San Clemente are the excavations *(scavi)* underneath the church. *Via di San Giovanni in Laterano, at Piazzale San Clemente.* ☎ *06/7045-1018. Free admission to church; 3€ for excavations. Mon–Sat 9am–12:30pm and 3:30–6:30pm (Oct–Mar till 6pm); Sun 10am–12:30pm and 3:30–6:30pm. Metro: Colosseo. Bus: 85, 87, 117, or 571. Tram: 3.*

FREE ➔**Santa Cecilia** This incredibly peaceful basilica—an 18th-century reworking of a medieval church—is dedicated to the patron saint of music, who was martyred here in the 3rd century A.D. Inside, altar mosaics dazzle, and fragments of Pietro Cavallini's wonderful 13th-century fresco of the *Last Judgment* can be seen at limited times. *Piazza Santa Cecilia, off Via di Santa Cecilia.* ☎ *06/581-9020. Free admission. Daily 7:30am–noon and 4–7pm. Bus: 23, 280, or 780. Tram: 8.*

FREE ➔**Santa Maria in Trastevere** ★ The first church in Rome dedicated to the Virgin Mary is spectacular inside and out, with a landmark Romanesque brick bell tower, colorful frescoes, mosaics, and loads of recycled ancient marbles. The basilica was built in the 4th century A.D. on the site of a *taberna meritoria,* a kind of VFW predecessor where ancient Roman veterans of foreign wars could come, drink, and regale each other with stories from the front lines of battle against Goths and Huns. Santa Maria in Trastevere is best visited just after Mass has let out (usually 6:15pm on weeknights), when the basilica is still fragrant with incense. *Piazza Santa Maria in Trastevere.* ☎ *06/581-9443. Free admission. Daily 7:30am–8pm. Bus: 23, 271, 280, or 780. Tram: 8.*

FREE ➔**Santa Maria Maggiore** ★ In this perfect example of the prototypical basilica, the main nave, flanked by two lower and narrower side aisles, terminates in a curved apse, which is decorated with dazzling polychrome and gold mosaics. Near the right side of the main altar, a modest marble slab marks the tomb of baroque superstar Gian Lorenzo Bernini; the epitaph, inlaid in bronze, is a pithy summary of his life: HE DECORATED THE CITY. One of Rome's four patriarchal basilicas. *Piazza di Santa Maria Maggiore.* ☎ *06/483-195. Free admission. Daily 7am–7pm (last admission 15 min. before closing). Metro: Termini or Cavour. Bus: 70.*

The University Scene

Head to San Lorenzo if you want to try to blend in with the city's left-wing university students—the city's main university accommodations (**University of Rome La Sapienza;** www.uniroma1.it) are centered around here. (The main campus is located by Termini Station.) Or simply try out one of the city's **centri sociali (social clubs).** Leftist high school and college students form these clubs and use them for hanging out, holding concerts, throwing parties, showing films, and so on. One centro sociale with a welcoming vibe is **Circolo degli Artisti** (Via Casilina Vecchia 42; ☎ **06/70-30-56-84;** bus: to Via Casilina; Tues–Sun 9pm–3am; cover varies), near the Termini in an old milk-production center, a good-size place with a bar, a video room, and two theaters. The music varies—although hip-hop and jungle are in abundance—as does what's going on: live performances, movie screenings, DJs, and such. The crowd is generally early 20s, some ghetto-brat types, hip-hop kids, and guys with no shirts and pierced septums. The best way to get information about a particular show is to call **Mondo Radio 90.9 FM** (☎ **06/207-32-32** or 06/70-30-56-84) for the pertinent details; they speak English.

ROME

Playing Outside

Biking

If you're going to ride a bike around Rome, stick to the peaceful confines of the Villa Borghese, or only ride on Sundays, when traffic is light in the centro. Otherwise, biking in Rome can be very stressful. On the other hand, it can be really enjoyable if you have a guide to lead the way through the traffic. **Enjoy Rome** (p. 791) runs a 3½-hour **bike tour** several days per week from March to November. The tours take you to the Villa Borghese, Piazza del Popolo, the Mausoleum of Augustus, the Spanish Steps, Piazza Venezia, the Mouth of Truth, the Circus

Good Places to chill: The Seven Hills

Starting in the north and moving around the city clockwise, the famous seven hills of ancient Rome were the **Capitoline (Campidoglio)**, the **Quirinal (Quirinale)**, the **Viminal (Viminale)**, the **Esquiline (Esquilino)**, the **Caelian (Celio)**, the **Aventine (Aventino)**, and the **Palatine (Palatino)**. The Quirinale and the Esquilino have long been covered by modern buildings, and the Viminale isn't even recognizable as a hill anymore. The other four, however, still retain a great ancient-feeling atmosphere. A spur of red tufa, the Capitoline was the citadel of Rome and perch for the city's most sacred temples (to Jupiter, Juno, and Minerva); it also formed the northern boundary of the Roman Forum. The Tarpeian Rock, the precipice on the steep western slope of the hill, is where, from ancient times right through the 1500s, traitors were hurled to their death.

The Capitoline lost most of its ancient appearance when it was extensively embellished in the 16th century by none other than Michelangelo, who designed the outstanding public square here (Piazza del Campidoglio) and the pink buildings that surround it (the Capitoline Museums and Palazzo Senatorio, or city hall). The travertine steps around Piazza del Campidoglio are a great place to get some sun and write postcards, but don't forget to check out the breathtaking views from the terraces that overlook the Forum on either side of Palazzo Senatorio. At the far end of the Forum, south of the Colosseum, the Celio hill is one of my favorite under-the-radar spots in all of Rome. With crumbling ruins and overgrown vegetation and some great old sun-baked churches, it has that strange but fabulous Roman quality of feeling more like it's out in the country than in the middle of a 3-million-person city.

The Celio's main attraction is its public park, the Villa Celimontana (bus: 81), which makes for great picnicking and chilling out after hitting the ancient sites. From the Celio, the green swath of archaeological parkland continues south to the Baths of Caracalla. West of the Celio (across the Circus Maximus), the Aventino was the favored residential area of the non-imperial wealthy citizens of ancient Rome, and it's still one of the most desirable (and leafiest) neighborhoods in central Rome today. Check out the Aventine's Giardino degli Aranci Park (bus: 175) for wonderful views over the river and Trastevere. Finally, the hill that's stayed truest to its ancient roots is the Palatine, forming the southwestern boundary of the Roman Forum. The Palatine is now a tree- and grass-filled archaeological site where you can climb all over extensive but rather confusing ruins of imperial palaces (the 8€ ticket also gets you into the Colosseum).

Sunday Soccer Games

To experience Roman culture at its most fervent, don't go to Mass—go to a ❚❚ **Best** soccer game ★★★. Full of pageantry, dramatic tension, and raw emotion, the home games of **AS Roma** (www.asromacalcio.it) and **SS Lazio** (www.sslazio.it), the city's two Serie A (Italian premier league) teams, can be far more spectacular than any fancy theater event.

All games are played at the **Stadio Olimpico,** Foro Italico, Viale dello Stadio Olimpico. The ticket office can be reached by phone at ☎ 06/323-7333. You can get to the games by taking bus no. 32, 271, or 280, or tram no. 2. Tickets go on sale at team stores exactly 7 days before game time and can be purchased at the Stadio Olimpico—on game day only—from the box office or *bagherini* (scalpers), or at tabacchi stores displaying the "Lottomatica" logo. For Roma games, you can buy tickets at the official **AS Roma store** (Via Colonna 360; ☎ 06/678-6514). For Lazio games, tickets are available at **Lazio Point** (Via Farini 34; ☎ 06/482-6768). They don't take credit cards, and tickets run between 15€ and 90€.

Maximus, and the Colosseum. The tours cost 20€ for riders age 26 and under; it's 25€ for over-26s. Tours are suspended during rainy weather; call the office for schedule details.

Boating

Rome's riverboat service, the **Battelli di Roma,** stops in the centro storico under Ponte Cestio, Ponte Sisto, and Ponte Sant'Angelo and travels north to the **Foro Italico.** The view is not always scenic (unless you consider half-submerged Vespas "scenic"), but your feet will welcome the alternative means of locomotion. Call ☎ 06/6938-0264 or go online to www.battellidiroma.it. Tickets are 1€ for the shuttle service and 10€ to 50€ for guided, wine-tasting, or dinner cruises.

FREE → **Foro Italico** ★★★ Underrated and undervisited, this massive 1930s sports complex below Monte Mario, on the western bank of the Tiber a few kilometers north of the centro, is Mussolini's gloriously over-the-top paean to the cult of athleticism. The esplanades are covered with hugely entertaining black-and-white **mosaics** ★ of good little fascists doing virtuous fascist things—gymnasts performing difficult stunts, sporty

guys doing calisthenics, soldiers riding on tanks tagged with VIVA MUSSOLINI graffiti. To the immediate north of here is the fabulously campy **Stadio dei Marmi** ★★★, the crown jewel of fascist art in the Foro Italico. In May, the Italian Open is held at the tennis center here. Plenty of umbrella pines and the lush green slope of Monte Mario make this a refreshing place to spend an hour or two. *Largo de Bosis, at Lungotevere Maresciallo Cadorna. No phone. Free admission. Bus: 32, 271, or 280. Tram: 2.*

Parks

Believe it or not, Rome has more trees and parkland per square kilometer than any other large city in Europe. The most central and most used park in the city is the ❚❚ **Best** **Villa Borghese** ★★ (www.villa borghese.it; Metro: Spagna or Flaminio; bus: 52, 53, 116, 490, or 910; tram: 3 or 19), which extends over 80 hectares (148 acres) of groomed green hills in the northeast part of the centro. Villa Borghese has lawns with spots of sun or shade where you can hang out and read, picnic, make out, and the like, and paved paths where you can go for a nice jog. There's also a little lake where you can

ROME

rent a rowboat, and kiosks throughout the park where you can rent inline skates and bikes. The view over the city from the Pincio terrace, on the western edge of the park, is one of the best in Rome. Clear across town, just west of the Gianicolo hill and Trastevere, the **Villa Doria Pamphilj** ★★ (bus: 44, 75, or 870) is the largest park in Rome, with vast regions that border on wilderness. In the more frequented parts of the park, there are jogging paths, soccer fields, a 17th-century villa, and a turtle pond. Villa Pamphilj is

the park you should use if you're planning on doing a full Renaissance-style picnic spread with wine. Open containers aren't technically allowed in Villa Pamphilj (neither is lying out in a bathing suit), but the mounted cops who patrol the park won't hassle you as long as you're not bothering anyone. Back in the centro, the **Villa Celimontana** (south of the Colosseum; Metro: Colosseo; bus: 60, 75, 81, or 175; tram: 3) is smaller but lovely, with paved paths, fragrant gardens, and pretty views.

Shopping

The **Spanish Steps** area (Via Condotti and the web of streets leading off Piazza di Spagna) is where all the fancy, big-name label stuff is—Gucci, Prada, *yada yada yada*—but chances are you didn't budget a 750€ pair of boots into the ol' travel finances. The good news is, you can also get some real shopping done in Rome, but you do need to know where to go. The tiny side streets off Campo de' Fiori, including **Via dei Giubbonari** and **Via dei Baullari,** have a high concentration of independent boutiques for young and hip urbanites, as well as a few hole-in-the-wall places selling trendy belts and accessories for 5€ or so.

Via del Governo Vecchio, to the west of Piazza Navona, has more of the same, although some shops there skew older, and are more bohemian and more expensive. Just south of the Vatican, **Via Cola di Rienzo,** is one of the Romans' favorite all-purpose shopping streets, with a wide array of chain boutiques for both sexes and all price ranges. The classic retail street in Rome is **Via del Corso.** All of Via del Corso is lined with shops, but the northern half, from Via del Tritone to Piazza del Popolo, is where most of the action is, with stores like Miss Sixty and tons of kids hanging out on their motorini. The scene is worth experiencing at least once.

Halfway down Via del Corso (opposite Piazza Colonna) is the **Galleria Colonna mall** (aka Galleria Alberto Sordi)—it's not very big, and the stores are nothing you couldn't find elsewhere in town, but its covered halls make it the only place in Rome where you can comfortably do retail damage during a downpour. Finally, as a last resort, you can also head to **Via Nazionale.** One of central Rome's grimier thoroughfares, Via Nazionale has most of the mass-market chain boutiques, plus some good cheap shoe stores, and an excellent dress shop, L.E.I.

➔ **Coin** ★★ Italy's biggest department-store chain, with two locations in Rome, has some great finds in the jewelry and accessories departments (including well-priced knockoffs of the latest European runway looks), but stay away from the clothing, which tends to be overpriced and inexplicably frumpy. *Via Cola di Rienzo 173.* ☎ *06/708-0020. www.coin.it. Metro: Ottaviano. Branch at Piazzale Appio 7 (Metro: San Giovanni).*

➔ **Disfunzioni Musicali** ★ In the left-wing university 'hood of San Lorenzo, "Musical Dysfunctions" is a place to pick up rare imports and cult recordings, and the dozens of flyers deposited here by various event promoters are a good way to get in on what's happening in the dance clubs and live venues. *Via degli Etruschi 4 (off Via Tiburtina).* ☎ *06/446-1984. www.dispu.com. Bus: 71 or 492. Tram: 3 or 19.*

→ **Ditta G. Poggi** ★★ This old-school artists' supplies and vintage stationery shop makes for a fascinating (and mercifully quiet) detour off the tourist path between Piazza Venezia and the Pantheon. Inventory from the past 50 years that never sold out can still be found here, often at the original price. *Via del Gesù 74–75 (off Via Plebiscito).* ☎ *06/678-4477. www.poggi1825.it. Bus: 46, 62, 64, 170, or 492 to Largo di Torre.*

→ **Energie** Supplying trendy teens and 20-somethings with flashy sportswear, jeans, shoes, and bags with a surfy, resorty feel, this techno-blaring mainstay on the upper half of Via del Corso is where you need to shop—over and over—if you're young and hoping to fit in with Rome's cool kids. *Via del Corso 408–409.* ☎ *06/687-1258. Bus: 117.*

→ **Ethic** ★★ The boutiques in this local chain are full of vintage-inspired styles and materials that will give you a more "downtown" Mary Kate Olsen type of look while still being practical. Especially good for skirts, wash-'n'-wear dresses, and knits in chic, jewel-tone colors. *Multiple locations around town. Branch at Via del Pantheon 46–47.* ☎ *06/6880-3167. Bus: 46, 62, 64, 170, or 492 to Largo di Torre.*

→ **La Feltrinelli** Italy's largest bookstore chain has recently gone Borders-style, launching a series of integrated book and media stores, including the Roman flagship at Largo Argentina, which has a good, if small, selection of English-language books (most are paperback bestsellers and books on Roman history and tourism). For a much more comprehensive selection of English (and Spanish, French, and German) titles, check out the branch at Via V.E. Orlando, near Piazza della Repubblica. *Largo di Torre Argentina 11.* ☎ *06/6866-3001. www.la* feltrinelli.it. *Bus: 30, 40, 46, 62, 64, 70, 87, 492, or 571. Tram: 8. Branch at Via V.E. Orlando 78–81.* ☎ *06/487-0171. Metro: Repubblica. Bus: 40, 64, 70, 170, 175, or 492.*

→ **Martina Novelli** ★★ Chicks with a shoe habit should not miss this tiny shop on Piazza Risorgimento, just outside the Vatican City walls. Some seasons feature stronger collections than others, but when you see the hot and truly unique styles, priced at a fraction of what other designer-ish boutiques are asking, well . . . *Piazza Risorgimento 38.* ☎ *06/3973-7247. Bus: 23, 81, 271, or 492. Tram: 19. Metro: Ottaviano.*

→ **Pink Moon** ★ An incredibly well-informed and friendly staff make it well worth the minor trek to this music store south of Trastevere. If you have a record player, there's a fantastic selection of 45s, covering music from the '40s to the '90s. *Via Pacinotti 3/c (off Viale Marconi).* ☎ *06/557-3868. www.pinkmoonrecords.com. Bus: 170 to Viale Marconi. Tram: 3 or 8 to Stazione Trastevere.*

→ **Posto Italiano** ★★ Amid all the narrow shop fronts on busy Via Giubbonari, this store is a must for any guys or girls looking for a cool pair of shoes at a great price (styles you won't find back home start at 69€). The selection is excellent for how tiny the space is—with comfy boots, sexy fuchsia stilettos, and leather sandals, there's not a dorky style in sight. There's a newer branch in Trastevere, too. *Via Giubbonari 37/a.* ☎ *06/686-9373. Bus: 30, 40, 46, 62, 64, 70, 87, 492, or 571. Tram: 8. Branch at Viale Trastevere 111.* ☎ *06/5833-4820. Bus: 23, 280, 780, or H. Tram: 8.*

→ **Prototype** Proof that the sexiness of Italian men can transcend the formal gear they're usually associated with, this unisex boutique has racks packed with cool and casual button-down shirts, cargo pants, and graphic T-shirts. *Via Giubbonari 50 (off Campo de' Fiori).* ☎ *06/6830-0330. Bus: 30, 40, 46, 62, 64, 70, 87, 492, or 571. Tram: 8.*

ROME

→ **Ricordi** Part of the Feltrinelli group, Ricordi is a mass-market record store with flashy video displays, CD bar-code scanning listening stations, and other mega-store fare. Like similar stores in the U.S., displays are set up according to the best-selling CDs, so if there's a current Italian chart-topper you're looking for, you'll be able to find it easily here. Europeans love dance and pop compilations, and Ricordi will not let you down on that front. The Via del Corso location also has a box office that handles ticket sales for most of the big-name music acts that come to Rome. *Via del Corso 506, near Piazza del Popolo.* ☎ *06/361-2370. Bus: 117.*

→ **Sole** ★ Belts inspired by papal vestments, mixed-media trenchcoats, and other edgy stuff only Italian chicks know how to rock—the women's garments and accessories at this friendly little boutique off Campo de' Fiori have tons of attitude. The only downside is that prices are a tad steep. *Via dei Baullari 21 (off Campo de' Fiori).* ☎ *06/6880-6987. Bus: 30, 40, 46, 62, 64, 70, 87, 492, or 571. Tram: 8.*

Markets

→ **Porta Portese** ★★ Rome's famous weekly flea market isn't always the most rewarding shopping experience, but as a cultural experience, however, Porta Portese is very worthwhile: You will see vendors hawking rusty Vespa parts and plumbing components from the 1930s (and miraculously enough, people buying them). Most tourists who brave the crowds and sheer size of the market are looking to score amazing vintage shoes and clothes, and if you arrive early enough in the morning (as in 7am) and are willing to dig through bins of used clothing, you will come upon the occasional Gucci jacket or fabulous 1970s polyester shirt. *Piazza di Porta Portese, Via Portuense, Piazza Ippolito Nievo, Via Ettore Rolli, Trastevere. No phone. Full market: Sun 7am–2pm. Fireworks, auto parts, lawn furniture (Via Portuense): Mon–Sat 9am–2pm. Bus: 75, 780, or H. Tram: 3 or 8.*

→ **Mercato di Testaccio** ★★ There are more "picturesque" markets in the city, but this food and dry goods bazaar, a covered maze-like space in the heart of the Testaccio neighborhood, is the real deal, and a colorful, convivial spectacle of Roman daily life. All around you, local residents of this tight-knit community chatter with each other as they wheel their canvas carts from stall to stall, stocking up on all the vegetables, cheeses, and meats they'll need for the next few days. All who enter can expect to be greeted with gusto, even if you're only a curious tourist. *Piazza Testaccio. Mon–Sat 7am–1pm. Metro: Piramide. Bus: 23, 75, 95, 170, or 280. Tram: 3.*

→ **Via Sannio** ★ The stands on this street just south of the church of San Giovanni in Laterano (St. John Lateran) are great for picking up knockoffs of the latest trendy belts and accessories, as well as decent-quality leather jackets, and soccer team jerseys. Like a kinder, gentler, less varied version of Porta Portese. *Via Sannio, off Piazzale Appio. Mon–Sat 9am–1pm. Metro: San Giovanni. Bus: 85, 87, or 850.*

Seville

Come to Seville if you love drama and romance. The locals here are passionate, whether they're cheering at bullfights in La Maestranza, dancing at the *peñas* in the La Macarena, pouring out of bars in Santa Cruz, or praying in one of the city's grandiose churches. Add to this the charm of Seville's labyrinthine passageways, the fragrant smell of orange blossoms, and the soft cadence of the Andalusian accent, and you're bound to fall victim to this quixotic town. If Madrid is the sexiest city in Spain and Barcelona the most cultured, Seville is the most sensual.

Seville's long history—it began about 600 B.C.—and its proximity to Africa means that you'll see a cultural mix here unlike any other. Look for Moorish influences everywhere, get lost in the old Jewish quarter whose streets were made to confuse outsiders, and take in the old church traditions of a Spain not yet totally lost to global golden arches and green-and-white disposable coffee cups.

Kids here embrace the past, but have both feet firmly in the future. Internet surfing, piercing, and spinning—they're as much a part of the culture here as bullfighting, flamenco dancing, and hanging out in cafes and eating tapas.

The climate here in "the frying pan of Spain" helps create the charged atmosphere: It gets hot, damn hot, especially in late summer, forcing the whole city out onto the streets. If you're getting too fried, do as the locals do and head to the cooler banks of the river. The Guadalquivir has always been the lifeblood of Seville, allowing it to prosper during the Age of Discovery when it was the city that launched 1,000 ships.

And Sevillians know how to celebrate their successes, large and small. The nightlife is as hot as the city's notoriously sultry weather. Spend enough time in Seville and you'll soon find yourself agreeing with King Alfonso X, who said of the place: *"No me ha dejado"* (It hasn't left me). Once Seville gets into your system, you simply can't sweat it out.

The Best of Seville

◌ **The Best Hotel to Practice Your Solo:** **Hotel Amadeus** is a musician's paradise, but the beautiful soundproof rooms guarantee a great siesta, even if your musical sense doesn't go beyond singing in the whirlpool shower. See p. 845.

◌ **The Best Bar for Flamenco Worship:** **El Tamboril**'s midnight flamenco performances are a breathtaking experience. (The dancing that follows will literally leave you breathless.) See p. 854.

◌ **The Best Place to Recover:** No matter what it is you're recovering from (a long day sightseeing, a broken love affair, a marathon), head to **Aire de Sevilla** to be refreshed. It is a modern spa built inside an ancient Arab bath that will float away your cares. See p. 856.

◌ **The Best Place to be a Wallflower:** Actually, it's the best place to be a wallwatcher. **Alcázar**'s walls, floors, and ceilings have so many details that you can

Talk of the Town
Five ways to start a conversation with a local

1. **Where can I find the most beautiful Moorish tiles?** Locals are justly proud of their city, and beginning any conversation by complimenting the incomparable beauty of the architecture, women, men, sidewalks, lampposts, and so on, will get you in like Flynn.

2. **Where can I learn to dance the flamenco?** The *sevillana* is the distinctly local form of flamenco dancing, which almost all kids here learn in school at a young age. If you ask to learn a few steps, don't be surprised if the proper rhythms are not in your gene pool.

3. **What's your favorite festival?** Seville lives for its festivals, Semana Santa and Feria, and if you miss them, its residents will tell you what a fool you are and give you a play-by-play of the action.

4. **What do you think of bullfighting?** The establishment here is fiercely protective of its right to bullfight, no matter how outsiders view public displays of animal cruelty. So of course, the rebellious youth love to poke fun at it, because hey, in a place of perfect beauty and perfect weather you've got to have something to rebel against, right? Just don't refer to it as a sport.

5. **Do you think machismo is in the air here?** Machismo, that particular Spanish form of male chauvinism, is a touchy subject bound to get the passions flowing and give you a new insight into modern Spain. Be careful who you ask (a group of oldsters watching the bullfight on TV is not a good idea) and if you get a reply such as "What are you talking about?" or "There's no such thing," it's best to drop it.

easily spend a day picking out your favorites, including, perhaps, the doll heads at Patio de las Muñecas. See p. 856.

○ **The Best Pick-Up Place:** The neighborhood around Alameda has every type of bar and disco you can possibly imagine, from grungy to trendy, from gay to straight, and for amateurs and professionals. Sample a few. See p. 841.

Getting There & Getting Around

Getting into Town

BY PLANE

Seville's airport, **San Pablo** (☎ 95-444-9000; www.aena.es), is located 10km (6 miles) east of the city on the N-IV road to Cordoba. To get into the city, you can catch a public bus from TUSSAM (☎ 90-221-0317; 2.30€). It takes about 30 minutes to get to Puerta de Jerez and runs every 30 minutes between 6:15am and 11pm on weekdays and every hour on weekends and holidays. Or take a taxi (17€ to town during working hours, 22€ otherwise, plus baggage fees). Call **Tele Taxi** (☎ 95-462-2222) or **Radio Taxi** (☎ 95-458-0000) if you can't grab one in front of the airport.

BY BUS

There are two bus stations in Seville. **Estación de Autobuses El Prado de San Sebastián** (☎ 95-441-7111) is the base for buses going to Cádiz, Córdoba, Málaga, Granada, and other towns in the Cádiz province, Costa del Sol, and Mediterranean coast all the way to Barcelona.

At the **Estación de Autobuses Plaza de Armas** (Av. del Cristo de la Expiración; ☎ 95-490-7737), you can find 14 daily buses to Madrid and northwestern Spain. Also, the companies Alsa and Damas have buses to Lisbon and other destinations in Portugal.

BY TRAIN

Trains arrive to and depart from the modern **Estación Santa Justa** (Av. Kansas City; ☎ 95-441-4111). Spain's pride, the lightning fast AVE train joins Seville and Madrid in 2¹/₂ hours every day, or you can take an extra hour and save some money on the Talgo. There are also local Andalusian trains to Cádiz and Jérez de la Frontera every hour, to Córdoba every half-hour, along with trains to Málaga, Granada, Almería, and Mérida. Barcelona trains leave three times a day, including an overnight hotel train, ideal for sleeping off wine and saving on a hotel night. For times and fares, contact **Renfe** (☎ 90-224-0202; www.renfe.es). Bearers of the Carnet Joven Euro under 26 get a 20% discount.

To get to the city center, exit the station and walk toward your right for about 20 to 25 minutes. If your bags are too heavy for all that walking, you can get bus 32 (1€) to Plaza Encarnación.

Getting Around

BY CAR

A car is not a good idea in Seville. The streets are made for horses, so you'll find yourself making three-point turns on almost every corner of the old city. The traffic is therefore a bit of a medieval nightmare and getting stuck behind a garbage truck or even an idle taxi can ruin your afternoon, not to mention that parking on the streets is out of the question, so you'll have to add parking fees to the already expensive renting rates. However, if you can't live without the CO_2 emissions, there are a couple of rental agencies by Puerta de Jérez, such as **ATA Rent A Car** (Almirante Lobo 2; ☎ 95-422-1777) and, of course, your friendly local **Avis** at the airport (☎ 95-444-9121) and Santa Justa train station (☎ 95-453-7861).

SEVILLE

BY BUS

The subway system in Seville has been in the works for decades and is supposed to be opening soon, but it won't be ready anytime in the near future. Meanwhile, try using the decent public bus system called **TUSSAM** (☎ 90-245-9954; www.tussam.es), with four buses that do two circular itineraries around the city center passing by the transport terminals. The C1 and C2 go clockwise and counterclockwise from Estación Santa Justa around the old town passing by Parque de María Luisa, Triana, La Cartuja, and La Macarena. The C3 and C4 do a smaller circle around the center passing by Puerta la Carne, Puerta de Jerez, Plaza de Armas, Avenida Torneo and Macarena. At night they change the letter C for an A. Other buses go inside the center, but we don't recommend you take them unless you like to watch people make fun of you as they walk past you at twice your speed. Each bus has a TV screen where, besides some hideous commercials, they show you the route step by step, or should I say stop by stop, making the experience simple in even the worst states of consciousness. The ride costs 1€ and you can also get unlimited passes at the main station in Plaza de Armas.

BY BICYCLE

Seville is the perfect size for riding a bike—if only it weren't for those cobblestones. The hot summers can be a problem, too, but ask at the bike shop for a local route that suits your experience and wishes. **Cyclotour,** on Torre del Oro (☎ 95-427-4566; www.cyclotouristic.com) rents bikes for 18€ a day (you can also get silly-looking four-wheel pedal carts) at the parque María Luisa.

ON FOOT

You can pretty much walk everywhere in Seville. One of the best walking routes is the barrio Santa Cruz, with its maze of cobblestone streets and whitewashed houses. Planning a walk here is impossible, though, because the whole point is to get lost.

Seville Basics

Orientation: Seville Neighborhoods

Seville promises great rewards if you give it time and attention. A good pair of walking shoes will come in handy, too. Geographically flat, it lacks the dramatic first impression of other great cities; it's what stoners might call a "creeper." But in the crooked paths of Santa Cruz, the banks of the river Guadalquivir, and the rambling alleys of the Centro and Macarena, the city finds itself, at times strolling, most often strutting.

To orient yourself, use the Gothic **Catedral** as your reference point; it's the heart of the city and easily identifiable by its tower, the Giralda, the tallest thing in town, with the spinning gold weathervane on top. From there, these are the neighborhoods:

SANTA CRUZ   East of the Catedral, lies Santa Cruza, also known as the **Judería (old Jewish quarter),** with its serpentine cobblestone streets, flower-filled plazas, and charmingly overpriced restaurants. This is the oldest area of town, which means, of course, that tourists are everywhere. Still, you should find surprises around many corners: Look up and you'll see a street covered by a roof of ivy, make the right turn, and you'll bump into some Roman columns in somebody's backyard.

ARENAL   West of the Catedral, on the east banks of the river Guadalquivir, is the lively Arenal. This neighborhood is marked by the other Sevillian cathedral and the legendary bullfighting arena, **Plaza de Toros de Real Maestranza.** Just as picturesque as Santa

Cruz, though not as well preserved but much less touristy, it's full of great sights and better deals for eating, quality and price-wise.

CENTRO   North of the Catedral, the main drag **Avenida de La Constitución** takes you to the commercial center of Seville, the appropriately named Centro. Daytime activity gives the big, tree-lined **Plaza Nueva** its buzz, but if you go at night, head east to **Plaza Salvador** and nearby **Plaza Alfalfa.** North of Plaza Nueva stretches the shopping district, where you can stroll the pedestrian-only streets **Calle Sierpes** and **Calle Tetuan.** There are no cars or tricked-out scooters here to interfere with the capitalist machinery of chain stores.

MTV Best ALAMEDA   If you walk a few minutes farther north of Centro, along the funkified **Calle Amor de Dios,** you'll end up in the artsy-but-still-sketchy-enough-to-be-interesting area around Alameda de Hércules, which everyone just calls "the Alameda." It used to be "Barrio de Putas," which is a colorful way of saying it's the red-light district. You still might see some working girls or boys at night. The whole area surrounding Alameda, and particularly **Jesús del Gran Poder,** is bursting with new bars and cafes that stay open until the wee hours and cater to the bohemian, gay, and alternative crowd.

LA MACARENA   Farther east is the Macarena, a classic working-class neighborhood that's following Alameda's transformation, with trendy bars, restaurants, and urban-street-wear stores along and around its main drag, **Feria.** Together with Alameda, this is also the neighborhood where most flamenco *peñas* are found.

TRIANA   Across the river from El Arenal, Triana was historically the home of sailors leaving for or arriving from the New World. Later a Roma (gypsy) neighborhood, it's the birthplace of many famous flamenco luminaries, although not many are left. Now highlighted by **Calle del Betis,** the street that runs along the river north from Puente San Telmo (that's a bridge) to Puente Isabella II, Triana is an essential spot for summertime cruising and boozing.

ISLA DE CARTUJA   Also on this side of the river are the fairgrounds for April's annual Feria, to the south; to the north is **Isla Cartuja,** a marginal neighborhood until the '90s, revamped for the Expo '92, and now sort of dormant again, save for a theme park and a monastery where Chris Columbus used to hang with pals before discovering America.

SOUTH OF SANTA CRUZ   South of the Catedral, wide avenues take you past **Universidad de Sevilla** and to the very attractive **Parque María Luisa,** where you'll come across canals you can row through and couples making out on nearly every bench. Next to the Parque is **Plaza Real,** and, across the street, the Antigua Fábrica de Tabacos.

Be forewarned that many maps of Seville, including those given out by the tourist offices, have a strange affliction: Due North is not at the top of the map, but somewhere off to the left. Make sure to find the compass on your map and don't end up in the Indies when you're looking for India.

Tourist Offices

The main tourist office in Seville is at Av. de la Constitución 21 (☎ **95-422-1404**); ask for **Puerta de Jerez** and go from 9am to 7pm on weekdays, 10am to 7pm on Saturdays, and 10am to 2pm on Sundays. There are several more with less accommodating hours at the train station (☎ **95-453-7626**), airport (☎ **95-444-9128**), Puente Isabel II (called Puente de Triana by the locals), and Parque María Luisa.

Recommended Websites

○ **www.turismo.sevilla.org:** The city's official website in six languages.

SEVILLE

○ **www.seviquorum.com**: Cultural goings on in Seville.

○ **www.discoversevilla.com**: Advice for life and partying in the city.

Culture Tips 101

A cloud of smoke does not envelope Seville as it does other southern European cities, but the young folks here do like their hash, especially in the Alameda, where most anything goes (if no one's looking). Be aware that hash is always rolled with tobacco, so if you pull out your pipe and load it up, you are suddenly a drug abuser and will be kindly asked to leave the premises. Or worse—see the Barcelona and Madrid chapters for more on Spain's drug laws.

As in the rest of Spain, the cops are pretty mellow here, but they also know they have Seville's reputation to protect. So, while you will probably never have any contact with them, you will also notice that Seville is one of the few European cities that doesn't have a vibrant street performance scene in its center. They won't break your legs for playing guitar on the street or anything, but they definitely might discourage you from distracting the shoppers on Calle Sierpes with your performance art.

Drinking is part of life here, but drunkenness is not. The rule is: If you're casual, it's casual.

Recommended Books, Movies & Music

Seville's charm has been the source of inspiration for artists from the beginning of time and so are its characters. You'll find an overwhelming number of books, movies, and albums about Don Juan, Carmen and the Barber, and, of course, flamenco dancers, but there's a slew of more contemporary-themed books, DVDs, and CDs to sift through, too.

BOOKS

The mother of all Spanish novels is *Don Quixote* by Miguel de Cervantes, and it's certainly worth a read to appreciate Spain's windmill-chasing history. A more recent but no less romantic novel is *Driving Over Lemons: An Optimist in Andalucia,* by Chris Stewart, which tells the story of an English sheep shearer, who buys an isolated farmhouse in the mountains of Granada. Gustavo Adolfo Bécquer's love poems were forged in the streets of Seville and are to romantic writing what Seville is to romantic cities. Check out his *Rhymes* and get in the mood for some old-style loving. Better yet, read them all in Spanish, if you can.

MOVIES

In Luis Buñuel's *That Obscure Object of Desire,* the master of surrealism shows Seville like no one else could in this odd story of love, passion, and sick jealousy. For a more contemporary film, try something—anything!—by Pedro Almodóvar. The funny Spanish filmmaker's *Tie Me Up, Tie Me Down!; Talk to Her;* and *All About My Mother* are centered around fantastical scenarios but offer quite truthful takes on modern-day Spanish culture.

MUSIC

Flamenco is the word. Get something by Camarón, who was originally from Cádiz but spent a lot of time here, and then go to La Carbonería, where he used to make everybody's neck hair raise to the tin roof. For a more modern, international version of flamenco, try Ketama. Also listen to *Carmen,* by Carlos Saura. Not to be confused with the terrible Plácido Domingo adaptation of the opera, this album with Spanish guitar god Paco de Lucía is not only a great ode to flamenco but to a Spain that had just come out of decades of dictatorship and was rediscovering its own culture.

Seville Nuts & Bolts

Cellphone Providers & Service Centers   The main cellphone providers in Spain are **Amena** (www.amena.com), **Movistar** (movistar.es), and **Vodafone** (www.vodafone.com). You can find them all over the Centro and along Amor de Dios in Alameda or Feria in La Macarena.

Currency   You'll get the best exchange rate at ATMs, which are all over the center of town, especially on Avenida de la Constitución and in the shopping district. If you have cash and you need to exchange it, any major bank branch (Mon–Fri 9am–2pm) will give you a much better deal than the small booths on the streets. For traveler's checks, there's only one place to go for no-fee exchanging: **American Express** (Plaza Nueva 7; ☎ 95-421-1617; Mon–Fri 9:30am–1:30pm and 4:30–7:30pm, Sat 10am–1pm).

Embassies   Get your passport's worth at the **U.S. consulate** in Seville (Paseo de las Delicias 7; ☎ 95-423-1885). The nearest **British consulate** is in Málaga, but there is an **Australian consulate** at Federico Rubio 14 (☎ 95-422-09-71; Mon–Fri 10am–noon). All embassies are in Madrid (p. 592).

Emergencies   For any emergency, dial ☎ 112. For major medical emergencies, go to **Hospital Virgen del Rocío** (Av. Manuel Siurot s/n; ☎ 95-424-8181). For smaller cuts and scrapes there's a first-aid post just east of the Alcazar on the other side of the road from Jardines de Murrillo (Av. Málaga; ☎ 95-441-1712).

Internet/Wireless Hot Spots   **Internetia** is the no-nonsense mac-daddy of Internet stores in Seville. With 80 computers at 4mbps, surfing is made quick and easy—there's almost no waiting in lines. Prices range from .60€ to 1.90€ an hour. You can also bring your own laptop or use their Macs if you are picky. It's located at Av. Menéndez Pelayo 46 (☎ 95-453-4003; daily 24 hr.).

Sevilla Internet Center is another option. It has fewer computers and worse hours, but it's steps away from the Catedral and other tourist attractions. It's at Almirantazgo 2 (☎ 95-456-1881; Mon–Fri 9am–10pm, Sat–Sun 10am–10pm).

Laundry   There's a notable dearth of places to wash those atmosphere-soaked clothes in Seville; the one exception is **AutoServicio de Lavandería Seville** located in the Arenal just off Calle Adriano. Here, for 6€ a load, you will get your duds washed, dried, and folded, no questions asked. It's at Castelar 3 (☎ 95-421-0535; Mon–Fri 9:30am–1:30pm and 5–8:30pm, Sat 9am–2pm).

Luggage Storage   At the Estación Santa Justa, you'll find lockers available for 2€ to 5€ for 24 hours. They're the kind that print out a code that anyone can use to open it, so they're ideal to leave stuff for other people to pick up.

Pharmacies   Neon-green crosses mark the *farmacias,* which can be found all over town. No single one is open 24 hours a day; instead, farmacias rotate the all-night responsibility. Each one posts a schedule indicating who will be open on what night.

Post Offices   **Postal de Correos** (Av. de la Constitución 32; ☎ 95-421-9585; Mon–Fri 8:30am–8pm, Sat 9:30am–2pm) is right near the Catedral and the main tourist office. If you are sending a letter, it is a good idea to drop it at the office as mailboxes don't tend to be checked all that often.

Restrooms   As in most of Spain, the words "public restrooms" in Seville are more associated with a dark alley, corner, or tree than an actual facility. Restaurant owners are very nice, though, and a simple *"Puedo usar el lavabo?"* and a smile will usually get you in.

Safety   Like many other cities in Spain, Seville has become considerably safer in the last couple of years. However, there is still a fair amount of petty theft. Take the same precautions you would in any large city. Try to leave your passport in the hotel and make sure you have your credit card numbers somewhere else, in case you have to cancel them. Beware of the old gypsy ladies that offer you free stuff—just say no. Make sure you keep your valuables close at all times and be careful with the groups of drunk teenagers by the riverside at night; though mostly harmless, they can be scary. Women should not walk alone at night if it can be avoided.

Telephone Tips   There are plenty of pay phones around town, most of which accept coins (but won't always give them back) and all of which take telephone cards. You must dial the prefix **95** for any number in Seville. But keep in mind that calling a cellphone number from a pay phone in Spain will cost you the same or more as calling your buddies back in the States.

Tipping   Waiters here get paid decent wages so tipping is 10% or less. Only foreigners tip at bars and you don't tip the masseuse. Cabbies are sometimes tipped .50€.

Sleeping

Finding a room in Seville during the summer can be a pain, and during Semana Santa and Feria, it's nearly impossible even if you're willing to pay the jacked-up rates (about double the low season's) unless you've booked months in advance. The rates here are for low (June–Feb) and high season (Mar–May).

Hostels

→ **Hostal Gravina** To find a cheaper room in Seville you would probably have to steal castañuelas from a flamenco dancer and spend the night in jail. The rooms are very simple, clean, and well preserved, with a sink, closet, and decent beds. The friendly and efficient twin brothers that own it also have another three hostels, all with private bathrooms and more amenities (and higher prices), that cater to all sorts of pockets and needs. The website is good, although the pictures are a little nicer than reality. *Gravina*

46. ☎ 95-421-6414. *www.hostales-sp.com. 20€–25€ single, 30€–35€ per person double. Amenities: Safe; shared bathrooms.*

→ **Pensión Vergara** A backpacker's favorite, this old Sevillian house is in the heart of Barrio Santa Cruz, above a souvenir shop, 4 short blocks from the Catedral. It's the bright interior patio, with tons of plants and atmosphere, that may make you feel as if you've gone back in time a bit. Inside are spacious, brick-walled rooms with floral bedcovers, and 8 of the 12 have a view over the cobblestone street. *Ximénez de Enciso 11.* ☎ *95-421-5668. pensionvergaraseville@yahoo. es. 20€–30€ per person. Amenities: Shared bathrooms.*

Cheap

→ **Espacio Azahar** A little farther away from the Catedral and the American tourists there, you'll find this hotel, at one end of the

Alameda, where you'll probably be spending your nights among Seville's hipsters. The same architect who concocted the Plaza de España designed this classic Sevillian house, converting it into something so hip that it's not a hotel but a "space." A trendy young staff can inform you where in town to go, but the ethnic dinner parties and drinks on the roof with its handcarved wood chairs and the outdoor Jacuzzi may be one of the best options on any given night. Take advantage of this place while the neighborhood is still cheap. It won't last. *Jesús del Gran Poder 28.* ☎ *95-438-4109. www.espacioazahar.com. 56€ single, 66€ double. Amenities: Restaurant; bar; Jacuzzi; wheelchair friendly; Wi-Fi. In room: A/C, TV, minibar.*

→ **Hotel Aacr Museo** This spanking-new hotel looks more like New York than Andalucía. The loftlike lobby/bar/reception area with slick minimalist decor, a huge skylight, and some paintings reminiscent of Rothko manages to be cozy. The breakfast room can be a little claustrophobic with no windows, but the beds are huge, the rooms have parquet floors and full bathrooms, and some even sport a small balcony. The staff is very professional and the prices wouldn't get you a bed in a trailer in the Big Apple. *Pedro del Toro 9.* ☎ *95-450-2231. www.hotel esensevilla.info. 67€–81€ single, 81€–95€ double. Amenities: Breakfast room; bar; A/C; laundry service; lounge; wheelchair friendly; Wi-Fi. In room: TV.*

MTV **Best** → **Hotel Amadeus** ★ You don't have to be Wolfgang to appreciate these 18th-century Sevillian family houses that have been tastefully converted into a music-themed hotel. You'll appreciate its soundproof common spaces and rooms lined with pianos, violins, and other shiny instruments. Each of the 19 unique rooms features different comforts, in some a terrace, whirlpool, or sauna shower, and 2-inch-thick

wooden window shutters. Prices vary with the rooms but not with seasons except, of course, Semana Santa and Feria. Adding a third bed won't cost you a penny. *Farnesio 6.* ☎ *95-450-1443. www.hotelamadeussevilla. com. 65€ single (in a double room), 80€– 130€ double. Amenities: Restaurant/lounge; wheelchair friendly; Wi-Fi. In room: A/C, TV, minibar, safe, sauna.*

→ **Hotel Casona de San Andrés** It's late, you're tired, and you've had too many glasses of wine sitting outside in the beautiful plaza. Don't worry, home is a step away. Another gracefully restored 19th-century house in the middle of the Centro, this place offers an especially good value if you get one of the four rooms with balconies that open out to the plaza or one of the two with a private terrace. Dark wooden furniture, intricate tiles, colorful stained-glass doors, and big patios with fountains round out the picture. Yes, it's painfully romantic, but what else would you expect from Seville? *C. Daioz 7* ☎ *95-450-2231. www.casonadesanandres. com. 45€–50€ single, 85€–100€ double. Rates include breakfast. Amenities: Restaurant; bar; wheelchair friendly. In room: A/C, TV, hair dryer, Internet, safe.*

→ **Hotel Puerta de Seville** This modern, modest hotel on a main street in Santa Cruz offers all the comfort and amenities of its higher consecrated competitors and more. The classical oil paintings and antiques in the lobby and Andalusian poems on every door are almost too picture perfect. Think the smell of orange blossoms (goodbye, musty hostel), wafting through your ample Provençal-style room. The über-helpful staff can tell you legends of the city to get in full Seville mood. *Santa María La Blanca 36.* ☎ *95-498-7270. www.hotelpuertadesevilla. com. 50€–55€ single, 65€–85€ double. Amenities: Laundry services; wheelchair friendly. In room: A/C, TV, safe.*

SEVILLE

Seville

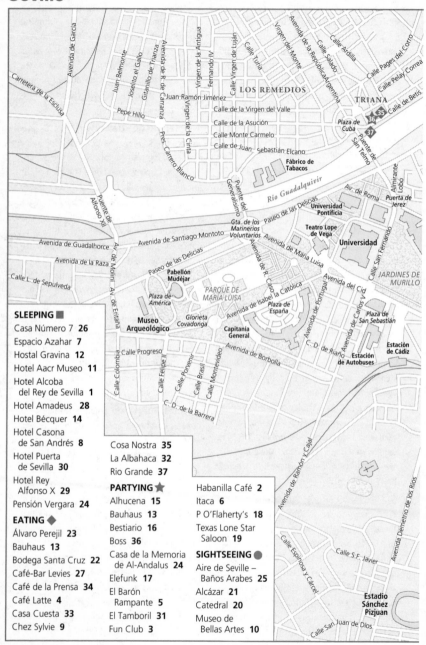

SLEEPING ■

Casa Número 7 **26**
Espacio Azahar **7**
Hostal Gravina **12**
Hotel Aacr Museo **11**
Hotel Alcoba
  del Rey de Sevilla **1**
Hotel Amadeus **28**
Hotel Bécquer **14**
Hotel Casona
  de San Andrés **8**
Hotel Puerta
  de Sevilla **30**
Hotel Rey
  Alfonso X **29**
Pensión Vergara **24**

EATING ◆

Álvaro Perejil **23**
Bauhaus **13**
Bodega Santa Cruz **22**
Café-Bar Levies **27**
Café de la Prensa **34**
Café Latte **4**
Casa Cuesta **33**
Chez Sylvie **9**

Cosa Nostra **35**
La Albahaca **32**
Rio Grande **37**

PARTYING ★

Alhucena **15**
Bauhaus **13**
Bestiario **16**
Boss **36**
Casa de la Memoria
  de Al-Andalus **24**
Elefunk **17**
El Barón
  Rampante **5**
El Tamboril **31**
Fun Club **3**

Habanilla Café **2**
Itaca **6**
P O'Flaherty's **18**
Texas Lone Star
  Saloon **19**

SIGHTSEEING ●

Aire de Seville –
  Baños Arabes **25**
Alcázar **21**
Catedral **20**
Museo de
  Bellas Artes **10**

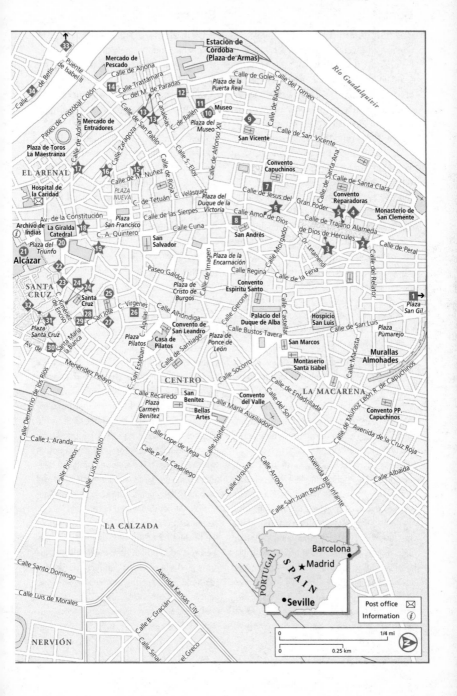

Doable

➔ **Hotel Alcoba del Rey de Seville** You don't need a genie to grant your wishes to experience the luxury of this Moorish Sevillian–inspired boutique hotel at the edge of La Macarena. It's not as close to the Catedral, but the cedar-wood furniture and doors with Moorish arches, handmade brass kitchen sinks, round or square marble bathtubs, and Hermès bath products make it worth the trip even without a magic carpet. While away some time watching belly dancers perform under a Persian tent or chilling with hookahs on the roof and a whole array of spa treatments available. Get a feeling for each of the 15 unique rooms on the website (never mind the lame photos), but be careful not to get stuck here for a 1,001 nights. *Bécquer 9.* ☎ *95-491-5800. www. alcobadelrey.com. 100€–172€ single (in a double room), 119€–191€ double. Amenities: Restaurant; bar; breakfast lounge; wheelchair friendly. In room: A/C, TV, Internet, safe.*

➔ **Hotel Rey Alfonso X** As you walk into the bright quiet lobby you might think, "Okay, not a place for frat parties." The Alfonso X could be in Soho, were it not for the touches of Sevillian tilework in the front lobby of this elegant modern hotel. The entrance lounge and restaurant feel more business than backpacker, with their comfortable white chairs and glass walls. The 35 modern and spacious rooms (some with a terrace) overlook a large internal patio, also available for guests to loll about in, making the rooms very sunny and quiet. Another huge plus is that it shares a pool with the hotel Fernando III across the street. *Ximénez de Enciso 35.* ☎ *95-421-0070. www.reyalfonso x.com. 80€–139€ single (in a double room), 80€–158€ double. Call for seasonal rates. Amenities: Restaurant; wheelchair friendly. In room: A/C, TV, Internet.*

Splurge

➔ **Casa Número 7** If you want to experience what nobility feels like, pull out your credit card and walk through the door of this tastefully restored, luxurious, six-room 1824 Sevillian house, complete with inner courtyard. An eclectic mix of antique furniture and oil paintings makes the house feel as if you're slumming at an ambassador's party. A rooftop from where you can almost touch the Giralda, a lounge room with a fireplace, and a butler with white gloves serving you a decadent breakfast will make you redefine your notion of "classy." Check out the gun room with the family tree and picture yourself planning a trip to the Indies. Sorry, no TV. *Vírgenes 7.* ☎ *95-422-1581. www.casa numero7.com. From 181€ double. Amenities: "Honesty" bar; laundry service. In room: A/C, hair dryer.*

➔ **Hotel Bécquer** Though it seems as if it's a branch of the Marriot, this hotel does offer more bang for the buck, especially when it comes to extra goodies like the full-service spa offering individual attention in the ways of chocolate wraps, facials, hydromassage, and the like at 20% off the regular price for its clients. There are many large indoor and outdoor communal spaces for lounging; at presstime, a new rooftop pool and solarium were being built. The well-kept and comfortable rooms are large with king-size beds and slick new bathrooms. The only drawback to this conveniently located hotel is its lack of Andalusian charm, except when it comes to the hospitality of the staff and the delicious food served in one of its many lovely restaurants and cafes. *Reyes Católicos 4.* ☎ *95-422-8900. www.hotelbecquer.com. 115€–210€ double. Amenities: Restaurant; bar; Internet; pool; spa; solarium; wheelchair friendly. In room: A/C, TV, safe.*

Eating

Seville is not the kind of place where you can indiscriminately stumble on unique, tasty, and cheap food; it takes a little bit of research. Almost any bar or restaurant can offer decent tapas such as the humble tortilla española, a tuna sandwich, or the inevitable gazpacho. But if you aren't careful, you can spend your time in Seville eating authentic but uninspired food, and paying 8€ for a 3€ ham sandwich. Follow our recommendations for finding exotic delights at value prices. Tapas, which are the best way to try all sorts of different dishes in 1 night, are generally between 1.50€ and 3€ each, the value therefore depends on the portion size. A shrimp (gambas) tapa can mean 3 gambas at one place or 10 at the other.

Hot Spots

→**Bauhaus** ★ MODERN MEDITERRANEAN One of those hard-to-classify places, Bauhaus is everything: Nice restaurant with a creative menu for lunch and dinner, trendy cafe bar in the early evenings, cool lounge in the early night with a small dance floor that gets moving later on. The varied menu includes mouthwatering creations such as foie gras with red fruits and ginger sauce and also fun vegetarian options such as coconut milk croquettes and great salads and juices. Get their flyer to find out the activities for the month. *Marqués de Paradas 53.* ☎ *95-422-4210. www. bauhauscafe.com. Lunch menu 9.50€; main courses 8€–15€. Daily noon–4am.*

→**Cosa Nostra** ★★ ITALIAN If you are sick of traditional tapas bars (hey, it could happen), slick your hair back, put on your linen slacks, and take your date to Triana for the ultimate Italian-chic experience, care of Neapolitans Rafaelle Melloni and Giuseppe Batista. Black-and-white celebrity fashion photos welcome you to the main dinning room. From some seats, you can watch the pizza chef whip out killer pies. Or order specialties straight from the muthaland, such as mozzarella di buffalo from Napoli or prosciutto from you know where. But before you attempt some face-to-face with your honey, go by the restrooms and grab a disposable toothbrush from the expendables machine; Neapolitans sure know how to use their garlic. *Betis 52.* ☎ *95-427-0752. Main courses 6€–15€. Daily Tues–Sun 1:30–4.30pm and 8:30pm–midnight.*

Cheap

→**Alvaro Perejil** SANDWICHES Walking down Mateos Gago by the Catedral, you'll see a storefront size locale with approximately five times its capacity of people hanging out outside. Work up your courage and dive into the fray, and you'll be rewarded with delicious *salmorejo* and tuna *montaditos.* Sevillians from all over town come for the ambience and the sweet orange wine—and, brace yourself, to sing their lungs out. It's the most authentic place in this tourist infested neighborhood. *Mateos Gago 20. Tapas 2€. Daily noon–4pm and 7pm–close.*

→**Bodega Santa Cruz** ANDALUSIAN TAPAS Raise your elbows and make yourself some space by the bar at this old bodega a few feet away from the Catedral. It gets packed at lunch and at night with tourists, but they only add to the liveliness of the place. The sassy bartender will keep track of your bill by making chalk marks on the wooden bar in front of you; of course, that's if you make it to the bar. Skip the average potatoes and try something more adventurous, like the eggplants with honey, the best *croquetas* in town or the *cazón en adobo.* Get some of the very decent house wine (don't you love Spain?) to wash it down. ***Warning:*** You'll have to scream to get your food and you'll scream after you try it. *Rodrigo Caro 1 at Mateos Gago.* ☎ *95-421-3246. Tapas 1.50€–2.20€. Daily 9am–midnight.*

→ **Café-Bar Levies** MODERN TAPAS As you enter this average, student hangout—looking place (you know, lame art and decor, small tables, and so on), you'll wonder how so many young Spaniards can look so happy all crammed in together. When you finally get seated and the tapas arrive, you'll understand. The portions are huge (for tapas, of course) and delicious, with vegetarian options that could convert any carnivore. There's outdoor seating in a quaint plaza and the service is lightning fast by Spanish standards. Then you get the check and you'll wonder, like that time your friend took care of the bill at the end, "Why didn't I order more?" *San José 15.* ☎ 95-421-5308. *Tapas 2.60€; combination platters 6€. Daily 9pm–1am.*

→ **Chez Sylvie** FRENCH TAPAS You don't have to be Sartre to feel at home at this bohemian French enclave in El Centro. Its welcoming owner, Sylvie, keeps the spirit of '68 alive in her French books, songs, and movies on the TV screen, not to mention the multinational backpackers and musicians at the tables and Internet-ready computer. Have a little French wine while you wait for your salmon crepe or the toasted goat cheese with duck ham and a nice salad. Ask Sylvie where to go and what to do in Seville and, if you are lucky, she will point you to some of the most authentic spots in town. Seville may be the Spanish capital of romance, but when it comes to *l'amour,* nobody knows it like the French. *San Vicente 11.* ☎ 95-437-5412. *Tapas 1.75€–5€. Mon–Wed 8:30am–7pm; Thurs–Fri 8:30am–11pm.*

Doable

→ **Casa Cuesta** ★ ANDALUSIAN If Triana can claim to be the birthplace of flamenco, this restaurant can very well claim to have invented tapas. Converted from an 1880 winery, Casa Cuenta has managed to keep the old-school ambience intact, with Moorish tiles, huge windows, and turn-of-the-century dark-wood furniture. This is a homey place to take a wine and tapas break during your Triana walking tour, or sit down for a fancy home-made dinner around the tree trunk that dominates the center of the dining room. Tapas not to miss are the outstanding jamón Ibérico and a *salmorejo* that puts gazpacho to shame. If you're hungrier, try the *cazuela del tío,* featuring shrimp, mushroom, and ham stewed in a sherry sauce, or one of their wide selection of fish and meat dishes. *Castilla 1.* ☎ 95-433-3335. *Tapas 1.80€–2.50€; main courses 9€–19€. Daily noon–1am.*

Splurge

→ **La Albahaca** ★ BASQUE FRENCH This very elegant and quiet restaurant is in a beautiful old palace with Sevillian tile work, antique furniture, and classic oil paintings. Once you find it in the famous Plaza Santa Cruz, sit in one of the dark Victorian rooms that have seen illustrious visitors ranging from Charlton Heston to real-life royalty. The venison with mushrooms and almonds and roasted pheasant breast with Iberian bacon are unforgettable, as are desserts such as the fig soufflé or bitter orange mousse. *Plaza Santa Cruz.* ☎ 95-422-0714. www.andalunet.com/la-albahaca. *Main courses 18€–24€. Mon–Sat 1–4pm and 8pm–midnight.*

→ **Río Grande** ★★ NOUVEAU SPANISH They say aristocrats and even the Queen mother used to frequent this stunning all-white terrace restaurant on the Triana side of the river and it is hard to doubt it. Expect an innovative and exquisite seafood menu by star chef Nacho Martínez and views that will compete for your attention. Monkfish in foie gras sauce or gazpacho cream with Bogavante taste even better than they sound. Choose from one of their 110 wines, including some jewels older than your parents. Bring your blue-blooded date here. *Betis s/n.* ☎ 95-427-3956. www.riogrande-sevilla.com. *Main courses 12€–25€. Daily 1–4pm and 8pm–midnight.*

Cafes & Tearooms

→ **Café de la Prensa** CAFE The atmosphere here is all about wooden benches, flyers on the wall, and all the Enya you can handle—but don't let that dissuade you. During the day, it's a good place to get a *cortado* (a shot of espresso with milk) and read the paper. At night, young intellectuals killing their brain cells pack the outside tables for the great views across the river. *Betis 6.* ☎ *95-433-3420. Daily 1pm–3am.*

MTV Best → **Café Latte** ★★ CAFE In the trendiest neighborhood of Seville, this cafe caters to the hipster's need for caffeine and fun. Triangular tables and designer chairs in reds and browns, loud music, and a long bar make it a fun place for breakfast, afternoon macchiatos, or even early evening drinks. A big screen shows music videos and the occasional movie. It's a good place to go with a date and mingle as you wait for the bars in Alameda to get busy. *Jesús del Gran Poder 83. No phone. Daily 8:30am–1pm and 4pm–closing.*

Partying

If Andalucía is one of the great world headquarters of hanging out, Seville is the plush couch in the CEO's office. If you get a coffee or beer at a cafe, lingering is not only encouraged, it's required. The service is usually quite laid-back, so you may have to beg and plead for your check, but you'll never be asked to leave. So relax, Columbus's remains will still be there tomorrow. The locals already understand this, which is why you'll find them lingering over a 12-ounce soda for 1¹/₂ hours. Really. The most popular neighborhood for tourists to *tomar algo* is Santa Cruz; for students, it's Centro (especially little Plaza Alfalfa); down-to-earth (stony) artist types flock to Alameda; and the locals head over to La Macarena or Triana.

For nighttime hanging out, especially in spring, summer, and fall, the place to be is Plaza Salvador. Here young people practice the custom of the *botellón,* which means bring your own bottle and chill outside with your homeys; the church steps are a favorite spot. Or, order a drink to go from one of the bars on the southeast side of the plaza. The plaza is packed on weekends with everyone from sketchers to yuppies until about 1am, when the action moves to the nearby bars of Plaza Alfafa or up to the Alameda. In the summer, when the city is baking, the party moves across the Guadalquivir, especially to

Calle Betis. A ton of bars line the esplanade along the river, many with outside tables. Just remember, if a bar sells its own T-shirts in the windows, it's probably best to go elsewhere.

As for clubs, don't think of going before midnight: Things don't get really cooking until 2am.

Nightclubs

Seville doesn't have the thriving dance scene or world-class DJs of other places in Spain. But after one too many flamenco shows, that may not matter. The bouncers are generally muscle-bound but fair, and if you were lucky enough to be born with breasts, or have a really convincing drag outfit, you won't have to pay a cover. Don't think of going before midnight: Things don't get really cooking until 2am.

→ **Bestiario** If you are wondering what the word *pijos* (conservative kids) means, put away your dictionary, tuck in your polo shirt, and walk into this lively lounge/club any day of the week. Boasting many levels, it resembles a Spanish small-town version of a place you'd see in *Sex and the City.* Lots of cushy seats and a crowd of 30-somethings complete the decor. If you are into Spanish pop, you will find yourself in Gypsy Kings heaven here. Free admission and reasonably priced drinks make it a worthy cultural experience, if nothing else. It's closed in July and August. *Zaragoza 33.* ☎ *95-421-3475.*

➔ **Boss** Across the river, in Triana, is Boss— one of the top dance spots in town. But before making the journey, remember that you'll have to get pass the bouncers to get inside, so dress to impress. If you're successful, you'll find yourself entering a huge space, complete with four different bars with different decors to ensure that you'll always find one suiting your tastes. On Wednesday nights, a special party called "funky" (creative, huh?) pumps up international, hiphop, and R&B tunes. It's a great night to meet other Sevillians. On weekends, house music is the focus, and it gets even harder to get in with more house music and more local pijos (aka conservative, and sometimes snobby, rich kids). Try to get a pass and get there before 1am (although nobody will be there) for free admission. *Betis 67.* ☎ *95-499-0104.*

➔ **Elefunk** Feel like a fish out of water in this flamenco and Spanish music-fueled world? Then head over to Arenal for alternative haven, where goldfish swim under every lamp and cool psychedelic graffiti by Ed Zumba grace the walls and give the place an ultimate urban atmosphere. DJs spin electronic, hip-hop and, obviously, funk, and the ambience stays lively until very late. Thankfully, there are couches to rest your tired feet on after all that humping among people of many colors and shapes. *Adriano 10. No phone. www.elefunk.org.*

➔ **Fun Club** ★ Less Americanized and scrappier, in the tradition of its location, Fun Club smokes on weekends in the Alameda until very, very late. Come here if you're still dying to try out your "running man" and it's 5am in the morning. The music is also varied and less strictly dance; there's live music early on Fridays and Saturdays and DJs the rest of the time. Next to the DJ booth, a pair of double doors leads to the chill room,

where it's a little quieter for conversation. You can spend a whole night here just watching pie-eyed rookies push as hard as they can on the double doors to try to get back into the main room (pulling works much better). *Alameda de Hércules 85.* ☎ *95-425-0249.*

Bars & Lounges

➔ **Alhucena** Struggling with Habanilla for the title of cutest bar in town, but much smaller and quainter, this shabby chic place is the best spot around to bring your love interest. Super-mellow bartenders serve homemade vermouth, while chill electronic music softens the background noise caused by chatty hipsters. The decor alone is worth the visit; you'll want to soak in every detail, from the relief tiles to the ornate wooden shelves, to the lamps, to the bar (the same one since 1927). *Carlos Cañal 2.* ☎ *95-506-3517.*

➔ **Bauhaus** ★ Bauhaus is a little of everything: Nice restaurant with a creative menu for lunch and dinner, trendy cafe bar in the early evenings, cool lounge in the early night with a small dance floor that gets moving later on. The slick decoration with Philip Stark furniture and lamps by Arturo Alvarez mixed with a hip and nice staff, plus one of the coolest DJ lineups in town make this place a great option for any time of the day. House music sounds Thursday through Saturday nights and electronic lounge dominates on Sundays to start the week in a chill mood. *Marqués de Paradas 53.* ☎ *95-422-4210. www. bauhauscafe.com.*

Ⓜ **Best** ➔ **Habanilla Café** ★★ On the northern end of the Alameda, this former whorehouse may appear unassuming, but is in fact a supercenter of good times: coffee during the day, tapas in the afternoon, and drinking at night, when the crowds spill out onto the street. A series of little carved hands (don't ask) holds up the railing of the classic long wooden bar, a gigantic lamp made of empty beer bottles hangs over your head, and a collection of coffeemakers shimmers above the bar. The scene is fueled by acidic jazz and trippy jam music, and it attracts visionary malcontents of all ages, from rockers, to punks, to hippies (and even a few leftover beatniks). *Alameda de Hércules 63.* ☎ *95-490-2718.*

→ **P O'Flaherty's** This Irish pub lays claim to one of the best locations in Spain, right across from the Catedral. Yes, a pint here is expensive, but it is Guinness, which is worth at least two Spanish beers. Plus, the outdoor tables are right in the thick of the action for people-watching, and it's a good place to meet other foreigners as well as locals trying their first stout ("*Que fuerte!*" is the most common reaction). *Arenales 7.* ☎ *95-421-0451.*

→ **Texas Lone Star Saloon** Just north of the Catedral, you'll find this little slice of Texas. Well, there's a Texas flag and a giant-screen TV, although you'll be watching more European soccer matches than American sporting events on the tube. Y'all ready for some *fútbol*? You can down Bass, Bud, and Corona, but no Shiner Bock. Even though they dared mess with Texas, this place gets packed with young foreigners and even some locals at night, grooving to throbbing pop/dance music that would make Willie Nelson pee his Wranglers. As of yet, no one has put a shotgun rack on their scooter. *Placentines 25.* ☎ *95-421-0384.*

Gay Bars

→ **El Barón Rampante** Tucked into a small street off Alameda de Hércules and next door to another gay bar, this unassuming spot with a large bar is a prime meeting place. Loud house music attracts guys of varied ages, who mingle at the tables in the bar or drink standing outside. The vibe is very laid-back and open. *Arias Montano 3.* ☎ *95-491-5830.*

→ **Itaca** ★ Not the Greek town. This Itaca is the quintessential Spanish gay club: buff staff, loud house music until the early morning, and, of course, a very busy and dark room where anything could happen. Females are not admitted beyond the modest-size front bar, which works out great if you are a SWGM traveling with your mom, but leaves half of the gay population out of the fun. The venue is weekends-only, when it tends to be very crowded with high-testosterone 20- and 30-somethings who come to dance, dance, dance. *Calle Amor de Dios 31. No phone. Cover 6€.*

Pub-Crawls

Seville has an endless number of areas to pub-crawl, but for the sake of organization, it's best to visit the city's three major strips. First, you'll want to tackle **Plaza Alfalfa** and particularly, calle Pérez Galdos. The vibe here is mainly that of students crowding bars that are a little too small. So you'll soon want to venture across the river to **Triana's Calle Betis,** which is great in the summer, with amazing views of the river and preferred by locals. Here, though, the bars are a little large, and American in style. Feeling like Goldilocks yet? You might just find your perfect bowl of porridge at **Alameda de Hércules.** The bars here are the coolest in the city, with a more artsy, gay/straight mixed crowd. Check out the bar section above for our favorites, or try them all and find the one that fits you just right.

Performing Arts

Keep an eye out for classical concerts that are sometimes presented in the cathedral of Seville, the church of San Salvador, and the Conservatorio Superior de Música at Jesús del Gran Poder. A variety of productions in Spanish, including some plays for the kids,

Seville's Music Scene

Seville has world-class flamenco. If you want to see some rock 'n' roll . . . Seville has world-class flamenco. If you want to see jazz, blues, reggae . . . let us repeat: Seville has world-class flamenco. If it ain't flamenco, the live-music scene here compares to what you'd find at any college watering hole. There's a bunch of overproduced, overpriced, overacted, and I'm-so-over-them flamenco shows that you can find everywhere in the Santa Cruz neighborhood. If you want to go for them, book in advance and be ready to deal with the old English ladies telling you to sit down before you even enter the hall. A better option in that category is the shows at Casa de la Memoria de Al-Andalus (see below), which are more authentic, and still don't involve dark alleyways. Our recommendation is that you get over your fear of darkness and find out about the *peñas,* where, again, you may find the next Camarón or get stuck with something that sounds more like a cat in heat, but you'll have spent the night in a place that you can proudly tell your friends in Madrid about. To do this (*peñas* take place in different places every night—gypsies, remember?), pick up a copy of El Giraldillo and find out what's going on where. Some of the *peñas* are Cantes al Aire (Castilla 47), Cerro del Aguila (Tomás Pérez 61), Torres Macarena (Torrijano 29), or Jumosa 3 (Av. Ciudad de Chiva s/n). They're usually free and a lot of fun. Some more predictable places are listed below.

are presented at **Teatro Alameda** (Crédito; ☎ 95-438-8312). The venerable **Teatro Lope de Vega** (Av. María Luisa; ☎ 95-459-0853), is the setting for ballet performances and classical concerts, among other events. Near Parque María Luisa, this is Seville's leading stage.

Flamenco

→ Casa de la Memoria de Al-Andalus
This traditional and small theater with a great patio in the Barrio Santa Cruz offers more authenticity than its neighbor's nightly shows in a cultural center with art and exhibitions. The quality may vary, but you should find something interesting, from guitar and voice concerts to dance and castañuelas; check the daily program. The prices are also below the average tourist fare. Shows start at 9pm and sell out way before that, so get your tickets early. *Ximénez de Enciso 28.* ☎ *95-456-0670. Admission 9€–11€.*

📺 Best **→ El Tamboril** ★★ Okay, this is not your average, polka-dot dress with the big hair flamenco you know from movies and tourist brochures. One glance at the beautifully odd decor, including orange walls and a weird altar, tells you you're in for a unique experience. The space merely consists of a little dance floor with bench-like chairs behind it, but when the lights go out and the performers start belting out tunes to the glass-encased shrine, the space will become irrelevant. After this heart-wrenching ceremony, dry your eyes and get ready to test your newly learned flamenco moves—you'll have the opportunity to dance after the performance. *Plaza de Santa Cruz, s/n. No phone. Daily varied hours and prices.*

→ La Carbonería On the edge of the barrio Santa Cruz, housed in what used to be a coal yard, this venue will always be cool no matter how many tourists tramp through it for the free nightly flamenco music and dance performances. These hit-or-miss shows go from around 9pm until midnight in the German-beer-hall–style room in the back, which stays open until much later with an ongoing great atmosphere that makes it always worth it. In the front room, sloping up from the street, with cobblestone walls and high ceilings, live jazz and/or folk acts of dubious quality go on every night except for Monday and Wednesday, starting at approximately 9pm. *Levíes 18.* ☎ *95-421-4460. Mon–Sat 8pm–3:30am; Sun 8pm–2:30am. Admission varies.*

➔ **Los Gallos** Los Gallos borders on the ultratouristy, but it has better-quality shows than the average touristy spot in Santa Cruz. It also is a small and, therefore, more intense theater than the norm. The shows consists of the whole nine yards of flamenco: Guitar, *cante* (singing), dancers, and castañuelas, Get there early; you don't want to be stuck in the top floor. There are daily shows at 9 and 11pm. *Plaza Santa Cruz 11.* ☎ *95-421-6981. Admission 27€ (drink included).*

Opera

➔ **Teatro de la Maestranza** ★★★ It wasn't until the 1990s that Seville got its own opera house, but it quickly became one of the world's premier venues for operatic performances. Naturally, the focus is on works inspired by Seville itself, including Verdi's *La Forza del Destino* and Mozart's *Marriage of Figaro.* Jazz, classical music, and even the quintessentially Spanish *zarzuelas* (operettas) are also performed. The opera house can't be visited except during performances. Tickets (which vary in price, depending on the event staged) can be purchased from the box office in front of the theater. *Paseo de Colón 22.* ☎ *95-422-6573. Prices vary. Box office: daily 10am–2pm and 6–9pm.*

Sightseeing

Hopefully, we've hammered it into your little heads that Seville is about atmosphere, not about hopping from monument to museum. Still, some manmade structures here are worth entering, and the biggies (Catedral and Alcázar) demand to be seen—even if it means missing out on that important siesta.

Festivals

The two spring monster-fiestas, which draw crowds from all over the world, are taken seriously in Seville.

March & April

Semana Santa. Features spectacular religious processions that inch through the streets with music, people in pointed white hoods, and, most importantly, floats with giant recreations of 17th-century images of the Christ and the Virgin Mary. The parades leave from various churches around the city and go right through the center of town, ending at the Catedral, while thousands of onlookers trample (sometimes literally) their way for a closer look. The atmosphere is somewhat solemn and reverent, but this

is still Spain, so the bars do a good business as well. Holy Week from Palm Sunday to Good Friday.

🎬 Best **Feria de Abril.** An all-day and all-night blow-out that takes place 2 weeks after Easter, on the fairgrounds in the Los Remedios district. During the day, men in full costume ride horses, and girls from 7 to 85 appear in their best flamenco dresses to dance the *sevillana,* the local, joyous form of flamenco. The most prestigious bullfights also take place during this week. Nighttime is for more dancing, eating, and drinking in the hundreds of *casetas,* or tents, each of which is run by a different family or organization and requires an invitation to enter. Except for a few public casetas, the event feels like a giant family reunion mixed with a county fair, leaving the visitor to stand around and gape; you might even get a sight of that rare species: drunk Spanish people. Also be warned that all hostels and hotels will double their rates, and that the center of the city becomes a ghost town. 2 weeks after Easter.

Free & Easy

› If you're short on Es (euros, that is), the best thing to do in Seville is to keep walking—there are always new barrios to explore, especially if you haven't been to **La Macarena** or **Triana.**

› Or take a stab at getting through some of the 4 million documents that record the discovery of the Americas in the **Archivo General de Indias** (Av. de la Constitución 3; ☎ 95-421-1234; free admission; Mon–Sat 10am–4pm, Sun 10am–2pm); this collection includes letters from Columbus to Queen Isabella, some of which are displayed in glass cases.

› **Parque María Luisa** is also always free and great for strolling, sleeping, rowing, PDA, even architecture appreciation at Plaza de España and Plaza de América.

Historic Buildings

▥ **Best** →**Aire de Sevilla—Baños Arabes** ★ Are you exhausted from walking around the cathedral? Do you long for a massage, but feel guilty taking valuable tourist time out to indulge your whims? Well, you are in luck; history meets heaven at Aire de Sevilla. This luxurious spa and bathhouse is located at the site of an Arab bath dating back to the 16th century. The Almudeha-style palatial house with gilded wood ceilings offers four baths of varying temperatures, one of which sits where the original ancient bath did. Top off your salty soak with a massage and an exotic tea, and you will fully understand what Arab hospitality is all about. *Aire 15.* ☎ *95-501-0025 or 95-501-0026. www. airedesevilla.com. Thermal bath and aromatherapy 15€–18€. Daily 10am–midnight.*

▥ **Best** →**Alcázar** ★★★ Just behind the Catedral is this palace that, since the 11th century, has housed everyone from ruthless Muslim rulers to ruthless Christian rulers; each addition to the building since then highlights architectural trends over the ages. It's not a bad idea to get the 3€ audio tour because you may not notice the millions of details otherwise. As in all great palaces, you can't help but fantasize about the intrigue, treason, and romance that these walls have witnessed over the years. The backyard is pretty nice, too—an amazingly verdant series of maze-like gardens that stretches as far as the nose can smell. It's a great place to contemplate your own next conquest, whether it be man, woman, or tortilla. *Plaza del Triunfo.* ☎ *95-450-2323. Admission 5€; free for students. Apr–Sept Tues–Sat 9:30am–8pm, Sun 9:30am–6pm; Oct–Mar Tues–Sat 9:30am–6pm, Sun 9:30am–1:30pm.*

→**Catedral** ★ Depending on who's doing the measuring, Seville's cathedral is one of the three biggest churches in Europe, right up there with St. Peter's in Rome and St. Paul's in London. According to the locals, if you measure cubic centimeters rather than just the area of the floor, it's actually the biggest, although we can't imagine how you'd get a tape measure up in the vaunted Gothic ceiling. Maybe they can just fill all three of them with water and decide once and for all. Anyway, don't get so caught up with the size of the thing (you know who you are) that you miss the stunning stained-glass windows or giant canvases depicting violent scenes from the Bible. You also must make a trip up to the top of La Giralda, the tower that was originally built by the Moors in the 12th century and which the Christians had the good taste not to tear down. You'll walk up La Giralda on a long series of ramps that were put in place for some very lucky horses—they got to enjoy the stunning 360-degree vistas of the city without having to

12 Hours in Seville

1. **Climb La Giralda.** This tower attached to the Catedral is on all the post-cards and is the highest point in town. So climb to the top, survey your kingdom, and plan your attack.

2. **Get lost in Barrio Santa Cruz.** Some complain that the Judería (Jewish Quarter) has been a little too well restored, but all the tour groups in the world can't suck the charm out of this place. And you can still get so lost in the cobblestone maze that you won't even be able to hear German being spoken.

3. **Chill in the Alameda.** The antidote for Santa Cruz is Alameda, the center for alternative living. Get tattooed, buy health food, smoke a *porro,* watch an indie movie—basically just act as if you were at home. Late at night, Fun Club is the discoteca you most certainly do not have at home (at least not at 5am).

4. **Enjoy some tapas.** Seville brings cheap bar food to a new level, if you know where to go. *Cazón en adobo* at Bodega Santa Cruz and *papas al mojo* at Café Levies are essential.

5. **Experience Plaza Salvador at night.** B.Y.O.B. and anything else you want to share, and make new amigos on the steps of the church.

6. **Walk along Calle Betis.** This is not a pub-crawl, nor *la marcha,* but a bar stroll down the esplanade along the river Guadalquivir.

7. **Take in a bullfight.** The pageantry, the drama, the moral conundrum—do you root for the matador or the bull?

8. **Top off the evening at La Carbonería.** Join the tourists for the spicy flamenco show in the back, or hang with the locals in the front room for live folk or jazz.

SEVILLE

elbow so many gasping-for-breath tourists out of the way. *Plaza Virgen de los Reyes.* ☎ *95-421-4971. Admission 7€ adults, 1.50€ students; free on Sun. Sept–Jun Mon–Sat 11am–6pm, Sun 2:30–7pm; July–Aug Mon–Sat 9:30am–4:30pm, Sun 2:30–7pm.*

Museums

→**Museo de Bellas Artes** Here you'll discover important religious works by Spanish masters you've probably never heard of, such as Murillo and Zurbarán. The visit is worth it for Sala V alone, which has a gorgeous ceiling and giant Murillo canvases depicting religious figures with scary things (like rabid dogs) lurking in the shadows. The Museo can't match any of the major museums of Madrid (its modern art collection is forgettable), but the air-conditioning is just as strong on hot summer days. *Plaza del Museo 9.* ☎ *95-422-1829. Admission 1.50€. Tues 3–8pm, Wed–Sat 9am–8pm, Sun 9am–2:30pm.*

The University Scene

The **University of Seville** (www-en.us-es), located south of the Cathedral, attracts a ton of foreign exchange students. One benefit of all the young internationals studying in Seville is the easy availability—you think you know where we're going with this, but you're wrong—of books in English. Right across from the university, **Librería Vertice** (San Fernando 33–35; ☎ **95/422-97-38;** Mon–Fri 9:30am–2pm and 5–10:30pm, Sat 11am–2pm) has a good selection of Penguin Classics.

Located near Plaza Salvador, **Catedral Club** (Cuesta del Rosario 12; ☎ 95/422-85-90; daily midnight–8am) has no connection whatsoever with the Gothic cathedral of the same name, though the dance floor is only slightly smaller. So please don't go banging on the door of the church at 2am. This is a popular club with the international set (especially Americans), and local and guest DJs spin a lot of hip-hop and some house, depending on the night. Consult the free English guide *The Tip*, which usually contains a back-page ad listing the upcoming parties. Everyone pays 6€ unless they're female or they got a free pass beforehand from an Internet cafe or hostel. The scene at 3:30am is studenty, bouncy, sweaty, and black-clad.

Playing Outside

Whether solo or with a love, head to **Parque de María Luisa** and **Plaza de España**, a beautiful and impressive green complex that's a perfect setting for PDA. The park has 3,500 trees, which means there are 3,500 shady spots where you can rest from the stifling heat. If you feel like spending a buck to impress him/her, go for the 24€ carriage ride. Along the way, you can see the park's fancy buildings, plus you can stop at the northeast side of the park at Plaza de España, a huge semicircular structure with a little canal where you can rent a boat to make the date end in a perfect (semi) circle. It's at Avenida de María Luisa and Avenida de Isabel la Católica.

Biking

Bike Sevilla Mágica (Calle Miguel de Manana; ☎ 95-456-3838) will rent you a bike; prices vary, so call for info. It's open daily 10am to 2pm and 5 to 8:30pm.

The Scent of a City

Seville is famous for many things—flamenco, bullfights, tapas—but did you know that it smells? In a good way: If Seville had a signature scent, it would be orange blossoms. These great trees were planted all over town as a way to fight scurvy centuries ago, but now their main claim to fame is to keep the city smelling wonderful, especially during spring. But don't fall to the temptation of trying the fruit. Tired of people eating oranges and dropping them on the streets, the city government decided to mix the oranges with lemons. This resulted in a unique breed of bitter oranges, good for marmalade and perfume, but not too tasty.

Shopping

Every Spanish city seems to have a centrally located shopping district set on pedestrian-only cobblestone streets, and Seville is no exception. On Calle Sierpes, Calle Tetuan, Calle Cuna, and the streets that run between the three, you can find your friendly neighborhood chain stores, such as the Body Shop, but also classy local joints that specialize in flamenco dresses and accessories. If your home needs a little spiffing up or you want to impress your friends, pick up some traditional Sevillian crafts in a few decent boutiques hidden away between the souvenir shops in barrio Santa Cruz, or else hit the intersection of Calle Alfalferia and Calle Antillano Campos in the Triana district and discover the eclectic abundance of ceramic tiles and gifts.

No matter if your style is skater, goth, or hipster, you'll find something to fill your backpack with in the Alameda district. *El Jueves,* the Thursday flea market on Calle Feria in the Macarena district, has been a

Feeling Bullish

From Easter until late October, some of the best bullfighters in Spain appear at the **Plaza de Toros Real Maestranza** (Paseo de Colón 12; ☎ 95-422-4577; www.maestranza.com). One of the leading bullrings in Spain, the stadium attracts matadors whose fights often receive TV and newspaper coverage throughout Iberia. Unless there's a special festival going on, *corridas* (bullfights) occur on Sunday. The best are staged during Feria de Abril celebrations.

Just so you have no misconceptions about going to a bullfight here, know in advance: The bull will be tortured and killed, there will be lots of blood, and the animal will be dragged unceremoniously out of the ring by a team of horses. (If it's any consolation, he is taken to the butcher.)

But by all means, you must go to truly get under the skin of Spanish tradition. A bullfight in Plaza de Toros, one of the most famous arenas in Spain, is a colorful spectacle like no other: a brass band playing, the costumed matador's macho stare, men shaking their heads at less-than-perfect swipes of the cape, and overly made-up, bloodthirsty women chanting "*olé*," waving their white hankies, throwing roses, jackets, and hats at the matador's feet. There is also the extremely miniscule chance that, if the bull puts up a good enough fight or sticks his horn through the matador's leg, he will be spared for breeding purposes. It does happen, if only rarely. So root for the bull, just not too loudly. Bullfights are at 6:30pm on Sundays, every day during Feria de Abril.

Sevillian tradition for centuries. Some of the second-hand clothes and antiques look as if they've been around about that long, though there are some real finds here, especially if you want recuerdos of Andalucía.

Wherever you are, remember that siesta thing: The iron gates come down at 2pm and don't go back up until 5pm.

→ **Campillo** Get your fill of European and American high fashion for men and women at this designer brand superstore. *Rosario 9.* ☎ 95-456-1711.

→ **Discos Latimore** ★ New and used music in all its forms dominate in this retro store. Aficionados of '70s LPs will not be disappointed. *Javier Lasso de la Vega 4.* ☎ 95-438-2161.

→ **El Corte Inglés** One place that doesn't close for siesta is this gargantuan department store, kind of like Wal-Mart without the auto parts. Before you disregard this cathedral of capitalism, realize that if you stay long enough in Seville, you will end up

looking for something you need here. If you have a place to cook, it has, hidden in its basement, the biggest and most modern supermarket in town, including a wide selection of local wines. The sports outlet across the plaza has a decent, if pricey, selection of camping supplies. *Plaza Duque 6.* ☎ 95-422-0931.

→ **Exotic Zones** This street wear store in La Macarena is officially ready for action. Get your Electra bike, throw on a hoodie from the owners own Panava line, along with a pair of Le Coq Sportif kicks, and you'll be on your way. *Peris Mencheta 31.* ☎ 95-490-8900.

→ **Flamenco Cool** ★ Stop here to load up on kitsch. You'll find locally made and imported gifts, including polka-dot magnets, hot-pink bull heads, and a pair of flamenco shoes more apt for RuPaul than Carmen. *Amor de Dios at San Andrés.* ☎ 95-491-5194. *www.flamencocool.com.*

→ **Juan Foronda** This chain store deals with exquisitely embroidered mantillas and flamenco accessories. *Tetuan 28.* ☎ *95-422-6060.*

→ **Munda Interiores** Home decor and objects d'art of such tasteful and modern quality you just can't fathom they could be useful. Check out the white-washed serving trays with just a spill of color down the sides, handcrafted by the owner. *Bailen 22.* ☎ *95-456-5066.*

→ **Raquel** For offbeat and traditional flamenco gear such as Hawaiian prints on classic ruffled dresses. Pick a style off the rack and they will alter it to fit you nice and tight. *Cuna 51.* ☎ *95-421-7293.*

Road Trip

It may not be the closest option for a road trip, but every minute of the $1^3/_4$ hours that the train takes to get to **Cádiz** will be worth it.

Getting into Town

GETTING THERE

There are 15 trains a day leaving from **Estación Santa Justa** (p. 839) about every hour from 6am to 10pm and the ticket is 8.65€ each way. The train will drop you off at the train station in Plaza de Sevilla (☎ 95-625-4301). You can also catch a bus at the **Estación del Prado de San Sebastián;** the Comes bus company has a bunch of daily services to Cádiz, and drops you off right by Plaza de España and the port of Cádiz.

GETTING AROUND

Possibly the oldest town in the western world, charming Cádiz was founded by the Phoenicians as an important trade colony, and later taken over by the Carthaginians, the Romans, and the Moors. Geographically blessed, it is a little peninsula, almost an island surrounded by the sea. As you get off the train, follow the main drag to the Ayuntamiento, where you can find the tourist information office.

Exploring Cádiz

The best way to tour this town is to simply wander and get lost among its little streets, but make sure you find your way to the **Torre Tavira** (Marqués del Real Tesoro 10; ☎ 95-621-2910; www.torretavira.com; admission 3€; June–Sept daily 10am–8pm; Sept–June daily 10am–6pm). Of the many merchant-house watchtowers that grace Cádiz, Torre Tavira is the tallest one and the only one open to the public. Walk up for the breathtaking 360-degree views of the city and make sure you catch the *camara obscura* show.

After seeing the Torre Tavira, walk to the **Parque Genovés** and then go by the sea up to the **cathedral,** which boasts architectural details that span the two different periods in which it was built. You will notice that this area of Cádiz looks a lot like La Habana. So did the producers of James Bond movies, who shot scenes from *Die Another Day* at **Playa de la Caleta.** After all this walking, go a little further to **Playa de Santa María del Mar** and take a well-deserved bath in the Atlantic waters.

Stockholm

To begin to understand Sweden, start with three of its most successful imports: the Nobel prize, IKEA, and H&M clothing stores. All three imports represent functionality and a cheap, simple formula (Nobel earned his fortune by inventing dynamite), and they point to how the Swedes have proven themselves to be trend-setters, of a sort. Despite isolation from mainland Europe, dreadfully dark winters, and shocking prices for everything from homes to beer (caused, happily, by high taxes used to pay for Sweden's superior social services), Swedes, particularly those living in Stockholm (pop. 1.8 million), are also some of the most happening and friendliest folks you'll meet in Europe.

The city of Stockholm is made up of islands on a lake—14, to be exact—with 57 bridges connecting them. Like other cities in Europe, Stockholm has a medieval town center—Gamla Stan—with narrow alleyways and castles from later eras, but it also has handled its recent growth well, using urban planning to build a modern, lively, and architecturally vibrant city. Wander through the narrow alleys of the old part of the city known as Gamla Stan, and you'll be transported back in time several hundred years—until you stumble upon streams of tourists along the town's main arteries. The neighborhoods surrounding Gamla Stan are packed with young profes-sional Swedes, who have come here from all over the country, creating a hip cafe culture and urgent nightlife scene. Whether you come for the innovative museums, the abundance of urban green space, or just the electric atmosphere, Stockholm won't disappoint.

The Best of Stockholm

- **The Best Cheap Meal:** With several locations throughout the city, **Jerusalem Kebab** is a local favorite for quick, cheap eats. The portions are huge, the food is tasty, and the price is right. See p. 871.

- **The Best Splurge Meal: Koh Phangan** delights in many of Thailand's stereotypes, especially those of the notoriously outlandish party islands. Think of it as dining and amusement all in one. See p. 871.

- **The Best Museum:** If you've ever wondered what Sweden looked like a few hundred years ago, roam through **Skansen,** the world's oldest open-air museum where 18th- and 19th-century Sweden is resurrected. See p. 876.

- **The Best Shops:** Taking pride in its home mega-industries, Stockholm boasts an **H&M** on almost every corner. See p. 878.

- **The Best Outdoor Activity:** Island-hopping in the **Archipelago** is what locals do. Follow in their footsteps. Visit one island or several, using the efficient ferry service to get to iconic villages and cliffside beaches. See p. 878.

- **The Best Festival to Celebrate Spring:** Sweden's main university city, Uppsala, goes all out to welcome the sun on **Walpurgis Eve** (Apr 30). The whole academic community turns out and tumbles into the streets, in an increasingly frenzied affair. The locals know that the night originates in the deep, Viking past when their ancestors made sacrifices to the Norse gods. See p. 880.

Getting There & Getting Around

Getting into Town

BY AIR

Flights arrive at **Arlanda** airport (☎ 08/797-60-00 or 08/797-61-00 for flight info), about 40km (25 miles) north of Stockholm. A long, covered walkway connects the domestic and international terminals. The easiest way to get to and from the airport is on the **Arlanda Express** train (☎ 02/022-22-24; www.arlandaexpress.com), which takes about 20 minutes to the central train station, runs every 15 minutes from 5am to midnight, and costs 180SEK for adults, 90SEK for students (unless you have a rail pass; see p. 40 for more info on rail passes throughout Europe). Or, you can catch an airport bus (☎ 08/60-01-00) that takes about 40 minutes to get to the train station and costs 89SEK (free for those under 16). A taxi should cost between 400SEK and 500SEK (see "By Taxi," below, for more info).

BY TRAIN

Trains arrive at **Centralstationen (Central Station;** ☎ 07/717-57-575), in the city center. From there, follow the signs for the T-bana (TUNNELBANA) to catch the subway or take a city bus to most points. (See "By Public Transportation," below, for more info.) Exchange services, luggage storage, and various restaurants are available. The ticket office is on the ground floor. For info on the Scanrail Pass, see p. 223 in the Copenhagen chapter.

BY BUS

Cityterminalen (City Terminal; ☎ 08/440-85-70), the central bus hub, is in the train station, upstairs on the north end. **Eurolines** (☎ 46/8762-5960; www.eurolines.com) runs buses from many European destinations, such as Copenhagen (248SEK), and Berlin (590SEK).

BY FERRY

Three major ferry companies operate out of Stockholm: Both **Silja** (Kungstgatan 2; ☎ 08/22-21-40; www.silja.com) and **Viking** (in train station; ☎ 08/452-40-00; viking line.fi) sail from various Finnish destinations into the terminal at Stadsgården, near the junction of Södermalm and Gamla Stan (to get there, take the subway to Slussen). **Tallink** (☎ 08/666-60-01; www.tallink.se) offers service from Estonia.

BY CAR

Getting to Stockholm by car is relatively easy, but finding a parking space once you've arrived is relatively hard. If you must come by car, expect to pay for a garage. The hotel's staff can direct you to parking. International car-rental agencies there, such as **Avis** (☎ 08/20-20-60), **Europcar** (☎ 08/20-44-63), and **Hertz** (☎ 08/79-799-00), are set up at Arlanda airport and in central Stockholm.

Getting Around

BY PUBLIC TRANSPORTATION

Stockholm has an efficient subway system that will get you to most places in the city. You can also catch a city bus—the ordinary red kind, or the more modern blue lines. When purchasing tickets at subway stops, inform the teller where you want to go, and he or she will calculate the price. Tickets can also be purchased from bus drivers. Stockholm runs on a zone system. For most trips you will need to buy two coupons (30SEK), which gives you an hour of travel time. You can also buy ticket strips at a discount: 10 tickets for 80SEK or 20 tickets for 145SEK. Another option is the Stockholm Card (p. 874), which offers unlimited travel on regular public transportation, transport on the ferry to Djurgården, free entrance to the Transport Museum, and discounts on a few attractions. For more information on Stockholm's public transport call ☎ 08/60-01-00 or visit www.sl.se.

BY BICYCLE

Although Stockholm can be a little intimidating on a bike, a ride through one of the city's parks is a pleasant way to spend an afternoon, especially through Djurgården. To rent a bike visit **Djurgårdensbrons Sjöcafé** (Djurgårdsbron; ☎ 08/660-57-57). Rentals are from 250SEK per day. It's open May through August daily from 9am to 9pm.

ON FOOT

An old-fashioned walk is a wonderful way to explore Stockholm, and it never takes too long to walk anywhere. When your feet get tired, simply hop on a nearby subway.

BY TAXI

Taxis are expensive—in fact, they're the most expensive in the world—with the meter starting at around 36SEK. A short ride can easily cost 100SEK. If you're willing to splurge, taxis displaying the LEDIG sign can be hailed, or you can order one by phone. **Taxi Stockholm** (☎ 08/15-00-00) is one of the city's larger, more reputable companies.

Stockholm Basics

Orientation: Stockholm Neighborhoods

Gamla Stan, the old city, is Stockholm's most visited neighborhood, and it's usually crowded with visitors strolling down the cobblestone streets to visit the Kungliga Slottet (Royal Palace). To the south lies **Södermalm,** once a run-down district but today, home to many young Stockholmers and much of the city's nightlife. North of Gamla Stan is the busy **Norrmalm** area, which is especially crowded along the pedestrian street Drottninggatan. The train station is in the southern end of Norrmalm, and Stockholm's clubs are in the eastern end. To

STOCKHOLM

Talk of the Town

Six ways to start a conversation with a local

1. **Do you think Stockholm has more bachelors and bachelorettes than any other capital in the world?** Ask your new friend this and you may get an earful.

2. **What do you do at night in the winter?** Be prepared: On the longest day of the year, the sun rises at 3:31am and sets at 9:08pm, although it never gets completely dark. On the shortest day of the year, the sun rises at 8:44am and then sinks below the horizon at 2:49pm, and the sky never gets completely light.

3. **Do you have a favorite park?** Stockholm has over 35 parks, which account for a whopping 30% of the city's area. Water takes up another 30%, and the last third is roughly living space.

4. **Where's the best street art?** Stockholm's subway is the world's longest art gallery: Nearly all of its stations are decorated with paintings, sculptures, and other works of locally produced art.

5. **Any new ABBAs on the horizon?** Sweden is the third largest exporter of music in the world, after the U.S. and the U.K.

6. **Can I camp here?** Swedes employ a medieval right called the Right to Public Access, which renders the phrase "no trespassing" meaningless. Basically, you are entitled to walk or jog on anyone else's land as long as you do no damage.

the north and west of Norrmalm is **Vasastaden,** which, like Södermalm, is a trendy residence for young professionals. To the south, the once-industrial **Kungsholmen** is another trendy nook. A promenade stretches along the south shore, leading to City Hall to the east. In the center of Stockholm lies **Östermalm,** once home to the royal family. The neighborhood still retains an official feel, with embassies and municipal administrative buildings. In the southwest corner of the city, **Djurgården** is the center of recreational activities, and also home to a few popular museums. Finally, the city's newest hipster neighborhood is **Hornstull**, to the west of the center city.

Tourist Offices

Stockholm Tourist Center offers a huge amount of information, including online resources, books, tours, and hotel information.

It's at Hamngatan 27 but enter at Kungsträdgården (☎ 08/789-24-00 or 08/789-24-90; Mon–Fri 9am–7pm; Sat 10am–5pm; Sun 10am–4pm).

Recommended Websites

○ **www.stockholmtown.com**: This is the official Stockholm website. The section for young and budget travelers is especially helpful.

○ **www.visitsweden.com**: Sweden's tourist website offers general information on the country as well as travel tips.

Culture Tips 101

In the land that invented schnapps, alcohol is the drug of choice. The minimum legal age for buying alcohol is 21. Drinking in a club, if you're younger and try to pass, can be a little tricky. Some places say you have to be 18 to get in;

others say 21, 23, or even 27. Also, cops are really tough on drunk drivers. Checkpoints aren't uncommon on weekend nights.

Police are also allowed to stop anyone who they think is under the influence of drugs; they can demand a visit to the local police station and a test. Drugs are illegal and police crackdowns will result in large fines and deportation or jail time. The laws in the last few years have become more draconian than in a number of other European cities. One report stated that passing a joint is considered trafficking, with a mandatory jail sentence.

Recommended Books, Movies & Music

For pop, listen to ABBA, Roxette, or Ace of Base. For punk, check out The Hives. To get a taste of a hugely popular Swedish-language rock band, tune in to Kent.

In the movie arena, watch anything by Ingmar Bergman, especially *Fanny and Alexander,* and the *Seventh Seal.*

Astrid Lindgren's children's books (*Pippi Longstocking* series) are a must-read. Also check out Frans G. Bengtsson's Viking adventure stories, as well as Karin Boyes' poetry and dystopic novel, *Kallocain.*

Stockholm Nuts & Bolts

Cellphone Providers & Service Centers   **Telenor** is the largest mobile-phone provider in Sweden. Their main center in Stockholm is at Artillerigatan 24 (☎ 0709-61-45-57).

Currency   The Swedish krona (SEK) is issued in notes in denominations of 20, 50, 100, 500, 1,000, and 10,000. Coins are issued in denominations of 50 oüre, and 1 and 5SEK. You can exchange money at foreign exchange bureaus throughout the city, including in the train station, as well as at all banks. We recommend **Forex,** at the Central Station (☎ 08/411-67-34); it's open daily from 7am to 9pm. There are also numerous ATMs in the city.

Embassies   **U.S.** citizens, head to Dag Hammarskjölds väg 31 (☎ 08/783-53-00). For **Australia,** to Sergels Torg 12 (☎ 08/613-29-00); for the **U.K.,** to Skarpögatan 6–8 (☎ 08/71-30-00); and for **Canada,** to Tegelbacken 4 (☎ 08/45-33-00).

Emergencies   In an emergency, dial ☎ 112. For an emergency doctor, call the medical hot line at ☎ 08/32-01-00. The main hospitals are **Karolinska** (☎ 08/51770000), and **Sankt Göran** (☎ 08/58701000). But call the English-speaking operator at **Medical Care Information** (☎ 08/320-100) to find out which hospital is closest to you.

Internet/Wireless Hot Spots   Ridiculously overpriced Internet access is available at the **Stockholm Tourist Center.** Cheaper options include **Sidewalk Express Internet Café,** where you can purchase a time card from the machines (Central Station; Internet 19SEK per hour; daily 7am–9:30pm). **7-Eleven** branches (especially those on major streets) also have Internet access. Try the one across from the train station on Centralplan (19SEK per hour; 24 hr.). Also see "Kulturhuset" on p. 874.

Laundry   **City Kemtvatt** will not only do your laundry for you, but also neatly fold the freshly cleaned clothes; the cost is 50SEK per kilo (about 110SEK per pound). They're located at Drottningsholmsvagen 9 (☎ 08/654-95-34), and they're open Monday

STOCKHOLM

through Friday 7am to 7pm and Saturday from 10am to 2:30pm. You can even get same-day service if you bring in your clothes before 10am. Just don't wait until Sunday to get your duds done because they're closed.

Luggage Storage   There are lockers at the Central Station, lower concourse: You can rent them for 25SEK to 50SEK (depending on the size) for 24 hours.

Post Office   The Central Station Post Office is on Centralplan (☎ 08/781-24-25). It's open Monday through Friday from 7am to 10pm, Saturday and Sunday from 9am to 6pm.

Restrooms   There are numerous public toilets throughout the city, such as in the central station and subway stations, and along major streets and squares.

Safety   Stockholm, like the rest of Scandinavia, is generally safe. Use common sense when traveling—whether alone or in groups—and watch out for pickpockets and petty thieves on public transportation and around major tourist attractions.

Telephone Tips   It is now almost impossible to find a coin-operated pay phone in Stockholm: Buy local or long-distance phone cards from newsstands and tobacco shops. Cards start at 50SEK.

Tipping   Restaurants usually add a service charge to the tab, so there is no obligation to leave any extra tip. A lot of locals, however, round the bill up a bit if the service is good. Hotels include a 15% service charge in the bill. Taxi drivers are entitled to 8% of the fare, and cloakroom attendants usually get 65SEK.

Sleeping

If you arrive in Stockholm and have a hard time finding a place to stay—which often happens during the summer—try **Hotellcentralen** (☎ 08/50828508; hotels@svb.stockholm.se), the hotel booking service in the central station. They're open 24 hours a day, and will reserve a hostel or hotel room for a small fee (hotel room 60SEK, hostel bed 25SEK).

Hostels

MTV Best ➔ Hostel **Af Chapman/ Skeppsholmen (HI)** ★ A landmark in Stockholm, the hostel offers beds in both a building on land—where rooms are large and bright—or on board the *Af Chapman* boat—where rooms are tiny, but cool. *Flaggmansvägen 8 (Skeppsholmen).* ☎ *08/463-22-66. www.stfchapman.com. 155SEK dorm, 460SEK double. Hostelling International membership required. Breakfast buffet 60SEK. Bus: 65. Amenities: Internet; kitchen; laundry; minimarket; pool table; TV (in common room).*

➔ **City Backpackers** This is a fully loaded hostel, with free Internet and free morning sauna (you have to pay 20SEK in the evening), two kitchens, a television room with comfy sofa, an outdoor courtyard, and a lounge area with international newspapers. Though rules abound (no shoes in the hostel and door codes for everything), the staff is both friendly and full of helpful advice. Rooms are small but bathrooms are numerous. *Upplandsgatan 2A (Norrmalm).* ☎ *08/ 20-69-20. www.citybackpackers.se. 190SEK– 230SEK dorm (depending on number of people in dorm room), 500SEK double. Bus: 47, 53, or 69. Amenities: Free coffee, tea, and pasta (you bring the sauce!); Internet; 2 kitchens; laundry facilities (50SEK for wash and dry); lockers; luggage storage; patio; sauna; TV (in common room); Wi-Fi. In room: A/C, duvet, pillow, sheets (50SEK), towels (15SEK).*

→ **City Lodge** Another centrally located hostel, with spare, bare-bones, clean bathrooms, and good facilities. *Klara Norra Kyrkogatan 15.* ☎ *08/22-66-30. www.city lodge.se. 175SEK–650SEK dorm (depending on number of people in dorm room), 550SEK cabin (bunk beds), 700SEK double. Breakfast available for 60SEK. T-bana: Centralen. Amenities: Alarm clock; hair dryer; free Internet TV; laundry; lockable cabinets; kitchen. In room: Sheets (50SEK), towel (10SEK).*

Cheap

→ **A&Be Hotel** Definitely no frills here, but bathrooms are clean, rooms are comfortable enough, and the hotel is located close to the lushly green Humlegården in Östermalm. *Grev Turegatan 50.* ☎ *08/660-21-00. www.abe hotel.com. 490–790SEK single, 590–890SEK double, 200SEK extra bed. Breakfast available for 50SEK. T-bana: Stadion. Amenities: Internet; kitchen; laundry; mini-market; pool table; TV (in common room).*

→ **Colonial Hotel** This government-rated two-star hotel is located in a quiet part of Norrmalm, steps from many sights. The hotel's colors are warm, and the house dates back to the 1880s. The standard rooms are comfortable, with a private bathroom, TV, and radio. Budget rooms have none of these amenities. *Västmannagatan 13.* ☎ *08/21-76-30. www.colonial.se. 495SEK budget single, 795SEK standard single; 590SEK budget double, 890SEK standard double; 735SEK budget triple, 1,150SEK standard triple. Breakfast is included in rates. T-bana: Centralen. Amenities: Internet; kitchen; laundry; minimarket; pool table; TV (in common room). In room: Standard rooms have TV, CD player, and radio; budget rooms require sheet rental (35SEK).*

Doable

→ **Hotel Oden** ★ A friendly staff and 138 comfortable rooms make this hotel a civilized oasis, centrally located on Odenplan

square. Rooms are a bit small but bright, and some come equipped with kitchenettes. *Karlbergsvägen 24.* ☎ *08/457-97-00. www. hoteloden.se. Weekday 1,195SEK single, 1,495SEK double, 1,930SEK suite; weekend 820SEK single, 990SEK double, 1,380SEK suite; summer 770SEK single, 950SEK double. Rates include breakfast buffet. T-bana: Odenplan. Amenities: Cafeteria; exercise room; Internet; sauna; solarium; wheelchair friendly; Wi-Fi (120SEK for 24 hr.). In room: Fridge, kitchenette (in some), safe.*

→ **Rex Hotel** Boasting comfy rooms with private bathrooms decorated in vibrant colors, this hotel is housed in a newly remodeled 19th-century building. The general vibe is very Scandinavian—think practical but stylish. *Luntmakargatan 73.* ☎ *08/16-00-40. www.rexhotel.se. From 900SEK single, from 1,450SEK double. Summer and weekend discounts available. Breakfast buffet available for 50SEK. T-bana: Rådmansgatan. Amenities: Breakfast room; bar; wheelchair friendly. In room: TV, hair dryer, Internet, towel warmer.*

Splurge

→ **First Hotel Reisen** ★★ Perfectly situated on the water in Gamla Stan, this place dates from the 17th century, when it used to serve as a coffee house. Today, it's been newly renovated, with dark wood and lush fabrics, and it now serves up stylish, decent-sized rooms to a hip, young clientele. *Skeppsbron 12.* ☎ *08/22-32-60. www.first hotels.com/reisen. Weekday 2,199SEK single, 2,599SEK double; weekend and summer 1,258SEK single, 1,498SEK double. Check website for package deals. Rates include breakfast. Bus: 43, 46, 55, 59, or 76. Amenities: Bar; dry cleaning; laundry service; nonsmoking rooms; pool; room service (limited); sauna. In room: TV, Internet, ironing board, minibar, trouser press.*

MTV Best → **Nordic Sea Hotel** ★★ There's nothing in Scandinavia quite like this

Stockholm

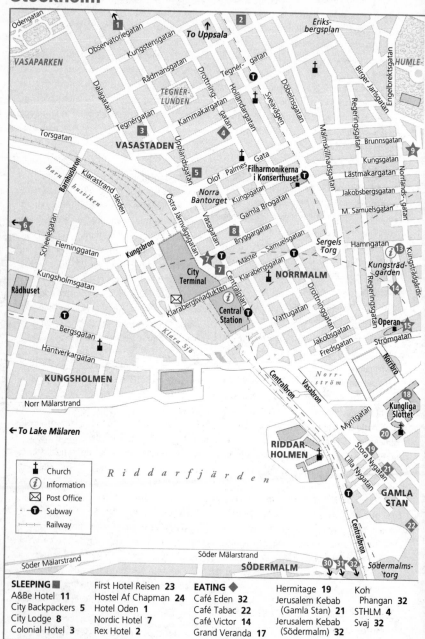

SLEEPING ■
A&Be Hotel **11**
City Backpackers **5**
City Lodge **8**
Colonial Hotel **3**

First Hotel Reisen **23**
Hostel Af Chapman **24**
Hotel Oden **1**
Nordic Hotel **7**
Rex Hotel **2**

EATING ◆
Café Eden **32**
Café Tabac **22**
Café Victor **14**
Grand Veranda **17**

Hermitage **19**
Jerusalem Kebab
(Gamla Stan) **21**
Jerusalem Kebab
(Södermalm) **32**

Koh
Phangan **32**
STHLM **4**
Svaj **32**

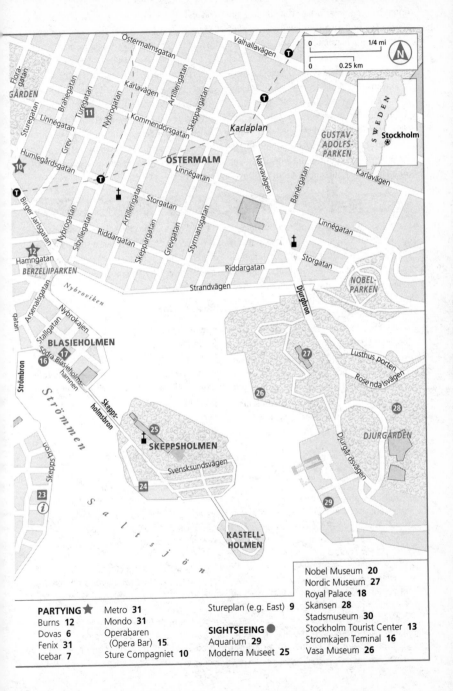

PARTYING ⭐
Burns **12**
Dovas **6**
Fenix **31**
Icebar **7**
Metro **31**
Mondo **31**
Operabaren
(Opera Bar) **15**
Sture Compagniet **10**

Stureplan (e.g. East) **9**

SIGHTSEEING ●
Aquarium **29**
Moderna Museet **25**

Nobel Museum **20**
Nordic Museum **27**
Royal Palace **18**
Skansen **28**
Stadsmuseum **30**
Stockholm Tourist Center **13**
Stromkajen Teminal **16**
Vasa Museum **26**

hotel. Located next to the train station, the Nordic Sea Hotel features luxuries including a fitness center, sauna, bar, and restaurant; this hotel is also home to the Absolut Icebar, where you can buy the world's most expensive drink for a mere 23,450SEK! Luckily, rooms are a bit more affordable. The Nordic Sea Hotel is actually part of a complex that also includes the Nordic Light hotel—while the Nordic Sea turns to the water for its inspiration, the Light is filled with sun-shape projections that guarantee bright light even on the darkest winter's day. *Vasaplan 2–4.* ☎ *08/50563000. www.nordicseahotel.com. Weekdays from 1,290SEK single, from 2,400SEK double; weekends from 790SEK single, from 1,390SEK double; summer from 690SEK single, from 1,190SEK double. T-bana: Centralen. Amenities: Restaurant; 2 bars; dry cleaning; fitness center; laundry service; nonsmoking rooms; sauna; spa treatments; steam bath; wheelchair friendly. In room: TV, coffeemaker, Internet, ironing board and iron, minibar.*

Eating

It's a good thing that Stockholm has developed a diverse international culinary scene, as some of its traditional dishes are not at all appealing. Consider a traditional Swedish breakfast: cereal with curdled milk, liver pâté on toast, and to finish things off, blood pudding sweetened with jam. Yum!

The fame of the smorgasbord is justly deserved. Using a vast array of dishes—everything from Baltic herring to smoked reindeer—the smorgasbord can be eaten either as hors d'oeuvres or as a meal in itself. Just remember: Don't mix fish and meat dishes. It is customary to begin with *sill* (herring) followed by other treats from the sea (jellied eel, raw pickled salmon); diners then proceed to the cold meat dishes, such as baked ham. Fortunately for vegetarians, these are usually accompanied by vegetable salads and cheese and crackers.

Hot Spots

The center of action in Gamla Stan, **Stortorget** is a beautiful square lined with cafes. It's a great place to take a break and watch the square's pedestrian action unfold before you, but unless you're willing to shell out the cash, plan on just having a drink here. A full meal can cost upward of 150SEK.

Picnic Fare & Where to Eat It

Fast-food eateries and fresh-food markets abound in Stockholm, especially in the center of the city, around Hötorget. Here you can visit **Hötorgs Hallen,** a fresh-food market where you can buy the makings of an elegant picnic. Recently arrived immigrants sell many Turkish food products here, including stuffed pita bread.

For the most elegant fare of all, however, go to **Östermalms Hallen,** at the corner of Humlegårdsgatan and Nybrogatan, east of the center. Here, stall after stall sells picnic fare, including fresh shrimp and precooked items that will be wrapped carefully for you.

With your picnic fixings in hand, head for **Skansen** or the wooded peninsula of **Djurgården.** If you like to picnic with lots of people around, go to **Kungsträdgården,** "the summer living room of Stockholm," in the center of town.

Svaj ★★ CAFE Hang out with the city's alternative and hip folks in this dark, funky place on a quiet street in Södermalm. Music plays a critical role: DJs spin throughout the day and the cafe features an attached record shop. *Bjurholmsg. 18. www.svaj.com. Mon–Fri 2–9pm, Sat–Sun noon–7pm. T-bana: Skanstull Station.*

Cheap

The cheapest way to eat and eat well is to go for a hot dog straight off the grill at one of the many stands around town (from around 20SEK). If you're lucky, you can even find a veggie dog.

🅼 Best → **Jerusalem Kebab** ★ MIDDLE EASTERN Reportedly the best kebab stand in the city, and definitely popular with locals, this place serves up huge plates of "kebab" (slivers of rotisserie meat), falafel, and other Middle Eastern treats—and it's all cheap. Locations are throughout the city, but we particularly like the Gamla Stan one. *2A Gasgrand in Gamla Stan. No phone. Kebabs and falafel from 28SEK; full plate dinners from 65SEK. Daily 11am till late. T-bana: Medborgarplatsen Station.*

Doable

→ **Café Eden** ITALIAN This cafe is a good option for a coffee break, with a great location in trendy Södermalm, at the intersection of the main drag (Götgatan). It helps that the goods are relatively cheap—even for a big lunchtime meal. *Folkungagatan 48 (at Götgatan). Lunch from 60SEK; dinner from 51SEK. Mon–Thurs 9am–11pm; Fri 9am–1am; Sat 10am–1am; Sun 10am–11pm. T-bana: Medborgarplatsen Station.*

→ **Hermitage** VEGETARIAN In a city focused on fish dishes, it's good to know that this excellent vegetarian restaurant is around.

Offering a daily selection of pastas and rice items, it's also one of the more affordable options in Gamla Stan. *Stora Nygatan 11 (at Gåsgränd). Lunch 65SEK; dinner 80SEK. Daily 11am–8pm. T-bana: Gamla Stan Station.*

→ **STHLM** ITALIAN STHLM is one of the more affordable places to eat along Drottningholm, with space both inside and outside for dining (and some prime peoplewatching). The sandwiches and pasta dishes make a tasty lunch or early dinner meal. *Drottningholm 73c. ☎ 08/22-56-66. Main courses 65SEK–75SEK. Mon–Fri 8am–8pm; Sat 10am–8pm, Sun 10am–6pm. T-bana: Rådmansgatan Station.*

Splurge

🅼 Best → **Grand Veranda** ★★ SWEDISH Located inside the swank Grand Hotel, this restaurant opens onto a stunning view of the harbor and the Royal Palace across the water. Try the traditional Swedish cuisine (if you've ever had a hankering for reindeer, this is the place to satisfy your curiosity) a la carte, or imitate most locals and hit the lavish all-you-can-eat buffet. *Södra Balseiholmshamnen 8. ☎ 08/679-35-86. Main courses 115SEK–295SEK; buffet 350SEK. Daily 7am–11pm. Bus: 46, 55, 62, or 76.*

🅼 Best → **Koh Phangan** ★ THAI Thailand gone wild. Who knew you can dine under the faux stars on a Thai beach without ever leaving Stockholm? Black lights bring the fluorescent decor to life, and servers sport shirts with Thailand's unofficial catchphrase "same but different." Thankfully, the food lives up to the high concept—order any of the grilled fish, and you're bound to be happy. *Skånegatan 57 (Södermalm). ☎ 08/642-50-40. Main courses 135SEK. Mon–Thurs 11am–11pm; Fri–Sun 2–11pm. T-bana: Medborgarplatsen Station.*

Partying

Stockholm has a vibrant nightlife, due to the huge number of young Swedes who migrate from the far reaches of Sweden to its capital, both permanently or just for the weekend. Most of the hipsters live on and around Södermalm, so that's where you'll find many nightlife options. Gamla Stan's alleys house small pubs, and to the north, Norrmalm (especially around Stureplan) is home to posh clubs.

Bars tend to fill up by around 11pm and then quiet down on the weekends when people migrate to the clubs; it's a good idea to arrive before the crowd if you want to avoid the lineup. Even during the week, the popular establishments stay busy until at least 2 or 3am. If you plan on partaking in a little bit of alcohol-infused debauchery in the privacy of your home, there are two important things to know: First, in order to buy spirits, you need to seek out a Systembolaget, one of the state-run liquor stores, open Monday to Friday from 9am to 6pm. They're often closed on the weekends (some will open until 3pm on Sat), so stock up earlier in the week. Second, you'll find beer sold in supermarkets.

where to Find out what's on

What's On Stockholm magazine (www.stockholmtown.com) gives a rundown of entertainment listings. If you care to decipher Swedish, both *Nöjesguiden* (also online at www.nojesguiden.se) and *QX* (online at www.qx.se) are publications that provide lists of current happenings.

At many of the fancier clubs, bouncers will literally pick and choose from the crowded mob out front, deciding who they'll allow to enter. Girls have an easier time getting in, as do those dressed stylishly and with an attitude. Just be prepared to wait.

Nightclubs

→ **Mondo** Five bars, four dance floors, three stages, and a variety of music—if you can't find it here, you'll have to go to another city. *Medborgarplatsen 8.* ☎ *08/673-10-32. Cover from 40SEK. T-bana: Mariatorget Station.*

[MTV] Best → **Operabaren (Opera Bar)** ★★ Not what you'd picture for an establishment attached to Stockholm's opera house. Operabaren is the opposite of stuffy—odds are you won't spend your night discussing your opera favorites. This place is a bar before 10pm, after which it gets packed with dancing hipsters. *Kungsträdgården.* ☎ *08/676-58-07. Cover 100SEK after 11pm. T-bana: Kungsträdgården Station.*

→ **Sture Compagniet** ★ Stockholm's biggest club boasts 50m (164 ft.) ceilings, which give it a church-like atmosphere, with an added bonus—you'll do things in here you'd never try in the house of the Lord. *Sturegatan 4.* ☎ *08/611-78-00. T-bana: Östermalmstorg Station.*

Bars

In addition to the below options, you might want to try **Dovas** (Sankt Eriksgatan 53, Kungsholmen; no phone; T-bana: Fridhemsplan Station) if you're in the mood for a real dive bar. (Come here for cheap beer, not decor.)

→ **Berns** Facing Berzellparken, this is a great place for a drink with a view—although it'll cost you; beer starts at 50SEK and drink prices go up from there. It's popular with the older tourist crowd. *Berzelii Park 9.* ☎ *08/56632222. T-bana: Kungsträdgården Station.*

→ **East** There are several trendy bars around Stureplan in Norrmalm, all attracting a bit of an older, upscale crowd. East is the best of the lot. It's normally packed even during the week and has a good-size terrace with its own outdoor bar. *Stureplan 13.* ☎ *08/611-49-59. Drinks from 45SEK. Open until 3am. T-bana: Hötorget Station.*

→ **Fenix** This large bar in the heart of Södermalm boasts a 1950s inspired decor, such as checkered tiles and photos of that era's movie stars. If you tire of the throwback theme, have a seat at the bar along the open window and watch the parade of locals walk along the busy street fronting this space. *Götgatan (at Högsbergs)* ☎ *08/640-45-06. T-bana: Medborgarplatsen Station.*

📺 **Best** → **Icebar** ★★ Located in the Nordic Sea Hotel (p. 867), this is Stockholm's "coolest" bar. The world's first permanent ice bar opened in 2001 in the heart of Stockholm. Amazingly, the interior is kept at temperatures of −5°C (27°F) all year. The decor and all the interior fittings, right down to the cocktail glasses themselves, are made of pure, clear ice shipped down from the Torne River in Sweden's Arctic north. Dress as you would for a dogsled ride in Alaska. In the bar you can order any drink from a Bahama Mama to an Alabama Slammer, although you may have to order liquor-laced coffee to keep warm. *Vasaplan 4–7.* ☎ *08/217177. T-bana: Centralen.*

→ **Metro** ★ This was formerly a theater but is now a trendy spot with cool decor, such as fountains in the washrooms, and a lounge area with comfy armchairs. Utterly dead during the week, this place is packed with wannabe stars and starlets on the weekends. *Götgatan 93.* ☎ *08/442-03-30. Medborgarplatsen Station.*

Gay Bars

Looking for a nonconfrontational bar peopled with regular guys who happen to be gay? Consider a round or two at **Sidetrack** ★★ (Wollmar Yxkullsgatan 7; ☎ **08/641-1688**; T-bana: Mariatorget). Small, and committed to shunning trendiness, it's named after the founder's favorite gay bar in Chicago. Tuesday seems to be something of a gay Stockholm institution here. Other nights are fine, too—something like a Swedish version of a bar and lounge at the local bowling alley, where everyone happens to be into same-sex encounters.

To find a Viking, or Viking wannabe, in leather, head for **SLM** (Scandinavian Leather Men; Wollmar Yxkullsgatan 18; ☎ **08/643-3100**; T-bana: Mariatorget). Technically, this is a private club. If you look hot, wear just a hint (or even a lot) of cowhide or rawhide, or happen to have spent the past 6 months felling timber in Montana, you stand a good chance of getting in. Wednesday, Friday, and Saturday from 10pm to 2am, the place functions as Stockholm's premier leather bar. You'll find lots of masculine-looking men on the street level and a handful of toys and restrictive accouterments in the cellar-level dungeon. On Saturday from 10pm to 2am, a DJ spins highly danceable music. It's closed on other nights.

If you need a caffeine fix and a slice of chocolate cake before all that leather and latex, you might want to drop into Stockholm's most appealing, best-managed gay cafe, **Chokladkoppen** (Stortorget 18–20; ☎ **08/203170**; T-bana: Gamla Stan). Open daily from 9am to 11pm, it specializes in sandwiches, gorgeous pastries, and all manner of chocolate confections that appeal even to straight people. The staff is charming, and the clientele more gay than not.

STOCKHOLM

Performing Arts

Kulturhuset ★★ This center has a little bit of everything. Founded 25 years ago as a sort of cultural supermarket, Kulturhuset hosts writers from across the globe who lecture about current events, photographic exhibitions, musicians, modern dance, experimental theater, and more. The website (www.kulturhuset.stockholm.se) has a great calendar in English.

More than a million visitors each year flood through the building to take in the various exhibits here. Two large galleries house shows ranging from interactive filmmaking to Harley-Davidson motorcycles. There's an Internet cafe, a library with audio listening stations, video rental, magazine racks, and **Lava,** an all-purpose activity room for young Stockholmers complete with cafe, video

lounge, and a stage open to performers of all ilk. This is definitely the place to hang if you're looking for feedback on that indie film script you just happened to bring along to Scandinavia. *Kulturhuset: Sergels Torg.* ☎ *08/508-31-508. Lava: Sergels Torg 3.* ☎ *08/508-31-44. Tues–Fri 2–9pm; Sat–Sun 1–6pm. Admission 50SEK adults; free for 18 and under. Prices per show vary. T-bana: T-Centralen.*

Moderna Dansteatern A progressive dance center, Moderna Dansteatern gives creative voice to established and struggling choreographers, dancers, and performing artists. *Torpedverkstan, Skeppsholmen.* ☎ *08/611-14-56. www.mdt.a.se. Prices and times vary. Bus: 65.*

Sightseeing

Stockholm has some great, varied museums, from the formal National Museum and the Nobel Museum, to the unique Skansen open-air museum. The city is also an excellent

place to stroll around and soak up the vibrant Swedish atmosphere, especially through Gamla Stan and along the waterfront.

The Stockholm Card
....

If you plan on visiting several museums in the city, this may be a money-saver: It includes free admission to 75 museums and attractions, free travel on local buses and metro, free boat sightseeing on selected tours from April to December, free parking in the city center, and discounts on other attractions including bus tours. A 24-hour card costs 260SEK; a 48-hour card costs 390SEK; and the 72-hour card costs 540SEK. Pick one up at the tourist information center, the airport, various hotels, or online at www.stockholmtown.com/stockholmcard.

Festivals

July & August

🅼 Best Stockholm Jazz Festival. This event draws international acts from the jazz circuit. Check out the website www.stockholmjazz.com for the exact lineup. Late July.

Stockholm Pride. Stockholm's annual gay pride celebrations includes a week of films, art exhibits, workshops, parties, lectures, and culminates in the extravagant Pride Parade. Look for more information online at www.stockholmpride.org. Late July into August.

Stockholm Cultural Festival. This is a 3-day folk festival celebrating Swedish culture with dancing, street theater, and musical performances. To read about it online at

Free & Easy

→ Do as the Swedes do and get out of bed at 3am to **watch the summer dawn** as the sky turns from the eerie blue of the midnight north to a peachy sunrise color.

→ Take **bus no. 4,** which rings the city and offers some great views of the Gamla Stan.

→ The **Museum of Modern Art** is free every day, so there's no excuse to miss it.

→ The **changing of the guard** takes place Monday to Saturday at 12:15pm and Sunday at 1:15pm in front of the Royal Palace.

→ Take a nighttime stroll through the **Gamla Stan.** Walk the narrow cobblestone streets of Old Town at night, and you'll feel like you've traveled back in time. It's that quaint.

www.kultur.stockholm.se, just click on the British flag. Last week of August.

September & October

Stockholm Beer and Whisky Festival. This event treats visitors to tastes of an international selection of beers, whiskies, and ciders. You can find a little more information at www.stockholmbeer.se (although at press time, it didn't have much more than a bunch of snapshots of some *really* happy looking people). End of September into October.

Top Attractions

MTV Best → **Kungliga Slottet (Royal Palace)** ★★ This is the official address of Sweden's royal family, but the family prefers to live in the Drottningholm palace, and these days this palace is mainly used for official functions. View the state apartments for a lesson in how to live like a king; see the crown jewels and other royal bling in the treasury; check out 17th-century carriages, weapons, and armor in the Royal Armory; or peruse Gustav III's collection of sculptures from the Roman Empire in the Museum of Antiquities. Be sure to catch the changing of the guard at noon: The Royal Guard parades through the city, often accompanied by a band, for the daily ceremony at the palace. *Gamla Stan.* ☎ *08/402-61-30. www.royalcourt.*

se. Admission for each sight 80SEK adults, 35SEK students; combination ticket 120SEK adults, 65SEK students. State apts and Treasury: daily May 15–Aug 10am–4pm (June 27–Aug 14 till 5pm); Sept–May 14 Tues–Sun noon–3pm. Royal Armory daily June–Aug 10am–5pm; Sept–May Tues–Sun 11am–5pm (Thurs till 8pm). Museum of Antiquities: daily May 15–Aug 10am–4pm (June 27–Aug 14 till 5pm). Gamla Stan Station.

FREE → **Moderna Museet (Museum of Modern Art)** ★ A good overview of both Swedish and international contemporary art, with works by such artists as Matisse, Picasso, Dalí, Max Ernst, and Andy Warhol. Other exhibits and activities highlight contemporary Swedish design and culture. *Skeppsholmen.* ☎ *08/519-552-00. Free admission. Tues–Wed 10am–8pm; Thurs–Sun 10am–6pm. T-bana: Kungsträdgården Station.*

FREE → **Nationalmuseum (National Museum of Art)** ★★ Sweden's largest art museum, housing works from the Middle Ages to the 21st century. Founded in 1792, it's one of the oldest museums in the world. Exhibits include notable paintings by big shots such as Rembrandt, Rubens, and Giovanni Bellini, as well as more contemporary artists like Manet, Degas, and Renoir. *Södra Blasieholmen* ☎ *08/519-543-00. www.nationalmuseum.se. Free admission. Tues and*

Thurs 11am–8pm; Wed and Fri–Sun 11am–5pm.
T-bana: Kungsträdgården Station.

→**Nobel Museum** For an educational
and inspirational experience, explore this
museum's multimedia displays, which give
information on the history of the prestigious
Nobel prize and various Nobel Laureates (for
more information on the prize and its namesake, see the box below). Listen to speeches
and interviews, view films, and check out the
cableway of Laureate photos. _Stortorget,_
Gamla Stan. ☎ _08/23-25-07. www.nobelprize._
org/nobelmuseum. Admission 50SEK adults,
40SEK students, 20SEK youth (ages 7–18). Free
guided tours daily at 10:15am and 3pm.
Mid-May to mid-September daily 10am–5pm
(Tues till 8pm); mid-September to mid-May
Tues 11am–8pm, Wed–Sun 11am–5pm. T-bana:
Gamla Stan Station.

→**Nordiska Museet (Nordic Museum)**
★★ This museum contains all you've ever
wanted to know about Scandinavian culture,
with over a million objects on display from
Viking paraphernalia to ultramodern furniture, and everything imaginable in between.
Djurgårdsvägen 6–16 (Djurgården). ☎ _08/_
519-560-00 or 08/457-06-60. www.nordiska
museet.se. Admission 75SEK adults, 60SEK
students. Mon–Fri 10am–4pm; Sat–Sun
11am–pm. Bus: 44, 47, or 69.

→**Skansen** ★★ Ever imagined what
Sweden used to look like? Roaming through
the world's oldest open-air museum here
offers a quick time warp, with more than 150
historical buildings from 18th- and 19th-cen-
tury Sweden that you can enter and explore,
complete with actors in full period costume.
If you arrive at an opportune time, you'll
catch demonstrations of traditional Swedish
handicrafts such as glassblowing and metal-
working (this is what silversmiths do, right?),
as well as folk dancing and musical concerts.
Djurgårdsvägen 49–51 (Djurgården). ☎ _08/_
442-80-00. www.skansen.se. Admission June–
Aug 70SEK; Sept–May 50SEK. Park May
10am–8pm, June–Aug 10am–10pm, Sept
10am–5pm, Oct–Apr 10am–4pm; historical
buildings May–Sept 11am–5pm, Oct–Apr
11am–3pm (some buildings closed). Bus: 47
from central Stockholm. Ferry from Slussen.

→**Stadsmuseum (Stockholm City**
Museum) The exhibitions here trace the
history of the city in a general, easy to follow
way. Most interesting are the maps showing
how the city has grown through the centuries,
and the early-20th-century photographs
superimposed on contemporary ones of
the same subject, to highlight the changes.
Definitely check out the third floor: Walking
around the re-created town and inside the
homes, it's as if you've traveled back in time

Alfred Nobel & His Prize

Alfred Nobel was born in 1833 in Stockholm, a descendant of a famous 17th-
century technical genius. He earned his fortune as a scientist and businessman,
establishing companies and laboratories in over 20 countries. When he died
in Italy in 1896, his will provided for the establishment of an annual prize for
achievements in physics, chemistry, medicine, literature, and peace (years later,
economics was added to the list).

Oddly enough, Nobel gave the responsibility of selecting the winners to the
Norwegian Parliament. Winners are announced every October, and receive a
special medal, a diploma, and a cash prize (now about 10 million SEK, or over
$1 million) at a special awards ceremony in December. Past winners of the prize
include Albert Einstein (1921, Physics), Ernest Hemingway (1954, Literature),
and the Dalai Lama (1989, Peace).

12 Hours in Stockholm

1. **Walk along Stockholm's waterfront.** Journey from Gamla Stan, from Öster-långgatan (lots of restaurants and shops) to Katarinav street to the water at Södermalm and its main drag, Götgatan. At noon, check out the changing of the guard at the Royal Palace.

2. **Take a coffee break at one of the cafes near Stortorget.** Once you've rested, get ready for some major sightseeing.

3. **Head over the bridge to Skeppsholmen and start touring.** This area is literally stuffed with museums. After you've visited one or two, continue along Svensksundsvägen to the eastern shore of the island. Then catch one of the frequent ferries over to Djurgården. Here, the opportunities are numerous: Visit the excellent Vasa Museum, take a stroll around the inner ring road, or find a shady spot and rest your feet.

4. **Ride an Icelandic pony or take a sauna.** See p. 878 for info.

to the 19th century. *Ryssgården.* ☎ *08/508-31-602. www.stadsmuseum.stockholm.se. Admission 60SEK adults, 50SEK students and seniors. Tues–Sun 11am–5pm (Thurs till 8pm). T-bana: Slussen Station (Södermalm).*

→ **Vasamuseet (***Vasa* **Museum)** ★★★
This museum is home to the royal warship *Vasa,* intended to play a major role in the Swedish Navy, which instead sank in 1628 shortly after embarking on its maiden voyage. After more than 300 years underwater, the vessel was resurrected, and is now displayed here. Adjacent exhibits portray life on the boat, and during that time period in general. *Galärvarvet (Djurgården).* ☎ *08/519-548-00. www.vasamuseet.se. Admission 80SEK adults, 40SEK students. Daily Jan 1–June 9 10am–5pm (Wed till 8pm); daily June 10–Aug 20 9:30am–7pm; daily Aug 21–Dec 31 10am–5pm (Wed till 8pm). Bus: 47 or 49. Ferry from Slussen year-round, from Nybroplan in summer only.*

The University Scene

In nearby Uppsala (p. 879), life centers around the university.

STOCKHOLM

Playing Outside

If you go to the official website (p. 864) for Stockholm, you'll find someone's thoughtful, very inclusive list of sports in town from badminton to windsurfing, parachuting, climbing, paintball, tennis, and about 10 more activities.

GARDENS & PARKS   A huge national park right in the city, **Djurgården** houses attractions like the Vasamuseet, the Nordiska Musset, and Skansen. The park is worth a visit if only because it's darn peaceful—it's also a perfect spot to spend an afternoon bike riding, strolling, picnicking, or just hanging out.

Another great place to while away some spare time is on southern **Kungsholmen,** where a pedestrian walkway takes you along the shore of the island. Beginning from Norr Malarstrand, at the foot of Sankt Eriksgatan, a trail leads through tiny parks and grassy knolls along the water. Past the gas station around Kungsholmstorg, the trail transitions into a brick lane lined with old fishing boats and industrial ships that private owners have refurbished. (Plaques in front of each give the history of the boats.) The path eventually leads to city hall, which occupies the eastern corner of the island.

The city's best outdoor playground, however, is the islands of Stockholm's archipelago (see information under "Road Trips," below).

 Best HORSEBACK-RIDING★★ Hop on an Icelandic horse—relax, they're known for being gentle and small—at the **Haniwnge Iceland Horse Center** at Hemfosa (37km/23 miles south of Stockholm; ☎ **08/500-481-81**). For 400SEK, you can ride for 2½ hours; the price includes a picnic lunch. Aside from walking, galloping, trotting, and cantering, the horses have another gait, the *tölt,* a kind of equine speed walk that has no English translation.

SAUNA & SWIMMING A combination sauna, outdoor heated pool, and children's paddling pool, **Vilda Vanadis** is at Vanadislunden (☎ **08/30-12-11**), near the northern terminus of Sveavägen, within easy walking distance of the Oden Hotel and the city center. This really is an adventure park, with a variety of attractions, as well as a sauna and a restaurant. The entrance fee is 55SEK, but once you're inside, the attractions are free. It's open daily from early May until the end of August, from 10am to 6pm.

Shopping

Shop at two of Sweden's biggest international chain stores in their native country: **Best** H&M ★★ is located on almost every corner in the city, and **IKEA** runs a free shuttle bus to its store (from Regeringsgatan 17; Mon–Fri 11am–5pm) once an hour; it departs for IKEA on the hour and from IKEA on the half-hour.

The main pedestrian shopping street in Stockholm is **Drottingholm,** which runs through Norrmalm and offers clothing shops, souvenir shops, cafes, and restaurants. In Gamla Stan, tourists flock to **Vasterlanggatan,** a pretty street that winds through the old town, stuffed full of souvenir stands and unique craft stores selling such items as hand-woven and knitted clothing, silver jewelry and—of course—Swedish clogs. Another good shopping option is along Gotgatan, in Södermalm. Here you'll find used bookshops

Market Value

Loppmarknaden i Skärholmen (Skärholmen Shopping Center) At the biggest flea market in northern Europe, you might find a pleasing item from an attic in Värmland. You might indeed find *anything.* Try to go on Saturday or Sunday (the earlier the better), when the market is at its peak. Admission is 10SEK for adults (15SEK on Sun). *Skärholmen.* ☎ *08/710-00-60. Bus: 13 or 23 to Skärholmen (20 min.).*

and record stores, as well as clothing stores. Finally, **Vastermalmsgallerian** is a new large shopping mall on Sankt Eriksgatan in Kungsholmen. For a list of stores, visit the website www.vastermalmsgallerian.se.

Road Trips

The Archipelago

If you thought Stockholm was comprised of a lot of islands, wait until you see this! Just outside the city lies the **Best** **Archipelago** ★★★, with more than 24,000 islands.

No need to explore them all; just make like the locals and head to one—or all—of the most popular ones. Each island has its own charm, many with pretty historic buildings and even prettier beaches, as well as ritzy restaurants and hotels. Formal dining on the islands will cost you—plan ahead and pack a picnic lunch. Hotels are also quite pricey, and hostels are usually booked way in advance. Unless you'd like to exercise your right to public access and pitch a tent in an open spot, it's best to visit the Archipelago as a day trip from Stockholm.

GETTING THERE & GETTING AROUND

Waxholmsbolaget ferry service runs boats to the Archipelago from Stockholm: Catch one at Stromkajen terminal on Balseiholmshamnen in Norrmalm (marked on the map; ☎ o8/ 679-58-30; www.waxholmsbolaget.se). You can purchase tickets at the terminal or on board the ferry. Single ticket costs vary depending on the destination (see prices in listings, below). Alternatively, you can buy a Boat Hiker's Card at the terminal, giving you 5 days of unlimited travel for 300SEK. Another option is to purchase a cash card, which can be used as a debit card on board to pay for single trips: 750SEK gets you 1,000SEK worth of tickets, but this is only worth it if you plan on making many trips, or have a large group. You can either island hop, taking the ferry from one island to another, or visit each island separately from Stockholm.

SIGHTSEEING

VASHOLM   This is the archipelago's capital, and the most visited island. Restaurants and craft shops line the harbor, and art galleries and old hotels line its narrow streets. Up until 1912, any material other than wood was prohibited as building material, so that in case of a siege the town could simply be torched instead of falling into enemy hands. Luckily, that never happened, and the wooden town still stands today. Ferries to Vaxholm cost 65SEK and take 1 hour.

GRINDA   This tiny island (you can traverse the entire thing on foot in 30 min.!) boasts some of the archipelago's best swimming—the water may be ice cold, but the setting can't be beat—which you can do from both sandy beaches and cliffs. Ferries from Stockholm cost 85SEK and take 1½ hours; from Vaxholm the cost is 50SEK and it takes 45 minutes.

FINNHAMN   On the border between the middle and outer archipelago, Finnhamn actually consists of three islands attached together. The sheltered bays make for excellent fishing spots. You can also rent a rowboat and explore the cliff-lined shore. Ferries from Stockholm cost 120SEK and take 2 hours; from Grinda they cost 65SEK and take 1½ hours.

SANDHAMN   One of the area's quieter islands, Sandhamn was once the meeting point for seafarers in the 18th century, and it eventually became a summer resort. Gingerbread-style houses and handicrafts, such as hand-knitted clothing and metalworks, attract visitors here, as do the nice sandy beaches along the eastern tip of the island: Trouville beach is usually packed in the summer. Ferries from Stockholm cost 120SEK and take 3 hours; from Finnhamn, the cost is 65SEK and it takes 1 hour.

Uppsala

Uppsala ★★★ has two claims to fame: Its 15th-century cathedral and Uppsala University. During the Viking period, Uppsala was the site of numerous animal and human sacrifices. The locals were tamed, for a period, with the establishment of the Catholic Church. Today, Uppsala can once again get a little wild, with over 40,000 students in residence.

UPPSALA BASICS

Trains run from Stockholm about once an hour, and take 45 minutes to reach Uppsala. Eurolines (☎ 46/8762-5960; www.eurolines. com) also runs a bus service between Stockholm and Uppsala several times a day (65SEK or 50SEK with student ID). The Tourist Information Office is on Fyris Torg 8

ᴍᴛᴠ**U** University Nights

Uppsala University dates from 1477 and, before then, Uppsala was a religious and pagan center, a scene of animal sacrifices in honor of the Norse gods. Some ancient traditions still carry on here today, especially so during **Walpurgis Eve** (Apr 30), a celebration of the rebirth of spring. Students gather in front of the library precisely at 3pm and don their white university caps all at the same time, and then, after singing and a toast, they run down the hill into town for further revels. Balloons, herring lunches, bonfires, and a torchlight parade follow. Check the university website (http://info.uu.se/fakta.nsf/sidor/visitors.id3E.html) for additional info on the school and how to become an exchange student there.

(☎ **018/727-48-00;** www.uppland.nu). It's open Monday through Friday from 10am to 6pm, Saturday from 10am to 3pm, and Sunday from noon to 4pm in July and August only.

TOP ATTRACTIONS

If you have time to do sightseeing after all the Walpurgis celebrations, head to the nearby **Museum Gustavianum** (Akademigatan 3; ☎ **018/471-75-71**). The odd exhibits include a dissection "theater" from 1663, an art cabinet, and mummies. Join a guided tour on Saturday or Sunday at 1pm or book your own for another day. The museum is open Tuesday to Sunday from 11am to 4pm and costs 40SEK or 30SEK for students. The university is justly proud of its restored Linnaeus garden, a botanical garden, the Museum of Evolution, and the Natural History museum. Also check out the **Uppsala Domkyrka** ★ (Domkyrko-plan 2; ☎ **018/18-72-01;** bus: 1), the largest cathedral in Scandinavia, built in 13th century and then rebuilt in the late 19th century after it was destroyed by fire. Several notable Swedes are buried here, including St. Erik, the patron saint of Sweden, and Linnaeus. The cathedral is open daily 8am to 6pm and admission is free.

Venice

Y ou know, of course, that Venice is a magical, canal-filled city whose 1,500-year existence seems to defy logic. So, we're going to cut to the fine print and tell you upfront the things you need to know to make the most of your (too short) visit to this extraordinary place.

The average backpacker's first foray into Venice should not include a hot, disorienting walk that ends at the Piazza San Marco, dodging pigeons, and seeking out a McDonald's. We know you are *not* the average backpacker, so take some time here.

You need to spend the night—not to partake of any wild nightlife (there is none in Venice) but because cruise-ship day-trippers maraud the city until 5 or 6pm every day. When they scurry back aboard their 2,400 passenger behemoths, Venice exhales and is infinitely more enjoyable for those who've stayed behind. Even if you only have 12 hours to devote to Venice, make them the night shift. Next, accept immediately that you will pay through the nose for *everything* in Venice—just make it a part of your budget, and it won't stress you out.

Venice is a charmer, all right: There's a mystical quality that touches everything here, including tired and sweaty backpackers who don't have the time or money to do it "right." So, even if the gondola ride and the violin concerto on Piazza San Marco elude you, that last *vaporetto* run of the night, past the moonlit palazzi of the Grand Canal, strains of diesel engine humming in the background, isn't such a bad substitute.

The Best of Venice

❍ **The Best Way to Spend Your Evening:**
Skip the full, sit-down dinner (unless you've got money to burn). Instead, hit up the **lounges** and **bars** in Campo Santa Margherita (in Dorsoduro) or Campo San Giacometto (in San Polo off the Rialto Bridge) for drinks and small plates. At around 11pm, head for the docks at Piazza San Marco and find one of the few gondoliers who hasn't gone home for the night. With the money you saved on not having a real dinner, the price of a **nighttime gondola ride** is a bit less outrageous. Late at night, Venice belongs to you: There is no traffic on the canals, and gondoliers will usually let the passably sober try their hand at *voga veneziana* (Venetian-style rowing) on the Grand Canal. Totally unforgettable, and so freakin' romantic that same-sex heterosexual traveling companions may well want to make out with each other. See p. 904

❍ **The Best Hangout:** The **Piazza San Marco** may be tourist central, but the hordes come here for a reason: The view of the Basilica di San Marco, with the exotic Palazzo Ducale shimmering in the sunlight in the background, is overwhelmingly beautiful. (By this logic, the pigeons of the world must be real aesthetes because they all seem to live in this square.) For an entirely different atmosphere, come here early in the morning or around dusk, when the grand piazza is eerily quiet and wonderfully peaceful—even the pigeons seem to have taken a breather. See p. 913

❍ **The Best Low-Key but Glamorous Escape:** It's 5pm, and *ugh, there are so many tourists around!* The only solution: Duck into **Harry's Bar** ★★. True, you'll be surrounded by more tourists, but the bar is cozy (with no windows, no canal views—which is why it's an escape) and utterly unpretentious. Do put on your cleanest clothes before visiting, however. At Harry's, the drink *de rigueur* is the Bellini—a blend of white peach nectar and sparkling prosecco wine that was apparently invented here—at 14€, it may be the most expensive cocktail you'll ever throw back, but believe us, it will probably be the most delicious as well, so make it last! See p. 904

❍ **The Best Place to Veg Out and Rest Your Feet:** Board the water bus (vaporetto) no. 1 or 82, grab an outside seat on the prow, and go for a round-trip **vaporetto ride on the Grand Canal** ★★★. The mesmerizing motion picture that will play out before your eyes—Venetian-Gothic palazzi, candy-striped boat-docking pylons, police boats and garbage scows, flotillas of singing gondoliers—is sure to stick with you for a lifetime. If you have any Vivaldi on your iPod, even better. At any Grand Canal vaporetto stop, board a boat traveling toward the train station *(ferrovia);* hop off and travel back down the canal's inverted S-curve; and finish up with the monumental views as the Grand Canal opens up into the *bacino* (basin) of San Marco. See p. 885.

❍ **The Best Cafes for People-Watching:**
The best cafes in the city are those that line **Piazza San Marco,** and are worth the splurge for the experience alone. From here, you have a front-row seat to the action in the square, and the view of its stunning surroundings. For a fabulous, romantic (and for now, insider) canal-side setting, **Naranzaria** ★★ (p. 905) and **Bancogiro** ★★ (p. 903) on Campo San Giacometto (north of the Rialto Bridge in San Polo) can't be beat.

Getting There & Getting Around

Getting into Town

BY AIR

Venice's **Aeroporto Marco Polo** (☎ 041/ 260-6111; www.veniceairport.it) is in Mestre, the mainland section of the town. In the arrivals area, you'll find ATMs, currency exchange, and a tourist information center that also books accommodations.

The cheapest, but least exciting, way to get into town is by taking the orange **city bus,** which costs 1€ and takes about 30 minutes, or the blue **shuttle bus** (www.atvo.it) which costs 2€ but only takes 20 minutes. These buses drop passengers off at Piazzale Roma, from which it's usually a vaporetto ride to your hotel. To arrive in style from the airport, take a **water bus** (marked Alilaguna ACTV/Cooperativa San Marco; www.alilaguna.it) to either Fondamenta Nuove (on the north end of Cannaregio) or Piazza San Marco; the 45-minute ride costs 10€. Tickets for the shuttle buses and water buses can be bought in the arrivals hall of the airport.

BY TRAIN

Venice has two train stations, so be sure to get off at **Venezia-Santa Lucia** (Piazzale Roma in Venice proper; ☎ 892021) and not Venezia-Mestre, which serves the ugly industrial mainland of greater Venice. A few Venice-bound trains will actually end at Mestre instead of going one more stop to Santa Lucia—in that case, take one of the frequent shuttle trains—it's only a 10-minute ride between Mestre and Santa Lucia. The ticket office opens at 6am and stays open until 9pm. In the train station, you'll also find a tourist office, currency exchange, luggage storage, and several restaurants.

On exiting Santa Lucia train station, you'll find the Grand Canal in front of you, a sight that makes for a heart-stopping first impression. You'll find the docks for a number of vaporetto lines (the city's public ferries, or "water buses") to your left and right. Head to the booths to your left, near the bridge, to catch either of the two lines plying the Grand Canal: the no. 82 express, which stops only at the train station, S. Marcuola, Rialto Bridge, S. Tomà, S. Samuele, and Accademia before hitting San Marco (26 min. total); and the misnamed no. 1 accelerato, which is actually the local, making 14 stops between the station and San Marco (a 31-min. trip). Both leave every 10 minutes or so, but every other no. 82 stops short at Rialto, meaning you'll have to disembark and hop on the next no. 1 or 82 that comes along to continue to San Marco.

BY BUS

ACTV buses (www.actv.it) arrive in and depart from Venice at Piazzale Roma, serving such Veneto cities as Treviso and Padua. If you're heading to one of those places next, and you want to see what it's like to bus it in Italy (it's not that exciting), you can purchase tickets at the office in the square. For

OKKIO! Don't Go the Wrong Way on the No. 82

The no. 82 goes in two directions from the train station: Left down the Grand Canal toward San Marco— which is the (relatively) fast and scenic way—and right, which also eventually gets you to San Marco (at the San Zaccaria stop) but takes more than twice as long because it goes the long way around Dorsoduro, *not* along the Grand Canal, and serves mainly commuters. Make sure the no. 82 you get on is headed to "San Marco."

VENICE

Getting Lost in Venice

It's a given. With street names that are spelled one way on a map and another way in person, street numbers that follow no conventional order, and alleys that wind around and around only to stop at dead ends, pretty much everyone finds themselves lost at some point. Here are a few tips to help you find your way:

→ First, invest in a good **map**. Buy one from a tourist stand, about 2.50€.

→ Next, if you're looking to find a specific address such as a restaurant or hotel, figure out what **district** *(sestiere)* it's located in. Keep in mind that (1) addresses are usually given as a number and district—there *are* "street" names in Venice, but for some reason, they usually don't appear in any official printed addresses; and (2) address numbers repeat in each district.

→ Use the **signs!** If you do find yourself lost in a labyrinth of alleys, look up for the quasi-handmade signs pointing in the direction of such major landmarks as Piazza San Marco, the Rialto Bridge, the Accademia, and the *Ferrovia* (train station). These signs work wonders in getting you untangled.

→ Most important, if you find yourself lost, **don't panic!** Venice is safe, and getting hopelessly disoriented here is part of the fun. (And don't ever think about that movie *The Comfort of Strangers*.) Remember that whatever direction you walk in, you will eventually hit water, as well as a vaporetto stop.

information and schedules, contact the ACTV office at Piazzale Roma (☎ 041/272-211).

BY CAR

The only wheels you'll see in Venice are those attached to luggage. Venice is a city of canals and narrow alleys. No cars are allowed—even the police and ambulance services use boats. Arriving in Venice by car is problematic and expensive—and downright exasperating if it's high season and the parking facilities are full (they often are). You can drive across the Ponte della Libertà from Mestre to Venice, but you can go no farther than Piazzale Roma at the Venice end, where many garages eagerly await your euro. Do some research before choosing a garage—the rates vary widely, from 19€ per day for an average-size car at the communal **ASM garage** (☎ 041/272-7301; www.asmvenezia.it) to 26€ per day at private outfits like **Garage San Marco** (☎ 041/523-2213; www.garagesanmarco.it), both in Piazzale Roma. If you have reservations at a hotel, check before arriving: Most of them offer discount coupons for some of the parking facilities.

Vaporetto nos. 1 and 82, described under "By Train," above, both stop at Piazzale Roma before continuing down the Grand Canal to the train station and, eventually, Piazza San Marco.

Getting Around

Two words: (1) walk and (2) vaporetto. (Romantic as they are, gondolas are ridiculously expensive and should never be used as a practical means of transportation from point A to point B.)

ON FOOT

Venice is small enough that you can walk wherever you need to go—that is, if you're able to find it (see "Getting Lost in Venice," above). You might be surprised at how few bridges there are for pedestrians to cross the canals. The **Grand Canal** only has three bridges: the **Ponte degli Scalzi** in front of the train station, the shop-lined **Ponte di Rialto** in the center of the city, and the wooden **Ponte Accademia** in the south, not far from Piazza San Marco. This makes getting to the other side of the main waterway a bit of a problem, right? Fear not: *Traghetti* are gondola-style "ferries" that shuttle people across the Grand Canal where there are no bridges around. Look for them under signs that say "Calle del Traghetto." The .50€ fare is payable to the gondolier when you step aboard. To make the crossing like a true Venetian, do it standing up—although this is perhaps not advisable in choppy water on the Grand Canal, or if you've just had a few too many *spritz* at the local bar.

Whether or not you really *need* to take a traghetto, it's fun: For the experience, try the "Santa Sofia" crossing that connects the Ca' d'Oro (Cannaregio) and the Pescheria fish market (San Polo), opposite each other on the Grand Canal just north of the Rialto Bridge—the gondoliers expertly dodge water traffic at this point of the canal where it's the busiest and most heart-stopping.

VAPORETTO

Get to know your new best friend, **the vaporetto (water bus)** ★. They may not be as graceful as gondolas, but the sputtering hum of these clunky boats is a welcome sound when you've spent a long day walking. Vaporetto stops are easy to spot—they're modern glass-and-steel shelters with yellow signs. Not only are they a convenient way to move up or down the Grand Canal, vaporetti offer some gloriously cinematic views as they snake their way down the reverse S-curve of Venice's "main street." The ticketing system (see below) is confusing, but unless you're only staying in Venice for a few hours, the **11€/24-hour Grand Canal ticket** is the one you'll want because it permits unlimited trips on the Grand Canal. If you're staying for more than 2 days, it's worth forking over the 22€ for the 72-hour Grand Canal ticket. Though most people don't pay it (and don't end up in jail), there is a 3.50€ charge for luggage.

Comprehensive maps of the vaporetto system are available at the tourist office and at vaporetto stops. In general though, the

boats will either run through the city along the Grand Canal, or around the perimeter of the city. The only vaporetti most visitors need are nos. 1 or 82, which ply the Grand Canal every 15 minutes from 7am to midnight (every hour midnight–7am).

If you decide to make the trek out to the islands of Murano, Burano, or Torcello, a number of vaporetti make the trip from Fondamenta Nuove, on the north side of Castello. Only the no. 12 vaporetto goes all the way to Burano and Torcello. To cross the lagoon to the beaches of the Lido, hop on the vaporetti no. 1, 6, 52, or 82 from the San Zaccaria-Danieli stop (near Piazza San Marco).

Ticket prices are as follows: A 24-hour ticket including Grand Canal is 11€; a return ticket with one Grand Canal trip is 7€; a Grand Canal single trip is 5€; a single-fare ticket with no Grand Canal trip is 3.50€; a return ticket with no Grand Canal trip is 6€; a 72-hour pass including Grand Canal is 22€; and the luggage charge for any trip is 3.50€. (You'll also see a much lower price bracket posted on the vaporetto ticket info boards, but this reduced rate is only available for full-time residents of Venice—and, no, you can't pretend to be one.) For more information on public transportation in Venice, go online to www.actv.it.

USING STREET MAPS & SIGNAGE

The free map offered by the tourist office and most hotels has good intentions, but it doesn't even show—much less name or index—all the *calli* (streets) and pathways of Venice. For that, pick up a more detailed map (ask for a *pianta della città*) at news kiosks (especially those at the train station and around San Marco) or most bookstores.

The best (and most expensive) is the highly detailed **Touring Club Italiano map,** available in a variety of forms (folding or spiral-bound) and scales. Almost as good, and easier to carry, is the simple and cheap **1:6500 folding map** put out by **Storti**

Figuring Out *Casas, Calles* & *Canales*

Venice's colorful 1,000-year history as a once-powerful maritime republic has everything to do with its local dialect, which absorbed nuances and vocabulary from far-flung outposts in the East and from the flourishing communities of foreign merchants who, for centuries, lived and traded in Venice. A linguist could gleefully spend a lifetime trying to make some sense of it all. It's been a successful one, though. From Venetian dialect we've inherited such words as *gondola* (naturally), *ciao, ghetto, lido,* and *arsenal.*

But for the Venice-bound traveler just trying to make sense of Venetian addresses, the following should give you the basics.

Ca': The abbreviated use of the word "casa" is used for the noble palazzi, once private residences and now museums, lining the Grand Canal: Ca' d'Oro, Ca' Pesaro, and Ca' Rezzonico. There is only one palazzo, and it is the Palazzo Ducale, the former doge's residence. However, as time went on, some great houses gradually began to be called "palazzi," so today you'll also encounter the Palazzo Grassi or the Palazzo Labia.

Calle: Taken from the Spanish (though pronounced as if Italian: "*cah*-leh"), this is the most commonplace word for street, known as "via" or "strada" elsewhere in Italy. There are numerous variations. "Ruga," from the French word "rue," once meant a calle flanked with stores, a designation no longer valid. A "ramo" (literally, "branch") is the offshoot of a street, and is often used interchangeably with "calle." "Salizzada" once meant a paved street, implying that all other, less important "calles" were once just dirt-packed alleyways. A "stretto" is a narrow passageway.

Campo: Elsewhere in Italy it's "piazza." In Venice the only piazza is the Piazza San Marco (and its two bordering "piazzette"); all other squares are "campi" or the diminutive, "campielli." Translated as "field" or "meadow," these were once small, unpaved grazing spots for the odd chicken or cow. Almost every one of Venice's campi carries the name of the church that dominates it (or once did) and most have wells, no longer used, in the center.

Canale: There are three wide, principal canals: the Canal Grande (affectionately called "il Canalazzo," the Canal), the Canale della Giudecca, and the Canale di Cannaregio. Each of the other 160-odd smaller canals is called a "rio."

Fondamenta: Referring to the foundations of the houses lining a canal, this is a walkway along the side of a rio (small canal). Promenades along the Grand Canal near the Piazza San Marco and the Rialto are called "riva" as in the Riva del Vin or Riva del Carbon, where cargo such as wine and coal were once unloaded.

Piscina: A filled-in basin, now acting as a campo or piazza.

Ramo: Literally, "branch;" a small side street.

Rio Terà: A small canal that's been filled in with earth. Literally, "buried canal."

Salizzada: The word originally meant "paved," so any street you see prefaced with "salizzada" was one of the first streets in Venice to be paved.

Sottoportego: An alley that ducks under a building.

Edizioni (its cover is white-edged with pink, which fades to blue at the bottom). See "Getting Lost in Venice," above, for more navigation tips.

Venice Basics

Over 100 small islands comprise Venice, which is divided into six districts, or *sestiere*.

CANNAREGIO   In the northern part of the city, it's probably the least scenic and most grungy part of Venice, but also the most convenient place to base yourself: From the train station, head down busy Lista di Spagna to find cheap accommodations and food, services geared toward budget travelers such as laundry and Internet facilities, and a decent nightlife scene.

CASTELLO   The largest district, in the east of Venice, this is primarily a residential and working district, and is also home to pricey hotels and restaurants, many lined up along Riva degli Schiavoni, a popular promenade.

SAN MARCO   This is the core of Venice, and tourists know it: There is a constant crowd along its shop-filled alleys and in its restaurants and piazzas. Piazza San Marco sits in the south of the district, and around it you'll find designer boutiques, ritzy restaurants, and pricey accommodations.

DORSODURO   To the south and east of San Marco, this quiet, sunny section of town is filled with museums and small hotels. It is becoming more of an artsy, trendy area to live, especially among the university population. Consequently, the neighborhood's Campo San Margherita is a buzzing place at night. The Zattere, a 16th-century quay, is also a popular place for a stroll, offering up stellar views of the lagoon and its islands.

SANTA CROCE   Between Dorsoduro and Cannaregio, this is probably the least-visited district, which makes it a quiet place for a stroll if you're looking to experience Venice without a mob of tourists in front of you. Stick to the eastern side, as the western part of the district is mainly industrial and not at all interesting.

SAN POLO   The smallest of Venice's districts, sitting between San Croce and San Marco, this is the commercial heart of the city, with its produce markets and store-lined Rialto Bridge. Here, you'll also find moderately priced hotels and restaurants, as well as the new crop of cool wine bars off Campo San Giacometto.

Tourist Offices

In general, tourist offices function mainly as hotel and tour booking venues, with very little general information available. On the positive side, however, there are various branches scattered throughout the city:

○ The **airport** branch: Located in the arrivals hall. Open daily 9:30am to 7:30pm.

○ **Train station** branch: Open daily 8am to 6:30pm.

○ **Piazzale Roma** branch: Open daily 9:30am to 3:30pm.

○ **San Marco** branch: Open daily 9am to 3:30pm.

For all branches dial ☎ 041/529-8711 or go online to www.turismovenezia.it.

The tourist office's *LEO Bussola* brochure is useful for museum hours and events, but their map only helps you find vaporetto lines and stops (it's well worth buying a street map at a news kiosk; see "Getting Around," earlier in this chapter). More useful is the info-packed monthly *Un Ospite di Venezia* (www.unospitedivenezia.it); most hotels have a handful of copies. Also keep an eye out for the ubiquitous posters around town with exhibit and concert schedules. The classical concerts held mostly in churches are touristy but fun and are advertised by an army of costumed touts handing out leaflets on highly trafficked streets.

Recommended Websites

○ **www.veniceworld.com**: Venice World provides general information on things to see and do in Venice, as well as a directory of websites related to travel in Venice.

VENICE

Another Money-Saving Pass

The **VeniceCard** (www.venicecard.it) is a good investment if you plan on visiting several museums and taking frequent rides on the vaporetti. The **orange** VeniceCard entitles you to unlimited travel on the vaporetto system, free entry at Venice's civic museums (including Palazzo Ducale, Museo Correr, Ca' Rezzonico, the Glass Museum on Murano, and the Lace Museum on Burano, and others), free use of the public toilets (otherwise 1€ each time you have to pee), and discounts at many restaurants. The cheaper **blue** VeniceCard gets you free travel on the vaporetti, use of the toilets, and some restaurant discounts (but not free entry to the museums). The cards are divided into two age brackets—junior (29 and under) and senior (30 and over)—and they come in 1-, 3-, and 7-day validities.

→ **1-day orange card:** 22€ junior; 29€ senior. **1-day blue card:** 15€ junior; 17€ senior.

→ **3-day orange card:** 44€ junior; 53€ senior. **3-day blue card:** 29€ junior; 33€ senior.

→ **7-day orange card:** 65€ junior; 75€ senior. **7-day blue card:** 46€ junior; 50€ senior.

○ **www.doge.it**: Venezia Net provides information on culture, events, and tourist resources. There's an excellent map, and lots of information on events in the city.

Culture Tips 101

The permanent population of Venice is half of what it was in 1945. Venetians have moved onto the mainland to make room for paying visitors (and for the benefits of more solid ground). The few locals who still live on the lagoon mostly work in the tourist trade. So there's a lot more English spoken in Venice than in the rest of Italy, though it's usually being used to sell you something.

The thing about Venice is that it's so otherworldly that it attracts everyone. Yet don't expect a traditional party scene. Venetians are serious wine drinkers, and you can be, too, but what nightlife there is tends to stay mellow and end early. Not that the city is catatonic after dark, but Venice is the leg on your whirlwind Italian tour where you get your good night's sleep.

See p. 795 in the Rome chapter for advice on drinking laws in Italy.

Recommended Books, Movies & Music

Two heavy-hitting pieces of literature set in Venice are William Shakespeare's *Merchant of Venice* and Thomas Mann's *Death in Venice*. You can always rent the screen versions instead, or try the 2005 movie *Casanova*, which offers some breathtaking views of the city.

See p. 795 in the Rome chapter for more book, movie, and music recommendations.

Venice Nuts & Bolts

Cellphone Service & Providers There's a **Vodafone** store on San Marco, 5169–5171. Visit www.190.it or call ☎ **041/5239016** for info.

VENICE

Currency   Money can be changed at the train station (though with a hefty commission charge), and at various banks and exchange centers throughout the city. ATMs are located on the streets around San Marco, San Polo, and the train station.

Embassies   The **U.K.** consulate (Piazzale Donatori di Sangue 2/5, Mestre; ☎ **041-5055990**) is open Monday to Friday 10am to 1pm. The **U.S., Canada,** and **Australia** have consulates in Milan. See p. 617.

Emergencies   If you fall into a canal (or have any other serious emergency) and have a phone handy, call ☎ **112** for the Carabinieri (Italian military police), ☎ **113** for the regular police, ☎ **118** for an ambulance, and ☎ **115** for the fire department.

Internet/Wireless Hot Spots   The cheapest Internet cafes are in Cannaregio:

- **Casanova:** A 15-minute session costs 2.50€ (1.50€ with student discount) at this Internet point, but it gets less expensive as your time online increases: 30 minutes is 4€ (2.50€ with student discount) and 60 minutes is 7€ (4€ with student discount). It's located at Lista di Spagna 158A, Cannaregio (☎ **041/275-0199**), and it's open daily late into the night (attached to disco).

- **VeNice:** This Internet cafe charges 2.50€ for 15 minutes, 4.50€ for 30 minutes, and 8€ for an hour. They offer a student discount, but only for local students. They have fax, Webcam, and CD-burning services. It's at Lista di Spagna 149, Cannaregio (☎ **041/275-8217**), and is open daily from 9am to 11pm.

- **Planet Internet:** For 3€, you get 15 minutes to check your e-mail; for 5€, you can take 30 minutes and respond to it; and for 8€ for an hour, you can do both and see what's in the news in your hometown. There's a student discount of 50%. Printing and fax services are also available. It's at Rio Terà San Leonardo 1519, Cannaregio (☎ **041/524-4188**), and is available daily from 9am to midnight.

Laundry   There's a **Speedy Wash** where you can get your duds washed for 5€ and dried for an additional 3€ for 15 minutes; detergent is 1€. Go to Rio Terà San Leonardo 1520, Cannaregio. It's open from 8am to 10pm.

Luggage Storage   Luggage storage is available in the train station (p. 883). It's open daily 6am to midnight. Storage costs 3.80€ for the first 5 hours and .60€ per hour after that. You can store your luggage for a maximum of 5 days.

Post Office   The main post office is near the Rialto Bridge on Salizzada Fondaco dei Tedeschi 5554, San Marco (☎ **041/271-7111**). It's open Monday through Saturday from 8:15am to 6pm.

Restrooms   There are clean public toilets all over the city, charging 1€.

Safety   Venice is generally a safe city. As always though, guard your valuables and watch out for pickpockets in crowded areas like Piazza San Marco, and on busy vaporetto lines, like the nos. 1 and the 82.

Tipping   In most tourist-oriented restaurants, a service charge is usually included in the bill. Feel free to add a little extra (5%–10%) for deserving service, if not already included in the bill.

VENICE

Sleeping

Though Venice is chock-full of hotels, finding accommodations any time of the year can be a problem—to avoid roaming the streets in search of any empty bed, book a place to stay as far in advance as possible; a month or two in advance is not unreasonable. If you do arrive without a reservation, seek out the A.V.A. (The Venetian Hoteliers Association), which helps with finding accommodations, although it may not be as cheap as you'd like. There are offices in the airport, the train station, and at Piazzale Roma. Call ☎ **800/ 843-006** (toll free within Italy) or ☎ 041/ 522-2264 from abroad; you can also check out the info-loaded website, **www.veniceinfo. it**. Simply state your budget, and they'll do their best to confirm a hotel while you wait.

Because Venice is small, and everything's a relatively short walk or vaporetto ride away, it doesn't matter much where you stay (as long as you're not on the island of Giudecca, which is inconvenient, or Mestre, which is inconvenient *and* ugly). **San Marco** is many visitors' top choice for accommodations, but it's the busiest and most heavily trodden sestiere—you'll be in the heart of the action, but you might find yourself wishing you could escape it. For budget accommodations, your best bet is **Cannaregio,** where there are a ton of decently priced hotels within a 10-minute walk of the train station. For convenience to San Marco and atmosphere, I am partial to **Dorsoduro.**

Hostels

→**Ostello di Venezia (HI)** Inconveniently located on Giudecca Island, with the sterile environment typical of HIs, this hostel nonetheless provides a clean, cheap option if you're just looking for a place to lay your head and don't mind commuting to and from Venice proper (which can be a costly affair if you weren't already planning on buying a 24-hr. vaporetto ticket). The hostel offers a

quiet garden and TV room for relaxing at the end of the day, and a restaurant with mediocre food. *Fondamenta delle Zitelle 86, Giudecca.* ☎ *041/523-8211. www.ostellionline. org. 19€ dorm bed. Rates include breakfast. Hostelling International membership required. Vaporetto: Zitelle. Amenities: Breakfast room/ restaurant; shared bathrooms; TV room.*

→**Ostello Santa Fosca** ★ Venice's best hostel option, especially if you're looking for ambience: Near the Rialto Bridge, the hostel is a garden oasis providing sanctuary from the city's heat and crowds. Rooms are spacious and clean and shared bathrooms are numerous. Try to score a room on the top floor: The others are a bit dark and dingy. *Cannaregio 2372 (off Campo Santa Fosca), Cannaregio.* ☎ *041/715-733. www.santafosca.it. 19€ dorm bed, 22€ single, 44€ double. Rolling Venice and student discount. Vaporetto: San Marcuola. Amenities: Internet; kitchen (summer only); shared bathrooms.*

Cheap

→**Albergo ai do Mori** ★★ Antonella, the young hands-on owner/manager, creates an efficient yet comfortable ambience here. The more accessible lower-floor rooms (there's no elevator and the hotel begins on the second floor) are slightly larger and offer rooftop views, but the top-floor rooms boast views of San Marco's cupolas and the Torre dell'Orologio, whose two bronze Moors ring the bells every hour (the large double-paned windows help to ensure quiet). You'll also find tiled bathrooms (with heated towel racks), and firm mattresses. Every room but two has a private bathroom, and a 2001 renovation revealed the rest of the wood beams on the ceilings. The walls were painted bright colors and comfy new furnishings were added. Room nos. 4 (a small double) and 5 (a triple) share a bathroom and a small hallway and can be turned into a suite. Additionally,

Antonella has now opened a four-room annex nearby. This hotel is entirely non-smoking. *San Marco 658 (on Calle Larga San Marco), San Marco.* ☎ *041/520-4817 or 041/528-9293. www.hotelaidomori.com. 15 units. 60€–95€ double with shared bathroom, 80€–140€ double with private bathroom, 180€–220€ suite (up to 5 people). Off-season discounts available. Vaporetto: San Marco. Amenities: Bar; concierge. In room: A/C, TV, hair dryer, safe.*

→ **Albergo San Samuele** ★ This friendly guesthouse is a steal considering the central location near Piazza San Marco. The rooms' decor is an attempt at elegance—with floral wallpaper and satin bedspreads—and most units have views of the street below. And there's only 10 of them, so be sure to book *way* in advance any time of year. The hotel is nonsmoking. *Salizzada San Samuele 3358, San Marco.* ☎ *041/522-8045. www.albergo sansamuele.it. 26€–46€ single with shared bathroom; 36€–75€ double with shared bathroom; 46€–105€ with private bathroom; 60€–135€ triple. Breakfast 4.50€. Vaporetto: San Samuele.*

→ **Gerotto Calderan** Through the big brass doors (you'll need to buzz to get in) you'll find an efficient hotel with friendly service, facing busy Campo San Geremia. Rooms are a bit small and you'll have to lug your baggage up several flights of stairs but the clean rooms, especially those with views of the square, are worth the effort. For a cheap option, the hotel often offers dorm-style accommodations, which is essentially a bed in a five-bed room, and may involve sleeping extremely close to fellow travelers. There's a credit card or deposit required for reservation, as well as a 12:30am curfew and a lockout from 10am to 2pm. *Campo San Geremia 283, Cannaregio.* ☎ *041/715-562. www. casagerottocalderan.com. 25€ dorm bed, 41€–55€ single, 60€–98€ double, 84€–108€ triple. Vaporetto: Ferrovia. Amenities: Internet.*

→ **Hotel Bernardi-Semenzato** ★★ The exterior of this weather-worn palazzo belies its charming interior, which offers exposed hand-hewn ceiling beams, air-conditioned rooms outfitted with antique-style headboard/spread sets, and bathrooms modernized and brightly retiled. The enthusiastic young English-speaking owners, Maria Teresa and Leonardo Pepoli, offer government-rated three-star style at one-star rates (prices get even better in the off season). Upstairs rooms enjoy higher ceilings and more light. The *dépendance* (annex) 3 blocks away offers the chance to feel as if you've rented an aristocratic apartment, with parquet floors and Murano chandeliers—room no. 5 is on a corner with a beamed ceiling and fireplace, no. 6 (a family-perfect two-room suite) looks out on the confluence of two canals, and no. 2 overlooks the lovely garden of a palazzo next door. The Pepoli family recently opened yet another annex nearby consisting of just four rooms, all done in a Venetian style, including one large family suite (two guest rooms, one of which can sleep four, sharing a common bathroom). *Cannaregio 4366 (on Calle de l'Oca), Cannaregio.* ☎ *041/522-7257. www. hotelbernardi.com. For Frommer's/MTV Europe readers: 60€ double without bathroom, 90€ with bathroom; 2€ triple without bathroom, 98€ with bathroom; 90€ quad without bathroom, 108€ with bathroom. Rates include continental breakfast. 10% less in the off season. Vaporetto: Ca' d'Oro. Amenities: Concierge; tour desk; room service (limited). In room: A/C, TV, hair dryer, Internet, safe.*

→ **Hotel Dolomiti** For those who prefer to stay near the train station, this is an old-fashioned, reliable choice. Because it has large, clean but ordinary rooms spread over four floors (no elevator), your chances of finding availability are better here—one of the larger places I suggest. It's been in the Basardelli family for generations—the current head manager, Graziella, was even born

Venice Sleeping & Eating

SLEEPING ■

Ostello di Venezia (HI) **20**
Ostello Santa Fosca **3**
Albergo ai do Mori **22**
Albergo San Samuele **12**
Hotel Bernardi-Semenzato **29**
Hotel Dolomiti **1**
Hotel Galleria **16**
Hotel San Geremia **2**
Hotel Tivoli **8**
Hotel Ai Due Fanali **4**
Hotel American-Dinesen **19**
Locanda Fiorita **13**
Pensione Accademia **18**
Hotel Ala **9**

EATING ◆

Accademia Foscarini
    Snack Bar **17**
Brek **2**
Cantina do Mori **6**
Osteria alle Botteghe **14**
Pizzeria ae Oche **5**
Pizzeria/Trattoria al
    Vecio Canton **24**
Rosticceria Teatro Goldoni **25**
Ai Tre Spiedi **28**
Cantina Do Spade **27**
Osteria Vivaldi **7**
Trattoria da Remigio **21**
Trattoria alla Rivetta **23**
Bistrot de Venise **26**

Pal. Giovanelli

S. Felice ✝

CANNAREGIO

Pal. Zen

Fond. Nove

Palazzo Seriman

Pal. Fontana

29

Ca' d'Oro

S. Sofia

Pal. Sagredo

Pal. Brandolin

Pescaria

Pal. Mangilli

Ca' da Mosto

Ss. Apóstoli ✝

Pal. Widman

Pal. Grifalconi

H

Ospedale Civile

S. Maria ✝ d. Pianto

Fábbriche Nuove

28

Pal. Falier

27

✝ S. Canciano

S. Maria d. Miracoli

Pal. Soranzo-Van Axel

Ss. Giovanni e Paolo (S. Zanipolo)

S. Giovanni Crisostomo

Teatro Málibran

Pal. Pisani

Pal. Morosini

Palazzo Dieci Savi

Fóndaco d. Tedeschi

Pal. Cavazza-Foscari

Campo S. Marina

Palazzo Ruzzini

Pal. Donà

Pal. Cavignis

Pal. Muazzo

S. Aponàl ✝

S. Silvestro ✝

Riva del Vin

S. Bartolomeo ✝

Palazzo Dolfin-Manin

26

✝ S. Lio

Salizzada S. Lio

Campo S. Maria Formosa

S. Maria Formosa

Palazzo Cappello

Pal. Donà

S. Lorenzo

Pal. Bembo

S. Salvador

Pal. Tasca Papafáva

C. Bande

24

Ruga Giuffa

Questura

CASTELLO

Palazzo Grimani

Ca' Farsetti

25

S. Luca

Cínema Rossini

Campo Manin

Palazzo Contarini d. Bovolo

SAN MARCO

S. Gallo

S. Zulián ✝

C. Guerra

Palazzo Soranzo

Palazzo Trevisan-Cappello

✝ S. Giovanni Novo

23

Pal. Priuli

Pal. Zorzi

S. Giorgio dei Greci

Ateneo Véneto

S. Fantin ✝

Pisc. di Frezzeria

Torre d. Orologio

Campanile

Basilica di San Marco

S. Zaccaria

Convento

21

La Pietà ✝

22

Museo Corrèr

Piazza San Marco

Pal. d. Prigioni

Teatro La Fenice

S. Moisè ✝

S.S. Moise

Piazzetta

Palazzo Ducale (Doge's Palace)

Molo

Riva d. Schiavoni

S. Zaccaria

C. Larga XXII Marzo

Giardini ex Reali

Capo di Porto

Ponte d. Sospiri (Bridge of Sighs)

Palazzo Tiépolo

Palazzi Contarini

Pal. Gritti

Palazzo Treves d. Bonfili

S. Marco

Pal. Genovese

Salute

Dogana da Mar

Punta d. Dogana

Bacino di San Marco

S. Maria d. Salute ✝

Seminario Patriarcale

Ex Ospizio

20

| 0 | | 1/8 Mi |
| 0 | | 1/4 Km |

N

in a second-floor room—and they and their efficient polyglot staff supply dining suggestions, umbrellas when necessary, and big smiles after a long day's sightseeing. Rooms without bathrooms always come with sinks. The Basardellis are slowly renovating the guest rooms; those that don't have air-conditioning now will soon. *Cannaregio 72–74 (on Calle Priuli ai Cavalletti), Cannaregio. ☎ 041/ 715-113 or 041/719-983. www.hoteldolomiti-ve.it. 60€–90€ double with shared bathroom, 80€–140€ with private bathroom; 84€–111€ triple with shared bathroom, 120€–180€ with private bathroom. Extra bed 20€. Discounts available in the off season. Rates include continental breakfast. Closed Nov 15–Jan 31. Vaporetto: Ferrovia. Amenities: Bar; concierge; tour desk. In room: A/C (newest rooms), hair dryer (newest rooms).*

→ **Hotel Galleria** ★★ If you've always dreamed of flinging open your hotel window to find the Grand Canal in front of you, choose this 17th-century palazzo. But reserve way in advance—these are the cheapest rooms on the canal and the most charming at these rates, thanks to owners Luciano Benedetti and Stefano Franceschini. They overhauled the hotel in 2004, keeping a sumptuous, 18th-century look in public spaces and giving a cozier look to the new bedrooms. Six guest rooms overlook the canal; others have partial views that include the Ponte Accademia over an open-air bar/cafe (which can be annoying to anyone hoping to sleep before the bar closes). Breakfast, with oven-fresh bread, is served in your room. *Dorsoduro 878A (at foot of Accademia Bridge), Dorsoduro. ☎ 041/523-2489. www.hotelgalleria.it. 110€ double without bathroom, 120€–155€ with bathroom. Rates include continental breakfast. Vaporetto: Accademia. Amenities: Concierge; room service (limited); tour desk. In room: Hair dryer.*

→ **Hotel San Geremia** ★ If this gem of a government-rated two-star hotel had an elevator and was in San Marco, it would cost twice as much and still be worth it. Consider yourself lucky to get one of the tastefully renovated rooms—ideally one of the seven overlooking the campo (better yet, one of three top-floor rooms with small terraces). The rooms have blond-wood paneling with built-in headboards and closets or whitewashed walls with deep-green or burnished rattan headboards and matching chairs. The small bathrooms offer hair dryers and heated towel racks, and rooms without bathrooms were recently renovated. Everything is overseen by an English-speaking staff and the owner/manager, Claudio, who'll give you helpful tips and free passes to the winter Casino. *Cannaregio 290A (on Campo San Geremia), Cannaregio. ☎ 041/716-245. For Frommer's/MTV Europe readers: 77€ double with shared bathroom, 114€ with private bathroom. Ask about rates/availability for singles, triples, and quads and off-season rates (about 20% cheaper). Rates include continental breakfast. Vaporetto: Ferrovia. Amenities: Concierge; room service (breakfast); tour desk. In room: TV, hair dryer, safe.*

→ **Hotel Tivoli** Located in the northern part of Dorsoduro, close to the Grand Canal. Rooms are a bit dark but nonetheless attractively furnished with dark wooden bed frames and armoires. There's also a charming communal garden area perfect for kicking back at the end of the day. *Ca' Foscari 3838, Dorsoduro. ☎ 041/524-2460. www.hotel tivoli.it. Low season: from 31€ single without bathroom, 50€ single with bathroom, from 68€ double; high season from 122€ single, from 144€ double. Rates include breakfast. Vaporetto: San Tomà. Amenities: Shared bathrooms (in some). In room: TV, hair dryer.*

Doable

→ **Hotel Ai Due Fanali** ★★ The 16th-century altar—turned—reception desk is your first clue that this is the hotel of choice for lovers of aesthetics with impeccable taste and restricted budgets. The hotel is located on a quiet square in the residential Santa Croce area, a 10-minute walk across the Grand Canal from the train station but a good 20-minute stroll from the Rialto Bridge. Signora Marina Stea and her daughter Stefania have beautifully restored a part of the 14th-century *scuola* of the Church of San Simeon Grando with their innate *buon gusto*, which is evident wall to wall, from the lobby furnished with period pieces to the third-floor breakfast terrace with a glimpse of the Grand Canal. Guest rooms boast headboards painted by local artisans, high-quality bed linens, chrome and gold bathroom fixtures, and good, fluffy towels. Prices drop considerably from November 8 through March 30 with the exception of Christmas week and Carnevale. Ask about the four equally classy waterfront apartments with a view (and kitchenette) near Vivaldi's Church (La Pietà) east of Piazza San Marco, sleeping four to five people at similar rates per person. *Santa Croce 946 (Campo San Simeone Profeta), Santa Croce.* ☎ *041/718-490. www.aiduefanali. com. 95€–210€ double, 119€–262€ triple, 185€–380€ apt. Rates include breakfast. Closed most of Jan. Vaporetto: Riva di Biasio. Amenities: Bar; concierge; dry cleaning; laundry service; room service (limited). In room: A/C, TV, hair dryer, Internet, minibar, safe.*

→ **Hotel Al Piave** The Puppin family's tasteful hotel is a steal: This level of attention coupled with the sophisticated *buon gusto* in decor and spirit is rare in this price category. You'll find orthopedic mattresses under ribbon candy–print or floral spreads, immaculate white-lace curtains, stained-glass windows, new bathrooms, and even (in a few rooms) tiny terraces. The family suites—with two bedrooms, minibars, and shared bathrooms—are particularly good deals, as are the small but stylishly rustic apartments with kitchenettes and washing machines (in the two smaller ones). A savvy international crowd has discovered this classy spot, so even with renovations that have expanded the hotel's size, you'll need to reserve far in advance. *Castello 4838–40 (on Ruga Giuffa), Castello.* ☎ *041/528-5174. www.hotelalpiave.com. 100€–210€ double, 150€–230€ triple, 160€–240€ suite for 3, 200€–265€ suite for 4, 220€–300€ suite for 5. Ask about discounts in the off season. Rates include continental breakfast. Closed Jan 7–Carnevale. Vaporetto: San Zaccaria. Amenities: Concierge; tour desk. In room: A/C, TV, fridge (family suite), hair dryer, minibar, safe.*

→ **Hotel American-Dinesen** ★★★ I'll take the American over the astronomically expensive Cipriani, the Gritti, or the Danieli any day. For its friendliness, style, and location—on the lovely San Vio canal, which meets the Grand Canal only 100m (338 ft.) away—this place is a dream. With Oriental carpets, plush armchairs, marble flooring, and polished woods, the lobby feels like a real lobby, not just an afterthought with a makeshift reception desk (as is the case in too many moderate Italian hotels). The staff is ever bright and hospitable, and there's always a charming member or two of the Sutera family, who manages the hotel, on hand to greet guests, too. Of the hotel's 30 rooms, the best choices are the larger corner rooms and the 9 rooms overlooking the canal; some even have small terraces where you can stand, turn to the right, and watch the passing traffic on the Grand Canal. Every room is outfitted with traditional Venetian-style furnishings that usually include hand-painted furniture and Murano glass chandeliers. Bathrooms are small but immaculate, and outfitted with all the comforts and amenities you'll need. If it's late spring, don't miss a drink on the second-floor terrace beneath a wisteria arbor dripping with plump violet blossoms. This hotel enjoys great word-of-mouth among Venice habitués, so book early. *Dorsoduro 628 (on Fond. Bragadin), Dorsoduro.* ☎ *041/520-4733. www.hotelamerican.com. 130€–250€ double,*

180€–300€ with canal view. Rates include buffet breakfast. Extra person 60€. Vaporetto: Accademia. Amenities: Bar; concierge; car-rental desk; Internet; laundry service; non-smoking rooms; room service (limited); tour desk. In room: A/C, TV, hair dryer, Internet, minibar, safe.

➔**Locanda Fiorita** ★ The owners have created a pretty little hotel in this Venetian red palazzo, parts of which date from the 1400s. Its overall style is 18th-century Venetian. The wisteria vine partially covering the facade is at its glorious best in May or June, but the Fiorita is excellent year-round, as much for its simply furnished rooms boasting new bathrooms (now with hair dryers) as for its location on a *campiello* off the grand Campo Santo Stefano. Room nos. 1 and 10 have little terraces beneath the wisteria pergola and overlook the campiello: They can't be guaranteed on reserving, so ask when you arrive. Each of the two rooms without bathrooms has its own private facilities down the hall. Just a few meters away is **Ca' Morosini** (☎ **041/241-3800;** www.ca morosini.com), the Fiorita's three-star annex. There you'll find more rooms with views of the campo. *San Marco 3457a (on Campiello Novo), San Marco. ☎ 041/523-4754. www.locandafiorita.com. 110€ double with shared bathroom, 145€ with private bathroom. Rates include continental breakfast. Vaporetto: S. Angelo. Amenities: Concierge; nonsmoking rooms; room service (limited); tour desk. In room: A/C, TV, Internet (annex only), hair dryer, minibar (annex only), safe (annex only).*

➔**Pensione Accademia** ★★ This pensione is beloved by Venice regulars. You'll have to reserve far in advance to get any room here, let alone one overlooking the breakfast garden, which is snuggled into the confluence of two canals. The 17th-century villa is fitted with period antiques in first-floor "superior" rooms, and the atmosphere is decidedly old-fashioned and elegant (Katharine Hepburn's character lived here in the 1955 classic *Summertime*). Formerly called the Villa Maravege (Villa of Wonders), it was built as a patrician villa in the 1600s and used as the Russian consulate until the 1930s. Its outdoor landscaping (the Venetian rarities of a flowering patio on the small Rio San Trovaso that spills into the Grand Canal and the grassy formal rose garden behind) and interior details (original pavement, wood-beamed and decoratively painted ceilings) still create the impression of being a privileged guest in an aristocratic Venetian home from another era. *Dorsoduro 1058 (Fondamenta Bollani, west of the Accademia Bridge), Dorsoduro. ☎ 041/521-0188 or 041/ 523-7846. www.pensioneaccademia.it. 130€– 185€ double, 170€–235€ superior double.*

Kickin' It, Lido Style

The Lido (p. 919)—you know, where those pictures of Nicole Kidman during the Venice Film Festival are taken—offers an entirely different Venice experience. The city is relatively close, but you're really here to stay at an Italian beach resort and day trip into the city for sightseeing. Although there are a few lower-end, moderately priced hotels here, they are entirely beside the point of the Lido and its jet-set reputation. If you are looking for a more reasonable option—and one that's open year-round—check out the modern **Hotel Belvedere** (Piazzale Santa Maria Elisabetta 4; ☎ **041/526-0115;** fax 041/526-1486; www.belvedere-svenezia.com). It's across from the vaporetto stop, has been in the same family for nearly 150 years, and sports a good restaurant and a free beach cabana. It charges 44€ to 229€ per double. See "Playing Outside," later in this chapter.

Off-season discounts available. Vaporetto: Accademia. Amenities: Bar; concierge; dry cleaning; laundry service; massage; room service (limited); tour desk. In room: A/C, TV, hair dryer, Internet, minibar, safe.

Splurge

→ **Hotel Ala** ★★★ This government-rated three-star hotel is in the heart of Venice, only a few minutes' walk from Piazza San Marco, yet it seems far removed from the hysteria that predominates on that square. Devotees of Venice return year after year to Ala's comfortable precincts, which—while not spectacular—are tasteful and well maintained. For nearly 2 decades, the hotel has been owned by the Salmaso family. The much-restored property dates back to the early 18th century, and, in fact, appears in a work painted by Canaletto. The decor of the bedrooms is a marriage of modern functionality with lacquered Venetian baroque style. Some of the units have a Jacuzzi, and a beautiful and spacious suite has been installed in the attic. **Tarnowska's American Bar** is named for the Russian countess Maria Tarnowska (one of her lovers was murdered inside the building in the 1800s). *Campo S. Maria del Giglio, San Marco.* ☎ *041/520-8333. www.hotelala.it. 80€–190€ single, 110€–340€ double, 150€–310€ triple, 180€–340€ junior suite. Rates include buffet breakfast. Vaporetto: Giglio. Amenities: Tearoom; piano bar; cigar corner; dry cleaning; laundry service; nonsmoking rooms. In room: TV, minibar.*

Eating

Venetian cuisine, though not without its delicacies—including such fish specialties as *saor* (whole sardines marinated in vinegar)—is hardly the stuff Italian food legend is made of; let's be frank, you came to Venice for the canals, not the weird seafood. If you do choose to eat at Venetian restaurants, you can often eat very well, although you will usually pay a hefty price for doing so—you can either suck it up and deal with it, or you can forgo traditional sit-down meals and grab some *cicchetti* (finger foods) from the local *bacaro* (wine/snack bar) instead. Restaurants near tourist attractions often offer a special tourist menu, which is usually overpriced and so should be avoided. Most restaurants also tack on a cover charge and service charge, though cheaper eateries draw in customers by advertising no cover or service charge. Venice also has some of the best gelato in all of Italy, one indulgence in this city that you *can* afford.

Hot Spots

On the San Polo side of the Grand Canal, right where it bends west above the Rialto Bridge, a number of very hip (and for now, very Venetian) wine bars have opened in Campo San Giacometto (or Giacometo, depending on whose spelling you go with), in the medieval buildings that once belonged to Venice's fruit-and-herb market. **Naranzaria** and **Bancogiro** (see "Partying," below) are more popular for drinks, but both serve food (antipasti and other light fare) and have convivial indoor bar areas as well as cozy upstairs seating. Best of all are the chic outdoor tables, set up on broad, otherwise empty swathes of esplanade that face the Grand Canal. So much unused space right on the Grand Canal, all for your enjoyment. Does it get any better than this?

Cheap

→ **Accademia Foscarini Snack Bar** ★ ITALIAN A cheap canal-side option, located more centrally on the Grand Canal next to the Accademia Bridge. After a tiring exploration of the Accademia, stop in to re-energize: Definitely go for the pizza. Try to get a seat right by the water for maximum scenery and gondola viewing. *Dorsoduro 878C.* ☎ *041/522-7281. Toast, panini, and other snacks 2.50€–6€; pizza 7€–10€. Includes cover and*

VENICE

Dining on a Budget in Venice

Pizza is the fuel of Naples and bruschetta and *crostini* (small, open-face sandwiches) the rustic soul food of Florence. In Venice it's *tramezzini*—small, triangular white-bread half-sandwiches filled with everything from thinly sliced meats and tuna salad to cheeses and vegetables; and *cicchetti* (tapaslike finger foods such as calamari rings, speared fried olives, potato croquettes, or grilled polenta squares), traditionally washed down with a small glass of wine, or *ombra* ("shade from the sun"). Venice offers countless neighborhood bars called *bacari* and cafes where you can stand or sit with a *tramezzino*, a selection of *cicchetti*, a *panino* (sandwich on a roll), or a *toast* (grilled ham-and-cheese sandwich). All of the above will cost approximately 1€ to 3€ if you stand at the bar, as much as double when seated. Bar food is displayed on the countertop or in glass counters and usually sells out by late afternoon, so you can't always rely on it for a light dinner, though light lunches are a delight. A concentration of popular, well-stocked bars can be found along the Mercerie shopping strip that connects Piazza San Marco with the Rialto Bridge, the always lively Campo San Luca, and Campo Santa Margherita. Avoid the tired-looking pizza (revitalized only marginally by microwaves) you'll find in most bars; informal sit-down neighborhood pizzerias everywhere offer savory and far fresher renditions for less, plus your drink and cover charge—the perfect lunch or light dinner.

10% service charge. Daily 7am–9pm. Vaporetto: Accademia.

→ **Brek** ★ITALIAN CAFETERIA Good old Brek, a chain of cafeteria-style restaurants serving up hearty and cheap pastas and salads. The Venice branch serves mainly the hungry masses of people waiting for their train or budget travelers who lodge on Lista di Spagna. Pick up items in the cafeteria, grab a flask of cheap wine, and check out with the cashier before sitting down. The bar in the front serves up coffee drinks and pastries. *Lista di Spagna 124A.* ☎ *041/244-0158. www.brek.com. Main courses from 3€. Daily 8:30am–11pm. Vaporetto: Ferrovia.*

→ **Cantina do Mori** ★★WINE BAR/SANDWICHES Since 1462 this has been the local watering hole of choice in the market area; legend even pegs Casanova as a habitué. *Tramezzini* are the fuel of Venice—sample them here where you're guaranteed fresh combinations of thinly sliced meats, tuna, cheeses, and vegetables, along with tapaslike

cicchetti. Venetians stop to snack and socialize before and after meals, but if you don't mind standing (there are no tables), for a light lunch this is one of the best of the old-time *bacari* left. And now that it serves a limited number of first courses like *melanzane alla parmigiana* (eggplant Parmesan) and *fondi di carciofi saltati* (lightly fried artichoke hearts), my obligatory stop here is more fulfilling than ever. *San Polo 429 (entrances on Calle Galiazza and Calle Do Mori).* ☎ *041/522-5401. Sandwiches and cicchetti 1€–2€. Mon–Sat 8:30am–9:30pm. Vaporetto: Rialto.*

→ **Osteria alla Botte** CICCHETTI It's a grease-fest, but far preferable to McDonald's. They offer awesome fried calamari. The hot guys in red T-shirts working the bar will choose a wine for you: They're all good, and all cheap. It's a hard place to find, in a portico maze east of Rialto Bridge, but you should make the effort. A crowd of students and young locals spills out into a secluded alleyway, and perch their glasses on nearby building ledges. There's a good selection of hand-cut cheeses and meats, as well as pasta dishes, and the wine list has more than 100 selections. *Campo San Marco 5482.* ☎ *041/520-0279. www.osteriaallabotte.it. Vaporetto: Rialto.*

→ **Osteria alle Botteghe** PIZZA/ITALIAN Casual, easy on the palate, easy on the wallet, and even easy to find (if you've made it to Campo Santo Stefano), this is a great choice for pizza, a light snack, or an elaborate meal. You can have stand-up *cicchetti* and fresh sandwiches at the bar or windowside counter, while more serious diners head to the tables in back to enjoy the dozen pizzas, pastas, or *tavola calda*, a glass counter–enclosed buffet of prepared dishes like eggplant parmigiana, lasagna, and freshcooked vegetables in season, reheated when you order. *San Marco 3454 (on Calle delle Botteghe, off Campo Santo Stefano).* ☎ *041/522-8181. Primi 4.15€; secondi 7€–8€; menù turistico 8.80€. Mon–Sat 11am–4pm and 7–10pm. Vaporetto: Accademia or Sant'Angelo.*

→ **Osteria Enoteca Ai Artisti** LIGHT ITALIAN This little restaurant proves that it is in fact affordable to dine at an outdoor table right alongside a canal, if you can manage to snag one of the few tables. Otherwise, grab something to go from the bar inside and munch away while walking along the water. Don't let the name of the canal—Rio della Toletta (and not, as some mistakenly read, Toilette)—dissuade you. *1169A Dorsoduro. Toast 2.20€–2.50€; panini 3.50€; pizza 6€–7€. Cover 1.50€. Daily 7:30am–9pm. Vaporetto: San Tomá.*

MTV Best → **Pizzeria ae Oche** ★★ PIZZERIA/ITALIAN This American-style tavern sports wooden beams and booths decorated with classic 1950s Coca-Cola signs and the like. Italians are zealously unapologetic about tucking into a pint of beer (with more than 20 served) and—count 'em—85

varieties of imaginative pizza. The clientele is a mixed bag of young and old, students and not, Venetians and visitors. If you come on a weekend, you may want to make reservations. *Santa Croce 1552 (on Calle del Tintor south of Campo San Giacomo dell'Orio).* ☎ *041/524-1161. Pizza 4.30€–7.40€; primi 5.20€–6.30€; secondi 5.80€–7.50€. Tues–Sun noon–midnight (daily in summer). Vaporetto: Rio San Biasio or San Stae.*

→ **Pizzeria/Trattoria al Vecio Canton** PIZZA/ITALIAN Good pizza is hard to find in Venice, and I mean that in the literal sense. Tucked away in a northeast corner behind Piazza San Marco on a well-trafficked route connecting it with Campo Santa Maria Formosa, the Canton's wood-paneled tavernalike atmosphere and great pizzas are worth the time you'll spend looking for the place. There is a full trattoria menu as well, with a number of pasta and side dishes (*contorni*) of vegetables providing a palatable alternative. *Castello 4738a (at the corner of Ruga Giuffa).* ☎ *041/528-5176. www.alveciocanton.com. Primi and pizza 6€–9€; secondi 11€–18€. Wed 7–10:30pm; Thurs–Mon noon–2:30pm and 7–10:30pm. Vaporetto: San Zaccaria.*

→ **Rosticceria Teatro Goldoni** ITALIAN/INTERNATIONAL Bright and modern (though it has been here for over 50 years), this showcase of Venetian-style fast food tries to be everything: bar, cafe, rosticceria, and *tavola calda* (hot foods deli) on the ground floor and pizzeria upstairs. A variety of sandwiches and pastries beckons from a downstairs display counter, and another offers prepared foods (eggplant parmigiana, roast chicken, pasta e fagioli, lasagna) that'll be reheated when ordered; there are also a dozen pasta choices. A number of combination salads are a welcome concession to the American set and are freshest and most varied for lunch. This won't be your most memorable meal in Venice, but you won't walk

VENICE

away hungry or broke. *San Marco 4747 (at the corner of Calle dei Fabbri).* ☎ *041/522-2446. Pizza and primi 6€–15€; secondi 8€–20€; menù turistico 14€. Daily 9am–9:30pm. Vaporetto: Rialto.*

Doable

→**Ai Tre Spiedi** ★★ VENETIAN   Venetians bring their visiting friends here to make a *bella figura* (good impression) without breaking the bank, then swear them to secrecy. Rarely will you find as pleasant a setting and appetizing a meal as in this small, casually elegant trattoria with reasonably priced fresh-fish dining—and plenty to keep meat-eaters happy as well. The *spaghetti O.P.A.* (with parsley, peperoncino, garlic, and olive oil) is excellent, and the *spaghetti al pesto* is the best this side of Liguria. Follow it up with the traditional *bisato in umido con polenta* (braised eel). This is one of the most reasonable choices in town for an authentic Venetian dinner of fresh fish. *Cannaregio 5906 (on Salizzada San Cazian).* ☎ *041/520-8035. Primi 4.50€–12€; secondi 9.50€–18€; menù turistico 15€–20€. Tues–Sat noon–3pm; Tues–Sun 7–10pm. Closed July 20–Aug 10. Vaporetto: Rialto.*

→**Cantina Do Spade** ★★★ WINE BAR/ VENETIAN   Since 1415, workers, fishmongers, and shoppers from the nearby Mercato della Pescheria have flocked to this wine bar. There's bonhomie galore here among the locals for their daily *ombra* (glass of wine)—a large number of excellent Veneto and Friuli wines are available by the glass. A counter is filled with *cicchetti* (potato croquettes, fried calamari, polenta squares, cheeses) and a special picante panino whose secret mix of superhot spices will sear your taste buds. Unlike at most *bacari,* this quintessentially Venetian cantina has added a number of tables and introduced a sit-down menu, accounting for my star here over its competitor, Cantina do Mori (above), which is a better choice for stand-up bar food.

San Polo 860 (on Sottoportego do Spade). ☎ *041/521-0574. www.dospadevenezia.it. Primi 6€–10€; secondi 7€–10€; menù fisso (fixed menu) 13€–18€. Mon–Wed and Fri–Sat 11:30am–3pm and 6–11:30pm; Thurs 9am–3pm. Closed Jan 7–20. Vaporetto: Rialto or San Silvestro.*

→**Osteria Vivaldi** VENETIAN   Rumored to be where composer Vivaldi once lived, the building now houses a cozy restaurant resembling a rural wine bar. For a special treat, try the grilled lobster: a steal at only 17€. *San Polo 1257.* ☎ *041/523-8185. Pasta from 6€–12€; main courses 9€–17€. Cover charge 1.50€. Daily 10:30am–2:30pm and 5:30–10:30pm. Vaporetto: Rialto.*

→**Trattoria alla Rivetta** ★ SEAFOOD/ VENETIAN   Lively and frequented by gondoliers (always a clue of quality dining for the right price), merchants, and visitors drawn to its bonhomie and bustling popularity, this is one of the safer bets for genuine Venetian cuisine and company in the touristy San Marco area, a 10-minute walk east of the piazza. All sorts of fish—the specialty—decorate the window of this brightly lit place. Another good indicator: There's usually a short wait, even in the off season. *Castello 4625 (on Salizzada San Provolo).* ☎ *041/528-7302. Primi 6€–10€; secondi 10€–15€. Tues–Sun noon–2:30pm and 7–10pm. Vaporetto: San Zaccaria.*

→**Trattoria da Gianni** VENETIAN   One of the more affordable restaurants along busy Lista di Spagna, with a cozy terrace and friendly service. A good place to sample traditional Venetian cuisine, such as *saor* (sardines marinated in vinegar), served here with a dollop of polenta, as well as seafood dishes, which may be disappointing if you've previously splurged on high-quality food in the city. *Cannaregio 4377.* ☎ *041/523-7268. Seafood appetizers 6€; primi 8€; seafood secondi 11€–16€. Vaporetto: Ferrovia.*

The Incredible Sinking City
....

The fact that Venice is sinking is nothing new: Scientists have noted the strange phenomenon for hundreds of years, caused by the fact that Venice is built on marshy ground, which sinks in the same way a sponge does when you apply pressure. The problem is the rate at which Venice is sinking. Venice typically sinks at a rate of about 7 centimeters (2¾ in.) a century—not a very worrisome amount—but scientists now say that the city has sunk 24 centimeters (9½ in.) in the past 100 years alone.

Anyone who has visited Venice during high tide has witnessed the consequence of this sinking: enormous flooding that is doing serious damage to the city's famous landmarks. Take St. Mark's Basilica: Due to its sinking foundation, the building now leans slightly to the left. Numerous projects have been suggested to fix the problem, such as the **Moses Project (Progetto Mosè;** www.progettomose.com), a dam project aptly named after the famous biblical character. The idea is to build gates at points where seawater enters the lagoon so that when water levels rise, the gates can be shut and prevent water from flooding the city. Environmentalists, however, argue against this project as the closed gates will prevent water from moving out of the city as well, causing a backlog of water pollution, and harming the fish and plant life in the water. A controversial new plan has recently been proposed. This plan aims to solve the flooding problem by not only preventing Venice from sinking further, but actually seeks to raise the city. The 93-million euro project involves digging enormous holes under the city and then pumping them full of water. This extra water will expand the layer of sand lying underneath the city and will push the city higher up, at a rate of around 3 centimeters (1¼ in.) a year. It still remains to be seen how the city will deal with these problems, but the fact remains that if it doesn't do something soon, Venice may very well end up underwater.

VENICE

→ **Trattoria da Remigio** ★ITALIAN/VENETIAN Famous for its straightforward renditions of Adriatic classics, Remigio is the kind of place where you can order simple *gnocchi alla pescatora* (homemade gnocchi in tomato-based seafood sauce) or *frittura mista* (a cornucopia of seafood fried in clean oil for a flavorful but light secondo) and know that it will be memorable. It bucks current Venetian trends by continuing to offer exquisite food and excellent service at reasonable prices. The English-speaking headwaiter, Pino, will talk you through the day's perfectly prepared fish dishes or dozen meat choices. Dine in one of two pleasant but smallish rooms. If you need directions, ask a local, but make reservations before you head out, 'cause they're required. *Castello 3416 (on Calle Bosello near Scuola San Giorgio dei Greci).* ☎ *041/523-0089. Primi 3.50€–8€; secondi 8€–20€. Wed–Mon 1–3pm; Wed–Sun 7–11pm. Vaporetto: San Zaccaria.*

Splurge
- - - - - - - - - - - - - - - - - - - -

→ **Bistrot de Venise** ★★ VENETIAN An upscale restaurant with traditional Italian atmosphere, often housing exhibitions from local artists in the dining room. This is a good place to come for a sampling of traditional Venetian cuisine: The restaurant offers set menus that are pricey but well coordinated with a good sampling of the city's best cuisine. *Calle dei Fabbri 4685.* ☎ *041/523-4740. www.bistrotdevenise.com. Primi 10€; secondi 15€–17€; Classic Venetian menù fisso 38€;*

Historic Venetian menù fisso 55€. Daily noon–11pm. Vaporetto: Rialto.

Cafes & Snacks

For a true Venetian experience, take a coffee break in a cafe in one of the city's piazzas or campos—try **Piazza San Marco** for the ultimate experience (p. 913), **Campo Santa Margherita** for something affordable (p. 911), or the stylish, Art Deco **Bar Accademia** (immediately east of the Accademia bridge, on the Dorsoduro side), to mix with gondoliers on break.

→ **Caffè Florian** ★★ On the south side of the piazza, is Venice's most famous and most theatrical cafe. It's a bit heavy on nostalgia, but we like having a Bellini (prosecco and fresh peach nectar) at the back bar for half what you'd pay at an indoor table; alfresco seating is even more expensive when the band plays on, but it's worth every cent for the million-dollar scenario. It's said that when Casanova escaped from the prisons in the Doge's Palace, he stopped here for a coffee before fleeing Venice. *San Marco 56A–59A.* ☎ *041/520-5641. Thurs–Tues 10am–midnight. Closed week before Christmas and Jan 7–13, and Wed in winter. Vaporetto: San Marco.*

→ **Caffè Quadri** ★ They claim to be the first to introduce coffee to Venice. There's a restaurant upstairs that sports Piazza San Marco views. At all spots in the cafe, a cappuccino, tea, or Coca-Cola at a table will set you back about 5€. *San Marco 120.* ☎ *041/522-2105. www.quadrivenice.com. Daily 9am–midnight. Closed Mon in winter. Vaporetto: San Marco.*

Partying

In general, Venice's less-than-booming nightlife ends early. Most people usually have a drink at a campo cafe, and then walk around for a bit, soaking up the dreamy atmo before heading to bed. The best places for this are Piazza San Marco, the campi on either side of the Rialto Bridge, and for a slightly more boisterous, international-budget-traveler scene, Cannaregio's Lista di Spagna.

Those looking for a party can check out the following bars and clubs, mostly located around Campo Santa Margherita (lively and unpretentious) in Dorsoduro, and Lista di Spagna (backpacker-oriented, but borderline tacky) in Cannaregio. You can also ask any of the younger staff members at your hotel—they'll be able to tell you where to go for the current hot hangouts ("hot" being a relative term in serene Venice).

Finally, just because Venice is not a city of velvet ropes and bouncers does not mean it's acceptable to wear flip-flops and shorts out on the town at night. The look you're going for is casual but chic, which means wearing your cleanest and least wrinkled pair of jeans or other pants, and a "real shirt" of some sort (that is, not a graphic T-shirt). Women, if you've brought a skirt or dress, now would be a good time to bust it out. (But keep the shoes flat—most people look ridiculous trying to walk around Venice in heels.)

There's not a general rule of thumb for what days/nights these bars and clubs are open. In Venice, there's no one set closing day because their "work week" is not like most cities; it revolves around tourism and the esoteric Venetian people who still live in Venice.

Finding Out What's On

Check out the free magazine *A Guest in Venice* for festival, concert, and nightlife listings. While bars are busy from early evening onward, Venice's clubs don't really get going until around midnight. Check out **www.unospitedivenezia.it** for information.

Bars

For tourists and locals alike, Venetian nightlife mainly centers on the many cafe/bars in one of the world's most remarkable piazzas: Piazza San Marco. Even Napoleon called it the most beautiful drawing room of the world. It is also the most expensive and touristed place to linger over a Campari or cappuccino, but a splurge that should not be dismissed too readily.

➜ **Bacaro Jazz** It's a mix of recorded jazz (played a bit too loud), rough plank walls, industrial-steel tables, and a corrugated aluminum ceiling at this happening cocktail bar. The happy hour specials (4–7pm; BOGO Heineken for 7€, cocktails from 8€) make this a good place to stop for a post-sightseeing or pre-dinner drink, or a late-night snack. The kitchen serves pasta, seafood, and snacks till closing. (Not to be confused with the pricey and pretentious Bacaro Lounge, which should be avoided.) *San Marco 5546.* ☎ *041/528-5249. www.bacarojazz.com.* ☎ *041/528-5249. Thurs–Tues 4pm–2am. Vaporetto: Rialto.*

MTV Best ➜ **Bancogiro** ★★ At this cool, modern osteria, set in the arcades of the old fruit-and-herb market west of the Rialto Bridge, you'll find *cicchetti, spritz, ombre,* and boozy locals eating plates of who-knows-what at the bar. You can have a full, creative Venetian meal in the vaulted upstairs room, or a drink and snack at the tables set up behind the bar outside, on a broad (and remarkably underused) stretch of fondamenta right on the Grand Canal. *San Polo 122.* ☎ *041/523-2061. Tues–Sat until midnight or later; Sun for lunch only. Vaporetto: Rialto.*

➜ **Centrale Lounge** This sleek and sexy bar in the heart of San Marco has its own private boat dock, for those who are arriving by gondola or water taxi. For the rest of us, there's a pedestrian entrance on Piscina Frezzeria. Every night, a DJ spins a mix of

chill-out, house, and lounge music. The crowd is a young and good-looking mix of locals and out-of-towners. Some of the bartenders are clearly hoping to be discovered by visiting talent agents and will act snobby toward non-Hollywood types. The best nights here are Thursdays—from 7pm on, there's a free buffet, a friendly vibe, and jazz and Latin tunes. *San Marco 1659B.* ☎ *041/296-0664. www.centrale-lounge.com. Wed–Mon 6:30pm–2am. Vaporetto: Vallaresso.*

➜ **Devil's Forest** As popular with tourists as it is with real Venetians, this Italian version of the classic Irish pub, in an alley off Campo San Bartolomeo, has such quintessential features as Irish brew on tap (pints from 4.50€), *calcio* on the big screen, and even an authentic red phone booth. Backgammon and chess boards are also available for patrons, making this a great place to kick back and warm up if you're in Venice during the biting cold of winter. *Calle Stagneri 5185.* ☎ *041/520-0623. www.devilsforest.com. Daily 8am–12:30am. Vaporetto: Rialto.*

MTV Best ➜ **Duchamp** ★★ Rumored to be named after a controversial French Dada artist, this casual bar across the campo from Orange Bar caters to a more bohemian

We Heart Gondolas!

So what if a 50-minute ride costs more than several days' meals? Riding a
📺 Best gondola ★★★ is one of the most magical, memorable experiences
you'll have in all of Europe. We are the first to call out any overrated tourist
attractions, but when it comes to the gondola, I guarantee you that any guidebook or so-called Venice expert who dismisses it as overrated has never tried
it. Yes, it's touristy, and no, you'll never see Venetians riding around in them,
but a ride in a 12m (39 ft.) sleek black gondola is truly as romantic as it looks—
especially if you go at night.

There are major gondola *stazi* near all the Grand Canal bridges and off
Piazza San Marco, as well as some smaller moorings on side canals. Look for
the "Servizio Gondole" signs and the telltale striped shirts (yes, they all wear
them). The straw hats come out in summer. While the prices are all the same
from gondolier to gondolier, it doesn't hurt to do some tire, er, gunwale-kicking:
The older gondoliers tend to be the charmers, the romantic real Venetians who
will serenade you (and any passing women) with lilting gondola barcarole. (The
younger guys tend to be too cool to bust out the barcaroles.) On the other
hand, the younger gondoliers are the ones who work the later shift and are
therefore your best bet if you want to pilot a gondola on the Grand Canal at
midnight.

> **When to gondola:** If I can give you one piece of advice about Venice, it's
> this: Do not waste your precious euros on a broad-daylight gondola ride.
> During the day, the most picturesque canals (in the sestiere of San Marco)
> are a logjam of gondolas, each filled with six middle-aged day-trippers. A
> good time to board your gondola is late afternoon, just before sundown,
> when the light does its magic on the canal reflections, and most of the
> day-tripper crush has cleared out of the city. Even better, go between
> 10pm and midnight at the absolute latest.

crowd, though the city's trendsetters have also deemed this place as cool. The place is especially popular at the start and end of the night. *Dorsoduro 3019.* ☎ *041/528-6255. Daily 10am–2am. Vaporetto: Ca' Rezzonico.*

📺 Best ➜ **Harry's Bar** ★★ In 1932, famed restaurateur and hotelier Giuseppe Cipriani opened this now-legendary watering hole near the Vallaresso vaporetto stop. Named for his son Arrigo (Italian for Harry), it has been a preferred, if overpriced, retreat for everyone from Hemingway—when he didn't want a Bloody Mary, he mixed his own drink: 15 parts gin, 1 part vermouth—to Woody Allen. Regulars prefer the close and elegant front room to the upstairs dining

room (decent cooking, and they invented *carpaccio,* a dish of thinly sliced raw beef now served throughout Italy). Harry's is most famous for inventing the Bellini, a mix of champagne and peach juice. Prices—for drinks and the fancy cuisine—are rather extravagant, with the house Bellini priced at 14€. *Calle Vallaresso. San Marco 1323;* ☎ *041/528-5777. Vaporetto: Vallaresso.*

➜ **Hotel Monaco** ★ When it comes to setting, the Hotel Monaco beats Harry's Bar hands down. The splendid waterfront restaurant here has some of the most prized real estate in Venice, with postcard views of La Salute church across the Grand Canal, and San Giorgio Maggiore across the lagoon.

- **Where to gondola:** The most magical canals and romantic canal-side buildings are in San Marco; you're bound to cruise down a lot of them if you board your gondola from the *stazi* in front of Piazza San Marco, Campo San Moisè, or the Rialto Bridge. Try to minimize your gondola time on the Grand Canal; its choppy waters are better suited to larger craft like vaporetti. However, the Grand Canal is the one place where gondoliers sometimes let you drive—late at night, its wide open waters mean that you can flail around, drop the oar, or whatever, and not run the risk of crashing into a wall and ending up a splintery wreck.
- **What to bring:** Booze. Yes, it's allowed, and even encouraged—but do the classy Venetian thing and get a bottle of *prosecco* (a sparkling white wine) as opposed to a flask of Jägermeister. Stop off at a local cafe or grocery store before your ride to buy a chilled bottle, and be sure to grab at least some plastic cups. (If you can find some, bring real glasses.) Bottoms up: You only have 50 minutes.
- **What to pay:** Though it's often quoted in print at differing official rates, expect to pay 62€ for up to 50 minutes (77€ 8pm–8am), with up to six passengers, and 31€ for another 25 minutes (39€ at night). Any gondolier will always quote much higher rates when negotiating a fare with tourists, but as long as there are other gondoliers around willing to take your euros, he can be bargained down to somewhere near the "official" rate. Late at night, when he's the last gondolier around, good luck paying less than 100€ for 50 minutes. ***Note:*** Gondoliers do not take Visa, Amex, or Mastercard. It's cash only, and at these ridiculously inflated prices, there is definitely no need to leave a tip.

All Venetian gondolas are regulated by the **Ente Gondola (☎ 041/528-5075; www.gondolavenezia.it)**, so call if you have any questions or complaints.

VENICE

Eating here is outrageously expensive, but you can come before the dinner hour (6–7pm) for an aperitivo, or after dinner (10pm) for a nightcap. If you're unsure, just ask the friendly guys in the lobby if it's a good time to stop in for a drink. Expect a crowd of older luxury-hotel types, although this spot is also popular with the younger international jet-set. *San Marco 1332. ☎ 041/520-0211. www.hotelmonaco.it. Daily 12:30–2:30pm and 7:30–10:30pm. Vaporetto: Vallaresso.*

MTV Best → **Naranzaria** ★★★ We challenge you to find a more fabulous, unpretentious spot for a few cocktails than this wine bar with 50 exclusive-feeling seats on the wide-open Erbaria esplanade, facing the Grand Canal just north of the Rialto Bridge. The 16th-century building here used to be the citrus market of Venice (*naranza* means "orange" in Venetian), where scurvy-prone sailors would come to fuel up on vitamin C after long stints on the high seas. Nowadays, a friendly, young, and hip crowd comes here to fuel up on sushi and sashimi (prepared by Japanese chef Akira) and light fare from northern Italy. The kitchen's only open until 11pm, but you can drink *ombre* of fantastic wines from the Veneto and Friuli regions, spritz, or after-dinner digestivi until 1 or 2am most nights—all the while taking in an unbelievably uncluttered Grand Canal view. *San*

Polo 130. ☎ *041/724-1035.* *www.naranzaria.it.*
Tues–Sun 10am–midnight (or later, depending
on the night). Vaporetto: Rialto.

MTV Best → **Orange Bar** ★★ It doesn't
take a genius to figure out where they got
the name for this hip restaurant and champagne lounge on Campo Santa Margherita:
Everything is orange! Grab a drink at the
curvy bar in the main room and plant yourself by the window, or on one of the orange
patio chairs in front. Upstairs, a roof terrace
offers a great view of the masses in the lively
campo below. For a quieter setting, take a
seat on the terrace in the back. With a name
like this, there's only one drink imaginable:
an orange, Aperol-based *spritz.* *Dorsoduro*
3054A. *www.orangebar.it.* ☎ *041/523-4740.*
Daily 7am–2am. Vaporetto: Ca' Rezzonico.

→ **Senso Unico** A favorite of American students (and the young-to-old real Venetians
who are fascinated by them), this cozy
British-style pub, just 2 minutes from the
Guggenheim and the Accademia, is a relaxed
and friendly place to have a glass or pint
of something after gawking at the art in

the nearby museums. *Dorsoduro 684.* ☎ *041/*
2410770 Wed–Mon 10am–1am. Vaporetto:
Accademia.

→ **Torino@Notte** When you're wandering
around after dinner in the sestiere of San
Marco, join the party that spills out from the
plate-glass windows of this bar in Campo
San Luca. "Torino at Night" has brought this
square to life after dark with live jazz many
nights, unusual beer from Lapland, and good
panini. *San Marco 459.* ☎ *041/522-3914. Tues–*
Sat 7pm–2am. Vaporetto: Rialto.

Nightclubs

→ **Casanova** ★ Techno beats pound in this
moderately popular club, frequented by
both locals and tourists, which doubles as an
Internet cafe during the day. And no need to
worry about appropriate attire here: In the
darkness, and the borderline-tacky environs
of Lista di Spagna, nobody will notice that
stain on your shirt or the dirt on your jeans.
Cannaregio 158A. ☎ *041/275-0199. Cover 13€*
Fri (includes 1 drink), 10€ Sat. Daily 10pm–
4am. Vaporetto: Ferrovia.

Performing Arts

In January 1996, a fire left the fabled **Teatro
La Fenice** ★★★ (Campo San Fantin;
(☎ **041-786511;** www.teatrolafenice.it), the
city's main venue for performing arts, a
blackened shell and a smoldering ruin.
Opera-lovers around the world, including
Luciano Pavarotti, mourned its loss. The
Italian government pledged $12.5 million for
its reconstruction, and the theater reopened
on November 12, 2004, presenting *La
Traviata* by Verdi. The total cost of the renovation came to $90 million. New seating
gives the renovated hall a total of 1,076
seats, and the stage curtain was donated by
Italian fashion designer Laura Biagiotti.
Tickets and subscriptions can be purchased
in person from the following Ve.La box
offices in Venice: **Calle dei Fuseri,** San

Marco 1810 (Mon–Sat 8:30am–6:30pm);
Piazzale Roma (daily 8:30am–6:30pm);
Ferrovia Scalzi (daily 8:30am–6:30pm, only
tickets). For further information call **Ve.La**
(☎ **041-2424**).

On the seaside street looking north to the
Canale delle Fondamenta Nuova, **Teatro
Fondamenta Nuova** (Fondamenta Nuova,
5013 Cannaregio; ☎ **041/522-44-98;** hours
and ticket prices vary) is the city's main
venue for avant-garde theater and conceptual art. It also stages modern dance performances on a regular basis.

Take a short walk southeast from the
Rialto bridge to find the **Teatro Goldoni**
(Calle Goldoni, 4650B San Marco; ☎ **041/
520-54-22** or 041/520-52-41; vaporetto:

VENICE

Rialto; box office: Mon–Sat 9am–1pm and 3–7pm; ticket prices vary widely) home to the local theater company, as well as visiting performers and huge concerts.

Sightseeing

Venice has enough historic and artistic treasures to keep visitors busy for weeks. In all likelihood, however, you'll only be here for a day and a half, which is just enough time to squeeze in the main attractions. A visit to Piazza San Marco is a must—you could easily spend a day exploring its historic buildings

Free & Easy

→ Proving that Venetians have a knack for flair in virtually everything they do, the island-cum-cemetery of **San Michele** is the final resting place for Venetians, and makes for a quiet escape from the city. When Napoleon brought his army to town, he ordered Venetians to haul their dead across the lagoon instead of burying them in the city. The tradition continues today, and 200 years of funerals have resulted in a severe shortage of space. The city has come up with some pretty gory solutions: The dead are allowed to rest peacefully for 12 years—just enough time to decompose. The remains of those with wealthy relatives are then sealed in a metal box and put in storage, while the less fortunate are merely tossed in the nearby bone yard. Seek out the grave of Greek Orthodox composer Igor Stravinsky and Protestant poet Ezra Pound. To get here, take vaporetto no. 41 or 42 heading toward Murano.

→ One of the most interesting (and photographed) sights you'll see in Venice is **Squero di San Trovaso** ★★ (Dorsoduro 1097, on the Rio San Trovaso, southwest of the Accademia Gallery; no phone), a small boatyard which first opened in the 17th century. Just north of the Zattere (the wide, sunny walkway that runs alongside the Giudecca Canal in Dorsoduro), the boatyard lies next to the Church of San Trovaso on the narrow Rio San Trovaso (not far from the Accademia Bridge). It is surrounded by Tyrolian-looking wooden structures (a true rarity in this city of stone built on water) that are home to the multigenerational owners and original workshops for traditional Venetian boats. Aware that they have become a tourist site themselves, the gondola-makers don't mind if you watch them at work from across the narrow Rio di San Trovaso, but don't try to invite yourself in. It's the perfect midway photo op after a visit to the Accademia galleries and a trip to the well-known gelateria, Da Nico (Zattere 922), whose chocolate gianduiotto is not to be missed.

→ An amazing spot from which to take in the full glory of Venice, the eastern tip of Dorsoduro is covered by the triangular **Dogana da Mar (Customs House)** ★★, which once controlled all boats entering the Grand Canal. It's topped by a statue of Fortune holding aloft a golden ball. Now it makes for remarkable, sweeping views across the *bacino* of San Marco, from the last leg of the Grand Canal past Piazzetta San Marco and the Doge's Palace, over the nearby isle of San Giorgio Maggiore, La Giudecca, and out into the lagoon itself.

VENICE

Venice Partying & Sightseeing

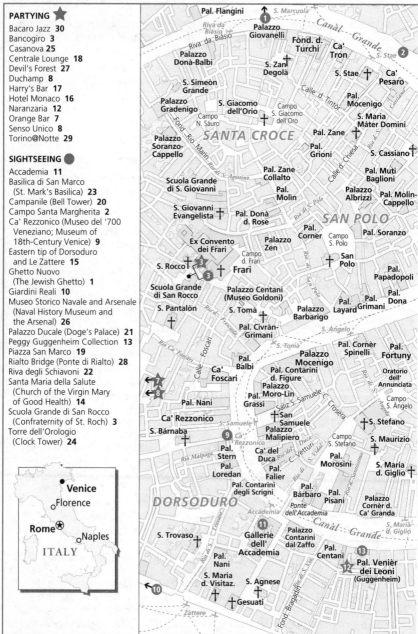

PARTYING ⭐

Bacaro Jazz **30**
Bancogiro **3**
Casanova **25**
Centrale Lounge **18**
Devil's Forest **27**
Duchamp **8**
Harry's Bar **17**
Hotel Monaco **16**
Naranzaria **12**
Orange Bar **7**
Senso Unico **8**
Torino@Notte **29**

SIGHTSEEING ●

Accademia **11**
Basilica di San Marco
   (St. Mark's Basilica) **23**
Campanile (Bell Tower) **20**
Campo Santa Margherita **2**
Ca' Rezzonico (Museo del '700
   Veneziano; Museum of
   18th-Century Venice) **9**
Eastern tip of Dorsoduro
   and Le Zattere **15**
Ghetto Nuovo
   (The Jewish Ghetto) **1**
Giardini Reali **10**
Museo Storico Navale and Arsenale
   (Naval History Museum and
   the Arsenal) **26**
Palazzo Ducale (Doge's Palace) **21**
Peggy Guggenheim Collection **13**
Piazza San Marco **19**
Rialto Bridge (Ponte di Rialto) **28**
Riva degli Schiavoni **22**
Santa Maria della Salute
   (Church of the Virgin Mary
   of Good Health) **14**
Scuola Grande di San Rocco
   (Confraternity of St. Roch) **3**
Torre dell'Orologio
   (Clock Tower) **24**

Venice
Florence
Rome
Naples
ITALY

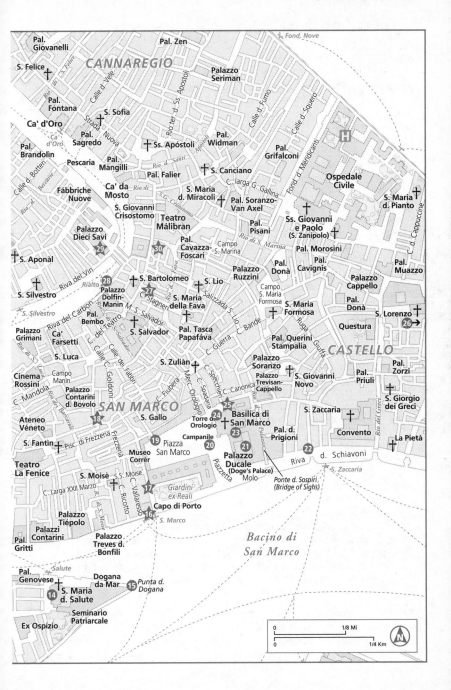

The Big Festival: Carnevale a Venezia

....

[TV] [Best] **Carnevale** ★★ is the ultimate shindig in Venice, with 2 weeks of pre-Lent debauchery (usually in Feb) including masked balls (with tickets costing upward of 500€!), concerts, and fireworks. No matter how you partake, a mask—if not a full-fledged costume—is mandatory. See **www.carnevale.venezia.it** for details.

Venetians once more are taking to the open piazzas and streets for the pre-Lenten holiday. The festival traditionally was the unbridled celebration that preceded Lent, the period of penitence and abstinence prior to Easter, and its name is derived from the Latin *carnem levare,* meaning "to take meat away."

Today Carnevale lasts no more than 5 to 10 days and culminates in the Friday to Tuesday before Ash Wednesday. In the 18th-century heyday of Carnevale in La Serenissima, well-heeled revelers came from all over Europe to take part in festivities that began months prior to Lent and crescendoed until their raucous culmination at midnight on Shrove Tuesday. As the Venetian economy declined, and its colonies and trading posts fell to other powers, the Republic of Venice in its swan song turned to fantasy and escapism. The faster its decline, the longer, and more licentious, became its anything-goes merry-making. Masks became ubiquitous, affording anonymity and the pardoning of 1,000 sins. Masks permitted the fishmonger to attend the ball and dance with the baroness, and the properly married to carry on as if they were not. The doges condemned it and the popes denounced it, but nothing could dampen the Venetian Carnevale spirit until Napoleon arrived in 1797 and put an end to the festivities.

Resuscitated in 1980 by local tourism powers to fill the slower winter months when tourism comes to a screeching halt, Carnevale is calmer nowadays, though just barely. Politicians and city officials have adopted a middle-of-the-road policy that helped establish Carnevale's image as neither a backpacker's free-for-all outdoor party nor a continuation of the exclusive private balls in the Grand Canal palazzi available to a very few.

Whether you spend months creating an extravagant costume, or grab one from the countless stands set up about the town, Carnevale is about giving in to the spontaneity of magic and surprise around every corner, the mystery behind every mask. Masks and costumes are everywhere, though you won't see anyone dressed up as generic 1970s vintage store grab-bags. Emphasis is on the historical, for Venice's Carnevale is the chance to relive the glory days of the 1700s when Venetian life was at its most extravagant. The places to be seen in costume (only appropriate costumes need apply) are the historical cafes lining the Piazza San Marco, **Caffè Florian** (p. 902) being the unquestioned command post. Don't expect to be seated in full view at a window seat unless your costume is straight off the stage of the local opera house.

and hours soaking up the atmosphere in the square. The city's best museums are close together in Dorsoduro, offering up artwork that's old and new and all excellent. Be sure to make time to amble through the city's winding alleyways away from the tourist crowds, and don't be afraid to get lost (see sidebar for tips on finding your way). Don't leave the city without a cruise or three along the Grand Canal from an outside seat on a vaporetto.

Festivals

April

The Feast Day of San Marco. Celebrates the patron saint of Venice. April 25.

May to October

Biennale d'Arte. A showcase of international modern art—with dance performances, theater, film, and art exhibitions—fills the pavilions of the public gardens at the east end of Castello and in the Arsenale. Many great modern artists have been discovered at this world-famous show. In the past, awards have gone to Jackson Pollock, Henri Matisse, Alexander Calder, and Federico Fellini, among others. Tickets (10€) can be reserved online (www.labiennale.org) or by calling ☎ 199/199-100 in Italy. From late May to October every odd-numbered year.

Voga Longa. An annual rowing race open to the public, where participants race to Burano and back, and crowds on the shore cheer in support. Mid-May.

July

The Festa del Redentore. Stupendous fireworks mark the celebration of the end of the plague that hit Venice in 1576. The festival is centered on the Palladio-designed Chiesa del Redentore (Church of the Redeemer) on the island of Giudecca: A bridge of boats across the Giudecca Canal links the church with the banks of Le Zattere in Dorsoduro, and hundreds of boats of all shapes and sizes fill the lagoon. It's one big floating *festa* until night descends and an awesome half-hour *spettacolo* of fireworks fills the sky. Third weekend in July.

August

Venice International Film Festival. Screenings of Italian and international films in various venues throughout the city. A few Hollywood big-names make an appearance on the Lido each year. Late August to early September.

Rolling Venice Saves You Money

Anyone between 16 and 29 is eligible for the terrific **Rolling Venice pass**, which gives discounts in museums, restaurants, stores, language courses, hotels, and bars across the city (it comes with a thick booklet listing everywhere it entitles you to get discounts). It's valid for 1 year and costs 2.60€. Year-round, you can pick one up at the **Informagiovani Assessorato alla Gioventù** (Corte Contarina 1529, off the Frezzeria west of St. Mark's Sq.; ☎ 041/274-7645 or 041/274-7650), which is open Monday to Friday 9:30am to 1pm, plus Tuesday and Thursday 3 to 5pm. July to September you can stop by the special Rolling Venice office set up in the train station daily 8am to 8pm; in winter you can get the pass at the **Transalpino travel agency** just outside the station's front doors and to the right, at the top of the steps; open Monday to Friday 8:30am to 12:30pm and 3 to 7pm and Saturday 8:30am to 12:30pm.

September

The Regata Storica. Venice's version of the Rose Parade, during which various boats decorated to the nines file in procession along the Grand Canal. First Sunday in September.

Top Attractions

FREE ➔ **Campo Santa Margherita**
★★ Aaahh, without a gondola or canal in sight, this elongated rectangle is one of the last vestiges of unpretentious, authentic daily life in old Venice. During the day, it's a mix of dapper elderly local men in felt hats and wool vests shooing pigeons and shooting the breeze with the news agent, and a younger set of Venetian and international

VENICE

students and artists who hang out at the myriad hip cafes on the square. At night, this is where most of the alcohol is consumed in Venice, so if you're looking for a lively, fun-loving atmosphere (albeit one that's not as picturesque as the more watery parts of the city) come to Campo Santa Margherita. *Vaporetto: Ca'Rezzonico.*

MTV **Best** → **Canal Grande (Grand Canal)** ★★★ A leisurely cruise along the 3.2km-long (2-mile) "Canalazzo," from Piazza San Marco to the Ferrovia (train station), or the reverse, is an absolutely spellbinding moving picture that just doesn't seem real—and one of life's great experiences. Hop on the vaporetto no. 1 in the late afternoon (try to get one of the coveted outdoor seats in the prow), when the weather-worn colors of the former homes of Venice's merchant elite are warmed by the soft light and reflected in the canal's rippling waters, and the busy traffic of delivery boats, vaporetti, and gondolas that fills the city's main thoroughfare has eased somewhat. The sheer number and opulence of the 200-odd palazzi, churches, and imposing republican buildings dating from the 14th to the 18th centuries is enough to make any boat-going visitor's head swim. Many of the largest are now converted into imposing international banks, government or university buildings, art galleries, and dignified consulates. They unfold along this singular ribbon of water that loops through the city like an inverted S, crossed by only three bridges (the Rialto spans it at midpoint) and dividing the city into three sestieri neighborhoods to the left, three to the right. Some of the waterfront palazzi have been converted into condominiums where lower water-lapped floors are now deserted, and the higher floors are still the coveted domain of the city's titled families; others have become the summertime homes of privileged expatriates. The two most popular stations are Piazzale Roma/Ferrovia (train station) and Piazza San Marco. See "Getting Around,"

earlier in this chapter, for vaporetto ticket prices. *Vaporetto: 1 or 82.*

FREE → **Eastern Tip of Dorsoduro and Le Zattere** ★★ When you want to people-watch, simply grab a gelato and head across the Grand Canal from San Marco to make your way to the eastern tip of Dorsoduro, the "frontier" of old Venice. The esplanades in front of **La Salute** church and the triangular **Dogana da Mar** (the old Customs House), which sits at the pointy extremity of Dorsoduro, provide breathtaking (and sometimes blustery) vistas over the lagoon and some of the more memorable moments you can have in Venice, especially at sunset. Along the southern side of Dorsoduro, the **Zattere** promenades offer the famous **Gelateria Da Nico** (Fondamenta Zattere, Dorsoduro 922, ☎ 041/522-5293) and views across the Giudecca Canal to—you guessed it—the island of Giudecca. The Zattere are an especially exciting place to be when Death Star–size cruise ships pull down the canal, threatening to steamroll any gondolas in sight. (Thousands of "storm trooper" passengers aboard the ships lay siege to Piazza San Marco and the Rialto Bridge during the day.) *Vaporetto: San Tomá.*

→ **Palazzo Ducale (Doge's Palace)** ★★★ Looking more like a Turkish palace than the former residence of the Venetian doges, or mayors, the stunning palazzo shimmers like a mirage in the piazzetta right next to St. Mark's Basilica and gives you a good idea of the sumptuousness of Venice's glory days. The "Doge house" was originally built in the 13th century and then rebuilt in the 16th century after most of it was destroyed in a fire; this was perhaps a blessing because when it was reconstructed, the great Venetian painters of the time were invited to contribute artwork. Today, the palace is essentially a museum housing this art collection. Upstairs, check out the works by Veronese and Tintoretto. Then venture downstairs into

12 Hours in Venice

1. **Hop on vaporetto no. 82.** Soak in the views along the **Grand Canal** before jumping off at Piazza San Marco.

2. **Experience San Marco.** Get a cup of coffee at **Caffè Florian** and then revel in the splendor of the **Basilica di San Marco.**

3. **Go to Dorsoduro.** Get lost in the Venetian painting craze at the **Accademia.**

4. **Stop at Campo Santa Margherita.** Sidle into **Duchamp** for a little well-earned downtime. Continue north to San Polo, and stop for a meal at **Naranzaria.**

5. **Take a traghetto.** Head to the other side of the Grand Canal and wander up and around the **Rialto Bridge.** Then head north through **Cannaregio,** following the Strada Nova, stopping in at **Casanova** for a little dancing and wine.

the old apartments of the doges for a glimpse into the life of these city rulers, and stop into the Grand Council chamber for a view of Tintoretto's massive *Paradise.* The notorious Council of Ten used to operate in this room, where they would sentence criminals to horrendous forms of punishments. The nearby Ponte dei Sospiri, or **Bridge of Sighs** ★, connects the palace with the old prison blocks, and is aptly named for the reaction of the prisoners as they crossed the bridge to meet their sad fate. See "Who Let the Doges Out?" (below) for info on the highly recommended guided tours of the palace. *Admission 11€ adults; 5.50€ students, E.U. citizens over 65, and Rolling Venice cardholders. Admission also buys entry into the Museo Correr, the Museo Archeologico Nazionale, and the Monumental Rooms of the Biblioteca Nazionale Marciana. Audioguide 5€. Palace Nov 1–Mar 31 9am–5pm (ticket office 7am–4pm); Apr 1–Oct 31 9am–7pm (ticket office 7am–6pm). Vaporetto: San Marco.*

📺 Best FREE ➔ **Piazza San Marco** ★★★ The classiest and usually most congenial place to hang out in Venice is undoubtedly Piazza San Marco. You could spend hours just sitting on the steps, watching all the action in the square. Amid the hordes of tourists that cram into the piazza,

flocks of pigeons feed on breadcrumbs and dodge playful children. The piazza is flanked by the most popular tourist attractions in the city—most tourists spend virtually their entire visit here.

Sip on an overpriced coffee at one of the historic cafes lining the piazza, or simply sit on the steps and listen to the live orchestra music for free. The truly sadistic can buy a pack of birdseed for 1€ and get swarmed by overfed birds. *Vaporetto: San Marco.*

➔ **Rialto Bridge (Ponte di Rialto)** ★★ One of the great icons of Venice, this elegant marble arch over the Grand Canal is lined with overpriced boutiques and is teeming with tourists. Until the 19th century, it was the only bridge across the Grand Canal, originally built as a pontoon bridge at the canal's narrowest point. Wooden versions of the bridge followed; the 1444 one was the first to include shops, interrupted by a drawbridge in the center. In 1592 this graceful stone span was finished to the designs of Antonio da Ponte, who beat out Sansovino, Palladio, and Michelangelo with his plans that called for a single, vast, 28m (92 ft.) wide arch in the center to allow trading ships to pass. The name "Rialto," which—like other Italian place names such as "Capri"—has come to be synonymous with glamour, is derived from

VENICE

Who Let the Doges Out?

For an insider look at and tons of fascinating anecdotes about the Doge's Palace, I cannot recommend highly enough the **"Itinerari Segreti" (Secret Itineraries)** ★★★ guided tours. The tours offer an unparalleled look into the world of Venetian politics over the centuries and are the only way to access the otherwise restricted quarters and hidden passageways of this enormous palace, such as the **doges' private chambers** and the **torture chambers** where prisoners were interrogated. The story of ladies' man extraordinaire Giacomo **Casanova's imprisonment** in, and famous **escape** from, the palace's prisons is the tour highlight (though a few of the less-inspired guides harp on this aspect a bit too much). I strongly recommend you **reserve in advance,** by phone, if possible—tours are often sold out at least a few days ahead, especially from spring through fall—or in person at the ticket desk. Guided tours that promise to take visitors into "the most secret and fascinating rooms in the Palace" run daily at 9:55, 10:45, and 11:35am. Book at the museum information desk by calling ☎ 041/520-9070. The Secret Itinerary tour costs 13€ for adults; 7€ for students, E.U. citizens over 65, and Rolling Venice cardholders.

rivus altus ("high bank"). Flotillas of singing gondoliers are common in the waters around the Rialto Bridge, making for a great (and very self-aware) photo op. *San Polo and San Marco. Vaporetto: Rialto.*

FREE → **Riva degli Schiavoni** Known for being the toniest waterfront promenade in Venice, the "Bank of Slaves" stretches north from Piazza San Marco into the sestiere of Castello. Here, the Grand Canal ceases to exist, having already spilled into the *bacino di San Marco,* so the spectacular views from here take in the monumental structures on the islands of San Giorgio Maggiore and Giudecca, across the water in the middle of the lagoon. Riva degli Schiavoni is also a great vantage point for observing the circus that attends the arrival of the monstrous cruise ships that drop anchor in the lagoon on a daily basis. Thousands of day-trippers stream in from the floating apartment buildings on shuttle boats and proceed to flood St. Mark's Square and the Rialto Bridge until it's time for them to set sail again in the late afternoon. Otherwise, Riva degli Schiavoni is the place where older tourists—or those with enough cash to afford the luxury hotels on this strip—shuffle along, past kitschy souvenir stands, congratulating themselves on how fabulous they are. *Vaporetto: 1 or 82.*

Historic Buildings, Areas & Monuments

The most important and most popular historic buildings are all conveniently located in or around Venice's monumental main square: St. Mark's.

MTV **Best** → **Basilica di San Marco (St. Mark's Basilica)** ★★★ Stepping into Piazza San Marco, you are automatically struck by the beauty of the basilica; on a hot, hazy day it shimmers like a mirage and is utterly surreal. Legend has it that the basilica was built in the 9th century after the body of St. Mark, patron saint of Venice, was smuggled out of Alexandria in a pork barrel and secretly brought to Venice. The interior of the church is stuffed with ornate mosaics depicting the life of St. Mark and scenes from the Old Testament, as well as various treasures looted when Venice took part in the medieval Crusades. Off the main nave are the baptistery, the treasury, and the presbytery, which holds St. Mark's sarcophagus on an altar. Behind the altar is the Pala d'Oro, an altar screen encrusted with a dizzying amount of jewels. Upstairs, you'll find the Marciano Museum, whose main attraction is the Triumphal Quadriga: a 4th-century quartet of bronze horses snatched up by crusaders in Constantinople. Also upstairs, step out onto the Loggia dei Cavalli, a balcony offering a bird's-eye view of the piazza below. Free guided tours Tuesday and Wednesday at 11am (highly recommended). *Piazza San Marco.* ☎ *041/522-5697. Free admission to the Basilica; 1.50€ Museo Marciano (St. Mark's Museum, also called La Galleria, includes Loggia dei Cavalli); 2€ Tesoro (Treasury); 1.50€ baptistery. Basilica, Tesoro, and Pala d'Oro Mon–Sat 9:45am–5pm; Sun 2–5pm (winter hours usually shorter by an hour); Museo Marciano daily 9:45am–5pm (winter hours usually shorter by an hour); baptistery 9:45am–5pm. Vaporetto: San Marco (Vallaresso or Giardinetti).*

→ **Campanile (Bell Tower)** ★★ What may seem like a simple tower, no different from so many others in the country, is actually a structure with quite the notorious history. The campanile was first built in the 10th century (and modified in the 16th c.) as a military watchtower, and its bells were originally used to signal various events, such as the start and end of the workday, the summoning of senators to the Doge's Palace, and to announce the execution of prisoners who were kept hanging from the tower in cages before having their heads chopped off. In 1902, Venetians received a huge shock when the bell tower gracefully crumbled into the piazza below, miraculously killing no one (although one unlucky *gatto* was flattened in the debacle—meow). Ten years later, in 1912, the tower had been rebuilt (using many of the original materials), a replica of its former self with one new addition—an elevator. Today, the bells of the tower are rung just

for the amusement of the tourists who line up to ride the elevator to the top for the stellar views of the square and the lagoon beyond. *Piazza San Marco.* ☎ *041/522-4064. Admission 6€, audioguides 3€ (2€ with Rolling Venice card). Daily 9:30am–4pm (July–Sept till 8pm). Vaporetto: San Marco (Vallaresso or Giardinetti).*

FREE → **Ghetto Nuovo (The Jewish Ghetto)** ★★ The original European *ghetto* (the term is derived from the Venetian word for foundry) was founded in 1516 by the city not because of any ill-will towards Jewish Venetians but as a way to get the Roman Catholic Church off their backs, who at this point in history were expelling Jews from a good part of western Europe. At its heyday, persecuted Jews from all over Europe flocked here, creating a multicultural community whose diversity is still evident today. The ghetto contains five synagogues: the German Synagogue, the Spanish Synagogue, the Italian Synagogue, the Levantine (aka Turkish) Synagogue, and the Canton Synagogue. When Napoleon brought down the Venetian Republic in the early 19th century, the ghetto was dismantled and the city's Jews merged with the mainstream population. Today, only about 30 of Venice's 500 Jewish people still live in the ghetto, but the lively atmosphere still remains. The center of the action is around Campo del Ghetto Nuovo, flanked by the German, Levantine, and Spanish synagogues, as well as the Museo della Comunità Ebraica (Museum of the Jewish Community), housing various historical artifacts from the ghetto. Walk through the square, and its radiating alleyways with Jewish shops, kosher eats, and the Holocaust memorials, and you'll wonder if you're in Italy or Israel. For those with a serious interest, the museum offers in-depth walking tours of the ghetto. The ghetto is best avoided on Saturdays, the Jewish Sabbath, when everything is closed and there is not a soul in sight. *Campo di Ghetto*

VENICE

Nuovo 2902B. ☎ *041/715-359. 10€ (includes museum entrance). Sun–Fri 10am–7pm June–Sept; 10am–4:30pm Oct–May. Walking tours are 10€ (includes museum entrance) and depart hourly from the museum starting at 10:30am. Vaporetto: San Marcuola.*

→ **Santa Maria della Salute (Church of the Virgin Mary of Good Health)** ★ The only great baroque monument built in Italy outside of Rome, the octagonal Salute is recognized for its exuberant exterior of volutes, scrolls, and more than 125 statues and rather sober interior, though one highlighted by a small gallery of important works in the sacristy. (You have to pay to enter the sacristy; the entrance is through a small door to the left of the main altar.) A number of ceiling paintings and portraits of the Evangelists and church doctors are all by Titian. On the right wall is Tintoretto's *Marriage at Cana*, often considered one of his best. *Dorsoduro (on Campo della Salute).* ☎ *041/522-5558. Free admission to the church; sacristy 1.50€. Daily 9am–noon and 3–5:30pm. Vaporetto: Salute.*

→ **Torre dell'Orologio (Clock Tower)** Only 20 years after it was supposed to be finished (in time for the 500-year anniversary of its 1496 construction)—the clock tower *finally* reopened to the public on May 27, 2006. The famous tower stands on the north side of Piazza San Marco, next to and towering above the Procuratie Vecchie (the ancient administration buildings for the republic). The tower's actual clock mechanism is original from the Renaissance and still keeps perfect time (although it recently received a cleaning by luxury timepiece maker Piaget). The two bronze figures, known as "Moors" because of the dark color of the bronze, pivot to strike the hour. The base of the tower has always been a favorite *punto di incontro* ("meeting point") for Venetians, and is the entranceway to the ancient Mercerie, the principal souk-like retail street of both high-end boutiques and trinket shops that zigzags its way to the Rialto Bridge. *San Marco, Piazza San Marco. www.torreorologio.it. At press time, it was possible to request a guided tour of the clock tower via the website, but information about opening hours and admission fee (if any) was not available. Vaporetto: San Marco (Vallaresso or Giardinetti).*

Museums & Galleries

Ⓜ **Best** → **Accademia** ★★★ Venice's most famous and crowded gallery, this is *the* place to come to view spectacular Venetian art. Even if you have little interest in 13th-century paintings depicting Christ in various poses of near-death, of which there are too many here, the paintings in this museum are still worth a visit, simply for their opulence and amazing state of preservation. The collection follows a chronological order, beginning with those done in the 13th century, and ending with 18th-century works. The majority of the paintings are religious-themed: Besides Christ, other featured stars include the Madonna, the Madonna and Bambino, and various angels and saints. Giorgione's *Tempest* is the most famous painting in the gallery (in Room 5), but to the average eye, there is really nothing too impressive about this painting. Others that do stand out, and are worth a glance, include Giovanni Bellini's series of Madonna and Bambino paintings, Lorenzo Lotto's gloomy *Portrait of a Young Man*, Paolo Veronese's *Feast In the House of Levi*, and both Bellini and Carpaccio's versions of the *Miracle of the True Cross*—which take place at the San Lorenzo and Rialto bridges, respectively—for great depictions of 14th- and 15th-century daily life in Venice. *Campo della Carità, Dorsoduro.* ☎ *041/522-2247. Admission 6.50€. Tues–Sun 8:15am–7:15pm; Mon 8:15am–2pm. Tours are offered Fri 11am–1pm, Sat 3:30pm–5pm, Sun 10am–noon and*

3:30pm–5pm. Call ahead to reserve. Vaporetto: Accademia.

→**Ca' Rezzonico (Museo del '700 Veneziano; Museum of 18th-Century Venice)** ★ This museum, in a handsome palazzo on the Grand Canal, reopened after a complete restoration in late 2001. It offers an intriguing look into what living in a grand Venetian home was like in the final years of the Venetian Republic.

Begun by Baldassare Longhena, 17th-century architect of La Salute Church, the Rezzonico home is a sumptuous backdrop for this collection of period paintings (most important, works by Venetian artists Tiepolo and Guardi, and a special room dedicated to the dozens of works by Longhi), furniture, tapestries, and artifacts. This museum is one of the best windows into the sometimes frivolous life of Venice of 200 years ago, as seen through the tastes and fashions of the wealthy Rezzonico family of merchants—the lavishly frescoed ballroom alone will evoke the lifestyle of the idle Venetian rich. The English poet Robert Browning, after the death of his wife Elizabeth Barrett Browning, made this his last home; he died here in 1889. *Dorsoduro (on the Grand Canal on Fondamenta Rezzonico).* ☎ *041/241-0100 or 041/520-4036. Admission 6.50€ adults; 4.50€ students. Wed–Mon 10am–6pm. Vaporetto: Ca' Rezzonico.*

→**Museo Storico Navale and Arsenale (Naval History Museum and the Arsenal)** The Naval History Museum's most fascinating exhibit is its collection of model ships. It was once common practice for vessels to be built not from blueprints, but from the precise scale models that you see here. The prize of the collection is a model of the legendary *Bucintoro,* the lavish ceremonial barge of the doges. Another section of the museum contains an array of historic vessels. Walk along the canal as it branches off from the museum to the Ships' Pavilion, where the historic vessels are displayed.

To reach the arsenal from the museum, walk up the Arsenale Canal and cross the wooden bridge to the Campo dell'Arsenale, where you will soon reach the land gate of the Arsenale, not open to the public. Occupying a fifth of the city's total acreage, the arsenal was once the very source of the republic's maritime power. It is now used as a military zone and is as closed as Fort Knox to the curious. The marble-columned Renaissance gate with the republic's winged lion above is flanked by four ancient lions, booty brought at various times from Greece and points farther east. It was founded in 1104, and at the height of Venice's power in the 15th century, it employed 16,000 workers who turned out merchant and wartime galley after galley on an early version of massive assembly lines at speeds and in volume unknown until modern times. *Castello 2148 (Campo San Biasio).* ☎ *041/520-0276. Admission 3€. Tues–Sun 9:30am–12:30pm; Tues–Sat 3:30–6:30pm. Vaporetto: Arsenale.*

→**Peggy Guggenheim Collection** ★★ About as different as you can get from the Accademia, and perhaps a bit of a shock to the senses if you go from one to the other, this gallery houses the collection of well-known art curator Peggy Guggenheim, of the same Guggenheims behind the Guggenheim museums in New York, Bilbao, Berlin, and Las Vegas. The building—Palazzo Venier dei Leoni—is not only the former residence of the curator but it also houses Peggy Guggenheim herself—or at least her final resting place, in a corner of the sculpture garden next to a tree donated by Yoko Ono! The gallery itself contains various modern works, from cubists Picasso and Gris, to Italian futurists Balla and Boccioni, to surrealists like Giorgio De Chirico and Salvador Dalí, as well as Peggy's ex-husband Max

Ernst. Jackson Pollock is also well represented here—but don't look too long at his intense paintings or you'll hurt your eyes. Works by Miró, Kandinsky, Chagall, and the wonderful Pegeen Vail (Peggy's daughter) are also on display. When you're finished strolling through the gallery, have a seat at its canal-side entrance and watch the traffic go by. *Palazzo Venier dei Leoni.* ☎ *041/240-5411. www.guggenheim-venice.it. Admission 10€ adults; 5€ seniors and students. Wed-Mon 10am–6pm. Vaporetto: Accademia.*

→ **Scuola Grande di San Rocco (Confraternity of St. Roch)** ★★ This museum is a dazzling monument to the work of 16th-century Venetian painter Tintoretto—it holds the largest collection of his work anywhere. The series of the more than 50 dark and dramatic works took the artist more than 20 years to complete, making this the richest of the many confraternity guilds, or *scuole*, that once flourished in Venice.

The downstairs room is fine, but you won't really be blown away until you walk upstairs and feast your eyes on the truly wow-inducing Sala dell'Albergo, where the most notable of the enormous, powerful canvases is the moving *La Crocefissione (The Crucifixion)*. In the center of the gilt ceiling of the great hall, also upstairs, is *Il Serpente di Bronzo (The Bronze Snake)*. Among the eight huge, sweeping paintings downstairs, each depicting a scene from the New Testament, *La Strage degli Innocenti (The Slaughter of the Innocents)* is the most noteworthy, so full of dramatic urgency and

energy that the figures seem almost to tumble out of the frame. As you enter the room, it's on the opposite wall at the far end of the room.

There's a useful guide to the paintings posted inside on the wall just before the entrance to the museum. In the upstairs and downstairs halls, there are large mirrors that you can walk around with and angle up for better viewing of the ceiling paintings. There are a few Tiepolos among the paintings, as well as one work by Titian. Note that the enormous works (recording Venice being saved from yet another plague) on or near the staircase are not by Tintoretto. *San Polo 3058 (on Campo San Rocco adjacent to Campo dei Frari).* ☎ *041/523-4864. www.scuolagrande sanrocco.it. Admission 5.50€ adults; 4€ students. Daily 9am–5:30pm (winter hours usually shorter by about an hour). Vaporetto: San Tomà.*

The University Scene

The **University of Venice** lies on the Grand Canal, between the Rialto and San Marco, and the main building on campus is the Ca' Foscari (Foscari House). Most students live around the artsy, trendy Dorsoduro area, so you're bound to bump into local coeds at any of the cafes or bars there. Try Accademia Foscarini Snack Bar or **Orange Bar** (p. 906), depending on your mood. If you'd rather *become* a student, check out www.unive.it or call ☎ **041/2347540** for info on the university's exchange programs.

Playing Outside

Gardens & Parks

FREE → **Giardini Reali** ★ In a city with a serious lack of green space (unless, of course, you count the algae-infested sections of canal water), this tiny patch of solitude behind bustling Piazza San Marco is a blessing. Yes, it's small and dirty and overcrowded, but if

you can manage to snag a seat at one of the shady benches, you'll appreciate this little oasis that provides an often-needed respite from the heat and tourist crowds. Before settling in, purchase an ice cream or cold beverage from one of the vendors at the park gates and then give your feet a deserved

VENICE

rest. *Vaporetto: San Marco (Vallaresso or Giardinetti).*

Lido Beaches

Once a retreat enjoyed only by the upper strata, the Lido is a resort island to the south of Venice, and is usually overrun with tourists, particularly those with a lot of money. It's not the most gorgeous stretch of beach in Italy, and the polluted waters don't make for the most pristine swimming environment, but the sandy beaches do make for a nice place to soak up some Italian rays. Even if you only come for a few hours, the Lido is a nice break from the museums and monuments of Venice proper—they're not going anywhere. While the Lido has gotten a bit more democratic since its days as a *beau-monde* refuge, you should definitely pack a lunch to avoid the still-absurd prices at the island's restaurants. The nicest beach area is, of course, the privately owned stretch in front of the ritzy hotels; although it's technically reserved for guests, you probably won't be hassled if you inconspicuously set up camp here. Otherwise, try the free but dirtier public bathing beach at the end of Lungomare Gabriele d'Annunzio, at the eastern end of the island. To get to the Lido take vaporetto no. 1, 52, or 82.

A Picnic Where?

Eat alfresco, and you can observe the city from a slightly different perspective. Plus, doing your own shopping for food can be an interesting experience—the city has very few supermarkets as we know them, and small *alimentari* (food shops) in the highly visited neighborhoods (where few Venetians live) are scarce.

You'll have to deal with not much green space (it's not worth the boat ride to the Giardini Pubblici past the Arsenale, Venice's only green park). An enjoyable alternative: Some of the larger piazzas or campi that have park benches, and in some cases even a tree or two to shade them, such as Campo San Giacomo dell'Orio (in the quiet sestiere of Santa Croce). The two most central are **Campo Santa Margherita** (sestiere of Dorsoduro) and **Campo San Polo** (sestiere of San Polo).

For a picnic with a view, scout out the **Punta della Dogana area (Dogana da Mar/Customs House)** ★★ near La Salute Church for a prime viewing site at the mouth of the Grand Canal. It's located directly across from the Piazza San Marco and the Palazzo Ducale—pull up on a piece of the embankment here and watch the flutter of water activity against a canvas-like backdrop deserving of the Accademia Museum. In this same area, the small **Campo San Vio** near the Guggenheim is directly on the Grand Canal (not many campi are) and even boasts a bench or two.

If you want to create a real Venice picnic, you'll have to take the no. 12 boat out to the near-deserted island of Torcello, with a hamper full of bread, cheese, and wine, and reenact the romantic scene between Katharine Hepburn and Rossano Brazzi from the 1950s film *Summertime*.

But perhaps the best picnic site of all is in a patch of sun on the marble steps leading down to the water of the Grand Canal, at the foot of the **Rialto Bridge** on the San Polo side. There is no better ringside seat for the Canalazzo's passing parade.

VENICE

Shopping

Hands down the best place to shop in Venice, especially if you can't afford the swank boutiques around Piazza San Marco, is the **Rialto Market.** And even if you're not looking for anything in particular, window-shopping here—if you can deal with the crowds—is a fun way to spend an afternoon. Tiny stores cover the length of the Rialto Bridge, and then continue along the streets leading from the bridge all the way through Campo San Polo and up to the train station. Here, you will find glassware, masks, jewelry, shoes, fresh produce, and the usual tourist kitsch (such as random T-shirts of kittens wearing gondolier get-ups). Stores usually open around 10am, and the bridge becomes utterly crowded by midafternoon with window-shopping tourists, and then quiets down again in the early evening as shops close.

Markets

MERCATO RIALTO

Venice's principal open-air market is a sight to see. It has two parts, beginning with the produce section, whose many stalls, alternating with that of souvenir vendors, unfold north on the San Polo side of the Rialto Bridge (behind these stalls are a few permanent food stores that sell delicious cheese, cold cuts, and bread selections). The vendors are here Monday to Saturday 7am to 1pm, with a number who stay on in the afternoon.

At the market's farthest point, you'll find the covered **fresh-fish market,** with its carnival atmosphere, picturesquely located on the Grand Canal opposite the magnificent Ca' d'Oro and still redolent of the days when it was one of the Mediterranean's great fish markets. The area is filled with a number of

VENICE

Road Trip

When Venice's crowds and—in summer—smelly canals become overwhelming, a mere 30-minute train ride will magically transport you to **Padua,** which may lack some of the beauty of its neighbor, but is nonetheless a cool, peaceful haven with enough of its own parks, sights, and piazzas to warrant at least a day's exploration. If you do visit Padua, you'll often find yourself surrounded by religious pilgrims, who flock to the **Basilica di Sant'Antonio** in droves from all over the world.

Padua is also a well-established university town; the **University of Padua** (www.unipd.it) was founded in 1222. Students in the past have included the likes of Dante, Galileo, and Donatello. This leads to an interesting mix of people, as pilgrims and ancient-looking monks and nuns mix with crowds of students hanging out in between classes.

It's easiest to arrive here by **train** if you're coming from Venice, Milan, or Bologna. Trains depart for and arrive from Venice once every 30 minutes (trip time: 30 min.), costing 7.50€ one-way. For information and schedules, call ☎ 892021 in Italy. Padua's main rail terminus is at **Piazza Stazione,** north of the historic core and outside the 16th-century walls. A bus will connect you to the center. The IAT Information Office is in the train station, offering very little paper material in English but a good free map, and the helpful staff members are happy to answer questions (☎ 049/8752077). It's open Monday through Saturday 9:15am to 7pm and Sunday 9am to noon.

small *bacari* bars frequented by market vendors and shoppers where you can join in and ask for your morning's first glass of *prosecco* with a *cicchetto* pick-me-up. The fish merchants take Monday off (which explains why so many restaurants are closed on Mon; those that are open are selling Sat's goods—beware!) and work mornings only.

CAMPO SANTA MARGHERITA

On this spacious campo, Tuesday through Saturday from 8:30am to 1 or 2pm, a number of open-air stalls set up shop, selling fresh fruit and vegetables. You should have no trouble filling out your picnic spread with the fixings available at the various shops lining the sides of the campo, including an exceptional *panetteria* (bakery), Rizzo Pane,

at no. 2772, a fine *salumeria* (deli) at no. 2844, and a good shop for wine, sweets, and other picnic accessories next door. There's even a conventional supermarket, Merlini, just off the campo in the direction of the quasi-adjacent campo San Barnabà at no. 3019. This is also the area where you'll find Venice's heavily photographed **floating market** operating from a boat moored just off San Barnabà at the Ponte dei Pugni. This market is open daily from 8am to 1pm and 3:30 to 7:30pm, except Wednesday afternoon and Sunday. You're almost better off just buying a few freshly prepared sandwiches (panini when made with rolls, tramezzini when made with white bread).

Vienna

Vienna is impossible to describe in terms other than cosmopolitan. It boasts a number of great hotels, a fast and reliable subway system, renowned international restaurants, sexy nightclubs, and the sort of hustle and bustle you'd expect from any booming city. It has been shaped by hundreds of cultures and lived through more wars and changing empires than almost anywhere else in Europe. The result is a worldly city that enjoys its mix of Gothic, baroque, and Art Nouveau architecture, prides itself on its narrow cobblestone roads in the picturesque Inner City, and takes pleasure guiding visitors to stellar sites like St. Stephan's Cathedral and Schönbrunn Palace.

But to get a real feel for Viennese culture, simply step into one of its cafes. Cafe culture was born here, and no visit to the city is complete without sipping a cup of coffee and watching your neighbors, the city's sophisticated cafe clientele. We advise drinking your coffee slowly—and visiting the city *slowly*. Vienna has too much going for it not to be savored properly.

The Best of Vienna

- **The Best Cheap Meal:** The meat-lovers pizza at **Pizza Bizi** kept me coming back for more. The large pizza slices come covered with peppers, pepperoni, ham, and garlic. Calzones and sandwiches are also available. See p. 934.

- **The Best Bar:** A great place to chill with your friends after a day of sightseeing,

Excess is a favorite local dive. Here you can party in the downstairs basement to DJs spinning the latest American hits. The dance floor is small but cozy—you're certain to make friends by the end of the night. See p. 936.

- **The Best Night Club:** Get ready to dance all night at **Empire Club,** a multiplatform, always-packed dance club. With DJs spinning everything from the latest singles to old-school hits, the club plays something for every personality. This is a great place to watch the Viennese move it, and it doesn't hurt that the bartenders are sexy as all get out. See p. 937.

○ **The Best Top-of-the-World Sight:** At **St. Stephan's Cathedral,** you can climb the south tower of the cathedral (or take an elevator) for a panoramic view of the city like no other. See p. 940.

Getting There & Getting Around

Getting into Town

BY AIR

Vienna's international airport, **Wien Schwechat** (☎ **01/70070** for flight information; www.viennaairport.com), is about 19km (12 miles) southeast of the Inner City. Inside the airport is the **Vienna Tourist Information Office** (www.info.wein.at), which is open daily June to September from 9am to 10pm, October to May from 8:30am to 9pm.

A one-way **taxi** ride from the airport into the Inner City is likely to cost 32€, or more if traffic is bad. It's better to take the bus. Regular **bus** service connects the airport and the **City Air Terminal,** which is adjacent to the Vienna Hilton and directly across from the **Wien Mitte/Landstrasse** Rail Station, where you can easily connect with subway and tram lines. Buses run every 20 minutes from 5:30am to 11:30pm, and then every hour from midnight until 5am. The trip takes about 25 minutes and costs 5€ per person. Tickets are sold on the bus and must be purchased with Austrian money.

There's also local **train** service, Schnellbahn (S-Bahn), between the airport and the **Wien Nord** and **Wien Mitte** rail stations. Trains run hourly between 4:30am and 9:30pm and leave from the basement of the airport. Trip time is 40 to 45 minutes, and the fare is 3€.

BY TRAIN

There are four major train stations in Vienna. Train information for all stations is available at ☎ **05/1717** or www.wienerlinien.co.at.

Westbanhof (West Railway Station) This is the main station in Vienna, with trains connecting to other European destinations as well as Salzburg and Innsbruck. It also connects with the U-Bahn lines U3 and U6. This station is located at Europlatz.

Südbahnhof (South Railway Station) This station mainly runs to destinations in Austria, Italy, and Hungary, and also links with some local bus/tram routes. It's located at Sudtirolerplatz.

Franz-Josef Bahnhof This station is mainly for local lines. You can hop on the D tram line and that will take you right into the city center. It is located at Franz-Josef Platz.

Wien Mitte This station has trains that will take you to the Vienna Airport and also runs to the Czech Republic. It is located at Landstrasser Hauptstrasse 1.

BY BUS The **City Bus Terminal** is at the Wien Mitte rail station, Landstrasser Hauptstrasse 1. This is the arrival depot for Eurolines, all of Austria's postal and federal buses, and private buses from other European cities. The terminal has lockers, currency-exchange kiosks, and a ticket counter open daily from 6:15am to 6pm.

BY CAR

If you're interested in renting a car, contact one of the following: **Avis** (Opernring 1; ☎ **01/700-732-700**), **Budget Rent-a-Car** (Hilton Air Terminal; ☎ **01/714-6565**), or **Hertz** (Marriott Hotel Parking 12A; ☎ **01/512-8677**). Try to stay away from renting cars at the airport—they tack on an extra 6% charge. To rent a car you need a passport and a driver's license that is at least 1 year old.

Getting Around

A uniform fare applies to all forms of public transport. Very few buses and streetcars sell tickets on board, having replaced humans long ago with coin-operated machines. A ticket for the bus, the subway, or the tram will cost 1.50€ if you buy it in advance at a Tabak-Trafiks (a store or kiosk selling tobacco products and newspapers), or 2€ if you buy it aboard the bus or tram. Remember that no matter what means of transport you use, once a ticket has been stamped (validated) by either a machine or a railway attendant, it's valid for one trip in one direction, anywhere in the city, including transfers. *Note:* Although some locals sneak onto public transport without paying, keep in mind that you can be hit with a hefty fine if you try the same.

Visit a **Vienna Public Transport Information Center (Informationdienst der Wiener Verkehrsbetriebe)** for maps and more info on the city's transport. The five largest locations are in the Opernpassage (an underground passageway adjacent to the State Opera House); the Karlsplatz; the Stephansplatz, near Vienna's cathedral; the Westbahnhof; and the Praterstern. For information about any of these outlets, call ☎ **01/790-9105** or go online to http:// progs.wiennet.at.

BY SUBWAY

The **U-Bahn** is Vienna's incredibly clean and reliable underground subway system—it's also the quickest and most convenient way to get around town. It consists of five lines labeled **U1, U2, U3, U4,** and **U6** (there is no U5). Karlsplatz, in the heart of the Inner City, is the most important underground station for visitors: The U4, U2, and U1 converge there. The U2 traces part of the Ring, the U4 goes to Schönbrunn, and the U1 stops

Discount Tickets

The **Vienna Card** is the best ticket to use when traveling within the city limits. At 17€, it's extremely flexible and functional for tourists because it allows 3 days of unlimited travel, plus discounts at various city museums, restaurants, and shops (see all that it covers at www.wien.info). You can purchase a Vienna Card at tourist information offices, public transport centers, and some hotels, or order one over the phone with a credit card (☎ **01/798-400-128**).

You can also buy tickets that will save you money if you plan to ride a lot on the city's transport system. A ticket valid for unlimited rides during any 24-hour period costs 5€; an equivalent ticket valid for any 72-hour period goes for 12€. There's also a green ticket, priced at 24€, which contains eight individual partitions. Each of these, when stamped, is good for 1 day of unlimited travel.

in Stephansplatz. The U3 also stops in Stephansplatz and connects with the Westbahnhof.

The U-Bahn schedule runs from 6am to midnight.

BY BUS

Buses traverse Vienna in all directions. They operate Monday to Saturday from 6am to 10pm and Sunday from 6am to 8pm. Bus nos. 1A, 2A, and 3A will get you around the Inner City. Convenient night buses are available on weekends and holidays starting at 12:15am. They go from Schwedenplatz to the outer suburbs (including Grinzing). Normal tickets are not valid on these late "N" buses. Instead, you pay 1.50€ on board.

BY STREETCAR

Riding the red-and-white trams (Strassenbahn) is not only a practical way to get around but also a great way to see the city. Tram stops are well marked. Each line bears a number or letter. Lines 1 and 2 will bring you to all the major sights on the Ringstrasse. Line D skirts the Outer Ring and goes to the Südbahnhof, and line 18 goes between the Westbahnhof and the Südbahnhof. Trams run daily from 6am to midnight.

BY TAXI

Cab service is a very convenient way to get around in Vienna, but it's also expensive. Taxi stands are marked by signs, or you can call ☎ 01/31300, 01/60160, 01/81400, 01/91011, or 01/40100. The basic fare is 4€, plus 1.09€ per kilometer. A 10% tip is the norm. Trips at night (after 11pm) and on Sundays and holidays carry a surcharge of 1€. There is an additional charge of 2€ if you phone for a taxi. The fare for trips outside the Vienna area (for instance, to the airport) should be agreed on with the driver in advance.

BY CAR

If you drive to Vienna, park the car. Much of Vienna is not accessible by car, and the

streets make for confusing driving. It's much easier to get around by subway or on foot.

ON FOOT

Hoofing it around town is often the best way to see Vienna, especially the Inner City. Just prepare for the cobblestone streets by leaving your flips-flops or heels at home.

BY BICYCLE

You'll find some great cycling paths down by the Danube River. You can rent bikes near the river or at many pensions/B&Bs, or they can be rented at **Pedalpower** (Ausstellungsstrasse 3; ☎ 01/729-7234; www.pedalpower.at). They usually cost around 10€ to 15€ per day.

BY HORSE-DRAWN CARRIAGE

Vienna's *Fiakers,* or horse-drawn carriages, have transported people around the Inner City for some 300 years. You can clip-clop along for about 30 minutes at a cost of 45€, 70€ for 1 hour—way too expensive and touristy, in my opinion.

VIENNA

Vienna Basics

Orientation: Vienna Neighborhoods

Vienna is divided into 23 districts. Most tourists and attractions can be found in the Inner Stadt (Inner City). Many of Vienna's hotels and restaurants are conveniently located in or just outside the first district, which is basically one large circle known as Kärntnerstrasse. The Strassenbahn (streetcar) is arranged so that it circles around the first district. Other rings loop around the Middle Ring.

INNER STADT (FIRST DISTRICT) This compact area, bounded on all sides by the legendary Ring, is at the center of Viennese life. The Inner City has dozens of streets devoted exclusively to pedestrian traffic, including **Kärntnerstrasse,** which bypasses

the Vienna State Opera House, and the nearby **Graben,** which backs up to Stephansplatz, home to the famous cathedral. Competing with both the cathedral and the Opera House as the district's most famous building is the **Hofburg,** the Habsburg palace that's now a showcase of tourist attractions, including the National Library, the Spanish Riding School, and six museums. Other significant landmarks include the Rathaus (City Hall), Parlament (Parliament), the Universität (University of Vienna), the Naturhistorisches (Natural History), the Kunsthistorisches (Art History) museums, and Stadtpark.

LEOPOLDSTADT (SECOND DISTRICT) Once inhabited by Balkan traders, this area doesn't physically border the Ringstrasse but lies on the eastern side of the Danube Canal, just a short subway ride (U1) from the Inner City. Here you'll find the massive **Prater Park,** which boasts an amusement park, miles of tree-lined walking paths, and numerous sports facilities, including a large stadium. Vienna's renowned trade fair exhibition site is also in this district, which has seen a spree of development along the canal in recent years.

LANDSTRASSE (THIRD DISTRICT) The bucolic **Stadtpark** spreads into this district, where you'll see more of Vienna's imperial charm. Streets are dotted with churches, monuments, and palaces, such as the grand **Schwarzenberg Palace** and the looming **Konzerthaus (concert house).** However, the top attraction remains Prince Eugene Savoy's **Belvedere Palace,** an exquisite example of baroque architecture. Several embassies are in a small section of Landstrasse that's known as Vienna's diplomatic quarter. The **Wien Mitte Rail Station** and the **City Air Terminal** are also here.

WIEDEN (FOURTH DISTRICT) This small neighborhood extends south from Opernring and Kärtnering, and it's just as fashionable as the first district. Most activity centers on **Karlsplatz,** a historic square that features its domed namesake, Karlskirche. Also around this hub are Vienna's **Technical University** and the **Historical Museum of the City of Vienna.** Kärnerstrasse, the main boulevard of the city center, turns into **Wiedner-Hauptstrasse** as it enters this district, and the **Südbahnhof,** one of the two main train stations, lies at its southern tip.

MARGARETEN (FIFTH DISTRICT) Southwest of the fourth district, Wieden, this area does not border the Ring and thus lies a bit farther from the Inner City. You'll start to see more residential neighborhoods, representing the continual growth of Vienna's middle class. The historic homes of composers Franz Schubert and Christoph Gluck still stand here among modern apartment complexes and industrial centers.

MARIAHILFERSTRASSE (SIXTH DISTRICT) One of Vienna's busiest shopping streets, **Mariahilferstrasse,** runs through this bustling neighborhood. The sprawling, lively **Naschmarkt (produce market),** selling fresh fruits, vegetables, breads, cheeses, and more, is an ideal place to people-watch. On Saturdays, the adjacent **Flohmarkt (flea market)** adds to the lively but sometimes seedy atmosphere as vendors sell antiques and junk. The surrounding streets are packed with *beisls* (small eateries), theaters, cafes, and pubs. As you go farther from the city center, you'll find that the landscape becomes more residential.

NEUBAU (SEVENTH DISTRICT) Bordering the expansive Museum Quarter of the Inner City, this is an ideal place to stay, as it's easily accessible by public transportation. The picturesque and once neglected **Spittelberg quarter** lies atop a hill just beyond Vienna's most famous museums. The vibrant cultural community is popular with both young and old visitors. The old Spittelberg houses have been renovated into boutiques, restaurants, theaters, and art galleries—a perfect backdrop for an afternoon stroll.

JOSEFSTADT (EIGHTH DISTRICT) The smallest of Vienna's 23 districts is named after Habsburg Emperor Joseph II and was once home to Vienna's civil servants. Like Neubau, this quiet, friendly neighborhood sits behind the City Hall and the adjacent grand museums of the Ringstrasse. You'll find everything from secluded parks to charming cafes to elaborate monuments and churches. Vienna's oldest and most intimate theater, **Josefstadt Theater,** has stood here since 1788. Josefstadt's shops and restaurants have a varied clientele, from City Hall lawmakers to university students.

ALSERGRUND (NINTH DISTRICT) This area is often referred to as the academic quarter, not just because of nearby **University of Vienna** but also because of its many hospitals and clinics. This is Freud territory, and you can visit his home, now the **Freud Museum,** on Berggasse. Here you'll also stumble upon the **Lichtenstein Palace,** one of Vienna's biggest and brightest, which today houses the federal **Museum of Modern Art.** At the northern end of Alsergrund is the **Franz-Josef Bahnhof,** an excellent depot for excursions to Lower Austria.

Tourist Offices

A **Vienna Tourist Information Center** is located inside the airport (p. 923). Once you've arrived, head for either of two information points that make it their business to have up-to-the-minute data about what to see and do in Vienna. The more centrally located is the **Wien Tourist-Information** office (at Albertinaplatz, directly behind the Opera House, on the corner of Philharmonikerstrasse; ☎ 01/211-140; tram: 1 or 2). Located in the heart of the Inner City, it's open daily from 9am to 7pm. The staff will make free hotel reservations for anyone in need of lodging. Larger and more administrative, but also willing to handle questions from the public, is the headquarters of the **Vienna Tourist Board** (Obere Augartenstrasse; ☎ 01/2111-4412; tram: 31).

For information on Vienna and Austria, including day trips from the city, visit the **Austrian National Tourist Office** (Margaretenstrasse 1, A-1040; ☎ 01/58866; www.Austria-tourism.net). The region surrounding the city (Lower Austria, or *Niederösterreich*) contains dozens of worthwhile attractions. The **Vienna Tourist Board**'s website is www.info.wien.at.

Culture Tips 101

Although German is the official language of Austria, English is commonly spoken throughout the county because the high schools teach it.

Many locals prowl the city's nightclub areas, asking partygoers if they'd like to smoke grass or hash or if they'd like to take ecstasy. Though you'll often see younger people smoking outside on the streets, always remember that these drugs are illegal here. You'll be fined or jailed if you're caught using or carrying. On the other hand, Vienna imposes few restrictions on the sale of alcohol; except in alcohol-free places you should be able to order beer or wine with your meal—even if it's 9am.

Recommended Books, Music & Movies

BOOKS & MOVIES

Carol E. Schorske's *Fin-de-Siècle Vienna: Politics and Culture* is a landmark book that takes you into the political and social world of Vienna at the end of the 19th and beginning of the 20th century. Also read Graham

VIENNA

Talk of the Town

Three ways to start a conversation with a local

1. **What's the best coffee house around here?** Café Sacher is justly famous, but ask a native, and you'll probably be steered toward a smaller, less touristy haunt.
2. **Id or ego?** Vienna is Freud's town, so brace yourself for some psycho babble.
3. **Mozart versus Haydn versus Strauss?** Vienna is the heaviest hitting classical music venue around, and you'll be missing out if you don't compare and contrast its more famous hometown composers.

Greene's *The Third Man*. Greene based this novel about intrigue and mystery in postwar Vienna on his screenplay for Carol Reed's famous 1949 film starring Orson Welles and Joseph Cotten.

The mild-mannered playwright, **Arthur Schnitzler**, who died in 1931, was the quintessential Viennese writer. Through his works he gave the imperial city the charm and style more often associated with Paris. Our favorite is *Reigen*, on which the film *La Ronde* was based.

A more recent film to rent is 1995's *Before Sunrise*, about strangers who meet on a train and end up spending the night in Vienna. I guarantee that you'll find the scenes shot in Vienna to be romantic, even if you don't feel the same way about the plot.

MUSIC

The classical period was a golden age in Viennese musical life. Two of the greatest composers of all time, **Wolfgang Amadeus Mozart** (1756–91) and **Franz Joseph Haydn** (1732–1809) lived and worked in Vienna.

Franz Schubert (1797–1828), was the only one of the great composers born in Vienna. He turned *lieder*, popular folk songs often used with dances, into an art form. His *Unfinished Symphony* remains his best-known work, but you also might want to give his chamber music and song cycles a listen.

After 1850, Vienna became the world's capital of light music, especially the waltz. **Johann Strauss** (1804–49) composed more than 150 waltzes and helped spread the art form throughout Europe. Vienna did not lack for important serious music in the late 19th century, though; **Gustav Mahler** (1860–1911) composed evocative music, much of it set to poetry, and **Arnold Schöneberg** (1874–1951) developed a 12-tone musical technique known as "dodecaphony."

Its amazing classical music history aside, don't forget that Vienna is also home to "Rock Me Amadeus." Back in the 1980s, pop singer **Falco** gained worldwide acclaim for this ditty, inspired by the movie *Amadeus* (another flick that's worth renting).

Vienna **Nuts & Bolts**

Cellphone Providers & Service Centers   There's a **T-Mobile** store at Wienerbergstrasse (☎ 602/1357; www.t-mobile.at).

Currency   Bankomat and Bank of Austria are the two most popular banks in Vienna—you'll find locations pretty much everywhere. The most convenient **American Express** office in Vienna is at Kärntnerstrasse 21–23 (☎ 01/5154-0770; Mon–Fri 9am–5:30pm, Sat 9am–noon).

Embassies   The main building of the **U.S. Embassy** is at Boltzmanngasse 16 (☎ 01/31339). The consular section, which handles lost passports, tourist emergencies, and other matters, is at Gartenbaupromenade 2–4 (☎ 01/31339). Both the embassy and the consulate are open Monday to Friday 8:30am to noon and 1 to 4pm.

The **Canadian Embassy** (Laurenzerberg 2; ☎ 01/531-380) is open Monday to Friday from 8:30am to 12:30pm and 1:30 to 3:30pm; the **U.K. Embassy** (Jauresgasse 12; ☎ 01/716-130) is open Monday to Friday 9am to 1pm and 2 to 5pm; the **Australia Embassy** (Mattiellistrasse 2–4; ☎ 01/50674) is open Monday to Thursday 8:30am to 1pm and 2 to 5:30pm, Friday 8:30am to 1:15pm; and the **New Zealand Embassy** (Springsiedelgasse 28;

☎ 01/318-8505) is open Monday to Friday from 8:30am to 5pm, but it's best to call to see if it's open. The **Irish Embassy** is at Hilton Center (Landstrasser Hauptstrasse 2; ☎ 01/715-4246) and is open Monday to Friday 9 to 11:30am and 1:30 to 4pm.

Emergencies   Dial ☎ **144** for an ambulance, ☎ **133** for the police, and ☎ **122** for a fire. The hospital, **Allgemeines Krankenhaus,** is located at Währinger Gurtel 18–20 (☎ 01/40400).

Internet/Wireless Hot Spots   Internet cafes can be found all around town. Most hotels and pensions and even hostels also have some sort of Internet connection available. I recommend **Café Stein** (Währingerstrasse 6; ☎ 01/319-7241), which offers Internet service for 3€ per half-hour. The cafe is open daily from 5 to 11pm.

Laundry   There's a shortage of laundromats in the city, so your best bet is to do your wash at a hotel. If you need a tailor, head to **Lacosto** (Ringstrassen Gallerian 134; ☎ 5050888).

Luggage Storage   Most hotels and pensions will store your luggage for you if you need to hold it for a day or so. Otherwise, all of the four train stations in Vienna have lockers available. They cost 3€ for a 24-hour period.

Post Offices   Every district in Vienna has a post office, usually in the middle of the district. Look for signs that read "post." The central post office is called Hauptpostamt and is located at Barbaragasse 2 (☎ 01/515-090). Most post offices are open Monday to Friday from 8am to 6pm.

Restrooms   Vienna has a number of public toilets, labeled WC (water closet), scattered at convenient locations throughout the city. Don't hesitate to use them, as they are clean, safe, and well maintained. All major sightseeing attractions also have public facilities.

Safety   Vienna has an almost non-existent crime rate. I felt extremely safe walking around by myself day and night. Still, you'll need to beware of pickpockets in the more touristy areas.

Tipping   Tips are often included in your meal; if not, then a 15% to 20% tip is customary. Remember to always tip bellhops and taxi drivers a few euros.

Sleeping

If you're looking to cut costs, staying outside the Inner City is not a bad option. You can expect to pay 20% to 25% less for a hotel outside the Ringstrasse. High season in Vienna encompasses most of the year: from May until October or early November, and during some weeks in midwinter when the city hosts major trade fairs, conventions, and other cultural events.

Hostels

→**Wombat's Hostel** ★ This ultrahip hostel was deemed the Cleanest Hostel in 2003 by hostelworld.com, and the decent-sized rooms *are* spotless. The no-age-limit policy allows for some weirdos, but in general you'll encounter young students from all over the world eager to go out together. Upon your arrival, the friendly staff will

Vienna

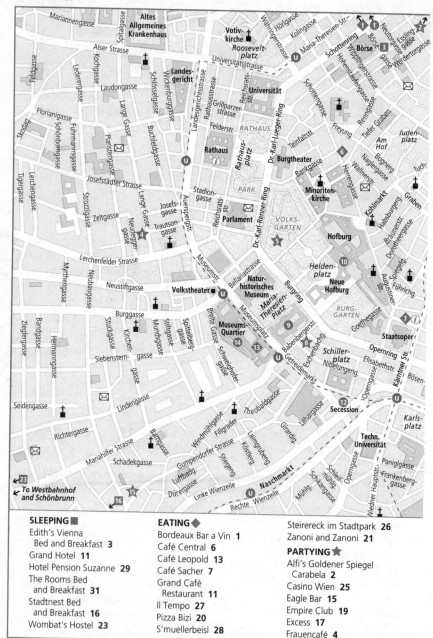

SLEEPING ■

Edith's Vienna
  Bed and Breakfast **3**
Grand Hotel **11**
Hotel Pension Suzanne **29**
The Rooms Bed
  and Breakfast **31**
Stadtnest Bed
  and Breakfast **16**
Wombat's Hostel **23**

EATING ◆

Bordeaux Bar a Vin **1**
Café Central **6**
Café Leopold **13**
Café Sacher **7**
Grand Café
  Restaurant **11**
Il Tempo **27**
Pizza Bizi **20**
S'muellerbeisl **28**

Steirereck im Stadtpark **26**
Zanoni and Zanoni **21**

PARTYING ★

Alfi's Goldener Spiegel
  Carabela **2**
Casino Wien **25**
Eagle Bar **15**
Empire Club **19**
Excess **17**
Frauencafé **4**

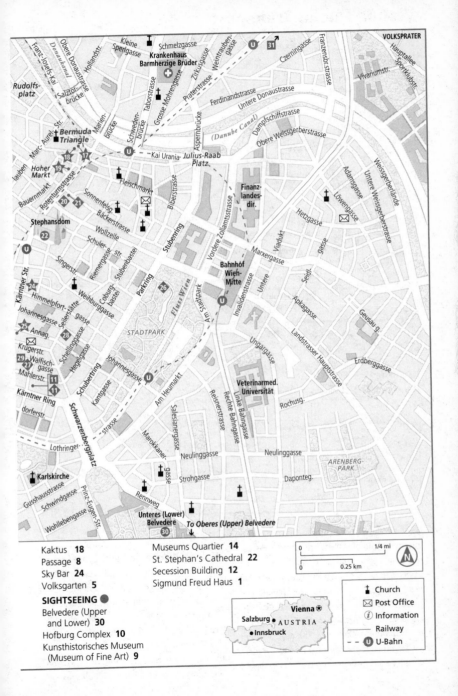

Kaktus **18**
Passage **8**
Sky Bar **24**
Volksgarten **5**

SIGHTSEEING ●
Belvedere (Upper
  and Lower) **30**
Hofburg Complex **10**
Kunsthistorisches Museum
  (Museum of Fine Art) **9**

Museums Quartier **14**
St. Stephan's Cathedral **22**
Secession Building **12**
Sigmund Freud Haus **1**

0 ⊢———————⊣ 1/4 mi
0 ⊢———————⊣ 0.25 km

✝ Church
✉ Post Office
ⓘ Information
——— Railway
- - Ⓤ U-Bahn

Vienna ⊛
Salzburg • AUSTRIA
  • Innsbruck

Vienna Public Transport

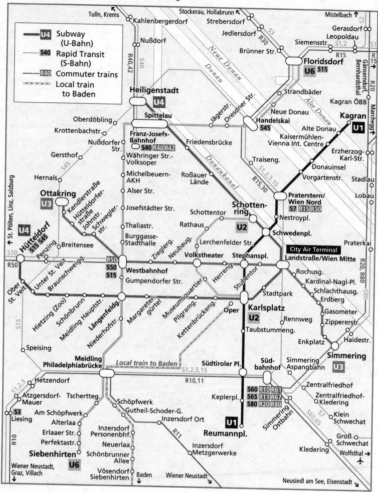

greet you with a free drink—you can draw out the hospitable vibe in the hostel's restaurant and bar. *Grangassee 6.* ☎ *043/897-2336. www.wombats.at. Low season 16€ dorm bed (4–6 people), 42€ single, 21€ double; high season 18€ dorm bed (4–6 people), 48€ single, 24€ double. Breakfast 3.50€. Tram: 5 or 18 to Westbahnhof. Amenities: Bar; cafe; foosball table; inline skate rental; Internet; kitchen; laundry facilities; pool table. In room: Locker, sheets.*

Cheap

→ **Edith's Vienna Bed and Breakfast** ★
This family-owned bed-and-breakfast has been around longer than my grandparents and is filled with antique Austrian treasures. It has three guest rooms, each decorated differently, but all sized for three or more people. The rooms also boast plenty of lighting and a library of reading materials on Vienna. The innkeeper, Ms. Edith, doubles as the

maid and receptionist; she's fluent in English and can offer directions and travel tips. As if the woman didn't have enough to do, Ms. Edith also cooks a breakfast every morning with coffee/tea, juices, an assortment of meats, vegetables, and freshly baked rolls with jelly and butter. *Borseplatz 3.* ☎ *043/533-6877. www.ibbp.com/europe/austria/edith svienna.html. 75€–115€ double. U-Bahn: Schottentor. Amenities: Exercise equipment; Internet; TV (in common room). In room: Hair dryer, Internet (in 1 room).*

→**Hotel Pension Suzanne** This pension is not as well known as it should be, considering that it has one of the best locations in Vienna—behind the Grand Hotel Wein and close to the Ringstrassen Galleries, El Tempo, and the Inner Stradte. It's run by delightful individuals who will even offer a tour of the pension before you pay. Rooms are somewhat small and the exterior is a bit dated, but comfort is guaranteed. There's usually a ton of students staying here. *Walfischgasse 4.* ☎ *043/513-2507. www.pension-suzanne.at. 77€ single with tub, 96€ double with shower, 108€ double with tub, 117€ apt with tub. Rates include breakfast. U-Bahn: Karlsplatz. Amenities: Tour desk. In room: TV.*

Doable

MTV **Best** →**The Rooms Bed and Breakfast** ★★ This bed-and-breakfast is a dream-come-true for both the owners and its guests. Almost every part of the retreat is handmade, from the wooden plank patio, to the beautiful downstairs eating area, to the three themed bedrooms—including an Indian-influenced room with canopy beds and hand-sewn pillows, and similarly cushy Asian and Mediterranean rooms. A hot breakfast is served daily; I recommend the delicious homemade pancakes. Although the B&B isn't in the center of town, it's right next to the U-Bahn—this means you can tour the city during the day, and look forward to retreating to this relaxing area afterwards.

Schlenthergassee 17. ☎ *043/644-431-2830. www.therooms.at. 50€–60€ single, 80€–90€ double. Extra person 15€. Rates include breakfast. U-Bahn: Kagran. Amenities: Breakfast room; bicycle rentals. In room: TV.*

→**Stadtnest Bed & Breakfast** ★ The Stadtnest is owned by one of the sweetest innkeepers I've met, Barbara Lenz—who built this place according to her own scrupulous travel demands. The modern rooms are spacious and kept extremely clean, and Barbara is quick to offer recommendations and directions to guests. She also keeps the kitchen healthy by only serving organic products, including homemade bread. The bed-and-breakfast is about 20 minutes' walking distance from the Opera House and extremely close to Mariahliferstrasse, the main shopping road. *Stumpergasse 29.* ☎ *043/545-4938. www.stadtnest.at. 68€ single, 82€ double. Rates include breakfast. U-Bahn: Nestroyplatz. Amenities: Breakfast room; Internet; kitchen; library. In room: TV, DVD (on request), Internet, movies (free from DVD library), safe.*

Splurge

→**Grand Hotel Vienna** ★★ Step into this luxurious hotel and an attentive and knowledgeable staff will guide you past the stunning lobby—think chandeliers and beveled mirrors—to your room. The equally stunning rooms are spacious and have large bathrooms with a tub/shower combination and separate toilet area. The hotel is equipped with three restaurants, all of which are gorgeous but a little pricey. The cafe downstairs in the lobby is definitely worth stopping in to grab a quick caffe latte. The location is unbeatable as it leads right into the Inner City and is attached to the Ringstrassen Galleries. *Kaerntner Ring 9.* ☎ *043/515-1313. www.grandhotelVienna.com. 380€–460€ double. U-Bahn: Karlsplatz. Amenities: Restaurant; 2 bars; cafe; business center; health club; Internet; laundry service; limo service; on-call*

VIENNA

doctor; postal service; shopping arcade; wheel-chair friendly, Wi-Fi. In room: A/C, TV, fax, hair dryer, Internet, Lifecycle (on request), minibar,

radio (satellite), safe, trouser press, voice mail, Wi-Fi.

Eating

Although Viennese meals are traditionally big and hearty, innovative chefs throughout the city now turn out lighter versions of the old classics. Even so, the Viennese love to eat, often as many as six times a day. Breakfast usually consists of bread with butter, jam, or cheese along with milk and coffee. Around 10am is *Gabelfrühstück* (snack breakfast), when diners usually savor some type of meat, perhaps little finger sausages. Lunch at midday is normally a filling meal, and the afternoon *Jause* consists of coffee, open-face sandwiches, and the luscious pastries that the Viennese make so well. Dinners can also be hearty, although many locals prefer a light evening meal.

Because Vienna cherishes its theaters, concert halls, and opera houses, many locals choose to dine after a performance. *Après-théâtre* is all the rage in this city, and many restaurants and cafes stay open late to cater to cultural buffs.

Unlike those in other western European capitals, many of Vienna's restaurants observe Sunday closings (marked by SONNTAG RUHETAG signs). Also beware of summer holiday closings, when chefs would rather rush to nearby lake resorts than cook for Vienna's tourist hordes. Sometimes restaurants announce vacation closings only a week or two before shutting down.

Make sure you try at least two different types of Wiener schnitzel while you're visiting Vienna. This Austrian specialty is basically a big chicken nugget that's made with pork instead of chicken. You should also pick up a kebab at some point during your travels—this street food makes for a perfect late-night meal.

Hot Spots

📺 **Best** → **Café Leopold** ★★ CAFE
This cafe inside the Leopold Museum at the Museum Quarter became a word-of-mouth sensation before it even opened its doors. The trendy restaurant functions as a cafe during the day and as a late-night eatery, complete with DJ music 3 nights a week. The food is international cuisine with an emphasis on Thai dishes. Note that the crowd skews a bit older, and it can get pricey. *Museumsplatz 1.* ☎ 01/523-6732. *Main courses 4.50€–11€. Daily 9am–2am. U-Bahn: Babenbergstrasse or MuseumQuartier.*

Cheap

📺 **Best** → **Pizza Bizi** ★★ PIZZA/ITALIAN This chain restaurant serves the best pizza in Vienna—actually, I rate it among the best pizza I've ever tasted. I highly recommend the meat-lovers pizza with pepperoni and ham. If you aren't into pizza, they have some sandwiches and meat dishes as well. Pizza Bizi is located right near Stephansplatz in the Inner City, and close to the Bermuda Triangle bars. *Rotemturmstrasse 4.* ☎ 513/3705. *www.pizza-bizi.at. Pizza 3.50€. Daily 11am–midnight. U-Bahn: Stephansplatz.*

→ **Zanoni and Zanoni** SNACKS This is a must-stop for gelato in the Inner City. Grab one of the outside or tent tables and take your pick of flavors from chocolate to mint chip. No matter what you order, the gelato is sure to please. Just avoid coming here during the weekend if you hate crowds. *Lugeck 7. Gelato 2€.* ☎ 512/7979. *www.zanoni.co.at. Daily 7:30am–midnight. U-Bahn: Stephansplatz.*

Doable

➜**Bordeaux Bar a Vin** AUSTRIAN This cafe is nestled along a small side street, a few minutes away from Vienna's Inner City. The patio seating makes for a great spot to relax and enjoy a glass of wine, fresh bread, and one of the tasty pork chop dishes. The service is great at any time of day, but it's less rushed during lunchtime. *Servitengasse 2.* ☎ *315/6363. www.bordeauxbar.at. Main courses 4.50€–20€. Mon–Fri noon–4pm and 6pm–1am; Sat 6pm–1am. U-Bahn: Schottenring.*

➜**Il Tempo** ★ BISTRO This modern bistro is right nearby the Ringstrassen Galleries, Grand Vienna Hotel, and Opera House. It's a great little place to grab an afternoon coffee and linger at the outdoor tables, or to stop in for a drink at the full-service bar. It also has great pasta dishes, especially the pasta with shrimp. The English-speaking staff is friendly and really cares about quality service—they're happy to provide directions around the Inner City. Check out the selection of magazines in the back corner if you want to indulge in a quick scan of the European tabloids. *Walfischg 8.* ☎ *043/513-0315. Main courses 7€–16€. Mon–Fri 8am–midnight; Sat–Sun 10am–midnight. U-Bahn: Karlsplatz.*

➜**S'Muellerbeisl** AUSTRIAN This restaurant serves all of the Viennese usual suspects, from *gulasch* (Hungarian stew) to potato soup. I found the dishes to be a little on the heavy side, but that's to be expected with this type of food. The meats are cooked to perfection and, because it's tucked away on a quieter side street, you will get quick, courteous service. When it's nice, you can sit at the picnic-style tables outside. *Seilerstatte 15.* ☎ *043/512-4265. Meals 4.50€–20€. Daily 10am–midnight. U-Bahn Stephansplatz.*

Splurge

MTV **Best** ➜**Café Sacher** ★★★ CAFES/DESSERTS Chocolate lovers, take heed: When in Vienna, you must go to this cafe and order the original *sachertorte* (chocolate layer cake); it is a must. This cafe packs in tourists eager to try the famous chocolate treat, which was created here in the 1800s. There's also a gift shop where you can buy chocolate. *Philharmonikerstrasse 4.* ☎ *01/514560. Main courses 22€–38€. Dessert 1.50€–7.50€. Daily noon–3pm and 6–11:30pm. U-Bahn: Karlsplatz.*

Cafes

➜**Café Central** ★ CAFE Located right across from the Hofburg, this cafe is always buzzing with people enjoying their routine cup of coffee. A great location for people-watching, it sells delicious caffeinated drinks and assortments of cakes and gelato. Even though Café Central is popular with locals, it's highly recommended by tour guides, so you're bound to see other tourists. *Herrengasse 14.* ☎ *01/533-3763. Main courses 3.50€–11€. Mon–Sat 8am–10pm; Sun 8am–6pm. U-Bahn: Stephansplatz.*

➜**Familie Reitbauer/Steirereck im Stadtpark** ★★ CAFE This trendy but casual outdoor cafe sits right in the center of Stadtpark, and offers front-row views of the entire park. There's no better place to try traditional Wiener schnitzel than here—it's tender and flavored to perfection. Inside Stadtpark. *Rasumofsygsse 2.* ☎ *043/713-3168. www.steirereck.at. Main courses 15€–20€. Mon–Fri 10:30am–2pm and 7–11pm. U-Bahn: Stephansplatz.*

VIENNA

Partying

The nightlife scene in Vienna is smoking hot. Whether you are gay, straight, introverted, or outgoing, you will find great places to party in the city. If your time in Vienna is limited, I

Get Lost in the Bermuda Triangle

A triangular area roughly bordered by Judengasse, Seitenstättengasse Rabensteig, and Franz-Josefs-Kai, Vienna's **Bermuda Dreieck (Bermuda Triangle**; U-Bahn: Schwedenplatz) is a must-stop along any bar-crawl. It has everything from intimate watering holes to large bars with live music. Most of the places here are open until at least 4am and only start to get crowded at 11pm.

recommend checking out the Bermuda Triangle area and also visiting the nightlife venues along the Danube River on the weekend.

Bars and clubs get most hopping on Tuesday through Saturday. If you're in town and want to party on a Sunday or Monday, hit one of the smaller bars. Get ready to rock out till the wee hours because the city's nightclubs and bars are usually open until at least 4am, and some are open until 6am. Cover charges usually run about 10€ and drinks about 5€ each.

The style at Austrian clubs is rarely flashy or wild. At nightclubs and bars, jeans are fine for males and females, and I recommend wearing closed-toed shoes (but not sneakers). Men usually wear collared shirts with nice jeans and ladies wear tight pants or a skirt with a sexy top and heels. When going to hot spots like Passage, you should glam it up more, though.

Bars

→ **Carabela** This Latin-themed bar is the perfect place to relax with *muchos* drinks while gazing over the beautiful Danube River. Drink too many Coronas at the circular, open-air bar, and you just might find yourself dancing with one of the bartenders.

The place gets pretty crowded late at night, but it's also a great place to grab an early drink and chat before the real partyers arrive. *Donauinsein. No phone. U-Bahn: Reichsbrücke.*

MTV Best → **Excess** ★★ This smoke-filled nightclub/bar is the perfect Viennese dive bar. Head to the basement for the real action: It's where most of the dancing and drinking happens. Mondays are typically karaoke nights, but most evenings you can count on hearing dance music like 50 Cent and J.Lo. Don't be afraid to try the red "wodka" (vodka) concoction served in a wine glass—it tastes amazing. Excess is packed with friendly locals every night of the week, but the best nights are Sunday or Monday evenings. *Near Schwedenplatz on Bezirk 1 (Bermuda Triangle).* ☎ *0222/533-6956. U-Bahn: Schwedenplatz.*

→ **Kactus** This is a great spot to get a few drinks, but it may not be exciting enough to hold your interest all night. Try to stay long enough to take in the sexy go-go girls and hot selection of male bartenders. If you're feeling a little cramped in the bar area, head to the spacious main dance floor to groove to a mix of pop and rap music. *Seitenstettengass 5 (Bermuda Triangle). U-Bahn: Schwedenplatz.*

→ **Sky Bar** ★ If you're looking to party with a slightly older, cocktail-lounge crowd, come to Sky Bar. The drinks can get a bit pricey, but the view overlooking the entire Inner City is worth it. It's located right above the Steffl department store (p. 946). *Kartnerstrasse 19.* ☎ *043/513-1712. www.skybar.at. U-Bahn: Stephansplatz.*

Casinos

→ **Casino Vienna** This casino is normally filled with folks who have loads of money, so unless you are heir to a fortune, keep your bets low. They have slot machines, two blackjack tables, one roulette table, and some poker—the table minimum bets are usually 10€. Many of the dealers don't speak English, so make sure you understand the rules of the game before sitting down. *Karntner Strasse 41.* ☎ *043/1512-4836. www. Vienna.casinos.at. U-Bahn: Karlsplatz.*

Nightclubs

🅼 Best ➔**Empire Club** ✶ If you want to dance but can't be bothered by stuck up bouncers or a line, head straight to the Empire Club. Here you'll find a great crowd of university students, who really know how to shake it—be it on the huge dance floor, platforms, or right in their seats. Tables are also spread throughout so you can sit down whenever you need a break. Themed events rotate with a regular roster of rock, electronic, hip-hop, and techno songs. It doesn't really matter how you dress for this club as long as you look spiffy. The waitstaff is gorgeous and drinks are regularly priced. *Rotgasse 9A.* ☎ *043/664-131-916. www.empire.co.at. U-Bahn: Schwedenplatz.*

➔**Passage** ✶✶ What makes this ultra-trendy spot especially cool is knowing that the space is an old subway passage, transformed into a large nightclub with DJs spinning hip-hop music until the wee hours. Bouncers only let in the best looking and best dressed—this is where wealthy locals and most University of Vienna students hang out—so dress to impress. Once you've charmed your way in, you'll be greeted by a hot waitstaff and loaded bar. If the high-tech sound system doesn't blast you aboveground, be prepared for the crowd to get increasingly rowdier as the night wears on. *Center of Ringstrasse, Babenbergstrasse 4.* ☎ *043/961-8800. U-Bahn:*

➔**Volksgarten** This hot spot is right in the middle of one of the city's parks and features outdoor and indoor dance floors. The indoor club is usually packed with a mix of wealthy and not-so-wealthy college students. It's easy to get in during the week, but prepare to wait in line on the weekends. *Burgring 1.* ☎ *043/532-4241. www.volksgarten.at. Tram: 1, 2, or D.*

Gay Scene

➔**Alfi's Goldener Spiegel** The most enduring gay restaurant in Vienna is also the most popular gay bar. The place is very meat-market, and the bar is open Wednesday to Monday from 7pm to 2am. *Linke Viennazeile 46.* ☎ *01/586-6608. U-Bahn: Kettenbrückengasse.*

➔**Eagle Bar** This is one of the premier leather and denim bars for gay men in Vienna. There's no dancing, but virtually every gay male in town has dropped in at least once or twice for a quick look around. The bar offers a back room and distributes free condoms. Large beers begin at 2.60€. It's open daily from 9pm to 4am. *Blümelgasse 1.* ☎ *01/587-2661. U-Bahn: Neubaugasse.*

➔**Frauencafé** Frauencafé is a politically conscious cafe for gay and (to a lesser degree) heterosexual women. Established in 1977, in cramped quarters in a century-old building, it's filled with magazines, newspapers, and modern paintings, and it caters to locals and foreigners alike. Next door is a feminist bookstore with which the cafe is loosely affiliated. Glasses of wine begin at 2€. It's open Tuesday to Saturday from 6:30pm to 2am. *Langegasse 11.* ☎ *01/406-3754. U-Bahn: Lerchenfelderstrasse.*

VIENNA

Performing Arts

Cabaret

➔**First Floor** As its name implies, this worldly nightclub is one floor above street level, in an antique building in the city's

historic Jewish district. Most of the people in the metallic-looking, mostly blue space range in age from 25 to 45. There's a long, very active bar area along with a vast, artfully

Vienna Boys Choir

The 📺 Best Vienna Boys Choir ★★ was started over 500 years ago when Emperor Maximilan insisted that 12 boys become part of the court musicians and they quickly built up a reputation as world-class artists. Today, there's no better way to experience the renowned choir than to get tickets to one of their performances. They sing at locations all over Vienna, including Schönbrunn and Hofburg Palaces. Tickets can be bought online at www.wsk.at and run anywhere from 5€ to 29€ depending on the time of year.

illuminated aquarium. Mixed drinks cost 8€ to 14€ each. There's live music—usually only a piano and bass—on Monday night. Hours are Monday to Saturday 7pm to 4am, Sunday 8pm to 3am. *Seitenstettengasse 5.* ☎ *01/533-7866. U-Bahn: Schwedenplatz.*

Opera & Classical Music

→ **Musikverein** Consider yourself lucky if you get to hear the Vienna Philharmonic here. One of the Musikverein's two concert halls, the Golden Hall, has often served as the setting for TV productions. Out of the 600 or so concerts per season (Sept—June), the Vienna Philharmonic plays only 10 to 12. These are usually subscription concerts, sold out long in advance. Standing room is available at almost any concert, but you must line up hours before the show. *Karlsplatz 6.* ☎ *01/505-8190 (box office). www.musikverein.at. Tickets 3€—120€ for seats, 3€—7€ for standing room. Box office Mon—Fri 9am—7:30pm, Sat 9am—5pm. U-Bahn: Karlsplatz.*

→ **Weiner Staatsoper (State Opera)** Opera is sacred in Vienna—when World War II was over, the city's top priority was the restoration of the heavily damaged Staatsoper. With the Vienna Philharmonic Orchestra in the pit, the leading opera stars of the world perform at the legendary opera house. In their day, Richard Strauss and Gustav Mahler worked as directors. Daily performances run from September 1 until the end of June. Tickets are hard to get but worth the effort. *Opernring 2.* ☎ *01/514-442-960. www.Viennaer-staatsoper.at. Tickets 10€—178€. Tours 4.50€ per person. Check board outside the entrance for tour times. U-Bahn: Karlsplatz.*

Theater

→ **Theater in der Josefstadt** ★ One of the most influential theaters in the German-speaking world, this institution reached legendary heights of excellence under the aegis of Max Reinhardt beginning in 1924. Built in 1776, it presents a variety of comedies and dramas. *Josefstädterstrasse 26.* ☎ *01/42700. www.josefstadt.org. Tickets 3€—46€. Box office daily 10am—7:30pm. U-Bahn: Rathaus. Tram: J. Bus: 13A.*

→ **Vienna's English Theatre** This popular English-speaking theater was established in 1963. Many international actors and celebrities have appeared on the neo-baroque theater's stage. Princess Grace of Monaco once took part in a performance to raise money for charity. The theater occasionally presents works by American playwrights. *Josefsgasse 12.* ☎ *01/4021-2600. www.englishtheatre.at. Tickets 20€—36€. Box office Mon—Fri 10am—5pm, Sat 10am—4pm. U-Bahn: Rathaus. Tram: J. Bus: 13A.*

Sightseeing

It's possible to spend a week here and only touch the surface of this multifaceted city. We'll take you through the highlights, but even this venture will take more than a week of fast-paced walking. No matter how much time you have, don't miss the Inner

City, Schönbrunn Palace, Hofburg Palace, Belvedere Palace, Kunsthistorisches Museum, and St. Stephan's Cathedral.

The Inner City is truly the heart of Vienna. Here you'll find some of the city's best shopping, cafes, the casino, and St. Stephan's Cathedral. This area also features an array of street performers such as authentic Austrian singers, dancers, and instrumentalists.

Festivals

January & February

🎦 Best **New Year's Eve/Fasching.** The famed concert of the Vienna Philharmonic Orchestra launches Vienna's biggest night. The New Year also marks the beginning of **Fasching,** the famous Vienna Carnival season, which lasts through Shrove Tuesday (Mardi Gras). For tickets and information, contact the Viennaer Philharmoniker (Bösendorferstrasse 12; ☎ 01/505-6525; www.Viennaerphilharmoniker.at). The **Imperial Ball** in the Hofburg follows the concert. For information and tickets, contact the WKV (Hofburg, Heldenplatz; ☎ 01/587-3666; www.valhol.com/vienna ball.shtml). New Year's Eve/New Year's Day to Shrove Tuesday.

May to August

International Music Festival. This traditional highlight of Vienna's concert calendar features top-class international orchestras, distinguished conductors, and classical greats. You can hear Beethoven's *Eroica* as it was meant to be played, Mozart's *Jupiter Symphony,* and perhaps Bruckner's *Romantic.* The list of conductors and orchestras reads like a "who's who" of the international world of music. The venue and the booking address is Viennaer Musikverein (Lothringerstrasse 20; ☎ 01/242-002). Early May through late June.

Vienna Jazz Festival. This is one of the world's top jazz events, using the Vienna State Opera as its central venue. The program

calls for appearances by more than 50 international and local stars. For information and bookings, contact the Vienna Jazz Festival (Frankenberggasse 13; ☎ 01/503-561; www. viennajazz.org). Late June to early July.

Music Film Festival. Opera, operetta, and masterly concert performances captured on celluloid play free under a starry sky in front of the neo-Gothic City Hall on the Ringstrasse. Programs focus on works by Franz Schubert, Johannes Brahms, or other composers. You might view Rudolf Nureyev in *Swan Lake* or see Leonard Bernstein wielding the baton for Brahms. For more information, contact Ideenagentur Austria (Opernring 1R; ☎ 01/587-0150). July and August.

October & November

Vienna Modern. Celebrating its 20th year in 2007, the Vienna Modern was founded by Claudio Abbado and is devoted to the performance of contemporary music. You might catch works from Iceland, Romania, or Portugal in addition to Austria. Some of the composers make live appearances and discuss their compositions. Performances are at Verein Vienna Modern, Lothringerstrasse 20; the booking address is Viennaer Konzerthaus (Lothringerstrasse 20; ☎ 01/242-002; www. Viennamodern.at). Late October through late November.

Historic Buildings

🎦 Best ➔ **Belvedere Palace** ★★ This is one of the most famous baroque palaces in the world. It consists of an upper and lower half and magical gardens that wind between the two. The palace was first built for military strategist Prince Eugene of Savoy in the 18th century and it was the residence of Archduke Franz Ferdinand, whose assassination sparked World War I.

The **Oberes Belvedere (Upper Belvedere)** houses the **Galerie des 19. und 20. Jahrhunderts (Gallery of 19th- and 20th-Century Art)** ★. Here you also find the works by the artists of the 1897 Secessionist movement. Most outstanding are those by Gustav Klimt (1862–1918), one of the movement's founders. Notable works on display are *The Kiss, Adam and Eve,* and five panoramic lakeside landscapes from Attersee. Sharing almost equal billing with Klimt is Egon Schiele (1890–1918), whose masterpieces on display include *The Wife of an Artist.* Works by Vincent van Gogh, Oskar Kokoschka, James Ensor, and C. D. Freidrich are also represented.

Lower Belvedere houses the **Barock-museum (Museum of Baroque Art).** The original sculptures from the Neuer Markt fountain (replaced now by copies) and the work of Georg Raphael Donner, who died in 1741, are displayed here. **Museum Mittelalterlicher Kunst (Museum of Medieval Art)** is in the Orangery at Lower Belvedere. Here you'll see art from the Gothic period as well as a Tyrolean Romanesque crucifix that dates from the 12th century. Outstanding works include Rueland Frueauf's seven panels depicting scenes from the life of the Madonna and the Passion of Christ.

I recommend starting your tour of Belvedere at the top of the palace, where you can view the Art Nouveau artwork and then amble around the gardens on your way down to the lower palace. Belvedere is a bit of a walk from the Inner City, so a taxi might be a good option. *6 Rennweg.* ☎ *043/7955-7134. www.belvedere.at. Admission 7.50€. Tues–Sun 10am–6pm. Tram: D to Schloss Belvedere.*

→ **Domkirche St. Stephan (St. Stephan's Cathedral)** ★★ This cathedral is easily considered the best and most popular tourist attraction in Vienna. It's been around since the 12th century when it was built in the center of the Inner City. The original Dom was destroyed by fire in 1258, and toward the end of the 14th century, the cathedral was rebuilt using Gothic architecture. The steeple at the top of the cathedral rises 137m (450 ft.) into the air—making it a

great landmark for finding your way around the city.

You can take a guided or audio tour of the interior. Definitely climb up the 343-step tower at the back of the cathedral; the top boasts exhilarating views of the city. The climb is not for the claustrophobic, though—you'll have to work your way up a dark, windy, steep staircase. Also be prepared for bars and railings on top, which makes for a slightly blocked view. *Stephansplatz 1. (Center of the Inner City).* ☎ *01/515-5253. www.stephanskirche.at. Free admission to cathedral; guided tour for cathedral 3€; tower 3.50€. Daily 9am–5:30pm. U-Bahn: Stephansplatz.*

TV Best → Hofburg Palace Complex (Imperial Palace Complex) ★★★ Once the winter palace of the Habsburgs, the vast and impressive Hofburg sits in the heart of Vienna. This complex of imperial edifices, the first of which was constructed in 1279, grew with the empire, and today the palace is virtually a city within a city. Inside the Hofburg complex you will find the **Albertina Museum** (see below), the **Church of the Augustinians,** the **Imperial Apartments,** home of the Vienna Boys Choir (see the box, earlier in this chapter), the **Lipizzaner Museum** (see below), and the **Neue Hofburg museums.** The palace is also home to the **Schatzkammer,** the greatest treasury in the world.

Allow at least a few hours to wander around here. *Michaelerplatz.* ☎ *01/587-5554. Free admission (prices for attractions inside Hofburg listed below). Daily 9am–5pm. See hours for separate attractions below. U-Bahn: Stephansplatz, Herrengasse, or Mariahilferstrasse. Tram: D, J, 1, or 2.*

TV Best → Schönbrunn Palace ★★ Another day, another palace built for the Habsburg dynasty. This palace was constructed for Emperor Leopold I's son, Joseph I. Maria Theresa used this as her summer home for many years and Mozart played here at only 6 years of age. Nowadays, it's one of the best attractions in Austria. Imagine an ancient and super-size version of the White House and you'll get a sense of its appeal.

Though damaged in World War II, Schönbrunn has been restored to its original baroque splendor. Make sure to view the beautiful Imperial Gardens and to take in all the architecture and monuments. Also check out the State Apartments if you want to get a daily dose of bling—most are literally covered in gold. Tours run every half-hour and are about 50 minutes long. *Schönbrunn Schlosstrasse.* ☎ *01/8113. www.schoenbrunn. at. Admission 9.80€. Daily 9am–4:30pm. U-Bahn: Schönbrunn.*

→**Secession Building** ★ Come here if for no other reason than to see Gustav Klimt's *Beethoven Frieze,* a 30m-long (99-ft.) visual interpretation of Beethoven's *Ninth Symphony.* This building—a virtual art manifesto proclamation—was the home of the Viennese avant-garde, which extolled the glories of *Jugendstil* (Art Nouveau). A young group of painters and architects launched the Secessionist movement in 1897 in rebellion against the strict, conservative ideas of the official Academy of Fine Arts. Gustav Klimt was a leader of the movement, which defied the historicism favored by the Emperor Franz Joseph.

Today works by the Secessionist artists are on display in the Belvedere Palace, and this building is used for substantial contemporary exhibits. It was constructed in 1898 and is crowned by a dome once called "outrageous in its useless luxury." The empty dome—covered in triumphal laurel leaves—echoes that of the Karlskirche on the other side of Vienna. *Friedrichstrasse 12 (west side of Karlsplatz).* ☎ *01/5875-3070. www. secession.at/building/menu_e.html. Admission 5.50€ adults. Tues–Wed and Fri–Sun*

10am–6pm; Thurs 10am–8pm. U-Bahn: Karlsplatz.

Museums & Art Galleries

→**Albertina** This massive gallery is one of the most buzzed about in Vienna. Exhibits change every 3 months or so, but typically focus on modern and postmodern art. This place also holds the greatest collection of graphic art in the world. *Albertinaplatz.* ☎ *043/53483. www.albertina.at. Admission 9€. Thurs–Tues 10am–6pm; Wed 10am–9pm. U-Bahn: Stephansplatz, Herrengasse, or Mariahilferstrasse. Tram: 1, 2, D, or J to Burgring.*

→**Kunsthistorisches Museum (Museum of Fine Art)** ★ Come here to pay a visit to the remaining Habsburgs artwork collection. The museum is well known for its Egyptian and Greek influenced artwork and expansive Albrect Dürer (a famous German painter) collection. It's located right across from the Hofburg complex. *Maria-Theresien-Platz 5. Burgring.* ☎ *01/ 5252-4405. www.khm.at. Admission 9€ adults, 6.50€ students. Daily 10am–6pm. U-Bahn: Mariahilferstrasse. Tram: D.*

→**Lipizzaner Museum** The latest attraction at Hofburg Palace is this museum near the stables of the famous white stallions. This permanent exhibition begins with the historic inception of the Spanish Riding School in the 16th century and extends to the stallions' near destruction in the closing weeks of World War II. Paintings, historic engravings, drawings, photographs, uniforms and bridles, plus video and film presentations bring to life the history of the Spanish Riding School, offering an insight into the breeding and training of the champion horses. Visitors to the museum are able to see through a window into the stallions' stables while they are being fed and saddled. *Reitschulgasse 2, Stallburg.* ☎ *01/533-7811. www.lipizzaner.at. Admission 9€ adults. Daily 9am–6pm.*

VIENNA

The Museums Quarter

The **MuseumQuartier Complex** ★★, new to Vienna in 2001, is the cultural center of the city. One of the 10 largest cultural complexes in the world, it is like combining New York's Guggenheim Museum, Museum of Modern Art, and Brooklyn Academy of Music, plus a children's museum, an architecture and design center, theaters, art galleries, video workshops, and much more. There's even an ecology center, architecture museum, and, yes, a tobacco museum. Plan to spend *at least* half a day wandering through the different exhibits at all of the museums. Here are the highlights:

Kunsthalle This small museum is home to cutting-edge local and international contemporary art, focusing on photography, video, film, and new media. You'll find works by everyone from Picasso and Joan Miró to Jackson Pollock and Paul Klee, from Wassily Kandinsky to Andy Warhol and, surprise, Yoko Ono. *Museumplatz 1.* ☎ *01/521-8933. www.kunsthalleVienna.at. Admission 6.50€. Daily 10am–7pm (Thurs till 10pm). U-Bahn: MuseumQuartier.*

Leopold Museum Rudolph Leopold was a famous Austrian painter who specialized in collecting 19th-century and modern art. And what a collection it is: Austrian modernist masterpieces include paintings by Egon Schiele, Oskar Kokoschka, the great Gustav Klimt, Anton Romaki, and Richard Gerstl. Major statements in Arts and Crafts from the late 19th and 20th centuries include works by Josef Hoffmann, Kolo Moser, Adolf Loos, and Franz Hagenauer. *Museumsplatz 1.* ☎ *01/52570. www.Leopoldmuseum.com. Admission 6€ student, 9€ adults. Mon and Wed–Thurs 11am–7pm; Fri 11am–9pm; Sat–Sun 10am–7pm. U-Bahn: MuseumQuartier.*

Mumok This museum exhibits mainly American pop art, mixed with concurrent continental movements such as Hyperrealism of the 1960s and 1970s. *Museum of Modemer Kunst. Museumplatz 1.* ☎ *01/52500. www.mumok.at. Admission 8€. Daily 9am–6pm. U-Bahn: MuseumQuartier.*

→ **Sigmund Freud Haus** Walking through this museum, you can almost imagine the good doctor ushering you in and telling you to make yourself comfortable on the couch. Antiques and mementos, including his velour hat and dark walking stick with ivory handle, fill the study and waiting room he used during his residence here from 1891 to 1938. The museum also has a bookshop with a variety of postcards of the apartment, books by Freud, posters, prints, and pens. *Berggasse 19.* ☎ *01/319-1596. www.freud-museum.at. Admission 5€ adults, 3€ seniors and students. Daily 9am–6pm. Tram: D to Schlickgasse.*

University Scene

The Alsergrund (ninth district) is considered to be the city's main academic quarter, though the **University of Vienna (Universität Wien)** that's here also has a campus in the Inner City, and buildings elsewhere in the city. For info on becoming a student, visit the main info office at Dr. Karl Lueger, Ring 1 (☎ **314-2770;** www.univie.ac.at).

Hit **Mariahliferstrasse** in the sixth district for some seriously trendy shopping and to rub elbows with the city's university students. It's lined with the hottest fashions for young people, so it's not surprising that young people are everywhere. The nearby **Flohmarkt** (p. 946) is another good place to hobnob with local coeds.

12 Hours in Vienna

1. **Take in St. Stephan's Cathedral.** Climb up to the top of this cathedral for some gorgeous views of the city—it'll help you get the lay of the land before you plunge further into your visit.
2. **Visit Schönbrunn Palace or Hofburg Palace.** You can't go wrong with a trip to either of these lavish palaces, though you might find it hard to ignore the museums within and near the Hofburg even if you're strapped for time.
3. **Get your caffeine fix.** Spend some time sipping coffee or tea at one of the city's many outside cafes, and brace yourself for some major people-watching. While you're at it, go ahead and treat yourself to some cake—I hear the *sachertorte* isn't too shabby.
4. **Soak in some art.** Hit up either the **Belvedere Palace** or the **MuseumQuartier Complex** to satisfy your inner Art Nouveau fan.
5. **Play some pool:** Many of the bars you'll pass in the Inner City have billiards where you'll spot locals hanging out. Pick a pool table and start watching one game. Make eye contact and you're bound to be asked to join in.
6. **Get lost in the Bermuda Triangle.** Wander to whichever of the clubs or bars in the Bermuda Triangle has the most happening crowd. Still feel like catching that train after dancing with the hot locals?

Playing Outside

Biking

Vienna maintains almost 322km (200 miles) of bike lanes and paths, some of which meander through the most elegant parks in Europe. To find them, look for either a yellow image of a cyclist stenciled directly onto the pavement, or rows of red brick set amid the cobblestones or concrete of the busy boulevards in the city center. See "Getting Around: By Bicycle" earlier in this chapter for more information.

Hiking

You're likely to expend plenty of shoe leather simply walking around Vienna, but if you yearn for a more isolated setting, the city tourist offices will provide information about its eight **Stadt-Wander-Wege.** These marked hiking paths usually originate at a stop on the city's far-flung network of trams.

You can also head east of town into the vast precincts of the **Lainzer Tiergarten,** where hiking trails meander amid forested hills, colonies of deer, and tons of birdlife. To get there, first take the U-Bahn to the Kennedy Brücke/Hietzing station, which lies a few steps from the entrance to Schönbrunn Palace. Take tram no. 60, then bus no. 60B.

Parks & Gardens

📺 **Best** → **Praterverband (the Prater)** ★★ This extensive tract of woods and meadowland in the second district has been Vienna's favorite recreation area since 1766, when Emperor Joseph II opened it to the public. The Prater is probably the most loosely organized amusement park in Europe—it's more a public park that happens to have rides and food kiosks sprouting from the flowerbeds and statuary. Few other spots in Vienna convey such a sense of the decadent end of the Habsburg Empire—it's turn-of-the-20th-century nostalgia, with a touch of 1950s-era tawdriness.

VIENNA

The 65m-tall (213-ft.) 🎬 Best Prater Ferris Wheel is the highlight here—it's considered the second most famous attraction in Vienna after St. Stephan's. It takes 20 minutes to rotate around and was built in 1897—hence the old-style carts. *Prater 90.* ☎ *043/729-5430. www.wienerriesenrad.com. Free admission; pay for rides, games; Ferris wheel 7.50€. May–Sept daily 10am–midnight, Oct 10am–10pm, Nov–Dec 10am–8pm. U-Bahn: Praterstern.*

→ **StadtPark** Right off the Inner City is the entrance to Stadtpark, a lush stretch of green with benches, a cafe, and a playground. Once you enter the park, the hustle and bustle of Vienna seems to come to a halt—it's a great place to re-energize and literally stop to smell the flowers. (Flowers of every shade of pink, red, and purple are well maintained around the park's premise.) *Tram: 1, 2, T, or J.*

→ **Vienna Woods** The Vienna Woods (Viennaerwald in German) weren't something Johann Strauss (II) dreamed up to enliven his musical tales told in waltz time. The Viennaerwald is a delightful hilly landscape of gentle paths and trees that borders Vienna on the southwest and northwest. If you stroll through this area, a weekend playground for the Viennese, you'll be following in the footsteps of Beethoven, Strauss, and Schubert.

A round-trip through the woods, a distance of some 80km (50 miles), takes about $3^1/_2$ hours by car. Even if you don't have a car, visiting the woods is relatively easy. Board tram no. 1, going to Schottentor; there, switch to tram no. 38 (the same ticket is valid) going out to the village of **Grinzing,** home to the famous *heurigen* (wine taverns). If you can resist the heurigen, board bus no. 38A, which goes through the Viennaerwald up the hill to **Kahlenberg,** on the northeasternmost spur of the Alps (483m/1,585 ft.). The whole trip takes about 1 hour each way.

Skiing

Limited skiing is available on the **Hohe Wand,** west of town. To reach it, ride the U4 subway to the Hütteldorf station, then take bus no. 49B to the city's 14th district. The area around the Semmering (about an hour from the city) is a favorite quick skiing getaway. For information on skiing in Austria, contact the **Austrian National Tourist Office** (p. 927).

Cruising the Danube

Its waters aren't as idyllic as the Strauss waltz would lead you to believe, and its color is usually muddy brown rather than blue. But despite these drawbacks, many visitors to Austria view a day cruise along the Danube as a highlight of their trip. Until the advent of railroads and highways, the Danube played a vital role in Austria's history, helping build the complex mercantile society that eventually begat the Habsburg Empire.

The most professional cruise line is the **DDSG Blue Danube Steamship Co.** (Donau-Dampfschiffahrts-Gesellschafts "Blue Danube"; Fredrickstrasse 7; ☎ 01/588-800; www.ddsg-blue-danube.at). The most appealing cruise, through the Wachau region east of Vienna, operates from April to October between Vienna and Dürnstein. The cruise departs every Sunday at 8:45am from the company's piers at Handelskai 265, arriving in Dürnstein about 5¾ hours later. The one-way cost is 17€ for adults. To reach the Vienna piers, take U-Bahn line U1 to Vorgartenstrasse, about 7.2km (4½ miles) from St. Stephansplatz.

Swimming

Despite the popularity of certain beaches on islands in the Alte Donau Canal in summer, swimming in either the Danube or any of its satellite canals is not recommended because of pollution and a dangerous undertow in the main river.

Vienna has dozens of swimming pools, though. Your hotel's reception can tell you about options in your neighborhood. One of the most modern is in the Prater. For pool locations and information, contact Rathaus (City Hall; Friedrich Schmidt-Platz; ☎ **01/40005**).

Shopping

Vienna's main shopping streets are in the city center (first district). Here you'll find **Kohlmarkt,** between the Graben and Michaelerplatz (U-Bahn: Herrengasse); and **Rotenturmstrasse,** between Stephansplatz and Kai (U-Bahn: Stephansplatz). Both streets are destinations for more expensive, designer wares. Less high-market stuff can be found on **Kärntnerstrasse,** between the State Opera and Stock-im-Eisen-Platz (U-Bahn: Karlsplatz) and **Mariahilferstrasse** (p. 926), between Babenbergerstrasse and Schönbrunn.

Another famous shopping area in the city center is **Graben Street,** home to big-name international brands like Vuitton, Chanel, Monte Blanc, Gucci, and other major designers. This street is only a 5- or 10-minute walk from Stephansplatz. It's to be avoided or embraced, depending on your view of the world.

Shops are normally open Monday to Friday from 9am to 6pm, and Saturday from 9am to 1pm. Small shops close between noon and 2pm for lunch. Shops in the Westbahnhof and Südbahnhof railroad stations are open daily from 7am to 11pm, offering groceries, smokers' supplies, stationery, books, and flowers.

→**Arcadia Opera Shop** This respected record store is one of the best for classical music. The well-educated staff knows the music and performers (as well as the availability of recordings) and is usually eager to share that knowledge. The shop also carries books on art, music, architecture, and opera, as well as an assortment of musical memorabilia. The shop is on the street level of the Vienna State Opera, with a separate entrance on Kärntnerstrasse. Guided tours of the splendid opera house end here. *Viennaer Staatsoper, Kärntnerstrasse 40.* ☎ *01/513-9568.*

→**The British Bookshop** This is the largest and most comprehensive emporium of English-language books in Austria, with a sprawling ground-floor showroom loaded with American, Australian, and English books. There are no periodicals, and no cute gift displays. All you'll find is enough reading material to last you for the rest of your life, and educational aids for teaching English as a second language. *Weihburggasse 24–26.* ☎ *01/512-1945.*

→**Casselli** Young shop assistants throughout downtown Vienna swear by this place for both casual clothes and experimental evening wear. You might enjoy rummaging through the racks to discover an Italian made or Austrian find. *In the Ringstrassen Galleries, Kärntner Ring 5–7.* ☎ *01/512-5350.*

→**Humana** ★ If you're up for scrounging through the new and used clothing on the racks at this secondhand store, you'll likely find yourself a 1980s-ready T-shirt or two. Discriminating eyes may also spot some designer-worthy contemporary ware, at less than designer prices. *Perfektastrasse 86–88.* ☎ *869/3813.*

→**The Ringstrassen Galleries** This shopping complex is a great place to window-shop. Upstairs in the Ringstrassen you will find a few trendy boutiques that carry

VIENNA

designer brands like Miss Sixty, Seven, Juicy, and True Religion. Ringstrassen is located right next to the Grand Hotel at the Inner City. Each shop is operated independently, but virtually all of them conduct business Monday to Friday 10am to 7pm, and Saturday 10am to 5pm. Stores here of particular interest to fashion hounds include **Casselli** (p. 945). *In the Palais Corso and in the Kärntnerringhof, Kärntner Ring 5–13.* ☎ *01/512-8111.*

→ **Steffl** This big department store is a lot like Macy's, with a little of everything for men, women, juniors, and children. Downstairs is the pricey designer stuff (Miss Sixty, Diesel, Cavalli, Boss, and so on) and on the top level (seven) is the Sky Bar and Sky Café. It's a great place to snack on moderately priced grub while sitting outside and enjoying the great view of the city. *Kärntnerstrasse 19.* ☎ *01/514-310.*

Markets

→ **Flohmarkt** ★ You'll find a little of everything at this flea market near Naschmarkt.

It's held every Saturday from 6:30am to 6pm, except on holidays. Everything you've ever wanted is here, especially if you're seeking chunky Swiss watches from the 1970s, glassware from the Czech Republic, and even Russian icons. Believe it or not, some of this stuff is original; other merchandise is simply knockoff. *Linke Wienzeile. U-Bahn: Karlsplatz.*

MTV Best → **Naschmarkt** ★★ This colorful open-air market is quintessential Vienna. Come here on Saturday morning, and you'll see 3 blocks of vendors, all trying their hardest to seduce shoppers with their array of fresh vegetables, olives, fresh fruit, nuts, meats, and different trinkets. At the end of the strip of vendors, you'll find a section filled with old clothes and toys—thrift-shop paradise, for some. Located at Viennazeile in the sixth district. It's open Monday to Friday from 6am to 6:30pm and Saturday 6am to 5pm. Prices can be negotiated. *U-Bahn: Karlsplatz.*

Road Trip

Salzburg—home to Mozart and hills "alive with the *Sound of Music*"—is probably the quaintest city reviewed in this guide. If the city doesn't excel at cutting-edge museums or restaurants, however, its picturesque setting among Alpine peaks on both banks of the Salzach River more than makes up for it. Skiers who want some urban time can use Salzburg as a base and try out a different ski village each day of the week. When the weather's nice, the city livens up with outdoor music and art festivals. See how many royals and other upper crust folks, eager for an excuse to break out their gowns and jewels, you can spot at the most famous event—the classical music fest in August. Just remember that the city's not all about Mozart and musicals. Red Bull was invented around here, and you'll need some liquid

energy if you want to experience the city's growing nightlife scene. When the sun sets, the bars—especially beer gardens—*do* get crowded.

Getting into Town

GETTING THERE

The Salzbug Airport—WA Mozart (Innsbrucker Bundesstrasse 95; ☎ **662/ 8580;** www.salzburg-airport.com) is 3.2km (2 miles) from the city center. Bus no. 77 runs frequently from the airport to Salzburg's main train station. The ride is approximately 20 minutes, and costs 2.80€. You can walk right into town from the train station. A taxi ride into town is faster than the bus but costs much more—approximately 15€. You can call a taxi in advance at ☎ **662/8111.**

Salzburg's train station is **Salzburg Hauptbahnhof** (☎ 05/1717 for all rail information). Trains arrive from and depart for Vienna every half-hour between 5:05am and 8:05pm and take approximately 3¹/₂ hours; the one-way fare is 25€. Trains run to other major European cities, such as Munich, too.

GETTING AROUND

From the train station, buses depart to various parts of the city, including the Altstadt (Old Town). Or you can walk from the rail station to the Old Town in about 20 minutes. The rail station has a currency exchange, storage lockers, and ticket-selling windows.

Walking around Salzburg is one of the best ways to see the city, especially the Old Town and Residenz areas. Note that driving is pretty much impossible.

Salzburg Basics

ORIENTATION

Most of what visitors come to see lies on the left bank of the Salzach River in the **Altstadt (Old Town)**. If you're driving, you must leave your car in the modern part of town—the right bank of the Salzach—and enter the Old Town on foot, as most of it is for pedestrians only.

The heart of the inner city is **Residenzplatz**, which has the largest and finest baroque fountain this side of the Alps. On the western side of the square stands the **Residenz**, palace of the prince-archbishops, and on the southern side of the square is the **Salzburg Cathedral** (or Dom). To the west of the Dom lies **Domplatz**, linked by archways dating from 1658. Squares to the north and south appear totally enclosed. On the southern side of Max-Reinhardt-Platz and Hofstallgasse, edging toward **Mönchsberg**, stands the **Festspielhaus (Festival Theater)**, built on the foundations of the 17th-century court stables.

Discount Passes

The **Salzburg Card** lets you use unlimited public transportation, and it's an admission ticket to the city's most important cultural sights. With the card you can visit Mozart's birthplace, the Hohensalzburg Fortress, the Residenz gallery, the world-famous water fountain gardens at Hellbrunn, the Baroque Museum in the Mirabell Gardens, and the gala rooms in the Archbishop's Residence. The card is also good for sights outside of town, including the Hellbrunn Zoo, the open-air museum in Grossingmain, the salt mines of the Dürnberg, and the gondola trip at Untersberg. The card, approximately the size of a credit card, comes with a brochure with maps and sightseeing hints.

Cards are valid for 24, 48, and 72 hours and cost 19€, 27€, and 33€, respectively. You can buy the pass from Salzburg travel agencies, hotels, tobacconists, and municipal offices.

TOURIST OFFICE

The **Salzburg Information Office** (Mozartplatz 5; ☎ 662/8898-7330; www.salzburginfo.at; bus: 5, 6, or 51) is open in summer daily from 9am to 8pm and off season Monday through Saturday from 9am to 6pm. There's also a tourist information office on Platform 2A of the Hauptbahnhof, Südtirolerplatz (☎ 662/8888-7340).

Sleeping

📺 Best →**Goldener Hirsch** ★★★
This is one of Europe's most famous hotels, legendary for having pampered countless prestigious guests within its three medieval buildings over the years. Just a few doors away from the couture shopping and famous

attractions of Salzburg, the hotel's premier location matches its impressive guest list. If you really want to spend a chunk of money, this hotel is for you. Rooms are spacious and are decorated with a variety of antique and modern furniture and 15th-century accents. Goldener Hirsch also houses two amazing restaurants and a bar—perfect spots to hob-nob with rich folks from all over the world. *Getreidegasse 37, Salzburg.* ☎ *800/325-3535. www.goldenerhirsch.com. 157€–660€ double, 395€–1,110€ suite. Higher rates at festival time. Amenities: 2 restaurants; bar; babysit-ting; laundry service/dry cleaning; nonsmok-ing rooms. 24-hr. room service; In room: A/C, TV, dataport, hair dryer, minibar, safe.*

→ **Yoho International Youth Hostel** If you want to party and meet people in Salzburg, definitely stay at this backpacker's party haven. Although the bathrooms had some dust and toilet paper on the floor, Yoho is a good value for the money. There's a cheap restaurant and bar that is very accommodating to the many late-night partyers. Be prepared—evenings here get pretty loud. Though most of the party stays downstairs, this isn't the best place to go to bed at 10pm. The hostel is located within walk-ing distance to the Old Town. *Peracelsusstrase 9 Salzburg.* ☎ *662/819-649. www.yoho.at. Prices are per person and depend on room size. 28€ single, 21€ double, 19€ triple, 18€ quad, 17€ 6-person dorm, 16€ 8-person dorm. Showers are available within room for an extra 3€–4€. Amenities: Restaurant; bar; Internet; TV (in common room). In room: Shared bath-rooms, sheets (5€ deposit).*

Eating

→ **Café Tomaselli** ★ CAFE The oldest cafe in Salzburg, Café Tomaselli is a must-stop for tourists and locals, who come for the history but stay for the variety of tasty treats and piping-hot beverages. Its outside patio, smack dab in Old Town, allows for some of the best people-watching in the city. *Alter Markt 9, Salzburg.* ☎ *662/844-488. Snacks 2€ and up. Mon–Sat 7am–midnight; Sun 8am–9pm. Bus: 5, 6, or 55.*

→ **Ristorante Pizzeria al Sole** ITALIAN/ PIZZERIA I have to agree with the many tourists and locals who love this small, tradi-tional Italian restaurant. The pizza and pasta are great; the penne pasta with shrimp is my favorite, though this place is famous for its ham, salami, artichoke, and mozzarella pizza. The owner often stops by diners' tables to make recommendations. *Gstattengasse 15, Salzburg.* ☎ *662/843-284. Pizza/dishes 7€–9€. Daily 11:30am–2pm and 5:30pm–mid-night. Bus: 1, 27, or 49.*

Partying

The club/bar scene in Salzburg is much qui-eter and more casual than in Vienna. Salzburg excels in the bar department; the bar scene is hot from about 10pm to 4am, with some places open until 6am.

[MTV] [Best] → **Die Wiesse** ★★ Filled with young men dressed casually sexy and the occasional clan of sexy young women, this brewery is quite the pickup factory. It gets really buzzing around midnight, when the young set comes to chug a few down. This brewery was my favorite late-night spot in Salzburg because it's young and spirited yet laid-back—think many down-to-earth, good-looking people and no one trying too hard to fit in. It gets crowded, though; I recommend arriving around 10:30pm. During the day this place functions more as a restaurant. *Rupertgasse 10, Salzburg.* ☎ *662/872-2460.*

[MTV] [Best] → **Hangar 7** ★★ The Red Bull king, Dietrich Mateschitz (aka Red Bull founder and Salzburg socialite), built this bar/airplane hangar to house his private jets and array of Red Bull memorabilia. The space also happens to hold Austria's trendi-est bar. The bar on the third-floor balcony of the hangar overlooks the airplanes and has a touch-feature where you can send messages to other people seated around the bar—very flirtatious and very clever. Drinks are moderately priced and comfortable seating surrounds the bar, cafe, and restaurant. Dress to impress, and come prepared to pay to get here: Fittingly, it's located near the airport so you'll need to take a taxi, which can run 8€ to 25€. *Salzburg Airport, Wilhelm-Spazier-Str. 7A, Salzburg.* ☎ *662/2197. www.hangar-7. com.*

→**Rockhouse** The best alternative music club in town, Rockhouse also has a cafe. Local and European bands are booked to play this tunnel-like venue, which offers everything from blues, funk, and jazz to techno pop. Sometimes groups from the United States or even Africa appear here. The structure itself is from the 1840s, having once been a wine cellar and ice-storage depot. Call to see what's happening at the time of your visit. *Schallmooser Hauptstrasse 46, Salzburg.* ☎ *662/884-914. Cover 7€–20€ (depending on the act). Bus: 68 or 81.*

Performing Arts

→**Mozart Dinner Concert** ★★ One of the most culturally alive experiences I had in Salzburg was attending this dinner show, which takes place at beautiful and historic St. Peter's Church. You'll feel like you're at a gala dinner—which in fact, you are. The set-up for the night is music, food, music, food, and so on. You get a three-course meal that is absolutely delicious. The music is Mozart, played by students from the Salzburg school of music and accompanied by two opera singers. I usually snooze through classical music, but it really works in this setting. Dress up a little bit and call ahead for reservations. I recommend arriving 15 minutes prior to your reservation for the best house seating. *Peterplatz, Salzburg.* ☎ *662/828-695. www.salzburg-concerts.com. 45€ adults, 33€ students 26 and under.*

Sightseeing

📺 Best →**The Original** *Sound of Music* **Tour** ★★ "The hills are alive . . ." That's right, cheesy musical fans, this 4-hour tour pays homage to one of the most-watched American musicals ever, and by golly, it's a damn good time. The tour takes you into the mountains and past Nonnberg Abbey, one of the largest convents in Europe; Mirabell Gardens where Maria dances with the children; Leopoldskron Castle, which was used as the front of the Von Trapp home; Hellbrunn Castle where the glass pavilion from the movie was reconstructed; Wedding Church Mondsee where the wedding scene with Maria and the captain was filmed; and St. Gilgen and Lake Wolfgang in Salzkammergut—a small lakeside village where some scenes were shot. The English-speaking tour-guides are filled with fun facts and information about the movie—they even play the soundtrack as you tour around. Even if you hated the film, it's a great way to soak in Salzburg's natural beauty. ☎ *662/874-029. www.panoramatours. com. Tour 35€ adults. Tour hours 9:30am and 2pm. They will pick you up at your hotel; you can buy tickets at some hotels. Bus terminal: Mirabellplatz.*

VIENNA

Best Fest

Since the 1920s, the **Salzburg Festival** has been one of Europe's premier cultural events, boasting opera, chamber music, plays, and concerts by world-class artists, along with many other cultural presentations. Always count on stagings of Mozart operas. Performances are staged in July and August at various venues throughout the city. For tickets, write several months in advance to the Salzburg Festival at Postfach 140, A-5010 Salzburg (☎ 662/8045).

→ **Dom (Salzburg Cathedral)** Located where Residenzplatz flows into Domplatz, this cathedral is world renowned for its 4,000-pipe organ. Hailed by some critics as the "most perfect" northern Renaissance building, the cathedral has a marble facade and twin symmetrical towers. The mighty bronze doors were created in 1959. The themes are Faith, Hope, and Love. The interior has a rich baroque style with elaborate frescoes, the most important of which, along with the altarpieces, were designed by Mascagni of Florence. In the crypt, traces of the old Romanesque cathedral have been unearthed.

The treasure of the cathedral and the "arts and wonders" the archbishops collected in the 17th century are displayed in the **Dom Museum** entered through the cathedral. The **cathedral excavations** around the corner (left of the Dom entrance) show the ruins of the original foundation. *South side of Residenzplatz, Salzburg.* ☎ *0662/84-41-89. Free admission to cathedral; excavations 2€ adults; museum 5€ adults, 1.50€ children. Cathedral daily 8am–7pm (till 6pm in winter); excavations May–Sept Tues–Sun 9am–5pm (closed mid-Oct to Easter); museum Wed–Sun 10am–5pm, Sun 1–6pm. Closed Nov–Apr. Bus: 1, 3, or 5.*

→ **Residenz State Rooms/Residenzgalerie Salzburg** ★ This opulent palace, just north of Domplatz in the pedestrian zone, was the seat of the Salzburg prince-archbishops after they no longer needed the protection of the gloomy Hohensalzburg Fortress of Mönchsberg. The Residenz dates from 1120, but work on its series of palaces, which comprised the ecclesiastical complex of the ruling church princes, began in the late 1500s

and continued until about 1796. The 17th-century Residenz fountain is one of the largest and most impressive baroque fountains north of the Alps. The child prodigy Mozart often played in the Conference Room for guests. More than a dozen state rooms, each richly decorated, are open to the public via guided tour. On the second floor you can visit the **Residenzgalerie Salzburg** (☎ **0662/84-04-51,** ext. 24), an art gallery containing European paintings from the 16th century to the 19th century. Note the **glockenspiel** across from the Residenz—the bells chime at 7, 11am, and 6pm daily. *Residenzplatz 1, Salzburg.* ☎ *0662/80-42-26-90 or 0662/84-04-51. Admission to Residenz State Rooms: 5€ adults, 4€ students 16–18. Combined ticket to state rooms and gallery, 7.30€. Residenzgalerie: 5€ adults, 4€ students 16–18. Jan, Mar 26–Oct, and Nov 27–Dec daily 10am–5pm. Bus: 5 or 6.*

→ **Hohensalzburg Fortress** ★★ The stronghold of the ruling prince-archbishops before they moved "downtown" to the Residenz, this fortress towers 120m (400 ft.) above the Salzach River on a rocky dolomite ledge. The massive fortress crowns the Festungsberg and literally dominates Salzburg. Work on Hohensalzburg began in 1077 and wasn't finished until 1681. This is the largest completely preserved castle in central Europe. Visit Hohensalzburg even if you're not interested in the fortress, just for the view from the terrace. From the Reck watchtower you get a panoramic sweep of the Alps. *Mönchsberg 34, Salzburg.* ☎ *0662/84-24-30-11. Admission (excluding guided tour but including museum) 7.20€ adults. Fortress and museums Oct–Mar daily 9:30am–4:30pm; Apr–Sept daily 9:30am–5:30pm.*

VIENNA

Zurich

No doubt you've heard about the glories of Swiss precision while vegging out to those *The Fabulous Life of* reruns on VH1. You know, when that announcer with the ambiguous accent sings the praises of Diddy's latest Rolex watch, and how, because it's *fabulously* Swiss, it keeps time better than any watch you could ever imagine touching? That's because for ages, Switzerland has been hyped as the world's buttoned-up headquarters for *all* things perfection, from watch manufacturing to knife-making to banking to, well, neutrality. It may seem impossible for a place to really be so darn good at everything it sets out to do, but when visiting Zurich, Switzerland's largest city, prepare to be impressed—your lofty preconceptions are probably closer to the reality of the city than you'd have imagined.

Paris is often a foreigner's first choice when visiting Europe for the first time, but for those who have traveled a lot in both riverfront cities, Zurich is frequently the preferred choice. Round almost every corner and you can see a billowing red Swiss national flag, and it's no wonder the people here are so proud of their city and their country. Amazingly clean air and water, expansive and well-maintained streets, chic residents, intact centuries-old architecture, world-renowned shopping and cultural scenes—Zurich is really all that, plus it sells the best chocolates and cheese. Its fashionable and often quite wealthy residents ensure that Zurich operates on a tight leash, which is not exactly conducive to a wild, loud nightlife or party scene. Drinks are expensive, the hot-spot clubs can be impossibly exclusive, and everything closes pretty early. The increase in visitors in recent years has helped to somewhat loosen

Zurich's conservative nature, but don't expect to find too many policies that color outside of the lines. Zurich sips, it never chugs—not exactly a place for dancing on bars, but a scene that's fun to be a part of, nonetheless.

The Best of Zurich

○ **The Best Splurge:** Views from the bedrooms of this ultracool hotel look out into the city's historic core or into a beautiful inside courtyard. If that isn't enough—the 49 rooms in the **Widder Hotel** are in eight interconnected, architecturally redesigned town houses that showcase the best of modern design. You'll have fun bankrupting yourself here. See p. 958.

○ **The Best View of Zurich:** Enjoy the breathtaking cityscape at the **Jules Verne Wine Bar**—the scenery only gets more beautiful as the wine flows. See p. 962.

○ **The Best People-Watching:** Come to town during the annual **Street Parade** in August, one of the largest gatherings for electronic music lovers in all of Europe. Over a million dressed-to-impress people flood into the streets to enjoy the peaceful, open vibe. Colorful wigs, neon glowsticks, and ridiculous fake eyelashes abound. See p. 963.

○ **The Best Cheap Date:** Pick up some snacks at one of the many COOP grocery stores in the city and head to a spot along **Lake Zurich.** Snack and snuggle as you watch the chic locals talk business on lunch breaks or just check out the sailboats drifting along. See p. 966.

○ **The Best Way to Work Up a Sweat:** On a hot summer day, you might want to make the time—1½ hours approximately—to cycle 13km (8 miles) from shaded woods to a picnic spot on the shore of the Katzensee, a lake with a beach that provides a nice break from urban touring. See p. 966.

○ **The Best Sweet Thing:** The topic of which Swiss chocolate is best is about as hotly debated here as any election is in the states. Many people swear by the goodies from **Teuscher** chocolatier. The confections created at this Old Town shop are a far cry from your typical Hershey bar—think handmade champagne truffles instead. See p. 967.

Getting There & Getting Around

Getting into Town

BY PLANE

Kloten Airport (☎ 044/816-22-11; www.zurich-airport.com) is Zurich's international airport, the largest airport in Switzerland and approximately 7km (4¼ miles) north of the city center. The taxi into town costs a hefty 55CHF to 60CHF. If you're not completely saddled with baggage, consider the much cheaper train service from the airport offered by the Swiss Federal Railways for 8CHF. Press the solid red button on the automated ticket machine, and you'll arrive 10 to 15 minutes later at the Zurich Hauptbahnhof railway station in the center of town. From the train station you can walk or hop on a tram or bus to most hotels in less than 30 minutes. Alternatively, you can purchase a 24-hour version of the same ticket for 12CHF (press the solid red button followed by the silver button with arrows). The train runs every 15 to 20 minutes between 5:36am and 12:20am—follow the train signs (it's clearly marked) to get to the station from the airport. You can also take bus no. 768 (Zurich

Airport–Seebach), but you'll have to change to tram no. 14 to get to the center of town.

BY TRAIN

Train service in Switzerland is world famous for its punctuality and professionalism. A nonstop train departs Paris Gare l'Est station at 10:42pm daily, arriving in Zurich at 6:24am; another train leaves Paris daily at 9:46am, arriving at 5:58pm in Zurich. Other connections involve changing trains in Basel, and take a bit longer. Four trains depart daily from Munich bound for Zurich, for a 4¹/₂ hour trip. There is a daily direct service from Brussels as well, a little over 8 hours long. All trains arrive at the **Zurich Hauptbahnhof** (☎ **090/030-03-00**), Zurich's main train station, which is basically at the center of everything. The Bahnhofstrasse, Zurich's main road for commerce, shopping, and restaurants, extends from the station.

BY BOAT

If you're feeling old-fashioned and are traveling from within Switzerland, consider the **Zurichsee-Schiffahrtsgesellschaft** (Mythenquai 333; ☎ **014/82-10-33**), which offers service to the city on modern passenger ships as well as steamers from both sides of Lake Zurich.

Getting Around

BY BUS & TRAM

There is no subway in Zurich, but a comprehensive and well-run system of trams and buses runs from 5:30am to 12:30am. Fare payment is based on an honor system, and you have to buy a fare card from a machine located at each stop that you redeem by stamping it yourself from a machine on the bus or tram. Don't get over-confident, though—plainclothes transit cops patrol the lines often, and if you're caught without a ticket, you'll be fined 50CHF. All the trams and buses connect at the Hauptbahnhof

train station, in the center of Zurich. A day-long ride pass can be bought for 7.50CHF, and allows for unlimited use of the system for 24 hours. It's all run by **Zurich Public Transport** (☎ **012/12-37-37**; www.vbz.ch).

You might want to get acquainted with the city by taking a 2-hour tram trolley tour, with headset (no live tour guide). Between May and October, for a fee of 32CHF, you can sign up for a tour daily at 9:45am, noon, and 2pm. The tour takes in the commercial and shopping center and Old Town, and goes along the lakefront for a visit to Fraumünster or one of the famous guildhalls beside the Limmatquai.

BY TAXI

Taxis are ridiculously expensive in Zurich. Save your francs because Zurich is expensive as it is. If you really need a taxi, your hotel or hostel can call one for you, or you can contact **Taxi-Zentrale Zurich** (☎ **012/ 72-44-44**). The basic charge before you even step into one is 6CHF, plus 3.50CHF for each kilometer you travel (and, as you know, kilometers click off twice as fast as miles).

BY BICYCLE

MTV Best **Biking** is popular here, and you'll find many bike paths and trails. Bicycles can be rented at the baggage counter of the railway station, the **Hauptbahnhof** (☎ **051/222-29-04**), for 27CHF for a city bike per day or 21CHF for a half-day. Hours are daily from 7am to 7:30pm.

ON FOOT

If the weather is nice, there's really no better way to see the city than by walking. Many of the roads in the Old Town are narrow, cobblestone streets that are best explored the old-fashioned way. Most roads have sidewalks, and pedestrians have the right of way—just watch out for bikes, which, if you're not used to bike traffic, can seem to come out of nowhere.

ZURICH

Zurich Basics

Orientation: Zurich Neighborhoods

Zurich is split by the Limmat River into two areas, the Left and Right Banks. Sort of like the two banks of Paris along the Seine, each bank is differentiated from the other by a distinct personality and purpose within the city.

"WEST" OR "LEFT" BANK This district is anchored by Bahnhofplatz, the center of rail connections and public trams and buses, and Bahnhofstrasse, which is the wide main street that stretches away from the train station and is the center of shopping and banking in Zurich. Sort of like a mix of New York's Wall Street and Fifth Avenue, this street is the location of the world-renowned Swiss banking industry as well as the city's high-end luxury boutiques and department stores. The West Bank is also home to one of Zurich's two most famous churches, the baby blue steepled Fraumünster. You'll also find many of the city's clubs here.

"EAST" OR "RIGHT" BANK On the other side of the river, directly opposite the Fraumünster, stands the Grossmünster church. You will probably recognize its two Gothic towers, which define the Zurich sky-line. The East Bank is known as Zurich's "Old Town," home to the city's historic guildhalls and the Rathaus, the city's town hall, which dates back to the 17th century. Also here is the Neumarkt, one of the city's best-preserved old streets. Juxtaposed with all this historic architecture and flavor is the area called Niederdorf, with clusters of nightclubs and restaurants catering to the high school and collegiate partying crowd—and adults.

Tourist Office

The **Zurich Tourist Office** is conveniently located inside the main railway station (Bahnhofplatz 15; ☎ 012/15-40-00). It's open weekdays November to March from 8am to 8:30pm and weekends from 8:30am to 6:30pm; April to October Monday to Saturday from 8am to 8:30pm, and Sundays from 8:30am to 6:30pm. Here you'll find English-speaking staff members who can provide you with maps, brochures, and tips for current events going on during your stay.

Talk of the Town

Three ways to start a conversation with a local

1. **Do you love it here or what?** I didn't talk to a single young person from Zurich (or the entire country of Switzerland, for that matter) who gave the old "This place is such a drag" speech that so many young people recite when discussing their hometown. The Swiss are a seriously proud people, and it's inspiring to hear their reasons for loving their homeland. Watch out for envy overload, though—Swiss citizenship is notoriously next to impossible to get.

2. **Which way to the street parade?** Depending on your personality or music preferences, you'll either flock to or flee from Zurich's annual rave/techno dance party. Either way, you'll want to find out where it's being held.

3. **Zurich versus Geneva?** You probably know that Zurich boasts a German-inspired culture, in contrast to Geneva's more decidedly French society. Any local can fill you in on the finer differences, though.

Recommended Website

○ **www.zuerich.com**: The official website for tourism in Zurich is your best bet for surfing around for the latest museum, concert, events, weather, and transportation news. It also offers tips on accommodations and information about city tours.

Culture Tips 101

The legal minimum drinking age in Zurich is 16 for beer and 18 for spirits, but that doesn't mean that the city is a nonstop party. Any substances other than alcohol and cigarettes could get you in big trouble—the Swiss don't mess around when it comes to penalizing illegal drug possession. Penalties for infringements are actually more severe in Switzerland than they are in the United States and Canada. You could go to jail or be deported immediately.

The three main languages in Switzerland are German, French, and Italian. In the area around Zurich, the first language is Swiss German—but the Swiss variation and dialect of the language is so different from what's spoken in Germany that it's often not even understood by Germans. So even if you've studied German extensively, you might be better off just using English if you can. Tread lightly, though, and don't expect everyone to be accommodating. People in Zurich are proud of their city and their country, and they don't go out of their way to cater to the language limitations of arrogant tourists.

Switzerland is also known as "Confoederatio Helvetica," so CH is the official international abbreviation for the country. That should explain all the CH stickers posted everywhere.

Recommended Books, Movie & Music

BOOKS

Why Switzerland by Jonathan Steinberg provides a great look at Swiss society, culture, and history. Mark Twain's *A Tramp Abroad* is the eternal tongue-in-cheek travelogue for "innocents abroad" during the Swiss Alps. For some light reading, *Ticking Along with the Swiss* by Diane Dicks is an amusing collection of personal tales from travelers to Switzerland. F. Scott Fitzgerald called *Tender is the Night* his "confession of faith," a book evidently dear to his heart. Much of it is set in Zurich, and Fitzgerald's crisp, exacting prose paints a beautifully accurate picture of the characters' time spent in Switzerland.

MOVIES

Other than the very corny *Heidi*, there aren't many flicks set in Switzerland to add to your Netflix queue. Zurich is the setting for the beginning of Bourne's wild ride in *The Bourne Identity*, and it's a glossy take on the banking capital. Unfortunately, it also happened to be taped in Prague, so it won't give you a real feel for the place. Set in modern-day Zurich, *Snow White* (2005) is your standard edgy tale about a poor little rich girl gone bad. It stars Nico, a 20-year-old girl from upper-class Zurich who falls prey to a lifestyle of sex, drugs, and rock 'n' roll. It's an interesting portrait of what may lie beneath Zurich's squeaky clean, straight-edge image.

MUSIC

Switzerland, like Austria, has a long classical and folk music heritage (though the folk music here is heavy on the accordion). Come the 1960s, rock music took off throughout the country; the 1960s and early 1970s are known for notable releases by bands like the Hula Hawaiians (rockabilly tunes) and Rumpelstilz (reggae-infused rock). Prog rock took over in the 1970s and 1980s—bands like Krokodil and Brainticket dominated the scene—followed by hard rock (led by Krokus, Switzerland's most famous band). In the 1990s, rappers like Sens Unik Electronica and electronic artists like Armin van Buuren and DJ Tiesto made significant inroads into the Swiss music scene, and they continue to do so today.

ZURICH

Zurich Nuts & Bolts

Banks   Banks are generally open Monday through Wednesday and on Friday from 8:15am to 4:30pm and on Thursday from 8:15am to 6pm. Two well-known banks are the **Swiss Bank Corporation** (Bahnhofstrasse 70; ☎ 012/24-21-42) and **Swiss Bank,** with locations throughout Zurich. Swiss Bank has longer opening hours than many banks— Monday through Friday from 8am to 7pm. Some of the banks at the train station are also open on Saturday from 10am to 3 or 4pm.

Currency   The official currency in Zurich is the Swiss franc (CHF). The exchange rate at the time of this writing is about 1.30CHF to a dollar, but don't be fooled—you won't be living like a king here. The prices in Switzerland more than make up for it.

   The tourist office is a good place to change money and traveler's checks, as are banks. ATMs are easy to find—a great 24-hour one is at the bank adjacent to the Interlaken West train station.

Embassies   If you lose your passport or have another emergency, go to the **U.S. Consulate** (Durfourstrasse 101; ☎ 043/499-29-60). The **U.K. Consulate** is at Minervastrasse 117 (☎ 044/383-65-60). **Canadians** and **Australians** should contact their respective embassies in Bern, and **New Zealanders** should apply to their consulate-general in Geneva.

Emergencies   For the police, dial ☎ **117,** for an ambulance, dial ☎ **144.** For medical assistance, go to the **Zurich Universitätsspital** (**University Hospital;** Rämistrasse 100; ☎ **012/55-11-11**).

Internet/Wireless Hot Spots   A high-speed, cheap Internet and phone cafe is located within the Shopville mall underneath the train station at the Bahnhofplatz— access is about 2CHF per half-hour.

Laundry   In Zurich, laundromats are pretty much history—most visitors here are moneyed enough to have their laundry done by their hotel's service, and most residents are wealthy enough to have their own washing machines. I couldn't find a single self-serve laundromat in the entire city, and believe me, I tried. If you're really in need, your best bet is to ask your hotel or hostel for information—but don't be surprised if a couple of loads sets you back more than 20CHF.

Luggage Storage   There are lockers available at Zurich's main train station, the Hauptbahnhof. If you're bag won't fit into a locker, or if you want to leave a suitcase for more than 24 hours, follow the luggage sign to the bag-check office at the rear of the train station.

Pharmacies   A pharmacy is called an *apotheke* in German. Regular pharmacy hours are Monday to Saturday 9am to 6pm (some close earlier on Sat). For 24-hour service, go to **Bellevue Apotheke** (at Theaterstrasse 14, off Bellevueplatz; ☎ **012/66-62-22**).

Post Office   The main post office is the **Sihlpost** (Kasernenstrasse 95–97; ☎ **012/ 96-21-11**), across the Sihl River from Löwenstrasse; an emergency-service window is open from 6:30am to 10pm daily. Most post offices in the city are open Monday to Friday from 7:30am to 6:30pm and on Saturday from 6:30 to 11am.

Telephone Tips The telephone area code for Zurich is **01.** You need to dial the **001** area code both from inside Zurich and from elsewhere in Switzerland.

Tipping A 15% service charge is included in all hotel and restaurant bills, although some people leave an additional tip for exceptional service. For taxis a tip is usually included in the charges (a notice will be posted in the cab).

Sleeping

Swiss hospitality is the unspoken law of the land in Zurich, but a high cost of living has resulted in a lack of accommodations options for the traveler on a budget. As a center of European commerce, Zurich tends to have more wealthy business clientele than backpackers—so options for hostels and cheaper hotels are limited and often in need of renovation and attention. What's more, hostels in Zurich are expensive by most European standards. The upside? Although it may cost you a bit more than you'd like, Swiss standards nearly guarantee your bed will be clean and your breakfast satisfying. But if you're a traveler for whom money is no object, Zurich can be an accommodations paradise—in fact, it may be hard to find many other hotels on earth that can match what Zurich's finest offer in service, luxury, and taste.

Hostels

→**City Backpacker Hotel Biber** This hostel boasts a central location in Zurich's Old Town, only a 10-minute walk from the train station and smack in the middle of the bars and restaurants in the Niederdorf area. Street noise can be loud at night; this is definitely a place where people come to stay and have a good time. Amenities are pretty sparse—beds and little else—but hey, the beds are comfy. *FYI:* Pack light; the reception is up three flights of stairs and there is no elevator. Nevertheless, the place is the cheapest you'll find in Zurich, and the location in town can't be beat. Get there by 10pm because reception closes up tight at 10:01pm.

Niederdorfstrasse 5. ☎ 044/251-90-15. *www. city-backpacker.ch. 31CHF dorm bed with shared bathroom, 66CHF single with private bathroom, 92CHF double with private bathroom. Amenities: Internet, kitchen. In room: Sheets (3CHF rental fee).*

→**Zurich Youth Hostel** A huge, well-run, professionally managed hostel with 290 beds on five floors, this place is a favorite for families, business conventioneers, and budget travelers—so try to book well in advance. It's not in the main city center, which makes it quiet, so don't expect to find any nightlife right around the hostel. Service is impersonal but efficient. Rooms are all recently refurbished with new beds and furniture, and each has a locker and a desk. Because the volume of visitors is so high, it's a great place to meet fellow travelers. Dorm rooms have shared bathrooms, but all other rooms include a private bathroom. *Mutschellenstrasse 114.* ☎ *044/399-78-00. www.youthhostel.ch. 38CHF dorm bed (4-bed room), 56CHF with half-board. Rates include breakfast. Amenities: Restaurant; breakfast room; bar; Internet; laundry service; meeting rooms; 24-hr. reception. In room: Sheets.*

Doable

→**Hotel du Théâtre** ★ This modern hotel located just steps away from the train station used to be a Broadway-style theater in the 1950s. A far cry from the traditional Swiss cabin kitsch that many midpriced Zurich hotels rely on for decor, the rooms here are decorated in tribute to the Broadway stage, sleek and modern—far from campy. Whites and primary colors decorate the sunny rooms in a bright, Art Deco style, and the warm, upbeat staff is quite helpful. A decent assortment of audio books is available free of charge to carry on with the theater tradition—seems like you're never too old for a bedtime story. *Seilergraben 69, Centralplatz.* ☎ *044/267-267-0. www.hotel-du-theatre.ch. 135CHF–220CHF single, 195CHF–260CHF double. Buffet breakfast 15CHF. Amenities: Wi-Fi. In room: TV w/radio, hair dryer, Internet, minibar, safe.*

→ **Hotel Goldenes Schwert** The "Golden Sword" caters to a clientele that's almost exclusively out, proud, and eager to patronize some of the many nightlife options that ring it within this bustling neighborhood of Zurich's historic Alstadt. Two nightclubs inside are on its lowest floors, and you'll find comfortable bedrooms on floors 4, 5, and 6. Each of the 22 rooms is individually decorated from artfully minimalist to more cluttered and cozy. *Marktgasse 14.* ☎ *044/250-70-80. www.gayhotel.ch. 130CHF–160CHF single, 165CHF–235CHF double, 250CHF–378CHF suite. Amenities: Restaurant, bar. In room: TV, hair dryer, safe.*

MTV Best → **X-Tra Hotel Limmat** ★★ Another breath of fresh, performance-inspired air in the midpriced hotel range. The hotel's management, here since 1997, is also one of the biggest organizers of rock-'n'-roll concerts in all of Switzerland, and the restaurant/nightclub on the ground floor is often host to performances by the bands they work with. In the past couple of years the Dandy Warhols, Maroon 5, and Cake have all played here. Rooms are tastefully simple, spare, and modern, with no frills (perhaps in case you decide to really get all rock 'n' roll and try to trash the place). The clientele often includes faithful customers and friends of the management, so the place has a genuine rock-'n'-roll vibe, and you're liable to meet some characters if you stop into the nightclub for a drink or a look around—entrance is discounted for guests. *Limmatstrasse 118.* ☎ *044/448-15-95. www.x-tra.ch. 100CHF–115CHF single with shared bathroom, 128CHF–170CHF with private bathroom; 130CHF–150CHF double with shared bathroom, 154CHF–205CHF with private bathroom; 188CHF–235CHF triple with private bathroom. Rates include breakfast. Amenities: Restaurant; bar; discounted admission at a nearby health club; laundry facilities; nightclub. In room: TV, hair dryer (in private bathrooms), Internet, minibar, safe.*

Splurge

MTV Best → **Widder Hotel** ★★★ If you're looking for a place to have a Cosmo, peer out at the crowd from a half-open glass elevator, and just have a little fun and comfort while you bankrupt yourself, try this trendy hotel on the Left Bank. The Widder is actually eight interconnected town houses, including some associated with the city's medieval butchers' guild, clustered around a central courtyard in the capital's historic core. The architect, who put the complex together in the 1990s, successfully emphasized each building's individual characteristics in the redo. Great care was used to retain the original stone walls, murals, frescos, and ceilings. The result: a unique hotel in which each of the 49 rooms is different—sometimes radically so—from its neighbors. Furnishings range from metallic, minimalist, and modern to more traditional dark wood and upholstery. *Renweg 7.* ☎ *044/224-25-26. www.widderhotel.ch. 665CHF–790CHF double, 920CHF–1,510CHF suite. Rates include breakfast. Tram: 6, 7, or 11. Amenities: Restaurant; bar; dry cleaning; health club; laundry services; 24-hr. room service. In room: TV, coffeemaker, fax, hair dryer, minibar, safe (in some), Bang & Olufsen stereo, Wi-Fi.*

Zurich

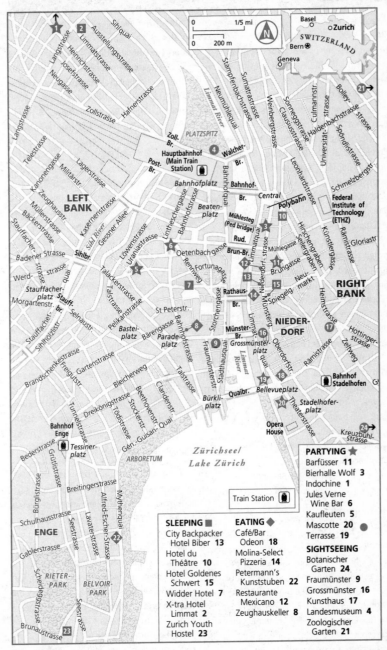

SLEEPING ◼
City Backpacker
  Hotel Biber **13**
Hotel du
  Théâtre **10**
Hotel Goldenes
  Schwert **15**
Widder Hotel **7**
X-tra Hotel
  Limmat **2**
Zurich Youth
  Hostel **23**

EATING ◆
Café/Bar
  Odeon **18**
Molina-Select
  Pizzeria **14**
Petermann's
  Kunststuben **22**
Restaurante
  Mexicano **12**
Zeughauskeller **8**

PARTYING ★
Barfüsser **11**
Bierhalle Wolf **3**
Indochine **1**
Jules Verne
  Wine Bar **6**
Kaufleuten **5**
Mascotte **20** ●
Terrasse **19**

SIGHTSEEING
Botanischer
  Garten **24**
Fraumünster **9**
Grossmünster **16**
Kunsthaus **17**
Landesmuseum **4**
Zoologischer
  Garten **21**

Eating

Zurich is not easy on the wallet by any stretch of the imagination, and this extends to its food scene as well. World renowned as it is for delectable cheeses and fine chocolates, Zurich also amazes people with its other world-class dining options, many of which are out of range for backpackers and kids on a budget. So, what to do if you're looking for a big, cheap meal? Not so easy to find. Check out the kebab and burger stands on the popular Niederdorfstrasse or the bratwurst stands at Bellevueplatz and Zurich Hauptbahnhof (train station) for a cheap bite. As far as sit-down meals go, though, you'll probably pay more than you'd like to.

Local specialties include *rösti* (potatoes grated and fried), *Züri-Gschnätzlets* (shredded veal cooked with mushrooms in a cream sauce laced with white wine), *Kutteln nach Zürcherart* (tripe with mushrooms, white wine, and caraway seed), and *Leberspiesschen* (liver cubes skewered with bacon and sage and served with potatoes and beans).

It's always interesting to try local wines with regional food. Here, the white Riesling Sylvaner is outstanding, as are the light Clevner wines (served chilled) that are made from the blue Burgundy grapes that grow around the lake.

Save your appetite, too, for that cheese and chocolates. If you haven't had enough at dinner, stroll down the Bahnhofstrasse for the city's best chocolate and cheese shops.

Hot Spots

→ **Café/Bar Odeon** ★ CAFE Okay, it's slightly overpriced, but its status as a legendary boho landmark dates back to 1912, and getting a front row seat to the antics of its stylish, gay-friendly, hipster/artist/actor/model/poseur clientele is definitely worth the few extra francs. The romantic, intimate atmosphere—low lighting and tiny tables—is perfect for a date or just a good chat. The staff is somewhat aloof, but service is good and there's no one pressuring you out the door. The only downside to the atmosphere is the cigarette smoke—don't even think about a nonsmoking section. *Limmatquai 2.* ☎ *044/251-16-50. Light meals 8.50CHF–26CHF; coffee 4CHF–6CHF. Mon–Thurs 6:30am–2:30am; Fri–Sat 7am–4:30am; Sun 9am–2:30am.*

Cheap

→ **Restaurante Mexicano** MEXICAN This festive, colorful restaurant might be a little below the standards of the hard-core Mexican food connoisseur, but for those hankering for a good fiesta atmosphere, hearty portions, and a break from Swiss noodles and cheese, this place is a dream come true. A laid-back, attractive, multilingual waitstaff serves a surprisingly good selection of Mexican beers, tacos, and fajitas while Latin music wafts through the candlelit and Christmas-light strewn dining room. The complimentary chips and salsa help you fill up cheaply—the chips are lightly seasoned and freshly made, tasting like a better version of Doritos Cool Ranch. *Niederdorfstrasse 13.* ☎ *044/260-56-46. Main courses 9CHF–17CHF. Mon–Sat 10am–2am.*

Doable

→ **Molina-Select Pizzeria** ITALIAN Genuine, affordable Swiss-Italian food, such as pizzas and sandwiches, with a gorgeous view of the Limmat. The place is small and cozy, and the wine list is good and relatively cheap. The only real downside is the slightly off-putting waitstaff, who seem almost like you're inconveniencing them by asking for, well, anything. Don't take it personally; the staff is pretty uniformly condescending. A favorite with locals, this slightly out-of-the-way place doesn't need to pander at all to tourists—which is actually a good thing. Any of their pizzas will give you the most bang for your buck. *Limmatquai 16.* ☎ *044/252-43-72. Main courses 15CHF–29CHF. Mon–Sat 4pm– 1:30am.*

➔**Zeughauskeller** ★ SWISS This mammoth restaurant dates from 1487 and was once an arsenal; its vast dining room now seats 200. Large wooden chandeliers hang from cast-iron chains, and medieval halberds and illustrations of ancient Zurich noblemen decorate the walls. A stein of local beer is a good accompaniment for the traditional, tasty Swiss dishes here, including calf's liver, Wiener schnitzel, and regional sausages. Hurlimann draft beer is poured from 1,000-liter barrels. For 77CHF, you can order a 1m-long (3$^1/_4$-ft.) sausage—enough to share with three other friends. Service is quick and efficient, and reservations are recommended. *Bahnhofstrasse 28a (near Paradeplatz).* ☎ *044/211-26-90. www.zeughauskeller.ch. Main courses 13CHF–44CHF. Daily 11:30am– 11pm.*

Splurge

MTV Best ➔**Petermann's Kunststuben** ★★★ CONTINENTAL Recently rated by Zagat as the best restaurant in Europe, Petermann's, run by chef Horst Kunststuben and his wife, Iris, has been a staple for Zurich's local elite and visiting luminaries since its debut in the 1980s. This kind of list-making excellence comes at a whopping price, to be sure—the restaurant also made *Forbes* magazine's 2005 list of the "World's Most Expensive Restaurants." The six-course dinner includes all the requisite hard-to-pronounce French and Swiss foodie delights, like fois gras and coquilles St. Jacques. The real value here is in the top-notch Swiss service. The illustrious staff dotes on each customer without being stifling or overly fawning. The small, 55-seat capacity ensures the quality of service; the pitch-perfect wine suggestions and course explanations are given in perfectly accented French, German, or English. If you've got the francs (and the reservations—they're required), come here to experience a restaurant confidently and comfortably on top of the game. *Seastrasse 160, in Küsnacht, outside of Zurich.* ☎ *019/10-07-15. Prix-fixe meals 125CHF–195CHF. Tues– Sat 11:30am–4pm and 6:30pm–midnight.*

ZURICH

Partying

If you're looking for a kegstand, Budweiser, or body-shot scene in Zurich, well, think again. The buttoned up business-like vibe of the city means nightlife never gets too wild. That's not to say there aren't plenty of great places to go; the best clubs and bars in Zurich are just as exclusive and chic as its hotels and shopping. Unless the bouncer at a club is on your MySpace page, I'd recommend greasing his palm (no less than 40CHF) or calling ahead to try to make a reservation. Clear your throat, try to sound important, and don't forget to walk up to the door like you belong there.

A more collegiate, frat-style party can be found at any one of the bars that line the funky Niederdorf area around Old Town— they're more or less interchangeable in terms of price and style. These are all decent places to throw back a few with other tourists and lose yourself for a night or two, but the only locals that frequent these places seem to be the lowlifes.

Party fashion in Zurich is all about minimalist chic—which means black clothes, well-cut simple items, and attention to detail when it comes to accessories. To get in and blend in, your best bet is well-fitting jeans and a dark top with some expensive (or expensive-looking) shoes. Ladies show less skin here than in other European cities, sporting well-cut trousers or designer jeans and conservative but snug tops, and most guys are dressed professionally, looking like they spent all day managing high-value investments (which they probably did).

Bars

→ **Bierhalle Wolf** With 160 seats, this is the best-known beer hall in Zurich, drawing people of all ages and all walks of life. Folk music is played by an oompah band in regional garb, and beer is available in tankards costing 6.50CHF and up. *Limmatquai 132.* ☎ *044/251-01-30. Cover 4CHF–5CHF.*

MTV **Best** → **Jules Verne Wine Bar** ★ For one of the best views of downtown Zurich in a bar that tends to fly under the tourism radar, head to the Jules Verne Wine Bar. To find the panorama-windowed bar, walk through the ground floor restaurant to the elevator, where you'll get off at the 11th floor. Though it's also a good spot for lunch, the view at night is just breathtaking. *Uraniastrasse 9.* ☎ *012/11-11-55.*

→ **Terrasse** ★ For a classy cocktail by the lake, head to fashionably minimalist Terrasse to lounge in a cushy, luxurious couch by the bar and indulge in the views of the lake and the bar/restaurant's clientele. The laid-back bar equivalent to upscale clubs like Indochine and Kaufleuten, Terrasse is Zurich's of-the-moment place to see and be seen for a drink or bite to eat before hitting the dance floor. Terrasse is open all day and hosts a well-heeled crowd in late mornings for brunch, mimosas, and gossip, but the real strutting of stuff starts as the sun goes down. *Limmatquai 3.* ☎ *012/51-10-74.*

Clubs

→ **Indochine** A supremely snobby crowd congregates at Indochine, an exclusive, dimly lit, sexy Southeast Asian–inspired club

filled with Zurich's most beautiful movers and shakers. Make sure to wear your best designer (or knockoff) shoes if you want to get in the door and hold a conversation with a hottie here. It's an adrenaline rush to be in such a buzzing, "in" place—and the cocktails are really well made. DJs spin a fusion of pop, electronic, and funk. *Limmatstrasse 275.* ☎ *444/48-11-11. www.club-indochine.com. Cover 20CHF.*

→ **Kaufleuten** ★★ The hottest spot in town (and probably the hardest to get into) is Kaufleuten, a stylish, upscale club where you'll feel nothing short of blessed if you're lucky enough to get into the door. Prince and Madonna have both made pit stops at Kaufleuten on trips to Zurich—does nightclub clientele get any more A-list? It helps to arrive with a small posse of attractive females. This in-spot includes a restaurant, a bar, a lounge, and an outdoor terrace and is an after-work hangout for hotshot bankers looking to unwind and trendy women wanting to show off this season's shoes and bag. *Pelikanstrasse 18.* ☎ *442/25-33-00. www. kaufleuten.com. Cover 15CHF–25CHF, depending on the night.*

→ **Macotte** This slightly less image-obsessed dance club thumps with progressive and house music. The inside is dark and packed with people—this place focuses less on sights and much more on sounds. Attracts some of the top European DJs. *Theaterstrasse 10.* ☎ *012/60-15-80. www.mascotte.ch. Cover varies.*

Gay Bars

Zurich's not the most alluring magnet for gay life, but it's got a number of clubs and bars that cater to gay men and lesbians, including those in the Hotel Goldenes Schwert (p. 958), and a tolerance that allows those out and proud to have a little fun.

→ **Barfüsser** This is the premier jeans-and-leather bar for gay men in the city, although plenty of gay women are sometimes in the mix. It proudly claims to be the oldest continuously operated gay bar in Europe, with a well-worn dark and woodsy decor and a loyal clientele who have patronized the place since its establishment in 1956. Most show up after 8pm, and it's especially popular on weekends. On-site is a sushi bar, which serves continuously throughout the day until 11pm. *Spitalgasse 14.* ☎ *442/51-40-64.*

Performing Arts

No special tickets are granted, but for regular tickets to operas, theaters, and concerts, go to **Billetzentrale** (**BiZZ** for short; Bahnhofstrasse 9; ☎ **044/221-22-83**), which is open Monday to Friday from 10am to 6:30pm and on Saturday from 10am to 2pm.

The Zurich opera is the most outstanding local company, performing at the Opernhaus. The Zurich Tonhalle Orchestra, performing at Tonhalle, also enjoys an international reputation.

➔**Opernhaus** Zurich Opera House, near Bellevueplatz in the center of the city, was founded in 1891. This history of the opera house forms part of the cultural history of Europe; the house was the venue of several world premiers. The opera house is also a repertory theater, hosting ballets, concerts, and recitals. The hall is dark in July and August. Box office open daily from 10am to 6:30pm. *Falkenstrasse 1.* ☎ *044/268-66-66. www.opernhaus.ch. Tickets 16CHF–230CHF.*

➔**Schauspielhaus** This is one of the most important theaters in Switzerland, generally performing plays in German that range from classic to modern. It's a repertoire theater that performs different works nearly every evening, not long-running shows. Box office open daily from 10am to 7pm. Closed mid-June to September. *Rämistrasse 34, at Heimplatz.* ☎ *044/268-66-66. www.schauspielhaus.ch. Tickets 23CHF–97CHF.*

Sightseeing

Zurich's clean streets and river-edge walkways make it a great city to explore on foot—the city's quays are sights in their own right. Zurich also boasts 20 museums, nearly 100 galleries, and 24 archives; highlights follow below.

Festivals

July

Züri Fäscht. This summertime citywide festival takes over Zurich with fairground revelry. Held every 3 years in early July; the next one takes place in 2007.

August

MTV Best Zurich Street Parade. The Zurich Street Parade is one massive rave/techno dance party that fills the streets for 1 day and 1 night each August. It's as over-the-top as Zurich gets. More than half a million visitors came in 2005 to celebrate love, peace, freedom, and tolerance. Modeled after Berlin's Loveparade, floats (lovemobiles) rumble by, each with its own music and dance theme. If you don't want to dance, find a table outdoors, order a beer, and take in some prime people-watching. As the party winds down, at about 3am, the city

That's the Ticket

The ZurichCARD offers 50% reductions on public transportation, free visits to 43 museums, reduced prices at the zoo, and a welcome drink at more than 2 dozen restaurants. The pass is sold at the Zurich Hauptbahnhof station, the airport, and at certain hotels. It costs 15CHF for 24 hours or 30CHF for 72 hours.

ZURICH

sends out another flotilla, this time of street-cleaning machines, that leaves the town spotless. Book very early (or plan to flee) or stay in a nearby town. For dates and details, visit the street parade's official website: www.streetparade.ch.

Top Attractions

FREE ➔ **Fraumünster** Although it's a staple on every walking tour of the city, the actual interior and architecture of this 13th-century church is quite simple. The real reason everyone piles into the iconic blue-spired building is to see the five extraordinary color-rich **stained-glass windows** ★ in the choir, painted by artist Marc Chagall in 1970. The three windows in the middle (the blue, green, orange and yellow panels) portray the life of Jacob, the life of Christ, and the road to Zion, respectively. The orange panel on the left tells the story of the prophets, and the blue window to the right represents biblical law. The Chagall windows are such a focal point that the rosette by Swiss artist Augusto Giacometti near the entrance is often overlooked—make sure you have a look on your way out. *Fraumünsterstrasse. No phone. Free admission. May–Sept Mon–Sat 9am–noon and 2–6pm, Sun 2–6pm; Oct and Mar–Apr Mon–Sat 10am–noon and 2–5pm, Sun 2–5pm; Nov–Feb Mon–Sat 10am–noon and 2–4pm, Sun 2–4pm.*

FREE ➔ **Grossmünster** Without a doubt, the double-towered Grossmünster church is Zurich's most recognizable landmark. Once you're inside, though, it's surprising how quiet and understated the church actually is—with unpainted wooden pews and little ornamentation on the altar and the windows. The windows, painted in 1933 by the Swiss artist Augusto Giacometti, provide the only display of ostentation. Descend the stairs in front of the altar into the crypt (consecrated in 1107), where you'll find a 16th-century statue of Charlemagne, Grossmünster's founder. *Grossmünsterplatz.*

☎ 012/52-59-49. *Free admission to the cathedral; towers 2CHF. Cathedral Mar 15–Oct daily 9am–6pm; Nov–Mar 14 daily 10am–4pm. Towers Mar–Oct daily (when weather permits) 9am–6pm, Nov–Feb daily (when weather permits) 10am–5pm.*

📺 Best ➔ **Kunsthaus (Fine Arts Museum)** ★★★ The Kunsthaus is Switzerland's undisputed top museum for fine art. Its permanent collection is like a greatest hits compilation of 19th- and 20th-century art, including works by Picasso, Chagall, Monet, and Rodin. There's also a great collection of Swiss art, including a newly finished wing dedicated to the skinny, dripping sculptures of Alberto Giacometti. But do pass up the restaurant—it's a rip-off, with a bland menu and overpriced dishes. *Heimplatz 1.* ☎ 012/53-84-84. *www.kunsthaus. ch. Tues–Thurs 10am–9pm; Fri–Sun 10am–5pm. Admission 7CHF adults; 5CHF with student ID.*

➔ **Landesmuseum (Swiss National Museum)** ★★ Dedicated to the history and culture of the Swiss people, this museum has a massive collection of artifacts from as far back as the 4th millennium B.C. The museum is in a palace-like 19th-century building behind the train station, a structure surrounded by beautiful, impeccably maintained gardens. Inside you'll find religious art and everyday pieces like silverware, furniture, clothing, and dollhouses. *Museumstrasse 2.* ☎ 012/18-65-11. *Admission 5CHF adults; 3CHF students. Tues–Sun 10:30am–5pm.*

The University Scene

Even though Zurich is a major center of international finance, it's certainly not just about commerce. The city has also long been a great center of liberal thought, attracting such scholars as Lenin, Jung, Joyce, and Mann; the Dadaist school was founded here in 1916. The scholarly tradition carries on

12 Hours In Zurich

1. **Window-shop along the Bahnhofstrasse.** Some people say this is the most beautiful shopping street in the world. See for yourself why.

2. **Zone out on Lake Zurich.** For a different perspective of the city, hire a boat for 1½ to 4 hours on the water. The boats leave from Bürkliplatz, the lake end of Bahnhofstrasse.

3. **Picnic at Uetliberg.** On a sunny day, take an electric train to this park-like, 840m (2,755-ft.) hill that's only 15 minutes from the city. From the station, a 10-minute hike will take you to the summit, where you can see as far away as the Black Forest. For more info about the train, call ☎ 442/06-45-11.

4. **Wander through the Kunsthaus.** Here you can stumble on Rodin's *Gates of Hell* and take in the Giacometti wing, with its eerie skinny sculptures.

5. **Stop for pastries.** Hit up **Confiserie Sprüngli** (on Am Paradeplatz; ☎ 442/24-47-31), an old-fashioned pastry shop founded in 1836 that still sells fine hot chocolate, coffee, and tea. It's open for fixed-price lunches (22CHF–29CHF) and tea or coffee (from 4CHF) Monday to Friday 7am to 6:30pm, and Saturday from 7:30am to 5:30pm.

6. **Walk the quays of Zurich.** Their promenades are beyond inviting. The most famous, Limmatquai, begins at the Bahnhof Bridge and extends east to the Rathaus (town hall) and beyond.

7. **Grab a tankard.** You can hoist one up at the local beer hall, **Bierhalle Wolf.** This place draws all kinds, offers folk music played by an oompah band in regional costume, and shows slides of Alpine scenery during the music breaks.

ZURICH

today at the main campus of the **University of Zurich** (☎ 044/634-22-36; www.unizh. ch/index.en.html), the largest university in Switzerland. It's centered around Rämistrasse 71 in Old Town, so you're bound to stumble upon some students if you walk through this quarter.

Playing Outside

On a beautiful day, there are few nicer ways to while away the time in Zurich than joining the scores of people getting some fresh air. Any spot along Lake Zurich is a good bet for feeding crumbs to the swans and soaking up the sun. For more organized fun outside, you can head to the ⟨MTV⟩ ⟨Best⟩ ⟨FREE⟩ **Botanischer Garten** ★ (Universität Zurich, Zollikerstrasse 107; ☎ 016/34-84-61), a site maintained by the University of Zurich that contains over 15,000 living species of plants. March through September it's open Monday to Friday from 7am to 7pm, Saturday and Sunday from 8am to 6pm; October through February it's open Monday to Friday from 8am to 6pm, Saturday and Sunday from 8am to 5pm. To get there, take tram no. 11 to Hegibachplatz, or no. 2 or 4 to Höschgasse; or take bus no. 33 to Botanischer Garten.

Alternatively, check out the pricier (but worth it) **Zoologischer Garten** (Zurichbergstrasse 221; ☎ 012/54-25-00). It's one of the most famous zoos in Europe, and about 2,200 animals representing 260 species call it home. March through October it's open daily from 8am to 6pm; November

Life's a Beach, or a Lake, or a River

If you land in Zurich in the summer heat and all you crave (besides chocolate) is a cold dip and a suntan, I highly recommend heading to Zurich's waterside playgrounds. When Zurich residents can't jet off to the Greek Islands or the French Riviera, they bring the beach (and the beach party) home. Many of these diverse river and lakeside spots are collectively called *Lidos,* and the fun heats up after the sun goes down.

One type of *Lido* is a *Strandbad,* a sectioned-off spot along a lake where people go to swim and romp in the sun. These meticulously clean and well-maintained grounds usually provide grassy areas to lay out, concession stands, showers, and bathrooms and various other perks like picnic tables, grilling stations, and volleyball nets. You'll also find a different type of *Lido* (also labeled *Flussbad,* or *Seebad*) that are structures built out onto the lake or river, a sort of large, floating dock with concessions, bathrooms, and showers. You can either lay out on wooden planks (more comfortable than it sounds, trust me) or recline in a rented lounge chair in between dips.

Day passes for all *Lidos* are cheap; you'll only pay around 5CHF to 7CHF (3CHF–6CHF for students under 20) for the privilege of swimming and sunbathing here. It's the drinks or the concession food prices that will break the bank, so bring your own to save pennies—you'll want them later that night, when many *Lidos* turn their sundecks into alfresco bars. The drinks are pricey, but you'll be outside, on a waterside deck, probably staring out at landmarks and bridges alight and glittering off the water—many, like the Fraumünster cathedral, are spectacular at night. For a complete list of *Lidos* with and without bars, and more details, see www.zuerich.com/zurich/sport_fun/badi_bar. I really liked Strandbad Tiefenbrunnen during the day and the swank Rimini Bar (www.rimini.ch) at night.

Caroline Sieg

through February it's open daily from 8am to 5pm. Admission is 22CHF. To get there, take tram no. 6 from the Hauptbahnhof; the zoo is in the eastern section of the city, called Zurichberg.

BIKING Urban Zurich is seldom overwhelming, but a nice alternative to the city's gentle bustle is to hop on a bike to tour the countryside. The lake at Katzensee is a lovely destination. Start at Seeback station, cycle to Katzenruti (a picnic spot in the shady woods), and then cycle to the lake itself; it's only about 1 ¹/₂ hours away (13km/8 miles). Return via Affolten.

BOATING If the weather's nice, you can rent a canoe or paddleboat at one of the many rental places along. **Best** Lake

Zurich. Prices vary, but expect to pay around 31CHF for 3 to 4 hours.

A steamer ride is also a kick. You'll spot steamers plying the waters from May to September; all have simple restaurant facilities inside and boast two or three deck levels with lots of windows. A full-length, round-trip tour of the lake from Zurich to Rappersil takes 2 hours each way, plus whatever exploring you'll be doing on shore (20CHF in second class, 33CHF first class). Shorter boat rides go from 5.40CHF.

HIKING Zurich has seven "Vita-Parcours," or keep-fit trails, which vary in difficulty. Someone at the Zurich Tourist Office (p. 954) can show you the trails on a map. In addition

ZURICH

to hiking, exercise enthusiasts can also utilize the various fitness stations along the way.

SWIMMING One of Lake Zurich's best beaches is the **Tiefenbrunne,** which is popular with the gay crowd. On a hot summer day, you'll find local 20-somethings hanging out, swimming in the lake (though be warned the temperature hovers around 68°F/20°C during the summer), picnicking, recovering from last night's party with a nap, and generally sharing good times and laughter. People simply spread out their towels wherever there is free space—on waterside grassy spots or concrete/rocky areas. To get there take tram no. 4 from central Zurich to Tiefenbrunnen

Bahnhof, about a 15-minute ride. There's also a public pool at Sihlstrasse 71 with a sauna.

We also recommend the leafy, park-like setting along the **Seefeldquai** (pedestrian-only trail hugging the lake) between Feldeggstrasse and Fröhlichstrasse. Look for the wide grassy field flanking a striking red Chinese Pagoda, the **Chinagarten** (www.chinagarten.ch), home to—you guessed it—a Chinese garden. The field is perfect for throwing a Frisbee, or you might encounter an impromptu soccer or rugby match in the works. If this is your thing, maybe you can play. Joining a game is a great way to interact with the locals, and the lake will be even more inviting after you work up a sweat.

Shopping

Bahnhofstrasse is the center for most things in Zurich: transportation, banking, and, most famously, shopping. Cars are not allowed on Bahnhofstrasse, so pedestrians and trams move freely along the wide roadway and cafe clientele spill out to alfresco tables during spring and summer months. Here you'll find a dizzying selection and some of the most well-maintained stores in the world—Zurich is right up there with Paris when it comes to serious shopping. Clothing shops include midpriced chains like H&M, Benetton, and Diesel, along with high-end shops like Armani and Chanel. Jewelry stores abound, including all the heavy hitters like Cartier, Chopard, and Tiffany & Co.

Most shops are open Monday to Friday from 8am to 6:30pm and on Saturday from 8am to 4pm. Some of the city's larger stores stay open until 9pm on Thursday, and other shops are closed on Monday morning.

Chocolatiers like 📺 Best **Teuscher** ★ are interspersed with cafes and restaurants, so you can keep your energy up to shop till you drop (or till that exchange rate really starts to set in). For a full list of stores, restaurants, and services in the area, check out www.bahnhofstrasse-zuerich.ch.

A quirkier shopping experience can be found in the area around Niederdorfstrasse, where a lot of backpackers and college-aged people hang out. On weekends, you'll often find open-air markets selling jewelry and your typical tie-dyed fare here. One store I really liked in this area was **Booster** (Stussihofstatt 6; ☎ 013/53-73-79). It stocks both vintage and new unique T-shirts, sneakers, flip-flops, and jewelry, and boasts an independent and laid-back vibe.

ZURICH

Appendix

Tourist Offices

AUSTRIAN TOURIST OFFICE
www.Austriatourism.com; info@oewnyc.com
In the U.S.: 120 W. 45th St., New York, NY
10036 (☎ 212/944-6880)
In the U.K.: 14 Cork St., London W1X 1PF
(☎ 020/7629-0461)

BELGIAN TOURIST OFFICE
www.visitbelgium.com or www.belgiumthe
placeto.be; info@visitbelgium.com
In the U.S.: 220 E. 42nd St., New York, NY
10017 (☎ 212/758-8130)
In Canada: P.O. Box 760 NDG, Montreal, H4A
342 (☎ 514/457-2888)
In the U.K.: 217 Marsh Wall, London E14 9FJ
(☎ 020/7531 0391)

VISIT BRITAIN
www.visitbritain.com or www.travelbritain.
org; travelinfo@bta.org.uk
In the U.S.: 551 Fifth Ave., Suite 701, New
York, NY 10176-0799 (☎ 800/462-2748 or
212/986-2266)
In Australia: Level 16, Gateway, 1 Macquarie
Place, Sydney, NSW 2000 (☎ 02/9377-4400)
In New Zealand: Fay Richwhite Blvd., 17th
Floor, 151 Queen St., Auckland 1 (☎ 09/
303-1446)

CZECH TOURIST AUTHORITY
www.czechtourism.com or www.czech
centrum.cz; travelczech@pop.net
In the U.S.: 1109 Madison Ave., New York,
NY 10028 (☎ 212/288-0830)
In Canada: 401 Bay St. Suite 1510, Toronto,
ON M5H 2Y4 (☎ 416/363-9928; ctacanada@
iprimus.ca)

FRENCH GOVERNMENT TOURIST OFFICE
www.franceguide.com; info@francetourism.
com
In the U.S.: 444 Madison Ave., 16th Floor,
New York, NY 10022 (☎ 212/838-7800); 875
N. Michigan Ave., Suite 3214, Chicago, IL 60611
(☎ 312/751-7800); 9454 Wilshire Blvd., Suite
715, Beverly Hills, CA 90212 (☎ 310/271-
6665). To request information at any of these
offices, call the **France-on-Call Hot Line** at
☎ 900/990-0040 (50¢ per min.).
In Canada: Maison de la France/French
Government Tourist Office, 1981 av. McGill
College, Suite 490, Montreal, PQ H3A 2W9
(☎ 514/876-9881)
In the U.K.: Maison de la France/French
Government Tourist Office, 178 Piccadilly,
London W1J 9AL (☎ 0906/824-4123)
In Australia: French Tourist Bureau, 25 Bligh
St., Sydney, NSW 2000 (☎ 02/9231-5244)

GERMAN NATIONAL TOURIST OFFICE

www.cometogermany.com; gntony@aol.com

In the U.S.: 122 E. 42nd St., 52nd Floor, New York, NY 10168-0072 (☎ **800/637-1171** or 212/661-7200)

In Canada: 480 University Ave., Suite 1410, Toronto, ON M53 1V2 (☎ **416/968-1685**)

In the U.K.: P.O. Box 2695, London W1A 3TN (☎ **020/7317-0908** or 020/7495-6129)

In Australia: P.O. Box A980, Sydney, NSW 1235 (☎ **02/9267-8148**)

GREEK NATIONAL TOURIST ORGANIZATION

www.gnto.gr or www.greektourism.com; info@greektourism.com

In the U.S.: 645 Fifth Ave., Suite 903, New York, NY 10022 (☎ **212/421-5777**)

In Canada: 91 Scollard St., Toronto, ON M5R 1G4 (☎ **416/968-2220**)

In the U.K.: 4 Conduit St., London W1S 2DJ (☎ **020/7734-5997**)

In Australia: 51–57 Pitt St., Sydney, NWS 2000 (☎ **02/9241-1663**)

HUNGARIAN NATIONAL TOURIST OFFICE

www.gotohungary.com; info@gotohungary.com

In the U.S. and Canada: 150 E. 58th St., 33rd Floor, New York, NY 10155 (☎ **212/355-0240**)

In the U.K.: c/o Embassy of the Republic of Hungary, Trade Commission, 46 Eaton Place, London, SW1X 8AL (☎ **020/7823-1032**)

ICELANDIC TOURIST BOARD

www.goiceland.org

In the U.S.: 655 Third Ave., New York, N.Y. 10017 (☎ **212/885-9700**)

IRISH TOURIST BOARD

www.ireland.travel.ie or www.tourism ireland.com; info@tourismireland.com

In the U.S.: 345 Park Ave., New York, NY 10154 (☎ **800/223-6470** or 212/418-0800)

In the U.K.: British Visitors Centre, 1 Regents St., London SW1Y 4XT (☎ **0800/039-7000**)

In Australia: 36 Carrington St., 5th Floor, Sydney, NSW 2000 (☎ **02/9299-6177**)

ITALIAN GOVERNMENT TOURIST BOARD

www.enit.it or www.italiantourism.com; italy@italiantouristboard.com

In the U.S.: 630 Fifth Ave., Suite 1565, New York, NY 10111 (☎ **212/245-4822**); 500 N. Michigan Ave., Suite 2240, Chicago, IL 60611 (☎ **312/644-0996**); 12400 Wilshire Blvd., Suite 550, Los Angeles, CA 90025 (☎ **310/820-1898**)

In Canada: 175 Bloor St. E., South Tower, Suite 907, Toronto, ON M4W 3R8 (☎ **416/925-4882**)

In the U.K.: 1 Princes St., London W1R 8AY (☎ **020/7408-1254**)

MONACO GOVERNMENT TOURIST OFFICE

www.monaco-tourism.com; Monaco@Monaco.co.uk

In the U.S. and Canada: 565 Fifth Ave., New York, NY 10017 (☎ **800/753-9696** or 212/286-3330)

In the U.K.: 3–8 Chelsea Garden Market, Chelsea Harbour, London, SW10 0XF (☎ **0500/006-114** or 020/7352-9962)

NETHERLANDS BOARD OF TOURISM

www.holland.com; info@goholland.com

In the U.S. and Canada: 355 Lexington Ave., 19th Floor, New York, NY 10017 (☎ **888/464-6552** or 212/557-3500)

In the U.K.: Imperial House, 7th Floor, 15–19 Kingsway, London, WC2B 6UN (☎ **020/7539-7950**)

PORTUGUESE TRADE & TOURISM OFFICE

www.portugal.org or www.portugalinsite.com; tourism@portugal.org

In the U.S.: 590 Fifth Ave., 3rd Floor, New York, NY 10036 (☎ **212/354-4403**)

In Canada: 60 Bloor St. W., Suite 1005, Toronto, ON M4W 3B8 (☎ **416/921-7376**)

In the U.K.: 22 Sackville St., 2nd Floor, London W1S 3LY (☎ **020/7494-5720**)

SCANDINAVIAN TOURIST BOARDS (DENMARK & SWEDEN)

www.goscandinavia.com, www.visitdenmark. com, or www.visit-sweden.com; usa@nortra. no, info@gosweden.org, dtb.london@dt.dk, or greatbritain@nortra.no

In the U.S. and Canada: P.O. Box 4649, Grand Central Station, New York, NY 10163-4649 (☎ 212/885-9700)

In the U.K.: Danish Tourist Board, 55 Sloane St., London SW1X 9SY (☎ 020/7259-5959); Swedish Travel & Tourism Council, 5 Upper Montagu St., London W1H 2AG (☎ 020/7870-5604).

TOURIST OFFICE OF SPAIN

www.okspain.org; oetny@here-i.com

In the U.S.: 666 Fifth Ave., 35th Floor, New York, NY 10103 (☎ 212/265-8822); 845 N. Michigan Ave., Suite 915E, Chicago, IL 60611 (☎ 312/642-1992); 8383 Wilshire Blvd., Suite 956, Los Angeles, CA 90211 (☎ 323/658-7188); 1221 Brickell Ave., Suite 1850, Miami, FL 33131 (☎ 305/358-1992)

In Canada: 2 Bloor St. W., 34th Floor, Toronto, ON M5S 1M9 (☎ 416/961-3131)

In the U.K.: 22–23 Manchester Sq., London W1M 5AP (☎ 020/7486-8077)

SWITZERLAND TOURISM

www.switzerlandtourism.com; info.uk@switzerlandtourism.ch or info.usa@switzerland.com

In the U.S.: 608 Fifth Ave., New York, NY 10020 (☎ 877/794-8037 or 212/757-5944).

In the U.K.: Swiss Centre, 10 Wardour St., London, W1D 6QF (☎ 020/7292-1550).

TURKEY TOURISM

www.turkey.org; www.tourismturkey.org

In the U.S.: 821 United Nations Plaza, New York, NY 10017 (☎ 212/687-2195). New Yorkers can now stop off at the bright new information office on the ground floor (☎ 212/687-2194; Mon–Fri 9am–5pm).

In the U.K.: 170–173 Piccadilly, London WV1 9DD (☎ 44-207-629-7771 or 089-188-7755 at 50p per min.).

Airlines

Major North American Airlines

Air Canada
☎ 888/247-2262
www.aircanada.ca

American Airlines
☎ 800/433-7300
www.aa.com

Continental Airlines
☎ 800/525-0280
www.continental.com

Delta Airlines
☎ 800/221-1212
www.delta.com

Northwest KLM Airlines
☎ 800/225-2525
www.nwa.com

US Airways
☎ 800/428-4322
www.usairways.com

European National Airlines

Not only will the national carriers of European countries offer the greatest number of direct flights from the United States (and can easily book you through to cities beyond the major hubs), but because the aim of their entire U.S. market is to fly you to their home country, they often run more competitive deals than most North American carriers.

APPENDIX

AUSTRIA
Austrian Airlines
In the U.S. and Canada: ☎ **800/843-0002**
In the U.K.: ☎ 020/8897-3037
www.austrianair.com

BELGIUM
SN Brussels Airline
In the U.S. and Canada: ☎ **322/723-2323**
In the U.K.: ☎ 0845/601-0933
www.flysn.com

CROATIA
Croatia Airlines
In Croatia: ☎ **01/481-96-33**
www.croatiaairlines.hr.

CZECH REPUBLIC
CSA Czech Airlines
In the U.S.: ☎ **800/223-2365**
In Canada: ☎ 514/844-4200
In the U.K.: ☎ 0870/4443-747
In Australia: ☎ 02/9247-7706
www.csa.cz

FRANCE
Air France
In the U.S.: ☎ **800/237-2747**
In Canada: ☎ 800/667-2747
In the U.K.: ☎ 0845/0845-111
In Australia: ☎ 02/9244-2100
In New Zealand: ☎ 064/9308-3352
www.airfrance.com

GERMANY
Lufthansa
In the U.S.: ☎ **800/645-3880**
In Canada: ☎ 800/399-LUFT
In the U.K.: ☎ 0845/773-7747
In Australia: ☎ 300-655-727
In New Zealand: ☎ 0800/945220
www.lufthansa-usa.com

GREECE
Olympic Airways
In the U.S.: ☎ **800/223-1226**, or 718/
269-2200 in New York
In Canada: ☎ 514/878-3891 in Montreal, or
905/676-4841 in Toronto
In the U.K.: 0870/606-0460

In Australia: ☎ 02/9251-1044
www.olimpic-airways.gr

HUNGARY
Malev Hungarian Airlines
In the U.S.: ☎ **800/223-6884**, or 212/
566-9944 in New York
In Canada: ☎ 800/665-6363
In the U.K.: ☎ 020/7439-0577
In Australia: ☎ 02/9244-2111
In New Zealand: ☎ 09/379-4455
www.malev.hu

ICELAND
Iceland Air
In the U.S. and Canada: ☎ **800/223-5500**
In the U.K.: ☎ 020/7874-1000

IRELAND
Aer Lingus
In the U.S.: ☎ **866/IRISH-AIR**
In the U.K.: ☎ 0845/084-4444
In Australia: ☎ 02/9244-2123
In New Zealand: ☎ 09/308-3351
www.aerlingus.com

ITALY
Alitalia
In the U.S. and Canada: ☎ **800/223-5730**
In the U.K.: ☎ 0870/544-8259
In Australia: ☎ 02/9244-2445
www.alitalia.com

THE NETHERLANDS
Northwest KLM
In the U.S. and Canada: ☎ **800/374-7747**
In the U.K.: ☎ 08705/074074
www.klm.com

PORTUGAL
TAP Air Portugal
In the U.S.: ☎ **800/221-7370**
In the U.K.: ☎ 0845/601-0932
www.tap-airportugal.pt

SCANDINAVIA (DENMARK & SWEDEN)
SAS Scandinavian Airlines
In the U.S.: ☎ **800/221-2350**
In the U.K.: ☎ 0870/6072-7727
In Australia: ☎ 1300/727-707
www.scandinavian.net

SPAIN

Iberia

In the U.S. and Canada: ☎ **800/772-4642**

In the U.K.: ☎ 0845/601-2854

www.iberia.com

SWITZERLAND

Swiss International Airlines

In the U.S.: ☎ **877/FLY-SWISS**

In Canada: ☎ 877/359-7947

In the U.K.: ☎ 0845/601-0956

http://yourcountry.swiss.com

TURKEY

Turkish Airlines

In the U.S. and Canada: ☎ **800/874-8875**

www.turkishairlines.com

UNITED KINGDOM

British Airways

In the U.S. and Canada: ☎ **800/247-9297**

In the U.K.: ☎ 0870/850-9850

In Australia: ☎ 02/8904-8800

www.britishairways.com

Virgin Atlantic Airways

In the U.S. and Canada: ☎ **800/862-8621**

In the U.K.: ☎ 01293/450-150

In Australia: ☎ 02/9244-2747

www.virgin-atlantic.com

European Budget Airlines

Aer Arann

Based in Ireland, with flights around the U.K.

www.aerarann.com

Air Berlin

Hub in Berlin, Germany.

www.airberlin.com

Air Scotland

Flights from Edinburgh or Glasgow to the Mediterranean.

www.air-scotland.com

Bmibaby

A British Midland's budget airline; leaves from Manchester, East Midlands, and Cardiff in England.

www.bmibaby.com

easyJet

Main hubs in Luton, Bristol, Gatwick, and Stansted in the U.K.

www.easyjet.co.uk

Germanwings

German-based airline with hubs in Cologne and Stuttgart, and flights throughout Europe.

www.germanwings.com

Hapag-Lloyd Express

Main hubs in Dublin, Newcastle, and Manchester with flights throughout Europe.

www.hlx.com

Iceland Express

Flights to Iceland.

www.icelandexpress.com

Jet 2

U.K.-based budget carrier with flights to southern destinations.

www.jet2.com

Ryanair

Main hubs in Dublin, London, Stockholm, Brussels, Milan, Barcelona, and Rome, with flights to 16 countries and 88 airports around Europe.

www.ryanair.com

Sky Europe Airlines

Central Europe's main low-cost airline, with hubs in Budpaest, Vienna, and Bratislavia.

www.skyeurope.com

Snowflake

A budget offshoot of Scandinavia Airlines, with hubs in Stockholm and Copenhagen.

www.flysnowflake.com

Sterling Airlines

Flights to central and southern Europe from Denmark, Sweden, and Norway.

www.sterlingticket.com

Thomson Flights

Budget flights out of the U.K. to central and southern Europe.

www.thomsonfly.com

Transavia
Flights from its hubs in Amsterdam and Rotterdam throughout Europe.
www.transavia.com

Wizz Air
Eastern European carrier with flights throughout Europe.
www.wizzair.com/index.shtml

Volareweb.com
Budget flights out of Italy, including Venice, Milan, and Rome.
http://buy.volareweb.com

Rail & Ferry Lines

National Railways

Country	Website	Phone Number
All countries	www.raileurope.com	☎ 1/877-272-RAIL
Austria	www.oebb.at	☎ 43/1 930 000
Belgium	www.b-rail.be	☎ 32/2 528 2828
Croatia	www.hznet.hr	☎ 060/333-444
Czech Republic	www.cdrail.cz	☎ 420/2 2422 5849
Denmark	www.dsb.dk	☎ 45/70 13 14 16
Finland	www.vr.fi	☎ 358/307 20 902
France	www.sncf.com	☎ 33/1 53 90 10 10
Germany	www.bahn.de	☎ 44/870 243 53 63
Greece	www.ose.gr	☎ 30/210 529 7777
Hungary	www.mav.hu	☎ 36/1 461 5500
Ireland	www.irishrail.ie	☎ 353/1 836 6222
Italy	www.trenitalia.it	☎ 39/89 20 21
Luxembourg	www.cfl.lu	☎ 352/49 90 49 90
Netherlands	www.ns.nl	☎ 31/900 92 96
Norway	www.nsb.no	☎ 47/815 00 888 x 4
Portugal	www.cp.pt	☎ 351/213 215 700
Spain	www.renfe.es	☎ 34/93 490 11 22
Sweden	www.sj.se	☎ 46/771 75 75 75
Switzerland	www.sbb.ch	☎ 41/512 20 11 11
Turkey	www.tcdd.gov.tr	☎ 866/674-3689 in the U.S., or 0845/077-2222 in the U.K.
United Kingdom	www.nationalrail.co.uk	☎ 44/845 7 48 49 50

Major European Ferry Lines

Countries	Ferry Line	Website	Phone Number
Denmark–Norway	Color Line	www.colorline.com	☎ 47/810-00-811
France–Corsica	SNCM	www.sncm.fr	☎ 33/8 91 701 801
France–England	SeaFrance	www.seafrance.com	☎ 44/8705-711-711
Germany–Estonia	Finnjet	www.silja.com	☎ 800/533-3755, ext. 113

continues

APPENDIX

Countries	Ferry Line	Website	Phone Number
Germany–Finland	Superfast Ferries	www.superfast.com	☎ 30/210-891-9130
Germany–Finland	Finnjet	www.silja.com	☎ 800/533-3755, ext. 113
Germany–Sweden	Scandlines	www.english.scandlines.dk	☎ 45/33-15-15-15
Germany–Sweden	Travemünde TT Line	www.ttline.com	☎ 49/40-36-01-442
Greece–Italy	HML	http://hml.gr/HML.htm	☎ 30/210 422 5341
Greece–Italy	Blue Star	www.bluestarferries.com	☎ 30/210-414-1314
Greece–Italy	Superfast Ferries	www.superfast.com	☎ 30/210-969-1190
Ireland–France	Irish Ferries	www.irishferries.com	☎ 772/563-2856 in U.S.
Italy–Sicily	Trenitalia	www.trenitalia.com	☎ 39/89-20-21
Netherlands–England	Stena Line	www.stenaline.com	☎ 44/8705-70-70-70
Spain	Trasmediterranea	www.trasmediterranea.com	☎ 34/902-45-46-45
Spain–Morocco	Trasmediterranea	www.trasmediterranea.com	☎ 34/902-45-46-45
Sweden–Denmark	Scandlines	www.english.scandlines.dk	☎ 45/33-15-15-15
Sweden–Finland	Silja Line	www.silja.com	☎ 800-533-3755

Conversion Charts

Apparel Sizes

Women's Clothing

American	8	10	12	14	16	18
Continental	38	40	42	44	46	48
British	10	12	14	16	18	20

Women's Shoes

American	5	6	7	8	9	10
Continental	36	37	38	39	40	41
British	4	5	6	7	8	9

Men's Shirts

American	$14\frac{1}{2}$	15	$15\frac{1}{2}$	16	$16\frac{1}{2}$	17	$17\frac{1}{2}$	18
Continental	37	38	39	41	42	43	44	45
British	$14\frac{1}{2}$	15	$15\frac{1}{2}$	16	$16\frac{1}{2}$	17	$17\frac{1}{2}$	18

Men's Shoes

American	7	8	9	10	11	12	13
Continental	39 $^{1}/_{2}$	41	42	43	44 $^{1}/_{2}$	46	47
British	6	7	8	9	10	11	12

Liquid Volume

To convert	Multiply by
U.S. gallons to liters	3.8
Liters to U.S. gallons	.26
U.S. gallons to imperial gallons	.83
Imperial gallons to U.S. gallons	1.20
Imperial gallons to liters	4.55
Liters to imperial gallons	.22

1 liter = .26 U.S. gallons; 1 U.S. gallon = 3.8 liters

Distance

To convert	Multiply by
Inches to centimeters	2.54
Centimeters to inches	.39
Feet to meters	.30
Meters to feet	3.28
Yards to meters	.91
Meters to yards	1.09
Miles to kilometers	1.61
Kilometers to mils	.62

1 mile = 1.6 kilometers; 1 kilometer = .62 mile; 1 foot = .30 meters; 1 meter = 3.3 feet

Weight

To convert	Multiply by
Ounces to grams	28.35
Grams to ounces	.035
Pounds to kilograms	.45
Kilograms to pounds	2.20

1 ounce = 28 grams; 1 gram = .04 ounce; 1 pound = .4555 kilograms; 1 kilogram = 2.2 pounds

A

AAA (American Automobile Association), 46
AB (Ancienne Belgique; Brussels), 184
Abbey Theatre (Dublin), 292
The Abbotsford (Edinburgh), 349
Above and Beyond Tours, 49
Accademia (Florence), 385–386
Accademia (Venice), 916–917
Accademia Foscarini Snack Bar (Venice), 918
Access-Able Travel Source, 48
Accessible Journeys, 48
Accommodations, 12, 23
    booking online, 27
    tips on, 26–29
    websites, 52
ACEA–Centrale Montemartini (Rome), 828
The Acropolis (Athens), 114
Acropolis Archaeological Museum (Athens), 115
Action Bar (Budapest), 209
Ad Hoc (London), 578
Adolfo Domínguez (Barcelona), 142
Adventure Café (Bath), 582
African-American travelers, 50
After Line (Milan), 623
Agência 117 (Lisbon), 538
AghaRTA (Prague), 754
The Agora (Athens), 115–116
Ägyptisches Museum (Berlin), 166
Aire de Sevilla–Baños Arabes (Seville), 856–857
Airfares, 12, 38, 39
Airlines, 36–37, 46–47, 970–973
    bankrupt, 39
    booking online, 38–39
Air Travel Advisory Bureau, 47
Akkusativ, 51
AKM (Istanbul), 508
Akmerkez Shopping Center (Istanbul), 513
Akt.Records (Budapest), 219
A la Mort Subite (Brussels), 183–184
Albergue de Juventud Kabul (Barcelona), 4
Albert Cuyp Market (Amsterdam), 84
Albert Heijn (Amsterdam), 73

Albertina (Vienna), 941
Alcázar (Seville), 856
Aldstadt (Munich), 632
Al Faia (Lisbon), 530
The Alfama (Lisbon), 521, 534
Alfi's Goldener Spiegel (Vienna), 937
Alhucena (Seville), 852
Alibi (Rome), 816
Allatkert (Zoo; Budapest), 215
Alley (Galway), 312
All-Ireland Hurling and Gaelic Football Finals (Dublin), 294
Alsergrund (Vienna), 926–927
Alte Nationalgalerie (Berlin), 167
Alte Pinakothek (Munich), 648
Altes Residenztheater (Munich), 646–647
Altstadt (Old Town), Salzburg, 947
Amalfi, 679–682
The Amalfi Coast, 679–688
Amalienborg Slot (Amalienborg Castle; Copenhagen), 237–238
American Automobile Association (AAA), 46
American Express
    Brussels, 178
    Madrid, 592
    traveler's checks, 24
American Foundation for the Blind, 49
Amnesia (Ibiza), 475
Amsterdam, 54–85
    accommodations, 55–56
    best of, 55–56
    bicycling, 60, 78
    brown cafes and tasting houses, 74
    cellphones, 64
    consulates, 64
    culture tips, 63
    drugs and drinking, 63, 65
    eating, 71–73
    emergencies, 64
    festivals, 78–79
    free activities, 78
    getting around, 58–60
    Internet/Wi-Fi access, 65
    laundry, 65
    luggage storage, 65
    movies, 64
    museums, 79–81
    neighborhoods, 61

    partying, 73–77
    performing arts, 77
    pharmacies, 65
    picnic fare and spots, 73
    playing outside, 81–82
    post offices, 65
    recommended books, 62–64
    Red-Light District, 76
    restrooms, 65
    safety, 65
    shopping, 82–85
    sightseeing, 77–81
    sleeping, 66–71
    smoking coffee houses, 63
    starting a conversation with a local, 62
    taxis, 59
    telephone, 66
    tipping, 66
    tourist offices, 61
    traveling to, 56–58
    12 hours in, 80
    university scene, 78
    walking, 60–61
    websites, 62
    for women, 76
Amsterdam Pride, 79
Amsterdam Roots Festival, 79
AmsterUit Buro (AUB) Ticketshop (Amsterdam), 74
Ancient Akrotiri (Santorini), 451
Ancient Thira (Santorini), 451
Andrews Lane Theatre (Dublin), 292
Anema e Core (Capri), 676
Angel (Budapest), 209
Ann Demeulemeester (Antwerp), 100
Anne Frankhuis (Anne Frank House; Amsterdam), 79
Annual Tattoo Expo (Athens), 114
Antiques Market (Antwerp), 100
Antre Bloc (Paris), 727
Antwerp, 86–100
    best of, 87
    cellphone providers, 90
    culture tips, 89–90
    currency, 90
    drugs and alcohol, 94
    eating, 93–94
    eats, 87
    emergencies, 90
    festivals, 97
    gay clubs, 95

getting around, 88
Internet access, 90
laundry, 90
luggage storage, 90
orientation, 88–89
partying, 94
performing arts, 96–97
pharmacies, 90
playing outside, 99
post office, 90
red-light district, 96
restrooms, 90
safety, 90
shopping, 99–100
sightseeing, 97–99
sleeping, 91–93
starting a conversation with
  a local, 89
telephone tips, 91
tipping, 91
tourist information, 89
traveling to, 87–88
12 hours in, 99
university scene, 98
websites, 89
Antwerp Tourist Office, 89
Apartment rentals, 27
Apollo Belvedere (the Vatican),
  827
Apostasy (Galway), 313, 314
Appian Way (Rome), 821–822
Aqua Club 2000 (Prague),
  753–754
Aquarium and Maritime
  Museum (Dubrovnik), 330
Aquarius (Dubrovnik), 332
The Aragonese Castle of Ischia,
  688
Aragon House (London), 566
Ara Pacis (Rome), 823
Arcadia Opera Shop (Vienna),
  945
Arc de Triomphe (Paris), 720
Archaeological Museum
  (Mykonos), 464
Archa Theater (Prague), 756
The Archipelago (near
  Stockholm), 878–879
Archivo General de Indias
  (Seville), 856
Area Sacra (Rome), 822
Arsenale (Venice), 917
Art Café (Rome), 816
Art Deco Galerie (Prague), 765
Art galleries, Paris, 717

Astra Apartments (Santorini), 5
Astra Bar (Ios), 458
Asturias (Madrid), 590
A Tasca Tequila Bar (Lisbon),
  530
Atatürk Museum (Istanbul), 510
Athenaeum Boekhandel B.V.
  (Amsterdam), 83
Athena Nike (Athena of Victory;
  Athens), 114
Athens, 101–117
  best of, 102
  culture tips, 104–105
  currency, 106
  drugs and drinking, 104–105
  eating, 111–112
  embassies and consulates, 106
  emergencies, 106
  festivals, 114
  free activities, 115
  getting around, 103–104
  Internet/Wi-Fi access, 106
  laundry, 106
  luggage storage, 106
  neighborhoods, 104
  partying, 112–113
  performing arts, 113
  pharmacies, 106
  playing outside, 117
  post offices, 106
  recommended books and
    movies, 105
  restrooms, 107
  safety, 107
  shopping, 117
  sightseeing, 114
  sleeping, 107–110
  taxis, 103
  tipping, 107
  tourist offices, 104
  traveling to, 102–103
  12 hours in, 105
  websites, 104
Athens and Epidaurus Festival,
  114
Athens International Airport
  Eleftherios Venizelos, 102
A-38 (Budapest), 2, 208
ATMs (automated teller
  machines), 23
Atoll, 51
Atölye Mountaineering &
  Climbing (Istanbul), 512
Atomik Café (Munich), 2, 645
Atomium (Brussels), 187

Attanasio (Naples), 6
Auditorium (Rome), 818
The Auld Dubliner (Dublin), 290
Au Printemps (Paris), 727
Automático Bar (Madrid), 6
Avalanche (Glasgow), 439
The Aventine (Rome), 832
Avinguda Diagonal (Barcelona),
  122
Avis Rent a Car, for customers
  with special travel needs,
  48–49
Ayasofya (Istanbul), 509
Ayios Sostis (Mykonos), 464

B

Babbity Bowster (Glasgow), 432
Babylon (Bath), 582
Bacaro Jazz (Venice), 903
Bağdat Caddesi (Istanbul), 495
Bagni Nettuno (Capri), 678
Bagni Tiberio (Capri), 678
Bahnhof Zoologischer Garten
  (Berlin), 170
Bairro Alto (Lisbon), 521
Baixa (Lisbon), 521
Balmer's Herberge
  (Inter-laken), 4
Bamboo (Glasgow), 431
Ba Mizu (Dublin), 288
Banana Brothers (Glasgow),
  430–431
Banana Cabaret (London), 570
Bancogiro (Venice), 903
Bang Bang (Barcelona), 134
Banje (Dubrovnik), 331
The Bank (Dublin), 288
Bar Bar (Rome), 813–814
The Barbican (London), 568
Barcelona, 118–143
  best of, 119
  cafes and tearooms, 132–133
  currency, 124–125
  drugs and drinking, 124
  eating, 131–133
  emergencies, 125
  festivals, 137
  getting around, 121
  hanging out, 142
  Internet access, 123
  laundry, 125
  luggage storage, 125
  neighborhoods, 121–122
  partying, 133–136

Barcelona (Cont.)
 playing outside, 141
 post offices, 125
 recommended books and
  movies, 124
 restrooms, 125
 safety, 125
 shopping, 142–143
 sightseeing, 136–141
 sleeping, 126–131
 starting a conversation with
  a local, 120
 telephone tips, 125–126
 tipping, 126
 tourist offices, 123
 traveling to, 119–121
 12 hours in, 136
 websites, 124
Barcelona (Copenhagen),
 235–236
Barcelona Card, 122
Bar del Fico (Rome), 814
Bar Directo (Amalfi), 682
Barfly (Glasgow), 433
Barfüsser (Zurich), 962–963
Bargello (Florence), 386
Bar Jardí (Barcelona), 132
Barmacy (Ios), 458
Bar Magenta (Milan), 622
Barockmuseum (Vienna), 940
Bar Quisi (Capri), 675
Barri Gòtic (Barcelona), 122
Barrowland Ballroom
 (Glasgow), 433
Bars and pubs, best, 2–3
Bar 10 (Glasgow), 431
Bar Tiberio (Capri), 675
Bartolucci (Florence), 390
Bar Zuka (Ibiza), 473
Basilica da Estrela (Lisbon), 534
Basilica di San Marco (Venice),
 914
Basilica di Sant'Antonio
 (Padua), 920
Basilique du Sacre-Coeur de
 Montmartre (Paris), 721
Bastille Day (Paris), 719
Bateau Concorde Atlantique
 (Paris), 715
Bath, 581–584
Baths of Caracalla (Rome), 819,
 821
Batofar (Paris), 715
Battistero (Baptistery),
 Florence, 382
Bauhaus (Seville), 852

Bayswater (London), 552
Bazaar P&J-P.Truhlář (Prague),
 766
Beach Bar 23 (Barcelona), 135
Beaches, 10
 Barcelona, 141
 Cannes, 415
 Capri, 678–679
 Copenhagen, 241
 Dublin, 301
 Dubrovnik, 331–332
 Galway, 317
 Hvar, 257
 Ibiza, 477
 Lisbon, 536–537
 Monaco, 416
 Mykonos, 464
 Nice, 406
 St-Tropez, 409–410
 Santorini, 452
 Split, 254
 Venice, 919
 Zurich, 966
Beaufort House (London), 566
Beaujoulais Nouveau (Paris),
 720
Beckett's Irish Bar (Budapest),
 208
The Beehive (Rome), 4
Beer
 Belgian, 181
 Prague, 751
Beer Saloon (Berlin), 161
Before (Nice), 404
Belém (Lisbon), 521
Belgravia (London), 551
Bellagio, 626
Bell Tower (Venice), 915
Beltane (Edinburgh), 351
Belvedere Palace (Vienna),
 939–940
Belvedere Torso (the Vatican),
 827
Benelux Tourrail pass, 174
Berlin, 144–171
 bars, 161–162
 best of, 145
 cabaret, 164–165
 cellphones, 150
 culture tips, 149–150
 currency, 151
 eating, 159–161
 embassies, 151
 emergencies, 151
 festivals, 165
 on foot, 148

 free activities, 165
 gay nightlife, 163
 getting around, 147
 Internet/Wi-Fi access, 151
 laundry, 151
 luggage storage, 151
 neighborhoods, 148–149
 partying, 161–163
 playing outside, 170
 post offices, 151–152
 recommended books, movies,
  and music, 150
 restrooms, 152
 safety, 152
 shopping, 170–171
 sightseeing, 165–170
 sleeping, 152–159
 starting a conversation with
  a local, 146
 telephone tips, 152
 tipping, 152
 tourist offices, 149
 traveling to, 145–147
 12 hours in, 169
 university scene, 167
 websites, 149
Berliner Ensemble (Berlin),
 163–164
Berlin-Mitte, 149
Berlin Philharmonic Orchestra
 (Philharmonisches
 Orchester), 164
Berlin Wall, 168
Berlin Zoo/Aquarium, 165
Bermuda Dreieck (Vienna), 936
Berns (Stockholm), 872
Bertramka (W. A. Mozart
 Museum; Prague), 762
Beşiktaş, 495
Bestiario (Seville), 851–852
Betsy Palmer (Amsterdam), 83
Beulé Gate (Athens), 114
Beyoğlu (Istanbul), 495
Biblioteca Laurenziana
 (Florence), 384
BiddingForTravel, 39
Biennale d'Arte (Venice), 911
Bierhalle Wolf (Zurich), 962,
 965
Biffi (Milan), 628
Big Ben Bookshop (Prague), 757
Big Big World Festival
 (Glasgow), 434
Big Brother Records (Dublin),
 304
Big Mama (Rome), 815

Bikers Caffe (Dubrovnik), 328
Biking
    Amsterdam, 60, 78
    Antwerp, 88, 99
    Barcelona, 121, 141
    Berlin, 147–148, 170
    Brussels, 189
    Copenhagen, 224–225, 241
    Dublin, 271, 301
    Edinburgh, 336
    Florence, 359
    Galway, 317
    Glasgow, 419
    Ibiza, 467
    Lisbon, 537
    Madrid, 588
    Munich, 651
    Reykjavík, 772
    Rome, 791, 832–833
    Seville, 840, 858
    Stockholm, 863
    Vienna, 925, 943
    Zurich, 953
Birdland Restaurant and Bar
    (Budapest), 209
Bird Market (Antwerp), 100
Bird-watching, Istanbul, 512
Bisevo, 258
Blackberry Fair (Dublin), 305
Black Bo's (Edinburgh), 348
Black Travel Online, 50
Bloemenmarkt (Amsterdam), 84
Blogs and travelogues, 53
Bloomsbury (London), 553–554
Bloomsday (Dublin), 294
Blue Grotto (Grotta Azzurra),
    677
The Blue Lagoon (Iceland), 786
Blue Mosque (Istanbul), 509
Blue Note (Galway), 312–313
The Boater (Bath), 582
Boating (boat rentals)
    Galway, 317
    Munich, 651–652
    Prague, 764
    Rome, 833
    Zurich, 966
Boat rides, 10
Boat tours
    Capri, 678
    Como, 627
    the Danube, 944
    Dublin, 303
    Lake Thun, 490
    Paris, 718
    St-Tropez, 407

    Santorini, 452
    Zurich, 966
Boboli Gardens (Florence), 389
Bocca della Verità (Rome), 823
Bodrum, 514–516
Bodrum Underwater
    Archaeology Museum, 516
Bois de Boulogne (Paris), 725
Bokar Fortress (Dubrovnik), 329
Bologna (city), 392–393
Bologna (shop; Florence),
    390–391
Bongo Club (Edinburgh),
    347–348
Bontonland Megastore
    (Prague), 764–765
Book market (Amsterdam), 84
The Book of Kells (Dublin), 295
Boom Chicago (Amsterdam), 75
Bora Bora (Ibiza), 473
Boss (Seville), 852
Botanic Gardens, Glasgow, 437
Botanischer Garten (Berlin), 170
Botanischer Garten (Zurich),
    965
Botticelli's *Birth of Venus* and
    Primavera (Florence), 387
Boudisque (Amsterdam), 83
Boujis (London), 565–566
Boutari Winery (Santorini),
    451–452
Brandenburger Tor
    (Brandenburg Gate; Berlin),
    168–169
Branislav-Dešković Modern Art
    Gallery (Brač), 261
Bray Head, 302
Brazen Head (Dublin), 290
Brel (Glasgow), 431–432
The Brick Lane Festival
    (London), 572
Brick Lane Market (London),
    580
The Bricklayers Arms (London),
    566
Bridge of Sighs (Brisbane), 913
Britart Showroom (London), 571
British Airways, 46
British Airways London Eye,
    573–574
The British Bookshop (Vienna),
    945
British Library (London), 574
The British Museum (London),
    574
Brittany Ferries, 37

Brixton Academy (London), 567
Bruges, 191–193
Brunswick Cellar (Glasgow), 432
Brussels, 172–193
    beer, 181
    best of, 173
    cafes and tearooms, 183
    cellphone providers, 178
    culture tips, 178
    currency, 178
    eating, 181–183
    embassies, 178–179
    emergencies, 179
    festivals, 186–187
    getting to and around,
        173–175
    Internet/Wi-Fi access, 179
    laundry, 179
    luggage storage, 179
    neighborhoods, 175
    partying, 183
    playing outside, 189–190
    post offices, 179
    recommended books, music,
        and movies, 178
    restrooms, 179
    safety, 179
    shopping, 190
    sightseeing, 186–189
    sleeping, 180–181
    starting a conversation with
        a local, 175
    tipping, 180
    tourist offices, 175, 178
    12 hours in, 188
    university scene, 189
    websites, 178
Brussels Jazz Marathon, 187
Brutus (Amsterdam), 83
Bruxelles (Dublin), 288
BT2 (Dublin), 304
Buchanan Galleries (Glasgow),
    439
Buckingham Palace (London),
    573
Buda Castle Labyrinth
    (Budapest), 211
"Budafest" Summer Opera and
    Ballet Festival (Budapest), 211
Budai Vigadó (Buda Concert
    Hall; Budapest), 216
Budapest, 194–220
    bathhouses, 218
    beer, 208, 209
    best of, 194–195
    cellphone providers, 200

Budapest (Cont.)
coffee houses, 210
culture tips, 199–200
currency, 200
eating, 206–207
embassies, 201
emergencies, 201
festivals, 210–211
free and easy activities, 211
gay nightlife, 209
getting to and around,
195–198
Internet/Wi-Fi access, 201
laundry, 201
luggage storage, 201
neighborhoods, 198–199
partying, 208
performing arts, 210–211,
216–217
playing outside, 217
recommended books, movies,
and music, 200
restrooms, 201
road trips from, 219
safety, 201
shopping, 218–220
sightseeing, 210–216
sleeping, 202–206
starting a conversation with
a local, 196
tipping, 201
tourist offices, 199
12 hours in, 215
university scene, 216
websites, 199
Budapest Art Weeks, 211
Budapest Spring Festival, 210
Budda Bar (Glasgow), 432
Bulldog (Amsterdam), 63
Bull Dog (Ios), 458
Bulldog Palace (Amsterdam), 63
Bullfighting
Lisbon, 537
Madrid, 587
Seville, 859
Bundestag (Reichstag; Berlin),
169–170
Burns Night (Edinburgh), 351
The Burrell (Glasgow), 435
Busker Brownes (Galway), 313
Bus travel, 38, 47

C
Ca'Bianca Club (Milan), 623
Cabiria Cafe (Florence), 385

Cacilhas (Lisbon), 521
Cádiz, 860
Café Chris (Amsterdam), 74
Café Cozy (Reykjavík), 780
Café d'Anvers (Antwerp), 2, 94
Café del Rio (Budapest), 208
Café du Journal (Galway), 314
Café en Seine (Dublin), 288
Café Konvikt (Prague), 761
Café Latte (Seville), 7
Café Local (Antwerp), 95
Café Mambo (Ibiza), 474–475
Cafe Royal Circle Bar
(Edinburgh), 349
Café Sacher (Vienna), 7
Café Slavia (Prague), 6, 749
Café t'Veurleste (Antwerp), 95
Caffè Florian (Venice), 902,
910, 913
Cağaloğlu Hamami (Istanbul),
513
Cala Xarraca Beach (Ibiza), 477
Caledonia Books (Glasgow), 439
Camaldoli Park (Naples), 671
Camden (London), 556
Camden Arts Centre (London),
571
Camden Market (London), 580
Camera Obscura (Edinburgh),
352–353
Çamlica (Istanbul), 495
Campania, best of, 655–656
Campania Artecard, 667
Campanile (Venice), 915
Campidoglio (Rome), 832
Camping, St-Tropez, 408–409
Camp Nou (Barcelona), 136
Campo de' Fiori (Rome), 813
Campo di Marte (Florence), 389
Campo San Polo (Venice), 919
Campo Santa Margherita
(Venice), 911–912, 919, 921
Campo San Vio (Venice), 919
Canal Bike (Amsterdam), 82
Canal Bus (Amsterdam), 59–60
Canal Café Theater (London),
570
Canal Grande (Venice), 912
Candela (Madrid), 605
The Candy Bar (London), 567
Cannaregio (Venice), 887
Cannes, 410–415
Can Pou Bar (Ibiza), 474
Caparica, 536–537
Capitoline (Rome), 832
Capitoline Hill (Rome), 820

Capitoline Museums (Rome),
828
Capocaccia (Florence), 376
Cappella dei Principi
(Florence), 383
Cappelle Medicee (Florence),
383
Capri, 671–679
Carabela (Vienna), 936
Caravaggio, 296, 387, 388, 669,
824, 827, 829, 830
Ca' Rezzonico (Venice), 917
The Carlsberg Visitors Center
(Copenhagen), 240
Carnaby Street (London), 580
Carnevale (Venice), 910
Carnival, 1
Athens, 114
Copenhagen, 237
Croatia, 245
Carpe Diem Cocktail Bar/
Nightclub (Hvar), 2, 256–257
Car rentals, 45–46
Carrer Aragó (Barcelona), 140
Car travel, 38, 44–45
Caryatids (Athens), 114
C.A.S.A. (Dublin), 304
Casablanca Café (Milan), 623
Casa de Campo (Madrid), 608
Casa de la Memoria de
Al-Andalus (Seville), 854
Casa Del Libro (Madrid), 609
Casa Milà (La Pedrera;
Barcelona), 138, 140
Casanova (Venice), 906
Casa Patas (Madrid), 606
Cash, 22–23
Casino Barrière de Cannes
Croisette (Cannes), 414
Casino Ruhl (Nice), 405
Casinos
Cannes, 414
Monte-Carlo, 416
Nice, 405
Vienna, 936–937
Casino Vienna, 936–937
Casselli (Vienna), 945
Castel dell'Ovo (Naples),
667
Castello Nuovo (Naples),
667
Castello Sforzesco (Milan), 624
Castelo de Sao Jorge (Lisbon),
534
Castel Sant'Angelo (Rome),
823–824

Castel Sant'Elmo (Naples), 668
Catacombes de Paris, 720–721
Catacombs of San Callisto (Rome), 9, 822–823
Catacombs of San Gennaro (Naples), 668
Catacumbas Jazz Bar (Lisbon), 530
Catedral (Seville), 856
Catedral Club (Seville), 858
Catedral de Barcelona, 138
Cathédrale des Saints Michel et Gudule (Brussels), 187
Cathedral of St. Marco (Korčula), 264
Cavalcalario Club (Bellagio), 627
C.C. Bloom's (Edinburgh), 348
Ceilidh Culture Festival (Edinburgh), 351
Cellphones, 35–36
Celtic Connections (Glasgow), 434
Celtic Park (Glasgow), 438
Çemberlitaş Hamamı (Istanbul), 513
Center for Comic Strip Art (Brussels), 188
Centers for Disease Control and Prevention, 30
Centraal Station (Amsterdam), 57
Central (Athens), 112
Central Bookstore (Barcelona), 142
Centrale Lounge (Venice), 903
Central Park (Florence), 378
Central Park (Galway), 312
Central Station (London), 568
Central Wine Bar (Bath), 582
Centre Belge de la Bande Déssinée (Brussels), 188
Centre de Cultura Contemporània de Barcelona (CCCB), 139
The Centre for Contemporary Art (Glasgow), 435
Centre International d'Antibes (C.I.A.), 51
Centre Pompidou (Paris), 723
Centro Comercial Barceló (Madrid), 609
Centro Cultural de Belém (Lisbon), 532
Centro di Musica Antica Pieta dei Turchini (Naples), 666
Centro Storico (Rome), 792

Certosa di San Giacomo (Capri), 676
Certosa-Museo di San Martino (Naples), 668
Český Krumlov, 766–769
Český Krumlov Château, 767
Cevahir Shopping Center (Istanbul), 513
Changing of the Guard (London), 573, 575
Chapel of San Gennaro (Naples), 668
Chapel of the Princes (Florence), 383
Chaplin's Pub/The English Inn (Sorrento), 684
Charles Bridge (Prague), 759, 760
Charlie Byrne's Bookshop (Galway), 318
Charlie Rocket's (Bruges), 4
Charlottenburg Palace (Berlin), 166
Charter flights, 46
Chateau (Prague), 750
Chelsea (London), 551
Chelsea Flower Show (London), 571–572
Chemical Tattoo (Madrid), 609
Chester Beatty Library (Dublin), 295
Chez Wayne's (Nice), 404
Chiado (Lisbon), 521
Chiaia Beach (Forio), 688
Chinesischer Turm (Munich), 651
Chioschetto Ponte Milvio (Rome), 814
Chokladkoppen (Stockholm), 873
Christ Church Cathedral (Dublin), 295
Christiania (Copenhagen), 238–239
Christianshavn (Copenhagen), 226
Christopher Street Day (Munich), 647
Christopher Street Day Parade (Berlin), 165
Chueca (Madrid), 589–590
Church of the Annunciation (Brač), 261
Church of the Assumption (Dubrovnik Cathedral), 329

C.I.A (Centre International d'Antibes), 51
Ciánkáli (Budapest), 219
Cimetière du Père-Lachaise (Paris), 721
Cinema Astro (Florence), 379–380
Circus Maximus (Rome), 821
Citadella (Budapest), 212
Citadium (Paris), 728
The City (London), 554
City codes, 34–35
City Hall (Barcelona), 134
City Halls and Old Fruitmarket (Glasgow), 433
City Park (Budapest), 217
City Theatre (Reykjavík), 781
City Wall, 329
CJP (Cultural Youth Pass; Amsterdam), 74
Claddagh Records (Dublin), 304
Claude Monet Foundation (Giverny), 731
Clerkenwell (London), 554–555
Clock Tower (Dubrovnik), 329
Clock Tower (Venice), 916
Club 14 (Istanbul), 507
Club Industria (Antwerp), 95
Club Metro (Interlaken), 486
Club Nautica (Hvar), 257
Club Purple (Istanbul), 507
Club Stella (Prague), 754
Club Vega (Istanbul), 507–508
Coach travel, 38, 47
The Cobblestone (Dublin), 290
Coccodrillo (Antwerp), 100
Cockney, 548
Coin (Florence), 391
Coin (Rome), 834
Colete Encarnado (Lisbon), 534
Colosseum (Rome), 820
Comedy Café (London), 570
Comedy Store (London), 570
Come on Eileen (Paris), 728
Como (city), 626
Como, Lake, 626–627
Concertgebouw (Amsterdam), 77, 78
Condomerie Het Gulden Vlies (Amsterdam), 83
Condoms, 31, 32
Confiserie Sprüngli (Zurich), 965
Confraternity of St. Roch (Venice), 918
Conservation International, 51

Consolidators, 39

Constantine, colossal statue of (Rome), 829

Constantine Column (Istanbul), 509

Contemporary Music Weeks (Budapest), 211

Conversion charts, 974–975

Cooking schools, 50

Copacabana Beach (Dubrovnik), 331–332

Copenhagen, 221–243
  best of, 222–223
  culture tips, 226–227
  currency, 227
  discount cards, 224
  eating, 233–235
  embassies, 227
  emergencies, 228
  famous Danes, 222
  festivals, 237
  free and easy activities, 238
  gardens and parks, 241
  getting to and around, 223–224
  Internet/Wi-Fi access, 228
  laundry, 228
  luggage storage, 228
  neighborhoods, 225–226
  partying, 235–236
  performing arts, 236
  post offices, 228
  recommended books, movies, and music, 227
  restrooms, 228
  road trip from, 242–243
  safety, 228
  shopping, 242
  sightseeing, 237–241
  sleeping, 229–233
  starting a conversation with a local, 227
  telephone tips, 228
  tipping, 228
  tourist offices, 226
  12 hours in, 240
  university scene, 240
  websites, 226

Copenhagen International Film Festival, 237

Copenhagen Jazz Festival, 237

Copenhagen JazzHouse, 236

Copper Face Jacks (Dublin), 288

Cornetto Free Music Festival (Rome), 818

Corniche (Edinburgh), 354

Corso Buenos Aires (Milan), 628

Coses de Casa (Barcelona), 142

Country codes, 34–35

The Courtauld Institute (London), 571

The Court Bar (Glasgow), 432

Covent Garden (London), 554

Cow's Lane Market (Dublin), 305

Cox (Paris), 716

Coxx Club (Budapest), 209

The Crane (Galway City), 4, 314

Crash (Munich), 644

Crawdaddy (Dublin), 290

Crazy Larry's (London), 566

Credit cards, 24

Cricket, London, 578

Crisco (Florence), 379

Croatian National Theater (Split), 251

Crypt of the Capuchin Monks (Rome), 830

Cuba (Galway), 312

Cube (Glasgow), 432

Cultural differences, 12–13

Cultural Information Desk (Antwerp), 97

Cumhuriyet Bayrami (Republic Day; Istanbul), 508–509

Cumpa' Cosimo (Ravello), 686

Curia (Rome), 821

Curlers Bar (Glasgow), 432

Curling, Glasgow, 438

Currency and currency exchange, 21–22

Customs regulations, 20–21

Cuvillies Theater (Munich), 646–647

Cycling. See Biking

Cyclorent (Antwerp), 99

Czech Philharmonic Orchestra at Rudolfinum (Prague), 756

D

Dachau Concentration Camp, 653

Dalkey Hill, 302

The Dalmatian Coast, 244–265
  best of, 244
  festivals, 245–246

D'Alt Villa (Ibiza), 468

Damascus (Dublin), 304

Dance clubs. See "Partying" under specific cities

Dante Alighieri language school, 51

Danube River, cruising, 944

Data (Florence), 391

Davy Byrnes (Dublin), 289

Days of European Film (Prague), 759

DC-10 (Ibiza), 475

De Dampkring (Amsterdam), 63

De Drie Fleschjes (Amsterdam), 74

De Duivel (Amsterdam), 75

Delos, 463–464

De Muze (Antwerp), 96

Den Lille Havfrue (The Little Mermaid) Statue (Copenhagen), 239

De Pijp (Amsterdam), 61

Der Weinkeller (Berlin), 171

De Sade (Milan), 623

DeSingel (Antwerp), 97

Det Kongelige Teater (Copenhagen), 236

Deurne Airport (Antwerp), 87

Deutsche Guggenheim (Berlin), 166

Deutsches Museum (Munich), 648

Deutsche Staatsoper (Berlin), 164

Devil's Forest (Venice), 903

De Windroos (Antwerp), 99

Diamondland (Antwerp), 98

Die Badeanstalt (Munich), 645

Diesel Lisboa (Lisbon), 538

Die Stachelschweine (Berlin), 164

Die Wiesse (Salzburg), 948

Dig a Little Deeper (Berlin), 171

Dining, 23
  best cheap, 5–7
  tips on, 28

Diocletian's Palace (Split), 246, 251–253

Disabilities, travelers with, 48–49

Disco 7 (Cannes), 414

Disco Gaudi (Korčula), 264

Discotheque (Barcelona), 134

Disfunzioni Musicali (Rome), 834–835

Dissolvenze (Florence), 380

Ditta G. Poggi (Rome), 835

Dive Center Hvar, 258

Diversions Temple Bar (Dublin), 294

Diving
  Hvar, 258
  Ibiza, 478
  Mykonos, 464
  Nice, 406
  Split, 254
Diwali (London), 572
Djurgården (Stockholm), 877
Docklands (London), 555
Dock's (Lisbon), 531
Dogana da Mar (Venice), 907, 912, 919
Doge's Palace (Venice), 912–913
Dohány Synagogue (Budapest), 214
Doheny and Nesbitt (Dublin), 289
Dom (Salzburg Cathedral), 950
Dôme Bar (Ibiza), 477
Dominican Monastery (Brač), 261
Dominican Monastery and Museum (Dubrovnik), 330–331
Domkirche St. Stephan (Vienna), 940
Dom Museum (Salzburg), 950
Donmar Warehouse (London), 568–569
Don Quijote, 51
Doors Open Days (Glasgow), 434
Dorsoduro (Venice), 887, 912
Dos de Mayo (Madrid), 606
Dos Locos (Korčula), 264
Dovas (Stockholm), 872
Dragon's Cave (Brač), 262
Dr. Jives, a vintage boutique (Glasgow), 439
Drottingholm (Stockholm), 878
Drug laws, 30
Drugs, Amsterdam, 63, 65
Druid Theatre Company (Galway), 315
Dublin, 266–305
  bars and wine bars, 288–289, 297
  best of, 267–268
  cellphones, 274
  comedy clubs, 292
  culture tips, 273
  currency, 274–275
  eating, 281–285
  embassies and consulates, 275
  emergencies, 275
  festivals, 293–294

gay and lesbian travelers, 276, 291
  getting to and around, 268–271
  hanging out with students, 297
  Internet/Wi-Fi access, 275
  laundry, 275
  luggage, 275
  music bars and clubs, 290
  neighborhoods, 271–272
  organized tours, 299–300
  partying, 285–292
  performing arts, 292–293
  pharmacies, 275
  playing outside, 300–303
  post offices, 275
  pubs, 289–290, 300
  recommended books, movies, and music, 273–274
  shopping, 303–305
  sightseeing, 293–300
  sleeping, 276–280
  taxis, 270
  telephone, 275
  tipping, 276
  tourist offices, 272–273
  12 hours in, 294
  websites, 273
  youth information services, 276
Dublin Castle, 295
Dublin Experience, 295
Dublin Film Festival, 294
Dublin Theatre Festival, 294
Dublin Writers Museum, 297
Dubrovacka kuca (Dubrovnik), 332
Dubrovnik, 320–332
  best of, 320
  culture tips, 322–323
  eating, 326–327
  embassies, 323–324
  emergencies, 324
  festivals, 328
  getting to and around, 321
  Internet/Wi-Fi access, 324
  luggage storage, 324
  neighborhoods, 321–322
  partying, 327–328
  performing arts, 328
  post offices, 324
  recommended books, movies, and music, 323
  restrooms, 324
  road trips from, 332

  safety, 324
  shopping, 332
  sightseeing, 328–331
  sleeping, 324–326
  starting a conversation with a local, 322
  tipping, 324
  tourist office, 322
  12 hours in, 331
Dubrovnik Cathedral (Church of the Assumption), 329
Dubrovnik International Film Festival, 328
Dubrovnik Summer Festival, 328
Duchamp (Venice), 903
The Duke of Clarence (London), 566
Dulcenea (Istanbul), 506
Duomo
  Amalfi, 682
  Florence (Santa Maria del Fiore), 360, 382–383
  Milan, 625
  Naples, 668
Duomo Works Museum (Florence), 386
Duplex (Prague), 752
Dynamic Earth (Edinburgh), 352

E

Eager Beaver (Dublin), 297, 304
Eagle Bar (Vienna), 937
Eamonn Doran's (Dublin), 290
Earl's Court (London), 552
East (Stockholm), 873
The East End (London), 555
Eastwest Beach Club (Dubrovnik), 332
EasyJet, 46
Eats, best cheap, 5–6
Ecotourism, 50–51
Ecotravel.com, 51
Ecseri Flea Market (Budapest), 220
E.D. (Paris), 707
Edinburgh, 333–354
  best of, 334–335
  cellphones, 339
  culture tips, 338
  currency, 339
  eating, 344–346
  embassies, 339
  emergencies, 339

Edinburgh *(Cont.)*
festivals, 351
gay bars, 349
getting to and around,
335–337
Internet/Wi-Fi access, 340
laundry, 340
luggage storage, 340
neighborhoods, 337
partying, 346–349
pharmacy, 340
post offices, 340
recommended books, movies,
and music, 338–339
restrooms, 340
safety, 340
shopping, 354
sightseeing, 350–354
sleeping, 340–344
starting a conversation with
a local, 334
taxis, 336
telephone tips, 340
tipping, 340
12 hours in, 353
university scene, 350
websites, 337–338
youth information service
offices, 340
Edinburgh Castle, 351
Edinburgh International Jazz &
Blues Festival, 351
Edinburgh University, 350
EFTI (Escuela de Fotografía y
Centro de Imagen; Madrid),
607
Egon Schiele Foundation and
the Egon Schiele Centrum
(Český Krumlov), 768
Egyptian Obelisk (Istanbul), 509
Egyptian Spice Bazaar
(Istanbul), 514
Eiger, 488
Eklektika Café (Budapest), 208
Elafiti Islands, 332
Elaine's Vintage Clothes
(Edinburgh), 354
El Barón Rampante (Seville),
853
El Café que Pone Muebles
Navarro (Barcelona), 132
El Corte Inglés (Seville), 859
El Divino (Ibiza), 475
Elefunk (Seville), 852
El Encants (Barcelona), 143

Elevador de Santa Justa
(Lisbon), 533
El Mercadillo (Barcelona), 142
El Prat de Llobregat Airport
(Barcelona), 119–120
El Rastro (Madrid), 609
El Raval (Barcelona), 122
El Retiro (Madrid), 608–609
Els Quatre Gats (Barcelona),
132–133
El Tamboril (Seville), 4, 854
ELTExpress, 39
El Viajero (Madrid), 604
Email Café (Nice), 400
Emerging Horizons, 49
Eminönü (Istanbul), 494
Empire Club (Vienna), 937
Energie (Rome), 835
Englischer Garten (Munich),
648, 651
English, teaching, 52
Enigma (Santorini), 450
Enjoy Rome, 819
Enoteca Belledonne (Naples),
665
Erechtheion (Athens), 114
Ergostasio (Athens), 113
Ermita de San Antonio de la
Florida Panteón de Goya
(Madrid), 606
Erotik Museum (Berlin),
166–167
Érra Café (Prague), 750
Es Cavellet Beach (Ibiza), 477
Escorted tours, 40
Estates Theatre (Prague), 756
Ethic (Rome), 835
Etnomusic (Barcelona), 142
Etruscan Museum (the Vatican),
827
Eurailpass, 40, 41
The euro, 21–22
EuroArte (Lisbon), 532
Eurolines, 47
Europe by Air, 46
E-vision (Florence), 391
Excess (Vienna), 936

F
Fabric (London), 2, 566
Faces Disco (Brač), 261
Facultad de Bellas Artes
(Madrid), 607
FA Cup Final (London), 571

Fado, 532
Fallers of Galway, 319
Fame Music (Amsterdam), 83
Fasching (Munich), 647
Fasching (Vienna), 939
Fashion Gallery (Prague), 765
Fashion Week (Paris), 719
Fast Flying Ferries
(Amsterdam), 85
Fatih (Istanbul), 494–495
Fat Tire Bike Tour (Berlin), 170
Fauchon (Paris), 728
Fauno Bar (Sorrento), 684
The Feast Day of San Marco
(Venice), 911
Feast of St. Blaise (Dubrovnik),
328
Feast of St. Domnius (Split), 246
Febiofest (Prague), 759
Feira de Ladra (Lisbon), 539
Fenix (Stockholm), 873
Feria de Abril (Seville), 855
Ferries, 37, 47
Festa de la Mercé (Barcelona),
138
Festa del Redentore (Venice),
911
Festa di San Giovanni
(Florence), 380–381
Festa Major de Gràcia
(Barcelona), 138
Festas dos Santos Populares
(Lisbon), 534
Festival Month (Edinburgh), 351
The Festival of the Sea
(Reykjavík), 782
Fete de la Musique (Paris), 719
Fete de St-Sylvestre (Paris), 720
The Fez Club (Bath), 582
Fiddler's Elbow (Florence), 377
Fiesole, 389
The Fifth Bar (Paris), 711
Figueres, 143
Filmfest München (Munich),
647
Finalmente (Lisbon), 531
Fine Arts Museum (Zurich), 964
Finnegan (Rome), 814
Finnhamn, 879
First Floor (Vienna), 937
Fish & Chips (Antwerp), 100
Fishing
Dublin, 301
Galway, 317
5.Kat, 506

Flaminio (Rome), 794
Flea markets
    Amsterdam, 84
    Athens, 9, 102, 105, 117
    Budapest, 220
    Lisbon, 539
    Nice, 406
    Vienna, 946
Flip (Dublin), 304
Flohmarkt (Vienna), 946
Florence, 355–393
    best of, 356
    cellphones, 363
    consulates, 363
    culture tips, 362
    eating, 372–376
    emergencies, 364
    farm stays, 368
    festivals, 380
    gay bars, 379
    gelato, 375
    getting to and around,
        356–359
    Internet/Wi-Fi access, 364
    laundry, 364
    luggage storage, 364
    partying, 376–379
    performing arts, 379–380
    playing outside, 389–390
    post offices, 364–365
    recommended books,
        movies, and music,
        362–363
    restrooms, 365
    safety, 365
    shopping, 390–392
    sightseeing, 380–388
    sleeping, 365–371
    starting a conversation with
        a local, 361
    telephone tips, 365
    tourist offices, 361
    12 hours in, 388
    university scene, 385
    websites, 362
    youth information services,
        361–362
Flying Wheels Travel, 48
FNAC (Antwerp), 100
FNAC (Paris), 729
Focus Theatre (Dublin), 292
Foire du Trône (Paris), 719
Fonó (Budapest), 209
Fontana di Trevi (Rome), 825

Football (soccer)
    Barcelona, 136
    Brussels, 189–190
    Florence, 389
    Istanbul, 512
    Lisbon, 537
    London, 571, 578
    Milan, 627
    Munich, 651
    Rome, 833
Forbidden Planet (Dublin), 304
Forio, 688
Formentera, 478–479
Formula One Grand Prix
    (Budapest), 211
Formula One Grand Prix
    (Monaco), 396
Foro Italico (Rome), 833
Fortnum & Mason (London),
    578
The Fortress Citadel (Hvar), 257
Forum of Trajan (Rome), 821
Fountain of the Four Rivers
    (Rome), 824
Frágil (Lisbon), 531
Franciscan Monastery
    Dubrovnik, 331
    Hvar, 257
Frank, Anne, House
    (Amsterdam), 79
Frauencafé (Vienna), 937
Frauenkirche (Munich),
    648–649
Fraumünster (Zurich), 964
Freischwimmer (Berlin), 162
The French Institute (Prague),
    755
The French Riviera, 394–416.
    See also specific destinations
    best of, 395
    business hours, 396, 398
    culture tips, 396
    emergencies, 398
    festivals, 395–396
    free and easy activities, 396
    telephone, 398
    tipping, 398
Freni e Frizioni (Rome), 815
Friday Market (Antwerp), 100
Friends (Prague), 754
The Friends Pub (Florence), 378
Frihedsmuseet (The Museum of
    Danish Resistance 1940–1945;
    Copenhagen), 241
Fringe Festival (Edinburgh), 347

Frituur N81 (Antwerp), 5, 93
Fritz Hot Club (Barcelona), 134
Front Door (Galway), 313
The Front Lounge (Dublin), 291
Fruitmarket Gallery
    (Edinburgh), 352
Fun Club (Seville), 852
Fundació Joan Miró
    (Barcelona), 140

G
Gaiety (Dublin), 292
Galata (Karaköy; Istanbul), 495
Galerie de la Java (Paris), 729
Galerie MXM (Prague), 755
Galeries St-Hubert (Brussels),
    190
Galleria Borghese (Rome), 829
Galleria Vittorio Emanuele II
    (Milan), 625
Galleries Lafayette (Paris),
    729–730
Gallery of Modern Art
    (Glasgow), 435
Galway
    laundry, 308
    luggage storage, 308
    pharmacies, 308
    post offices, 308
    telephone tips, 308
Galway Arts Centre, 316
Galway Arts Festival, 316
Galway City, 305–319
    best of, 267
    crisis centers, 307
    culture tips, 307
    eating, 310–311
    emergencies, 308
    festivals, 316
    gay bars, 314–315
    getting to and around, 306
    Internet/Wi-Fi access, 308
    neighborhoods, 307
    partying, 311–315
    performing arts, 315–316
    playing outside, 317–318
    shopping, 318–319
    sightseeing, 316–317
    sleeping, 308–310
    starting a conversation with
        a local, 306
    youth information service,
        308
Galway Film Fleadh, 316

Galway International Oyster Festival, 316
Galway Irish Crystal Heritage Centre, 316
Galway Market, 318
Galway Races, 316
The Garage (Glasgow), 431
Garricks Head (Bath), 582
G'Art (Florence), 391
The Gate (Dublin), 292–293
Gaudí i Cornet, Antonio, 139
G-A-Y (London), 568
Gay and lesbian travelers, 49–50
  Amsterdam, 79
  Antwerp, 95–96
  Barcelona, 136
  Berlin, 163
  Brussels, 185
  Dublin, 276, 291–292
  Edinburgh, 349
  Florence, 379
  Galway, 314–315
  Glasgow, 432
  Ibiza, 477
  Ireland in general, 315
  Istanbul, 507
  Lisbon, 531
  London, 567–568, 572
  Milan, 623
  Munich, 646
  Naples, 666
  Nice, 405
  Paris, 716
  Prague, 753–754
  Reykjavik, 781
  Rome, 816–817
  Seville, 853
  Stockholm, 873, 874
  Vienna, 937
  Zurich, 962–963
Gay.com Travel, 49
Gay Pride Parade (Paris), 719
Gelateria Italiana Peppino (Amsterdam), 73
Gelato, 5
Gellért Bathhouse (Budapest), 218
General Post Office (GPO; Dublin), 297–298
The George (Dublin), 291
Gerbeaud's (Budapest), 210
German State Opera (Berlin), 164
Geyser National Park (Iceland), 785

Ghetto Nuovo (Venice), 915–916
Ghosts and Gore (Edinburgh), 9, 337
Gianicolo (Rome), 820
Giardini Pubblici (Milan), 626
Giardini Reali (Venice), 918–919
Gigasport (Prague), 765
Giverny, 731
Glasgay! (Glasgow), 435
Glasgow, 417–439
  best of, 418
  cafes and tearooms, 430
  cellphones, 422
  coffee houses, 430–431
  culture tips, 420–421
  currency, 422
  eating, 428–430
  emergencies, 422
  festivals, 434
  gay bars, 432
  getting to and around, 418–420
  Internet/Wi-Fi access, 422–423
  laundry, 423
  luggage storage, 423
  neighborhoods, 420
  partying, 431–433
  performing arts, 433
  playing outside, 437–438
  post offices, 423
  recommended books, movies, and music, 421–422
  safety, 423
  shopping, 438–439
  sightseeing, 434–437
  sleeping, 423–428
  spectator sports, 438
  starting a conversation with a local, 421
  taxis, 419
  telephone tips, 423
  tipping, 423
  tourist offices, 420
  12 hours in, 437
  university scene, 435
  websites, 420, 434
Glasgow Comedy Festival, 434
Glasgow Green, 437–438
Glasgow Science Centre, 435–437
Glasgow University, 435
Glastonbury, 583
Glastonbury Tor, 583
Glenlee, S.V., the Tall Ship at Glasgow Harbour, 437

Globe Bookstore and Coffeehouse (Prague), 757
Globus/Cosmos, 40
Glyfada (Athens), 112
The Golden Circle (Iceland), 785–786
Golf, Lisbon, 538
Government websites, 52–53
GPO (Galway), 312
Gràcia (Barcelona), 122
The Grand Bazaar (Istanbul), 9, 492, 514
Grand Canal (Venice), 912
Grand Escurial (Nice), 404
Grand Ole Opry (Glasgow), 433
Grand-Place (Brussels), 187
Grand Rokk (Reykjavík), 780
Grands Appartements (Monaco), 416
Grand Veranda (Stockholm), 7
Great Spitalfields Pancake Race (London), 571
GREC Festival (Barcelona), 137–138
Greek Folk Art Museum (Athens), 116
The Greek Islands, 440–464. *See also specific islands*
  best of, 440–442
  island-hopping by boat, 441
Greene's Bookshop Ltd. (Dublin), 304
Green Park (London), 577
Grinda, 879
Grindelwald, 489
Grinzing, 944
Grossmünster (Zurich), 964
Grotta Azzurra (Blue Grotto), 677
Grunewald (Berlin), 170
GUBU (Dublin), 291
The Gues't (Nice), 404
Guinness Storehouse (Dublin), 298–299
Gullfoss waterfall (Iceland), 785
Guy Fawkes Night (London), 572

H

Habanilla Café (Seville), 3, 852–853
Hadrian's Arch (Athens), 116
Haggis, 344
Hagia Sophia (Istanbul), 509

Halászbástya (Fisherman's Bastion; Budapest), 212
Hallgrímskirkja (Reykjavík), 782
Hall of Emperors (Rome), 828–829
Hall of Mirrors (Versailles), 731
Halt Bar (Glasgow), 432
Hamley's (London), 579
Hammam (Istanbul), 513
Hampstead (London), 556
H&M (Stockholm), 878
Hangar (Rome), 817
Hangar 7 (Vienna), 948–949
Ha'Penny Laugh Comedy Club (Dublin), 292
Harem (Istanbul), 510
Harlem Jazz Club (Barcelona), 136
Harlequin (Dublin), 297
Harrods (London), 579
Harry Potter books, 338
Harry's Bar (Venice), 882, 904
Harvey Nichols (Edinburgh), 354
Hash Marijuana & Hemp Museum (Amsterdam), 80
Hatchard's (London), 579
Havel's Market (Havelský trh; Prague), 765
Health concerns, 29–30
Heilig Bloed Basiliek (Bruges), 192–193
Heimatwerk Interlaken, 487
Heineken Experience (Amsterdam), 9, 56, 79–80
Heineken Music Hall (Amsterdam), 77
The Helix (Dublin), 293
Hercules, statue of (the Vatican), 827
Herend Porcelain Company, 220
Hessenhuis (Antwerp), 95
Het Grote Avontuur (Amsterdam), 83
Highgate (London), 556
High Holborn Residence (London), 576
The High Kirk of St. Giles (Edinburgh), 352
High season, 13
Hiking and walking
    Dublin, 301–303
    Nice, 406
    Reykjavík, 784

St-Tropez, 409
Santorini, 452–453
Vienna, 943
Zurich, 966–967
Hippodrome (Istanbul), 509
Hippy Market (Ibiza), 478
Hisar (Istanbul), 512
The Hive (Glasgow), 435
Hodges Figgis (Dublin), 305
Hofbräuhaus (Munich), 3, 644
Hofburg Palace Complex (Vienna), 925, 940
Hogmanay (Edinburgh), 351
Hogmanay (Glasgow), 435
Höhenpromenade (Interlaken), 487
Hohensalzburg Fortress (Salzburg), 950
Hohe Wand (Vienna), 944
Höheweg (Interlaken), 487
Holala! (Ibiza), 479
Holborn (London), 554
Holburne (Bath), 582–583
Holdudvar (Budapest), 208
Hole in the Wall (Galway), 313
Holland Festival (Amsterdam), 78–79
Hollywood (Milan), 623
Homer's Grave (Ios), 459
The Honeycomb (Edinburgh), 348
Hoppe (Amsterdam), 75
Horseback riding
    Galway, 317
    Ibiza, 478
    Stockholm, 878
Horse racing, Galway, 317–318
Horse riding, Dublin, 301
The Horse Shoe Bar (Glasgow), 432
Horse-trekking, Reykjavík, 784
Hósök tere (Hero's Square; Budapest), 212
Hostel Af Chapman/ Skeppsholmen (Stockholm), 4
Hostelling International, 26
Hostels, 26
    Amsterdam, 66–67
    Antwerp, 91
    Athens, 107, 110
    Barcelona, 126–127
    Berlin, 152, 154
    best, 4
    Bruges, 191
    Brussels, 180

Budapest, 202–203
Cannes, 411
Copenhagen, 229
Dublin, 276, 278
Dubrovnik, 324
Edinburgh, 341
Florence, 365
Galway, 308–309
Glasgow, 423–428
Interlaken, 483–484
Ischia, 687
Istanbul, 499
Lisbon, 524, 526
London, 559–560
Madrid, 593, 597
Milan, 618
Munich, 636
Naples, 662
Nice, 401–402
Paris, 701, 704
Prague, 743, 746
Reykjavík, 775–776
Rome, 799, 802
Salzburg, 948
Santorini, 447–448
Seville, 844–845
Split, 249–250
Stockholm, 866–867
Venice, 890–891
Vienna, 929, 932
Zurich, 957
Hotel Amadeus (Seville), 5
Hotel Arena (Amsterdam), 5
Hotel Burchianti (Florence), 5
Hôtel Byblos (St-Tropez), 5
Hôtel des Invalides/Napoleon's Tomb (Paris), 721
Hotel La Palma (Capri), 675
Hotel mitArt (Berlin), 4
Hotel Monaco (Venice), 904–905
Hotel Růže (Rose Hotel; Český Krumlov), 768
Hotels, best, 5
Hot Springs Party (Ischia), 687
House of Marco Polo (Korčula), 264
Hoverspeed, 38
H2O2 (Florence), 378
Hugh Lane Municipal Gallery of Modern Art (Dublin), 295–296
Huis Marseille (Amsterdam), 80
Humana (Vienna), 945

Humboldt University (Berlin), 167

Hungarian National Museum (Budapest), 212–213

Hurling, 302

Hüsi Bar-Cafè (Interlaken), 486

Hvar, 254–258

Hyde Park (London), 577

Hype (Ibiza), 474

I

Ibiza, 465–479
  best of, 466
  culture tips, 469
  drugs, 469
  eating, 472–473
  emergencies, 469
  gay bars, 477
  getting to and around, 466–467
  hanging out, 474
  Internet access, 473
  neighborhoods, 467
  partying, 473–477
  performing arts, 477
  pharmacies, 469
  playing outside, 477–478
  shopping, 478
  sleeping, 469–471
  telephone tips, 469
  tourist offices, 468
  websites and magazines, 468

Ibiza Town, 467

Ibrox Stadium (Glasgow), 438

ICan, 49

Icarus (Mykonos), 463

Icebar (Stockholm), 873

Icelandic Dance Company (Reykjavík), 781

Icelandic Opera (Reykjavík), 781

Ice-skating
  Amsterdam, 82
  Antwerp, 97
  Copenhagen, 242
  Glasgow, 438

Icon (Berlin), 162

IKEA (Stockholm), 878

Ile Ste-Marguerite, 415

Ile St. Honorat, 415

Iles de Lerin, 415

Il Locale (Rome), 815–816

Il Salvagente (Milan), 628

Imperial Forums (Rome), 820–821

Imperial War Museum (London), 571

Indochine (Zurich), 962

Inkadelic (Ibiza), 478

In-line skating, Amsterdam, 82

Inner City (Vienna), 925

Interlaken, 480–490
  best of, 481
  currency, 482
  eating, 485–486
  emergencies and safety, 482
  getting to and around, 481–482
  Internet/Wi-Fi access, 483
  language, 483
  partying, 486
  post office, 483
  road trips, 488–490
  shopping, 487–488
  sightseeing and playing outside, 487
  sleeping, 483–485
  telephone tips, 483
  tourist office, 482
  website, 482

International Arts Biennale, 508

International Association for Medical Assistance to Travelers (IAMAT), 30

International Bar (Dublin), 292

International Driver's License, 46

The International Ecotourism Society (TIES), 50

International Film Festival
  Berlin, 165
  Cannes, 414

International Gay and Lesbian Travel Association (IGLTA), 49

International Istanbul Film Festival, 508

International Istanbul Music Festival, 508

International Jazz Festival
  Glasgow, 434
  Prague, 760

International Music Festival (Vienna), 939

International Society of Travel Medicine, 30

International Storytelling Festival (Edinburgh), 351

International Student Identity Card (ISIC), 48

International Youth Travel Card (IYTC), 48

Internet access, 33

Internet/Wi-Fi access
  Amsterdam, 65
  Antwerp, 90
  Athens, 106
  Barcelona, 123
  Berlin, 151
  Brussels, 179
  Budapest, 201
  Copenhagen, 228
  Dublin, 275
  Dubrovnik, 324
  Edinburgh, 340
  Florence, 364
  Galway City, 308
  Glasgow, 422–423
  Ibiza, 473
  Interlaken, 483
  Istanbul, 498
  Lisbon, 523
  London, 558
  Madrid, 592
  Milan, 617
  Munich, 635
  Naples, 660
  Paris, 700
  Reykjavík, 775
  Rome, 797–798
  Santorini, 447
  Seville, 843
  Stockholm, 865
  Venice, 889
  Vienna, 929

In The Park (Glasgow), 434

Ios, 453–459

Irish Film Centre (Dublin), 298

Irish Music Hall of Fame (Dublin), 298

Irók Boltja (Budapest), 220

Isaacs Hostel (Dublin), 4

Isar River (Munich), 651

Ischia, 685–688

Isla Cartuja (Seville), 841

The Island Brač, 258–262

Island Central (Athens), 113

The Island Korčula, 262–265

Islington (London), 556

Istanbul, 491–516
  ATMs, 497
  best of, 491–492
  cellphones, 497
  culture tips, 496
  eating, 503–505
  embassies, 497–498

emergencies, 498
festivals, 508
gay nightlife, 507
getting to and around,
492–494
Internet/Wi-Fi access, 498
laundry, 498
luggage storage, 498
neighborhoods, 494
partying, 505–508
performing arts, 508
playing outside, 512
post offices, 498
recommended books, movies,
and music, 496
restrooms, 498
road trip from, 514
safety, 498
shopping, 512–514
sightseeing, 508–512
sleeping, 499–503
soccer, 512
starting a conversation with
a local, 497
tipping, 498
tourist offices, 496
12 hours in, 511
university scene, 511–512
websites, 496
Istanbul Archaeology Museum,
509, 510
Istanbul University, 511–512
Itaca (Seville), 853
Itineraries, 36
Itinerary tips, 13

J

Jaap Edenbaan (Amsterdam), 82
Jackson Hall (Athens), 113
Jáma (Prague), 750–751
Jamboree (Barcelona), 136
James Bond, 490
James Joyce (Istanbul),
506–507
Jardim Zoológico de Lisboa
(Lisbon), 537–538
Jardin des Tuileries (Paris), 726
Jardin du Luxembourg (Paris),
725, 727
Java (Galway), 313
Jazz & Image (Rome), 818
Jazz-Fest Berlin (Berlin), 165
Jenners (Edinburgh), 354
Jenny Vander (Dublin), 305

Jerusalem (London), 567, 576
The Jewish Ghetto (Venice),
915–916
Jewish Museum (Prague), 760
Jimmy's Inferno (Athens), 117
Jimmy Woo (Amsterdam), 75
Jiří Švestka Galerie (Prague),
756
John Anthony (Bath), 583
Jolly's (Bath), 584
Jongleurs (Edinburgh), 349
Jongleurs Comedy Club
(Glasgow), 433
The Jordaan (Amsterdam), 61
Jordaan Festival (Amsterdam),
79
Jo's Bar (Prague), 761
José Alfredo (Madrid), 604
Josefov (Prague), 737
Josefstadt (Vienna), 926
Jules Verne Wine Bar (Zurich),
962
Jungfrau, 488
Jungfraujoch, 488
Jungle Montmartre (Paris), 715

K

Kaaitheater Studios (Brussels),
185
Kactus (Vienna), 936
KaDeWe (Berlin), 171
Kaffee Burger (Berlin), 162
Kaffi Hljomalind (Reykjavík),
6–7, 779
Kaffibrennslan (Reykjavík), 780
Kahlenberg, 944
Kaiser Wilhelm Church (Berlin),
168
Kalamajka Dance House
(Budapest), 217
Kalamoto, 332
Kalerie (Berlin), 171
Kamari (Santorini), 452
Kapital (Madrid), 603
Karaköy (Galata; Istanbul), 495
Karma (Dublin), 288
Kaštelet (Split), 252
Kaufhaus Schrill (Berlin), 171
Kaufleuten (Zurich), 962
Káva Káva Káva (Prague), 761
Kavárna Obecní dům (Prague),
749
Kelvingrove Park (Glasgow), 437

Kelvin Hall International Sports
Arena (Glasgow), 438
Kemanci (Istanbul), 505
Kemwel, 39
Kenny's Book Shop and Gallery
(Galway), 318
Kensington (London), 551–552
Kensington Gardens (London),
577
Keyser Soze (Berlin), 162
Killiney Hill, 302
Kilmainham Gaol Historical
Museum (Dublin), 296
King Döner (Barcelona), 5
King's Head (Galway), 313, 314
The King's Head (London), 569
King Tut's Wah-Wah Hut
(Glasgow), 433
Kinki (Amsterdam), 83
Kinky (Naples), 665
Kiraly Bathhouse (Budapest),
218
Királyi Palota (Buda Palace;
Budapest), 214
Kira Thira Jazz Bar (Santorini),
450
Kitesurfing, Dublin, 303
Kit Kat Club (Berlin), 162
Kleine Scheidegg, 488
Klub Lávka (Prague), 752
Knightsbridge (London), 551
Kolonaki (Athens), 117
Koninklijk Ballet van
Vlaanderen (Antwerp), 96–97
Koninklijk Museum voor
Schone Kunsten Antwerpen
(Antwerp), 98
Konzerthaus Berlin, 164
Koo Club (Santorini), 450
Korčula, 262–265
Korčula Museum, 264–265
Kozmic Music (Brussels), 190
Központi Vásárcsarnok (Central
Market Hall; Budapest), 220
The Kulminator (Antwerp), 95
Kultfabrik (Munich), 645
Kulturhuset (Stockholm), 874
Kungliga Slottet (Stockholm),
875
Kungsholmen (Stockholm), 877
Kunst-& Antiekcentrum De
Looier (Amsterdam), 84
KunstenFESTIVALdesArts
(KFDA; Brussels), 187

INDEX

Kunsthalle (Vienna), 942
Kunsthaus (Zurich), 964
Kunsthistorisches Museum
 (Vienna), 941
Kurfürstendamm (Ku'damm;
 Berlin), 148
Kuzelky (Prague), 764
K.V. (Istanbul), 512

L

La Base (Rome), 816
La Bodeguita (Lisbon), 530–531
La Boqueria/Mercat de Sant
 Josep (Barcelona), 133
Labyrinth (Dubrovnik), 327–328
La Carbonería (Seville),
 854–855
The Lady and the Unicorn
 Tapestries (Paris), 724
La Feltrinelli (Florence), 391
La Feltrinelli (Rome), 835
La Fiorentina (Florence), 389
La Fontelina (Capri), 678
La Font Màgica (Barcelona), 138
Lagoon Leisure Centre
 (Glasgow), 438
Lainzer Tiergarten (Vienna), 943
La Latina (Madrid), 589
La Locomotive (Paris), 715
La Maison (Rome), 816
La Mela (Naples), 666
Landesmuseum (Zurich), 964
Landhuis van het Brugse Vrije
 (Bruges), 192–193
Landstrasse (Vienna), 926
The Language Center (Istanbul),
 512
Language courses, 51
Language Courses Abroad, 51
Laocoön (the Vatican), 827
La Paloma (Barcelona), 134–135
La Petit Fer à Cheval (Paris), 711,
 714
Largo das Portas do Sol
 (Lisbon), 534
La Rinascente (Florence), 391
La Rinascente (Milan), 628
La Risacca (Amalfi), 682
La Riviera (Madrid), 605
La Scala (Milan), 624
Las Ramblas (Barcelona), 9, 121
Las Salinas Beach (Ibiza), 477
Last Blast (Milan), 622
L'Atelier-Palm Beach (Cannes),
 414

L'Atelier Privé des Langues, 51
La Terrrazza (Barcelona), 135
Latin Club Fuego (Dubrovnik),
 327
Laugardalshöll (Reykjavík), 781
Laundry Day (Antwerp), 97
Laurentian Library (Florence),
 384
Lava (Stockholm), 874
Lavapies (Madrid), 589
La Venencia (Madrid), 604
La Vía Láctea (Madrid), 605
La Vineria (Rome), 814–815
La Voile Rouge (St-Tropez), 410
Lazzarella (Naples), 665–666
Leader Price (Paris), 707
Le Blue Boy (Nice), 405
Le Blue Note (Paris), 4, 715
Le Botanique (Brussels), 184
Le Carré (Paris), 716
Le Cithéa (Paris), 714
Le Club 55 (St-Tropez), 410
Le Fumoir (Paris), 6, 710
Le Fuse (Brussels), 184
Le Garage (Madrid), 603
Le Graal (Galway), 313
Leicester Square (London), 553
Le Klub (Nice), 405
Leonardo da Vinci
 Annunciation (Florence), 387
 The Last Supper (Milan), 625
Leopold Museum (Vienna), 942
Leopoldstadt (Vienna), 925–926
Le Progress (Paris), 714
Le Reflet (Paris), 724
Le Rendez-vous des Amis
 (Paris), 715–716
Le Scimmie (Milan), 623
Les Deux Magots (Paris), 710
Les Distilleries Ideal (Nice), 404
Le 6 (Nice), 405
Les Puces de Nice (Nice), 406
Levant (Istanbul), 495
Le Whisky à Gogo/Ladybird
 (Cannes), 414
Le You (Brussels), 184
Le Zattere (Venice), 912
L'Hôtel (Paris), 5
Liberation Day (Amsterdam), 78
Liberation Monument
 (Budapest), 212
Liberty of London, 579
Liberty Travel, 39
Libro Azul (Ibiza), 479
The Lido (Venice), 896, 919
Lifestyle websites, 53

Lighthouse (Glasgow), 434
Likavitos Festival (Athens), 114
Lillie's Bordello (Dublin), 291
Limelight (London), 566
Lipizzaner Museum (Vienna),
 941
Liquid (Galway), 314–315
Lisboa Card, 533
Lisbon, 517–540
 best of, 518
 cafes and tearooms, 529
 cellphones, 522–523
 culture tips, 522
 eating, 527–529
 embassies, 523
 emergencies, 523
 festivals, 533–534
 gay bars and clubs, 531
 getting to and around,
  518–521
 hanging out, 530
 Internet/Wi-Fi access, 523
 laundry, 523
 luggage storage, 523
 neighborhoods, 521
 partying, 530–532
 performing arts, 532–533
 playing outside, 536–538
 post offices, 523
 recommended books, movies,
  and music, 522
 restrooms, 523
 road trip, 539–540
 safety, 523–524
 shopping, 538–539
 sightseeing, 533–536
 sleeping, 524–527
 starting a conversation with
  a local, 519
 taxis, 520
 tipping, 524
 tourist offices, 521–522
 12 hours in, 536
 university scene, 536
 websites, 522
Literární kavárna G plus G
 (Prague), 758
*The Little Mermaid (Den Lille
 Havfrue)* Statue
 (Copenhagen), 239
Little Venice (Mykonos), 463
Live music, best, 3–4
Livraria Bertrand (Lisbon), 538
Livraria Britanica (Lisbon), 538
Loft (Cannes), 414
Lokrum Island, 331

London, 541–584
  best of, 542
  cellphones, 557–558
  coffee houses, 565
  culture tips, 556–557
  eating, 562–565
  embassies, 558
  emergencies, 558
  festivals, 570–572
  free and easy activities, 571
  gay bars, 567–568, 572
  getting to and around, 543,
    548–550
  Internet/Wi-Fi access, 558
  laundry, 558
  luggage storage, 558
  neighborhoods, 550–556
  partying, 565–568
  performing arts, 568–570
  playing outside, 577–578
  post offices, 559
  recommended books, movies,
    and music, 557
  road trips from, 581–584
  safety, 559
  shopping, 578–581
  sightseeing, 570–577
  sleeping, 559–562
  spectator sports, 578
  starting a conversation with
    a local, 543
  taxis, 549
  tipping, 559
  tourist offices, 556
  Travelcards, 550
  12 hours in, 573
  university scene, 576
  websites, 556
The Long Hall (Dublin), 2, 289
The Long Hop (Paris), 714
Loonees (Florence), 378
Loppmarknaden i Skärholmen
  (Stockholm), 878
Lopud, 332
Los Gallos (Seville), 855
Louise Gallery (Brussels), 185
Louisiana Bistro (Milan), 622
The Lounge (Florence), 377
Love Parade (Berlin), 166
Lovrijenac Fortress
  (Dubrovnik), 329
Lucerna Music Bar (Prague), 754
Lucky's, (Santorini), 6
Ludwig-Maximilians-University
  of Munich, 650–651

Lunatheater (Brussels), 185
Lux (Lisbon), 531

M

Macho 2 (Brussels), 185
Macnas (Galway), 315
Macotte (Zurich), 962
Madame Tussaud's
  (Amsterdam), 79
Madrid, 585–610
  best of, 586–587
  cellphones, 591
  culture tips, 590
  currency, 591–592
  eating, 599–602
  embassies, 592
  emergencies, 592
  festivals, 606
  getting to and around,
    587–589
  glossary of common slang
    terms, 610
  Internet/Wi-Fi access, 592
  laundry, 592
  luggage storage, 592
  neighborhoods, 589–590
  partying, 602–605
  performing arts, 605–606
  pharmacies, 592
  playing outside, 608–609
  post offices, 592
  recommended books, movies,
    and music, 590–591
  restrooms, 592
  safety, 592–593
  shopping, 609–612
  sightseeing, 606–608
  sleeping, 593–599
  starting a conversation with
    a local, 587
  tapeos, 604
  telephone tips, 593
  top 10 local favorites, 591
  tourist offices, 590
  12 hours in, 608
  university scene, 607
  websites, 590
Maggio dei Monumenti
  (Naples), 666
Maggio Musicale Fiorentino
  (Florence), 380
Magic Fountain (Barcelona), 138
Magnet (Berlin), 162

Magyar Allami Operaház
  (Hungarian State Opera
  House; Budapest), 216
Maison du Football (Brussels),
  189–190
Maki Beach (Bodrum), 516
Malasaña (Madrid), 589
Malá Strana (Lesser Town;
  Prague), 736–737
Malostranská Beseda (Prague),
  754
Mamacas (Athens), 113
Manganari Beach (Ios), 459
Manneken-Pis (Brussels), 173,
  187–188
Manto's (Mykonos), 463
Manuel Contreras II, Luthier
  (Madrid), 609
Manzana de la Discordia
  (Barcelona), 140
Mapa Mundi (Ibiza), 479
Marais Plus (Paris), 730
Marató de L'Espectacle
  (Barcelona), 137
Marché à la Brocante (Nice), 406
Marché-aux-Puces (Brussels),
  9, 189
Marché aux Puces St-Ouen de
  Clignancourt (Paris), 9, 729
Marco Polo, House of (Korčula),
  264
Margareten (Vienna), 926
Margaret Island (Budapest), 217
Mariahilferstrasse (Vienna),
  926, 942
Marina Grande (Sorrento), 685
Marina Piccola (Capri), 678–679
The Market Bar (Dublin), 288
Markets
    Amsterdam, 84
    Antwerp, 100
    Barcelona, 133, 143
    best, 9
    Dublin, 305
    Florence, 390
    Galway, 318
    Lisbon, 539
    London, 580
    Munich, 652
    Paris, 729
    Prague, 765
    Rome, 836
    Venice, 920, 921
    Vienna, 946

INDEX

Marmontova Street (Pazar; Split), 252
Marquis de Sade (Prague), 751
Martina Novelli (Rome), 835
Marylebone (London), 552–553
Matilda Club (Sorrento), 684
Mátyás Templom (St. Matthias Church; Budapest), 214
Mausoleum of Halicarnassus (Bodrum), 516
Max Emanuel Brauerei (Munich), 644
Maximillianstrasse (Munich), 632
Maximum Underground (Prague), 765
Mayfair (London), 552
The Mazet (Paris), 714
Mecca (Prague), 752
Meccanò (Florence), 378
MEDEX Assistance, 31
MedicAlert identification tag, 30–31
Medici Chapels (Florence), 383
Megaron Musikis (Athens), 113
Meiringen, 488–489
Melkweg (Amsterdam), 3, 77
Mercado da Ribeira (Lisbon), 539
Mercado Fuencarral (Madrid), 609–610
Mercato di Testaccio (Rome), 836
Mercato La Loggia (Florence), 390
Mercato Rialto (Venice), 920
Mercurio, 42
Merlin Theater (Budapest), 217
Mestizaje, 134
Meštrović Gallery (Split), 252
Metaverso (Rome), 817
Metro (Stockholm), 873
Michelangelo, 827, 832
    Holy Family (Florence), 387
    Pietà (the Vatican), 826
    Rondanini Pietà (Milan), 624
Michelin maps, 46
Midsummer's Night (Copenhagen), 237
Mike's Bike Tours (Amsterdam), 60
Milan, 611–628
    best of, 612
    cafes and tearooms, 622
    cellphones, 617
    culture tips, 616

currency, 617
eating, 620–622
embassies, 617
emergencies, 617
gay nightlife, 623
getting to and around, 612–613, 616
Internet/Wi-Fi access, 617
laundry, 617
luggage storage, 618
neighborhoods, 616
partying, 622–623
performing arts, 624
playing outside, 626–627
post offices, 618
restrooms, 618
safety, 618
shopping, 627–628
sightseeing, 624–627
sleeping, 618–620
spectator sports, 627
tourist offices, 616
12 hours in, 625
university scene, 626
websites, 616
Milan International Film Festival, 624
Milk and Honey (London), 567
Millenium Monument (Budapest), 212
Mini-Europe (Brussels), 188
Minority travelers, 50
Mirador de Colón (Barcelona), 138
Mljet, 258
Mobile phones, 35–36
Moby Dick Bar (Brač), 261
Moderna Dansteatern (Stockholm), 874
Moderna Museet (Stockholm), 875
Mogador (Antwerp), 95
Mojo Blues Bar (Copenhagen), 236
Molecule Man (Berlin), 169
Moles (Bath), 582
Mommy (Athens), 113
Monaco, 415–416
Monastiraki Flea Market (Athens), 9, 102, 105, 117
Mönch, 488
Mondo (Stockholm), 872
Mondo at Stella (Madrid), 603
Mondo Culto! (Florence), 381
Money matters, 21–24
    websites, 53

Monroe's (Galway), 314
Monte-Carlo Casino, 416
Monte Solaro chairlift (Anacapri), 678
Montuno's (London), 567
Moog (Barcelona), 135
Moore Street Market (Dublin), 305
Morrison's Music Pub (Budapest), 209
MossRehab, 49
Mosteiro dos Jerónimos (Lisbon), 534–535
Mother Red Caps Market (Dublin), 305
The Moulin Rouge (Paris), 717–718
Mozart, Wolfgang Amadeus, Museum (Prague), 762
Mozart Dinner Concert (Salzburg), 949
Mucsarnok Múzeum (Museum of Modern Art; Budapest), 212
Mulligan (Galway), 318–319
Mumok (Vienna), 942
Münchner Philharmoniker (Munich), 647
Munich, 629–654
    best of, 629–630
    Catedral, 633
    cellphones, 634–635
    consulates, 635
    culture tips, 634
    currency, 635
    eating, 642–643
    emergencies, 635
    festivals, 647
    gay nightlife, 646
    getting to and around, 630–632
    Internet/Wi-Fi access, 635
    laundromats, 635
    luggage storage, 635
    neighborhoods, 632–633
    partying, 643–646
    performing arts, 646–647
    playing outside, 651–652
    post offices, 635
    recommended books, movies, and music, 634
    restrooms, 636
    road trips, 653–654
    safety, 636
    shopping, 652
    sightseeing, 647–651
    sleeping, 636–642

spectator sports, 651
tourist offices, 633
12 hours in, 650
university scene, 650–651
websites, 633–634
youth information, 636
Munich Philharmonic
    Orchestra, 647
Murphy's (Santorini), 450
Musée d'Art Américain Giverny,
    731
Musée d'Art Ancien (Brussels),
    188
Musée d'Art Moderne
    (Brussels), 188–189
Musée d'Art Moderne et
    Contemporain (Nice), 405
Musée de la Castre (Cannes),
    414–415
Musée de la Mer (Ile
    Ste-Marguerite), 415
Musée de la Ville Brussels, 189
Musée d'histoire Naturelle
    (Nice), 405–406
Musée d'Orsay (Paris), 723
Musée du Cinéma (Brussels),
    185–186
Musée du Louvre (Paris), 723
Musée Matisse (Nice), 406
Musée National du Moyen Age
    Thermes de Cluny (Paris), 723
Musée National Picasso (Paris),
    724
Musée Océanographique et
    Aquarium (Monaco), 416
Musée Rodin (Paris), 724
Museo Archeologico (Florence),
    386
Museo Archeologico Nazionale
    (Naples), 656, 668–669
Museo de Bellas Artes (Seville),
    857
Museo del '700 Veneziano
    (Venice), 917
Museo dell'Opera del Duomo
    (Florence), 386
Museo del Prado (Madrid), 607
Museo e Gallerie di
    Capodimonte (Naples),
    669–670
Museo Nacional Centro de Arte
    Reina Sofía (Madrid), 607
Museo Nazionale di San
    Martino (Naples), 668
Museo Nazionale Romano
    (Rome), 829

Museo Storico Navale and
    Arsenale (Venice), 917
Museo Tattile di Pittura Antica
    e Moderna (Bologna), 393
Museu Calouste Gulbenkian
    (Lisbon), 535
Museu d'Art Contemporani
    (MACBA; Barcelona), 141
Museumboot (Amsterdam), 60
Museum Gustavianum
    (Uppsala), 880
Museum Haus am Checkpoint
    Charlie (Berlin), 167
Museum Het Rembrandthuis
    (Rembrandt House Museum;
    Amsterdam), 61
Museuminsel (Berlin), 167
Museum Kampa–Sovovy mlýny
    (Prague), 762
Museum Mittelalterlicher Kunst
    (Museum of Medieval Art;
    Vienna), 940
Museum of 18th-Century
    Venice, 917
Museum of Baroque Art
    (Vienna), 940
Museum of Ethnography
    (Budapest), 213
Museum of Fine Art (Vienna),
    941
Museum of Folklore (Mykonos),
    464
Museum of Modern Art
    (Stockholm), 875
Museum of Prehistoric Thira
    (Santorini), 452
Museumplein (Amsterdam), 61
MuseumQuartier Complex
    (Vienna), 942
Museums, top 17, 8
Museu Nacional d'Art de
    Catalunya (MNAC;
    Barcelona), 141
Museu Nacional dos Coches
    (Lisbon), 535–536
Museu Picasso (Barcelona), 141
Music Film Festival (Vienna),
    939
Musiekgebouw (Amsterdam), 77
Musik Unter den Gleisen
    (Berlin), 171
Musikverein (Vienna), 938
Múvész Kávéház (Budapest), 210
Muziektheater (Amsterdam), 78
Mykonos, 459–464
Mystic SK8s (Prague), 765

N

Nachtwerk (Munich), 645
Nagy Cirkusz (Great Circus;
    Budapest), 215
Napier University (Edinburgh),
    350
Naples, 655–671
    culture tips, 659
    currency, 660
    eating, 663–665
    embassies and consulates,
    660
    emergencies, 660
    getting to and around,
    656–658
    Internet/Wi-Fi access, 660
    laundry, 660
    luggage storage, 660
    neighborhoods, 658
    partying, 665–666
    playing outside, 670–671
    post offices, 660
    recommended books, movies,
    and music, 659
    restrooms, 660
    safety, 660
    shopping, 671
    sightseeing, 666–670
    sleeping, 660–663
    starting a conversation with
    a local, 659
    tipping, 660
    tourist offices, 658–659
    12 hours in, 669
    websites, 659
Napoleon's Tomb (Paris), 721
Naranzaria (Venice), 3,
    905–906
Národní třída (Prague), 759
NASA (Reykjavík), 780
Naschmarkt (Vienna), 9, 946
Nasti Club (Madrid), 605
National and International
    Dance Festival (Milan), 624
National Archaeological
    Museum (Athens), 116
National Coach Museum
    (Lisbon), 535–536
National Concert Hall (Dublin),
    293
National Cycling Day
    (Amsterdam), 78
National Etruscan Museum at
    Villa Giulia (Rome), 829–830
The National Gallery (London),
    574

National Gallery of Ireland (Dublin), 296
National Gallery of Photography (Reykjavík), 783
National Gallery of Scotland (Edinburgh), 335, 351–352
National Garden (Athens), 117
National Jewish Festival (Budapest), 211
Nationalmuseet (Copenhagen), 241
National Museum (Dublin), 296
National Museum (Prague), 762
National Museum (Reykjavík), 783
Nationalmuseum (Stockholm), 875
National Museum of Art (Stockholm), 875–876
National Museum of Scotland (Edinburgh), 352
The National Portrait Gallery (London), 574–575
National Theater (Prague), 756–757
National Theatre (Reykjavík), 781
National Trust for Scotland (Glasgow), 439
Natural History Museum (London), 574
Nature (Madrid), 603
Nautical Museum of the Aegean (Mykonos), 464
Naval History Museum and the Arsenal (Venice), 917
Naval Museum (Santorini), 452
Navigaytion (Antwerp), 97
Negroni and Zoe (Florence), 377
Nelly's (Reykjavík), 780
Nemzeti Múzeum (Budapest), 212–213
Néprajzi Múzeum (Budapest), 213
Ness (Edinburgh), 354
Neubau (Vienna), 926
Neue Pinakothek/Pinakothek der Moderne (Munich), 649
Neuschwanstein Castle, 653
New Joli Coeur (Rome), 817
New Sacristy (Florence), 383
New Valentino (Ischia), 687
New Year's Eve
  Antwerp, 98
  Paris, 720
  Vienna, 939

New York Café Jazz Club (Brussels), 184
Nice, 398–406
Nice Carnaval, 395
Nice Festival du Jazz, 396
Nice 'n' Sleazy (Glasgow), 433
Nightclubs, best, 2
Nightflight (Munich), 645–646
Nimmo's Long Walk Wine Bar (Galway), 314
Nobel, Alfred, 876
Nobel Museum (Stockholm), 876
Nobel Prize, 876
Nordiska Museet (Stockholm), 876
Norrebro (Copenhagen), 226
Notre-Dame (Paris), 722
Notting Hill (London), 552
Notting Hill Carnival (London), 572
Nova (Brussels), 186
Nové Město (New Town; Prague), 737
Now, Voyager, 49
No. 1 Royal Crescent (Bath), 582
Number Two (Capri), 676
Nuova Idea International (Milan), 623
Ny Carlsberg Glyptotek (Copenhagen), 241
Nyhavn (Copenhagen), 225–226

O

Obchodní Centrum Novy Smíchov (Prague), 766
Océade (Brussels), 189
Oceanario de Lisboa (Lisbon), 535
O'Ché's (Galway), 313
Octagon Bar (Dublin), 288–289
Odeon (Amsterdam), 75
Odeon Cinehall (Florence), 379
O'Donoghue's (Dublin), 289
O Faia (Lisbon), 532
Off season, 16
O Guarracino (Capri), 676
O'Hara's Irish Pub (Barcelona), 135
Okresní Muzeum (Česky Krumlov), 768
Oktoberfest (Munich), 647
Old Christmas (Croatia), 245

Old English Store (Florence), 391
Old Fashion Café (Milan), 623
Old Fortress (Ibiza), 468
The Old Jameson Distillery (Dublin), 299
Old Mrs. Henderson (Munich), 646
Old Town Hall (Prague), 761
Olivia Cruises & Resorts, 49
Oltrarno (Florence), 361
Olympia (Dublin), 292
Olympiapark (Munich), 632–633, 652
Olympic Stadium (Barcelona), 139
151 (London), 565
100 Club (London), 567
O'Neill's Irish Pub (Nice), 405
One World Shop (Edinburgh), 354
Onofrio's Fountain (Dubrovnik), 328
Onze-Lieve-Vrouwekathedraal (Antwerp), 98
Onze-Lieve-Vrouwekerk (Bruges), 193
Opal Lounge (Edinburgh), 348
Open House (London), 572
Opening hours, 12
Open World, 49
Opera Assos Odeon (Athens), 113
Operabaren (Stockholm), 872
Opernhaus (Zurich), 963
Orange Bar (Venice), 906, 918
Original Sound of Music Tour (Salzburg), 9, 949
Orlando's Column (Dubrovnik), 330
Orsanmichele (Florence), 383–384
Orsanmichele, Church of (Florence), 380
Ortaköy (Istanbul), 495, 511
Oschen Garten (Munich), 646
Ostiense (Rome), nightlife, 817
Ostiense, Goa (Rome), 817
O'Sullivan's (Paris), 716
Our Lady Cathedral (Antwerp), 98
Out & About, 49
Outdoor activities, best, 10
The Outhouse (Edinburgh), 348
Outlook Tower and Camera Obscura (Edinburgh), 352–353

Out on the Liffey (Dublin), 292
Over Het IJ Festival
  (Amsterdam), 79
Overstock (Barcelona), 143
Oxegen (Dublin), 294
Oxfam (Dublin), 304
The Oxford (Nice), 405
Oxford/Cambridge Boat Race,
  571

P

Pacha (Madrid), 603
Pachá (Ibiza), 2, 475–476
Package tours, 39
Packing tips, 21
Paddington (London), 552
Padrao dos Descobrimentos
  (Lisbon), 535
Padua, 920–921
Pakleni Otoci, 257
Palác Akropolis (Prague), 754
Palace of Holyroodhouse
  (Edinburgh), 352
Palace of the Liberty of Bruges,
  192–193
Palacio Gaviria (Madrid),
  603–604
Palácio Nacional de Pena
  (Sintra), 540
Palácio Nacional de Sintra, 540
Palacio Real (Madrid), 606
Palais des Festivals (Cannes),
  414
Palais du Luxembourg (Paris),
  725
Palais Princier (Monaco), 416
The Palatine (Rome), 832
Palazzo Ducale (Venice),
  912–913
Palazzo Nuovo (Rome),
  828–829
Palazzo Pitti (Florence), 388
Palazzo Reale (Naples), 668
Palazzo Vecchio (Florence), 381
Pallas Theater (Athens), 113
Pampelonne, 409, 410
PAN Club and Café
  (Copenhagen), 235
P&O Ferries, 37
Panini and Web (Nice), 400
Panorama Bar (Berlin), 163
Panoramas, best, 8
Panormos (Mykonos), 464
Pantheon (Rome), 822

Papeneiland (Amsterdam), 75
Paradiso (Amsterdam), 75–76
Paradox (Amsterdam), 63
Parc André Citroen (Paris), 726
Parc d'Atraccions Tibidabo
  (Barcelona), 141
Parc de Bercy (Paris), 726
Parc de la Ciutadella
  (Barcelona), 141
Parc Güell (Barcelona), 139
Parco della Floridiana (Naples),
  671
Parco della Musica (Rome),
  817–818
Parco delle Cascine (Florence),
  389
Parco Forlanini (Milan), 626
Parco Sempione (Milan), 626
Parioli (Rome), 794
Paris, 689–730
  best of, 690–691
  cafes, 710–711
  cellphones, 699
  culture tips, 697
  currency, 699
  eating, 707–711
  embassies, 699–700
  emergencies, 700
  festivals, 719–720
  free and easy activities, 719
  gay nightlife, 716
  getting to and around,
    691–693
  Internet/Wi-Fi access, 700
  laundry, 700
  luggage storage, 700
  neighborhoods (arrondisse-
    ments), 694–696
  partying, 711–716
  performing arts, 716–718
  picnics, 707–708
  playing outside, 725–727
  post office, 700–701
  recommended books, movies,
    and music, 697–699
  safety, 701
  shopping, 727–730
  sightseeing, 718–724
  sleeping, 701
  starting a conversation with
    a local, 698
  tipping, 701
  tourist offices, 696–697
  tours, 718
  12 hours in, 722

  university scene, 724
  websites, 697
Paris Roller Rando, 726
Park Hotel (London), 577
Parkour (Paris), 725
Parks, best, 10
Parliament (Budapest), 214
Parque de Retiro (Madrid), 608
Parque Eduardo VII (Lisbon),
  539
Parque Genovés (Cádiz), 860
Parque Juan Carlos I (Madrid),
  609
Parque María Luisa (Seville),
  856
Passage (Vienna), 937
Passeig de Gràcia (Barcelona),
  140
Passports, 19
Pavilhao Chinês Bar (Lisbon),
  2, 531
Pazarin (Pazar; Split), 252
The Peacock (Dublin), 293
Peggy Guggenheim Collection
  (Venice), 917–918
Peluso (Florence), 391
Pension Unitas (Prague), 5
People (Brussels), 184
Pergamon Museum (Berlin),
  167–168
Perissa (Santorini), 452
Peter Stücken (Munich), 652
Petticoat Lane (London), 580
Philharmonisches Orchester
  (Berlin Philharmonic
  Orchestra), 164
Phoenix Park (Dublin), 296
Piazza dei Martiri (Bologna),
  392–393
Piazza del Campidoglio (Rome),
  832
Piazza della Signoria (Florence),
  360, 381
Piazza del Popolo (Rome), 824
Piazzale Michelangelo
  (Florence), 389
Piazza Maggiore (Bologna), 392
Piazza Mino (Fiesole), 389
Piazza Navona (Rome), 824
Piazza San Marco (Florence),
  360
Piazza San Marco (Venice), 882,
  887, 913
Piazza San Pietro (the Vatican),
  825–826

Piazza Santa Trinità (Florence), 360–361
Piazza Stazione (Padua), 920–921
Piazza Tasso (Sorrento), 684
Piazza Venezia (Rome), 824
Piccadilly Circus (London), 553
Piccadilly Sound (Florence), 391
Picnic fare, 7
Pierro's (Mykonos), 463
Pile Gate (Dubrovnik), 329
Pinacoteca (the Vatican), 827
Pinakothek der Moderne (Munich), 649
Pincio (Rome), 820
Pingvellir (Iceland), 785–786
Pink Moon (Rome), 835
Pizzafest (Naples), 667
Plaça Catalunya (Barcelona), 140
Place du Jeu de Balle (Brussels), 189, 190
Plage de la Bouillabaisse (St-Tropez), 410
Plage de Larvotto (Monaco), 416
Planet Out (Edinburgh), 349
Playa d'en Bossa (Ibiza), 468
Plaza de Toros Real Maestranza (Seville), 859
Ploce Gate (Dubrovnik), 329
Poble Espanyol (Barcelona), 138–139
P O'Flaherty's (Seville), 853
The Point Depot (Dublin), 293
Polé Polé (Antwerp), 97
Pollok Country Park (Glasgow), 438
Pompeii, 670
Po Na Na (Edinburgh), 348
Pond Bar (Edinburgh), 348
P1 (Munich), 646
Ponte di Rialto (Venice), 913–914
Ponte Vecchio (Florence), 381–382
Pop Boutique (London), 579
Populart (Madrid), 605
Porta Portese (Rome), 836
Portas Largas (Lisbon), 531
The Porterhouse (Dublin), 5
Portobello Market (London), 9, 552, 580
Portobello Road (London), 580
Poseidon (near Forio), 688
Poseidon's Temple (Athens), 116–117

POSITIVeinfach Café & Cocktail Bar (Interlaken), 486
Posto Italiano (Rome), 835
Potsdamer Platz (Berlin), 149
Potterow (Edinburgh), 350
Powerscourt Townhouse Centre (Dublin), 303
Praça de Touros de Lisboa (Lisbon), 537
Prague, 732–769
   best of, 733
   bookstores, 757–758
   cafes, 749–750
   cellphones, 740
   culture tips, 738–739
   currency, 740
   eating, 747–750
   embassies, 741
   emergencies, 741
   festivals, 759–760
   free and easy activities, 759
   gay bars and clubs, 753–754
   getting to and around, 733–736
   hanging out, 759
   laundry, 741
   luggage storage, 741
   movie theaters, 757
   neighborhoods, 736–737
   partying, 750
   performing arts, 755–757
   pharmacies, 742
   playing outside, 763–764
   post offices, 741
   recommended books, movies, and music, 739–740
   restrooms, 742
   safety, 742
   shopping, 764–766
   sightseeing, 758–763
   sleeping, 743–747
   starting a conversation with a local, 736
   taxis, 734, 736
   telephone tips, 742
   tipping, 742
   tourist offices, 737–738
   12 hours in, 763
   university scene, 761
   websites, 738
Prague Autumn, 760
Prague Castle, 760
Prague House of Photography (Prague), 756
Prague Spring Festival, 759
Prague State Opera House, 757

Prague Symphony Orchestra in the Municipal House, 757
Prater Ferris Wheel (Vienna), 944
Praterverband (the Prater; Vienna), 943–944
The Prati (Rome), 793
Pravda (Reykjavík), 2, 780
Prescription medications, 31
Pride London (London), 572
Prince's Palace (Monaco), 416
Princes Square (Glasgow), 439
Prinzknecht (Berlin), 163
Privilege (Ibiza), 476
Project: Dublin, 292
The Proms (London), 572
Protestant Cemetery (Rome), 825
Prototype (Rome), 835
Puerta del Sol (Madrid), 589
Puffin Island, 784
Pulalli (Capri), 675–676
Pulp Bar (Bath), 582
Punta della Dogana area (Venice), 919
Pussy Galore's Flying Circus (Copenhagen), 236

Q
Q Jazz Bar (Istanbul), 507
The Quays (Galway), 313
The Queen Adelaide (London), 577
Queen Bar (Istanbul), 508
Queen Elisabeth Concert Hall (Antwerp), 97
Queens (Lisbon), 531
Queen's Day (Amsterdam), 78
Queen's Hall (Edinburgh), 349
Quintas de Regaleiga (Sintra), 540
The Quirinale (Rome), 793, 832

R
Radnice (Town Hall; Český Krumlov), 768
Radost/FX (Prague), 752, 765
Rag Republic (Munich), 652
Raid Bar (Paris), 716
Rail Europe, 41–42
Rail passes, 37, 40–42
Rastoni (Santorini), 450
Ravello, 686

Raveman Records (Lisbon), 538–539
Razzmatazz (Barcelona), 3, 135
Rector's Palace (Dubrovnik), 330
Red & Blue (Antwerp), 95–96
Red Garter (Florence), 377
Red-Light District (Amsterdam), 76
Regata Storica (Venice), 911
Regatta on the Arno (Florence), 380
Regent's Park (London), 577
Reichstag (Bundestag; Berlin), 169–170
Reina (Istanbul), 506
Relève de la Garde (Monaco), 416
Rembrandt, 80–81
Rembrandt House Museum (Museum Het Rembrandthuis; Amsterdam), 80–81
Rendez-Vous Electroniques Festival (Paris), 720
Rent a Skate (Amsterdam), 82
Residents, The, 239
Residenz (Munich), 649
Residenzgalerie Salzburg, 950
Residenz State Rooms (Salzburg), 950
Restaurants, 23
    best cheap, 5–7
    tips on, 28
Revelin Fort (Dubrovnik), 329
Rex (Reykjavík), 780
Reykjavík, 770–786
    best of, 771
    cellphones, 774
    culture tips, 773
    eating, 778–779
    embassies, 774
    emergencies, 775
    free and easy activities, 782
    gay bars, 781
    getting to and around, 771–772
    Internet/Wi-Fi access, 775
    neighborhoods, 772
    partying, 779–781
    performing arts, 781
    playing outside, 784–785
    recommended books, movies, and music, 774
    road trips, 785–786
    shopping, 785
    sightseeing, 781–784
    sleeping, 775–778
    starting a conversation with a local, 773
    tourist offices, 772–773
    12 hours in, 783
    websites, 773
Reykjavík Art Museum, 782, 783–784
Reykjavík Dance Festival, 782
Reykjavík Gay Pride Festival, 782
Reykjavík International Film Festival, 783
Reykjavík Jazz Festival, 782
Reykjavík Museum of Photography, 782, 784
Rialto Bridge (Venice), 913–914, 919
Rialto Market (Venice), 920
Ribeira Nova (Lisbon), 539
Ricordi (Rome), 836
Rijksmuseum (Amsterdam), 81
The Ringstrassen Galleries (Vienna), 945–946
Rí-Rá (Dublin), 291
Rise (London), 572
Riva degli Schiavoni (Venice), 914–915
River strolls, 10
Road Records (Dublin), 297
Robbie Burns Night (Glasgow), 434
Robot (Munich), 652–653
Rock Café (Prague), 754–755
Rock climbing, Paris, 726–727
Rock en Seine (Paris), 720
Rockhouse (Salzburg), 949
Rodgers Travel, 50
Roisín Dubh (Galway), 314
Rokerij (Amsterdam), 63
Rolling Stone (Milan), 623
Rolling Venice pass, 911
Roman Forum (Rome), 821
Rome, 787–836
    best of, 788
    cafes, 812
    culture tips, 795
    currency, 796–797
    eating, 806–812
    embassies and consulates, 797
    emergencies, 797
    festivals, 818
    free and easy activities, 820
    gay nightlife, 816–817
    gelaterias, 808
    getting to and around, 789–791
    Internet/Wi-Fi access, 797–798
    laundry, 798
    luggage storage, 798
    museums and galleries, 828–830
    neighborhoods, 792–794
    partying, 812–817
    performing arts, 817–818
    pizzerias, 810–811
    playing outside, 832–834
    post offices, 798
    recommended books, movies, and music, 795–796
    safety, 798
    seven hills of, 832
    shopping, 834–836
    sightseeing, 818–831
    sleeping, 799–806
    starting a conversation with a local, 796
    taxis, 791
    tipping, 799
    tourist offices and information, 794
    12 hours in, 830
    university scene, 831
    websites, 794–795
Rookies (Amsterdam), 63
Roosevelt Tér (Budapest), 217
Rosenborg Slot (Rosenborg Castle; Copenhagen), 239
Rose Street (Edinburgh), 348–349
Roskilde, 242–243
Roskilde Domkirke (Cathedral), 242
Roxy (Prague), 751, 753
Royal Academy of Arts (London), 575
Royal Air Force Museum (London), 571
Royal Albert Hall (London), 4, 568
Royal Concert Hall (Glasgow), 433
Royal Flanders Ballet (Antwerp), 96–97
Royal Highland Show (Edinburgh), 351
Royal Museum of Fine Arts (Antwerp), 98
Royal National Theatre (London), 569

Royal Palace (Stockholm), 875

Royal Scottish Academy of Music and Drama (Glasgow), 433

Roy d'Espagne (Brussels), 184

Rubens, Peter Paul, 98–99

Rubenshuis (Rubens's House; Antwerp), 98–99

Rust (Copenhagen), 235

Ruta del Modernisme (Barcelona), 138, 140

Ryanair, 46

S

Saatchi Gallery (London),The, 575

Safety tips, 32–33

Sagrada Familia (Barcelona), 139, 140

Sagrestia Nuova (Florence), 383

Sailing, Split, 254

St. Blaise, Church of (Dubrovnik), 329

St. James's (London), 553

St. James's Park (London), 577

St. John (Dubrovnik), 329

St. Marco, Cathedral of (Korčula), 264

St. Mark's Basilica (Venice), 914

St. Michan's Church (Dublin), 298

St. Nicholas, Church of (Prague), 760–761

St. Nicholas' Collegiate Church (Galway), 316–317

Saint Nicholas' Day (Prague), 760

St. Patrick's Dublin Festival, 293

St. Paul's Cathedral (London), 572

St. Peter Castle (Bodrum), 516

St. Peter's Basilica (the Vatican), 826

St. Peter's Square (the Vatican), 825–826

St. Peter's tomb (the Vatican), 826

St. Savior Church (Dubrovnik), 330

St. Stephan's Cathedral (Vienna), 940

St. Stephen's Basilica (Budapest), 214–215

St. Stephen's Cathedral (Hvar), 257

St. Stephen's Day (Budapest), 211

St-Tropez, 406–410

St. Vitus Cathedral (Český Krumlov), 768

Salamanca (Madrid), 590

Salotto 42 (Rome), 815

Salvatian Army (London), 579

Salvation (Barcelona), 136

Salzburg, 946–950

Salzburg Festival, 949

San Antonio (Ibiza), 467

San Clemente (Rome), 831

Sandhamn, 879

San Gennaro Festival (Naples), 666

San Isidro Festival (Madrid), 606

San Lorenzo (Florence), 360, 384

San Lorenzo street market (Florence), 9

San Michele (Venice), 907

San Polo (Venice), 887

San Rafael (Ibiza), 468

Santa Cecilia (Rome), 831

Santa Croce (Florence), 360, 384–385

Santa Croce (Venice), 887

Santa Eularia (Ibiza), 468

Santa Gertrudis (Ibiza), 468

Sant'Agnese in Agone (Rome), 824

Santa Maria della Salute (Venice), 916

Santa Maria delle Grazie/*The Last Supper* (Milan), 625–626

Santa Maria del Popolo (Rome), 824

Santa Maria in Trastevere (Rome), 831

Santa Maria Maggiore (Rome), 831

Santa Maria Novella (Florence), 359–360, 385

Sant'Ambrogio (Florence), 390

Sant Joan (Barcelona), 137

Sant Jordi (Barcelona), 137

Santorini, 442–453

  eating, 449–450

  emergencies, 446–447

  getting to and around, 442–445

  Internet/Wi-Fi access, 447

  laundry, 447

  neighborhoods, 445–446

  partying, 450

  playing outside, 452–453

  post office, 447

  shopping, 453

  sightseeing, 451

  sleeping, 447–449

  taxis, 445

  tourist offices, 446

  websites, 446

Sanz Sans (Paris), 714

Sao Jorge Movie Theater (Lisbon), 532–533

Sa Penya (Ibiza), 467–468

Saponeria (Rome), 817

SATH (Society for Accessible Travel & Hospitality), 49

Sauna Marco (Prague), 754

Scanrail Pass, 223

Schauspielhaus (Zurich), 963

Schipol Airport (Amsterdam), 56–57

Schloss Charlottenburg (Berlin), 166

Schönbrunn Palace (Vienna), 940–941

Schwabing (Munich), 633

Scottish National Gallery of Modern Art (Edinburgh), 353

Scuba diving

  Hvar, 258

  Ibiza, 478

  Mykonos, 464

  Nice, 406

  Split, 254

Scuola Grande di San Rocco (Venice), 918

Sé (Cathedral; Lisbon), 535

Seasons, 12, 13, 16–17

Secession Building (Vienna), 941

The Secret Book and Record Store (Dublin), 297

Sefahathane Bar (Istanbul), 507

The Seine (Paris), 722

Selfridges (London), 579

Semana Santa (Seville), 855

Senso Unico (Venice), 906

Serpentine Column (Istanbul), 509

Seville, 837–860

  best of, 838–839

  cellphones, 843

  consulates, 843

  culture tips, 842

  currency, 843

  eating, 849–851

  emergencies, 843

festivals, 855
free and easy activities, 856
gay bars, 853
getting to and around,
    839–840
Internet/Wi-Fi access, 843
laundry, 843
luggage storage, 843
neighborhoods, 840–841
partying, 851–853
performing arts, 853–855
pharmacies, 843
playing outside, 858
post offices, 843
recommended books, movies,
    and music, 842
restrooms, 844
safety, 844
shopping, 858–860
sightseeing, 855–858
sleeping, 844–848
starting a conversation with
    a local, 838
telephone tips, 844
tipping, 844
tourist offices, 841
12 hours in, 857
university scene, 857–858
websites, 841–842
Sexmuseum Amsterdam, 81
Shakespeare & Company
    (Paris), 730
Shakespeare's Globe Theatre
    (London), 569
Sheperds Bush Empire
    (London), 567
Sherlock Holmes Museum
    (Meiringen), 489
Shooters Bar (Ios), 458–459
Shoulder seasons, 16
Shrove Tuesday (London), 570
Siamsa, The Galway Folk
    Theatre (Galway), 315
Sidetrack (Stockholm), 873
Sigmund Freud Haus (Vienna),
    942
Single travelers, 48
Sinksenfoor (Antwerp), 97
Sinners (Amsterdam), 76
Sintra, 539–540
Sipan, 332
Sir John Soane's Museum
    (London), 575
Sirkeci (Istanbul), 494
Siroco (Madrid), 605

The Sistine Chapel (the
    Vatican), 827–828
Six Nations Rugby Tournament
    (Dublin), 293
Skansen (Stockholm), 876
Skärholmen Shopping Center
    (Stockholm), 878
Skateboarding
    Dublin, 301
    Lisbon, 538
The Skeff (Galway), 313
Skiing
    Munich, 651
    Reykjavík, 784
    Vienna, 944
Skinny Bridge (Amsterdam), 78
Sky Bar (Vienna), 936
Sleeping, 12, 23
    booking online, 27
    tips on, 26–29
    websites, 52
SLM (Stockholm), 873
Slovansky ostrov (Prague), 759
S'move Light Bar (Naples), 666
Soccer (football)
    Barcelona, 136
    Brussels, 189–190
    Florence, 389
    Istanbul, 512
    Lisbon, 537
    London, 571, 578
    Milan, 627
    Munich, 651
    Rome, 833
Société Lutèce (Rome), 815
Soho (London), 553
Sole (Rome), 836
Soma Store (Munich), 653
Sónar (Barcelona), 137
Sorbonne, College de (Paris),
    724
Sorrento, 682–685
Sortie (Istanbul), 506
Soundgarden (Amsterdam), 76
Sounds of the Universe
    (London), 579
South Bank (London), 555
South Kensington (London),
    551–552
Space (Ibiza), 476
Space Electronic (Florence),
    378–379
Spanish Steps (Scalinata di
    Spagna; Rome), 792, 825, 834
Speakers Corner (London), 577
Spiritual Café (Barcelona), 133

Spitalfields (London), 580–581
Spitalfields Festival Fringe
    (London), 571
Split, 246–254
Split Summer Festival, 246
Sponza Palace (Dubrovnik), 330
Sprite Urban Games (London),
    577
Square (Bath), 583
Squero di San Trovaso (Venice),
    907
Staandard (Antwerp), 100
Stadhuis (Bruges), 193
Stadio Comunale Artemio
    Franchi (Florence), 389
Stadio dei Marmi (Rome), 833
Stadio Olimpico (Rome), 833
Stadium of Domitian (Rome),
    824
Stadsmuseum (Stockholm), 876
Stadsschouwburg (Antwerp), 97
Stadt Café (Munich), 644
Stadtmuseum (Munich),
    649–650
StadtPark (Vienna), 944
The Stand (Edinburgh), 349
The Stand (Glasgow), 433
Staré Město (Old Town;
    Prague), 737
Starry Starry Night (Glasgow),
    439
STA Travel, 39, 48
Statue Park (Budapest), 213
Stedelijk Museum CS
    (Amsterdam), 81
Steffl (Vienna), 946
Steinberg and Tolkien
    (London), 580
Stoa of Attalos (Athens), 116
Stockholm, 861–880
    best of, 862
    cellphones, 865
    culture tips, 864–865
    eating, 870–871
    emergencies, 865
    festivals, 874–875
    free and easy activities, 875
    gay bars, 873
    getting to and around,
        862–863
    Internet/Wi-Fi access, 865
    laundry, 865–866
    luggage storage, 866
    neighborhoods, 863–864
    partying, 872–873
    performing arts, 874

Stockholm *(Cont.)*
  picnic fare, 870
  playing outside, 877–878
  post office, 866
  recommended books, movies,
    and music, 865
  shopping, 878
  sightseeing, 874
  sleeping, 866–870
  starting a conversation with
    a local, 864
  tipping, 866
  tourist offices, 864
  12 hours in, 877
  university scene, 877
  websites, 864
Stockholm Cultural Festival, 874
Stockholm Jazz Festival, 874
Stockholm Pride, 874
Stohrer (Paris), 710–711
The Strand (London), 554
Stroget (Copenhagen), 225
Stromovka Park (Prague), 764
Stúdentakjallarinn (Reykjavík),
  780
Studenterhuset (Copenhagen),
  236
Sture Compagniet (Stockholm),
  872
The Sub Club (Glasgow), 431
Sultanahmet (Istanbul), 494
Summer of Antwerp, 97
Sunset Café (Ibiza), 474
Supperclub (Rome), 7
Surfing, 10
  Galway, 318
  Munich, 651
S.V. *Glenlee,* the Tall Ship at
  Glasgow Harbour, 437
Swimming. *See also* Beaches
  Dublin, 301
  Munich, 651–652
  Stockholm, 878
  Vienna, 945
  Zurich, 967
Swingcafe (Antwerp), 96
Swiss National Museum
  (Zurich), 964
Sword Dance Festival, 246
Széchenyi Lánchíd (Chain
  Bridge; Budapest), 213
Szechnyi Baths & Thermal Pools
  (Budapest), 218
Szentendre, 219
Szépmúvészeti Múzeum
  (Budapest), 213

T

Tabasco (Florence), 379
Taboo Records (Antwerp), 100
Tacheles (Berlin), 163
Tahe Audley (London), 567
Taiza (Prague), 765
Taksim, 495
Tanec Praha (Prague), 759
Tantra (Cannes), 414
Tantra (London), 566
Tate Britain (London), 575–576
Tate Modern (London), 576
Tchai Ovna (Glasgow), 430
Tea Room Luthi (Interlaken),
  488
Teatre-Museu Dalí (Figueres),
  143
Teatro Comunale di Firenze
  (Florence), 380
Teatro da Trinidade (Lisbon),
  533
Teatro degli Arcimboldi (Milan),
  624
Teatro de la Maestranza
  (Seville), 855
Teatro della Pergola (Florence),
  380
Teatro dell'Opera (Rome), 818
Teatro Nacional de Sao Carlos
  (Lisbon), 533
Teatro Olimpico (Rome), 818
Teatro Pereyra (Ibiza), 475
Teatro Romano (Fiesole), 389
Teatro Scribe (Florence), 377
Teatro Verdi (Florence), 380
Telephones, 34–35
Temple Bar Book Market
  (Dublin), 305
Temple Bar Food Market
  (Dublin), 305
Temple Bar Gallery and Studios
  (Dublin), 298
Temple Bar Music Centre
  (Dublin), 290
Temple of the Olympian Zeus
  (Athens), 116
Tenax (Florence), 379
Terrasse (Zurich), 962
Terror Háza (House of Terror;
  Budapest), 213
Testaccio (Rome), nightlife, 817
Teviot (Edinburgh), 350
Texas Lone Star Saloon
  (Seville), 853
Texxt (Munich), 653

Theater in der Josefstadt
  (Vienna), 938
Théâtre de la Ville (Paris), 717
Théâtre des Champs-Elysées
  (Paris), 717
Théâtre Toone VII (Brussels),
  185
Thermal pools, Reykjavík, 784
Thesion (Temple of Hephaistos
  and Athena; Athens), 116
Thieves' Market (Lisbon), 539
Thiossan (Barcelona), 135
Thomas Cook European
  Timetable, 42
Thor (Nice), 405
3D.Com (Nice), 400
3W Kafé (Paris), 716
Thun, Lake, 489–490
Thunersee (Lake Thun),
  489–490
Thyssen-Bornemisza Museum
  (Madrid), 607–608
Tibidabo, Mount (Barcelona),
  141
Tiergarten (Berlin), 149, 170
Tigh Neachtain (Galway), 313
Time Out magazine (London),
  570
Time zones, 33
Tinderbox Espresso Emporium
  (Glasgow), 431
Tingl Tangl (Prague), 754
Tipping
  Amsterdam, 66
  Antwerp, 91
  Athens, 107
  Barcelona, 126
  Berlin, 152
  Brussels, 180
  Budapest, 201
  Copenhagen, 228
  Dublin, 276
  Dubrovnik, 324
  Edinburgh, 340
  The French Riviera, 398
  Glasgow, 423
  Istanbul, 498
  Lisbon, 524
  London, 559
  Naples, 660
  Paris, 701
  Prague, 742
  Rome, 799
  Seville, 844
  Stockholm, 866
  Venice, 889

Vienna, 929
Zurich, 957
Tivoli (Dublin), 292
Tivoli Gardens (Copenhagen),
225, 238
TODINE/TONIGHT
(Amsterdam), 77
Tom's Bar (Berlin), 163
Topkapi Palace (Istanbul), 510
Topography of Terror (Berlin),
168
Top Shop (London), 580
Torino@Notte (Venice), 906
Torre de Belém (Tower of
Belém; Lisbon), 535
Torre dell'Orologio (Venice),
916
Torre Tavira (Cádiz), 860
Tour de France (Paris), 719
Tour Eiffel (Paris), 722–723
Tourist offices, 968–970
Tours, best offbeat, 9
Tower of London, 573
Town Hall Theatre (Galway),
315–316
Town Treasury (Korčula), 265
Trafalgar, 40
Trafalgar Weekend/Trafalgar
Day Parade (London), 572
Train travel, 37, 40–44, 973
Transportation, websites, 53
Trash (Berlin), 171
Trastevere (Rome), 792–793
Travel Assistance International,
31
Travel Bar (Barcelona), 135
Travel CUTS, 48
Traveler's checks, 24
Travel Guard International, 45
Trevi Fountain (Rome), 825
Triburbana (Madrid), 610
Tricker's (Bath), 583–584
Trinity College (Dublin), 271, 297
accommodations, 279
Trinity College (Rome), 814
Tropical Bar (Santorini), 3, 450
Trubadur (Dubrovnik), 328
Tulle (Dublin), 305
22 (Reykjavík), 780

U

Uetliberg (Zurich), 965
Uffizi (Florence), 387
UGC de Brouckère (Brussels),
185

U Kotvy (Prague), 761
Ultra (Florence), 392
U Malého Glena (Prague), 755
U medvídků (Prague), 751
Universidade de Lisboa
(Lisbon), 536
Universiteit Antwerp, 98
Université Libre de Bruxelles
(Brussels), 189
University College Dublin, 297
University College London, 576
University of Bologna, 393
University of Copenhagen, 240
University of Dubrovnik, 331
University of Milan, 626
University of Naples, 670
University of Padua, 920
University of Prague, 761
University of Seville, 857
University of Venice, 918
University of Vienna
(Universität Wien), 942
University of Zurich, 965
Unterseen church (Interlaken),
487
Uppsala, 879–880
Uppsala Domkyrka, 880
Uppsala University, 880
Usher Hall (Edinburgh), 349
U Vystřelenyho oka (Prague),
751

V

Vacation Together, 39
Valentim de Carvalho (Lisbon),
539
Van Gogh Museum
(Amsterdam), 81
Varadero Bar Lounge (Brač), 261
Vasamuseet (Vasa Museum;
Stockholm), 877
Vasholm, 879
Vasterlanggatan (Stockholm),
878
Vastermalmgsgallerian
(Stockholm), 878
The Vatican, 793–794, 825–828
Vatican grottoes, 826
Vatican Museums, 827
The Vault (Glasgow), 433
Vega (Copenhagen), 235
Veletržní Palace–National
Gallery Collection of Modern
and Contemporary Art
(Prague), 762–763

Velryba (Prague), 756
Velvet (Naples), 666
Veneranda (Hvar), 257
Venice, 881–921
best of, 882
cellphones, 888
culture tips, 888
districts, 887
eating, 897–902
emergencies, 889
festivals, 911
free and easy activities,
907
getting to and around,
883–885
gondolas, 904–905
Internet/Wi-Fi access, 889
laundry, 889
local dialect, 886
luggage storage, 889
money-saving passes, 888,
911
partying, 902–906
performing arts, 906–907
picnics, 919
playing outside, 918
post office, 889
recommended books, movies,
and music, 888
road trip, 920
shopping, 920
sightseeing, 907–918
sinking problem, 901
sleeping, 890–897
tipping, 889
tourist offices, 887
12 hours in, 913
university scene, 918
websites, 887–888
Venice International Film
Festival, 911
Venue (Edinburgh), 348
Versailles, 730–731
Verso (Antwerp), 100
Vesterbro (Copenhagen), 226
Via Sannio (Rome), 836
Via Veneto (Rome), 793
Vicar Street (Dublin), 290
Victoria (London), 554
Victoria & Albert Museum
(London), 576–577
Victoria Café (Milan),
622–623
Vidám Park (Amusement Park;
Budapest), 215

Vienna, 922–950
  best of, 922–923
  cafes, 935
  cellphones, 928
  culture tips, 927
  currency, 928
  eating, 934–935
  embassies, 928–929
  emergencies, 929
  festivals, 939
  gay scene, 937
  getting to and around,
    923–925
  Internet/Wi-Fi access, 929
  laundry, 929
  neighborhoods, 925–927
  partying, 935–937
  performing arts, 937–938
  post offices, 929
  recommended books, music,
    and movies, 927–928
  restrooms, 929
  road trip, 946–950
  safety, 929
  shopping, 945
  sightseeing, 938–942
  sleeping, 929–934
  starting a conversation with
    a local, 927
  tipping, 929
  tourist offices, 927
  12 hours in, 943
  university scene, 942
Vienna Boys Choir, 4, 938
Vienna Card, 924
Vienna Jazz Festival, 939
Vienna Modern, 939
Vienna's English Theatre, 938
Vienna Woods, 944
Viking Diving Center (Hvar), 258
Viking Ship Museum
  (Vikingeskibshallen;
  Copenhagen), 243
Viktualienmarkt (Munich), 652
Vilda Vanadis (Stockholm), 878
Villa Borghese (Rome), 833–834
Villa Celimontana (Rome), 834
Villa Cimbrone (Ravello), 686
Villa d'Este (Paris), 718
Villa Doria Pamphilj (Rome),
  834
The Village (Dublin), 290
Villa Jovis (Capri), 676–677
Villa Rufolo (Ravello), 686
Vineria Reggio (Rome), 814–815
Virgin Express, 46

Visas, 19
Visegrad, 219
Vittoriano (Rome), 820, 824
Vivoli (Florence), 5
Vlaamse Opera (Antwerp), 96
Vltava River (Prague), 764
Voga Longa (Venice), 911
Volcano Show (Reykjavík), 781
Volksgarten (Vienna), 937
Vondelpark (Amsterdam),
  81–82
Voodoo Lounge (Dublin), 289
Vrije Universiteit Brussel, 189
Vroni's Wine Bar (Glasgow), 431
Vrouwenhuis (Amsterdam), 76
Vyšehrad (Prague), 761–762

W

Wake Up! London, 4
Waldwirtschaft Grosshesselohe
  (Munich), 645
Walpurgis Eve, 862, 880
Watch This Space (London), 569
Water bikes, Amsterdam, 82
Waterlooplein Flea Market
  (Amsterdam), 84
Watersports. See also specific
  sports
  best, 10
  Brač, 262
  Dublin, 303
  Glasgow, 438
  Interlaken, 487
Wax (Paris), 714–715
WE (Amsterdam), 84
Weather, 16–17
Websites, 52–53
Weihenstephan Brewery,
  Freising, 653–654
Wembley Arena (London), 567
Westend City Center
  (Budapest), 220
Westminster (London), 554
Westminster Abbey (London),
  572
Whale-watching, Reykjavík, 9,
  771, 784–785
Whelan's (Dublin), 290–291
Where the Monkey Sleeps
  (Glasgow), 430
Whitechapel Art Gallery
  (London), 571
The White Horse (London), 567
Wieden (Vienna), 926

Wiener Staatsoper (Vienna),
  938
Wi-Fi access, 33–34
Wild at Heart (Berlin), 163
The Willow Tea Rooms
  (Glasgow), 430
Wimbledon (London), 571, 578
Windsurfing
  Brač, 262
  Galway, 318
Wini (Amsterdam), 84
Wins Bar/Café (Budapest), 210
Wintergarten Varieté (Berlin),
  164–165
Winter Lights Festival
  (Reykjavík), 782
Wireless Festival (London), 577
Women travelers, 50
Words'Worth (Munich), 653
Work and volunteer programs,
  51
World Pipe Band
  Championships (Glasgow),
  434

X

X-Tra Hotel Limmat (Zurich),
  5, 958

Y

Yab Yum (Florence), 379
Yacht Club (Mykonos), 463
Yerebatan Cistern (Istanbul),
  509–510

Z

ZAM–Zentrum für
  Aubergewöhnliche Museen
  (Munich), 650
Zanzibar (Dublin), 289
Zebra (Brussels), 183
Železné dveře (Prague), 751
Zeneakadémia (Ferenc Liszt
  Academy of Music;
  Budapest), 216–217
Zhivago Records (Galway), 319
Zipper (Amsterdam), 84–85
Zlatni Rat, 258
Zomer van Antwerpen
  (Antwerp), 97
Zoo Antwerpen (Antwerp), 99
ZooBar (Rome), 817

Zoologischer Garten (Zurich),
    965–966
Zoos
    Berlin, 165, 170
    Budapest, 215
Zrce beach (Pag), 262
Zurich, 951–967
    banks, 956
    best of, 952
    consulates, 956
    culture tips, 955
    currency, 956
    eating, 960–961
    emergencies, 956

festivals, 963–964
gay bars, 962–963
getting to and around,
    952–953
laundry, 956
luggage storage, 956
neighborhoods, 954
partying, 961–963
performing arts, 963
pharmacies, 956
playing outside, 965–967
post office, 956
recommended books, movie,
    and music, 955

shopping, 967
sightseeing, 963–965
sleeping, 957–958
starting a conversation with
    a local, 954
telephone tips, 957
tipping, 957
12 hours in, 965
university scene, 964–965
Zurich, Lake, 965
Zurich Street Parade, 963
Züri Fäscht (Zurich), 963

YOU DON'T HAVE TO BE
ON CAMPUS TO WATCH mtvU.

MTVU **Über**™

MUSIC ABOVE ALL - IN YOUR CONTROL

Streaming 24/7, 1000s of music videos,
student-produced content and more.

LOG ON TO mtvU.com